# Canada

## a travel survival kit

### Mark Lightbody
### Tom Smallman

PIONEER

CN
CN

**Canada – a travel survival kit**

**5th edition**

**Published by**
**Lonely Planet Publications**
Head Office:   PO Box 617, Hawthorn, Vic 3122, Australia
Branches:       155 Filbert St, Suite 251, Oakland, CA 94607, USA
                      10 Barley Mow Passage, Chiswick, London W4 4PH, UK
                      71 bis rue du Cardinal Lemoine, 75005 Paris, France

**Printed by**
Colorcraft Ltd, Hong Kong

**Photographs by**

| | | |
|---|---|---|
| Mark Lightbody (ML) | Tom Smallman (TS) | Richard Everist (RE) |
| Deanna Swaney (DS) | Michael Abraham (MA) | The Province of British Columbia (PBC) |
| Colleen Kennedy (CK) | James Lyon (JL) | |

Front cover: Lake Peyto along Lake Columbia Icefields Highway, Jasper National Park,
                   Wally Hampton, Scoopix Photo Library
Back cover: Totem pole (PBC)
Title page: Grain elevators, Saskatchewan (DS)

**First Published**
March 1983

**This Edition**
September 1994

**Although the authors and publisher have tried to make the information as accurate as possible, they accept no responsibility for any loss, injury or inconvenience sustained by any person using this book.**

National Library of Australia Cataloguing in Publication Data

Lightbody, Mark.
       Canada – a travel survival kit.

       5th ed.
       Includes index.
       ISBN 0 86442 216 4.

       1. Canada – Guidebooks. I. Smallman, Tom. II. Title.
       (Series : Lonely Planet travel survival kit).

917.104647

text & maps © Lonely Planet 1994
photos © photographers as indicated 1994
climate charts compiled from information supplied by Patrick J Tyson, © Patrick J Tyson, 1994

## Mark Lightbody

Mark was born and grew up in Montreal. He was educated there and in London, Ontario, and he holds an honours degree in journalism. Among a variety of occupations, he worked for a while in radio news. Mark has travelled in nearly 50 countries, visiting every continent but Antarctica. He made his first foray across Canada at the age of four. Since then he has repeated the trip numerous times using plane, train, car and thumb.

Besides writing the Lonely Planet guide to Canada, Mark has worked on former editions of LP's travel survival kits *Papua New Guinea; Australia; Malaysia, Singapore & Brunei* and on *South-East Asia on a shoestring*. He now lives in Toronto.

## Tom Smallman

Tom was born and raised in the UK where he was educated. He now lives in Melbourne, Australia. He has had a number of jobs including dishwasher, labourer, hospital theatre technician and high school teacher. Tom has travelled in Europe, North America, the Middle East and Asia. He joined Lonely Planet as an editor in 1988.

## From the Authors

**From Mark Lightbody** It's very gratifying to have a book reach its fifth edition, to see that it has successfully met the test of time and the critical eyes of real travellers. But along with the satisfaction comes the increased challenge to improve, distill and concentrate further. In my research I'm always looking for the hole, the gap, for what is essential and may have been missed. These now, I trust, are few but I'm convinced the more you travel around Canada, the bigger it gets.

For this edition Tom Smallman and I covered much of the country, from the Atlantic to the Pacific, talking and walking through towns and cities as much as possible, hopping ferries along the coasts and spending many hours on the roads.

Special thanks go to Colleen Kennedy for research assistance, editorial help, a range of suggestions and countless phone calls. Diane Carpentier supplied much help with the Montreal chapter as did Jill Sechley in Ottawa. Mary Theresa Lawlor added considerably to the northern Ontario section. Particular thanks also go to Bill Butler of the St John's City Tourism Office and Nina Chung of Hostelling International – Canada in Ottawa. Also thanks to Michael Abraham for hospitality and recommendations and to my mother and father for answering so many questions.

Again, warm thanks to those who sent letters, many of whom will see that their information was not only interesting but helpful and useful.

**From Tom Smallman** Tom wishes to thank the following for supplying so much useful information so readily: Julie Matson at the Canadian Consulate in Sydney, Tony Bulman of Alberta Tourism, Maya Araki of Tourism Victoria, Andres Arabski of the

Northwest Territories' Visitor Information Centre at the 60th parallel, the staff at the Visitor Reception Centre in Watson Lake, Carolyn Thompson of Yukon Tourism in Whitehorse, Sue of the Yukon Conservation Society, Tourism BC in Victoria and Hostelling International in Vancouver.

Special thanks to Bert Noble and Gwen Going for their hospitality and for sharing part of the journey with me; to David, Robyn and Carly Edwards for the overnight stay; to Joy, Bill and the rest of the Derry clan; to Lindy Mark for helping to organise things so efficiently; to Heather Noble; the Gowan-McKenna family; and finally to Sue Graefe for her patience and support.

## This Book

The first three editions were researched and updated by Mark Lightbody, the fourth edition and this edition were updated by Mark Lightbody and Tom Smallman.

## From the Publisher

At Lonely Planet in Melbourne, Australia, this edition was edited by Steve Womersley and Sharan Kaur. Thanks also goes to Alison White and Frith Pike for additional copyediting; to Tom Smallman for proofing; to Sharon Wertheim for helping with the index, and Sandy Laughren (Canadian High Commission, Canberra) for providing useful information.

Richard Stewart, Adam McCrow, Michelle Stamp and Indra Kilfoyle did the mapping; Richard Stewart, Tamsin Wilson,

Rose Keevins and Tracey O'Mara did the illustrations and Tamsin Wilson was responsible for cover design. Richard Stewart took charge of the overall layout of the book.

## Thanks

The response from readers in quantity and calibre of letters has continued to mount and this information is invaluable. Whether it's a mountain hike, a quirky airline regulation or a downtown restaurant please continue to let us know what you find. The stories of interesting and/or funny experiences are always great to receive as well. Have a good trip. (A list of thanks to readers is on page 928.)

## Warning & Request

Things change – prices go up, schedules change, good places go bad and bad places go bankrupt – nothing stays the same. So if you find things better or worse, recently opened or long since closed, please write and tell us and help make the next edition better.

Your letters will be used to help update future editions and, where possible, important changes will also be included in a Stop Press section in reprints.

We greatly appreciate all information that is sent to us by travellers. Back at Lonely Planet we employ a hard-working readers' letters team to sort through the many letters we receive. The best ones will be rewarded with a free copy of the next edition or another Lonely Planet guide if you prefer. We give away lots of books, but, unfortunately, not every letter/postcard receives one.

# Contents

# Map Legend

## BOUNDARIES

International Boundary

Provincial Boundary

## ROUTES

Trans Canadian Highway

Freeway

Highway

Major Road

Unsealed Road or Track

City Street

Railway

Underground Railway

Tram

Walking Track

Walking Tour

Ferry Route

Cable Car or Chairlift

## AREA FEATURES

Park, Gardens

National Park

Provincial Park

Marine Park

Built-Up Area

Pedestrian Mall

Market

Cemetery

Beach or Desert

## HYDROGRAPHIC FEATURES

Coastline

River, Creek

Intermittent River or Creek

Lake, Intermittent Lake

Canal

Swamp

## SYMBOLS

| | | |
|---|---|---|
| ✪ CAPITAL | National Capital | |
| ◉ CAPITAL | Provincial Capital | |
| ▨ City | Major City | |
| ● City | City | |
| ● Town | Town | |
| ● Village | Village | |
| ■ | Hotel, Pension (Place to Stay) | |
| ▼ | Restaurant (Place to Eat) | |
| � | Pub, Bar (Place to Drink) | |
| ✉ ☎ | Post Office, Telephone | |
| ❶ ❸ | Tourist Information, Bank | |
| ⊖ P | Transport, Parking | |
| 🏛 ▲ | Museum, Monument | |
| ⌖ ⛺ | Caravan Park, Camping Ground | |
| † ⛫ † | Church, Cathedral | |
| ☪ ✡ | Mosque, Synagogue | |
| ⚊ ☸ | Buddhist Temple, Hindu Temple | |

| | | |
|---|---|---|
| ⊕ ★ | Hospital, Police Station |
| ✈ ✝ | Airport, Airfield |
| ▥ ✿ | Swimming Pool, Gardens |
| ❖ 🐘 | Shopping Centre, Zoo |
| ⚲ ⛱ | Winery or Vineyard, Picnic Site |
| ← 125 | One Way Street, Route Number |
| ⚱ | Archaeological Site or Ruins |
| ☗ ⚑ | Bike Hire, Ski Field |
| ⌖ ▣ | Castle, Tomb |
| ⌂ ⌂ | Cave, Hut or Chalet |
| ▲ ☀ | Mountain or Hill, Lookout |
| ⚑ ⚓ | Lighthouse, Shipwreck |
| )( ⚬ | Pass, Spring |
| | Ancient or City Wall |
| | Rapids, Waterfalls |
| | Cliff or Escarpment, Tunnel |
| | Railway Station |

Note: not all symbols displayed above appear in this book

# Introduction

Canada is big, spacious, rugged, uncluttered and tremendously varied. With the break-up of the Soviet Union, it has become the largest country in the world. You can stand in places where perhaps nobody else has ever stood and yet the cities are large and modern, offering art and culture as a balance.

From the Atlantic Ocean it's over 7000 km to the Pacific coast. In between you can have a coffee and a croissant at a sidewalk café or canoe on a silent northern lake. You can peer down from the world's tallest building or over the walls of a centuries-old fort. You can hike amid snowcapped peaks or watch the sunset where it's an unobstructed 30 km to the horizon.

The four very different seasons can bring the winters Canada is known for, but also sweltering hot summer days.

It's said that the national personality has been shaped by life in a northern frontier; people constantly come from the wild to the settled areas and back again. Because the country is so young, a modern identity is still forming. But it's there, distinctly different from that of Canada's neighbour to the south.

The cultural mix of Canada is said to form a mosaic, not the melting pot of America. This patchwork of peoples is made up of British, French and many others, ranging from Europeans to those from the Far East as well as the original Native peoples.

Inflation has dropped to about 2% in the past few years, so prices haven't been rising dramatically. The Canadian dollar remains low compared with the US greenback, making exchange rates excellent for Americans while holding steady for many other currencies. For Canadians, this is another good reason to see the homeland.

With its history, people, land and nature, Canada has a lot to offer the traveller.

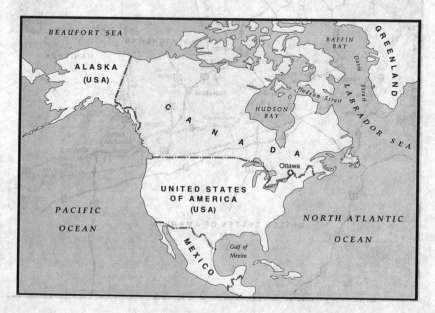

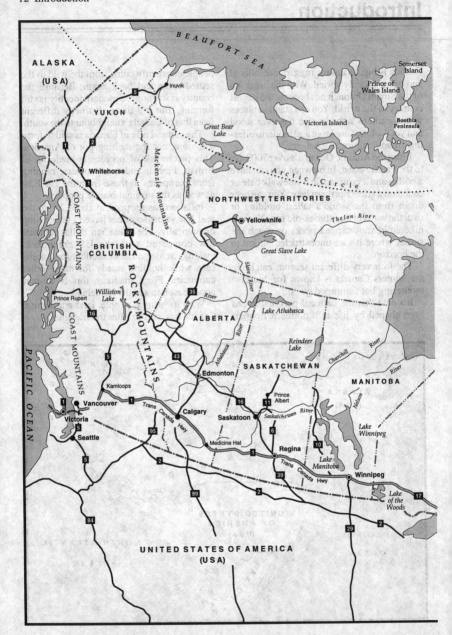

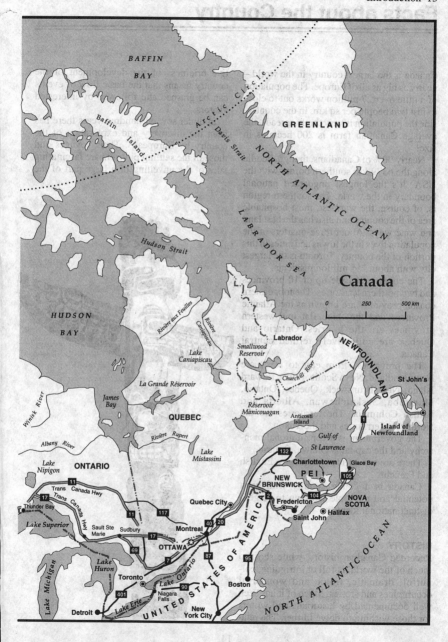

Canada

BAFFIN
BAY

Arctic Circle

GREENLAND

Baffin Island

Davis Strait

NORTH ATLANTIC OCEAN

LABRADOR SEA

Hudson Strait

HUDSON
BAY

Rivière aux Feuilles

Rivière Caniapiscau

Labrador

Smallwood Reservoir

Churchill River

NEWFOUNDLAND

0    250    500 km

Lake Caniapiscau

La Grande Réservoir

James Bay

Winisk River

Albany River

Lake Nipigon

ONTARIO

Réservoir Manicouagan

St John's

QUEBEC

Rivière Rupert

Lake Mistassini

Anticosti Island

Gulf of St Lawrence

Island of Newfoundland

1

Trans Canada Hwy
11

Trans Canada Hwy
11

117

132

Charlottetown

Glace Bay

NEW
BRUNSWICK

P·E·I

105

Thunder Bay

Sault Ste Marie

Sudbury

Quebec City

2

Fredericton

104

NOVA
SCOTIA

Lake Superior

17

69

40  20

Montreal

Saint John

Halifax

Lake Michigan

7

OTTAWA

87

95

Lake Huron

Toronto

Lake Ontario

UNITED STATES OF AMERICA

Boston

401

Niagara Falls

90

NORTH ATLANTIC OCEAN

Detroit

Lake Erie

New York City

# Facts about the Country

Canada is the largest country in the world – nearly as big as all of Europe. The population of a little over 27 million works out to close to just two people per sq km. In the countryside the population is very thinly spread – the average Canadian farm is 200 hectares in size!

Nearly 90% of Canadians, though, huddle along the 6379-km southern border with the USA. It's the longest unguarded national boundary in the world. The southern region is, of course, the warmest, most hospitable area of the country and also has the best land and waterways. About three-quarters of the population lives in the towns and cities in this portion of the country. Toronto is the largest city with about 2½ million residents.

The country is made up of 10 provinces and two northern territories. The four eastern coastal provinces are known as the Atlantic Provinces and the three flat mid-western provinces are the prairies. Ontario and Quebec are collectively termed central Canada.

The provinces (from east to west) are Newfoundland, Nova Scotia, Prince Edward Island, New Brunswick, Quebec, Ontario, Manitoba, Saskatchewan, Alberta and British Columbia. The territories are the Northwest Territories and the Yukon.

The government is a constitutional monarchy and the capital is Ottawa, Ontario.

There are two official languages, English and French.

Canada is a young country with great potential and a people working to forge a distinct national identity.

## HISTORY

Recorded Canadian history, while short to much of the world, is full of intriguing, colourful, dramatic, tragic and wonderful occurrences and stories. Much of it has been well documented by historians and writers for those wishing to delve further. The rela-tive briefness of the development of the country means that the basic flow of events can be grasped and followed by interested visitors.

In under several hundred years there has been the discovery and exploration of the country by Europeans. Their voyages and those of the settling pioneers are fascinating tales of the unveiling of a large part of the

globe. The Native Indian cultures they met and dealt with through the years of the fur-trade and beyond make up contrasting chapters of the story. Battles between French and English, British and Americans are other major themes.

Canadians have recently come to appreciate and admire their nation's history. National Historic Sites and buildings of every description can be found across the country and are well worth discovering.

## Original Inhabitants

When Columbus 'discovered' America in 1492, thinking he had hit the lands south of China, vaguely called 'the Indies', he sensibly called the people he found 'Indians'.

Ironically, he was nearly correct, for the Native Indians had come from Asia, across the Bering Strait, after the last great ice age – about 15,000 years ago. The earliest occupation site in Canada yet found is the Bluefish Caves of the Yukon.

By the time Columbus arrived the descendants of these people had spread throughout the Americas, from Canada's frozen north to Tierra del Fuego at the southern tip of Argentina and Chile.

The major American Indian cultures – Mayan, Aztecan and Incan – developed in Central and South America. Although no comparably sophisticated Indian societies sprang up in Canada, partially due to the climate, the Canadian Indian tribes had evolved dramatically through prehistory. When the Europeans arrived Native People across the country had developed a multitude of languages, customs, religious beliefs, trading patterns, arts & crafts, highly specialised skills, laws and government.

At this time, around the early 1500s, six distinct groupings of people could be discerned each with its own language and customs. These six major groups are classified by their geographic location.

The Arctic peoples lived in the far north. The subarctic group were found across the country from Newfoundland to British Columbia. The Eastern Woodlands tribes lived across the top of the Great Lakes, along the St Lawrence River and in what was to become Nova Scotia, New Brunswick and Prince Edward Island. The Plains people roamed across the prairies from Lake Winnipeg to the foothills of the Rocky Mountains. The Plateau area covers those groups in central southern British Columbia and the North-west group ranges from Vancouver to Alaska along the Pacific coast and includes all the ocean islands of British Columbia.

Most of these peoples depended on hunting, fishing and gathering. The more complex societies lived either on the mild west coast or around the fertile southern Ontario and St Lawrence Valley region in the east. The Eastern Woodland Indians had developed agriculture and lived in more-or-less permanent settlements. The tribes of the north and midwest lived a more hand-to-mouth existence. The Inuit (meaning 'people', and once called the Eskimos) eked out an existence in a world virtually unchanged until the 1950s.

Within each grouping were numerous

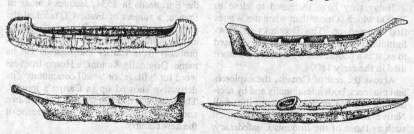

Ancient canoes

tribes which in turn were comprised of numbers of smaller bands who came together to winter or in times of celebration or hardship and when marriage partners were sought. Even today, 53 distinct indigenous languages are spoken and many of these have various dialects. Other languages are now extinct. The existing languages fall into 11 broader families, most of which are independent from all the others. North America is generally considered as one of the most complex linguistic regions in the world. About half of Canada's Native people can today speak their original language.

The Inuit, who arrived from Asia after the forefathers of all other US Indians, are a separate people. There are about 100,000 of them in the Arctic areas of the USA, Russia, Greenland (Denmark) and Canada. Canada is home to roughly 25% of the total population.

The peaceful Inuit had little to do with the more southerly Indian groups and, other than meetings with European explorers around the north-east coast, remained in relative isolation. They were the last group of Native Canadians to give up the traditional, nomadic way of life, although, despite more modern housing many remain primarily hunters. Though having to face brutal weather conditions and frequent starvation, the Inuit were a remarkably healthy lot and the pristine conditions helped protect them from disease and sickness. The arrival of European bugs and germs reduced their numbers dramatically to the point where their very survival was in question.

Today they have increased to close to 30,000 which is more than when the Whites first showed up. The Beothuks of Newfoundland did not fare so well. They ceased to exist as a people when the last two women died in the early 1800s.

Across the rest of Canada, the explorers and pioneers, both intentionally and by accident, brought to an end the way of life of all Native Indian people. The eastern tribes, such as those of the Iroquois Confederacy, had to side against each other with the French or English in their seemingly never-ending battles and ended up losing all their land. The Plains people, such as the Cree and Blackfoot, with their teepees, horses, bows and arrows and spectacular feathered headdresses, perhaps the archetypal North American Indian, were forced into the Europeans' world by the virtual destruction of the buffalo.

The west coast tribes such as the Haida, fared a little better, their isolation, strong tradition of independence and long, stable history affording some protection.

Overall, the European discovery and settlement of the country reduced Native Indians from about 350,000 to 100,000. Through treaty arrangements, the formation of reservations (now called reserves) and strong policing, notably by the RCMP, the remaining groups were provided some measure of protection. Canada never had the all out wars and massacres that marred the American clash of cultures.

### European Exploration

The first European visitors to Canada were the Vikings from Iceland and Greenland. There is evidence that they settled in northern Newfoundland at the eastern edge of Canada around 1000 AD. How long they stayed, how much they explored and what happened to them is unknown.

It was around 1500 AD that the action around the Americas started to heat up. The Spanish, French, British and Italians all wanted in.

In Canada, it was the French who got first licks. After a few earlier exploratory visits by the Europeans in 1534, Jacques Cartier of France, a subject of Francis I, reached the gulf of the St Lawrence River and claimed all the surrounding area for France. It was probably from Cartier that Canada got its name. Originally *Kanata*, a Huron-Iroquois word for 'village' or 'small community', its derivative showed up in Cartier's journal. The name was used for the St Lawrence area and eventually became the official name of the new country.

The French didn't bother much with this new colony throughout the 1500s, but the pattern of economic development which began then has continued through to the present. This is, put bluntly and simply, the selling of its resources to whoever is buying, thus enabling the country to pay for everything else it needs. The first commodities prized by the French were the fish of the east coast and furs for the fashion-conscious of France.

Samuel de Champlain, another Frenchman, began further explorations in the early 1600s. He settled Quebec City, and Montreal was founded soon after in 1642 as a missionary outpost. Throughout the 17th century fur-trading companies dominated this new world. In 1663 Canada became a province of France. There were about 60,000 French settlers by then – they are the ancestors of a good percentage of today's French Canadians.

Throughout the 1600s the French fought the Native Indians, who soon realised that they were getting a raw deal in the fur trade and through development of their lands. The French kept busy, too, with further explorations. They built a long chain of forts down to Louisiana – another major settlement – in what is now the southern USA. In the 1730s another of the major explorers, Pierre Gaultier de Varennes, Sieur de la Vérendrye, was responsible for another series of forts. This one stretched across the south of what are now the provinces of Ontario, Manitoba and Saskatchewan.

### The Struggle for Power

Of course, the British weren't just sipping pints through all this. Though concentrating on the lands of America's east coast, the Hudson's Bay Company (still one of Canada's main department-store chains) had moved into the Hudson Bay area in northern Ontario around 1670.

The British soon muscled into settlements on the Canadian east coast. By 1713 they had control over much of Nova Scotia and Newfoundland. And then, for a while, there was peace.

In 1745 a British army from New England, America, moved north and cap-

tured a French fort in Nova Scotia. The struggle for control of the new land was on. What is known as the Seven Years' War began in 1754. The French held the upper hand for the first four years. In one of Canada's most famous battles, the British defeated the French at Quebec City in 1759. Both General Wolfe, leader of the British, and the Marquis de Montcalm, who led the French, were killed in battle. After this major victory, the British turned the tide. At the Treaty of Paris in 1763, France handed Canada over to Britain.

The British, however, didn't quite know how to manage the newly acquired territory. The population was nearly exclusively French and at that time in Britain, Roman Catholics had very few rights – they couldn't vote or hold office. In 1774 the Quebec Act gave the French Canadians the right to their religion, the use of French civil law in court and the possibility of assuming political office. The British, however, maintained positions of power and influence in politics and business. It was during this period that the seeds of the Quebec separatist movement were sown.

During the American Revolution (1775-83) against Britain, about 50,000 settlers – termed 'Loyalists' due to their loyalty to Britain – shifted north to Canada. They settled mainly in the Atlantic Provinces and Ontario.

This migration helped to balance the number of French and British in Canada. Soon after, Quebec and Ontario were formed with their own governors. Throughout the late 1700s and into the 1800s Canada's frontiers were pushed further and further afield. Sir Arthur Mackenzie explored the north (Mackenzie River) and much of British Columbia. Simon Fraser followed the river which was named after him to the Pacific Ocean. David Thompson travelled the Columbia River, also in British Columbia. In 1812, Lord Selkirk formed a settlement of Scottish immigrants around the Red River Valley near Winnipeg, Manitoba.

Also in 1812, the last war between Canada and the USA, the War of 1812, began. Its causes were numerous, but the US attempt to take over its northern neighbour was only part of the campaign against Britain. Each side won a few battles, and in 1814 a draw was declared.

## The Dominion Period

With the end of the US threat and the resulting confidence in themselves, many of the colonists became fed up with some aspects of British rule. Some spoke out for independence. In both Upper (Ontario) and Lower (Quebec) Canada, brief rebellions broke out. In 1840 both areas united under one government. But by this stage, the population in Upper (British, mainly) outnumbered that in Lower Canada (French) and wanted more than a half-say. The government became bogged down, with Britain attempting to work out something new. Again you can see the historical disputes between the British and French.

Britain, of course, didn't want to lose Canada, as it had the USA, so it stepped lightly and decided on a confederation giving a central government some powers and the individual colonies others.

In 1867 the British North America Act (BNA Act) was passed by the British government. This established the Dominion of Canada and included Ontario, Quebec, Nova Scotia and New Brunswick. The BNA Act became Canada's equivalent to a constitution, though far less detailed and all-inclusive than that of the USA.

John Alexander Macdonald became Canada's first prime minister. The total population was 3½ million, nearly all living in the east and mostly on farms. It had been decided at the Act's signing in 1867 that other parts of the country should be included in the Dominion whenever possible.

The completion of the Canadian Pacific railway – one of Canada's great historical sagas – joined the west coast with the east, linking those areas with the Dominion. By 1912 all provinces had become part of the central government except Newfoundland, which finally joined in 1949.

In the last few years of the 19th century

Canada received large numbers of immigrants, mainly from Europe.

The government continued to grapple with French and British differences. These reached a peak during WW I, which Canada had entered immediately on Britain's behalf. In 1917, despite bitter French opposition in Quebec, the Canadian government began a military draft.

## The Modern Era

After WW 1 Canada slowly grew in stature and prosperity, and in 1931 became a voluntary member of the Commonwealth.

With the onset of WW II, Canada once again supported Britain, but this time also began defence agreements with the USA, and after the attack on Pearl Harbor, declared war on Japan.

In the years after WW II Canada experienced another huge wave of European immigration. The postwar period saw economic expansion and prosperity right across North America. The 1950s were a time of unprecedented wealth. The middle class mushroomed.

The 1960s brought social upheaval and social-welfare programmes with their ideals and liberalism. Canada's first Bill of Rights was signed in 1960. Nuclear-power generators and US nuclear warheads became major issues in Canada.

The Quebec separatist movement attracted more attention. A small group used terrorism to press its point for an independent Quebec. In 1976 the Parti Québecois (PQ), advocating separatism, won the provincial election. Since that time, though, sentiments on the issue have risen and fallen. In 1980, a Quebec referendum found most Quebeckers were against independence and the topic was more or less dropped.

In the early 1990s separation is once again a hotly debated possibility and another provincial referendum may be in the offing. Currently, the PQ is not in power in Quebec but is once again finding favour across the province. It seems at the moment that most Canadians would prefer Quebec to stay, while about half of Quebeckers feel the formation of a separate, distinct political entity is preferable and even inevitable.

In 1967 the country celebrated its 100th anniversary with the World's Fair in Montreal – Expo – as one of the highlights.

Well-known Pierre Elliot Trudeau, a Liberal, became Canada's prime minister in 1968 and, except for a brief period in 1979, held power until his retirement in 1984. Despite great initial support and international recognition, Trudeau was, to be kind, not a popular man at the end of his stay.

During his leadership, however, he was largely responsible for the formation of a Canadian Constitution, the last step in full independence from Britain. It came into being in 1982 along with a Charter of Rights and Freedoms. Quebec, however, never ratified the agreement and it was passed without their participation. They wanted to be recognised as a 'distinct society' with special rights. Later talks to bring them into the fold and thus make the agreement more national have failed. Constitutional matters have now been put aside for what many see as more practical, less divisive topics. The issue will not go away however and played a part in the startling election of 1993.

The 1984 election saw the Progressive Conservatives, led by Brian Mulroney, sweep into power with a tremendous nationwide majority, slamming the door on the Trudeau era. The 1988 World Economic Summit of the seven major industrial nations was held in Toronto and the winter Olympics were hosted in Calgary, each bringing increased prestige and favourable attention to Canada's somewhat fragile international self-image. The government was re-elected to another five-year term in 1988.

Following the customary pattern this government, too, fell from grace with a large thump. Among the major issues through the later Mulroney years were the very controversial free-trade alliance with the USA and the attempt to reach a consensus, known as the Meech Lake Accord, on overhauling the distinctions between provincial and federal powers, rights and jurisdictions. Another live wire was the introduction of a Goods & Services Tax (GST). Mounting concern over the colossal national debt and the massive annual federal government deficit also plagued the government. Further difficulties were encountered in attempting to deal with the Native peoples of the country, their land claims and search for more power.

In the early 1990s Canadians are fed up with politicians in general, the poor economy, high unemployment and perhaps more than anything else their own pessimism. Prime Minister Mulroney quit and the party's first woman, Kim Campbell was chosen as the new leader at a Conservative convention in the spring of 1993. Her term as Canada's first prime minister was to be very short-lived. The federal election in October saw the most dramatic change in Ottawa in history as the country sought a way out of the tangle of so many heavy-duty problems.

The Liberals, led by Quebecker Jean Crétien, routed the Conservatives. Crétien, a one time associate of Trudeau, has been around a long time, knows the ropes and appeals with his lack of artifice and posturings. The country wants to rally behind him but he has a lot of unappetising food on his plate to chew through.

The Americans pushed for an extension to the disliked free-trade agreement (FTA) which included Mexico in the North American Free Trade Agreement (NAFTA). Big business likes the deals but many Canadians see them as killing jobs not creating them. Canada, after asking for some modifications, ratified the agreement. Crétien also has to comes to terms with the economics which alienated the people from the Conservatives. It will not be an easy road.

The social programmes including the 'free' universal medicare system, unemployment insurance and welfare for the needy of which Canadians are justifiably proud and protective, are coming under ever-increasing threat from a cash-strapped country. Canadians are already feeling overburdened with taxes and won't take another grab without howling long and hard. Other major areas to be considered are defence and immigration.

Nobody really seems to know what to do with the military and its high costs in light of the end of the Cold War with the Soviet bloc. Equally contentious is the issue of too much immigration and the thorny allegations of racism which surround it.

The Liberals also face a new-look parliament with the traditional opposition parties, the Conservatives and the New Democrats virtually absent. They both suffered resounding defeats in the election and were replaced with two fractious regional parties, the Reform Party from the west and the separatist Bloc Québecois (federal party) from Quebec (see under Political Parties later for more details). The latter, led by Lucien Bouchard, is now the official opposition after coming second in the number of representatives elected.

Internationally, Canada maintains its position in NATO and as one of the so-called G-7 countries. (The G-7 group of Germany, France, the USA, the UK, Japan, Italy and Canada meet regularly to develop major economic policies.)

Canadian troops continue to be among the world's foremost peacekeepers, working not only in the Middle East, Cyprus and traditional trouble spots but also playing leading roles in battle-torn Somalia, Kuwait and the provinces of former Yugoslavia.

## GEOGRAPHY

Canada is about 7730 km from east to west. Its only neighbour is the USA, which includes Alaska in the north-west. With such size the country can boast a tremendous variety of topography.

Though much of the land is lake and river-filled forest, there are mountains, plains and even a small desert. Canada has (or shares with the USA) seven of the world's largest lakes and also contains three of the globe's longest 20 rivers. The country is blessed with the most freshwater of any country. About 25% of the country is covered in forest. Canada's highest mountain, Mt Logan at 5951 metres, is found in the south-west Yukon.

Despite being bordered on three sides by oceans Canada is not generally viewed as a maritime country. This is in part due to the large, central regions which contain the bulk of the population and dominate in so many ways. Also the Rocky Mountains and Niagara Falls, the country's two best known and most visited geographic features, are found inland.

From eastern Quebec to the eastern edge of the country the Atlantic Ocean plays a major part in the population's day-to-day life and offers the visitor much to discover and explore. The same can be said of British Columbia to the west with Vancouver Island and many other smaller islands in the Pacific Ocean.

Canada can be divided into seven geographic regions each with its own characteristic scenery and landforms.

The far eastern area, the Appalachian Region, includes Newfoundland, Prince Edward Island, New Brunswick, Nova Scotia and the part of Quebec south of the St Lawrence River. The land is mainly hilly and wooded.

The St Lawrence-Great Lakes Lowland is roughly the area between Quebec City and Windsor, Ontario, and includes most of the large towns, cities and industry. In all, about half of Canada's people live here. The land, originally forested, later nearly all used for farming, is generally flat.

Centrally, below vast Hudson Bay, the most dominant characteristics of the Canadian map, are the Hudson Bay and Arctic Lowlands. This region is mainly flat, bog and muskeg – little-inhabited or visited with the notable exception of Churchill, Manitoba.

Most of the north is taken up by the Canadian Shield, also known as the Precambrian Shield, formed 2.5 billion years ago. This geographic area covers all of northern Manitoba, Ontario and Quebec and stretches further east across Labrador and west to the northern edge of Alberta. It's an enormous ancient, rocky, glacially sanded region of typical Canadian river and lake-filled timberland. It is also rugged, cool and little-developed, with mining and logging the two primary ingredients in human settlement. This semi-remote area is best explored by visiting and/or camping in the government parks throughout the region.

The fifth region, the Great Plains, runs through Manitoba, Saskatchewan and parts of Alberta. The plains, formerly grasslands, make up a huge, flat region now responsible for Canada's abundant wheat crop.

The sixth geographic area is the Mountain or Western Cordillera Region covering British Columbia, the Yukon and parts of Alberta. Mountains dominate this region. The Rocky Mountains form the eastern edge of the area rising from 2000 to 4000 metres. Between them and the coastal peaks lie a series of lesser mountain ranges and valleys. Among the latter is the long, narrow valley called the Rocky Mountain Trench.

The interior of British Columbia consists of countless troughs, plateaus, hills, gorges, basins and river deltas. The province is by far the most scenically varied and spectacular in the country. Further north, the twenty highest mountains in the country are found in the Yukon.

Lastly, there is the far north, the Arctic region. The northernmost section of the north is made up of islands frozen together for much of the year.

## CLIMATE
### Seasons

| | |
|---|---|
| Summer | June-August |
| Fall (Autumn) | September-October |
| Winter | November-March |
| Spring | April-May |

Canada has four distinct seasons all of which occur right across the country although their arrival times vary. The single most significant factor in climate and even day to day weather is latitude. In just a few hours travelling north by road a drop (sometimes a considerable one) in temperature can often be felt.

The warmest area of Canada is along the US border. It's no accident that nearly everybody lives in this southernmost region. The overall warmest areas of the country are British Columbia's south and central coast and southern Ontario particularly around the Niagara Peninsula. These districts have the longest summers and the shortest winters.

July and August are the warmest months across the country and generally they are reasonably dry. Along the US border, summer temperatures are usually in the mid and upper 20°Cs. Each year there are a few days in the 30°Cs. Manitoba through to central British Columbia gets the hottest summer temperatures as well as the most

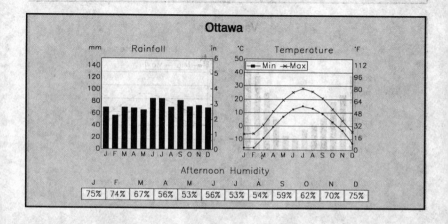

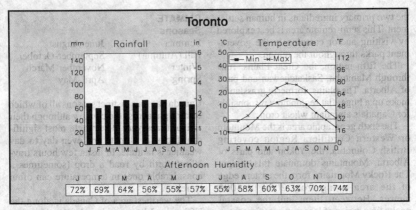

## Toronto

### Rainfall

| | | | | | | | | | | | |
|---|---|---|---|---|---|---|---|---|---|---|---|

### Temperature

Min  Max

### Afternoon Humidity

| J | F | M | A | M | J | J | A | S | O | N | D |
|---|---|---|---|---|---|---|---|---|---|---|---|
| 72% | 69% | 64% | 56% | 55% | 57% | 55% | 58% | 60% | 63% | 70% | 74% |

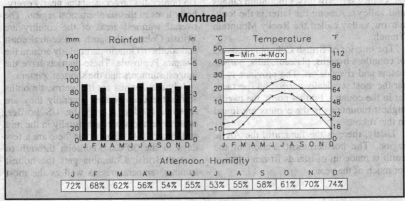

## Montreal

### Rainfall

### Temperature

Min  Max

### Afternoon Humidity

| J | F | M | A | M | J | J | A | S | O | N | D |
|---|---|---|---|---|---|---|---|---|---|---|---|
| 72% | 68% | 62% | 56% | 54% | 55% | 53% | 55% | 58% | 61% | 70% | 74% |

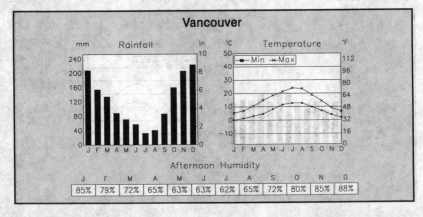

## Vancouver

### Rainfall

### Temperature

Min  Max

### Afternoon Humidity

| J | F | M | A | M | J | J | A | S | O | N | D |
|---|---|---|---|---|---|---|---|---|---|---|---|
| 85% | 79% | 72% | 65% | 63% | 63% | 62% | 65% | 72% | 80% | 85% | 88% |

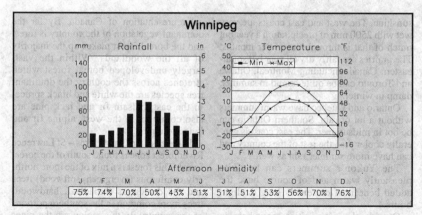

## Winnipeg

Rainfall / Temperature

Afternoon Humidity

| J | F | M | A | M | J | J | A | S | O | N | D |
|---|---|---|---|---|---|---|---|---|---|---|---|
| 75% | 74% | 70% | 50% | 43% | 51% | 51% | 51% | 53% | 56% | 70% | 76% |

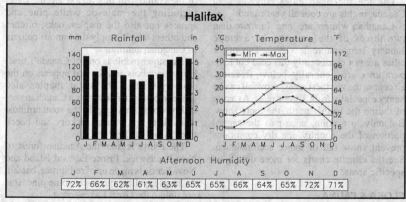

## Halifax

Rainfall / Temperature

Afternoon Humidity

| J | F | M | A | M | J | J | A | S | O | N | D |
|---|---|---|---|---|---|---|---|---|---|---|---|
| 72% | 66% | 62% | 61% | 63% | 65% | 65% | 66% | 64% | 65% | 72% | 71% |

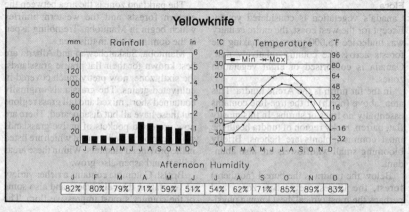

## Yellowknife

Rainfall / Temperature

Afternoon Humidity

| J | F | M | A | M | J | J | A | S | O | N | D |
|---|---|---|---|---|---|---|---|---|---|---|---|
| 82% | 80% | 79% | 71% | 59% | 51% | 54% | 62% | 71% | 85% | 89% | 83% |

sunshine. The west and east coasts are very wet with 2500 mm of precipitation a year but much of that is through the winter months. The prairies are fairly dry all year but south-eastern Canada including Montreal, Ottawa and Toronto can be quite humid in summer, damp in winter.

Ontario and Quebec have warm summers without a lot of rain. Southern Ontario can be hot in midsummer. The east coast is generally cooler than the rest of the country and can have more summer rain as well.

The Yukon's summers can be quite pleasantly warm and of course have the added benefit of extremely long daylight hours.

Outside the main cities, anywhere in Canada, nights are cool all year round.

Canadian winters are long. In more than two-thirds of the country the average January temperature is -18°C. The major cities are not consistently this cold but temperatures are generally below freezing. Except in the warmest areas, snowfall can be heavy especially from Toronto east. As a rule of thumb the further north, the more snow. But only to a point, once past the central portion of the country, the dry conditions prevent snow fall of major accumulation. See the climate charts for more details on specific areas.

## FLORA & FAUNA
### Flora

Canada's vegetation is considered young. Except for the west coast, the entire country was under ice 15,000 years ago making the forests across the country relatively new. Canada is comprised of eight vegetation zones.

In the far north is the Arctic tundra. This area, above (north) of the tree-line contains essentially no trees or shrubs. In this mostly flat, barren, rocky region of tundra heath the most common plants are lichens. Briefly blooming small wildflowers are also abundant.

Below the tundra is the boreal (northern) forest, the largest vegetative zone, and perhaps the most typical, best known physi-

cal representation of Canada. By far the dominant vegetation of the country is forest and the boreal forest makes up the majority of all the woodlands. Within the vast, largely undeveloped boreal forest which stretches across the country the dominant tree species are the white and black spruce. In the east, balsam fir and jack pine are also common, in the west, alpine fir and lodgepole pine.

In the east, the Great Lakes – St Lawrence River forest zone is found south of the boreal forest. This forest is a mix of the more northerly coniferous (evergreen, softwood) trees and the deciduous (broadleaf, hardwood) trees more common in the southern portions of the country. In this region are the pines including the majestic white pine and spruces but also the maples, oaks, birches and others which supply the famous colours of Canadian autumns.

The sugar maple is one of Canada's best-known symbols and the leaf appears on the country's flag. The sugar maples also produce edible maple syrup, a Canadian speciality worth sampling. In the southernmost areas there are walnut, hickory and beech trees as well as fruit trees.

The fourth region, the Acadian forest of New Brunswick, Prince Edward Island and Nova Scotia is made up of red spruce, balsam fir, maple, yellow birch and some pine. It is not unlike the Great Lakes forest.

The parkland zone is the area between the eastern forests and the western prairies which begin in Manitoba. Trembling aspen is the dominant tree in this area.

Manitoba, Saskatchewan and Alberta are best known for their flat prairie grasslands, the sixth zone, now pretty much covered in cultivated grains. The grasslands originally contained short, mixed and tall grass regions but these have all but disappeared. There are now protected pockets of native grasslands which can be visited some of which are listed in the provincial chapters. Within these areas willow and aspen also grow.

British Columbia contains a richer variety of vegetation than elsewhere and also some of the country's most impressive flora. The

Rocky Mountain forest consists of sub-alpine species such as Engelman spruce, alpine fir and larches. In areas of higher elevation there are lodgepole pine and aspen. Scattered around south-east BC forests also contain some of the species found at the coast but here they do not attain the dramatic size seen further west.

It is around the coastal areas though, in the Pacific Coast forest, that the truly awesome trees of the country may be seen. This last vegetation area is characterised by the ancient, gigantic western red cedar, Douglas fir, western hemlock and Sitka spruce. These are the forests which inspire the major environmentalist battles against the logging industry. These west coast forests are the oldest in the country with some specimens over 1000 years old.

Among the country's countless wildflowers, just a few favourites and commonly seen

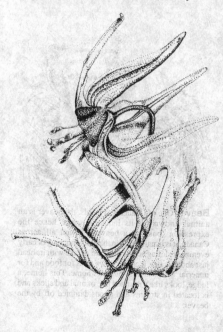

Avalanche lillies

ones are mentioned. For those with a keen interest, guide books to them all and to the country's trees are available at better bookshops.

Throughout the east, canoeists will appreciate the fragrant water lily, a large white flower with yellow centre surrounded by rounded flat leaves which sit on the water.

The trillium, the provincial flower of Ontario, is one of the most popular of wildflowers. Trilliums bloom in the spring in shaded areas of the Ontario and Quebec woods, their large white or pink flowers often nearly carpeting whole sections of the forest floor. They grow about 20 cm high and have three distinct petals.

The pitcher plant seen from Saskatchewan to Newfoundland and Labrador in bogs is carnivorous, that is, it feeds on insects. The leaves collect rainwater. Insects are attracted to the plant by its purplish-red colour and odour. They fall down the slippery leaves into the water where they drown and the plant then digests them. Even with all the protein the pitcher plant does not grow much taller than the length of an adult's hand.

The pickerel weed, with its deep-blue, purplish spiked flower and narrow, long, green leaves, grows around ponds and shallow streams from Ontario to Nova Scotia.

Loosestrife is a beautiful waist high bright pinky-purple plant seen along roadsides and in ditches and marshes across the country. Now considered a nuisance weed because of its rapid growth and spread which crowds out other native aquatic plants it was once sold as a garden ornamental. Across the Maritimes the lupine (blue, pink or somewhere in between) grows wild in fields and by the roadsides.

Sea blush cast a pink glow over the rocks along the southern west coast in spring. Even the early explorers wrote about their beauty as they travelled the Strait of Juan de Fuca.

The bright-red, common Indian paintbrush supplies wonderful contrast to the blues and greys of the Rocky Mountains.

Those with a keen eye who enjoy the less-travelled forest paths anywhere in the country may glimpse the Indian pipe or ghostly pipe. This uncommon plant forces its way up through the debris of the forest floor in shady moist areas. It is a ghostly, silvery white with no greenery and no coloured flowers. They grow about as long as a finger, with the top part nodding over (as in the shape of a pipe) when in bloom.

A delicious assortment of wild berries can be picked across the country. Blueberries are the most common and abundant. The blessed may happen upon a patch of wild raspberries, one of life's exalted moments. The forests, meadows and marsh areas all have plenty of other edible plants and mushrooms. They also have plenty of poisonous plants and mushrooms. Telling the difference is difficult at times even with years of experience and a good book. If in any doubt at all, don't take a chance. Some species can be fatal.

Less deadly but more irritating is the three-leaved but difficult to identify poison ivy found in wooded southern regions of the country. A brush against this small, nondescript plant will result in a skin reaction causing blisters and a very maddening itch.

## Fauna

Canada, with so much land and much of it relatively remote, is abundant in wildlife yet conservation is an ongoing necessity. Campers and hikers, with any luck at all, can see a number of different animals in the wild. The following are some of the most interesting and/or most common.

**Bears** These are Canada's largest and most dangerous animals. They are widely dispersed, and as there are four types, most of the country is populated with at least one kind. For detailed information on the hazards of bears, see the Dangers & Annoyances section in the Facts for the Visitor chapter.

**Grizzly Bear** This is the most notorious bear and is found on the higher slopes of the Rocky and Selkirk mountains of British Columbia, Alberta and the Yukon. The grizzly is big – standing up to 275 cm high. It can be recognised by the white ends of its brownish hair and the hump on the back behind its neck. It can't see well but makes up for that with its

excellent senses of smell and hearing. To make matters worse, it's a very fast animal. The best thing about a grizzly is that it can't climb trees. Like other bears, it is normally afraid of people but can be unpredictable and is easily provoked.

**Black Bear** This bear is found all across Canada and is the one you'll most likely spot. The black bear often mooches around campgrounds, cottages and garbage dumps. It is usually less than 150 cm high and 90 kg in weight. It's active during the day and unfortunately can climb trees.

**Brown Bear** Actually a black bear but brown in colour, the nocturnal brown bear is found mainly in British Columbia, Alberta and the Yukon.

**Polar Bear** The polar bear is very large – up to 680 kg – with thick, whitish fur. It is found only in the extreme north but can be viewed in Churchill, Manitoba and in zoos. A majestic animal, it is graceful in the water despite its size and apparent awkwardness. Due to hunting, it is now a protected animal.

**Beaver** One of Canada's symbols, the beaver is an animal known for its industriousness, hence the expression 'busy as a beaver'. Found all across Canada, it is usually seen in the early morning or early evening paddling across a stream or lake with its head just above water. It chews down trees for food and for material with which to build its home. This home, a lodge, looks like a rounded pile of mud and sticks and is located in streams and ponds dammed off by the beaver.

**Buffalo/Bison** The buffalo now exists only in government parks. It is a huge, mean-looking animal but is really little more than a cow. Its near-extinction has become symbolic of the Europeans' effect on North American Indians and their environment. Technically, Canadian buffalo are bison, not buffalo. There has recently been sporadic attempts to raise buffalo for their meat and it does occasionally show up on menus.

**Wolf** The wolf looks like a large, silver-grey dog. Its ferocious reputation is more misconception than fact. Hunting has pretty well banished this animal to the north land, but you may hear the wolf's howl late at night if you're in the bush. It usually hunts in packs and rarely harms humans.

**Coyote** More widespread than the wolf, the coyote is smaller and more timid, with an eerie howl or series of yaps used for communicating. It is often now more scavenger than hunter and is sometimes the victim of massive poison-bait campaigns by western ranchers and farmers.

**Deer** Various types of deer are plentiful in the woodlands of Canada, ranging across the entire width of the country. They are quiet and timid and the object of much hunting.

**Moose** This is one of the largest animals and again, a popular target for hunters. The moose is found in woods and forests all across Canada, particularly around swamps. Moose are, for the most part, a more northerly ranging animal than deer. They have large, thick antlers and are brown.

The moose is reclusive, generally solitary, and may be seen swimming to escape biting bugs. The male bellows in October and November in its search for a mate. At that time, their behaviour can be erratic and the normally timid moose can become aggressive. Both deer and moose can be road hazards, especially at night. Watch for them and the roadside signs warning of their presence.

**Elk** The elk, a cousin of the moose in the deer family, is found in Europe and Asia. They differ though from the North American elk which is also called the wapiti. Some of this species, a smaller relative of the moose, can be seen around the Rocky Mountains. They are striking animals and can appear quite tame often allowing visitors to approach for picture taking. This is not recommended as people have been attacked in either the rutting or calving seasons.

**Rocky Mountain Goat** This goat is as close as you can get to an all-Canadian animal. Found in British Columbia and the Yukon, it is white and hairy, has horns and looks like an old man. Around popu-

lated areas it is quite tame. Generally though, it prefers the higher, more remote mountain regions. One of its food staples is clay, and you may see one pawing at the ground and gobbling up clumps of earth – strange but true.

**Lynx** Another nearly exclusively Canadian animal, the lynx is a grey cat about 90 cm long and is found all across the undeveloped Canadian woodlands. It has a furry trim around its face and sharp pointed ears. The mainly nocturnal cat eats small animals. Although rarely seen, humans are its main enemy, largely by destroying its habitat. Larger, rarer and even less often seen is the majestic cougar, a full-sized cat.

**Skunk** The skunk resembles a large black cat but has a white stripe down its back and a big, bushy tail. It is seen everywhere – in woods, in larger city parks, even in residential suburbs and their household garbage. It's dangerous only in that its defence mechanism is the spraying-out of the foulest, longest lasting, clothes-clingingest smell you can imagine. The cure is a bath in tomato juice. Watch out!

**Porcupine** A curious animal about 90 cm long, the porcupine weighs 18 kg. It is grey, lives in the woods across Canada and feeds mainly on bark and tree buds. Its protection from abuse are its hollow, barbed quills which project from its body like long hair. They are easily dislodged, as many a dog will remember.

**Caribou** The barren-ground caribou live in herds in the far north and are still used by some Inuit for food and for their hides. Their numbers are now carefully monitored, as over-hunting and radioactive fallout have affected them.

A full herd on its seasonal migration is said to be a wondrous sight. There are some small groups of woodland caribou in more southern areas such as the Gaspé Peninsula of Quebec and the Lake Superior region of Ontario. A cousin of the North American caribou is the reindeer found in Europe and Asia.

**Birds** Five hundred species have been spotted in Canada but many of them are quite rare. One of the most notable among our feathered residents is the loon, a water bird with a mournful yet beautiful call which is often heard on the quieter lakes across the country in early morning or evening. It is most abundant in northern Ontario.

The Great Blue Heron, one of the country's largest birds, is a wonder to see when it takes off. Seen in quiet marsh areas it is very timid, taking to flight at the least provocation.

Canada geese are seen across the country,

especially during their spring and fall migration when the large V-shaped formations are not an unusual sight in the sky. Big, black and grey, these so-called honkers can be aggressive.

There are many varieties of duck, the mallard being the most common, the wood duck the most attractive and colourful. The whisky jack, found mainly in the Rockies, is a fluffy, friendly and commonly seen bird that will eat out of your hand. Bald eagles and ospreys are large, impressive birds of prey. Owls may be seen or heard in wooded areas across the country. Sparrows are the most common garden songbirds. Finches, blue jays, chickadees and cardinals are also readily viewed and/or heard.

Around the coasts there is a very interesting array of marine birdlife including puffins and razor-bills.

**Whales & Seals** Whale-watching has become so popular it is now a successful commercial enterprise (a point for the conservationists). A number of different species can be seen off the coast in British Columbia, in the St Lawrence River in Quebec, and in the Atlantic Ocean off the country's east coast. More details can be found in the text.

In the Atlantic Provinces the bloody, annual seal hunt (for pelts, boots, coats, etc) diminished following the European Union's ban on imports (another point for animal welfare). Indeed, tourists with the money can now fly out to the east-coast ice floes to see, touch and photograph the new-born calves.

a) Blue whale 30m
b) Finback whale 21m
c) Sperm whale 20m
d) Right whale 18m
e) Humpback whale 15m
f) Killer whale 9m

g) Minke whale 8m
h) Northern bottlenose whale 8m
i) Beluga whale 4.5m
j) White-sided dolphin 2.4m
k) Harbour porpoise 2m
l) Human 1.8m

**Fish** Northern pike, bass and various trout varieties are the most common freshwater fish. Salmon in large numbers and a range of species is found on the west coast. The Atlantic salmon of Quebec and the Atlantic Provinces is a highly sought after freshwater version. Arctic char, found only in the far north (and on some southern menus), is also fine eating. Fishing is a popular Canadian pastime and also attracts Americans in large numbers.

Off the coasts there is deep-sea fishing for both sport and table species.

## National Parks

Canada has 36 national parks, ranging from coast to coast and from the US border to the far north. Each has been developed to protect, preserve and make accessible a unique, special or otherwise interesting and significant environment. The number of parks is expanding. A few new ones are currently in the works. All of them are well-worth visiting. Environment Canada (☎ 1-800-668-6767), 351 Saint Joseph Blvd, Hull, Ontario K1A OH3 produces free brochures which outline the features and facilities of the parks.

Most have camping. Several are close to major population centres and are heavily used, others are more remote and offer good wilderness opportunities. Many manage to combine both characteristics. Among the most popular are the Cape Breton Highlands in Nova Scotia, Prince Edward Island in PEI, Riding Mountain in Manitoba, Pacific Rim on Vancouver Island and all of the parks in the western Rocky Mountains.

Some parks rent canoes and/or rowing boats. In parks with numerous lakes and rivers, a canoe is ideal; you can portage to different lakes. Doing this a few times may be hard work but you'll be rewarded with peace and solitude. At other parks, bicycles may be rented. Many have established walking or longer hiking trails. The towns of Banff and Jasper are within the boundaries of the mountain parks of the same names.

Entrance fees to national parks vary from park to park and from nil to several dollars. Some offer free day-use but charge, as they all do, for overnight camping. Some such as Cape Breton and the Rocky Mountain Parks have daily, multi-day and yearly permits. The latter is good for any park in the system.

In addition to national parks, the system contains over 70 national historic parks and sites. These are for 'day use only' and present various aspects of Canadian history, from forts to pioneer homesteads to early Viking settlements. Most include interpretation centres, some with costumed workers, which offer an accurate glimpse of life during an earlier era. Many have picnic areas.

For information on Canada's national parks, contact Environment Canada, formerly known as the Ministry of the Environment, (☎ 1-800-668-6767, 997-2800 Ottawa) at 351, Saint Joseph Boulevard, Hull, Quebec K1A 0H3. Another address worth contacting is 111 Water St East, Cornwall, Ontario, K6H 6S3. This Parks Canada office (☎ 613-938-5866), which may become known as Canadian Heritage under the new government, has information on the federal National Historic Sites and parks. There is currently some overlap in their duties but contacting them both should result in receiving the best information available.

For more information on the national and provincial parks, see Camping under Accommodation in the Facts for the Visitor chapter.

## Provincial Parks

Each province runs its own system of parks and reserves. These can vary dramatically in size, accessibility, characteristics and main purpose. Some are developed for recreation, others to preserve something of historical interest, still others to protect wildlife or natural geographic features of particular beauty or uniqueness.

Some of these provide camping and other conveniences, some do not. In many provinces day-use is free and admission is charged only for overnighters. Most parks have staff knowledgeable in the characteristics of their park who will answer questions and offer lectures, walks and other presentations. Some parks have a biologist or a naturalist on duty. Others are simply a sandy beach.

Provincial tourist boards and offices have free material available which provides some information on the parks under their jurisdiction. These outline camping facilities and basic features of the parks.

There is also a series of provincial historic sites across the country. These tend to be small and are meant, for the most part, to be visited for anywhere from an half an hour up to half a day. They usually deal with one significant event or period of the province's history.

### Crown Land, Reserves & Recreation Areas

Undeveloped crown land (government-owned land) can be used for hiking, canoeing and camping at no cost. Some national or provincial parks are adjacent to crown lands. Other crown lands are scattered over much of the northern areas of the provinces and in more inaccessible remote parts of the country. Some crown land areas do have basic campsites carved out of the woods or lake edges and/or portage routes and hiking paths.

Provincial nature reserves and designated wilderness areas can also generally be used by those seeking wilderness experiences. A careful scanning of provincial maps will often reveal some of these areas. Local people will be able to help with advice and access information. Be well equipped and be especially careful with fire when enjoying these undeveloped areas.

### World Heritage Sites

Canada has 10 sites designated by the World Heritage Convention of the United Nations. Seven of these are natural and all are either national or provincial parks. They are: Gros Morne National Park; Kluane National Park; Nahanni National Park; the Rocky Mountain National Park; Wood Buffalo National Park; Dinosaur Provin-

cial Park and Head-Smashed-In Buffalo Jump, Alberta.

The remaining three sites involve human endeavour: Anthony Island Provincial Park in the Queen Charlotte Islands in British Columbia, an old Haida Indian settlement; L'Anse aux Meadows in Newfoundland, a 1000-year-old Viking camp; and Quebec City, a European-style gem. All are definitely worth visiting.

### GOVERNMENT

The form of the government of Canada is a constitutional monarchy.

Canada is ruled by a parliamentary system with the head of state officially remaining the Queen of England. Within Canada the appointed Governor General is the Queen's representative. The upper house, or Senate, also made up of appointees, is deemed to be the house of review regarding potential legislation. Mostly it acts as a rubber stamp for the wishes of the elected lower house, generally known as the House of Commons. Senate reform or its abolition is an ongoing debate within the country.

The head of the political party with the most elected representatives in the House of Commons becomes the prime minister, the leader of the country. From the members of parliament within his own party he or she then selects a cabinet, which in effect runs the country and initiates any legislation. Federal elections occur at least once every five years and, unlike in the USA, leaders can run for as long as the people let them. Governments are elected for five years, but elections can be called earlier.

The 10 provinces are largely self-governing and are presided over by premiers, elected provincially. A lieutenant-governor appointed by the federal government represents the monarchy, but takes instructions from Ottawa. The lieutenant-governor calls the leader of the party which has won an election to form the government. That leader becomes premier and forms a ministry from other elected members of the party. The two northern territories are for the most part the domain of the federal government although more independence is being sought (and some has been granted to the eastern part of the Northwest Territories).

The constitution consists of both written proclamations under the Constitution Acts (1867 and 1932) and unwritten conventions. Updating, changing and clarifying constitutional matters and the balance of powers between the provinces and between them and the federal government are on-going contentious issues.

## Political Parties

Canadian voters were 'cranky' about entering the '90s as one recently losing politician lamented. This general widespread dissatisfaction has meant major changes in voting patterns.

The last federal election changed the scene in Ottawa more than anyone could have foretold. The lambasting that the Progressive Conservatives and their leader Kim Campbell took has resulted in fundamental alterations in parliament.

That the Liberals (Grits) won a landslide majority is not so unusual, even the Mulroney Conservatives (Tories) did that. It was more who else won and who lost. Now forming the official opposition, after garnering the second highest number of seats in the country is the Bloc Québecois party of Quebec. They have no members in any other part of Canada and their stated goal is to work toward the separation of Quebec from the rest of Canada. They rose dramatically and nearly swept the province of Quebec which, due to its large size and population, can supply enough seats to out-elect more widespread parties.

In third place, a mere two seats behind, another regional party, the Reform Party of Canada, based in Alberta, came out of nowhere. Their platform of fiscal restraint, deficit reduction and less government/more responsibility attracted voters across the country but in huge numbers in Alberta and British Columbia.

Between the overwhelming number of votes for the Liberals and the support given the two regional upstarts, the Conservatives and NDP (New Democratic Party) have found themselves without enough backing to even maintain official party status and the privileges that brings. The future of these two parties federally is in some doubt.

Until this upheaval, the party structure was somewhere between stable and staid. The three principal political parties were the Liberals (who for much of the country's history have virtually owned the reins of power), the Progressive Conservatives (not a lot unlike the Liberals but without the success) and the NDP (known as the 'socialist menace').

The Conservatives have been voted in every once in a while, apparently as an effort to keep the Liberals somewhat humble and honest. The NDP has never formed a federal government and always came up third. They have, however, ruled provincially in several provinces and generally accept their opposition status, considering themselves the 'conscience of the nation' keeping socialist-type initiatives on the burners.

Provincially, the three main parties are again the Liberals, the Progressive Conservatives and the NDP. In British Columbia the Social Credit Party periodically forms a government. The provincial parties generally keep their distance from their federal cousins and act independently from them. The voters, too, treat them differently and have elected the NDP in four different provinces within the past 10 years. The Parti Québecois (provincial party) of Quebec stresses Quebec rights and the possibility of separation from the rest of Canada.

## Flag & Anthem

Canada's current flag was proclaimed in 1965 after 2000 public design entries were hotly debated in parliament. The side bars represent the ocean boundaries and are not blue because an important reason for the entire procedure was to show independence from Britain and France. Both of their flags are red, white and blue. Before the new flag, between 1924 and 1965, the Red Ensign, which included a Union Jack, rippled over the country.

Each province also has its own flag most of which I dare say would not be recognised by many Canadians. The white and blue 'fleur de lys' of Quebec is probably an exception.

The national anthem, 'O Canada', was composed by Calixa Lavalée in 1880.

## ECONOMY

Canadians enjoy the high standard of living that major Western countries are accustomed to and tend to take for granted. Income and employment has fallen over the past 10 years so maintaining the wealth experienced by the previous generation is becoming ever more difficult, even elusive. Today nearly half the work force is women and by far the majority of households have two incomes, often by necessity.

The Canadian economy is based, as it always has been, on abundant natural resources; Canadians as hewers of wood, drawers of water. These natural renewable and non-renewable riches include fish, timber and wood products, minerals, natural gas, oil and hydroelectricity. Although only 5% of the land is arable, the agricultural sector, primarily in wheat and barley, accounts for much of the Canadian export total.

Manufacturing has long been a weak component of the economy and today employs just 14% of the country's workers. The most important manufactured product is motor vehicles. Hi-tech industries and developers in the space and computer fields are recent additions to this area but remain small thus far.

By far the largest part of the economy at a whopping 75% is in services which includes an enormous civil service. Banking, insurance, education, communication and consulting bring in foreign exchange. The rest of the service sector does not.

The country's major trading partner is the USA although business people are increasingly strengthening ties to Japan, China and all of the Pacific Rim. Mexico, too, is poised to become a major trading partner.

The high degree of foreign ownership of Canadian business has also been problematic, drawing profits away from the country. Overall, about 40% of the country's industry is owned by non-Canadians, led by the Americans.

Currently unemployment hovers around 10% with regional variations, and the inflation rate is about 2%.

Canada has an immense 'underground economy'. This does not refer simply to various, more or less traditional, criminal activities but the hidden transactions of legitimate businesses done in order to avoid paying tax. Estimates of the extent of this underground economy range to over 20% of the country's internal economic output! This is a staggering amount of taxes going unpaid which means rates have to go up. This means people feel hard done by and so redouble their efforts to avoid paying. The car mechanic offers a tune-up, you offer to fix his plumbing. You stay at my B&B, I'll design you a brochure, the variations are infinite. There are even 'contra' or service-exchange clubs to join. All by word of mouth, of course.

Many transactions are done 'under the table', meaning paid for in cash with no bills, receipts, written guarantees or paperwork generated. Offering to pay cash usually results in a lower price as well as the tax saving. On top of this there is all the cross-border shopping done in the USA with goods brought back hidden in the trunk or under the sleeping baby with no duty paid. And then there is the large-scale smuggling of liquor and cigarettes. Obviously, the government has a bit of a problem but answers are difficult to find.

## POPULATION & PEOPLE

Canada's population is now just under 27,000,000. About 40% Canadians are of British stock. French descendants of the original pioneers long made up about 30% of the population but this has dropped (and continues to fall) to about 25%. Most people of French descent live in Quebec but there are large numbers in New Brunswick, Ontario and Manitoba.

The English-speaking population has grown mainly by immigration from the old country and the USA. Over 3½ million Canadians are of Scottish or Irish ancestry.

Generally speaking, the French are Catholic, the British Protestant, but religion does not play a large part in Canadian life.

Early Central and Eastern European settlers went to the prairies but can now be found everywhere, particularly in the large cities. Canada's third-largest ethnic group is German. Other major groups are Italian, Ukrainian, Dutch, Greek, Polish and Scandinavian. More recently, Asians, particularly Chinese from Hong Kong, and to a lesser degree, Latin Americans and Blacks from the Caribbean have been immigrating in larger numbers. Canada receives refugees from around the world. Unlike the early days of rapid expansion and settlement, today's arrivals head for the large cities. Toronto, the centre for international immigration, is one of the most cosmopolitan cities in the world.

## Aboriginal Peoples

These now number about 330,000 Native Indians and 27,000 Inuit, roughly a third more than when White people first arrived. There are also approximately 400,000 Métis, the name used to denote those of mixed aboriginal and European blood. All together the three groups make up about 4% of Canada's total population today. The majority are found in the Yukon, Northwest Territories and Ontario but every province has some aboriginal communities.

Inuit is the general name for the Eskimo peoples in Canada. This is their preferred name, as it distinguishes them from the Eskimo of Asia or the Aleuts of the Aleutian Islands.

Collectively the three groups are also called Native Canadians. Another term which has gained currency is 'First Nations' which recognises the one-time independent status of individual aboriginal groups.

Since the early pioneering days the Native Indians' lot has been marked by sadness and tragedy. At first their numbers dropped dramatically with the influx of European diseases. Then they lost not only their power and traditions but also their land and eventually, in many cases, their self-respect.

Today, there are about 2250 reserves scattered across Canada and 600 government registered Native Indian 'bands' which has become a political and organisational term. Every Indian is officially affiliated with a band. Some bands can own more than one reserve.

About 72% of Native Indians now live on these government reserves, most in poverty and on some form of government assistance. In the cities, with little education and few modern skills, many end up on skid row. Infant mortality, life expectancy, literacy, income and incarceration rates all compare unfavourably with those of other Canadians.

Native Indian leaders have since the early 1980s become more political, making stands on constitutional matters, land claims and mineral rights. Today a range of national organisations such as the Assembly of First Nations keep Native Canadian interests from being pushed aside. It is through these channels, however slow-moving, that the Native Canadian voice will be heard in the future. Most Canadians now feel the aboriginal peoples have had a raw deal and sympathise with many of their complaints.

This, however, has not so far resulted in the introduction of many concrete attempts to improve the situation. Both provincial and federal governments are finding it less and less possible to ignore the state of affairs, and many issues regarding Native Canadian rights and claims are currently before the courts. Among the many issues to be dealt with is some form of self-government for aboriginal peoples. Native Canadian schools to provide control over religious and language instruction and a Native justice system are being discussed.

Native Canadians have also become more active in revitalisation movements which encourage original spirituality, Native culture, language and a respect for their history.

**Note**

In North America, Indians from the Asian subcontinent are often called East Indians to distinguish them from the indigenous peoples. People from the Caribbean countries are sometimes referred to as West Indians.

**EDUCATION**

Under the jurisdiction of the provinces, Canada provides free education from elementary right through to high school (secondary school). Beyond that tuition must be paid in what are known as community

colleges (CÉGEPS in Quebec) and university although the true cost is subsidised through taxes. Community colleges present one to three-year programmes in a range of fields from graphic design to jewellery-making to nursing. These are taught under the broad categories of Arts, Business, Science & Technology and Health Services. Universities provide higher academic and professional training.

At the early levels, there are two basic school systems, known as the public and the separate. Both are free and essentially the

---

**Canadian Firsts, Inventions & Discoveries**

Canadians can lay claim to quite an assortment of the products of human ingenuity. The Native Indians have given the world snowshoes and the birch-bark canoe; the Inuit developed the winter parka and accompanying boots known as mukluks and the kayak. More recent Canadian inventions include the electron microscope and the manipulable space arm used on the US space shuttle craft.

Canadians have been active in the food arena, too. Important research developed strains of wheat suitable to a variety of world climates. Pablum, a baby cereal, was created in Canada and perhaps even more significant, was the development of instant mashed potatoes. The country's most important, best-known fruit, the MacIntosh apple comes from a wild apple tree found in Ontario and which was reproduced through grafting. The chocolate bar was created by Ganong Brothers Ltd which still produces bars and chocolates in St Stephen, New Brunswick. Canada Dry Ginger Ale is well known throughout the world.

Other firsts include the paint roller (a simple yet great little device), the telephone, the wireless photograph transmitter, the friction match, the chainsaw and the snowmobile. To clear snow, the rotating snowplough was created in 1911 and ten years later the snowblower.

Canadians have pioneered the development of short take-off and landing (STOL) aircraft. For trains, the observation car known as the dome car, was designed in Canada.

The use of calcium carbide-acetylene gas for light was discovered by Canadian Thomas Wilson. It replaced kerosene, another Canadian invention, and led to the formation of the giant Union Carbide Company. Standard Time adopted around the world was devised in Canada.

In the world of fashion (or more critically, relations between the sexes) Canada can lay claim to both the push-up bra created by Canadelle in Montreal in 1963 and the clothes zipper.

Insulin was discovered by Banting and Best in 1921. The radiation source stronger than X-rays, cobalt, used to treat cancer around the world was developed in Canada.

The first batteryless radio was invented in Canada in 1925 and the first all electric, batteryless radio station followed two years later. It was called CFRB and to this day the station in Toronto is the most listened to in the country. The IMAX large format films and technology were developed by a Canadian company. Young Peoples Theatre (YPT) of Toronto pioneered true theatre geared to children using professionals who don't condescend to the audience.

Greenpeace, one of the world's predominant environmental groups was founded in Vancouver. On the other hand, the green, plastic garbage bag, seen all over North America, was also created in Canada.

Two Canadians created Trivial Pursuit, a board game which swept the world even outselling Monopoly. About 50 million have been sold.

The inexpensive Laser sailboat popular around the world was designed by Canadians. Ice hockey was developed in the mid-1800s. And perhaps to the chagrin of the country's US friends, it should be noted that the game of basketball was created in Canada. ∎

same but the latter is designed for Catholics and offers more religious education along with the three 'R's. Anyone can attend either one but the two systems do split pretty much along religious denomination.

French-immersion programmes, in which English children are taught all their courses in French, are quite popular across Canada.

There are also a number private schools but no real private system. Schools in this category include alternative educational methods such as Waldorf and Montessori.

The education system has been under constant scrutiny in recent years as students leaving high school have fared poorly in international testing, have been called essentially illiterate by universities and poorly prepared by business leaders. Educators cite lack of funding, poor facilities and the need to act as disciplinarians, counsellors and social workers as well as teachers as unsolved problems.

A national survey in 1989 found that 62% of Canadians had enough reading skills to get through an average Canadian day reasonably competently. Numeracy came out to about the same percentages.

Not quite half of all Canadians finish high school. About 10% have a university degree. Students from around the world attend Canadian universities.

## ARTS & CULTURE
### Literature

Canada has and is producing an impressive body of writing. Most of it has appeared since the 1940s.

Among the best known, most-read poets are E J Pratt, Earle Birney, Gwendolyn McEwen, Irving Layton, Leonard Cohen (who also wrote the less-known novel, *Beautiful Losers*, which I highly regard), BP Nichol for concrete poetry, Michael Ondaatje, Milton Acorn and Al Purdy.

Perhaps more familiar internationally are short story and novel writers such as Margaret Atwood, Mordecai Richler, Margaret Laurence, Marion Engel, Timothy Findley, Robertson Davis, Alice Munro, W O Mitchell and Morley Callaghan.

Canada seems to produce writers who excel in the short story so an anthology of these would make a good introduction to Canadian fiction. For a short story collection, try one of the anthologies regularly published by Oberon Press or by Penguin.

English writer Malcolm Lowry spent most of his productive writing years in British Columbia, many of them in a basic shack on the beach near Vancouver.

French Quebec writers who are widely read in English include Anne Hebert, Marie-Claire Blais, Roch Carrier, Gabrielle Roy and Mavis Gallant.

Two Native Canadian writers are George Clutesi and Markoosie.

Most good bookstores have a Canadiana section with both fiction and nonfiction works. Two publishers specialising in Canadian fiction are Oberon and House of Anansi. McClelland & Stewart is an important, large Canadian publishing house.

### Music

Canadian musicians have become increasingly well known in the past few decades with several achieving international stature. Many of the most established names have found it necessary to temporarily or permanently establish residency in the USA.

Canadians have perhaps been best known in the field of folk and folk rock. Among the top names are Gordon Lightfoot, Joni Mitchell, Neil Young, Bruce Cockburn, Leonard Cohen and Buffy Ste Marie. In more of a country vein there are KD Lang, Rita McNeil, Ian and/or Sylvia Tyson, Prairie Oyster, George Fox and Anne Murray. Sort of between the two categories are the Cowboy Junkies, Blue Rodeo, the Roches and Kate and Anna McGarrigle. Jeff Healy and Collin James both play scintillating blues guitar.

The country has always tended to produce individualistic musicians who emphasise lyrics and personal sentiments. In rock, Luba stands out in this mould. Brian Adams, Allanah Miles, Heart and Kim Mitchell have all deservedly come by their popularity as have newcomers the Tragically Hip. More corporate music successes include Loverboy and Glass Tiger.

Among Quebec singers who are rarely heard outside that province, except perhaps in France, Gilles Vigneault could be the biggest name. Others are Michel Rivard and Daniel Lavois but there are many more. The province has its own successful pop, rock and semi-traditional folk bands and artists.

The traditional Celtic-based music of the Atlantic Provinces of Canada remains very popular in that region and efforts to hear some are recommended.

In the classical field, three of Canada's best known artists are guitarist Liona Boyd, the late pianist Glen Gould and composer R Murray Schafer.

Pianist Oscar Peterson is the country's highest profile jazz musician.

## Painting
Artists began painting Canada as early as the 1700s and their work has grown to encompass a wide variety of styles and international influences. One of the earliest distinctive Canadian painters was Cornelius Krieghoff who used the St Lawrence River area of Quebec as his subject matter. Out west Paul Kane was equally captivated by the Native Indians and their way of life. Landscape painters travelled and explored the country often following the laying of railway lines.

Tom Thompson and the Group of Seven beginning just before WW I established the style and landscape subject matter which was to dominate Canadian art for about 30 years. The Group of Seven are: Franklin Carmichael, A J Casson, Lawren Harris, A Y Jackson, Arthur Lismer, J E H MacDonald and Frederick Varley. Their work, drawn from the geography of the eastern Canadian lakelands, is still the country's best known both inside and outside Canada. Emily Carr in a similar tradition painted the west coast, its forests and Native Indian villages and totems.

In the 1950s, another group of painters, which included Jack Bush, Tom Hodgson and Harold Town helped bring new abstract influences into Canadian painting. Joyce

Wieland and Michael Snow two of the best known among more contemporary visual artists grew out of this period. Well-known realists include Ken Danby, Alex Colville, Christopher and Mary Pratt and, for nature studies, Robert Bateman.

As with the previous music and literature sections, this is but a very brief overview of some of the country's artists.

## Film
Canadian film is well respected abroad primarily through the work of the National Film Board (NFB) whose productions are, perhaps surprisingly, little-viewed and scarcely known at home. Each year the film board, formed in 1939, releases a combination of animation, documentary and dramatic films. The film board is considered to have created the documentary genre. National Film Board offices can be found in many of the country's large cities. Films are often screened at the centres and, increasingly, videos of the vast collection can be rented.

Canada also has a commercial feature-length film industry. Its output is relatively small and the quality varies in the same way as Hollywood productions. In the past few years Quebec has been the most prolific and artistically successful in film. The better-known movies are subtitled and sometimes dubbed into English.

## Native Art
Among the country's most distinctive art is that of the Inuit of the north, particularly their stone and bone sculptures and carvings. These also represent some of the more affordable pieces, although their prices too can range into the stratosphere for larger works by well-established artists.

Materials used for Inuit carvings include bone, ivory, antler and occasionally horn or wood. By far the most common, though, is a group of rock types known generically as soapstone. They include the soft steatite and harder serpentine, argillite, dolomite and others. Quarried across the far north, the stone material can vary from black to grey to green and may be dull or highly polished.

Carving styles vary from one isolated community to the other across the far north with some better known than others. Almost all work is done completely by hand with low-tech tools. Northern Quebec tends to produce realistic, naturalistic work such as birds or hunting scenes. Baffin Island sculpture is more detailed and finer often with varying depictions of people. The central Arctic area art embraces spiritual themes, and whalebone is often employed.

As a result of interest and appreciation in Inuit carvings there are now mass-produced imitations which are widely seen and sold. Genuine works are always marked with a tag or sticker with an igloo symbol on it. Many are also signed by the artist. The type of retail outlet is also an indicator. A reputable store and not a souvenir kiosk will likely be stocking the real thing. Aside from the maker and the quality, imitations are not often even made of the true raw material and really are of no value or interest.

Inuit artists also produce prints which are highly regarded. Subject matter often is taken from mythology but other works depict traditional day-to-day activities, events and chores.

The best of Native Indian art is also in printmaking although there is some fine carving and basketry. The country's best-known Indian paintings are those by artist Norval Morrisseau. The carvings and totems of Bill Reid from the west coast have established him as a major international figure. Across the country much of what is sold as Native Indian art & craft is pretty cheap and tacky and a poor likeness to the work which was done at one time and to what can still be found with some effort.

Some of the most interesting and best quality items from either Inuit or Native Indian artisans are the clothes: moccasins (*mukluks*), knitted sweaters (from Vancouver Island, known as Cowichan sweaters) and parkas (warm winter coats). Some interesting jewellery and beadwork can also be found.

## Sports

Canada's official national sport is lacrosse, an old Native Indian game similar to soccer but played with a small ball and sticks. Each stick has a woven leather basket in which the ball is caught and carried.

The sport that really creates passion, however, is ice hockey. This is especially true in Quebec, home of the Montreal Canadiens, a hockey legend and one of the most consistently successful professional sports teams anywhere. If you're in Canada in winter, a National Hockey League (NHL)

Native Indian mask

game between good teams is recommended. The season runs from October to April. There are teams in eight Canadian cities and twice that many in US cities although most of the players are from Canada. In Canada, NHL teams are found in Quebec City, Montreal, Ottawa, Toronto, Winnipeg, Calgary, Edmonton and Vancouver. Many other cities have minor league teams.

US-style football, with some modifications, is played in the Canadian Football League (CFL). There are eight teams across the country. Although the Canadian game is faster and more interesting, its popularity has sunk so low that the survival of the league is in question. The championship game, known as the Grey Cup, is played sometime in November.

US baseball has gained a good following especially now that there are teams in Montreal (the Expos), and Toronto (Blue Jays). Toronto earned the World Series Championship in 1992 and 1993.

Soccer and basketball have never been able to catch on and are strictly small-time in Canada. The American professional basketball league, known as the National Basketball Association (NBA), hoping to change that, is planning on expanding into Canada within the next few years.

Skating on frozen rivers and outdoor ice rinks is a common, pleasant way to exercise. Joggers are a familiar sight and roller blades have caught on in the past several years, too. Tennis and golf are actively participated in. Curling is popular across the country as a winter sport for both men and women. The popularity of cycling increases each year.

Both the summer and winter Olympics are participated in and watched with much interest.

More details on spectator sports are given in the relevant province chapters in the book.

## RELIGION

Canada was settled by Christians, primarily the Roman Catholics of France and Ireland and the Protestants of England and Scotland. Even today the largest single religious group is the Catholic but it has been bolstered by

the addition of other Europeans such as the Italians, Greeks and Poles.

Within the Protestant group, the Anglicans form the largest denomination, followed by the United Church. Montreal, Toronto and Winnipeg have considerable Jewish populations. More recent immigration has brought Hinduism and Islam to Canada. The Sikhs in Vancouver have a sizable community. The Chinese populations of Vancouver and Toronto maintain the Buddhist tradition. Canada also has small but determined pockets of rural, traditional religious sects such as those of the Mennonites, Hutterites and Doukobhors.

Regardless, formal religion plays an ever-diminishing role in Canadian life. Attendance at the established churches has declined steadily since WW II. Following in their peers' footsteps, the lack of interest in the religion by the children of immigrants seems cause for some family strife.

Among the Native population, most list their religion as Catholic, an indication of the efficiency of the early Jesuits. There is, however, a small but growing movement back to the original spiritual belief systems based on the natural world and words of the ancestors.

## LANGUAGE

English and French are the two official languages of Canada. You will notice both on highway signs, maps, tourist brochures and cereal boxes. In the west, the use of French is less visible. In Quebec, English can be at a premium. There, roadside signs and visitor information is often seen in French only. Outside Montreal and Quebec City some French or your own version of sign language will be necessary at least some of the time.

Many immigrants use their mother tongues, as do some groups of Native Indians and Inuit. In some Native communities though it is now only the older members who know the original indigenous language. Few White Canadians speak any Native Indian or Inuit language but some words such as igloo, parka, muskeg and kayak are commonly used.

The Inuit languages are interesting for their specialisation and use of many words for what appears to be the same thing; eg the word for 'seal' depends on whether it's old or young, in or out of the water. There are up to 20 or so words for 'snow' depending on its consistency and texture.

## Canadian English

Canada inherited English primarily from the British settlers of the early and mid-1800s. This form of British English remains the basis of Canadian English. There are some pronunciation differences; Britains say 'clark' for clerk, Canadian say 'clurk'. Grammatical differences are few. The Canadian vocabulary has been added to considerably by the need for new words in a new land and the influence of the Native languages as well as the pioneering French.

Canada has never developed a series of easily detectable dialects such as those of England or Germany. There are, though, some regional variations in idiom and pronunciation. In Newfoundland, for example, some people speak with an accent reminiscent of the west country of England (Devon and Cornwall) and some use words such as 'screech' (rum) and 'shooneen' (coward).

The spoken English of the Atlantic Provinces, too, has inflections not heard in the west. The Ottawa Valley has a slightly different sound due mainly to the large numbers of Irish who settled there in the mid 1800s. In British Columbia some expressions reflect that province's history: a word like 'leaverite' meaning a worthless mineral is a prospecting word derived from the phrase 'Leave 'er right there'.

Canadian English has been strongly influenced by the USA, particularly in recent years via the mass media and the use of US textbooks and dictionaries in schools. Most spellings follow British English such as centre, harbour, cheque, etc but there are some exceptions like tire (tyre) and aluminum (aluminium). American spellings are becoming more common, to the consternation of some. Perhaps the best known difference between American and Canadian

English is in the pronunciation of the last letter of the alphabet. Americans say 'zee', Canadians say 'zed'.

Canadian English as a whole has also developed a few of its own distinctive idioms and expression. The most recognisable is the interrogative 'eh?' which sometimes seems to appear at the end of almost every spoken sentence. Although to many non-North Americans, Canadians and Americans may sound the same, there are real differences. Canadian pronunciation of 'ou' is the most notable of these: words like 'out' and 'bout' sound more like 'oat' and 'boat' when spoken by Canadians.

English Canadians have added to the richness of the global English language too with words like kerosene (paraffin), puck (from ice hockey), bushed (exhausted) and moose and muskeg from anglicised Native Canadian words.

## Canadian French

The French spoken in Canada is not, for the most part, the language of France. At times it can be nearly unintelligible to a Parisian. The local tongue of Quebec where the vast majority of the population is French is known as Québecois or *joual*, but variations on it occur around the province. English students in Quebec and even many or most French students are still, however, taught the French of France. This notwithstanding, where many around the world schooled in Parisian French would say *Quelle heure est-il?* for 'What time is it?', on the streets of Quebec you're likely to hear *Y'est quelle heure?* Most Quebeckers will understand a more formal French, it will just strike them as a little peculiar. Remember, too, that broken French can sound as charming as the French's broken English if said with a warm attitude.

Quebec French also often contains English words pronounced in a unique way or variations on them. Announcers and broadcasters on Quebec TV and radio tend to speak a more refined, European style of French. Visitors to the country and students without much real-use experience will have the most luck understanding them. Despite all this, the preservation of French in Quebec is a primary concern and fuels the Quebec separatist movement.

New Brunswick is, perhaps surprisingly, the only officially bilingual province. French is widely spoken, particularly in the north and east. Again, it is somewhat different from the French of Quebec. Nova Scotia and Manitoba also have significant French populations but there are pockets in most provinces.

The following is a short guide to some French words and phrases which may be useful for the traveller. The combination 'ohn' should sound very nasal. The 'n' shouldn't be pronounced. Quebec French employs a lot of English words although with unique pronunciations, so this may make understanding and speaking easier. The following is a guide.

## Greetings & Civilities

Yes.
    wee, often more        *Oui.*
    like 'why'
No.
    nohn                   *Non.*
Please.
    seel voo pleh          *S'il vous plaît.*
Thank you.
    mehr-see               *Merci.*
You're welcome.
    zhe voo-zohn           *Je vous en prie*
    pri, bee-ehn ven-      (often *Bienvene*).
    oo
Hello. (day)
    bohn-joor              *Bonjour.*
Hello. (evening)
    bohn-swar              *Bonsoir.*
Hello. (commonly)
    sa-loo                 *Salut*
How are you?
    common sa vah?,        *Comment ça va?*
    sa vah?                (often *ça va*)
I'm fine.
    sa vah bee-ahn         *Ça va bien.*
Excuse me.
    par-dohn               *Pardon.*

Welcome.
    bee-ahn ven-oo         *Bienvenu.*

## Useful Words & Phrases

big
    grond                  *gran-d*
small
    peh-tee                *petit*
cheap
    bohn mar-shay,         *bon marché,*
    pa sher, ceh           (often *pas chère*
    cheep                  or *c'est cheap*)
expensive
    share                  *cher*
here
    ee-see                 *ici*
there
    lah                    *là*
much, many
    boh-coo                *beaucoup*
before
    ah-vonh                *avant*
after
    ah-preh                *après*
tomorrow
    de-mahn                *demain*
yesterday
    yeah                   *hier*
toilet
    twah-leh               *toilet*
bank
    bohnk                  *banque*
travellers' cheque
    shek vwoy-yazh         *cheque voyage*
the bill
    la-dis-yohn, le        *l'addition, le reçu*
    reh soo
store
    mag-a-zahn             *magasin*
a match
    un feuh                *un feu*
museum
    mew-zay                *musée*
gas
    gaz                    *gaz*
lead-free (gas)
    sohn plom              *sans plomb*
self-serve
    sairvees lee-br        *service libre*

## Questions

where/where is...?
  oo/oo ehh...?          *où/où est...?*
what?
  commonh?               *comment?*
huh? (slang)
  kwah?                  *quoi?*
how much?
  kom-bee-ahn?           *combien?*

## Signs

entrance
  on-tray                *entrée*
exit
  sor-tee                *sorti*
platform
  kay                    *quai*
information
  ron-sayn-mohn          *renseignement*
no camping
  an-ter-dic-shion       *interdiction de*
  de compay              *camper*
no parking
  stas-iohn-mohn         *stationnement*
  ahn-ter-dee            *interdit*
tourist office
  bew-ro dew too-        *bureau du*
  rism                   *tourisme*

## Simple Sentences

I am a tourist.
  zhe swee toure-        *Je suis touriste.*
  est
Do you speak English?
  parlay vooz anglay?    *Parlez-vouz*
                         *anglais?*

I don't speak
  French.
  zhe neh parl pah       *Je ne parle pas*
  fronh-say              *francais.*

I understand.
  zhe com-prohn          *Je comprends.*
I don't understand.
  zhe ne com-            *Je ne comprends*
  prohn pah              *pas.*

## Accommodation

hotel
  o-tell                 *hôtel*

## YHA

  o-bairzh de zheuness   *auberge de*
                         *jeunesse*
room
  shombr                 *chambre*

## Food

restaurant
  rest-a-ronh            *restaurant*
snack bar
  kass krewt             *casse croûte*
eggs
  er                     *oeufs*
French fries (chips)
  pa-tat frit            *patates frites*
bread
  pahn                   *pain*
cheese
  fro-majh               *fromage*
vegetable
  lay-goom               *légume*
fruit
  frwee                  *fruit*

## Drinks

water
  low                    *l'eau*
milk
  leh                    *lait*
beer
  bee air                *bière*
wine
  vahn                   *vin*
red
  roozh                  *rouge*
white
  blohnk                 *blanc*

## Transport

bus
  auto-boos              *autobus*
train
  trahn                  *train*
ticket
  bee-yay                *billet*
plane
  a-vee-ohn              *avion*
return (ticket)
  alay eh reh-tour       *aller et retour*

train station
   lah gahr — *la gare*
bus station
   leh-stas-ion — *la station*
   d'auto-boos — *d'autobus, le terminus*

## Directions

left
   a go-shh — *à gauche*
right
   a drwat — *à droit*
straight ahead
   too drwat — *tout droit*

## Numbers

| | | |
|---|---|---|
| 1 | uhn | *un* |
| 2 | der | *deux* |
| 3 | twah | *trois* |
| 4 | cat | *quatre* |
| 5 | sank | *cinq* |
| 6 | cease | *six* |
| 7 | set | *sept* |
| 8 | weet | *huit* |
| 9 | neuf | *nerf* |
| 10 | dees | *dix* |
| 20 | vahn | *vingt* |
| 21 | vahnt-eh-un | *vingt et un* |
| 22 | vahn der | *vingt-deux* |
| 25 | vahn sank | *vingt-cinq* |
| 30 | tronht | *trente* |
| 40 | car-ohnt | *quarante* |
| 50 | sank-ohnt | *cinquante* |
| 60 | swa-sohnt | *soixante* |
| 70 | swa-sohnt dees | *soixante-dix* |
| 80 | cat-tr' vahn | *quatre-vingt* |
| 90 | cat-tr'vahn dees | *quatre-vingt-dix* |
| 100 | sohn | *cent* |
| 500 | sank sohn | *cinq cents* |
| 1000 | meel | *mille* |

# Facts for the Visitor

## VISAS & EMBASSIES

Visitors from nearly all Western countries don't need visas. Exceptions are citizens of Portugal and South Africa. Tourists from developing or Third World countries do require visas, as do residents of Eastern European countries and Hong Kong. Those from Communist nations definitely need one.

Visitor visas which are free, are granted for a period of six months and are extendable for a fee. Extensions must be applied for at a Canadian Immigration Centre. Visa requirements change frequently and since visas must be obtained before arrival in Canada, check before you leave – Europeans included. A separate visa is required for visitors intending to work or to go to school in Canada.

A passport and/or visa does not guarantee entry. Admission is at the discretion of the immigration officer at the border. This depends on a number of factors, some of which you control. An exit ticket is not officially required, nor a show of money, but you may be asked to present either. It's mostly common sense. If you turn up looking shabby with $20 for a six-month stay, forget it. Have a reasonable amount of money and an estimation of your daily expenses ready. If you have friends or relatives where you can stay, mention it. If you have a Hostelling International card, show it. Visitors from Western countries should have little difficulty.

If you are refused entry but have a visa you have the right of appeal at the Immigration Appeal Board at the port of entry. Those under 18 years of age should have a letter from a parent or guardian.

Aside from the necessary paperwork, admission to the country can depend on a number of factors including: being of good health; being law abiding; having sufficient money; and possibly being in possession of a return ticket out of the country. This latter requirement will not often be asked of any legitimate traveller, especially from a Western country.

### Canadian Embassies

Addresses of some of the Canadian embassies or government offices abroad are:

Australia
    High Commission, Commonwealth Ave, Canberra ACT 2600 (☎ 06-273-3844)
    Canadian Consulate General, 111 Harrington St, Level 5, Quay West, Sydney, New South Wales 2000 (☎ 364-3000); Visa Immigration Office (☎ 02-364-3050)
    Consulate of Canada, 11th Floor, National Mutual Centre, 111 St George's Terrace, Perth, Western Australia 6000 (☎ 321-1151)
Denmark
    Embassy, Kr Bernikowsgade 1, 1105 Copenhagan K (☎ 33-12-22-99)
France
    Embassy, 35 Avenue Montagne, 75008 Paris (☎ 44-43-29-00)
Germany
    Government Trade Office, Immermannstrasse 65D, 4000 Dusseldorf 1
Ireland
    Embassy, 65 St Stephen's Green, Dublin 2 (Note: the immigration section of this office has closed.) (☎ 3-478-1988)
Italy
    Embassy, Via G B de Rossi 27, 00161 Rome (☎ 6-44598.1)
Japan
    Embassy, 3-38 Akasaka 7-Chome, Minato-ku, Tokyo 107 (☎ 3-3408-2101-8)
Netherlands
    Embassy, Sophialaan 7, 2514 JP The Hague (☎ 70-361-4111)
New Zealand
    High Commission, 61 Molesworth St, Thorndon, Wellington (Note: visa and immigration inquiries are handled by the Consulate General of Canada in Sydney, Australia.) (☎ 4-473-9577)
Spain
    Embassy, Edificio Goya, Calle Nunez de Balboa 35, Madrid (☎ 1-430-4300)
Sweden
    Embassy, Tegelbacken 4 (7th Floor), Stockholm (☎ 8-613-9900)

Switzerland
   Embassy, Kirchenfeldstrasse 88, 3005 Berne
   (☎ 31-352-63-81)
Taiwan
   Trade Office, 13th Floor, 365 FU SING North
   Road, Taipei 10483
UK
   Canada House, Trafalgar Square, Cockspur St,
   London SW1Y 5BJ (☎ 258-6600)
USA
   Consulate General, 1251 Avenue of the Ameri-
   cas, New York City, New York 10020-1175
   (☎ 596-1600) (Note: the Canadian Consulate
   Generals in Buffalo, Los Angeles and Seattle can
   provide visa information; and the Consulate
   Generals in Atlanta, Boston, Buffalo, Chicago,
   Dallas, Detroit, Los Angeles, Minneapolis, New
   York, Seattle and Washington all offer tourist
   programmes.)

## Visa Extensions

An application for a visa extension must be
submitted before the current visa expires.
The fee for an extension is $60 per person.
For more information and to obtain an application call or visit a Canadian Immigration
Centre. These can be found in major cities.
Requirements for receiving an extension
include having a valid passport, onward
ticket and adequate finances.

## FOREIGN EMBASSIES, CONSULATES & HIGH COMMISSIONS IN CANADA

Australia
   Australian High Commission, 50 O'Connor St,
   Ottawa, Ont K1P 6L2 (☎ 613-236-0841)
Denmark
   Embassy, 85 Range St, Suite 702, Ottawa, Ont
   K1N 8J6  (☎ 613-2340-704)
France
   Embassy, 42 Sussex Drive, Ottawa, Ont K1M
   2C9 (☎ 613-789-1795)
Germany
   Embassy, 275 Slater St, Ottawa, Ont K1P 5H9
   (☎ 613-232-1101)
Ireland
   Embassy, 170 Metcalfe St, Ottawa, Ont K2P 1P3
   (☎ 613-233-6281)
Italy
   Embassy, 275 Slater St, 21th Floor, Ottawa, Ont
   K1P 5H9 (☎ 613-232-2401)
Japan
   Embassy, 255 Sussex Drive, Ottawa, Ont K1N
   9E6 (☎ 613-236-8541)

Netherlands
   Embassy, 350 Albert St, Ste 2020 Ottawa, Ont
   K1R 1AY (☎ 613-237-5030)
New Zealand
   High Commission, Metropolitan House, 99 Bank
   St, Ottawa, Ont K1P 6G3 (☎ 613-238-5991)
Spain
   Embassy, 350 Sparks St, Suite 802, Ottawa, Ont,
   K1R 7S8 (☎ 613-237-2193)
Sweden
   Embassy, 377 Dalhousie St, Ottawa, Ont K1N
   9N8 (☎ 613-241-8553)
Switzerland
   Embassy, 5 Marlborough Ave, Ottawa, Ont, K1N
   8E6 (☎ 613-235-1837)
UK
   High Commission, 80 Elgin St, Ottawa, Ont K1P
   5K7 (☎ 613-237-1530)
USA
   Embassy, 100 Wellington St, Ottawa, Ont K1P
   5T1 (☎ 613-238-5335)

## Side Trips to the USA

Visitors to Canada who are planning some
time in the USA should be aware of a few
things. First, admission requirements to the
USA when arriving by land can be significantly different than when arriving by air or
sea from your country of origin. These regulations are also subject to rapid change; it's
best never to assume. The duration of the US
visit, whether one afternoon or three months,
is inconsequential; the same rules apply. Visitors to the USA from most Western
countries do not need visas but there are
exceptions. These include Australia, Ireland
and Portugal.

Most visitors to the USA (by air or sea)
are required to have either a return or
onward ticket in their possession. These
tickets may be 'open', that is undated. Visitors entering the USA by land from
Canada are not required to have any ticket
but some show of finances may be
required as well as some indication of a
residence abroad, ie some document that
shows you have a home to return to. Residents of countries for whom US visas are
necessary must get them at home. They
cannot be given in Canada.

As mentioned, the border between Canada
and the USA has tightened up even for citizens of either of these countries. Anyone

travelling with young children should be aware of the extra need for good documentation. This is true whether on plane, bus, train or driving a vehicle. Because of the heightened fear of child abductions parents can find themselves in the unenviable position of having to prove that the baby in their arms is in fact their own.

This is particularly the case for single parents or anyone crossing the border without their spouse. In the latter case, a letter of consent, preferably notarised, from the missing partner should be considered. You may be asked to legally document custody of the child. Commercial carriers such as Amtrak and Greyhound are facing threats of heavy fines for carrying passengers without sufficient documentation and so have been forced to be more strict in requiring proper identification for crossing the border in either direction. Any potential trouble can also be minimised by having valid passports for all members of the family.

Also, for those wishing to visit duty-free shops and perhaps take advantage of the prices, you must be in the USA for a minimum of 48 hours to be entitled to use them. The selection and prices at these shops has never been all that impressive anyway and the concept is a bit overrated. Smokers may find the cigarettes aren't a bad buy.

Check that your entry permit to Canada, whatever it may be, includes multiple entry. For people holding passports to Western countries multiple entry is generally given. But check, because if not, you may find your afternoon side trip across the border to the USA involuntarily extended when Canadian officials won't let you back in!

Lastly, the time spent on a side trip to the USA will be included as time spent in Canada for the purpose of your time allotment upon arrival. For example, if you have been given a six-month stay in Canada and after three months you spend one month in California, upon your return to Canada you will only be permitted to stay the remaining two months.

## DOCUMENTS

Visitors from all countries but the USA need a passport. Two minor exceptions include people from Greenland (Denmark) and Saint Pierre & Miquelon (France) who do not need passports if they are entering from their areas of residence. Americans do need good identification, however, when visiting Canada. Formerly a driver's licence was all that was required (going in the other direction, too, for Canadians) but often this is no longer sufficient. A birth certificate or a certificate of citizenship or naturalisation if not a passport is highly recommended and may indeed be required in some cases before admission is granted. Americans arriving in Canada from somewhere other than the USA should have a passport. Americans travelling in Canada may want to investigate the Canadian Nonresident Interprovince Motor Vehicle Liability Insurance Card which is only available in the USA.

If you've rented a car, trailer or any other vehicle in the USA and you are driving it into Canada, bring a copy of the rental agreement to save any possible aggravation by border officials. The rental agreement should stipulate that taking the vehicle to Canada is permitted.

## CUSTOMS

How thoroughly customs will check you out upon arrival at a Canadian entry point depends on a number of things. First among them are point of departure, nationality and appearance. Arriving from countries known as drug sources or with a history of illegal immigration or refugees will add to the scrutiny. Always make sure the necessary papers are in order.

Don't get caught bringing drugs into Canada: this includes marijuana and hashish, as they are termed narcotics in Canada. The sentence is seven years minimum and it doesn't matter if you're a nice person – the judge has little choice by law.

If you're 19 years old or over you can bring in 1.1 litres (40 oz) of liquor or a case of 24 beers (it's cheaper in the USA) as well as 200 cigarettes, 50 cigars and one kg of tobacco (all also cheaper in the USA). You can bring in gifts up to $60 in value.

Sporting goods, including 200 rounds of ammunition, cameras and film and two days' worth of food can also be brought in without trouble. Registering excessive or expensive sporting goods, cameras, etc might save you some hassle when you leave, especially if you'll be crossing the Canadian-US border a number of times.

If you have a dog or cat you will need proof that it's had a rabies shot in the past 36 months. For Americans, this is usually easy enough; for residents of other countries there may well be more involved procedures. If you must bring a pet from abroad, to save a lot of potential headaches, check with the Canadian government or a representative before arriving at the border.

For boaters, pleasure craft may enter Canada either on the trailer or in the water and stay for up to one year. An entry permit is required and is obtainable from the customs office at or near the point of entry. All boats powered by motors over 10 horse power must be licensed.

Pistols, fully automatic weapons and any firearms less than 65 cm (26 inches) in length are not permitted into the country. Most rifles and shotguns will be admitted without a permit.

### Warning
Do not make any comments, jokes or movements indicating the existence of anything illegal, particularly a weapon and especially at an airport inspection point. Customs agents do not abide this and you will be whisked off, possibly in handcuffs, faster than you'd like. A few years ago a Canadian politician was charged and lost his post over a gun quip at the airport. Be patient and dump your pockets quietly.

### MONEY
### Currency
Canadian currency is much like that of the USA with some noteworthy variations. Coins come in one-cent (penny), five-cent (nickel), 10-cent (dime), 25-cent (quarter)

and $1 (loonie) pieces. The latter which replaced the dollar bill, is an 11-sided, gold-coloured coin known familiarly as the 'loonie' because the common loon (a species of waterbird) is featured swimming on it. There is also a 50-cent coin but this is not regularly seen. Western Canadians seem to use it somewhat more frequently, it is rare in Eastern Canada.

Everyday working bills come in $2 (there is no US two-dollar bill), $5, $10 and $20 denominations. The $50, $100 and larger bills are less common and could prove difficult to cash in smaller places or at night. Gas (petrol) stations, for example, are sometimes reluctant to deal with larger bills. Canadian bills are all the same size but vary in their colours and images. Some denominations have two styles as older versions in good condition continue to circulate.

All prices quoted in this book are in Canadian dollars, unless stated otherwise.

### Exchange Rates
| | | | |
|---|---|---|---|
| Australia | A$1 | = | C$0.99 |
| Germany | DM1 | = | C$0.83 |
| New Zealand | NZ$1 | = | C$0.80 |
| UK | UK£1 | = | C$2.09 |
| USA | US$1 | = | C$1.38 |
| Japan | ¥100 | = | C$1.36 |

Changing money is best done at companies such as Thomas Cook which specialises in international transactions. In some of the larger cities, such companies operate small exchange offices and booths along main streets. Second choice for changing money is the banks or trust companies. Lastly there are hotels (always open at least), stores, attractions and gas stations. The rates at the latter group are not likely to be in your favour.

American Express and Thomas Cook are the best travellers' cheques to use in either US or Canadian dollars. Some smaller places don't know exchange rates, so you'll have to pay for a call to find the rate as well as the mailing charges. Some banks now charge a couple of bucks to cash travellers' cheques, so ask first; if a charge is levied, cash several, as generally the charge remains the same whether it's one cheque or five. Despite this service charge, banks usually offer better rates than hotels, restaurants and visitor attractions, etc. The difference can be a few percentage points. Personal cheques are rarely accepted at any commercial enterprise.

Banking hours have loosened up considerably in the past few years. Many have evening hours or are open part-time on Saturdays. For more information see under Business Hours following.

### Credit Cards
Carrying a credit card (plastic) is a good idea in Canada. Their use is widespread and they can serve a number of purposes. They are good identification (ID) and are more or less essential for use as security deposits for such things as renting a car or even a bicycle. They are perfect for using as a deposit when making reservations for accommodation, even all the Hostelling International (HI) hostels will take credit-card reservations or payments. They can be used to book and purchase ferry tickets, airplane tickets or theatre tickets. Lastly, they can be used at banks to withdraw cash, termed cash advances.

Visa, MasterCard and American Express credit cards are honoured in many places in most larger centres. American Express has the advantage of offering a free mail pick-up service at their offices. In smaller communities, the use of travellers' cheques or cash is advisable.

### Automated Teller Machines (ATMs)
Automated teller machines (ATMs) are now common throughout Canada and as well as being located at banks can be found in some grocery stores, gas stations, variety stores, shopping centres, bus depots, train stations and elsewhere. Known in Canada as banking machines, these can be used day or night, any day of the week. Cards must be applied for at home through your own bank. Ask if the cards are good for use in the Canadian banking networks.

Americans should have little difficulty. Be sure to receive a list of addresses where banking machines can be found or the 800 toll-free telephone number which can be called to help locate one.

### Costs
Finding a place to sleep and eat is not a lot different here than in Europe or other Western countries. The Canadian lifestyle, like the Canadian personality, is a little bit British, a little bit American and somehow different from both. There are no formal social classes, but there are widely different incomes, and therefore a range in housing, eating and entertainment prices.

For most visitors, the biggest expense will be accommodation. There are, however, alternatives to the standard hotels which can make paying for a bed nothing to lose sleep over. The larger cities generally have the more expensive lodging prices, while those in country towns can be quite reasonable. In the far north, accommodation rates are a little more than in the south, only sometimes outlandishly so.

The heavily touristed areas such as Niagara Falls and Quebec City tend not to have really inflated prices because the volume of places to stay means plenty of competition, particularly when it's not peak season. An exception is Banff in the Rocky Mountains which is costly. As a rule, accommodation prices are a little higher in the summer months. After this period, asking about a discount if one is not forthcoming is well worthwhile.

Food prices are lower than those in much of Western Europe but are higher than those in the USA and about parallel to those in Australia.

Gasoline prices vary from province to province but are always more than US rates, sometimes shockingly so. Fill up before crossing the border. Canada's gasoline prices are, however, lower than those in most of Europe.

Within Canada the eastern provinces and the far north have the highest prices. Also, as a rule the more isolated the service station, the higher the prices will be. Alberta has traditionally had the lowest prices. Of course, these prices reflect on all transportation costs.

Buses are almost always the least expensive form of public transport. Train fares, except when using one of the various special price rates, are moderate. Again, they are more expensive than US fares, less than European ones and comparable to those in Australia.

Inter-provincial airfares are high. Distances are great and the competition minimal. Again, always inquire about specials, excursion fares, etc.

Most prices that you see posted do not include taxes, which can add significantly to your costs. See the following Consumer Taxes section. It's a good idea to ask if the price of something includes tax.

### Tipping

Normal tipping is 10% to 15% of the bill. Tips are usually given to cabbies, waiting staff, hairdressers, hotel attendants and bellhops. Tipping helps for service in a bar too, especially if a fat tip is given on the first order. After that you won't go thirsty all night.

A few restaurants have the gall to include a service charge on the bill. No tip should be added in these cases.

Canadians, it might be noted, have an international reputation as being lousy tippers. What's the difference between a Canadian and a canoe? A canoe tips.

### Consumer Taxes

**Provincial Tax** In most of Canada, provincial sales tax must be paid on all things purchased. Alberta has a sales tax only on accommodation in hotels and motels, but the other provinces also have sales taxes on most items bought in shops and on food bought at restaurants and cafés. The Yukon and Northwest Territories have no consumer sales tax.

Some provinces – Ontario, Manitoba, Nova Scotia, Newfoundland and Quebec – allow rebates on goods being taken out of Canada. Check with a provincial tourist

office for information and to obtain the necessary forms for reimbursement – it's worth the trouble on a tent, camera or similarly large purchase. Tax information is published in the provincial tourist information booklets.

Note, that you need to send the original receipts to obtain the tax refund. The originals are also required to receive the GST refunds. Get around this by applying first for the GST refund. The original will be returned. Receipts are not returned from provincial refund offices. Some conditions apply and the form must be posted to the provincial tax office after you return home. For information on Manitoba and Quebec refunds see below under GST.

**Goods & Services Tax** As of 1 January 1991 Canada's controversial Goods & Services Tax (GST) came into law despite massive repugnance by the citizenry and predictable outrage by the opposition parties of government. Known as the Gouge & Screw Tax, it replaces a largely hidden 13.5% federal sales tax on manufactured goods only, with a 7% tax to be applied to more or less every product, service and transaction. Even the government admits this has increased inflation, though by how much is debated.

Unfortunately for tourists, it hits the travel industry hard. Air, train and inter-city bus fares are all subject to the 7% increase. Ditto for taxi fares, gasoline, parking lot costs, tow truck charges, even bicycle repairs.

Perhaps worse, all hotel bills, campsite rentals, car, boat and equipment rentals (eg of skis) all went up by 7%.

Restaurant meals, all snack foods and drinks, alcohol, newspapers, pay phones, stationery and stamps, toiletries, golf fees, caddies and film and photo processing are also all fully taxed. And this GST tax is applied on top of the usual provincial sales tax. In Ontario, for example, this total can mean an additional 15% on a bill, so remember to calculate it in before reaching the checkout cash register.

For visitors or travellers who prepare their own food, there is no tax applied to groceries.

Some tourist homes (the small ones), guesthouses, B&Bs etc don't charge GST for rooms, and foreign visitors should try asking for an exemption from the GST on their hotel bill when making payment. If paid, the GST added to all other accommodation except campsites is refundable.

Several years after this tax's implementation, resentment remains and the new Liberal government has talked of trying to replace it.

A rebate or refund is available for visitors on nonconsumable goods bought for use outside Canada, provided the goods are removed from the country within 60 days. Tax paid on services or transportation is not refundable. The value of the goods taxed must be over $100 and you must have original receipts. Credit-card slips and photocopies are not sufficient. Most 'tourist' or duty-free shops have a GST rebate booklet and mailing form or you can contact Revenue Canada, Custom & Excise, Visitors' Rebate Program, Ottawa, Ontario K1A 1J5. The forms are also available at tourist information offices. The forms can also be used to apply for sales tax rebates on tax paid in the provinces of Quebec and Manitoba. See under provincial taxes above for more information.

**WHEN TO GO**
Spring, summer and fall are all ideal for touring. The far north is best in summer as the roads are open, ferries can cross rivers and it has long daylight hours. Many of the country's festivals are held over the summer, one notable exception being the Quebec Winter Carnival. If you're skiing or only visiting the cities, then winter's OK. Canada's ballet, opera and symphony season runs through the winter months.

Note that outside the main summer season which runs roughly from mid-June to mid-September, many visitor-oriented facilities, attractions, sights and even accommodation may be closed. This is especially true in the Atlantic Provinces. Advantages are the slower pace, lack of crowds, lower prices and perhaps more time for the people serving you. Spring and fall make a good compromise between the peak season and the cold of winter. For campers, though, July and August are the only reliably hot months. For more info, see the climate charts in the Facts about the Country chapter.

**WHAT TO BRING**
Travellers to Canada have no real need for any special articles. Those with allergies or any particular medical ailments or conditions should bring their customary medicines and supplies. Extra prescription glasses and/or contact lenses are always a good idea. A small travel alarm clock is useful and once in Canada extra batteries are not difficult to find.

Those planning trips out of the summer season should bring a number of things to protect against cold. Layering of clothes is the most effective and the most practical way to keep warm. One thin and one thick sweater and something more or less windproof is recommended. On particularly cool days a T-shirt worn under a long sleeved-shirt and then a combination of the above is quite effective. Gloves, scarf and hat should be considered and are mandatory in winter.

Even in winter a bathing suit which weighs next to nothing is always good to throw in the pack. Aside from possible ocean and lake summer swimming there are city, hotel and motel pools some of which are heated and others which are indoors. Some hotels have saunas etc which you may want to take advantage of. A collapsible umbrella is a very useful, practical accessory. A good, sturdy pair of walking shoes or boots is more or less essential for all but the business traveller with no spare time.

For English-language speakers planning on some time in Quebec, a French/English dictionary or phrase book should be considered although these are available in Montreal.

Drivers travelling long distances should have a few basic tools, a spare tyre that has been checked for pressure, a first-aid kit and a flashlight.

## TOURIST OFFICES
### Local Tourist Offices

Each province in Canada has a governmental ministry responsible for tourism and the major cities generally have an office for distributing provincial information. In addition, most cities and towns have at least a seasonal local information office. Many of these are mentioned in the text. The small, local tourist offices are the best place for learning specialised information on the area. As a rule they will have little knowledge or materials on other parts of the country.

### Provincial/Territory Tourist Offices The
provincial tourist offices can supply, at no charge, the basic information requirements including a map and accommodation and camping guides. They also have information on events scheduled for the current or upcoming year. On request, they will furnish more specialised information such as on a particular activity or on organised wilderness package tours. They do not have detailed information on any given area of their province or territory. For this, a city in your area of choice must be contacted by phone, mail or in person.

Each province has one or more major provincial tourist offices located within its borders. These may be in the major city, at provincial boundaries or at a major provincial attraction. These are listed in the text.

Newfoundland & Labrador
Newfoundland Department of Tourism & Culture, Visitor Services Section, P O Box 8730, St John's, Newfoundland A1B 4K2 (☎ 1-800-563-6353, free from continental North America)
Nova Scotia
Nova Scotia Department of Tourism & Culture, P O Box 456, Halifax, Nova Scotia B3J 3N8 (☎ 1-800-565-0000, free from anywhere in Canada; ☎ 1-800-341-6096, free from anywhere in the USA)
Prince Edward Island
Prince Edward Island Department of Tourism, Parks & Recreation, P O Box 940, Charlottetown, Prince Edward Island C1A 7M5 (☎ 1-800-565-7421, free from Nova Scotia & New Brunswick; ☎ 1-800-565-0267, free from everywhere else in North America)

New Brunswick
New Brunswick Tourism, Department of Economic Development & Tourism, P O Box 6000, Fredericton, New Brunswick A1B 4K2 (☎ 1-800-561-0123, free from anywhere in continental North America)
Quebec
Tourism Quebec, PO Box 979, Montreal, Quebec H3C 2W3 (☎ 1-800-363-7777, free from anywhere in continental North America)
Ontario
Ontario Travel, Queen's Park, Toronto, Ontario M7A 2E5 (☎ 1-800-668-2746, free from Canada, continental USA and Hawaii; ☎ 1-800-268-3736, in French – free from anywhere in Canada)
Manitoba
Travel Manitoba, Department 3219, 7th Floor, 155 Carlton St, Winnipeg, Manitoba R3C 3H8 (☎ 1-800-665-0040, free from anywhere in continental North America)
Saskatchewan
Travel Saskatchewan, 1919 Saskatchewan Drive, Regina, Saskatchewan S4P 3V7 (☎ 1-800-667-7191, free from anywhere in continental North America)
Alberta
Alberta Economic Development & Tourism, 3rd Floor, 10155-102nd St, Edmonton, Alberta T5J 4L6 (☎ 1-800-661-8888, free from anywhere in continental North America)
British Columbia
Tourism British Columbia, Parliament Buildings, Victoria, British Columbia V8V 1X4 (☎ 1-800-663-6000, free from continental North America, Hawaii & parts of Alaska)
Yukon
Tourism Yukon, P O Box 2703, Whitehorse, Yukon Territories Y1A 2C6 (☎ 403-667-5340)
Northwest Territories
Northwest Territories Economic Development & Tourism Marketing, P O Box 1320, Yellowknife, Northwest Territories X1A 2L9 (☎ 1-800-661-0788, free from anywhere in continental North America)

### Federal Tourist Offices/Reps Abroad Due
to government restructuring and cut-backs, there is no longer a federal tourism department which supplies information to the public. The Tourism Canada offices which were located in countries around the world have all been shut. As part of decentralisation, all tourism information is handled by the individual provinces.

For basic help in planning a visit to Canada, see your closest Canadian embassy, consulate or high commission, listed earlier in this chapter under Visas & Embassies. They can furnish details on entry requirements, the weather, duty regulations, where to get travel information and the like. Travel agents can also be consulted. Lastly, the provincial offices listed above can be contacted.

## USEFUL ORGANISATIONS
### Canadian University Travel Service

For budget, young or student travellers, this service, known as Travel CUTS offers a wealth of information. This is Canada's student travel bureau with offices in Halifax, Ottawa, Toronto, Saskatoon, Edmonton and Vancouver. Some offices are on university campuses, others have central downtown storefronts.

For student discounts you must have an International Student Identity Card (ISIC) available at these outlets. You must have proper ID though – this isn't Athens or Bangkok.

CUTS deal mostly in ways to get you out of Canada cheaply. They also sell European train passes, arrange working holidays and set up language courses. They can, however, provide tickets and advice for getting around Canada.

Within Canada, CUTS can arrange tours and canoe trips and help with domestic flights. They have a *Discount Handbook* which lists over 1000 stores and service establishments offering bargains to ISIC card holders.

### Hostelling International

Canada is a member of Hostelling International (HI) Canada. Besides offering economical beds, some of the hostels run field trips, operate travel agencies or have stores selling outdoor supplies and guide books. The hostels are also great sources of information through the guests, staff and bulletin boards. For more information on them, see under the Accommodation section in this chapter.

### Canadian Automobile Association

Known as the CAA, this organisation like its counterpart the American Automobile Association (AAA) provides assistance to member motorists. This is done in several ways.

Firstly, is the emergency roadside assistance. Anytime anywhere your car breaks down a call to the CAA will mean help is on the way. They will either get the car started or at no charge, tow it to somebody who will. That person must be paid, however. The CAA limits itself mainly to jumping batteries, fixing flat tyres and the like. This response service is offered 24 hours a day. Unfortunately the chances are that when you need them, everybody else does too: for example in a major snowstorm or when the weather is bitterly cold and nobody's battery will start.

In these cases, you may have to wait a long time. If, on the other hand, you get a flat tyre or run into some other problem in the middle of the night on some lonely highway you won't have trouble waiting your turn and the investment will seem a wise move indeed. Of course, you *do* have to get to a phone.

A second service is that of trip planning and advice. Agents at the local office will help lay out scenic or efficient routes to any given destination and offer maps and some guide books. The value of these varies.

Thirdly, the offices can supply travellers' cheques.

All in all, if you have a decent car the association's help will not be necessary. If you have bought a cheap, older car to tour the country, the fee may well be invaluable and after one or two breakdowns will have paid for itself as towing charges are high.

The head office (☎ 613-226-7631) is at 1775 Courtwood Crescent, Ottawa, Ontario, K2C 3J2. Each province has its own regional office and branches can be found in most major cities and towns. An annual membership costs $54.

## BUSINESS HOURS
### Banks

Banks have slowly been extending their often inconvenient opening hours, but these vary. As a rough guide, most banks are open

Monday to Thursday from 10 am to 4.30 pm, and from 10 am to 5 or 6 pm on Friday. Trust companies open for longer hours, perhaps to 6 pm daily and are often open at least in the morning on Saturday. Some banks now also open for shorter hours on Saturday. No bank is open on Sunday and the whole lot are always closed on holidays. Many banks now have automated teller machines (ATMs) known as banking machines in Canada, which are accessible 24 hours a day.

### Stores

Store hours in Canada are confusing. The issue of Sunday opening has been hotly debated for several years but no consensus has been reached. British Columbia, Alberta, the other western provinces to a lesser extent, plus Quebec and Ontario, tend to have limited Sunday shopping. Eastern Canada is basically closed up tight on Sundays.

In general, cities and their suburbs have the longest retail store hours. Opening time ranges from 9 to 10 am with closing time around 6 pm. Longer hours, until 9 pm, are usually kept on Friday and sometimes Thursday. Shopping malls, plazas, large department stores and downtown stores may remain open until 9 pm every day.

Smaller centres, towns and country villages generally have shorter hours with little evening shopping and nothing much available on Sunday except for milk, bread and movies.

Big cities and some large towns have a limited number of stores which remain open 24 hours. The vast majority of these are convenience shops which sell basic groceries, cigarettes and newspapers. In the country's largest, major cities the odd all-night chemist (drug store) can be found. To locate one, call a hospital or the police.

Major highways have 24-hour service stations for petrol and food.

### Bars

Hours vary according to the province. Most open at noon and close around 2 am. In Ontario last call is just before 1 am. In Quebec laws are more liberal; bars stay open

until 3 or 4 am. The larger cities usually have after hours bars which remain open for music or dancing but stop serving alcohol. Bars in Canada are not permitted to sell take-away alcoholic beverages.

## FESTIVALS & HOLIDAYS

The school summer holidays in Canada are from the end of June to Labour Day in early September. This is also the period when most people take their vacations. University students have a longer summer break running from some time in May to the beginning or middle of September. Labour Day is an important holiday as this long weekend is unofficially seen as the end of summer. It marks the closing of many businesses, attractions etc and the beginning of a change of hours of operation for many others.

Although not officially a holiday, Halloween, 31 October, is a significant (and fun) Canadian celebration. Based on a Celtic pagan tradition, Halloween is a time of ghosts, goblins, witches and the like. Today, it is mainly geared to children who dress in costume and in the evening go door to door where they are given candy treats. Houses are decorated with candle-lit hollowed-out pumpkins. Adults, too, often have night-time costume parties around this time of year. Traditionally costumes have been based on the supernatural but nowadays anything may be seen. Most are homemade but fancy dress can also be bought or rented. In larger cities, the gay community has adopted Halloween as a major event and nightclubs are often the scene of wild costume parties.

### National Holidays

January
New Year's Day (1 January)
April-May
Easter (Good Friday, also Easter Monday for government & schools)
Victoria Day (Monday preceding May 24 except in the Atlantic Provinces)
July
Canada Day, called Memorial Day in Newfoundland (1 July)
September-October
Labour Day (first Monday in September)
Thanksgiving (second Monday in October)

November-December
  Remembrance Day (11 November – banks & government)
  Christmas Day (25 December)
  Boxing Day (26 December – many retailers open, other businesses closed)

## Provincial Holidays

February-March
  Alberta – Family Day, third Monday in February
  Newfoundland – St Patrick's Day (Monday nearest 17 March), St George's Day (Monday nearest 23 April)
June-July
  Quebec – Fête Nationale, formerly known as Saint Jean Baptiste Day (24 June)
  Newfoundland – Discovery Day (Monday nearest 24 June);
  Orangeman's Day (Monday nearest 13 July)
August
  Yukon – Discovery Day, third Monday in August
  All other provinces Civic Holiday (1 August or first Monday in August)

## CULTURAL EVENTS

Major events are listed in the text under the city or town where they occur. There are many others.

The provincial governments publish annual lists of events and special attractions as part of their tourism promotion packages. Each give dates, locations and often brief descriptions. Local tourist departments may print up more detailed and extensive lists of their own, which include cultural and sporting exhibitions and happenings of all kinds. Military and historic celebrations, ethnic festivals and music shows are all included. Some provinces produce separate booklets for summer and winter events.

Major provincial and national holidays are usually cause for some celebration, especially in summer when events often wrap up with a fireworks display. The 1 July festivities are particularly noted for this with the skies lit up from coast to coast.

## POST & TELECOMMUNICATIONS
### Post

The mail service is neither quick nor cheap but it's reliable. Canadian post offices will keep poste-restante mail marked 'c/o General Delivery' for two weeks and then

return it to sender. Some useful information follows:

Standard 1st-class air-mail letter is limited to 50 grams to North American destinations but as much as 500 grams to other international destinations. To the USA, heavier mail can go either by surface or, more expensively, by air in small packet mail. Anything over one kg goes by surface parcel post.

To other international destinations, letter packages, to a maximum of two kg, can be sent by air. Small packet mail up to the same weight can go by either surface or air. Packages over two kg are sent by parcel post and different rates apply. For full details go to a post office; full-page pamphlets which explain all the various options, categories, requirements and prices are available. Suffice it to say there are numerous methods for posting something, depending on the sender's time and money limitations: air, surface or a combination of these. Rates vary according to destination. Mail over 10 kg goes surface only – this is slow.

For added security, speed or other requirements there is registered mail, special delivery and both surface and air mail for packages. Canada Post also offers an international courier-style service.

Some countries require a customs declaration on incoming parcels. Check at the post office.

Aside from the post offices themselves, stamps and postal services are often available at other outlets such as chemists (drug stores) and some small variety stores. Finding them is a matter of asking around. Hotel concessions also often stock stamps.

## Postal Rates

1st-class letter or postcard within Canada: 43 cents (up to 30 grams; includes GST)

1st-class letter or postcard to USA: 49 cents (up to 30 grams)

1st-class letter or postcard to other destinations: 86 cents (up to 20 grams)

Aerogrammes (which are not common) cost the same.

## Telephone

Canada has an excellent telephone system. Rates tend to be low for local use and rather costly for long distances. Overall, the rates are about the same as in the USA but probably more expensive (at least for long distances) than in Europe. Public telephones are generally quite readily available and can be found in hotel lobbies, bars, restaurants, large department stores and many public buildings. Blue or red telephone booths can be found on street corners in cities and towns. Rotary dial phones are pretty much a

### Telephone Area Codes

| | |
|---|---|
| Yukon | 403 |
| Northwest Terrorities (West) | 403 |
| Northwest Terrorities (East) | 819-709 |
| British Columbia | 604 |
| Alberta | 403 |
| Saskatchewan | 306 |
| Manitoba | 204 |
| Toronto City | 416 |
| Greater Toronto | 905 |
| Western Ontario | 807 |
| Central Ontario | 705 |
| South-western Ontario | 519 |
| South-eastern Ontario | 613 |
| Quebec | 819 |
| Montreal | 514 |
| Eastern Quebec | 418 |
| Labrador | 709 |
| Island of Newfoundland | 709 |
| Prince Edward Island | 902 |
| New Brunswick | 506 |
| Nova Scotia | 902 |

thing of the past in Canada and the use of touch tone (push button) telephones has taken over.

The basic rate of a call varies but is generally 25 cents for a local connection. If you use the operator (dial ☎ 0) you do not even need any money. There is also no charge from a public phone for dialling ☎ 411, the telephone information number or for 911, the emergency number. For inquiries on long-distance calls, dial ☎ 1 (area code) 555-1212. There may be a small charge for this service.

Long-distance calls to anywhere in the world can be made from any phone but the rate varies depending on how it is done and when. A call made without the assistance of an operator is not only cheapest but quickest. This can be done if you know the area code as well as the number of the party to be reached. With operator assistance, calls in increasing order of cost are, station to station (no particular person to speak to required), collect (reverse charge) and person to person.

In Canada, long-distance rates are cheapest from 11 pm to 8 am daily. The second most economical time slot is from 6 pm to 11 pm daily except Sunday when this rate runs from 8 am to 11 pm.

The most expensive time to call is from 8 am to 6 pm Monday to Friday.

Reductions can also apply to calls to the USA or overseas. All international rates and codes are listed in the front pages of the telephone book.

The 1-800 numbers which many businesses, ferries, hotels and tourist offices operate are toll free, no long-distance charges apply.

All Canadian business and residential phones are paid for on a flat monthly rate system, the number of calls made is immaterial.

For those who will be using the telephone in hotels, motels, guesthouses, etc, note that many, if not most, places charge a service fee for the use of the phone on a per call basis even for local calls. At maybe 50 cents per call, this can add up resulting in a bit of a shock on the final room bill; especially if you didn't know it was coming!

Many Canadian businesses, tourist attractions and information offices have jumped right in to the use of the touch-tone menu information system. After dialling, the caller is given a range of options and recorded messages to listen to. This can be useful in learning the hours of operation of a museum, for example, but also frustrating because it's so difficult to reach a live person to whom you can direct specific questions. Good luck.

Canadians or visitors with telephone calling cards can make long-distance calls and have them charged to their home number to avoid having to feed the phone a pocketful of change or reverse the charges.

Bell Canada has launched a pre-paid long-distance phone pass. It is sold only in a $20 denomination and is valid for two years. The card should soon be available through vending machines at key locations such as airports and bus and train stations. Other companies are also quickly getting into this new market. Before purchasing any one of the passes be sure to check on how long it is good for and whether it can be used for calls in Canada only, across North America or internationally.

Something new to look for are CardCaller Canada (☎ 733-2163 Toronto) cards which are for sale at some convenience stores and some hostels. These cards available in various values of from $10 to $100 allow the holder to make long-distance calls from any phone quickly until the value of the card has been used up in charges. Calling the supplied number provides dialling instructions in one of six languages. Calls can be made from any touch-tone telephone 24 hours a day, seven days a week.

## Fax, Telex & Telegraph
Facsimile machines are now in wide usage in Canada. Fax machines accessible to the public are available at major hotels, big city post offices and at a range of small businesses in major centres. To locate one of the latter, check under facsimile or stationers or

mail box services in the yellow telephone pages.

Other than in some private businesses, telex is not readily available.

For sending a telegram, contact CN-CP Telecommunications listed in the telephone directory. They will be able to send to any location in Canada or overseas.

## TIME
Canada spans six of the world's 24 time zones. As shown on the map, the eastern zone in Newfoundland is unusual in that it's only a half-hour different from the adjacent zone. The time difference from coast to coast is 5½ hours.

Canada uses Daylight Saving Time during summer. It begins on the last Sunday in April and ends on the last Sunday in October. It is one hour later than Standard Time, meaning a seemingly longer summer day. Saskatchewan is the exception, using Standard Time all year round.

For details of each provincial time zone see the beginning of each province chapter.

Some examples for international time comparisons follow.

If it is noon in London (UST/GMT), it is 7 am in Toronto, 4 am in Vancouver or Los Angeles, 10 pm in Sydney and 9 pm in Tokyo. If it is midnight in London, it is 7 pm in Toronto, 4 pm in Vancouver or Los Angeles, 10 am in Sydney (the following day) and 9 am in Tokyo (also the following day).

## ELECTRICITY
Canada, like the USA, operates on 110-V, 60-cycle electric power. Non-North American visitors should bring a plug adapter if they wish to use their own small appliances such as razors, hairdryers etc. Canadian electrical goods come with either a two-pronged plug (the same as an American one) or sometimes a three-pronger with the added ground. Most sockets can accommodate both.

## LAUNDRY
All cities and major towns have central storefronts known as laundromats with rows of

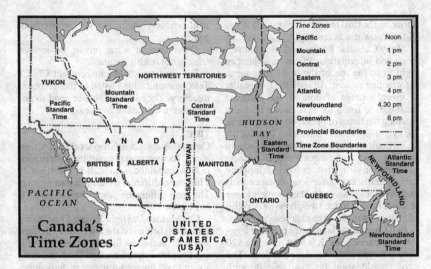

Canada's Time Zones

| Time Zones | |
|---|---|
| Pacific | Noon |
| Mountain | 1 pm |
| Central | 2 pm |
| Eastern | 3 pm |
| Atlantic | 4 pm |
| Newfoundland | 4.30 pm |
| Greenwich | 8 pm |
| Provincial Boundaries | |
| Time Zone Boundaries | |

coin-operated washing machines and dryers. These tend to be open all day until 10 or 11 pm seven days a week. There is rarely an attendant on the premises. Some have machines which will dispense change and others for soap. It is less trouble, more reliable, more convenient and cheaper to bring both. It's fine to go out for a coffee while the wash goes through its cycle but if you leave a load too long it may be dumped on top of a machine when somebody takes it over for their clothes. A wash and dry costs a couple of dollars, most often in one dollar or 25-cent coins.

Also common are dry cleaners, known simply as 'the cleaners', where shirts, dresses, pants and coats can be cleaned in about a day, sometimes two or three. Quick service is usually offered.

The better hotels will likely have an in-house service but rates will be higher than going to the cleaners on your own.

Many campgrounds and some B&Bs have a washer and dryer that guests may use, generally at an extra fee.

## WEIGHT & MEASURES

Canada officially changed from British imperial measurement to the metric system in the 1970s. Most citizens accepted this change only begrudgingly and even today both systems remain in use for many day-to-day uses. The use of imperial measurements has held on in some areas of the country more than others.

All roadway speed signs are in metric – do not go 100 mph! Gasoline is sold in litres but hamburger meat and potatoes are still often sold by the pound. Radio stations will often give temperatures in both Celsius and Fahrenheit degrees.

The expensive changeover has really resulted in a bit of a mess. The old system can never be done away with completely because the Americans, Canada's largest trading partner, still use it. Also, expressions such as 'you can see for miles on a clear day' just don't come out the same in metric.

For help in converting between the two systems, see the chart at the back of this book. Note that the US system, basically the same as the imperial, differs in liquid measurement, most significantly (for drivers) in the size of their gallons.

## BOOKS

Canada has a small but quality publishing industry which is very active in promoting books by and about Canadians.

## People & Society

For more information on Canada's Native People try *Native Peoples and Cultures of Canada* by Allan Macmillan which includes both history and current issues.

The classic book on Canada's Native People, *The Indians of Canada* was written in 1932 by Diamond Jenness. Originally from New Zealand, the author's life is an amazing story in its own right as he spent years living with various indigenous people across the country. The book has been reprinted many times.

*Who Has Seen The Wind* W O Mitchell's best-known book is about a boy growing up. Weyburn, Saskatchewan is the birthplace of the author and the setting for this book.

Canada's best known humorist, Stephen Leacock's *Sunshine Sketches of a Little Town*, based on Orillia (a town at the north end of Lake Simcoe in Ontario), has been called the most Canadian book ever written.

## History

Pierre Berton is Canada's best known chronicler of the country's history. He has written on a wide range of subjects such as the gold rush, the railways and the Depression in an entertaining and informative way. Peter C Newman writes on Canadian business but has also produced an intriguing history of the Hudson's Bay Company, *Caesar's of the Wilderness*, beginning with the early fur-trading days.

A basic primer on the country's history is *The Penguin History of Canada* by Kenneth McNaught.

## General

Among academic writers two who stand out are the late Northrop Frye for literary criticism and Marshall McLuhan for media observations.

John Robert Colombo has written a number of books of Canadian facts, figures and trivia and others on places in Canada such as *Canadian Literary Landmarks*. Mordecai Richler, well known for his fiction, also writes on a range of topics in his opinionated way. *Home Sweet Home: My Canadian Album* is a collection of essays on the country.

Ralph Nader (yes, the US consumer advocate) has put together an interesting and sometimes surprising list of many of Canada's achievements in the book *Canada Firsts*.

The *Canadian Encyclopedia*, a four-volume reference set published by Mel Hurtig and found in any decent Canadian library, is a wealth of information on the country.

For a brief guide to Canada's literature see under Arts & Culture in Facts about the Country.

## Travel Books

Jan Morris, a Welsh travel writer, who has written about many cities around the world, published *City to City* in 1990. Written after travelling Canada coast to coast it is a highly readable collection of essays of fact and opinion about 10 Canadian cities and their people. Note that this book was also published under the name *O Canada: Travels in an Unknown Country*.

The *Maple Leaf Rag* is a quirky collection of travel essays by Stephen Brook. Stuart McLean in *Welcome Home: travels in small town Canada* reveals much about the character of small-town life and describes in a very approachable style some of the changes taking place within them.

Kildare Dobbs wrote of a bus trip across the country in *Ribbon of Highway: The Trans Canada Hwy Coast to Coast*. John and Martha Stradiotta describe the many, accessible varied national and provincial parks across the country in *The Road to Canada's Wild's: parks along the Trans Canada Hwy*. *Canada's National Parks – A Visitor's Guide* by Marylee Stephenson is the most complete guide to the country's national parks and provides all the essential information.

Gary and Joanie McGuffin have written *Where Rivers Run: a 6000-mile exploration of Canada by canoe*. Also for adventurers is *Freshwater Saga: memoirs of a lifetime of wilderness canoeing* by Eric Morse. *Lords of the Arctic: A journey among the polar bears* by Richard Davids is based in Churchill which many travellers may visit.

Farley Mowat, with such books as *Never Cry Wolf*, writes about the north, wildlife, nature and speaks for their conservation.

*Wild is Always There: Canada through the eyes of foreign writers* is a collection of pieces by a variety of writers who have spent some time in the country. It is edited by Greg Gatenby of Toronto who puts together writer festivals and readings featuring writers from around the world.

### Bookshops

Any store of reasonable size will have a Canadiana section covering both fiction and nonfiction titles. Perhaps the country's best in this regard is Longhouse Book Shop in Toronto which specialises only in Canadian books. Other stores of note are mentioned in the text in the city sections.

### MAPS

Good provincial road maps are available from the respective provincial tourist offices. Bookstores generally sell both provincial and city maps. Gas stations often have road maps as well.

For a list and order form for topographic maps of anywhere in the country contact the Canada Map Office (☎ 613-952-7000), 615 Booth St, Ottawa, Ont K1A 0E9. Through this address any map can be ordered by mail. Although there is a retail outlet on the premises, it is small and deals only with Ottawa area maps. The main retail store with all the maps is well out of the centre south in Nepean at 130 Bentley St.

Canada Map Company (☎ 416-362-9297) in downtown Toronto at 211 Yonge St, downstairs, has a wide selection of maps of all kinds. Standard highway maps, city maps, fishing maps, nautical and aviation charts and topographic maps are all available. They will fill phone and mail orders. The postal code is M5B 1M4.

The Global Village Map & Travel store, (☎ 204-453-7081), 213 Osborne St in Osborne Village in Winnipeg has a very good selection of maps, particularly for western cities and regions.

### MEDIA
### Newspapers & Magazines

The *Globe & Mail* newspaper, sometimes termed Canada's newspaper, out of Toronto but available across the country daily, provides a well-written record of national affairs from politics to arts. Other principal newspapers are the *Toronto Star*, *Montreal Gazette*, *Ottawa Citizen* and *Vancouver Province*.

In Quebec readers of French should have a look at both the federalist *La Presse*, the largest circulation French daily and the separatist-leaning *Le Devoir*, although there are other French dailies as well. *Maclean's* is Canada's weekly news magazine in the style of America's *Time* magazine.

Each of Canada's major cities has one or two newspaper and periodical speciality shops where magazines and newspapers from around the world can be purchased. Staff of major hotels should be able to direct you to these central outlets. Some of the major hotels stock some foreign papers themselves. A selection of periodicals from abroad may also be available at major airport kiosks.

### Radio & TV

The Canadian Broadcasting Corporation (CBC) with both national and regional broadcasts in both radio (on AM and FM bands) and TV can be seen or heard almost anywhere in the country including some of the more remote areas. It carries more Canadian content in music and information than any of the private broadcast companies. CBC Radio, in particular, is a fine service which unites listeners across the country with some of its programmes.

Highly recommended is the Morningside show heard between 9 am and noon weekdays hosted by Peter Gzowski. It's entertaining, educational and offers listeners a well-rounded view of what's on and in the minds of Canadians. Unfortunately, it only runs from the beginning of September to the end of May. The summer substitute known as Summerside, which uses various hosts, is not quite the same but definitely worth listening to. It also replays some of the highlights from various Morningside shows.

The CBC also has a French radio and TV network, both going under the name Radio-Canada. These can also be tuned into anywhere across the country.

The other major national TV network is the CTV Television Network (CTV). It is the main commercial channel broadcasting a mix of local, US and national programmes. Its nightly national news show is seen across the country.

Most Canadians can readily tune into US TV and radio stations and often do.

## FILM & PHOTOGRAPHY

Camera shops in the major centres are good, well-informed and stock a range of products. All films including Ilford are available at these outlets. Big city stores also provide the freshest film (always check the expiry date) and the best prices.

Once widely and easily available, transparency film (slides) has become increasingly difficult to get without going to a real camera shop. Chemists, department stores and corner convenience shops generally no longer carry anything other than basic Kodak and Fuji print film.

Most film in Canada is bought with processing not included. An exception is Kodachrome which can be purchased with processing included (the cheapest option) or finishing extra. The main Kodachrome processing plant is in Toronto. Films can be mailed to them or taken to a camera store who will handle the delivery and return at a modest fee. Black's is a good retail outlet found across the country except in Quebec. They sell a good selection of film and offer quick processing, too.

Carrying an extra battery for your built-in light metre is a good idea because you know it will die at the most inopportune time.

Canadian airports use new X-ray scanning machines for security which should pose no problems (but can) to most films. Any given roll should not be scanned more than half a

dozen times to be on the safe side. Also with specialised film, for example film with an ASA (ISO) of 400 or higher, X-ray damage is a real threat. For those who do not want to take a chance with any film, good camera shops now offer lead-lined pouches which can hold several canisters of film and which provide total protection. And, no, they are not unduly heavy.

Many people around the world are now using video camcorders and Canada is no exception. There are four-size formats in use in the country; VHS, VHS C size, Beta and 8 mm. For best service and selection visit a camera store. They are also available at Radio Shack, a cross-country electronic retailer.

## HEALTH

Canada is a pretty safe place to visit and little is necessary in the way of preparation. Travel health depends on your predeparture preparations, your day-to-day health care while travelling and how you handle any medical problem or emergency that does develop.

While the list of potential dangers can seem quite frightening, with a little luck, some basic precautions and adequate information few travellers experience more than upset stomachs.

### Travel Health Guide

*Travel with Children*, Maureen Wheeler, Lonely Planet Publications, includes basic advice on travel health for younger children.

### Predeparture Preparations

**Health Insurance** A travel insurance policy to cover theft, loss and medical problems is a wise idea. There is a wide variety of policies and your travel agent will have recommendations. The international student travel policies handled by STA Travel or other student travel organisations are usually good value. Some policies offer lower and higher medical expenses options but the higher one is chiefly for countries like the USA which have extremely high medical costs. Check the small print:

- Some policies specifically exclude 'dangerous activities' which can include scuba diving, motorcycling, even trekking. If such activities are on your agenda, you don't want that sort of policy. A locally acquired motor-cycle licence may not be valid under your policy.
- You may prefer a policy which pays doctors or hospitals direct rather than you having to pay on the spot and claim later. If you have to claim later make sure you keep all documentation. Some policies ask you to call back (reverse charges) to a centre in your home country where an immediate assessment of your problem is made.
- Check if the policy covers ambulances or an emergency flight home. If you have to stretch out you will need two seats and somebody has to pay for them!

Check to see if your health insurance covers you during a visit to Canada and the precise details, limitations and exclusions of that coverage. Medical, hospital and dental care is excellent but very expensive in Canada. The standard rate for a bed in a city hospital is at least $500 a day and up to $2000 a day in the major centres for nonresidents!

The largest seller of hospital and medical insurance to visitors to Canada is John Ingle Insurance. They offer hospital medical care (HMC) policies from a minimum of seven days to a maximum of one year with a possible renewal of one additional year. The 30-day coverage costs $87 for an adult under the age of 65, $117 over the age of 65. Family rates are available. Coverage includes the hospital rate, doctors' fees, extended health care and other features. Visitors to Canada are *not* covered for conditions which they had prior to arrival.

Be sure to inquire about coverage details if you intend to make side trips to the USA, Mexico, the Caribbean countries or others.

They also offer insurance policies for foreign students (at reduced rates) and to those visiting Canada on working visas. Their policies may be very beneficial in filling in coverage gaps before either a government policy kicks in, in the case of students, or the employers' paid benefits begin, in the case of foreign workers. Again, the policies may vary depending where in the country you settle.

Ingle has offices in major cities across the country and representatives in the northern territories. The head office (☎ 416-961-0666, 1-800-387-4770) is at 800 Bay St, Toronto, Ontario, M5S 9Z9. They can supply information pamphlets in over 15 languages and in the office in Toronto, even speak most of them. The pamphlet includes an application form and payment can be made before or after arrival in Canada.

The Blue Cross is the best known of Ingle's competitors. Their medical travel insurance is called 'emergency coverage' and costs about $3 a day for a single up to age 54, $6 a day for a family but varies slightly depending on length of stay. These rates are for a maximum of up to three months. Rates jump for those between the ages of 55 to 69 and up once more for those older than that. Again, this insurance doesn't cover any expenses arising from a condition you had prior to arrival or due to pregnancy. The insurance can be purchased upon arrival or at home before leaving. For information write to the head office (☎ 416-429-2868, 1-800-268-3763) at 150 Ferrand Drive, Don Mills, Ontario, M3C 1H6.

Brochures for either company are available in Canada from the above offices or at post offices, banks, chemists, doctors' offices and some shopping centres. For either one read the information carefully. There are exclusions, conditions etc which should be clearly understood. Also check the maximum amounts payable, different policies allow for greater payments.

**Medical Kit** When doing a lot of driving, visiting less-populated areas or camping, hiking, canoeing, etc a good first-aid kit is recommended. A possible kit list includes:

- Aspirin or Panadol – for pain or fever
- Antihistamine (such as Benadryl) – useful as a decongestant for colds, allergies, to ease the itch from insect bites or stings or to help prevent motion sickness. Antihistamines may cause sedation and interact with alcohol so care should be taken when using them.

- Antibiotics – useful if you're travelling well off the beaten track, but they must be prescribed and you should carry the prescription with you. Some individuals are allergic to commonly prescribed antibiotics such as penicillin or sulfa drugs. It would be sensible to always carry this information when travelling.
- Kaolin preparation (Pepto-Bismol), Imodium or Lomotil – for stomach upsets.
- Rehydration mixture – for treatment of severe diarrhoea, this is particularly important if travelling with children, but is recommended for everyone.
- Antiseptic such as Betadine, which comes as impregnated swabs or ointment, and an antibiotic powder or similar 'dry' spray – for cuts and grazes.
- Calamine lotion – to ease irritation from bites or stings.
- Bandages and Band-aids – for minor injuries.
- Scissors, tweezers and a thermometer (note that mercury thermometers are prohibited by airlines).
- Insect repellent, sunscreen, suntan lotion, chapstick and water purification tablets.

Ideally, antibiotics should be administered only under medical supervision and should never be taken indiscriminately. Take only the recommended dose at the prescribed intervals and continue using the antibiotic for the prescribed period, even if the illness seems to be cured earlier. Antibiotics are quite specific to the infections they can treat. Stop immediately if there are any serious reactions and don't use them at all if you are unsure if you have the correct one.

**Health Preparations** Make sure you're healthy before you start travelling. If you are embarking on a long trip make sure your teeth are OK.

If you wear glasses take a spare pair and your prescription. Losing your glasses can be a real problem, although in many places you can get new spectacles made up quickly, cheaply and competently.

If you require a particular medication take an adequate supply, as it may not be available locally. Take the prescription or, better still, part of the packaging showing the generic rather than the brand name (which may not be locally available), as it will make getting replacements easier. It's a wise idea to have

a legible prescription with you to show that you legally use the medication – it's surprising how often over-the-counter drugs from one place are illegal without a prescription or even banned in another.

**Immunisations** Normally no vaccinations are required and there's nothing to recommend for protection here. You need shots for cholera and yellow fever if you're coming from an endemic area or have been in contact with these diseases.

**Basic Rules**
**Water Purification** Canadian tap water from coast to coast is safe to drink. The following information is for those who intend to be out in the woods or in the wilds on outdoor excursions using lake and river water. Since most extended adventure trips are taken in government parks, ask the ranger about local water quality. The simplest way of purifying water is to boil it thoroughly. Vigorously boiling for five minutes should be satisfactory even at high altitude. Remember that at high altitude water boils at a lower temperature, so germs are less likely to be killed.

Simple filtering will not remove all dangerous organisms, so if you cannot boil water it should be treated chemically. Chlorine tablets (Puritabs, Steritabs or other brand names) will kill many but not all pathogens, including giardia and amoebic cysts. Iodine is very effective in purifying water and is available in tablet form (such as Potable Aqua), but follow the directions carefully and remember that too much iodine can be harmful.

If you can't find tablets, tincture of iodine (2%) or iodine crystals can be used. Two drops of tincture of iodine per litre or quart of clear water is the recommended dosage; the treated water should be left to stand for 20 to 30 minutes before drinking. Iodine crystals can also be used to purify water but this is a more complicated process, as you have to first prepare a saturated iodine solution. Iodine loses its effectiveness if exposed to air or damp so keep it in a tightly sealed container. Flavoured powder will disguise the taste of treated water and is a good idea if you are travelling with children.

**Nutrition** If your food is poor or limited in availability, if you're travelling hard and fast and therefore missing meals, or if you simply lose your appetite, you can soon start to lose weight and place your health at risk.

Make sure your diet is well balanced. Eggs, tofu, beans, lentils and nuts are all safe ways to get protein. Fruit you can peel (bananas, oranges or mandarins for example) is always safe and a good source of vitamins. Try to eat plenty of grains (rice) and bread. Remember that although food is generally safer if it is cooked well, overcooked food loses much of its nutritional value. If your diet isn't well balanced or if your food intake is insufficient, it's a good idea to take vitamin and iron pills.

**Everyday Health** A normal body temperature is 98.6°F or 37°C; more than 2°C higher is a 'high' fever. A normal adult pulse rate is 60 to 80 per minute (children 80 to 100, babies 100 to 140). You should know how to take a temperature and a pulse rate. As a general rule the pulse increases about 20 beats per minute for each °C rise in fever.

Respiration (breathing) rate is also an indicator of illness. Count the number of breaths per minute: between 12 and 20 is normal for adults and older children (up to 30 for younger children, 40 for babies). People with a high fever or serious respiratory illness (like pneumonia) breathe more quickly than normal. More than 40 shallow breaths a minute usually means pneumonia.

**Medical Problems & Treatment**
Potential medical problems can be broken down into several areas. First there are the climatic and geographical considerations - problems caused by extremes of temperature, altitude or motion. Then there are diseases and illnesses caused through poor environmental sanitation, insect bites or stings, and animal or human contact.

Simple cuts, bites or scratches can also cause problems. Self-diagnosis and treatment can be risky, so wherever possible seek qualified help.

Help can be found at the emergency department of any hospital although a lengthy wait may be necessary for non-critical attention. This is when that medical insurance really comes in handy.

## Climatic & Geographical Considerations

**Sunburn & Windburn** Sunburn and windburn should be primary concerns for anyone planning to spend time trekking or travelling over snow and ice. The sun will burn you even if you feel cold and the wind will cause dehydration and chafing of skin. Use a good sunscreen and a moisture cream on exposed skin, even on cloudy days. A hat provides added protection and zinc cream or some other barrier cream for your nose and lips is recommended if you're spending any time on ice or snow.

Reflection and glare from ice and snow can cause snow blindness so high-protection sunglasses should be considered essential for any sort of glacier visit or ski trip. Calamine lotion is good for mild sunburn.

**Cold** Despite the perception by some that Canada is a perpetually ice-bound wasteland, health problems due to extreme cold are not likely to be suffered by many people. On winter days when frost bite is a possibility (due almost always to a combination of low temperature and high wind, the result of which is a reading known as the wind-chill factor) you will be aware of it. Everybody will be discussing it, the radio will broadcast warnings about how many minutes of exposed skin is acceptable and...it will be bloody cold.

If you are trekking at high altitudes or simply taking a long bus trip over mountains, particularly at night, be prepared. You should always be prepared for cold, wet or windy conditions even if you're just out walking or hitching.

Hypothermia occurs when the body loses heat faster than it can produce it and the core temperature of the body falls. It is surprisingly easy to progress from very cold to dangerously cold due to a combination of wind, wet clothing, fatigue and hunger, even if the air temperature is above freezing. It is best to dress in layers; silk, wool and some of the new artificial fibres are all good insulating materials. A hat is important, as a lot of heat is lost through the head. A strong, waterproof outer layer is essential, as keeping dry is vital. Carry basic supplies, including food containing simple sugars to generate heat quickly and take lots of fluid to drink.

Symptoms of hypothermia are exhaustion, numb skin (particularly toes and fingers), shivering, slurred speech, irrational or violent behaviour, lethargy, stumbling, dizzy spells, muscle cramps and violent bursts of energy. Irrationality may take the form of sufferers claiming they are warm and trying to take off their clothes.

To treat hypothermia, first get the person out of the wind and/or rain, remove their clothing if its wet and replace it with dry, warm clothing. Give them hot liquids – not alcohol – and some high-kilojoule, easily digestible food. This should be enough for the early stages of hypothermia, but if it has gone further it may be necessary to place victims in warm sleeping bags and get in with them. Do not rub victims but place them near a fire or remove their wet clothes in the wind. If possible, place a sufferer in a warm (not hot) bath.

**Altitude Sickness** Acute Mountain Sickness or AMS occurs at high altitude and can be fatal. The lack of oxygen at high altitudes affects most people to some extent.

A number of measures can be adopted to prevent acute mountain sickness:

- Ascend slowly – have frequent rest days, spending two to three nights at each rise of 1000 metres. If you reach a high altitude by trekking, acclimatisation takes place gradually and you are less likely to be affected than if you fly direct.

- Drink extra fluids. The mountain air is dry and cold and moisture is lost as you breathe.
- Eat light, high-carbohydrate meals for more energy.
- Avoid alcohol as it may increase the risk of dehydration.
- Avoid sedatives.

Even with acclimatisation you may still have trouble adjusting - headaches, nausea, dizziness, a dry cough, insomnia, breathlessness and loss of appetite are all signs to heed. Mild altitude problems will generally abate after a day or so but if the symptoms persist or become worse the only treatment is to descend - even 500 metres can help. Breathlessness, a dry, irritative cough (which may progress to the production of pink, frothy sputum), severe headache, loss of appetite, nausea, and sometimes vomiting are all danger signs. Increasing tiredness, confusion, and lack of coordination and balance are real danger signs. Any of these symptoms individually, even just a persistent headache, can be a warning.

There is no hard and fast rule as to how high is too high: AMS has been fatal at altitudes of 3000 metres, although 3500 to 4500 metres is the usual range. It is always wise to sleep at a lower altitude than the greatest height reached during the day.

**Motion Sickness** Eating lightly before and during a trip will reduce the chances of motion sickness. If you are prone to motion sickness try to find a place that minimises disturbance – near the wing on aircraft, close to midships on boats, near the centre on buses. Fresh air usually helps, reading or cigarette smoke doesn't. Commercial anti-motion-sickness preparations, which can cause drowsiness, have to be taken before the trip commences; when you're feeling sick it's too late. Ginger is a natural preventative and is available in capsule form.

**Diseases Spread by People & Animals**

**Giardiasis** If you're going to do a lot of camping, particularly in the backcountry and woods of Alberta or British Columbia, you should take precautions against an intestinal parasite *(Giardia lamblia)* which causes giardiasis, known colloquially as 'beaver fever'. This intestinal parasite is present in contaminated water.

The symptoms are stomach cramps, nausea, a bloated stomach, watery, foul-smelling diarrhoea and frequent gas. Giardiasis can appear several weeks after you have been exposed to the parasite. The symptoms may disappear for a few days and then return; this can go on for several weeks. Tinidazole, known as Fasigyn, or metronidazole (Flagyl) are the recommended drugs for treatment. Either can be used in a single treatment dose. Antibiotics are of no use. About 10 years ago the condition was considered rare and nobody had ever heard of it, but in the past few years it has been causing more and more hikers a lot of discomfort.

**Rabies** This isn't a major problem, but rabies is something to be aware of when spending any time in the woods or undeveloped areas. Animals most likely affected are the squirrel, skunk, racoon and particularly, the fox. Paradoxically, all of the above animals have learned to adapt quite well to populated regions, and may be seen in city parks and recreation areas, wooded areas around rivers and streams and even along residential streets after dark. Especially on garbage nights!

Rabies is caused by a bite or scratch by an infected animal. Any bite, scratch or even lick from a mammal should be cleaned immediately and thoroughly. Scrub with soap and running water, and then clean with an alcohol solution. If there is any possibility that the animal is infected, medical help should be sought immediately. Even if the animal is not rabid, all bites should be treated seriously as they can become infected or can result in tetanus. A rabies vaccination is now available and should be considered if you are in a high-risk category – eg, if you intend to explore caves (bat bites could be dangerous) or work with animals.

**Sexually Transmitted Diseases (STDs)** In common with other Western countries, Canada has its share of sexually transmitted diseases. As might be expected, the rates for such conditions are highest in the large cities. Sexual contact with an infected sexual partner spreads these diseases. While abstinence is the only 100% preventative, using condoms is also effective.

Gonorrhoea and syphilis are the most common of these diseases; sores, blisters or rashes around the genitals, discharges or pain when urinating are common symptoms. Symptoms may be less marked or not observed at all in women. Syphilis symptoms eventually disappear completely but the disease continues and can cause severe problems in later years. The treatment of gonorrhoea and syphilis is by antibiotics.

There are numerous other sexually transmitted diseases, for most of which effective treatment is available. However, there is no cure for herpes and there is also currently no cure for AIDS. Using condoms is the most effective preventative. Current Canadian government advertising, promoting the use of condoms, encourages young women to lay down the law: 'no glove, no love'.

*HIV/AIDS* HIV, the Human Immunodeficiency Virus, may develop into AIDS, Acquired Immune Deficiency Syndrome. HIV is a major problem in many countries. Any exposure to blood, blood products or bodily fluids may put the individual at risk. In many developing countries transmission is predominantly through heterosexual sexual activity. This is quite different from industrialised countries where transmission is mostly through contact between homosexual or bisexual males or contaminated needles in IV drug users. Apart from abstinence, the most effective preventative is always to practise safe sex using condoms. It is impossible to detect the HIV- positive status of an otherwise healthy-looking person without a blood test.

HIV/AIDS can also be spread through infected blood transfusions; most developing countries cannot afford to screen blood for transfusions. It can also be spread by dirty needles – vaccinations, acupuncture, tattooing and ear or nose-piercing can potentially be as dangerous as intravenous drug use if the equipment is not clean.

## Cuts & Bites

**Lyme Disease** Less of a threat but still something to be aware of is the relatively recent threat of Lyme disease (doesn't it seem as though there's always something new out there to get you?).

Since the late 1980s each summer sees more of this disease although the vast majority of North American cases have occurred in the USA. The disease is really more of a condition transmitted by a certain species of deer tick, similar to a tick found on a dog but smaller. The tick infects the skin with the spirochaete bacterium which causes the disease.

The disease was first identified on the continent in 1975 in Lyme, Connecticut, hence the name. Most cases still go undetected, misdiagnosed or unreported. It is a difficult disease to diagnose because symptoms vary widely. Consult a doctor if you experience the following:

Sometime within 30 days after being bitten a small red bump appears surrounded by a rash often but not always accompanied by flu-like symptoms.

Treatment with antibiotics is simple and effective, if the disease is caught at this early stage. Later symptoms can be quite severe and include a form of arthritis which affects the knees.

The best way to avoid the whole business is to take precautions in areas where it has been reported. So far, the few Canadian cases seem to be in the far west or in the far east. California, Washington, Minnesota and New England have had most of the US cases. If you hear anything about it in an area where you are hiking or walking in the woods, cover the body as much as possible, use an insect repellent containing diethyl-metatoluamide (DEET) and at the end of the day check yourself, children or pets for the ticks. DEET is not recommended for use on children, however, so a milder substitute will

have to do. Chances are that you will not feel it if bitten. Of course, most ticks are not the right sort to pass on the disease and even most of the nasties do not carry the harmful bacteria.

**Snakes** To minimise your chances of being bitten always wear boots, socks and long trousers when walking through undergrowth where snakes may be present. Don't put your hands into holes and crevices, and be careful when collecting firewood.

Snake bites do not cause instantaneous death and antivenenes are usually available. Keep the victim calm and still, wrap the bitten limb tightly, as you would for a sprained ankle, and then attach a splint to immobilise it. Then seek medical help, if possible with the dead snake for identification. Don't attempt to catch the snake if there is even a remote possibility of being bitten again. Tourniquets and sucking out the poison are now comprehensively discredited.

**Bedbugs & Lice** Bedbugs live in various places, but particularly in dirty mattresses and bedding. Spots of blood on bedclothes or on the wall around the bed can be read as a suggestion to find another hotel. Bedbugs leave itchy bites in neat rows. Calamine lotion may help.

All lice cause itching and discomfort. They make themselves at home in your hair (head lice), your clothing (body lice) or in your pubic hair (crabs). You catch lice through direct contact with infected people or by sharing combs, clothing and the like. Powder or shampoo treatment will kill the lice and infected clothing should then be washed in very hot water.

## Women's Health

**Gynaecological Problems** Poor diet, lowered resistance due to the use of antibiotics for stomach upsets and even contraceptive pills can lead to vaginal infections when travelling in hot climates. Keeping the genital area clean, and wearing skirts or loose-fitting trousers and cotton underwear will help to prevent infections.

Yeast infections, characterised by a rash, itch and discharge, can be treated with a vinegar or even lemon-juice douche or with yoghurt. Nystatin suppositories are the usual medical prescription. Trichomonas is a more serious infection; symptoms are a discharge and a burning sensation when urinating. Male sexual partners must also be treated, and if a vinegar-water douche is not effective medical attention should be sought. Metronidazole (Flagyl) is the prescribed drug.

**Pregnancy** Most miscarriages occur during the first three months of pregnancy, so this is the most risky time to travel as far as your own health is concerned. Miscarriage is not uncommon, and can occasionally lead to severe bleeding. The last three months should also be spent within reasonable distance of good medical care. A baby born as early as 24 weeks stands a chance of survival, but only in a good modern hospital. Pregnant women should avoid all unnecessary medication, but vaccinations and malarial prophylactics should still be taken where possible. Additional care should be taken to prevent illness and particular attention should be paid to diet and nutrition. Alcohol and nicotine, for example, should be avoided.

Women travellers often find that their periods become irregular or even cease while they're on the road. Remember that a missed period in these circumstances doesn't necessarily indicate pregnancy. There are Family Planning clinics in many small and large urban centres where you can seek advice and have a urine test to determine whether you are pregnant or not.

## WOMEN TRAVELLERS
While not yet common, more and more women are travelling alone in Canada. This goes for vacationers, visitors and women on business.

There are no overriding differences for men and women travelling in Canada and as a Western country there are no particular cultural or traditional pitfalls which females need to be aware of.

As in so much of the world, though, women do face sexism and the threat of violence is certainly felt more by Canadian women than men. The following tips to consider have been suggested by women.

When travelling, try to arrive at your destination before dark. If arriving at a bus or train station (bus stations in particular are often not in the best parts of town) take a taxi to the place where you're spending the night. In some of the larger cities, the bus and/or train station is connected to the subway system. Subways in Canada are clean and safe. Once close to your destination, catch a taxi from the subway stop.

Some parts of the downtown areas of major cities should be avoided at night especially on a Friday or Saturday. Where applicable these areas are noted in the text.

If driving, keep your vehicle well maintained and don't get low on gas. If you do break down on the highway, especially at night, a large pre-made sign placed in the window reading 'Call Police' is not a bad idea. I recently saw such a sign, stopped to call police and was told they already had a dozen calls and a car was on the way, so motorists do respond to this. It is not advisable for women to get out of their broken car and wait beside it, especially at night. Wait inside with the doors locked. In cities avoid underground parking lots, these are uniformly creepy.

Care should be taken when hitchhiking, especially if you're travelling alone – use common sense and don't be afraid to say no to lifts. It is rare indeed to see women alone hitching and it can't be recommended. Mixed sex couples are the better way for women to thumb if they are determined to travel this way.

Women alone may be more comfortable with their room booked before arriving in a new town. Many women prefer to simply use an initial with their surname, S Smith, as opposed to Susan Smith, Miss Smith, Ms Smith, etc when making reservations or appointments. Many of the chain hotels and motels have 800 telephone numbers which allow for free long-distance reservation-making.

Hostels and B&Bs are good, safe choices. Many Canadian B&Bs are run by couples or women. In B&Bs and guesthouses, ask whether the rooms have locks – some do not.

When checking into a motel, ask to see the room first and make sure the doors and windows can be secured. Nearly all motel rooms have a telephone in the room.

A few of the cheaper inner-city hotels listed in the text are not suitable for women alone. Where these places are mentioned it is suggested that accommodation should be sought elsewhere.

Unaccompanied women in nightclubs or bars will quickly find they get a lot of attention (and possibly drinks) whether they want it or not.

For women who enjoy the outdoors, the smell of perfumes and fragrant cosmetics attracts bears so, if you're likely to be in an area where they're around, it's best not to wear any. Insects, too, are said to find perfume a pleasant lure.

## DISABLED TRAVELLERS

Canada has come a long way in making day-to-day life less burdensome to the physically disabled, most notably the wheelchair bound. In general, Canada has gone further in this regard than the vast majority of the world's countries and this process continues. Most public buildings are wheelchair accessible, including major tourist offices. Ditto for major museums, art galleries and principal attractions. All the above and many restaurants also have washroom facilities suitable for wheelchairs. Major hotels are often equipped to deal with wheelchairs and some less-expensive motel chains such as the countrywide Journey's End (frequently mentioned through the text) has wheelchair access through ramps.

Many of the national and provincial parks have accessible interpretive centres and even some of the shorter nature trails and/or boardwalks have been developed with

wheelchairs or self-propelled mobility aids in mind.

The VIA Rail system is prepared to accommodate the wheelchair bound but advance notice of 48 hours should be given. All bus lines will help passengers and take chairs or any other aids providing they collapse and will fit in the usual luggage compartments. Canadian airlines are accustomed to dealing with disabled passengers and provide early boarding and disembarking as standard practice.

In major cities, parking lots all have designated parking spots for the physically disabled, usually marked with a painted wheelchair. These spots, located closest to the door or access point of the place being visited can not be used by others under threat of serious fine.

Car-rental agencies can provide special accessories such as handcontrols but again, advance notice is required. Toronto's public transportation system, the TTC, has a special bus service around town with lifts for wheelchairs.

## SENIOR TRAVELLERS

Visitors over the age of 65, and sometimes 60, should take advantage of the many cost reductions they are offered in Canada. Canadians of this age are classed as 'seniors' and it is this term that is seen frequently. Seniors' discounts are offered on all means of transportation and can mean substantial savings. Many of the government parks have reduced rates as do most of the country's attractions, museums, historic sites, even movie houses. Some hotels and motels may provide a price reduction – it's always worth asking.

Elderhostel with branches in many countries is also found in Canada. It specialises in inexpensive, educational packages for those over 60 years of age. The standard type of programme consists of mornings of talks and lectures followed by afternoon field trips and visits to related sights. Participants are accommodated in university dorms. There is generally a full-package price which includes meals, lodging and some transportation. The courses are of varying lengths but may be several weeks long. Subject matter is drawn from history, nature, geography and the like. The head office for Elderhostel Canada (☎ 613-530-2222) is at 308 Wellington St, Kingston, Ontario K7K 7A7.

## DANGERS & ANNOYANCES
Check the Health section earlier for some of the health risks you should be aware of. See also Road Rules & Safety in the Getting Around chapter for tips about driving.

### Fire
When bedding down outside legitimate campgrounds do not start a fire. This is extremely dangerous and could cause untold amounts of devastation during the dry summer months.

One couple did so and when nailed by the local authorities pointed to this book and said 'He said we could set up camp anywhere!' So please give both yourself and me a break.

**Mark Lightbody**

In designated campgrounds make sure that anything that was burning is put out completely when you've finished with it, including cigarettes.

### Bears
A serious problem encountered when you're camping in the woods is the animals – most importantly bears – who are always looking for an easy snack. Keep your food in nylon bags; a sleeping-bag sack is good. Tie the sack to a rope and sling it over a branch away from your tent and away from the trunk of the tree as some bears can climb. Hoist it up high enough so a standing bear can't reach it, say three metres. Don't leave food scraps around the site and never, ever keep food in the tent.

Don't try to get close-up photographs of bears and never come between a bear and its cubs. If you see any cubs, quietly and quickly disappear. If you do see a bear, try to get upwind so it can smell you and you won't startle it. While hiking through woods or in the mountains in bear country, some people

wear a noise-maker, like a bell. Talking or singing is just as good. Whatever you do, don't feed bears – they lose their fear of people and eventually their lives to park wardens.

### Blackflies & Mosquitoes
In the woods of Canada, particularly in the north, the blackflies and mosquitoes can be murder – they seems to get worse the further north you get. There are tales of lost hikers going insane from the bugs. This is no joke – they can make you miserable. The effect of a bite (or sting, technically, by the mosquito) is a small itchy bump. The moment of attack is itself a very minor, passing pain. Some people are allergic to blackfly bites and will develop a fair bit of swelling. But other than the unsightly welt, there is no real danger. The potential trouble is in the cumulative effects of scores of them and even this hazard is mainly psychological.

As a rule, darker clothes are said to attract biting insects more than lighter ones. Perfume, too, evidently attracts the wrong kind of attention. Take 'bug juice' liquid or spray repellents widely available at chemists (drugstores, pharmacies). Two recommended names are Muskol and Off; the latter also has an extra strength version known as Deep Woods Off. An ingredient often used in repellents known as DEET should not be used on children. There are brands without it. Try to minimise the amount of skin exposed by wearing a long-sleeved shirt, long pants and a close-fitting hat or cap.

June is the worst month, and as the summer wears on, or if things are dry, the bugs disappear. Some years they are not much of a problem but during other years it's very bad, depending on weather and other conditions.

The bugs are at their worst deep in the woods. In clearings, along shorelines or anywhere there's a breeze you'll be safe, except for the buzzing horseflies, which are basically teeth with wings.

Mosquitoes come out around sunset, building a fire will help keep them away. For campers, a tent with a zippered screen is pretty much a necessity.

If you do get lost and are being eaten alive, submerge your body if there's water around. This will enable you to think clearly about where you are and what to do. Lemon or orange peel rubbed on your skin will help if you're out of repellent.

## Other Stings & Bites

Canada is relatively problem-free regarding stings and bites. There are no poisonous spiders or insects. Rattlesnakes do live in parts of Ontario and British Columbia but are rarely seen – even by serious hikers – and actually are generally timid. Still the bite is a matter of concern and immediate medical attention is essential. The normal run of bees, wasps and hornets is found across the country. Those with allergies should carry kits outside of urban areas.

In some areas, sand gnats and 'no-see-ums', bugs so called because you never see them but rather just feel their bites, may be encountered. There is not much to be done about it; fortunately neither are overly common. Campers should have very finely meshed tents to prevent a possible night noseeum invasion. All this insect generated horror just mentioned really isn't so bad but it's better to hear the worst than be innocently caught. Millions spend time in the bush each year and actually live to tell about it. And besides, this is the only kind of terrorism you have to concern yourself with in Canada – bugs are better than bombs.

## Campsite Pests

Campers are unlikely to encounter bears but squirrels, chipmunks, mice and racoons are common. And they all love human food. They will spend a lot of time tearing through any bags of food or garbage you leave about and even smack pots and pans around making a heck of a clatter in the middle of the night. The best defence is not to feed them, no matter how cute, and store all food securely.

## EMERGENCY

In most of the country, particularly urban areas, telephone 911 for all police, fire, accident and medical emergencies. See under the province introductions for details. In all other areas or when in doubt, call 0 and ask the operator for assistance. You will then be put through to the appropriate service. Dialling 911 results in a faster response. For non-emergency police matters, consult the local telephone book. Police numbers are listed on one the first few pages.

Should your passport get lost or stolen, contact your nearest consulate. They will be able to issue a temporary replacement and inform you when and how to go about getting another. You may not need another depending on your travel plans.

For lost or stolen travellers' cheques, contact the issuer or their representative. Upon purchase of the cheques you should have received a list of telephone numbers to call in case of loss. To make matters as easily as possible do record which cheques you cash as is suggested. If you supply a list of which cheques are gone, a refund should be forthcoming with minimal inconvenience.

For anything stolen for which an insurance claim will be filled you should call the police and have them make a record of the theft. Ask for their reference number on their report – you may be asked for it.

## STUDY & WORK

Student and work authorisations must be obtained outside Canada and may take six months. A work permit is valid for one specific job and one specific time, for one specific employer. If you want to study here, get the information and apply in your own country.

It is difficult to get a work permit: opportunities go first to Canadians. However, employers hiring casual, temporary, service workers (hotel, bar, restaurant) construction, farm or forestry workers often don't ask for the permit. Visitors working here legally have Social Insurance numbers beginning with '9'. If you don't have this, and get caught, you will be told to leave the country.

Many young European women come to Canada as nannies. Many countries have agencies where details on these arrangements can be found.

## Student Work Abroad Programme (SWAP)

Of particular interest to Australian students may be the SWAP. Organised by Student Services Australia (SSA) and the Canadian Federation of Students (CFS), the programme allows Australians between the ages of 18 and 25 to spend a year in Canada on a working holiday. This programme only has space for 100 people a year and applicants must be enrolled in a post-secondary educational institution.

After an orientation programme in Vancouver you find your own job with help from CFS. Most jobs are in the service area – as waiters, bar attendants, cleaners and maids, particularly in the snowfields over winter – although SWAP participants have worked in other kinds of jobs ranging from farmhands to bell-hops. You are issued with a one-year, nonextendable visa which allows you to work anywhere in the country. 'Swappers' must be Australian citizens and pass a medical check-up.

SSA, in conjunction with STA Travel, arranges group departures at reduced fares leaving from Sydney, Melbourne and Brisbane in November and December. Independent departures leave throughout the rest of the year. Participants are given orientation information and a copy of this Lonely Planet book prior to departure.

For full details contact Student Services Australia (☎ 03-348 1777), PO Box 399, Carlton South, Victoria, 3053.

## Working Holiday Programme

This is another programme, which is open to all Australians between the ages of 18 and 25 and they need not be enrolled in a post-secondary educational institution. This programme has a quota of 3000 annually. Application forms can be obtained by contacting the Canadian Consulate General in Sydney, Australia. See under Visas &

Embassies earlier in this chapter for the address. Applications for this programme take up to two months to process.

## ACTIVITIES

Canada's greatest attribute is its natural environment. This, for the most part, is what it has to offer visitors, what makes it unique. Much of Canada's appeal lies in the range of physical activities possible. Hiking, canoeing, fishing, skiing and observing flora & fauna quickly come to mind.

There are wilderness trips of all types, organised or self-directed. Provincial tourist offices have information on activities in their region and also details on the hundreds of private businesses, operators and outfitters offering adventure tours and trips. Many provinces have booklets and maps on canoeing and hiking. All have information on national and provincial parks, many of which can be highlights of a trip to Canada. A good many national and provincial parks are detailed in the text.

Long-distance cycling has become more popular recently. There is downhill skiing in many parts of the country – slopes in the Rockies are excellent and higher than any in the European Alps. Hang gliding is always gaining converts. People even surf off the west coast. And if you want to try your luck, you can pan for gold. Although the season is short, boating is very popular across the country. It has been said there are more boats per capita in Canada than anywhere except Sweden.

The clean, safe and vital cities are also enticing and you will find arts and cultural activities if the outdoors starts to wear you down.

Entering the various lotteries is a less rigorous but favourite Canadian pastime. Bingo is another favourite form of small-time gambling. A whimsical variation is cow-pie bingo played in some rural areas often as a fundraiser for charity.

This involves dividing, marking and numbering a pasture into equal-sized sections. Each participant then selects one of these squares to bet on. A cow is let into the field. The 'owner' of the square upon which the cow relieves itself is the winner; good wholesome, if not necessarily clean, fun.

## Hiking

Canada offers both long and short, rugged and gentle, mountain and coastal when it comes to hiking and walking paths. Almost all of the country's trails, and certainly most of the best, are found in either the provincial or national parks.

The majority of parks have some type of walking trail although some may be no more than a short nature trail. The larger the park, as a rule, the longer the trail. Some require one or more nights camping out to complete. Conservation areas, wildlife reserves and sanctuaries also often have marked trails. Throughout the text, parks with trails are discussed and some individual trails are outlined.

Prime hiking is found throughout the Rockies in all of the several national parks in Alberta and British Columbia. Other mountainous regions with good trails include Gros Morne National Park in Newfoundland, Cape Breton National Park in Nova Scotia, Gaspésie Park and Mont Tremblant Park in Quebec. In Ontario, Killarney Provincial Park has a long-distance trail around the tops of its rounded mountains. In Manitoba, Riding Mountain Park also has a series of trails.

Among the toughest of trails are the coastal hike on the west coast of Vancouver Island in Pacific Rim National Park and another multi-day coastal trail, the one in Pukaskwa National Park on Lake Superior in Ontario.

Outside the two park systems there are also some extended trails running through a mix of public and private lands. A few to consider are the following. The Bruce Trail of southern Ontario, described in the text runs from Lake Ontario 700 km north to Georgian Bay. Under Gros Cap in Sault Ste Marie, Ontario, details on the long-distance Voyageur Trail, as yet unfinished, can be found. Two in New Brunswick are the Dobson Trail (see around Moncton) and the

trail between St Martins and Fundy National Park (see under St Martins).

Another is the historic gold-rush Chilkoot Trail from near Skagway in Alaska to the Yukon.

## Canoeing

The possibilities for canoeing are almost limitless from an easy half-day paddle to some of the most challenging white waters. Again, the government parks are a good place to start and many of them are quite accessible. Some have outfitters able to supply all equipment, at others private operators do much the same thing just outside the park boundaries.

Many of the major cities have operators who can help organise trips as well as excellent outdoor sporting equipment stores. Provincial tourist boards will be able to help with information on canoeing areas and outfitters. Better bookstores and outdoor stores sell good guides to canoeing in Canada.

Some of the country's main canoeing areas follow. Details for many can be found through the text. In Nova Scotia try Kejimkujik National Park or inquire about the numerous inland nature reserves. In Quebec there are a series of canoe routes in La Mauricie National Park, La Verendrye Provincial Park and excellent coastal canoeing or kayaking at Mingan Archipelago National Park.

Ontario offers terrific canoeing at accessible Algonquin Provincial Park, Killarney Provincial Park and at Temagami and its adjoining wilderness areas.

Across the prairies, the northern sections are vast, undeveloped lake-filled forest. Prince Albert National Park in Saskatchewan is one area to look into.

British Columbia has a well-known weeklong canoe circuit around Bowron Lake Provincial Park near Barkerville. Wells Gray Provincial Park also has fine flat water canoeing. The coastal areas around the Gulf islands offer sea canoeing and kayaking.

Many of the country's rivers and the far north regions offer the experienced challenging, white-water opportunities. One of the most spectacular of these trips is in Nahanni National Park of the Northwest Territories.

## Fishing

Freshwater fishing is abundant and popular across the country with both residents and visitors. Casting a line is one of the country's basic outdoor activities. In winter many northern areas set up and rent 'huts', small wooden shacks, out on frozen lakes. Inside there is a bench, sometimes a heater, a hole in the ice and often more than a few bottles of beer.

See under Fauna in the Facts about the Country chapter for fish species information. Anglers must purchase fishing licences which vary in duration and price from province to province. Any tourist office can help with information and advice on where to buy one. At the same time pick-up a guide to the various 'open' seasons for each species and also a guide to the eating of fish. In southern regions there are recommended consumption guidelines due to pollution and natural contaminants such as mercury which are important especially for pregnant women and young children. Also be sure to check on daily limits and if there are any bait restrictions. In some areas live minnows or other bait is prohibited.

## Swimming & Beaches

Although Canada is surrounded on three sides by ocean, by far the majority of the swimming is done inland, in the much warmer freshwater lakes and rivers. Still, Canadians do swim at places in the oceans during July and August and it is along the coastal areas where some of the country's finest beaches can be enjoyed. Beaches are popular summer gathering and relaxing places even when the water is too cold for the vast majority to venture into the water. With very few exceptions (mainly gay-oriented places) Canada does not have nude or topless beaches. Below are some of Canada's best strips of sand.

At the eastern end of Canada, Ingonish Beach just out of Cape Breton National Park,

Nova Scotia is a fine arch of sand surrounded by green hills where, in the middle of a good summer, the swimming can be quite pleasant. For warmer waters, Melmerby and Caribou beaches near Pictou and New Glasgow are long, wide and reap the spin-offs of the Gulf Stream, meaning the waters reach 19°C.

Rissers Beach south of Halifax is easy paced, relatively quiet, close to town and is edged with some dunes, too.

The north coast of Prince Edward Island is lined with good beaches notably best-known Cavendish which may get slightly warmer than those of Nova Scotia.

In New Brunswick, Parlee Beach, east of Moncton, draws people from around the province for the relatively warm waters and party atmosphere.

Ontario has some of the finest beaches. Wasaga north of Toronto on Georgian Bay is the big city's closest real beach and gets jam packed on summer weekends. Longer, wider and quieter is beautiful Sauble Beach on Lake Huron with warm, shallow waters and superb sunsets. Immense sandy beaches can also be found at popular Sandbanks and Presqu'ille provincial parks near Belleville on Lake Ontario. Sandbanks also boasts some of the country's largest sand dunes.

North of Winnipeg in Manitoba, Grand Beach on Lake Winnipeg is also one of the country's best and attracts people all summer long. Interior British Columbia has a fine central, urban beach in Kelowna where the surroundings and warm blue skies make a day at the beach well worthwhile.

Kitsilano Beach in Vancouver is a classic strut-and-preen beach and can attract thousands on any given hot, summer day. The water though is not as clean as the others mentioned but who is here to swim? Rough, wild Long Beach in Pacific Rim National Park on Vancouver Island is at the other end of the spectrum – natural as opposed to cultural.

Way up in the Yukon, the small beach at Kookatsoon Lake offers very fine scenery, warm summer temperatures and sun nearly all day and night in July and August.

Perhaps the finest swimming of all is enjoyed on a northern lake with its surface a sheet of glass when you find yourself alone but for the moon at the end of a day of canoeing. And there are thousands of these across the country.

## Skiing

Canada is justly known for its downhill skiing. There are four main alpine ski centres. The slopes of the Laurentian Mountains are found within two hours or less driving north of Montreal and Quebec City in Quebec. South of Montreal there are also ski centres which are part of the Appalachian Mountains; well known to skiers in Vermont and New Hampshire.

Secondly, north of Toronto toward Georgian Bay between the towns of Barrie and Collingwood there are good downhill runs although hills are not found in the same number or at the same elevations as those in the prime Laurentian districts. There is also downhill skiing in the Thunder Bay region of Ontario. See Montreal and Toronto in the text for more ski information. Equipment can be rented at the slopes.

Thirdly, and most grand, are the Rocky Mountains with truly international status skiing based in Banff and Lake Louise. Calgary is under two hours by car to the east.

The Whistler ski area north of Vancouver is a major and still-growing resort which has hosted international competitions.

The provincial tourist boards produce guides to skiing and travel agents can arrange full-package tours which include transportation or accommodation. As the country's major ski resorts are all close to cities, it is quite straightforward to travel on your own to the slopes for a day's skiing and head back to the city that same night.

Each of these areas and many more offer cross-country skiing as well.

## Ecotourism

Long before the environmental movement Canada was into what has become known as ecotourism. It just wasn't called that and, for the most part, still isn't as Canadians are neither quick nor inclined to adopt marketing trends and aggressive promotion methods. It just isn't Canadian. With the country as large and undeveloped as it is, wilderness trips and lodges, outdoor resorts and remote escapes have long been part of the travel opportunity package.

There have been some changes and innovations. Rather than hunting with guns, some tour operators specialising in wildlife are now geared to shooting with cameras. Seeing the polar bears in Churchill, Manitoba is popular with travellers from around the world and is relatively accessible. Perhaps the perfect example of ecotourism are the trips operated to the Magdalen Islands of Quebec to see and photograph baby seals. It was publicity surrounding the bloody slaughter of the seal pups (activist Brigitte Bardot was seen on the icefloes with the seals and their hunters) which brought to an end the controversial hunt which had long been part of the fur fashion business.

As is often the case with ecotours around the world, these trips are somewhat exclusive and very costly. Run by Nortour, the trips from Montreal can be arranged through travel agents or call Tourism Quebec.

## HIGHLIGHTS
### Newfoundland & Labrador

Hilly, chilly St John's with a fabulous, storied harbour tucked beside rocky Signal Hill is the headquarters of the distinctive Newfoundland culture. A night out for music or satirical theatre has to be included here.

Twillingate and the islands of Notre Dame Bay provide some of the best of Newfoundland's coastal features including drifting icebergs.

Gros Morne National Park offers fjords, mountain hiking and other geographic and historic features. Beyond it, at the northern tip of the island, is a 1000-year-old former Viking settlement. The isolated fishing villages of the south coast are unique in North America.

Remote but increasingly road and ferry accessible Labrador presents the determined visitor with the grandeur and solitude of the

Canadian north. Outdoor adventures and isolated villages are attractions which take some pre-planning in this corner of the country. For suggestions on travel routes here see the Newfoundland introduction.

## Nova Scotia

Nova Scotia is best known, and rightly so, for its rugged Cape Breton Island reminiscent of the Scottish Highlands. Traditional Scottish arts can be seen at Ste Anne's and Gaelic can still be heard in various smaller communities. The best of the region is protected within Cape Breton National Park. The Cabot Trail around a magnificent coastal stretch of the mountainous park is one of the most scenic stretches of roadway in Canada. The park also contains some excellent hiking trails. Also on Cape Breton is Louisbourg National Historic Site, an early French fort and now home of one of the best Canadian re-creations of periods passed.

Historic Halifax, the capital, is green, attractive, compact and well preserved with fine lodging, dining and a lively music scene. The Citadel, a massive 18th-century British fort dominates the central area of the city.

Digby Neck, stretching out into the Bay of Fundy, is a good place to hop aboard whale-watching boat tours. In Digby, a meal caught by the local scallop fleet should be considered.

The Annapolis Valley, site of the first European settlement, offers some fascinating history particularly that involving the Acadians, the early French farmers, and their expulsion by the British in the mid-1700s. The apple-growing valley is at its best in spring when the apple blossoms are in bloom and visitor numbers are below the peaks of midsummer.

## Prince Edward Island

Among the island's low-key charms are the north-coast beaches and the pastoral Anne of Green Gables house and property, the setting for the internationally known stories. Also not to be missed are the casual, fun, exceptional-value lobster suppers held around the province. In Charlottetown, known as the birthplace of Confederation, visit Province House where the representatives of the British colonies began working out the details for the formation of the country. Try to catch one of the costumed re-enactments.

A short tour could begin at Summerside near one of the ferry landings to the national park beaches and then on to Charlottetown. From nearby another ferry can be caught to Nova Scotia or Summerside can be revisited.

## New Brunswick

This is Canada's only truly bilingual province. Mt Carlton in the north is a huge, undeveloped park with some excellent hiking and fine wildlife viewing possibilities. The Trans Canada Hwy extends from the north-west corner of the province down along the green, fertile Saint John River Valley which the British Empire Loyalists settled after the American Revolution. Historic sights which make an educational comparison are two re-created pioneer villages; Loyalist King's Landing near Fredericton and Acadian Historic Village near Caraquet on the French Acadian Peninsula. The river ends at the Bay of Fundy where the world's highest tides can be seen. Out in the bay, the Fundy Isles are a peaceful ocean retreat.

## Quebec

Montreal is a blend of French and British sophistication. Chuck the budget and splurge on a meal, wander the cobblestone streets of Old Montreal on a warm night or have a drink somewhere along Rue Saint Denis. A hockey game at the Forum is something many Canadians would cherish. From Montreal it's only three hours to Quebec City, the only walled city in North America and an historic gem designated as such by the United Nations. This is the centre of French culture in Canada. The country's largest winter festival, the Quebec Winter Carnival is held each February. For breakfast have a bowl of café au lait and a croissant and spend the day on the battlefield that might well have determined the history of the country.

From Quebec travel down the St Lawrence River to Tadoussac and the fjord of the Saguenay River. There is great walking in the area and whale-watching tours where the two rivers meet. Drivers could take the ferry across the river, visit Rivière-du-Loup and return to Quebec or Montreal along the south side of the river.

If more time is available, the Gaspé Peninsula at the eastern extremity of southern Quebec is recommended for fine coastal and mountain topography, small typically Quebecois communities and the excellent, uncrowded provincial and national parks which are good for camping, hiking and flora & fauna. Impressive Percé Rock is one of the country's best known geographic features.

For those going to or from New Brunswick, the road through Quebec's Matapédia Valley is suggested as a route. It can be used as the western portion of a circular tour around the Gaspé Peninsula.

Travellers heading to Quebec from anywhere in New England can easily spend a couple of days around the Eastern Townships south of Montreal en route. This is one of the province's top ski regions as well as a summer holiday area.

## Ontario

Ottawa, the country's capital, has nearly a dozen museums and galleries including some of Canada's most important. Added to these are the edifices of power: the Parliament Buildings; the Supreme Court; and others. Ottawa, Montreal, Quebec City make a short circuit which manages to cover both British and French centres as well as some of the country's oldest and most important history.

From Ottawa, a short tour of Ontario can take in handsome Kingston, an old military town and sight of a major university on the way to Toronto, Canada's largest city. In the big city, easily the country's most ethnically varied, distinct 'neighbourhoods' provide sights, sounds and foods from around the world. A recent United Nations report stated Toronto was the most culturally diverse city in the world. A major league baseball game featuring the Blue Jays can be seen or the

entire city from the top of the world's tallest structure, the CN Tower. A short ferry ride leads to the quiet Toronto Islands giving a cheap skyline view and harbour cruise at the same time.

Two hours to the south-west is one of Canada's top attractions, Niagara Falls. Walk along the undeveloped gorge for an inkling of how this world-renowned site appeared to the Native peoples of the region. A short tour of South-Western Ontario can take in the Niagara wine district, German and Mennonite Kitchener, Shakespearean Stratford and the rural tourist centre of Elora. A side trip from Toronto going north could include Midland with its Huron Indian sites and Georgian Bay with its classic rocky, pine-edged shorelines. From here it is not far to another of the country's best-known nature areas, Algonquin Provincial Park with excellent camping, canoeing and wildlife viewing possibilities. From Algonquin, Ottawa is about as far as Toronto, so it can be included in a circular tour of southern Ontario.

## Manitoba

The Museum of Man in Winnipeg is a major Canadian museum worth a couple of hours. On the outskirts of Winnipeg, Canada's largest folk festival is held each summer. South of town, fields of three-metre-high sunflowers as far as the eye can see are both unique and unusual. In the far north at Churchill, at the edge of Canada's tree-line, nature in a variety of guises can be experienced. The aurora borealis, seals, whales and the big draw – polar bears. There is also plenty of the country's early history to learn here as well.

## Saskatchewan

The flat wheatfields and skyscapes of the central prairies are the dominant feature of the open space of southern Saskatchewan. The Wanuskewin Heritage Park north of Saskatoon is a must for its blend of geography, history and Native peoples' culture. From here a side trip to Prince Albert National Park, with its western Canadian Shield topography and features can be added. A walking trail or canoe route leads to the former home of Grey Owl, one of the country's most intriguing adventurers and one of the first international conservationists.

## Alberta

Alberta with the famous resort towns of Banff and Jasper is best known for its Rocky Mountain western border region. Busy Lake Louise and less-known Peyto Lake are two of the undeniable beauty spots in the mountains. The drive or cycle along the Icefields Parkway takes in some supreme alpine scenery and is one of the best remembered strips of pavement in Canada.

The south-central badlands and former dinosaur stomping grounds around Drumheller should not be missed either. The Royal Tyrell Museum of Palaeontology, north-west of Drumheller, has some magnificent exhibits and is a must.

The Calgary Stampede is one of the country's best-known events and continues the province's western traditions. Calgary's Glenbow Museum is a primer to understanding some of the Canadian history and culture.

## British Columbia

Vancouver is Canada's third and fastest growing city and has been booming along while the rest of the country has suffered through the international recession. It's blessed with the best setting of Canada's main population centres with the ocean at its side and mountains hovering nearby. Victoria prides itself on its British roots and acts as a base for any explorations of Vancouver Island and environs, which should include seeing the ancient trees of Canada's original growth forests.

The western region of the province is dominated by the Columbia and Rocky Mountain chains which can be explored in a number of government parks. A soak in one of the regional hot springs early in the morning when the air is cool and fellow travellers are not yet out and about is a highlight, as is a walk in the bugaboos although

picking a site for hiking here is a fool's game; there are hundreds of memorable trails.

The interior of the province around the Okanagan region is geographically similar to the south of France with its appealing scrubby, dry rounded hills, orchards and vineyards.

## Yukon & Northwest Territories

In the Yukon you can hike amid some of the highest mountains in Canada in Kluane National Park, or along the Chilkoot Trail once followed by gold seekers, or stroll around Dawson City which still has many of the original buildings from the gold-rush days.

In the Northwest Territories you can visit the pristine wilderness of Nahanni National Park, see the wildlife of the Mackenzie Delta or take a boat out on the Arctic Ocean to see beluga whales and other marine life.

In summer the hours of daylight are long and in spring and autumn the aurora borealis puts on a magnificent display at night.

## ACCOMMODATION
### Camping

There are campgrounds all over Canada – federal, provincial and privately owned. Government sites are nearly always better and cheaper and, not surprisingly, fill up the quickest. Government parks are well laid out, green and well-treed. They are usually quiet, situated to take advantage of the local landscape, and offer a programme of events and talks. The private campgrounds are generally less geared to tenters, more to those with trailers or recreational vehicles (RVs) of one sort or another and often have more mod cons and services available as well as swimming pools and other entertainment facilities.

RVs are mobile homes which range from moderate campers, basically a small apartment on a pick-up truck, to full-sized motor homes. The majority you'll see are from the USA, but many RVs are also rented in Canada – at rental outlets in places like Whitehorse, Vancouver and Edmonton – by non-Canadians to use as their mobile vacation hotels. If you're surprised by the size and features of some of these suckers you should be: they come with price tags of up to half a million dollars.

In national parks, camping fees range from $9 to $15 for an unserviced site, and to as high as $19 for sites with services like electricity. See under Tourist Offices earlier for more information.

Provincial-park camping rates vary with each province but range from $8.50 to $18. Interior camping in the wilderness parks is always less, about $4. Commercial campgrounds are generally several dollars more expensive than either provincial or national parks.

Government parks start closing in early September for the winter. Dates vary according to the location. Some remain open for maintenance even when camping is finished. Sometimes they let you camp at a reduced rate; maybe the showers or something are turned off. Other places, late in fall or early in spring, are free. The gate is open and there is not a soul around. Still others block the road and you just can't enter the campgrounds although the park itself can still be visited. So, out of the main summer season, you have to investigate but using the parks after official closing can save the hardy a fair bit of money.

There are also campgrounds every 150 km or so along the Trans Canada Hwy.

Lastly, many people travel around the country camping and never pay a dime. For those with cars or vans, using roadside rest areas and picnic spots is recommended. I've done this many times. If there are signs indicating no overnight camping, don't do something like set up a tent. If you're asleep in the car and a cop happens to wake you, just say you were driving, got tired, pulled over for a quick rest and fell asleep: 'What time is it, anyway?'. For less chance of interruption, little side roads and logging roads off the highway are quiet and private.

For cyclists and hitchhikers, just walking off into the woods or fields from the roadside and rolling out the sleeping bag is good enough. It's done all over the country. This is a bit of a hassle on the prairies where there's not much to disappear behind, but it can be done.

## Hostels

There are some excellent traveller's hostels in Canada much like those found in countries around the world. The term hostel in Canada, however, has some unfortunate connotations for travellers as well as those running them and working in them. The term has long been and continues to be used in reference to both government and private shelters for the underprivileged, sick and abused. There are, for example, hostels for battered women who have been victimised by their mates and hostels for recovering drug addicts. So, if you get a sideways glance when you smilingly say you are on the way to spend the night at the hostel now you know why. Indicating traveller's hostel or international hostel should help.

There are now two hostelling associations operating in Canada geared to low-budget visitors. They represent the cheapest places to stay in the country and are where you'll probably meet the most travellers.

**Hostelling International** By far the largest is Hostelling International (HI) Canada. This well-established organisation is part of the internationally-known hostelling network. It was formerly known as the Canadian Hostelling Association which operated in conjunction with the then International Youth Hostels Federation (IYHF). The hostels are no longer known as youth hostels, although they are sometimes still referred to in this way, but rather are known simply as hostels. Through the text of this book these hostels are referred to as HI Hostel (eg the HI Niagara Falls Hostel). Their symbol is an evergreen tree and stylised house within a blue triangle.

HI Canada has about 80 hostels with members in all parts of the country. Nightly costs range from $10 to $20 with most $12 to $15. At many, nonmembers can stay for an additional $2 to $5. A membership, obviously, can quickly pay for itself.

Most of the main cities have a hostel and some provinces have quite a few scattered around more or less randomly. There are fortunately quite a few places in and around the Rocky Mountain national parks.

In July and August space may be a problem at some Canadian hostels particularly in the large cities and in some of the small mountain places. In Montreal, Quebec, Toronto and Vancouver calling ahead a couple of days is a good idea. Ottawa and Victoria are also busy. Reservations for North American hostels can be booked through hostels in Europe, Australia, New Zealand and Japan using computer systems and faxes. This can be convenient for those flying into 'gateway' cities who don't want to hassle for a bed upon arrival.

Outside July and August, traffic thins and getting a bed should not be difficult. Many Canadian hostels are closed in winter but this is generally the case for the smaller ones in secondary towns or more rural areas.

Hostel members are entitled to lower overnight costs but in addition, members can often take advantage of discounts offered by various businesses, including outdoor equipment and sundry travel supplies. Local hostels should have a list of where the various bargains can be had.

Guidebooks, sleeping sheets and other travel accessories can also be purchased at one of half a dozen hostel shops across the country.

At some of the regional offices or hostels themselves outdoor activities such as canoeing, climbing or skiing are organised. Others offer such things as guided walks around the city.

Membership costs $25 for an adult and is good around the world for a year. Less expensive family and senior memberships are also available. Many hostels now have family rooms set aside. For those under the age of 18 there are also discounts. This is the American Express Card of budget travel: don't leave home without it. It's usually cheaper and more convenient to get a membership in your own country.

With a membership comes a handbook listing the hostels' addresses, dates of operation, hostel etiquette, reservation systems etc. Don't rely solely on the information in the handbook as details can change quickly.

The national office is in a suburb of Ottawa. The address is: Hostelling International (HI) Canada (☎ 613-748-5638; fax 613-748-5750), National Office, 1600 James Naismith Drive, Suite 608, Gloucester, Ontario K1B 5N4.

One-year memberships are available through this office or at the various provincial offices. Each province has its own regional office. Any hostel will be able to direct you to it.

**Backpackers' Hostels** The second hostel group is an affiliate of Backpackers' International and is called Backpackers' Hostels Canada. Their symbol is the circled howling wolf with a map of Canada in the background. For information on this group and its members in Canada contact the Longhouse Village Hostel (☎ 807-983-2042), R R 13, Thunder Bay, Ontario, Canada, P7B 5E4. Aside from hostels, they also have campgrounds, motels, campuses, tourist homes etc which will give budget travellers a price reduction. No formal membership is required for users of these hostels.

**Other Hostels** In addition to these two organisations, independent hostels may be found here and there around the country but their numbers are small. Most of these will be found by word of mouth through other travellers. The province of British Columbia has an informal network of privately run hostels which charge about the same rates as the 'official' ones. Quebec, too, is most likely to have some of the unofficial variety although they can be found anywhere.

**Salvation Army** Male travellers who are really on a shoestring or are looking for some 'edge', may find a place at Salvation Army hostels for a couple of nights. They're often free or close to it and they throw in meals, but remember that they're not operated to cater for travellers. The Salvation Army (Sally Ann) hostels or residences are mainly populated by unemployed men – often alcoholics – and the environment isn't particularly pleasant. Many of Canada's larger cities have a Salvation Army Men's Hostel and they are usually in the heart of downtown.

**YM-YWCA** The familiar YM-YWCAs are slowly getting out of the accommodation end of their operations in Canada. They are now tending to concentrate more on fitness, recreation and various other community-oriented programmes. That said, many still offer good lodging in a style between that of a hostel and a hotel, but prices have been creeping up. In YM-YWCAs where complete renovations have occurred, costs can now be as high as those of a bottom-end hotel. Sharing a double with a friend or stranger can bring the price down to quite a reasonable level. Also, some places permit couples and these doubles are fair value.

YM-YWCAs are clean and quiet and often have swimming pools and cheap cafeterias. They are also as a rule very central which is a big plus. Another is that they are open all year. Some offer hostel-style dormitory accommodation throughout the summer. Many are mentioned through the text under hostels in the accommodation sections.

The average price for men is from $24 to $32 a single, and usually a bit more for women.

For information write to: YMCA Canada, 2160 Yonge St, Toronto, Ontario M4S 2A9. The telephone number is ☎ 416-485-9447. They may have a printed sheet on the country's Y's offering accommodation although the last one available was outdated.

**Universities** Many Canadian universities rent out beds in their residence dormitories during the summer months. The 'season' runs roughly from May to some time in August with possible closures for large

academic conferences, etc. Prices average $30 a day and, at many places, students are offered a further reduction. Campus residences are open to all including families and seniors.

Reservations are accepted but aren't necessary. Breakfasts are sometimes included in the price but if not, there is generally a cafeteria which cooks up low-priced meals. The other campus facilities such as swimming pools are sometimes available to guests.

Sometimes annual directories of the various residences are published and may be available on the campus through the residence manager, the alumni association or general information.

Campus accommodation is listed in the text under hostels.

This form of budget accommodation seems to be somewhat unknown in Canada and at most places finding a room even in peak season should not be a problem.

**Efficiency Units**
Efficiencies may also be called housekeeping units or may be described as rooms having cooking facilities, kitchens, kitchenettes or light housekeeping.

This type of overnight option is usually found at motels where some of the rooms have been converted or enlarged for this purpose and for which the owners can ask a few more dollars. A few guesthouse or B&Bs have a room or two with cooking facilities.

This form of accommodation includes a small kitchen and basic cooking supplies such as pots and pans and dishes although often equipment and accessories are minimal. For example, wine drinkers may find they are without a corkscrew. Many have stove tops but no standard oven but these days microwave ovens may be included.

In the country's larger cities some apartment complexes have been set up to offer this type of lodging. They may be called suites. These are primarily aimed at the business traveller or those in town for a week or longer on a course or some type of exchange programme but are available to other travellers.

## Guesthouses & Tourist Homes

Another alternative is the simple guesthouse or tourist home. These may be an extra room in someone's home but are more commonly commercial lodging houses. They are found mainly in places with a large tourist trade such as Niagara, Banff, Victoria, Quebec City and Montreal. In Quebec's principal centres they are popular and plentiful, and usually the best places to stay.

Rooms range in size and have varying amenities. Some include private bathrooms, many do not. The standard cost is about $40 to $65 a double, but could be a bit lower or a lot higher.

Some so-called tourist homes are really rooming houses rented more often by the week or longer and usually have shared kitchens. These places are normally used by local people but can be good for long stays. Rates are lower for long-term rentals.

## B&Bs

B&Bs have caught on in Canada only in the past dozen years or so, but they have sprung up quickly and continue to grow in number. Their popularity is due to offering a decent, more personal alternative to the standard traditional motel/hotel accommodation picture.

Many of the larger cities have associations which manage local member houses; other places are listed directly with tourist offices and are run independently. Some operate as businesses, others just provide their operators with part-time income for a few months in the summer. This type of lodging can be found in all provinces and both in towns and the countryside.

More and more business travellers are finding them both a more comfortable and economical choice. Conveniently, many urban B&Bs are centrally located, often within walking distance of downtown sights. Prices of B&Bs vary quite a bit, ranging roughly from $30 for a single to $80 a double

with the average being from $45 to $65 for two people.

The more expensive ones generally provide more impressive furnishings and decor, often including antiques. Many are found in classic heritage houses, particularly in the east where there is more history. Rooms are almost always in the owner's home and are clean and well kept. Note that smoking is almost always prohibited. Some places will take children and the odd one will allow a pet.

Breakfast can vary from light or continental to what is termed full breakfast which generally means the typical Canadian weekend breakfast of eggs, bacon, toast and coffee. It's worth inquiring about the breakfast before booking.

Several guidebooks dealing exclusively with B&Bs across the country are widely available in Canadian bookstores.

## Hotels

Good, inexpensive hotels are not a Canadian strong point. Though there is a wide range of hotel types, the word usually means one of two things to a Canadian – a rather expensive place to stay or a cheap place to drink. Most new hotels are part of international chains and are designed for either the luxury market or for businesspeople.

Canadian liquor laws have historically been linked to renting beds, so the older, cheap hotels are often principally bars, and quite often low-class bars at that. This latter are found all over the country. For the impecunious, who don't mind some noise and a somewhat worn room, these hotels can come in handy.

Prices usually range from $25 to $35 a single, but rooms are often taken by more permanent guests on a monthly basis. There are some places in this category which are quite alright and which are mentioned in this book. They are not suitable for families or females travelling alone but couples and single males may find these basic hotels more than adequate at least one occasion.

Between the very new and the very old hotels, there are places to be found in the smallish band in between. In the larger cities in particular, you can still find good older, small hotels which mainly rent rooms. Prices vary with the amenities and location and range from about $30 to $75 for singles or doubles.

Overall in Canada, Quebec excepted, there are few of the quaint, charming old hotels you come across in European cities. An encouraging sign is that there are a few more now than when the first edition of this guide appeared. The alternatives to the hotels are motels, B&Bs, tourist homes, and various types of hostels. It is these places which are stressed in this book.

## Motels

In Canada, like the USA (both lands of the automobile), motels are ubiquitous, and until the early-1980s represented the only uniformly acceptable type of moderately priced accommodation. Mostly they are simple and clean, if somewhat nondescript. Many can be found dotting the highways and clustered on the main road routes on either side of larger towns and cities. They usually range from $35 to $70 for singles or doubles with an average being about $50.

Outside the cities, prices drop so motels can be a bargain, especially if there are two or more of you. Before entering a big city it's a good idea to get off the main route and onto one of the smaller, older roads. This is where you'll find motels as cheaply as they come. The less-travelled parts of the country tend to have lower prices, too.

Prices tend to go up in summer or when a special event is on. Off-season bargaining is definitely worthwhile and acceptable. This needn't be haggling as in a Moroccan market; just a simple counter-offer will sometimes work. Unlike many hotels, motels are still pretty much 'mom and pop' operations and so retain more flexibility and often reflect more of the character of the owners.

One motel chain which is seen from coast to coast is Journey's End, which is also seen under the names of Comfort Inn, Quality Inn and Econolodge. They are moderately

priced, not the cheapest, not the most expensive but always reliable. The rooms are plain and simple but spotless and always well maintained. The benefit of the chain system is that it allows for reserving a room anywhere through their ☎ 1-800-668-4200 toll-free telephone number.

Some motels offer 'suites'. This usually means there is a separate second bedroom (good for those with children) but may mean there is a sitting room with TV and chesterfield set apart from the bedroom. In the more costly hotels, a suite usually means there are two rooms, one for sleeping and another set up with a desk where work may be done or clients met.

## Farm Vacations

Each province has a farm vacation programme enabling visitors to stay on working farms for a day, a week or longer. The size and type of farm vary considerably, as do the activities you can take part in. There are usually chores you can help out with and animals to tend. In the west there are ranches to stay at. Rates range from roughly $30 to $35 for singles, $40 to $65 for doubles depending on meals taken. There are also family rates and reductions for children. Details of these programmes are available from provincial tourist boards.

## FOOD

Canadian gastronomy was long based on the British 'bland is beautiful' tradition (although it never quite reached the unimaginative depths of British food). While there are still no distinctive national dishes or unique culinary delights, good food is certainly plentiful. The large numbers of varying ethnic groups spread across the country continue to have a large hand in epicurean improvements. In addition, speciality shops, increased sophistication and knowledge (often through travel) and the natural and health-food movements have all cut into the mainstream and taken business from the ever-present and internationally familiar giant fast-food outlets.

In most cities it's not difficult to find a

Greek, Italian, East Indian or Chinese meal. Small bistro-type places, often with lots of plants, are found across the country with menus emphasising freshness, spices and the latest trends. They tend to fill the gap between the low-end 'greasy spoons' and the priciest restaurants. Many of these, as well as a range of soup-and-salad bars, provide good-value lunches as they compete for office workers' appetites. In the country's largest cities, vegetarian restaurants, although not abundant, can be found. Many are discussed in the text. Such places may be known as natural food or health-food restaurants. East Indian restaurants also offer a selection of vegetarian dishes.

On the east coast of Canada, through all the Atlantic Provinces, deep-fried food is common; all too common for many. It does not hurt to ask for an alternative cooking method or pick from menus carefully.

The common 'spoons', the equivalent of the American diners, are found throughout Canada with names like 'George's' or 'Linda's Place'. Little changed since the 1930s, these small, basic places are the blue-collar workers' restaurants. Some are excellent, some bad news, but they're always cheap. There's usually a breakfast special until 11 am for about $3, followed by a couple of lunch specials. A fairly balanced, if functional, meal costs around $6.

Canadian bread, as a rule, is pathetic. For some improvement from the packaged stuff go to a baker, delicatessen or health-food store.

Fruit, in summer, is a bargain and the apples, peaches, cherries, etc are superb. In June watch for strawberries; in August, blueberries. Farmers' stands are often seen along highways and secondary roads.

Canada produces some very good cheeses, in particular, cheddars – mild, medium and old. Oka from Quebec is a more expensive, subtler and very tasty cheese developed by Trappist monks.

On both coasts, seafood is plentiful, delicious and affordable. On the west coast the salmon in several varieties is a real treat, fresh or smoked and crab is plentiful. The east coast has the less-known but highly esteemed freshwater Atlantic salmon which some consider the finest of them all. The Atlantic region is also famous for lobster and scallops. In the far north, Arctic char is a speciality. The king of inland fish gastronomically is the walleye, often called pickerel.

Canadians' favourite locally produced chocolate bars, available at any corner store, are Caramilk and Crispy Crunch. The latter was in 1991 introduced to the US market in the hopes that they will feel the same way about it.

Lastly, one truly Canadian creation must be mentioned: the butter tart. This delectable little sweet can best be described as...well, just get on the outside of one and you'll see.

## French Food

Most of the country's few semi-original repasts come from the French of Quebec. French pea soup is thick, filling and delicious. The *tourtières* (meat pies) are worth sampling. Quebec is also the world's largest producer of maple syrup, made in the spring when the sap is running, and it's great on pancakes or ice cream.

French fries (chips) in Quebec, where they are known simply as *frites* or *patates*, especially those bought at the small roadside chip wagons are unbeatable – the world's best. Further east into the Atlantic Provinces the Acadian French carry on some of their centuries-old culinary traditions in such dishes as rapie pie *(paté à la rapure)* – a type of meat pie (maybe beef, chicken or clam) topped with grated paste-like potato from which all the starch has been drawn.

## Native Indian Food

Native Indian foods based on wild game such as deer (venison) and pheasant are something to sample if the opportunity presents itself. Buffalo meat, just beginning to be sold commercially in a few places, turns up on menus occasionally. It's lean and has more protein and less cholesterol than beef.

The fiddlehead is a distinctive green, only edible in springtime. It's primarily picked from the woodlands of the Maritime Provinces.

Wild rice, with its black husks and almost nutty flavour is very tasty and often accompanies Native Indian-style meals. Most of it is picked by hand around the Ontario and Manitoba borders but it's widely available in natural-food shops.

## Markets

Many cities have farmers' markets one or more days a week where fresh produce can be bought at good prices. Roadside stands offering the crops of the season can be found in all rural areas. Corn is something to look for and is easy to prepare. On the coasts, seafood can often be purchased at the docks.

## Prices

The variety and quality of meals available across the country has risen appreciably since the first edition of this book (1983). Of course prices have gone up, too, but are not out of line compared with what you'd pay elsewhere. As with most things, food is costlier than in the USA. If you're from Europe, though, or are travelling with a strong currency, you'll find prices reasonable.

Generally, for dinner, under $8 is a major deal, from $8 to $15 is cheap, from $15 to $25 moderate, $25 to $40 getting up there, and anything higher than that is expensive. Except for the lowest price these rates would include some wine. Lunches are a lot less, almost always under $10. Most of the places mentioned in this book fit into the first three categories but some costlier places are listed for treats and splurges.

## DRINKS
### Alcohol

Getting a drink can be a little difficult or at least inconvenient due to a range of laws and regulations concerning alcohol. Alcoholic beverages as a rule must be bought at government stores which are usually closed at night and always on Sundays and holidays. In Quebec, beer and wine can be bought in grocery stores. In other parts of Canada, government stores are being privatised.

Closing time for bars and nightclubs is generally 1 or 2 am. In Quebec it's 3 or 4 am. Some bars in the large cities remain open later but cannot serve booze past the 'closing hour'. The drinking age in most provinces is 19 years.

Restaurants with applicable licences, and this includes all the better ones and those in hotels, serve liquor but must conform to the same hours as drinking establishments.

**Beer** Canadian beer, in general, is good, not great. It's tastier and stronger than US brands and is always served cold. Lagers are by far the most popular beers but ales, light beers, porters and stouts are all available. The two big companies are Molson and Labatts, with the most popular beers being Molson Export Ale and Canadian Lager, or Labatts 50 Ale and Blue Lager.

A welcome trend is the advent of small breweries producing real or natural beers and pubs brewing their own for consumption on the premises. Both these new breaks from tradition are developing rapidly across the country but are most evident in the large cities.

In a bar, a pint (340 ml) ranges from $1.75 to $4.50. Draught beer, sold only in bars, is the cheapest way to drink; a 170-ml glass can cost as low as $1.20. In places featuring live music, prices usually go up after the night's entertainment arrives. Retail, beer in cases (bottles or cans) costs about $1.25 a bottle.

**Wine** Canadian wine has long had a deservedly poor reputation. Recently the product has improved, in some cases considerably, but the stigma continues undiminished. True, cheap wines are the domestics and they taste as cheap as the price. But most of the Canadian wineries now also take great care with at least some of their brands.

The country has two main wine-producing regions, Ontario's Niagara Peninsula with by far the largest share and British Columbia's Okanagan Valley. Wineries can also be found in southern Quebec, elsewhere in Ontario and in Nova Scotia. The best-known ones are the ones of the Niagara district.

In southern Ontario there are three viticultural areas, the Niagara Peninsula, the Lake Erie Shoreline and Pelee Island which is out in Lake Erie. These areas now have their own Vintners Quality Alliance (VQA) grading and classification system, meant to establish and maintain standards for the better wines in much the same way as is done in Europe. Wines sporting the VQA label are among the ones recommended to sample.

Red, white, dry and sweet are all produced as are some sparkling wines, but the dry whites and the very expensive ice wines are Canada's best.

Import duties keep foreign wine prices up to protect the Canadian wine industry but you can still get a pretty low-priced bottle of French wine.

**Spirits** Canada produces its own gins, vodkas, rums, liqueurs, brandies and coolers. But Canadian whiskey, generally known in the country as rye, is the best-known liquor and the one with the biggest reputation. Canadian Club and VO rye whisky are Canada's most famous drinks – good stuff. Rye is generally taken with ginger ale or soda but some like it straight with ice. Canadian whiskey has been distilled since the mid-1800s and has been popular in the USA as well as Canada from the early days of production. Most of the high price of spirits in Canada is attributable to tax.

### Nonalcoholic Drinks

The fruit-growing areas of Quebec, Ontario and British Columbia produce excellent apple and cherry ciders, some with alcohol, some without. In Quebec and the Atlantic Provinces, visitors may want to sample a local nonalcoholic brew called spruce beer. It's produced in small batches by individuals and doesn't have a large commercial base but is sold in some local stores. It varies quite a bit and you can never be too sure what will happen when the cap comes off, but some people love the stuff.

Canadian mineral and spring waters have become quite popular and are now readily available. Bottle waters from Europe, especially France are also readily available.

A cup of standard Canadian coffee is not memorable but it isn't expensive either. If fresh it can be fairly decent. Restaurant coffee is almost always a filtered brew. In the western provinces it is not uncommon to be offered free refills (sometimes multiple) with every purchased cup. This is not the case in the rest of the country. True coffee drinkers should not under any circumstances buy a coffee from a vending machine. Big city cafés and restaurants often offer espresso, cappuccino and the like. Speciality coffee bars such as those operated by The Second Cup are becoming increasingly popular across the country and offer a selection of good coffees. A good cup can also be found at the ubiquitous doughnut shops found everywhere across Canada.

True to the British heritage, tea is also common. It is served hot with milk (add your own) unlike in America where tea often means iced lemon tea. In restaurants it is always made with bags and generally is not of the highest calibre but certainly comparable to what is generally brewed around the world. It is often served in a small, steel pot which is impossible to pour without spilling.

### ENTERTAINMENT

Entertainment in major Canadian cities is top rate. Theatre, ballet, opera and symphony orchestras can be enjoyed across the country although the main 'cultural' season is from November to May when most Canadians are home, back at work and spending time indoors. Still, first-rate productions are performed through the summer as well.

Toronto and Vancouver (the largest English-speaking cities) have particularly noteworthy theatre and dinner theatre scenes.

Montreal is the capital of French theatre and performance arts. Nightclubs and bars present nightly jazz, blues, rock of widely varying calibre. National and international names perform regularly in the main centres. Most large cities and towns now have a comedy club or two. Long illegal, casinos are in the nascent stage in Canada with Winnipeg, Calgary and Montreal in full swing and Windsor, Ontario and others about to open.

Spectator sports including professional hockey, baseball and football can be seen in most of the larger cities and are outlined in the text.

For more information on Canadian arts and sports see under Arts & Culture in the Facts about the Country chapter.

## THINGS TO BUY

Despite being a Western consumer society largely filled with the goods of the international market place, Canada does offer the discriminating a number of interesting or unique things to buy.

Outdoor or camping specialists may turn up something you haven't seen before and some of the outdoor clothing is particularly good – durable, well-made and not too bad to look at. One Canadian name to look for is Tilley. These clothing products are not cheap but their longevity pays off.

For edibles, the British Columbia smoked salmon is a real treat and from west coast outlets fresh salmon can be packed to take on flights home. In Quebec there is maple syrup and maple sugar which make different, inexpensive gifts. The wines of the Niagara region can be very good, advice is available at liquor outlets in southern Ontario. Rye whiskey is a Canadian speciality.

Most good bookstores have a Canadiana section for books on Canada or Canadian literature. Likewise, record shops offer tapes of Canadian music. Traditional folk music is especially abundant in Eastern Canada.

At art gallery gift shops prints of the work of Canadian painters can be found.

Wood carving has a long tradition in Quebec notably at the town of Saint Jean Port Joli. Another area for this but to a lesser degree is along the French Shore of Nova Scotia. Also in this province but at Cheticamp there are some fine handmade rugs available.

In the west, British Columbia jade can be bought in a number of ways including jewellery. Saskatchewan and Alberta have a Western tradition which reveals itself in leatherwork – tooled belts, vests, etc as well as leather cowboy-style boots and hats can make good, interesting buys.

Traditional Hudson Bay blankets and coats of 100% wool can be bought at The Bay department stores run by Canada's oldest company. For both these items look for the tell-tale green, red, yellow and black stripes on a white background. Classic cloth lumberjack jackets in either red or blue checks are cheap and distinctive if not elegant.

Crafts shows, flea markets and speciality shops showcase the work of Canadian artisans. Potters, weavers, jewellers etc turn out some fine distinctive articles.

For information on the worthwhile Native arts & crafts to consider as purchases see under Native Art in the Art & Culture section. These represent some of the best value, most 'Canadian' souvenirs.

Shops designed to serve tourists at the country's attractions such as Niagara Falls are not the place to look for a meaningful keepsake. Canadiana kitsch in the form of plastic Mounties, cheap pseudo-Indian dolls, miniature beavers and tasteless T-shirts is good for a smirk and nothing more.

# Getting There & Away

## AIR

The most common way to enter Canada is via its well known neighbour to the south, the good ol' USA. Apart from American visitors reaching Canada overland or flying in, many overseas flights to North America go to the USA, with New York, San Francisco and Los Angeles as the major destinations. You can then either fly to a major Canadian city, such as Montreal or Vancouver, or catch a bus or train. Often though, flying directly into Canadian gateway cities such as Halifax, Montreal, Toronto and Vancouver can be more or less the same price as first arriving in American cities.

Also, from Europe anyway, getting a reasonably priced ticket has become increasingly straightforward. The budget airlines and the lesser-known, smaller airlines out of countries such as Iceland or Belgium have given way to the competitive

---

**Air Travel Glossary**

**Apex** Apex, or 'advance-purchase excursion' is a discounted ticket which must be paid for in advance. There are penalties if you wish to change it.

**Baggage Allowance** This will be written on your ticket: usually one 20-kg item to go in the hold, plus one item of hand luggage.

**Bucket Shop** An unbonded travel agency specialising in discounted airline tickets.

**Bumped** Just because you have a confirmed seat doesn't mean you're going to get on the plane – see Overbooking.

**Cancellation Penalties** If you have to cancel or change an Apex ticket there are often heavy penalties involved, insurance can sometimes be taken out against these penalties. Some airlines impose penalties on regular tickets as well, particularly against 'no show' passengers.

**Check In** Airlines ask you to check in a certain time ahead of the flight departure (usually 1½ hours on international flights). If you fail to check in on time and the flight is overbooked the airline can cancel your booking and give your seat to somebody else.

**Confirmation** Having a ticket written out with the flight and date you want doesn't mean you have a seat until the agent has checked with the airline that your status is 'OK' or confirmed. Meanwhile you could just be 'on request'.

**Discounted Tickets** There are two types of discounted fares – officially discounted (see Promotional Fares) and unofficially discounted. The lowest prices often impose drawbacks like flying with unpopular airlines, inconvenient schedules, or unpleasant routes and connections. A discounted ticket can save you other things than money – you may be able to pay Apex prices without the associated Apex advance booking and other requirements. Discounted tickets only exist where there is fierce competition.

**Full Fares** Airlines traditionally offer first-class (coded F), business-class (coded J) and economy-class (coded Y) tickets. These days there are so many promotional and discounted fares available from the regular economy class that few passengers pay full economy fare.

**Lost Tickets** If you lose your airline ticket an airline will usually treat it like a travellers' cheque and, after inquiries, issue you with another one. Legally, however, an airline is entitled to treat it like cash and if you lose it then it's gone forever. Take good care of your tickets.

**No Shows** No shows are passengers who fail to show up for their flight, sometimes due to unexpected delays or disasters, sometimes due to simply forgetting, sometimes because they made more than one booking and didn't bother to cancel the one they didn't want. Full-fare passengers who fail to turn up are sometimes entitled to travel on a later flight. The rest of us are penalised (see Cancellation Penalties).

**On Request** An unconfirmed booking for a flight, see Confirmation.

**Open Jaws** A return ticket where you fly out to one place but return from another. If available this can save you backtracking to your arrival point.

---

prices of airlines such as Air Canada and British Airways.

Still, whether you fly directly or indirectly, shopping for airfares can be a bit of a confusing adventure. Trying to track down prices and deals can sometimes be compared to trying to pin jello to the wall. Things change and prices go up and down by the day, even by the phone call. Nothing is consistent and deals come and go.

The best advice is to suggest you ask a lot of questions of the airline and a number of travel agents: as always, persistence, ingenuity and luck will get you everywhere. This is particularly true for those heading to Canada

from anywhere other than one of the Western countries.

If it's possible, shop for a ticket in a city that has a high number of budget travellers passing through; you'll find the best bargains in such cities. The most famous of these are London, Athens and Bangkok. Sydney, Hong Kong, Kuala Lumpur and Manila are others. If these departure points are not feasible, shop around the travel agents at home. There are often travel agencies which specialise in trips to North America and which will know of organised charters or good deals.

One of the basics in air travel is that most

---

**Overbooking** Airlines hate to fly empty seats and since every flight has some passengers who fail to show up (see No Shows) airlines often book more passengers than they have seats. Usually the excess passengers balance those who fail to show up but occasionally somebody gets bumped. If this happens guess who it is most likely to be? The passengers who check in late.

**Promotional Fares** Officially discounted fares like Apex fares which are available from travel agents or direct from the airline.

**Reconfirmation** At least 72 hours prior to departure time of an onward or return flight you must contact the airline and 'reconfirm' that you intend to be on the flight. If you don't do this the airline can delete your name from the passenger list and you could lose your seat. You don't have to reconfirm the first flight on your itinerary or if your stopover is less than 72 hours. It doesn't hurt to reconfirm more than once.

**Restrictions** Discounted tickets often have various restrictions on them – advance purchase is the most usual one (see Apex). Others are restrictions on the minimum and maximum period you must be away, such as a minimum of 14 days or a maximum of one year. See Cancellation Penalties.

**Standby** A discounted ticket where you only fly if there is a seat free at the last moment. Standby fares are usually only available on domestic routes.

**Tickets Out** An entry requirement for many countries is that you have an onward or return ticket, in other words, a ticket out of the country. If you're not sure what you intend to do next, the easiest solution is to buy the cheapest onward ticket to a neighbouring country or a ticket from a reliable airline which can later be refunded if you do not use it.

**Transferred Tickets** Airline tickets cannot be transferred from one person to another. Travellers sometimes try to sell the return half of their ticket, but officials can ask you to prove that you are the person named on the ticket. This is unlikely to happen on domestic flights, on an international flight tickets may be compared with passports.

**Travel Agencies** Travel agencies vary widely and you should ensure you use one that suits your needs. Some simply handle tours while full-service agencies handle everything from tours and tickets to car rental and hotel bookings. A good one will do all these things and can save you a lot of money but if all you want is a ticket at the lowest possible price, then you really need an agency specialising in discounted tickets. A discounted ticket agency, however, may not be useful for other things, like hotel bookings.

**Travel Periods** Some officially discounted fares, Apex fares in particular, vary with the time of year. There is often a low (off-peak) season and a high (peak) season. Sometimes there's an intermediate or shoulder season as well. At peak times, when everyone wants to fly, not only will the officially discounted fares be higher but so will unofficially discounted fares or there may simply be no discounted tickets available. Usually the fare depends on your outward flight – if you depart in the high season and return in the low season, you pay the high-season fare. ■

airlines, particularly the larger ones (including the Canadian companies flying internationally), provide the greatest discount on return tickets rather than on one-way fares. Some travellers get around this by buying a return ticket, using it to get to Canada, then selling the unused portion – naturally, this is highly improper. However, tickets are still rarely checked for names. One-way tickets provide the greatest flexibility. On the other hand, pre-booked returns with a range of possible restrictions provide, as a rule, the best prices.

## To/From the UK & Europe

The key to cross-Atlantic flights is timing. In either direction, the season is the price guide. That said, how high and low seasons are defined varies with particular airlines, the day of the week, the duration of the stay and other factors.

Generally, one-way fares are no bargain and if they are less than a return, it is not by much. In such cases, many people sell the other half of their return ticket when they get to Canada if they plan on overstaying the ticket's validity or are going elsewhere. Those looking for tickets should note, of course, that this means these tickets can also be purchased, sometimes at less than face value. This is usually done through newspaper ads, university and hostel bulletin boards and the like.

Many of Europe's major centres are served by at least one of Canadian Airlines or Air Canada. They arrange return fares starting on either side of the Atlantic.

For example, Air Canada flies from London, Paris and Frankfurt (among many others) to Toronto. The cheapest return flights are from London with a maximum stay of six months. Fares vary a lot depending on the time of year, with the summer months and Christmas being the most expensive season. In any case an advance booking of 21 days is required for the best prices. From London, return fares can vary from as low as UK£299 in low season.

Air Canada flies one way London to St John's, Newfoundland twice a week for UK£350 (C$693) or UK£700 (C$1386) return on a regular economy, no advance notice fare. With a 14-day advance booking this return fare drops to high season UK£477 (C$949) and low season UK£318 (C$632).

This is a flight to consider for a couple of reasons. It's one of the so-called open jaw return tickets which allow for landing in one city and departing from another, sometimes at no extra charge, sometimes with a small additional payment required.

The fare to Toronto is the same price so you can fly into St John's make your way across eastern Canada and head home from Toronto. Another benefit to this particular flight is that transportation from mainland Canada to Newfoundland, for example, is costly and time-consuming. This way you start there and move to the rest of Canada with no back-tracking.

Canadian Airlines has London, Amsterdam and Munich as major cities although they serve many other European cities, too. From Munich midweek, midsummer the return ticket costs DM1299, C$1009. The low-season rate for the above fare is about 30% less. Prices are highest between 15 June and 15 August.

Both Canadian companies offer youth fares to Canada from Europe.

The British Airways direct one-way flight London to Montreal is UK£350 (C$693) regular economy fare or double that for return. The advance booking return excursion fare is UK£459 (C$909) midweek, midsummer. British Airways offers neither youth nor standby fares. Alternatively, British Airways offers some one-way fares to John F Kennedy Airport, New York City, for UK£339 (low season). From New York City, it's about an eight-hour bus ride or a 10-hour train ride to Montreal.

None of the above airlines are currently offering any stop-over privileges in Canada for tickets such as London-Montreal-Toronto-Vancouver-London. A travel agent or bucket shop may be able to work something.

**Charters** If you are travelling between Europe and Canada you might investigate these. Most charter trips with a Canadian connection are between Canada and Europe. Other Canadian charters connect to US destinations, mostly Florida or Hawaii (the sunspots), or to the Caribbean.

Private Canadian charter companies operate flights to various European countries. Often a good place to look in Canada is at the travel agencies in an ethnic part of a major city where immigrants are often seeking cheap trips back to the homeland.

Some of the bigger, better established charter companies and tour wholesalers in Canada work in conjunction with one of the two principal Canadian airline companies. An example is Air Canada Vacations which puts packages together in Europe for visitors to Canada. Canadian charter companies don't seem to have either an easy or a long life so the names change frequently. In Canada or abroad, travel agencies and university student offices should have some information on potential charter trips.

There are probably good charters from France to the province of Quebec.

**Budget Airlines** The worldwide recession of the late 1980s and early 1990s has been hard on all international carriers and budget airlines created by flamboyant owners are nowhere to be seen. For a while, every couple of years a small upstart airline arrived on the scene creating a sensation with fares that undercut everybody else's on the cross-Atlantic route. Such airlines usually fly into and out of New York from a Western European city so keep your ears open. Unfortunately this has not occurred for some time now and the near future doesn't look too promising either. But, if you're very lucky, a new one will spring up just before you leave.

**To/From the USA**
Flights between US and Canadian cities are abundant and frequent. Between larger cities there are generally direct flights. Montreal, Toronto and Vancouver are the busiest Canadian destinations but all major cities are plugged into the extensive North American system.

Canadian Airlines flies from Los Angeles, California, to Vancouver for US$288 plus taxes, one way.

Air Canada flies in and out of New York City to Montreal and Toronto. A one-way New York City to Toronto ticket costs US$170. American Airlines also serves this route.

The *New York Times*, the *Chicago Tribune*, the *San Francisco Chronicle Examiner* and the *LA Times* produce weekly travel sections containing lots of ads with current airfares. You could also try CUTS or STA Travel which have offices in all the major cities.

**To/From Australia & NZ**
Continental Airlines, Canadian Airlines, United Airlines, Qantas and Air New Zealand offer regular flights to Vancouver from Australia and New Zealand.

Qantas offers standard economy airfares from Australia to Canada: a return ticket to Vancouver is a whopping A$4820 all year. However, there are much cheaper advance-purchase tickets available with varying conditions attached. These fares range from A$1621 in the low season to a high of $2345.

From Auckland the regular return economy fare with Air New Zealand is also huge at NZ$5308, but like Qantas it offers discounted advance-purchase airfares. These start from NZ$1899 in the low season, for a minimum stay of seven days and must be purchased 21 days in advance.

Coming from Australia, New Zealand or Asia, landing in the USA is often cheaper than flying directly to Canada. After arriving in Los Angeles, San Francisco, or possibly Seattle (Washington state) on the west coast, a train (as far as Seattle) or bus will take you to Vancouver.

Qantas and Air New Zealand flights from Australia to US cities (in California), are lower by up to A$150 or so. In addition, they often include many stopovers in the Pacific – Fiji, Rarotonga, Hawaii and even Tahiti.

The fares given are only the airlines' official fares. You will find the best deals by shopping around the travel agencies.

### To/From Asia

From Asia it's often cheaper to fly first to the USA rather than directly to Canada. Singapore Airlines and Korean Airlines run cheap flights around the Pacific, ending on the USA's west coast.

Check in Singapore and in travel agencies in Bangkok and Kuala Lumpur. You can probably find one-way fares from these centres to the USA's west coast, with up to five stops, for under US$750, and for under US$900 return.

From Hong Kong, one-way fares to Los Angeles, San Francisco or Vancouver are also reasonable and usually cheaper than going the other way. The cheapest one-way fare to Los Angeles is around US$430, to Vancouver US$395.

### Round-the-World Tickets

If you are covering a lot of distance, a Round-the-World (RTW) ticket could be worthwhile. A good ticket can include a lot of stops in places all over the world, with a maximum ticket validity of 12 months. Check out the huge variety of RTW tickets available.

Out of Canada, Air Canada in conjunction with other airlines offers such tickets. Air Canada uses just one other airline per ticket, but which airline that is varies. Depending on which you select the price of the fare will change. Two that are regularly part of such a deal are Singapore Airlines and Cathay Pacific.

Air Canada and Singapore Airlines offer a RTW fare of C$3131 for unlimited stopovers (their destinations only), going in one direction over a period of not more than 12 months. Side trips can be arranged in Europe at a reasonable cost. Similar fares are offered out of many countries but you should investigate in the country of first departure.

### LAND

### Bus

The Greyhound bus network connects the major continental US cities with most major destinations in Canada but with a bus transfer at the border or nearest town to it. Note, however, that the multi-day passes available in the USA cannot be used in Canada. If you're using a US pass, enquire as to how close you can get to your Canadian destination before having to buy a separate ticket.

There is one exception to this. Only one city in Canada is served by an American Greyhound bus and that is Montreal, Quebec. The last trip taken on an American Greyhound pass can be used to travel from New York City to Montreal. Other American bus lines do run directly to Canadian cities with no stop or need for a bus change.

Alaska's Gray Line buses connect Fairbanks, Anchorage, Skagway and Haines in Alaska with Whitehorse in the Yukon.

### Train

Amtrak has three main routes between the USA and Canada: these are New York City to Montreal (10 hours), New York City to Toronto (12 hours; via Niagara Falls) and Chicago to Toronto (11½ hours). On the west coast, Seattle is as far north as Amtrak reaches. Buses run from Seattle to Vancouver. For information about fares and schedules contact Amtrak (☎ 1-800-872-7245), 50 Massachusetts Ave NE, Washington, DC 20002, USA.

### Car

The highway system of the continental USA connects directly with the Canadian highway system along the border at numerous points, which then meet up with the Trans Canada Highway further north.

During the summer months, Fridays and Sundays can be very busy at major international border crossings what with shoppers, vacationers and visitors all travelling at the same times. Back-ups can be especially bad on the long summer holiday weekends. Waits at these times can be hours so avoid them if possible. The crossings at Detroit-Windsor, Buffalo-Fort Erie, Niagara Falls and NY-Niagara Falls, Ont and Rouse's Point, NY-Quebec, are especially prone to lengthy queues. The small, secondary border points elsewhere are always quiet. Sometimes so quiet the officers have nothing to do except tear your luggage apart.

Between Canada and Alaska the main routes are the Alaska, Klondike and Taylor highways.

Visitors with US or British passports are allowed to bring their vehicles in for six months.

## SEA
### Yacht
Many flights from Australasia stop off in Hawaii. With a bit of persistence and luck it might be possible to find someone with a yacht who needs a hand. Hawaii is a favourite vacation spot with Western Canadians, but don't count on hitting the jackpot.

If you're coming from the Caribbean you might also find a yacht there (it's been done). Most head for Florida and from there, some edge up the east coast. Experienced sailors and females have the best chance at getting a place on board.

### Passenger Ship
Regular, long-distance passenger ships disappeared with the advent of cheap air travel, to be replaced by a small number of luxury cruise ships. The standard reference for passenger ships is the *ABC Passenger Shipping Guide* published by the Reed Travel Group (☎ 0582-60-0111), Church St, Dunstable, Bedfordshire LU5 4HB, UK. Cunard's *Queen Elizabeth II*, sails between Southampton in the UK and New York 20 times a year; the trip takes five nights one way.

Seabourn Cruise Line (☎ 415-391-7444), 55 San Francisco St, San Francisco, California 94133, USA, offers cruises to and around Eastern Canada from Boston and New York. Both seven and 14-day trips are offered with stops in many Canadian ports ending up in Montreal. These trips are in the $1000 a day range.

Canada Travel Specialists (☎ 210-690-2514 and ☎ 1-800-829-2262) with the head office in Texas market various trips and tours of Canada to Americans. One is a 12-day

educational cruise run by Canadian-owned Adventure Canada of the British Columbia coast departing from Seattle. This cruise stresses wildlife, history and the environment and includes lectures and input by various guests on board. For more information contact 10999 IH 10 West, Suite 210, San Antonio, Texas, 78230.

### Freighter
A more adventurous, though not necessarily cheaper, alternative is as a paying passenger on a freighter. Freighters are more numerous than cruise ships and there are more routes from which to choose. Passenger freighters typically carry six to 12 passengers (more than 12 would require a doctor on board) and, though less luxurious than dedicated cruise ships, give you a real taste of life at sea.

The previously mentioned *ABC Passenger Shipping Guide* is a good source of information or contact the Freighter Travel Club of America, 3524 Harts Lake Rd, Roy, WA 98580.

### Ferry
On the west coast there are ferries between Washington state and Victoria on Vancouver Island. From Port Hardy on northern Vancouver Island ferries also head north along the Inside Passage to Alaska. See the Getting There & Away sections for Port Hardy and Victoria in the British Columbia chapter.

On the east coast, Canada is connected with the USA by several ferries. Yarmouth, Nova Scotia, is linked to both Bar Harbour, Maine, and to Portland, Maine, in the USA with two different ferry routes. See under Yarmouth for more details. From the south end of Deer Island, New Brunswick in the Bay of Fundy, another ferry runs to Eastport, Maine. A ferry at the north end of Deer Island connects it to the New Brunswick mainland.

## LEAVING CANADA
### Departure Tax
There is a departure/airport tax of $40 levied on all international flights out of Canada, other than those to US destinations. To

American destinations the tax is 7% of the ticket value plus $10 to a maximum of $40.

Most tickets purchased in Canada for international flights out of Canada include this tax; but tickets out of Canada, purchased in another country, usually don't include it. If you did buy your ticket in another country and it didn't include departure tax, you will be asked for this tax after you pass through customs and immigration. When you're changing money, consider saving enough to cover it.

Also, sales taxes and the GST may or may not be included in any quoted airline ticket in Canada so ask. In Vancouver there is an additional tax known as the airport improvement tax. A flight leaving Canada for an American destination is taxed at $10, every other international flight is taxed at $15. This tax is not included with the ticket purchase price and must be paid for at the airport. Save the cash for it or use a credit card.

Remember, too, that if you intend to apply for any GST rebate this is your last chance

to get a form (see under the Consumer Taxes section in the Facts for the Visitor chapter for more details).

## WARNING

This chapter is particularly vulnerable to change. Prices for international travel are volatile, routes are introduced and cancelled, schedules change, rules are amended and special deals come and go.

Airlines and governments seem to take a perverse pleasure in making price structures and regulations as complicated as possible and you should check directly with the airline or a travel agency to make sure you understand how a fare (and ticket you may buy) works.

The upshot of all this is that you should get opinions, quotes and advice from as many airlines and travel agencies as possible before you part with your hard-earned cash. The details given in this chapter should be regarded as pointers and are not a substitute for your own up-to-the-minute research.

# Getting Around

Within Canada, land travel is much cheaper and, of course, much more interesting than flying. The bus network is the most extensive public transportation system and is generally less expensive than the now limited train service. VIA Rail, the national passenger train service does, however, offer some multi-day passes as well as discount prices for travelling on specific days, for example during midweek. Train travel can also be quicker than riding the buses.

Although quite a bit higher than in the USA, driving costs are reasonable with gasoline prices considerably lower than those in Europe. Still, it's a big country and if you really want to get around quickly your wallet will be thinned.

Whether using the train or bus network or a combination of both, visitors should remember that despite Canada's size the population is small. In many ways this is an asset and part of the country's appeal but can also mean that transportation is not always frequent, convenient or even available. Hopping on a bus or train on a whim, as may be possible in much of Europe, is not realistic here unless you're in one of the main centres. However, as any traveller knows, the greater the hassle, the less likely the place will be inundated by tourists.

Air fares are expensive, but for those with a little extra money and not much time, the odd flight may be useful. Flying in Canada actually works out a few cents cheaper per km than owning and operating a car on a full-time basis. An open eye and ear can often turn up one of the ever-changing specials or 'seat sales' (last-minute ticket price reductions).

## AIR

Canadian airlines have been struggling for the past few years and this has meant the end of many and the amalgamation of others. The country has two major airlines both privately operated, Air Canada and Canadian Airlines International (formerly CP Air, Pacific Western, Eastern Provincial and several secondary carriers), usually referred to simply as Canadian. Both work in conjunction with a number of regional carriers known as partners. Canadian Airlines is also working on a deal with American Airlines of the USA which may see close ties develop between them. Air Canada has made some financial connections with Continental of the USA.

In recent years more flights by US carriers have been permitted in to Canada and talks continue on more movement in this direction. An 'open skies' policy – a sort of a free-trade of the air system – would mean even more US airlines in Canada and maybe lower fares. On the other hand, critics say, it would spell the end of Canadian airline companies which would be unable to match the lower prices.

Air Canada partners in Canada are Air Ontario, Air BC, Air Nova, Bearskin Airways, Northwest Territories Airlines, First Air (NWT) and Air Creebec (northern Ontario & northern Quebec). The Canadian Airlines partners have been amalgamated into Canadian Regional Airlines. Within this group are the former Air Atlantic, Time Air, Calm Air, Ontario Express and Inter-Canadienne. These names may still be heard although the airlines do not formally exist – just their routes do.

There are also some independent regional and local airlines which tend to focus on small specialised regions particularly in the north and other relatively remote areas.

Together all these airlines cover most small cities and towns across the country. On smaller airlines it's worth inquiring about student rates but you will need an International Student Identity Card (ISIC).

Domestic flights tend to be costly. The prices and schedules of flights change and fluctuate often. Phone an airline for information one week, and the next week they'll tell you something quite different. The best thing to do is shop around – directly with the airline or through a travel agent – and be as flexible as you can. Waiting a day or two or avoiding a weekend flight could save you a lot. If you have the time, advance-booking flights are always the most economical.

Air Canada may be cheap for one flight, Canadian Airlines for another, although each keeps pretty well abreast of what the other is up to.

In order to keep down the price of air travel there are a few general rules to follow. First, plan in advance because the best bargains are excursion fares, pre-booked return flights with minimum and maximum stays. Flights booked at least seven days in advance are lower than spur-of-the-moment prices. Booking either 14 or 30 days in advance may well result in further reductions. Secondly, don't fly at peak times, that is between 7 am and 7 pm. Thirdly, be prepared to make stops; direct flights may cost more.

Both airlines offer year-round youth fares on domestic flights. On Air Canada and Canadian those 24 years of age and younger are offered standby fares which mean reductions of about 30% or more. Standby policies come and go so be sure to ask.

Occasionally, there are short-term specials for promotion of a certain flight; these can be cheap but are irregular. Both Canadian airlines occasionally offer 'seat sales'.

Another thing to consider is getting a ticket from point A to B and stopping off in the middle. This can often be done for little more than the straight-through fare.

Canadian Airlines and Air Canada sometimes offer fly-drive packages which cover the air fare and car rental. The packages, only available on return flights, sometimes include accommodation. Other possibilities include reductions on cars, hotels and bus tours. The hotels used, however, are expensive. You just have to ask about the latest gimmicks and offers.

Travel agencies offer economical charters and package tours to various Canadian cities as well as US destinations. These turn up throughout the year but especially over Christmas and through the summer holiday season. Book well in advance to take advantage of these specials. There's a varying minimum and maximum stay on charter flights. No student or youth fares are offered on these types of tickets.

One way that travellers get cheap tickets to cities around the country, is by checking the classified ads in newspapers and city entertainment papers under 'Travel' or 'Business Personals'. These often involve the sale of the redundant half of a two-way (return) ticket, as return tickets are often the same price or even cheaper than one ways. These offers are also advertised on university and hostel noticeboards. It isn't strictly legal, as tickets are officially nontransferable, but it's done a lot.

Air fares in Canada are generally quoted as the base fare only. All taxes including the GST are added on top. Ticket agents will quickly total these for you, but you do need to ask. This is worth doing as taxes can add quite a bit to the bill, perhaps resulting in a rather nasty surprise. In Vancouver, passengers must pay an additional tax to help finance airport expansion. This is billed at $5 to fly within the province, $10 within North America and $15 to fly out of North America. This tax is not added on to the ticket price and must be paid at the airport so make sure to save the fee required. It can also be paid with a credit card if you don't have the cash.

The air fares listed in this book should be used as a rough guide as prices fluctuate regularly and taxes change with new governments – both provincial and federal. Prices of regular economy flights go up for the high seasons of Christmas and summer.

Canada is no exception when it comes to the beefed-up security of the 1990s. This all takes longer so arriving well before flight time is recommended although the two hours requested by some airlines is excessive.

Also, a note on confirming seats is in order. Canadian airlines, as is customary, do overbook their flights in the usually correct assumption that there will be no-shows (people who book a flight then don't turn up or arrive too late). At the times when almost everybody turns up some individuals are bumped from the flight and forced to await the next departure. This can be a real hassle and throw a spanner in the works. A so-called confirming of the ticket with a travel agent or the airline does not necessarily mean you are indeed a confirmed passenger and therefore not subject to the possible hassle. To guarantee yourself a seat ask for a specific seat number. This can be done at the time of booking or with a later call to confirm the flight. Once you've been given a designated seat number, you're safe.

## BUS

Buses supply the most extensive transportation routes across the country. They go nearly everywhere and are normally cheaper than trains. Buses are usually clean, safe and comfortable. They are also generally efficient and run on time.

The two biggies are Voyageur Colonial Ltd in Quebec and Ontario and Greyhound

from Toronto westwards. Other major companies include Greyhound-Gray Coach Lines in Ontario, Orleans Express in eastern Quebec, SMT in New Brunswick, Acadian Lines in Nova Scotia and Roadcruiser in Newfoundland. There are other provincial, regional and local lines. Bus services are covered in the text.

Travellers should know however, that services are not exhaustive nor always convenient. Routes between any two given destinations may not be too frequent and in some cases not even daily. Many routes are run on a three-times-a-week basis or something similar. In more out of the way places there may be no service at all.

Some bus lines offer reduced return fares and other specials some of the time. Always ask, the policies often change.

On long trips the journey can be broken any number of times. A one-way ticket is usually good for 60 days, a return for a year.

### Highway Distances between Major Cities (km)

| | Calgary | Charlottetown | Edmonton | Fredericton | Halifax | Montreal | Ottawa | Quebec | Regina | St John's | Saskatoon | Thunder Bay | Toronto | Vancouver | Victoria | Whitehorse | Winnipeg |
|---|---|---|---|---|---|---|---|---|---|---|---|---|---|---|---|---|---|
| Charlottetown | 4917 | | | | | | | | | | | | | | | | |
| Edmonton | 299 | 4949 | | | | | | | | | | | | | | | |
| Fredericton | 4558 | 359 | 4598 | | | | | | | | | | | | | | |
| Halifax | 5042 | 232 | 5082 | 346 | | | | | | | | | | | | | |
| Montreal | 3743 | 1184 | 3764 | 834 | 1318 | | | | | | | | | | | | |
| Ottawa | 3553 | 1374 | 3574 | 1024 | 1508 | 190 | | | | | | | | | | | |
| Quebec | 4014 | 945 | 4035 | 586 | 912 | 270 | 460 | | | | | | | | | | |
| Regina | 764 | 4163 | 785 | 3813 | 4297 | 2979 | 2789 | 3249 | | | | | | | | | |
| St John's | 6183 | 1294 | 6212 | 1622 | 1349 | 2448 | 2638 | 2208 | 5427 | | | | | | | | |
| Saskatoon | 620 | 4421 | 528 | 4070 | 4554 | 3236 | 3046 | 3507 | 257 | 5684 | | | | | | | |
| Thunder Bay | 2050 | 2878 | 2071 | 2527 | 3011 | 1693 | 1503 | 1963 | 1286 | 4141 | 1543 | | | | | | |
| Toronto | 3434 | 1724 | 3455 | 1373 | 1857 | 539 | 399 | 810 | 2670 | 2987 | 2927 | 1384 | | | | | |
| Vancouver | 1057 | 5985 | 1244 | 5634 | 6119 | 4801 | 4611 | 5071 | 1822 | 7248 | 1677 | 3108 | 4492 | | | | |
| Victoria | 1123 | 6051 | 1310 | 5700 | 6185 | 4867 | 4677 | 5137 | 1888 | 7314 | 1743 | 3174 | 4558 | 66 | | | |
| Whitehorse | 2385 | 7034 | 2086 | 6684 | 7168 | 5850 | 5660 | 6120 | 2871 | 8298 | 2614 | 4157 | 5528 | 2697 | 2763 | | |
| Winnipeg | 1336 | 3592 | 1357 | 3241 | 3726 | 2408 | 2218 | 2678 | 571 | 4855 | 829 | 715 | 2099 | 2232 | 2298 | 3524 | |
| Yellowknife | 1811 | 6460 | 1511 | 6109 | 6593 | 5275 | 5086 | 5546 | 2297 | 7723 | 2039 | 3582 | 4966 | 2411 | 2477 | 2704 | 2868 |

If a ticket is purchased for a destination beyond one bus line's territory and involves switching bus lines at some point, the connection made is generally free. Through tickets are sold for many routes in central and eastern Canada but generally not westward into Greyhound territory.

Some bus lines offer student fares on some routes, so ask. For example, Voyageur Colonial provides student (ID required) rates for trips from Toronto to either Montreal or Ottawa. There's a deal on some routes for students where two free tickets are given with every four purchased. There is no student age limit.

Some bus companies in larger towns offer sightseeing tours ranging from one day to several weeks in length. Some include accommodation, meals and admission fees to attractions. These can be good value but check prices carefully and exactly what you're getting. You need to make reservations for these types of trips.

### Bus Passes

There are some bus passes available in Canada which work much like the famous Eurail pass.

Greyhound has four different bus passes for travel within the Greyhound system in Canada. Their bus passes cannot be used on other bus lines. Each requires seven days' notice before it can be purchased. The main pass is known as the Canada Travel Pass which allows for unlimited travel. This pass comes in seven ($192), 15 ($256), 30 ($352) and 60-day ($459) variations. These are available all year except during major holiday times such as Christmas and Easter.

A second pass is the Excursion Pass which permits four stopovers on a return ticket. It must be used within 60 days. The cost is $298.

The third pass is the Companion Pass which is very good if there are two people travelling together. One person pays full fare and the second person pays 50% of that. This applies to both one-way and return fares.

Lastly, there is the Family Pass on which adults pay full fare and one child aged five to 15 years travels free and all other children pay half fare. All kids travel free if they are under the age of five.

There is also a pass offered by Voyageur Colonial called Tourpass Voyageur which is good for 14 consecutive days of unlimited travel in Quebec and Ontario from May to September. The cost is $170 with extra days possible at a daily rate. Many other bus lines in Quebec and Ontario honour this pass so free connections can be made out of Voyageur territory. Note that Greyhound does not accept the pass.

Travel agents in Europe may have Canadian bus passes for sale. Compare them carefully to those listed here. Representatives in Europe say the bus passes are likely to be not as good as what is available in Canada.

### Tips

All bus lines (except in rare cases) use the same central bus stations in any given Canadian city so you can change bus lines or make connections at the same place. Buses are also convenient because reservations are not necessary. Indeed, reservations are not offered. When one bus fills up another is added so waiting hours for the next one is not required. Always check this, however, as it may not be the case for all routes all the time. This does not apply unless you are getting on at the point of origin. For this reason, in a big city, if you have a choice of using the downtown station or a suburban stop, pick the downtown station. The bus may be full by the time it reaches the outskirts and you will be left waving good-bye. Seating is on a first-come first-served basis. Smoking is not permitted.

Arrive at the station about an hour or half-an-hour before the departure and purchase a ticket. Tickets can also be purchased hours or days or longer ahead of time if this is convenient. Beware that advance tickets do not apply to any specific bus and do not guarantee a seat. You still must arrive early and line up for your bus.

On holiday weekends especially Friday

Top: Husky puppy (TS)
Bottom: Flower farm near Saint John, New Brunswick (CK)

Top: View from the Top of the World Hwy, Yukon (TS)
Bottom Left: Market Square, Saint John, New Brunswick (ML)
Bottom Right: Break Neck Stairs, Quebec City, Quebec (ML)

nights or around major holidays such as Easter, the bus stations can get pretty crowded and chaotic. At these times arriving early or having bought a ticket beforehand is recommended as the ticket counters become very busy.

On longer trips always ask if there is a direct or express bus. On some routes some buses go straight through while others stop seemingly everywhere and these trips can be interminable. The price is generally the same and you may save hours.

In summer, the air-conditioners on buses can be far too effective. Take a sweater on board.

Take your own picnic whenever possible. Long-distance buses stop at highway gas-station restaurants where you pay an awful lot for plastic food.

Most of the larger bus stations have coin-operated luggage lockers. Many have small, simple cafeterias or restaurants for break-fasts and other basic, inexpensive meals. Some bus stations are not in the best areas of a city so some care should be taken after late-night arrivals.

## TRAIN

The railway was part of the formation of Canada and has played a major role in the country's history. It was the promise of a rail connection that brought the west into the Dominion of Canada and it was the same line which transported the first European settlers across the country. The saga of the construc-tion of this massive project is the subject of entire books (see any good bookstore). Because of the history of the Canadian Pacific railway (CPR) and because so many have worked for the huge company at one time, Canadians feel a special nationalistic attachment to the 'ribbons of steel' from coast to coast. Unfortunately, this does not mean they take the train very often. Lack of support is one cause of the slow dismember-ment of the train network.

However, despite stories of its total col-lapse, Canada still has a train system extensive enough to be useful as well as appealing. Some routes provide the only overland travel option but allow passengers a glimpse of otherwise unseeable country-side.

As a result of government cost-cutting measures, train travel in Canada has decreased markedly since the beginning of the 1990s. There are fewer lines and on those remaining lines the trains are less frequent. Still others are under threat. There are no passenger trains in Newfoundland (on the island) nor in the province of Prince Edward Island. But most of the country's major cities still operate a local train service.

Generally, long-distance train travel is more expensive than taking the bus, and reservations are important especially on weekends and holidays.

From my experience, the trains are not as reliable as the buses and are often late, but this has been an area of both management concern and improvement. On some routes there is food and bar service to your seat – this food is quite good but not cheap. The snack-bar food is usually lousy but the bar car, when there is one, can be fun. And of course, you can always get up and walk around the train.

Train service is best in the so-called Quebec City to Windsor, Ontario corridor. In this densely populated area of the country which includes Montreal, Ottawa, Kingston, Toronto and Niagara Falls, trains are fre-quent and the service is quick. On these trains, free meals brought to your seat, airline style, are included in the price. A first-class option available in the corridor includes plush waiting areas, pre-boarding, deluxe seating and more complete meals.

Canada has two main rail companies; the government-run Canadian National (CN) and the privately owned CPR. Yes, this is the same CPR that used to have the airline and still is into trucking, shipping, hotels, mining, etc. It is one of Canada's biggest, most pervasive companies. These are freight-only companies.

## VIA Rail

VIA Rail is a federal government agency. Except as noted below (and some urban commuter trains), VIA Rail operates all the passenger trains in Canada. The word VIA has become synonymous with train travel and the stations and their road side direction signs are labelled in this way. VIA uses CP and CN trains and lines but is responsible for the service independently.

For train schedules and routes, you can pick up the *National Timetable* booklet at any VIA Rail station.

In smaller towns the station may only be open at arrival and departure times and this may not be every day. Also when telephoning the station you may be speaking to someone in a central location in another part of the country who handles all questions and reservations.

The pricing policy at VIA Rail is essentially that every trip is considered to be a one-way fare. A return trip between points A and B is billed as a one-way fare A to B, and a one-way fare B to A. There are no return or excursion fares.

There are, however, ways to reduce your costs considerably. In Ontario and eastwards, full fare is paid on Friday, Sunday and holidays. Travel on any other day is discounted 40% if the trip is booked five or more days in advance. The discount does not apply to trains linking the Maritimes to Quebec during the summer months, but does include trains within each of these areas all year. In the provinces west of Ontario, tickets are reduced by 33% every day from the end of October to the beginning of May with seven days or more advance notice. More than the minimum advance notice is recommended.

The reason for booking well ahead is that a limited number of seats are offered at the discount rates. Once they are gone, you're back into the full fare. These bargains are also not available during peak periods such as Christmas.

Children, seniors (over 60) and students are entitled to discounts any time.

**Long-Distance Travel** For long-distance travel, VIA Rail offers several types of cars and different sleeping arrangements ranging from the basic seat to private rooms. The price of any sleeping arrangement above the basic coach seat is in addition to the travel fare or the multi-use pass. If you're going long distances you may want to take some of your own food. Train meals can be expensive and, as mentioned, the snack food is not particularly good.

The best known trains in Canada are the Transcontinentals that travel right across the country, formerly known as the Canadian (CPR) and the Continental (CN). This service, too, has been greatly cut back, but a rail ride right across much of Canada is still possible. The trip, taking approximately five days, takes in nearly all of Canada's provinces and vastly different scenery and some of it is spectacular. It can be a very pleasant, relaxing way to go, particularly if you have your own room. During the summer months this trip should be booked well in advance. There are a variety of sleeping arrangements from simply staying put in your seat, to upper-and-lower, pull-out berths to self-contained roomettes of varying sizes.

The longest continuous route in the country is from Toronto to Vancouver. VIA Rail now calls this train the *Canadian* but has restored more than the name. The train looks like the classic 1950s stainless steel original complete with the two-storey windowed 'dome' car for sightseeing. The route it takes passes through Sudbury, Sioux Lookout, Winnipeg, Saskatoon, Edmonton, Jasper and the Rocky Mountains. There are three of these four-day trips weekly. The coach fare for this is $443 and it remains constant throughout the year. If you want to begin further east and go all across the country, the train can be boarded in Halifax but you will have to change trains in Montreal and Toronto. The fare from Halifax to Vancouver is $181 plus the $443.

From the end of June to the end of August within the 'corridor' area mentioned above family fares are offered. Adults pay 40% of the full fare and children travel free.

**Canrailpass** For those who intend to travel a lot, or far, or both, VIA Rail offers the Canrailpass. The *National Timetable* booklet will help you plan your travel. The pass is available to anybody and is good for 12 days of coach-class travel within a 30-consecutive day period beginning on the day of the first trip.

The pass is good for any number of trips and stopovers from coast to coast. Reserving early is suggested, though, as the number of seats on the train set aside for pass holders is limited. You can buy the Canrailpass in Canada or in Europe (ask a travel agent for a VIA Rail outlet) but there's no difference in cost.

The Canrailpass comes in two price versions – low season and high season.

Low season is from roughly 6 January to 6 June and from 1 October to 15 December. The cost is $329 or $299 for those aged 24 and under or 60 and over.

High season is roughly 7 June to 30 September. At this time the pass is $489 full fare of $439 for those in the above age categories.

Canrailpass holders may be entitled to discounts at a car-rental agency; inquire if this bonus is in effect.

### Other Train Lines

Canada has a few, small, local train companies which may be of interest to the traveller and which are mentioned in the text. An example includes the Algoma Central Railway in Sault Ste Marie, Ontario which provides access to a northern wilderness area. Another is Ontario Northland which operates northwards from Toronto and includes the Polar Bear Express up to Moosonee on Hudson Bay.

The Quebec North Shore & Labrador Railway runs from Sept-Îles, Quebec north to Labrador.

British Columbia Rail runs from Vancouver north to Prince George.

### Luxury Trains

Canada has one luxury train and another in the works. The operating one has a route which travels along the country's most spectacular stretch of track, the old CPR line through the southern Rockies.

The trip runs on the 'Rocky Mountaineer',

between Vancouver and Banff taking in the best of mountain scenery. An extension to or from Calgary is an option. A second route runs between Vancouver and Jasper. Both routes pass through Kamloops where there is an overnight stay.

The Rocky Mountaineer is operated by the Great Canadian Railtour Company (☎ 1-800-665-7245), Suite 104, 340 Brooksbank Ave, North Vancouver, British Columbia V7J 2C1.

The trains run from the end of May to the beginning of October three times a week. The regular fare from Calgary to Vancouver or vica versa is $548. Price reductions to $448 are offered in two brief periods; from the end of May to mid-June and from the end of September to early October.

To be safe reservations should be made well in advance but openings are possible at any time.

A private tour company, Blyth & Company (☎ 1-800-387-1387) of Toronto, plans to run deluxe trips across the country and through the Rockies from Toronto to Vancouver beginning in 1995. Check it out when you get there.

It's expected that these trips will be far beyond the price reach of most travellers and will only cater to the well-heeled. Amenities will not be spared.

### Amtrak

Amtrak is the US equivalent of VIA Rail. Good-value passes and information on Amtrak's services are available at many Canadian train stations. See the Train section in the Getting There & Away chapter for more details.

### CAR

In many ways, driving is the best way to travel. You can go where and when you want, use secondary highways and roads and get off the beaten track. It's particularly good in summer when you can camp or even sleep in the car. Cars with reclining seats are great for this and surprisingly comfortable with a sleeping bag.

Canada's roads are good and well-marked. In Quebec, non-French-speaking visitors may have some difficulty with the French-only signs. Getting hold of a decent provincial highway map is advisable. Provincial tourist offices have both provincial and, often, national road maps – usually free. Service stations and variety stores sell similar maps.

There are few toll roads in the country although crossing some bridges requires a small payment.

The Trans Canada Hwy runs from St John's, Newfoundland across 7000-plus km to Victoria, British Columbia. There are campgrounds and picnic stops all along the route, often within 100 km to 150 km of each other. Rural routes are among the smallest road categories: they're found in rural Canada and are marked RR1, RR7, etc.

Drivers expecting to travel long distances or to more out-of-the-way areas may wish to bring along some audio tapes. The CBC radio network does cover much of the country but radio station options may be limited and in some areas nonexistent.

City rush hours – especially around 5 pm and on Fridays – can be bad, particularly in Montreal, Toronto and Vancouver. Toronto's main access routes are busy night and day and everybody is impatient. In Montreal drivers possessing nerves of steel, confidence and a devil-may-care attitude will fare best.

In places, there are no lines painted on the roads and driving becomes a type of high speed free for all. Guess what? The province of Quebec has the highest accident rate in the country. All told, avoiding city driving as much as possible is recommended, regardless of the time. Walking or even taking the bus is generally cheaper with today's hefty parking fees and it's a lot less wearing on your nerves.

### Road Rules & Safety Precautions
Canadians drive on the right, as in the USA, but they now use the metric system for measuring distance: 90 to 100 km/h = 60 mph,

50 km/h = 30 mph. The speed limit on highways is usually 100 km/h; in towns, it's 50 km/h or less.

The use of seat belts is compulsory throughout Canada. In some provinces, like Quebec and Ontario, fines for not wearing them are heavy. All traffic violations in money-short Quebec will cost you plenty, so take it easy there. Speeding fines are also costly in Ontario. Most provinces require motorcyclists and passengers to wear helmets and to drive with the lights on.

Traffic in both directions must stop when stationary school buses have their red lights flashing: this means kids are getting off and on. In cities with pedestrian crosswalks like Toronto, cars must stop to allow walkers across. Provided it is safe to do so, turning right at red lights (after first coming to a complete stop) is permitted in some provinces. Just watch what everybody else is doing or listen for the impatient blast of the horn behind you to figure things out.

Sleeping at roadside parks, picnic spots or other areas on the highways is OK, just don't set up a tent.

A valid driver's licence from any country is good in Canada for three months while an International Driving Permit, available in your home country, is cheap and good for one year almost anywhere in the world.

You can't drive in Canada without insurance and your home insurance may not cover you in a foreign land – investigate this beforehand.

Driving in Quebec and other areas with heavy snow is best avoided but if you do, it may mean having to buy snow tyres. Most cars have four-season, radial tyres now. If you get stuck, don't stay in the car with the engine going; every year people die of carbon monoxide suffocation by doing this during big storms. A single candle burning in the car will keep it reasonably warm.

When driving in the north of the provinces, the Yukon and Northwest Territories there can be long distances between service stations – try not to let your tank get much below half full and always carry extra gasoline. Make sure the vehicle you're driving is in good condition and take along some tools, spare parts, water and food.

On the gravel roads the biggest problems are dust and flying stones from other vehicles: keep a good distance from the vehicle in front of you and when you see an oncoming vehicle, slow down and keep well to the right (this also applies to ones overtaking you). If you have to overtake wait until you reach a signposted dust-free zone to do it. A bug and gravel screen is recommended, as are covers for your tank and lights, a spare tyre, fan belt and hose.

In much of the country, wildlife on the road, such as deer and moose are a potential hazard. Most run-ins occur at night when animals are active and visibility is poor. In areas with road-side signs alerting drivers to possible animal crossings keep your eyes scanning both sides of the road and be prepared to stop or swerve. Often a vehicle's headlights will mesmerise the animal leaving it frozen in the middle of the road. Try flashing the lights or turning them off as well as using the horn.

## Rental

Car-rental agencies are all across the country. The main companies are Hertz, Avis, Budget and Tilden but there are many more. The biggies can all book cars for you at any one of their outlets anywhere in the country. They also have rental outlets at almost all of the country's airports. To be certain of finding one and to save time, it is worthwhile making a reservation before your arrival.

Rent-A-Wreck is a well-known used-car-rental place and its rates are somewhat less.

Count on needing a credit card to rent a car in Canada. Cash is not considered good enough! There may be some companies here and there who will rent to those without plastic but even after the hassle of finding one, expect more problems. First the company will need a few days (at least) to check you out. If you're not working, things can be sticky: bring a letter from an employer or banker if you can, and lots of good identification. You may also need to leave a deposit, sometimes as much as several hundred dollars a day. And after all that you may still have to sign away your first child, too. It's not worth the headache.

Some companies require you to be over 21 years of age, others over 26. You may be asked to buy extra insurance depending on your age, but the required premiums are not high.

As far as prices go, it's best to shop around. Rates vary but really haven't changed much in the past few years. Most companies have a daily rate of about $35 to $40 plus a number of km fee. Others offer a flat rate which is nearly always better if you're travelling far. Note that it costs quite a bit extra, as much as hundreds of dollars, to drop a car off in a place other than where you got it, but this can be readily done. Weekly rates are generally 10% less than daily rates, and many companies offer special reduced weekend rates. Book early, especially for weekend use, and request a small, more economical car.

Beware that prices really creep up with rental cars. The daily rate may be an enticing $29 but by the time you finish with insurance, gas (fill it up before taking it back or you pay their prices plus a fee for doing it), the number of km, provincial sales tax, GST and this and that, you're handed a shock as well as a bill. So make sure you know all the extra costs.

Some companies now offer vans and, with a number of people sharing, this can work out quite economically. Campers, RVs and various trailers are other options in which some companies specialise.

Parents note, that children under 18 kg (40 lbs) are required to be in a safety car seat which must be secured by a seatbelt. The big-name rental companies can supply seats at a small daily rental fee. Out of the major cities it may take a couple of days for the outlet to come up with one but the cost is the same.

## Purchase

Older cars can be bought quite cheaply in North America. Look in the local newspaper or, in larger centres, the weekly *Buy & Sell*

*Bargain Hunter Press*, *Auto Trader* or an equivalent. In some cities there is also a weekly paper devoted to nothing but used-car sales. All the above are available at corner variety stores. Private deals with an individual buying a vehicle from another individual are nearly always the most economical way to buy a car. Many used-car businesses are no more reliable and must mark up the prices in order to make a profit. Some of the cheaper cars are the big gas-guzzlers people are trying to get rid of, but there are always bargains on the smaller cars and imports to be found.

For those who prefer a reasoned, semi-scientific approach take a look at Phil Edmunston's excellent *Lemon-Aid*, an annual book published by the Canadian Automobile Protection Association. It is available in stores and libraries and details all the used cars on the market and rates them and gives rough price guidelines. Haggling over car prices, whether at a dealership or at someone's home, is the norm. Expect to knock off hundreds or even a thousand dollars depending on the value of the car.

For a few months' driving, a used car can be an excellent investment, especially if there are two of you. You can usually sell the car for nearly what you paid for it. An old bomb can probably be had for around $1000. A fairly decent old car not meant to last for years should be available for under $4000. West coast cars last longer because salt doesn't have to be used on the roads in winter which means the cars rust less quickly.

I once bought a clunky old 1958 station wagon for $50 and got 19,000 km out of it in one summer before the transmission gave up, the wiring burnt out and the floor fell out.

**Mark Lightbody**

The potential problem for visitors is getting insurance at a reasonable rate. Most companies will offer a six-month term but costs vary widely and can change dramatically from province to province.

In 1990 an English couple reported they were told rates in Quebec were much less than in Ontario for such an arrangement. Checking into it they did indeed find the rate out of Montreal a little over a tenth the cost of their Toronto quotes! Quite a saving! And odd, because for residents, Ontario is much cheaper.

**Mark Lightbody**

Regardless of where you buy, it is useful to have proof of insurance from your homeland. In addition to making a transaction easier, this might well entitle you to some discount as it makes you a more credible risk. As a rule, the rates for women are noticeably less than for a man of comparable age and driving record. If you're planning a side trip to the USA, make sure the insurance you negotiate is valid over the border, too. Also remember that rates are linked to the age and type of car. A newer car may cost more to insure but may also be easier to sell.

## Drive-Aways

One of the best driving deals is the uniquely North American Drive-Away system. The basic concept is that you drive someone's car for them to a specific destination. Usually the car belongs to someone who has been transferred for work and has had to fly, or doesn't have the time, patience or ability to drive a long distance. Arrangements are made through a Drive-Away agency. The major cities have them.

After contacting the agency you are required to fill out an application stating where and when you would like to go. When a match is made to a suitable car you put down a deposit and are given a certain number of days to deliver the car. The security deposit runs from $300 to $500. If you don't show up with the car in the allotted time, the law is called in. Most outlets suggest a route to take and may give you a very rough km guideline.

Your services as a chauffeur are usually not paid (but may be if you really hit the jackpot and someone's in a rush) and generally you pay for gas. Sometimes a portion of the gas costs are paid and if you're lucky, again perhaps on a rush job, all the gas might be paid for. With two or more people, this can be an especially great deal. The company will want to know how many drivers there will be.

You'll require good identification, the deposit and a couple of photos. Look for Drive-Away companies under transportation or business personal ads in the newspaper classifieds or in the yellow pages of the phone book under Drive-Away Automobiles. Most big cities have at least one outlet. They exist all through the USA too. Some trips will take you across the border: from Montreal to Florida is a common route. About eight days is normal for a trip from the east to west coast. Try to get a smaller, newer car. They're less comfortable but cheaper on gas.

In summer when demand is highest, cars may be more difficult to obtain and you could be asked for a nonrefundable administrative payment, perhaps $100.

One thing to ask about is what happens if the car breaks down. Get this information in writing if possible. Generally minor car repairs of say $100 or less are paid for by you. Keep the receipt and you will be reimbursed upon delivery. If bad luck strikes and a major repair is required there may be hassles. The agency might get in touch with the owner and ask him or her how to proceed. This might take time and could involve some inconvenience.

Usually the cars offered with drive-aways are fairly new and in good working order. If not, the owner wouldn't go to the bother and expense and would rather just dump the car. Occasionally you hear of a Jaguar or something similar available – class on a shoestring.

### Car Sharing

Allo Stop, started in Quebec, is a company which acts as an agency for car sharing. It unites people looking for rides with people who have cars and are looking for company and someone to share gas expenses. It is a good service which has been around a number of years and which continues to expand.

There are now offices in Montreal, Quebec City, Toronto, Ottawa and many of the smaller towns around the province of Quebec. More information is given in the text under the Getting There & Away sections. Prices are good and destinations include Quebec, Ontario, further afield in Canada and even down to New York City.

Call them a couple of days before your planned trip and they will try to link you up with someone. Costs of the service are low.

A new service operating out of Montreal, Toronto and Ottawa takes passengers in vans between the cities. These van shuttle services ply the routes between these major cities on a regular, scheduled basis taking six to a dozen passengers at far below bus rates. Check hostel noticeboards and entertainment weekly newspapers for addresses, telephone numbers, etc for these essentially illegally operated services.

They work unofficially because only registered carriers have the right to take passengers for money. Also insurance coverage may not be sufficient in cases of accident or emergency. Nonetheless, these van trips are a popular, fun, casual way to get between some major cities. Some trips go to New York City as well. Call ahead a few days before your departure to book and get the full details.

### Gasoline

Gasoline (petrol) or simply gas (gaz in Quebec), varies in price across the country with the highest prices in the far north and on the east coast. In the east, prices are highest in Quebec, Newfoundland and Labrador. Drivers approaching Quebec from Ontario top up the tank before the border. Those arriving from the USA should always have a full tank as the low US prices will never be seen in Canada. Alberta's prices, with less tax, are relatively low. Fill up there before hitting British Columbia.

In general, the big cities have the best prices so fill up in town. The more remote a place, the higher the price. Major highway service stations offer no bargains and often jack up the price on long weekends and at holiday time in order to fleece the captive victims. Gas is always sold by the litre. On average a litre of gas costs about 60 cents, or about $2.70 per imperial gallon. The Canadian (imperial) gallon is one-fifth larger than the US gallon.

Credit cards are accepted at gas stations, many of which are now self-service and will not accept large bills at night. The large cities have some stations that are open 24 hours but you may have to search around. On the highways, truck stops stay open the longest hours and some have showers you can use.

## BICYCLE

This method of getting around long distances is becoming more and more popular in Canada. Obviously you'd need a lot of time to cover much of Canada. You can't really consider traversing vast regions, it's best to concentrate on one area. Some of the most popular are the areas around the Gaspé Peninsula in Quebec and all around the Atlantic Provinces, excluding Newfoundland. The Gaspé Peninsula is very hilly, Prince Edward Island is flat, and New Brunswick and Nova Scotia offer a fair bit of variety and are relatively small, with towns close together. You get a good mix of country and city. All these areas have good scenery.

The other major cycling area is around the Rocky Mountains and through British Columbia. The weather there in summer is fairly reliable and again there's grand and varied scenery.

Between these eastern and western sections of the country, cycling would be more of a chore than anything else and the landscape is similar for very long stretches. Still, each year cyclists peddle over the north of the Great Lakes across northern Ontario. Also in Ontario, the Bruce Peninsula is good for cycling as is the Thousand Islands Parkway area around Kingston.

VIA Rail allows passengers to take bicycles for free on trains that have baggage cars. This would mean pretty well any train going a fair distance. Local and commuter trains wouldn't be included. You don't have to pack the bike up or disassemble it, but then it may not be covered by insurance. For full protection bicycles must be boxed.

The provincial highway maps have more detail and secondary roads than the usual gas-station maps. You can pick them up at tourist offices. Bookshops may also have cycling guides, and cycling magazines might contain useful information.

Some cities such as Montreal, Ottawa, Toronto and Vancouver have routes marked around town for bikes only. The extent of these routes varies considerably. Toronto's is minimal, Ottawa's is good.

Most cyclists, at least for touring, now wear helmets although this is not mandatory. Ontario is intending to make the wearing of helmets the law. This may come into effect in 1995.

Canada has a number of cycling associations but these are mainly geared to competitive riders. For more casual cyclists or travellers, general information on cycling within a province is available through the provincial tourist office. In several of the large cities, the local city tourist office will have a cycling map and/or information on cycling within the city. Bicycle rentals, some routes and events are discussed in the text.

Bicycle shops are also good sources of information. Major cities have specialised stores where all manner of supplies and cycling gear can be purchased.

Bicycle couriers, practically their own sub-culture with radios, day-glo clothes, and individualistic headgear and jewellery, are a familiar sight speeding around inner cities delivering packages to businesses.

Provincial tourism offices and travel agencies can also help with finding companies which specialise in organising overnight and long-distance cycling trips. These have become increasingly popular in recent years. Accommodation, guidance and automobile support are usually part of the package.

## HITCHING

Readers' letters indicate there have been no problems hitching in Canada, however, hitching is never entirely safe in any country in the world, and we don't recommend it.

Travellers who decide to hitch should understand that they are taking a small but potentially serious risk.

I've always found hitching good in Canada. It's not the UK, which is a hitchhiker's dream, but thumbing a ride is still worthwhile. Many travellers depend on hitching at least for a portion of their trip. Transportation can be expensive but more often lack of buses or trains means the thumb can fill in a gap in the most convenient way. And of course you meet people you would otherwise never speak to. Two people, one of each gender, is ideal. Three or more and I'd forget it and ditto for single women.

If you feel you've waited a long time to be picked up, remember that the ride you get may take you over 1500 km.

Out of the big cities, stay on the main highways. Traffic can be very light on the smaller roads. Always get off where there's a gas station or restaurant and not at a side road or farmer's gate.

Around towns and cities, pick your spots carefully. Stand where you can be seen and where a car can easily stop. A foreign T-shirt, like one with 'University of Stockholm' on it, might be useful. Some people find a cardboard sign with large clear letters naming your destination city helps. I once used one saying 'Moscow' out on the prairies. I don't know if it got me a ride any quicker but a lot of people pointed and laughed.

If you're going into a large city, make sure the ride is going all the way. If it's not, get dropped where you can catch a city bus, especially after dark. When leaving a city, it's best to take a bus out a little way.

You must stay off inter-city expressways, though the feeder ramps are OK. In Toronto and Vancouver particularly, the police will stop you on the expressway.

Hitching in town is not recommended. A lot of prostitutes employ this technique and it's generally considered the inner-city hitcher is a less desirable breed than those out on the open roads and most people ignore them.

It's illegal to hitch within some city limits; fines can be steep. Generally, the scruffier you look, the more ID and documents you should have.

Around the large cities, there will be heavy traffic leaving on Friday and returning on Sunday. Despite the volume I find hitching difficult then because most cars are full with families. Weekdays are best, when you get salespeople and truckers on the road. Many companies forbid truck drivers to pick up people, though some do anyway.

If you're in a hurry, from Toronto to Vancouver shouldn't take longer than five days; I've done it in three.

One last tip: if you don't want to spend time in Northern Ontario, get a ride straight through from Sault Ste Marie to Thunder Bay. The same in reverse.

Wawa, a small town between the two, is a notorious waiting spot. Its reputation as a tough, anti-hitchhiker, mining and drinking town is pretty outdated, but it's still a small, cold, nothing-to-do place to try to hitch from. I once heard of a guy who waited so long he finally got a job then married and settled in Wawa. Southern Saskatchewan is also a place with a reputation for long waits.

**Mark Lightbody**

## BOAT

With oceans at both ends of the country and a lake and river filled interior some boat travel is often called for.

On the east coast, major ferries link provinces and islands to the mainland. New Brunswick and Nova Scotia are connected to Prince Edward Island. From Prince Edward Island, ferries connect with the Magdalen Islands of Quebec out in the Gulf of the St Lawrence. Nova Scotia is connected to Maine, USA, by two ferry routes and to New Brunswick across the Bay of Fundy by another. Newfoundland is connected to Nova Scotia.

Other ferries run around the edges of Newfoundland and up to Labrador. The major operator is Marine Atlantic (☎ 904-794-5700) in Canada. For information and reservations write to Marine Atlantic Reservations Bureau, PO Box 250, North Sydney, Nova Scotia B2A 3M3. Details are found under the Getting There & Away sections of the port towns.

Along the St Lawrence River the north and south shore of central Quebec is connected at several points.

Across the country various boat tours and ferry services both long and short are discussed in the text.

On Canada's west coast, ferries connect mainland British Columbia with Vancouver Island, the Gulf Islands and the Queen Charlotte Islands. For schedules and fares contact BC Ferries (☎ 604-386-3431, 24 hours; ☎ 604-669-1211 in Vancouver), 1112 Fort St, Victoria, British Columbia V8V 4V2.

## TOURS

Organised group tours are best arranged through bus companies, travel agencies or tour companies themselves. Many of the private specialised tour companies are listed in the tourist brochures available from provincial and territorial governments. The larger transportation companies are reliable and they're your best bet if you want a general type of organised tour.

Many of the larger regional bus companies offer trips of varying lengths, including transportation and accommodation. Some offer sightseeing as well.

AmeriCan Adventures is a private company which runs tours throughout the Americas for 18 to 35-year-olds. Most of the trips are two to five weeks long and are 'city & sights' oriented. Included are tours which cross Canada one way and return through the USA. Others are more slanted towards outdoor activities, with everything included but sleeping bags. These are expedition and camping-type trips. Participants must help with the chores and cooking. An example is an eight-day canoe trip in Ontario's Algonquin Park. For information contact AmeriCan Adventures (☎ 322-1034), 2300 Yonge St, Toronto, Ontario M4P 1E4.

The Canadian Outward Bound Wilderness School, with offices in Vancouver and Toronto, runs good, rigorous outdoor adventure trips which are more like courses than holidays. Ranging from seven to 24 days, they take place in various rugged parts of the country; many programmes include a solo portion. In Toronto (☎ 421-8111) it can be contacted at 150 Laird Drive and will send out a pamphlet outlining its programmes.

The Canadian Universities Travel Service Ltd (known as Travel CUTS), mentioned in the Facts for the Visitor chapter, runs various trips and outings that include activities like hiking, cycling and canoeing. It can also arrange ski and sun destination holidays. It has offices in every major city in Canada. In Toronto (☎ 979-2406), it is at 187 College St, M5T 1P7.

Hostelling International (HI) Canada also runs some tours and special-event trips featuring hiking, cross-country (nordic) skiing, etc. Check at hostels for organised activities.

There are many small companies across the country offering a variety of adventure trips of different lengths and difficulty. Good camping stores often carry pamphlets put out by such companies. You can also pick them up at hostels and tourist offices.

Major museums and art galleries also sometimes run specialised educational/recreational tours, for example to the Canadian Arctic and the Inuit carvers. These trips, when available and with lectures included, are interesting but can also be costly. If you have a particular interest a phone call may turn up the perfect opportunity.

Always make sure you know exactly what sort of tour you're getting and how much it will cost. If you have any doubts about the agency or the company it may be dealing with, pay your money into what is called the 'tour operators escrow account'. The law requires that this account number appear on tourist brochures (you may have to look for a while). Doing this protects you and your money should the trip fall through for any reason. It's a good idea to pay by cheque because cash is always harder to get back; write the details of the tour, with destination and dates, on the front of the cheque. On the back write 'for deposit only'.

# Newfoundland & Labrador

Entered Confederation: 31 March 1949
Area: 404,520 sq km
Population: 568,474 (2nd smallest province)
Provincial Capital: St John's

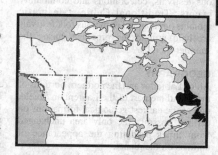

Unlike any other province, two distinct geographic areas make up this singular political entity. The residents, too, will remind you that Newfoundland (pronounced 'new-fen-LAND') is Newfoundland and Labrador is Labrador. The former is the island section of the province, the latter the larger northern mainland portion of the province and each is always referred to separately. Though they have much in common, there are cultural, historical, geological and developmental differences. By far the majority of the population lives in more accessible Newfoundland and this is the region most visitors see. The province was the last to join Canada, doing so as recently as 1949.

Newfoundland has a unique character, and even a brief encounter with it is gratify-

ing. It's a rugged, weather-beaten land at the edge of Canada, heavily influenced by the sea and the conditions of the not-too-distant far north. There are no skunks, snakes or ragweed pollen. The province has a rich aviation history hosting 40 pioneering trans-atlantic flights between 1919 and 1937 including the Lindbergh's and Amelia Earhart's. Tourist information booths across the province are known as 'chalets'.

From the often foggy shore, fishers head to waters legendary for cod and dozens of other kinds of fish. On the Grand Banks, lying south-east off the most populated region (the Avalon Peninsula), fishing boats gather from around the world as they have done since before Columbus even saw the 'New Land'. The early 1990s has seen the inevitable result of this with drastically reduced catches and the end of work for thousands of Newfoundland fishers. Fish stocks are now being monitored and the next few years may well determine the future of not only a good percentage of the local population but of the province itself. In 1992 cod fishing was banned around much of the province putting 25,000 rural Newfoundlanders on temporary government assistance. It is hoped the decimated cod schools will return and that in the mean time other species can tide the people over. Cod farming is also being attempted.

Sometime between April and June each year the province celebrates St George's Day. Throughout the year there are numerous festivals, celebrations and community events. Traditional Celtic-style music remains popular and numerous folk festivals are held around the province during the summer months.

## GEOGRAPHY

All of Labrador and the northern portions of the island are part of the Laurentian Shield, one of the earliest geological formations on earth – possibly the only area unchanged from times predating the appearance of animals on the planet.

Across the province, in both sections, the interior is mostly forested wilderness with many peat bogs and countless lakes and rivers. Almost all the people live along the coast, with its many isolated fjords, bays and coves.

## CLIMATE

Newfoundland's weather is cool throughout the year, Labrador's especially so, with the Arctic currents and north winds. There's heavy precipitation all year too, mainly around the coasts where fog and wind is not at all rare. Summer is short but July and August are generally quite warm. The sunniest and driest places are the central, inland areas.

## ECONOMY

Unemployment has been high for many years. The discovery of offshore oil around Newfoundland, particularly the huge Hibernia field in the south, has not yet lived up to expectations. This is partially due to low international prices, the tragic loss of an 'indestructible' oil rig and, the wrangling between the federal and provincial governments and the private development interests. If and when the wells become operational

Puffins

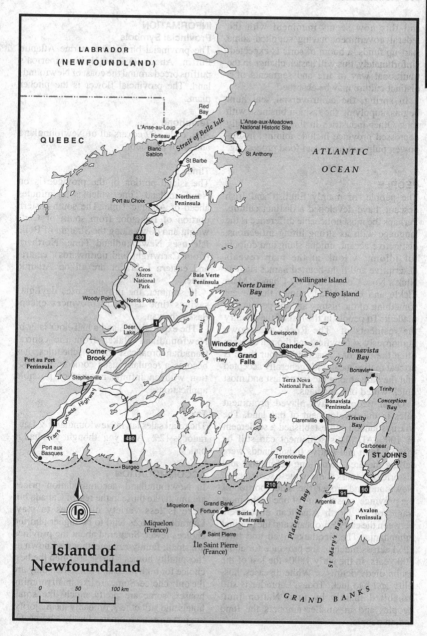

LABRADOR
(NEWFOUNDLAND)

QUEBEC

Red
Bay

L'Anse-au-Loup
Forteau

Blanc
Sablon

St Barbe

L'Anse-aux-Meadows
National Historic Site

St Anthony

ATLANTIC
OCEAN

Strait of Belle Isle

Port au Choix

Northern
Peninsula

430

Gros
Morne
National
Park

Baie Verte
Peninsula

Norte Dame
Bay

Twillingate Island

Fogo Island

Woody Point

Norris Point

Deer
Lake

1

Windsor

Lewisporte

Gander

Bonavista
Bay

Corner
Brook

Grand
Falls

Hwy

Bonavista

Port au Port
Peninsula

Stephenville

Trans Canada Highway

Terra Nova
National Park

Bonavista
Peninsula

Trinity

Conception
Bay

Trans Canada Highway

480

Clarenville

Trinity
Bay

Carbonear

ST JOHN'S

Port aux
Basques

Burgeo

Terrenceville

Placentia Bay

91    90

Argentia

Avalon
Peninsula

Miquelon

Grand Bank

Fortune

210

St Mary's Bay

Miquelon
(France)

Burin
Peninsula

Saint Pierre

Île Saint Pierre
(France)

Island of
Newfoundland

0    50    100 km

GRAND BANKS

and this now seems imminent with the federal government having supplied some start-up funds, a boom of sorts is expected. Unfortunately, this will hasten change in the traditional way of life and segments of a distinct culture may be absorbed.

In spring, the controversial seal hunt begins, supplying the fashion business with furs. Other industries in this economically depressed province include mining, hydropower, pulp and paper and food processing.

## PEOPLE

The people, of mainly English and Irish descent, have developed a distinct culture. Perhaps the most noticeable difference is the language with its strong lilting inflections, distinctive accent, unique slang and colourful idiom. A look at the map reveals descriptive and light-hearted names such as Nick's Nose Cove, Come-by-Chance, Main Tickle and Cow Head; names that reveal something of the history and the people that made it. To people in the rest of the country the residents of 'The Rock' are known humorously as Newfies, and though they are often the butt of Canadian humour there is no real malice meant: it's generally accepted that they are among the friendliest and most quick-witted of Canadians.

Other peoples have played prominent roles in the development of this land. The Vikings landed and established a settlement in 1000 AD. This settlement can still be visited. Inuit and Native Indian bands were calling the area home long before that and historic sites mark some of these settlements. Newfoundland proper, the island portion of the province, was the site of one of the most tragic of all North American encounters between the early Europeans and the original inhabitants. The Beothuks lived and travelled across much of the province for about 500 years. In the early 1800s the last of the group died, victims of White diseases, hostility and bad luck. Today, Labrador is still inhabited mainly by First Nation Inuit peoples and in smaller numbers the Innu Indian people.

## INFORMATION
### Provincial Symbols

The provincial bird is the marine Atlantic Puffin. About 95% of North America's puffins breed around the coast of Newfoundland. The provincial flower is the pitcher plant.

### Telephone

Area code 709 covers all of Newfoundland and all of Labrador.

### Time

The island portion of the province is on Newfoundland Time which is 30 minutes ahead of Atlantic Time. The south-eastern portion of Labrador from south of Cartwright and down along the Straight of Belle Isle uses Newfoundland Time. Northern (from Cartwright and northwards), central and eastern Labrador are all on Atlantic Time.

In summer, the province uses daylight-savings time as do all provinces except Saskatchewan.

The expression '...and a half-hour later in Newfoundland', taken from the central Canadian broadcast media schedules, has become a regularly used comedic interjection with an infinite number of possible applications.

### Tax

The retail sales tax in Newfoundland & Labrador is 12%. And *you* thought you had it bad.

### ACCOMMODATION

In Newfoundland, accommodation prices are much like those in the rest of Canada but there is less variety of places to stay. Labrador's prices tend to be higher and the choices fewer. Scattered about the province are small, family-run guesthouses known as 'hospitality homes'. These are often the best choice for both price and fun. Often they are the only choice. Some are like small rooming houses, some are pretty much like small hotels and still others, probably the majority, are just an extra room in a family's home. Of course these places vary a bit but are usually friendly, informative and economical and many offer meals of the kind not available in restaurants, featuring maybe homemade bread and jam or a traditional fish dish. The tourist office publishes lists but they are never complete. Other places can be found. In some of the small, out-of-the-way spots the pub manager might be able to suggest a couple of names.

The main alternatives to the types of places already mentioned are motel units. These are generally fairly new and reliable but more expensive and fairly uniform. The larger towns offer hotels as well.

Many visitors camp and the system of provincial parks is good, inexpensive and extensive with most parks within a day's trip of each other. Note that facilities at many of them are minimal. There are also some privately run campgrounds but nowhere near as many as you'll find in many other provinces. Potential tenters should have reasonably decent equipment as weather conditions don't allow a casual hammock-in-the-tree style of camping.

## GETTING AROUND

Getting around the province presents some peculiar problems. The ever-growing road network connects major towns and most of the regions of interest to visitors but remains sketchy in many areas. Outside the two cities of St John's and Corner Brook and a few largish towns, such as Gander and Port aux Basques, communities are small and the visitor traffic is light. Except for the one trans-island route, the public bus system consists of a series of small, regional services that usually connect with one or more major points. Although not extensive, this system works pretty well and will get most people where they want to go. Information on all these bus lines is sometimes hard to find but the ones of most interest are listed in the text.

There is no longer any train service on the island but one line in western Labrador still operates.

The 905-km-long Trans Canada Hwy is the only road linking St John's, the capital,

to Port aux Basques on the other side of the island. The road begins and ends at barren but strikingly attractive rocky coasts typical of the provincial shoreline. In between are vast areas of wooded lakeland, some of it quite scenic, and at the western end of the island there's a fertile valley edged by mountains.

It is a long haul from St John's to Port aux Basques, however, but there are a few places worth stopping at on the way, and several towns break up the trip.

For more interesting territory, head to the coastal bays and inlets. Bonavista and Notre Dame bays to the north and the Burin Peninsula to the south, with their many villages, shoreline scenery and views, are what this province is all about. Use the parks: they are good for information, walking and exploring as well as camping. They're often found in particularly interesting or scenic areas and there's no charge if you're not staying overnight.

One thing I love about Newfoundland is that you can pretty much wander about wherever you like. Find a spot by the side of the road or along a beach and spend half a day walking, taking pictures, swimming, picking berries, whatever. You can fish for salmon in pure waters running a few metres from the highway. There aren't signs everywhere saying no this, no that.

**Mark Lightbody**

For many of the small, isolated coastal villages known as 'outports', the only means of transportation and connection with the rest of the province is by boat. Some of these villages are connected by a surprisingly inexpensive ferry service which runs regularly in a couple of areas and is for passengers and freight only. A trip along one of these routes provides a chance to see some of the most remote communities in North America. Visitors are few, but mainstream culture is seeping in at an ever-increasing rate.

Budget travellers may forgo, perhaps reluctantly, a trip to the province fearing travelling costs and the need to retrace their tracks. However, consider the following:

Take the ferry from Nova Scotia to Port aux Basques – with no vehicle the cost is reasonable. From Port aux Basques take the inexpensive coastal ferry, on which you can sleep, along the southern shoreline. From Terrenceville catch a bus to St John's. After a couple of days there catch the bus back to Port aux Basques and the return ferry to Nova Scotia. This offers a good overall view of the province without transport of your own. Alternatively consider a visit up to Gros Morne from Port aux Basques and back.

# St John's

St John's, the province's capital and largest town is not to be confused with Saint John which is a city in New Brunswick. It is a city that manages to feel like a town: invigorating yet warm, busy yet homey, modern centre and fishing village. Its splendid geographical location and its tumultuous, romantic history make St John's an inviting tourist destination.

The land is inhospitable, the weather not much better and the economy still pretty much dependent on the whims of the sea. This may alter with the oil field's exploitation, and the past few years have seen some quickening of controversial downtown development. Unemployment, always high here has been exacerbated by both the recession of the early 1990s and the moratorium on cod fishing around the province. These factors have partially offset the nascent oil field benefits.

As the oldest city in North America and England's first overseas colony, the establishment of St John's has been said to mark the birth of the British Empire.

John Cabot in 1497 was the first to find the excellent and protective harbour that led to the city's development. As it's the closest point to Europe in the New World and as the famous Grand Banks teem with fish offshore, a European settlement sprang up in 1528. Unfortunately, this brought to an end not only the lifestyle but the very existence of the Beothuk Indians.

From its inception, the settlement was the scene of battles, raids, fires, pirates, deprivations and celebrations.

The Dutch attacked in 1665. The French ruled on three occasions, but each time the English regained the settlement from them. In the 1880s it became a centre for shipbuilding and for drying and smoking fish. Its location has inspired more than trade, warfare and greed, however. The first transatlantic wireless cable was received here; 40 pioneering aeroplane crossings – including Earhart's and Lindbergh's – used the site, and even Pan Am's inaugural transatlantic flight touched here.

The wharves have been lined with ships for hundreds of years and still are, acting as service stations to fishing vessels from around the world. As befits a port of adventurers and turbulent events, the tradition of raising a glass is well established. Eighty taverns were well in use as long ago as 1775, and in the early 1800s rum was imported to the tune of 220,000 gallons annually. Today the city might well lay claim to the most watering holes per capita.

St John's rises in a series of steps, sloping up from the waterfront. Everywhere there are stairs, narrow alleys and winding streets. Several of the downtown roads are lined with colourful, pastel clapboard town houses – the kind found all over the province. The more modern sections are mostly in the sprawling suburbs.

In 1892 the Great Fire, lit by a dropped pipe, burned down more than half the town. In 1992 another major downtown fire burned a considerable section of Harvey Rd and its many old houses. The city has an infill housing policy which stipulates that new housing be designed to blend in with the existing historic character of the street. Examples of this may be seen on New Gower St east of the City Hall.

There's lots of rain and fog, so pray for good weather.

## ORIENTATION

On the approach to St John's, the highway passes the newer subdivisions, the suburb of Mount Pearl and then some of the older

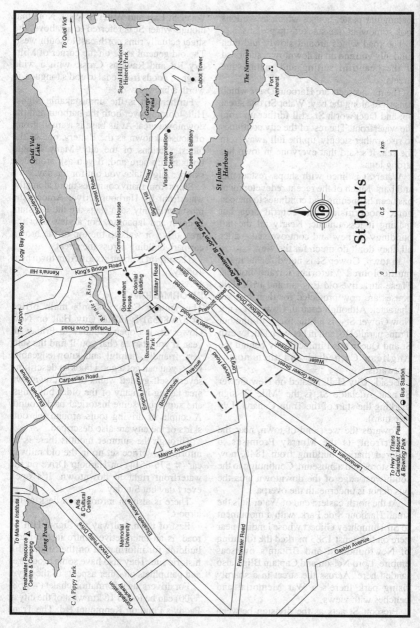

St John's

To Quidi Vidi

Signal Hill National Historic Park

George's Pond

Cabot Tower

The Narrows

Signal Hill Road

Forest Road

Visitors Interpretation Centre

Queen's Battery

St John's Harbour

Fort Amherst

Quidi Vidi Lake

The Boulevard

Logy Bay Road

Kenna's Hill

Commissariat House

King's Bridge Road

Colonial Building

Government House

Military Road

Dicksworth Street

Gower Street

Prescott Street

Harbour Drive

See Downtown St John's map

To Airport

Portugal Cove Road

Rennies River

Queen's Road

Long's Hill

New Gower Street

Water Street

Bus Station

Carpasian Road

Elizabeth Avenue

Empire Avenue

Bonaventure Avenue

Harvey Road

Bannerman Park

Mayor Avenue

Leamarchant Road

To Hwy 1 (Trans Canada), Mount Pearl & Bowring Park

To Marine Institute

Freshwater Resource Centre & Camping

Long Pond

C A Pippy Park

Arts & Cultural Centre

Memorial University

Elizabeth Avenue

Prince Philip Drive

Confederation Parkway

Freshwater Road

Cashin Avenue

0      0.5      1 km

rectangular pastel houses which in sections look somewhat like stacked-up prefabs.

The road winds around slowly and then suddenly you end up in downtown, surprised at the beautiful setting and picturesque streets.

The main streets are Harbour Drive which runs right along the bay; Water St, one street up; and Duckworth St, still further up from the waterfront. The rest of the city continues to rise, rather steeply, up the hill away from the sea. It's said that everyone in town has strong legs.

Water St is lined with shops, restaurants and bars. Much of the recent redevelopment has been happening and continues to happen here, modernising this central area but making it less unique. Nearly all the tall buildings are new and controversial – after all, they don't do much for the view.

In town, Gower St is noted for its many multicoloured Victorian terrace houses. These attractive old English and Irish style houses are now protected for their historic character. Although central, Gower St – not New Gower St – is a little tricky to find but it runs parallel to, and in between Duckworth St and Queen's Rd immediately behind the Anglican Cathedral and then north-eastwards.

Beside City Hall, located on New Gower St near Adelaide St, is the 'Mile O' sign marking the start of the Trans Canada Hwy (see map).

Towards the west end of town, near the waterfront, is the Murray Premises, a restored market building from 1846, now with stores and a museum. Continuing to the south-west edge of the downtown area the bus depot is underneath the overpass.

At the north-eastern end of Water St is the small Harbour Side Park, with a monument to Sir Humphrey Gilbert whose landing near here on 5 August 1583 marked the founding of Newfoundland and Britain's overseas empire. Lord Nelson and Captain Bligh also landed here. Across the street in a sharply rising park there's a War Memorial and benches with views.

Prescott St acts as the division between Water St East and Water St West. Note that though Water St is referred to as above, the street actually runs north-east to south-west. The old general store on the corner of Military Rd and Rawlins Cross, with a wide range of goods from coal to cod's tongues, is worth a browse.

Further east is the unmistakable Signal Hill, looming over both the harbour and the downtown area. At its base is a small group of houses known as the Battery, one of the oldest sections of the city. Many fishing boats tie up here and, if you ask around, a skipper might take you out for the day.

Ships from many countries moor along the waterfront by Harbour Drive. Among the most commonly seen flags are the Russian, Spanish and Japanese. For a view over the area, drive or walk to the top of the brown car-park building across the street.

The airport is about six km from town near Torbay.

## INFORMATION

The Tourist Commission's main office (☎ 576-8455) is in the City Hall on New Gower St. It's open Monday to Friday all year. If you start to chat you'll find the staff very friendly, helpful and knowledgeable. Here, you can get a good booklet describing several self-guided walks of the downtown area taking in many of the older buildings, and supplying some historical background. A couple of driving tours around the outskirts of the city are also described.

Through the summer months there is an information office set up in the old railway car (☎ 576-8514) on Harbour Drive on the waterfront right in downtown. It's open every day but Sunday.

There is also an information desk at the airport.

East of town, halfway up Signal Hill by road, is an interpretive centre in the parks building for information on the Signal Hill historic site. They also have some brochures and pamphlets on other aspects of the city.

For drivers, an information chalet (☎ 368-5900) can be found 16 km west of the city at Paddy's Pond on Kenmount Rd. The Trans

Canada Hwy eastbound becomes Kenmount Rd, then Freshwater Rd on its way downtown.

Breakwater Books at 100 Water St has a large and excellent selection of titles on the city and Newfoundland.

## NEWFOUNDLAND MUSEUM

Though small, the museum (☎ 729-2329) provides several good, worth-catching displays. There are a few relics and a skeleton – the only remains anywhere – from the extinct Beothuk Indian tribe who once lived here. Also on display are exhibits about the Vikings and the history of St John's. The museum, at 285 Duckworth St, is open every day except holidays. It is closed weekend mornings and weekdays from noon until 1 pm. Admission is free. A second portion of the museum is found in the Murray Premises (see below).

Incidentally, a fine attraction nearby is the now nearly extinct Canadian traffic cop, gesticulating on the corner of Prescott and Duckworth Sts.

## MURRAY PREMISES

Within this restored market building on the corner of Water St West and Beck's Cove are shops, a pub and the second branch of the Newfoundland Museum. The latter is larger than the original on Duckworth St with exhibits on three floors. Topics covered include the marine, military and naval history of the province. There's some interesting information on the Basques who came to the area in the early 1500s to whale. The museum entrance is marked by a fine portrayal of the huge Newfoundland dog. The hours and phone number are the same here as at the Duckworth St location and it is also free.

## JAMES O'MARA PHARMACY MUSEUM

At 488 Water St in Apothecary Hall, the original Art Nouveau building, the pharmacy museum (☎ 753-5877) is a replica of an 1885 drug store (chemist's) complete with vintage fixtures, cabinets, equipment and medicines. It's open from mid-June to mid-

September only and is free. Opening hours are from 11 am to 5 pm daily. At other times of the year, the interested may call for an appointment.

## COURT HOUSE

By the Duckworth St Newfoundland Museum, the working court house dates from 1904 and in the late 1980s had a major facelift. Now appearing pretty much as it did when first opened, it is one of the more imposing buildings in town.

## CITY HALL

On New Gower St, five blocks west of the court house, (Duckworth St runs into New Gower St) is the new City Hall and 'Mile 0' sign, from where the Trans Canada Hwy starts westwards on its 7775-km journey across Canada to Victoria, British Columbia.

## MASONIC TEMPLE

Up the hill from the Newfoundland Museum on Duckworth St you'll see the striking, renovated temple from 1897 and now a private men's club.

## ANGLICAN CATHEDRAL

Across the street from the temple is the Anglican Cathedral of St John the Baptist. Now a National Historic Site, the church was first completed in the mid-1800s. It was gutted in the Great Fire of 1892 and then rebuilt within the remaining exterior walls by 1905. Inside, note the stone walls, wooden ceilings and long, thin stained-glass windows. The address is 22 Church Hill. To enter, go to the side facing the harbour and into the doorway by the toilet. Ring the bell and someone will probably come to let you in. Tours are offered through the summer.

## BASILICA OF ST JOHN THE BAPTIST

Further north up Church St to Garrison Hill, and then right on Military Rd you'll find this Roman Catholic church, also a National Historic Site. Built in 1855, it's considerably more impressive from the outside than the cathedral and, in fact, the Gothic façade dominates the cityscape. Inside, however, it's rather plain although the Italianate ceiling with gold-leaf highlights will catch the eye's attention and the pipe organ is a 'beaut'. There is a small museum on the premises which has articles relating to the history of the church.

There're good views out over the bay from the front steps. Within walking distance, there are about half a dozen other churches.

## SIGNAL HILL NATIONAL HISTORIC PARK

The view alone makes this site a must. East of town along Duckworth St, this park rises up the hill forming the cliff edge along the channel into St John's Harbour. The view of the town and out to sea is superb night or day and many types of fishing vessels moving in and out of the port may be seen. Halfway up the road from the end of Duckworth St is the Visitors' Interpretive Centre with a small museum, where you can get information about the park. There is also information about the city in general.

During the Battle of Signal Hill in 1762 the English took St John's which pretty much ended French control of North America. The French had already lost the decisive battle of

Quebec in 1759. **Queen's Battery** further up the hill has some cannons and the remains of the British battery of the late 1700s. **Cabot Tower** at the top of the hill honours John Cabot's arrival in 1497. Built in 1900, this tower was where Marconi received the first transatlantic message in 1901 – the wireless broadcast was sent from Cornwall, England. There are guides and displays in the tower.

Admission is free and the park is open daily in summer until 8 pm. Near the tower is Ladies Lookout which, at an elevation of 175 metres is the highest point in the park, offers views over what seems like half the province.

Highly recommended in either direction is the 1.7-km walking trail connecting Cabot Tower with the Battery section of town down in the harbour. Going up, the trip takes about 90 minutes. This walk should not be considered in winter or when any ice lingers or in heavy fog or at night. A slight stumble and it's a long way down.

The tourist office has a map of the park.

## FORT AMHERST

Across the Narrows you can see the remains of this fort. With the Battery and the fort to

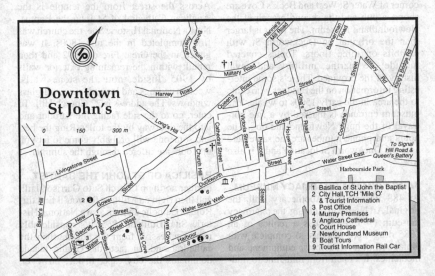

**Downtown St John's**

0    150    300 m

† 1

Military Road

Rennie's Mill Road

Bonaventure Avenue

Bannerman Road

Military Road

King's Bridge Rd

Harvey Road

Queen's Road

Bond Street

King's Street

Street

Long's Hill

Victoria Street

Prescott Street

Gower Street

Holloway Street

Cochrane Street

Street

Livingstone Street

Cathedral Street

Church Hill

5 †

Duckworth Street

7 ☷

Gower Road

Water Street East

Street

To Signal Hill Road & Queen's Battery

Harbourside Park

Barter's Hill

2 ❶

New Gower Street

Adelaide Street

Queen Street

George Street

Ayre Cove

Water Street West

Back's Cove

4 •

Harbour Drive

8 ❶ 9

1  Basilica of St John the Baptist
2  City Hall, TCH 'Mile O' & Tourist Information
3  Post Office
4  Murray Premises
5  Anglican Cathedral
6  Court House
7  Newfoundland Museum
8  Boat Tours
9  Tourist Information Rail Car

face, enemy ships wouldn't have had an easy time getting into the bay. On the point, on the fort side, the lighthouse dates from 1813. Here you're about as close to Europe as you can be without getting wet.

## OTHER HISTORIC SITES
### Commissariat House
On King's Bridge Rd near New Gower St, Commissariat House is one of the most complete historic sites. Built in 1818, the late-Georgian mansion was used by the supplies officer of the British military. When British forces left in 1870, the building was used as a church rectory, nursing home and children's hospital. It is now restored to reflect the style of the 1850s with many period pieces inside. The house is open daily in summer and by appointment at other times. Admission is free. There's an interpretive centre.

### Colonial Building
This building, nearby on Military Rd, was the seat of the provincial legislature from 1850 to 1960. It's built of stone from Ireland which was formerly used as ships' ballast and contains many of the province's old records. The building is open in summer Monday to Friday from 9 am to 4.15 pm and is free.

### Government House
Built in 1830, Government House, actually a residence, is beside Bannerman Park close to Commissariat House. The house was the official residence of the governor of Newfoundland until it became part of Canada and since then the lieutenant-governors have called it home.

## C A PIPPY PARK
The north-western edge of the city along or near Confederation Parkway contains a number of attractions. The dominant feature is the huge 1343-hectare C A Pippy Park. Within the park, recreational facilities include walking trails, picnic areas and playgrounds.

At Long Pond marsh the bird-watching is good and mammals as large as moose can sometimes be spotted in areas of the park. There is also a campground and snack bar.

The province's only university, **Memorial University** is here and provides some of its own points of interest. The university's **Botanical Garden** at Oxen Pond at the western edge of the park off Mt Scio Rd is both a cultivated garden and nature reserve. Together, these two areas provide visitors with a good introduction to the province's flora and varying natural habitats including boreal forest and bogs. The garden area is open from 1 May to 30 November, Wednesday to Sunday 10 am to 5.30 pm and currently is free although this may change in the near future.

### The Newfoundland Freshwater Resource Centre (NFRC)
Also in C A Pippy Park the NFRC (☎ 754-3474) is the striking hexagonal balconied building across the street from the campground. At the time of writing it was open but not completed so a full report is not possible. The main feature is the 25-metre fluvarium, a glass-sided cross-section of a 'living' river, in this case the Nagle's Hill Brook. Viewers can peer through the glass to observe the natural, undisturbed goings-on beneath the surface in a river ecosystem. Numerous brown trout and the occasional eel can be seen. How much activity there is can vary considerably. Also if the weather has been unsettled, with high winds or if there has been any rain the water becomes so cloudy that virtually nothing can be seen through the murkiness. You may want to call to check on visibility before you visit.

It seems as though a lot of work remains to be done in order to make this an informative and enjoyable place to spend a couple of hours. Aquariums, preserved samples exhibits and photo displays reveal and explain various aspects of marshes, ponds, bogs and other water environments.

In summer the centre is open daily from 9 am to 5 pm with a feeding time scheduled at 4 pm. Tours are offered hourly. The rest of the year it is closed on Wednesday, Sunday morning and the daily hours are reduced.

The rates are $2.75 for adults, less for seniors and children and a ticket includes a tour. Free parking is available. The site is run by a nonprofit environmental awareness group which has done some fine work along the Rennie River and Quidi Vidi Lake and are responsible for the development of some of the walking trails in the area.

## ARTS & CULTURAL CENTRE

The Arts & Cultural Centre (☎ 729-3900) complex about two km north-west from the downtown area on the corner of Allandale Rd and Prince Phillip Drive, beside the university contains the Memorial University Art Gallery. The art gallery displays mainly contemporary Newfoundland and Canadian painting and sculpture. It's free and open from Tuesday to Sunday, noon to 5 pm and

### Moose

Though the moose is a fairly common animal across the country it is mainly found in the less populated, heavily forested northern regions. Nowhere in Canada are you as likely to see one as in Newfoundland. There are some 40,000 of them here and many of them live close to towns and roads including the Trans Canada Hwy. This, of course, increases the chances of getting a good look at one but also presents some hazards. There is more than one moose/vehicle collision a day across the province and smacking into a beast the height of a horse weighing 400 kg with antlers nearly two metres across is more wildlife than most people care for.

Moose tend to like the highways for a number of reasons. The open space makes walking easy, there is usually more breeze and fewer insects and, in spring, the salt from winter de-icing makes a nice treat. For these reasons they also enjoy the train tracks, a habit which decreased their population at the rate of some 2000 per year until the train service was discontinued.

The areas of heaviest concentration are well marked and should be heeded particularly when travelling after dark when most accidents occur. Ninety per cent of the run-ins take place between 11 pm and 4 am. If you do see a moose on or beside the road, slow down and if it doesn't want to move approach slowly with the lights off as they seem to get mesmerised by the beams.

I've seen them during the day on the Trans Canada Hwy on each of my trips. Get out and take pictures if you like, moose are generally not aggressive and are very impressive, if unusual-looking animals. They can be unpredictable, however, and anything of this size should not be approached too closely or startled. During rutting (mating) season in October and November the males (bulls) can become very belligerent and downright ornery; it's a good time to stay in the car and well out of their way.

Calves are born in the spring, and throughout the summer it is not uncommon to see a cow moose with her young. Females and the young do not have antlers. Adult males grow a 'rack' each year in summer, only to have it fall off each fall. ■

on Thursday and Friday nights until 10 pm. There is also a theatre at the complex.

## CONFEDERATION BUILDING
Nearby, just off Confederation Parkway, east of the arts centre, is the home of the provincial government. You can visit the building and the small military museum inside for free. It's closed on weekends.

## THE MARINE INSTITUTE
Although misleadingly named, the Marine Institute (☎ 778-0372) may be considered more worthwhile than the NFRC. Really it's more like a science and technology museum. The institute features primarily interactive exhibits. Although not on the scale of such facilities in the country's larger cities there is enough for a visit of over an hour with exhibits on such matters as fibre optics.

The institute is open daily with tours available in summer twice every afternoon. Call to check hours of operation and the precise tour times. Also at the site is a planetarium which presents its own shows featuring the heavens. The address is 155 Ridge Rd (at the top of the hill) in Pippy Park. Call for current hours and prices.

## BOWRING PARK
West of the downtown area off Pitts Memorial Drive on Waterford Bridge Rd, this is another popular large city park. A couple of streams and walkways meander through the park. The Peter Pan Statue is a replica of the famous one in Kensington Gardens in London, England and was made by the same sculptor.

## OCEAN SCIENCES CENTRE
Tours can be taken at this research unit (☎ 737-3706), part of Memorial University's science department. Ongoing research examines the life cycle of salmon, seal navigation, ocean currents and many other aspects of life in the colder ocean regions. There is a visitor interpretive centre and guided tours of the facility which take about an hour. Seals can be seen and there is a hands-on tank where various creatures can be touched.

It's open everyday in July and August when tours are offered and from Monday to Friday for the rest of the year. Tours are offered every half an hour commencing at 10 am. Part of the tour is outside so bring appropriate clothes and footwear. Admission is $2.50. The centre is about eight km north of town just before Logy Bay at the end of Marine Lab Rd on the ocean. From town take Logy Bay Rd (Route 30) and then follow Marine Drive.

## NEWFOUNDLAND DOGS
The huge, black, cuddly Newfoundlands whose rescues and heroics are legendary and perhaps a little fanciful seem slowly to be fading into lore. These days they are rarely seen here or elsewhere – who can afford to feed them? The fortunate, however, may see one ambling through a seaside village somewhere in the province. For those who can't stand the long odds, there are breeders carrying on the tradition of raising these wonderful beasts. The owner of the Logy Bay Kennels (☎ 722-4799) permits visits but call first.

## QUIDI VIDI
Over Signal Hill, away from town, is the tiny, picturesque village of Quidi Vidi. This little fishing port has one of the oldest houses in North America, dating from the early 1700s. You can walk to the village from Signal Hill in about 20 minutes or go around by road from St John's. Take Forest Rd, which runs along the lake and then turns into Quidi Vidi Village Rd.

### French Battery
Built in 1762, this provincial historic site also known as Quidi Vidi Battery is up the hill from the village, guarding the bay. The French built it after taking St John's. It was later taken by the English and remained in military service into the 1800s. It's free to look around and costumed guides are on hand daily in summer.

## Quidi Vidi Lake

Inland from the village is this lake, site of the St John's Regatta, which is held on the first Wednesday in August. Records show that the event started in 1818 and it's probably the oldest continuing sporting competition in North America. For those seeking more information there is the Regatta Museum (☎ 576-8058) on the 2nd floor of the boathouse at the lake.

**Pleasantville**, now a suburb at the west end of the lake, was a US military base until the 1950s or '60s when they packed up and returned it to Newfoundland.

The Rennies River flowing into the west end of the lake is an excellent trout stream. A conservation group, the Quidi Vidi Rennies River Development Foundation, is developing the area and a three-km walking trail from the lake along the river to west Long Pond has been set up. The foundation's Freshwater Resource Centre is at Long Pond. Trout leap from the river in the autumn as they get ready for spawning. Other trails in the area such as around Quidi Vidi Lake are in the works. The tourist office has a pamphlet with a map of the river system.

## ORGANISED TOURS

For a relatively small city, the number and variety of tours available is noteworthy. The Newfoundland Historic Trust offers walking-tours of the old city twice daily in summer leaving from the Murray Premises. In addition, some years the city does much the same tour from mid-June to mid-September, leaving from City Hall, free. Call the tourist office (☎ 576-8455) for schedules.

McCarthy's Party (☎ 781-2244), a well established tour operator, offers three different excursions. The three-hour tour of the city costing $13 is good, but really doesn't provide too much that you can't do yourself for free. The other two, one to Cape Spear and one in the opposite direction along Marine Drive are more worthwhile. Plenty of humour, interesting historical tidbits and general information on the people and province is woven into the commentary.

Fleetline (☎ 722-2608) offers trips ranging from half a day around town to a full 10 days around the province which includes Saint Pierre and Miquelon islands. Another trip covers the Northern Peninsula. The company has an office in town but some trips leave from the major downtown hotels daily in summer.

There are other operators with a range of bus tours to various points around the province. The tourist office has complete details.

Other tours are done by boat. Dee Jay Charters (☎ 753-8687) is at the harbour near the rail car tourist chalet. They run a good-value three-hour trip from the waterfront out to sea in search of whales and icebergs for $20. Icebergs are most likely to be seen in June and sometimes early July near St John's. When there is one floating around out of the Narrows there will be a noticeable chill in the air around town. (The prime viewing area is around Twillingate on Notre Dame Bay in the north.) If the big highlights are not in the neighbourhood there is still bird-watching and sightseeing along the coast. Three trips are offered daily.

Try to pick a calm day as it allows the boat to travel further and also permits a little cod jigging. There are great views along the coastline, but it can get rough (this is the North Atlantic, after all – no reason to mention how I lost my breakfast overboard!) and cold, so take warm clothes – it may be balmy in the protected harbour but it's quite a different story once outside the Narrows. A sip of the Screech may help.

Bird Island Charters (☎ 753-4850) is similar but visits the **Sea Bird Sanctuary Islands** of the Witless Bay Sea Bird Ecological Reserve which includes the largest puffin colony on the east coast of North America. This sea bird reserve is one of the world's largest. Bird Island offers daily departures from Bay Bulls, south of town. There's a shuttle service from downtown hotels to get you to the dock.

Island Rendezvous (☎ 747-7253) based in suburban Mount Pearl but operating out of the village of Garden Cove two hours from town has a one-of-a-kind trip. Popular with local residents and taken mainly by couples, the two-day adventure visits one of the many now abandoned outport communities. Visitors are taken by boat to Woody Island, virtually a ghost town except for some people who use it as a base for seasonal fishing. Visitors are put up in a large old house run as a hospitality home. The days are spent poking around the old town and island and on a boat tour of Placentia Bay. The trip provides a glimpse into the traditional fishing village way of life as well as offering escape from what has replaced it. In town, the office is at 42 McCrath St in Mount Pearl.

Lastly, Canoe Newfoundland (☎ 726-5900) at 67 Circular Rd is recommended for those with an interest in outdoor trips. Although operated mainly for school groups, Stan Cook, who runs it, is a wealth of information and can offer all sorts of tips and advice on a range of canoe, kayak, wildlife and nature tours in the area or in other parts of the province.

The tourist office will have information on other tour possibilities.

## FESTIVALS
Some of the major festivals are listed here. For other festivals – there are several during summer – ask at the tourist office.

June
   *St John's Days Celebrations* – The celebrations are held from 18 June for two days to commemorate the city's birthday. Festivities include concerts (any Newfoundland event includes music), a parade, street dance and sporting events.
July-September
   *Craft Fair* – The Newfoundland & Labrador craft fair is held twice annually, once around the beginning of July and once in September in the St John's Memorial Stadium.
   *Signal Hill Tattoo* – This colourful event takes place from mid-July to mid-August twice a day on each of Thursday, Saturday and Sunday.
   *George Street Festival* – featuring music of all kinds this festival, performed on central George St, is held around the end of July.
   *The Provincial Folk Festival* – This three-day event, not to be missed for its great music; it takes place annually around the first week of August. Dancers and story-tellers also perform in their respective traditions. The event is held in Banner-

man Park with some portions held indoors if the weather is bad.
   *Quidi Vidi Regatta* – It's held on the first Wednesday in August.

## PLACES TO STAY
As might be expected, there are more accommodation possibilities here than anywhere else in the province and the price range is wide. Overall, prices are higher here than elsewhere but many of those that follow are close to average.

### Camping
Conveniently located right in the city by the university there is camping in *C A Pippy Park* (☎ 737-3655). They charge just $5.50 for tenting, $11 for unserviced sites and $15 for serviced ones. The campground is off Higgins Line at the north-western side of the park near the Confederation building.

### Hostels
The hostel situation in Newfoundland is very changeable and usually minimal. Currently there is no official hostel in St John's but read on.

There are rooms for rent, though, at *Memorial University*. Call Hatcher House (☎ 737-8000, 737-7590) through the summer months, mid-May to mid-August. Singles cost $13/16 for students/nonstudents with even cheaper doubles. Weekly rates are offered and all meals are available. There are buses to town but you can walk in less than half an hour, even if the roads are not direct. From the campus Newtown Rd leads downtown.

The owners of a private house on Lemarchant St, who have travelled on the cheap themselves, rent out a couple of rooms to backpackers and like-minded visitors. They have enough space for three guests at a time. I can't give out the address because they do not want a lot of attention drawn to their house and people waiting outside the door for long stretches as they are both out a lot during the day. Call either Donna or Jerry at (☎ 754-5626) for the specifics. The price is $25 per person including breakfast and they will pick-up from the bus depot or airport. The house is central, about a five-minute walk to City Hall.

The YM-YWCA in town has no accommodation.

## Tourist Homes & B&Bs

Aside from the established places listed here, the tourist office should have an up-to-date list of places available in people's homes although they change frequently. There are usually places not mentioned in the printed provincial accommodation guides and pamphlets. The tourist office also takes calls from local people throughout the day who call in to offer a room for the night – sort of a part-time hotel system. So, if things are busy and you're having trouble getting a room, call in more than once as the situation can quickly change. That said, there is usually not a major problem finding something anyway.

The year-round *Sea Flow Tourist Home* (☎ 753-2425, 781-2448) is at 53-55 William St. Mrs Hutchens has four simple rooms at singles/doubles for $30/35 and up. The cheapest room has no bath and one room, the most costly at $60 has kitchen facilities.

Gower St, not to be confused with New Gower St which runs into Gower at Bulley St, is an attractive, historic street and a fruitful place to look for a guesthouse as they line the length of it.

Centrally located near the Anglican Cathedral, at 180 Gower St, is the *Gower St House* (☎ 754-0047). All the rooms are good and come with private bathroom and one has a balcony. Check out the wood mosaic inlay of Cabot Tower in the floor beside the living room on the ground floor. Singles/doubles cost $40/50 with a full breakfast which may include some traditional fare. Overnight costs drop in autumn, winter and spring. Other benefits here include the use of kitchen, laundry and parking facilities.

Nearby at 5 Gower St, the *Fort William* (☎ 726-3161) is open all year with singles/doubles $46/62 and one housekeeping unit at slightly higher cost. The *Gables*

*Hospitality Home* (☎ 754-2318 at No 115 has singles/doubles at $45/55. Breakfast is included and there are laundry facilities. Ask for the room with the view.

The *Oh! What a View* (☎ 576-7063) at 184 Signal Hill Rd is recommended as a neat, clean B&B with a spectacular view over the harbour and city. To take advantage of the location a wooden outdoor deck has been built and guests can just sit and stare. There are four rooms at singles/doubles/triples $45/55/65 including a continental breakfast of bread and muffins. Two of the rooms are in the basement but they are modern and comfortable. City buses run nearby but it is only a 10-minute walk into town. Note that this guesthouse is only open during the summer.

The *Prescott Inn* (☎ 753-6036) is a long-running B&B at 19 Military Rd, centrally situated on the eastern side of the downtown area. It's a well-kept old house with balconies looking out over the harbour. Singles/doubles cost $46/62 with a full breakfast included, for an extra person add $10.

At 36 Kings Bridge Rd is the year-round *Kincora Hospitality Home* (☎ 576-7415). It's a well-appointed Victorian house furnished with antiques. Singles/doubles cost $50/60 (more for a private bath) and include a continental breakfast.

*Monroe House* (☎ 754-0610) from 1900 and once the home of a prominent Newfoundland politician is very comfortable. The rooms are spacious and tastefully decorated, the hosts friendly and the breakfasts substantial. It's on a quiet street just a few minutes walk from the centre at 8A Forest St behind the Newfoundland Hotel. If you seek some creature comforts and a little pampering this fits the bill. Singles/doubles cost $59/65.

Away from the centre is the *Bird Island Guest Home* (☎ 734-4850) at 150 Old Topsail Rd. From downtown take Cornwall Ave which turns into Old Topsail Rd. Rates for singles/doubles are $45/55 with a continental breakfast included.

Also out of downtown there's the low-priced *Fireside Guesthouse* (☎ 726-4869) at 28 Wicklow St near the Avalon Mall Shopping Centre. Call for directions. Including a full breakfast, singles/doubles cost $35/40, making it one of the better buys, and just a short walk from the house is an indoor swimming pool you can use.

## Hotels
Hotels are not St John's strong point but with the good guesthouses listed above this shouldn't pose any problems. As a rule the hotels are fairly pricey and business-oriented but there are still some good, inexpensive places around town.

For a plain but central, clean and inexpensive place, try the *Catherine Booth House* (☎ 738-2804), at 18 Springdale St, which is a short walk from the bus depot. Singles/doubles cost $34/39, and a family of four pays $45. Four adults can get a room for $48 and rates include breakfast and a snack at night. It's run by the Salvation Army. PS – there's no smoking, not even in the TV lounge.

The central *Rawlin's Cross Inn* (☎ 754-8989) is the big green, barn-like house with white trim at 118 Military Rd, corner of King's Rd. It was known as the Parkview Inn but changed hands during the update of this book and current details were not known although the name was said to have been changed to the above. Prices did range from $40 to $60 but also may have changed.

The *Olde Inn* (☎ 722-1171), run by Amon Rosato, is a lodge of 14 rooms with singles/doubles from $30/40 and good weekly rates. It's at 157 Lemarchant Rd, the black-and-white place built in 1892. It's a long walk from the centre but the bus goes along Lemarchant Rd.

Right in downtown and moving up-market a bit, the *Victoria Station Inn* (☎ 722-1290), at 290 Duckworth St, is not bad value for its 10 rooms with ensuite baths at singles/doubles $75/85. The rooms are nicely furnished and most have a fireplace. The inn also has a very good seafood restaurant and a coffee bar with a fine selection of cakes and desserts available any time.

The historic *Hotel Newfoundland* (☎ 726-4980) with the imposing stone façade on Cavendish Square at the end of Duckworth St is the top-end classic in town. Run by Canadian Pacific Hotels, it's very expensive but comes down on weekends to about $90 a double. About six km from downtown, at 102 Kenmount Rd is *Hotel St John's* (☎ 722-9330). About a third of its 85 rooms come with kitchen facilities. Singles/doubles go for $65/70 and up. Also on Kenmount Rd but at No 199 is the *Best Western Travellers Inn* (☎ 722-5540), one of a chain seen in many places across the country. They're fairly standard, reliable mid-range hotels. This one costs about $5 less than the St John's and children stay free.

Out by the airport on Airport Rd is the reasonable *Airport Inn* (☎ 753-3500) with singles/doubles at $45/50.

## Motels
Motels are priced in the middle range or higher. *1st City Motel* (☎ 722-5400) is at 479 Kenmount Rd, about six km from the city centre. Prices are $45 for a single and $5 more for the double and additional people.

The *Center City Motel* (☎ 726-0092) at 389 Elizabeth Ave is the same price and children stay free. Some of the newer rooms cost a little more.

Again about the same price is *Greenwood Lodge & Motel* (☎ 364-5300) towards Mount Pearl, off Route 60, close to town. They've got a games room, and housekeeping units are available at additional cost.

Less costly is the *Crossroads Motel* (☎ 368-3191) at the junction of routes 1 and 60. Rates for singles/doubles are $35/40 and this place has all the facilities.

## PLACES TO EAT
The city has a good array of places 'to have a scoff' to use a local term for eat. Seafood is widely available and there is an assortment of ethnic or international choices for diversity.

At 190 Duckworth St is the comfortable *Duckworth café* popular with the artsy and student crowds. They serve breakfast specials, good sandwiches, light meals, tea, coffee etc at reasonable prices and there are lots of newspapers to read.

Smaller, cozy *Stella's* across the street at No 183 serves natural foods and vegetarian plates in the $5 to $10 range. The Caesar salad is good.

Also cheap and busy is the *Ports of Food*, a food-booth assortment in the Atlantic Place Mall on Water St. It only has fast food – Chinese, soup and salads, doughnuts, etc, but it's open every day. The cafeteria in the discount *Woolco* store on Water St near Queen St west of the post office is also cheap and being in Newfoundland has lunch specials such as Arctic Char priced as low as $5! Everywhere else this delicacy goes for at least twice that.

*Mary Jane's,* at 377 Duckworth but with a back entrance off George St, is a health-food store with an eat-in sandwich counter and food can be taken out. It's also a bakery, ethnic craft outlet, bookshop and generally an interesting place for a browse. Light meals are served at the counter from 11 am to 3 pm and feature various homemade, natural and organic ingredients.

St John's has some of the best fish & chips in the world. Locals tend to have their favourites and competitions are held to determine popularity, but to me they were all top-rate. For a quick sampling head to the junction of Harvey, Lemarchant and Freshwater Sts, a short walk from the centre, where there is a real concentration. The ever popular *Ches's* is at 5 Freshwater Rd. The *Big R* is at 69 Harvey and *Scamper's* is at 1 Lemarchant. A fourth is *Leo's* with outlets at 27 Freshwater or in the centre at 586 Water St. The numerous pubs often serve fish & chips, too. People often bad mouth cod but it is *the* fish in this part of the world and fresh out of the sea it's excellent.

The *Cavendish Café*, at 73 Duckworth St, is good for a soup and sandwich and has an outdoor patio and view of the harbour area.

*House of Haynes* at 207 Kenmount Rd is a casual dining room, offering other seafood like salmon, scallops and a local dish called 'brewis'. The latter is a blend of fish, onion

and a bread-like mix that's soaked overnight. Another local speciality is cod tongues which are really closer to cheeks. They're often served deep-fried with very unimpressive results but, if you can, try them pan-fried.

*Casa Grande* is a nicely decorated Mexican restaurant at 108 Duckworth St. It holds about 10 small wooden tables encircled by wicker chairs and has dishes from around $6 and up. It's open daily, but does not offer lunch on Sunday.

For an East Indian meal try the *India Gate* at 286 Duckworth St which has a good-value lunch special Monday to Friday from noon until 3 pm for $7.

For fine dining, the *Stone House Restaurant* (☎ 753-2380) at 8 Kenna's Hill has long been considered the number one choice. Specialities at this expensive restaurant are seafood, game and traditional Newfoundland dishes. It's in one of the city's oldest homes.

Lastly, you may want to check out the *Fish Market* at the end of Harbour Drive at the western end of town.

## ENTERTAINMENT

St John's is a lot of fun at night. You won't have to search too long in this town if you're thirsty because, per capita, there must be more watering holes here than anywhere. Political correctness in the sphere of alcohol is pleasantly absent in these parts and makes a refreshing change (throwback?) from the constant didacticism found in much of Canada. The elsewhere often forbidden 'happy hour' here becomes stretched to a laughable misnomer lasting from as early as 11 am to as late as 7.30 pm! Two for one specials abound across town and establishments are busy through the day especially on weekends.

George St is pretty crazy with crowds and queues at a variety of bars. The *Corner Stone* on the corner of Queen St has videos and live rock, *Sundance* with a western slant has karaoke on Tuesday and Wednesday and others cater to different age groups and musical preferences. All are cheap or free to get in.

The *Ship Inn* down the steps beside the Arts Council, 245 Duckworth St, is good with live music.

*Bridgett's Pub* at 29 Cookstown Rd, but with the door on Freshwater Rd has meals and a variety of music – folk on Wednesday and anything from blues to traditional the rest of the time.

There are several pubs along Water St and one in the Murray Premises.

Try to seek out some live Newfie music – excellent folk music with Celtic origins, usually based on the fiddle. Pigeon Inlet Productions (☎ 754-7324) is a Newfoundland based company which records, produces, distributes and promotes the province's rich musical heritage. Their recordings on cassette or CD are available at Duckworth Distribution, 198 Duckworth St. Throughout the summer the Newfoundland Museum at 285 Duckworth offers free traditional music concerts on Sunday afternoons.

Apart from these suggestions, you can drink in the quiet lounges of the larger hotels or attend a theatre or dance performance at the Arts & Cultural Centre (☎ 729-3900) on Confederation Parkway.

The *LSPU Hall*, up the stairs from Duckworth St near the Arts Council, often has plays, concerts, comedy nights, etc. This place is worth checking out as it's the centre for the very active arts community.

You may also want to sample Screech – a particularly strong rum once available only here, but now widely available across Canada and still tasty.

## GETTING THERE & AWAY
### Air
Air Canada (☎ 726-7880) to Halifax costs $295, to Montreal $405. Canadian Airlines (☎ 576-0274) flies to Charlottetown for $301. The two biggies work with Air Nova and Air Atlantic respectively for local flights. For flights solely within the province also try Provincial Airlines (☎ 576-1804) and Labrador Airways (☎ 896-8113).

### Bus
The bus system is a little confusing but if you can track things down it can work fairly well for you. The system, unlike that in other provinces, isn't monopolised by one or two operators but consists of a lot of small local and regional services. Finding out who they all are and where they go can take some digging. I've now got many of them listed here and around the province but there are others, I'm sure. Some don't really have much of a depot so call to find out where the bus can be picked up.

The main bus depot (☎ 737-5912, open 7.30 to 5.30 pm; or for recorded information call ☎ 737-5911) is at the far south-west end of town at 495 Water St, underneath the overpass. It's about a 20-minute walk from town.

CN Roadcruiser, a division of Canadian National railways, operates from here running just one route. But it's the province's main one, running across Newfoundland along the Trans Canada Hwy to Port aux Basques and stopping at many places along the way. So many places, in fact, that the trip becomes somewhat of a marathon. There was at one time a direct bus too. Ask about it if you're going right through. To Port aux Basques there's one bus daily at 8 am which costs $80 one way. The trip takes about 14 hours. Two buses leave for Grand Falls at 8 am and 5.30 pm daily and cost $46. This distance takes about 6½ hours to cover. Note that across the province the CN Roadcruiser bus is often referred to as the CN bus.

For Argentia, Placentia and Freshwater there is Newhook's Transportation (☎ 726-4876) which runs buses down to the south-west Avalon Peninsula. There is an office on the corner of Prince and George Sts. Fleetline Bus Service (☎ 722-2608) goes to Carbonear and the lower Conception Bay area daily.

Bonavista North Transportation (☎ 579-3188) runs up to the Bonavista Bay area.

There are still others in St John's, for example, North Shore Bus Lines (☎ 722-5218) which runs to the Old Pelican area beyond Carbonear to the end of the north arm of the Avalon Peninsula. People at the main bus depot or the tourist office will be able to help with information but you may find it necessary to ask more than one person.

## Train

The last passenger trains in the province died in late 1984. It was the end of an era when the narrow-gauge trains, each car heated with its own oil stove, finally succumbed to economics. Now the final freight train has hauled its last load as well and even the tracks have been pulled up. Buses have become the sole means of public transportation.

## Taxi

Share-taxis also run between St John's and the ferry terminal. In Argentia (☎ 227-2552) you can make dockside arrangements for getting to St John's.

Cheeseman's Transportation (☎ 753-7022) runs a share-taxi service to points around the Burin Peninsula and has a depot in the town of Burin and one in St John's.

## Ferry

The Marine Atlantic ferry for North Sydney, Nova Scotia, docks at Argentia (☎ 227-2431) on the south-west coast of the Avalon Peninsula. Newhook's runs a minibus between Argentia and St John's. The fare is about $12 one way and they have an office in downtown St John's (see earlier under Bus for more details).

The MV *Joseph & Clara Smallwood* goes in each direction twice a week and runs from 1 June to 21 October only. It departs Argentia on Wednesday and Saturday, and North Sydney on Tuesday and Friday. The departure times vary according to the month so check. The crossing time is 14 hours which is about four hours shorter than it was in the early 1980s on the older ship although the price has not gone up dramatically since then. Still, an adult ticket is $46.25, a car $103. Rooms and beds are extra. Many people, your humble writer included, find this fare a bit steep and prefer instead to land in Port aux Basques and drive across the province twice to avoid it.

As on the sister ship to Port aux Basques, the MV *Caribou* (from Port aux Basques to North Sydney, Nova Scotia), however, passengers can enjoy the movie theatre, a bar with live band, a tourist booth, a children's play area, and the outdoor decks – in short, the works. On the night trips most people flake out anywhere they can including all over the floor. Bring a blanket or sleeping bag and join the slumber party.

In July or August reservations are a good idea in either direction: call ☎ 902-794-5700 in North Sydney from anywhere in Canada or ☎ 709-772-7701 in and around eastern Newfoundland. Usually one or two days' notice is all that is necessary.

If you're in a car, you'll get a free car wash as you board the ferry back to the Canadian mainland. This is to get rid of two bug varieties harmful to potatoes and found only in Newfoundland.

## Car & Motorbike

If you want a car when arriving at the airport (or in town) make sure you reserve in advance as it is not uncommon for every car, no, every vehicle, in town to be booked out, possibly for several days! Reservations can be made at branches of the international chains in Nova Scotia or elsewhere or you can phone the offices here in advance.

There are several car-rental agencies in town. Most can be found along Topsail Rd. Among the chains are: Budget (☎ 747-1234) at 954 Topsail Rd; Thrifty (☎ 576-4351) at 685 Topsail Rd; and Rent-A-Wreck (☎ 753-2277) with cheaper, used cars at 43 Pippy Place.

Gas (petrol) is expensive in Newfoundland – the costliest in Canada.

Also, if you drive a car one way between St John's and Port aux Basques, you'll have to pay a return charge of at least $150. Basically though, the rates are about the same here as anywhere else in Canada.

## GETTING AROUND
### To/From the Airport

There is no city bus to the airport, about six km north of town on Route 40 going towards

Torbay. Going by taxi, at about $12, is the only way. The official airport service is by Dave Gulliver Cabs (☎ 722-0003). Inquire about sharing and if you're lucky it may be cheaper.

### Bus
The St John's Transportation Commission runs the Metrobus (☎ 722-9400) city bus system. There are a few bus routes in and around town and together they cover most areas – No 1 does the central area. By transferring from this one to an adjoining loop, say the bus No 12 going west, you can get a pretty good city tour for just a couple of bucks. The bus No 2 goes to Bowring Park and to the Queen's Battery.

### Bicycle Rentals
For two wheels, try Canary Cycles (☎ 579-5972) 294 at Water St.

### AROUND ST JOHN'S
Marine Drive, north of St John's, up towards Torbay, goes past nice coastal scenery. There are rocky beaches at both **Middle Cove** and **Outer Cove** – good for a walk or picnic.

Offshore around **Torbay** is a good whale-watching area. Puffins live and feed here also. Marine Drive ends at **Pouch Cove** but a gravel road continues to **Cape St Francis** for good views. West of town, head to **Topsail** for a great view of Conception Bay and some of its islands.

Ten km south of St John's towards **Petty Harbour** don't miss Bidgood's, a supermarket with a twist. It's become known far and wide for its Newfoundland specialities. Popular with local residents, this is also the place where those back on a visit stock up on their favourite items before returning to jobs on the mainland. Recently more tourists have been showing up. Where else can you buy caribou steak, moose in a jar or seal meat pie? Depending on the time of year the selection may also include cod tongues, saltfish or lobster. There are jars of the province's distinctive jams – try partridge berry or the elite of the island's berries, bakeapple. You may

also want to take a gander at the bakery section which regularly sells out.

Further south, along the coast, about 13 km from town is **Cape Spear** where there is a national historic park centred around the lighthouse which dates from 1835. A guide will show you around and offer all sorts of information, like how many coats of wallpaper layer the inside walls (you won't believe it). Cape Spear is the most easterly point in North America: next stop, Ireland.

Continuing south, the area around **Goulds** has some unusual things to see – cows and fields of vegetables. This is one of the very few good farming districts in the province.

**Bay Bulls** and **Witless Bay** are excellent places from which to observe birds. Three islands off Witless Bay and southward are bird sanctuaries collectively known as an ecological reserve. Together they represent one of the top sea-bird breeding areas in eastern North America. Every summer thousands of puffins, kittiwakes, murres, cormorants, storm petrels and several other species make these rocky islands home and hatch their young there. Several operators run highly recommended trips out to the colonies.

No one is permitted on the islands but the boats do get close enough for you to consider taking ear plugs as well as camera and binoculars! The din overhead is incredible. The best months for visiting are June and July which is also good for whale-watching – humpback and minke are fairly common here. Whales are seen in the vicinity until early August and the humpback is the most spectacular of all whales for its breaching performances. If you really hit the jackpot, an iceberg might be thrown in too.

Out of Bay Bulls, Bird Island Charters (☎ 753-4850) has 2½-hour trips and passes by two of the islands. A good feature is that they also run a shuttle bus to the dock from the major hotels in St John's, 30 km away.

Gatherall's (☎ 334-2887) runs a similar boat tour and also has a guesthouse in Bay Bulls on the North Side Rd. The town was the site of a repair station for Allied ships in WW II and a German submarine actually surrendered here.

Cape Broyle further down the coast also has a bird-sanctuary trip run by Great Island Tours. Their trip includes a seaside view of an abandoned coastal village wedged into the cliffs. They also offer shuttle buses to and from the city.

Regardless of the weather take a jacket or sweater and, call me a wimp, a Gravol pill is not a bad idea either. I know.

A little further south, about 80 km south of St John's, at the town of **Ferryland**, also on the coast, is an on-going archaeological dig which can be visited. The site was one of the earliest English settlements in North America, dating from circa 1625. An interpretive centre contains some explanatory exhibits and artefacts uncovered thus far. An interesting concept is the 17th-century garden planted with species the colonists would have had. The dig and the field lab can be seen. The interpretive centre is open daily through the summer. The dig is closed on Sundays.

## AROUND THE AVALON PENINSULA

The peninsula, more like an island hanging onto the rest of the province by a thin strip of land, is the most densely populated area of Newfoundland: nearly half its population lives here.

**Conception Bay** is lined with scores of small communities but all around the coast you'll find fishing villages.

At **Argentia** in the south-west is the ferry depot connecting with Nova Scotia. The tourist office can suggest driving and camping tours around the peninsula.

### Southern Avalon

Despite its proximity to St John's this section of the province is very good for viewing wildlife and has several good parks. The coast has a long history having been visited and settled by various Europeans from the 1600s onward.

Down the coast at **La Manche Provincial Park** are two excellent, scenic walking trails: one to a waterfall, one to the remains of a coastal village.

In the interior is the huge **Avalon Wilder-**

**ness Reserve** with an increasingly large herd of woodland caribou which now numbers about 100,000. Permits, available in St John's at the government Parks Department, are required to visit the area for hiking or canoeing. Caribou, however, can sometimes be seen right at the edge of the road, on Hwy 10, between **Biscay Bay** and **Trepassey** at the bottom of the peninsula. (Trepassey was the launching place of Amelia Earhart's first-woman-across-the-Atlantic flight in 1928.)

Actually, keep your eyes open from the town of Cappahayden southbound all the way to Biscay Bay, too. It is worth asking the locals when you're down this way where the herd is. As migrating animals, caribou tend to move en masse, quite an experience to see. Even spotting a lone individual is a real treat as they are quite impressive beasts and rarely seen by those not living or working in the far north of Canada, Russia or Finland.

Camping is possible at Chance Cove south of Cappahayden. *Lawlor's Hospitality Home* (☎ 363-2164), open from June to August, is in Cappahayden with five rooms at singles/doubles $30/40. Breakfast is available but gets added to the bill.

Continuing up the coast, the area from St Vincent's to St Mary's provides an excellent chance of seeing whales, particularly the humpback which feeds close to shore. The best times are between mid-June and mid-July. A fishing boat may take you for a closer look at other whales including the fin, blue, sperm and minke.

On Hwy 90, **Salmonier Nature Park** is in the centre of the Avalon Peninsula, 12 km south of the junction with Hwy 1. Here you can see many animals found in the province, enclosed in the park's natural settings. A marked trail through the woods takes you past the animals – moose, caribou, beaver, etc – as well as indigenous flora. The park is open daily from June to September from noon; there's a small admission fee.

### Conception Bay Area

Like the rest of eastern Newfoundland, Con-

Top: Boya Lake, Northern British Columbia (DS)
Bottom: Grain silo in Denholm, Saskatchewan (DS)

Top: Québecois cowboy (RE)
Bottom Left: The Château Frontenac overlooking Quebec City's Lower Town, Quebec (R
Bottom Right: Former World's Fair pavilion, now a casino, Montreal, Quebec (JL)

ception Bay is rich in history and coastal scenery. The road winds along the densely populated coastline and passes through dozens of towns and villages. Much of the early history of Canada was played out here. **Bay de Verde** in the north can be reached in half a day's drive from St John's. But, if time permits, there are places to stay. Fleetline Bus Service connects St John's with Carbonear and makes stops along the way.

### Brigus

Despite its small size, Brigus, 80 km west from St John's, has quite a reputation for its pleasing old European atmosphere. Its distinctive character draws many visitors. A former resident, one Captain Bartlett, accompanied Peary on part of his 1909 voyage to the North Pole. Now his house is an historic site. Another thing to see is the tunnel, cut through rock in 1860, to make berths for Bartlett's ships. There are also a couple of craft shops in town.

With four places to stay and another one 20 km or so away there is more accommodation here than anywhere else on Conception Bay. The *Brittoner Guest Home* (☎ 528-3412), on Water St, is right in the middle of things and, with singles/doubles for $40/47 including full breakfast.

### Harbour Grace

Up past Cupid's where the first official English settlement of Newfoundland was attempted in 1610, is Harbour Grace where the Spanish and French had been since the early 1500s. In the 1700s it was used by pirates. The old Customs House is a museum.

Many of the first attempts to fly across the Atlantic began in Harbour Grace beginning in 1919. In 1932, four years after her flight from Trepassey on the Avalon Peninsula to Europe, Amelia Earhart took off from here and became the first woman to cross the Atlantic solo too. The airstrip is designated an historic site. Fish processing is the main economic activity.

### Carbonear Island

Carbonear Island has had a tumultuous history with international battles, pirate intrigues, shipwrecks and more recently, seal-hunt controversy. Carbonear Island is designated an historic site and there are many examples of old architecture in town. The annual summer folk music festival here is not to be missed.

### Other

EJ Pratt (1883-1964), one of Canada's best-known poets, was born in Western Bay and a national historic plaque here commemorates him. The following lines are from the poem *The Titanic* and describe the destructive beauty of the iceberg which sank the unsinkable ship.

But when the months of voyaging it came
To where both streams – the Gulf and Polar – met
The sun which left its crystal peaks aflame
In the sub-Arctic noons, began to fret
The arches, flute the spires and deform
The features, till the batteries of storm
Playing above the slow-eroding base,
Demolished the last temple touch of grace.

Further north up the coast, **Northern Sands Provincial Park** has beautiful beaches. On the inland side is a good spot for freshwater swimming, the ocean is too cold.

From **Lower Island Cove** there is some fine coastal scenery. At **Bears Cove**, near **Bay de Verde**, a short walk leads to dramatic views.

At the very tip, at **Grates Cove**, there is a rock on the shore into which, it is said, John Cabot scratched his name. I suppose this makes John Cabot the first person to graffiti the continent.

### Along Trinity Bay

On the other side of the peninsula are several towns which exemplify the wonderful place names so often seen and enjoyed around the province. How about the absolutely lovely **Heart's Delight** or **Heart's Content**?

In Heart's Content an historic site tells the story of the cable station here, where the first transatlantic cable was laid.

Both towns mentioned have a place to stay (appropriately, nearby Heart's Desire doesn't!) In Heart's Delight is *Legge's Hospitality Home*, at 2 Farm Rd, near the Irving Station. It's run by Mrs Gertie Legge (☎ 588-2577) who charges $30/35 for singles/doubles and a little more for breakfast. Heart's Content has the small, more costly *Legge's Motel* (☎ 538-2929) which consists of seven self-contained housekeeping units and two cheaper simple motel-style rooms.

At the bottom of Trinity Bay, **Dildo** (when you stop sniggering) is a good spot for whale-watching. Pothead whales come in by the school; humpbacks, a larger species, can also be seen in summer. Both can be viewed even from the shore.

### Argentia

The south-west portion of the Avalon Peninsula is known primarily for Argentia with the large ferry terminal for boats to Nova Scotia. For ferry information see St John's. Newhook's Transportation connects both Argentia (☎ 227-2552) and Placentia with St John's by road.

Since WW II, the USA operated a naval and air base here but it's been phased out in recent years. There isn't much to see in Argentia and, surprisingly, given the presence of the ferry dock, there's nowhere to stay.

### Placentia

Nearby in Placentia, settled in 1662, are the remains of a French fort at Castle Hill National Historic Site (☎ 227-2401), with a visitors' centre and fine views. In the early 1800s Placentia was the French capital of Newfoundland and French attacks on the English at St John's were based from here. There are picnic tables around the park and the site is open daily all year.

The old graveyard by the Anglican church offers more history as does the Placentia Area Museum (☎ 227-3621) found in O'Reilly House at 48 Riverside Drive. In a home built in 1902 and well restored in 1989, the museum offers details of both the house

and the area. It's open from June to September. The courthouse and the Roman Catholic church are other notable historic buildings. Plaques and cannons mark the sites of other former local fortifications. A boardwalk runs along the waterfront and there is a beach.

Near Placentia there is a section of the coast which is forested, a rather unusual sight here, as so much of the entire provincial coastline is barren and rocky.

Point Verde has a lighthouse first established in 1876 but now in a new incarnation.

Placentia has one hotel, the *Harold Hotel* (☎ 227-2107), five km from the ferry, with doubles at $54 and it has a restaurant. There is also the *Unicorn Guest House* (☎ 227-5424) at $47 double with a continental breakfast. It, too, is five km from the ferry.

### Cape St Mary's

At the southern tip of the peninsula is the **St Mary's Ecological Reserve**, an excellent place for seeing sea birds. An unpaved road leads the 16 km from Route 100 into the sanctuary where there is an interpretive centre and a lighthouse. A walk in from there taking about half an hour offers views of Bird Rock, the second largest gannet nesting site in North America. Throughout the summer the shoreline and cliffs are home to thousands of birds including kittiwakes, murres and razorbills. There is no admission charge and through the summer guides are present to answer questions.

# Eastern Newfoundland

This is the smallest region of the province and consists of the area just west off the Avalon Peninsula on the edge of the main body of the island. Geographically it is also distinguished from the central portion of the province by the jutting peninsulas at each end: the Bonavista to the north and the Burin to the south. Like the Avalon Peninsula area, Eastern Newfoundland was settled early and the convoluted coastlines are lined with historic old fishing villages.

The ferry for the islands of Saint Pierre and Miquelon departs from Fortune in the south. To this day, the islands are French possessions and certainly not in name only. Spending a couple of days here is like a mini trip to Europe.

Terrenceville is at one end of the south coastal ferry line which services outports all the way to Port aux Basques at the southwestern tip of the province. Leaving the Eastern region the principa

l road travels through Terra Nova National Park providing a microcosm of the area's varied topography and plant and animal life.

## BONAVISTA PENINSULA

The Bonavista Peninsula has some superb coastal scenery with many small, traditional fishing communities including some of the oldest in the province. Some people claim that historic Trinity is the oldest town in North America. Several companies around the peninsula offer boat tours and Terra Nova National Park preserves a section of the peninsula in its natural state.

### Clarenville

This is the access point to the peninsula and it's best to pass right through. In 1955, Clarenville became the North American terminal for undersea telephone cables connecting with Oban, Scotland. To the west are many small communities lining the three long arms to the sea. North of town along Hwy 230 is a bird sanctuary protecting large numbers of Canada geese which nest here.

### Up the Coast

Hwy 235, along the edge of **Southern Bay**, has some fine coastal scenery and a picnic spot with a view at Jiggin' Head Park. At the 300-year-old fishing village of **Keels,** boat tours of the rugged coastline are available.

Along the beaches here and around the Avalon Peninsula in late June and early July, millions of capelin – a small silver fish – get washed up on shore by the tides. This is

partially due to the spawning cycle and partially to being chased by hungry cod. Anyway, the shore is alive with the fish, and people go down with buckets and bags to scoop up a free meal.

### Bonavista

This largish town of 5000 residents is at the end of the peninsula where John Cabot landed on 24 June 1497 and first saw the 'new found land'. Later he drifted down to the St John's harbour and stopped there. For his troubles the King of England rewarded him with the royal sum of £10. It wasn't until the 1600s that Bonavista became a permanent village and from then on through the 1700s, the English and French battled over it like they did for other settlements along the coast.

Built over and around hills, Bonavista, with its narrow, winding streets is best explored by foot. Even the government tourist information says that street names are 'as rare as hen's teeth' and you'll likely get lost.

The **Bonavista Museum** in town on Church St and its staff offer all manner of information on the town and its history. In the garden at the old courthouse, is a whipping post where instant justice could be meted out. Another historic site is the Mockbeggar Property which, in a number of buildings, outlines aspects of traditional Newfoundland life.

The **lighthouse** at Cape Bonavista dating from 1843 has been restored and is now a provincial historic site with guides in 19th-century period costume. The scenery of the cape is dramatic. The **Dungeon** is an unusual rock formation on the shoreline. In early summer whales may be seen off the coast. In 1997 the area celebrates the 500th anniversary of Cabot's arrival at the cape. A statue of the explorer can be seen near the lighthouse.

Outside of town at the village of **Maberly** is a park with views over some of the islands where thousands of sea birds birds roost. Principal species are puffins, kittiwakes and murres. There is also a sandy beach at the provincial park

**Places to Stay** Despite being the major town on the peninsula there is a dearth of accommodation. The only choice at Bonavista is the *Hotel Bonavista* (☎ 468-1510) on Hwy 230. Doubles are $58 with children under 12 free. Hospitality homes can be found scattered around the peninsula, notably around the Trinity area.

**Getting There & Away** Newhook's Transportation runs a daily bus service between St John's and Bonavista.

### Port Union
The Fisherman's Protective Union was formed here in 1910 and a monument and a museum honour its founder. The province's largest fish-processing plant is here and one of Newfoundland's largest trawler fleets operates out of this ice-free port.

### Trinity
First visited by the Portuguese explorer Corte-Real in 1500 and established as a town in 1580, Trinity is one of the oldest settlements in the province and might be the oldest town on the entire continent. The village has a fascinating history which includes the first court in North America – convened in 1615. Many buildings along the town's narrow streets have been restored or renovated and indeed, much of the town has national heritage designation. An interpretive centre (☎ 729-2460) open daily in the summer has much information on the history, houses and buildings in town. Also see the Trinity Museum, Hiscock House Provincial Historic Site and the fort remains.

Also in town is Ocean Contact, a whale-watching and research organisation. They offer day expeditions, short holidays and all-inclusive, expensive week-long trips that take in other wildlife and local geographic and historic attractions. Aside from whales, other marine life includes porpoises and dolphins. Boat tours depart Trinity daily in the summer months.

There is another town of Trinity also on the Bonavista Peninsula which is smaller and of less interest. To avoid confusion, the one discussed above is known sometimes as Trinity, Trinity Bay or Trinity, TB.

**Places to Stay & Eat** Ocean Contact operates from the *Village Inn* (☎ 464-3269), a good place to stay with rooms from singles/doubles $40/50. Films and slides on whales and other sea life can be seen.

Alternately, there is *Trinity Cabins* (☎ 464-3657), with housekeeping cabins in the $40 to $45 range for two people. There's a swimming pool or, for the brave, a beach near by.

There are also two B&Bs in Trinity providing visitors with an unaccustomed and almost overwhelming accommodation decision. The more modest is the *Beach B&B* (☎ 464-3695) while the *Campbell House* (☎ 464-3377) is a beautifully restored historic house.

Lastly, in the village of Trinity East is the *Peace Cove Inn* (☎ 464-3738) in a restored turn-of-the-century house. A complimentary breakfast is included with a night's stay and lunch and dinner are available at extra charge.

### Terra Nova National Park
This east coast park (☎ 533-2801) split by the Trans Canada Hwy typifies the regional geography. The rocky, jagged coastline on beautiful Bonavista Bay gives way to long bays, inland lakes, ponds, bogs and hilly woods. There's canoeing, fishing, hiking, camping, sandy beaches, even swimming in Sandy Pond.

You can rent bicycles in the park – a good way to get around. Lots of wildlife may be seen – moose, bear, beaver, otter and bald eagles – and, from May to August, icebergs are commonly viewed off the coast. Both short and long hiking trails wind through portions of the park. A short one at Malady Head leads to good views.

At either of Newman Sound or Twin Rivers visitor centres staff will recommend activities depending on the length of your stay. The park's main campground at Newman Sound has a grocery store and bicycle rentals. A couple of km away at Sandy Pond canoes and kayaks may be rented.

Commercial lodging can be found outside the park in nearby communities.

Within the park is Ocean Watch Tours, recommended for their good-value boat tours. One trip explores the fjords and islands and sometimes stops in at old abandoned outports. Another trip specialises more in wildlife and seeks out whales, seals, birds etc. On either one, icebergs from as far away as Greenland may be sighted.

The tour boat also offers a fantastic ferry service to backcountry campers which means dropping you off at an otherwise inaccessible cove and picking you up at a predetermined time later. Hiking trails lead into the park from the two drop-off points. You do have to take one of the boat tours for the service but they are certainly no burden at all and backcountry camping is free!

The park is 240 km west of St John's and 80 km east of Gander.

## BURIN PENINSULA
Jutting south into the Atlantic Ocean, the peninsula has been the base for European fishing boats since the 1500s. The Grand Banks off the peninsula (part of the continental shelf) teem with fish. Or at least they did until the early 1990s when stocks plummeted. The hilly, wooded northern area supplied timber for building and ships; the southern end is mostly barren, glacier-stripped rock interspersed with bogs and marshes.

Cheeseman's Transportation with depots in St John's and Burin (☎ 891-1866), connects points around the peninsula and the big city by share-taxi.

### Terrenceville & Coastal Ferry
Terrenceville is the eastern port for the southern coast Marine Atlantic ferry which skips along the south of the province from Port aux Basques. This trip is one of the province's unique adventures and, with new roads always being built, is likely to be history within a decade. The ferry serves about 10 mostly otherwise isolated communities. It carries the sick to the doctor and later brings the bill in the mailbag. Each trip is somewhat different as the stops made vary. The trip is generally scheduled as taking 19 hours but it can be longer.

It's possible to break the journey and although none of the stops have official hotels, it's not uncommon to find someone to take you in for the night. The ferry fare is paid for according to distance at a rate of just 19 cents per nautical mile, less for seniors and children. It is 259 nautical miles to Port aux Basques. Cabin berths are available at additional cost but only in the winter. For reservations which can only be made in Newfoundland call Marine Atlantic (☎ 1-800-563-7381) toll free.

Ferries depart Terrenceville three times a week throughout the summer. (See under Outports for more information.)

In Terrenceville there is, unfortunately, no place to stay but the ferry arrives the night before the morning departure, so you can sleep on board.

### Marystown
Although the largest town on the peninsula, there is not much here for the visitor but Marystown does have a tourist office and the most shops and services in the area. There is camping and freshwater swimming at **Frenchman's Cove Provincial Park.**

### Burin
Settled by fishers from Europe in the 1700s, Burin is one of the oldest towns on the south coast. It is a pretty town or rather a series of villages sparsely scattered around coves and the lumpy, treeless hills.

Unlike some of the region's towns, Burin has maintained its important role in the Grand Banks and has a major trawler repair facility as well as a processing plant.

**Captain Cook's Lookout** provides good views of the harbour and area. The English built fortifications here in 1812. The French were based across the bay in Placentia.

Along the coast northward at **Tides Point** is a lighthouse.

**The Golden Sands** is a popular beach and there is camping at the provincial park.

### St Lawrence

A little further down the coast, St Lawrence is a mining town with the only deposits of fluorospar in Canada. It was once the world's largest producer and although this is no longer the case, the mine still operates and a small museum outlines its history.

### Grand Bank

Its role now diminished, this was one of the main centres of the early Grand Banks fishery and some of that history remains. The Burin Peninsula long-served as the base for the famous Banks fishing grounds. A walk through town shows the varied architecture of the 1880s in the homes, churches and Water St storefronts.

The Southern Newfoundland Seaman's Museum depicts both the era of the banking schooner and the changes in the fishery over the years. It's free and, in summer, open every day. You can't miss it – it's like a large white boat on Marine Drive.

If you're spending the night in Grand Bank the big, old *Thorndyke* (☎ 832-0820), a designated historic home, makes a fine place to stay. It's at 33 Water St, just 6.5 km from the Fortune ferry; the rooms are offered at good prices. It's busy, so call for reservations. From the roof there are views over the town and bay and there is a restaurant on the premises. There is also a motel in town.

### Fortune

Fortune is the jumping-off point for trips to Saint Pierre and Miquelon and 20,000 people a year pass through on their way to the islands. Aside from looking after visitors, many of the town's people are employed at the large fish-processing plant. There is also a shipbuilding and repair depot.

Foote's Taxi (☎ 832-0491) links Fortune with St John's. It's about a five-hour trip.

The *Eldon House* (☎ 832-0442) inn at 56 Eldon St is open from mid-June to early September. There are just three rooms which go for $40 double, including continental

---

### The Grand Banks

The fabulous portion of the Atlantic Ocean known as the Grand Banks, lying just south-east off Cape Race at the southern part of the Avalon Peninsula, is one of the prime reasons anybody ever bothered with the New World. After 500 years of serious plundering it remains one of the world's best fishing grounds. In the early 1990s the warning bells finally went off and when they did they rang long and loud. One species, the dominant one, cod, had finally been reduced to alarming lows.

Biologists, fishers and government have now combined forces to work out a plan to let the stocks replenish themselves.

The banks are a series of submarine plateaus stretching from north-west to south-east about 80 km out to sea from Cape Race. They extend to cover an area about 500 km long by 300 km wide with a depth ranging from just five up to 350 metres.

Though mostly in the Labrador Current, the waters are met by the Gulf Stream and this blending of the warm and cold gives rise to the legendary fogs. It also helps plankton, a surface plant, to thrive and it is this that results in the millions of fish. The main catch has always been cod but there is also halibut, flounder and herring among others. Boats come from around the world, notably from Norway, Japan, Portugal, Spain and Russia to fill their hulls. Canada has imposed restrictions and regulations but has an impossible task in trying to enforce its limits and authority.

It was John Cabot, an Italian working for England, who first put down a net and found his eyes bulging as much as the net did. From that time, 1497, Europeans began to arrive and set up fishing communities. As well as the fog, nasty storms and marauding icebergs are hazards that fishers have had to contend with through the centuries.

In the past 20 years, oil has been discovered on parts of the Banks and it is debatable what development will mean for the fishing grounds. ■

breakfast. The *Fair Isle Motel* (☎ 832-1010) with 10 rooms at $60 single or double is the alternative.

There is also a fairly large campground with sites for tents and trailers on the edge of town.

# Saint Pierre & Miquelon

This is probably the oddest side-trip in Canada. Once called the 'Islands of 11,000 Virgins', these two dabs of land, lying 16 km west off Newfoundland's Burin Peninsula, belong to France. The tiny islands represent the only French holdings left in North America. The 6000 residents drink French wine, eat baguettes and pay for it in francs.

First claimed by France in the 1500s, the islands were turned over to the English along with Cape Breton after the Seven Years' War. They were then ceded to the French by the British in 1783 under the Treaty of Paris. Battles over fishing rights continued with Newfoundland and the islands changed hands a couple of times until 1815. Since then they have remained under French control. The disputes persist, however, and in 1989 there was a fairly serious flare-up with France getting involved in the bickering over territorial fishing limits.

An interesting aside is Saint Pierre's role during the Prohibition period. Canada would legally export what amounted to oceans of booze to the French island where US rum runners would pick it up to take home.

A few days make a good visit – exploring, relaxing, enjoying a different culture. Like much of the Newfoundland coast, the islands are barren and rocky (although there are some relatively wild areas as well as cliffs and sandy beaches).

As in so much of Atlantic Canada, the main source of livelihood has always been fishing and the supplying of fishing boats. The closing of much of the region's fishery, most notably the moratorium on cod fishing, has seriously undermined the economic viability of the islands. France has been paying

some compensation to those put out of work and aims to boost the tourism industry. This money maker which has been increasing in importance for the past decade is where the island is placing its bets. France is building a new airport able to accommodate jumbo jets, and plans are being made to develop gambling casinos to lure even more visitors.

The archipelago consists of numerous islands. Saint Pierre, although not the largest, is the principal one; it's the most populated and its town of the same name is the largest on the islands.

Miquelon is actually two islands separated by a narrow isthmus of sand. The northern section, Great Miquelon, has pretty well all the people and a small town. The southern island called Langlade or Little Miquelon is quite wild. The remaining islands are all very small.

Canadian and US visitors need neither passports nor visas for a visit, but good ID such as a birth certificate or driver's licence with photograph is recommended. For citizens of the European Union (EU), Switzerland and Japan, passports are required. All other nationals need both a passport and a visa.

Note that the time on the islands is half an hour ahead of Newfoundland time. Also keep in mind that there is a duty-free shop for alcohol, cigarettes, etc.

## THINGS TO SEE

In Saint Pierre you can see the **museum** which outlines the island's history and the cathedral. Also, visit the interesting **French cemetery**.

Outside town there is a lighthouse at **Gallantry Head** and good views from **Cap aux Basques**. Out in the harbour, a 10-minute boat ride away, is **Île aux Marins** with a small museum. You can take a bilingual guided tour around the island which had its own fishing village at the turn of the century.

Miquelon, 45 km away, is less visited and less developed. The people here are largely of Acadian background while Saint Pierre's inhabitants are French (mainly from Brittany and Normandy), and Basque.

The village of **Miquelon**, centred around the church, is at the northern tip of the island.

From nearby **l'Étang de Mirande**, a walking trail leads to a lookout and waterfall. From the bridge in town a scenic 25-km road leads across the isthmus to **Langlade**. The island of Langlade remains pretty much the same as it has always been. There are some summer cottages but no year-round inhabitants – human ones, that is. There are some wild horses and smaller animals such as rabbits and around the rocky edges and lagoons you'll see seals and birds. Walks or horseback rides can be taken through the woods, along the beaches or through the sandy grasslands.

## FESTIVALS

Several annual holidays and festivals occur in July and August. On 14 July is Bastille Day. On 4 August, Jacques Cartier's arrival in the islands in 1536 is celebrated. The following week, a two-day festival on Miquelon recalls the Acadians' heritage and, later in the month, another two-day event on Saint Pierre celebrates the Basques' heritage. These, of course, are busy as well as interesting times to visit. From mid-July to the end of August folk dances are often held in Saint Pierre's square.

## PLACES TO STAY & EAT

Saint Pierre has about half a dozen hotels and the same number of guesthouses or pensions which are more reasonably priced and which generally provide breakfast. *Hotel Robert* (☎ 722-3892), on the waterfront with 54 rooms, is the largest place. The *Hotel Paris-Madrid* (☎ 412933) at 14 Quai de la République is much smaller, simpler and cheaper. *Motel Roger Rode* (☎ 722-3892) has five rooms with kitchens. For the pensions ask the tourist office for listings. At a couple of these places meals are available. Accommodation can be tight in high season so you may want to check before you go. A guide with the latest lodgings should be available at one of the Newfoundland tourist offices. If not the Saint Pierre Tourist office (☎ 412384) can help out.

Miquelon has one hotel, one pension and a small campground at l'Étang de Mirande near town.

As might be expected on French islands, restaurants are numerous relative to the size of the population, and the food is good. In both Saint Pierre and Miquelon there are several places serving traditional French food. *Chez Dutin* on Saint Pierre has been recommended by a traveller. Saint Pierre has more choice and a number of less-expensive places for sandwiches, pizza and the like. *Le Maringoiun'fre* has good crêpes.

## GETTING THERE & AWAY
### Air

Air Saint Pierre flies from Montreal, Halifax and Sydney (Nova Scotia) during the summer. Information and reservations can be had through Canadian Airlines International.

### Ferry

There are two ferries, neither taking vehicles, running between Fortune and Saint Pierre. Reservations are advised for both.

The MV *St Eugene 5* with a capacity of 200 passengers, does the trip in 55 minutes and costs $29 one way, $48 return, less for children. From June to the beginning of September (with some exceptions in early June and mid to late September) there is one trip a day in each direction departing in the early afternoon. If you're pressed for time, ask about the cheaper same-day return trip. For tickets and information call Lloyd Lake Ltd (☎ 832-2006) in Fortune.

The MV *Arethusa* also makes daily trips during the same period but also travels in May and the first half of June on a reduced schedule. The fare rates are the same as for the other boat. Although new and comfortable this boat is considerably slower, taking about 1¾ hours. This isn't necessarily a bad thing as there is an open upper deck and, besides the coastal views, you might be lucky enough to see a whale. For tickets and information, there is an office (☎ 832-0429) at the terminal in Fortune. There is also an office (☎ 738-1357) in St John's at 38 Gear

St. This office is open all year, the former one is seasonal.

To catch either boat, arrive at the dock close to an hour ahead of departure. The Fortune ferry terminal has a parking lot for those who have driven to the ferry. Check the arrival and departure times of both ferries as one may suit your plans better.

Several companies offer various package tours which may include the bus trip to the ferry, ferry crossings, hotel and sightseeing or some combination of the above. Two companies to try are the same outfits which run the ferries, Lloyd Lake Ltd in Fortune and SPM Tours in Fortune and St John's.

### GETTING AROUND
#### Between the Islands
The MV *St Eugene 5* travels to Miquelon and returns later the same day three times a week. The return fare is $30 (roughly, depending on the value of the franc) less for kids and the trip takes just under an hour.

#### Around the Islands
In Saint Pierre rent a 'rosalie', a four-wheeled bicycle that comes in two sizes, two and four-person models are available. There are regular bicycles as well or small motorbikes. In both Saint Pierre and Miquelon, tours on horseback are offered.

Also on Saint Pierre there are tours by bus and mini-train and on Miquelon a bus trip takes visitors around the island and across the isthmus to Langlade. In a couple of days much can be seen on foot.

# Central Newfoundland

The vast, little-populated central area is the largest geographic region of the island portion of the province. For the visitor it is the area of least interest, although there are still some fine places to see, particularly the Notre Dame Bay coast and its intriguing, small islands. From Lewisporte ferries depart for northern Newfoundland and Labrador. The southern area is mostly inaccessible, lake-filled woodland. One road leads down to the coast linking many small remote villages to the rest of the province.

## GANDER
Gander, with a population of 13,000, is at the crossroads of the east-west Trans Canada Hwy and Hwy 330 which leads to Notre Dame Bay. Though there isn't a lot to do, it is a convenient stopping point whichever way you're going. Gander is best known for its airport and a Canadian Forces base.

Gander served the first regular transatlantic flights and then, during WW II, was a major link for planes on their way to Europe. The first formation of bombers made in the USA for the UK left here in February 1940. The location was chosen because it is close to Europe and yet far enough inland to be free of the coastal fog which often plagues St John's.

Numerous US and Canadian airlines also used it for transatlantic flights beginning in the 1930s. The airport, a major Aeroflot refuelling stop, is known for being the site of thousands of defections from Russia, Cuba and former Eastern Bloc countries: the plane touches down and passengers ask for political asylum. These days it is more likely the hopeful arrivals seek refugee status which permits them to stay in Canada until their case is heard. The airport lies 3744 km from London, 2782 km from Chicago and 12,536 km from Tokyo.

There is a tourist chalet on the Trans Canada Hwy at the central exit into town. Airplane buffs will notice that almost all the street names are related to aviation and its history.

Gander is a main stop on the CN Roadcruiser (☎ 256-4874) bus route across the province. In Gander call for scheduling information.

### Aviation Attractions
There are three planes mounted and on display around town. On the west side of town is a Beech 18 from the Canadian navy. In the downtown area near the City Hall is a

McDonnell CF100 Voodoo and out at the airport is the third, a Hudson Bomber.

Also at the airport is a small aviation display on Gander's history and, of more interest, there's a huge tapestry depicting the history of flight. It's in the passengers' waiting lounge but, if you don't have a ticket, ask the security officials and they'll let you in for a look.

Just east of town, south off the Trans Canada Hwy, the Silent Witness Monument unveiled in June 1990 tenderly marks the site of an horrendous early morning crash in December 1985 in which 248 US soldiers returning home from the Middle East for Christmas were killed along with eight crew members. The possible causes are still debated. The size of the swath of forest taken out by the crash is astounding.

### Places to Stay

There is a campground 16 km north of town at Jonathan's Pond and another at Square Pond 34 km east of Gander. The *Cape Cod Inn* (☎ 651-2269) at 66 Bennet Drive is in a newish residential area close to downtown. A doubles ranges between $45 to $65, breakfast included. Other Newfoundland-style meals are available at extra cost.

There are numerous motels on the highway but they're decidedly pricey. The basic *Fox Moth* (☎ 256-3535) with some efficiency units is the cheapest with singles from $52. Also try *Skipper's Inn* (☎ 256-2534) where there is a dining room. Consider heading to Notre Dame Bay for the night where prices are lower.

### Places to Eat

On Airport Drive in town are the usual fast-food outlets. The Chinese restaurant, *Highlight*, is better. It's in the little mall strip on the corner of Elizabeth St and Airport Blvd, the two main streets of Gander. It's very popular and, though the food is good, I suspect some people come just for the remarkably lavish decor. Standard Canadian fare is also available.

Continuing east on Airport Blvd towards the airport turn south (left) at Bennet St. At

136 Bennet St, beside the Gander mall, is the *Bread Shoppe*, a good bakery with a wide selection of breads and pastries.

## NOTRE DAME BAY & AROUND

This coastal area north of Gander is the highlight of Central Newfoundland. Though relatively heavily populated it has typically rugged but especially scenic Newfoundland coastal topography. About 80 little villages are found around the bay nestled in small coves or clinging to the rocky shoreline. From Gander there are two road loops – one through Lewisporte, the other eastward to Wesleyville – which make good circular tours. A few of the towns have small museums dealing with various aspects of local history.

Offshore is a large cluster of islands, including New World, Fogo and Twillingate, which should not be missed and where whales and icebergs may be seen.

If you go north along Hwy 330 (watch for moose), you'll reach the coast at Gander Bay which has a good place to stay. *Doorman's Cove Lodge* (☎ 676-2254), in a century-old house, is across the street from the sea in the village of Doorman's Cove. Singles/doubles cost $35/40 and there is a triple room as well. Breakfast is included and the jams are terrific. Other meals are also available. The owners also run trips along the Gander River for nature watching, fishing or hunting. Canoes can be rented.

### Change Islands

These two islands, reached by ferry from Farewell at the end of a what seems a long road from the main highway, don't change much, name notwithstanding. There are five (four on Sunday) 20-minute trips in each direction daily costing $2 per car and driver and 50 cents per person. From Farewell the first ferry leaves at 8.30 am, the last at 9 pm with the others scattered evenly through the day. Check schedules as the times vary. There is no real town at Farewell but there is a restaurant at the ferry landing.

The two main Change Islands with a population of just 500 or so are connected by a short causeway at the northern end where the largest village is. The islands are quiet with many traditional wooden houses and some old fishing-related buildings painted in a red-ochre colour common to the area. At the northern end is a small store and one place to stay, the *Seven Oakes Island Inn & Cottages* (☎ 621-3256). Singles/doubles cost $50/60 in the rooms, the two-bedroom cottages are more costly. There is no smoking in any of the rooms. Meals are available and boat tours can be arranged.

### Fogo Island

Fogo, just to the east of Notre Dame Bay, is the largest of the area's islands. It is just 25 km long. Tread carefully because the Canadian Flat Earth Society has stated that Fogo is at the edge of the world! Indeed, say they, Brimstone Head is one of the four corners of the earth. Standing here looking out to sea it's not difficult to agree with them.

Like the Change Islands, Fogo is reached by ferry from Farewell. Again, there are five services daily (four on Sunday) leaving from early morning to evening. The fare is $4 for car and driver, $1 for adult passengers. This trip takes about 45 minutes.

The island is pleasant for just exploring slowly and enjoying the coastal scenery. It has an interesting history being first settled by Europeans in the 1680s. There are about 10 villages on the island, together making up a population of about 4500. There is a provincial park for picnicking and maybe a quick dip, a couple of fine walking trails, a sandy beach at **Sandy Cove** and a small herd of caribou and some free roaming ponies on the island. At **Burnt Point** is a lighthouse. There are several fish plants on the island and visitors can have a look around them.

Icebergs can often be seen and in July there's a folk festival. Lastly, a heritage house, once the residence of a merchant, has been converted into the small **Bleak House Museum** in Fogo and, of course, you can pick berries.

**Places to Stay** For those wishing to stay, *Payne's Hospitality Home* (☎ 266-2359) in

the town of Fogo, is one of the best bargains in the province. Singles range from $32 to $40, doubles from $52 to $60 depending on facilities and these rates include all three meals. Alternatively, there is the *Quiet Canyon Hotel* (☎ 627-3477) not far from the ferry terminal at Stag Harbour. They offer 11 rooms and have a restaurant. Singles/doubles cost $55/59. *Fogo Island Motel* (☎ 266-2556) rounds out the accommodation situation. It's a good idea to book ahead before arriving in July and early August.

### New World Island

From the mainland, causeways almost imperceptibly connect **Chapel Island**, tiny **Strong's Island**, New World and Twillingate islands.

At **Newville** is a tourist office with maps of the area, advice on what to see and a sheet describing some of the trails and walks on Twillingate which are well worth taking advantage of.

There is a good, central provincial park, **Dildo Run**, with camping and picnicking, set in a wooded area by a bay. Due to currents, swimming is not recommended.

The western section of New World Island is far less visited and has some of the area's older houses in the small fishing villages clinging to the rough, rocky edges of the sea. At **Moreton's Harbour** is a small museum in an old-style house furnished in much the manner it would have been when the town was a more prosperous fishing centre than it is today. There is one small, basic store in town but not much is stocked.

There are several very small parks around where picnicking and even camping are possible although facilities are minimal. One of them is **Wild Cove Park**, not far north of Moreton's Harbour: look for the clearing surrounded by rocky hills right by the water on the left-hand side of the road.

### TWILLINGATE ISLAND

Actually consisting of two islands, north and south Twillingate, this is the area in all of Notre Dame Bay that gets the most attention and very deservedly so. It's stunningly beautiful, with every turn of the road revealing new ocean vistas, colourful fishing wharves or tidy groups of pastel houses perched on cliffs and outcrops.

### Long Point Lighthouse

The lighthouse is a spectacular place with dramatic views of the coastal cliffs. Tell me if this isn't the cleanest, clearest air you've ever had the privilege of looking through.

This is an ideal place to watch for icebergs which are fairly common in May and June and not unusual in July. Seeing one in August is possible too, but fairly rare. (I missed out by a week in mid-August once.) They tend to drift southward from Labrador then eastward towards Bonavista Bay slowly melting in these warmer waters. Icebergs of some size have been seen just outside of St John's.

In June and July whale-watching is very good here and all around the islands. If you miss both of these attractions, you can still see memorable sunsets which occur year round!

You can visit the 114-year-old lighthouse itself and take the winding stairs to the top. Note how all the buildings are connected by enclosed walkways, a clue to just how foggy and/or nasty the weather can be.

### Twillingate Museum

In Twillingate town, the museum in what was formerly the Anglican rectory provides an overview of the local history. Twillingate, one of the oldest towns in this part of the province, was settled by British merchants in the mid-1700s. One room displays articles brought back from around the world by local sea captains and includes a cabinet from India, a hurdy-gurdy from Germany and an Australian boomerang. Another room details the seal hunt and its controversy. There is also a craft shop at the museum. Next door is **St Peter's Church** dating from 1844, one of the oldest wooden churches in Newfoundland. Many other attractive churches are found around the island and, on the south island. The United church is a heritage site.

### Durrell

Don't neglect to tour around unbelievably scenic Durrell. What some people see out their window when they get up in the morning!

Many of the two-storey, box-like wooden houses are over 100 years old. The **Iceberg Shop**, for crafts, is here in a 130-year-old house. It also runs a recommended boat tour out to see whales, icebergs and along the jagged local shores.

Also here is the **Durrell Museum** perched way up on a hill with great views. It has displays on what the fishing community of the early 1900s was like. It's open daily and, as in all local museums, the admission fee is just a token.

Numerous walks are possible: see the tourist office map for ones to French Beach and the natural arch. Smith's Lookout provides a panoramic view of the island.

### Fish, Fun & Folk Festival

Held each year during the last week of July this four-day event is a 'don't miss' one if you're anywhere near the region. It features traditional music and dance some of which goes back to the 16th century. There are fishing exhibits, lots of great food and crafts as well. This is a busy time of year what with the possibility of whales and icebergs lurking offshore, so book early if possible.

### Places to Stay

For campers, there are sites at *Dildo Run Provincial Park*. *Sea Breeze Park* beside the Long Point Lighthouse is a glorious, very inexpensive place to bed down. It's also a good place for a picnic. Contact the tourist office for locations of some of the other small parks around the area.

The *Hillside B&B* is central at 5 Young's Lane (☎ 884-5761) in a house built in 1874. It features fine views of the harbour and lighthouse. Prices are good at $30/40 for singles/doubles with a light breakfast.

The *Anchor Inn* (☎ 884-2776), with views from on top of a hill, has some rooms in the lodge, some more motel-style rooms and some with cooking facilities. Singles/doubles cost $55/60 but for $5 more housekeeping units are offered. There is also a dining room where fish is featured on the menu.

Apart from staying at these few places, spending the night means going back to New World Island or beyond. For example, there is the *Friday's Bay Summer Cottage* (☎ 629-3459) in Virgin Arm on New World Island 20 km south of Twillingate. The cabin can be rented by the week as well as nightly and, if there are a few of you, it can be an excellent bargain as it has lots of space and a kitchen. It is only available in July and August.

### Places to Eat
The *R&J* has fish & chips and a great view of one of the many harbours. The *Anchor Inn* has a dining room and bar.

In Durrell, the *Bayside Restaurant* serves chicken or pizza, but again the fish is recommended.

### TWILLINGATE TO LEWISPORTE
From Twillingate the road leads through Birchy Bay past timber and farming districts once roamed by the Beothuk Indians. Near Campbellton watch for Indian Cove Neck, a small park with a beach and fine views of the shoreline. Anglers may want to try a cast into the Campbellton River for the chance of a salmon dinner.

### Lewisporte
Lewisporte with a population of 4500 is the largest town along the coast and is known primarily for its Marine Atlantic ferry terminal. Other than the boats, there really isn't much reason to visit – though as a distribution centre it does have all the goods and services. West of Lewisporte, the bay becomes less populated and, as the road network declines, less accessible.

The **Bye The Bay Museum** (☎ 535-2737) in the large wooden Women's Institute Building on Main St displays locally collected articles from the area's history. A pair of sunglasses from 1895 struck my fancy but the showpiece is a long, colourful handmade rug depicting various facets in the life and times of Lewisporte. The museum is closed

from late December to early June. The ground floor of the building is a craft shop stocked with items made by local residents.

Several people offer boat trips for some cod jigging or a visit to the quiet, rocky **Exploits Islands** where local people have summer cottages.

### Places to Stay & Eat
You can camp in town at the *Municipal Park* or at *Notre Dame Provincial Park* about 14 km from town. There are a few places where you can put up for the night including three guesthouses right on Main St. At No 92 *Northgate B&B* (☎ 535-2258), a short walk from the ferry terminal, offers singles/doubles at $40/50 including a breakfast of bread, muffins and homemade jams. The B&B is in an old house with views of the harbour. At No 313 is *Seaside Lodge* (☎ 535-6305) with five rooms from singles/doubles $40/45 and a balcony overlooking the street.

On the way into town from Hwy 341 is *Brittany Inns* (☎ 535-2533) with 34 hotel, motel and housekeeping rooms from $52. There is a dining room.

For other places to eat try the mall near the junction of Hwys 340 and 341. There is a bakery here and a Sobey's grocery store which could be useful if you're getting on board one of the ferries. Main St also has a Chinese restaurant.

### Getting There & Away
**Bus** The CN Roadcruiser bus running between Port aux Basques and St John's makes a stop at Notre Dame Junction at the Irving gas station south of town where Hwy 340 meets the Trans Canada Hwy. This is about 16 km from town and the ferry dock. The bus also pulls into the Brittany Inn which is only about three km to the centre. Taxis meet the bus arrivals.

**Ferry** Two Marine Atlantic ferries (☎ 535-6876) depart for points north. One, a car ferry, goes to Cartwright on the Labrador coast and then on Hamilton Inlet to large Lake Melville (which the Vikings may have visited) and on to Happy Valley-Goose

Bay in the heart of Labrador where there is an important military base.

With a vehicle you can go from here across central Labrador to Churchill Falls and beyond to Labrador City at the Quebec border. The road continues south through Quebec to Baie Comeau.

The ferry to Goose Bay is a serious ride taking about 38 hours and only making the one stop en route. A variation is the direct trip with no stop in Cartwright. This knocks about three hours off the total travel time.

A one-way ticket is $80; add $130 for a car. Reduced rates are offered for children and seniors. Cabins are available at additional charge. There are two ferries a week in each direction (one direct, one with the stop) from mid-June to approximately mid-September.

The other boat, opening up a different part of Labrador, provides the coastal service which runs up the Northern Peninsula making a stop at St Anthony and then heading over to the coast of Labrador for a series of outport stops. This is strictly a passenger and freight service – no cars. Of course, except in a couple of places, there are no roads at any of these destinations anyway: that is their appeal.

This is approximately a 14 to 16-day return trip with Nain, the northernmost point, about 2100 km from Lewisporte. The ferries run on this route from sometime in July to around mid-December when the coastal ice meets the Arctic pack ice and everything is sealed up until the summer thaw.

Towards the end of the season, throughout November and into December, the weather plays havoc with the schedule and the one-way trip can take weeks. With high winds and waves close to 15 metres high, the ship is often harbour-bound for days at a time.

Normally, it's a comfortable ship (actually there are two different ships which alternate trips) with four meals a day (you didn't forget 'night lunch' did you?) and a choice not unlike that found in any mainland restaurant but with prices slightly higher. Fares are low and determined by the number of nautical miles travelled. The rate is 19 cents per

nautical mile and an additional 18 cents per nautical mile for an economy two-berth cabin. To St Anthony it's 130 nautical miles, to Red Bay it's 194 and to Goose Bay it's 700.

There are 46 possible ports of call along the entire return route and the number of stops partially determines the length of the trip. You can get off at the village of your choice. Some of these places have accommodation but check to see when the ferry returns. You can always sleep on the boat – in or out of port.

The low prices make the trip a real bargain. Because of that, the chance to visit some of the country's most remote settlements and to see the fine scenery with granite cliffs and long fjords the trip has become popular with visitors. Space is limited and, as most of it is required for local residents and their gear (everything from food to music cassettes to snowmobiles to toasters), reservations for the trip must be made from within Newfoundland.

Be prepared when making a reservation to pay a 25% deposit. Most likely a credit card will be necessary unless you are at a Marine Atlantic office. Some conflicting information indicates that making reservations for the coastal ferries may still be possible from outside the province. If this is the case and a reservation will be accepted, be prepared to pay 100% of the ticket value at the time of booking.

If you are driving, you can leave your car at the ferry terminal in Lewisporte. There is a security guard but a waiver must be signed discounting responsibility.

There are four trips a month in July, August, September and October and two before mid-November.

For either of the two ferry routes, arrive 90 minutes before departure in either Lewisporte or Happy Valley-Goose Bay and make reservations. For these and all information call the number (given earlier) in Lewisporte or ☎ 709-772-7701 in eastern Newfoundland or ☎ 709-695-7081 in western Newfoundland.

On either trip huge icebergs are not uncommon sights.

The federal government, which has developed air links to these northern communities, is talking about trying to phase out the boat runs – in a few years the voyage may not be possible.

## GRAND FALLS & WINDSOR

These two small towns sit in pulp and paper country. Actually Windsor seems more like a suburb of Grand Falls and it is the latter which is of more interest to the visitor. The huge Abitibi-Price pulp mill sits in the centre of Grand Falls and offers tours in summer. Arrangements should be made at the tourist chalet.

The tourist chalet information booth (☎ 489-6332) is on the highway a couple of km west of town. The **Mary March Museum** on the corner of Cromer Ave and St Catherine St is good and among other things outlines the life of the extinct Beothuk Indians. They lived in this portion of the province before the Europeans arrived but the clash of cultures spelled the end for this tribe. The last two surviving women, who supplied much of the information used in the museum, died in the early 1800s. Mary March was the name given to one of them by the British; her Beothuk Indian name was Demasduit. The museum is open daily and is free.

Adjacent to the museum set in the woods is a re-creation of a **Beothuk Indian village**. It's also free but donations are accepted.

Not far west of town, **Beothuk Provincial Park** has an exhibit simulating a turn-of-the-century logging camp.

### Places to Stay & Eat

There are a couple of expensive motels in town or the *Poplar Inn* (☎ 489-2546), a B&B at about half the rate with doubles at $40. It's at 22 Poplar Rd which runs off Lincoln Rd behind the Mt Peyton Hotel which is visible from the Trans Canada Hwy. The CN Roadcruiser stop is walkable, about three km away. The Poplar Inn is open all year.

In Grand Falls there's the obligatory Chinese restaurant on Church Rd (the main

street) and a pizza place. There are other places on the highway.

### Getting There & Away

The CN Roadcruiser bus stops in town on Main St in Windsor. The Bay d'Espoir Bus Service links Grand Falls to St Alban's way down Hwy 360 south. There are also other small services based here so ask around if you have a particular destination in mind.

## SOUTH OF GRAND FALLS

One fairly recent road runs 130 km through the centre of the province to the south coast. It's a long way down to the first settlements at the end of **Bay d'Espoir**, a huge fjord. The cliffs at **Morrisville** offer the best views. **St Alban's** is the main town and is connected with Grand Falls by bus. **Conne River** is a Micmac Indian town. The region supports itself with a large hydroelectric plant, forestry and salmon farming. There is one motel and a campground around the end of the bay.

Going further south you'll find a concentration of small, remote fishing villages, some connected with still less-accessible ones by the south coast ferry. The scenery along Hwy 364 is particularly impressive.

### Places to Stay & Eat

Harbour Breton has a motel but a better choice is the cheaper *Olde Oven Inn* (☎ 888-3461) with doubles at $50 in little English Harbour West which is noted for its knitted sweaters. Breakfast is included and other meals are offered.

## RED INDIAN LAKE

Set in a huge wilderness area west of Grand Falls, the lake is the centre of a prime fishing and wildlife region with large concentrations of moose and caribou. Mining and lumbering support the local towns.

## BAIE VERTE PENINSULA

Little-visited Baie Verte (Green Bay) is a traditional region of small fishing and mining villages with a long history of human habitation. The Maritime Archaic Indians originally settled the edges of the peninsula and were followed by the Dorset Inuit who had a camp at and around **Fleur de Lys** from 1000 BC for several hundred years. There is a soapstone outcrop here from which the Inuit gouged the material for household goods such as lamps and for carvings. Evidence of their digging can be seen.

Around Baie Verte and the islands archaeologists have turned up Beothuk Indian artefacts. And as you'll notice by the town names, the French also were here in some number.

The Baie Verte area is pretty with green rounded hills edging the shore. Short ferry trips connect several of the islands. Springdale, the largest community in the area, has some accommodation.

At Baie Verte, a relatively sizeable town at the north-west end of the peninsula, see the **Miners' Museum** and **tunnel**. There is a tourist office in town. Just out of town, open-pit asbestos mining can be seen from an observation point off the main highway. The peninsula also has deposits of copper, gold, silver and zinc though much of it has been mined out. You can also visit some of the many abandoned mines nearby. In the past at little **Tilt Cove**, on the coast, 5% of the world's nickel was mined.

**La Scie** is another good place to see an iceberg; boat trips are available.

# Western Newfoundland

### DEER LAKE & AROUND
There is very little here for the visitor but it is the centre of a small farming area which appears so noticeable because agriculture is so uncommon across the province. It's also a convenient jumping-off point for trips up the northern peninsula.

In town the *Driftwood Inn* (☎ 635-5115), a large white, green-trimmed wooden building at 3 Nicholas Rd – an easy walk from Main St – is a good place to stay, although it's not cheap with rooms from $52 a single. It has a popular bar and restaurant. Also for eating, the *Tai Lee Garden* is a simple, cheap

### Beothuk Indians
Scattered around much of north central Newfoundland the Beothuks, a distinct cultural group, lived from about 500 years ago until 1829 when the last woman died. It was they, their faces painted red with ochre, who were first dubbed 'redmen' by the arriving Europeans, a name that was soon to be applied to all the Native peoples of North America. Semi-nomadic, they travelled the rivers, notably the Exploits, in birch bark canoes between the inland lakes and the sea at Notre Dame Bay. They were not a violent people and there weren't large numbers of them. With White hostility, firepower, and diseases the ultimate tragedy unfolded. Before anybody had enough gumption or time it was realised there were just a handful of Beothuk Indians left. By the early 1800s there were only two women alive to leave what knowledge they could.

There is a museum dedicated to them in Grand Falls and also a re-created village. The museum in St John's also has a display, including a skeleton – the only known remains anywhere. The Beothuk Trail, Hwy 380, leads through some of their former lands but otherwise is just a name. ■

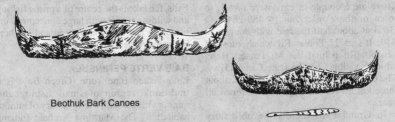

Beothuk Bark Canoes

Chinese place in the middle of Main St which serves up surprisingly good meals.

Between the town of Deer Lake and Corner Brook the road passes through scenic landscape alongside Deer Lake where many locals have summer cottages or trailers. Around Pasadena Beach there are some motels and cabins available for visitors.

## NORTHERN PENINSULA

From Deer Lake the immense northern peninsula extends 430 km northward to Labrador along one of the most extraordinary, beautiful, rugged, historic roads in eastern North America. Called the Viking Trail, the little-known Hwy 430, extends between the coast and the Long Range Mountains to two UNESCO world heritage sites (there are 10 in Canada), another National Historic Site, two provincial parks, wonderfully barren far north topography and views over the history-filled Strait of Belle Isle to the coast of remote Labrador. There's lots of wildlife, ranging from large mammals to specialised fauna, unbelievably various and abundant edible berries, spectacular fjords, excellent salmon fishing, small coastal fishing villages and very friendly people – some with accents so distinct an outsider can barely catch much of the conversation.

Even for those without a lot of time a trip from Port aux Basques to the northern peninsula if only as far as Gros Morne makes a memorable visit to Newfoundland. Many people make this region the focus of their trip to the Rock and never go further east than Deer Lake. L'Anse-aux-Meadows, a 1000-year-old Viking settlement (by far the oldest European landing site in North America, centuries ahead of Chris Columbus) has become somewhat of a pilgrimage site drawing a small but determined group from all over the USA and, to a lesser extent, Europe.

Despite my enthusiasm a few cautionary words are in order. Public transportation is minimal although a bus does do the entire route. There is only one road; it's long with some uninteresting stretches so the return

trip is somewhat redundant. In addition gas prices are outrageous and increase at each successive station as you head north until they reach exorbitant peaks at St Anthony. Services, while certainly adequate, are not overly abundant. There are not a lot of places to stay and food supplies are pretty basic. Probably most of the people who make the entire trip are campers but they mainly have vans or trailers of one sort or another. I tented like many others but it can be windy, wet, foggy and rather cool even in summer. There can be lots of bugs as well, so be prepared for maybe the odd night in a motel. If you're camping, it's a good idea to stock up on supplies in Corner Brook.

### Deer Lake to Gros Morne National Park

There are many berry farms just north of Deer Lake and if you're passing by in August (a late season compared to most of the country) take advantage of one of the pick-your-own farms offering raspberries, strawberries or blueberries. Roadside stands are common and a jar or two of homemade jam is worth stopping for.

At **Wiltondale** there is a small pioneer village, a reconstruction of an early 20th-century country community. There's also a tea room at the site.

### Gros Morne National Park

Gros Morne National Park is a must for its spectacular, varied geography which has earned it status as a world heritage site. Special features include fjords that rival Scandinavia's, the majestic barren Tablelands, excellent mountain hiking trails, sandy beaches and historic little fishing communities. There are rivers, lakes and highland tundra as well as plenty of wildlife including caribou and moose. Offshore there are seals and, occasionally, whales. Part of the UNESCO designation is due to the park's Precambrian, Cambrian and Ordovician rock and the evidence this rock supplies researchers with for the theory of plate tectonics. Another factor was the site's 4500 years of human occupation.

Woody Point, Norris Point and Rocky

Harbour are the principle commercial centres of Gros Morne National Park.

In the southern portion of the park, Hwy 431 leads to Woody Point and beyond to the Tablelands. The village of Woody Point with its large old houses makes a good centre for seeing some of the park.

There are five campgrounds, several more primitive camping areas, scattered picnic sites and a smattering of villages, towns and other areas that, while within the park boundaries, technically lie outside the park's jurisdiction. At these areas commercial establishments offer lodging, restaurants and other services. The park information centre (☎ 458-2066) is about 25 km in from the entrance on Hwy 430 but maps are available at the entrance to the park and at campgrounds. Actually there isn't that much at the centre but the attendants and rangers can answer questions about trails, wildlife, etc. There is also a booklet available describing and listing the various trails which range from easy and short (from one to two km) all the way up to strenuous three to four-day trips.

The main community in the park is Rocky Harbour, where there are all the amenities including a laundromat and grocery stores.

**Things to See & Do** The day hike up the James Callahan Trail to the peak of the park's namesake, Gros Morne, at 806 metres, provides spectacular views. It takes a full-day (16 km return) and is one of the park's most rigorous trails so be prepared for exertion as well as exhilaration. Caribou sometimes wander about the summit area.

More accessible but equally compelling are the **Tablelands**, by the road's edge, not far from Woody Point. This is a barren 80-km ledge of rock 700 metres high shoved up from beneath the ocean floor – a glimpse of the earth's insides. It often retains snow year round. Trails lead out to it and there are viewpoints along the road.

Going west, **Green Gardens** is a beach hike with camping a possibility. In **Trout River**, a small fishing community, the

*Seaside Restaurant* is good for fresh seafood.

From the government wharf in Norris Point two-hour boat trips of scenic **Bonne Bay** depart daily stopping over in **Woody Point** for more people to board before cruising the Arms. The Sunday trips are longer and include some live traditional music.

Back on Hwy 430 going north there are good views along the East Arm fjord. The James Callahan Trail up Gros Morne Mountain begins in this area.

Near Rocky Harbour is a recreation complex with a swimming pool and whirlpool. It's open everyday for a small fee and lockers are available.

Further up the coast past Sally's Cove, parts of the wreck of the SS *Ethie* which ran aground in 1919 can be seen on the beach. The storm and subsequent rescue sparked the writing of a song about the incident.

**Western Brook Pond** is the park's feature fjord with dwarfing cliffs nearly 700 metres high running vertically from the cool waters. Boat tours of the 15-km-long fjord are offered. I know, big deal – a little boat trip on a narrow lake. Many people say it's definitely recommended. This trip is like 2½ hours of the best Norway has to offer, with sheer cliffs towering at the water's edge. The trips are very popular. Make reservations at the park's interpretive centre or the Ocean View Motel (☎ 458-2730) in Rocky Harbour before going to the dock.

The tours run from 1 June to the end of September with three trips daily in the high season each taking up to 40 passengers. A ticket costs $20, less for kids. The dock is reached after an easy 30-minute walk from the road and is worth doing even if you're not boarding the boat.

The gentle, safe, sand-duned beach at **Shallow Bay** at the other end of the geographic spectrum seems almost out of place – as if transported from the Caribbean by some bizarre current. The water, though, provides a chilling dose of reality, rarely getting above 15°C.

At **Broom Point** restored fishing premises depicting the inshore fishery of the

1960s can be visited. The premises are open daily from June to September. Paleo Inuit used the site as a base for seal hunting from 300 BC to 600 AD.

St Paul's is a small fishing village now without a lot of work. Boat tours take passengers to Seal Island where seals and views of the Long Range Mountains can be seen. Several trips are run daily.

The most northerly community, **Cow Head**, has a small museum, hospitality home, walks along the shoreline and beach, and the *Shallow Bay Motel & Cabins* (☎ 243-2471) with a restaurant. The Viking Express bus makes a stop in Cow Head.

**Places to Stay & Eat** There are a couple of places to stay in Woody Point including the HI *Woody Point Hostel* (☎ 453-2442), a rare find in Newfoundland. At any rate this makes a great place for one. It's open from the end of June to the beginning of September. The small hostel with 10 beds charges $10 for members, a little more for nonmembers. It is on School Rd close to the bus depot and is open all day. There's a kitchen and boat rentals.

There is also the *Victorian Manor* (☎ 453-2485), a hospitality home with rooms in the nice old house or newer two-bedroom efficiency cabins where you can cook your own meals. In the main house, which has four rooms, singles/doubles cost $40/45 with a light breakfast included. Laundry facilities and bike and canoe rentals are also offered.

Across the bay in Norris Point there are more choices. *Shear's* (☎ 458-2275) has two rooms available from June to September for singles/doubles $35/40 including a light breakfast. A little more expensive is *Terry's B&B* (☎ 458-2373) but with the morning comes a full breakfast.

There are restaurants and grocery stores in both villages and a drug store (chemist) in Norris Point.

At Rocky Harbour, you could stay at *Gros Morne Cabins* (☎ 458-2020) in individual log cabins with kitchens and views over the ocean. Inquire at Endicott's variety store. The price is $55 for a one-bedroom place

large enough for up to two adults and two kids. There are also four other cottage or cabin rental places and the *Ocean View Motel* (☎ 458-2730) at $60 a double.

For a munch, *Jackie's* has good homemade French fries and fruit pies. More substantial meals are available elsewhere.

**Getting There & Around** Martin's Bus Service connects Woody Point with Corner Brook once daily Monday to Friday. In Woody Point, Martin's is at Martin's Auto Service (☎ 453-2207).

The Viking Express bus from Corner Brook via Deer Lake to St Anthony running three times a week makes stops at Norris Point (across Bonne Bay from Woody Point) and Rocky Harbour further north.

In Corner Brook both buses depart from the Millbrook Mall (see Corner Brook.)

From Woody Point a ferry runs across Bonne Bay to Norris Point allowing circular trips around the southern area of the park. The 20-minute ferry runs every two hours from each side between early morning and dinner time daily. The price is $10 per car and driver, $3 for passengers, and half-price for a return ticket.

**The Arches**

Out of the park back northward on Hwy 430, The Arches is worth stopping at for a stroll down to the beach which is littered with beautiful, smooth, coloured rocks about the size of footballs. The main attractions, though, are the three limestone arches and the remains of maybe three or four more formed some 400 million years ago. There are picnic tables overlooking the beach.

**Daniel's Harbour**

Just outside town the world's highest grade of zinc concentrate is mined, supplementing the fishing industry. The *Mountain View Motel* (☎ 898-2211) with a restaurant is here.

**Table Point Ecological Reserve**

North of Bellburns along the shore there are protected sections of limestone 470 million years old containing abundant fossils.

## River of Ponds Provincial Park

On the Pond River which is good for salmon, this is the only provincial government campground on the Northern Peninsula other than the one way up at the northern extremity. Swimming and canoeing are possible although, for canoeists, some parts of the river call for white-water experience.

## Hawke's Bay

Halfway to St Anthony from Deer Lake Hawke's Bay was a whaling station at the turn of the century. There are some excellent salmon waters here and at the salmon ladder, a device to aid the fish in getting upstream, they can be observed jumping on their difficult journey inland to spawn. Trout are also plentiful.

Just behind the tourist office there is a small campground from where the Hogan Trail along the Torrent River begins. Most of the six-km walking trail is on a boardwalk and leads over marsh and through the woods to the salmon ladder. There's a swimming area near the beginning and three lookout stations along the way where birds may be observed.

Hawke's Bay is one of the few places with any roads leading east towards the Long Range Mountains. If you have a good vehicle capable of handling some smaller, less-maintained roads there are 150 km of routes leading to small lakes and rivers. There is a tourist office which may have advice on places to visit, which roads are easily passable and which ones are rougher.

*Maynard's Motel* (☎ 248-5225) has 20 units and another half-dozen with housekeeping facilities. The regular rooms are not cheap, but average for the area; singles/doubles cost $54/62. There is a restaurant (watch for the steak specials on weekends), lounge, gasoline bar and laundromat. Also they can arrange salmon fishing trips.

## Port au Choix

Busy and interesting Port au Choix is one of the biggest towns between Gros Morne and St Anthony and a main stop for travellers on the Viking Trail. It is a major fishing port with boats down at the docks from all along the coast and across the strait in Labrador. Tours of the fish plant can be taken.

The principal attraction is the national historic park (☎ 623-2601) with its helpful staff. Admission to this two part park is free. Each section deals with different peoples who lived thousands of years apart. Downtown beside the museum and visitors' centre is the main site, a **Maritime Archaic Indian cemetery** dating from 3200 to 4300 years ago. The remains of about 100 individuals as well as tools, weapons and ornaments were discovered here accidentally in 1967. Some of these artefacts are on view in the museum. Not a lot is known about these people who lived in the region for many centuries but they did no farming and instead relied on the sea and on gathering for survival.

The other section of the park is a short distance away through town by road followed by a 20-minute walk along a trail. It deals with the Dorset Inuit people who settled on the Cape Riche Peninsula between 1500 and 2200 years ago. Excavation of this site, known as **Philip's Garden**, was done in the 1960s and revealed the remains of several ancient houses. Archaeologists are still working in this area and hope to unearth more articles and perhaps some clues to the Dorset's disappearance. Beyond the site, continue on to the **Point Riche lighthouse** which you can also reach by car going around the other way.

On one visit, later the same day I was there, a visitor saw a very large shark washed up on the beach not far past the historic site.

**Mark Lightbody**

For a little more recent history, just out of town is a plaque outlining some of the tussles (between the French and British for the fishing rights in the area) which continued from the 1600s until the 1900s. In 1904 yet another treaty was signed in which the French relinquished their rights here in exchange for the privilege in Morocco – ah, the days when all the world was a monopoly game. There is also a French cemetery from the 1700s in the area.

It's not difficult at all to spend a full-day or two in and around town.

**Places to Stay** In Port Au Choix the economical choice is the two-room *Jean-Marie Guest Home* (☎ 861-3023) located just off the Viking Trail. The singles/doubles which which are rented from mid-June to mid-September cost $35/45 including a light breakfast. An evening snack is included, too, and dinner is an extra option. To bolster the thin accommodation scene there is also a guesthouse in nearby Port Saunders. Try *Biggin's Hospitality Home* (☎ 861-3523) in downtown with singles the same price as above and doubles a little cheaper with a continental breakfast included.

In Port au Choix, is the more expensive but well-kept *Sea Echo Motel* (☎ 861-3777) with 19 rooms. The dining room is quite good, friendly and has good-value lunch specials that are sometimes based around fresh Atlantic salmon.

About 50 km north of town right beside the provincial picnic park is a private campground, *Three Mile Lake Campground*, which is modelled so much after a government park it might as well be one. It's quiet, wooded and has a beach on the lake. Take all necessary supplies as there is nothing at all available at the campground. There are 30 sites.

**North from Port au Choix**
Close to town the long, treeless mountain range to the east is quite close to the road although it's not as high as the peaks averaging 650 metres, in Gros Morne National Park. After this close encounter, the mountains veer off to the east and don't have the same presence. The landscape becomes more and more barren until it appears pretty much like that found in the far Canadian north – an essentially flat, pond-filled primeval expanse. There is probably no other place in the country where this type of rugged terrain is as accessible. There's a majestic simplicity and awe to it that, despite the harshness, makes it appear somehow less daunting than it should.

At **Plum Point** is a gas station and a motel but after this there is little until you reach St Anthony.

From Plum Point a gravel road connects with the eastern shore. At **Main Brook** there is *Tuckamore Lodge* (☎ 865-6361), an A-frame, B&B cottage with four guest rooms, a dining room, a fireplace and a sauna. Meals are available. Singles/doubles are priced at $45/55 with a light breakfast. Call ahead

---

**Wild Berries**
Delicious berries proliferate all over the province and should be picked and eaten with great gusto as much as possible. Compared with much of the country, the fruit season here is late with most types of berries ripening in August, some even later.

The variety seems almost infinite with many kinds which I, for one, had never heard of: crackerberries, dewberries, dogberries, marshberries, partridgeberries, red currants, squashberries as well as the more common blueberries, blackberries and raspberries. Strawberries are grown commercially and many farms have a pick-your-own deal.

The unofficial queen of all the berries seems to be the bakeapple which can sell for as much as $50 a gallon (4.5 litres)! It's a small, golden berry which grows close to the ground out on the barrens and is usually eaten in a parfait or as jam.

Seeing people bent over bushes or strolling through the landscape in rubber boots, pail in hand is very common. At picnic sites and campgrounds, fresh desserts and fruit on the breakfast cereal is the order of the day. Just ask what's what. Along the main roads berries are offered for sale and, in some areas, homemade jams too. Many craft stores and the shops at tourist offices also sell the jams. The red partridgeberry jam is a favourite. Lastly, many of the hospitality homes offer some form of a berry or two with their meals and restaurants often have pies on the dessert menus. ■

before driving across the peninsula because the lodge is mainly used as a base for multi-day package adventure tours which include trips to see birds, caribou, etc. It's also often used by hunters and anglers.

The main town over on this side is **Roddickton** and here, as in Main Brook, there are outfitters for hunting and fishing. It also has an expensive motel. There is also some hiking and a trip up **Cloud Hill** affords good views of the islands offshore.

Back on Hwy 430, **St Barbe** is the site of a ferry to Labrador (see the Labrador section later for details). From here on up the coast of Labrador is visible on clear days.

Just beyond Eddie's Cove at **Watt's Point**, off the main road, is another ecological reserve. This one protects limestone barrens where rare flowers persevere.

North from Eddie's Cove watch for the little vegetable plots etched into the terrain beside the road where the soil is drained and deep enough for garden vegetables such as potatoes. Many are marked by whimsical scarecrows, others simply by a name painted on a board, Christopher's or Matthew's. About halfway between Eddie's Cove and the other side of the peninsula is the first St Anthony airport. The one used now is at Hare Bay.

### Pistolet Bay Provincial Park

With about 30 sites in a wild but wooded area about 20 km from the main road and about 40 km from the Viking site, this is the place to stay if you're camping.

My first morning there, awakening at 6 am, I stepped out of the tent and stared right into the eyes of a fox four metres away.

**Mark Lightbody**

The park is not on the water but it's probably preferable to have the scrubby, stunted trees around to provide some windbreak. Be prepared for the mosquitoes and blackflies, they seem to have a real mean streak. There is a comfort station at the park with hot showers and laundry facilities and it's heated! What luxury!

Also on Pistolet Bay is the privately run *Viking Trailer Park* for camper vehicles.

### Raleigh

The closest little town for milk and bread (and beer) is Raleigh a fishing village where everybody runs to the dock to greet the incoming fishers and a couple of cows stroll freely around the streets like their Hindu counterparts. It's a treat to walk around and have a chat in the isolated villages at the end of the peninsula here with their traditional uncomplicated ways.

### Saint Lunaire to Straitsview

There are five small old fishing villages on the way to the historic site of L'Anse-aux-Meadows. You may see kids by the road's edge selling berries collected out on the barrens. In mid-August this will include the queen of all Newfoundland berries, the golden bakeapple sold here for $30 per gallon (4.5 litres – the people here still use imperial measurements, unlike those in much of the country) and fetching as much as $50 further south. No wonder free samples are not offered! Bakeapples are often used for jam and chances aren't bad that it may be offered for your morning toast at one of the B&Bs somewhere.

People living in these picturesque little communities have quite strong, almost British accents and you may catch some of the unique expressions for which the New-foundlanders are renowned.

St Anthony has a reputation for the warm parkas sold but they are also available in one shop in each of Saint Lunaire and Straitsview where they may be a little cheaper. In Griquet there is a restaurant which is open everyday from 11 am. Note that you can't get anything to eat or drink at the historic park.

At the village of Gunner's Cove, five km from the historic site, is the recommended *Valhalla Lodge* (☎ 623-2018) the closest accommodation to L'Anse-aux-Meadows. From 15 May to 1 October the six Scandinavian-themed rooms are rented, two with private bath facilities. The basic singles/doubles are $35/45 or $5 more with breakfast. Ask about the nearby nature trail.

## L'Anse-aux-Meadows National Historic Park

This is a fascinating place (☎ 623-2601) made all the more special by the unobtrusive, low-key approach of the park developers. In an unspoiled, waterside setting – looking pretty much like it did in 1000 AD when the Vikings from Scandinavia and Greenland became the first Europeans to land in North America – are the remains of their settlement. Replicas of the sod buildings complete with smoky smell almost transport you back in time.

These guys, led by Leif Eriksson, son of Eric the Red, built their own boats, sailed all over the North Atlantic, landed here, constructed houses which still remain, fed themselves and they were practically all just 20-something years old. Oops, let's not forget they smelted iron out of the bog and forged nails with it – 1000 years ago! And as far as I can tell, they did it for the hell of it. They weren't out to save souls or bring back gold riches for the monarch or lay claim to half the planet – not too shabby.

Allow from two to three hours to browse through the interpretive centre with its artefacts, see the film and walk around the eight unearthed original wood and sod buildings and the three reconstructions. Guided tours are offered and everything is free.

Also captivating is the story of Norwegian explorer Helge Ingstad who discovered the site in 1960 ending years of searching. His tale and that of his archaeologist wife is told in the interpretive centre. A short walk behind the replica buildings leads to a small graveyard where lies the body of local inhabitant George Decker who made Ingstad's day and this site by pointing out the mounds in the terrain.

The park is open 9 am to 8 pm daily from mid-June to the beginning of September (Labour Day) and from Labour Day to 1 October 9 am to 4.30 pm.

The park is 43 km from St Anthony's.

## St Anthony

You made it! Unfortunately it's a little anti-climactic. With a population of 3500, and as the largest town in the north of the northern peninsula, it's functional and an important supply centre and fish-processing depot but it's not what you'd call pretty. There are, though, a couple of things to see.

At the Viking Mall in downtown is a Sobey's grocery store for stocking up if you're taking the boat north or heading back down to Deer Lake.

**Grenfell Museum** Have a look around the former home (☎ 454-3333) of Sir Wilfred Grenfell, somewhat of a local legend and hero and, by all accounts, quite a man. Born in England and educated as a doctor, he first came to Newfoundland in 1892 and for the next 40 years built hospitals, nursing stations and organised much needed fishing cooperatives along the coast of Labrador and around St Anthony. The fine old house with a large wrap-around porch outlines his life and work and displays mementoes and artefacts collected over the years. One thing that struck me was the wooden coachbox used to transport patients to hospital by dogsled in 1930.

The museum is open daily from mid-June to the beginning of September and for a few days a week in May and late September. The display is well done and there is a small admission charge. The Grenfell Mission and the Curtis Memorial Hospital are still two of the largest employers in town. Near the museum is Teahouse Hill where Mr and Mrs Grenfell are buried. The site is marked with several plaques.

**Other Attractions** In August, watch for the annual cod filleting contest held in town. Admission is free. These guys can clean fish!

In the rotunda at the hospital is a series of ceramic murals done by Montreal artist Jordi Bonet in 1967 depicting life in the area and Labrador.

There are a few walking trails around the edges of town: they're marked on the map available at the museum.

**Places to Stay & Eat** There are two guest-houses and two motels in St Anthony. *Howell's Tourist Home* (☎ 454-3402), at 76B East St, has been here for a while and has four rooms at a good rate of singles/doubles $28/35. Meals are available and it's open all year. A second choice is the *Olde House B&B* (☎ 454-3974) at 9 American Drive. This one is open from May to October only. Rates are singles/doubles $35/42 with a full breakfast.

Alternatively *St Anthony Motel* (☎ 454-3200), at 14 Goose Cove Rd, has 22 rooms but is a little pricey at $65 a double. The newer, larger *Vinland Motel* (☎ 454-8843) costs less and also offers some housekeeping units as well as a few serviced trailer sites.

Both motels have restaurants. Other than those two, there aren't a heck of a lot of places for a bite. *Pizza Delight* has an outlet and there is the ubiquitous fried chicken takeout (I guess they all get enough fish at home).

**Things to Buy** There are three craft outlets in town including Grenfell Handicrafts with parkas embroidered by hand, whale-bone and ivory carvings, and other articles. The Mukluk Factory has sealskin leather goods and some carvings and jewellery. A mukluk is a traditional Inuit soft winter boot made of sealskin or caribou hide and sometimes fur lined. Northern Crafts has a bit of everything.

**Getting There & Away** This is the final stop for the Viking Express bus (☎ 454-8451) and the ferry from Lewisporte en route to communities along the Labrador coast can be picked up here. For ferry information see under Lewisporte. The bus departs St Anthony for Corner Brook three days a week. From Corner Brook connections can be made for the trans-island CN Roadcruiser bus to either Port aux Basques or St John's.

## CORNER BROOK

With 30,000 people, this is Newfoundland's second largest town and there are a few things to see and do in and around it. Up high beside the waters of Humber Arm, it is fairly attractive despite the often all-pervading smell – a reminder that the focus of the town is the huge pulp and paper mill. The Corner Brook area is likely the sunniest region of the province and the warm, clear skies of summer can be a real treat. There is some good walking in the area and freshwater swimming south of town at a couple of parks.

There are good views on the road through town and beyond along the Humber Arm leading to the sea. Big log booms can be seen out in the bay. Also, from Corner Brook there are boat and fishing trips; ask at the tourist office.

Part of the Memorial University of St John's including the Fine Arts Department is in Corner Brook. Downtown is Main St by Remembrance Square and up along maple tree-lined Park St towards the Heritage District. There are a few restaurants here, the post office and, further along, City Hall.

### Information

The large tourist office (☎ 634-5831) and craft shop can't be missed out on the Trans Canada Hwy near the turn-offs into town. They have lots of local information and are very helpful.

The More or Less store at 35 Broadway at the west end of town near the Valley Shopping Mall is good for hiking and camping foods.

### Captain James Cook Monument

North-west of downtown up on some cliffs overlooking the Humber Arm is a National Historic Site commemorating Captain Cook and affording excellent views of the city and area. A map from the tourist office is necessary as the road access is pretty convoluted. Mr Cook certainly got around. He surveyed this entire region in the mid-1760s and his names for many of the islands, ports and waterways such as the Humber Arm and Hawke's Bay remain. His work here was so successful it led to the voyages to New Zealand and Australia. Replicas of some of Cook's charts are displayed.

Corner Brook

## Sticks & Stones House

On the opposite side of town, in a residential area, sits this folk art masterpiece/one man's life obsession (☎ 634-3275) that must be seen to be believed. I don't know where to start. It seems that for 30 years the owner, Mr Clyde Farnell, spent every spare moment elaborately decorating the walls and ceilings of the house with found and discarded objects.

When he died and neighbours entered the house his secret floored them. The university was notified and soon the house became protected as a folk art museum. The primary material used in the densely packed visual feast is the popsicle stick – some 53,000 of them!

Students of psychology might find it intriguing (or downright creepy) to learn that Farnell was blinded in one eye as a child by a popsicle stick. Other materials include wittily used pebbles, ashtrays, glasses, buttons and a flashcube as the light in a lighthouse.

The house is open from 1 to 5 pm daily at 12 Farnell's Lane and is well worth the very small admission fee towards its upkeep.

## Heritage District

The older section of town dating from 1925 to 1940 surrounds Central St. It's primarily a residential area though there are some shops and a few restaurants.

## Old Railway Display

Even when the trains were in service in Newfoundland they operated on a different, narrower gauge than those in the rest of the country. On display is a train from before Confederation consisting of a steam locomotive and five various cars. It can be seen during the summer near Station Rd not far from the large gypsum plant in the eastern part of town. If you're lucky there'll be someone around to let you have a look inside too.

## Curling Kennels

This is not really a tourist attraction but a private kennel (☎ 785-2038) whose owner,

Gord Grant, breeds the well-known but now rarely seen Newfoundland dog. Visitors who just have to see these big beautiful, black beasts (or buy one to take home) can go to the kennels at 6 Clifton Ave. Though larger than St Bernards, the Newfoundland dogs are known for their gentleness as much as their love of water and traditional rescue heroics.

## Places to Stay & Eat

For camping, *Blow Me Down Park* is at the end of Route 450 which leads from town along the Humber Arm. Out here at the tip of the peninsula there some good views of the Bay of Islands.

Corner Brook has half a dozen small tourist homes with prices lower than those in much of the province; singles/doubles cost $25/30, sometimes including breakfast.

The central *Bell's B&B* (☎ 634-5736) is within walking distance of downtown at 2 Ford's Rd. It is open all year and has four rooms; singles/doubles cost $39/49, with continental breakfast.

Another place to try is *Brake's Hospitality Home* (☎ 785-2077) away from the centre west along the Humber Arm at Bartlett's Point. A city bus takes you almost to the door. The address is 25 Cooper's Rd. They have three rooms; singles/doubles cost $30/40, including breakfast. A good park with walking trails by the water is just up the road.

For more gracious accommodation the *Glynmill Inn* (☎ 634-5181), on Cobb Lane in downtown, is recommended. It's a large Tudor-style inn set off by surrounding lawns and gardens and offers a good dining room as well.

There are also a couple of motels in town not far from the main highway. The Heritage District has a few restaurants.

## Getting There & Away

The CN Roadcruiser depot (☎ 634-8244), for points east and west along the Trans Canada Hwy, is in the north-east section of town on the corner of the Lewin Parkway and Prince George Ave.

The Viking Express (☎ 634-4710) bus

which goes up the northern peninsula arrives and departs from the Millbrook Mall shopping centre not far from Main St in the centre of Corner Brook. Martin's Bus Service (☎ 634-4710) goes to Woody Point in Gros Morne National Park and also departs from the Millbrook Mall. There is one trip each way daily from Monday to Friday. Eddy's Bus Service (☎ 643-2134) runs to Stephenville daily. Devin's Bus Line (☎ 634-7777) heads to Burgeo on the south coast which is on the coastal ferry service route. For other destinations ask the Viking Express desk.

### Around Corner Brook

Boat tours tool up the Humber Arm and around the scenic **Bay of Islands**. Another, Goose Arm Boat Tours (☎ 688-2610), departs Cox's Cove for 2½-hour trips up narrow Goose Arm which is north of Corner Brook.

The **Humber River** which flows into the arm from Deer Lake is renowned for its salmon. The area from the beginning of the Humber Arm, a long narrow bay, back to **Little Rapids** is both pretty and rich in little fishing pools. *Log Cabin Lodge* (☎ 634-6087) in Spruce Brook caters for fishing and can arrange guides, etc.

**Marble Mountain**, in the Humber Valley eight km east of town, is becoming an established downhill ski centre; the area is also picturesque in the fall (autumn) with the colourful foliage. A trail less than 500 metres long leads from the rear parking lot of Marble Mountain to **Steady Brook Falls**. Another trail, which is 3.5 km one way, leads to the 500 metre summit of Marble Mountain.

For more serious walkers, including overnighters, there are numerous hikes in the **Blomidon Mountains** (also spelt 'Blow Me Down'), south of the Bay of Islands along Hwy 450 to Lark Harbour. These mountains were formed about 500 million years ago from brownish peridotite rock pushed up from the earth's mantle when the geographic plates of North America and Europe bumped together. What makes this special is that Newfoundland is one of the few places in the world where this type of rock is exposed and can be walked over.

Other features are the great views over the bay and islands and a small caribou population. Some of the trails especially ones up on the barrens are not well marked at all so bringing topographical maps and proper equipment is recommended. Ask at the tourist office for the small booklet on the local trails which shows the various access points.

One of the easiest as well as most popular trails begins at a parking lot on the left side of Hwy 450 (500 metres from the bridge which crosses Blow Me Down Brook). The trail can be taken for an hour or so or, for more avid hikers, it continues well into the mountains where you're on your own. At Blow Me Down Park near the end of Hwy 450 there are also well-used marked trails which still provide fine views of the coastline.

South of town there is very good freshwater swimming at **Stag Lake** and also fairly warm waters at the **Blue Ponds Provincial Park** a little further out.

### STEPHENVILLE

Formerly a large military base town with the decaying evidence visible from the road in, Stephenville with a population of 10,000, now relies mainly on the Abitibi-Price pulp mill which you can tour. The town sits on St George's Bay between Corner Brook and Port aux Basques and acts as entrance to French Port au Port. There is not much here for the visitor but information can be had from the Chamber of Commerce (☎ 643-5621).

The Stephenville Festival is a two-week English theatre event, usually held in late July with local and internationally known participants. The festival offers theatre ranging from Shakespeare to modern Newfoundlanders' plays. Good student reductions on tickets are offered. The festival is under some financial strain so look into the situation before planning a visit.

## Places to Stay & Eat

Main St offers a couple of places to eat, *Ildi's* for a coffee and two hotels for overnighters. Less expensive is the *Harmon House* (☎ 643-4673), a B&B, at 144 New Mexico Drive not far from the hospital. A bedtime snack and breakfast is included in the modest price and other meals can be provided upon request.

During lobster season (from April to July), the tasty devils are sold in the streets from trucks and trailers at good prices.

## PORT AU PORT PENINSULA

The large peninsula west from Stephenville is the only French area of the province and has been since the early 1700s when it became known as the **French Shore**. It was used by the French for fishing in the **Strait of Belle Isle** right up until the early 1900s. **Red Island** was at one time France's most important fishing base in the New World.

Today, the further west you go the stronger the French culture is. At the south-west tip of the Port au Port Peninsula in **Cape St George** the children still go to French school preserving their dialect which is now distinct from the language spoken in either France or Quebec. Mainland, Lourdes and Black Duck Brook are also very French. In late July or early August each year there is a major French folk festival held in Cape St George with lots of music and other events.

In **Port au Port West**, a small community not far from Stephenville the Our Lady of Mercy Church is worth a look. Begun in 1914, it is the largest wooden building in Newfoundland. During July and August, a guide is on hand to show you around and provide some details and stories about the church. On the way there from Stephenville after going across the small bridge continue straight on the small road, don't follow the road around to the left or you'll miss the church like everybody else does. There is also the small Lady of Mercy Museum with craft shop and tea room with a collection of local artefacts.

# South-Western Newfoundland

Within the small south-western corner of the province the visitor is offered a remarkable variety of geography and history. It is well worthwhile spending some time exploring it rather than just doing the usual mad dash to or from the ferry. Hilly Port aux Basques built up and around a jutting, jagged peninsula and offering all the services including a major tourist office is the centre of the region.

To the east a good glimpse of the coastal barrens and small fishing villages which surround much of the province is accessible by road before it ends at Rose Blanche. North from town, the treeless landscape gives way to one of the few farming areas in the province, the gorgeous Codroy Valley with some very fine walking trails.

## CODROY VALLEY

North of Port aux Basques beyond Cape Ray the broad green, fertile Codroy Valley runs from the coast north-east alongside the Long Range Mountains for about 50 km. This is one of the prime farming regions of the province and compared with the generally rugged, rocky landscape looks positively lush.

The Grand Codroy River and its many offshoots running through the valley make it especially pretty and there are some fine walks to enjoy. Probably the best of these start in Doyles at the southern end of the valley. Anyone around the valley or at the Port aux Basques tourist chalet will know the place. There is a campground nearby just off the Trans Canada Hwy and accommodation at the *Chignic Lodge* (☎ 955-2306) about 16 km further north.

A good spot for a view of the valley (accessible by car) is down near the sea by the town of **Searston**.

Further along, the road goes up a mountain at **Cape Anguille**; there are views as far as the mainland on a clear day. Back at the inlet, the estuary of the Grand Codroy River is an important wetland area for birds which is impressive at migration times when thousands of geese, black ducks and other species can be viewed. At Grand Codroy Park there is a beach and picnic areas.

Despite its long period of settlement and the many quiet farms, the valley does have a nasty side to it. It can be the windiest place in Newfoundland and that's saying something. Along the highway breezes can reach 200 km/h. They used to have to stop the trains at times to prevent them from blowing off the tracks – and you wanted to bring your bicycle!

Though now a blend of English, French, Irish and Scottish the population was at one time primarily Scottish. They developed a community tight enough that Gaelic was spoken until the 1950s. Now just a few of the older people know it but much of the song and dance of the area retains its Scottish roots.

## PORT AUX BASQUES
For many visitors this is the first glimpse of Newfoundland. Approaching by ferry from Nova Scotia, the rocky, barren treeless landscape can look a little forbidding but also appealing in a rough, undeveloped way. For the many people heading to the province to enjoy its ruggedness, this uncommercialised port is a welcome sight.

The town itself, at least the older section built on and around the hills to the left of the ferry as it approaches, is very attractive with narrow, winding roads edged with the traditional wooden houses offering different views and angles at every turn.

Port aux Basques was named by Basque fishers and whalers in the early 16th century who came to work the waters of the Strait of Belle Isle which separates the province from Quebec. The French and Portuguese also used the port as a fishing station centuries ago.

Today, Port aux Basques with a population of 6100, is the principal terminal for the Marine Atlantic ferry which links the island with the Canadian mainland.

The ferry company is now the largest employer in town, though there are also freight-handling and fish-packing industries.

The town is also sometimes known as Channel-Port-aux-Basques.

### Orientation
The ferry pulls into a small but well-protected bay. The town centre is to the east of the landing and back the way you came in. It consists of narrow, hilly streets overlooking the sea. They're lined with the brightly coloured wooden houses so common in the province.

To get to the old section of town, cross the bridge after leaving the ferry and turn left.

For the new part of town, turn right along the Trans Canada Hwy. Go past a number of gas stations and turn left at the Motel Port aux Basques on the corner of Grand Bay Rd and High St. This will take you to the shopping mall, the centre of the new district. If you have time to kill before the ferry, there's a movie theatre in the mall.

### Information
The tourist chalet (☎ 695-2262) with information on all parts of the province is on the Trans Canada Hwy a few km out of town on the way to St John's. It's on the eastern side of the highway.

### Port aux Basques Museum
In the old town, at 118 Main St near the corner of Avalon Lane, the two-storey museum (☎ 695-7604) is well done and for the price of $1 you can't really go wrong. The bulk of the collection is maritime artefacts of one sort or another – many from shipwrecks.

The showpiece of the museum is a navigational instrument from the 17th century known as an astrolabe. I know this doesn't sound fascinating, it didn't to me either, but it's actually quite interesting. The thing itself is a striking brass contraption about 17.5 cm in diameter made in Portugal in 1628. The design is based on a principal discovered by the ancient Greeks to allow for charting of the heavenly bodies. Variations on it have been used for nautical navigation since 1470.

This astrolabe is in remarkable condition and is one of only about three dozen in the world. It was found by a diver off Isle aux Morts, along the south coast from town in 1982, and is the only one in Canada although another, Samuel de Champlain's, was found in Ontario. Port aux Basques' astrolabe is believed to have been on board either a Portuguese or Basque fishing boat.

Among some of the other items are some old photographs of the Codroy Valley taken at the turn of the century and some soapstone relics taken from the Cape Ray Dorset Inuit site dating from around 100 to 500 AD.

### Places to Stay

Luckily, for campers, there is a good place close to town, in fact, close enough to be convenient when arriving late or leaving early. It's the *JT Cheeseman Provincial Park* north of town about 12 km along the Trans Canada Hwy.

At the *Heritage Home* (☎ 695-3240) guesthouse (three rooms) you can stay in bed almost until the ferry blows the whistle before getting up and walking down the hill and onto the boat. It's at 11 Caribou Rd beside the dock, and singles/doubles cost $37/42 with a continental breakfast.

Further out is *Caribou House* (☎ 695-3408), a B&B, at 30 Grand Bay Rd about three km from the ferry and bus terminals. Prices range from $40/$45 to $45/50 for singles/doubles.

*St Christopher's Hotel* (☎ 695-7034) with a fine view from its hilltop location on Caribou Rd is a larger, commercial hotel offering more amenities and a dining room. A double room costs $70.

There are also several motels in about the same price range as the above hotel. The *Grand Bay* (☎ 695-2105) is very close to downtown and the ferry near the shopping mall, and has a bar and restaurant.

The *Motel Port aux Basques* is even more expensive. The *Gulfside Inn* (☎ 695-7091) with 20 rooms is about four km from the ferry on the Trans Canada Hwy.

For more reasonable prices you'll have to hit the highway. *Tompkins Motel & Tourist Home* (☎ 955-2901) in Doyles, 34 km away, is a start with rooms in the house from just $20.

There are numerous places in the Codroy Valley. *Muise's Tourist Home* (☎ 955-2471) is in South Branch, 57 km from Port aux Basques and has single rooms from $28 breakfast included or full housekeeping cabins for $35 double.

### Places to Eat

The *Blue Rose Café* at 77 Main St beside Radio Shack in the old town, is a good little place for casual, inexpensive meals. They serve homemade bread, soups and desserts. In summer, to cater for visitors, they also offer fish platters and a distinctive Newfoundland offering, *brewis*, which involves bread being soaked in a broth overnight. The café is closed on Sunday.

The *Harbour Restaurant*, on Main St closer to the ferry terminal, is open later in the evenings. It is convenient and has good views of the waterfront if you're waiting for the midnight boat. The menu is mainly fried chicken or fish & chips.

At 116 Main St is the *San Yuan* for Chinese and not far away is a *Pizza Delight*.

In the shopping mall in the new part of town is an *A&W Restaurant* specialising in hamburgers and root beer.

### Getting There & Away

**Bus** The CN Roadcruiser bus service (☎ 695-2124) (known sometimes as the CN bus or occasionally listed as Terra Transport – a little confusing) leaves once a day at 7 am from the ferry dock terminal for the 904-km trip to St John's. The trip takes about 14 hours and costs $79.57 one way. You can stop at any of the towns along the way (and there are plenty of stops). Connections can be made in other towns with other, more local, bus companies which service destinations other than those on the main route to St John's covered by CN Roadcruiser. For example in Deer Lake, the Viking Express bus goes north up the peninsula. Corner Brook has a number of smaller lines and so is used as a transfer point as well.

**Train** There are no passenger trains in Newfoundland and even the freight service has ended.

**Ferry** Marine Atlantic (☎ 695-7081) operates both the ferry routes from Nova Scotia to Newfoundland: one going to Argentia and this one to Port aux Basques.

From the beginning of June to mid-September there is a minimum of one trip daily, it's more often two or three a day. During mid-summer, reservations are a good idea and can be made by calling the above number in Port aux Basques or Marine

Atlantic's North Sydney office (☎ 702-794-5700), Nova Scotia. Generally one or two-days' notice is sufficient. Early morning or late night trips are usually less busy and, if you're walking or cycling, there shouldn't be any trouble. During the rest of the year reservations are not required even though the ferry frequency drops. The boats do go all year.

The fare is $16.50, less for children and seniors, $51.50 per car, more with a trailer or camper. The night ferry saves you the cost of a night's bed because you can sleep anywhere and everywhere on board, and people

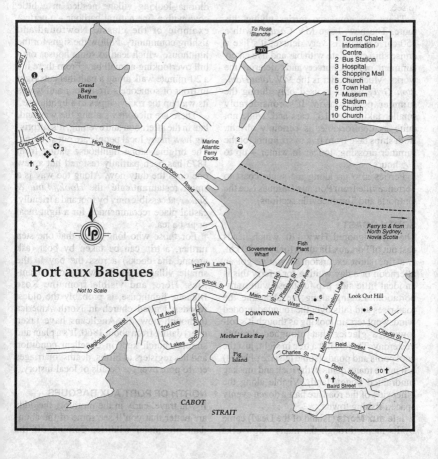

**Port aux Basques**

Not to Scale

1  Tourist Chalet Information Centre
2  Bus Station
3  Hospital
4  Shopping Mall
5  Church
6  Town Hall
7  Museum
8  Stadium
9  Church
10 Church

do just that. Upon boarding there is a rush to the decks to secure a comfortable, quiet location away from hallways and most traffic. Bring a sleeping bag or blanket – whatever you want – everybody does. When you get up in the morning, the bodies lying everywhere make you wonder if the food was poisoned! Of course it's not.

If it's a warm night the outside decks can be pleasant and there are a few benches that you can stretch out on. For those with extra cash, berths and cabins are also available. Whichever way you choose you miss nothing by going at night – there's nothing to see.

There are now two ferries plying this route. The new, large MV *Caribou* with a 350-car capacity is very deluxe; it's like a cruise ship complete with bar and live entertainment, movies, nursery and cafeteria – the works. Much smaller is the MV *John Hamilton Gray* which is used only during the summer peak season. It's considerably smaller taking just 165 cars and, while not quite as comfortable, is certainly alright. Both ships take from five to six hours for the summer crossing, longer in winter – up to 7½ hours.

Ferries also go along the south coast to Terrenceville from Port aux Basques (see the Outports and Terrenceville sections).

## SOUTH COAST

The often ignored Hwy 470, which heads east out of Port aux Basques for about 50 km, is a fine short excursion. If you've got an afternoon or a day waiting for a ferry this is an ideal little side trip for those with transportation. Edging along the shoreline the road rises and falls over the rounded, eroded windswept terrain looking as though it's following a glacier that ploughed through yesterday. There's not a tree in sight, just the cool pools and ponds (some the size of lakes) left in the many dents in the rock and muskeg (undrained boggy land). Visible along the other side of the road are half a dozen evenly spaced fishing towns.

**Isle aux Morts** (Island of the Dead) came by its name through the many shipwrecks just offshore which have occurred over some 400 years. The astrolabe, a navigational device and prize of the museum in Port aux Basques was found here. There's a restaurant in town offering the standards at reasonable prices.

Further east is **Otter Bay Provincial Park** with picnicking and some trails leading over the surrounding hills. It's a scenic and quiet spot; camping is possible but there are no facilities – I got my drinking water from a stream running through the park.

The highlight of the trip is the last village along the road, **Rose Blanche**, a pretty, traditional-looking village nestled in a little cove with a fine natural harbour – a perfect example of the classic Newfoundland fishing community. Follow the signs for the lighthouse which lead to some houses on a hill overlooking a small bay. From there it's a 20-minute walk along a path that cuts right in front of someone's front door and winds its way up the rocky slopes to a lighthouse.

There are nice views along the way and, late in the afternoon and evening, it's surprising how many local people are out strolling. The original stone lighthouse dating from 1873 has been partially restored but a new one does the duty now. Along the way is a small restaurant/café, the *Hook, Line & Sinker*, accessible only by foot and a friendly, casual place recommended for a light meal or just a tea.

For those who long to go that one step further, a trip can be taken by boat (ask around the docks) across the bay to the smaller village of **Petites** with about 30 families. Here, and visible from the Rose Blanche lighthouse, is probably the oldest wooden United church in North America (although now the Anglicans have taken over) dating from about 1860. It's a plain and simple church kept in excellent condition and has registers of births, deaths, marriages etc to pore over for details of local history.

## NORTH OF PORT AUX BASQUES

If you travel early in the morning, the odds are better that you'll see some of the abundant provincial wildlife. Coming off the ferry at 6 am on one trip, I saw within an hour of Port aux Basques half a dozen long-haired horses on the road and a cow moose with her calf.

Near Cape Ray, there is an excellent walk up Table Mountain which is a little over 518 metres high. Look for the sign across the street from the Cape Ray Rd turn-off. Cape Ray has a sandy beach and campground and was the site of a Dorset Inuit camp around 400 BC to 400 AD. A little further north is more camping at **Mummichog Park**.

# Outports

'Outport' is the name given to any of the tiny coastal fishing villages accessible only by boat. Some are on one of the three major intra-provincial coastal ferry lines, others are not. These little communities represent some of the most remote settlements left in North America. Change is coming at an ever quickening pace, but for the moment these outports harbour the rough Newfoundland life at its most traditional. Many of these places don't have TV or any outside contact, and some apparently have adult residents who have never seen a car. These villages clinging to the rocky coastlines are perhaps the best place to see the unique culture of the Newfoundland people of European blood born in Canada.

If you want to visit – now is the time, as this way of life inevitably erodes under the modern wave. More and more roads are being built to these out-of-the-way places while others wilt away due to lack of fish and the subsequent inability of the residents to make a living. Other areas remain isolated and difficult to reach as only private vessels supply them from other more accessible points.

There are really only two coastal services to choose from, both run by Marine Atlantic. One runs from Lewisporte on Notre Dame Bay up the coast of Labrador. This ferry carries passengers only. For details see the Labrador and Lewisporte sections. Another

trip also departs from Lewisporte but goes more or less directly to Happy Valley-Goose Bay which is hardly an outport, with soldiers from a handful of countries stationed there. This latter ferry takes vehicles and passengers.

The other major outport service runs along the southern coast from Port aux Basques to Terrenceville with about a dozen villages in between as possible stops. The trip takes about 19 hours and leaves Port aux Basques twice or three times weekly depending on the time of year. Ferries run all year. Throughout mid-summer a change of ferries is required as each of the two ferries is serviced in the middle of its voyage before returning to its port of origin. Through the rest of the year one boat travels the entire route. Fares are low at about 19 cents per nautical mile (2000 metres approximately), more for a cabin the price of which is also calculated on a mileage basis.

In summer the shortened trips only running part of the way may be taken, for example between Terrenceville and Burgeo or between Port aux Basques and Hermitage-Sandyville.

There is food service on board but you may want to bring some of your own too.

For places to stay on either the south or north coastal trip, ask around beforehand or just take a chance on arrival. You can always stay on the ferry if you're continuing on without a stopover. This can be tiring if you're doing it on the cheap: sleeping on the floor or in a chair can be pretty uncomfortable after a few days, especially if the sea is rough. On a longer trip consider a cabin, the prices actually are quite fair. Ask about stopovers and how long the ticket is good for.

An excellent and inexpensive circular trip around the province, including outports, can be done without the expense of a car. Take the ferry to Port aux Basques, then the coastal service to Terrenceville. Go on by public road transport to St John's or wherever and then catch the main cross-province bus back to Port aux Basques.

For details and schedules, call Marine Atlantic (☎ 695-7081) in Port aux Basques or Marine Atlantic (☎ 1-800-563-7381) from elsewhere in Newfoundland.

# Labrador

Labrador is that part of Newfoundland – three times the size of the island – that is adjacent to the Quebec mainland. The Strait of Belle Isle separates Labrador from the Newfoundland Island. This vast, rugged land is one of the last incompletely explored areas in the country and one of the largest, cleanest, natural areas anywhere. For this reason it is beginning to attract more and more visitors to its varied regions.

The geological base of Labrador is the ancient Laurentian Shield – possibly the oldest unchanged region on earth. It's thought the land looks much the same as it did before life on the planet began. Four great caribou herds, including the world's largest with some 750,000 head, migrate across Labrador to their calving grounds each year.

Until recently, small numbers of Inuit, Native Indians and longtime European descendants known as 'liveyers' were the only human residents. They lived in little villages dotted along the rocky coasts as they had done for centuries, eking out an existence fishing and hunting. The interior was virgin wilderness.

Today a new people, with a completely different outlook and lifestyle, has arrived. White southerners have been lured by the overwhelming and nearly untouched natural resources and potential they see.

And so, not far away from the more-or-less traditional way of life of the original inhabitants, lie some of the world's most modern, sophisticated industrial complexes. Most of the development has been far inland, near the border of Quebec. Labrador City and Wabush, with the latest technology, are two towns that produce half of Canada's iron ore. Churchill Falls is the site of an enormous hydroelectric plant that supplies power for north-eastern USA.

Happy Valley-Goose Bay is an older settlement first established as an air force base in WW II. It's now mainly a supply centre, you can get there from Lewisporte, Newfoundland by ferry. These four centres are home to more than half of Labrador's population of 30,000.

The east coast, accessible by boat from Newfoundland, is in its own way at least as interesting. Tiny villages dot the coast all the way to the far north. As in western Newfoundland, with some planning, you can take a unique trip on the supply ferries which could be excellent.

Camping is an option all across Labrador but is mostly done in a van or camper. Tenting is possible but be prepared: although summers can be pleasantly warm, even hot, this is often a cold, wet and windy place. The amount of accommodation is steadily increasing in all regions and the larger places all have hotels of one sort or another.

As a distinct entity from Newfoundland Island, Labrador has its own flag. The residents, too, consider themselves a breed apart.

## LABRADOR STRAITS

Lying 18 km across the Strait of Belle Isle and visible from the northern peninsula of Newfoundland, this region of Labrador is in some ways the most accessible. It is also the oldest settled area of Labrador. There are about half a dozen small, permanent communities connected by road along the historic coast here. Many of the inhabitants are the descendants of the European fishers who crossed from Newfoundland to fish in the rich strait centuries ago. Attractions include the simple but awesome far north landscape, icebergs, sea birds and whales and the historic Basque site at Red Bay. The region from Blanc Sablon up to around and Cartwright has some wooded areas especially in the northern section. Beyond this point, trees are pretty scarce along the coast.

The ferry from Newfoundland docks at **Blanc Sablon**, which is in Quebec right at the provincial border. There are a couple of fairly priced guesthouses in Blanc Sablon and Tilden has an outlet for rental cars. From

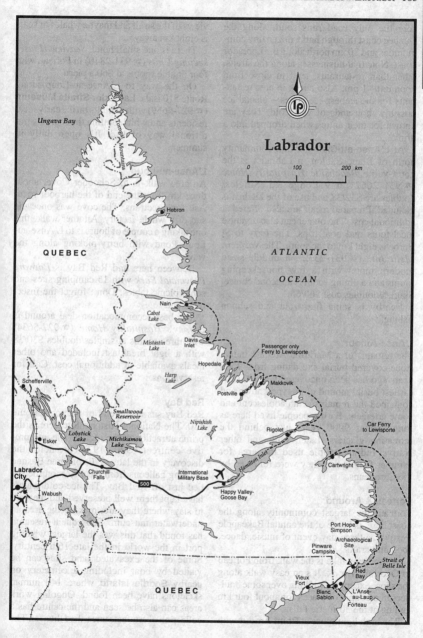

Ungava Bay

Torngat Mountains

QUEBEC

Hebron

ATLANTIC

OCEAN

Labrador

0      100      200 km

Cabot
Lake

Nain

Mistastin
Lake

Davis
Inlet

Passenger only
Ferry to Lewisporte

Harp
Lake

Hopedale

Makkovik

Postville

Scheffetville

Smallwood
Reservoir

Nipishish
Lake

Rigolet

Car Ferry
to Lewisporte

Esker

Lobstick
Lake

Michikamau
Lake

Hamilton Inlet

Cartwright

Labrador
City

Wabush

Churchill
Falls

500

International
Military Base

Happy Valley-
Goose Bay

Port Hope
Simpson

QUEBEC

Archaeological
Site

Pinware
Campsite

Red Bay

Strait of
Belle Isle

Vieux
Fort

Blanc
Sablon

L'Anse-
au-Loup

Forteau

here the only road runs south along the Quebec coast through half a dozen tiny communities and 80 km north along the Labrador coast. Note that businesses along the straits, other than restaurants, tend to close from noon until 1 pm. Also check in area restaurants for the iceberg ice cubes – glacial ice possibly thousands of years old. They are known for their antics when dropped into a drink.

At **L'Anse-au-Clair** the first community north of Blanc Sablon in Labrador is the good-value *Beachside Hospitality Home* (☎ 931-2662) at 9 Lodge Rd. Singles/doubles are $32/38 and use of the kitchen is included. Prepared meals are also offered at additional cost. The owner can also organise local tours and boat trips. The ferry to St Barbe is eight km to the south. The *Northern Light Inn* (☎ 931-2332), a middle-sized modern motel with a few housekeeping rooms and a dining room is a second choice. Singles/doubles cost $60/65.

Nearby is some fine trout and salmon fishing.

### L'Anse-Amour

The remains of a Maritime Archaic Indian stone-covered burial site dating from 7500 years ago has been uncovered here. It is the earliest burial mound of its type known and contained the remains of an adolescent and some artefacts. Earlier people lived here as long ago as 9000 years just behind the retreating glaciers. Later, Inuit and other Native Indian people used the area for summer fishing and they were followed by the Europeans.

### Forteau & Around

Forteau, the largest community along the coast here, is home of the annual Bakeapple Festival, a three-day event of music, dance, food and crafts.

A good area hike is the walk from Forteau to Overfalls Brook. It's an easy walk along the shore except for walking over some boulders in a couple of places for about four km ending at the 30-metre falls.

The high lighthouse at **Point Amour** with

views of the strait and maybe whales or seals is eight km away.

There is one small hotel, *Seaview House-keeping Units* (☎ 931-2840) in Forteau with four double rooms at $60 a piece.

On the way to L'Anse-au-Loup along Route 510 is the **Labrador Straits Museum** (☎ 927-5659) with exhibits on the early local residents and which outline the region's traditional way of life. It's open daily in summer.

### L'Anse-au-Loup

An area walk is to Schooner Cove, about three km from the end of the harbour road. Ask for directions. The cove was once the site of a whale factory. Another walk, this one taking a couple of hours is to L'Anse-au-Loup Pond with berry-picking along the way.

Between here and Red Bay is *Pinware Provincial Park* with 15 camping sites and some picnic tables. Don't forget the insect repellent.

The best accommodation deal around is *Barney's Hospitality Home* (☎ 927-5634) with three rooms at singles/doubles $30/38 with a light breakfast included and other meals available at additional cost. Call for reservations.

### Red Bay

Red Bay sits at the end of the road, Route 510. The National Historic Site here is the prime attraction of the region. The interpretive centre (☎ 920-2197) chronicles the discovery in the late 1970s of three Basque whaling galleons from the 1500s on the sea bed just off Red Bay. The ice-cold waters have kept them well preserved and they are to stay where they are, making the area an underwater museum. Subsequent research has found that this was the largest whaling port in the world in the late 16th century. Some of the excavated land sites can be visited by boat including a cemetery on nearby **Saddle Island** where 140 human skeletons have been found. Ongoing work areas can also be seen and the centre has a collection of artefacts unearthed thus far. The park is open daily throughout the summer and is free.

The Red Bay Visitor's Centre has more information on the Basque whaling port. Also ask about the hike up to the top of Tracey Hill from where there are fine views of the coast and town.

Red Bay is also on the Marine Atlantic coastal ferry service route from Lewisporte and St Anthony.

### Getting There & Away

**Air** Air Nova, an Air Canada partner, has flights from Deer Lake, Newfoundland, to Blanc Sablon. Also try Provincial Airlines from Corner Brook, Deer Lake or Happy Valley-Goose Bay. Blanc Sablon is also connected to Quebec destinations such as Sept Îles and Quebec City by Canadian Airlines and their partner Air Atlantic.

**Ferry** From 1 May to the end of the season in November, a vehicle and passenger ferry runs from St Barbe (Newfoundland) to Blanc Sablon (Quebec). It is operated by Puddister Trading Company (☎ 722-4000) out of St Barbe. During the 80-minute crossing you may see ice floes drifting southward to the melting warmer waters. Whales may also be seen. Shrimps grow like crazy in these waters. From the beginning of July to the end of August when things are at their busiest the boat runs two or three times a day, at other times service drops to once or twice daily. Every day though, a ferry leaves at 8 am, other times vary. The cost is $8.50 per person, $16 for a car and more for trailers, vans etc.

A coastal freight service, the *Nordic Express*, operated by Relais Nordik Inc (☎ 968-4707 in Sept-Îles or ☎ 1-800-463-0680 from anywhere in north-western Quebec) runs up the Quebec coast from Sept-Îles on the Gulf of St Lawrence to Blanc Sablon with stops along the way.

The Marine Atlantic coastal service from Lewisporte on Notre Dame Bay, Newfoundland or St Anthony, Newfoundland up the Labrador coast makes a call at Red Bay as

well but it's a passenger-only service. For details see the Lewisporte section.

**Road** The road running up and down the coast from Blanc Sablon is unconnected to further destinations in either Quebec or Labrador. The only road link is across the straight by ferry on the Northern Peninsula of Newfoundland.

### NORTHERN COAST

Beyond Red Bay all the way up to **Ungava Bay** are dozens of small semi-traditional communities and settlements accessible only by sea or air along the rugged, jagged and in some parts unspoiled mountainous coast. This area of Labrador doesn't get a lot of visitors but offers the persistent a look at some of the most remote regions of North America.

The original people were Inuit and they still make up a large part of the population. About 200 years ago Europeans began to settle and fish, which remains the principal way of making a living. Moravian missionaries established missions from as early as 1765 along this coast and their schools, churches and influence continue to play a part in the local culture.

Living off the land completely has pretty much disappeared especially now that the fishing industry has all but gone belly up. Between government moratoriums and lack of fish, making a wage from the sea is almost impossible. Some hunting and trapping is still carried on but these days unemployment is high and many people rely on government funds in one way or another. Still, the lifestyle remains unchanged in many ways due simply to the isolation and the small size of the villages. The people are a determined lot, they have to be.

The accommodation situation is a bit of an unknown as most travellers use the ferry as a floating hotel. For those wishing to get off and hang around somewhere until the next boat, it means winging it and asking around town for a spare bed. Although not often listed in provincial tourist information lists, there are guesthouses in some places but, of course, they come and go.

Some of the points of interest beyond Cartwright and Hamilton Inlet are listed below.

At **Makkovik**, an early fur-trading post, is a traditional fishing and hunting community. Both new and old-style crafts and materials can be bought there.

In **Hopedale** a National Historic Site preserves the old wooden Moravian mission from 1782. The site includes a store, residence, some huts and of course, the church. The *Hopedale Lodge* (☎ 933-3770) provides beds and meals. Singles/doubles are $74/94 with any or all meals at extra cost.

The Native coastal people are generally Inuit. This is not the case at **Davis Inlet**, home to a different group of Native Canadians, the Indian Innu (sometimes known as the Naskapi or the Montagnais Innu). They tended traditionally to inhabit the interior rather than the coast. It was the Canadian government who brought them to Davis Inlet in a relocation programme. This has been a pretty shameful affair and the legacy of hardship, erosion of traditions and the resulting problems continue. As late as the early 1960s many of these people were nomads roaming the interior with tents. Drugs, alcohol and among the young in particular, solvent abuse, petrol sniffing and suicide indicate a community crisis. Leaders hope that land-claim settlements will help their people regain some purpose and optimism.

Crafts can be purchased here too, including some interesting work with grass.

### Nain & Around

This is the last stop on the Marine Atlantic ferry and with a population of 1000 is the last town of any size as you go northward. Fishing is the main industry and the processing plant is an important employer. As in the other smaller settlements, after the fishing season hunting and trapping continue as they have for centuries. The **Piulimatsivik-Nain Museum** in one of the old mission houses, outlines both Inuit and Moravian history with artefacts relating to both traditions.

Again, there is a craft outlet and Nain has a hotel, the *Atsanik Lodge* (☎ 922-2910) at singles/doubles $73/83. There is often a guesthouse or two here as well.

North, beyond here is another Moravian historic site in **Hebron**. Close to the northern tip of Labrador the wild **Torngat Mountains** are popular with climbers because of their altitude (some of the highest peaks west of the Rockies) and their isolation.

### Getting There & Away

The Marine Atlantic passenger-only (no vehicles) ferry from Lewisporte, calls in at St Anthony on Newfoundland's northern tip and then 'bounces' along the Labrador coast from Red Bay, up into Goose Bay and then as far north as the town of Nain. Private vessels can be hired to reach still further north. This trip is really the only way to see something of isolated coastal Labrador and its changing older settlements. The trip length varies but is at least a week in each direction as the ferry drops in at somewhere between two dozen and over 40 communities unloading supplies and freight of every

---

**The Moravian Church**
The Moravians developed in the mid-1400s as the Church of the Brotherhood. They broke from the Church of Rome and had to flee persecution in their place of origin, the then largely German-speaking provinces of Bohemia and Moravia, Czeckoslovakia. A strong evangelical movement, they set up missions in Asia, Africa, the West Indies and North and South America. Starting in the late 1700s they began ministering to the Inuit of the New World, doing some good but attempting to diminish native spirituality and culture at the same time. They were a prominent European group all along the Strait of Belle Isle on both the Newfoundland side and most notably on the coast of Labrador. They maintained an extensive mission community here until the 1950s. Many of their former buildings are still in use, some as historical sites. ■

description. Space on this ferry is very limited and reservations must be made in Newfoundland. (If you know your schedule, a call to the Lewisporte reservation office may be worthwhile from outside the province, the rules on booking from out of the province don't seem totally fixed.) Highlights are the coastal scenery and icebergs. See Lewisporte in the Central Newfoundland section earlier for details.

## CENTRAL LABRADOR

Making up the territorial bulk of Labrador, the central portion is an immense, very sparsely populated and ancient wilderness. Paradoxically, it also has the largest town in Labrador, Happy Valley-Goose Bay, in the south with a population of 7000.

### Happy Valley-Goose Bay

Goose Bay was established during WW II as a staging point for planes on the way to Europe and has remained an aviation centre. Today there is a Canadian military base used by pilots from around Canada and Europe for testing high-tech planes, in particular controversial low-flying jets which the Innu say disturb their way of life.

The town has all the services including hotels but for the outsider there is not a lot to see or do and it is very isolated. The remote, forested landscape, however, attracts many anglers and hunters and there are numerous fly-in possibilities for camping.

For tourist information call the Mokami Regional Development Association (☎ 896-3100).

The **Labrador Heritage Museum** (☎ 896-2762) outlines some of the history of the area and includes a trapper's traditional shelter, samples of animal furs and some of the minerals found in Labrador. The museum is on the north side of town on the former Canadian Forces base. At the **Northern Lights Military Museum** (☎ 896-5939), 170 Hamilton River Rd, some of the military history of the city is displayed. Also at the Northern Lights building visit the free **Trappers Brook Animal Displays**, lifelike displays of many of the animals and birds found in the region. Both exhibits are closed on Sunday.

### Places to Stay & Eat

The city has three fair-sized hotels, none of them cheap. The *Royal Inn* (☎ 896-2456) with singles/doubles from $56/67 is the most economical. It's at 5 Royal Ave and it also has some housekeeping units at a higher rate. There are also some hospitality homes but these seem to change quickly so try the tourist office lists and ask around. The *79 MacDonald* (☎ 896-5031) at 79 MacDonald St has two rooms; singles/doubles cost $35/45 with a full breakfast included. Bicycles are available. A reader has suggested the *Labrador Friendship Centre* in Happy Valley which acts as a drop-in and community centre primarily for the Native population but where inexpensive rooms are available as well as meals such as caribou stew.

### Getting There & Away

**Air** Goose Bay is well served by air. Provincial Airlines serves Blanc Sablon and Goose Bay from Newfoundland's major towns. Labrador Airways connects to St Anthony and covers all the small communities along the Labrador coast.

**Road** From Happy Valley-Goose Bay, a new road, Hwy 500, which is unsurfaced (ie gravel), runs westward through the heart of Labrador to Churchill Falls and then forks. The No 500 continues south to Wabush, Labrador City and Fermont Quebec.

With this road the entire inland area becomes auto accessible for the first time. Drivers can take vehicles on the ferry from Happy Valley-Goose Bay to Newfoundland allowing for a complete circuit of the region. Potential users note that this road should only be travelled between June and October and that services are minimal. In fact between Happy Valley-Goose Bay and far western Labrador services are available only at towns. There are no road-side gas stations or the like. This makes for some pretty long stretches without a coffee or any other critical requirements.

The drive from Goose Bay to Labrador City takes about nine hours. The section between Goose Bay and Churchill Falls is rough and slow.

Cars can be rented in Happy Valley-Goose Bay at Avis and Tilden both with desks at the airport. Reserve before arrival through any one of their outlets elsewhere in Canada.

**Ferry** The slow coastal service from Lewisporte ties in here but there is also a more direct car ferry from Lewisporte which makes the trip to Goose Bay direct or with just a stop at Cartwright on the way. See Lewisporte in the Central Newfoundland section for details on this marathon 35 to 38-hour ferry ride.

## WESTERN LABRADOR

Accessible from Quebec, everything in this area of Labrador is oversized in the extreme: mega-developments in a mega-landscape which the visitor can explore relatively easily.

Remember that there is a one-hour time difference between Quebec and Labrador City.

### Labrador City/Wabush

These twin mining cities with a collective population of 12,000, just 15 km from Quebec, represent modern, industrial Labrador. The largest open-pit iron ore mine in the world is in Labrador City. Since 1958 a modern town has developed around this mine. Another open-pit mine operates in Wabush. You can tour both facilities. All the resource development in this part of the world is colossal in scale as the tours will reveal. Eighteen-metre-long dumptrucks with three-metre-high tyres are almost like absurd works of art.

There is a regional tourist chalet (☎ 944-7132) in Labrador City in the Arts & Cultural Centre which will help with information on Churchill Falls and other local spots as well as answering questions about the cities here.

The **Height of Land Heritage Centre** (☎ 944-2209) in a former bank is a museum.

Also, paintings by Tom Thompson may be seen in the Labrador City Town Hall.

Most people want to see the land away from town and you don't have to go far to do that. The landscape, a vast expanse of low, rolling, forested mountains interspersed with areas of flat northern tundra, was scraped down by glaciers.

The **Wapusakatto Mountains** are just five km from town and parts have been developed for skiing. About 10 km from Labrador City is **Duley Lake Provincial Park** which even has a wide, long sandy beach and good swimming. There are 100 camping sites here too. Another park, 43 km from Wabush, on the Trans-Labrador Hwy is **Grand Hermine** also with a beach, camping and some fine scenery.

The 15-km-long Menihek hiking trail goes through wooded areas with waterfalls as well as open tundra. Outfitters can take anglers to excellent fishing waters.

Bus tours of the towns or surroundings are available. A real treat is the free lightshow – the aurora borealis, also called the northern lights – about two nights out of every three. Northern Canada is the best place in the world to see them because the magnetic north pole is here. Evidently these otherworldly coloured, waving beams are charged particles from the sun which are trapped in the earth's magnetic field.

Personally, I vote for the spirit theories of the Native peoples. Various possibilities have been recorded. One such Inuit belief is that the shimmering lights are the sky people playing a game of ball. Another is that the lights are unborn children playing. The Ojibway called the lights Waussnodae and believed them to be torches held by their dead grandfathers to light the way along the Path of Souls. The souls of the recently deceased walked this path, the Milky Way, to their final resting place.

**Mark Lightbody**

### Places to Stay & Eat

There are several somewhat pricey hotels and motels some with dining rooms. In Labrador City on Avalon Drive is the *Two Seasons Inn* (☎ 944-2661) with doubles for $83 so you get the idea. The *Carol Inn*

(☎ 944-7736) at 215 Drake Ave has 23 housekeeping units where you can do your own cooking and singles/doubles cost $75/85. The *Wabush Hotel* (☎ 282-3221) is the costliest commercial place at $90 a double. Advance booking is recommended for all places. Ask around for guesthouses but don't bet on finding one.

Most of the eight or so restaurants are in Labrador City and include a couple of pizza places and *Ted's Pub*. Fish and sometimes caribou show up on menus.

## Churchill Falls

Not quite halfway to Goose Bay, modern Churchill Falls developed in the early 1970s is built around one of the largest hydroelectric generating stations in the world. The diverted Churchill River falling over a 300-metre ledge powers the underground turbines and kicks out 550 megawatts, enough to supply almost the entire needs of the New England states. It's quite a piece of engineering. Tours (☎ 709-925-3211) are offered but must be booked at least one day in advance.

The town is connected by road, Hwy 500, to Goose Bay to the east and to Wabush to the west.

Banking, laundry, car repair and gas can all be taken care of in Churchill. This is the only place between Goose Bay and Labrador City with any services or supplies so stock up.

For accommodation there is the central *Churchill Falls Inn* (☎ 925-3211) with a coffee shop and bar; booking ahead is recommended. A single is a relatively low $59, the doubles start at $65.

## Getting There & Away

Transportation here in central and western Labrador, while improving in giant strides, is still an adventure in itself.

**Air** Several airlines connect with Labrador City including Canadian Airlines with their regional partner Air Atlantic from Newfoundland and the rest of Canada. Air Alliance flies in from Quebec City.

**Road** Hwy 500 from Happy Valley-Goose Bay continues from just west of Churchill south to Wabush and Labrador City and then to Fermont, Quebec. From there it becomes mainly surfaced Hwy 389 and continues for 581 km south through the little-developed northern Manicougan District of Quebec, past Manic 5 with its huge dam to Labrador City. It can be driven in one day but it's a long day. Some sections are slow due to roughness or the narrow winding road. Some small bridges are one-way traffic only.

There are motels and campgrounds along the way, for example at Manic 5, and a motel, restaurant and gas station at Bassin Manic 5. For those going north from Baie Comeau, road conditions can be checked with the provincial police in that town. For those going south, if you are in any doubt or are wondering about updates or road improvements the police in Labrador can help.

Back at the Hwy 500 fork at Churchill Falls, a northern branch the No 501, continues to Esker. Esker halfway between Labrador City and Schefferville where the road ends, is really nothing more than a train station.

Tilden and Avis both have offices in Wabush.

**Train** Western Labrador is also accessible by rail. The route begins at Sept-Îles, Quebec (even further east than Baie Comeau). From there catch the Quebec North Shore & Labrador railway to Labrador City or beyond to Esker and Schefferville back in Quebec.

There are no other train routes in Labrador. With the opening of the road from Happy Valley-Goose Bay to Labrador City/Wabush the train is accessible to the eastern portion of Labrador.

In Labrador City the Quebec North Shore and Labrador railway (☎ 944-8205) is at Airport Rd. The one-way adult fare to Sept-

Îles is $48. Through the summer there are two departures weekly. The train has a snack car for light lunches.

See Sept-Îles in the Quebec chapter for more details of the train and trips around the Labrador City area.

# Nova Scotia

Entered Confederation: 1 July 1867
Area: 55,491 sq km
Population: 899,942
Provincial Capital: Halifax

In Nova Scotia, you're never more than 56 km from the sea, a feature which has greatly influenced the history and character of the province.

When Europeans first arrived in what was to become Nova Scotia, much of the land was inhabited by the Micmac nation, the dominant people of the Atlantic region.

For generations the rugged coastline, with its countless bays and inlets, has provided shelter for small fishing villages, especially along the southern shores.

It was here that the first settlers and pirates came, followed by Loyalists and immigrants from across Europe. Fishing remains important, with Lunenburg maintaining a significant east coast fleet and šerving fabulous fresh fish. The *Bluenose*, the boat seen on the Canadian 10-cent coin (dime), was built here.

The typical Maritime scenes and towns along the coast give way to Halifax-Dartmouth, one of the country's most attractive major metropolitan areas – a modern, cosmopolitan urban centre that retains an historic air.

## CLIMATE

The sea tends to keep the weather moderate. Summer and autumn are usually sunny, though the eastern areas and Cape Breton are often windy. Rain is heaviest on the east coast. The entire southern coast from Shelburne to Canso is often wrapped in a morning fog, which may take until noon or later to burn off. Winters can be very snowy.

## ECONOMY

A visitor may not notice it but manufacturing is the most important industry. Shipbuilding, dairy products and paper plants are significant economically. Fishing, of course, is a major business – the catch includes cod, lobster and scallops. Nova Scotia, along with Newfoundland, has been hit hardest by the recently documented decline in fish stocks and the resulting lowering of catch quotas.

## PEOPLE

Today many of the Micmac people remain on their original lands in Cape Breton. The majority of the province's people are now of English, Scottish, Irish and French ancestry.

The Highland Scots landed in familiar-looking Cape Breton in 1773 and thousands more Scots followed to settle Nova Scotia, which means 'New Scotland'. In some areas you can still hear Gaelic spoken; in other areas French culture and language live on.

## INFORMATION
### Provincial Symbols

The provincial flower is the mayflower, the bird, the osprey (unofficial).

### Telephone

The area code for the province is 902.

### Time

The entire province is within the Atlantic time zone.

### Tax

The provincial sales tax is 11%.

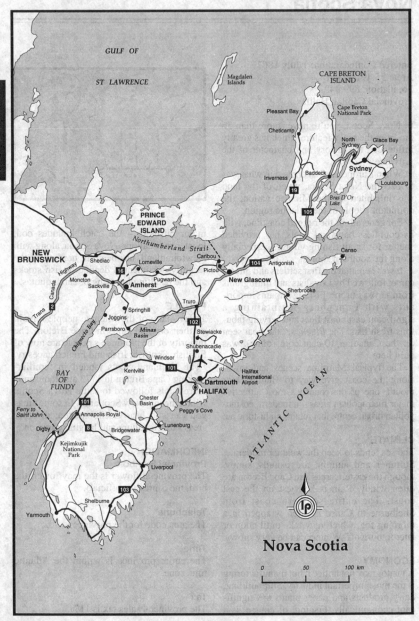

GULF OF
ST LAWRENCE

Magdalen
Islands

CAPE BRETON
ISLAND

Pleasant Bay

Cape Breton
National Park

Cheticamp

North
Sydney

Glace Bay

Inverness

Baddeck

Sydney

19

Louisbourg

Bras D'Or
Lake

105

Canso

PRINCE
EDWARD
ISLAND

Northumberland Strait

NEW
BRUNSWICK

Shediac

Lomeville

Caribou

104

Antigonish

Moncton

Pugwash

Pictou

New Glasgow

Sackville

Amherst

Canada
Highway

Trans

2

Springhill

Truro

Sherbrooke

Joggins

102

Parrsboro

Minas
Basin

Stewiacke

Chignecto Bay

Shubenacadie

Windsor

Halifax
International
Airport

BAY
OF
FUNDY

Kentville

101

Dartmouth
HALIFAX

ATLANTIC OCEAN

Ferry to
Saint John

101

Chester
Basin

Peggy's Cove

Digby

8

Annapolis Royal

Bridgewater

Lunenburg

Kejimkujik
National
Park

Liverpool

103

Shelburne

Yarmouth

Nova Scotia

0          50          100 km

## HIGHLIGHTS

Inland, much of the province is covered with forest, while low hills roll across the north. The Annapolis Valley, famous for its apples, is gentle, scenic farm country – beautiful in springtime with pink and white blossoms. The area contains some of Canada's oldest and most captivating historical features.

The Bay of Fundy region is dominated by the world's highest tides. As a consequence, the rivers carry brackish waters far inland to connect with the 400 or so lakes. Due to the vast number of waterways, canoeing in the province is excellent. Diving all around the coast is also good.

Along the Northumberland Strait, wide sandy beaches washed by the warmest waters around the province offer a place to relax for a day or two.

Visiting rugged, mountainous Cape Breton Island, which shows another side of the varied topography, is the highlight of a trip to Nova Scotia.

The Nova Scotia tourist office has designated 10 different road routes through the province which best show the scenery and sights. These routes are generally on older, smaller roads, not the main highways, and each is marked with roadside symbols. A free booklet detailing all the routes is available and is worth having, although at times it's prone to hyperbole.

Tourists who spend three or more days in the province may become members of the Order of the Good Time. This social organisation was founded at Port Royal (now called Annapolis Royal) in 1606 by the French explorer Samuel de Champlain. Ask about it at information offices. They can also tell you about the provincial farm vacation programmes.

Nova Scotia gets more visitors annually than any of the other Atlantic Provinces and its excellent travel-information network is well geared to tourists. In general prices are a little higher here than in much of the Atlantic region and many of the lodgings and restaurants are a little more up-market and sophisticated.

## ACCOMMODATION

As is the case across all of eastern Canada, the visitor season is quite short, with July and August bringing most travellers. During these two months, accommodation can be scarce in much of the province. It just doesn't pay anyone to add more rooms because of the eight months or so when a room can't be given away. The central and South Shore regions of the province are not as popular as the other areas, where finding a room each night before dark is recommended. From October to May the visitor may find attractions, campgrounds and guesthouses closed.

# Halifax

With a population of 114,450 and nearly three times that in the metropolitan area, Halifax, the capital of Nova Scotia, is the largest city east of Montreal. The city was the home of Canada's first representative government, first Protestant church and first newspaper. Residents are known as Haligonians.

The port here is the busiest on the east coast because it's a year-round harbour – ice forces most others to close in winter. Canada's largest naval base is also here.

Halifax's interesting history is longer than that of other Canadian cities. The area was first settled by Micmac Indians, and Halifax itself was founded in 1749 as a British stronghold with the arrival of 2500 people. The town was actually to be a military base counterbalancing the French fort at Louisbourg on Nova Scotia's south-east tip.

The harbour was used as a British naval base during the American Revolution (1775-83) and the War of 1812. During both World Wars, Halifax was a distribution centre for supply ships heading for Europe, a function which brought many people to the city.

In 1917 a French munitions ship carrying an enormous cargo of TNT collided with another foreign ship in the harbour. The result was the biggest unnatural explosion ever, prior to the A-bombs' being dropped on

Japan in 1945. It is now known as the Great Explosion. Half the city was flattened, 2000 people were killed and windows were broken as far away as Truro. Today the military contributes much to the economy, with six bases nearby. Other major industries are manufacturing, oil refining and food processing.

## ORIENTATION

Halifax sits by one of the world's largest natural harbours, midway along Nova Scotia's south Atlantic shore.

The city lies on a peninsula between the harbour and an inlet called the North West Arm. The downtown area is hilly and the city has parks everywhere. They're best seen from Citadel Hill, which provides views of the town and waterfront if the city is not lost in one of the frequent fogs.

The downtown area, dating from the earliest settlement, extends from Lower Water St on the waterfront and west up to the Citadel, a star-shaped fort on the hill. Cogswell St to the north and Spring Garden Rd to the south mark the other boundaries of the capital's core. Conveniently, much of what is of interest to visitors is concentrated in this area, making walking the best way to get around.

Restoration is a hallmark of the city, particularly down along the water in the Historic Properties area. This is a lively place with restaurants and bars in and amongst some of Halifax's original buildings. Two of the city's strengths are in this blending of the old and the new and in the attractive natural ocean setting. It's a pleasant, worthwhile place to visit.

From this central area the city spreads in three directions. At the extreme east end of the downtown area is the water and the area known as the Historic Properties. This is the original commercial centre of town, now restored and containing offices, shops, restaurants, the tourist office, etc. It's a busy, visitor-oriented place, good for getting a feel for the city.

Up from the Historic Properties there's an interesting mix of historic and contemporary buildings. The streets are wide and there are plenty of trees. At the end of Granville St, Duke St is a small but pleasant pedestrian mall, lined with fine old buildings in Italiante-style dating from about 1860.

Main streets leading west up from the shoreline are Sackville St and Spring Garden Rd. The latter is lined with shops, including grocery stores, restaurants and malls. At the corner of South Park St and Spring Garden Rd are the large Public Gardens, an attractive Victorian city park diagonally opposite Citadel Hill.

Many of the stores, hotels and other complexes of central Halifax, around the juncture of Barrington and Duke Sts, are connected by a completely indoor system of walking paths known as pedways. A map of these connections can be picked up at any tourist office. The city gets its share of inclement weather, and at these times the visitor may find the system helpful.

South of town, at the end of the peninsula and adjacent to North West Arm, is Point Pleasant Park, the city's largest park, which is pleasant indeed, with woods and beaches. South Park St, which becomes Young Ave, will take you there from the downtown area past the very large houses of the city's wealthy district.

Dartmouth, a twin city, lies east across the harbour and has business and residential districts of its own.

Two bridges span the Halifax Harbour, connecting Halifax to Dartmouth and leading to highways north (for the airport) and east. The Macdonald Bridge, running from the eastern end of North St, is closest to downtown. There is a 75 cents toll for cars. You can walk and take a bike, but bicycles can not be ridden. Further north is the MacKay Bridge. A passenger ferry also links the two downtown areas.

The airport is 40 km north-west of town on Hwy 102.

## INFORMATION
### Tourist Offices

You won't have any trouble getting information or maps in Halifax. Outside town is the

NOVA SCOTIA

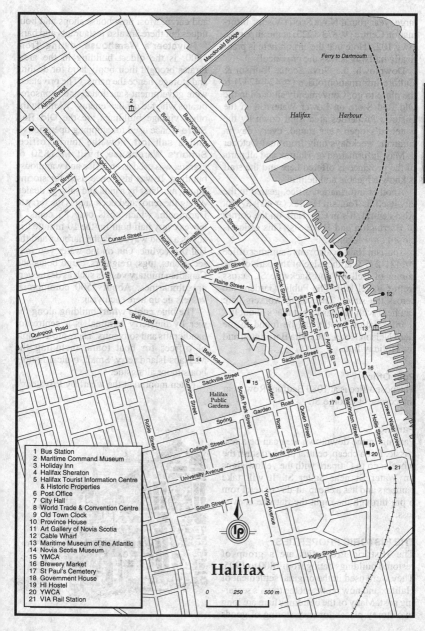

1 Bus Station
2 Maritime Command Museum
3 Holiday Inn
4 Halifax Sheraton
5 Halifax Tourist Information Centre & Historic Properties
6 Post Office
7 City Hall
8 World Trade & Convention Centre
9 Old Town Clock
10 Province House
11 Art Gallery of Novia Scotia
12 Cable Wharf
13 Maritime Museum of the Atlantic
14 Novia Scotia Museum
15 YMCA
16 Brewery Market
17 St Paul's Cemetery
18 Government House
19 HI Hostel
20 YWCA
21 VIA Rail Station

Halifax

0    250    500 m

large, year-round Nova Scotia Visitor Information Centre (☎ 873-1223) at the airport on Hwy 102. (Note that the airport here is practically halfway across the province!)

Downtown, the Nova Scotia Tourism & Culture information office (☎ 424-4247) is the place to go. Conveniently situated in the Old Red Store on Lower Water St, in the Historic Properties area right down by the water, it's open year round, every day in summer, weekdays only from mid-October to May. Information on Halifax and all parts of the province is offered here and the staff is knowledgeable and helpful.

Another information office, geared to the city itself, is Tourism Halifax (☎ 421-8736). Also central, it's in City Hall, on the corner of Barrington and Duke Sts. This office is closed on weekends.

Tourism Halifax also runs a summer office (☎ 421-2772) at the edge of the park on the corner of Bell Rd and Sackville St, across from Citadel Hill. The Public Gardens are across the street. The young workers here can help with the basics but that's about it.

Information booths can be found in the Lord Nelson Hotel, the Delta Barrington and the Holiday Inn.

### Post Office
The post office is at 1080 Bedford Row, near the corner of George St.

### Parking
Parking in the downtown area can be a real hassle. For a cheap, central place to stash the wheels, go to Citipark with the yellow signs on Water St near Salter St. It will take campers and has a cheap all-day ticket. From 6 pm through the night the flat rate is even less.

### THE HISTORIC PROPERTIES
The Historic Properties are a group of restored buildings dating from 1800 to 1905. They were used in the original settlement of Halifax and now represent the town's seafaring past. Many of the buildings here are long two-storey places for easy storing of goods

and cargo. Most now house shops and boutiques but there are also restaurants and bars.

**Privateer's Warehouse**, dating from 1800, is the oldest building in the area. Pirates brought their booty here for dealing and storage, hence the name. (The privateers were government-sanctioned and sponsored pirates who fed off the 'enemy'.) Among the other vintage buildings are the **Old Red Store** – once used for shipping operations – and a **sail loft**, now the tourist office. **Simon's Warehouse**, built in 1850 of granite, was used as an office and warehouse building. It was also once used for storing liquor, and later by a junk and salvage dealer. Along the renovated dock area is the ferry to Dartmouth, which costs only 85 cents. It leaves every half hour for the 10-minute trip and is a good way to see the harbour and the Halifax skyline. Out on the water you may see yachts, tugs, freighters, cargo boats and Canadian military vessels such as destroyers or submarines. About 3500 commercial vessels tie up here each year.

The blue **cable wharf** building along the pier by the ferry terminal is a centre for handicrafts and souvenirs. There are a couple of offices for boat tours, including the McNabs Island ferry. Small, typical fishing boats moor alongside.

Often moored at the wharf by Privateer's

Warehouse is the *Bluenose II*, a replica of Canada's best-known boat.

The original *Bluenose* schooner was built in 1921 in Lunenburg. She never lost a race in her 20-year racing career, and in tribute, the 10-cent coin bears her image. The *Bluenose* has become nearly as familiar a Canadian symbol as the maple leaf. The vessel spends a lot of time goodwill touring. The years and waves have taken their toll and there has been some talk of having to consider a third incarnation.

The *Bluenose II* was launched in 1963 and now has a permanent berth at the Historic Properties when not on display at another Canadian port. Two-hour harbour tours are given on her, but when she's docked you can walk on board, free, to look at this beautiful piece of work.

## MARITIME MUSEUM OF THE ATLANTIC

The large Maritime Museum of the Atlantic (☎ 424-7490) is a must for boat buffs but also has enough interesting displays to warrant a peek by anyone. It's spacious and contains full-scale examples of many regional vessels, with plenty of models, photographs and historical data as well. The lens from a Halifax lighthouse is impressive, but I particularly liked the painted figureheads taken from various ships, many of them wrecks. Also good is a portion of a boat you can enter which sways realistically as though out on the sea. There is a display on the ever-interesting *Titanic* and another on the Great Explosion.

Outside at the dock you can explore the CSS *Acadia*, a retired survey vessel from England. The museum is open from 9.30 am to 5.30 pm Monday to Saturday (until 8 pm on Tuesday) and from 1 to 5.30 pm on Sunday. It's at 1675 Lower Water St, to the west of the Historic Properties, and admission is free.

Also docked here is the HMCS *Sackville*, the last of 122 warships of its kind. It can be boarded daily, with donations going to its much-needed restoration work.

## OCEAN TOUCH TANK

Located near the Sackville ship (see above)

at the dock area at the foot of Price St, the small but popular touch tank affords landlubbers the opportunity of feeling a range of live sea mammals and plants. University students are on hand to answer questions and make handling suggestions. The tank is open every day from 10.30 am during good weather from June to August.

## BREWERY MARKET

Also part of the restored waterfront, this complex is in the Keith's Brewery building, dating from 1820, at 1489 Hollis St. It now contains boutiques, restaurants and a pub or two. It's all new-looking, and seems a bit contrived and lacking in atmosphere compared to what else is around. A farmers' market is held on the lower level on Friday and Saturday from 7 am to 1 pm in summer, on Saturday only the rest of the year.

## HISTORIC DOWNTOWN AREA

The tourist office has maps for a self-guided walking tour of the Historic Properties, the waterfront boardwalk and the old buildings west up the hill from the water. Most of the buildings which made up the early commercial area are marked with plaques giving a brief history.

The brochure adds a few details and makes them easier to find. Using the map, it take about an hour to do the circuit. Descriptions of some of the best spots follow.

### Province House

On Hollis St near Prince St, this fine example of Georgian architecture has been the home of Canada's oldest provincial legislature since 1819. There are free guided tours Monday to Friday from 9 am to 5 pm and on weekends from 10 am to 4 pm.

### Government House

This is between Hollis and Barrington Sts, near the corner of Bishop St. Government House has been the residence of the provincial lieutenant-governor since 1807 (making it Canada's oldest). It was built by Governor John Wentworth.

**NOVA SCOTIA**

## St Paul's Cemetery

Also known as the Old Burying Ground, the cemetery is across the street from Government House, on Barrington St. First used in 1749, it has graves of people from all faiths, many of whom died young. Numerous soldiers, sailors and stories lie buried here.

## St Paul's Church

St Paul's is on Barrington St near Prince St. It was the first Protestant church in Canada (dating from 1749) and the first church of British origin in the new land. It's open to visitors Monday to Friday from 9 am to 5 pm. A guide is on hand to answer questions. There are some intriguing curiosities here, such as the silhouette cast by a certain hole in the stained glass. Another is the piece of metal lodged above the door in the north wall, inside the porch. This is a piece of the *Mont Blanc*, the munitions ship which exploded three km away in Halifax Harbour in 1917.

## City Hall

Built in 1890 at the opposite end of the sunken courtyard from St Paul's Church, City Hall is a gem of Victorian architecture. In summer, visitors may join the mayor for tea Monday to Friday from 3.30 to 4.30 pm.

## Old Town Clock

At the top of George St, at Citadel Hill, stands one of the city's most distinct symbols, the Old Town Clock. The inner workings arrived in Halifax in 1803 after being built in London, England. The tower was erected to a design by Prince Edward, the Duke of Kent, then Commander of the Citadel.

## CITADEL NATIONAL HISTORIC SITE

The Citadel (☎ 425-3923), a huge, oddly angled fort on top of Halifax's big central hill, has always been the city's towering landmark. In 1749, with the founding of Halifax, construction of a citadel began.

In the mid-1750s, the British realised that the crunch was coming with France over possession of the new land. Halifax was a good location for British purposes: it could be used as a centre for ruling over Nova Scotia and, more importantly, as a military base from which to deal with the French, who had forts of their own in Louisbourg and Quebec City.

The fort visible today, built between 1828 and 1861, is actually the fourth one on the site. It is open daily from 9 am to 6 pm in summer, and from 9 am to 5 pm from early September to the middle of June. Admission is $2 in summer, free the rest of the year. I recommend the guided tours, which include theatrical presentations; the movie is also worthwhile. The guide will explain the fort's shape and how, despite appearances, it was not very well designed or constructed.

Also in the compound is the Army Museum, with exhibits relating to Atlantic Canada's military history.

Citadel Hill is a good park in itself and a popular sunbathing spot. There are excellent views in all directions – of the city, Dartmouth and waterfront areas.

## NOVA SCOTIA MUSEUM

The Nova Scotia Museum is not actually a single museum but rather a series of them scattered around the province. This one (☎ 424-7353), at 1747 Summer St, near the corner of Sackville St, south-west of the Citadel, is considered the headquarters of the provincial system. History, wildlife, geology, people and industry are all covered. The three-dimensional animal exhibits are excellent – you feel you can reach out and touch the displays. The fish of Nova Scotia exhibit is also well presented. There's a good history section, with an old stagecoach and a working model of a late-1800s sawmill. Also worth noting is the excellent mushroom display and the collection of Micmac artefacts.

From 1 June to 15 October it is open Monday to Saturday from 9.30 am to 5.30 pm (Wednesday to 8 pm) and on Sunday from 1 to 5.30 pm. Through the above months, admission is charged. The rest of the year it's free but closes at 5 pm each day and is closed all day on Monday.

## MARITIME COMMAND MUSEUM

This museum (☎ 427-8250) is on the Canadian Forces Base (CFB Halifax), off Gottingen St between North and Russell Sts, near Macdonald Bridge. It's in the fine-looking stone building on large grounds protected by numerous cannons. You'll see mementoes like uniforms, medals, etc from the military past of the Maritimes. It's open Monday to Friday from 9.30 am to 6 pm, Saturday and Sunday from 1 to 5 pm.

## TITANIC COLLECTION

Unknown to many, the people of Halifax had a role in another one of the great disasters of the century. Five years before the Great Explosion of 1917, the 'unsinkable' *Titanic* sank off the coast of Newfoundland after hitting an iceberg on her maiden voyage from Southampton, England to New York. Ships from Halifax took part in the rescue operation, although only 705 passengers of the 2227 on board survived. Over 150 recovered bodies were brought to Halifax to be buried.

In the Roy Building, at 1661 Barrington St, the Titanic Collection consists of artefacts from survivors, debris from the wreck, photographs and other matter relating to the saga. The original distress signal sent out from the damaged ship is part of the exhibit.

The Bedford Institute of Oceanography of Nova Scotia (see under Dartmouth later) has for years been involved in *Titanic* research. Expeditions in mini-submarines down the two km to the wreck have taken pictures and even retrieved materials, samples and artefacts. Late in 1993, the Bedford Institute together with the French Institute for Marine Research & Exploration released a report after analysing steel samples of the ship taken from the sea floor. Their conclusion was that the grade of steel used for the ship was as much to blame for the disaster as was the collision with the iceberg. Evidently that type of steel is brittle, and in the cold North Atlantic the resulting structural weaknesses proved catastrophic.

Note that the collection is in a space shared with the Atlantic Arts Alliance Cooperative, so it may be that sign which you see.

## ART GALLERY OF NOVA SCOTIA

The provincial Art Gallery (☎ 424-7542) is housed in the restored heritage Dominion Building of 1868 (once used as the post office), at 1741 Hollis St, across from Province House. Provincial and other Canadian works make up much of the large collection. There are both permanent and changing exhibits. Admission is $2.50 (free on Tuesday). The gallery is open Tuesday to Saturday from 10 am to 5.30 pm. On Sunday it is open in the afternoon only.

## MICMAC HERITAGE GALLERY

Owned and operated by the Micmac people, the gallery exhibits and sells a range of traditional and contemporary work by Native craftspeople, artisans and artists. Two traditional skills, basketry and decorating with porcupine quills, are shown to good advantage in a number of different applications. The contemporary art gallery shows work from across the country.

The gallery is found in the Barrington Place Shops complex on the Granville Level, 1903 Barrington St.

## DISCOVERY CENTRE

The new Discovery Centre (☎ 492-4422) is a hands-on science centre on the upper level of the Scotia Square complex, at the corner of Barrington and Duke Sts. A range of participatory displays and exhibits entertain and educate in matters of chemistry, physics and the like. It is mainly geared to kids but has something for everyone.

The centre is open Tuesday to Saturday from 10 am to 5 pm and on Sunday and Monday from 1 to 5 pm. Outside the summer season, it is closed on Monday (unless it is a school holiday). Admission is $4 per adult, $2.50 for children.

## NOVA SCOTIA SPORT HERITAGE CENTRE

Essentially a sports hall of fame, the centre (☎ 421-1266) is in the World Trade &

Convention Centre, 1800 Argyle St, Suite 403, between George and Prince Sts. It deals with provincial heroes and teams through displays of trophies and photographs. Some of the old equipment is fun to look at. It's open Monday to Friday from 9 am to 4 pm and admission is free.

## HALIFAX PUBLIC GARDENS
The public gardens are a small but pleasant well-kept formal Victorian city park on the corner of South Park St and Spring Garden Rd. The park has a reputation as one of the finest Victorian-style gardens in North America. Bands give concerts in the gazebo on Sunday afternoons throughout the summer.

## POINT PLEASANT PARK
Point Pleasant Park is highly recommended. Walking trails, picnic spots, a restaurant, a beach and an old Martello tower – a round defence structure – are all found within this 75-hectare wooded sanctuary. There are lots of joggers and sunbathers in the popular park, and good views all the way around the perimeter. No cars are allowed.

The park is at the far southern end of town, at the tip of the peninsula. The No 9 bus links the park with the downtown Scotia Centre until 9 pm, or you can drive to the park's edge. Whichever way you come, check out the size of the houses along Young St.

At the city edge of the park is the Port of Halifax, a very busy terminal with containers piled high and ships from everywhere steadily coming and going. Walk out to the lighthouse by the port for great views and a peek at the shipping activity; kids will be tossing in lines hoping for the big catch.

An interesting historical aside is that the park still belongs to the British Government, who have rented it out on a 999-year lease at the rate, to Canadian taxpayers, of 10 cents per year.

## YORK REDOUBT
The remains of a 200-year-old fort make up this National Historic Site which overlooks the harbour from a bluff just south of the North West Arm (south of the centre). It was designed to protect the city from attack by sea and is built at the narrowest point of the outer harbour. The site was used in various capacities by the military as late as 1956.

Aside from the view, there are mounted guns, a Martello tower and historical information and displays. The grounds are open all year but the buildings are open only from 15 June to Labour Day, 10 am to 6 pm.

## SEAVIEW PARK & AFICVILLE
At the north end of Barrington St, under the MacKay Bridge to Dartmouth, Seaview affords good views of the Bedford Basin. Footpaths wind through the largely open-style park. The park also has an interesting historic side to it. In the 1840s a Black community, known as Africville, was established here. Many of its members were former slaves from the USA. It remained until the 1960s, when the area was demolished and the residents moved south toward central Halifax. A visit after dark is not recommended.

## MCNABS ISLAND
Out in the harbour and easily seen from York Redoubt, this small island makes a good break from the busy and/or hot city. The island offers guided walks, beaches, picnic tables and hiking. There's also a teahouse for basic snacks or seafood. Ferries depart for the island through the day from the dock area, and tickets ($8) can be bought at the little office by Cable Wharf Market.

## HEMLOCK RAVINE
A system of linked walking trails winds through this large wooded estate once called home by Edward, Duke of Kent, Queen Victoria's dad. It includes a view of Bedford Basin, and amidst the gardens are some very impressive 30-metre-tall trees. To reach it by car, drive along the Bedford Hwy (Hwy 2) past Birch Cove and then look for the signs. It's not far and, once there, feels a long way from a city.

**BEACHES**

If you're looking for a beach, try Black Rock Beach, in Point Pleasant Park; Crystal Beach, 20 km west of town, with some areas for nude sunbathing; or Queensland Beach, 35 km west of town.

**ACTIVITIES**

**Canoeing**

To rent a canoe in Halifax for exploring nearby waterways, try the Trail Shop (☎ 423-8736). They can also give you some tips on good spots to go. The tourist office has information on canoeing too. The city's Recreation Department offers canoe rentals on the North West Arm, along which you can paddle.

**Diving**

There are about 50 wrecks at the mouth of Halifax Harbour and good diving along the coast. For information and equipment rentals, try the Aqua Dive Shop (☎ 469-6948), at 77 Prince Albert Rd in Dartmouth.

**ORGANISED TOURS**

A wide selection of tours by bus, boat or on foot is available. See the tourist office for a complete list, but some of the more established and interesting ones follow.

Gray Line (☎ 454-9321), a tour bus company represented across Canada, also has tours in and around town and they will pick you up from your hotel. Gray Line always has competitive fares and is reliable. The 2½-hour town tour is $15 and takes in many of the essential sites. They also have trips further afield.

Double Decker (☎ 420-1155) offers tours in London-style buses which leave from the Historic Properties several times a day. A ticket costs $13, less for kids and seniors. The tours run from the middle of June to the middle of October.

Cabana Tours (☎ 455-8111) can supply guides, and has city bus trips but also offers good, longer day trips to various points around the province (such as Peggy's Cove, Lunenburg and the Annapolis Valley) for relatively small groups. The Peggy's Cove

trip, for example, takes four hours and costs $22. Full-day trips are about $50. They pick up from many points and hotels around town.

The beauteous *Bluenose II* (☎ 422-2678), perhaps the country's best known boat, takes visitors out on two-hour harbour sailing cruises for a very reasonable $14. Usually the sails are not unfurled until the boat is at the outer reaches of the harbour, and it only leaves on clear days. Ask about tickets at the dock or at the Red Store tourist office, or call the above number and book ahead of time.

Murphy's on the Water (☎ 420-1015), from Cable Wharf at the Historic Properties, has various boat tours of the Halifax Harbour. The two-hour narrated trip aboard the *Harbour Queen* goes past both new and old city landmarks and at $13.50 is pretty good value. The boat carries 200 people and has both open and closed decks, a snack counter and a bar. From 15 June to 25 August there are four runs daily. Out of peak season there are two trips daily, and in winter they close down completely. Dinner cruises are an option. A different boat provides a more extensive tour taking in a wider area. Murphy's also operates the *Mar II*, a very handsome sailboat, for trips around the harbour.

A number of private entrepreneurs offer fishing trips, tours of the harbour or charters on yachts, the latter especially on weekends and holidays (in summer). Shop around the boats tied along the wharf area. There's likely to be one with moonlight sailings or some other unique angle which may appeal. Some offer whale-watching, but personally I'd be a bit sceptical, as this is not a prime area for that possibility. If you have time, try the trips from Digby Neck in north-western Nova Scotia.

Halifax Ghost Walk (☎ 469-6716) provides a two-hour evening walk beginning at 8.30 pm through July and August, from the Old Town Clock. The tour features tales of pirates, buried treasure and ghosts from the old city's lore.

More matter-of-fact walking tours around

the historic sections of the city are offered very cheaply by D Tours (☎ 429-6415). Also, the tourist office has a self-guided walking-tour brochure which denotes the historical and architectural highlights. Free-wheeling Adventures (☎ 857-3600), RR1, Hubbards, Nova Scotia B0J 1T0, operates well-organised, multi-day, all-inclusive bicycle tours to a number of the special places around Atlantic Canada, such as the Cabot Trail. Good meals and accommodation are included. Most of the tours are in the $1000 vicinity.

## FESTIVALS
July

*Nova Scotia Tattoo* – This event is held in Halifax during the first week of July (or close to it) every year. It's called the province's 'greatest entertainment extravaganza'.

*Halifax Natal Day* – A major event held at the end of July, featuring a parade, street parties, boat races, bridge walk, concerts and a fireworks display.

*Schooner Races* – The city also hosts these races in July.

*The DuMaurier Atlantic Jazz Festival* – This festival takes place at the end of July.

August

*Halifax Buskers Fest* – This festival now held annually draws street entertainers from far and wide to perform at a number of places around town, mainly along the waterfront, and is a lot of fun. These guys are no slouches! It runs for 10 days in August.

## PLACES TO STAY
### Camping

You can camp right in the city of Dartmouth at the *Shubie Municipal Campground* (☎ 464-2334) in Shubie Park, on the shore of Lake Charles. It's on Jaybee Drive near the Shubenacadie Canal – call for precise directions.

Laurie Provincial Park (☎ 861-1623) is on Route 2 six km north of Hwy 102, at the village of Grand Lake on the lake called Shubenacadie Grand Lake. It's strictly first come first served – no reservations are taken.

Going west along Hwy 333 there are several campgrounds within 25 km of town. *Seaside Camping* (☎ 823-2732), on Route 333 at Glen Margaret, is open from the beginning of June to the end of September. Also at Glen Margaret is the large *Wayside Camping Park* (☎ 823-2547, 1-800-565-7105), with both tenting and RV areas. *King Neptune Campground* (☎ 823-2582) is three km west of Peggy's Cove, at Indian Harbour.

*Woodhaven Park* (☎ 835-2271) is in Hammond Plains, a small town near Bedford just off Hwy 213, about 15 minutes' drive north of Halifax.

### Hostels

The newly moved HI *Halifax Heritage House Hostel* (☎ 422-3863) is perfectly located in a fine historic house at 1253 Barrington St which was formerly operated as a B&B. The hostel is an easy walk to the VIA Rail station or to downtown and the waterfront. There's room for 50 guests and features include cooking facilities, an outdoor patio and small travel shop. Family rooms are available. Prices are $12.75 for members, $15.75 for nonmembers, and check-in is from 5 to 9 pm. The hostel is open all year. From the airport, the shuttle bus goes to the nearby Hilton Hotel. From the bus depot, take the No 7 bus south from the corner of Robie and Almon Sts to the corner of Barrington and South Sts. The hostel can be seen from this corner.

The HI (Hostelling International) Canada office (☎ 425-5450) office for the province is at 5516 Spring Garden Rd, for any information on hostelling in the region.

The *YMCA* (☎ 422-6437) is in an excellent location at 1565 South Park St, across from the public gardens and very near Citadel Hill. Single rooms for men and women are $26 and a room for couples goes for $35. The weekly rate is cheaper. There's a small, cheap cafeteria and you can use facilities like the gym and swimming pool. It's open all year.

The *YWCA* (☎ 423-6162), for women only, is at 1239 Barrington St, between the city centre and the VIA Rail station. There are 30 rooms; singles/doubles cost $22/34 or you can take half a double for $17 and they'll pair you up. Good weekly rates are available.

Halifax has the highest ratio of educational facilities per capita on the continent. This is good for the traveller, not just in the enjoyment of the erudite citizenry but in being able to take advantage of the abundance of economical rooms offered in dormitories during the summer months.

At *Dalhousie University*, rooms are available from mid-May to mid-August in the Howe and Sherref Hall residences. Contact Room 120 in the Dalhousie Student Union Building (☎ 494-3831), 6136 University Ave. Both are on the campus: Howe residence is on the corner of Coburg Rd and LeMarchant St; Sherref Hall is on the corner of South and Oxford Sts. Reservations are required. Singles/doubles cost $29/38 with breakfast. For students with ID, singles/doubles cost $17/22 without breakfast. All three meals are available inexpensively.

Rooms may also be available from mid-May to mid-August at *Fenwick Place*, an off-campus, high-rise residence at 5599 Fenwick St. For information call the Accommodation Office (☎ 424-2075) in the building. It's central and close to the university. If you cannot get an answer, try the Dalhousie number.

The *Technical University of Nova Scotia*, or TUNS (☎ 420-7780), also has rooms from mid-May to the end of August. Singles/doubles cost $23/38; students pay $20/34. It's off Barrington St on Bishop St, a 10-minute walk east from the downtown core. Free laundry services are included and there is a cafeteria.

*Mount St Vincent University* rents rooms from 15 May to 15 August; contact the Conference Officer (☎ 457-6286) at 166 Bedford Hwy (Hwy 2) on the campus. Student rates are $20/32; others pay $26/39. They also offer excellent weekly and monthly rates, especially for students. Meals are available and there is a coin laundry. The university is a 15-minute drive west of town on the Bedford Hwy and overlooks the Bedford Basin.

Yet another university with accommodation is *St Mary's University* (☎ 420-5486), which is also cheap and not far from the

centre, at 923 Robie St. Singles/doubles are $22/32 and there are two-room self-contained units, which are good for families at $60.

## B&Bs, Tourist Homes & Hotels

Halifax is blessed with plentiful, moderately priced, central, good-value accommodation. In fact, for quality and selection downtown, it's one of the country's best cities. There are many B&Bs and guesthouses in town and over in Dartmouth as well. Some especially fine ones, though more costly, are found in heritage houses and mansions.

Unlike many cities, there are no B&B agencies in Halifax, but everybody does quite well working independently. Through the summer months, this popular town does fill up, so don't leave finding a place until too late in the day.

The *Old 362* (☎ 422-4309), at 1830 Robie St, is top choice for a low-price B&B. It's small, with just three rooms, and isn't fancy but is pleasant and comfortable in an understated way. Owner Carolyn Smedley has done some travelling of her own and understands what a budget traveller is looking for. Singles are $30 to $40 and doubles are $45, including a good, complete breakfast. Guests may also use the upstairs facilities to make their own tea and coffee.

The plain, straightforward *Fountain View Guesthouse* (☎ 422-4169) is the bright blue place with white trim at 2138 Robie St, between Compton Ave and Williams St, across from the park and west of Citadel Hill. It's reliable, consistent and, like the Old 362, open all year. Halifax Common is across the street and the Citadel is within walking distance. The seven simple rooms, all with TV, go for $24 to $28 a single, $24 to $30 a double, plus tax. Each extra person costs an additional $5. It's popular, so try in the morning after guests may have left. The owner, Helen Vickery, can often fix you up somewhere nearby if she's booked out.

The well-established *Waken 'n' Eggs B&B* (☎ 422-4737) is within walking distance of the downtown area, in a restored house at 2114 Windsor St. Singles/doubles cost

$35/45 with shared bath, $5 more for private facilities. All prices include breakfast.

At 1520 Robie St, the *Illusions Tourist Home* (☎ 425-6733) is reasonably priced, with singles from $30 to $35 and doubles for $40. It's open only from April to October. This is one of the few guesthouses which permits smoking. Guests share the bath. Again, this is a central location.

Also open for the summer only is the *Birdland B&B* (☎ 443-1055), at 14 Bluejay St. It's out of the centre, close to Mt St Vincent University, but it's quiet and the prices are low. Singles/doubles are just $25/35 and that includes a full breakfast. Triples are especially good value at $45 or $50. It's open from June to October. Cyclists, children and pets are all welcome. The hostess, Diana, knows the city and environs and can make suggestions and recommendations.

The *Running Lights Inn* (☎ 423-9873) is a three-storey house at 2060 Oxford St, just off Quinpool Rd. It's neat and clean, but a little overpriced for its style. Singles/doubles are $32/39 without bath, $48/60 with. A simple continental breakfast is included. The more expensive top-floor unit comes with kitchenette. Smokers can indulge without being asked to step outside. This one is also open year round.

The spacious, comfortable *Fresh Start B&B* (☎ 453-6616) is in a big, old house at 2720 Gottingen St. It's tastefully decorated but not prissy, well kept but relaxed. There are five rooms, priced from $40/45 a single/double. Rooms with private bath are more costly. Prices include an excellent, huge hot and cold breakfast served in the roomy dining room. It's open all year and prices drop after the summer season.

The only drawback to this recommended place is the neighbourhood. The B&B's immediate surroundings are fine but much of Gottingen St and its side streets can be seedy. Some people will feel uncomfortable walking to and fro, and women alone, especially, should probably not consider doing so after dark. If you're driving, though, don't think twice about it, and there is on-site

parking. Also, buses do run up and down Gottingen St.

*Twin Elms Hotel* (☎ 423-8974), at 5492 Inglis St, near the park, has rooms at $42/53 for singles/doubles and offers good weekly rates for the singles. The same owners operate the good-value *Harvey House Inn* (☎ 423-4140), at 5220 Harvey St. The huge front rooms with shared kitchen and bathroom are $40 and include two double beds and three sofas!

The following places are in the next bracket up and tend to be larger, more expensive and often in heritage or historical houses or buildings.

For hotels try the *Gerrard* (☎ 423-8614), at 1234 Barrington St. It's a small place in a good location, and the building is an historic residence built in 1860. There are nine rooms ($35/50 a single/double) and free coffee and parking are offered.

The *Queen St Inn* (☎ 422-9828) is at 1266 Queen St, near Morris St. It's also an old house dating from about 1860, with six tastefully decorated rooms, all different. Singles/doubles cost $40/45.

The *King Edward Inn* (☎ 422-3266, 1-800-565-5464) is an impressive-looking restored Victorian inn looking almost out of place standing graciously at 2400 Agricola St. There are over 40 well-decorated singles/doubles from $50/85, with continental breakfast. The Citadel is an easy walk.

Immaculately kept and finished is the *Halliburton House Inn* (☎ 420-0658), at 5184 Morris St, built in 1820. It has antiques, a library and a pleasant garden. The 30 rooms start at $85/100 for singles/doubles, with suites at additional cost. Most rooms come with private bath and all prices include a continental breakfast.

A number of the more traditional, large corporate hotels are also in the central core. The *Prince George* (☎ 425-1986), for example, is ideally situated, on the corner of George and Price Sts, close to the Citadel and the waterfront. A double here will set you back $160 a night.

There are also places of various sorts way out at the airport, if you have to be out this far.

## Motels

Motels tend to be a little expensive and are clustered along the No 2, Bedford Hwy, north-west of town along the bay called Bedford Basin. They offer good views of the bay and cool breezes; bus Nos 80 or 81 go into town, a 15-minute drive away.

The *Travellers Motel* (☎ 835-3394, 1-800-565-3394), open year round, is right at the city limits. The small, simple cottages (rather than the modern motel units) are the best buy, at $35 for two people with shower, TV and pool.

The *Econo Lodge* (☎ 443-0303, 1-800-561-9961), the big brown place at 560 Bedford Hwy, has 33 fully equipped rooms at $51/58 for singles/doubles. Breakfast is available and there's a pool.

A third choice is the *Bluenose Days Inn* (☎ 835-3388), at 636 Bedford Hwy. Singles/doubles cost $50/58. Breakfasts, at extra cost, are served from 7 to 11 am. Off-season rates are available from 1 October to 15 May. It's away from the road and is quiet.

Further out is *Stardust Motel* (☎ 835-3316), 1067 Bedford Hwy, which has 51 rooms, 31 with kitchenette. Singles/doubles cost $50 to $55, more with cooking facilities.

## PLACES TO EAT

Halifax has a good selection of restaurants offering a variety of foods in all price ranges, and generally the quality is high.

For breakfast, the *Athens*, on the corner of Barrington and Blowers Sts, offers the works for $2.99; or try *Smitty's* across from the Public Gardens, on the corner of Tower and Spring Garden Rds, for inexpensive pancake breakfasts and limitless coffee refills.

Down Spring Garden Rd, an area of recent regentrification, the cheap food market in the Spring Garden Place Mall, on the corner of Dresden Place, is a cut above the usual mall fare, with soups, salads and sandwiches. The Greek place has some tasty dishes.

At *Juicy Jane's*, 1723 Barrington St, they sell good sandwiches to take out.

The *Midtown Tavern*, on the corner of Prince and Grafton Sts, is highly recommended – a good example of the Canadian

workers' tavern. It's packed with locals at lunch and is noisy, friendly and cheap. An excellent sirloin steak with vegetables, French fries and coleslaw all washed down with draught by the glass won't even dent the wallet.

The *Bluenose*, on the corner of Duke and Hollis Sts, is another place packed with locals at lunch. It's cheap, casual, good for kids and has all the basics.

Halifax is well blessed with pubs, and many are good for a meal. The *Thirsty Duck* is at 5470 Spring Garden Rd; go through the store and up the stairs. They've got burgers, fish & chips, etc, and draught beer at low prices. There's an outdoor patio too.

The *Granite Brewery*, at 1222 Barrington St, is more up-market and brews its own beer, which is very good. The food, too, should not be ignored; try the jambalaya.

Several other pubs can be found in the mall area of Granville St on the corner of Duke St. Both the *Split Crow* and the *Peddlar's Pub* have outdoor sections and the latter has live music on Saturday afternoons. The Peddlar's serves mainly a variety of hamburgers, at $3 to $4.

Also for lunch or dinner, *Satisfaction Feast* is a well-established vegetarian restaurant. It's at 1581 Grafton St, in the pale blue building, open from 11 am to 9 pm. It's recommended and a meal is always under $10. The spinach-and-cheese curry is definitely worth considering. They now also have a Sunday brunch ($8) and even offer a children's menu.

*Lawrence of Oregano* has a spaghetti special that's hard to beat if you're economising: from 4 to 8 pm, dinner with garlic bread is just $3.95. Other Italian dishes cost about $7. It's at 1712 Argyle St, opposite the park.

There are two places for East Indian food. The *Guru*, 1580 Argyle St, is good, but with the cheapest dishes at $7, it has become a little expensive. Still, you can't argue with the quality. The all-you-can-eat lunch buffets are very good value, particularly the vegetarian one, which is $5.50. It's closed on Sunday and Monday and there is no lunch on

Saturdays. Cheaper is the *Chicken Tandoor*, open for dinners only, with dishes from $6. It's downstairs at 1264 Barrington St and is closed on Tuesday.

Halifax also has a good Vietnamese restaurant. The casual *King Spring Roll* is at 1284 Barrington St, out towards the train station. It offers tasty food, an extensive menu and low prices and serves reasonably priced curry dishes, some with vermicelli noodles and some with a favourite South-East Asian ingredient, lemon grass. A meal can be had for under $10. It's open daily from 11.30 am to 10 pm.

Another fine, inexpensive place to check out is *Kit's Ethnic Delight*, found incongruously in the Park Lane Shopping Centre, 5657 Spring Garden Rd. Most of the food is Sri Lankan but there are some East Indian and Singaporean-style dishes, too. The food is very good and the prices are low. It's closed on Sundays.

Continuing with the ethnic places there is the small, cosy but much more expensive *Czech Inn*, a local favourite, at 5237 Blowers St, with schnitzels, borscht and the like. A full meal for two with wine and dessert will set you back about $70. Nearby, at 5215 Blowers St, downtown, the lower-priced *Hungary Hungarian* (run by the same man) specialises in goulashes.

And there is seafood here, of course. For a splurge night out there is the *Silver Spoon*, on the 2nd floor of the stone building at 1813 Granville St. The menu is extensive and includes a range of seafoods. This is not an inexpensive restaurant but the food is prepared with interesting sauces and spices and in unusual combinations. It's closed on Sundays. The good desserts can be enjoyed on their own in the downstairs café. The huge *McKelvie's*, at 1680 Lower Water St, and the *Five Fishermen*, 1740 Argyle St, are also established seafood places with meals from $14 and up. McKelvie's has a cheaper dinner menu offered from 4 to 6 pm.

The *Sheraton*, beside the Historic Properties, has a $15 lobster buffet outside on the patio every evening through the summer, with entertainment provided.

Cogswell St and its continuation, Quinpool Rd, are commercial streets with plenty of eating spots. If you crave fish & chips, the place is *Camille's*, at 6443 Quinpool Rd.

All over town you'll see chip wagons, which are always good for a quick snack of decent French fries. Try in particular *Bud the Spud*, who parks on Spring Garden Rd outside the library, near Grafton St.

The *Trident Booksellers & Café*, at 1570 Argyle St, with the large stained-glass piece in the window, is unbeatable for lingering with a coffee or pot of tea. The various Italian coffees, from espresso to lattes, are good and cheap, and when you've finished with the newspaper, the other half of the café has a fine selection of books, new and used. This very comfortable refuge is open every day.

Lastly, the *Cave*, tucked in the little doorway at 5244 Blowers St, is open until 4.30 am on weekends. Down in the basement, this small bistro offers good desserts and is particularly well known for its cheesecake.

For do-it-yourself ocean fare, go to *Fisherman's Market*, in the white building beside the ferry terminal. Boiled lobster is $6.99 a pound (500 grams) – a one-pounder being the usual meal and as small as they can legally catch them (they're also available live). *Mary Jane's Alternative Tastes* is a health-food store at 1313 Hollis St, near Morris St.

## ENTERTAINMENT

Halifax is lively at night and has an active pub and music scene.

*Privateer's Warehouse*, in the Historic Properties (near the *Bluenose II's* docking area, on the waterfront), with two restaurants, also has a busy, inexpensive bar on the lower level. The *Lower Deck* often presents Maritime folk music – good stuff. The long wooden tables are like those in an old-style beer house.

*Scoundrels*, at 1786 Granville St, is a popular pub-style spot with no cover charge. *Secretary's*, on Sackville St near Granville

St, is definitely not highbrow, with lots of contests and hijinks for young drinkers.

The *Misty Moon* (☎ 422-5871), on the corner of Barrington and Sackville Sts, is one of the best known rock bars. Sometimes it stages well-known bands from across Canada, and they're nearly always good ones. The Moon is open seven days a week until 3 am. Admission varies but can be high.

The large, loud *New Palace Cabaret* (☎ 429-5959), 1721 Brunswick St, across from the Citadel, has rock and blues bands nightly.

There are several pubs with no admission fees in the downtown Historic Properties section – along and around Hollis and Granville Sts.

The Harbour Folk Society (☎ 425-3655) presents informal concerts on the first Saturday of every month as well as an open mike Wednesday evenings at the *Earl of Dalhousie Pub*. Call for details.

### Performing Arts
The Symphony Nova Scotia plays the *Rebecca Cohn Auditorium* (☎ 421-7311), at 1646 Barrington St. The *Dalhousie Arts Centre* (☎ 424-2646) at the university is a major performance venue for theatre, dance, etc. International Artists perform at the *Halifax Metro Centre* (☎ 451-1221), at 5284 Duke St.

The *Neptune Theatre* (☎ 429-7070) is the city's leading theatre venue.

### Cinema
For repertory films there's *Wormwood's Cinema* (☎ 422-3700), 2015 Gottingen St.

### GETTING THERE & AWAY
#### Air
Air Canada (☎ 429-7111) has services to Montreal ($280) and Toronto ($360). Canadian Airlines (☎ 427-5500) and Air Canada also both fly to St John's, Newfoundland.

#### Bus
The principal Nova Scotian bus line is the Acadian line, which connects with the New Brunswick SMT lines. There are also a couple of smaller, regional lines which service specific regions only. They all use the Acadian bus depot (☎ 454-9321) at 6040 Almon St, which runs south off Robie St, west of the Citadel. The No 3 city bus on Robie St goes from the depot into town and back.

One Acadian line runs through the Annapolis Valley and down to Yarmouth. Others cover the central region, the Northumberland Shore and parts of Cape Breton.

Following are the one-way fares to several destinations. To North Sydney (one express service daily and other milk runs) it's $42, to Yarmouth $37, Amherst $25, Saint John in New Brunswick $52 and Fredericton $58.

The MacKenzie Bus Line serves Nova Scotia's South Shore between Halifax, Lunenburg, Bridgewater and Yarmouth.

Zinck's bus company runs services along the Eastern Shore from Halifax to Sherbrooke, stopping at all the small villages along the way. It runs once a day (except Sunday) eastbound and every day (except Sunday and Monday) westbound.

#### Train
The VIA Rail station (☎ 429-8421, 1-800-561-3952) is a bit of a walk, six blocks out along Hollis St, from the downtown area. It's on Terminal Rd by the big old Halifax Hilton Hotel and is a beautiful example of Canadian train-station architecture. Here as elsewhere, however, services have been cut considerably, and the train is more useful for reaching out-of-province destinations than for getting around Nova Scotia. Services to Saint John, New Brunswick ($55) depart on Monday, Thursday and Saturday at 1 pm. Trains to Montreal ($143) depart at 2 pm daily (except Tuesday), passing through Maine, USA, and arriving the next morning, about 20 hours later. To avoid unnecessary complications, make sure your visas and documents are in order if you're not North American.

Big money can be saved by booking a week ahead.

#### Car
Byways (☎ 429-0092), at 2156 Barrington

St, charges $43 per day with unlimited free km or $230 a week with no km charge at all.

Other car-rental places in town are Budget (☎ 454-8501), at the corner of Hollis and Sackville Sts in the Ultramar gas station, and Avis (☎ 423-6303), on Scotia Square. Both have offices at the airport, where there are also several other car-rental places.

## GETTING AROUND
### To/From the Airport
It's a long way out on Hwy 102, north towards Truro.

There are no city buses to the airport There is, though, the Aerocoach City Shuttle (☎ 468-1228, 873-3525). It runs between the airport and the downtown centre, with stops at several of the major central hotels. The fares are no bargain, at $11/18 one way/return. On weekends and holidays, call ☎ 454-2490. The 33-km trip takes about 45 minutes. Allow 90 minutes before flight time.

An alternative is Share-A-Cab (☎ 429-5555). Call at least three hours before flight time and they'll find other passengers and pick you up. The price works out about the same as the bus.

### Bus
Metro Transit (☎ 421-6600) runs the good, inexpensive city bus system. Call for route and schedule information.

The No 1 bus goes from Halifax Shopping Centre, through town and along the Bedford Hwy, where the motels are. Bus Nos 7 and 80 leave from town for the bus depot.

### Ferry
A ferry runs continuously from near the Historic Properties dock across the bay to the city of Dartmouth. A ticket is 85 cents one way and the ride makes a nice, short mini-tour of the harbour. Ferries run every 15 minutes until 6 pm, then every 30 minutes. The last one is at 11.30 pm. On Sunday they run from noon to 5.30 pm.

### Bicycle
Bicycles can be rented at the Trail Shop

(☎ 423-8736), 6210 Quinpool Rd. They have hourly or daily rentals. The Trail Shop is also good for camping supplies.

For any bike information or to join a bicycle tour of the city or Halifax region, call the Velo Bicycle Club (☎ 443-5199).

### Rickshaw
Powered by muscular young men, real old-style Asian rickshaws can be hired around the downtown area.

## DARTMOUTH
Dartmouth is Halifax's counterpart, a short distance north-west across the Halifax Harbour. However, the similarities end with the waterfront location of the central area. Dartmouth is its own city of 70,000 people spread over a large area, and compared with Halifax, is more residential and the city centre is less commercial. The downtown area lacks the history, charm and bustle of Halifax. With a few exceptions, there is little to interest the visitor on this side of the harbour. The redeveloped waterfront and older section near the Halifax-Dartmouth ferry terminal are of minor appeal. The large ferry terminal complex is known as Alderney Gate.

The fact that the city has 23 lakes within its boundaries will suit those seeking accessible water activities. Many of these lakes are good for swimming, seven have supervised beaches, some are stocked with fish and there's in-town boating and canoeing. Most popular of the beaches are Birch Cove and Graham's Grove, both on Lake Bannock.

The city was founded in 1750, one year after Halifax, when Governor Cornwallis sent troops over to get wood for construction and fuel. Sort of makes you wonder how congenial a guy he was, doesn't it?

Today the two are connected by passenger ferry and two bridges – the 'old' Macdonald Bridge and, further inland, the 'new' MacKay Bridge.

The ferry from Halifax lands you at the centre of things in Dartmouth.

## Orientation

Alderney Gate houses, in addition to the ferry terminal, the Dartmouth Public Library, city offices, a food court and some shops.

Portland St, running up from the ferry terminal, is the main street. Several years ago it was completely overhauled, with trees planted and the sidewalks widened. Unfortunately there isn't much along it and the stores and businesses seem to be having a tough time. What there is includes several inexpensive restaurants, pizza joints, a couple of antique/junk shops and a bar or two of dubious character.

There are, though, a number of historic sites near the waterfront and the neighbouring downtown area. You can pick up a walking-tour guide at a tourist office in either city. Buildings in old Dartmouth are primarily made of wood, rather than of brick or stone as in Halifax.

Beside the large ferry terminal is a small park with good views. A walking path leads along the water from either side of the terminal but extends further on the park side. From the park, Halifax-Dartmouth Industries, a shipyard, can be seen.

Beside the docks shipyard in Dartmouth Cove is the home of Canada's largest coastguard base. The distinctive red-and-white ships are used for search and rescue, icebreaking, maintaining coastal navigational aids and responding to any ocean emergency. Also based at the site is a fleet of helicopters, which has been in Dartmouth for about 90 years.

Micmac Mall is the largest shopping centre in the Maritimes.

## Information

There is a tourist booth for Dartmouth in the ferry terminal on the Halifax side, near where the tickets are bought. The main Dartmouth information office, Dartmouth Tourism (☎ 464- 2220), is at 100 Wyse Rd, on the corner of Alderney Drive, to the west of the downtown area in Dartmouth. It is right beside the Dartmouth Heritage Museum.

## Shubenacadie Canal

A little further around the corner from the shipyards is the Shubenacadie Canal Interpretive Centre, at 140 Alderney Drive. The canal connects Dartmouth (through a series of waterways, lakes and locks) with the Bay of Fundy, on the other side of the province. Built in the mid-1800s along an old Micmac portage route, much of the canal has now been restored. It's used by canoeists, but parks and various historic sites along it can be reached by road.

The interpretive centre has some information on the whole system but mainly deals with the historic marine 'railway' which moved vessels from the harbour inland a couple of hundred metres to where the interconnecting water system really began. It's open every day from May to September (afternoons only on weekends) and admission is free.

For more details on the entire canal and its history and a look at two of the restored locks, visit the **Fairbanks Centre** (☎ 462-1826), 54 Locks Rd, at Lake Charles in north Dartmouth. It's open daily through the summer (afternoons only on weekends).

## Dartmouth Heritage Museum

The museum is at the junction of Alderney Drive and Wyse Rd, about a 15-minute walk left off the Halifax ferry. It houses an eclectic collection pertaining to the city's natural and human history and includes some Native Indian artefacts and crafts, various tools and fashions and industrial bric-a-brac. The museum is free and is open all day Monday to Friday, and on Saturday afternoons. Next door is the tourist office.

## Evergreen House

Built for a judge in 1862, Evergreen House, part of the Heritage Museum, is a fine example of a 19th-century house for the well-to-do. Many of the 20 rooms are open to the public and have been furnished in the style of the 1880s. Admission is free and the house is open daily in summer (afternoons only on weekends). The address is 26 Newcastle St, which is in the vicinity of the Shubenacadie Interpretive Centre.

## Other Historic Places

At 59 Ochterloney St, near the museum and tourist office and within walking distance of the ferry, is the **Quaker Whaler House**, the oldest house in the Halifax area, having been built in 1786. The Quakers came to the region as whalers from New England. Guides in costume lead visitors around the house.

There is a **farm museum** at 471 Poplar Drive, out of the centre.

## Moosehead Brewery

Free tours of the plant (☎ 468-7040), at 656 Windmill Rd, are offered through the summer months. Look for the big moose.

## Bedford Institute of Oceanography

Just outside Dartmouth is this large government marine research centre (☎ 426-4093), which has set up a free self-guided tour for visitors. A walk around the exhibits concerning the fishery and various ocean studies takes a little less than an hour. There is also a video and some aquarium specimens to see. This is the country's leading oceanographic facility and as such has international standing and often carries out research with similar institutes from other countries. The centre is open Monday to Friday only, from 9.30 am to 4.00 pm. To get there from Dartmouth by car, take Windmill Rd to the Shannon Park exit, which is near the MacKay Bridge, or get a bus from the Dartmouth ferry terminal.

## Black Cultural Centre

Described as the first of its kind in Canada, the centre (☎ 434-6223) is a museum, cultural and educational facility all in one. Its principal aim is to preserve and present the history of Black people in Nova Scotia. Perhaps surprisingly, Nova Scotia was an early centre for Black communities in Canada and a significant depot of the Underground Railway (see Windsor, Ontario and surroundings). There are various small exhibits, including some African musical instruments and a video. Of more interest may be the scheduled events, lectures, concerts, etc, so call for information.

For those more interested in Black history in the province, pick up a copy of the Black Heritage Trail pamphlet here or at one of the major tourist offices. It lays out various routes around the province, detailing points of note, and provides some little-known historical information.

The centre is open year round from 9 am to 5 pm Monday to Friday and from 10 am to 4 pm on Saturdays. It's in Westphal, just past the eastern border of the city of Dartmouth on Route 7, Cherrybrook Rd. This is about six or seven km south-east of central Dartmouth.

## Shearwater Aviation Museum

South of town on Pleasant St, at the Canadian Forces Base (CFB Shearwater), the aviation museum (☎ 466-1083) details the history of Canadian maritime military aviation. Some aircraft are on display, as well as pictures, uniforms and other salient objects. A visit is free. It's open on weekends through July and August. At other times, call for information.

The Shearwater International Airshow is held here annually, usually in September.

## Activities

The city's lakes are used for fishing, swimming and boating.

The Shubenacadie Canal connects Dartmouth with the Minas Basin in the Bay of Fundy. The Micmacs once used it as a route across the province; it's now interrupted in places but is a fine canoe route (with some portages needed).

## Festivals

Festivals include the Tattoo Festival, held along the waterfront in July; the Maritime Old-Time Fiddlers' Contest in early July; the Dartmouth Natal Day Celebration in early August; and the 10-day Winter Carnival in early February. A three-day multicultural festival is held in June along the waterfront, featuring ethnic foods and arts. The Olands

Grand Prix Hydroplane Regatta, held in early August down at the waterfront, has become a major event, featuring some of the world's fastest boats – 260 km/h!

### Places to Stay

There are places to stay on this side of the bay as well. They tend to be more scattered and less central than in Halifax. There is camping in the Shubie Beach Park.

Close to the harbour is *Martin House B&B* (☎ 469-1896), at 62 Pleasant St, with rooms from $45 to $58. Less expensive is *Caroline's* (☎ 469-4665), with three rooms at $25/30 a single/double, including a continental breakfast. It's at 134 Victoria Rd, not far from the Macdonald Bridge.

### Places to Eat

Aside from the fast-food places with a view in the ferry terminal complex, there are a couple of places in the old section near the dock. *Tea and Temptations*, at 44½ Ochterloney St, east of the ferry landing, is good for an afternoon break. *Incredible Edibles*, at the corner of King and Portland Sts, has good soup-and-sandwich lunches at about $5.

There are a couple of takeout places up Portland St, and the park next to the ferry terminal is not a bad spot for a picnic lunch.

# Central Nova Scotia

The central part of Nova Scotia, in geographic terms, essentially takes in the corridor of land from the New Brunswick border down to Halifax. With a few exceptions it's an area to be passed through on the way to somewhere else. For many coming by road from elsewhere in Canada, this is the introduction to Nova Scotia. But don't turn against the province because of what you see from the Trans Canada Hwy, as it passes through flat, uninteresting terrain on the way to the province's main highway at Truro, which makes a beeline to Halifax. Springhill is an interesting stop south of Amherst and

there is some good scenery to the west along the shores of the Bay of Fundy.

### AMHERST

Amherst is the geographic centre of the Maritimes, and a travel junction. For anyone heading into Nova Scotia, passing by is a necessity, and Route 104 leads south towards Halifax and then cuts east for Cape Breton Island. Also from Amherst, it's not far to the Northumberland Shore and the north coastal route across the province. Route 16 to the ferry for Prince Edward Island is just across the border in New Brunswick.

The tourist office (☎ 667-1888) is in a railway car built in 1905 and now parked on LaPlanche St, from exit 2 off the highway.

There's not much to do or see, but it's a pleasant town with some fine buildings, and many from the 19th century have been restored. You'll find a number of these along Victoria St, the main street, whose intersection with Church St is the primary one in town. In the 19th and early 20th centuries, Amherst was a busy manufacturing centre.

The **Cumberland County Museum** is at 150 Church St.

The **Amherst Point Migratory Bird Sanctuary** is not far from town, south-west along the marshy coast of Cumberland Basin, part of the Bay of Fundy. Much of the area is a national wildlife area but it's really only of interest to serious bird-watchers. The sanctuary is difficult to find: look for the small blue signs along the edge of Hwy 6. There are various trails through the woods and around the ponds. The tourist office has a pamphlet detailing it. Amherst Marsh actually part of the Tantramar marsh which is considered the world's largest.

On the east coast there is a good beach at Lorneville on Northumberland Strait.

### Places to Stay

There are a few tourist homes in town and motels on the outskirts. There are also several campgrounds nearby, three of them south off the Trans Canada Hwy.

*Brown's Guest Home* (☎ 667-9769) is at 158 East Victoria St and is reasonably priced, with singles for $28 and doubles for $30 to $35. There are three rooms for one to three people. For a motel, since my former choice the *Tantramar* seems to have lost it, try *Victorian Motel* (☎ 667-7211), at 150 East Victoria St. Unlike the guesthouse, the motel is open all year.

## Places to Eat

The classic *Hampton Diner* is recommended for good, cheap food and quick, courteous service. They've been open every day from 7 am to 9 pm since 1956! You can't miss it as you come into town from the highway off exit 2.

Right in the middle of town, at 125 Victoria St, the *Country Rose Tea Room* is very good for salads and sandwiches. It's a small, quiet place with pine furniture and lace curtains, well suited to the afternoon teas it serves.

## Getting There & Away

The Acadian bus lines terminal is a couple of blocks from Church St, on the corner of Prince Arthur and Havelock Sts. There are three buses a day for Halifax; points east and west are served as well.

## CHIGNECTO

For lack of a better name to call the region south and west of Amherst, I've named it after the bay, the cape at the western tip and the large game sanctuary in the middle of it. This is one of the least visited, least populated areas of the province. The road network is minimal, although the Glooscap Trail tourist route goes through the eastern portion. It's an area with some very interesting geology and ancient history, which attracts dinosaur detectives, fossil followers and rockhounds. The Minas Basin shore has some good scenery and shoreline cliffs. The tides of the Minas Basin are high even by Fundy standards.

## Joggins

A short distance from Amherst on Chignecto Bay is the village of Joggins, known for its seaside cliff full of fossils. It exposes one of

the world's best Carboniferous-period fossil collections, consisting of trees, insects, reptiles and others 300 million years old. There is a footpath down to the beach and along the 50-metre sandstone cliffs but you're better off first visiting the Fossil Centre (☎ 251-2727) on Main St, which is open daily from 9.30 am to 6.30 pm from 1 June to 30 September. Here you'll see samples of what there is, including fossilised footprints, and learn more about the site. Admission is $3.50.

Guided tours of the fossil cliffs are not cheap, at $10, but they do last two hours and mean almost certain success in finding something of interest. One tour is offered daily but the times vary and are tied to the tides. The tourist office in Amherst might have a schedule for the tours; if not, they will know the times of low tide, so you'll be able to have a look around on your own. This is a protected area, but small fossils which you find can be kept.

## Cape d'Or

If you make it way down to the end of the peninsula, don't miss Cape d'Or Park at the lighthouse, and walk out to the point for a really spectacular view over the Minas Channel and Bay of Fundy.

## Diligent River

At Diligent River there is a two-km walking trail worth taking to Ward's Falls to see the waterfalls and gorge.

## Parrsboro

Parrsboro is the largest of the small towns along the Minas Basin shore in this relatively little-visited region of Nova Scotia. There is a tourist office in the centre of town, beside the Town Hall. Two Islands Rd, on the east side of the harbour, affords good views of the Minas Basin across to Cape Blomidon.

The area is interesting geologically and is known for its semiprecious stones, fossils and dinosaur prints. Rockhounds scour the many local beaches and rock faces for agates and amethyst and attend the annual Rock Hound Roundup, a get-together for rock, mineral and fossil collectors, with displays, demonstrations, guided walks, boat tours, concerts, etc. The August event is now over 25 years old.

See the Fundy Geological Museum: Landscape & Life (☎ 254-3814), with its collection of the various stones of the region and fossils. It's open every day and is on Two Islands Rd. Guided fossil and mineral tours are offered. There are other geological museums, too. The largest batch of fossilised bones ever discovered in North America was found nearby at **Wassons Bluff** in 1986, and along the shoreline thousands of prehistoric footprints have been seen.

**Partridge Island**, on the coast, is good for rock collecting, with exposed rock 200 million years old.

There are several B&Bs in town, including the *White House* (☎ 254-2387), on Upper Main St, with singles for $25, doubles or triples for $40, including a continental breakfast. There is also a motel and a more expensive inn.

### Five Islands Provincial Park
East of Parrsboro, the park offers camping, a beach and picnicking possibilities. Walking trails show the terrain's variety, some leading to the 90-metre-high cliffs at the edge of the Minas Basin, with views of the islands. Nearby tidal flats are good for clam-digging.

The town has a few simple restaurants and not much else.

### Economy & Around
Closer to Five Islands than the town of Economy, Economy Mountain, at over 200 metres, affords good views. Six km north of Economy on River Phillip Rd, a walking path leads to Economy Falls, where the river flows from the Cobequid Mountains toward the Minas Basin. Lots of blueberries and a good view are the rewards.

South of town, Economy Point Rd leads to the marsh area at the coast where the Economy River meets the salt water of the Bay of Fundy. At the end of the road, at Thomas Cove, there is a sandy beach, some

sandstone cliffs and, at low tide, vast mudflats, which are perfect for clam-digging.

### SPRINGHILL
Springhill is a small, modest, working-class town known to many Canadians for two things: horrendous coal-mining disasters and as the birthplace of one of the country's most popular singers, Anne Murray.

The stories of both are told in museums. Springhill is also said to be the first town in the world to be thermally heated using flooded coal mines.

### Anne Murray Centre
More or less right in the middle of town, on Main St, is the centre honouring Springhill's best-known offspring. It's pretty well just for real buffs, though, with a rather high (relative to most provincial attractions) entrance fee of $4.50. For that you learn details of Anne Murray's successful career through pictures, videos, gold records and awards. There's also a gift shop.

The centre's open from May to October every day, 10 am to 7 pm.

### Miners' Museum
Three km from the Anne Murray Centre (follow the signs), this site is a story of obvious bravery, toil, guts and tragedy – life and death. A visit is worthwhile: interesting, educational and perhaps emotional. The displays brought tears to the eyes of a couple of visitors on my tour.

Springhill became a centre of the dirty coal-mining business as early as 1834. From 1872 when large-scale operations began, the black stuff was dug out and shipped out in large amounts. Major accidents in 1891 and again in 1956 claimed a total of 164 lives.

Two years later North America's deepest mine (4.3 km!) had a 'bump', a cave-in – disaster had struck again. Seventy-five miners were killed in this, one of the continent's worst mining accidents. Newspaper headlines far and wide told the story of the dead and the search for survivors until, 6½ days later, 12 men buried underground were found alive.

That, finally, was the end of that section of

the mine, and in 1970 all the other mining operations here ceased.

Today the Miners' Museum allows visitors a first-hand look down a mine, as well as displaying equipment, tools, photographs, etc. The guides, all retired miners, lead the tour with a beautifully warm, human grace.

Admission is just $2 for seeing all the above-ground displays and $3.50 for the complete tour, which includes the guided talk and a trip down a shaft. Go for the latter – when you feel the cold, damp air at the opening, you'll be glad you're not going to work.

The museum is open daily from the middle of May to the middle of October.

### Miners' Monument
In the centre of town, by the Miners' Hall, is a monument to all those who have died. Many die still, from bad lungs and other coal-related illnesses.

### TRURO
Truro, with its central position in the province, is known as the hub of Nova Scotia. The Trans Canada Hwy passes through the north and east of town; Hwy 102 goes south to Halifax. The VIA Rail line goes by and Truro is also a bus transfer point.

The main part of this town, with its population of 13,000, is around the corner of Prince and Inglis Sts, where some redevelopment has gentrified the streets.

The tourist office is in Victoria Square, at the eastern end of the downtown area, by the corner of Prince and Commercial Sts.

### Victoria Park
If you're making a stop in Truro or just passing through, a trip to large Victoria Park is worthwhile. There are hundreds of wooded hectares, with walking trails, two small waterfalls, a stream and a swimming pool.

It's a good place to break up a day of cycling or driving. Getting there is a little complicated, but from Bible Hill, the city landmark, anyone will be able to direct you. The park closes at 10 pm.

### Colchester Museum
At 29 Young St, in the centre of town, this small museum in the large building has exhibits on the region's and town's natural and human history.

### Tidal Bore
The Bay of Fundy is known for having the highest tides in the world, and an offshoot of these is a tidal wave or bore which flows up the feeding rivers when high tide comes in. The advancing tide is often pretty small but, with the right phase of the moon, can be a metre or so in height and runs upstream, giving the impression of flowing backwards. You can have a look for free at a few spots in and around town. The closest place is at the Salmon River, which runs through the north part of town. Another is not far from town, on the Shubenacadie River at Tidal Bore Day Park, off Hwy 215. Tide schedules are available at the tourist office.

### Millbrook Indian Reserve
This reserve is just south of town on Hwy 102. The Micmac Indians here sell handicrafts, notably baskets.

### Festivals
Nova Scotia's largest provincial exhibition and agricultural and amusement fair is held here in August.

### Places to Stay
There are several B&Bs in Truro and a number of motels on the outskirts. The YMCA in town has no rooms to rent and the nearest hostel is near Wentworth, on the way to Amherst. As you come into Truro via Bible Hill, you'll find *Foothill Motel & Cabins* (☎ 897-4143), seven km east of town. It's a cheap place to stay, offering cabins with cooking facilities at $40 for two people, and is open from 1 May to 31 October. Nearby is a bakery with homemade treats.

Better is the Victorian *Blue House* (☎ 895-4150), at 43 Dominion St, one of several B&Bs which have opened in the past few years to fill a gap in the low-priced end of the market. It's central, has three rooms and offers good value, at $34/45 a single/double, including a full breakfast and tea in the evening. The host will meet the train or bus if you give a call.

The best deal amongst the more expensive motels is *Berry's Motel* (☎ 895-2823), at 73 Robie St. It has 31 units, at $40 a single or $50 a double/triple.

The HI *Wentworth Hostel* (☎ 548-2379), in a 100-year-old farmhouse, is not quite halfway to Amherst, near Wentworth on Valley Rd. It's open all year and costs $9.50 for members, $11.50 for nonmembers. The bus stop is three km away. For drivers, turn off the Trans Canada Hwy at Valley Rd. About two km on, where the pavement turns to gravel, look for another road. The hostel is down that one; look for signs. There's good hiking nearby. Family rooms are available and there are kitchen facilities.

### Places to Eat

At 517 Prince St, the *Iron Kettle* is a friendly, inexpensive restaurant in a building dating from 1875. The breakfasts are good, but it is closed on Sundays.

The *Chow Family Restaurant*, at 344 Prince St, is the place for standard Chinese fare. There is a new eatery and a couple of pubs in the renovated warehouse complex at the corner of Inglis Place and Esplanade, in the centre.

Just off the Trans Canada at exit 14 into Truro along Hwy 2 (which becomes Robie St in town) are a number of the standard chain restaurants. *Smitty's* for pancakes and *Ponderosa* for cheap steak and an excellent all-you-can-eat salad bar are good choices. Also nearby is *Deluxe*, part of a small, local chain often seen in New Brunswick, which is known for its fish & chips.

### Getting There & Away

**Bus** The bus depot (☎ 895-3833) is at 280 Willow St. It's near the hospital along the motel strip – you'll see the blue-and-white Acadian bus terminal sign. There are three buses a day to Halifax ($10) and four a day, with different stops, to Sydney ($33). To Saint John, New Brunswick ($43), there's

one morning and one afternoon bus daily, with a stop in Amherst.

**Train** The train station (☎ 1-800-561-3952) is in town on Esplanade St, near the corner of Inglis St. All trains into and out of Nova Scotia pass through Truro, so connections can be made for Halifax, various points in New Brunswick and to Montreal via one of two different routes. Trains to Halifax ($15) depart once daily (except Wednesday) and to Saint John, New Brunswick ($42) on Monday, Thursday and Saturday.

### MAITLAND & SHUBENACADIE CANAL

To the west of Truro on the Bay of Fundy is the little town of Maitland, at the mouth of the Shubenacadie River. Extending south along the river then through various locks and lakes, the continuous water system eventually leads to the city of Dartmouth and the ocean.

Opened in 1861, the canal is now a National Historic Site and has a variety of sites and parks that can be visited along its course, including the Tidal Bore Day Park (mentioned under Truro). It is also used by boaters and canoeists. Maps available at tourist offices list all the points of interest, walking trails, etc.

The main interpretive centre is in Dartmouth, on the harbour.

### STEWIACKE

At this little town south of Truro, you're halfway between the North Pole and the Equator.

### SHUBENACADIE

South of Truro down Hwy 2 toward Halifax, Shubenacadie is one of the better spots to view the Fundy Tidal Bore. There are observation decks set up at Tidal Bore Park. The bore here can vary in height from about 30 cm to three metres. Rubber-rafting trips along the river on the tidal bores are offered. A side benefit is that the river is home to a lot of bald eagles. For more information on the tides and bores, see the section on Moncton, New Brunswick.

Shubenacadie Wildlife Park is a provincial park housing examples of Nova Scotia's wildlife, including birds, waterfowl, foxes and deer, in large enclosures. It's off Hwy 102 at exit 10, 38 km south of Truro, just north of the town of Shubenacadie. It is open every day during daylight hours from mid-May to mid-October and admission is free.

# South Shore

The South Shore refers to the area south and west of Halifax stretching along the coast to Yarmouth. It contains many fishing villages and several small historic towns. Some of the coastal scenery is good – typically rocky, jagged and foggy. The latter qualities have made the coast here and along the Eastern Shore as much a favourite with modern-day smugglers transporting illegal drugs as it once was to rum runners.

The first one-third of the area, closest to Halifax, is the city's cottage country and is quite busy. The tourist route through here, on the older and smaller roads, is called the Lighthouse Route and is probably the most visited region of Nova Scotia other than Cape Breton. Various museums and points of interest are found along the route, which was named for the many lighthouses along the shore. Accommodation is not plentiful considering the traffic in high season, so plan to find a place before dark each night. For eating, as might be expected, fresh seafood is abundant and excellent.

MacKenzie buses service the region from Halifax to Yarmouth, with at least one and usually two departures in each direction daily. Yarmouth can also be reached via a northern route through the Annapolis Valley from Halifax on the Acadian bus line.

## PROSPECT
South-west of Halifax is the quiet and little-visited Prospect, a small but attractive old coastal village. The view from the cemetery at the top of the hill on the approach to town

is very impressive, especially if the fog bank is obscuring some of the islands and shore-line. There is a wharf, rocks to clamber over along the shore and a lighthouse.

## PEGGY'S COVE
Canada's best known fishing village lies 43 km west of Halifax on Hwy 333. It's a pretty place, with fishing boats, nets, lobster traps, docks and old pastel houses that all seem perfectly placed to please the eye. Although not unlike many other such communities, Peggy's Cove does have a quintessential postcard quality about it.

The 415-million-year-old granite boulders (known to geologists as erratics) littering the surroundings add an odd touch.

The smooth shoreline rock all around the lighthouse just begs to be explored (but do not get too close – every year visitors are swept into the cold waters by unexpected swells). The ambience-creating fog completes the enticing effect. Count on the fog, too: it enshrouds the area at least once every three days and is present most mornings.

Peggy's Cove is a popular destination – probably one of the most visited in the Atlantic Provinces – and it's close to the capital too, so there are crowds which detract from its appeal. The best time for a visit is before 10 am; second best is later in the afternoon. Many full tour buses arrive in the middle of the day.

Surprisingly the village, which dates from 1811, has just 60 residents and most of them are fishers.

See the pictorial in-the-rock monument done by local artist DeGarthe near the provincial parking lot at the entrance to Peggy's Cove.

Down near the lighthouse is a restaurant and coffee counter with a variety of souvenirs. The lobster dinner is said to be good and comes with eating instructions. The lighthouse is now a small post office which uses its own lighthouse-shaped stamp cancellation mark.

## ST MARGARET'S BAY
A little beyond Peggy's Cove, large St

Margaret's Bay is an area of small towns, craft shops and small sandy beaches, with a number of motels, campgrounds and cottages, and some visitors prefer to use it as a base for exploring the Halifax/Peggy's Cove region. It's a developed area where many people who work in the city live or have summer places.

Near the head of St Margaret's Bay is the start of the Bowaters Hiking Trail, which can be used for a couple of hours or a full day's walk. At the top of the bay are the beaches. Queensland Beach, the one furthest west, is the largest and busiest and has a snack bar.

### Places to Stay

One of the most attractive places to spend a night or two is the *Baybreeze Motel & Cottages* (☎ 826-2213), nicely laid out by the water in Boutilier's Point. The cottages tend to be rented by the week but the motel units go from $38 to $50 a double nightly. The cottages are self-contained and some can sleep as many as seven.

## MAHONE BAY

Mahone Bay, with its islands and history, has become a sort of city escape, with the town of the same name acting as the recreation/accommodation centre. It's a popular destination for a Sunday drive from Halifax, about 100 km away, or for an afternoon tea. The town has antique and craft shops and a decided tourist orientation. There's often a flea market set up on summer weekends. The approach from Halifax is noteworthy for the view of the three church spires by the roadside. You can see fine examples of Victorian gingerbread-house architecture around town, and the cemetery is interesting, with many gravestones inscribed in German.

At 578 Main St is the **Settlers' Museum & Cultural Centre**, which deals mainly with the first German settlers to the area. Displays in two rooms cover the 1850s period. Admission is by donation.

### Places to Stay & Eat

There are a dozen B&Bs, an indication of the trendiness and popularity of the Mahone Bay

area. They tend to be average-priced, or maybe a little more expensive than those found elsewhere.

The *Fairmont B&B* (☎ 624-6173), 654 Main St, is central and reasonable. The three rooms offered from May to October cost $35 to $45 for singles, $45 to $55 for doubles. The higher-priced rooms have their own bathroom.

Also in the centre of town is the *Heart's Desire B&B* (☎ 624-8766), at 686 Main St.

Among the shops are two pubs, a café and, at 662 Main St, *Zwicker's Inn* – a busy but not inexpensive restaurant with a range of seafood and pasta dishes which are highly regarded.

## CHESTER

Chester, an old village with 1000 residents, overlooks Mahone Bay. Established in 1759, it has had a colourful history as the haunt of pirates and Prohibition bathtub gin smugglers. It's now a small summer resort, and although there isn't a lot to do in town, a lot of visitors pass through each summer.

The centre of town is along Pleasant St between King and Queen Sts. The Chester Playhouse, which runs inexpensive comedies, musicals and dramas through July and August, is on Pleasant St.

### Tancook Island

Offshore is Tancook Island, which can be reached by a very inexpensive 45-minute passenger-only ferry ride departing from the Chester wharf several times a day. Chester also has a back harbour, which is used mainly for pleasure craft. The islands – there is a **Big & Little Tancook** – are primarily residential but visitors are welcome to stroll around. Big Tancook has a tourist office, a B&B and a simple food outlet. A walking-tour brochure available at the Chester tourist office outlines the paths which lead over much of the island.

The island is known for its plentiful cabbage and sauerkraut. Distinctive little cabbage-storage houses can be seen around the island. There are also some old homes on the island, including a Cape Cod cottage dating from 1790.

## Places to Stay

There is a provincial park with camping just east of town.

At 78 Queen St, *Mecklenburgh Inn B&B* (☎ 275-4638) is a nice-looking place set in an old house built before the turn of the century. Some rooms have private adjacent balconies. Prices are $50/60 for singles/doubles and include breakfast. For exploring, bicycles and a rowboat are available. It's open from mid-May to mid-October. Owner, Suzi Fraser, has been a Lonely Planet traveller herself, so you may be able to swap some stories.

Another place to stay is the cheaper *Casa Blanca Guest House & Cabins* (☎ 275-3385), 463 Duke St, close to the centre. A single with shared bath is $35, including breakfast.

## Places to Eat

For a casual bite, there's the *Fo'c's'le Tavern*, and *Rosie Grady's* restaurant, on the corner of Pleasant and Queen Sts.

At 69 Queen St is the *Thirsty Thinker's Tearoom*, affiliated with a charity group, and along the waterfront is the *Rope Loft*, with a varied menu – if you want to save a bit of money, they'll supply the food and you can cook it yourself.

## NEW ROSS

At this small lumbering town in the interior of the province, 26 km north-west of Chester, you can see a **living agriculture museum** set up like a working 19th-century farm.

## GOLD RIVER

Not far west of Chester, the salmon fishing is said to be very good here.

## OAK ISLAND

What a story! This is treasure island with no treasure – so far. Said to be the burying place of the treasure of the infamous Captain Kidd or Blackbeard or Captain Morgan – maybe of Inca gold taken by the Spanish or...the list goes on.

Despite nearly 200 years of digging, it's still up for grabs and has become one of the country's biggest and most captivating ongoing mysteries.

Three farmboys stumbled upon a deep shaft in 1795, and since then, six lives and millions of dollars have been lost in the world's longest-running and most costly treasure hunt.

Before you grab your shovel and rush over, you need a permit you can't get. The search – now using a lot of sophisticated equipment – is carried on by an international consortium determined to solve the mystery of the money pit once and for all.

The exploration company runs tours of the site which explain some of the history and the incredible shafts, tunnels and chambers with their flooding systems. Some of the articles found thus far in the investigations are also shown. To get to the island, turn off Hwy 3 at Oak Island Rd. Several books have been written on the matter; local bookshops should have something.

## LUNENBURG

This attractive town of 3000 residents is best known for building the *Bluenose* sailing schooner in 1921, which can be seen on the Canadian dime. Always a shipbuilding and fishing town, it is now the centre of the provincial fishing industry and has one of the major fleets of the north Atlantic seaboard. The largest fish-processing plant in North America, employing 1000 people, is here. From it come the Highliner supermarket seafood products. Nova Scotia, like Newfoundland, has been hard hit by the dwindling fish stocks and severely curtailed limits recently imposed by the federal government. What lasting effect this will have on communities such as Lunenburg is as yet unknown.

Lunenburg is an old town where Acadians lived until the mid-1700s. It was officially founded in 1753 when the British encouraged Protestants to emigrate from Europe. It soon became the first largely German settlement in the country. This now diminished German heritage is reflected in some of the local foods.

## Orientation & Information

The town's main street is Lincoln St. Montague St, running parallel to the harbour, is the street of most interest to the visitor. Along it are many of the town's commercial enterprises, including a few places to eat and a couple of places to stay. There are some interesting stores with gifts, crafts, antiques and prints for sale.

Many of the restaurants along Montague St have patios out the back facing Bluenose Drive, which runs right along the wharves. The Lunenburg Fisheries Museum is here, as are the boat tours. In the evening people catch mackerel from the various docks where smaller fishing vessels moor. Further east along Montague are the shipyards and commercial docks for the bigger trawlers. The principal intersection is with King St.

King St contains several banks, including the Royal with a 24-hour banking machine. Pelham St, one street back up the hill from Montague St, also has a number of shops. At No 134 is the oldest house in Lunenburg, Bailly House, constructed in 1760. This is where Earl Bailly lived and had his studio. He was one of the area's best known seascape painters, despite having had polio and having to wield his brush in his teeth. His brother now lives in the house, which can be visited to view some of the paintings.

Going up the hill along Lincoln St to Blockhouse Hill Rd is the tourist office and a great view of the area.

The Koch-Solomon House, built at 69 Townsend St in 1775, is considered one of the town's finest 18th-century houses.

Despite Lunenburg's popularity, the residential streets are surprisingly quiet and free of tourists. Strolling around turns up many fine wooden houses. Some are made in the old shingle style and many are brightly painted. There are also some huge Victorian gingerbread places which really can only be termed mansions.

The town is built on a peninsula and has a back harbour, as well as the main one across the bay, from which the golf course on Kaulback Head can be seen. The back harbour, in a mainly residential area, is used primarily for pleasure boats and some inshore fishing vessels.

## Lunenburg Fisheries Museum

The interesting provincial museum is down on the waterfront, on Bluenose Drive. It has one building, and two ships in the water for inspection: a dragger and a fishing schooner. In the building are exhibits on fishing and fish processing, and a 25-minute film on marine life. There's also an aquarium. It's open daily from mid-May to September and admission is $2. There is a lot to see, so a visit could easily take a couple of hours.

## Churches

For a small town the churches are impressive, and there are five of them in the downtown area. St John's Anglican, on the corner of Duke and Cumberland Sts, is a real stunner. The beautiful black-and-white wooden place dates from 1753 and is one of the oldest churches in Canada. Tours are given through the summer. The Lutheran church on the corner of Cornwallis and Fox Sts isn't much younger, having been built in 1772. St Andrew's Presbyterian is the oldest Presbyterian church in the country.

The Zion Lutheran church has its own claim to fame. Although the congregation began as early as 1772, this church is only about 100 years old. In it, however, is one of the original bells from the fort at Louisbourg on Cape Breton Island. When at one time the federal government was considering ordering its return to the National Historic Site, it was removed from the church and hidden at the bottom of Lunenburg's back harbour.

## Lunenburg Academy

The Academy, a school, is the huge black-and-white turreted structure on a hill seen rising above the town on your way in from Halifax. Built entirely of wood in 1895, as a prestigious high school, it is one of the rare survivors of the academy system of education. Though now a National Historic Site, it is still a working school and therefore can not be entered.

Beside it is a cemetery, with many graves from the 1800s.

## Activities
The public swimming pool is on Knickle Rd south-west of the centre.

The Dory Shop (☎ 634-9146), at Railway Wharf, rents boats by the hour or day – row, sail or motor, depending on your energy level.

Jo's Dive Shop (☎ 634-3443), at 296 Lincoln St, has everything for the diver. A new underwater park is being created in the clear waters off Lunenburg.

Bicycles can be rented and repaired at the Bicycle Barn (☎ 634-3426).

## Organised Tours
Several boat cruises are offered from down by the docks. Anchor Boat Tours has a 2½-hour trip around the point to Blue Rocks. Others offer deep-sea fishing or sailing on a traditional-style schooner.

Walter Flower Charters (☎ 527-3123) offers whale-watching trips departing from the Lunenburg harbour.

At times through the summer, the *Bluenose II*, built in 1963 in Lunenburg, docks here for a few days.

## Festivals
In July, a craft festival is held, and a month later, the justly popular Folk Harbour Festival (☎ 634-3180) is a weekend of traditional music and dance. Book early, as accommodation is very scarce on this weekend.

## Places to Stay
Lunenburg is a popular destination, and during midsummer making reservations early in the day is not a bad idea. During the folk festival, in particular, accommodation will be scarce. There is a good variety of places here, though, from camping to classic old Maritime inns.

**Camping** Right in town beside the tourist office, with great views, there is a little campground for trailers or tenters, operated by the Board of Trade. It's an ideal, incredi-

bly convenient place which charges $9. It does get full so arrive early. Too bad more towns don't have something similar. There are three or four other, privately run campgrounds near town.

**Hostel** At 9 King St, in a house from 1879, the HI *Lunenburg Hostel* (☎ 634-9146) has eight beds in four rooms, each with its own bathroom. Bicycles are on hand for guests' use. Check-in is from 4 to 8 pm and a bed will cost members $12.50. Nonmembers can stay at slightly higher cost. Manager, David Callan, is knowledgeable about the town and area and can offer advice and answer questions. Note that this hostel is open from May to September only.

**B&Bs** The *Snug Harbour B&B* (☎ 634-9146) is operated at the same address as the hostel. Three rooms are available on the 3rd floor, one with private bath, and a sundeck provides views of the harbour. Singles cost $35 to $40 and doubles are $40 to $55, including breakfast. English, French and German are spoken.

The *Margaret Murray B&B* (☎ 634-3974), a short distance west of the centre, off Dufferin St at 20 Lorne St, is good value at $30/40 with a full breakfast.

Out on Blue Rocks Rd, 1.3 km from town, *Lamb & Lobster B&B* (☎ 634-9146) is appropriately named when you know the owner, William Flower, is a lobster fisherman and a shepherd. In the evening guests may be shown how the family collies round up the sheep. Singles/doubles are $35/45.

**Inns** There are several more up-market guesthouses or, rather, inns, formed out of the larger, gracious, historic properties around town.

Right in the middle of town is the *Compass Rose Inn* (☎ 1-800-565-8509), at 15 King St. It's a attractive old place with a good restaurant and the rooms are priced below what might be expected, with singles/doubles at $50 to $60, including a light breakfast and in-room tea or coffee.

*Bluenose Lodge* (☎ 634-8851), at 10 Falk-

NOVA SCOTIA

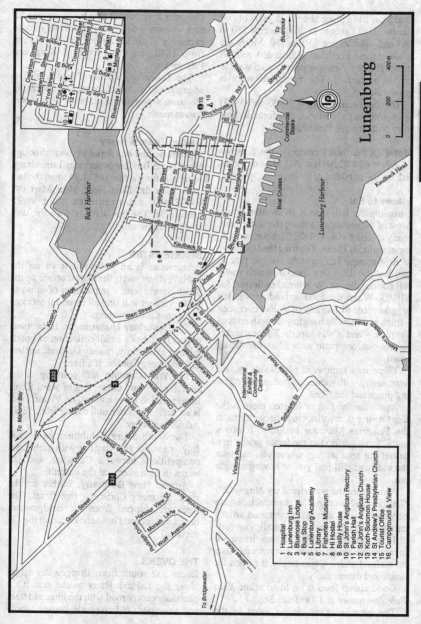

Lunenburg

Black Harbour

Lunenburg Harbour

Kaulback Head

Mason's Beach

To Mahone Bay

332

3

324

To Bridgewater

1  Hospital
2  Lunenburg Inn
3  Bluenose Lodge
4  Bus Stop
5  Lunenburg Academy
6  Library
7  Fisheries Museum
8  HI Hostel
9  Bailly House
10 St John's Anglican Rectory
11 Parish Hall
12 St John's Anglican Church
13 Koch-Solomon House
14 St Andrew's Presbyterian Church
15 Tourist Office
16 Campground & View

land St, is a big place about 125 years old on the corner of Lincoln St. Singles cost $50 to $65 and doubles are $50 to $70. Meals are available and breakfast is included with an overnight stay. Non-guests may also want to try the restaurant. The breakfast buffet is good value.

The *Lunenburg Inn* (☎ 1-800-565-3963) is another large, historic, comfortable hostelry with antique furnishings.

**Motel** In the motel category, the *Ranch-o Motel* (☎ 634-8220) is at 303 Masons Beach Rd, on the outskirts of town.

### Places to Eat

Sampling the fish here is an absolute must. Most of the restaurants along the waterfront, many offering views of the harbour, specialise in seafood. Three of us tried the *Dockside*, at 90 Montague St, one of the cheaper places, and had the daily fish special, which was a full halibut dinner, from bread to dessert for $10.95. When the food arrived, it was the biggest piece of fish any of us had ever seen – thick and literally hanging off both ends of the plate – and it was superb. The restaurant has an outdoor patio as well as the dining room.

There are a number of places side by side here, many with menus posted, some offering pizza and the like.

Again for the fish or lobster, there is the *Capt'n Angus*, overlooking the water from the Fisheries Museum building. It offers good, fresh seafood at moderate prices in a casual but nice setting, where you can take the kids and still feel you're having a night out.

Away from the waterfront try *Magnolia's Grill*, at 128 Montague St, the eclectic inside of which is like a cross between an artist's café/bistro and someone's small, comfortable country cottage. They have an inexpensive menu. There's some emphasis on seafood with a Cajun angle. It's open for lunch and dinner daily.

Good cheap food is on hand at the *Knot Pub*, downtown at 1 Dufferin St.

The more elegant dining room in the

*Compass Rose*, which also has accommodation, is very good but considerably more expensive. It's in a beautiful building (dating from 1830) on the corner of King and Pelham Sts.

The *Lunenburg Dinner Theatre*, at 116 Montague St, presents comedies concerning the town's past, together with good four-course meals.

### Getting There & Away

There is no real bus depot in town although MacKenzie Bus Lines services Lunenburg. From Halifax the fare is $11. In town the bus pulls in at the Blue Nose Mini Mart (☎ 634-8845), a convenience store at 35 Lincoln St. The bus also runs all the way along to Yarmouth.

### BRIDGEWATER

Bridgewater is an industrial town on the LaHave River and is the largest centre on the South Shore, with a population of close to 7000. Visitors will find all essential services and a couple of museums.

The **Desbrisay Museum**, on 10 hectares of parkland, has a small collection of goods relating to the early, mainly German, settlers of Lunenburg County. It's free.

The **Wile Carding Mill** (carding is the straightening and untangling of wool fibres in preparation for spinning), on Victoria Rd, is an authentic water mill dating from 1860. Admission is free.

The South Shore Exhibition, held each July, is a major five-day fair with traditional competitions between Canadian and US teams in such events as the ox pull.

Around **New Germany**, further up the river, are many Christmas tree farms. The trees are shipped from the Bridgewater docks to expectant households along the US seaboard.

### THE OVENS

Route 332 south from Bridgewater edges along the LaHave River to the sea. It's a pleasant country road with the huge old trees and mammoth old riverside houses fondly associated with the history and good life of the Maritimes.

At the end of the road is The Ovens (☎ 766-4621), a sort of combination nature park and campground, which is highly recommended for its scenery and general easy-going atmosphere.

Gold was found here in 1861 and still can be found on Cunard Beach. Rent a dish at the office and try panning. There's plenty there – I saw several people pocketing small nuggets. In a different area, a trail leads along the shore past (and into) numerous caves. The camping is very good, with many sites right by the shore with fine views over the ocean and a rocky ledge to explore at low tide.

There are also a couple of cottages for rent, a swimming pool, and a comfortable little restaurant which serves up inexpensive and delicious fish & chips.

## LAHAVE

From Riverport a 50-cent, five-minute ride by cable ferry takes you across the river to the town of LaHave, where a stop at one of the best bakeries (physically and gastronomically) in the country is a must. You can't miss it – it's just to the south of the ferry landing, on the main street.

Upstairs, the small HI *LaHave Marine Hostel* (☎ 688-2908), is a hostel for cyclists, backpackers or any like-minded soul looking for a good cheap place to spend the night. It's open from May to October. Also based at the bakery is LaHave Outfitters, who run coastal boat excursions.

On the outskirts west of the village is **Fort Point Museum**, a National Historic Site. It was here in 1632 that the first batch of French settlers soon to be known as Acadians landed from France. A fort, Sainte-Marie-de-Grâce, was built later the same year but very little of it remains today. The site was supplanted by Port Royal on the north coast and never became a major centre. A museum in the former lighthouse keeper's house at the site tells more of this early settlement and its leader, de Raizilly. It's open daily through the summer months.

From LaHave the gentle, green landscape continues towards Liverpool, the slow coastal road passing through a series of villages. At **Petite Rivière** is a pioneer cemetery, on the west side of town on top of the hill.

**Rissers Provincial Park** has a very busy campground and an excellent long, sandy beach, although the water is none too warm. There is also a saltwater marsh with a boardwalk trail.

At **Broad Cove** there is an inn with a tea room.

## MILL VILLAGE

In the midst of all the South Shore history, this town offers an odd attraction – the **Mill Village Satellite Earth Station**, an international telecommunications centre. Free 45-minute guided tours include a look at the control room, three large dishes or antennas and a film. It's open from mid-June to the beginning of September.

The Medway River here is considered one of the province's top salmon streams.

## LIVERPOOL

Situated where the Mersey River meets the ocean, as it does in Britain, Liverpool is another historic English-style town with an economy based on forests and fishing. The tourist office on Henry Hensey Drive, just off Main St, in Centennial Park, has a walking-tour pamphlet which guides you past many of the notable houses and buildings in the downtown area and along the waterfront.

**Perkins House**, built in 1766, is now a museum with articles and furniture from the colonial period. Next door, the **Queen's County Museum** has some Native Indian artefacts and more materials relating to town history, as well as some writings by early citizens.

At **Fort Point**, marked with a cairn, is the site where Samuel de Champlain landed from France in 1604. There is also a memorial to the British privateers who were active in the local waters at the beginning of the

1800s, protecting the British trade routes from American incursions.

There are four sandy **beaches** nearby: Beach Meadows, White Point, Hunt's Point and Summerville. All are within 11 km of town, and there are others further west.

A 10-km hiking trail at the Anglican Church begins on Bog Rd off White Point Rd, which is Route 3 toward Yarmouth. It's actually an old railway road and is gravelled. It runs through woods, crossing a brook and Five Rivers, and eventually ends at the coast near White Point.

### Places to Stay & Eat

For spending the night, there are B&Bs and nearby motels. *Lane's Privateer Inn* (☎ 354-3456), 33 Bristol Ave, is the white wooden building with balconies built in 1798 on Hwy 3 by the bridge over the Mersey River, just east of the centre. A double with continental breakfast is $45, and there is a good restaurant which specialises in seafood. There are a couple of more modest places but with a saving of just $5, the style and location of Lane's is worth the extra.

On the corner of Bristol Ave and Main St is the *Lunch Kettle*, which offers inexpensive homemade food.

The *Liverpool Landing Pub* is on Legion St, across from the Canadian Tire store.

### SEASIDE ADJUNCT KEJIMKUJIK NATIONAL PARK

The main body of this large national park is in the interior north-west of Liverpool, south-east of Digby, but in 1985 this undeveloped region of the south coast between Port Joli Bay and Port Mouton (ma-TOON) Bay was made part of the same park. The 'Keji Adjunct' protects a beautiful, wild stretch of shoreline and the animals, most particularly the endangered piping plover bird, within it.

Services are nonexistent – no campground (although there are some tent sites), no toilets, no drinking water and no fires allowed. What you will find is pristine coastline, with two great beaches, coves, vistas, rock formations and lots of birdlife.

Two trails, one leading in from each end, provide the only access. Both tend to be a little wet. From **South West Port Mouton**, an eight-km track leads to Black Point and the shore. From **St Catherine's River**, a little village, a three-km walk leads to the sea on the western side.

The **Port Joli Basin**, which is adjacent to the above park, also contains other sites of interest to nature lovers. The basin is composed of the harbour, Port Joli Bay, and the two coastal headlands which enclose it. On the west side of the bay is **Thomas Raddall Provincial Park**, a natural environment park with camping, which can act as a base for exploring this wild area. Trails lead to the coast and around bogs. The park contains a lot of wildlife, including moose, and an interpretation centre to help show you what to look for. At the end of the natural harbour, near the village of Point Joli, is the **Point Joli Migratory Bird Sanctuary**. Birders will find waterfowl, shorebirds and others in number, especially during migration periods. There are no facilities but visitors can explore on their own. In Port Joli ask for directions to the park. At the park, rangers will be able to help with some information on the bird sanctuary.

### LOCKEPORT

At the end of a jutting arm is the little town of Lockeport, with what is known as an historic streetscape. The town was founded by New Englanders in the 1700s but became prosperous in the mid-1800s through fishing and, more importantly, as a trading centre with the West Indies. It was during this time that the wealthy built the large, ostentatious homes seen at the waterfront. One street has five such homes, all impressive in their own way and all built by members of the Locke family between 1836 and 1876, using different architectural styles. The short street has been designated an historic site, although none of the houses is open to visitors.

Coming into town over the causeway there is a tourist office and, next door in a former one-room schoolhouse, a small museum with local relics, including a replica of a 19th-century classroom. Just behind is a large crescent-shaped sandy beach. A short visit will suffice, as there is little else in town and nowhere to eat. If it's time to consider quitting for the day, there is now one option for spending a quiet night. The *Locke's Island B&B* (☎ 656-3222), about 16 km down from Hwy 103, can't be missed. It's open all year and has three rooms, at $30/40 a single/double, with a light breakfast included.

A small tea room is open through the day for guests or visitors.

## SHELBURNE

For my money this is one of the most attractive and interesting towns anywhere on the South Shore. The whole place is pretty much like a museum, with fine buildings and historic sites at every turn. It sits on a hill overlooking a good harbour, with a nice waterfront area and some good places to eat and stay, and you can walk to everything along tree-lined streets.

This shipbuilding town with a population of 2200 is known as the birthplace of yachts. As well as the prize-winning yachts, though, it produces several other types of boats. Shelburne also boasts a towncrier, Perry Wamback, who has won national and international competitions.

Shelburne, like many towns in the Fundy region, was founded by Loyalists, and in 1783 had a population of 10,000, making it the largest community in British North America. Many of its inhabitants were former members of the New York aristocracy. Some of the Loyalist houses still stand. The so-called Loyalists were residents of America who maintained their allegiance to Britain during the period of the American Revolution. Life was not easy for those with loyalty to the Queen, and thousands left for Canada.

Water St, the main street, has many houses from 100 to 200 years old, and quite a few of the two-storey wooden homes are marked with dates.

Dock St along the harbour features several

historic buildings and museums and the tourist office.

The commercial fishing wharf is interesting in the mornings, when the cod are unloaded from the ships into ice-filled bins and reloaded onto trucks. This is a major port, and boats from Quebec's Gaspé and the Magdalen Islands, from New Brunswick and Prince Edward Island, may be moored here. Recent cutbacks in fishing quotas have resulted in a marked decline in fishing activity. Individuals still cast for mackerel right off the dock, though. A little further out are the shipyards where repairs to the Marine Atlantic ferries and other vessels are carried out.

### Ross-Thompson House

Built in 1784, this house (which has an adjacent store) belonged to well-to-do merchants who arrived from Britain via Cape Cod, and now acts as a small museum. Furniture, paintings, artefacts and original goods from the store may be viewed. The house is surrounded by gardens, as it would have been formerly. It's open daily from May to October and is free, as are all the places on Dock St.

### Shelburne County Museum

Nearby is this Loyalist house dating from 1787, with a collection of Loyalist furnishings, displays on the history of the local fishery and other articles from the town's past. The oldest fire engine in Canada, a wooden cart from 1740, is quite something. There is also a small collection of Micmac artefacts, including fine, typical porcupine-quill decorative work. The museum is on the corner of Dock St and Maiden Lane.

### Dory Shop

Shelburne has long had a reputation for its dories, small boats first used for fishing from a mother schooner and in later years for inshore fishing and as lifeboats. Many were built here from the 1880s until the 1970s. At the museum you can learn about them and their history and see examples still being made in the workshop upstairs.

The large building across the street was once used as a warehouse and was also, at one time, one of the country's largest department stores.

## Places to Stay

Just a few km west of town is a good provincial park, the *Town Islands*. The campsites are in mature forest and there is swimming too. It's quiet during the week but unfortunately has a bit of a problem on weekends with area rowdies who prefer loud drinking parties to sleeping. Ask if the situation has been cleared up or be prepared to join in.

The *Bear's Den* (☎ 875-3234) is a small, attractive and economical B&B on the corner of Water and Glasgow Sts. You'll pass it on the way into the centre of town. Singles/doubles cost $30/40, which includes a complete breakfast.

The *Toddle In* (☎ 875-3229) B&B is central, on the corner of Water and King Sts. Singles/doubles start at $40/50, plus $10 for a private bath. Breakfast is served in the pleasant dining room downstairs, where lunch is available, too.

The *Cooper's Inn* (☎ 875-4656) and the *Loyalist Inn* (☎ 875-2343), both in larger, fine historic buildings, are slightly more expensive choices.

There are also a few motels at the edge of town, including the attractive *Cape Cod Colony Motel* (☎ 875-3411), at 234 Water St.

## Places to Eat

The *Toddle In* has a small, cosy and friendly dining room for inexpensive, fresh breakfasts and lunches.

*Claudia's Diner*, on Water St, open every day, is a low-priced restaurant with style and standard fare. The cinnamon rolls are good.

For a bit of a splurge the dining room in the *Coopers Inn* (dating from 1785) is very good. They offer just four dishes and four desserts nightly and do them well. Of course, seafood is on the menu but there's always an alternative. *Hamilton House* is also said to be a cut above the others.

*Bruce's Wharf* is a pub on the water along Dock St.

## Getting There & Away

MacKenzie Bus Lines running between Halifax and Yarmouth stops at Donna's Kitchen in the Shelburne Mall, the town's only shopping mall.

## BARRINGTON

The small village of Barrington has four museums, all within walking distance of one another. The tourist office, in the middle of things, has an example of the Cape Island boat, the classic small fishing boat of the North Atlantic, originating on Cape Sable Island and now seen all around eastern Canada.

The **Barrington Meetinghouse** reflects the town's early Quaker influence and was used as both church and city hall. The **Woollen Mill** is representative of a small manufacturing mill of the late 1800s. It was the last woollen mill of its age to cease operating; it ran until 1962.

The **Seal Island Light Museum** is a replica of the lighthouse found on Seal Island, 30 km out to sea, and is a record of the original and its keepers. From the top there's a vista of Barrington Bay.

Across from the Historical Society Centre, the **Western Counties Military Museum** has uniforms, medals and other artefacts.

Aside from the museums, which are all free, there are many heritage buildings in town; get details of them from the walking-tour guide published by the local tourist office.

The tourist office should also have information on some of the local walking trails, including the one which runs along the old railway line from Yarmouth to Halifax.

In Barrington Passage is the *Old School House Restaurant*, with a natural food store and a bakery too. Good sandwiches and salads are offered, with more substantial meals also available. The menu changes daily and everything is made fresh. The above-mentioned trail passes right by the restaurant. It might be possible here to exchange some work for a night's lodging, as the place is run on a sort of commune/kibbutz philosophy. The restaurant and bakery is open all year but is closed from Friday evening until Sunday noon.

From Barrington there is not much of interest until Yarmouth. **Cape Sable** and **West Pubnico** were both once Acadian settlements and each has a small general museum. Pubnico remains French and is considered the oldest village in Canada still lived in by the descendants of its founders. Fishing remains important in the many traditional local villages.

# Yarmouth to Windsor

This region of Nova Scotia stretches from Yarmouth northward and along the south shore of the Bay of Fundy to Windsor and the Minas Basin. It consists, primarily, of two distinct geographical and cultural regions.

The area between Yarmouth and Digby was one of the first European-settled areas in Canada. This municipality of Clare formed part of Acadia, the French region of the New World colonies. The 'French Shore' and its history are still very much in evidence today.

The best-known area, however, is the scenic valley of the Annapolis River, which runs more or less from Digby to Wolfville. It's famous for apples, and in springtime the blossoming valley is at its best.

The Evangeline Trail tourist route passes through the entire region, taking in both these disparate districts.

## YARMOUTH

With its population of nearly 9000, Yarmouth is the largest town in western Nova Scotia. It's also a transportation centre of sorts, where aside from the main highway and the district airport, ferries from Portland and Bar Harbour in Maine, dock. It's an old city, and recent town improvements have stressed this heritage and historical side. A number of souvenir shops and other businesses have also recently opened to cater for visitors. Whichever way you're going,

chances are you'll be passing through, and this is a good place to stop.

There's a huge tourist office down at the ferry docks, at 228 Main St, with both local and provincial information available. They have a walking-tour guide of the city with a map and some historical information. The office remains open from 1 May to 31 October.

Every Saturday through the summer, a farmers' market and flea market is held at the Centretown Square, on the corner of Main and Central Sts.

On the corner of Main and Brown Sts is Toots, a shop you won't want to miss if you're getting on the ferry. It has a large selection of candy and an absolutely mammoth magazine selection.

## Yarmouth County Museum

Open every day in summer (on Sunday from noon only), the museum (☎ 742-5539) at 22 Collins St, in a grey stone building that was formerly a church, is quite good and worth a look. Admission is very cheap and the staff is friendly and helpful.

Most of the exhibits are to do with the sea – ship models, a large painting collection, etc. Many articles were brought back by sea captains from their travels in the Far East, and include things such as ebony elephant carvings from Ceylon (now Sri Lanka) and fine ivory work from Japan. There are also some rooms done in various period styles.

One of the highlights is a runic stone found near town in 1812 and believed to have been carved by Viking Leif Erikson some 1000 years ago. Other evidence has been discovered which suggests that the Vikings were indeed in this area. Ask for the pamphlet on all the theories connected with the stone.

Another interesting item is the 'pleasure vehicle' which, perhaps disappointingly, is only an electric car from 1915.

In summer, the museum is open Monday to Saturday from 9 am to 5 pm and on Sunday from 1 to 5 pm; in the off season, hours are shorter and it's closed on Monday. Admission is $1.

### Firefighters' Museum

This museum (☎ 742-5525) at 431 Main St has a collection of beautiful fire engines dating from the 1930s. They look like the ones in children's stories that have personalities and abused emotions. Admission costs $1; it's open from 9 am to 9 pm (until 5 pm on Sunday).

### The Wharves

As a major fishing port, Yarmouth's waterfront is lined with wharves. Beside the ferry terminal for the boats to Maine is the Public Wharf, where numbers of the local fishing boats tie in. Many of the small boats of the herring fleet depart from here at around sundown. Another good place to watch this floating parade is Fish Point, with a monument to those who work the seas. Also at the Public Wharf, vessels from around the world can sometimes be seen.

Next wharf over to the east is the new Killam Brothers Wharf, used mainly by visiting yachts and sailboats and with a number of places to eat.

For those with more than a passing passion, serious fishing wharves can be seen near town in Lower West Pubnico and at the Port Maitland Wharf.

### Places to Stay

For a fairly small town there is no shortage of accommodation, with a choice of some pretty good places. There are half a dozen B&Bs or guesthouses, a couple of hotels and plenty of motels.

Just one block from the ferry is *Murray Manor Guest House* (☎ 742-9625), at 225 Main St. There are three rooms and a kitchen guests may use. With breakfast, singles/doubles are $40/50. The Murray is a seasonal operation and is shut at the end of summer.

In an historic house at 109 Brunswick St is the *Victorian Vogue B&B* (☎ 742-6398). This one is open all year and is quite good value – singles/doubles cost $30/45 and a room for four is $60. The price includes a full breakfast.

At 21 Clements St is *Clementine's*

*B&B* (☎ 742-0079), with singles at $35 but doubles a might pricey at $60. Breakfast is included.

The *Mid-Town Motel* (☎ 742-5333) is central, at 13 Parade St, and charges $52 a double with a free coffee in the morning. Aside from the 21 standard rooms, there are a couple of efficiency units with kitchens.

The *Rodd Colony Harbour Inn* (☎ 742-9194, 1-800-565-RODD), right across from the ferry terminal, is a large and modern hotel/motel with prices to match. It has all the amenities, including a restaurant and bar.

The most economical of the motels is the *Lakelawn* (☎ 742-3588), 641 Main St, where breakfast is available. It's open from May to October only.

### Places to Eat

*Dawn's*, an all-purpose place at 351 Main St, is good for breakfast and also serves pizza. The *Lotus Garden* has straightforward Chinese food at honest prices. The cafeteria in the *Met*, a Woolworth's-style store at 386 Main St, near Lovitt St, is extremely inexpensive for Canadian basics, with everything under $6.

Not far away, in the big gabled place at 577 Main St, *Captain Kelley's* is a pub-style place which specialises in fish and beef. Best of all is *Harris' Quick 'n' Tasty*, four km from town on Route 3 (Main St) towards Digby. It's a busy, good and reasonably priced seafood spot.

There are both more expensive and cheaper places in town. At 3 Jenkins St, in the downtown area, is a natural-foods outlet with a good bakery.

### Getting There & Away

**Bus** The bus depot is now in the old train station, which wasn't needed when the train service to the area was cancelled in the late 1980s.

Acadian bus lines (☎ 649-2621), Nova Scotia's biggy, has two trips daily to Halifax, taking five hours via Digby and the Annapolis Valley. The morning trip is called 'the limited' and makes about a dozen stops along the way. The other trip, 'the regular', leaves

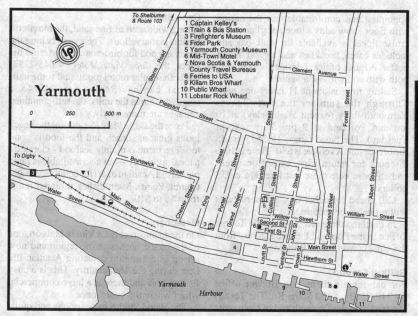

**Yarmouth**

0    250    500 m

1 Captain Kelley's
2 Train & Bus Station
3 Firefighter's Museum
4 Frost Park
5 Yarmouth County Museum
6 Mid-Town Motel
7 Nova Scotia & Yarmouth
  County Travel Bureaus
8 Ferries to USA
9 Killam Bros Wharf
10 Public Wharf
11 Lobster Rock Wharf

To Shelburne
& Route 103

To Digby

Yarmouth Harbour

NOVA SCOTIA

around noon and stops everywhere – at any little junction someone asks for. To Digby, the fare is $10.75; to Halifax it's $33.

MacKenzie Bus Line (☎ 742-5011) also runs to Halifax, but uses the South Shore route through Shelburne, etc. These buses arrive at and depart from the Texaco gas station on the corner of Main and Beacon Sts, opposite the train station.

**Train** There is no longer any train service to this part of the province.

**Ferry** There are two major ferry routes in and out of Yarmouth, both to the state of Maine in the USA; one connects with Bar Harbour and the other with Portland.

The Marine Atlantic (☎ 742-6800 in Yarmouth; 1-800-341-7981 elsewhere) ferry, the MV *Bluenose* to Bar Harbour, Maine, takes about six hours to travel the 160 km. It leaves Yarmouth at 4.30 pm daily during the summer months, less frequently

the rest of the year. The basic one-way fare is $45 per adult, $60 per car and $10 per bicycle. The prices go down quite a bit from October to May. There is also a bargain on a one-day return trip which is offered at half-price and really amounts to a 12-hour cruise. Private cabins are available at additional cost. Another option from Bar Harbour includes an overnight stay in Yarmouth. Ask Marine Atlantic for details.

The other ferry is operated by Maine's Prince of Fundy Cruises (☎ 742-6460 in Yarmouth; 1-800-341-7540 elsewhere in Canada) and it sails back and forth to Portland, Maine. The trip to Portland is 320 km – double the distance and therefore about twice the duration and more expensive – but you could win back the fare in the casino! This is a popular trip and for many is as much a holiday cruise as simple ferry transportation. Quite a few people just go and come back without even bothering to leave ship in port. Like the Bar Harbour boat, this is well appointed and comfortable, but the casino with floor show adds a touch of glamour. A cruise ticket is available for walk-ons and includes cabin, breakfast and a good dinner buffet. A range of ticket options is available, both with and without a vehicle.

Sailing time is about 11 hours one way. Through the summer the ferry leaves Yarmouth daily (except Wednesday) at 10 am and Portland at 9 pm daily (except Tuesday). The basic fare is US$55, less in the off season. A vehicle is $80. There is 10% discount for return trips, except on weekends. Please note these last fares are in US dollars.

Call ahead for either trip, as reservations will probably be required.

In Portland there is a Nova Scotia Tourist Office in the Portland Pier area, across from the old Thomas Block Building.

### Getting Around

For car rentals there is a Budget office (☎ 742-9500) at 150 Starrs Rd. The Texaco gas station at the far south end of town rents cars.

### FRENCH SHORE

From roughly Salmon River for 50 km up the coast along St Mary's Bay towards Digby is Old Acadia, also known as the Municipality of Clare. This is also where the province's largest, mainly French-speaking Acadian population lives. It's an interesting region where traditional foods and crafts are available, a few historic sites can be seen and, in summer, festivals are held in some of the small villages. The generally flat topography of the region is not of much appeal, and because the towns are small, a visit through the area can be done quite quickly.

The history and sights of the area are detailed in a booklet titled the *Acadian Shore*, available from the tourist office. Among the crafts offered out of people's houses along the way, the best two are the quilts and the woodcarvings, both of which have earned good reputations.

For campers, there are several campgrounds between Yarmouth and Digby.

### Cape St Mary's

A long wide arch of fine sand, the **Mavillette Beach** is marvellous. The marsh behind the beach is good for bird-watching. Across the street, the *Cape View Motel* (☎ 645-2258) has both regular motel rooms and some individual cabins. Prices are $40/45 a single/double in the units; the self-contained cottages are more costly.

From the *Cape View Restaurant* the beach looks great at sunset, and the food is good too. The menu is mainly seafood – clams are a local speciality – but also available is rapie pie, an old Acadian dish (for details see under Church Point). Main dishes at dinner range from $8 to $10.

### Meteghan

On the main street is **La Vieille Maison**, one of the oldest houses in the region and now set up as a museum depicting Acadian life here during the 18th century. This is a busy fishing port and there is a large commercial wharf where the boats moor.

The Wood Studio has carvings and quilts to see or buy.

For accommodation try the *Anchor Inn* (☎ 645-3390), a B&B in a big old house, which is low priced at $20/30 a single/double. The *Blue Fin Motel* (☎ 645-2251) charges about twice as much as the B&B.

For a light meal there is the *Meteghan Tea House* or the *Café Terrasse du Vieux Marin*.

### Comeauville

This is one of Canada's major mink-farming areas. A visit to a mink ranch can be arranged through one of the local tourist offices.

### Church Point (Pointe de l'Église)

Église Sainte Marie towers over the town and most other churches too. Built between 1903 and 1905, it is called the tallest and biggest wooden church in North America. It has an impressive multi-spired steeple and a very bright, airy interior.

In the corner by the altar is a small museum which contains articles from the church's history, including various vestments and chalices. A guide will show you around and answer any questions.

Nearby is the **Université de Sainte Anne**, the only French university in the province and a centre for Acadian culture.

The oldest of the annual Acadian cultural festivals, Festival Acadien de Clare, is held here during the second week of July.

**Places to Stay & Eat** There is an inexpensive B&B here, *Chez Benoit Stuart* (☎ 769-2715). For camping there is *Belle Baie Park* (769-3160), just out of town, where the best spots along the shore are saved for overnight tenters.

Just beyond the church, towards Yarmouth on the coast side of the road, with the Acadian flag outside, *Rapure Acadienne* is the place where all the local establishments get their rapie pie *(paté à la rapure)*. Inside, several women are busy preparing the three varieties: beef, chicken or clam. The result is difficult to describe but it's a type of meat pie topped with grated paste-like potato from which all the starch has been drawn. They are bland, filling and inexpensive and can be bought piping hot. In fact, they are all you can get here; you can't even find a coffee. Many of the French Shore restaurants offer this pie, often as an appetiser, but it's less than half the price right here.

### Belliveau Cove

There is a wharf on the attractive little harbour here, where the tides are particularly high. Stop at the pleasantly old-fashioned *Roadside Grill*, a comfortable local restaurant/diner with low prices for sandwiches and light foods but also lots of seafood – try the steamed clams, a local speciality, or the rapie pie. The walls are adorned with stuffed animals and various memorabilia.

There are a few wood-carving outlets here, but if you have any interest in these do not miss Clement Belliveau's shack, as he calls it, across the street from the Roadside. Despite constantly whittling the blocks of pine that have made him a big reputation, he enjoys a conversation.

### St Bernard

Here the grandest of the coast's churches stands – a mammoth granite Gothic-style monument which took 32 years to complete, beginning in 1910. A guide is on hand to show visitors around.

### DIGBY

An old, attractive town with 2500 residents, Digby was built around a hill in the Annapolis Basin, an inlet of the Bay of Fundy. It's famous for its scallop fleet and busy with its terminal for the *Princess of Acadia* ferry, which plies the waters between Digby and Saint John, New Brunswick. The town is also well known for its 'Digby chicks', a type of smoked herring. In summer, historic Water St has a bit of a resort flavour, with many visitors spending a day or so having a look around and feeding on scallops.

The town was founded by United Empire Loyalists in 1783, and since then its life has been based on fishing. The central area is small enough for walking to be the best way of getting around. At Loyalist Park on Water St is the town tourist office. Up Mount St from here is Trinity Anglican Church and its graveyard. A couple of blocks away, at the south edge of the downtown section, is the old Loyalist cemetery on Warwick St.

From the top of the hill by the high school on King St between Church and Mount Sts, five blocks back from Water St, there is a good view of the area.

From the ferry landing, it is about five km to Water St in downtown Digby.

### Admiral Digby Museum

At 95 Montague Row, this small museum displays articles and photographs pertaining to the town's marine history and early settlement. It's open daily in July and August but is closed on Sunday during other months. Admission is free.

### Places to Stay

For a place to sleep, the *Admiral's Landing B&B* (☎ 245-2247) is perfectly located at 115 Montague Row, opposite the Digby Bandstand, with views of the waterfront.

Singles/doubles start at $36/43. Most rooms are equipped with at least a sink, and some have TV. It's open all year and the rates are lower after October.

*Westway House* (☎ 245-5071) is a B&B at 6 Carlton St, a quieter street but still within walking distance of things to see. Singles/doubles are $30/37, including full breakfast, and outside there is a barbecue and picnic table to use. They also have a triple room and an available crib.

The *Thistle Down Inn* (☎ 245-4490), another B&B, is the big old white house at 98 Montague Row. There are chairs out the back on the lawn from where you can watch the harbour. It's a little more expensive than the others.

*Lovett Lodge Inn* (☎ 467-3917) includes the morning meal in its rates of $30/37. It's eight km east on Hwy 101, in Bear River.

Also out of town but in Sandy Cove is *Wingberry House* (☎ 834-2516), at $40 a double, including breakfast. There is swimming nearby. To get there, take Hwy 217 west from Digby. Turn left at the bottom of the first long hill in Sandy Cove and go to the end of the road. Turn right and it's at the end of the street. There are also three motels in town and a few private campgrounds around Digby.

### Places to Eat

There are a few seafood places where you can take advantage of the scallops and other local sea creatures. *Fundy Restaurant*, at 34 Water St, is not cheap but the food is good and the two outdoor balconies provide views over the harbour area. If it is too hot on the patio, there is a pleasant and cooler solarium, from where the ocean can still be viewed.

The *Captain's Cabin*, on the corner of Water and Birch Sts, is more casual but nice and offers similar seafood. Meals here range from $10 to $15. Steak is offered as an alternative to fish.

Also on Water St is the *Red Raven Pub*, for low-cost meals and a brew.

A walk over to and along First St between Church and Sydney Sts often turns up a small, modest place for a bite away from the main action, but they never seem to endure.

Lastly, consider buying some seafood fresh at the *Royal Fundy Seafood Market*, by the docks on Prince William St. The selection is wide and the prices low. If you're camping or have cooking facilities at the motel, even a bag of scallops can make a remarkably cheap and delicious dinner. Boil them until they turn white and then sautée them in butter. And that's it – pig out. Of course there is also shrimp available and lots of fish, including different types of smoked fish, which keeps for a few days without refrigeration. The Digby chicks, the heavily smoked herring for which the town is well known, will last up to two weeks.

### Getting There & Away

**Bus** The bus depot is at the Irving gas station on the corner of Montague Row (an extension of the main street, Water St) and Warwick St, a short walk from the centre of town. There are two buses a day to Yarmouth ($11) and two the other way to Halifax.

**Ferry** In summer, Marine Atlantic (☎ 245-2116) runs three ferry trips from Digby to Saint John, New Brunswick, daily, except Sunday when there are just two. One of the daily trips is at around midnight. The crossing takes a little more than 2½ hours. Prices are a bit steep – $20 per adult passenger and $45 per car, with bicycles $10. Reservations are a very good idea for this trip, and arrive at the dock an hour before departure. Rates go down between September and the end of June but trips are not as frequent during these months.

A one-day walk-on return ticket saves nearly 40% off the full fare and makes a five-hour Bay of Fundy minicruise.

The boat has a cafeteria, bar, video arcade and sun decks.

It will probably be cheaper to drive around in a small car but it takes longer because you must go right around the bay and up through Moncton, New Brunswick.

**NOVA SCOTIA**

## DIGBY NECK

The long, thin strip of land which protrudes into the Bay of Fundy from just north of town is known as Digby Neck and is visible from much of the French Shore. At the far end are Long and Brier islands, the two sections that have become split from the main arm. Short ferry rides connect them, so a road links Westport (on Brier Island, at the far end) to Digby. The many small villages along the way are primarily fishing ports and there is some good scenery.

Tiverton has a small museum, which includes a tourist information desk. Ask about balancing rock, a seaside oddity, and how to find it.

Brier Island has three lighthouses, with picnic tables and shoreline views and numerous walking trails. Agates can be found along the beaches.

What draws many people, though, is the sea life off **Long and Brier islands**. From June to October whale and bird-watching boat cruises run from Tiverton and Westport. Conditions make it a good location for seeing whales; the season is relatively long, beginning in May, building up through June and remaining steady, with a good population of three whale species – finback, minke and humpback – as well as dolphins, porpoises and seals, through August. Right whales are also sometimes seen.

All in all, the whale-watching trips here are the best and most successful of any in Nova Scotia.

There is a lot of other sea life to be seen, and over a dozen sea bird species are found in the area. Fall migration is the best time for bird-watchers.

Three operators run whale-watching tours. Reservations are a good idea and can be made by phone. Brier Island Whales & Seabird Cruises (☎ 839-2995) is in Westport and works in conjunction with BIOS, the Brier Island Ocean Study, a research organisation. The other two tours are based out of Tiverton, on Long Island. One of them, Ocean Explorations (☎ 839-2417), doesn't use a boat but rather a Zodiac, which being small, allows for pulse-quickening close encounters and a manageable-sized tour group.

Hopeful passengers should take plenty of warm clothing (regardless of how hot a day it seems), sunblock and binoculars, if possible. An antimotion-sickness pill taken before leaving the dock may not be a bad idea, either.

Westport is about 90 minutes from Digby, so leave with plenty of time if you've a boat to catch and remember there are two ferries. They are timed so that if you drive directly there is no wait for the second one. If you call one of the whale-watching companies for a reservation, double-check the ferry schedule at the same time.

There's is no public transportation along Digby Neck so you'll need a car or have to rely on hitching a lift.

To make things a little less hectic, there are three places to stay in Westport. Most economical is the *Westport Inn* (☎ 839-2675), with three rooms ($35/45 for singles/doubles). All three meals are available, and for whale-watching, a box lunch is offered.

The *Brier House* (☎ 839-2879), also with three rooms, is on top of a 40-metre bluff; singles/doubles cost $55/65 with a full breakfast.

With the same rates is the *Brier Island Lodge* (☎ 839-2300). At this much larger place there are 10 rooms, and a restaurant open to non-guests. The menu offers a range of fresh seafood – try the fishcakes – but even hamburgers are available. They also have bicycles for rent, and a good idea that I hadn't heard of before – camcorder rentals, ideal to take along on the whale trips.

All three places are open from May to the end of October only.

## ANNAPOLIS VALLEY

The Evangeline Trail through the valley is really not as scenic as might be expected, although it does pass through or by all the major towns and the historic sites. To really see the valley, though, and get into the countryside, it is necessary to take the still smaller roads parallel and either north or south of

Route 1. From here the farms and orchards, generally hidden from the main roads, come into view.

There are a number of quiet, pretty towns through the valley, as well as some fascinating history in such places as Port Royal and Grand Pré.

For those seeking a little work in late summer, there should be some jobs available picking apples. Check in any of the valley towns – Bridgetown, Lawrencetown, Middleton, etc. Line things up a couple of weeks before picking time, if possible. MacIntosh apples arrive first, at the end of August, but the real season begins around the first week of September.

## ANNAPOLIS ROYAL

Known as Canada's oldest settlement, Annapolis Royal is one of the valley's prime attractions and is certainly worth a visit for the plentiful history. It's also a pretty little town to which many are attracted for the fine eating and lodging establishments.

The site of Canada's first permanent European settlement, founded by Samuel de Champlain in 1604, is actually out of town at nearby Granville Ferry. As the English and French battled over the years for the valley and land at the mouth of the Annapolis River, the settlement often changed hands. In 1710, the English had a decisive victory and changed the town's name from Port Royal to Annapolis Royal (in honour of Queen Anne).

Despite the town's great age (in Canadian terms) the population is under 800, so it is quite a small community and easy to get around. It's a busy place in summer, with most things of interest located on or near the long, curving St George St. There is a waterfront boardwalk behind King's Theatre on St George St, with views over to the village of Granville Ferry.

A farmers' market is held every Saturday morning in summer.

A well-informed Nova Scotia Tourism Information Centre (☎ 532-5454) can be found at the Tidal Power Project site by the Annapolis River Causeway. Pick up a copy of the historic walking-tour pamphlet.

### Fort Anne National Historic Park

Right in the centre of town, this park preserves the memory of the early Acadian settlement plus the remains of the 1635 French fort. Two gunpowder magazines can be entered and the ground fortifications of mounds and moats observed. A museum has replicas of various period rooms, artefacts, uniforms and weapons; the Acadian room was transferred from an old homestead. The museum is open daily from May to October, on weekdays only for the rest of the year, and there is no admission charge.

### Lower St George St

One of the oldest streets in the country is St George, along the water. It contains many historic buildings, with three different centuries represented. The **O'Dell Inn Museum**, the former stagecoach stop, and **Robertson McNamara House**, once a school, both provide historic displays, the former of the Victorian era, the latter of local history. Admission to both is free.

Other places of note around town are the **de Gannes-Cosby House** (1708), the oldest wooden house in Canada, and the **Farmer's Hotel** (1710), also one of the oldest buildings in English Canada.

**Runciman House**, dating from 1817 and furnished in Regency style, is run by Heritage Canada and offers glimpses of former years.

### Historic Gardens

Numerous distinct types of garden, including Acadian and Victorian, are set out in the green 400-hectare grounds. There is an interpretive building, a restaurant, a gift shop and, adjacent, a bird sanctuary. Admission is charged. The gardens are not far from the centre of town, on St George St near the corner of Prince Albert Rd, and are open daily from May to October.

### Tidal Power Project

At the Annapolis River Causeway, this project offers visitors the chance to see a hydroelectric prototype harnessing power from the Bay of Fundy tides. There's also an interpretive centre that explains how it works. The site is free and is open every day in summer.

### Places to Stay

All budget categories of places to stay are well represented here, from inns to motels to cabins by the sea. There are a good half dozen B&Bs in or near town and a couple of motels along the primary routes.

About 25 km from Annapolis Royal is the HI *Sandy Bottom Lake Hostel* (☎ 532-2497), in South Milford on Hwy 8. It's open from mid-May to mid-October and there are nine beds, which cost $8/10 for members/non-members. Very conveniently, the hostel, which is right on the water, rents canoes. It is in the Beachside Park Campground; to get there, turn west in South Milford onto Clementvale-Virginia Rd and look for the signs.

Right in town, at 372 St George St, is the

*Turret B&B* (☎ 532-5770), an historic property with three rooms at just $30/40 a single/double with a full breakfast.

At the east end of the town at Aulden Hubley Drive, just off Route 201, is the *English Oaks B&B* (☎ 532-2066). Singles/doubles are $35/40 with full breakfast. Guests have use of a barbecue and picnic tables.

At 82 Victoria St is the *Bread & Roses Contry Inn* (☎ 532-5727), in a large restored Victorian house built in 1882. Singles/doubles are $55/70 and are for adults only. Evening tea is served.

About one km east of town on Hwy 201, Rural Route 1, *Helen's Cabins* (☎ 532-5207) cost $30 for singles/doubles and $48 for triples, with hot plates included for quick cooking. They are open from 1 May to 1 October.

The *Auberge Sieur de Monts* (☎ 532-5832), right beside the Habitation National Park in Port Royal, has two completely

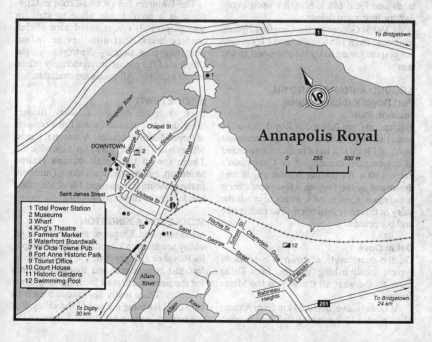

**Annapolis Royal**

0    250    500 m

1 Tidal Power Station
2 Museums
3 Wharf
4 King's Theatre
5 Farmers' Market
6 Waterfront Boardwalk
7 Ye Olde Towne Pub
8 Fort Anne Historic Park
9 Tourist Office
10 Court House
11 Historic Gardens
12 Swimmimg Pool

To Bridgetown

To Bridgetown
24 km

To Digby
30 km

self-contained houses for rent at $50 a night. Each sleeps four people and comes with kitchen, sitting room and bathroom. One has a fireplace, too.

At Victoria Beach, 26 km from Annapolis Royal, are the *Fundy View House & Cabins* (☎ 532-5015), with rooms in the house or in cabins with kitchens. Singles range from $25 to $30, doubles from $33 to $39. This place is open from 15 June to 15 September and there's swimming and fishing.

### Places to Eat
The *Ye Old Town Pub*, on Church St just off St George St, by the wharf, is a busy place for lunch and a brew. The *Fort Anne Café*, on St George St opposite the historic site, is cheap and basic and good for breakfast. At lunch try the soups or a sandwich nearby at *Leo's Café*, 22 St George St.

Expensive and decorative *Newman's*, at 218 St George St, has a good reputation for its varied menu, which includes fresh fish, lamb and local black bear. It's open every day for lunch and dinner.

At 350 St George St, the *Garrison House*, in a house from 1854, is also good. It's pricey but you may want to try the afternoon cream teas.

### AROUND ANNAPOLIS ROYAL
### Port Royal Habitat National Historic Park
Fifteen km from Annapolis Royal, this is the actual site of the first European settlement north of Florida. It has a replica, constructed in the original manner, of de Champlain's early 1600s fur-trading habitation. It was destroyed by the English a few years after it was begun. Costumed workers help tell the story of this early settlement. The park is free and is open daily.

### Delap Cove
On the coast north of town is a series of typical small fishing villages, from Delap Cove to the west all the way to the Minas Basin.

At Delap Cove, about 24 km from Annapolis Royal, a 12-km hiking trail runs through woods, along the shoreline and across the beach while providing a cross-section of the provincial coastal scenery. There are streams and waterfalls at various places and an assortment of birds and animals. Just west of Delap Cove is an interpretive office (where you can get a map) and there are a couple of toilets where the trails start, but that's it for amenities.

### KEJIMKUJIK NATIONAL PARK
This park contains some of the province's least-touched wilderness. It's an area of glacial lakes, good for canoeing, and evergreen forests, where the hiking is easy on the gentle, rolling hills. Some portage routes are marked; many were used by the Micmac Indians. Lots of frogs and reptiles inhabit the many bogs and deer also abound in the park.

There are primitive campsites along the trails and a main campground at Jeremy's Bay. Access north or south is by Hwy 8. Canoes are available for rent.

The *Whitman Inn* (☎ 682-2266) in Caledonia is a comfortable place to stay for noncampers. It's a restored turn-of-the-century house that now has an indoor swimming pool, saunas – the works – yet the simplest of the rooms are moderately priced at $50 a double. All meals are available.

### BRIDGETOWN
Back along the Annapolis Valley, Bridgetown has many trees and some fine examples of large Maritime houses. A seasonal tourist office is in Jubilee Park, on Granville St. There's also the small **James House Museum**, among the shops along Queen St. In the museum is a tea room for an afternoon break. Try the rhubarb pie.

### MIDDLETON & KINGSTON
Middleton and Kingston, two of the larger valley towns, aren't as attractive as Annapolis Royal or Bridgetown. They are more or less just commercial and shopping centres for the numerous small local farming communities. There really isn't much reason to stop until reaching the end of the valley. For scenery try getting off Route 1 through the

central region. This is the area where soil and climate combine to create one of the best orchard districts in the country. Aside from apples and other fruits, the area is noted for grains, vegetables and dairy cows. Roadside stands offer the fresh crops at good prices.

## COLDBROOK

This village is home to Scotian Gold, a large apple-processing facility where juice and apple sauce are produced. The plant offers visitors a look around in late summer and fall, when things are really getting cranked up.

## KENTVILLE

Kentville, with a sizeable population of 5000, marks the east end of the Annapolis Valley and acts as a focal point to a couple of nearby places of interest.

The town itself is functional and not of particular note but there are a few places to stay or eat. There is a military base outside town and its vehicles are often encountered on the roads.

At the eastern end of town is the **Agriculture Research Station**, with a museum related to the area's farming history and particularly to its apples. There is a pleasant walking trail through the woods – woods that contain old growth – one of the few areas in the province with original forest.

Neighbouring **New Minas** is strictly a shopping town, with a couple of malls and a branch of every chain restaurant you care to name.

Kentville is about a two-hour drive from Digby and about one hour from Halifax.

### Places to Stay & Eat

Highly recommended is the *Camelot Campground* (☎ 678-3343), which feels miles from anywhere with its peaceful woods and bubbling brook but is just 1.6 km from the main intersection in town – the junction of Main and Cornwallis Sts. The warm swimming pool surrounded by trees is perfect at the end of a day.

There are also some other conveniently central places to choose from. The *Wildrose*

*Inn* (☎ 678-8466), at 160 Main St, just out of the downtown area towards New Minas, is the very attractive old grey and pink house. Singles/doubles are $35/40, which includes a full breakfast as well as use of the swimming pool.

There are also two motels in town. Not far away, on Main St in Port William, the *Country Squire* (☎ 542-9125) is similar to the Wildrose.

The *King's Arms Pub* is on Main St, while *Paddy's*, a similar place, is over on Aberdeen St. Both provide inexpensive lunches.

## NORTH OF KENTVILLE

The area up to Cape Blomidon, on the Bay of Fundy, makes for a fine trip for half a day or longer, with good scenery, a memorable view of much of the valley and a couple of beaches. At Cape Split there is an excellent, dramatic hiking trail high above the Minas Basin and Channel.

### Canning

There is a guesthouse and a small, simple restaurant in Canning, where the main street through the tiny town is dark on a sunny day because there are so many large, overhanging trees.

### The Lookoff

From the road's edge at nearly 200 metres high, this could well be the best view of the soft, rural Annapolis Valley, its rows of fruit trees and farmhouses appearing like miniatures. Across the street is a campground and snack bar.

### Blomidon

At the provincial park here, there is a beach and camping. As at Kingsport's sandy beach further south, the water can get quite warm.

### Scots Bay

The road continues north to Scots Bay, with a large pebbled beach. From the end of the road, a spectacular 13-km hiking trail leads to the cliffs at Cape Split. Hikers note that this is not a loop trail, so you must retrace your steps.

## Halls Harbour

On the often foggy coast, Halls Harbour to the west is a classic, scenic little lobster village with a pier and a lobster pound where they cook live lobsters from 1 to 6 pm and sell them at the best prices you'll ever find. All that's sold is the lobster, rolls and butter. There are picnic tables around the dock area.

There are some very nicely kept and decorated houses in town and a small variety store opposite the wharf for drinks, etc. The tides are very high, leaving the entire wharf area high and dry when the water's out.

Along Hwy 359 to Halls Harbour, you may see some of the small local tobacco crop growing.

## WOLFVILLE

Wolfville is a quiet, green university town best known as the home of artist Alex Colville. With its art gallery, comfortable inns and impressive historic homes, there is a wisp of culture in the air.

The tourist office is in Willow Park, at the east end of Main St. The bus stop for Acadian bus lines is in a place called Nowlan's Canteen, at the far west end of town, on Main St on the corner of Hillcrest Ave. It's a bit of a walk into town.

St Andrew's United Church on Main St strikes me as being a particularly attractive structure.

### Acadia University Art Gallery

The gallery (☎ 542-2201) in the Beveridge Arts Centre building, on the corner of Main St and Highland Ave, exhibits mainly the work of other Maritime artists. It also has a collection of the work (mostly serigraphs) of Alex Colville, some of which is always on display. Admission is by donation.

### Carriage House Gallery

In the middle of Main St, this commercial gallery has the works of local artists for sale, as well as some Colville prints.

### Randall House Museum

Set in a house dating from the early 1800s, the museum (☎ 542-9775) deals with the early New England planters or colonists who replaced the expelled Acadians and the Loyalists who followed later. It is at 171 Main St and is open every day through the summer. Admission is free.

### Chimney Swifts

Ask at the tourist office about the town chimney swifts. From May to August, these birds collect and glide and swoop by the hundreds at dusk, before disappearing into a chimney. There is an interpretive display on the phenomenon on Front St.

### Places to Stay

The residences at the central Acadia University (☎ 542-2201) are open to visitors through the summer and are not expensive.

Modest *Birchcliff B&B* (☎ 542-3391), at 84 Main St, has two rooms offered through the summer, at $30/40 a single/double, which includes a full breakfast.

*Victoria's Inn* (☎ 542-5744), 416 Main St, is a very ornate place, with rooms in the lodge or in a motel section. The best deal is on rooms with shared bathrooms in the main lodge ($49 for singles and $59 for doubles or triples). They also have a dining room.

There are also three up-market inns in town.

### Places to Eat

Main St has both cheap places and more expensive ones offering seafood. The *Colonial Inn*, with historic decor and waitresses in period costume, has a good varied menu of standard dishes and does them well. It's open for all three meals and isn't too badly priced either.

For a real splurge *Chez La Vigne*, at 17 Front St, is recommended. It's open every day for lunch and dinner but is closed on Monday through the winter. The owner/chef has been voted Canadian chef of the year.

## GRAND PRÉ

Now a very small English-speaking town, Grand Pré was the site of one of the most dramatic stories in eastern Canada's history. The details of this sorry but fascinating tale can be learned at the National Historic Site north of the main highway and town, five km east of Wolfville.

## Grand Pré National Historic Park

Grand Pré means 'great meadow' and refers to the farmland created when the Acadians built dykes along the shoreline, as they had done in north-west France for generations. There are 1200 hectares below sea level. It's a beautiful area and one you wouldn't want to leave involuntarily, especially after the work that made it home. The park is a memorial to the Acadians, who had a settlement

### The Acadians

The story of the Acadians is one of the most interesting, dramatic and tragic in Canada's history. It was played out in what are now five of the country's provinces, the USA, the West Indies and Europe. And although it began in the 1600s it is not over.

When the French first settled the area around the south Minas Basin shore of the Bay of Fundy in 1604 they named the land Acadia. By the next century these settlers thought of themselves as Acadians. To the English, however, they were always to be 'the French'. The rivalry and suspicion between these two powers of the New World began with the first landings and was only to increase in hostility and bitterness.

The population of Acadia continued to grow through the 17th and 18th centuries and, with various battles and treaties, changed ruling hands from French to English and back again. Finally, in 1713 with the Treaty of Utrecht, Acadia became English Nova Scotia. The Acadians refused to take an oath of allegiance although for the most part they weren't much interested in France's point of view either and evidently wanted most of all to be left alone. Things sort of drifted along in this state for a while and the area around Grand Pré became the largest Acadian community. By this time the total regional population was not far off 10,000 with 3500 more people in Louisbourg and still others in Prince Edward Island.

Unfortunately for them tensions once again heated up between England and France with squabbles and trade-offs taking place all over the east coast. When a new hardline lieutenant-governor Charles Lawrence was appointed in 1754 he quickly became fed up with the Acadians and their supposed neutrality. He didn't trust them and decided to do something about it. He demanded an oath of allegiance and, as the game had always been played, the Acadians said forget it. This time, though, the rules had changed.

In late August 1755 with the crowns of France and England still locked in battle and paranoia increasing, what was to become known as the Deportation or the Expulsion began. All told, about 14,000 Acadians were forced out of this area. Villages were burned, the people boarded onto boats.

The sad, bitter departure was the theme for Longfellow's well known lengthy narrative poem, *Evangeline*, titled after its fictional heroine. Many Acadians headed for Louisiana and New Orleans, where their name became Anglicised to 'Cajun' (often heard in songs and seen on restaurant menus). The Cajuns, some of whom still speak French, have maintained aspects of their culture to this day. Others went to various Maritime points and north-eastern America, others to Martinique, Santo Dominigo, back to Europe, some even to the Falkland Islands. Nowhere were they greeted warmly with open arms. Some hid out and remained in Acadia. In later years many of those people deported returned.

Today, most of the French people in Canada's Atlantic Provinces are the descendants of the expelled Acadians and they're still holding tight to their heritage.

In Nova Scotia the Cheticamp area in Cape Breton and the French Shore north of Yarmouth are small strongholds. A pocket in western Prince Edward Island and the Port au Port peninsula in Newfoundland are others. New Brunswick has a large French population stretching up the east coast past the Acadian Peninsula at Caraquet and all around the border with Quebec.

There has recently been an upsurge in Acadian pride and awareness and in most of these areas you'll see the Acadian flag flying and museums dealing with the past and the continuing Acadian culture. There is another major National Historic Site dealing with the Acadians and their expulsion near St Joseph, New Brunswick, not far from the Nova Scotia border – a visit is recommended. Festivals held in some of these areas provide an opportunity to see traditional dress, sample foods and hear some of the wonderful fiddle-based music. ■

here from 1675 to 1755 and then were given the boot by the British.

It consists of an information centre, church, gardens, space and views.

Free tours of the site are offered, and if all the guides are as humorous as the young woman I had, then the tours are a good laugh as well as being informative. The worthwhile gift shop has a selection of books on the Acadians, among other things.

A new stone church, built in the Acadian style, sits in the middle of the site as a monument to the original inhabitants. Inside, the history of those people is depicted in a series of colourful paintings done in 1987 by New Brunswick painter Claude Picard.

Walk down through the gardens to the old blacksmith's shed, where there are views of the surrounding gorgeous, fertile farmlands and pastures with green hills in the background, the air an aromatic mix of sea breeze and worked fields.

In the gardens are a bust of Longfellow, honoured for his poem which chronicles the Acadian's saga, and a statue of Evangeline, now a romantic symbol of her people.

The park is open daily from June to September and admission is free. Acadian Days, an annual festival held sometime towards the end of July, consists of music, storytelling, arts & crafts. Many of the events are held at the historic park.

### Grand Pré Winery

The winery is one of only two in the province, the other being at Jost, near Malagash on the Northumberland Shore. It sits adjacent to the main road through town and can be visited.

A self-guided tour around the grounds and to the edge of the vineyards explains the history and wine-making procedures. In the cellar a variety of wines may be sampled free of charge and favourites can be purchased upstairs.

### WINDSOR

Windsor is a small town on the Avon River, halfway between the North Pole and the Equator. At one time it was the only British

stronghold in this district of French power and Acadian farmers.

Hwy 1 becomes Water St in town and the main intersection is with Gerrish St. Nearby, off King St, there's an old blockhouse still intact amid portions of the British fort at **Fort Edward National Historic Site** (dating from 1750). It was used as one of the assembly stations during the expulsions of the Acadians.

Another site is **Haliburton House**, once the home of Judge Thomas Chandler Haliburton, one of the founders of written American humour. He created the Sam Slick character in Mark Twain-style stories. Although these aren't read much now, many Haliburton expressions, such as 'quick as a wink' and 'city slicker', are often used today. Haliburton's large estate is open to visitors, free, from mid-July to mid-September. It's on Clifton Ave, which runs off Grey St, itself leading from Gerrish St just north of Lake Pesaquid, in the eastern section of town.

**Shand House**, part of the provincial museum system, is a small museum on Water St evoking the life of a well-to-do family at the turn of the century. It's open daily (except Sunday) and is on Ferry Hill. Admission is free.

Windsor has an internationally performing puppet theatre, the **Mermaid Theatre**, and the window of the theatre on Gerrish St is worth a look whether you're seeing a show or not.

The farms in the Wolfville/Windsor area regularly produce some of the world's largest pumpkins. These are serious pumpkins – I mean you could use a chain saw to carve a Halloween face in these guys. Watch for the Pumpkin Festival held here each year on Thanksgiving (in October). But don't get too close!

### Tides

The tides in the bay and Avon River near Windsor are impressive – falling and rising up to 12 metres. At Poplar Grove, off Hwy 14 East, you can view a tidal bore. Ask at the tourist office for good times and locations for observing this phenomenon because it varies a lot. Port Williams, near Wolfville, is also a good place to see the difference between high and low tides.

### Places to Stay

The *Meander Inn* (☎ 798-2325), at 153 Albert St, is a place for overnighters, with singles/doubles from $30/45. There are also other B&Bs and a motel here.

### Getting There & Away

Acadian bus lines from Halifax to Windsor continues on to Yarmouth, making numerous stops through the Annapolis Valley.

# Northumberland Shore

This is the north coastal district of the province, from the New Brunswick border to Cape Breton Island. The Northumberland Strait is between this shore and Prince Edward Island and has some of the warmest waters north of the US Carolinas. Hwy 6, also called the Sunrise Trail tourist route, runs along this strip of small towns, beaches and Scottish history.

On Hwy 104 right at the New Brunswick border is a large tourist office with maps and overviews of the driving trails around Nova Scotia.

Although there are no major attractions along this shore, it is busy, and as accommodation is not plentiful, places to stay fill quickly. It's strongly recommended that you find a place by lunch time in July and August.

## PUGWASH

On the coast along the Sunrise Trail from Amherst is this small port, with good beaches nearby. On average, the water temperature along this coast is slightly over 20°C in summer. Pugwash's two claims to fame are the large salt mine, which produces boatloads of salt to be shipped from the town docks, and the colourful Gathering of the Clans festival, which takes place each year on 1 July. Street names in town are written in Gaelic as well as in English.

Pugwash once hosted the International Thinkers' Conferences, organised by Cyrus Eaton, a Nova Scotian and one of America's top financiers.

There are several craftspeople in town and their wares are sold along the main street.

## WALLACE

There is no reason to stop here really but there is an interesting town tidbit. The sandstone from the quarry just out of town has been used to build many fine buildings, including the Parliament Buildings in Ottawa and Province House in Nova Scotia.

## MALAGASH

The Jost Winery (☎ 257-2636) off Route 6 is one of only two vineyards in Nova Scotia, the other being at Grand Pré in the Annapolis Valley. Run by a German family, the winery began operation in 1970 and now, with 13 hectares, produces several varieties, with the riesling style perhaps the best known. Free tours are offered at 3 pm through the summer and there is a store on the premises. Jost products can also be bought at the government liquor outlets, with the best selection being in the local ones.

## TATAMAGOUCHE

Despite having a population of just 550, Tatamagouche is somewhat of a visitor centre, with a lot of people passing through and a few things to see. Pretty well everything is along Main St, which is really the highway going east and west.

Not to be missed is the quirky **Fraser Culture Centre**, a sort of museum-cum-art gallery. The showpiece is the room dedicated to Anna Swan who, at 2.4 metres tall and weighing 187 kg, was known as the giantess of Nova Scotia and who went on to achieve some celebrity. Born in one of the surrounding villages in 1896, she parlayed her size into a lucrative career with Barnum & Bailey's circus and even ended up meeting Queen Elizabeth II in London, where Anna was married. Clothes, newspaper clippings and photographs tell the big story.

Next door a room houses two stuffed

calves – each with two heads. (I told you it was quirky.) But actually there is more to it, including some historical artefacts and paintings in the gallery section.

There is an inexpensive, pleasant little tea room, with home baking in one of the rooms too. The tourist office is also here, in another of the many rooms.

A few doors down is the less idiosyncratic **Sunrise Trail Museum** of local history, with emphasis on the shipbuilding industry, once of major importance here. Other items pertain to household and farmyard tools, with articles including a dog-powered churn. The Acadian French settled this area in the 1700s and a display tells of them and their expulsion.

In Tatamagouche an annual Octoberfest is held at the end of September or beginning of October.

### Places to Stay & Eat

For a place to sleep in town, the *Train Station Inn* (☎ 657-3222), in the old train station on Main St, is good and not overpriced (from $40/50 a single/double with full breakfast and evening tea). It's open all year round. There is also a café on the premises.

Ten km away at Brule Beach are the *Brule Shore Cabins* (☎ 474-7240), which are small, basic and have seen better days. They fill up most nights, however, and have a certain appealing funky charm – and they're cheap ($34 a double or triple). Forget the advertised ocean swimming though – the beach area isn't even pleasant to walk on, let alone swim at.

Aside from the café in the museum if you're looking for a bite, the *Villager Inn & Restaurant* has inexpensive specials, some seafood and quite good chowders.

German food is available at the *Balmoral Motel* dining room. Also in town is a pizza place and a submarine-sandwich shop.

The Tatamagouche farmers' market takes place on Saturday mornings through the summer.

### AROUND TATAMAGOUCHE

There are a couple of other small museums in the region. South down Route 311, **Balmoral Mills** has one of the province's oldest grist mills, which opened in 1874. You can't miss the bright red building down by the stream. Demonstrations show the flour (oatmeal, barley, wheat) milling process from start to finish and the completed products are even offered for sale. It's open daily from 15 May to 15 October and admission is free; there are some picnic tables by the creek.

Nearby, outside the village of Denmark, the **Sutherland Steam Mill** was built in 1894 and was run continuously by family members until 1953. The sawmill is no longer a commercial entity but the machinery and steam engine are still operational.

This part of the province has a bit of a German colony, and at the *Bavarian Garden Restaurant* in Denmark, various made-on-the-premises German foods are offered. It's open every day in July and August but only on weekends in May, June and September. The Pork Shop next door sells a wide variety of German sausage, kassler, hams, etc.

At **River John** look for the community lobster dinners held from May to July and the chicken barbecues in August. The lobster boats operate out of the small pier with its nearby storage shanties at **Cape John**.

### CAPE SKINNER

Back at the coast, Cape Skinner has a small wharf with boats that are engaged in the collection of Irish moss. This is a type of seaweed from which a gelatin, carrageenin, is extracted for use in making ice cream and other products that require a gel emulsifier.

### PICTOU

Pictou (pronounced 'pik toe'), one of the most attractive and interesting towns along the North Shore, was where the Highland Scots first landed in 1773, to be followed by thousands in the settling of 'New Scotland'. They spread from the Northumberland Shore through Cape Breton, reminded of home by the landscape and weather. In town, among the many older structures, are several buildings and historic sites relating to the early Scottish pioneers. Pick up a walking-tour brochure at the tourist office at the rotary (roundabout) north-west of the town centre.

Water St, with most of the commercial enterprises, is the main street and reflects the architectural style of the early Scottish builders. Above it Church, High and Faulkland Sts are lined with some of the old, very large houses for which the town is also noted.

There's a farmers' market, where you'll find baked goods and farm produce, every Saturday from April to December in the Community Centre on Front St.

The deCoste Entertainment Centre on Water St is the site of a range of live performances, which take place through the year.

The ferry to Prince Edward Island leaves from just north of town at Caribou. For details see the Charlottetown Getting There & Away section, in the Prince Edward Island chapter.

### Hector Heritage Quay
Part of the waterfront has been redeveloped to preserve both history and access. At the boatyard, a full-size replica of the first ship to bring the Scottish settlers, the three-masted *Hector*, is being constructed. Begun in 1993, it will take about a decade to complete. Guides tell the story of the crossing and settlement and will answer questions.

Other features include an interpretive centre (☎ 485-8028), with varied displays and dioramas depicting the life and times of the initial Scottish immigrants. Also included is an historic blacksmith shop and a collection of shipbuilding artefacts. There is also a marina and gift shop.

### Olde Foundry Art Centre
On Front St, this restored old complex houses the workshops and stores of local artisans and craftspeople and a number of antique dealers.

### Grohmann Knives Ltd
The small family-run business (☎ 485-4224) at 88 Water St has a well-deserved reputation

for the very fine outdoor and kitchen knives it produces. One of them, a classic belt knife available in many countries, is in the Museum of Modern Art in New York.

Many of the production stages are done by hand, as they were when the operation began in the mid-1950s, and can be seen on the free tours around the plant offered three times a day Monday to Friday from May to September. You'll observe an interesting procedure which in one stage employs thick walrus-hide belts for polishing. The tour highlight, though, is watching the guide's hands as he sharpens a knife to a razor's edge.

There is a wide and very tempting selection of knives for sale. (Yes, I did...a Russell.)

### Northumberland Fisheries Museum
On Front St in the old train station, the museum tells the story of the area's fishing, both past and present. The fisherman's bunkhouse is a good display. Shipbuilding remains important – the yards are nearby – and is also depicted in the museum. It's open seven days a week in July and August and admission is free.

### Hector National Exhibit Centre
Away from the town centre but within walking distance on Haliburton Rd, a continuation westward of High St, this centre (☎ 485-4563) presents a variety of ever-changing shows. On one visit it featured the tartans of Scotland and their histories. It's open daily and is free. The pond, just to one side of the museum, is home to a seemingly limitless number of frogs.

### McCullogh House
Open every day from May to October, the house built in 1806 for Tom McCullogh, a minister and important educator, now displays articles pertaining to his career and life but also items relating to other early Scottish settlers. The house is the one just up the hill from the Hector National Exhibit Centre.

### Beaches
There are a couple of very good beaches

outside Pictou. The most popular, and something of an 'in place', is **Melmerby Beach** ('the Merb'), which is actually north of New Glasgow but draws visitors from far and wide. It's a long, wide sandy beach; there is a basic hamburger stand but no shade.

My choice is **Caribou Beach**, which is equally sandy with gradually deepening water but is more scenic, with picnic tables along a small ridge above the beach and trees for when the sun gets too intense. It is much closer to town, north of Pictou near the Prince Edward Island ferry terminal. Both beaches are free and the water along this strip of ocean is as warm as any in Nova Scotia, heated by the Gulf Stream to around 19°C in midsummer – not bad at all if you keep moving.

### Festivals

The Lobster Carnival, a three-day event at the beginning of July, marks the end of the lobster season with music, parades and the like.

The Hector Festival in mid-August is four days of celebration of the area's Scottish heritage, including concerts.

### Places to Stay

Pictou has about a dozen possibilities for spending the night. Bear in mind that, while not crowded, the town has a steady stream of people passing through and most accommodation is full (or close to it) through the summer.

Most economical and central is *Munro's* (☎ 485-8382), at 66 High St, a tree-lined street within walking distance of the harbour. There are three rooms available from June to October for $25/30 a single/double, and that includes a full breakfast.

The *Willow House Inn* (☎ 485-5740) is a grander B&B developed in a large historic house dating from 1840 and once belonging to the mayor. It, too, is very central, at 3 Willow St. There are 10 rooms, the more expensive of which have private bath facilities. Singles/doubles cost $35/40 and up.

Away from the downtown area, near the tourist office by the traffic rotary, is *Johnston's Motel* (☎ 485-4157). It has some newish motel units and a number of older individual cabins with their own kitchens, some with two bedrooms which can make for a pretty good bargain. Singles are $45 but doubles and triples are just $5 extra. If this place is full, there is another just down and across the road towards town.

### Places to Eat

For breakfast go to *Smith's*, on Church St, which is one block back from and parallel to Water St. It's open from 6 am every day but Sunday.

Right in the centre, at 11 Water St, is the *Stone House Café & Pizzeria*, where the food isn't great but the selection is wide. There is a nice outside patio and local entertainment is often on tap in the evenings. A meal costs about $6.

The *Golden Boat* Chinese place, at 93 Water St, is open until midnight all week.

For a splurge amidst the surroundings of a very tasteful, warm, country lodge, step into the *Braeside Inn*, up the hill at 80 Front St, overlooking the water. The food is very good and the menu is varied, with a slant towards seafood. Built in 1938, the inn has been redone and has 20 overnight guest rooms.

Though out of the way and virtually impossible to reach without a car, one of the best known restaurants in the area is the *Lobster Bar*, across the bay from Pictou in Pictou Landing, where there is a Native Indian reserve and not a lot more. Driving involves a rather circuitous route over one of the bridges towards New Glasgow – get the map distributed at the Pictou tourist office.

It's a pleasantly casual (take the kids), busy and not badly priced seafood house specialising in lobster. A full lobster meal costs about $16. There is no help-yourself buffet as at some lobster-supper places, but portions will satisfy most people. They've been serving up fish, clams and all the rest since the late 1950s and have fed former US president Jimmy Carter as well as former prime minister Brian Mulroney and his wife Mila.

## NEW GLASGOW

With a population of 10,000, New Glasgow is the largest town along the Northumberland Shore. It originally was, and remains, a small industrial centre. There is little to see in town, but it can be useful as a stopping point as it's close if you're coming or going to the ferry for Prince Edward Island.

Provost St, the main retail and shopping avenue, has a couple of restaurants. Temperance St, parallel to Provost St and up the hill from the river, is attractive, with lots of trees, some large older houses, a couple of churches and **Stewart House**. The latter, at 86 Provost St, is an historic building housing a small museum illustrating the town's history in shipbuilding and coal mining.

Railway buffs should not miss the **Samson**, the first steam locomotive in North America. It operated nearby in 1837 and has been restored to its odd-looking glory. It sits encased in glass beside the library on Archimedes St.

**Fraser's Mountain**, not far from town, offers excellent views of the entire region. Drive east through town on Archimedes St and turn right on George St. Continue up the hill, veering left around the church, and keep going straight to the summit.

Out of town at nearby Abercrombie St, towards Pictou, the **Sobey Collection of Canadian Art** features some of the country's best known 19th and 20th-century painters. There is no admission charge.

### Places to Stay

For spending the night, the *Wynwood Inn* (☎ 752-4527), a B&B since 1930, makes a fine choice. Actually an attractive old house, it's central, at 71 Stellarton Rd, and has a nice balcony. Rates are $28 to $38 for singles, $32 to $40 for doubles, including a light breakfast. One room has a private bathroom.

*Mackay's B&B* (☎ 752-5889), at 44 High

St, is also central but is more modest. Prices are about the same ($30/40 for singles/doubles).

There are motels on the highway on the way in and out of town.

## ANTIGONISH

If you're coming from New Brunswick or Prince Edward Island, this is the place to spend the night or even a couple of days. Antigonish (pronounced 'An-tee-guh-NISH') is also a good stop between Sydney and Halifax. A pleasant, small town with a few things to see, it has some good places to stay and the beach is nearby. It's a university and residential town with no industry.

### Information

The tourist office is just off the highway at the west entrance to Antigonish, coming from New Glasgow at exit 32.

### St Ninian's Cathedral

This is the seat of the Catholic diocese for the adjoining three counties and all of Cape Breton. It was begun in 1868 and is built of blue limestone and granite from local quarries. Work in the interior comes from a variety of sources, including Quebec, New Hampshire and Europe. St Ninian was an obscure priest from Ireland who travelled and taught in the Scottish Highlands in the 4th century.

### St Francis Xavier University

The attractive campus of this 125-year-old university is behind the cathedral near the centre of town. It's a pleasant place to walk around just for a look-see.

### County Courthouse

In 1984 this 129-year-old building was designated a National Historic Site. Restored in 1970 although it was in good repair, it still serves as the county's judicial centre. The design (by Alexander Macdonald) is typical of many of the province's courthouses from the mid-19th century.

### Heritage Association

The association has put together a collection of pioneer artefacts, old town records from the schools and cemeteries, and maps and photos to present an historical record of the town. The old train station at 20 East Main St has found a new purpose as the home for this exhibit. It's free and is open every day but Sunday.

### Festivals

Antigonish is known for its annual Highland Games, held in mid-July. These Scottish games have been going on since 1861. You'll see pipe bands, drum regiments, dancers and athletes from far and wide; there are competitions, performances, singing, dancing, fiddling and a pipe band tattoo. The events last a week. The international Gathering of the Clans took place here in the summer of 1983. There is also a theatre programme through the summer.

Festival Antigonish is a summer theatre festival, with all performances held at one of the university auditoriums.

### Places to Stay

West of town, near Addington Forks and just off the Trans Canada Hwy, *Beaver Mountain* (☎ 863-3343) is a very quiet provincial park, good for camping. It's up on a hill in the woods and there is hardly anyone ever there.

*Whidden's Campground & Trailer Court* (☎ 836-3736), right in town on the corner of Main and Hawthorne Sts, is an unusual accommodation complex. It's a very large place and offers a real blend of choices. Camping costs $14 for a tent but just half that for hikers, cyclists or, basically, anybody else without a car. Serviced sites cost more. Then there are motel apartments with kitchens (from $60) and mobile homes with complete facilities ($65 a double plus $5 for each additional person). The grounds have a swimming pool and a laundromat for all guests to use.

For rooms at the central *University* from mid-May to mid-August, call the Residence Manager (☎ 867-3970, 867-2258). It has a

dining room, laundromat and pool. Singles/doubles are $24/32 and good weekly rates are available.

There are also numerous inns, motels, cottages and a couple of B&Bs. *Green Haven* (☎ 863-2884) is a central B&B at 27 Greening St. It's close to the bus depot and has singles/doubles at $25/35.

Another is the *Old Manse* (☎ 863-5696), in a house dating from 1874 at 5 Tigo Park, a couple of blocks from the corner of Main and West Sts.

*Hillside Housekeeping Cottages* (☎ 232-2888), 19 km east of town at Tracadie, are a better bargain than motels in the area. Basic cottages cost $34/40 for singles/doubles, $40/46 with cooking facilities. The cottages are 10 minutes from the beach.

### Places to Eat

A stroll down Main St and around the town will turn up several places for a bite. At *Adam's Bakery* there's decent food and prices. The *Sunshine Café* at 194 Main St is good for soups, salads and sandwiches under $5. The bran muffins are also very good. It's closed on Sundays. Next door the health food store has a fine selection of breads and pita.

*Farmer Brown's*, in the big red-and-white barn by the old train station, is the place for breakfast and offers quick meals of burgers and the like through the day. *Wong's* is friendly and provides the local Chinese option, with the standard dishes moderately priced at under $7 or so. The *Venice* has a few Greek dishes among the mainly Italian fare.

West out of town along the Trans Canada Hwy, the more costly *Lobster Treat* restaurant is good for seafood and steaks.

### Getting There & Away

**Bus**  The bus depot (☎ 863-6900) is on the Trans Canada Hwy at the turn-off for James St into town, on the west side of the city, and is within walking distance of the downtown area. Buses include those to Halifax (once a day, $23), to Sydney (one morning and one afternoon trip, $20) and to Charlottetown (at 1.15 pm daily, $30 including the ferry).

**Train** The train service has been discontinued.

## AROUND ANTIGONISH
### Monastery
East of town in the small village of Monastery, the old monastery is now home to the Augustine Order of monks. It was originally a Trappist monastery established by French monks in 1825. Visitors are welcome and a tour of the buildings and grounds is offered.

### Beaches
There are some good sandy beaches on the coast east or north from town. For the eastern ones, take Bay St out of town.

### Driving Tours
There are several driving tours of the area, each no more than 80 km – a descriptive pamphlet is available from the tourist office. They try to take in some good scenery and points of historical note. One recommended 'off-the-track' route goes north along the coast to Cape George on Hwy 337, with some fine shoreline views. At Crystal Cliffs, along the way, there are huge cormorant roosts.

# Eastern Shore

The 'Eastern Shore' designation refers to the area east from Dartmouth to Cape Canso, at the extreme eastern tip of the mainland. It's one of the least-visited regions of the province; there are no large towns and little industry, and the main road is slow, narrow and almost as convoluted as the rugged shoreline it follows. As in much of the province, the population is clustered in small coastal villages. Marine Drive, the designated tourist route, is pretty much the only route through the area, but despite its descriptions and alleged beauty spots, it is neither very scenic nor particularly interesting. There are a few good things, nonetheless, and these are emphasised here.

There are some campgrounds and good beaches along the coast but the water on this edge of the province is prohibitively cold.

## MUSQUODOBOIT VALLEY
A side trip away from the coast follows the course of the Musquodoboit River into the forested interior and along the valley's farming regions to the village of Upper Musquodoboit. Despite its light population, this was an area settled by Europeans as early as 1692. The following century saw people arriving from Ireland and New England.

There isn't a lot to do, although there are some walking trails. Consider it as an alternative route to the north coast, as it leads quite directly to New Glasgow.

## MARTINIQUE BEACH PROVINCIAL PARK
Martinique, 4.8 km south of the village of Musquodoboit Harbour, is the longest beach in the province and a good place for a break.

## JEDORE OYSTER POND
Quite the name for a town, I'd say. See the small **Fisherman's Life Museum** – it's a model of a typical 1900s fishing family's house. It's open every day through the summer and admission is free. Also here on the water is the *Golden Coast Restaurant*, for seafood.

## CLAM HARBOUR
There is a good beach with a small, basic restaurant and a picnic area. In mid-August each year, a sand-sculpting contest is held.

## SHIP HARBOUR
Off the shore here you'll see the buoys and nets of the local aquaculture industry. This is North America's largest mussel-farming centre. Fish-farming of every description is poised to become ever more significant as the natural stocks show the effects of centuries of indiscriminate hauling.

## TANGIER
A visit to **Willy Krauch's Smokehouse**, a short distance from the main road in Tangier,

NOVA SCOTIA

is worthwhile. Begun by Willy, a Dane, and now run by his sons, it's a small operation that has rightly earned a big reputation. They smoke Atlantic salmon, mackerel and eel, but to my tastebuds, the ultimate is the Cape Breton smoked trout – easily the best smoked fish I've ever had. It's great stuff for travelling too, because you can keep it without refrigeration. It can also be mailed, as it has been to Queen Elizabeth at Buckingham Palace.

The shed is open every day until 6 pm. Ask the person at the counter if you can watch the fish being smoked out the back.

Also in town is Coastal Adventures Sea Kayaking (☎ 772-2774), for lessons, rentals and tours to offshore islands.

## TAYLOR HEAD PROVINCIAL PARK

Just east of the village of Spry Harbour, this day-use park has a very fine, sandy beach fronting a shallow protected bay. The water, though, doesn't seem to warm up much. A walking trail (about a two-hour walk) runs along the shore and through the woods. At some points are good examples of Krummholz vegetation – trees and plants stunted and twisted by the poor, seaside conditions. Near the parking lot are a few picnic tables under the trees. The park is free.

## LISCOMB PARK GAME SANCTUARY

North of Sheet Harbour lies this large preserve, 518 sq km in area. There's lots of wildlife and some good canoeing, swimming, fishing and hiking. Sheet Harbour has a decently priced motel of the same name.

## PORT DUFFERIN

Tiny Port Dufferin, population 157, is mentioned for the *Marquis of Dufferin Seaside Inn* (☎ 654-2696), a highly regarded retreat featuring coastal views, breezes and tranquility. Rooms are in a new motel-like strip alongside the original house. Singles/doubles are $65/75 and include a good-size continental breakfast. The dining room in the restored house of 1859 serves good Maritime-style meals which often feature

seafood. The inn is closed from May until October.

Port Dufferin is about two hours' drive from Halifax, Antigonish or the Halifax International Airport.

## LISCOMB MILLS

In a green wooded area where the Liscomb River meets the sea is one of the provincial government's luxury resort lodges, *Liscomb Lodge* (☎ 779-2307). It has all the amenities, and prices to match, but you may want to have a look or a tea or splurge on one of the seafood meals.

## SHERBROOKE

Inland towards Antigonish, the pleasant little town of Sherbrooke is overshadowed by its historic site, which is about the same size.

**Sherbrooke Village** excellently recreates life of around 125 years ago through buildings, demonstrations and costumed workers. It's called a living museum, which means that almost all of the houses, stores, various workshops and buildings are the original ones and stand in their original locations. The green, quiet setting helps to evoke a real sense of stepping back in time.

The site is open daily from 15 May to 15 October and is a real bargain at the amazingly low price of $2.25. The hotel on the site serves snacks and simple lunches.

About half a km away is the **Sherbrooke Village Sawmill**, the former town mill, which is in working order and has a guide to answer questions, free. Across the street and a nice walk through the woods along a stream is a cabin in which the workers at the mill would have lived.

Sherbrooke itself, although not the major centre it was at the turn of the century, is one of the biggest towns in the area, so stop here for tourist information, groceries and gasoline. There are a few picnic tables by the tourist office and a couple of craft shops to have a look at.

Nearby St Mary's River is one of the province's top salmon rivers. A day-use provincial park by the river and with picnic tables is just 400 metres north of town.

### Places to Stay & Eat

If you're spending the night, consider the central *St Mary's River Lodge* (☎ 522-2177), with singles/doubles from $24/28 with shared bath facilities. Breakfast is available.

Something else to look for is the *Bright House* restaurant in town. In a bright yellow inn dating from 1850, it specialises in roast beef and fresh seafood and does them well. It's open daily for lunch, maybe a chowder, and dinner. It's not cheap but is not expensive either, with meals around $8 to $10 at lunch time.

Regardless of whether you are going to partake in the dining room, do visit the adjacent bake shop for cinnamon buns, muffins, pies and various other sweets. It's open from May to October.

There is camping nearby, with one place north of town and one place south to choose from.

### CANSO

With a population of just 1200, this town at the edge of the mainland is probably the largest on the whole eastern shoreline. Since the first attempted settlement in 1518, Canso has seen it all: Native Indian battles, British and French landings and captures, pirates, fishing fleets and the ever-present difficulties of life ruled by the sea.

A museum, **Whitman House**, on the corner of Main and Union Sts, has reminders of parts of this history and offers a good view from the roof.

An interpretive centre on the waterfront tells the story of the **Grassy Island National Historic Site**, which lies just offshore and can be visited by boat. In 1720 the British built a small fort here to offer some protection from the French, who had their headquarters in Louisbourg. Despite all the turmoil and events which took place here, or perhaps because of them, there isn't much of anything now on the barren island and the fort ruins are minimal.

# Cape Breton Island

Cape Breton, the large island adjunct at the north-east end of Nova Scotia, is justly renowned for its rugged splendour. It's the roughest, highest, coolest, most remote area of the province and is the one area a visitor should not miss. The coast is rocky and rugged, the interior a blend of mountains, valleys, rivers and lakes. The nearly 300-km-long highway, the Cabot Trail, around the Cape Breton Highlands National Park is one of Canada's grandest and best-known roads. It winds and climbs to 500 metres between mountain and sea, providing access to a variety of physical, historical and cultural attractions.

The island offers more than natural beauty – it has a long and captivating human history encompassing the original Native Canadians, the British, the French and, especially, the Scottish. It was this part of the province, with its strong resemblance to the Scottish Highlands, that drew numerous immigrants from that country.

Though not so true now, Cape Breton has long conjured up notions of remote isolation. Except for the industrial centres of Sydney and Glace Bay, most towns do remain small enough to be considered villages. People in some areas still speak French; in others, even Gaelic can be heard. Life is hard here and unemployment is very high. Fishing and mining have long been the main industries and both are in trouble.

For the visitor it is a very appealing, relatively undeveloped area, with the excellent national park in the highlands and a top historic site in Louisbourg.

Seafood is plentiful, the salmon fishing is memorable, the beaches have water warm enough for swimming, the walking trails are fine and the music is irresistible. And remember if you want to call home, the telephone was invented by Alexander Bell, who lived in Baddeck on Bras d'Or Lake, where there is now a major museum in his honour.

NOVA SCOTIA

North Sydney is the terminal for ferries to Newfoundland.

The Cabot Trail, understandably the most popular area, can be busy, even a little crowded in July and August, but it isn't difficult to get away if solitude is what you seek. The words most often used to describe the weather are windy, wet, foggy and cool. Summer days, however, can be warm and sunny. The sketchy public transportation system makes getting around Cape Breton difficult without a vehicle. From Port Hawesbury and Canso, the Inverness (McKinnin) bus runs as far as Inverness on the north-west coast, going by Long Point and Mabou on the way. Acadian Bus Lines run from Halifax or New Glasgow and Antigonish to Baddeck. Transoverland Ltd runs a bus route from Baddeck to Cheticamp through the Margaree Valley and from Baddeck to Sydney. Buses also run from Halifax to Sydney.

## INFORMATION

As you cross the Strait of Canso onto the island, you'll be charged $1.50 for using the causeway. (It's free on the way back – they say that's why the locals who leave never return.) A big and busy tourist office sits on the east side of the causeway, and from here you can pick up information on all parts of Cape Breton. Smaller offices are found in many towns, and the national park has its own information centres. If you need to make ferry reservations for a trip to Newfoundland, do it a few days before your planned departure.

There is a B&B programme in Cape Breton – the tourist office should have a complete list. There are many private and some government campgrounds besides those in the national park. In addition, there is sometimes an international hostel or two around the island, but they never seem to last more than a couple of years in the same place.

## NORTH COAST

From the Canso Causeway, Hwy 19, known as the Ceilidh (pronounced 'KAY-lee') Trail,

goes up the northern side of the island to the highlands. The first part of the route is not very interesting but it still beats the Trans Canada Hwy (No 105), which goes straight up the middle.

At **Mabou**, things pick up. It's a green, hilly region with valleys following numerous rivers and sheltering traditional towns. This is one of the areas on Cape Breton where Gaelic is still spoken and actually taught in the schools. Right in the centre of little Mabou is the Gaelic & Historical Society Centre, in a storefront. Aside from information they have books, tapes and various items relating to their Scottish heritage. On 1 July a Scottish picnic is held, with music, dancing, etc. There is a restaurant in town.

At the coast, off the main road, around Mabou Harbour and Mabou Mines, the **Mabou Highlands** offer some good walking trails.

Between Mabou and Inverness on Hwy 19, the thirsty may wish to stop at **Glenora Falls**, where North America's only single-malt Scotch whisky is made, at the Glenora Distillery. You can have something to eat or drink at the distillery's pleasant inn and tour the whisky operation.

## INVERNESS

This is the first town of any size on the northern shore. There are miles of sandy beach with some nice secluded spots and few people and, surprisingly, the water temperature is not too bad, reaching temperatures of 19°C to 21°C, which is about as warm as it gets anywhere around the Atlantic Provinces – cool but definitely swimmable. Pilot whales can sometimes be seen off the coast.

In town there's not a lot to see, but notice, on the north side of the street under the trees, the old houses which were originally built by the mining company for its workers. The mine is now closed but there is a small museum depicting those days.

### Places to Stay & Eat

The *Inverness Lodge* (☎ 258-2193), in the centre, is a hotel and motel offering

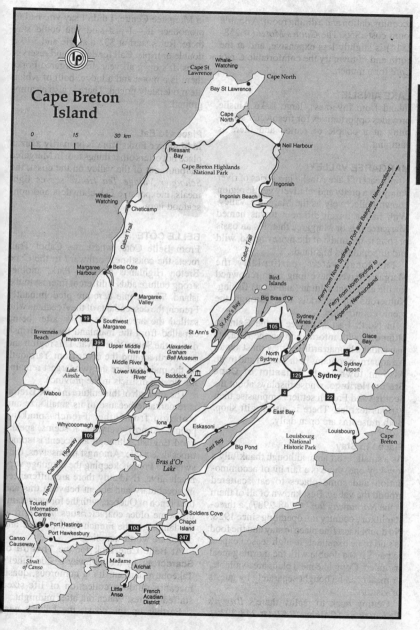

# Cape Breton Island

Whale-Watching
Cape St Lawrence
Cape North
Bay St Lawrence
Cape North
Neil Harbour
Pleasant Bay
Cape Breton Highlands National Park
Ingonish
Ingonish Beach
Whale-Watching
Cheticamp
Cabot Trail
Bird Islands
Margaree Harbour
Belle Côte
Big Bras d'Or
Margaree Valley
19
Southwest Margaree
St Ann's
St Ann's Bay
Sydney Mines
105
Inverness Beach
Inverness
395
Upper Middle River
Middle River
Lower Middle River
Alexander Graham Bell Museum
North Sydney
Glace Bay
4
Sydney Airport
Lake Ainslie
Baddeck
125
Sydney
Mabou
Iona
4
East Bay
22
Whycocomagh
105
Eskasoni
Louisbourg
Canada Highway
Trans
East Bay
Big Pond
Louisbourg National Historic Park
Cape Breton
Bras d'Or Lake
Tourist Information Centre
Port Hastings
Port Hawkesbury
104
Soldiers Cove
Chapel Island
247
Canso Causeway
Strait of Canso
Isle Madame
Arichat
Little Anse
French Acadian District

Ferry from North Sydney to Port aux Basques, Newfoundland
Ferry from North Sydney to Argentia, Newfoundland

0    15    30 km

**NOVA SCOTIA**

accommodation and a dining room. A double room costs $50. The *Gables Motel* (☎ 258-2314) is slightly less expensive, and at the north end of town try the comfortable *Cayly Café* for a munch.

## LAKE AINSLIE

Inland from Inverness, large Lake Ainslie provides opportunities for freshwater swimming at a couple of parks, and there is camping.

## MARGAREE VALLEY

North-east of Lake Ainslie in a series of river valleys is a pretty and relatively gentle region known collectively as the Margaree Valley. With half a dozen different towns named Margaree this or Margaree that, it's an oasis of sorts in the midst of the more rugged, wild and unpopulated highlands.

The local waters, particularly the Margaree River, have long been renowned for the excellent salmon (and trout) fishing. Numerous hiking trails lead through the scenic countryside.

In North East Margaree is the **Salmon Museum**, with information on the river, its fish and the human artifices they must avoid. An aquarium contains both salmon and trout. Also in town is the **Museum of Cape Breton Heritage**, whose displays about the Scottish and French settlers emphasise their various textiles. There is also a gift shop. Both museums are open daily.

### Places to Stay

As a small resort area, although thankfully a low-key one, there is a fair bit of accommodation and some places to eat scattered around the valley. Best known of all of them is the *Normaway Inn* (☎ 248-2987), a three-star luxury country inn operating since 1928. No doubt it is a fine place to stay and the food is said to be excellent. In high season expect to pay $100 a double with the morning meal included. Complete meal plans are available, or meals can be bought separately by guests or visitors.

Getting back to reality there's *Brown's Brunaich na H'Aibhne B&B* (☎ 248-2935),

in Margaree Centre. I didn't say you had to pronounce it – I just said you could stay there. Rates start at $32 a single and $40 a double or triple. Call for details and reservations. It's open all year. In Margaree Forks there is a motel and a lodge, both of which are moderately priced. There is also a campground.

### Places to Eat

In Margaree Forks *Van's* is primarily a pizza place but offers other things too. In Margaree Harbour, out of the valley on the coast, the *Schooner Village Tea House* serves light meals, inexpensive fish chowders and non-seafood items.

## BELLE CÔTE

From Belle Côte, where the Cabot Trail meets the coastline, northward to the Cape Breton Highlands National Park, another strong culture adds a different interest to the island. The people here are predominantly French, the descendants of the Acadians who settled the area in the 1750s after being expelled from the mainland by the British during the Seven Years' War. This region and one north around the coast from Yarmouth on the mainland are the two largest remaining French districts in the province.

The strength of this culture in Cape Breton is remarkable because of its small size and isolation from other French-speaking people. Almost everyone, it seems, speaks good English, although an accent is sometimes detectable. Amongst themselves, they switch to French, keeping the language very much alive. Evidently there are differences in vocabulary and accent between this and the French of Quebec, with the former retaining some older characteristics. Aside from the language, the French foods, music and dance are worth sampling.

At Belle Côte look for the **Theatre of Scarecrow**, by the highway beside Ethel's Takeout restaurant. It's a humorous, quasi macabre outdoor collection of life-size stuffed figures. Watch out after midnight.

Further up the coast, the bakery near

Grand Étang is good with huge loaves of bread as well as other things.

## CHETICAMP

Just before the Cape Breton Highlands National Park, Cheticamp (population 3000) is the centre of the local Acadian community. It's a busy little town through which many visitors pass on their way to the park. From Cheticamp the Cabot Trail becomes more scenic, with great views and lots of hills and turns as you climb to the highest point just before Pleasant Bay.

The church, St Pierre, dominates the town, as is so often the case in French centres. It dates from 1883 and has the characteristic silver spire. Feel free to have a look inside.

From the Government Wharf, across and down from the church, whale-watching cruises are run. The three-hour boat excursions by Whale Cruisers (☎ 224-3376) are pretty good value. The most common species in the area is the pilot whale, also called the pothead, but fin whales and minkes are sometimes seen, as are bald eagles and a couple of species of sea birds. And there's always the mountainous shoreline for a scenic backdrop. The tours are run from May until the end of September. Through midsummer there are three daily: morning, afternoon and evening.

Over on Île de Cheticamp, Plage Saint Pierre is a good sandy beach with picnic tables and camping. The island is connected by road to the mainland at the south end of town.

The Country Music Store is an excellent place for records and tapes of traditional and contemporary Maritime music – French, English, Scottish and Cape Breton fiddle. They'll also mail things home for you.

The Acadians have a tradition of handicrafts, but in this area one product, hooked rugs, has long been viewed as of particular beauty and value. Many of the local women continue this craft; their wares are displayed and sold in numerous outlets in and around town. A good rug costs $200 to $300 and up, so they aren't cheap but they are distinctive and attractive. Each is made of wool, and to complete the intricate work takes about 12 hours per 30 sq cm.

### Les Trois Pignons

At the north end of town, this cultural centre and museum shows, among other things, the rugs and tapestries of many local people, including those of Elizabeth Lefort, who has achieved an international reputation. Her detailed representational rugs and portraits in wool hang in the White House, the Vatican and Buckingham Palace. Admission is a couple of dollars.

Also here is a library, shop and information and genealogical centre to promote the Acadian heritage.

### Musée Acadienne

In the middle of town don't miss the Acadian museum, which has a small but interesting display of artefacts, furniture and some older rugs. It's interesting to see how the old motifs and designs are incorporated into the rugs made today.

Upstairs from the museum is a craft shop where some of the nicest rugs for sale are the ones with the traditional geometric patterns. Flora's, south of town, is the largest and most promoted craft store in the area. It has a good large assortment of textiles, including some small, less expensive pieces. Besides the textiles, though, most of the stuff is not of much interest.

Perhaps the highlight of the Acadian museum is its restaurant, with a large menu of mainly standard items, the low prices and freshness separating them from what's offered in run-of-the-mill places. The best dishes are the three or four traditional Acadian ones, all of which are excellent. The soup and meat pie make a great lunch. Fish cakes may be sampled (here, as in Newfoundland, fish means cod; other types are called by name). The desserts, which are all freshly made, include gingerbread and a variety of fruit pies. Everything is good and cheap (under $6); the women who run the place and do the cooking and baking wear traditional dress.

The museum and restaurant are open daily

from the middle of May to the end of October.

## Places to Stay

Throughout July and August accommodation is tight, so calling ahead or arriving early in the afternoon is advisable. This is particularly true if the weather is poor and campers are being forced out of the woods or if there is an event on of some sort. Almost all the lodging is in motels.

Cheapest of the lot ($40 a double) and good is *Albert's Motel* (☎ 224-2936), on Main St, but it has few rooms. Just before the park, *Les Cabines du Portage* (☎ 224-2822) has six housekeeping cabins (includes kitchen), each with two double beds, at $50 a single or double plus $5 for each extra person. There are also three bigger, slightly more expensive cabins, each with two bedrooms. Weekly rates are offered for all the cabins. The *Cheticamp Motel* (☎ 469-3380), on Main St on the south side of town, is well kept and friendly and has a dining room for breakfast. Doubles/triples here are $40 to $50. There is also one housekeeping unit.

As mentioned, there is camping at Île de Cheticamp.

## Places to Eat

Aside from the museum restaurant, there are quite a few other places for a small town. One of the main catches here is crab, which turns up on several menus. *Wilf's Restaurant*, at 838 Main St, is reasonably priced for seafood or chicken, with dishes around $8. For more of a night out, try the *Harbour Restaurant*, which has a view to complement the food. Lobster is offered thrcugh the summer and there is a kid's menu. Very highly rated but more expensive again is the dining room at *Laurie's Motel*, which has been operating since 1938.

## Getting There & Away

Cheticamp is connected to Baddeck by bus with Transoverland Ltd. The buses also run from Baddeck to Sydney. The schedule can vary seasonally and buses may not run every day. There is, unfortunately, no bus service

through or around the park but bicycles can be rented in Cheticamp for trips further into the park.

## CAPE BRETON HIGHLANDS NATIONAL PARK

In the middle of the highlands, this park not only has some of the most impressive terrain in the area but is also one of the most scenic places in Canada.

A one-day park entry pass is $5 and longer-term passes are available. Summer conditions tend to be rather rainy, foggy and windy even while remaining fairly warm. The driest month is generally July, with June and September the runners-up. Maximum temperatures in midsummer usually don't exceed 25°C and minimums are around 15°C.

At either of the entrances, Cheticamp or Ingonish, there are information centres for maps (including topographical ones), hiking brochures and advice. Both have a wide selection of nature books for sale too. Mountain bikes can be rented.

The Cabot Trail, one of the best-known roads in the country, gets its reputation from the 106-km park segment of its Cape Breton loop. It's at its best along the northern shore and then down to Pleasant Bay. The road winds right along the shoreline between mountains, across barren plains and valleys up to **French Mountain**, the highest point (459 metres). Along the way are lookout points, the best of which is at the summit. If possible save the trip for a sunny day, when you can see down the coastline. From French Mountain the road zigzags through switchbacks and descends to Pleasant Bay, just outside the park. If you're driving, make sure your brakes are good and can afford to burn off a little lining. Despite the effort required, the park is a popular cycling destination. However, it is not suggested that it be used as your inaugural trip.

Hiking trails abound and are, of course, the best way to see the park and perhaps glimpse some of the wildlife. Black bears, lynx, fox, otter and moose are some of the animals you might see, along with 185 species of birds. Most of the trails are short and close to the road. For longer, overnight camping hikes, ask for advice at the information offices. Always check in with a warden before starting off on an overnight trek.

Among the longer trails, No 22 from Ingonish to Lake of Islands (14 km one way) is good. A topographic map (they are available but quite expensive) is not necessary. The simple give-away map will suffice.

There are eight campgrounds in the park, some for tenters only. These tend to be small, with space for 10 to 20 people. Camping is $12 for a tent with any number of people. In the campgrounds, pick a site and set up. A warden will come around, probably in the evening, to collect the money.

Coming from Cheticamp there are a few park highlights to watch for. The top of **Mackenzie Mountain** affords great views of the interior. The **Grande Anse Valley** contains virgin forest.

In the small town of **Pleasant Bay**, the *Black Whale* restaurant is recommended for good, fresh seafood at reasonable prices in a casual, pleasant setting. The menu has everything from lobster to fish & chips; you can sit on the patio and watch for the regularly seen pilot whales just offshore. A lunch of fresh fish costs about $9, depending on the species. There are other places to eat, also specialising in seafood, and a couple of motels, both considerably more expensive than what's available in Cheticamp.

Towards Ingonish, the short **Lone Sheiling Trail** leads through 300-year-old maple trees to a replica of a Scottish Highland crofter's hut, a reminder of the area's first settlers. Other short trails lead to waterfalls at a couple of points along the road.

From the village of **Cape North** out of the park, the extreme northern portion (also called Cape North) of Cape Breton can be visited. In Cape North village there is a gas station and food store. Not i r north from here, at Cabot's Landing Provincial Park on Aspey's Bay, is the spot where John Cabot is believed to have landed in 1497. A re-enactment is held annually every 24 June on the beach at Sugarloaf Mountain. At Bay St

Lawrence **whale-watching boat tours** are run several times daily through the summer months.

A side trip is recommended to **Neil Harbour**, an attractive little fishing village. In fact, it's one of the nicest you're likely to see in Nova Scotia. Down at the wharf you can buy fish and lobster. Or try something at the inexpensive *Chowder House*, by the water at the lighthouse.

At the eastern entrance to the park are **Ingonish** and **Ingonish Beach**, two small towns with accommodation and basic supplies. There are several campgrounds, both government and private ones, as well as motels and a park information office.

The beach at Ingonish Beach is a wonderful place, with a long, wide strip of sand tucked in a bay surrounded with green hills. The water can get pleasantly warm here after a few sunny days and the beach really catches the late afternoon light in a special way.

See Getting There & Away under Cheticamp earlier for details of the limited bus service to the park.

### Places to Stay & Eat

Eight km north of the park entrance, near Igonish, is *Driftwood Lodge* (☎ 285-2558), run by Mrs Kulig. Rooms in the older building are cheapest and start at $35 for doubles without bath; if you want the view you'll pay more. Off-season rates apply in early June and from September to October. Breakfast is served and a German-Polish lunch and dinner are available.

Also in Ingonish, the *Sea Breeze Cottages & Motel* (☎ 285-2879) has a dozen cottages of varying sizes and amenities, some completely self-contained. The six motel units are rented at $48 a double.

Ingonish Centre also has a few places, mostly cabins, as does Ingonish Beach, where up on the hillside is the very expensive luxury government hotel, the *Keltic Lodge* (☎ 285-2880). Other than the Keltic, the prices aren't too bad.

For a place to eat, the coffee shop downstairs at *Doucette's Variety Store*, near

Ingonish Beach, has good soups, sandwiches and pies.

## CAPE SMOKEY

From Ingonish south and up to Cape Smokey there is some fine scenery. At the peak on Cape Smokey, at a small park with picnic tables, there are very good sea and coastal views. Walking trails leading both north and south offer even better viewing points.

The road descends sharply from here (smell those brakes!) leading out of the highlands.

## ST ANN'S

The interesting preserver and promoter of Scottish heritage, the **Gaelic College of Celtic Arts & Crafts** , is at the end of St Ann's Bay. Founded in 1938 and the only one of its kind in North America, the college offers programmes in the Gaelic language, bagpipe playing, Highland dancing, weaving and kilt-making and other things Scottish to students of all ages from across the land. Drop in any time during summer and the chances are you'll hear a student sing a traditional ballad in Gaelic or another play a Highland violin piece; mini-concerts and recitals are performed throughout the day. You can stroll around the grounds, see the museum with its historical notes and tartans or browse the giftshop for books, music tapes or kilts. There is also a cafeteria serving light meals or tea.

A Scottish festival, the Gaelic Mod, is held during the first week of August each year, with events daily.

The campus is pretty much the town – there really isn't anything else here.

## BIG BRAS D'OR

After crossing the long bridge over an inlet to Bras d'Or Lake on the way towards Sydney, a secondary road branches off and leads to the coast and the village of Big Bras d'Or. Offshore are the cliff-edged **Bird Islands**, Hertford and Ciboux. The islands are home to large colonies of razorbills, puffins, kittiwakes, terns and several other species. Boat tours run from town from May to September. The islands are about 1.6 km from shore and take about 40 minutes to reach. The entire boat trip takes 2½ hours. Nesting time is June and July, so these are the prime months for a visit, but plenty of birds can be seen any time from May to September. Bald eagles can also be seen, as they nest in the vicinity as well. Binoculars are handy, but not necessary (they can be rented) as the tour boats go to within 20 metres or so of the islands.

The boat tours depart from *Mountain View By The Sea* (☎ 674-2384), where there are housekeeping cabins for rent, B&B rooms and a campground.

## NORTH SYDNEY

Small and nondescript, North Sydney is important as the Marine Atlantic terminal for ferries to either Port aux Basques or Argentia, Newfoundland. For details see under those destinations.

There isn't much in town but it makes a convenient place to put up if you're using the ferry. Tourist information is available at the ferry landing or you can also call the Cape Breton Tourist Association (☎ 539-9876).

The main street in town is Commercial St, where you'll find the stores and places to eat. For drivers, there is public parking behind the Town Hall, on Commercial St near the corner of Blowers St. On the waterfront off Commercial St, right in the centre of town at the foot of Caledonia St, is a boardwalk leading to the Ballast Grounds harbour area. From here the busy waterfront can be purveyed. Sailing and fishing boats, freighters and the ferries for Newfoundland can all be seen plying the surrounding waters. On one visit the Coast Guard and police vessels had just lugged in and hauled out a rusty tub filled with illegal drugs.

### Places to Stay

North of town off the Trans Canada Hwy are a few privately owned campgrounds. The *Arm of Gold Campground* (☎ 736-6516), mainly for trailers, is closest to the ferry, at just 3.2 km away.

With a view over the water, *Alexandra Shebib's B&B* (☎ 794-4876) is two km west of the ferry terminal. It's at 88 Queen St, which is called Commercial St in town. This is a nice place, open all year and reasonably priced (singles from $30 to $35 and doubles for $40).

Other than this there are several motels in the vicinity at about twice the above rate. One to try is the *Clansman Motel* (☎ 794-7226), on Peppett St, off exit 2 on Hwy 125.

### Places to Eat

There are a few basic restaurants in town, such as *Papa J's*, which is not bad for submarine sandwiches and Italian fare. Order spaghetti for $5.50 and the portion will feed half the restaurant. *Rollie's Wharf* restaurant and lounge is on the water near the ferry dock. Nearby, at the ferry landing on Commercial St, is *Robert's Home-style Bakery*, where you can pick up a few things for the ferry trip.

Out of town beside the highway towards Baddeck is the widely known, notoriously named *Lick-a-Chick*, a chicken takeout place.

### Getting There & Away

**Bus** There is no real bus depot in North Sydney; the depot proper is in Sydney. However, the Acadian line bus between Sydney and Halifax can be picked up at the North Star Inn, beside the ferry terminal, three times a day. There is also a local bus which runs back and forth between Sydney and North Sydney for $2.50. It, too, can be caught at the ferry dock, or at some points along Queen St. See Getting There & Away under Sydney later for information on the Transoverland buses to Baddeck.

**Train** The train service in Cape Breton has been cut entirely.

**Ferry** For detailed information on ferry crossings, see the St John's and Port aux Basques sections in the Newfoundland chapter. Reservations may be required and are recommended in midsummer; call

Marine Atlantic (☎ 794-5700) in North Sydney. The ferry terminal is central, at the end of Commercial St at Blowers St. The Trans Canada Hwy (Route 105) leads straight into or out of the ferry terminal.

### SYDNEY MINES

Long known simply as the Mines, this small coastal town north-east of North Sydney was a depressed and dirty mining centre from as early as the 1700s. The mines were operating until recently and working in them was no picnic. Most of the shafts were out under the sea – one ran 6.4 km from shore below the ocean floor. Imagine working at that every day. After closing, a portion of the mine functioned as a museum, but this too has now closed and there really isn't much reason to visit. Glace Bay has a mining museum, as does Springhill, near the New Brunswick border.

### SYDNEY

Sydney is the third largest town in the province, the only real city on Cape Breton and the centre of the island's industrial sector. It's a very old town and, as the heart of a coal-mining district, has seen its share of grief and hardship. Until quite recently it was a drab, rather grim town with a hard-drinking, if warm and friendly, population. The people haven't changed but the appearance of the place has – there is more pride in the past and hope for the future. Though still somewhat at the whim of economic vagaries, it has the largest self-contained steel plant in North America, and numerous other industries, including machine works, foundries and pulp and paper manufacturing. Heritage buildings have been preserved and there is a variety of hotels and restaurants for visitors.

The main street downtown is Charlotte St, which has or is close to many of the stores and things of interest (or necessity) for the traveller. The Sydney River runs along the western edge of the downtown area. There isn't a lot to do, but with the ferry to the north and Louisbourg to the south, many people do pass by.

There is a tourist office south of town on

King's Rd, the motel strip, also known as Hwy 4.

### Northend

Just north of the city centre on Charlotte St, the Esplanade (which runs parallel to the river) and the adjoining streets is the old historic part of town, with half a dozen buildings from the 1700s and many built during the 19th century. The tree-lined streets make for pleasant walking, and if you're keen on history, a few places can be seen from the inside too. On the Esplanade across from the Government Wharf, you can visit the oldest Roman Catholic Church in Cape Breton, **St Patrick's**, dating from 1828.

**Cossit House**, on Charlotte St, dates from 1787 and is the oldest house in Sydney. It's now a museum with period furnishings. Nearby **St George's**, an Anglican church, is the oldest of all the churches on Cape Breton. There are three more heritage churches in Whitney Pier, an old residential part of town near the steel plant where early immigrants from Poland, the Ukraine and the West Indies found homes and work and then built their houses of worship.

At the Lyceum, the former cultural centre, 225 George St, is the **Centre for Heritage & Science**. This museum on the human and natural history of this part of the province also has an art gallery. The centre is open daily through the summer and for reduced hours the rest of the year.

Action Week is an annual event held in the first week of August. Festivities include music, sports and various other goings-on.

### Places to Stay

Right in town is *Paul's Hotel* (☎ 562-5747), at 10 Pitt St. It has 24 rooms, some with shared facilities and the more expensive ones with private bath. Rates range from $28 to $40.

Also quite central, at 169 Park St, is the *Park Place* (☎ 562-3518), a turn-of-the-century B&B with low rates (singles/doubles are $32/40).

The *Mansion Tourist Home* (☎ 539-

5979), 259 Kings Rd, has 10 rooms, as well as a wedding chapel just in case the urge arises. Doubles cost $45 and each room has a private bath. Continental breakfasts are included.

The larger, more modern choices are mostly along Kings Rd, which runs south of the centre along the Sydney River towards Hwy 125. Here you'll find numerous motels, most with restaurants attached. *Journey's End Motel* (☎ 562-0200), at 386 Kings Rd, is the modest in appointments and price ($60 a double).

### Places to Eat

*Jasper's*, with several locations around town, including a central one on the corner of George and Dorchester Sts, is an inexpensive family restaurant good for any meal of the day. Even at dinner, there is nothing over $13 on the large menu.

*Joe's Warehouse*, at 424 Charlotte St in the centre, has a varied menu featuring steak or beef and a large salad bar. There's also an outdoor patio with views of the water.

### Getting There & Away

**Bus** The Acadian bus line's depot (☎ 564-5533) is away from the centre a bit (walkable if necessary), across the street from the big Sydney Shopping Centre Mall on Terminal Drive. There are five buses a day to Halifax: the first at 8 am, the last at 6 pm. The charge is $35.50. One bus in the morning is direct, and three others go to the ferry terminal in North Sydney and make many other stops along the way.

For Charlottetown, Prince Edward Island, the fare is $40 and the bus leaves at 8 am.

Transoverland Ltd runs buses to Baddeck, via St Anne's, and from there north through the Margaree Valley and up the coast to Cheticamp.

**Train** There is no longer any train service, due to government cutbacks.

### GLACE BAY

As part of the Sydney area's industrial region, the difficulties of Cape Bretoners have been and are reflected here. The district has a long, bitter history of hard work – when there is any – with low pay and poor conditions and, regularly, one of the highest unemployment rates in the country. On top of all that, there's a high degree of work-related illness. The hardships, however, have resulted in a people able to smile at misfortune and be generally friendly and hospitable to strangers.

Glace Bay is one of the places where the coal-mining tradition survived until recently, but the mines are currently shut. The town's livelihood has always depended on the luck of the miners, so things are not looking too rosy and the population has decreased over the past decades.

The **Miners' Museum** (☎ 849-4522), less than two km east from the town centre in Quarry Point, at 42 Birkley St off South St, provides a look at the history of local coal mining, with equipment displays and a recreated village depicting a miner's life at the beginning of the century. The highlight, though, is a 20-minute underground tour led by a retired miner. It's $5 for the complete tour, less if you forgo (but don't) the mine visit. There is a restaurant at the site. The museum is open all year, daily from June to September and on weekends only for the rest of the year.

The **Marconi National Historic Site** marks the place where, in 1902, Italian Gugliemo Marconi sent the first wireless message across the Atlantic. It was received in Cornwall, England. There is a model of the original transmitting station, and other information on the developments in communications that followed. The site is on Timmerman St at the area of Glace Bay referred to as Table Head.

## MARCONI TRAIL

The coastal road south of Glace Bay leads past small fishing villages and rocky beaches to the town of Louisbourg and its top-rate historic site. The main, more direct route running south of Sydney has half a dozen campgrounds along it.

## LOUISBOURG

At the edge of the ocean with an excellent harbour sits Louisbourg (population 1400), the largest of the region's fishing towns and now famous for its adjacent historic fort. There is no public transportation down this way but hitching is pretty easy.

There's still a fair-sized fishing fleet and the processing plant is an important employer. Aside from the park there are a couple of other things to see in the old town.

The **Sydney & Louisbourg Railway Museum** and the tourist office are at the entrance to the town. The museum has displays pertaining to the railway, which ran up to Sydney from 1895 until as late as 1968, shuffling fish one way and coal the other. Entry is free.

In an historic building on Main St is the **Atlantic Statiquarium Marine Museum**, with exhibits on the fishery, artefacts recovered from wrecks, and marine life, including some live specimens. There is a small admission fee. Both museums are open daily through the summer.

The local heritage society has an exhibit in the impressive **Victorian rectory** beside the Anglican church.

Along the waterfront, examples of crafts can be seen and bought. At the **House of Dolls** is a collection of nearly 2000 miniature people. South of town are the ruins of Canada's oldest lighthouse, and an interpretive display.

### Places to Stay & Eat

For those wishing to do more than a day trip, Louisbourg is good for inexpensive accommodation, with four B&Bs.

On Main St (you can't miss it), *Ashley Manor* (☎ 733-3268) has three rooms, at $32/40 a single/double or triple. *The Manse* (☎ 733-3155), 10 Strathcona St, has identical prices and again includes a full morning meal. Another option is the large *Louisbourg Motel* (☎ 733-2844), at 1225 Main St.

There are a couple of places to eat with varied, reasonably priced menus which include numerous things from the sea. Beside the tourist office is *Anchor's Aweigh*

– good for breakfast as well as the other meals. The chowders are pretty good. A stroll down Main St will turn up the alternatives. The *Grubstake* is the place for a good seafood dinner but it is not in the low-budget category.

## LOUISBOURG HISTORIC NATIONAL PARK

This excellent, historic fort site (☎ 733-2280) about 50 km south of Sydney on the south-east tip of Cape Breton Island is worth the trek. The park is open daily in summer and admission is $7.

After the Treaty of Utrecht in 1713, the French lost their bases in Newfoundland. This left them Prince Edward Island, Saint Pierre and Miquelon islands, and Cape Breton Island, which became the centre for exporting cod to France. It was also chosen as the spot to build a new military base. Louisbourg, a massive walled fort and village complex, was worked on continually from 1719 to about 1745. It looked daunting but was poorly designed, and the British took it in 46 days during 1745 when it was barely finished. It was returned to the French under the terms of another treaty, only to fall with the British siege of 1758. In 1760, after Wolfe (who had led the Louisbourg onslaught) took Quebec City, the walls of Louisbourg were all destroyed. It was abandoned and, having no commercial use, began to decay.

In 1961, with the closing of many Cape Breton coal mines, the federal government began a make-work project: the largest historical reconstruction in Canada. Today the site depicts in remarkable detail what French life was like here in the 1700s. All the workers, in period dress, have taken on the lives of typical fort inhabitants. Ask them anything – what the winters were like, what they ate, what that tool is for, how this was made, who they had an affair with – and they'll tell you. There are many interesting buildings with appropriate contents. The restaurant serves food typical of the time. Definitely go to the bakery and buy a one-kg loaf of soldiers' bread. It's delicious; one

piece with cheese makes a full meal. (But take a plastic bag – they won't give you one because they didn't have plastic in 1750!)

You'll need a lot of time to see the park properly – plan on spending about half a day at the site. The best times to visit are in the morning – when there's more going on and fewer tourists – and during June or September. It's a popular site, so it's good to go there early in the day or outside the peak months of July and August, when the workers are not as harried and have more time to talk. Regardless of this, a visit is most interesting. Take in the movie in the interpretive centre first. Free guided tours around the site are offered through the day.

The weather here is very changeable and usually bad. Take a sweater and raincoat even if it's sunny when you start out, and be prepared for lots of walking. As well as the fort area itself, there are hiking trails around the grounds.

## AROUND BRAS D'OR LAKE
### Baddeck

An old resort town in a pastoral setting, Baddeck is on the north shore of the lake, halfway between Sydney and the Canso Causeway.

It's small but is a visitor centre of sorts as nearly everyone travelling Cape Breton spends some time here. This is making it a little too touristy, but it remains attractive and the **Graham Bell Museum** is still interesting and extensive.

Chebucto St, the main thoroughfare, has more or less everything on it and makes for a pleasant walk. On Water St, along the waterfront, the Government Wharf is lined with pleasure craft, tour sailing boats and, occasionally, the *Bluenose*, which will take passengers out for a spin around Bras d'Or Lake. Worse ways of spending a sunny afternoon could be found. In midsummer there is a free shuttle-boat service across the bay to **Kidston Island** just offshore, where there is good swimming.

Acadia buses serve New Glasgow and Antigonish and also run to Baddeck from Halifax. From Baddeck, Transoverland Ltd buses run north through the Margaree Valley and then up the coast to Cheticamp. Transoverland also goes from Baddeck to North Sydney and Sydney.

Buses out of town depart from the Ultramar gas station at the east end of the central town area. To New Glasgow, the fare is $24.

### Alexander Graham Bell National Historic Site

Alexander Graham Bell, the inventor of the telephone, had a summer place in Baddeck. This large museum is dedicated to him and his work. It's a national historic park that covers all aspects of this incredible man's inventions and innovations. Written explanations, models, photographs and objects detail his varied works. On display are medical and electrical devices, telegraphs, telephones, kites and seaplanes. You'll need a few hours if you want to see it all. Admission is free and it's open daily until 9 pm in summer.

The museum is set on a hillside amidst gardens and picnic tables, and there is a good

view of the bay and part of the saltwater Bras d'Or Lake from the roof.

**Places to Stay** There are a few B&Bs in and around town and half a dozen or so rather costly motels. All the central places are expensive.

The *Duffus House Inn* (☎ 295-2172), on Water St, has nine rooms furnished with antiques. Rates start at $50 a double with shared bath and go way up.

For a motel, the *Telegraph House* (☎ 295-9988), right in the centre of town, is very attractive in grey with white shutters, but a double with breakfast is in the $60 to $80 range. Others are closer to a measly $75.

Lowest priced is the *Restawhyle Tourist Home* (☎ 295-3428), on Shore Rd, with singles/doubles from $25. Call for directions and information.

The *Eagle's Perch B&B* (☎ 295-2640) is away from the centre, off Hwy 105 at exit No 9. Turn left at the stop sign and go for about five km. It's right on the Baddeck River and has canoes and bicycles for rent, so do-it-yourself transportation is not too much of a problem. Singles/doubles are $35/45 with a full breakfast.

**Places to Eat** Baddeck has a wide selection of good-quality eating places which tend to be a bit pricey. The best, and one that offers some cheaper possibilities while maintaining high standards, is the *Highwheeler Café/Deli/Bakery*, with a mouth-watering selection of things to eat there or to take on picnics. It has the simple basics, or smoked salmon and brie to go with the bagels.

The *Old Chowder & Dessert Bar*, off the main street, one block back and parallel to Chebucto St, has good soups at good prices. Moving up-market, the *Bell Buoy*, by the wharf, is good for seafood but is not cheap. Lobster suppers, with a one-pounder and everything else you can eat from the buffet, are available in the centre of town in the old Legion Hall, on Ross St. At $25, they don't compare with the value of the real Prince Edward Island lobster suppers but the food is good and plentiful. The meal includes

Alexander Graham Bell

chowder, mussels, rolls, salad, dessert and beverages. They're open daily from June to October. Lunch specials are offered from 11.30 am to 1.30 pm. Dinners are served from 4 to 9 pm.

A surprise is the Indian restaurant the *Taj*, in the grounds of the Bell Museum, with dishes from $6 to $9.

Don't bother with the fish & chips from the dock takeout place, where the food is all appearance and potential, but proves 'once frozen now greasy'.

Recommended is the *Herring Chokee* deli, near Baddeck in the community of Nyanza ( 1½ km west of the Cabot Trail turn-off), for healthy, tasty, cheap food. There is also a bakery in-house.

### Iona

This is a small village south of Baddeck, on the south side of the peninsula, by Barra Strait in Bras d'Or Lake (on Hwy 223). Iona is a bit out of the way but may appeal for that reason. The **Highland Village Museum** depicts the life of the Highland Scots at home, and here as pioneers. The ten historic buildings include an example of the smokey peat-heated homes of the Scottish Highlanders in the early 1800s, the first pioneer houses in the new land, and later ones in which new skills and materials were employed.

A Highland festival held on the first Saturday in August features the Celtic-based music of the island. Special events are scheduled through the summer, and something to watch for are the traditional suppers.

Next to the museum is the *Highland Heights Inn* (☎ 725-2360), a motel with rooms at the rather hefty rate of $70 a double.

In this area as well as in other rural parts of Victoria County, you may still hear Gaelic spoken.

A short ferry ride connects with roads for the south side of Bras d'Or Lake.

### SOUTH OF BRAS D'OR LAKE

This is a little-visited, sparsely inhabited area of small villages, lakes and hills. It's a farming and forestry region where many of the roads have not been paved.

### Eskasoni

Not far from the ferry on the edge of East Bay, Eskasoni is the largest Micmac Indian reserve in the province. The Micmacs were the largest Native Indian group in the Atlantic area when the Europeans arrived and they are still found in all four eastern provinces. Their language is still spoken by some people in Nova Scotia and their basketry is available at roadside shops on some reserves (for example, the one near Whycocomagh on the busy Trans Canada Hwy).

### Big Pond

On the south shore of East Bay, Big Pond has *Rita's Tea Room*, run by the hometown Cape Breton singer Rita MacNeil and helpers. If she is not away touring or recording, you'll probably get a chat while you're sipping. Every July, the Big Pond Concert, a sizeable annual Cape Breton music event, is held.

### Soldiers Cove

Further east along Route 4, at Soldiers Cove and Chapel Island, is another Micmac reserve, in an area they have long occupied. Each year on the last weekend of July, a major cultural festival takes place.

### The French Corner

The extreme south-west corner of Cape Breton, like the Cheticamp area, is largely French. The region all around Île Madame was settled by Acadians who had first tried to make Martinique in the West Indies home after the Expulsion but later returned to Nova Scotia. Arichat, on the ocean, is the largest town and has a restaurant and a traditional-style wooden Acadian inn called *L'Auberge Acadienne* , whose dining room offers some Acadian dishes. The LeNoir Forge museum on Route 320 is a restored 18th-century French blacksmith shop, open from May to September.

Just down the road, Petit-de-Grat holds an Acadian festival every August, with music, food, etc. This small town is the oldest on Île

Madame and was a busy trading port during Prohibition. Now it is a fishing centre.

There is a campground near Arichat and several parks with shoreline to explore. From Little Anse, a trail leads to a lighthouse.

### Port Hawkesbury

Though a fairly large town, there is little here for the visitor; it's essentially a modern shopping and industrial centre for the district.

### Sable Island

Lying south of Cape Breton, about 150 km from the mainland, this is the 'graveyard of the Atlantic'. Countless ships from the 1500s to the present have gone down around the island, with its rough seas and hidden sandbars. The island, 32 km long by 1½ km wide, is little more than a sandbar itself, with no trees or even shrubs. There are about a dozen inhabitants, a small herd of tough, wild ponies and lots of cranberries. The people maintain the two lighthouses, a meteorological station and a few other installations. The ponies are believed to be descendants from survivors of a 16th-century shipwreck.

# Prince Edward Island

Entered Confederation: 1 July 1873
Area: 5657 sq km
Population: 129,765
Provincial Capital: Charlottetown

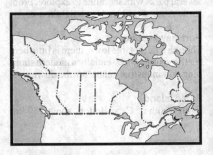

The Micmac Indians say Glooscap, a god, painted every beautiful place on earth. Then he dipped the brush in all the colours and created this, Abegweit, his favourite island.

Visitors may find it a favourite as well. If you're suffering big city burn-out or any kind of modern malaise and want to put a few years back on your life, this is the place to spend some time. If you can't unwind here, I'm sorry, you're a terminal case.

Now known as the Island, or PEI, Prince Edward Island is a pastoral, peaceful, wonderfully Irish-green expanse of quiet beauty. Mainlanders are seen on roadsides all over the island trying to capture the landscape on film: a few black and white cows here, some purple lupines there, perhaps a wave of sea in the distance. The pace of life here is slow. Laws against billboards further add to the old-country flavour of the island. Indeed, in some ways it has changed little from the descriptions in the internationally known novel *Anne of Green Gables*, written here after the turn of the century.

This is not an exciting place; there is not a lot to do, particularly after dark, when the province basically closes, and if you get a week of rain, you'll be more than a little restless. But for a really lazy holiday take the chance. The island is popular with cyclists, families and anybody else looking for an inexpensive change of scenery – prices are among the lowest in the country.

Prince Edward Island is the smallest and most densely populated province. You'd never guess this, however, as it's rural and the towns aren't big at all, though countless little-used roads crisscross every segment of land.

In March 1993, the province became the first in Canadian history to elect a woman premier. Catherine Callbeck led the Liberals to victory with a convincing 31 of 32 seats.

## CLIMATE & WHEN TO GO

Conveniently, July and August are the driest months of a fairly damp year. Because of warm ocean currents, the province has a milder climate than most of Canada and the sea gets warm enough for swimming. As in all of the Atlantic Provinces, the visiting season is short. This is perhaps noticed here more than anywhere, with many attractions, tour operations and guesthouses open only during the two midsummer months.

## ECONOMY

PEI is primarily a farming community, with the main crop, potatoes, being sold all over the country. The rich, distinctively red soil is the secret, the locals say. Fishing, of course, is also important, particularly for lobsters, oysters and herring. The tasty, reasonably priced lobster suppers held throughout the province have become synonymous with the island.

There is little manufacturing, as transportation costs are prohibitive. Nor has industry been helped by the lack of energy sources.

Late in 1993, the federal government was set to sign a controversial contract with a private company to build a bridge (termed the fixed link) connecting the province to New Brunswick. This has been an ongoing issue for several years. There is plenty of opposition to it, from fishers worried about possible negative impacts on the catch, to environmentalists, to those in favour of saving the enormous cost. Some feel it would spur much-needed economic activity. Personally, I find the beauty of islands is that they are separate from the mainland. Whether the bridge proposal will go ahead remains to be seen.

The quiet, gently rolling hills edged with good beaches have made tourism a reliable moneymaker.

## PEOPLE
Europeans of French, Scottish and Irish

background make up nearly 90% of the population. The Native inhabitants at the time of colonisation, the Micmacs, now represent about 4% of the island's people. Aboriginal peoples have been here for about 11,000 years, from before the land was separated from the mainland! The Micmacs, a branch of the Algonquin nations, arrived at about the time of Christ.

## INFORMATION
### Provincial Symbols
The provincial flower is the common lady's slipper and the provincial bird is the blue jay.

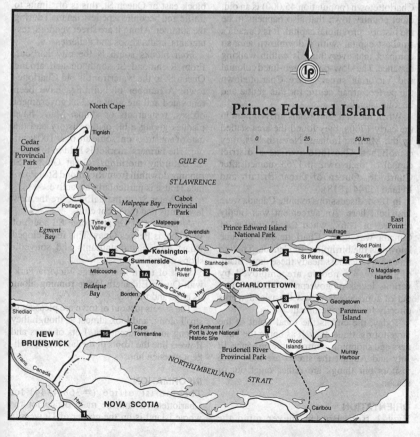

Prince Edward Island

0    25    50 km

GULF OF ST LAWRENCE

North Cape

Tignish

Cedar Dunes Provincial Park

Alberton

Portage

Malpeque Bay

Cabot Provincial Park

Tyne Valley

Egmont Bay

Malpeque

Cavendish

Prince Edward Island National Park

Naufrage

East Point

Red Point

Kensington

Summerside

Stanhope

St Peters

Souris

Miscouche

Hunter River

Tracadie

To Magdalen Islands

Bedeque Bay

Borden

Trans Canada Hwy

CHARLOTTETOWN

Shediac

Cape Tormentine

Orwell

Georgetown

Panmure Island

NEW BRUNSWICK

Fort Amherst / Port la Joye National Historic Site

Wood Islands

Murray Harbour

Trans Canada

Brudenell River Provincial Park

NORTHUMBERLAND STRAIT

NOVA SCOTIA

Caribou

**Telephone**
The area code for the entire province is 902. In the event of emergency dial 0. In pay phones no money is required for these calls.

**Time**
PEI is on Atlantic Time.

**Tax**
The provincial sales tax is 10%.

# Charlottetown

Charlottetown (population 45,000) is an old, quiet country town that also happens to be the historic provincial capital. It is Canada's smallest capital, with a downtown area so compact that everything is within walking distance. The slow-paced, tree-lined colonial and Victorian streets make Charlottetown the perfect urban centre for this gentle and bucolic island.

When the first Europeans arrived here in the early 1700s, they found the area settled by the Micmac Indians. Nevertheless, they established Charlottetown as a district capital of their own in 1763, named after Charlotte, Queen of Great Britain and Ireland (1744-1818).

In 1864, discussions to unite Canada were first held here. An agreement was finally reached in 1867, when the Dominion of Canada was born; Charlottetown became known as the birthplace of Canada. Though times are much less heady these days, many of the town's people are employed by various levels of government. Indeed, one out of four people across the island works directly for the government.

Today, the city is the focal point of the large tourist trade as well as being the business and shopping centre for the province. In July and August the streets are busy with visitors but things are rather quiet out of season.

**ORIENTATION**
Hwy 1 from Borden (never mind the

approach into town – it's the only ugly stretch of road on the island) becomes University Ave, the city's main street. University ends at Grafton St and the large war memorial statue depicting three soldiers. Behind it, the entire block is taken up with the Provincial Archives, Province House National Historic Site and the large Confederation Centre of the Arts complex.

Half a block west along Grafton is Queen St, parallel to University Ave. This is the other main street of Charlottetown and of more interest to visitors.

Off Queen St, south behind the Confederation Arts Building, is Richmond St. For one block east of Queen St, this is off limits to traffic and becomes a pedestrian mall during the summer. Along it are street vendors, restaurants, crafts shops and galleries.

Four blocks south is the city harbour. From Richmond St south on and around Queen St to the waterfront is old Charlottetown. A number of buildings have been renovated and are now used as government offices, restaurants or shops. Many have plaques giving a bit of the history and the date of construction; some are over 100 years old. The farmers' market is held in this area on Saturday mornings. Great George St running downhill from Richmond St at Province House is particularly attractive.

On Water St, at the harbour, are the new law courts and the yacht club.

At the foot of Great George St, south of Water St, is Peakes Quay. This redeveloped wharf now has restaurants and souvenir shops geared to tourists.

West of town is the large Victoria Park, with Queen Elizabeth Drive running along its edge and the bay.

The streets just out of town are pleasant to stroll along, and look almost as though they belong in a different era. Lots of trees and flowers line the fronts of the large, old, well-kept wooden houses.

**INFORMATION**
The tourist office (☎ 368-4444) for Charlottetown and the main office for the whole island is on the corner of University

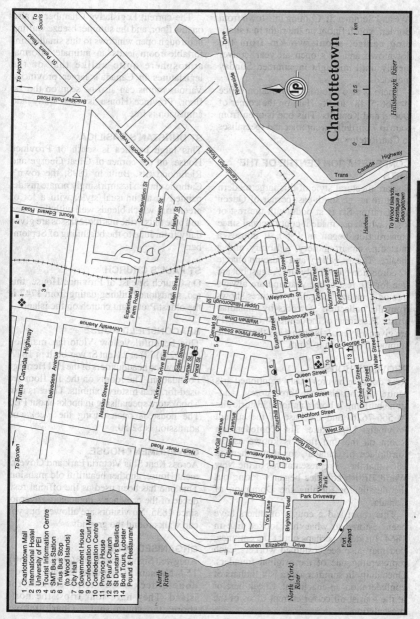

PRINCE EDWARD ISLAND

Charlottetown

To Souris

To Airport

St Peters Road

Bradley Point Road

Riverside Drive

Hillsborough River

Trans Canada Highway

To Wood Islands, Montague & Georgetown

Harbour

Kingston Road

Confederation St

Gower St

Harley St

Mount Edward Road

Langworth Avenue

Experimental Farm Road

University Avenue

Belvedere Avenue

Nassau Street

Kirkwood Drive East

North River Road

Trans Canada Highway

To Borden

Fitzroy Street

Kent Street

Grafton Street

Richmond Street

Sydney Street

Water Street

Weymouth St

Hillsborough St

Prince Street

Euston Street

Allen Street

Upper Hillsborough St

Upper Prince Street

Walthen Drive

Gerard St

Eden Street

Pond St

Summer St

Gt George St

Queen Street

Pownal Street

Rochford Street

Dorchester Street

King Street

West St

McGill Avenue

Highland Avenue

Greenfield Avenue

Churchill Avenue

Goodwill Ave

York Lane

Brighton Road

Pond Road

Park Driveway

Victoria Park

Fort Edward

Queen Elizabeth Drive

North River

North (York) River

0   0.5   1 km

1 Charlottetown Mall
2 International Hostel
3 University of PEI
4 Tourist Information Centre
5 SMT Bus Station
6 Trius Bus Stop
  (to Wood Islands)
7 City Hall
8 Government House
9 Confederation Court Mall
10 Confederation Centre
11 Province House
12 St Paul's Church
13 St Dunstan's Basilica
14 Boat Tours, Lobster
   Pound & Restaurant

Ave and Summer St. Coming into town from Borden, you'll find it on the right in a shopping centre, about two km from the downtown area. It's open all year, conveniently until midnight in summer, Sunday included.

There is also a tourist information office (☎ 566-5548) at City Hall, on the corner of Queen and Kent Sts. This one is open from 8 am to 7 pm daily in summer and specialises in Charlottetown.

## CONFEDERATION CENTRE OF THE ARTS

The architectural style of this large modern structure at the south-east corner of Queen and Grafton Sts is at odds with the rest of town, which has made it controversial since construction began in 1960. It houses a museum, an art gallery, a library and a theatre. The art gallery and museum charge $2 admission fees in July and August but are free for the rest of the year and are always free on Sunday. The gallery features shows from the collection of works by Canadian artists. Free tours of the centre (☎ 628-6111) are given all year. It is open daily through the summer from 9 am to 8 pm.

## PROVINCE HOUSE

Next door to the previously mentioned arts centre, this neoclassical, three-storey, sandstone building is both a national historic site (☎ 566-7626) and the base of the current Provincial Legislature. The Confederation Room on the 2nd floor is known as the 'birthplace of Canada', for it was here in 1864 that the 23 representatives of the New World British colonies began working out the details for forming the Dominion of Canada.

This room and a couple of others have been restored to what they looked like in 1864. Inside or perhaps out at the entrance, you may also see costumed workers, each representing one of the original founders. Once daily in summer, there is a 'fathers of confederation' re-enactment. Check here or at the tourist office for current times of the presentation.

The current Legislative Chamber is also on this floor, and the summer breeze wafting in through open windows to this small, comfortable room lends an intimate informal atmosphere quite unlike that of the legislatures in Canada's larger provinces. Various rooms can also be seen on the 1st floor. Province House is open daily and admission is free.

## ST DUNSTAN'S BASILICA

This large basilica is south of Province House, on the corner of Great George and Richmond Sts. Built in 1898, the town's Catholic church is surprisingly ornate inside, painted in an unusual style, with a lot of green trim which blends well with the green and blue tints in the marble. Masses are given daily from June to the beginning of September.

## ST PAUL'S CHURCH

On Church St east of Province House, this red, sandstone building dating from 1747 is the oldest Protestant church on the island.

## BEACONSFIELD HOUSE

This beautiful yellow Victorian mansion (☎ 892-9127) at 2 Kent St was built in 1877. It is now the headquarters of the PEI Heritage Foundation. The rooms on the 1st floor are used for local history exhibits. There is also a bookstore specialising in books about PEI. The house is open during the week and admission is $2.50.

## GOVERNMENT HOUSE

Across Kent St is Victoria Park and Government House, another beautiful old mansion. This one has been used as the official residence of the province's lieutenant-governor since 1835. No visitors are allowed but you can walk around the grounds.

## ORGANISED TOURS

Abegweit Sightseeing Tours (☎ 894-9966), 157 Nassau St, Charlottetown, offers double-decker bus trips around the island. They have four trips: the north shore, the south shore, Charlottetown itself and a new one, the Anne of Green Gables Tour.

The first three each take in some of the commercial attractions of the area visited. The north shore trip takes about six hours and costs $27 all-inclusive. The city tour takes just an hour and costs $5.50. The south shore trip makes a stop at Fort Amherst National Historic Park.

The Anne of Green Gables mega tour takes seven hours and takes in Green Gables, the birthplace of Lucy Maud Montgomery and the Anne of Green Gables Museum.

If you just want to go to the beach for the day, you can take the North Shore Tour bus. They'll pick you up on the way back. The cost is $7 or $8 one way, $9 or $10 return. The extra dollar is charged for trips to Cavendish Beach.

There are a number of boat-tour possibilities out of Charlottetown. A long-standing, reliable operator is Little Ferryboat Tours (☎ 368-2628). Their 1½-hour $16 tours include pulling up a lobster trap and sampling delicious, fresh steamed mussels. On Saturday afternoons they have a special family outing, and once a week a diving trip is offered, with all equipment available for rent. Boats depart from the Prince St wharf.

For charters or cruises aboard a 12-metre yacht, contact Gordon Miller (☎ 675-3666). Other sailing vessels and tour operators can be found around the docks at the city harbour.

Bike tours can be arranged through Gordon McQueen at McQueen's Bike Shop (☎ 368-2463), 430 Queen St.

Finally, walking tours of the historic Charlottetown area commence at City Hall (☎ 566-5548) every hour in summer, beginning at 9.30 am. Alternatively, the self-guided tour brochure available at the tourist office covers the waterfront area and Peake's Wharf.

## FESTIVALS

All across the province, look for the local ceilidhs: mini-festivals at which there is always some music (usually of the traditional Celtic-based variety) and dancing. There is almost one a week. Ticketworks (☎ 566-1267), a ticket agency, has information and tickets for shows across the province. Some of the major events held in PEI are:

June-September

*Charlottetown Festival* – This festival is held each year from mid-June to mid-September. It's a theatrical event with drama and musicals; each year, *Anne of Green Gables* is performed. It's called 'Canada's favourite musical' and is a family show. Tickets to any of the plays are available at the Arts Centre and range from $9 to $18 for most plays, $16 to $30 for 'Anne'.

In recent years some less-conservative, contemporary plays have been added to the programme – one about Elvis Presley a couple of years ago stirred up some controversy due to its colourful language. There are also summer theatre and dance programmes, both in town and around the province.

*Blue Grass Music Festival* – A new tradition seems to be developing: this festival is held annually in July. It's a two-day camping event held at a park or campground. Tickets are not costly.

*Provincial Exhibition* – This event is held in the first week or two of August, features tractor pulls, a carnival with rides, harness racing, entertainment and games of chance.

*National Milton Acorn Festival* – It's a unique event worth considering. Sometimes known as Canada's People's Poet, Acorn was born and raised on PEI. The festival, held in the third week of August, includes poetry readings and music.

**Ceilidh**
Pronounced KAY-lee, this Gaelic word meaning an informal gathering for song and story (a party, basically) is used across the province for the many evening events or concerts to which all are welcome. They are sometimes known as house parties. Featuring, as tradition dictates, music, dance and singing, there seems to be one somewhere on the island nearly every third night. The Celtic-based music is terrific, the atmosphere casual and friendly. They can be held in churches, community halls, provincial parks, sports fields – just about anywhere. ■

PRINCE EDWARD ISLAND

## PLACES TO STAY
### Camping
The island is covered with campgrounds – private, provincial and one national. Provincial parks charge $10 or so for an unserviced site, depending on facilities. Privately owned places charge more but accept reservations. Government parks, which operate on a first-come, first-served basis, are usually better and are often full by the end of the day in July and August. The tourist office can give you vacancy reports.

Half a km outside Charlottetown there's the *Southport Trailer Park* (☎ 569-2287), at 20 Stratford Rd, overlooking the Hillsborough River. The nightly rate is $15, less if you're tenting or staying a week or longer. This is the only campground near town.

### Hostels
The good, friendly HI *Charlottetown Hostel* (☎ 894-9696), at 153 Mount Edward Rd, is about three km from the downtown area and close to the university. The barn-shaped building has room for 54 people and there's a kitchen with microwave available for light cooking. Rates are $12.50 for members, $15 for nonmembers. To get there, follow University Ave north from town towards Borden. Turn right at Belvedere Ave. The hostel is near Mount St Mary's Convent. The hostel is open from the beginning of June to the beginning of September. Some years, there may be an additional hostel somewhere around the island – they seem to come and go (mostly go).

The *University of PEI* (☎ 566-0442) itself has rooms from mid-May to the end of August. Reservations are a good idea. The rate of $21.50 per person includes breakfast. There is a useful kitchenette to use as well.

Charlottetown has a YMCA-YWCA and a Salvation Army, but neither of them rents rooms.

### Tourist Homes
Across the province there are few hotels, but fortunately the city, like the entire island, has an abundance of guesthouses. The quality is generally high and the prices excellent. PEI guesthouses and tourist homes offer some of the best accommodation deals in Canada. A double room averages about $25 or $30 and rarely goes above $40, and sometimes that includes breakfast. Much accommodation is in beautiful old wooden homes in the east coast style. The tourist office has a complete list of these places and will make reservations for you. In town, there are quite a few. Here are several to try.

Very central, at 234 Sydney St, the unassuming *Aloha Tourist Home* (☎ 892-9944) is in a large old house and has four rooms to rent. Two people in the room with a double bed pay $32. The single is $28. There is a large kitchen that visitors can use. There isn't much privacy at the shared washroom off the kitchen but the owner, Maynard MacMillan, is an affable, helpful host. Cyclists can stash their bikes in the garage.

Also central is the *Blanchard* (☎ 894-9756), at 163 Dorchester St. Here singles/doubles cost just $20/30.

In behind the tourist office, at 18 Pond St, is the spotless and friendly *Cairn's Tourist Home* (☎ 368-3552), in a modern house on a residential street. The rate is $26 for a double and an extra $5 per additional person.

*Morais' Guest Home* (☎ 892-2267), at 67 Newland Crescent, near the tourist office, will pick you up from the airport or bus depot. The owner speaks English and French. A double here goes for $32.

Some of the least expensive choices are on the eastern side of downtown, close to the racetrack. You might check along Edward St or York Lane. Houses here are smaller and less gracious than many but the area is still conveniently walkable to the city centre.

### B&Bs
In this category are many places much like the tourist homes but offering the morning meal. As a rule, they tend to be outside the city centre and in newer houses but there are also several more central, up-market places established in fine heritage homes and decorated with antiques and collectables.

The *Duchess of Kent* (☎ 566-5826), in a

heritage house from 1875 and with period furnishings, is at 218 Kent St, in the centre of town. The seven rooms of varying features range in price from $45 to $60 a double, including the morning meal. Washrooms are shared, but there are so many that this is no hardship.

Some of the larger historic places have been converted to inns. One such is the *Dundee Arms Inn* (☎ 892-2496), at 200 Pownal St, in an impressive, restored turn-of-the-century mansion complete with antiques, dining room and pub. A double here will cost $95 with a continental breakfast included.

## Motels

There are motels along Hwy 1 west of Charlottetown towards Borden. Also on this commercial strip are drive-in movies, restaurants and gas stations. Motels here usually cost at least $50 a double. The ones further from town tend to be more modest in appearance, amenities and price. Those in town provide more comforts and the price goes up accordingly.

Close to town on the south side is the *Garden Gate Inn* (☎ 892-3411). It's small and well off the highway but, like many of the motels, expensive – $58 for singles or doubles.

Three km from town on the Trans Canada Hwy is the *Queen's Arms Motel* (☎ 368-1110), with a heated pool. Rooms cost about $55 and up for two people and housekeeping units are also available.

Further out, near the Hwy 2 junction, the brown *Banbridge Inn* (☎ 892-2981) offers doubles for $65 and rooms with kitchens for $85. There is a laundromat.

## PLACES TO EAT

For a small city there are a surprising number of quality restaurants but these mostly fall into the higher price bracket. Still, with the ocean minutes away, a fresh seafood dinner is not too outrageous and the low prices elsewhere around the island make up for costs here.

*Cedar's Eatery*, open every day and right in the middle of town on University Ave, is a fine little place. At the chunky wooden tables the speciality is Lebanese food, ranging from felafels to more expensive kebabs. But there is also standard Canadian fare: soups, salads, sandwiches, steaks and Old Abbey, a local beer. Cedar's stays open late, one of the few places which does.

For breakfast, a simple meal or snack, the cheap and unpretentious *Town & Country*, at 219 Queen St, fills the bill with its basic Canadian menu. Also small and cheap but with a certain charm is *Linda's Old Town Coffee Shop*, at 32 Queen St.

The *Potato Blossom Tea Room*, at 104 Water St (the original still operates in the town of York), is recommended for lunch. Within the cool green-and-white interior of an old house diners, are proffered a menu on which nearly every dish is made with potatoes, the island's principal crop. The cheese soup with grated potato together with a spud scone makes a tasty and filling lunch. The sandwiches served on huge slices of homemade bread are also tempting. Lunches range from $4 to $7.

The *Old Dublin Pub*, upstairs at 131 Sydney St, has pub meals from $6, an agreeable outside deck and live entertainment at night.

There are a couple of inexpensive Chinese places around town; my choice would be the *King's Palace*, on Queen St on the corner of Grafton St, with its good-value lunches.

In Confederation Court Mall, on the corner of Kent and Queen Sts, the 2nd floor has a collection of cheap fast-food outlets offering pizza, chicken, burgers, etc.

*Pat's Rose & Grey Room*, on Richmond St behind the Confederation Arts Building with the great front window, is highly regarded and also has a nice bar section. The tasty lunch specials change daily. At night, features include pastas and steaks, but note that this is decidedly not for those on a low budget.

Again in the splurge category, the dining room of the *Dundee Arms Inn*, at 200 Pownal St, offers fine eating in a traditional setting with top-notch service.

PRINCE EDWARD ISLAND

Among the pricier seafood spots in town are *Samuel's* in the Inn on the Hill, and the *Claddagh Room* in the old historic area, downstairs at 131 Sydney St. At the latter a seafood dinner is $20. Down at Charlottetown's waterfront on the Prince St wharf is *Mackinnon's*, where you can buy fresh mussels, clams and oysters, as well as live or cooked lobster.

You can get an inexpensive feed in the *university cafeteria*. It's open Monday to Friday from 7.30 am to 6 pm, Saturday and Sunday from 10 am to 6 pm. Full meals are served. It's near the Charlottetown Hostel, across the field off University Ave.

Back in town, along Sydney St or around the Confederation Centre of the Arts building, you'll always be able to find a café for a cappuccino.

*Cows*, now an island institution, has a location on Queen St near Grafton St. It is not a large place but it turns out good homemade ice cream. There are also outlets, open in summer only, in Cavendish and North River. People across Canada can be seen sporting the colourful, humorous Cows T-shirts.

A 10-minute drive west to Cornwall on the way to Borden is the *McCrady's Green Acres Motel & Restaurant*. Run by an English couple, the restaurant serves afternoon English cream teas from 1 to 4 pm. Other menu items, like steak & kidney pie, are also good. Actually if you're considering a motel, this is not a bad place to spend the night, at a lower than average $45 a double.

## ENTERTAINMENT

Charlottetown may be the capital city but it's really a country town and therefore doesn't have much action at night.

*Myron's*, at 151 Kent St, off University Ave, is a popular spot, with different types of music featured each night. Further down Kent St is the *Tradewinds*, a much spiffier dancing spot which is open until 1 am.

A Friday night spent at the Irish Hall (☎ 566-3273), 582 North River Rd, is a lot of fun, with traditional Irish and Scottish music and dance. Things start around 8 pm

on a regular basis through the year, but not every Friday – call to confirm.

## GETTING THERE & AWAY
### Air

Charlottetown has a small airport, north of the city west off Hwy 2, about six km from the centre. Air Canada and Canadian Airlines connect PEI with the major Canadian cities and some New England US points like Boston. Air Canada flies one way to Toronto for $399 and Canadian Airlines flies to St John's, Newfoundland for $329 and to Montreal for $310. Prince Edward Air (☎ 436-9703) has a daily connection to Halifax.

### Bus

There are once-daily buses to and from PEI using each of the two ferries. Trius Bus Lines (☎ 566-5664), using the Wood Islands ferry, goes to New Glasgow, Nova Scotia, from where connections can be made to Acadian buses for points around Nova Scotia. The depot, in the VIA Rail building, is at 308 Queen St, on the corner of Queen and Euston Sts.

SMT Bus Lines (☎ 566-9744) uses the Borden ferry and connects with Moncton, New Brunswick. Tickets include the price of the ferry. For Moncton, a ticket is $28. The SMT depot is at 330 University Ave.

### Train

There is no passenger train service to, from or on the island. The VIA Rail system will get you to Amherst or Truro, Nova Scotia, or to Moncton, New Brunswick, from where buses travel to Charlottetown. The ferry across the Northumberland Strait is included in the fare.

### Ferry

Most people get to PEI by ferry, from either New Brunswick or Nova Scotia. There are two ferries linking the island with the mainland. They take cars, buses, bicycles and pedestrians.

One ferry links Cape Tormentine, New Brunswick with Borden in south-west Prince

Edward Island. This 14-km trip takes 45 minutes and is run by Marine Atlantic, a government ferry system. The fare is $6.75 per person return, $17.50 per car and $3 per bicycle. There are nearly 20 crossings a day between June and September, slightly fewer the rest of the year.

In peak season, arrive before 10 am or after 6 pm to avoid long delays. Still, this is one of Canada's busiest ferry routes and having to wait for two or even three ferries is not uncommon. Reservations are not taken for this route but calling in will give you an idea of the situation. In Borden, call ☎ (902) 855-2030. In Cape Tormentine call ☎ (506) 538-7873. Sometimes mini-concerts are staged by the waiting queues to help the time pass. The ferry has a cafeteria.

Charlottetown is about 60 km from Borden and the drive takes about 40 minutes.

The other route, run by Northumberland Ferries, joins Wood Islands (in the eastern section of PEI province) to Caribou, Nova Scotia. This 22-km trip takes 1½ hours and costs $8 per person return, $25.75 return per car and $3.75 per bicycle. In summer there are 20 runs in each direction daily. This route, too, is busy – during peak season you may have a one or two-ferry wait. There's a cafeteria on board. The head office is in Charlottetown, at 54 Queen St, or call ☎ 1-800-565-0201 for reservations.

### Car

A car, for better or worse, is the best and sometimes only means of seeing much of the island. There are several outlets in the capital. The supply of cars is limited and with the local bus system shut down, getting a car is not easy. They can all be booked up for a week, so try to reserve well ahead through an office of one of the major chains in whatever city you're in prior to your PEI visit.

Avis Rent-A-Car (☎ 892-3706) is on the corner of University Ave and Euston St. Their cars cost $34 to $40 per day, depending on the size, with 200 free km. Without a credit card, you'll have to pay in advance and put a deposit on top of that.

## GETTING AROUND
### To/From the Airport

As there is no airport bus in town, the only transportation is a cab. It's only a few km to the airport so a taxi is about $5.

See also Bus, Bicycle and Hitching in the following Around the Island section.

## AROUND CHARLOTTETOWN
### Micmac Indian Village

While not far at all by boat south from the city across the Charlottetown Harbour, the village site (☎ 675-3800) is a somewhat circuitous but scenic half-hour drive from Charlottetown on Hwy 19. Together with the historic site, it can make a worthwhile half-day trip from the city. The village re-creation is small and unsophisticated but this is part of its charm – it was run for ages by an old Micmac man and his homemade approach is in evidence.

A path winds through the woods past teepees, dugout canoes and sweat lodges, some of which have informative notes

---

**Milton Acorn**

Born in 1923 in Charlottetown, Acorn was to become somewhat the bad boy of Canadian literature. Despite living and working as a poet, he did not fit the usual academic mould and was always known for voicing his firmly held left-wing opinions. He supported a range of radical causes and his poems often reflected his political biases as well as his unwavering support of the working person. Spending much of his life in Montreal, Toronto and Vancouver, he became known as the People's Poet after being honoured as such by fellow poets. He died in his home town in 1986.

*Dig up my Heart: Selected Poems 1952-1983* is the most complete and representative collection of Acorn's poetry, offering a good sampling of his subject matter and style. Personally, I prefer his numerous nature and reflective poems, some of which have a wonderful, easy lyricism. ■

accompanying them. A series of traps reveals traditional hunting techniques. The simple museum contains such things as arrowheads, baskets and clothing. A visit takes 30 minutes to an hour and costs $3.25. There is also a simple gift shop.

### Amherst National Historic Park

Very close to the Micmac Indian Village and Rocky Point is the site of the old French capital and more recently Fort Amherst (☎ 675-2220), built by the British in 1758 after they had taken over the island. There isn't really anything left to see other than foundations but the interpretive centre features exhibits and an audiovisual show. There are views of the city and three lighthouses and a beach within the park area. Admission to the park is free.

### Charlottetown Harbour

An old docker with gutted cheeks,
time arrested in the used-up knuckled hands
crossed on his lap, sits
in a spell of the glinting water.

He dreams of times in the cider sunlight
when masts stood up like stubble;
but now a gull cries, lights,
flounces its wings ornately, folds them,
and the waves slop among the weed-grown piles.

**Milton Acorn**

# Around the Island

The island is small and, with a car, easy to get around. In one day it's possible to drive from Charlottetown up to the beaches for a swim, along the north coast all the way up to North Cape, then back along the western shoreline, over to Summerside and down to Borden to catch the evening ferry. And you're not even rushing!

There are about 12 tourist offices around the island, including one at each of the ferry terminals. Any one of them can arrange accommodation anywhere on the island within an hour.

Prince Edward Island offers a wide variety

of attractions: oddities, local museums, historical sites and many child-oriented activities. You can get a list at the information offices or just check these things out as you come across them.

Three equal-sized counties make up the island: Prince in the west, Queen's in the middle and King's to the east. Each county has a scenic road network mapped out by the tourist bureau. Though far from the only options, these routes do take in the better-known attractions and the historical and geographical points of note.

### ACCOMMODATION & FOOD

Tourist homes are found in towns and on farms all over the province and are generally reasonably priced. Get details at the tourist offices.

Around the north coast by the national park are scores of cabins and cottages for rent. Features and prices vary but many places are rented by the week.

There are 15 provincial parks with campgrounds and these charge $12.50 for unserviced sites, $15 for trailers. There are plenty of privately owned campgrounds too, often offering more extras, such as recreational facilities. Prices are up to $15 (but usually less) for unserviced sites, $12 to $18 for hook-ups.

There are nearly 40 outlets around the island for buying fresh seafood – good if you're camping and can cook your own food. Some guesthouses offer cooking facilities or use of barbecues.

Also look for the famous lobster suppers held in church basements or community halls or restaurants – these are usually buffet style and good value. Perhaps not as much fun, the restaurants offering lobster suppers at least do so on a regular basis and are reliable, whereas the others are sometimes hit and miss. In the past couple of years more and more lobster supper venues have sprung up in response to the popularity and reputation of these casual seafood-based meals. Some of the newer ones unfortunately do not offer the value and quality of the originals. I have recommended the more established sites, but keep your ears open for a bargain.

## GETTING AROUND
### Bus
Island Transit, the provincial bus service operated out of the VIA Rail station (☎ 892-6167), 308 Queen St, shut down late in the summer of 1993. This came as a bit of a shock, even to the locals, and has left the province with virtually no public transportation. Ask about it though – with any government funds freed up, perhaps at least a limited service will resume.

Visitors can use the handy beach bus shuttle offered by Abegweit Tours. It runs between Charlottetown and the north coast beaches of the National Park. See Organised Tours under Charlottetown earlier for details.

### Bicycle
The island is popular with cyclists, as it is crisscrossed by narrow roads running through peaceful, unhurried countryside. The gently rolling landscape offers no major hardship for cyclists, and it's here you see the island at its most natural, with few or no tourists.

Daily and weekly bicycle rentals can be arranged at McQueen's Bike Shop (☎ 368-2453), 430 Queen St in Charlottetown.

Rent-A-Bike is at the junction of routes 6 and 13, in Cavendish village at the Petro Can gas station, near the beach, and has hourly and daily rates. It's open every day in summer. There's some good riding in this area, such as along the Gulf Shore Parkway. Rentals are also available in Stanhope, at the Stanhope Beach Lodge.

### Hitching
Thumbing around the island is common, accepted and often done by residents. The island is relatively free of violence and you can generally hitch without expecting trouble. Your safety cannot be guaranteed, however, and hitching is not be recommended without some reservations. Caution is advised.

## NORTH OF CHARLOTTETOWN
The area north of the capital in Queen's County is where all the action is on Prince Edward Island (refer to the Cavendish Region map). The national park is here, with its camping and beaches, and most of the island's main attractions are in this area. To feed and house the vacationers, many of the province's lodging and dining establishments are found not far from the north coast. After York, my description covers areas from east to west *outside* the park, and then, again in the same direction, areas *within* the park boundaries.

### York
Not far from Charlottetown, the *Potato Blossom Tea Room* in York makes a pleasant afternoon stop for a sip and snack. It's at the **Jewell's Country Gardens**, which has a small pioneer village and glass museum.

### Grand Tracadie
Little more than a crossroads at the southeastern edge of the national park and not far from the entrance to it on Route 6, this is a 'must stop' for *Beulah's Bake Shop*, a tiny shed beside the house and kitchen where all the cooking is done. The strawberry and raspberry pies are unbelievable (I confess to having eaten a whole raspberry one at a sitting) and are cheap to boot. There are other things too, including bread and a variety of buns. Campers at Stanhope, stock up here.

### Stanhope
There is really nothing in this town, but near the park entrance are a couple of restaurants. There is one basic place, and another, more up-market one in the old-time *Stanhope by the Sea* hotel, dating from 1817 and refurbished in 1988. You can also get a bite at the golf course, or at *Captain Dick's Pub*, next door to the hotel, which is open only on Friday nights (and even then not every week).

Stanhope is one of the major accommodation centres, with dozens of places renting cottages, often by the week or longer. Weekly rates vary but most are between $300 and $450. The daily rate for most of the housekeeping units is around $50.

*Campbell's Tourist Home* (☎ 672-2421) in Stanhope is a B&B with a double for $35.

From Stanhope to Cavendish there are about 10 privately operated campgrounds. (See also information on places to stay *within* Prince Edward Island National Park in that section later.)

### Winsloe North

South of Brackley is a dairy farm where gouda cheese is produced. It sounds interesting but there is nothing at all to see and the various cheeses which can be purchased on the premises are expensive.

### North Rustico

There is a post office and a government liquor store here. Across the province, these liquor stores are the outlets for beer, wine and all alcoholic beverages.

PEI is the home of *Fisherman's Wharf Lobster Suppers*, probably the best known, busiest restaurant in the province. It's huge but in peak season it still gets crowded, with queues from 6 to 8 pm. It's a fun, casual, holiday-style restaurant offering good-value dinners. For $22 you get served a half-kg lobster and can help yourself to an impressive salad bar, unlimited amounts of chowder, good local mussels, rolls and a variety of desserts. If you get really lucky, along the back wall are tables with a view of the ocean.

Less commercial is the *Barn*, south along Route 6 out of town for a few km, with all-you-can-eat chicken dinners at $11. Everything is homemade – you can see the local women carrying in their designated dishes at opening time. It's just like going home for a Sunday meal. A late report indicates that this place may have closed – another recession victim?

At **Rusticoville** fishing charters can be arranged down at the quay and you can buy fresh lobster and fish.

Outside South Rustico on the small Route 242 is, for me, the quirkiest of island attractions, **Jumpin' Jack's Old Country Store Museum**. It's in the middle of nowhere and doesn't charge admission – on our visit the only person about was an old man waiting patiently to show someone around. The museum is a junk collector's dream – an old two-storey house jammed with dust-covered articles of every description and function collected from far and wide for who knows how many years. It's open daily (except Mondays) through July and August. On Sundays, it is closed in the morning, opening at 1 pm.

North Rustico also has a lot of accommodation, including many tourist homes where it's possible to get something for less than a week fairly easily. A double room in someone's home can be had for $25 to $35.

North Rustico Harbour is a tiny fishing community with a lighthouse which you can drive to from North Rustico or walk to from the beach once you're in the national park.

The Rustico area is the base for one of the largest of the province's fishing fleets. Prince Edward Island's fishing industry is inshore (as opposed to offshore), meaning that the boats head out and return home the same day.

### Cavendish

At the junction of routes 6 and 13 south of the park, this little town is the area's commercial centre. You're in the centre of town when you see the gas station, Cavendish Arms Pub, the church and the cemetery!

Just east of town is a restaurant complex all done in cedar shakes. It contains a few fast-food places, including one for breakfasts. *Thirsty's*, across the street, is a bar. Nearby is a bicycle-rental outfit.

The Cavendish Tourist Mart is a grocery store open from 8 am to 10 pm daily, good for all essential supplies, and there is a bakery a few doors away.

East of Cavendish is a large **amusement park** and close by are a **wax museum, go-kart tracks** and other newish diversions, including (for some reason) a life-size replica of a space shuttle. At Stanley Bridge the **Marine Aquarium** has live samples of some of the native fish and a few seals. It isn't large, so to broaden the appeal there is a pinned butterfly display and a collection of

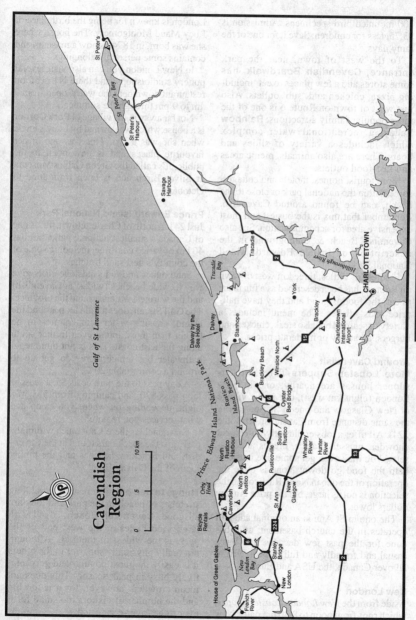

PRINCE EDWARD ISLAND

## Cavendish Region

Gulf of St Laurence

St Peter's

St Peter's Bay

St Peter's Harbour

Savage Harbour

Tracadie

Tracadie Bay

CHARLOTTETOWN

Hillsborough River

York

Brackley

Dalvay

Stanhope

Dalvay by the Sea Hotel

Brackley Beach

Winsloe North

Charlottetown International Airport

Prince Edward Island National Park

Rustico Island Beach

North Rustico Harbour

Oyster Bed Bridge

Wheatley River

Hunter River

North Rustico

South Rustico

Rusticoville

New Glasgow

Orby Head

St Ann

Bicycle Rentals

Cavendish

House of Green Gables

Stanley Bridge

New London Bay

New London

French River

0   5   10 km

700 mounted bird specimens. Admission is $3.75, less for children. Save it for one of the rainy days.

To the west of town, near the park entrance, **Cavendish Boardwalk** has some stores and a few places to eat, including pizza, chicken and 'sub' outlets. Also just west of town on Route 6 is one of the more popular family attractions: **Rainbow Valley**, a recreational water complex which includes a variety of slides and boats. There are also animals, picnic areas and fast-food outlets.

More tourist homes, motels and cottages, some within the national park or close to the beach, can be found around Cavendish. Remember that this is the busiest and most expensive area for accommodation. See also Cavendish Beach & Campground in the description of Prince Edward Island National Park.

Fiddles 'n' Vittles, three km west of town on Route 6, has been described as a fun place to eat; the food is good and they have half-price kids' dishes. The menu includes a variety of seafood but also steak, chicken and burgers, all at low or moderate prices.

### Around Cavendish
**More Lobster Suppers** Three lobster-supper houses are nearby: one in New London (eight km west), one in the village of New Glasgow and one in St Ann (about the same distance from Cavendish on Route 224). All offer a lobster plus all-you-can-eat chowder, mussels, salads, breads and desserts. You may even get some live music to help the food go down. None is quite the operation of the one in North Rustico and the selection is not as large, but the price is a few dollars lower.

The one in St Ann is an original and still operates in the church basement, as it has done for the past few decades. It's busy, casual and friendly and full of people from all over Canada, the USA and Europe.

### New London
Aside from the *New London Lobster Supper*, which runs from noon to 8.30 pm daily, New London is known for being the birthplace of Lucy Maud Montgomery. The house where she was born, in 1874, is now a museum and contains some personal belongings.

In New London you can also visit several pottery studio/shops, and there is a seafood restaurant down near the water, open from 9 am to 9 pm through the summer.

Not far away in the village of **Park Corner** is a house which was owned by Lucy's uncle when she was a girl. This was one of her favourite places and is now open to the public. It's called the Green Gables Museum at Silver Birch and is open from June to October.

### Prince Edward Island National Park
Just 24 km north of Charlottetown, this is one of Canada's smallest national parks but has 40 km of varied coastline, including some of the country's best sand beaches.

Sand dunes and red sandstone cliffs give way to wide beaches (widest at Cavendish) and the warmest waters around the province. The Gulf Stream does a little loop around the island, causing water temperatures to be higher than those found even further south along the east coast. This is not quite tepid bathwater but temperatures do get up to around a comfortable 20°C.

A day pass to the park costs $5, a season-long pass $20, and camping from $13.50 a night, depending on where you camp and what services you require.

For munchies there's not much within the park, just the snack bars found at the Cavendish and Brackley beaches and the dining room of the Dalvay Hotel.

**Things to See & Do** There are several long stretches of beach in the park and they are all good. **Cavendish Beach**, edged with large sand dunes at the west end of the park, is the widest of them all. Although not really physically superior to the others it is easily the most popular and gets relatively busy in peak season. This does not mean crowded, however, for it is too big and the number of visitors too small for it ever to get over-congested.

**House of Green Gables** in the park near Cavendish town is, apart from the national park itself, the most popular attraction in the province.

The house is known as the place where Anne, the heroine of many of Lucy Montgomery's books, lived. The surrounding property was the setting of the 1908 novel *Anne of Green Gables* – a perennial favourite not only in Canada but around the world, having been translated into nearly 20 languages. The warm-hearted book tells the story of a young orphan, Anne, and her childhood tribulations in turn-of-the-century Prince Edward Island in a way that makes it a universal tale.

Lucy Maud Montgomery was born down the road in New London. In *Anne of Green Gables* and many subsequent novels, she painted a world based on the land, life and times of this quiet, staid region.

Everything relating to either the story or the author anywhere on the island has now pretty well become part of the Green Gables industry, but despite that, the original charm of place and character do remain.

At House of Green Gables, actually a rather attractive and comfortable place, the overpopularisation reaches its zenith, with tremendous crowds arriving daily all through the summer. Busloads arrive at the door continuously. Visiting first thing in the morning is highly recommended. It's free,

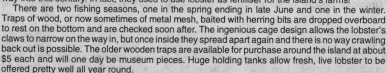

### Lobster

Unfortunately for this mottled green or bluish or blackish prehistoric wonder somebody realised it tasted bloody good. This has meant that we've learned a lot about it. But the facts on this 100-million-year-old crustacean read like a joke book. It tastes with its feet, listens with its legs (of which there are 10), and has teeth in its stomach (which is found just behind the head). The kidney is in the head, the brain in the neck and the bones (shell) are on the outside.

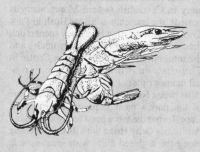

Lobster is widely associated with the east coast of Canada but perhaps Prince Edward Island, with its famous lobster suppers, is most closely linked with this symbol of gourmet dining. It's now hard to believe but there wasn't much interest in the delicate meat until a good way into this century. In fact, they used to use lobster as fertiliser for the island's farms!

There are two fishing seasons, one in the spring ending in late June and one in the winter. Traps of wood, or now sometimes of metal mesh, baited with herring bits are dropped overboard to rest on the bottom and are checked soon after. The ingenious cage design allows the lobster's claws to narrow on the way in, but once inside they spread apart again and there is no way crawling back out is possible. The older wooden traps are available for purchase around the island at about $5 each and will one day be museum pieces. Huge holding tanks allow fresh, live lobster to be offered pretty well all year round.

The standard restaurant lobster in Canada weighs a pound or a little less than half a kg. Two and three pounders are often available but bigger ones are not often seen. Along the Quebec coast of the St Lawrence around Rivire-du-Loup I've seen five and six pounders (2.5 kg) for sale but tell me who's gonna pick one of those suckers up and put it in a pot of hot water?

Most people are satisfied with the regular portion as it seems to be a rich food. The meat is lean, however, and is permitted on low cholesterol diets. Hold the butter.

Lobster can be baked, broiled, even barbecued but the best method is boiling. They should be cooked in boiling, salted fresh water for 12 to 15 minutes for the first pound, adding four minutes for every extra pound (half-kg). When done, the lobster has the characteristic orangey-red shell, not unlike that of some of the bathers at Cavendish beach. Most meaty is the tail, followed by the larger claws. Though most people quickly discard it, the green mushy liver known as tomalley, is considered a delicacy and one of the choicest parts to savour. ∎

and worth a visit for the period furniture and the feeling it gives of life here in the late 19th and early 20th centuries. The house is open from 9 am to 8 pm in high season, till 5 pm otherwise.

Also worthwhile are the quieter trails from the house through the green, gentle creek-crossed woods. 'Lover's Lane', particularly, has maintained its idealistic childhood ambience.

Not far away, near the United Church in the town of **Cavendish**, you can visit the site of the house where Lucy Montgomery lived with her grandparents. *Anne of Green Gables* was written here. The farmhouse no longer stands, just the stone foundations and surrounding gardens.

Other Anne-related sites include the cemetery in Cavendish (where Montgomery is buried), the museum at Silver Bush in Park Corner on Route 20 (where Lucy spent much time when it was owned by her uncle) and the museum in the Confederation Centre in Charlottetown (which contains some original manuscripts).

Between Rustico and Cavendish is some of the park's most impressive terrain. At Cape Turner there is a good look-out area but don't miss **Orby Head** with its trails leading along the high red cliffs with great seaside views. There are other stopping-off points along this stretch of coastal road.

**Brackley Beach**, in the middle of the park, is also well attended, the others less so. Long, wide Brackley Beach backed by sand dunes is popular with locals, young people and visitors. There is a snack bar and change rooms by the boardwalk to the beach. Lifeguards are on hand but watch out for riptides.

**Stanhope Beach**, opposite the campground of the same name is similar to the more popular ones in appearance but seems to mainly attract the people of the nearby campground. There are no cliffs or dunes here, the landscape is flat and the beach is wide. At the entrance to the beach is a snack bar and change rooms with showers. A boardwalk leads to the beach which has lifeguards on duty through the day.

**Dalvay Beach** is the easternmost beach and a couple of short hiking trails begin in the area. One called Long Pond is quite good with a small graveyard, some remnants of old stone dykes and a spring for a cool drink found along the way.

An appealing landmark is the **Dalvay by the Sea Hotel** built in 1895 and looking like something out of F Scott Fitzgerald. For a splurge this Victorian seaside lodge offers a varied menu – lobster bisqué to coq au vin. Reservations are required.

If you're thinking of spending the night, the price of a double room (from $150 and up) includes dinner and breakfast.

There is virtually no shade to be had at any

---

**A Yen for Anne**

Although Prince Edward Island is generally little known internationally, up to 10,000 of the island's annual visitors are now from Japan. This makes it easily one of the country's top destinations for the Japanese traveller. There is even a direct Tokyo-Charlottetown flight. Banff and the Rockies are also a major lure.

The attraction is partly because Charlottetown has become the twin city of Ashibetsu, a rural city in northern Japan. Student exchanges have taken place, as well as a number of tourist-related activities.

The main draw, however, is the Japanese fascination with *Anne of Green Gables*. The book has been found on Japanese school curriculums since the 1950s, and Anne's story has found a spot in the national psyche, especially among women, who identify strongly with Anne's character.

Also many Japanese now come to PEI to marry. Weddings and marriages in Japan can be prohibitively costly and are often difficult to prepare. Here couples enjoy the quiet countryside and, in some cases, the Christian church and ceremony to which many young people are attracted. Quite a few couples are married at Silver Birch in Park Corner, where Montgomery herself was married. Arrangements are handled by the local tourism ministry. ∎

of the beaches, so consider using an umbrella or lots of sunscreen lotion.

All the north coast beaches tend to have red jellyfish. They are known locally as bloodsuckers but they aren't. Most are much smaller than a closed fist and, while unpleasant, are not really dangerous, although brushing against one can irritate the skin. Most years the jellies are not overly abundant and don't pose much of a problem. The beaches of the southern coast don't have these jellyfish but they don't have the sand either – some tend to be rather rocky, with debris and logs scattered around.

**Activities** Windsurfing equipment can be hired and lessons are available within the park at the Stanhope Beach Lodge. It costs $10 an hour for a board, less by the day. Canoes and sailboats are also for rent. On Thursday nights surfboard races are held, with prizes offered.

**Places to Stay** Overnight camping costs range from $13.50 per night and up. The more services, the higher the price. Tent sites are cheapest. Those looking to save some dollars should check Rustico Campground (see below). Reservations are not taken for the campgrounds, so it's strictly first come, first get. In July and August try to arrive by mid-afternoon. After Labour Day, the park is free to visit but camping must still be paid for. All three campgrounds use the same number; if you want to check availability call ☎ 672-6350.

The *Cavendish Beach Campground* (☎ 672-6350) at the centre of things with nearby attractions and restaurants as well as the beach is usually full. If this is where you want to stay, check the office early in the morning for available spaces which are $13.50 unserviced. The campground is three km west of Cavendish.

The relatively isolated *Rustico Campground* is on an island. It has good camping, again with lots of trees, but the beach was entirely washed away in a storm in the summer of 1987. A walk along the shoreline with its debris and upturned trees shows how

nasty the sea can get – there is literally no sand left. The campground has no showers either, but these drawbacks result in a reduced fee – camping costs just $9 a site.

*Stanhope Campground* also within the park is recommended for good sites with lots of trees and a fine sandy beach opposite. An unserviced site is $13.50 and there is a well-stocked store. Arrive early in the day, as it may be full for the night by 3 or 4 pm.

Outside the park and occasionally adjacent to it are many private campgrounds supplementing the ones inside the park. *Marco Polo* (☎ 964-2960), near Cavendish, has a range of amenities, including two swimming pools. At the other end of the national park, near Grand Tracadie on Route 6, the much smaller *Ann's Whispering Pines* (☎ 672-2632) has tent and trailer sites. Both take reservations.

Some of the many local rental cottages are in the park or back onto it. Many visitors do rent a cottage for a week or two but the places just a short walk from the beach tend to be pricier. There are also many tourist homes near the park, but without a car or bicycle, it's difficult to get around.

## WEST OF CHARLOTTETOWN
### Lady Slipper Drive

The western third of the island is made up of Prince County. Lady Slipper Drive is 288 km long and is the marked tourist route around this portion of the island, pretty much circumnavigating the region.

The northern section of Prince County is, like so much of the province, pretty farm country, but the southern portion is rather flat, less scenic and possibly the least visited part of the island. The southernmost area, along Egmont and Bedeque bays, retains some evidence of its Acadian French history.

### Summerside

The second largest city in the province, Summerside has a population of 10,000. At one time residents of the capital would move to this side of the island in the hot months. Now Summerside is more a town in its own right, although the closure of the large military base here has caused a major economic setback.

The approach along Hwy 1A is much like that to Charlottetown, lined with motels, hamburger joints and a few campgrounds.

It's a quiet village with quaint old homes on streets trimmed with big trees. There are a couple of things to consider having a peek at but not a lot for the visitor to do. The one main street, Water St, has most of the commercial establishments.

The **Lady Slipper Visitor Information Centre** is on Route 11, off Hwy 1A two km east of Summerside. Here there is a display of photographs, maps, etc which outline the attractions along Lady Slipper Drive. The walking-tour pamphlet of historic Summerside details some of the town's finer buildings from 1850 to the turn of the century.

Go behind the centre and there is a good chance you'll see great blue herons standing fishing, especially if the tide is on the way out. Black cormorants may also be seen.

Watch for the International Highland Gathering at the end of June at the College of Piping & Celtic Performing Arts.

For a week in mid-July each year there's the Lobster Carnival, with nightly feasts, contests, games and music. At the end of the month there is a hydroplane regatta. Sleman Park is the site of an airshow at the end of August.

South of Summerside, **Borden** is the terminal for ferries to Cape Tormentine, New Brunswick.

### International Fox Museum & Hall of Fame

The interesting though perhaps controversial story of island fox farming is told at 260 Fitzroy St (☎ 436-2400), one block from Water St.

In 1890, using two wild silver foxes captured on the island, a breeding and farming operation was begun. It was the first anywhere to successfully breed wild fur-bearing animals in captivity. The principles learned are now used around the world. Through the 1920s fortunes were made in Summerside in shipbuilding and in fur farming. For a time,

the latter was Prince Edward Island's most important economic activity.

From May to September, the museum, created in Holman Homestead, a beautiful historic house with a lovely garden, is open from 9 am to 6 pm. Holman himself was a fox breeder, and there are still fox farms on the island today. One of them, Anglo Farms (☎ 882-2825) in the village of Anglo Tignish, is also a B&B.

### The College of Piping & Celtic Performing Arts

The school (☎ 436-5377), at 619 Water St, provides visitors with nearly continuous entertainment through the day – bagpipes, singing, dancing. Drop in any time Monday to Friday from 11 am to 5 pm and see what's happening. There are also exhibits such as fiddle-making and there is a lunch room for light meals. A ticket is $3, or $6 for the special Thursday night Scottish Ceilidh shows. The Thursday performance is usually held outdoors at the back of the building – bring a sweater!

### EPTEK National Exhibition Centre & PEI Sports Hall of Fame

Free and open daily in the summer, the centre (☎ 888-8373) presents small, changing art and history exhibits. A section on provincial sports figures is permanent. The centre is at the waterfront near Spinnaker's Landing, a new tourist shopping area.

### Harbour Cruises

These depart from the Spinnaker's Landing Information Centre at the waterfront.

### Places to Stay

Accommodation is sufficient if not abundant in Summerside, but there are many places to stay in the surrounding area during the busy periods, should the need arise. The nearby villages of St Eleanors and Miscouche have tourist homes.

For campers, there is *Linkletter Provincial Park* (☎ 436-7438), on Route 11 eight km west of Summerside. There's a beach and a store for basic supplies.

In town, *The Arbor Inn* (☎ 436-6847) is a B&B at 380 MacEwan Rd. It has seven

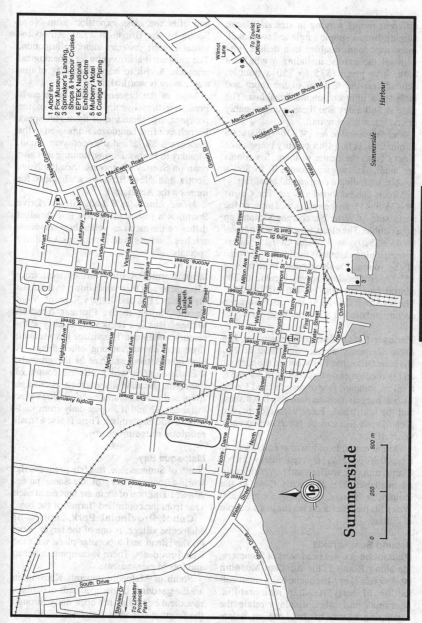

PRINCE EDWARD ISLAND

**Summerside**

1 Arbor Inn
2 Fox Museum
3 Spinnaker's Landing,
  Shops & Harbour Cruises
4 EPTEK National
  Exhibition Centre
5 Mulberry Motel
6 College of Piping

To Tourist
Office (2 km)

Wilmot Lane

Glover Shore Rd

MacEwen Road

Heckbert St

Maple Grove Road

MacEwen Road

Kenmore Ave

High Street

Lefurgey Ave

Arnett Ave

Linden Ave

Victoria Road

Granville Street

Arcona Street

Ottawa Street

Green St

Water Street

Central Avenue

Highland Ave

Schurman Street

Queen
Elizabeth
Park

Green Street

Convent Street

Milton Ave

Harvard Street

Russell St

King St

East St

Belmont St

Granville Street

Hanover St

Fitzroy St

Spring St

Winter St

Summer St

Church St

First St

Second Street

Water Street

Harbour Drive

Summerside

Harbour

Maple Avenue

Chestnut Ave

Willow Ave

Cedar Street

Duke
Street

Elm Street

Brophy Avenue

Market
Street

North
Street

Notre
Dame
Street

Northumberland St

Greenwood Drive

West St

Water Street

South Drive

Bayview Dr

To Linkletter
Provincial Park

Spinx Drive

0    250    500 m

different rooms varying in size and decor, ranging from a simple single and two small, share-washroom doubles to a deluxe suite with all the extras, including a whirlpool bath. The price ($35 to $50 a double) depends on the features of the room and includes a light continental breakfast. The suite is $80 a day and there is a reasonably priced housekeeping unit.

The *Summerside Inn* (☎ 436-5208), at 98 Summer St, is in a 19th-century house three blocks from the centre of town. Six rooms are available, ranging from $40 to $60 a double, including a continental breakfast.

Motels can be found as well. The *Cairns* (☎ 436-5841), on the east side of town on the north side of Water St, charges $35 and up for a double. The clean, new *Mulberry Motel* (☎ 436-2520), at 6 Water St East, offers housekeeping (kitchen) facilities with some of the rooms. Doubles range from $38 to $55. A coffee shop serves breakfast. The central *Linkletter Inn* (☎ 436-2157), at 311 Market St, off Central St, is good no-surprise accommodation at $50 a double.

### Places to Eat
Of the several restaurants, *The Little Mermaid*, on the waterfront at 240 Harbour Drive, has fine views of the harbour and is recommended. At prices of $5 to $7, it offers standard fare of mainly fried foods, such as burgers, but there are also fish dishes, and the homemade French fries (chips) are great. Fresh fish can be purchased to cook yourself, too.

On the east side of town, at 652 Water St East, *Seafood Delights* is reasonably priced. Clams, mussels, scallops and fish & chips are all available. The *Dominion Café*, in the Dominion Square Shopping Centre, 250 Water St, has afternoon tea for just a couple of dollars.

### Around Summerside
**Miscouche** As you head west of Summerside along Route 2, the **Acadian Museum** (☎ 436-6237) in Miscouche has a small collection of early Acadian memorabilia. Dioramas and other displays relate the engrossing history of the Acadians before and after the mass expulsion from Nova Scotia by the British in 1720. An audiovisual exhibit provides more information. The museum is also a centre for genealogical research. A visit to learn something of this tragic story is worthwhile.

Most of the descendants of these early French settlers live in this section of the province. Six thousand of them still speak French as a first language. Admission to the museum is $2.75 and it's open year round, Monday to Friday. During summer it is also open on Sunday afternoons. (See the Nova Scotia and New Brunswick chapters for more on the Acadians.)

*Mémé Jane's*, at 8 Lady Slipper Drive South, is a restaurant with a few Acadian dishes on the menu as well as burgers, sandwiches, salads and inexpensive daily specials.

**Mont Carmel** A little further west from Miscouche and then south down to the coast on Route 11 is the little village of Mont Carmel, home to the **Pioneer Acadian Village**. This is a replica of an early 19th-century settlement. The village has a school, store and church, among other things. A highlight is the restaurant in the grounds, *L'Étoile de Mer*, which offers a couple of traditional Acadian dishes, such as chicken fricot and paté à la rapure. Admission to the village is $2 and it's open daily from mid-June to mid-September. There is also a small **religious museum** nearby.

### Malpeque Bay
North of Summerside, this bay produces the world-famous oysters of the same name. About 10 million of them are harvested each year from the controlled 'farms' of the bay.

**Cabot Provincial Park**, north of Malpeque village, is one of the larger parks on the island and a popular place with the island residents. There is camping, a beach and lots of picnic areas.

South of Malpeque towards Kensington are the **gardens**, landscaped beds of dahlias, roses and begonias. It's open daily through the summer and admission costs $2.50.

## Continuing Around Prince County

If you're in the vicinity, **Tyne Valley** is worth a visit. There are also a few craft places to visit, including a pottery. Also here, the *Doctor's Inn* (☎ 831-2164) is a fine country B&B whose good dining room is able to take full advantage of its surrounding organic garden.

The *West Island Inn* (☎ 831-2495) is also an attractive-looking historic place, with a big balcony and a gazebo with hot tub. A small double goes for $38, less in May, June, September and October. There is also one housekeeping unit, which is $35 for two people plus $6 for each additional person.

A band of about 50 Micmac families live on **Lennox Island**, in Malpeque Bay. The scenery is good, and there's a museum dealing with the history of the people who were the first in Canada to be converted to Christianity. St Ann's Church, dating from 1875, can be visited, along with an Indian craft shop. Artefacts and some art work can be viewed on weekdays at the office complex. The island is connected by road from the west side of the bay, near the village of East Bideford, north of Tyne Valley.

The inland town of **O'Leary**, right in the middle of Prince County, is a small commercial centre which sees few tourists. Partially in response to that, there is the new **PEI Potato Museum** (☎ 859-2039), on Parkview Drive in Centennial Park. Those looking for all kinds of fascinating trivia and lore surrounding the lowly tuber will be disappointed. The small museum deals mainly with local history through the work of late resident photographers, farm tools, etc.

Also in town are several craft outlets, with the primary article being knitted goods. The **Macausland's Woollen Mill**, an old town business, remains in operation and can be toured. Pure woollen goods can be bought at the mill. There is also another church lobster supper here.

If you're near **Tignish** at meal time, drop in at the Royal Canadian Legion. It's cheap, and you're bound to find conversation. The Parish of St Simon and St Jude Church has an impressive pipe organ built in Montreal and installed here in 1882. It employs 1118 pipes, ranging in size from a few cm to five metres.

Near the village of Norway (ask for directions), **Elephant Rock**, a large erosion formation at the seashore, is worth a look.

Up at the northern tip, **North Cape** is a wind-blown promontory with a lighthouse. A wind turbine station has been set up to study the efficacy of wind-powered generators. The interpretive centre provides information. Along the east side of the cape in particular are some fairly high cliffs, and there is a rock reef at North Cape which can be explored at low tide – look for sea life in the pools and watch for coastal birds. North Cape also has a restaurant.

About midway down the coast on the western shore along Route 14 is the village of Miminegash, in one of the more remote sections of the province. Out of town, at the Government Research Centre on Route 152, is the **Irish Moss Interpretative Centre** (☎ 882-2920), in an old fishing boat. It was begun by local women whose families have long been involved in the collecting or harvesting of the moss, a type of seaweed.

Visitors passing by were always curious about the green stuff and the people and horses mucking it up along the beach, and the centre is meant to answer a lot of questions. Traditional and newer methods of collecting are explained, as are the uses of the moss. It is the main source of carrageenin, which is used as an emulsifier in the making of commercial ice cream, toothpaste and cough syrup. Recipes are available at the centre for other, tastier uses. Almost half the world's supply of Irish moss comes from PEI.

**Cedar Dunes Provincial Park**, at the south-east tip of Prince County, has a lighthouse, restaurant and beach. The lighthouse, dating from 1875, has been restored, and there is now a museum outlining its history. Overnight guests can stay in the inn, *West Point Lighthouse* (☎ 859-3605), part of the former lightkeeper's premises. Alternatively there is camping, or a less-expensive B&B

called *Red Capes Inn* (☎ 859-3150), four km away on Route 14.

## EAST OF CHARLOTTETOWN
### The King's Byway

The 374-km-long, circular sightseeing route around King's County (the eastern third of the province) is called the King's Byway. It's a lightly populated, rural region of farms and fishing communities. Much of this section of the province is peopled by ancestors of Scottish settlers rather than by the French of the western side or the Irish of the central district. The ferry to Nova Scotia is on the south coast, while the ferry to the Magdalen Islands is at Souris, on the east coast.

The shoreline is a mixture of parks, beaches, fishing ports and a few larger but quiet towns. The interior is crisscrossed with roads between farms.

### Orwell

Just out of town is the **Orwell Corner Historic Village** (☎ 651-2013), a restored and preserved 19th-century community. Originally settled by Scottish immigrants in 1766, the village includes a farm, blacksmith's, post office and store among other buildings still in their initial settings. It's open every day in summer and costs $3. Concerts are held on Wednesday evenings.

### Wood Islands

Down on the south coast, 'Woods' is where you'll find the PEI-Nova Scotia ferry terminal, and as such it's a busy visitor centre even though there isn't much in town itself. The mainland is 22 km (75 minutes) across the Northumberland Strait.

The *Cozy Nest* (☎ 962-2030) is a B&B one km from the ferry landing, on the Trans Canada Hwy towards Charlottetown. A double room costs $22 and breakfast is a few dollars more. There is also a motel, which is two km west of the ferry. In town there are about half a dozen places to eat.

### Murray Harbour

Little visited and tucked out of the way, Murray Harbour is a fishing town with its own canning plant. A boat tour out to watch seals departs from the town wharf. There is also a small museum on the outskirts.

### Brudenell River Provincial Park & Around

The campground in the park is just a bare field, but there's a lodge and a golf course for those not roughing it. At **Panmure Island Provincial Park**, just south down the coast, there is a good beach, swimming and picnicking.

**Georgetown** is a shipbuilding and repair depot. **Cardigan**, an old shipbuilding centre north of the park, has a lobster-supper house right down by the harbour; it's open daily from June to October. The hours are early: 4.30 to 8.30 pm.

### Bay Fortune

The dining room at *The Inn at Bay Fortune* (☎ 583-2928) is considered to be one of the finest in the province. There are also 11 comfortable guest rooms at this expensive country inn.

### Fortune River

The Fortune River flowing near Hwy 2 which cuts across the island is another good place for canoeing.

### Souris

With a population of 1500, Souris feels like a real town after you've passed through so many small villages. It's actually one of the larger towns of the province and is the shopping and supply centre for the eastern region. First settled by the Acadian French in the early 1700s, it was named Souris, meaning 'mouse', due to several plagues of the little creatures. Today the name has been anglicised and the last 's' is pronounced. The town is an important fishing and processing port and is also important for the ferry (☎ 986-3278) which departs for the Magdalen Islands of Quebec, five hours and 134 km north in the Gulf of St Lawrence. See under Magdalen Islands in the Quebec chapter for more information on the ferry.

Main St, a strip with buildings from the

1920s and 1930s as well as some older distinctive architecture, is pleasantly slow, with cars stopping to let pedestrians cross. The shops, the newspaper office and a few simple restaurants are found here.

**St Mary's Roman Catholic Church**, built of island sandstone in 1901, is off Main St on Pacquet St and is the dominant structure in town. However, the **Town Hall** on Main St, the Georgian-style **Beacon House** and several other buildings are worth a look on the way by.

There is a tourist office down at the beach at the south-west corner of town. Across the small bay, at the breakwater on the other side of town, is the large fish-processing plant and the dock for the red-and-white coastguard ship.

**Places to Stay** For a small town, Souris gets quite busy due to the ferry traffic. There is one B&B in town, the *Matthew House Inn* (☎ 687-3461) on Breakwater St, one block from the ferry. With period furnishings, ensuite bath and more, this large restored Victorian home is not in the low-budget category. Doubles range from $50 to $125, including continental breakfast.

The good *Hilltop Motel* (☎ 687-3315), although not cheap either, gets full with ferry traffic even when the ferry arrives from Quebec at four or five in the morning. Checking in at that hour is OK, but call from the Magdalen Islands for a reservation before leaving or someone will probably beat you to the available bed. The motel has a restaurant that is good for breakfast. It's on the east side of town. If calling from Quebec, add 1-902 before dialling the telephone number. Rates are $60 a double.

At half the price is the *Souris West Motel* (☎ 687-2676), three km west of the ferry terminal on Route 2.

### Red Point Provincial Park

Red Point is a small park with a sandy beach and some pleasant shaded tent sites. The beaches around here are known for the squeaking sound they make when you walk on them.

### Basin Head

Not even really a village, Basin Head is at the ocean's edge, with a fisheries museum displaying equipment, a beach, a few old fishing buildings, a snack bar and a canoe rental outlet. There is a fair bit of inland water here to paddle around and explore.

### East Point

At East Point, the north-east tip of the island, cliffs are topped by a lighthouse, which can be climbed as part of a little tour for $2.50. Until the late 1980s it was run by a keeper, but is now automated like almost every other lighthouse in Canada. The old assistant's house nearby has a restored radio room and there is a gift shop. It's expected that in a few years the whole thing will have to be moved (as the lighthouse has been moved previously) because of the creeping erosion of the shoreline. The lighthouse is open from 10 am to 6 pm daily from 1 June to the end of September.

The north shore area of King's County all the way along towards Cavendish is more heavily wooded than much of the island but that doesn't mean the end of farms and potatoes altogether. Notice that many of the beautiful old cedar shake farmhouses are now being supplanted by modern, more energy-efficient bungalows not unlike those you can see in suburban Toronto. The older places often sit empty, quietly decaying or being suffocated by the lilac bushes.

There is a lot of fishing done along the coast here – you could try a charter in search of tuna. Inland there are a couple of trout streams worth investigating.

The people of the north-eastern area have a fairly strong, intriguing accent not unlike that heard in Newfoundland.

### North Lake

This is one of the four fishing centres found along the north coast of King's County. Although small, the dock area and its lobster traps, storage sheds and boats is always good for a poke around. There is some irresistible potential for picture-taking. Commercial boat operators may take passengers along for a little deep-sea fishing. With autumn comes tuna season and quite a busy sport-fishing period, drawing anglers from abroad. Some of the world's largest bluefin tuna have been caught in these waters. Indeed the world-record catch, a 680-kg behemoth, was reeled in off North Lake in 1979.

### Campbell's Cove Provincial Park

Quiet and relaxing through the day, this small park, the best one in the county, fills up by evening in July and August. As always shade is at a premium, with about half the campsites offering some sun relief. Most campers are tenters and there are no electric hook-ups. Facilities are minimal so bring all necessary supplies.

The beach is good, with cliffs at each end.

### St Margaret's

At the big church in St Margaret's, lobster suppers are held from Thursday to Sunday and cost a few bucks less than the ones

around the Cavendish area. Aside from the deep-sea fishing, there are some good trout streams along the road, and one of them, the **Naufrage River**, is just west of town. At the village of **Naufrage**, on the coast, there is another lighthouse and some colourful fishing boats around the wharf area.

### St Peter's

The nets for commercial mussel farming can be seen stretched around St Peter's Bay. In town don't miss *Wilma's Bake Shop*, for bread, muffins and cinnamon buns.

### Midgell

On Hwy 2 south of St Peter's Bay is the Midgell Centre (☎ 961-2963). Set up principally for the guests of the Christian centre, visitors are welcome to stay overnight at the hostel. There are 60 beds at $10 each. Light cooking is possible and there are showers and a lounge. It's open to visitors from 1 June to 1 September.

# New Brunswick

Entered Confederation: 1 July 1867
Area: 73,437 sq km
Population: 723,900
Provincial Capital: Fredericton

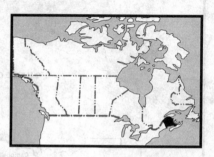

New Brunswick, which celebrated its 200th birthday in 1984, is (along with Nova Scotia and Prince Edward Island) one of Canada's three Maritime Provinces. It was also one of the four original members of the Dominion of Canada established in 1867. Despite its long history, the province's essential characteristic is that it remains largely forested. Yet, for most visitors, it is the areas apart from the vast woodlands that have the most appeal.

From the Quebec border the gentle, pastoral farming region of the Saint John River Valley leads to the Bay of Fundy with its cliffs, coves and tidal flats caused by the world's highest tides. Saint John, the largest city, and Fredericton, the capital, both have intriguing Loyalist histories. The eastern shore offers warm, sandy beaches and, some of the finest salmon-fishing rivers anywhere flow out of the forested interior. The wooded highlands of the north contain one of the highest mountains in eastern Canada and provide opportunities for a variety of outdoor activities.

What is now New Brunswick was originally the land of the Micmacs, and, in the southern areas, the Maliseet (Malecite) and Passamaquoddy Native peoples. Today their numbers are small and the majority of the population has British roots. Roughly 60% of the province's residents live in urban areas. You may be surprised at how much French you hear spoken. Around 37% of the population have French ancestors and, even today, 16% speak French only. New Brunswick is Canada's only officially bilingual province.

New Brunswick has never had a very strong image and, although many people pass through, it is nowhere near as popular a vacation destination as Nova Scotia or Prince Edward Island, having neither the tourist orientation nor the volume of visitors of these two neighbours.

Along the Trans Canada Hwy across the province it is impossible to miss the odd and considerable array of goods the locals offer for sale right at the roadside. You may see signs advertising eggs, rabbits, dogs, quilts, cars, fruits, vegetables and used books for sale!

## CLIMATE
Summers are usually not blisteringly hot and winters are very snowy and cold. The driest month of the year is August; generally, there is more rain in the south.

## ECONOMY
Lumber and pulp and paper operations are two of the main industries. Manufacturing and minerals are also important, as are mixed farming and fishing.

## INFORMATION
### Provincial Symbols
The provincial flower is the purple violet and the New Brunswick bird is the chickadee.

### Telephone
The area code for the entire province is 506. For emergencies call 911 or 0.

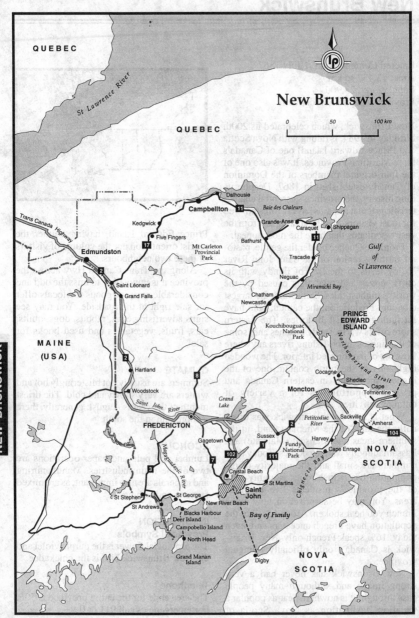

QUEBEC

St Lawrence River

QUEBEC

**New Brunswick**

0        50        100 km

Dalhousie

*Baie des Chaleurs*

Trans Canada Highway

Kedgwick

**Campbellton**        11

Five Fingers

Grande-Anse        Caraquet        Shippagan

17

**Edmundston**

Mt Carleton Provincial Park

Bathurst        11

*Gulf of St Lawrence*

2

Saint Léonard

Tracadie

Grand Falls

Neguac

*Miramichi Bay*

Chatham

Newcastle

**PRINCE EDWARD ISLAND**

**MAINE (USA)**

Kouchibouguac National Park

*Northumberland Strait*

Hartland

8

Cocagne

Shediac

Cape Tormentine

2

Woodstock

*Saint John River*

Grand Lake

**Moncton**

*Petitcodiac River*

Sackville

Amherst        104

**FREDERICTON**

Gagetown

Sussex        1

Fundy National Park

Harvey

Cape Enrage

**NOVA SCOTIA**

102        7

111

Crystal Beach

*Magaguadavic River*

3

St George

New River Beach

St Martins

**Saint John**

*Chignecto Bay*

St Stephen

St Andrews

Blacks Harbour

Deer Island

Campobello Island

North Head

*Bay of Fundy*

Digby

**NOVA SCOTIA**

Grand Manan Island

## Time

The province is on Atlantic Time – coming from Quebec or Maine, move your watch ahead one hour.

## Tax

The provincial sales tax is a whopping 11%.

# Fredericton

Fredericton is the queen of New Brunswick's towns. Unlike most, it is non-industrial and a very pretty, genteel, quiet place. The central area has some visible history to explore.

Three hundred years ago, the Maliseet and Micmac Indians lived and fished in the area. In 1762 the British founded a town over the abandoned French settlement. They named it in honour of Prince Frederick, the second son of King George III. When the American Revolutionary War ended in 1783, about 6000 people arrived in town. Two years later it became the capital of the newly formed province which had just been created by splitting away from Nova Scotia.

Long ago the town produced Canada's first English-speaking poet, Loyalist Jonathan Odell. Later, Lord Beaverbrook, who was to rise to international prominence, was born here. Today, Fredericton still presides over high society as home of the province's lieutenant-governor, the Legislature and the university dons.

About a fifth of the 45,000 residents work for the government, because Fredericton has remained the capital of New Brunswick. Of the light industries here, food processing, woodworking and the manufacturing of leather goods are the most important.

Some remarkable old buildings and beautiful houses remain, the river runs gently by and the streets are tree-lined, prompting the title 'City of Stately Elms'. Fredericton makes a nice spot to relax for a day or two.

## ORIENTATION

The centre of the city is on a small, rounded peninsula which juts into the south side of the Saint John River. The city extends to the north side of the river, too, but this area is mainly residential and of little interest to visitors. There are three bridges: two for cars and the middle one for trains only.

The Westmorland St Bridge connects the downtown area with the north shore. From the downtown side some fine big houses and a couple of church spires are visible across the river.

Further east along the river, the Princess Margaret Bridge, as part of the Trans Canada Hwy, links the two segments of the highway as it swings around the eastern edge of the city and over the river enroute to and from Moncton. Not far beyond the bridge are the green woods and farmlands typical of the Saint John River Valley.

Coming into town from the west along the Trans Canada Hwy, take exit 292B (Regent St). Regent St will take you straight down to the centre of town.

In town, King St and the parallel Queen St are the main streets, just a block up from the river. Northumberland and Saint John Sts are the west and east edges of the small downtown area. The park on the corner of Queen and Regent Sts, called Officers' Square, is pretty much the centre of things.

As you head east from Queen St, out of the downtown area, there's a small strip of park known as The Green between the road and the river. This park extends eastwards for several blocks. Near the art gallery is a statue of Scottish poet Robbie Burns. There are good views along the river here, and big shade trees to relax under. Several points of interest lie in The Green.

As you go further east, Queen St becomes Waterloo Row. Here it's the houses on the other side of the street that deserve your attention. Each is different from its neighbour and all are large and well maintained. Some have grand balconies, turrets and bizarre shapes. Nos 50, 82 and 146 particularly impressed me. The residence of the lieutenant-governor is around here; look for the coat of arms. There aren't too many streets in the country like this one.

Back on The Green you'll pass the Loyalist Memorial beside Waterloo Row, commemorating the British founders. Not far away, on Brunswick St, is the old Loyalist Cemetery, similar to the one in Saint John. The tombstones show that many of these people were born in England, Ireland or other foreign countries, and died young. Strangely, the inscriptions make the pioneers and their hardships come alive.

Church and Brunswick Sts, branching out from near Christ Church Cathedral, also have numerous large brick or wooden houses. The grey one at 767 Brunswick St dates from 1784.

## INFORMATION
The Visitors' Centre (☎ 452-9500) is in City Hall on Queen St. It's open Monday to Friday year-round from 8.30 am to 5 pm but keeps later hours during the summer.

There's a tourist bureau (☎ 458-8331) on the Trans Canada Hwy near Hanwell Rd, exit 289. It's open daily from early June to late September, from 9 am until 7 pm.

Tourism New Brunswick (☎ 800-561-0123) will also help with information about most places in the province.

Downtown, the post office, open Monday to Friday, is at 527 Queen St not far from Regent St.

A good thing to know if you're driving is that there is free parking behind the Legislative Assembly Building on Queen St. Just tell the attendant you're a visitor from out of town.

## HISTORIC WALKING TOUR
A roughly six-square block area of central Fredericton contains most of the city's attractions and is also the most attractive and architecturally appealing portion of the city. A walking tour around some of the following places plus other historical sites is outlined on the map of Fredericton, available at the tourist office. A booklet gives descriptions of the various sites. The walking tour includes 24 spots in the historic downtown area, starting from City Hall.

## OFFICERS' SQUARE
This is the city's central park – on Queen St between Carleton and Regent Sts. The square was once the military parade ground and still sits amongst several military buildings.

At 11 am and 7 pm Monday to Friday, from mid-July to the third week in August, you can see the full-uniform Changing of the Guard ceremony.

Also in the park, on Tuesday and Thursday evenings in summer at 7.30 pm, free band concerts attract crowds. There might be a marching, military or pipe band, and sometimes classical music is played too. In the park is a statue of Lord Beaverbrook, the press baron and the province's most illustrious son.

On the west side of the square are the former Officers' Barracks, built between 1839 and 1851. The older section, closest to the water, has thicker walls of masonry and hand-hewn timbers. The other, newer end is made of sawn timber.

## YORK-SUNBURY HISTORICAL MUSEUM
This museum (☎ 455-6041) is in the old officers' quarters off the park, a building typical of those designed by the Royal Architects during the colonial period. The museum has a collection of items from the city's past: military pieces used by local regiments and by British and German armies from the Boer and both world wars; furniture from a Loyalist sitting room and Victorian bedroom; Native Indian and Acadian artefacts and archaeological finds.

The highlight of the museum is a stuffed 19-kg frog. It was the pet of a local innkeeper. Nineteen kg! Perhaps he fed it the patrons who were incapable of walking home.

Opening hours in summer are Monday to Saturday from 10 am to 6 pm but Tuesday and Thursday from 10 am to 8 pm; Sunday from noon to 6 pm. During the winter it's open only Monday, Wednesday and Friday from 11 am to 3 pm. The admission fee is just $1.

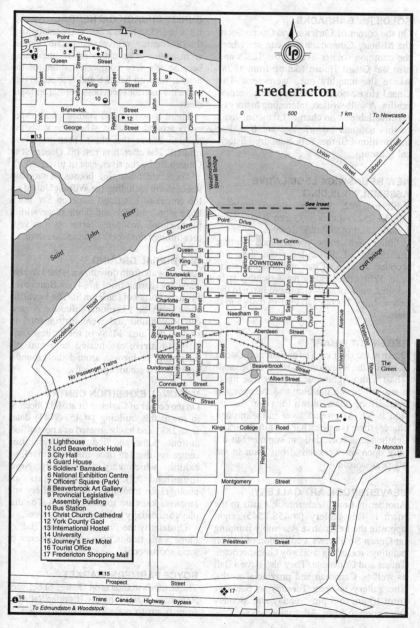

# Fredericton

0        500        1 km

**To Newcastle**

DOWNTOWN

**See inset**

**To Moncton**

**To Edmundston & Woodstock**

Trans Canada Highway Bypass

1  Lighthouse
2  Lord Beaverbrook Hotel
3  City Hall
4  Guard House
5  Soldiers' Barracks
6  National Exhibition Centre
7  Officers' Square (Park)
8  Beaverbrook Art Gallery
9  Provincial Legislative
   Assembly Building
10 Bus Station
11 Christ Church Cathedral
12 York County Gaol
13 International Hostel
14 University
15 Journey's End Motel
16 Tourist Office
17 Fredericton Shopping Mall

**NEW BRUNSWICK**

## SOLDIERS' BARRACKS

On the corner of Carleton and Queen Sts in the Military Compound you can see where the common soldier lived in the 1820s and also the Guard House (dating from 1828) where the naughty ones were sent. The Guard House now contains military memorabilia. A well-written, interesting history of it is available at no charge. Likewise, visits to this national historic site are free. For information call the York-Sunbury Historical Museum.

## NEW BRUNSWICK LEGISLATIVE ASSEMBLY BUILDING

Built in 1882, this government building (☎ 453-2527) stands on Queen St near Saint John St, east of Officers' Square.

Guides will show you around, pointing out things of particular merit, like the wooden Speaker's Chair and the spiral staircase. When the Legislative Assembly is in session, visitors are welcome to listen to the proceedings. It's open to visitors daily and is free.

## REGENT ST WHARF

Down at the river with an entrance off Queen St beside the Beaverbrook Hotel is the small wharf with a lighthouse and pier. The lighthouse contains a museum and the open top level affords views down the river. Admission is $2. At ground level (no admission charge) there is a snack bar and gift shop. The lighthouse is open daily in summer but it's only open on weekends from noon in the off-peak season.

## BEAVERBROOK ART GALLERY

Another of Lord Beaverbrook's gifts to the town is this gallery (☎ 458-8545), right opposite the Legislative Assembly Building on Queen St. There's a collection of British paintings including works by Gainsborough, Turner and Constable. They also have a Dali as well as Canadian and provincial works. The gallery is open Tuesday to Saturday from 10 am to 5 pm, Sunday and Monday from noon to 5 pm. Admission is $3.

## CHRIST CHURCH CATHEDRAL

Built in 1853, this is a fine early example of the 19th century revival of decorated Gothic architecture. The cathedral is interesting because it's very compact – short for the height, yet with balance and proportion that make the interior seem both normal and spacious.

There is some good stained glass, especially around the altar, where the walls are painted above the choir. Free tours are offered. The church is just off Queen St at Church St, by the river, east of town.

There are other fine houses of worship about town, including the Wilmot United on the corner of King and Carleton Sts. It's a huge wooden black and white place with a plain, simple wooden interior open to visitors through the week. Use the side door.

## OLD BURIAL GROUND

An easy walk from downtown is the Loyalist cemetery (dating from 1784) on Brunswick St on the corner of Carleton St. The Loyalists came from the 13 colonies after the American Revolution and were instrumental in settling this area. Many of the earliest Loyalists to arrive are buried here and it's interesting to browse around the grounds, open from 8 am to 9 pm daily.

## NATIONAL EXHIBITION CENTRE

On the corner of Carleton St at 503 Queen St in town, this building (☎ 453-3747) dates from 1881 and has been used as a post office, customs house and library. The exhibition centre on the 1st floor displays travelling exhibits which vary dramatically. Newfoundland folk art, hooked mats, art photographs from the National Gallery and Japanese kites are some examples. The displays are usually good and always free.

Upstairs is the Provincial Sports Hall of Fame with tidbits about achievements of local sportspeople.

## BOYCE FARMERS' MARKET

The farmer's market is on George St between Regent and Saint John Sts. It's open Saturday from 6 am to noon. A secondary opening with not as much activity is on Wednesday evening beginning at 4.30 pm. On Saturday there are nearly 150 stalls selling fresh fruit, vegetables, meat and cheese, and also hand-icrafts, homemade desserts and flowers. There is a restaurant here, too, open for breakfast/brunch.

## CONSERVER HOUSE

Near the corner of Brunswick St, at 180 Saint John St, is this house (☎ 458-8747) dating from 1890, now used as a model and infor-mation centre for energy conservation. Tours and advice are free. The house is open Monday to Friday from 9 am to 5 pm.

## POWER ELECTRICITY MUSEUM

If you got a charge from the above attraction, a visit to the museum (☎ 458-6805) at 514 Queen St will be worthwhile. Rather than the future and latest technologies, displays here feature primarily antique and obsolete equip-ment from the early days of electricity onwards. It's closed on Sunday.

## PARKS

In addition to the riverfront park and several smaller city parks, you can visit the follow-ing two. **Odell Park**, south-west of the downtown centre off Smythe St, covers 175 hectares and contains some primeval provin-cial forest. There are picnic tables, a kids' zoo and walking paths. **Killarney Lake Park** is about five km from town over the Westmor-land St Bridge. A spring-fed lake is used for swimming and fishing.

## TULA FARM

A 20-minute drive west of Fredericton on the Trans Canada Hwy leads to the Tula sustain-able agriculture education centre (☎ 459-1851). At the 29-acre project on Keswick Ridge overlooking the Saint John River Valley, visitors can witness ecologi-cally sound farming practices. Displays explain how farmers actually produce food and how this can be done using nature, rather than fighting it. Wearing boots or other suit-able footwear is suggested. Call to check current hours and for directions. It is not far

from the Mactaquac/Keswick Ridge turn-off from the Trans Canada Hwy.

## ACTIVITIES

Rent a canoe for drifting along the river. One place they're available is A to Z Rentals (☎ 452-9758), 128 Prospect St. Another is at McGivney Boat & Canoe (☎ 472-1655), Lower St Marys, five km east of Howard Johnson's on the Trans Canada Hwy.

The Small Craft Aquatic Centre (☎ 458-5513) offers guided canoe tours from one hour to three-day river ecology trips. Instruc-tion is offered in either canoeing or kayaking. Call Kerry Smith for the full range of options on getting out on the river and maybe spotting some of the wildlife that calls it home.

There are free swimming pools at Henry Park and Queen Square. At the YM-YWCA, 28 Saunders St, there is a small admission fee.

Eastern Canada Outdoor (ECO) Tours (☎ 452-0995) outside the city at Site 19 RR5, Fredericton offers two and three-day back-packing tours. One is a trek along the Fundy shoreline; another hikes up Mt Carleton, the highest peak in the province. The walks are considered moderate so some reasonable level of physical condition is expected but little outdoor experience is required. Educa-tion is part of the trip. If needed, all equipment can be supplied. German is spoken.

## ORGANISED TOURS

Throughout July and August, a member of an actors' group wearing historic costume leads a good free one-hour walking tour around town, beginning at City Hall, three times a day. Ask at the tourist office for details.

Trius Tours (☎ 459-3366) offers inexpen-sive car tours around town (for larger groups a van is used). Note that Trius is primarily a taxi company.

## FESTIVALS

Fredericton is a centre of the old craft of pewtersmithing. Examples can be seen any

NEW BRUNSWICK

time of year at Aitkens Pewter, downtown at 81 Regent St, or you can arrange tours of the main plant there. Other craftspeople in the town do pottery and woodcarving. Some of the major events and festivals celebrated in the province are listed here.

May-September
*Playhouse Theatre* – Various country music artists from Atlantic Canada perform at this theatre each Saturday from May to September.
*Canadian National New Brunswick Day Canoe Race* – It is held annually in early August in the Mactaquac Headpond.
*Handicraft Show* – A free provincial handicraft show is held at Mactaquac Park on the weekend before Labour Day. All types of handicrafts are exhibited and sold.
*The Fredericton Exhibition* – It is an annual six-day affair starting on Labour Day (the first Monday in September). It's held at the exhibition grounds, on the corner of Smythe and Saunders Sts. The exhibition includes a farm show, a carnival, harness racing and stage shows.
*Scottish Highland Games Festival* – It's a two-day Scottish festival with music, dancing and contests held each summer.

## PLACES TO STAY
### Camping
The best place nearby is *Mactaquac Provincial Park* (☎ 363-3011), 20 km west off the Trans Canada Hwy on Hwy 105, on the north side of the river. A tent site costs $12. There's swimming and a grocery store. Another provincial park is just south of King's Landing on Lake George.

There are several camping places closer to Fredericton, though they're not as nice as the parks. They're OK for stopping overnight or short stays. There are three privately owned sites on the Trans Canada Hwy before you reach Hanwell Rd.

*Hartt Island Campground* (☎ 450-6057) is 10 km west of Fredericton on the Trans Canada.

South-east 30 km from town is the *Sunbury Oromocto Provincial Park* (☎ 357-3708) campground on Waterville Rd at French Lake, off Hwy 7.

### Hostels
Fredericton has a member HI hostel, the HI

*York House Hostel* (☎ 454-1233), and it's a good one. It's centrally located in a big, old schoolhouse at 193 York St on the corner of George St, by the church. It's within easy walking distance of the bus station. Rates are $9 members, $12 nonmembers for each of the 30 beds. Breakfasts cost $3 and dinners are available although there are kitchen facilities. The hostel opens at 4 pm. It's open from early June to the beginning of September. The staff is friendly and helpful and the hostel has the strangest toilets I've yet seen.

There's no accommodation in the YMYWCA building here.

The *University of New Brunswick* (☎ 453-4891) rents single and double rooms in the dorms, available from mid-May to mid-August. For tourists singles/doubles are $27/40, and for students the price drops to $13/23. Contact the Director of Housing at the above number. Facilities include a pool. The campus is within walking distance of the downtown area in a south-east direction. It runs south of Beaverbrook St about five blocks from Regent St.

### Hotels & Tourist Homes
There isn't a vast selection of budget places in town, but the ones that exist are good.

The *Manger Inn* (☎ 454-3410) is the nice yellow-and-black house at 269 Saunders St. This is a tree-lined residential street two blocks south of Brunswick St. Rates are $30 singles, one bed (two people) $35, two beds (two people) $40; kitchen facilities are available at an additional cost.

The *Carriage House B&B* (☎ 452-9924) is over at 230 University Ave, also central but more expensive at singles/doubles $40/50 and up with breakfast included. There's a shared TV room.

Moving up-market, the venerable *Lord Beaverbrook* (☎ 455-3371), at 659 Queen St, is relatively moderate for a place of its class at singles/doubles $60/70. It has 165 rooms with all the amenities used mainly by business and government people.

## Motels

The bulk of the city's accommodation is in motels around the edges of town.

On the west side of town on Rural Route 6, which is the Trans Canada Hwy West, there are several places. The *Roadside Motel* (☎ 450-2080) is along this strip with singles/doubles $38/40. On the east side of town on Rural Route 8 (also known as Hwy 2 or the Trans Canada Hwy for Moncton) is the *Norfolk Motel* (☎ 472-3278). Singles/doubles here are only $27/30.

Just off the highway before Princess Margaret Bridge, east of the university, is Forest Hill Rd. At No 502 is the *Fredericton Skyline Motel* (☎ 455-6683), with singles/doubles $35/45. To get there, head for the highway over the bridge towards Moncton; Forest Hill Rd runs east of the highway. A taxi fare here from the centre of town costs $5.

The *Comfort Inn by Journey's End Motel* (☎ 453-0800) has large and clean singles/doubles from $65. Part of a widespread chain, it's at 255 Prospect St, one block north of the Trans Canada Hwy towards town off Regent St. There are a few places to eat within walking distance.

The *Town & Country Motel* (☎ 454-4223) at 967 Woodstock Rd, about two km south from the Trans Canada, offers housekeeping units at $58 a double.

Across the river in North Fredericton *Fort Nashwaak Motel* (☎ 472-4411) at 15 Riverside Drive has good views, and housekeeping units or individual cabins at $45 a double.

## PLACES TO EAT

The *JM&T Deli*, a small but comfortable and casual delicatessen with an interesting noticeboard, sits at the bottom of Regent St at No 62. It serves all the standards, including smoked meat from Montreal's Ben's. Various sandwiches, bagels and cheeses are served at the stools for about $3.50 and up. It's not open on Sunday.

At 349 King St is *Dimitri's*, good for an inexpensive Greek lunch or dinner of souvlakia, pita, brochettes, moussaka and the like.

On Queen St in the centre by the post office is the *Capital Garden*, which serves Chinese food. From 11.30 am to 2.30 pm, Monday to Friday there is an all-you-can-eat buffet for $7.50. It includes ribs, chicken balls, egg rolls and rice. On Saturday and Sunday nights, dinner is $9.50.

*Mei's*, at 73 Carleton St, is better and offers some Sichuan-style dishes. Dinner for two is in the $25 range and they now have a sushi bar.

The *Subway*, a small place not bad for sandwiches, is mentioned because it's one of the few places in the centre open on a Sunday. It's on King St near Westmorland St.

In the enclosed King's Place shopping mall on the corner of Brunswick and York Sts is *Crispins* which has cheap cafeteria-style lunches.

The *Lunar Rogue*, at 625 King St and open every day, is a pub with above average food. There are daily specials, British beers on tap and in fine weather, an outdoor patio. Live music is often presented at night, too.

At 594 Queen St, on the corner of Regent St, is *La Vie en Rose Café*, a snazzy little place for desserts and coffee.

For a tea try *Keay's*, at 72 York St, a sort of old-style counter eatery in a fruit market.

Away from the centre near the Trans Canada Hwy, have a look along Prospect St West off Regent St South. The Fredericton Mall is here with a grocery store, *Sobey's*, and there is a liquor outlet. Further along is *O'Tooles*, a pub-style place. On the corner of Smythe St the *Ponderosa* has good-value steak or shrimp and all you can eat from the variety of salads for $8. The no-meat buffet with salads, vegetables, pasta, soups and rolls at $5 is a real bargain.

For do-it-your-selfers with transportation, take a trip over the Westmorland St Bridge to Main St in North Fredericton. Just over the bridge there is a bakery and shop with a vast array of fresh fruits and vegetables. Next door, at 230 Main St, there's another place for meats, fish and cheeses. They're open every day. The quality is high, the prices low.

**NEW BRUNSWICK**

## ENTERTAINMENT
At 625 King St is the *Lunar Rogue*, a pub which often presents live Celtic music. Also on King St, but between Regent and Carleton Sts, is the *Club Cosmopolitan* which has a fairly expensive restaurant, a lounge and the local singles disco.

The University of New Brunswick often has concerts and folk performers. Cheap films are also shown at the university in the Tilley Hall Auditorium.

## GETTING THERE & AWAY
### Air
Fredericton is a small city, but as the provincial capital it does get a fair bit of air traffic. Many flights in and out are stopovers between various other points. Air Canada (☎ 458-8561) serves the city and has one nonstop flight daily from Toronto.

### Bus
The SMT bus station (☎ 458-6000) is on the corner of Regent and Brunswick Sts. Schedules and fares to some destinations include:

Moncton – 10.25 am, 2.30 pm daily ($25)
Quebec City via Campbellton – 2.30 pm, 8 pm ($59)
Halifax – same as Moncton ($58)
Amherst – same as Moncton ($34)

### Train
There is no longer any passenger service to or from Fredericton. But there is a bus service run by Trius (☎ 459-3366) which connects with trains at Fredericton Junction about 40 km south of town. For information and tickets, there are several agents in town including Blaine Thomas, at 99 York St, and Maritime Marlin Travel, in the King's Place Shopping Mall downtown. Buses leave from the Beaverbrook Hotel and from the Student Union Building at the university, so you could enquire at these points as well.

### Car & Motorbike
For car rentals, Budget (☎ 452-1107) is at 407 Regent St. Their rate is $36 a day with 100 free km. Weekly rates with 1000 free km are also offered.

Delta (☎ 458-8899), at 304 King St, is slightly cheaper at $33 a day with 100 free km, then 12 cents per km. There is also a good weekend package available. Tilden on Prospect St is a third possibility.

Distances in the Atlantic region are small; a few hours of driving will take you across any of the provinces. Cape Tormentine is 300 km away via the Trans Canada Hwy, and Hwys 16 and 2. To Halifax (415 km) take Hwys 102, 104 and then the Trans Canada Hwy. To Quebec City (576 km) take the Trans Canada Hwy, known here as Hwy 2.

## GETTING AROUND
### To/From the Airport
The airport is 16 km south-east of town. There's an airport bus from the Lord Beaverbrook Hotel before and after flights. It leaves from 45 to 60 minutes before flight time and costs $6.50. Generally there is no service on Sunday and holidays. A taxi to the airport costs around $15.

### Bus
The city has a good system, Fredericton Transit (☎ 458-9522), and fares include free transfers.

The university is a 15-minute walk from the downtown area; if you want to take the bus, take No 16S south on Regent St. It runs about every 20 minutes.

For hitching on the Trans Canada Hwy you want the Fredericton Mall bus, which is also the 16S.

For heading back into the city from these places catch the 16N.

### Car
Free tourist parking passes are available from the Visitors' Centre, City Hall; these enable you to park in lots and at meters free.

### Bicycle
Rentals at good prices either hourly or daily are available at Savage's (☎ 458-8985), 449 King St.

## SOUTH-EAST OF FREDERICTON
### Gagetown

Gagetown refers to both a small town and the largest military base in the Commonwealth of Nations. This is the source of all the military vehicles you've probably seen on the highways. Both are down the Saint John River a short distance from Fredericton. At Camp Gagetown, the base, you can visit the military museum which has articles from both world wars, the South African War and the Korean War. Admission is free. Along the way from Fredericton are farmers' markets and roadside stalls offering fresh produce.

Gagetown itself, on the river, has numerous craft outlets and good examples of earlier architecture, some dating from the 1700s.

### Grand Lake

From Hwy 2, along the river east of town, there's beautiful farmland and eventually you reach the dairy centre of Sussex. Other than the views though, there is very little along the way.

Grand Lake, the province's largest lake, is a busy summer resort area with lots of cottages and a couple of provincial campgrounds. At Cambridge Narrows on nearby Washademoak Lake is the *Lake Resort*, a well-known R&R spot with European-style saunas and spas. *Café Mozart* here is a very good restaurant and the German tortes have quite a reputation.

### Sussex

Sussex is a small country town in the middle of some pastoral and productive dairy lands. Fortunately all the local cows aren't the size of the one seen on the outskirts of town.

On Hwy 2 at the exit into the centre is a tourist office run by volunteer seniors. In town one of the streets, Queen St, has been somewhat remodelled and is reminiscent of earlier decades. It's off Main St opposite the VIA Rail station. Here you'll find the licensed *Broadway Café*, a little sanctuary from the standard small-town greasy spoons, offering good, inexpensive lunch specials in a comfortable and casual atmosphere complete with 'tasty' recorded music. It's also open for breakfasts and until 9 pm Friday and Saturday.

The *Pine Cone Motel* (☎ 433-3958), on Hwy 2, is good at $42 a double. For camping try *Lakeside Provincial Park* on Grand Lake along Hwy 2 near Waterborough.

The surrounding King's County has 17 of the appealing old wooden covered bridges often situated so prettily they look like pictures from a calendar.

On towards Moncton, also look for the old potato-storage houses and barns half-buried in the ground.

## SOUTH-WEST OF FREDERICTON
### Mactaquac Provincial Park

Twenty-two km west of Fredericton is New Brunswick's biggest provincial park (☎ 363-3011). It runs along the 100-km-long pond formed by the Mactaquac Power Dam. The park offers swimming, fishing, picnic sites, camping and boat rentals. There's also a golf course where you can rent all equipment. It's a busy campground through the summer and is often full but there are a couple of others not too far away: the attendants will have some suggestions.

### Mactaquac Power Dam

The Mactaquac Dam across the park is responsible for creating the small lake and therefore the park's location. Its 400,000 kilowatt output is the largest in the Maritime Provinces. Free tours, lasting about 45 minutes, include a look at the turbines and an explanation of how they work. The site is open seven days a week from 9 am to 4.30 pm.

### Woolastock Wildlife Park

Just a few km west of the Mactaquac Park, Woolastock Wildlife Park (☎ 363-2352) is open daily from 9 am to sunset. The park has a collection of Canadian animals, many typical of this region. You'll see moose, bears, wolves, coyotes, foxes, caribou, hawks, owls and more. There are also some water slides, picnic areas and camping spots. If you camp, the wildlife section is free. Up the river around here are several camp-

NEW BRUNSWICK

Bald eagle

grounds and many touristy attractions. For example, there's horse riding, craft shops and small museums.

### King's Landing Historical Settlement

The settlement (☎ 363-5805) is 37 km west of Fredericton, on the way to Woodstock. Take exit 259 off the Trans Canada Hwy. Here you can get a glimpse of (and taste) pioneer life in the Maritimes. A community of 100 costumed staff inhabits 11 houses, a school, church, store and sawmill typical of those used a century ago. The staff will answer questions about their chores, the tools, or life in general in such a village. The *King's Head Inn* serves traditional foods and beverages.

The settlement is open all year. From the end of June to just after Labour Day in September the opening hours are from 10 am to 6 pm daily. The rest of the year, it closes an hour earlier at 5 pm. Admission is $7.50 with children's and family rates offered. On weekends in July and August and on Sunday only in June, there's a bus from the SMT terminal in Fredericton. It leaves for King's Landing at 10 am and 1 pm and costs $6.50 return. With the bus ticket, admission to the site is only $6.

A good tip to consider is that the ticket for King's Landing entitles you to free entrance to the Acadian Historic Village near the town of Caraquet.

### Saint Croix Waterway Recreation Area

This area of 336 sq km is south-west of Fredericton near the Maine USA border. The town of McAdam is pretty much the commercial centre of this little-developed territory of woods and lakes. In McAdam itself, check out the Canadian Pacific railway station dating from 1900. It's one of the finest in Canada and was made a National Historic Site in 1983.

Sixteen km from McAdam is **Spednic Provincial Park**, with rustic camping and access to some of the Chiputneticook chain of lakes. The Saint Croix River is good for white-water canoeing. Other canoe routes connect lakes, and about 100 km of hiking trails wind through the area. There's another campground at Wauklehegan.

# Fundy Shore

Almost the entire southern edge of the province is presided over by the ever-present, constantly rising and falling, always impressive waters of the Bay of Fundy.

The fascinating shoreline, the English-style resort town of St Andrews, the wonderful quiet Fundy Isles, the city of Saint John and the Fundy National Park make this easily one of the most appealing and varied regions of New Brunswick. Despite the features which make it the best known and one of the most visited areas of the province, it usually isn't very busy.

## ST STEPHEN

Right at the US border across the river from Calais in Maine, St Stephen is a busy entry point for US visitors coming east. It's a small, old town that forms the northern link of what is known as the Quoddy Loop – a circular tour around south-eastern New Brunswick and north-western Maine around Passamaquoddy Bay. From St Stephen the loop route goes to St Andrews, St George and then on to Deer Island and lastly to Campobello Island which is connected by bridge to Maine. It's a popular trip taking anywhere from a day or two to a week, and includes some fine seaside scenery, interesting history and a number of pleasant, easy-going resort-style towns. In St Stephen the Festival of International Cooperation is held in August with concerts, parades and street fairs. Note that there is a duty-free shop for alcohol and cigarette bargains opposite the Canadian Customs building.

St Stephen also has quite a reputation as a chocolate mecca due to being the home of **Ganong's** (a family chocolate business since 1910), whose products are known all around eastern Canada. Some say the chocolate bar was invented by the Ganong brothers and they are credited for developing the heart-shaped box of chocolates now seen everywhere on Valentine's Day. You can visit the old factory on the main street of town, Milltown Blvd. It's just a store now with not much to see but plenty to buy ranging from boxed chocolates to bars such as Pal O' Mine, a very sweet little number. The modern factory is away from the centre towards St Andrews on Chocolate Drive near the Charlotte Mall. In typical low-key Canadian style it is not open to visitors and there

are no tours except during the annual Chocolate Fest which occurs in August.

Around the bay a little north and west of St Stephen on the border is **Milltown**, with one of the continent's oldest hydroelectric plants, operated by Power NB of New Brunswick. Free tours are given from 1 June to 31 August, 9 am to 4.30 pm daily.

Nearby at 443 Milltown Blvd, 2.8 km from the border-crossing, is the **Charlotte County Museum** with exhibits concerning the history of 200 years of settlement including the Loyalists and other ties with the USA. There are displays on shipbuilding and lumbering as well as other local industries. The museum is closed on Sunday and is in a substantial house built in 1864.

For a place to eat, there is the straightforward *Carman's Diner* in town on Main St or outside town on the way to St Andrews, the *Lobster House*.

Also out of town in this direction are a number of motels and, by the corner of Milltown Blvd and King St near the turn-off for Fredericton or St Andrews, a large tourist office.

## ST ANDREWS-BY-THE-SEA

As its name suggests, this is a summer resort of some tradition and gentility. Together with a fine climate and picturesque beauty, St Andrews has a long, charming and often visible history – it's one of the oldest towns in the province and for a long period was on equal terms with Saint John. Today the wealthy and the less fortunate, provincial residents and visitors alike, have made St Andrews' summer both popular and well known.

### History

The aboriginal Indians were the Passamaquoddies, a very few of whom still live in the area.

White settlement began in 1783 after the American Revolution. Many British pioneers, wanting to remain loyal, deserted their new towns and set up home in the British territory around the fort in Castine, Maine – a very pretty area.

The British-American border was changed with the war's end and these people once again found themselves on American soil. The tip of the bay across the water was scouted and agreed upon as being a place of equal beauty. So the pioneers loaded up ships and headed out, some even dragging their houses on rafts behind them, and St Andrews was founded in 1784.

Prosperity came first with shipbuilding and, when that was dying, continued with tourism. Oceanic research is now also a prominent industry. In the early part of the century, the Canadian Pacific railway owned and ran the Algonquin Hotel, which more or less started St Andrews as a retreat. Soon moneyed Canadians and Americans were building luxurious summer cottages alongside the 19th-century mansions of the lumber trade and shipbuilding barons. Nearly 100 of the beautiful houses first built or brought here from Maine are still used and main-tained in excellent condition. Though many well-known families keep houses here, the casual visitor is now also important to the town's affairs.

## Orientation & Information

Water St, the main street, is lined with res-taurants, souvenir and craft shops and some places to stay. King St is the main cross-street; one block from Water St, Queen St is also important. There are information offices in town and near the junction of Hwys 1 and 127.

## Walking Tour

There are more than 200 houses over a century old in town, many marked with plaques. A lot of them are real gems. Pick up the walking guide from the tourist office – it includes a map and brief description of 35 particularly interesting places.

Even without the guide, walking around

Native Indian family

the residential streets with their well-looked-after, colourful wooden houses and flower gardens is worthwhile.

### Algonquin Hotel

Also worth a look is the classic 1899 resort hotel with its veranda, gardens, tennis courts and pool. Inside, off the lobby, are a couple of places for a drink, be it tea or gin.

Opposite the hotel you may want to take a peek at the English-style thatched-roof cottage called Pansy Patch with its surrounding garden.

### Blockhouse Historic Site

The restored wooden guardhouse (☎ 529-4270) is the only one left of several that were built here for protection in the War of 1812. As it turned out, they weren't needed. Made of hand-hewn timber, structures like this were easy to construct, practical to live in, and strong enough to withstand most attacks. Down towards the shore is a battery of three cannons. The blockhouse is open daily in summer. Admission is free, and there are some good views through the gun holes on the 2nd floor. The park is at the north-west end of Water St.

### Huntsman Marine Science Centre

Out past the Blockhouse and then the Fisheries & Oceans Biological Station is the Huntsman Marine Science Centre (☎ 529-4285) with research facilities and labs. It's part of the Federal Fisheries Research Centre – St Andrews' most important business. Some of Canada's leading marine biologists work here, supplying knowledge to international markets.

At the Huntsman lab there's an aquarium open to the public as well as a small museum. The aquarium displays most specimens found in the local waters, including seals. There is a good seaweed display and one pool where the various creatures can be touched, even picked up. It's quite interesting and great for kids too. The centre, west of town on Brandy Cove Rd, is open daily from May to October and admission costs $3.75.

### Ross Memorial Museum

The Ross Memorial Museum (☎ 529-3906) is in a neoclassical house of some size on the corner of King and Montague Sts, downtown. It features the furniture, metal objects and decorative arts collections of two of its former owners, Mr & Mrs Ross, who lived in the house until 1945. It's open daily through the summer but afternoons only on Sunday.

### Sheriff Andrew House

On the corner of King and Queen Sts is this restored middle-class home (☎ 529-4470) dating from 1820 and now redecorated in period style (even down to the paint colours) and attended by costumed guides. The back garden is also typical of this past era.

### Sunbury Shores Arts & Nature Centre

This is a non-profit educational and cultural centre (☎ 529-3386) offering instruction in painting, weaving, pottery and other crafts in summer, as well as natural science courses. Various changing exhibits run through the summer. It is based in Centennial House, an old general store at 139 Water St.

The centre has a nearby conservation area through which there is a walking trail.

### Katy's Cove

Just north of town, this sheltered bay is good for swimming.

### Minister's Island Historic Site

Minister's Island was bought and used as a summer retreat by William Cornelius van Horne, builder of the Canadian Pacific Railway across the country and the company's first president and later Chairman of the Board. The island and his cottage of 50 rooms can now be visited.

Minister's Island is accessible at low tide, even by car, when you can drive on the hard-packed sea floor. A few hours later this route is under three metres of water. Guided tours of the property are offered for those with their own cars – ask at the tourist office for details. HMS Transportation (☎ 529-3371) has tours for those without cars or

NEW BRUNSWICK

drivers who do not wish to use their own transportation.

## Atlantic Salmon Centre

North of town about six km, in the village of Chamcook, the Salmon Centre (☎ 529-8899) tells the story of Atlantic salmon, prized by anglers and gourmets. Displays, including live fish, show the fish's history and life cycle. The centre's open from May to September daily, 10 am to 6 pm, and is designed to encourage knowledge and preservation of this fine creature.

## Dochet's Island

In the Saint Croix River, eight km from town on Hwy 127, is Dochet's Island with a national historic site marking the place where in 1604 French explorer Samuel de Champlain spent his first winter in North America. The island itself is inaccessible without a boat, but looking at it from the shore makes an excuse for a good, quick sunset drive. There is also a plaque on the Maine shoreline across from the island.

## Organised Tours

**Whale-Watching Tours** Cline Marine (☎ 529-4188) runs very good whale-watching trips from the town wharf. The same outfit also runs out of both Deer and Campobello islands. Because the waters best for whale-watching are further out in the bay, the trip from St Andrews is longer and therefore more expensive. A six-hour trip costs $40 and goes in search of humpback, right, fin and minke whales – sightings are generally assured. There's also a shorter tour around the shoreline in more sheltered waters, and a sunset cruise. Whichever trip you choose, take plenty of warm clothes and make reservations a day ahead.

## Places to Stay

As a small but busy resort town St Andrews has plentiful accommodation with quite a range in type and price including many guesthouses and B&Bs. Motels can be found on Reed Ave and Mowat Drive.

**Camping** There are several places to choose from. At the far east end of town on Indian Point is *Passamaquoddy Park* (☎ 529-3439) run by the Kiwanis Club, for tents and trailers.

Near St Andrews are two provincial parks with beaches. *Oak Bay* (☎ 466-2661) is eight km east of St Stephen, north of St Andrews. There is a protected bay where the water warms up nicely for ocean swimming and there's shoreline to explore at low tide. Further afield is *New River Beach* (☎ 755-3804), a little more than halfway to Saint John. They have 115 camping spots.

**B&Bs & Hotels** The central *Heritage Guesthouse* (☎ 529-3875) is a modest but very appealing place at 100 Queen St that has the added benefit of having been around for years. It is priced about average with singles/doubles for $38/40. Breakfasts are offered.

At 159 Water St is *McNabb House* (☎ 529-4368) with three rooms and charging about the same rates but a little less for singles, a little more for doubles. Some housekeeping rooms are available.

A few doors down at the water's edge at 153 Water St is *Snore by the Shore* (☎ 529-4255) which would deserve mention for its name even if it wasn't the decent place it is. Rates here range (with breakfast included) from as low as singles/doubles $30/40 to $40/60.

A new entry is the *Puff Inn B&B* (☎ 529-4191), at 38 Ernest St, which is the cheapest place in town with nine rooms at singles/doubles from $25/26 and up. Even the most expensive room does not exceed $40 a double and the beach is very close.

The *Shiretown Inn* (☎ 529-8877), run by Best Western, has been a hotel since 1881 and now is a blend of the old with modern conveniences and a dining room. It's right in the middle of town at 218 Water St and is a little pricier at singles/doubles $45/65 and up.

The classic Canadian Pacific-run *Algonquin Resort Hotel* (☎ 529-8823) has rooms that start at $110 (you pay for the charm of a former era and the amenities). A walk through the lobby or maybe a drink on the porch will give non-guests a sense of the atmosphere.

## Places to Eat

For decent, plain and cheap food there is the *Copper Grill* on Water St. It's closed on Sunday, and is otherwise open from 7 am to 7 pm daily.

Right in the middle of town with a pleasant patio on the water, the *Smuggler's Wharf* has a bit of everything. Also with outdoor tables, the *Brass Bull* has pub meals at around $6.

The *Shiretown Inn*, dating from 1881, is a very well-kept place and has more expensive seafood meals. Perhaps the best meals are at the cosy *L'Europe*, a German-style white stucco place on King St which is open for dinner only. Lobster is the main dish at the *Lighthouse Restaurant*. Through the summer, the *Algonquin Hotel* has a deluxe Sunday brunch for $16.

### Whales

Whales, the great mammals of the depths, first re-discovered by non-hunters in California then later up the coast in British Columbia, have now become major attractions around Atlantic Canada. Tours out to sea to photograph the awesome creatures depart from ports in places ranging from Quebec's Gulf of St Lawrence to Newfoundland's east coast. From most accounts, the trips are generally successful and well worth the uniformly reasonable cost, averaging $25 for a couple of hours.

Some of the best areas for such a trip are around the Bay of Fundy islands in New Brunswick or from the tip of Digby Neck in Nova Scotia. Also in Nova Scotia the north shore of Cape Breton up around the national park is good. Over in Newfoundland the region of Notre Dame Bay is a 'fruitful' one, with some tours based out of Twillingate. Whales can even be seen up and down the coast out of St John's from where more tours originate.

In the St Lawrence River, Quebec, boat tours operate in the Saguenay River area. Although the huge blue, finback and minke whales are seen here, probably the principal species is the beluga, whose numbers are declining alarmingly due to horrendous pollution levels. Regulations now suggest that no boat approach belugas too closely as these whales have enough problems to deal with.

So you're much better off in the Bay of Fundy or on the open ocean in one of the Atlantic Provinces. Around the Grand Manan region the most commonly seen whales are the fin (or finback), one of the world's largest at 20 metres; the humpback (12 metres); the right (12 metres and less commonly seen); and the minke (eight metres). In addition porpoises and dolphins are plentiful. In this area the best whale-watching begins in early August and lasts until September.

From Westport at the tip of Digby Neck the season seems to begin a little earlier with good sightings reported in late June although by mid-July there are good numbers of all species.

The humpback, one of the larger whales of the east coast, is the one to put on the best show, breaching and diving with tail clearly visible above the surface.

Up around Cape Breton and in Newfoundland the smaller pilot or pothead whales, also sometimes known as blackwhales, are common and they're sometimes even seen from shore. Finbacks frequent these waters as well. In the latter two regions, operators run trips pretty well only in July and August.

Regardless of the weather or time of year take plenty of clothing, perhaps something for seasickness and lots of film! ■

## Getting There & Around

SMT Bus Lines connects St Andrews and the surrounding area to Saint John with one bus trip daily which takes $1\frac{1}{2}$ hours. For information contact HMS Transportation (see following).

The Algonquin Hotel runs a more expensive service, which they call the airport shuttle, to downtown Saint John and its airport for $35 one way, less if you're a guest at the hotel.

HMS Transportation (☎ 529-3371) at 260 Water St rents cars and runs tours. The Carriage House store at 153 Water St has bicycles for rent.

## ST GEORGE

St George, 40 km east of St Stephen on the Magaguadavic River, is a small town with 1500 residents. The river gorge and falls near the tourist office between the highway and the centre of town make a local beauty spot. A salmon ladder has been built to facilitate the fish's upstream struggle over the gorge and dam,, and the salmon can be seen jumping its stages in summer.

In town the Presbyterian kirk dating from 1790 is one of the oldest churches in Canada. The Protestant cemetery at St Mark's Anglican church is of similar vintage. O'Neill House at 7 Main St was built in 1835 and is now an antique shop and café. The restaurant is a good little place for breakfast or lunch and for sampling the town water – said to be the best in the country. It comes from deep artesian wells and is indeed absolutely delicious.

There is freshwater swimming north of town on sandy beaches at Lake Utopia.

## Places to Stay & Eat

Across the street is the *Town House* B&B (☎ 755-3476), an attractive large home dating from the 1840s with singles/doubles at $35/45.

Another good place to stay is the *Fundy Lodge Motel* (☎ 755-2963) about 15 minutes' drive west of town. It has a pretty location on the water; the rooms are entirely lined with pine, inside and out. It's not really cheap at $55 a double but that's about par for the area. It's better than most places and includes a help-yourself continental breakfast with fresh muffins.

## FUNDY ISLES
### Deer Island

From Letete on the mainland south of St George a free 25-minute government ferry runs to Deer Island, the closest of the three main Fundy Isles. Ferries run every half-hour. Deer Island is, as it has been for centuries, a modest fishing community. Lobster is the main catch. Around the island are half a dozen wharves and the net systems used in aquaculture (fish farming). There is not a lot to see on the island as it is primarily wooded and residential. Roads run down each side towards Campobello Island.

There is a tourist booth at the ferry landing. At **Northern Harbour** is a huge (it could well be the world's largest) lobster pound which sometimes during the year contains 400 kg of live lobster.

**Whale-Watching Tours** Whale-watching is a popular activity from the islands. Cline Marine Charters (☎ 747-2287), with an office in Leonardville but departing from Richardson on Deer Island, offers whale-watching tours for $12 an hour. There's a minimum of three hours, which is standard. Cline Marine has offices in St Andrews and on Campobello Island as well. Three other operators, all on Grand Manan Island, also offer various whale cruises.

At the other end of the island is 16-hectare **Deer Island Point Park** where whales and **Old Sow** (the world's second largest natural tidal whirlpool) can be seen offshore.

**Places to Stay & Eat** Nearby in Fairhaven is the *49th Parallel Restaurant & Motel*, the only sit-down place to eat on Deer Island. Fairhaven also has two B&Bs and the *Deer Island Log Guest House by the Sea* (☎ 747-2221) which is a fine place and priced fairly at singles/doubles $40/50 with a continental breakfast.

In **Lambertville** is the *Darby Hill B&B*

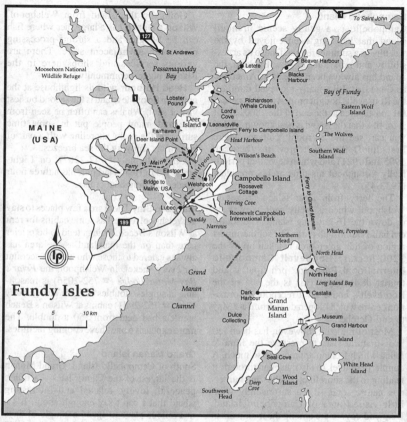

Fundy Isles

(☎ 747-2069) 800 metres from the ferry landing. A double costs $40.

At **Leonardville**, halfway down the island, is *Camick's* (☎ 747-2929) where you can rent a stationary camper van for $22 a night with crockery and bedding included.

**Getting There & Away** Two privately operated ferries leave from Deer Island Point: one for Campobello Island which is connected by bridge to the US mainland and one to Eastport, Maine.

The ferry to Campobello costs $2 per

person, and from $12 to a maximum of $16 per car. It's basically a floating dock strapped to an old fishing boat. It's a very scenic 45-minute trip past numerous islands and Eastport, an attractive seaside town where you may see freighters moored.

During the summer there are six trips a day between 9 am and 6.15 pm. For Eastport the ferry leaves every hour on the hour and is a bit cheaper than the one for Campobello. Either ferry can be used as part of the circular Quoddy Loop tour around Passamaquoddy Bay through both Canada and the USA.

## Campobello Island

Campobello is a gently scenic, tranquil island that has long been enjoyed by the wealthy as a summer retreat. Due to its accessibility and proximity to New England, the island has always been at least as American as Canadian. Like many moneyed families, the Roosevelts bought property in this peaceful coastal area at the end of the 1800s and it is for this that the island is best known. Today you can see the 34-room 'cottage' where Franklin D Roosevelt grew up (between 1905 and 1921) and which he visited periodically throughout his time as US president (1933-45).

The ferry from Deer Island arrives at Welshpool which is pretty well halfway up or down the 16-km-long island. The southern half is almost all park. The southernmost region of this green area is taken up by the 1200-hectare **Roosevelt Campobello International Park**, the principal island tourist destination. This is the site of the Roosevelt's house nd a reception-information centre which is open daily from late May to mid-October.

Most of the park, however, has been left in its natural state to preserve the flora & fauna which Delano appreciated so much. A couple of gravel roads meander through it leading to the shoreline, beaches and numerous nature trails. It's a surprisingly wild, little-visited area of Campobello Island. Deer and coyote are among the mammals in the park, and seals can sometimes be seen offshore on the ledges near **Lower Duck Pond**. Among the many birds along the shoreline are eagles, ospreys and loons.

Below the park at the southern tip of the island, a bridge connects with Lubec, Maine. On the Campobello side is a tourist office with a moneychanging desk.

Along the international park's northern boundary is New Brunswick's **Herring Cove Provincial Park**. Here too are several seaside walking trails and paths as well as a campground and a picnic area on an arching 1.6-km-long beach. It makes a fine, picturesque place for lunch and again is remarkably quiet.

Going up the island from Welshpool, **Wilson's Beach** has a large pier where fish can be bought, and a sardine-processing plant with an adjacent store. There are various services and shops here in the island's biggest community.

**Head Harbour** with its lighthouse at the northern tip of the island is the second busiest visitor spot. Whales can often be seen from here and many people put in some time sitting on the rocky shoreline with a pair of binoculars enjoying the sea breezes.

Cline Marine (☎ 747-2287), on Lighthouse Rd in Head Harbour, has a three hour whale-watching boat cruise.

**Places to Stay** There are a few places to stay in Welshpool as well as some cabins for rent at Wilson's Beach. Things tend to be pricier here than on the mainland as the area has always catered to those who needn't account for every shekel. In Welshpool, the *Friar's Bay Motor Lodge* (☎ 752-2056) is reasonable at singles/ doubles $25/35. The *Quoddy View* (☎ 752-2981) cabins at Wilson's Beach aren't a bad deal from $50 a double. The more expensive ones have cooking facilities.

## Grand Manan Island

South of Campobello Island, Grand Manan is the largest of the Fundy Isles – a quiet, peaceful, lovely, relaxed and interesting island that I can't say enough about. It's a marvellous place to spend a couple of days or a week away from the rest of the world observing nature on the land, at sea, and where the two meet. As the woman at the campground office told me, 'people like Grand Manan because you can park anywhere you want and you can walk anywhere you want'. And that perfectly accurately sums it up.

There is some spectacular coastal topography, excellent bird-watching, fine hiking trails, sandy beaches and a series of small fishing villages along the island which is approximately 30 km long.

On one side are ancient rock formations estimated to be billions of years old. On the other side, due to an underwater volcano, are volcanic deposits *only* 16 million years old, a phenomenon which draws many geologists.

In 1831, James Audubon first documented the many birds which frequented the island. About 312 species, including puffins and Arctic terns, live or pass by each year, so bird-watchers come in numbers as well. If possible, try to catch the puffins' fishing act.

Offshore it's not uncommon to see whales feeding on the abundant herring and mackerel. Whale species include the humpback, finback (rorqual), minke and pothead. Tours are offered in several places.

Despite all this, the relative isolation and low-key development mean there are no crowds and little obvious commercialisation. It's a good place for cyclists and it's not uncommon to see riders along the roads.

One thing of possible interest to sample on the island is the dulce, an edible seaweed, for which Grand Manan Island is renowned. It's a very popular snack food around the Maritime Provinces and most of it (and the best, say connoisseurs) comes from this island. Dulce is sold around the island mostly from people's homes. Watch for signs.

**North Head** The ferry terminal is at North Head. There are more business establishments in this village than elsewhere on the island but it is still small enough to walk through.

There are a few craft and tourist-oriented stores along the main drag but of most interest is the **Whale & Sea Bird Research Station** with a lot of good information on the marine life of the surrounding waters. Exhibits include skeletons and photographs and there are some books on whales and the island in general.

Ocean Search (☎ 662-8488) offers a different sort of whale-watching tour. Firstly they use a sailing schooner, secondly a marine biologist is on board to answer questions and, thirdly at least some of the trips include an evening lecture. These up-market, more in-depth tours are, naturally, more expensive than others but will be of interest to keen whalewatchers.

**North End** Some of the most popular of the numerous short walking trails around the island are in this area, particularly the one to 'Hole in the Wall', an unusual rock formation. It begins north of North Head at the site of the old airport and leads through the woods to a natural arch at the cliff's edge. There are also great views of the coast from this vantage point.

Highly recommended is the somewhat pulse-quickening (especially in the fog) trail and suspension bridge out to the lighthouse at Swallow Tail on a narrow cliff-edged promontory. Further up-island, the rock formations (reaching 80 metres high at Seven Days' Work) and the lighthouse at Northern Head are also fine walks with seaside vistas. From either of the lighthouses whales may be seen, most easily on calm days when they break the surface most conspicuously.

**Grand Harbour** At Grand Harbour is the **Grand Manan Museum** (☎ 662-3524) open from mid-June to 30 September daily but only during the afternoon on Sunday.

It has a marine section, displays on the island's geology, antiques and reminders of the Loyalist days but the highlight is the stuffed-bird collection with examples of species seen on the island.

US writer Willa Cather worked here for many years and some of her personal belongings, including a typewriter, are still here. There is also a good book selection, including one on trails around the island. Bird checklists are available too. Admission is $2.25.

**Dark Harbour** This, the only village on the west side of the island, is the centre of the dulce industry. The seaweed is hand-picked at low tide along the shores of the island. It is then dried in the sun and is ready to eat.

A trail to Little Dark Harbour provides fabulous coastal views.

**Ross Island** Uninhabited Ross Island can be visited at low tide. Or rather you can walk there at low tide, spend about four hours exploring the place, and then return before

Seal pup

the tide gets too high. The island was the site of the first settlement on Grand Manan, established when Loyalists arrived from the USA in 1784.

**Seal Cove** In this small community is Sea Watch Tours (☎ 662-8296), one of the island's principal whale and bird-watching boat-tour companies. They've been around for 25 years and know the waters. Most of the trips are long (around six hours), so take lunch, a gravol antimotion sickness pill and a warm sweater. Apart from whales there are seals and porpoises to see, a variety of sea birds and the coastal landscapes. Peak whale-watching begins in early August and continues through September.

Down at the docks the tasty island-smoked herring can be bought at Helshiron Sundries, a small all-purpose store. Smoked fish is also available at a couple of other places around the island. You could try MG Fisheries in Grand Harbour.

Anchorage Park in Seal Cove is good for bird-watching – wild turkeys and pheasant are common. Also watch for the rabbits which are abundant and half tame.

**Southwest Head** The walk to the lighthouse and beyond along the edge of the 180-metre cliffs here should not be missed. With the sun out and ocean air drifting in, bending the

flowers of high summer – thistles, butter-cups, daisies – time can be made to stand still for part of an afternoon.

**Places to Stay** The good news just doesn't stop here. There are over two dozen places to stay and the prices tend to be low. They're not slick and glitzy but homey and comfort-able places; many of the cabins have a really unpretentious country feel to them. Many of the places to stay are in the Seal Cove area but others are scattered around the island.

The *Cross Tree Guesthouse* (☎ 662-8263) in Seal Cove has just three rooms and charges $30/40 for singles/doubles or $45 for two people with two beds. Dinner is available at extra cost. Also in Seal Cove are the *Spray Kist Cottages* (☎ 662-8640), run by Mrs M Laffoley. Her four units cost from $50 per day for a double or $265 per week. Nearby, and the same price, are the *Cliff by the Sea Cabins* (☎ 662-3133), five unique places scattered amongst the trees in a superb setting. At both these places cooking facili-ties come with the cabins.

There are several places at North Head. The *Fundy Folly Guesthouse* (☎ 662-3731) is a good-value B&B at singles/doubles $30/40 with a full breakfast. The beach is within walking distance of the century-old house.

Lastly, at Grand Harbour the *Drop Anchor*

*Cottages* (☎ 662-3394) have been recommended as being good value, completely self-contained units for $45 a night with weekly rates offered. There are many other places to stay on the island, and most are very reasonably priced. Weekly rates for the various cabins and cottages are around $250.

For camping the only place is the good *Anchorage Provincial Park* (☎ 662-3215) where, even though it's not large, they never turn anyone away. Most people are tenters and, if you arrive early, there are some nice sites with trees edged into the woods. Otherwise you'll be out in the field where it can be very breezy. You should guy-wire out the tent. There is a kitchen shelter for rainy days, a playground and a very long sandy beach. The park is near Seal Cove.

**Places to Eat** Restaurants are not overly numerous on the island but there are enough casual, friendly and reasonably priced places.

North Head village has the widest selection with a couple of takeout places, two or three regular restaurants and a finer dining room in the *Marathon Inn*. The *Griff-Inn*, good for breakfasts and light lunches, is the kind of place where the island's cop comes in for a coffee.

There are two more places in Grand Harbour halfway up the island, one of which serves lobster.

In Seal Cove is the small, plain *Water's Edge* which is not on the water but does have good food. There are burgers and pizza and other basic Italian dishes such as lasagne for $9 which are all homemade, or there are more costly full-course fish dinners. A speciality is the lobster trap, a puff-pastry shell stuffed with chunks of lobster and covered in a creamy garlic sauce.

**Getting There & Away** The ferry (☎ 662-3724) operated by Coastal Transport Ltd is from Blacks Harbour, south of St George on the mainland to North Head on Grand Manan Island. Actually, there are two ferries – one old and one new. The *Grand Manan V* which began sailing in July 1990 is larger and

quicker, knocking half an hour off the two-hour trip. Both ferries have snack bars, outdoor decks, inside chairs, and are operated by the government. The trip is a very agreeable little cruise with good scenery, particularly near Blacks Harbour as the boat drifts by various islands and bays. Seeing a whale is not uncommon and on one trip I saw several groups of porpoises.

In summer, there are six trips on weekdays and five on weekends, but there are still usually queues if you have a car and there is no reservation system. For walk-ons, bicycles, etc there is no problem. From September to the end of June the number of trips drops markedly. There are advance-ticket sales for the trip back, but only for the first trip of the day, and tickets must be bought at North Head on Grand Manan Island.

For either boat the return fare is $8 per adult, less for children and $24 for a car. For camper vans and trailers you pay according to their length.

**Getting Around** Three operators run boat tours for viewing whales, birds and the dramatic coastlines. For details see the previous text.

In Grand Harbour, Avis Green Taxi Service offers sightseeing tours of the island or you can arrange to be taken anywhere for hiking, etc.

Seahawk Enterprises (☎ 662-3464) in North Head rents bicycles.

### White Head Island

White Head Island, connected by a no-charge car ferry from Ingalls Head, is the only other inhabited island in the archipelago. A few families on the island make a living fishing. There are six of the 20-minute ferry services daily. The island has a good long sandy beach, another lighthouse to visit and some plant and animal life not found on Grand Manan. Note that the last ferry back leaves at 4.30 pm.

### Machias Seal Island

Sixteen km south-west of Grand Manan is

the small island bird sanctuary Machias Seal Island. Unlike at many other sanctuaries, visitors are permitted on shore here accompanied by a wildlife officer, but the number is limited to 25 people per day. The feathered residents include terns, puffins, razorbacks and several others in lesser numbers. Sea Watch offers trips to this island too, if the seas aren't rough.

## BEAVER HARBOUR
If the islands cannot be visited but you still want a chance to see some whales, check out Rawja Tours in the village of Beaver Harbour back on the mainland. There are two-hour trips daily out to The Wolves, five small islands, around which whales feed.

## NEW RIVER BEACH
Between St Stephen and Saint John, about 35 km from the latter, New River is one of the best beaches along the Fundy Shore and there is camping.

## SAINT JOHN
Historic Saint John (whose name is always spelt out in full, never abbreviated, to avoid confusion with St John's, Newfoundland) is the province's largest city and leading industrial centre. Sitting at the mouth of the Saint John River, on the bay, it is also a major port able to remain open all year.

In the past dozen years the city has undergone considerable refurbishing (a process still continuing) and the downtown area is much improved.

As well as the restorations, Saint John has a proud past. Known as 'the Loyalist City', it is the oldest incorporated city in the country. Evidence of this Loyalist background is plentiful and often very visible. The town museum, dating from 1842, is Canada's oldest.

The Maliseet Indians were here when the British and French began squabbling about furs. Samuel de Champlain had landed in 1604, and soon a fort was built and was changing hands between these two old-world enemies. However, the area remained pretty much a wilderness until 1755, when

about 4000 British people loyal to the homeland and fleeing the revolutionary America arrived.

They built up and incorporated the city in 1785. It soon became a prosperous shipbuilding centre. Though now using iron and steel rather than wood, shipbuilding is still a major industry in town. The dry dock is one of the world's largest. Fishing is also important.

In 1985 the city marked its 200th birthday as Canada's first incorporated city and also hosted the Canada Games – a sort of mini-Olympics involving young Canadian athletes. A swimming pool complex – the Aquatic Centre – was completed near City Hall for the games.

Fog very often blankets the city, particularly in the mornings. This helps to keep the area cool, even when the rest of the province is sweating it out in midsummer.

### Orientation
Saint John sits on the waterfront at the mouth of the Saint John River. The downtown area, Saint John Centre, lies on a square peninsula jutting into the bay east of the river.

King Square, a small and pleasant park, marks the centre of town. Its pathways are placed to duplicate the pattern of the Union Jack. To the east of the square, across the street, is the Loyalist burial ground with graves dating from 1784. Streets on the east side of the park are designated that way, eg King St East.

Going west from the square are the principal downtown streets – Charlotte, Germain, Canterbury and Prince William – running south off King St. Modern Brunswick Square, a major city shopping mall, is on the corner of King and Germain Sts. One block further west at Water St is the Saint John Harbour. Here is the redeveloped waterfront area and Market Square with shops, restaurants and the Trade & Convention Centre. Across the street east from Market Square is City Hall.

South from King Square a few blocks is Queen Square, laid out in the same fashion. The district below the square is known as the

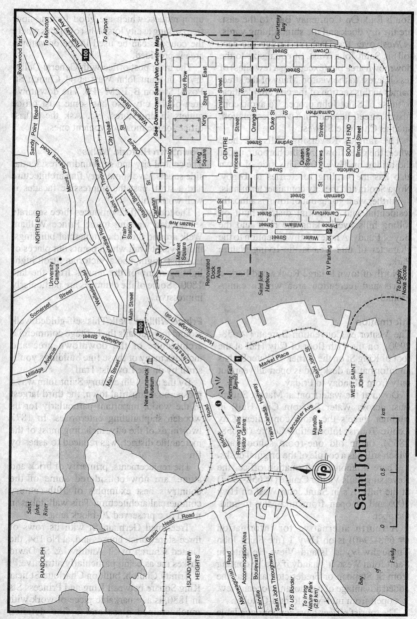

NEW BRUNSWICK

South End. On Courtenay Bay, to the east, are the dry dock and the shipbuilding yards.

West over the Harbour Bridge (25-cent toll) is Saint John West, of equal size to the downtown area but (excepting a few sites) of less interest to the visitor. Many of the street names in this section of the city are identical to those of Saint John proper. To avoid confusion, streets here end in a west designation, such as Charlotte St West.

The famous Reversing Falls are here where the river flows into the harbour, under the bridge on Hwy 100. This side of town also has the landing for ferries to Digby, Nova Scotia and the city container terminals.

Further west going out of town is a mostly residential and industrial district built on rolling hills overlooking the river and the Bay of Fundy. A noteworthy exception to the character of this area is the Irving Nature Park.

North of town is large Rockwood Park, a sports and recreation area with a campground.

### Information
The Visitor & Convention Bureau (☎ 658-2990), on the 11th floor of City Hall at the foot of King St on the corner of Water St, has an information desk and is open all year but only from Monday to Friday.

Down at the waterfront at Market Square (just across Water St from City Hall) in summer there's the more convenient City Centre Tourist Information Centre (☎ 658-2855), in an old one-room schoolhouse which still has a couple of the original desks.

There is another information office, the Reversing Falls Visitor Centre (☎ 658-2937) at the falls. It's in Saint John West on Hwy 100, and is open from mid-May to mid-October.

A fourth alternative for information (☎ 658-2940) is on Hwy 1 (the Saint John Throughway) at Island View Heights in Saint John West. It's handy if you're coming from St Stephen or Fredericton and has the added advantage of a panoramic ocean view. It's open from mid-May to mid-October.

The tourist offices have coupons available upon request which are good for one-hour free parking at city lots. A list of places where the coupons can be used in the downtown area is provided.

The main post office with General Delivery is in Saint John West at 41 Church St, Postal Station B, E2M 4P0. The downtown area of the city also has some post office outlets in drugstores, etc. Ask the tourist office for the most convenient ones.

### Downtown Historic Walks
The central city and surrounding residential side streets have some very fine architecture and a stroll past the impressive façades is well worthwhile.

The tourist office produces three separate self-guided walking tours: Prince William Walk around the old commercial buildings, the Loyalist Trail which points out places of Loyalist origin, and a Victorian Stroll highlighting many of the houses from the late 1800s. Some of the churches are particularly impressive.

**Prince William Walk** This self-guided walk around town details the heritage commercial architecture of the downtown area and includes many of those fine buildings you'll stroll by on the Loyalist Trail.

By the mid-19th century Saint John was a prosperous industrial town, the third largest in the world, important particularly for its wooden shipbuilding enterprises. In 1877 two-thirds of the city, including most of the mercantile district, was reduced to ashes by fire.

The replacements, primarily of brick and stone, are now considered some of the country's best examples of 19th-century commercial architecture. This walk takes in much of a preserved 20-block area.

Tree-lined Germain St with its rows of three-storey brick houses and, at No 164, the United Church of St Andrew & St David strikes me as being particularly attractive.

Trinity Church, built on Charlotte St near King Square between King and Princess Sts in 1880, is a remarkable piece of work with much stained glass and a fine detailed wooden ceiling. A very congenial and knowledgeable guide is on hand to lead visitors around, offering interesting bits of history and pointing out details.

Historic Trinity Royal is the area around the corner of Prince William and Princess Sts, where many businesses have set up in the restored old buildings.

**Loyalist Trail** The British Loyalists were really the founders of Saint John, turning a fort site into Canada's first legal city. Some of the early landmarks are still visible and interesting. The walking-tour pamphlet has a map and details of the best historical spots in the downtown area. Many of the places mentioned are no longer there; you just see the site of such and such – which is not exactly helpful unless you have a very active imagination – but some things do remain to see or visit.

Also, following the route is a good excuse to look at the many fine old buildings around the city, contrasting effectively with the modern ones. A good many old buildings have been or are now being restored.

**Victorian Stroll** Lasting about 1½ hours, this walk takes in the area south and west of King Square away from the commercial area and includes primarily Victorian houses, many of them very substantial dwellings.

**Reversing Falls**
The Bay of Fundy tides and their effects (see Tides in the Moncton section) are unquestionably an interesting and predominant regional characteristic. The falls here are part of that phenomenon and are not only the biggest attraction in the city but one of the best known sites in the province. However, 'reversing falls' has to be a misnomer at best and at worst a bit of a joke. When the high Bay of Fundy tides rise, the current in the river reverses, causing the water to flow upstream. When the tides go down, the water flows in the normal way.

By no stretch of the imagination could this trickle be termed 'falls' and it always strikes me, at least, as somewhat incredible to see so

many people crowding to look at this non-attraction. Since you'll probably go anyway, at least it's free and the tourist office here is worthwhile and helpful. A possible plus is that seals can sometimes be spotted in the river at high tide. Consult the tourist office for the tide schedule and optimum time to view the waters. At various points around the bay, you can see the tides to better advantage.

**Loyalist House**
On the corner of Union and Germain Sts, the Loyalist House (☎ 652-3590) dating from 1810 is the city's oldest unchanged building. The Georgian-style place is now a museum depicting the Loyalist period and contains some fine carpentry. This attraction is open every day in midsummer, weekdays only in June and September, and by appointment through the winter. Hours are from 10 am to 5 pm and admission is $2.

**Loyalist Burial Ground**
This interesting site is just off King Square, in a park-style setting in the centre of town. Here you can see tombstones, dating from as early as 1784, slowly eroding and falling to the earth.

**Chubb Building**
Back in the town core, on the corner of Prince William and Princess Sts, is the Chubb Building erected in the late 1800s. Chubb, the owner, had likenesses of all his children and half the town's politicians placed on the façade in little rosettes. Chubb himself is immortalised as a grinning gargoyle.

**Old Courthouse**
The County Court of 1829 is noted for its spiralling stone staircase, rising three storeys without any support.

**Old Market**
On Market St between Germain and Charlotte Sts is the colourful, interesting market which has been held here in the same building since 1876. Outside the door on Charlotte St, see the plaque outlining some of the

NEW BRUNSWICK

market's history. Overhauled and renovated in 1990, the heavy old roof beams
with the shipbuilding design influences
can still be seen – only now there is no
threat of collapse from the heavy winter
snows! A drawback, though, some locals
say, is that the newly installed heating
system is detrimental to the quality of the
vegetables and fruits.

Inside, the atmosphere is friendly but
busy. Apart from the fresh produce stalls,
most active on Friday and Saturday when
local farmers come in, there are several good
eating spots, a deli and some antiques for
sale. Good bread is sold and dulce and cheap
cooked lobster are available.

An underground walkway leads to Brunswick Square.

### Market Square

At the foot (western end) of King St is the
redeveloped waterfront area known as
Market Square. It offers views over the
working dockyards and container terminals
along the river. In summer there is an information booth here.

In the adjacent complex is a major hotel,
a convention centre and shopping and restaurant hub. The indoor mall is one of the best
designed I've seen and is actually pleasant to
be in. There are about 15 restaurants in here
although many are simple takeout counters
at the food court. Several of the better restaurants are along the outside wall and have
patios under umbrellas in summer. There is
also a library, art gallery, craft shop and some
benches for just sitting. An enclosed
walkway connects with City Hall across the
street.

### Barbour's General Store

This is a renovated old general store at
Market Square. Inside it's packed with the
kind of merchandise sold 100 years ago,
including old stoves, drugs, hardware and
candy. Most items are not for sale. Beside it,
the Old School is now a tourist information
kiosk.

### Partridge Island National/Provincial Historic Site

Out in the bay, Partridge Island (☎ 635-
0782) was once a quarantine station for the
Irish who were arriving after fleeing the
homeland's potato famine. There are the
remnants of some houses and a few old gun
placements on the island.

In summer, 2½-hour tours which include
the boat trip are offered out to the island.
They leave from the Market Square wharf
but service often seems sporadic – the boat
doesn't go unless enough people show up.
Ask about the boat trip at the tourist office
down by the wharf. At last visit, all tours
were suspended while various levels of government dickered over ownership and
operation of the site.

### City Hall

On King St near Prince William St in the
modern section of town is the new City Hall.
On the top floor is an observation deck with
a good view (on fog-free days!) of the city
and harbour. Go to the 15th floor and you'll
find the 'deck', an unused office, open from
8.30 am to 4.30 pm Monday to Friday.

### New Brunswick Museum

West of town at 277 Douglas Ave, near the
Reversing Falls, this is an eclectic place
(☎ 658-1842) with an odd collection of
things – some interesting, some not. There's
a very good section on marine wildlife, with
some aquariums and information on lobsters
(you may as well know about what you'll
probably be eating). There's a collection of
stuffed animals and birds, mostly from New
Brunswick. The displays on the marine
history of Saint John are good, with many
excellent models of old sailing ships.

In the other half of the museum is an art
gallery which includes local contemporary
work. Museum hours are from 10 am to 5 pm
daily from May to September. It's closed on
Monday for the rest of the year. Admission
is $2, students 50 cents.

### Carleton Martello Tower

Also in Saint John West, the national historic

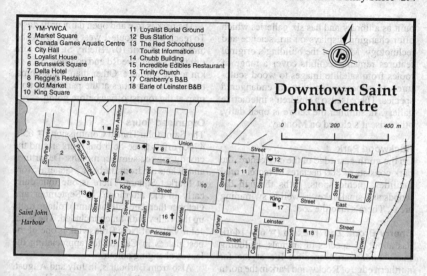

| | |
|---|---|
| 1 YM-YWCA | 11 Loyalist Burial Ground |
| 2 Market Square | 12 Bus Station |
| 3 Canada Games Aquatic Centre | 13 The Red Schoolhouse |
| 4 City Hall | Tourist Information |
| 5 Loyalist House | 14 Chubb Building |
| 6 Brunswick Square | 15 Incredible Edibles Restaurant |
| 7 Delta Hotel | 16 Trinity Church |
| 8 Reggie's Restaurant | 17 Cranberry's B&B |
| 9 Old Market | 18 Earle of Leinster B&B |
| 10 King Square | |

**Downtown Saint John Centre**

site Carleton Martello Tower (☎ 636-4011) is just off Lancaster Ave, which leads to the Digby ferry terminal. It's on Fundy Drive. Look for the signs at street intersections. A Martello tower is a circular two-storey stone coastal fortification. They were first built in England and Ireland at the beginning of the 19th century. In North America the British built 16 of them during the early 1800s. You can see others in Halifax, Quebec City and Kingston, Ontario. There are guides to show you around, answer questions, and give you some background information. Go when there's no fog because the view from the high promontory is good. The tower is open daily from 1 June to 31 September, free.

### Moosehead Brewery
While you're over here in Saint John West delving into history you might as well check out Moosehead Brewery (☎ 635-7000), the country's oldest independent beer maker. It dates back to 1867, the year of Confederation. It's at 89 Main St and offers tours through the week during summer.

### Telephone Pioneers' Museum
This museum (☎ 694-6388), in the lobby of

1 Brunswick Square, is small but good with an extensive collection of telephone equipment from the earliest models to the latest technology. It's open Monday to Friday from 10 am to 5 pm from mid-June to mid-September and is free. To find it, enter the mall off Germain St opposite Reggie's Restaurant.

### Jewish Historical Museum
Now a diminishing ethnic group in the city, the Jewish community was a sizeable and vital one from the 1920s until the 1960s. The museum (☎ 633-1833) is designed to preserve this heritage. There is a collection of articles used in the faith at home and in the synagogue and an outline of local Jewish history. The museum, at 29 Wellington Row, is open every day except Saturday in summer (limited Sunday hours are from 1 pm to 5 pm) but is closed on weekends during the rest of the year.

### Aitken Bicentennial Exhibition Centre
The centre (☎ 633-4870), also known as the City of Saint John Gallery, is at 20 Hazen Ave near the YM-YWCA in an attractive rounded sandstone building dating from 1904. It was

built as a library and has six galleries which offer changing displays on art, science and technology. Many of the building's original features remain. Exhibits cover a range of topics from satellite images to wood sculptures to superconductivity to endangered species. There is also a children's interactive gallery. In summer the centre is open daily, otherwise it's closed on Monday.

### Rockwood Park

On the north-east edge of the city centre, the park consists of 800 hectares of recreational facilities, picnic spots, paths through the woods and small lakes as well as swimming areas. There's also the zoo.

**Cherry Brook Zoo** The zoo (☎ 634-1440) has about 25 species of animals, including many endangered species. It's at the far northern edge of Rockwood Park in the north of the city and opens every day from 10 am to dusk. Admission costs $3.25, students $2.25

### Lakewood Beach

On Route 111 south-east of town (15 minutes by car) there is swimming and a sandy beach at Lakewood Reservoir Park. Route 111 is called Loch Lomond Rd in town.

### Irving Nature Park

For those with vehicles and an appreciation of nature, the park is a must (well worth the 20-minute drive south-west from the centre) for its rugged, unspoiled coastal topography. It is also a remarkable place for bird-watching, with hundreds of species regularly reported. Seals may be seen off-shore, too. Though the park is said to be on Taylors Island, this is not an island at all but rather a 225-hectare mountainous peninsula protruding into the Bay of Fundy. Four trails of varying lengths lead around beaches, cliffs, woods, mudflats, marsh and rocks. Good footwear is recommended. Also be careful along the ocean side on the rocks, as very large waves can occasionally catch the unsuspecting. The perimeter can be driven on a dirt road.

The park is free and open daily until dusk. To reach it take Route 1 west from town and turn south at Exit 107, Bleury St. Then turn right on Sand Cove Rd and continue for two km to the entrance. Other than washrooms, there are no facilities at the park. Pick up a map at the tourist office before going.

### Organised Tours

The Saint John Transit Commission (☎ 658-4700) offers three-hour bus tours around the city during the summer months. Departures and tickets are from Barbour's General Store at Market Square. There is one tour daily early in the afternoon. In September and October there are fall (autumn) foliage tours up the valley with lunch included. The Saint John Valley of New Brunswick is one of the best places in Canada for appreciating the leaves changing colour.

Also from Barbour's, in July and August, free guided walking tours are offered around the historic portions of downtown.

There are no longer any harbour boat tours but a pleasant day's outing is to take the boat over to Partridge Island (see the previous Partridge Island section).

For longer, more involving tours, Covered Bridge Bicycle Tours (☎ 849-9028) has different multi-day cycling trips around the region. Some even go out of the province.

### Festivals

Loyalist Days, a five-day event held annually during the third week of July, celebrates the city's Loyalist background. Featured are a re-creation of the first arrival, period costumes, parades, arts and crafts, music recitals, lots of food and performances. It all ends with fireworks, as do many Canadian events, on the last night of the festival.

Each August the city hosts the very popular, highly regarded Festival by the Sea. For 10 days (the dates change) this performing arts event presents hundreds of singers, dancers and other performers from across Canada in concerts and shows put on throughout the city night and day. Many of the performances staged in parks and along the harbourfront are free.

**Places to Stay**

**Camping** Just north of Rothesay Ave, north of the downtown area, is huge *Rockwood Park* (☎ 652-4050) with its small lakes, picnic area, golf course and part of the University of New Brunswick's campus. It's an excellent place to camp, with pleasant sites and a view of the city. It could not be more convenient – close to the downtown area and the main roads out of the city. If only more cities had something similar!

The rate for tenters is $11, less for longer stays and the ticket office is also a mini tourist centre.

**Hostels** The HI *Hostel* (☎ 634-7720) in Saint John is in the now amalgamated YM-YWCA at 19-25 Hazen Ave. It actually isn't a hostel at all, but hostel members can get a discount off the regular rates which fortunately are quite low. The hostel is central and clean with private single rooms for $28, or $21 for hostel members. You can use facilities like the pool, common room and snack bar with its cheap food. There are 30 rooms; you get your own room key and the lobby is always open.

For women travellers, there is the new *Salvation Army Evangeline Home* (☎ 634-76360), at 36 Saint James St on the corner of Canterbury St in the South End. They charge just $8 for a private room or $16.50 with meals! It's a nice place. A drawback is that this is not the best part of town and women alone may be uncomfortable walking at night.

**B&Bs** Right in town at 96 Leinster St, a short walk from King Square in a turn-of-the-century three-storey building, the *Earle of Leinster B&B* (☎ 693-3462) is that wonderful rarity – cheapest and best. There are seven rooms, all very comfortable and a good full breakfast is included for $39 a single or double. Single people can also ask for the small room, the only one without an ensuite bathroom, for $30. The outdoor courtyard with sandbox is good for those travelling with kids. Other features are the laundry facilities, fridge and microwave. Calling

ahead is a good idea as the place tends to fill up in summer.

The smaller *Cranberry's B&B* (☎ 657-5173) is also a well-cared-for historic place in the centre of town. Built in the late 1800s, this Victorian home is very convenient at 168 King St East. Singles/doubles on the 2nd floor are $50/55 with a satisfying breakfast of fruit, cereal and varying home-baked goods included. The very pleasant basement suite at $65 comes with a kitchenette and children aged under 10 years can stay for no charge. Owner Janice MacMillan is helpful and knows the city.

A little further out is the *Country Wreath 'n' Potpourri* (☎ 636-9919) at 125 Mt Pleasant Ave, a quiet tree-lined street in the north end of the city towards Rockwood Park. It's about a 10-minute walk to the train station, 20 minutes to the centre of town. Singles/doubles in this turn-of-the-century three-storey countrified house go for $45/50 with breakfast.

Over in Saint John West at 238 Charlotte St West is the *Five Chimneys B&B* (☎ 635-1888) with singles/doubles for $40/45. This is about a 10-minute drive from the centre of town over the Harbour Bridge but a bit of a hassle by bus. It's four blocks from the ferry terminal for Digby, Nova Scotia and within easy walking distance to the Reversing Falls. Call and the owner will be able to recommend the suitable bus route.

Manawagonish Rd has long been an important accommodation street in Saint John. Along this road are guesthouses, B&Bs, cabins and motels charging varying but mostly reasonable prices. The hassle is that it is a long way west of the downtown area beyond Saint John West, parallel to and north of Hwys 1 and 100. City buses do come and go into town from Manawagonish Rd but even in a car it's a 20-minute trip.

One place to try is the *Tartan B&B* (☎ 672-2592) with singles/doubles from $25/30 to $50 for the queen-size double with private bath. The address is 968 Manawagonish Rd.

**Hotels** There are actually few hotels in Saint

John and they tend to be in the middle or upper-price brackets. The *Courtenay Bay Inn* (☎ 657-3610) with 125 rooms is central at 350 Haymarket Square and is not badly priced with doubles starting at $50. *Keddy's Fort Howe* (☎ 657-7320) with singles/doubles for $64/70 is very good. It's on the corner of Main and Portland Sts. The *Hilton* (☎ 693-8484), on Market Square, charges $120 for a double.

**Motels** There are many motels along Manawagonish Rd and they tend to be less expensive than average. At times other than June to September prices tend to fall even further.

*Fundy Ayre Motel* (☎ 672-1125), at No 1711, is small with only nine units, but they go for just $40 a single or double with one bed. As with other motels, it costs more if two people use two beds. The rooms are tucked away off the road so they are quiet, and the very fine views of the Bay of Fundy and Taylors Island are a bonus. There are also rooms with kitchenettes available.

Second choice is the *Island View* (☎ 672-1381) across the street at 1726 Manawagonish Rd. They also have some kitchenettes as well as a heated swimming pool. Singes/doubles are $40/45.

Further out, still heading west, the road becomes Ocean West Way. Here at No 2121 you'll find the *Regent Motel* (☎ 672-8273). They have 10 rooms for $35 a single or double.

On the east side of town is a strip of motels along Rothesay Ave on Hwy 100, which leads out to Moncton. It's north-east of the city centre but a little closer to it than Manawagonish Rd. Most of the places out this way are more expensive.

An exception is the small *Bonanza Motel* (☎ 633-1710), 594 Rothesay Ave, which is OK at singles/doubles $25/27.

**Places to Eat**

Saint John is limited when it comes time to tie on the bib. There are few adventurous or noteworthy places which might go beyond stopping the hunger and there's little ethnic diversity.

There are no complaints, though, about *Reggie's Restaurant*. At 69 Germain St near the Loyalist House, this is a classic downtown no-nonsense diner which specialises in smoked meat from Ben's, a famous Montreal deli. Also on the menu are lobster rolls – a local favourite – and chowders at $3. It's a good, casual place open at 6 am for breakfast specials.

*Incredible Edibles*, at 42 Princess St in the Brodie Building, is a nice spot for a bit of a splurge. It offers pastas, curries, omelettes and is the only place with some vegetarian dishes. Specialities are the local desserts such as blueberry cobbler – a fruit-based sweet with a crispy cake crust, usually topped with milk or cream. Yummy! Dinner for two is, however, unlikely to be under $50.

The market is a good place to be when hunger strikes. Aside from the produce there are a few small restaurants or takeout counters. The *Whale of a Café* is good for a coffee and snack or the soups; *Jeremiah's* is a deli and sandwich bar. On the east side is a salad-to-go booth with lots of cheeses too. The market is closed in the evenings and on Sunday.

For Italian food there's *Vito's*, a reliable and steady eatery on Hazen Ave on the corner of Union St. Dishes are in the $10 to $12 range but on Monday night there's an economical all-the-spaghetti-you-can-eat deal.

Market Square has a number of restaurants, several of which have pleasant outdoor patios during the warm months. *Grannan's*, not strictly budget but not expensive either, has a good selection of seafood with steaks too. There is a bar in the downstairs section. *Keystone Kelly's* is less expensive and more casual with various finger foods at $8 to $12 for a meal. On the lower level with tables and chairs outside are a couple of other places which stay open for drinks later in the evening.

In the *Food Hall* at one corner of the main floor are about 10 fast-food places with shared tables. They offer unmemorable but cheap food including burgers, fish & chips and doughnuts. A plate of rice with vegetables and chicken from the Chinese place is $4.50.

The *Bamboo East* at 136 Princess St offers Chinese food. The weekday buffet is $7.95, weekend dinner buffet $9.95 and there's dim sum at noon on Sunday. Food is available à la carte, but it's not cheap.

Lastly, *La Belle Vie*, at 325 Lancaster Ave by the Reversing Falls, is a more elegant choice with a very expensive and well respected continental menu.

### Entertainment

Market Square also has a number of nightspots, some with live music and dancing; several places here have outdoor sections.

The *Harbour View Lounge* in the same complex, but near the Hilton Hotel in the Trade & Convention Building, is a place for a quiet drink.

At 30 Water St, busy *Thumpers* is good for jazz and blues. The *Imperial Theatre* is the new performing arts centre on King Square.

### Getting There & Away

**Air** Air Canada (☎ 632-1500) to Montreal costs $244. Canadian (☎ 657-3860) flies to St John's, Newfoundland for $331.

**Bus** SMT Bus Lines (☎ 648-3555) is the provincial carrier. The station is at 300 Union St on the corner of Carmarthen St, a five-minute walk from the town centre. SMT Bus Lines connects with Orleans Express lines in Rivière du Loup, Quebec for Quebec destinations. For cities in Nova Scotia, SMT connects with Acadian Bus Lines.

To Fredericton there are three trips daily costing $15. That same bus is used for connections for passengers carrying on to Quebec City, for which the fare is $60. The bus to Moncton leaves at 10 am and 3.15 pm and the fare is $20. For Cape Tormentine (to Prince Edward Island), go to Moncton and transfer from there.

**Train** The VIA Rail station (☎ 642-2916 or 800-561-3952 after 5 pm), on Station St, is a 10-minute walk from the downtown area,

north-west of King Square near the Loyalist House and the YM-YWCA. Fares listed are one way. To Quebec City, the train goes to Lévis (across the river from Quebec City) three times a week for $105. To Fredericton it's $18 (including a bus into town from the Fredericton Junction rail station) with the same schedule as above. Trains to Truro in Nova Scotia cost $45 and leave on Tuesday, Friday and Sunday. To Montreal (via Maine) there are services (costing $104) on Monday, Thursday and Saturday.

**Ferry** The Marine Atlantic ferry (☎ 636-4048), the *Princess of Acadia*, sails between Saint John and Digby, Nova Scotia, across the bay. Depending on where you're going, this can save a lot of driving around the Bay of Fundy through Moncton and then Amherst, Nova Scotia, but the ferry is not cheap. In comparison with the other Marine Atlantic routes around the region, and for the distance covered, the price is inexplicably high.

This route is heavily used by tourists which could be one explanation. Fares are $20 per person one way and $45 per car. Bicycles are $10. There is a very slightly reduced return passenger-only fare if you want to make a day cruise out of a trip there and back. Also, prices go down outside the summer season which is from the middle of June to the first week of September.

Crossing time is about 2½ hours. In summer there are three services daily: one in the morning, one in the afternoon and one at night. Arrive early or call ahead for reservations, as the ferry is very busy in July and August. Even with a reservation, arrive an hour before the ferry sails or your space may be given away. Walk-ons and cyclists should be OK. There's a restaurant and a bar on board.

Driving around the bay with a small car will save money but take more time.

**Car & Motorbike** There are several choices for rentals. Delta (☎ 634-1125), at 378 Rothesay Ave, is open seven days a week. They charge $29.95 with 100 free km, then

12 cents per km. There is also a weekly price of $149 with 1000 free km.

Avis (☎ 634-7750) is located conveniently right behind the market building at 17 North Market St. For a middle-sized car, the rates are pretty much the same as the above. Ask about the weekend special which is quite good value. A third option is Econo Leasing (☎ 632-8889), at 390 Rothesay Ave, where the daily rate is approximately the same.

Drivers should note that west of the town centre, Hwy 1 crosses over the Saint John River. There's a toll bridge where you pay 25 cents. Further out westward, connections can be made with Hwy 7 (northward) for Fredericton.

### Getting Around
**To/From the Airport** The airport is east of town out along Hwy 111. There is an airport bus costing $6.50 that leaves, approximately 1½ hours before all flights, from top hotels like the Hilton on Market Square and the Delta Brunswick on Brunswick Square. For a share taxi call Vets (☎ 634-1554).

**Bus** For information on local routes and times call Saint John Transit (☎ 658-4700) or ask at the tourist office.

### NORTH OF SAINT JOHN
North out of the city is a green rural area interspersed with deeply indented bays, rivers and islands, eventually leading to Grand Lake and Fredericton. It's prime New Brunswick cottage country. The Saint John River flows south through here to its mouth at the Bay of Fundy and the ferries connecting roads in the area are all free. The **Kingston Peninsula**, not far from Saint John, has scenery typical of the river valley landscapes and is particularly beautiful in the fall with the leaves changing colour. **Crystal Beach** is a popular spot for camping and swimming. If you're driving to Fredericton, don't take dull Hwy 7. Go along Hwy 102, which winds along by the river through small communities. At **Gagetown** there is a huge Canadian Forces base.

### ST MARTINS
A rather uninteresting 2½-hour drive east of Saint John will take you to the worthy destination of St Martins, one of the province's historic towns, situated on the Bay of Fundy. It's a small, pretty, out-of-the-way place that was once the centre of the wooden shipbuilding trade. On entering the town you'll see a quintessentially Maritime, picturesque scene: **Old Pejepscot Wharf** edged with beached fishing boats waiting for the tide, two wooden covered bridges and a lighthouse. (If on the other hand, the tide is in, the boats will likely be out, working.) The **Quaco Museum** depicts the shipbuilding period. But keep going over one of the bridges and around the corner where a vast expanse of beach opens up. At the far end there are a couple of caves cut into the shoreline cliffs to explore. At the parking lot is a snack bar, right by the beach.

### Hiking
The cliff-edged coastal region between St Martins and Fundy National Park and inland towards Sussex is a rugged undeveloped section of the province which has spectacular, wild beauty. Experienced hikers may wish to investigate the trail which runs mainly along the shoreline and extends some 40 km to the park. The hike takes three to five days.

From the park, another long-distance trail leads to the town of Riverview near Moncton.

### Places to Stay & Eat
Back in town there is the *Fundy Breeze Lodge* (☎ 833-4723) for spending the night or having a meal in the restaurant. There is also a B&B, the *Bayview* (☎ 833-4723) or camping just out of town at the *Seaside Tent & Trailer Park* (☎ 833-4413). All three places are on Main St.

### FUNDY NATIONAL PARK
Fundy National Park (☎ 887-2000) is one of the country's most popular parks. Aside from the world's highest tides, the park on the Bay of Fundy has about 80 km of hiking trails and

some dirt roads for touring around in your car. Irregularly eroded sandstone cliffs and the wide beach at low tide make a walk along the shore interesting. There's lots of small marine life to observe and debris to pick over. The park is home to a fair bit of wildlife – on one visit I nearly drove into a deer, and it was high noon! The ocean is pretty cool here, so there is a saltwater swimming pool (not far from the eastern entrance to the park) where you can have a dip, but you must pay for the privilege. There's also an arts & crafts school amongst the more developed attractions.

You can reach the park, 129 km east of Saint John and about halfway to Moncton, by following Hwy 114.

### Places to Stay

The park has five campgrounds charging from $6 for a tent on an unserviced site to $15 for a full serviced trailer site at the Headquarters campground.

Aside from the campgrounds, there are sites along the back-packing trails. In addition to the camping possibilities, there are motel-style rooms and chalets at the *Caledonia Highlands Inn* (☎ 887-2930) within the park. The chalets have cooking facilities and are very comfortable. The *Fundy Park Chalets* (☎ 887-2808) cost about $15 less at $45 for doubles and also contain cooking facilities.

At the small town of **Alma**, just east of the park on Hwy 114, you absolutely *must* stop at the *Home of the Sticky Bun* and buy an armful.

### CAPE ENRAGE

Heading east to Moncton take the smaller road, Hwy 915, as it detours closer to the coast and offers some fine views. At Cape Enrage, out on the cliffs at the end of the peninsula, the power of the elements is often strongly and stimulatingly in evidence.

### SHEPODY NATIONAL WILDLIFE AREA

South of the town of Riverside-Albert and the village of Harvey at Marys Point on the Bay of Fundy is this gathering place for literally hundreds of thousands of shore birds. From mid-July to mid-August the beach is almost obliterated by huge numbers of birds, primarily semi-palmated sandpipers. Along the dykes and marsh there is a nature trail.

# South-East New Brunswick

The corner of New Brunswick leading to Nova Scotia and Prince Edward Island is most interesting for its various geographic or topographic attributes. The regional centre is Moncton whose two principal attractions are places where nature appears to defy gravity. Outside the city are some fine, sandy beaches and, on the Petitcodiac River, the Rocks are the impressive result of seaside erosion.

### MONCTON

Moncton, with a population of 60,000, is the third city of the province and a major transportation and distribution centre for the Atlantic Provinces. It's near the ferry for Prince Edward Island and the train to Nova Scotia passes through it. Moncton is small and nondescript, but a much-needed face-lift has improved the downtown area. Despite the recession, some aggressive marketing and a bilingual workforce have resulted in the city's experiencing considerable economic growth and development. And due to a couple of odd attractions – Magnetic Hill and a tidal bore – it's worth a brief stop on your way by.

The first Europeans to settle in the area were Germans from Pennsylvania. Initially the town was called 'The Bend', after the turn in the Petitcodiac River, and specialised in shipbuilding. There's a fairly large French population and many people speak both of Canada's official languages. The Université de Moncton is the only French university outside Quebec province.

## Orientation

The small downtown area extends north and south off Main St. The river lies just to the south and the Trans Canada Hwy runs east-west north of town. Between Duke and Foundry Sts along Main St, the sidewalks have been gentrified and many of the old buildings have been re-done to contain restaurants and nightspots. Unfortunately, since my last visit, opposing forces have had a deleterious effect on these worthwhile efforts. For in Moncton, as in several other towns around the province (or indeed, in many across the country), growth means new shopping malls and the national (or international) chains taking root. Business is drawn away from local, privately-owned enterprises, restaurants and accommodations, sometimes contributing to closures. In Moncton, alone, there are 13 Tim Horton doughnut shops! Often, as is the case here, the downtown core suffers as consumers file to the malls and the development around the perimeter. Just to the east of the downtown centre across the bridge on Champlain St, an extension of Main St, is a mega-mall complex.

Lengthy Mountain Rd leading in and out

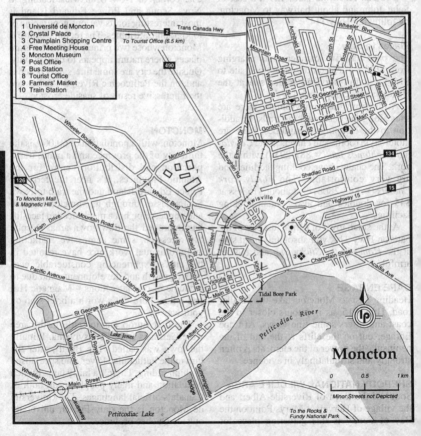

1  Université de Moncton
2  Crystal Palace
3  Champlain Shopping Centre
4  Free Meeting House
5  Moncton Museum
6  Post Office
7  Bus Station
8  Tourist Office
9  Farmers' Market
10  Train Station

**Moncton**

0        0.5        1 km

Minor Streets not Depicted

of the west side of town from the Trans Canada Hwy is also a main street for gas stations, chain restaurants, fast food joints and the same franchises seen in most Canadian cities. There are also some motels along here.

### Information

There are several tourist offices. The central summer information centre (☎ 853-3540) is at 581 Main St on the corner of Lewis St. This seasonal office location, however, is not stable from year to year although a nearby central spot on or near Main St is rented each summer.

From September to May, the visitors' centre is in City Hall (☎ 853-3596), 774 Main St, but it's closed on weekends. A third information office, and the largest, is right beside Magnetic Hill where Mountain Rd meets the Trans Canada Hwy, north-west of the downtown area.

There's another office south across the Gunningsville Bridge in Riverview.

### Magnetic Hill

This is the best known attraction (☎ 384-0303) in the area and is worth a visit. Gravity here seems to work in reverse: start at the bottom of the hill in a car or on a bike and you'll drift upward. Go as many times as you like, and maybe you'll figure it out. The hill is on the corner of Mountain Rd (Hwy 126) and the Trans Canada Hwy; it's free and the kids will like it. In recent years the hill has become the centre of a variety of attractions which now include a small zoo next door, a water park with slides of various sorts, restaurants and stores. A mini-train links the different diversions.

### Tidal Bore Park

The tidal bore is a twice-daily incoming wave caused by the tides of the Petitcodiac River, which are in turn related to the tides in the Bay of Fundy – known as the world's highest tides. The bore rushes upstream and sometimes raises the water level in the river by six metres in a few minutes. The wave itself varies in height from a few cm to over 30 cm.

A good place to watch for it is in Tidal Bore Park at the east end of Main St where there is a large, bright bore timetable display. The pleasant park is filled with old men sitting on the benches until close to bore time when the water's edge gets really crowded with expectant visitors. Don't anticipate anything spectacular though – mostly the wave is not at all impressive. This is so frequently the case that often street performers are now on hand to entertain the watchers – the performers that I've seen have been quite good and invariably steal the show from mother nature. The bore is best in spring and fall, if it's raining or if the moon is right.

### Moncton Museum

At 20 Mountain Rd near Belleview St, the museum (☎ 856-4383) has a collection of memorabilia covering the town's history, from the time of the Micmac Indians and early settlers to the present. Displays show the influence of shipbuilding and the railway on the area and an old-style street has been re-created. The museum's free and open daily in summer, but is closed on Monday for the rest of the year. Next door is the oldest building in town, the **Free Meeting House** dating from 1821, used by numerous religious congregations over the years.

Ninety-minute guided walking tours of the city commence at the museum from Tuesday to Friday at 9.30 am through the summer.

### Acadian Museum

On the university campus, this museum (☎ 858-4088) has a collection of artefacts belonging to the Acadian people, the first French settlers of the Atlantic region. The displays offer a brief history and chronicle aspects of the day-to-day life of these people who were driven out of Nova Scotia to New Brunswick and abroad by British troops. The museum's free and open daily but on weekends it's open only during the afternoons.

## Tides

The tides of the Bay of Fundy are the highest in the world. This constant ebb and flow is a prime factor in the life of the bay, the appearance of the shoreline and even how residents set shipping and fishing schedules.

The explanation for these record tides is in the length, depths and gradual funnel shape of the bay. As the high tide builds up, the water flowing into the narrowing bay has to rise on the edges. It is pushed still higher by the shallowing sea bed. A compounding factor is called resonance. This refers to the sloshing or rocking back and forth from one end to the other of all the water in the bay like in a giant bath tub. When this mass swell is on the way out of the bay and meets a more powerful incoming tide head on, the volume of water increases substantially.

The eastern end of the Bay of Fundy and around the Minas Basin is where the contrasts between the high and ebb tide are most pronounced with tides of 10 to 15 metres twice daily about 12½ hours apart. The highest tide ever recorded anywhere was 16.6 metres (54 ft), the height of a four-storey building, at Burncoat Head near the village of Noel, Nova Scotia. Other places around the world with noteworthy (that is, over 10 metres high) tides are Bristol in England, the Bay of St Malo in southern France, and Turnagain Arm in Alaska.

All tides, large and small, are caused by the rise and fall of the oceans due to the gravitational pull of the sun and the moon. Consequently, the distance of the moon and its position to earth relative to the sun determine tidal size. When the moon is full or new the gravitational forces of the sun and moon are working in concert, not at cross purposes, and the tides at these two times of the month are higher than average. When one of these periods coincides with the time (perigee, once every 27½ days) when the moon is at its closest to earth the tides are at their most dramatic.

Throughout the centuries various methods have been used around the bay to tap the tides as an energy source. Simple but successful grist mills spurned dreams of grandiose generating stations feeding the eastern seaboard. There is still no commercial electricity production but there is an experimental and working tidal power plant which can be visited at Annapolis Royal, Nova Scotia.

The times and heights of the tides change around the bay but local schedules are available at many tourist offices in the region.

## Tidal Bore

A feature related to the tides is the tidal bore, a daily occurrence in some of the rivers flowing into the Bay of Fundy, most notably the Saint John River running through Saint John, the Petitcodiac River in Moncton and the Salmon River in Truro, Nova Scotia.

As the tide advances up a narrowing bay it starts to build up on itself forming a wave. The height of this oncoming rush can vary from just a few cm to about a metre. The power behind it forces the water up what is normally a river draining to the sea. This wave flowing upstream is called a tidal bore.

The size and height of the bore is determined by the tide, itself regulated by the moon. In the areas where the bore can be most interesting it is not difficult to get hold of a bore schedule. Like with the tides, there are two bores a day, roughly 12 hours apart. While this is an interesting occurrence, especially in theory, the bores are not often overwhelming experiences to observe. Notice I resisted the term 'boring'. ■

**NEW BRUNSWICK**

### Thomas Williams's House

Built in 1883, this 12-room Victorian Gothic-style house remained in the family as a home until 1983 when it was bequeathed to the city as a heritage house. Much of the fine original work remains intact both inside and out, and the furnishings add to the overall effect. The tea room on the veranda is fun.

The house is open Tuesday to Sunday from June to September. It's at 103 Park St in the downtown area.

### Crystal Palace

Just north-east out of the downtown core, at 499 Paul St near Hwy 15 to Shediac, is Crystal Palace, an indoor amusement park complex with adjacent hotel and shopping centre. There are rides, including a roller coaster, and games.

## Farmer's Market

On Saturday, from 7 am to 1 pm, a produce market is set up on Robinson St south of Main St.

## Festivals

In early May there's the Acadian Art Festival, and in July a bluegrass and old-time fiddle-music festival is held.

## Places to Stay

**Hostels** The *YWCA* (☎ 855-4349) is near the bus and train stations in an attractive, three-storey old stone house on the corner of Highfield and Campbell Sts. It has its 2nd floor set up as a hostel. These dorm rooms are $12 if you need sheets, or $8 if you have your own bedding. Upstairs, private rooms are $20 or if you share a double, $15 per person. Note that accommodation is for women only. The cafeteria serves low-priced, good-value meals. The house was partially renovated in 1993.

The *Université de Moncton* (contact Housing Services on ☎ 858-4008) rents rooms during summer in two of the residences. They have shared washrooms and there is a cafeteria. Singles/doubles cost $23/28 and for students and seniors singles/doubles are $15/18. Very good weekly rates are available.

**Tourist Homes** The lack of hotels is partially offset by quite a few guesthouses and B&Bs. During the summer, these are often full by the end of the day.

*McCarthy's* (☎ 383-9152), at 85 Peter St, with three rooms is good and inexpensive with singles/doubles at $25/35. Note that it is open only from May to September. Peter St is just under two km north of the downtown centre.

Within walking distance (but a fair jaunt of seven or so blocks) is the *Bonaccord House B&B* (☎ 388-1535) at 250 Bonaccord St. It's the appealing yellow-and-white house on the corner of John St with a porch to sit out on. There are four comfortable rooms, complete with good reading material, at singles/doubles $35/45 and a family room

at $55. Unfortunately, on a recent visit, the breakfast had been prepared early and had sat a while before being served.

Very central at 101 Alma St is the *Downtown B&B* (☎ 855-7108), open all year with three rooms at singles/doubles $40/50.

*Mountain View Tourist Home* (☎ 384-0290) is at 2166 Mountain Rd. They have three rooms at the reasonable price of singles/doubles $30/35. It's a simple, no-frills place but is good.

**Hotels** At 46 Archibald St in a central location near Main St, is the yellow, wooden *Canadiana Inn* (☎ 382-1054). It's a beautiful place – as if you've stepped back in time – with wood everywhere and hanging lamps and, indeed, it's more than 100 years old. There are over a dozen rooms beginning at singles/doubles $50/$55.

The *Hotel Beauséjour* (☎ 854-4344) on Main St is the largest and most expensive place in town and is primarily for business clientele.

**Motels** There's no shortage of motels, and a fair range of prices.

Not far from town is the good *Beacon Light Motel* (☎ 384-1734), at 1062 Mountain Rd, reached by taking Hwy 126. Doubles cost $48 and there are some kitchenette rooms available. Mountain Rd has a couple of other places as well.

On Hwy 2 near Magnetic Hill are numerous motels. The *Atlantic* (☎ 858-1988) charges singles/doubles $42/47. The *Restwell* (☎ 858-0080) in the other direction (east) is from $40 to $45 a single or double. Features here include a pool and some kitchenette rooms.

Also decent is the *Moncton Motor Inn* (☎ 382-2587), an older place but clean and well kept, with a view of the river. It has a swimming pool and, at 1905 Main St, is just a five-minute drive into town. A double here is $48.

Right in the centre of town within walking distance to either the bus or train station, is the *Midtown* (☎ 388-5000) which is in a quiet location at 61 Weldon St. It's pricier with singles/doubles for $54/59 and also has some kitchenette rooms.

There are several other motels strung out along Rural Route 1, towards and in River Glade.

## Places to Eat
At 700 Main St, *Crackers* is a nice place for sandwiches, salads, ribs or Italian food. The large Caesar salad at $5 makes a good lunch and there is a wide selection of tempting desserts. At night it becomes a sort of club and is open very late on weekends. Across the street is *Spanky's*, a cleaned-up tavern with inexpensive food and beer, and late-afternoon happy hours.

*Len's* at 840 Main St is a classic workers' restaurant, open every day and packed for lunch, with everything under $6 or so. The *Traveller's Café* in the bus station has cheap breakfasts.

In summer, a couple of takeout booths pop up in the little mall area on the corner of Main and Robinson Sts in the centre of town, where there are benches to sit at. The food counter at the *Metropolitan* store at the High-field Mall on Main St has the lowest prices in town with meals at about $5.

Probably the best known restaurant is *Cy's*, a very well established seafood place at 170 Main St. It is not cheap and may be a little over-rated, but it's certainly alright.

Mountain Rd has quite a number of eating spots, including *Ming Garden* for Chinese food at No 797. Vast Chinese buffets are popular in town and the Ming claims a selection of 100 items on its all-you-can-eat tables – not bad value at $8. The inexpensive and recommended *Ponderosa* has good-value steak dinners at under $8 and the all-you-can-eat salad bar, which they now call the hot and cold (meatless) buffet, available with or without a meal. The latter can be had for just $5 and there is a lot of food to attempt to devour. The address is 956 Mountain Rd.

For things like pizza and spaghetti try *Vito's* at 726 Mountain Rd.

*Deluxe French Fries* is a local fresh-cut fries institution with burgers, fish and other seafood too. They've been around for over 40 years and have several locations about town including those on the corner of St George Blvd and Church St and the corner of Mountain Rd and Connaught Ave.

## Entertainment
The *Urban Corral*, 6 Duke St, has live country and western music from 9 pm to 1 am, except on Sunday. *Ziggy's* at 730 Main St attracts the young with a different diversion each night. The *Coliseum* is home to major shows, concerts and sporting events.

The impressive Capitol Theatre on Main St, a 1920s vaudeville house, has been restored and is now the city's Performing Arts Centre.

## Getting There & Away
**Bus** The station for SMT Bus Lines (☎ 859-5060) is at 961 Main St between town and the train station on the corner of Bonaccord St. Some schedules follow with one-way ticket prices:

Fredericton – 11.15 am & 5.45 pm daily ($25)
Saint John – 1.15 & 6 pm daily ($20)
Halifax – 1.45 & 6 pm daily ($33)
Prince Edward Island – 1.15 & 6 pm ($28)

**Train** The train station (VIA) (☎ 857-9830) is south-west of the downtown area near Cameron St off Main St. Look for it behind the building at 1234 Main St or behind Sobey's grocery store at the Highfield Mall. The station is a couple of hundred metres off Main St. It's only open from 10 am to 6.30 pm. Regular one-way fares include to Halifax $38 and to Saint John $23. There's a service to Montreal every day except Wednesday for $117.

To Montreal, there are two different trains using different routes. One train, the *Atlantic*, goes through Maine three times a week; the other, the *Ocean*, goes through northern New Brunswick including Campbellton and Quebec, also three times a week.

If you take the US route, note that you must have proper ID and comply with US immigration requirements although the situation now seems less stringent and actually passing through customs is unnecessary if you don't get off the train.

## AROUND MONCTON
### Covered Bridges

Within 100 km of Moncton, 27 of the province's historic covered bridges can be seen. They were known as 'kissing bridges', because you and yours could tuck the old horse and buggy in there away from curious eyes. Two driving trips south of Moncton, called the Scenic Trail and the Covered Bridge Trail, take in many of these bridges.

### Dobson Trail

Just south of Moncton in Riverview, this 60-km hiking trail leads you through the Albert County hills and maple forests down to Fundy National Park. For information contact the Trailmaster, Edwin Melanson (☎ 855-5089) in Riverview.

### Hillsborough

Hillsborough, about 20 km south-east of Moncton, is a small town overlooking the Petitcodiac River. From here a restored steam engine (☎ 734-3195) pulls antique coaches along the river to Salem, about eight km away. It takes an hour for the return trip. The fare is $6, less for kids, and half-price on rainy days. The schedule is very limited; through July and August the train runs once on Sunday afternoons.

### The Rocks Provincial Park

Continuing south-east from Hillsborough, you'll encounter the park at Hopewell Cape, the point at which the river meets the Fundy waters in Shepody Bay. The 'rocks' are unusual erosion formations known as 'flowerpots'. The shore is lined with these irregular geological forms, caves and tunnels created by erosion from the great tides. An exploratory walk along the beach at low tide is well worthwhile – check the tide tables at any tourist office. You can't hit the beach at high tide but the rock towers are visible from the trails above. Camping is not allowed but there are picnic areas and a restaurant.

### Saint Joseph

Here, 24 km south of Moncton, the Acadian Odyssey National Historic Site (☎ 758-9783) opened in the summer of 1990. It had been housed in what was one of the buildings of College Saint Joseph, where many Acadians were educated until its recent closure. The museum-style displays tell the enthralling but difficult history of the Acadians, the early French settlers of the Bay of Fundy region, most of whom were expelled by the British in 1755. The exhibits, including paintings, crafts and life-size models, are well done and, unlike those at many such history-based sites, also devote some attention to the subjects' lives through the years to the present.

Saint Joseph is in the Memramcook Valley, the only area near the Bay of Fundy where some Acadians live on what was the land of their forebears before the mass banishments.

The site is open from 15 June to 15 September, from 9 am to 5 pm daily and entry is free. It's between Moncton and Dorchester off Route 106 and, if you're interested in the Acadians or will be seeing some of the other sites relating to them, it's worth the slight detour.

## SACKVILLE

Sackville is a small, staid university town. While there isn't a heck of a lot here, it seems to be in the right place for a pit-stop on the way through. The park in the university grounds right in the centre of town is good for stretching the legs. The art gallery on campus displays the work of students.

Along some of the side streets a number of huge homes from the 1800s can be seen; a couple of them have been restored and converted to an inn and a B&B.

On the way into town off the Trans Canada Hwy along East Main St look for the Booster Pump by the edge of the road. All the locals stop here for a drink or to fill a jug with the ever flowing, excellent pure water.

Around Sackville are the **Tantramar Marshes**, an expanse of a couple of thousand hectares of wetlands, home to great numbers of waterfowl which have made the area of some interest to bird-watchers. Twenty-four species of ducks and other marsh birds live in or visit the area.

On the edge of town, off East Main St, is the **Sackville Waterfowl Park** on a major bird migration route. Boardwalks have been built over portions of it and there is another trail and some interpretive signs. Also in the Sackville area is the **Tintamarre National Wildlife Reserve**. Biologists at the Wildlife Service in Sackville will offer information for those wishing to know or see more.

On the road south from town all the antennae are part of the CBC's international short-wave broadcasting equipment.

### Places to Stay & Eat

*Mt Allison University* (☎ 364-2251), right in the centre of town, opens rooms to overnight guests from May to August. Singles/doubles cost $25/35, a few dollars less for students. They also serve inexpensive meals.

There's a good B&B at 146 West Main St called the *Different Drummer* (☎ 536-1291). It's a fine old Victorian house; each of the four rooms is furnished with antiques and has a bath. Breakfasts include homemade muffins and bread. Prices could be a little lower though: singles/doubles cost $40/48. *Borden's Motel* is slightly less.

At the *Marshland's Inn* at 59 Bridge St, you can get a very good dinner whether you're spending the night there or not. Ask about the chef's special. Meals are not cheap but are good value. Lodging is in the range of $60 a double. *Borden's Motel*, which you can see from the highway, offers good cheap meals and the lobster rolls have been recommended. On York St, across from the university, the little *Vienna Coffee House* is the place for a coffee and snack.

### FORT BEAUSÉJOUR NATIONAL HISTORIC PARK

Right by the Nova Scotia border at the shoreline, the park (☎ 536-0720) preserves the remains of a French fort built in 1751 to hold the British back. It didn't work. Led by Colonel Monckton, the fort was taken over

before it was even finished. Later it was used as a stronghold during the American Revolution and the War of 1812. There are some pretty good displays within the fort and some evocative pictures set in the surroundings. A museum provides more details and guides will answer questions. The park is free and open daily. The views over the marshy end of the Bay of Fundy alone make a trip out here worthwhile. Picnic tables are provided.

### SHEDIAC

Just 22 km north-east of Moncton on the coast, Shediac is a popular summer resort town with a population descended mainly from the Acadian French. The beaches along the Northumberland Strait are blessed with warm waters, but especially so here because of sand bars and shallow water. Most popular are **Parlee Beach** (east of Shediac) and **Pointe du Chêne**, with water temperatures of around 20°C all summer. The waters of the Northumberland Strait are possibly the warmest north of the US Carolinas.

There are other beaches on the small coastal roads and north and south of Shediac, and lots of camping places.

The area also is a lobster centre of some repute and Shediac is home to the annual lobster festival in July. Watch out for the 10-metre-long clawed beast which may be seen around town. Many restaurants offer seafood all through the summer.

There is little to see in town itself, but at night the many lights and the decorative seagulls add a festive touch. **Pascal Poirier House**, built in 1835 is the oldest house in town and is now open as a small museum.

The big white Hotel Shediac (dating from 1853) is prominent, and the dining room offers both seafood and steaks.

### Places to Stay & Eat

For camping there is a lot of choice in the area but best is probably *Parlee Beach Park* (☎ 532-1500), beside the provincial beach where it's $11 for one person with tent. Reservations should be made for holiday weekends, but for any weekend, arrive as early as possible on Friday.

Aside from camping, the aforementioned *Hotel Shediac* (☎ 532-4405) is a central, middle-range place to spend a night or two. Doubles cost $50. Accommodation is not plentiful, but one less expensive option is the *Neptune Motel* (☎ 532-4299) with singles/doubles $35/45. There are also a couple of places with cabins rented by the week.

East of town is a strip of eateries and takeout joints. You'll find clams and lobsters, cooked or fresh, dead or alive. *Fisherman's Paradise* packs 'em in with fair (but that doesn't mean cheap) prices. The *House of Lobster* with a large smorgasbord of seafood is an all-you-can-eat buffet. *Shediac Pizza* is good and inexpensive, try the pizza burger. Also along the strip are a couple of motels, a bar or two and a new water-slide complex.

Lobsters can be bought at various outlets and at the wharves. Boil them in ocean water and, with a bottle of wine and some French bread, you've got a cheap deluxe meal. Dig for clams and mussels too.

## CAP-PELÉ

East of Shediac there are a series of less used beaches such as the one at Cap-Pelé where there is also a water slide. Further south at Murray Corner is a provincial park with more sandy beach.

## CAPE TORMENTINE

Further east of Shediac and also on the coast is Cape Tormentine with the terminal for the ferry to Borden, Prince Edward Island.

Just north of Bayfield is a very long, almost empty beach with the remains of an old wreck at one end.

# North & East New Brunswick

North of Fredericton and Moncton lie the province's vast forests. Nearly all the towns are along the east coast or in the west, by the Saint John River along the US border. The interior of northern New Brunswick is nearly inaccessible rocky, river-filled timberland.

Inland, highways in this area can be quite monotonous with thick forest lining both sides of the very straight roads. It's like driving down unending corridors, most particularly on the routes south from Campbellton to Saint Léonard, from Bathurst to Chatham and from Chatham to Moncton.

Fortunately these routes need not often be used. In the eastern section of the province the coastal roads are where pretty well everything of interest lies. Kouchibouguac National Park protects a variety of littoral environments and their natural flora & fauna. Most of the larger towns of the east coast are pulp and paper centres with not a lot to hold the visitor's attention. Newcastle sticks out as a place to break up the trip.

The Acadian Peninsula with its little-touristed islands and French population based around Caraquet is one of the most geographically appealing regions with the Baie des Chaleurs shoreline. The peninsula also has a major historic attraction.

Campbellton and Dalhousie at the edge of the northern uplands are access points to the province of Quebec. The Miramichi and Restigouche rivers are both widely known, highly respected and very fetching salmon-fishing nuclei.

## COCAGNE

North up the coast from Shediac, Cocagne hosts a hydroplane regatta around the second week of August.

## KOUCHIBOUGUAC NATIONAL PARK

The highlights of this park (☎ 876-2443) (pronounced 'koo she boo gwak') are the beaches, lagoons and offshore sand dunes stretching for 25 km. The sands are good for beach-combing, bird-watching and digging clams. Seals are often seen offshore. For swimming, the water is warm but much of it is too shallow for adults. There are, though, a number of designated swimming areas with deeper waters.

Inland there is canoeing (with rentals), hiking trails, both short and long, and quiet roads for cycling. Bikes can also be rented and make a fine way to get around the very flat landscape. Telescopes along the bike route by the sea offer close-ups of the many great blue herons.

There's freshwater fishing for a variety of fish; the park also has moose, deer, black bears and smaller mammals. Other features are the salt marsh and a bog with an observation platform. Moose can often be seen from the bog boardwalk in early morning or in the evening.

The camping season is from May to October, based primarily at a large campground with firewood supplied. There are also less-expensive campsites for backpackers and canoeists.

At Ryan's there is a modest restaurant with some Acadian specialties and the bicycle rental booth. At Kelly's by the main beach is a takeout food counter with the usual beach fare.

The park is very popular and busy throughout July and August, particularly on weekends. Get there early in the day to obtain a campsite for about $11. The park is 100 km north of Moncton. If it is full, a good alternative is the Daigles private campground which is two km outside the park.

## MIRAMICHI BAY

North of the national park in and around Miramichi Bay are more beaches. Folks here, like those further south and in north Prince Edward Island and Nova Scotia, claim the waters are the warmest north of either Virginia or the US Carolinas depending on who you hear it from. In any case, the water at all these places is quite suitable for swimming in, having been warmed by spin-off currents of the Gulf Stream.

## CHATHAM

This was a prosperous town when it was the centre of the wooden shipbuilding industry, but the development of steel ships put an end to that. Since WW II there has been a Canadian Forces base here. Government spending cuts have now meant the end of this economically important facility. There is little to

recommend for visitors, but the revamped downtown area along Water St by the Miramichi River is pleasant enough in a quiet way.

Two blocks away from the waterfront the **WS Logge Cultural Centre**, in a restored Victorian house at 222 Wellington St, is primarily a locally oriented art gallery.

At 149 Wellington St on the corner of University Ave, the **Natural History Museum** has a small idiosyncratic collection which is open from mid-June to the end of August.

There is quite an Irish history here and, to commemorate this, a sizeable Irish festival is held annually usually in July with music, dance, food, film, crafts, a parade and even genealogy experts to help trace your Irish roots. There are a few B&Bs in and around town.

In **Douglastown**, halfway between the Chatham bridge and Newcastle is a tourist office and the **Rankin House Museum.**

## NEWCASTLE

Though the site of another huge paper mill, Newcastle is a pleasant little town – a good place to break up the trip north or south. Around the attractive town square are some fine old wooden buildings and shops, some unpainted and ancient-looking, others well tended.

In the central square park bounded by Castle and Henry Sts is a statue to Lord Beaverbrook, one of the most powerful press barons in British history and a statesman and philanthropist of no small reputation. Beaverbrook was born Max Aitken in 1879 and spent most of his growing years in Newcastle. Among the many gifts he lavished on the province are the 17th-century English benches and the Italian gazebo in the square here. His ashes lie under the statue presented as a memorial to him by the town.

Most of the shops are around the square and along Water St. South of town off Hwy 8 is another of Lord Beaverbrook's gifts – a forest park called **The Enclosure**, now part of a provincial park. If you just want to look around The Enclosure, tell them at the gate and you won't have to pay the park fee. From 19 June to 15 September there is camping and swimming in the park. Archaeologists have been working at the park, which has been occupied on and off by a number of different peoples for about 2000 years. There is a historic cemetery.

Each summer the Miramichi Folk Song Festival, now over 30 years old and the oldest one in North America, is held. Through traditional song, the local history and culture are preserved. It's good fun, and worth catching.

Just off the park on the corner of Castle and Pleasant Sts is an odd-looking but good place to stay. It's called *Castle Lodge* (☎ 622-2442). Inside the old vine-covered, red-and-green wooden house are five rooms rented out by, yes, an old lady. Singles/doubles cost $28/34 and you share the one bathroom. An alternative is *Governor's Mansion* (☎ 622-3036), across the river in Nelson-Miramichi. Also good value, they have five rooms for singles/doubles $35/40.

For a bite there is a quick little coffee shop in *Barett's Store* by the town square.

## MIRAMICHI RIVER
South-west of Newcastle, the Southwest Miramichi River extends beyond Doaktown, about halfway to Fredericton. The river runs 800 km and the waters are crystal clear. The area, in particular the main river, is renowned for Atlantic salmon fishing. Together with the Restigouche and Saint John rivers, it has gained the province an international reputation amongst serious anglers. Even Prince Charles has fished the Miramichi! Both residents and visitors need licences and there are special regulations for nonresidents. Check at the tourist office or the Forest Service of the Department of Natural Resources.

**Doaktown** has become more or less the unofficial fishing centre for the region.

Also in town is the **Atlantic Salmon Museum**, which is actually pretty interesting and includes pools of live salmon ('king of the freshwater game fish') on the 1.5-hectare grounds. One of Canada's best fly-fishing

shops is here, W W Doak & Sons. They sell about 60,000 flies a year, many tied on the premises. Other points of interest include the **Glendella Mansion** (a rather unexpected sight) and **Doak Historic Park**, concerning local history and with a preserved house from the 19th century and costumed interpreters for the farm section. Near town is a 1870s **covered bridge**, one of the province's oldest. And, oh yeah, don't miss the moose on the east side of town.

### Places to Stay
There are numerous fishing lodges and outfitters in and around town as well as motels and B&Bs. Serious salmon stalkers should consider *Pond's Resort* (☎ 369-2612) on Porter Cove Rd in nearby Ludlow. The owners have rights to 36 km of the Miramichi with some very memorable fishing pools. Most of the guests at the Pond's are repeat visitors and are not on very tight budgets. It's a large place with a range of options so call or write in advance for details.

## ACADIAN PENINSULA
The large peninsula, extending from Chatham and Bathurst out to two islands at the edge of the Baie des Chaleurs, is a predominantly French area which was first settled by the Acadians who were the unhappy victims of the colonial battles between Britain and France in the 1700s. The descendants of Canada's earliest French settlers proudly fly the Acadian flag around the region and many of the traditions live on in music, food and the language which is different to that spoken in Quebec.

For visitors, by far the most interesting section is around Caraquet and the scenery is better there too.

### Tracadie
From Neguac, north of Chatham, the road passes by a mixture of old houses and modern bungalows. It's not a wealthy area and there isn't much to see as the road is too far inland for coastal views. In the little town of Tabusintac is a small museum and, down

a few doors, a B&B which is open in the summer months only.

In Tracadie notice the Quebec-style double silver-spired Saint Jean Baptiste church and the *La Boîte à Pain* bakery.

## Shippagan

At the tip of the mainland, Shippagan has a **Marine Centre**, the highlight of which is the aquarium. Examples of many of the species, including seals, found in the Gulf of St Lawrence region are displayed There is also a freshwater exhibit. Other displays show all the electronic equipment used by today's fishing industry and other information related to the fishery.

The centre is also used for ongoing research. It's open every day from 10 am to 6 pm during the summer. The admission price is low.

Adjacent to the centre is a **marina** with a restaurant and gift shop.

A causeway connects **Île Lamèque**, a boggy island where the collection and shipping of peat competes in importance with fishing. **Île Miscou**, reached by a short free ferry ride, is less populated with quiet stretches of sandy beach. At the far tip is a lighthouse.

## Caraquet

The oldest of the Acadian villages, Caraquet was founded in 1757 and is now the main centre of the peninsula's French community. Stretched out more or less along one street, it has one of the oldest churches in the province, Sainte Anne du Bocage. Down at the dock area on Boulevard Saint Pierre Est is a big fish market with fresh, salted, and frozen seafood for sale. Also there is a seafood restaurant.

**Acadian Museum** In the middle of town, with views over the bay from the balcony, is the museum (☎ 727-3269) with a neatly laid out collection of artefacts donated by local residents. Articles include household objects, tools, photographs and a fine wood stove in the corner. What most impressed me was the desk/bed which you can work at all

day and then fold down into a bed when exhaustion strikes. Is there a workaholic in your life? It belonged to a superior at the Caraquet Convent in 1880.

The museum is open daily in summer, closed Sunday in the off-season and has a modest entry fee.

**Other Attractions** Behind the museum is the **Théâtre Populaire d'Acadie** which puts on shows in midsummer. In August there is an Acadian Festival with a variety of events. A few km east out of town near Caraquet Park is the **Sainte Anne du Bocage** religious shrine.

**Places to Stay** Back a bit from the street at 143 Boulevard Saint Pierre Ouest is the *Hotel Paulin* (☎ 727-9981), an old red house with a green roof, by the water. It's open all year, a double is $30 and there is a restaurant for lunches and dinners.

Out close to the shrine is *Maison Touristique Dugas* (☎ 727-3195) with rooms at $34 a double or much less costly campsites. It's at 683 Boulevard Saint Pierre Ouest, also called RR2. Also for camping there is a provincial park close to the shrine.

**Getting There & Away** Transportation around this part of the province is very limited although there is some service. SMT Line buses which cover pretty well the entire province are not seen in this region at all. Instead, a couple of individuals run vans around the Acadian Peninsula from Monday to Friday.

The Gloucester Coach Lines (☎ 395-5812) runs between Tracadie and Bathurst via Shippagan and Caraquet once each way every week day. In Caraquet, the bus stops at the Irving gas station on Boulevard Saint Pierre Ouest. In Bathurst the SMT station is the depot and from here the necessary information can be obtained.

The Tracadie Coach Lines (☎ 395-5639) covers the route between Newcastle/Chatham and Tracadie.

The drivers for both of these coach lines can be reached at these numbers only in the evenings and on weekends – the rest of the time they are out driving the routes.

## Acadian Historic Village (Village Historique Acadien)

Fourteen km west of Caraquet is this major historic museum (☎ 727-3467), set up like a village of old, with 17 buildings and workers in period costumes reflecting life from 1780 to 1880. The museum depicts daily life in such a typically simple post-expulsion Acadian village and makes for an intriguing comparison to the obviously prosperous English King's Landing historic village outside Fredericton.

A good two hours is required to see the site, and you'll want to eat. For that there are two choices: a cafeteria or restaurant, the latter serving Acadian dishes.

The museum is open from 10 am to 6 pm daily in summer. It's on Hwy 11 towards Grande-Anse. An adult ticket is $7 and there is a reduced family or senior rate. A ticket purchased here is also good for a visit to the King's Landing site.

The previously mentioned Gloucester Coach Lines van from Bathurst goes right by the door.

## Grande-Anse

This small town boasts the popular **Pope's Museum**, which houses images of 264 popes from St Peter to the present one, as well as various religious articles. There is also a detailed model of the Basilica and St Peter's Square in Rome.

The *Auberge de l'Anse* (☎ 732-5204) is a B&B on the main route, eight km from the Acadian Historic Village site, or there are a couple of inexpensive motels and a restaurant.

## GRANDE-ANSE TO BATHURST

All along the route from Grande-Anse to Bathurst the scenery is good, with cliffs, views of the bay and across to it to the mountains of the Gaspé Peninsula. There are some beaches (the one at **Maisonnette** is good), picnic sites and, at **Pokeshaw Provincial Park**, coastal erosion features to see. If you're making a return trip to Bathurst, follow this same route both ways, as going around the rest of the peninsula is not worthwhile. Note that many of the small towns may not have either a gas station or a grocery store.

Near **Janeville** there is a restored grindstone mill which can be visited. For an overnight camping place *Chapman's Tent & Trailer Park* (☎ 546-2883), 14 km east of Bathurst on Hwy 11, is highly recommended for its open sites overlooking the beach and ocean.

## BATHURST

Bathurst, yet another industrial town, but based on extremely rich zinc mines as well as lumber and pulp and paper, has little to recommend it to the casual visitor. Really quite small with about 15,000 people, the town is split into three sections: South, East and West Bathurst by the Nepisiguit River and the Bathurst Basin. The principal street is Main St in South Bathurst and this is where a couple of restaurants can be found.

St Peter Ave has the range of food-chain places, gas stations and grocery stores.

On the coast north-east of the harbour at the edge of the city is the **Daly Point Reserve**, a good place for observing birds. There are several trails through the woods or by the salt marsh. An observation tower provides views to the Gaspé Peninsula and along the Acadian Peninsula shoreline.

North of town towards Dalhousie in **Petit-Rocher** on the coast is the **New Brunswick Mining & Mineral Interpretation Centre** (☎ 783-8714). This mining museum has various exhibits, including a deep shaft to descend, and features the local zinc-mining industry. The site is open every day during summer and a tour takes about 45 minutes. It's on Route 134.

## Getting There & Away

You can walk to the old downtown section at the end of Nepisiguit Bay from the VIA Rail station (☎ 546-2659) which is at 690 Thornton Ave on the corner of Queen St. The station is open only when there is a train –

NEW BRUNSWICK

just once a day except on Wednesday, when there aren't any trains. Three times a week the VIA Rail train goes north and south. SMT Bus Lines (☎ 546-4380), at 15 St Peter Ave on the corner of Main St, can be called for information on travelling to the Acadian Peninsula.

## DALHOUSIE

Dalhousie is a small, sort-of-stretched-out but agreeable town on the north-east coast of New Brunswick on the Baie des Chaleurs opposite Quebec. The town's main industry is newsprint, but Dalhousie 'wears it well' and there are a few things to do.

William St and the parallel Adelaide St near the dock are the two main streets with most of the commercial enterprises. On the corner of Adelaide St at 437 George St is the **Restigouche Regional Museum**.

### Organised Tours

Boat tours leave from the town wharf at the foot of Renfrew St.

The cruise boat *Chaleur Phantom* departs from here on scenic cruises of either the bay or along the Restigouche River. Various coastal rock formations can be seen as well as sea birds and some historic sites. Other trips offer fishing opportunities at reasonable rates. Two km east from the ferry dock at the end of Victoria St is **Inch Arran Park** right on the water with camping sites, a swimming pool, the tourist office, the beach and fine views across the bay.

Between Dalhousie and Campbellton, Hwy 134 offers good views of the bay and the very green, lumpy hills of the Gaspé Peninsula's south shore. All along the Baie des Chaleurs there are lots of camping spots and motels.

### Getting There & Away

You can take a car ferry from across the bay to Miguasha, Quebec. The ferry, which leaves every hour on the hour from 9 am to 9 pm about 70 km off the driving trip around the bay. The trip takes about 15 minutes and costs $12 with a car – good if you're heading for the Gaspé Peninsula. It

runs from the end of June to sometime in September.

## CAMPBELLTON

Campbellton, on the Quebec border, is in the midst of a scenic area at the edge of the Restigouche Highlands. The Baie des Chaleurs is on one side and green, rolling irregularly shaped hills seem to encase the town on the remaining sides. Across the border is Matapédia and Hwy 132 leading to Mont Joli, 148 km into Quebec.

The last naval battle of the Seven Years' War was fought in the waters just off the coast here in 1760.

Main streets in this town of about 10,000 residents are Water St and Roseberry St, around which the commercial centre is clustered. Campbellton is truly a bilingual town with store cashiers saying everything in both French and English.

Nearby, **Sugarloaf Mountain**, rising nearly 400 metres above sea level and dominating the skyline, is the principal attraction and provides excellent views of the town and part of the Restigouche River. It looks remarkably like its namesake in Rio. From the base, it's a half-hour walk to the top; another trail leads around the bottom. From the tourist office a chairlift runs up another, lower nearby mountain.

There's camping in **Sugarloaf Park** and skiing in winter. The tourist office also has a small museum with interesting exhibits on the Atlantic salmon.

About 10 km west of town towards Matapédia is **Morrisey Rock**, another place for a good view of the scenic river area.

The **Restigouche River**, named by the Micmacs, is excellent for salmon fishing. It runs south-west from Campbellton. All along the river there are fishing camps, clubs, supply stores and some fishing pools (or holes) open to the public.

### Places to Stay

There is little to see or do in town and no reason to stay. But if you need accommodation there are a few places to choose from. There is an HI member, the *Campbellton Lighthouse Hostel* (☎ 753-7044), at 1 Ritchie St in the central waterfront district along the Restigouche River. It's open from early June to September. There are only 20 beds in this converted lighthouse, so calling ahead to check availability is advisable, but generally space should not be a problem.

The *Caspian Motel* (☎ 753-7606), on Duke St, is a good choice if you'd like to be right in the centre of town. There are several other places to stay; check along Roseberry St. Between here and Dalhousie on Hwy 134 are numerous motels and campgrounds, many with attractive seaside locations. Others are found on Hwy 134 West. *Sanfar Cottages* (☎ 753-4287) is west of town at Tide Head on Route 134. There are 12 cabins here, at $38 for two people, and a light breakfast is included.

As mentioned above, there is camping at Sugarloaf Provincial Park on Route 270, off Hwy 11.

### Places to Eat
In the centre is *Dixie Lee*, a fried-chicken outlet commonly seen around the province. An alternative is *Pizza Delight*. Better restaurants will offer salmon and, in spring,

another local delicacy, fiddleheads – a wild and very tasty green.

### Getting There & Away
The bus station or rather the SMT bus stop is at the Pik-Quik variety store on Water St near Prince William St. The VIA Rail station is conveniently central on Roseberry St. There are three trains a week going south to Moncton and Halifax and three heading the other way to Montreal.

### MT CARLETON PROVINCIAL PARK
Access to Mt Carleton Provincial Park (☎ 551-1377), the largest and wildest in the province, is from **Five Fingers**, a town south-west of Campbellton along the Restigouche River. The park is roughly 130 km south of Campbellton.

The central northern section of the province known as the **Restigouche Highlands** is a mountainous, river-crossed, largely uninhabited region. From the town of **Kedgwick** a superb 85-km canoe trip for a couple of days can be taken along the Restigouche River to Campbellton. The Mt Carleton Provincial Park, surrounded by a large tract of unspoiled land used only by loggers, encloses Mt Carleton (820 metres), one of Atlantic Canada's highest mountains. There is little development in the park and

---

**Atlantic Salmon**
The Atlantic Salmon of Eastern Canada are renowned as a sport fish and prized at the table for their delicate, refined flavour. They are also well known for their spectacular leaping during the journey up stream to spawn. In Canada, they are found in rivers from Ungava Bay in the north southward along the coast of Labrador and Newfoundland to the eastern seaboard of New Brunswick. To anglers, the Restigouche and Miramichi rivers are two of the most revered places. There are also some landlocked Atlantic salmon found in lakes around the Maritimes and Quebec. The species is part of the Salmonidae family which includes the well-known Pacific salmon, char, trout and whitefish.

Eggs are hatched in fresh water. After three years, the young salmon, known as smolts, migrate to the ocean. Here they spend anywhere from a year or three growing rapidly. Many from the New Brunswick waters travel as far as Greenland. After this period, the salmon return to their natal river or stream to spawn. Unlike their Pacific-coast cousins, the Atlantic salmon do not die after spawning but return to the ocean to begin the cycle again.

Spawning occurs in October and November although the 'early run' to the fresh water rivers takes place in spring or summer. The stragglers, arriving towards the end of summer or early autumn, make up the 'late run'. It is during these upstream migrations that the rivers attract anglers and spectators in appreciable numbers. ■

gas and groceries are not available, but there are maintained hiking trails and camping areas. Canoe rentals are available at Riley Brook and Nictau.

# Saint John River Valley

The Saint John River which has been likened to the Rhine begins in Maine, USA, on the north-western corner of New Brunswick and flows south for over 700 km before entering the Bay of Fundy at Saint John.

It winds along the western border of the province past forests and beautiful lush farmland, through Fredericton between tree-lined banks, and then around rolling hills to the bay. The valley that protects it is one of the most scenic places in the province. It's particularly picturesque and gentle from just north of Saint John to near Woodstock.

There are bridges and ferries across the river at various points. The Trans Canada, Hwy 2, follows the river up to Edmundston and then crosses into Quebec. In earlier days the river was the highway for the local Native Indians.

Because of its soft, eye-pleasing landscape and because the main highway connecting the Atlantic Provinces with central Canada runs along the river, not surprisingly, it is a busy route in summer. So much so that accommodation, which is limited at the best of times, can be difficult to find in July and August. It is advisable to stop early or use the tourist office toll-free reservation service to book ahead. In the off-peak season there is no problem at all.

On one trip south I started looking at dusk in the Edmundston area and was told everything was booked down the road as far as Woodstock. Eventually I and a group of weary travellers of every description were found overpriced rooms in the basement of an old folk's home in Grand Falls.

**Mark Lightbody**

Aside from the bigger centres, some small towns along the route have a B&B or two. There are also campgrounds along the way.

There is a choice of two routes, the quicker Trans Canada Hwy mostly on the west side of the river, or Hwy 105 on the east. The slower route is not any more scenic but does go right through many of the smaller villages.

## WOODSTOCK

A small town set in a rich farming area, Woodstock acts as a tourist crossroad. The Trans Canada Hwy goes through town, as does the road to Maine, USA. Hwy 95 to Bangor, Maine, and then Hwy 2 is an alternative and shorter route to Montreal than going north through Edmundston and then along the St Lawrence River. Main St through Woodstock has some fine, old large Maritime houses.

There is a bluegrass music festival held in town in summer.

### Places to Stay & Eat

For spending the night, there is a bit of choice here and prices aren't bad. At 133 Chapel St is the *Queen Victoria B&B* (☎ 328-8382) for adults only at singles/doubles $45/50.

Away from the centre but with a quiet, country location is the *Froelich's Swiss Chalet B&B* (☎ 328-6751). The house looks as though it might have been lifted from the Alps. A double is $39 and includes breakfast. It's about 15 km from town on Route 105, nine km south of the Grafton Bridge. Among the motels there's the *Motel Haven* (☎ 272-2100) on Route 2 with singles/doubles for $28/30.

On the north side of town is the *Hometown* (you can't miss it), a good spot for a meal.

## HARTLAND

Hartland is an attractive little town with a nice setting and, though there is not much else to see, it does have the grand-daddy of New Brunswick's many wooden covered bridges, now considered historic sites. This bridge at 400 metres long is the longest in the world. There are 74 of these bridges dotted around the province; the tourist office has a complete listing if you're interested. The bridges were covered to protect the timber beams used in the construction. With such protection from rain and sun, a bridge lasts about 80 years. They are generally high and wide because cartloads of hay pulled by horses had to pass through. Nearly all of the bridges that remain are on secondary or smaller roads.

Halfway between here and Grand Falls is a provincial park at Kilburn.

### Places to Stay & Eat

The *Ja-Se-Le Motel* (☎ 375-4419) (named with letters from the names of the original owner's daughters), north of town, is the only local motel. It's average-priced and has a pretty good restaurant serving mainly German food, but you can get the standard Canadian breakfast of eggs, bacon and toast.

### GRAND FALLS

A town with 7000 residents, Grand Falls consists essentially of one main street and the falls which make it an interesting short stop.

In a park in town, the falls drop about 25 metres and have carved out a gorge 1.5 km long with walls as high as 70 metres. At the site is an interpretive building and several trails, with lookout points, which lead along the gorge. Entrance to the park is $2 per adult and there are picnic tables, a restaurant and a place to swim.

The falls are best in spring or after a heavy rain. In summer, much of the water is diverted for generating hydroelectricity. The dam for this also takes away from the rugged beauty the site once would have had. The area at the bottom of the gorge reached by a staircase is more scenic than the falls themselves and permits a glimpse of how the pre-development days would have looked.

The town celebrates its primary resource, the potato, in a festival each year around 1 July.

### Places to Stay & Eat

At 142 Main St is the *Maple Tourist Home* (☎ 473-1763), a B&B. Along the highway on both sides of town are several motels and camping is possible near the falls.

For something to munch there are a couple of quick places down the main street, Broadway. *Bob's Deli* has salads and baked goods. The *Patricus* south of town on the Trans Canada Hwy is good for breakfast. The *Chinese Village* restaurant in town is not recommended.

### AROUND GRAND FALLS

East of Grand Falls around the farming community of New Denmark is the largest Danish population in North America. In the middle of July there's a festival celebrating all things Danish. In New Denmark is a restaurant which serves Danish foods all year.

Hwy 108, the Plaster Rock Hwy, cuts across the province to the east coast. The highway sluices through forest for nearly its entirety. Animals such as deer and moose are commonly seen on or beside the road – take care at night. There are some camping spots along the way.

### SAINT LÉONARD

As the name suggests, Saint Léonard is primarily a French town, like many in this region. Some are old Acadian settlements although the Acadian descendants are more concentrated in the north-east of the province.

In Saint Léonard is the Madawaska Weavers group, formed in 1939 and still using hand looms to make fabric for items such as ponchos and scarves. The centre at 739 Main St can be visited.

From here, Hwy 17 runs north-east through the dense forests of northern New Brunswick. Near Saint Quentin, Hwy 180 branches off eastwards and leads to Mt Carleton Provincial Park.

### EDMUNDSTON

If you're coming from Quebec there's a good chance this'll be the first town in the Maritimes you get a look at, as the border is only about 20 km away. At the border is a large, helpful tourist office. From here it is three hours' drive to Fredericton. Maine is just across the river and there is an international

**NEW BRUNSWICK**

bridge on Dupont St at the south end of town not far from City Hall.

Edmundston is an industrial pulp and paper centre with numerous mills in and around town. It's split pretty well in half by the Madawaska River and the old central district on the west side of the river is built around some low hills which give it a little character.

The population of about 13,000 is 85% French-speaking. Nearly all of them, like most of New Brunswick's French, speak English.

Where there are French people there are impressive churches and cathedrals, and Edmundston is no exception. Their cathedral here is the Roman Catholic Cathedral of the Immaculate Conception, quite an impressive sight up on a hill at the end of Church St near the centre of town.

The main intersection downtown is that of Church St and Canada Rd. Within a couple of blocks of this corner are many of the shops, a couple of restaurants, City Hall plus an indoor shopping mall. Victoria St, between the highway and this central section, is also a busy commercial street.

Clustered around exit 18 from the highway is the tourist office, a shopping mall, some fast-food restaurants, a Canadian Tire store (hardware, sports and automotive parts) and a nearby motel.

There is no inner-city bus service so you'll have to do some walking here, but the distances are not great.

The local citizens have a somewhat whimsical notion of Edmundston as the capital of a fictitious country known as Madawaska whose inhabitants are known as Brayons. Evidently this traditional community-uniting concept has historical origins in a period during the late 1700s when the region existed in a sort of political vacuum between the border-bickering of the American and British governments.

### Information
The local tourist office (☎ 735-2747) is in the museum building on the corner of Boulevard Pichette parallel to (and beside) the Trans Canada Hwy and Boulevard Hébert, the street which leads into the centre.

### Madawaska Museum
At 195 Boulevard Hébert on the corner of Boulevard Pichette by the Trans Canada Hwy, across from a shopping centre, is the Madawaska Museum (☎ 737-5064) which outlines the human history of the area from the time of the original Maliseet (Malecite) Indians through colonial times to the present. The museum also has displays on local industries such as the timber trade. It's open daily in summer, but closed on Monday during the rest of the year. There's a nominal admission fee.

### Festivals
Each year on the nine days preceding the first Monday in August is the 'Foires' Festival, which celebrates the physically nonexistent republic of Madawaska. The local people with various national ancestries term themselves Brayons, the inhabitants of Madawaska. There are cultural, social and sporting activities as well as some good traditional Brayon cooking to sample.

### Places to Stay
On Power Rd, in the north-west section of the city just off Hwy 2, are a couple of cheap tourist homes open through the summer months only.

The *Modern Tourist Home* (☎ 739-5236), 224 Power Rd, charges singles/doubles $20/22. The *City View* (☎ 739-9058), at No 226 next door, has five rooms for $20/22 singles/doubles.

*Le Fief* (☎ 735-0400), at 87 Church St, is a central B&B open all year. The four rooms tend to fill up in midsummer. The double rate of $55 includes a full breakfast.

There are also plenty of motels around town. *La Roma* (☎ 735-3305), about 1.5 km south of town, look for the sign along the highway, charges $45 a double and there are larger family rooms available. *Motel Le Brayon* (☎ 263-5656), also south but closer to St Basil, is new.

More expensive, the *Wandlyn Inn* (☎ 800-

561-0000, for toll-free calling and reservations) is relatively good value with a sauna, pool and restaurant. Singles/doubles are $60/70. It's located at 919 Canada Rd, north of the city and visible from the Trans Canada Hwy. There are several other places in this busy border stopover town and also a couple of provincial parks within 15 km.

## Places to Eat

The central downtown area has very few restaurants. The *Bel Air*, with the sign that can't be missed, is on the corner of Victoria St and Boulevard Hébert on the way into the centre from the highway. It's been here for 36 years, is open 24 hours a day, and has become a city landmark. The extensive menu offers Italian, Chinese, seafood or basic Canadian fare to choose from. The barbecue chicken is good. If you're wallet is thin, be careful not to enter the building at the wrong end, for a new expensive seafood restaurant has opened right next door!

There are also a couple of Chinese places along Victoria St. *Pizza Delight* has a large outlet at 180 Boulevard Hébert at exit 18 just off the Trans Canada Hwy.

The locals flock to *Belzile Restaurant*

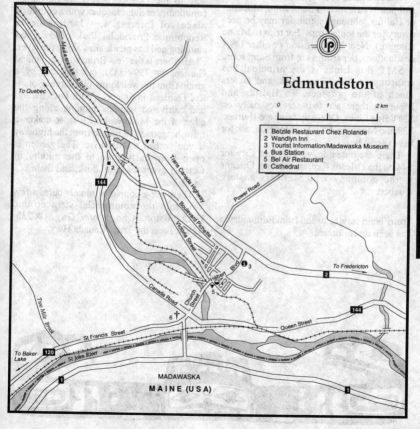

## Edmundston

0    1    2 km

1 Belzile Restaurant Chez Rolande
2 Wandlyn Inn
3 Tourist Information/Madawaska Museum
4 Bus Station
5 Bel Air Restaurant
6 Cathedral

**NEW BRUNSWICK**

*Chez Rolande*, a 10-minute drive from the centre at 815 Victoria St, for sandwiches, burgers etc and a couple of French Canadian specialties, poutine (fries topped with melted cheese curds and gravy) and their 'famous' sugar pies.

### Getting There & Away

**Bus** The SMT terminal (☎ 739-8309) is across the street from the Bel Air restaurant, at 169 Victoria St near the corner of Boulevard Hébert at the bridge. It's a little hard to find and not clearly visible from the restaurant, but it is there around the back.

You can catch buses here for Quebec City and points east such as Saint John, Moncton or Halifax, although a transfer may be necessary for the longer trips. For trips to Maine (Bangor), New York, Boston or other USA destinations, departures are from Saint John.

SMT Bus Lines is the principal bus company in New Brunswick and covers much of the province. To Halifax and Moncton there are two services daily on SMT Bus Lines. One-way fares are Halifax, $89 and Moncton, $57. For Moncton, ask for the express bus.

There are buses daily to Quebec City for $44 on the Orleans Express bus line. Orleans is the company which covers eastern Quebec.

**Train** Train service to and from Edmundston has been discontinued.

**Car** Heading to Quebec there is an alternative to the main route, the Trans Canada Hwy towards Cabano, Quebec and on to Rivière-du-Loup. Route 120 leads west out of town and then heads north through Baker Lake (Lac Baker) before reaching the Quebec border and going on to the St Lawrence River. In the interests of thoroughness and diversity I used this route on one trip and unreservedly class it as a lousy choice – it's slow, boring and without redeeming features along its entirety.

### SAINT JACQUES

North of Edmundston seven km, about half-way to the Quebec border, is the small community of Saint Jacques with a couple of places of interest. Les Jardins de la Republique Provincial Park offers good camping and has picnic sites along the river.

Also here is the New Brunswick Botanical Gardens (☎ 739-6335), put together by a group from the well known Montreal Botanical Gardens in Quebec. With both natural and cultivated sections running along the edge of the Madawaska River, it makes a refreshing, tranquil respite from the highway if you've had a long drive. The garden is open from early June to the middle of October every day until dusk, and there is a snack bar.

There are a couple of motels here, a few km from the commercial strip around Edmundston. One, *Motel Guy* (☎ 735-4253), is on the Trans Canada Hwy.

# Quebec

Entered Confederation: 1 July 1867
Area: 1,540,687 sq km
Population: 6,895,963
Provincial Capital: Quebec City

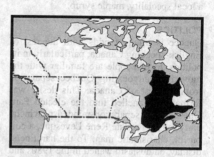

'Kebec', an Algonkian Indian word meaning 'where the river narrows' is the heart of French Canada. Explorer Samuel de Champlain of France first heard and recorded the word when he founded Quebec City in 1608. Jacques Cartier, another explorer, had landed here in 1534 (the 450th anniversary of the landing was celebrated in 1984) when the settlement was known as Stadacone. The region along the St Lawrence River from Ontario to Quebec City was at the time controlled by the Mohawks of the Iroquois Confederacy. North of and around Quebec City, the Montagnais were the principal Native group. Further north was and is Cree land and beyond that the Labrador Eskimo, Naskapi and Inuit peoples are dominant. The Montagnais and Naskapi are also known as Innu. Around the southern portion of the Gaspé Peninsula, the Micmacs, found around much of the Atlantic Provinces, were the principal aboriginal group and they still live in the region.

The province is Canada's biggest, and the now largely French population makes it quite different from other parts of North America. This is reflected in various aspects of life here including architecture, music, food and religion. About 90% of the population is Roman Catholic, though the Church's influence has declined sharply in recent decades.

Visitors will soon realise that Quebec is unlike English Canada and that the differences are not only in language. Even Montreal (Montréal, pronounced 'mor-eh-al'), where English is still widely used, has a decidedly different air to other Canadian cities, while historic Quebec City is noticeably European. But much of the beauty and appeal of the province lies outside these two intriguing population centres.

## GEOGRAPHY & CLIMATE

The Laurentian Mountains are a year-round resort. The L'Estrie or the Eastern Townships south of Montreal, settled by Loyalists, is a gentle, quiet region of farms, lakes and inns. The Gaspé region in the east with its rugged shoreline scenery is one of the overlooked areas of the country. The northern forests with their huge parks offer some excellent and accessible wilderness. Much of the far north is only now being developed. The provincial Ministry of Tourism has useful information booklets covering each of its regions.

The St Lawrence River (Fleuve Saint-Laurent) provides a link between the Great Lakes and the Atlantic Ocean, serving major Canadian and US ports. Along the river, where most visitors will go, summers can be hot and winters are always cold. Snow can be many metres deep. Generally, the further east and north you go, the colder it gets.

## ECONOMY

Quebec's wealth has long been as much potential as actual. Despite abundant natural resources, manufacturing is the prime industry. There are vast amounts of hydroelectric power and the province is the main paper

QUEBEC

producer in North America. Roughly half the province is forest. Other important industries are aluminium, minerals, timber, apples and a local speciality, maple syrup.

## POLITICS

Quebec is often at odds with the rest of English-speaking Canada, particularly in its politics. Most people are familiar with the movement advocating Quebec separation from the rest of Canada. This desire was formally channelled into the elected Parti Québecois, a separation-minded provincial party led by the late René Lévesque, a colourful, charismatic man. To the hardliners' dismay, enthusiasm waned in the 1980s and for some years separation was more or less a dead issue, deemed neither practical nor realistic.

Now in the 1990s, Quebec's leaving Canada in one form or another seems a serious possibility. This recent twist is in part due to Quebec's economic confidence which was in the doldrums for a number of years. But more so it is due to a sense that Quebec's differences and desires are neither understood nor appreciated by the rest of the country. Recent wrangling over constitutional matters and the failure of the Meech Lake Accord have brought these issues and sentiments to critical debate across Canada.

The federal election of October 1993 saw the Bloc Québecois party, which advocates separation, not only easily dominate but also become the official opposition in Ottawa. Speculation is that a provincial referendum on the matter will take place along with the next provincial election. Currently, the

---

### Quebec's Population Crunch or Who's Making Babies?

The dominant issue in Quebec and the one that fuels all the talk of independence is the threat, real or perceived, of cultural assimilation with and submersion into English North America. In this context the primary concern is the preservation, promotion and continuation of the all-critical component of any groups' cultural identity – their language. Hence we have the controversial provincial language laws meant to ensure the use of French in various aspects of life such as economic activity, education, etc.

Perhaps the most significant factor advancing the possibility of cultural decline (or extinction say some panicky demographers) is the little-discussed but inescapable fact of Quebec's disastrously low birth rates. With a fertility rate of 1.5 among women of childbearing age, it is one of the lowest in the Western world. A rate of 2.1 is considered necessary for replacing the existing population.

For generations, starting with colonisation in the 1500 and 1600s, Roman Catholic Quebec was synonymous with huge families. Couples with 10, 12, and even more children were by no means rare. Right up until the 1950s, French families of five and six kids were more or less the norm.

The changes occurring since then throughout the Western world have had a great impact on the women of Quebec. Those of child-rearing age in Quebec have been more inclined to want to shed the past with its dominance by the Church in things moral and by the English in things political and economic. Economic changes, the move to a less rural society, and the general loosening of traditional lifestyle constraints have also had their effect. Marriage rates dropped and births declined dramatically with the swing towards the search for independence and freedom, power and control, and personal satisfaction.

The provincial government has reacted in a number of ways to the alarming numbers. Quebec now has some generous financial packages including tax incentives and cash payments for couples considering children. The more children, the better the dollars become. There is large-scale luring of emigrants from French-speaking countries. It is quickly being discovered that French-speaking or not, people from nations as diverse as Senegal in West Africa, Vietnam in Asia and Haiti in the Caribbean instant Qubecoises do not make.

With a population of some five and a half million, French Quebec is not going to disappear overnight in any case. With a combina tion of schemes and plans and, most importantly, another societal attitudinal shift, the situation will probably resolve itself. It's just that it had best hurry up. ∎

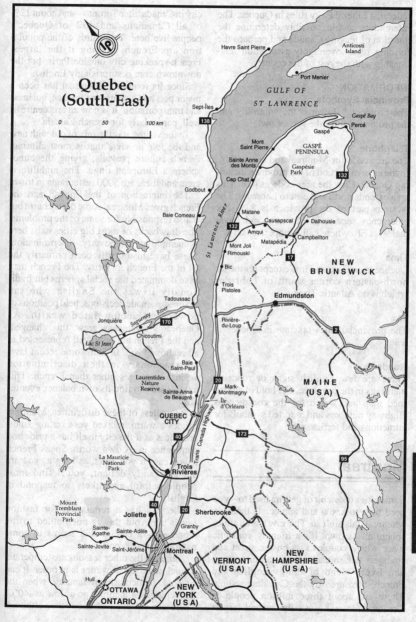

# Quebec
## (South-East)

0    50    100 km

**GULF OF
ST LAWRENCE**

Anticosti
Island

Havre Saint Pierre

Port Menier

Sept-Îles

Gaspé Bay

Gaspé    Percé

138

Mont
Saint Pierre    **GASPÉ
PENINSULA**

Sainte Anne
des Monts    Gaspésie
Park

Godbout    Cap Chat    132

Baie Comeau    Matane

Causapscal    Dalhousie

Amqui

Mont Joli    Matapédia    Campbellton

Rimouski    132    17    **NEW
BRUNSWICK**

Bic

Trois
Pistoles    Edmundston

Tadoussac

Rivière-
du-Loup

Jonquière    Saguenay River    170    2

Chicoutimi

Lac St Jean

Baie
Saint-Paul    **MAINE
(USA)**

Laurentides
Nature
Reserve    20

Sainte-Anne
de Beaupré    Mark-
Montmagny

Île
d'Orléans

**QUEBEC
CITY**    173

40

95

La Mauricie
National Park    Trois
Rivières

Mount
Tremblant
Provincial
Park    40    20

Joliette    Sherbrooke

Sainte-    Granby
Agathe    Sainte-Adèle

Sainte-Jovite    Saint-Jérôme    Montreal

Hull    **VERMONT
(USA)**    **NEW
HAMPSHIRE
(USA)**

OTTAWA

ONTARIO    **NEW
YORK
(USA)**

St Lawrence River

Trans Canada Highway

**QUEBEC**

federalist Liberal Party rules in Quebec. The referendum would possibly determine the question of leaving Canada and perhaps the forming of a sovereignty-association relationship with the rest of the country.

## INFORMATION
### Provincial Symbols

The provincial flower is the white lily and the provincial bird, the snowy owl.

### Telephone

The area code for Montreal and area is 514. In the eastern portion of the province including Quebec City, the area code is 418. This area extends north and east to Labrador. The western part of the province is 819. For emergency service in Montreal and Laval dial 911. Elsewhere call the operator on 0.

### Time

Quebec is on Eastern Time except for the far north-eastern corner south of Labrador which is on Atlantic Time.

### Tax

The provincial sales tax rate in Quebec is 8%.

### Roads

There are few English signs or roadside markings in the province. Get hold of a good road map and watch for the conspicuous Highway numbers and assorted symbols for attractions and ferries, etc.

# Montreal

Some cities take a bit of getting used to – you need time to know and appreciate them. In Montreal, this ain't so. This city has an atmosphere all its own. It's a friendly, romantic place where couples kiss on the street and strangers talk to each other – an interesting and lively blend of things English and French, flavoured by the Canadian setting. There are about three million people in Greater Montreal – it's the second largest

city in Canada after Toronto – and about 12% of all Canadians and 40% of Quebec's people live here. Two-thirds of the population are French, making it the largest French-speaking city outside Paris, but the downtown core is surprisingly English.

Since its founding, Montreal has been a major port and a centre for finance, business and transportation. It is now an arts centre as well, particularly for French Canada.

To the visitor, it is the mix of old with new and the *joie de vivre* that is most alluring. French culture prevails, giving the atmosphere a European tinge. The nightlife is great and there are 5000 restaurants in town.

The interaction of the English and the French gives Montreal some of its charm but is also responsible for some of the problems. The drawbacks of most big cities exist here – unemployment, poverty, discrimination. These have historically been primarily the lot of the French majority. The French may have dominated the social spheres but traditionally it was the English who ran businesses, made decisions, held positions of power and accumulated wealth. As Québecois awareness grew, this changed, and the French are now well represented in all realms of life. In fact, some recent laws are reactionary in their discrimination against languages other than French. This too, is likely to find its own balance eventually.

Regardless of these difficulties, Montreal exudes a warm, relaxed yet exciting ambience. It is as if the city itself has a pride and confidence in its own worth. Speak French if you can. If you can't, as long as you are not arrogantly defiant, you'll find most people helpful and likely to respond in English.

The city has a reputation for fashion savoir-faire, but this is not limited to the moneyed – a certain flair seems to come naturally to everyone.

Although the other seasons are temperate, a quick word about winter is in order. It can be cold, particularly in January, when the temperatures sometimes go as low as -40°C. There can be piles of snow too, although

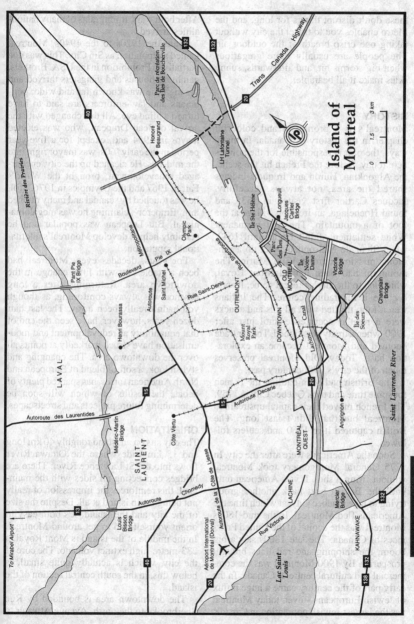

Island of Montreal

0   1.5   3 km

these don't disrupt things for long, and the Métro enables you to travel the city without taking one crisp breath of the outdoor air. The people are usually more gregarious when big storms hit, and afterwards, sunny skies make it all bearable.

## HISTORY

Montreal's is a prominent and colourful chapter in the history of Canada. In many ways, the past is responsible for the politics here today. Before the French hit the scene, the Algonkian, Huron and Iroquois Indians shared the area, not always peacefully. Jacques Cartier first visited in 1535 and found Hochelaga, an Iroquois village at the foot of a mountain. The first permanent White settlement didn't begin until 1642, when Sieur de Maisonneuve set up a religious mission named Ville Marie. The mountain had been named Mont Royal, which led to the city's present name. It soon became a fur-trading centre. The Indians weren't too thrilled with all this and attacks were a regular occurrence until just after 1700, when a treaty was signed. The fur trade boomed and Montreal became an exploration base. Today, Old Montreal preserves much of the city's 17th-century past.

The British had been battling the French for some time and took Quebec City in 1759. The French moved their capital upstream to Montreal but that didn't last long. The British captured it in 1760 and settlers followed.

Soon the Americans were after the city. In 1775 General Montgomery took Montreal without firing a shot. It was American only until the British beat back another group trying to take Quebec City, at which time the Americans fled Montreal. In the mid-1800s Montreal was the capital of the United Provinces of Canada. The late 1800s saw a big boom; the shipping and rail lines brought prosperity. By 1900 Montreal was the commercial and cultural centre of Canada. In the early part of the century came a huge influx of Jewish Europeans – even today Montreal has the largest Jewish population in Canada.

After both wars, immigrants of many nationalities arrived.

From the 1920s to the 1940s, Montreal gained a reputation as Sin City. This was due partially to Prohibition in the USA. Brothels, gambling houses and gangsters thrived and the nightlife was known far and wide; politicians and law-enforcers are said to have turned a blind eye. All this changed with the arrival of Jean Drapeau, who was elected mayor in 1954 and, except for a five-year period in the early '60s, was mayor right into the mid-80s. He cleaned up the city, encouraged redevelopment, brought the World's Fair in 1967 and the Olympics in 1976. Still, he was touched by scandal and many dubbed him 'Emperor', claiming he was megalomaniacal. But Drapeau was popular and he certainly helped develop Montreal's international reputation.

For years, decades even, Montreal had been a stable city with little change in the downtown area. Returning after a long absence was always comforting, as though you hadn't really been away. The last half dozen years, however, have seen the end of that equanimity as redevelopment and modernisation have struck markedly at points all over the downtown area. The changing and stylish look, a sort of blend of European and North American forms, has sparked plenty of debate the results of which will soon be determining future projects and streetscapes.

## ORIENTATION

The city sits on an island roughly 40 km long and 15 km wide where the Ottawa River flows into the St Lawrence River. There are bridges connecting all sides with the mainland; this reinforces the impression of really not being on an island at all. Despite the size of the city and the island, it's both easy to orient yourself and to get around Montreal. In the middle of the island is Mont Royal, a 233-metre-high extinct volcano. The core of the city, which is actually quite small, is below this, in the south central section of the island.

The downtown area is bounded by Rue Sherbrooke to the north, Avenue Atwater to the west, Rue Saint Antoine to the south and Boulevard Saint Laurent to the east. This is the busy area of skyscrapers, shops, restaurants, offices and luxury hotels.

The small park, **Square Dorchester** (formerly Dominion Square, and often still called that), marks the centre of downtown. It's a peaceful spot surrounded by some new and many old buildings, some with green oxidised copper roofs.

The tourist office is on the north side of Square Dorchester along with the horse-drawn carriages, known as *calèches*, which can be taken around parts of town or up the mountain. On the south-west corner is Windsor Station, the venerable Canadian Pacific (CP) railway terminal. To the south is the top-end CP hotel, Château Champlain, where you probably won't be staying. On the east side is the stone Sun Life Insurance building.

The Cathedral of Montreal (Marie-Reine-du-Monde Cathédrale, or Mary Queen of the World Cathedral) with its pastel, gilt-trimmed interior is on the corner of Boulevard René Lévesque (formerly Dorchester Boulevard) and Rue de la Cathédrale to the east of the square.

Just to the east of the cathedral is the Queen Elizabeth Hotel below which is the CN-VIA Rail Central Station from where most passenger trains now depart. South, down the hill from the square on Rue Peel, is the main post office (☎ 846-5390) at 1025 Saint Jacques St Ouest. The postal code for sending mail to the post office is H3C 1G0.

North, a block up Rue Peel from the square, is Rue Sainte Catherine, the principal east-west artery. This is the main shopping street where the department stores and many cinemas are. It's one-way only, for eastbound cars.

North of Rue Sainte Catherine is Boulevard de Maisonneuve and then Rue Sherbrooke, the two other main east-west streets. All three run a long way in each direction.

At 2025 Rue Peel is the Canadian Guild of Crafts which has interesting Native Indian, Inuit and Québecois crafts.

If you keep walking uphill on Rue Peel for a number of blocks you'll finally come to Avenue des Pins, across which is the edge of Parc du Mont Royal. You'll see some steps. At the top is an excellent view of the city, the river and the surroundings to the south – great day or night. This is the city's largest park and is pleasant to stroll in on a warm day. The cross, on top and lit at night, is a city symbol.

Other good vantage points for views over the city are the Olympic Stadium Tower (charging an admission fee), the bar at the top of the Château Champlain hotel and the restaurant on top of the Radisson Hotel, 777 Rue University. There are also pretty good views from St Joseph's Oratory and from various points along the road around Mont Royal.

At 705 Rue Sainte Catherine Ouest by the corner of Rue University, is one of the city's largest shopping complexes, the new and modern showpiece, the Eaton Centre – almost (I hate to say it) an attraction in its own right. The Promenade de la Cathédrale is an underground portion of the complex which runs beneath a church! The old and new houses of worship?

Avenue McGill College, north of Rue Sainte Catherine was once a narrow student ghetto but has recently (and controversially) been opened up and now presents an imposing boulevard edged with some of the city's newest corporate architecture. Structures aside, the channel of space leading from the city's main street to the campus of McGill University and beyond to the mountain is certainly impressive. A number of statues and sculptures including the eye-catching 'Illuminated Crowd' are found along the avenue. Inside the Place Montreal Trust building, along Avenue McGill College, are five levels of shopping lit by windows.

The area downtown and west to Loyola Campus on Rue Sherbrooke is pretty much English and residential. Westmount at the foot of the mountain is one of the city's wealthiest and most prestigious districts.

Running north and south of Rue Sainte Catherine west of Rue Peel are Rue Bishop,

Rue Crescent and Rue de la Montagne – the centre of one of the nightlife areas. There are many restaurants, cafés and discos here. The two big cafés on Boulevard de Maisonneuve between Rue de la Montagne and Rue Crescent are a good place to get a feel for the area.

Below and parallel to Rue Sainte Catherine is Boulevard René Lévesque, a wide street known for its high buildings. Place Ville Marie (sometimes referred to as the PVM) on the corner of Rue University across from the Queen Elizabeth Hotel, is one of the city's best known buildings. It's in the shape of a cross and is another landmark.

East along Rue Sainte Catherine you'll see Phillips Square, a meeting place where guitarists busk and bask. Further east, just past de Bleury, is Place des Arts, a complex for the performing arts. A few more blocks east is Boulevard Saint Laurent (St Lawrence Blvd) known as **The Main**. This is one of the city's best known streets, with an interesting history and ethnic make-up, and lots of inexpensive restaurants. It is long and changes complexion in different areas but is always interesting and lively and gets relatively few tourists.

To the east of Boulevard Saint Laurent, Rue Sainte Catherine Ouest becomes Rue Sainte Catherine Est. East of Saint Laurent, streets are given the Est (East) designation, west of Saint Laurent they include the Ouest (West) designation in their name. All streets, in fact, are divided in this way. East of Boulevard Saint Laurent the area has traditionally been predominantly French and it remains this way.

About 10 blocks east (you can get a bus) is **Saint Denis**, which has been transformed into a Paris-style café district. Saint Denis was originally an all-student area, but more expensive establishments are moving in. However, there is still something for everyone. Little bars, some with jazz, abound. French is the tongue spoken here but don't let that deter you – it's a good chance to practise.

From Saint Denis east along Rue Sainte Catherine to Rue Papineau is Montreal's developing gay town. New restaurants and

| 1 | Lookout |
| 2 | Montreal International Hostel |
| 3 | McGill University |
| 4 | Museum of Fine Arts |
| 5 | McCord Museum |
| 6 | Canadian Centre for Architecture |
| 7 | Tourist Office/Infotouriste |
| 8 | Square Dorchester |
| 9 | Place Ville Marie |
| 10 | Place Phillips |
| 11 | Place des Arts/Contemporary Art Gallery |
| 12 | Bus Terminal |
| 13 | Place du Canada |
| 14 | Mary Queen of the World Cathedral |
| 15 | Central Station (VIA) |
| 16 | Chinatown |
| 17 | Windsor Station |
| 19 | Main Post Office |
| 18 | Place Banaventure |
| 20 | Dow Planetarium |

stores have opened in this long neglected part of town and a number of bars and nightclubs catering to homosexuals and lesbians can be found in the district. There have been some incidents of bashing in the neighbourhood; just don't go wandering through parks alone in the middle of the night.

Two blocks east of Saint Denis is Rue Berri. Terminus Voyageur, the city's main bus station with US and Canadian destinations is a block north on Rue Berri at Boulevard de Maisonneuve. A major transfer point of the Métro system, the Berri-UQAM station is also here and city buses roll in all directions from this subway stop.

Old Montreal is south-east of the downtown area; both Boulevard Saint Laurent and Rue Saint Denis lead into it.

There is a small but determined Chinese community clustered along Rue de la Gauchetière between Rue Saint Urbain and Boulevard Saint Laurent. Rue de la Gauchetière runs east-west past the train stations.

The streets of east-end Montreal and parts of the northern section are lined with distinctive two or three-storey apartments with outside staircases. Such housing, peculiar to

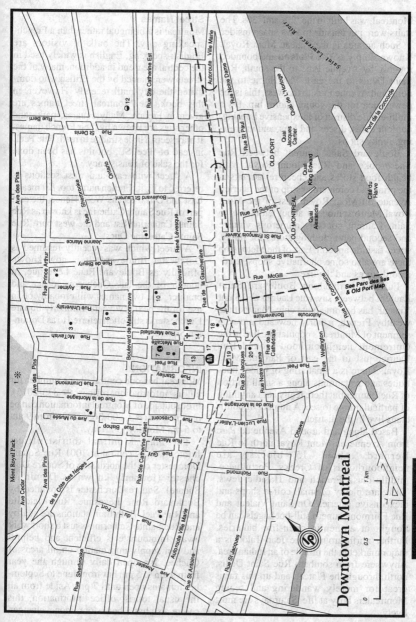

# Downtown Montreal

QUEBEC

0     0.5     1 km

Montreal, was built in the '20s and '30s. The stairs were put outside to save space inside.

Such an area is the Plateau Mont Royal. Known simply as **The Plateau** and bounded roughly by Avenue Pine to the south, Rue Saint Denis to the east, Van Horne to the north and Avenue Park to the west, this is the newer area for the young and/or hip. It's a multi-ethnic district of inexpensive housing, outdoor cafés, discos and bars, and interesting, funky shops.

Boulevard Saint Laurent between Rue Sherbrooke and Rue Mount Royal with health food stores and cheap restaurants is the principal commercial strip of the district. Avenue du Mont Royal west of the Mont Royal Métro station for about ten blocks to Saint Laurent contains numerous vintage and second-hand clothing stores for funky, street-fashion apparel. East of the Métro stop there are also some alternative shops, used-record stores and the like.

Further north along Boulevard Saint Laurent between, say, Rue Laurier and Saint Viateur, has become quite chic. Many of the wealthy French, a fairly new and growing segment of Montreal's population, live in the Outrement neighbourhood around Rue Laurier just to the east of Parc du Mont Royal. There is a smattering of pricey boutiques and restaurants along a small portion of Rue Laurier but there really isn't anything of particular note to see. A number of politicians live in the district.

Based along and around Avenue du Parc from Avenue du Mont Royal north to Rue Bernard (about 15 blocks) are neighbourhoods of Greeks, Portuguese, middle-class French and Hasidic Jews. There are plenty of small coffee shops and inexpensive eateries. On Saint Viateur and Rue Fairmont, superb still-hot bagels can be bought at authentic open-fire bakeries. Further north around Rue Jean Talon is a major market in the middle of an Italian area. Anywhere from southern Rue Saint Denis, north through the Plateau and up this far is great for merely wandering and seeing Montrealers busy at life. Saturdays are most lively.

## Street Names

Montreal is a bilingual rather than a French-speaking city. The bulk of visitors are English-speaking, English is widely used in the central area, and in addition, many of the streets were named by the British who dominated the city until recently. However, in this book, the Montreal street names are given in French. Many squares, parks and other sites are known by their French names. It may seem a little strange to read 'Rue Peel' instead of 'Peel St', but this has been done for the sake of consistency.

A street with east and west sections is referred to by its French name too. *Est* means East and *Ouest* means West. Hence, the east part of Rue Sainte Catherine is known as Rue Sainte Catherine Est and the west part, Rue Sainte Catherine Ouest.

A street which was recently renamed is Dorchester Boulevard. It is now known officially as Boulevard René Lévesque, in honour of the late Québecois leader and premier. The two names will probably be in use for the next few years. Similarly Square Dorchester is still often referred to as Dominion Square.

## INFORMATION

Montreal has one central phone number for all its information offices (☎ 873-2015). From outside of Montreal information can be obtained on (☎ 1-800-363-7777) from 9 am to 5 pm Monday to Friday.

The main Montreal tourist office, Infotouriste, is central at 1001 Rue Square Dorchester on the north side of Square Dorchester (formerly known as Dominion Square). Square Dorchester is bounded by Boulevard René Lévesque, Rue Metcalfe and Rue Peel. Both train stations are nearby and Rue Sainte Catherine is just a short walk away. Infotouriste is efficient and helpful and can supply information on all areas of Quebec. It's open daily through the year from 9 am to 5 pm but from June to September remains open until 7 pm. Aside from all the usual tourist office information, this centre also has a bookstore, moneychanger, souvenirs, post office and a fax machine, and can arrange sightseeing tours.

The other main information centre is also well located at 174 Rue Notre Dame Est in Old Montreal, not far from Place Jacques Cartier. It's busy but helpful, open from 9 am to 7 pm daily in season, 9 am to 5 pm with an hour and a quarter for lunch at 1 pm the rest of the year. This one deals mainly with Montreal.

The airports also have information kiosks which are open all year round. The Convention & Tourist Bureau (☎ 871-1129) is at 1555 Rue Peel in Suite 600, H3A 1X6.

Metropolitan News at 1109 Rue Cypress, west off Peel near Square Dorchester in the centre of downtown sells newspapers from around the world seven days a week.

Coles Bookstore on the corner of Rue Stanley and Sainte Catherine has a vast selection of English books including a good travel section.

For free accommodation reservations call ☎ 878-1000.

Note that Montreal's museums tend to be closed on Monday.

### Warning

Pedestrians, beware in Montreal! Might is right and drivers take full advantage of this. The careless may not get a second chance.

### OLD MONTREAL (VIEUX MONTRÉAL)

This is the oldest section of the city, dating mainly from the 1700s. The square **Place Royale**, is where Ville Marie, Maisonneuve's first small fort-town, was built, when fighting with the Iroquois Confederacy was both lengthy and fierce.

The narrow, cobblestone streets divide old stone houses and buildings, many of which now house intimate little restaurants and clubs. Throughout the area are squares and churches and the waterfront is never far away. Old Montreal is a must for romantics, though it's unfortunately a bit crowded in peak season. With all the activity and history, it's a perfect area for just wandering where your feet take you. Do yourself a favour and

don't bring your car down here – it's too busy and you won't find a parking spot.

The main streets are Rue Notre Dame and Rue Saint Paul. The area is bounded by Rue McGill on the west, Rue Berri on the east, Rue Saint Antoine on the north and the river on the south, with Boulevard Saint Laurent dividing the area east from west. The Métro stops in Old Montreal are Place d'Armes or Champs de Mars.

Near **Hôtel de Ville** (City Hall) and the Rue Notre Dame tourist office is the square **Place Jacques Cartier**, the centre of the area which in summer is filled with visitors, vendors, horse-drawn carriages and musicians. At the tourist office nearby, there's an *Old Montreal Walking Tour* booklet available, which is free and has all sorts of interesting historical tidbits, and points out the most noteworthy spots.

Many buildings are themselves marked with informative plaques. Some descriptions of the highlights follow.

### Place d'Armes & Basilica

The other major square in the area is Place d'Armes. A monument to Maisonneuve stands in the middle. On the square is Basilica Notre Dame, which you shouldn't miss. Built in 1829 and big enough to hold 5000 people, the church has a magnificently rich interior. The masses around Christmas, particularly Christmas Eve are worth a special trip. There's a small museum at the back.

### Église de Notre Dame de Bonsecours

This church is on Rue Saint Paul. It's also known as the Sailors' Church and has several models of wooden ships hanging from the ceiling. From the tower in the church there's a good view. The vignettes in the small museum are also quite good. They tell the story of Marguerite Bougeoys, the first teacher in Montreal and founder of the Congregation of Notre Dame order of nuns.

### Calvet House

Across from the church, Calvet House (☎ 282-1725) which dates from 1725 has been restored and is now a museum showing the furnishings of that time. It's free but closed on Mondays.

### Château de Ramezay

On Rue Notre Dame, across from the Hôtel de Ville, is the Château de Ramezay (☎ 861-3708) which was the home of the city's French governors for about 40 years in the early 1700s. The building has housed a great variety of things since, but is now a museum with a collection of artefacts, tools and miscellanea from Quebec's early history. The house is closed on Sunday mornings and all day on Monday. Admission is $5, students $3.

### Montreal History Centre

Also in Old Montreal is the Montreal History Centre (☎ 872-3207) in the old fire hall on Place d'Youville. Audiovisuals and displays depict some of the city's history, with tours running every 20 minutes. It's closed on Monday and public holidays and costs $4.50.

### Musée Marc Aurèle Fortin

Not far away is the Musée Marc Aurèle Fortin (☎ 845-6108), at 118 Rue Saint Pierre, which is less of a museum than a gallery dedicated to this Quebec landscape painter who lived from 1888 to 1970. Other painters are also represented in the changing exhibitions. Again, this one is closed on Monday. Admission costs $3.

### Sir George-Étienne Cartier National Historic Park

The Sir George-Étienne Cartier National Historic Park (☎ 283-2282) consists of two historic houses owned by the Cartier family. One details the life of the prominent 19th-century lawyer and politician and the changes in society in his lifetime, and the other offers a glimpse of a middle-class home during the Victorian era. It's at 458 Rue Notre Dame Est. The park is free and open every day in summer, and from Wednesday to Sunday for the rest of the year.

Parc des Îles & Old Port

### Pointe-à-Callière (Museum of Archaeology & History)

Situated on the very spot where Sieur de Maisonneuve and Jeanne Mance founded the first European settlement, on the south side of Place Royale, this museum (☎ 872-9150) is an interesting archaeological and historical study of the beginnings of the city of Montreal.

For the most part, the museum is underground, in the actual ruins of buildings and an ancient sewage/river system. The first European cemetery is here, established just a few years after the settlement itself. Grave sites can be seen and it is intended that this portion will be developed into a working dig for visitors to observe.

Artefacts are cleverly laid out on levels of shelving according to their time period just as they would be unearthed, the oldest items from Montreal's prehistory on the bottom. There are also a few interactive exhibits, the best of which is a video monitor which

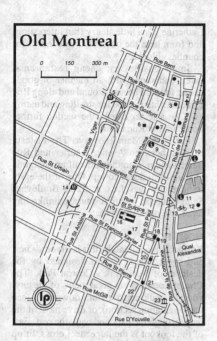

# Old Montreal

0    150    300 m

| | |
|---|---|
| 1 | Sir George Etienne Cartier National Historic Park |
| 2 | Notre Dame de Bonsecours Church/Marguerite Bourgeoys Museum |
| 3 | Calvet House |
| 4 | Bonsecours Market/ Palais de la Civilisation |
| 5 | Champ de Mars Métro Station |
| 6 | Hôtel de Ville City Hall |
| 7 | Château Ramezay |
| 8 | Place Jacques Cartier |
| 9 | Infotouriste |
| 10 | Tourist Information |
| 11 | Tourist Information |
| 12 | Imax Cinéma |
| 13 | Vélo Aventure (Bicycle Rentals) |
| 14 | Place d'Armes Metro Station |
| 15 | Place d'Armes |
| 16 | Notre Dame Basilica |
| 17 | Centaur Theatre |
| 18 | Place Royale |
| 19 | Pointe á Calliére |
| 20 | Place d'Youville |
| 21 | Montreal History Centre |
| 22 | Place d'Youville |
| 23 | Marc Aurèle Fortin Museum |

allows visitors to have a 'conversation' with some of the original inhabitants via a ghost-like image.

The lookout at the top of the tower in the new building provides an excellent view of the Old Port. The tower can be visited without paying the museum entry fee.

The museum is at 350 Place Royale, use the Place d'Armes Métro stop. It is open from Tuesday to Sunday 10 am to 8 pm in summer, until 5 pm the rest of the year. Admission is $6 for adults, free for kids under 12 but from 5 pm to 8 pm on Wednesdays it's free for all.

### Old Port (Vieux-Port)

The Old Port waterfront is a district of riverside redevelopment south of Place Jacques Cartier which is still evolving and changing as construction and ideas continue. It covers 2.5 km of riverfront and is based around four quays (*quais*) or piers. The Promenade du Vieux Port is a wide promenade along the river from Rue Berri Ouest to Rue McGill. An information booth (☎ 496-PORT) can be found at the entrance to Quai King Edward, pretty much in the centre of things. A number of the permanent features are listed here but each year, particularly through the summer, the port features a range of different temporary exhibits, shows and events. Check prices of the main attractions with the information number as they are not cheap and may be prohibitive to some.

At the far eastern edge of the historic port on Victoria Pier is **Sailors' Memorial Clock Tower** now used as an observation tower open to the public and with a history exhibit. Boat tours of the river depart nearby.

Quai Jacques Cartier includes an art gallery, restaurants, a large open flea market (*marché aux puces*) and a handicraft centre. Trolley tours of the port area depart from here. Also from Quai Jacques Cartier, a ferry goes over to **Parc de la Cité du Havre**,

**QUEBEC**

where there's a restaurant and some picnic tables. A ferry also runs to Parc des Îles.

On Quai King Edward at the foot of Boulevard Saint Laurent is **Images du Future**, a centre for holography, computer-generated films, satellite images and various other high-tech novelties, games and art forms. Quai Alexandra, a block east of Rue McGill, is the site of the IMAX Theatre and **S O S Labyrinthe**, a two-km maze which is definitely not just for kids. An acquaintance was in there for three days! And no, it was not Tony Wheeler.

The huge present-day port and container terminal is found at the foot of Rue McGill. Also there is the Iberville Passenger Terminal, the dock for cruise ships which ply the St Lawrence River as far as the Magdalen Islands out in the Gulf of St Lawrence.

### RUE SAINT DENIS

East of Boulevard Saint Laurent, this street, between Boulevard de Maisonneuve and Rue Sherbrooke, is the centre of a café, bistro and bar district with lots of open-air places and music. Snoop round in the side streets too. Some places are cheap. Many students still frequent the area which is lively at night. There are also some good small hotels in the area.

Going south along Rue Saint Denis will lead you into Old Montreal. North, up Rue Saint Denis just beyond Rue Sherbrooke, is Place Saint Louis, a small park dating from 1876 surrounded by fine Victorian homes built for the French elite of the time. West of the square is Rue Prince Arthur – with good, varied ethnic eating places.

### BOULEVARD SAINT LAURENT

Still called St Lawrence by some and known by many as The Main, Boulevard Saint Laurent has always been an interesting, busy commercial street. Stores are topped by apartments in the two to four-storey rows that line both sides of the street. Boulevard Saint Laurent running north-south divides the city into east and west, historically French and English, and has long had a multiethnic make-up. Around Rue Sainte

Catherine it's a little sleazy (but interesting) and from here the boulevard runs north for countless blocks.

Small businesses, cheap restaurants, cafés, and shops with all manner of goods can be found. The area around and along Rue Prince Arthur is good for strolling and eating as is, to a lesser extent, the section further north around Rue Duluth.

The Upper Main known as The Plateau, running between Avenue Laurier and Rue Saint Viateur, is in the midst of an energetic change from decay to hip. One of the early trendsetters was Lux at 5220 Boulevard Saint Laurent, a café/restaurant unlike any other and open very late.

### MONT ROYAL

Known as the mountain, this is the city's best and biggest park. It was designed by the designer of New York's Central Park. The **Chalet Lookout** has great views of the city: you can walk up to it from downtown (see the Orientation section), or drive most of the way through the park and walk the rest. East of the lookout is the huge steel cross, lit up at night and visible from all over the city. Within the park is **Beaver Lake** (Lac des Castors), a depression-era 'make work' project. The park has lots of trees and is used in summer for walking, picnicking, horse riding and frisbee throwing. In winter there is skating, tobogganing and skiing. There are walking trails, some with views. Calèches can be hired for rides up to the lookout or around the park's trails.

If you're driving here, take Rue Guy from the downtown area to Chemin de la Côte des Neiges and then look for signs. To the left is another small park called **Parc Summit**. There is another good lookout here; this one has a view of the western residential districts.

### UNDERGROUND CITY

To alleviate congestion and to escape the harsh winter, Montreal created a huge underground city in the city centre. Though much of it is actually underground, the term really covers anything connected by underground passageways. Thus you can go to the train stations, find a hotel, see a movie, eat out, go dancing or shopping, all without taking a step outside.

The notion is functional and innovative, but there's really not much to see. The shops are all modern and most of the system looks no different from a contemporary shopping mall, the differences being this is bigger and has the Métro going through it.

Major building complexes like Place Ville Marie, Place Bonaventure and Place du Canada are all connected and within easy walking distance. Others, like Place des Arts and Complèxe Desjardins, are a Métro ride away. The Eaton Centre is also part of the network. The tourist office has a good map of the entire system; it may prove useful on rainy or snowy days.

## MUSÉE DES BEAUX ARTS (FINE ARTS MUSEUM)

Beaux Arts (pronounced 'bose-ar') as it is known, is the city's main art gallery (☎ 285-1600), with both modern and pre-Columbian works. Europe, Africa, the Middle East and other areas are covered. There's also a display of Inuit art and special shows from time to time. Like many of Montreal's museums, this one is closed on Monday and open from 11 am to 6 pm on other days. It's at 1379 Rue Sherbrooke Ouest on the corner of Rue Crescent. Admission is a steep $9.50, students and seniors $4.75; more if there's a major travelling exhibition. Consider a visit on Wednesday when it is free from 5.30 to 9 pm. The architectural style of the new gallery annexe across the street is also worth a look.

## CONTEMPORARY ART GALLERY

With a new location in the centre of town by the Place des Arts Complex at 185 Rue Sainte Catherine, the gallery (☎ 847-6212) displays art from 1939 to the present with its substantial permanent collection and temporary shows. This is a much larger space than the gallery previously had and the extra space has meant a much more organised layout and presentation.

It's the only public gallery in the country which specialises exclusively in contempo-

rary art, and displays both Canadian and international work. On Tuesday and from Thursday to Sunday, the gallery is open from 11 am to 6 pm. It remains open on Wednesdays until 9 pm and is free from 6 pm onwards. It is closed on Monday. Admission is $4.75; students and seniors pay less. There is a simple restaurant within the gallery.

## SAIDYE BRONFMAN CENTRE

For a further look at contemporary art, this museum (☎ 739-2301), at 5170 Chemin de la Côte Sainte Catherine, on the west side of Mont Royal, has a collection to view. It's free and open from Sunday to Thursday.

## CANADIAN CENTRE FOR ARCHITECTURE

Opened in 1990 the centre (☎ 939-7000) is both a museum and working organisation promoting the understanding of architecture, its history and future. The numerous exhibition rooms feature permanent and changing shows of local and international architecture, urban planning and landscape design. It may sound dry but most people will find at least some of the displays (incorporating models, drawings or photographs) of interest.

A portion of the centre has been created in and around Shaughnessay House, built as home for a wealthy businessman in 1874 of the characteristic grey limestone seen so often around the city A wander around its 1st floor is interesting for the details and architectural features. A highlight is the solarium garden and the wonderfully ornate tea room with intricate woodwork and fireplace (sorry, no refreshments served).

There is a busy bookstore in the centre with books on famous architects and topics ranging from international styles to photography.

Don't miss the sculpture garden and lookout on the other side of Boulevard René Lévesque. About 15 sculptures of varying styles and sizes are scattered about a terrace overlooking parts of south Montreal. Directional markers set in the border wall point out various buildings of note below. The old banks, mills, etc provide intriguing evidence of the centre's conviction that the study of architecture is the study of history and civilisation.

The centre's open from 11 am to 5 pm daily, until 8 pm on Thursday and closed on Monday and Tuesday. Admission is $5, $3 for students and seniors. On Thursday it's free all day for students and for everybody else from 6 to 8 pm. The address is central at 1920 Rue Baile near the corner of Boulevard René Lévesque and Fort. The Métro stop is Atwater and there is parking available.

## McCORD MUSEUM

Renovated and re-opened in 1992, the McCord is the city's main history museum (☎ 398-7100). It is not large; budget 60 to 90 minutes for a visit. Located at 690 Rue Sherbrooke Ouest, the two-level museum is well laid out, with exhibits dealing for the most part with Eastern Canada's early European settlement. One room exhibits the history of Quebec's First Nations. Other displays highlight the museum's collection which includes Native Indian and Inuit works, early Canadian costume and textiles, folk art and 700,000 photographs! There are both permanent and changing exhibits.

A highlight is the collection of photographs by William Notman, who, with his sons, photographed Canadian people, places and activities from 1850 to about 1930.

The 2nd-floor room entitled 'Turning Point: Quebec 1900' neatly encapsulates French Canadian history in Quebec. The gift shop has some quality items and interesting reading material.

Admission is $5, less for students. Thursday evenings from 6 to 9 pm there is no charge. Opening hours are Tuesday to Friday 10 am to 6 pm and on weekends 10 am to 5 pm; it's closed Monday. If you tire before seeing the entire photo collection (don't panic they are not all on display), there is a tea room, but don't plan to eat a full meal as food prices are high.

## MARGUERITE D'YOUVILLE MUSEUM

Mentioned more for the building itself, rather than the small museum (☎ 937-9501),

this is a fine example of early Quebec stone architecture, particularly of the convents seen in number across the province. Founded by Mother d'Youville, this was and is home to the Grey Nuns, an active and hardy group from the colonial era. It was they who set out by canoe for what was to become Manitoba and founded a mission in St Boniface there. That nunnery of 1850 is now a museum in the middle of the largest French community of western Canada.

The museum here, open from Wednesday to Sunday from 1.30 to 4.30 pm contains Marguerite's tomb and some religious artefacts and other related articles. It's centrally located at 1185 Rue Saint Mathieu.

## MT STEPHEN CLUB

Funded by the George Stephen House Foundation, this Renaissance-style mansion (☎ 849-7338) dating from 1880 was built for the man who gave it his name, the first president of the Canadian Pacific Railway. The 15 rooms inside are rich with quality materials and skilful artistry. The woodwork is tremendous. Long the home of the private Mount Stephen Club, it is open to the public for a small fee from Thursday to Sunday, noon to 4 pm during July and the first week of August only. It's at 1440 Rue Drummond.

## CHÂTEAU DUFRESNE MUSEUM OF DECORATIVE ARTS

Château Dufresne displays decorative art and handicrafts (☎ 259-2575). It's a fine building dating from 1916-18. Each room is furnished with objets d'art and finery and is open daily from 11 am to 5 pm except Mondays and Thursdays. Admission is $3. The museum is in front of the Botanical Gardens on the corner of Boulevard Pie IX (pronounced 'pee nerf').

## ST JOSEPH'S ORATORY

The impressive modern-style basilica (☎ 733-8211), completed in 1960 and based on and around a 1916 church, honours St Joseph, patron of healers and patron saint of Canada, and Brother André, a monk said to have had the power to cure illness. Piles of

crutches testify to the strength of this belief. Brother André's heart, which is on view here – a display ranking with the weirdest – was stolen a few years ago but was finally returned intact.

You can see the dome of the oratory from anywhere in the south-west of Montreal. From the dome, the view of that part of the city is good. The site is open daily and is free. There is a small museum dedicated to Brother André. On Sunday there are free organ concerts at 3.30 pm.

The oratory is at 3800 Chemin Queen Mary, off the western slope of Mont Royal. From downtown, take the Métro to Guy, then transfer to bus No 65.

For those seeking a quiet night, it is also possible to stay here, see under Accommodation.

## CATHEDRAL OF MONTREAL

The Cathedral of Montreal or Marie-Reine-du-Monde (Mary, Queen of the World), is a smaller version of, and is modelled on, St Peter's Basilica in the Vatican. The cathedral was built between 1870 and 1894. It's situ-ated on Boulevard René Lévesque just off Dorchester Square near the Queen Elizabeth Hotel. Note the unusual canopy over the altar.

## ST JAMES UNITED CHURCH

This church, at 463 Rue Sainte Catherine Ouest, is unusual in that the portals open onto the street but have stores and offices built in beside them. The church is actually behind the street.

## OLYMPIC PARK

Ask any Montrealer and you'll find that the scandal, indignation and tales of corruption and government incompetence surrounding the buildings of the Olympic Sports Complex are as great as the structures themselves. Nevertheless, the complex (☎ 252-8687), created at enormous cost for the 1976 Olympic Games, is magnificent.

The showpiece is the multipurpose **Olympic Stadium** able to hold 80,000 spectators. It certainly is a grand structure, even if it did take until 1990 to get it finished. The

**QUEBEC**

infamous retractable roof eventually arrived from Paris, France in late 1981 (five years after the Games) and then sat for several years before the money was found to hoist it into place. It then took yet more time to get it operating. The kevlar it is made with has ripped many times resulting in expensive repairs.

Plans have now been made to give up on it and replace it with a nonretractable steel roof. This is to cost $57 million. In 1991, part of the roof support system collapsed sending chunks of concrete weighing 55 tonnes tumbling to the ground. I'm not making this up! Luckily no one was killed but they had to shut it down again and thoroughly safety check the place. Once again, it is operating.

In summer, major league professional baseball (the Expos of the National League) is played in the stadium and it is also used for concerts.

Also on the grounds is the **Biodome** (see below), another boldly designed stadium, originally built for cycling and later used for roller-skating.

The **swimming complex**, also impressive, has seven pools including a 20-metre-deep scuba pool. Public swimming costs $3 at this huge, clean facility. The Métro stop for the pool is Viau. You are not going to believe this but, in September 1993, part of the floor of one of the pools fell in, causing a few moments of panic during a therapy session with elderly nonswimmers. This area has been closed indefinitely but other sections remain open.

A new attraction is slated to open in 1994. The Space Centre, if it gets off the ground, is to contain a museum and displays on space technology.

Also in the complex is **Olympic Village**, the housing sector with apartments and restaurants.

Guided tours of the site in French and English (☎ 252-TOUR) leave from the lobby of the swimming complex every day. The fee of $7 chisels away at the local citizens' debt. It's worth it for those with a special interest in either architecture or sport

but otherwise I'd say give it a miss at that price.

A cable car runs up the arching tower which overhangs the stadium to a glassed-in observation deck which provides outstanding views of the city and beyond for a distance of 80 km. A ticket to the top is $7.

There is an information centre by the Biodome which includes a souvenir shop.

The entire site is in Parc Maisonneuve on the extreme eastern side of the city, off Rue Sherbrooke on the corner of Boulevard Pie IX (pronounced 'pee nerf'). The Métro stop is Viau (pronounced 'vee o'). A free shuttle bus runs from the Olympic site at the Biodome over to the Botanical Gardens.

## BIODOME
Housed in the former Velodrome cycling stadium at the Olympic Complex, the Biodome (☎ 868-3000), 4777 Avenue Pierre de Coubertin, is a captivating environmental museum which re-creates four distinct ecosystems, homes to 4000 animals and 5000 plants. Under one roof visitors can enjoy, learn about and appreciate the necessity of the environments, the rainforest, the polar regions, the Laurentian Shield woodlands and the Gulf of St Lawrence ocean environment.

The rainforest section is particularly encompassing, with monkeys in huge live trees and alligators in rivers. Other highlights include the underwater views of riverscapes where ducks may be seen competing with fish for food, the ocean microcosm and colourful tidal pools. The penguins are a natural favourite, too. Admission is $8.50 for adults, $6 for seniors and from $4 to $6 for children depending on their ages. Under age five, kids are free. A good visit takes two hours. A combination ticket is available for $12.50 which includes the Biodome, Botanical Gardens and Insectarium.

It is a popular attraction, far exceeding attendance expectations. Plan to go on a weekday, if possible, and avoid midday. You can bring your own lunch, there are picnic tables near the cafeteria. The gift/bookshop is quite tempting – beware.

A free bus shuttle runs between here, the Botanical Gardens and the Insectarium.

## BOTANICAL GARDENS

The 81-hectare gardens (☎ 872-1400) are the third largest in the world after those in London and Berlin. Some 26,000 types of plants are grown in 30 garden settings and various climate-controlled greenhouses. The collection of 700 orchid species is particularly impressive, as are the Japanese Garden and bonsai and Chinese *penjing* with plants up to 100 years old. The new Ming Dynasty style Chinese Garden is also a must. Other displays change with the seasons.

The gardens are open every day from 9 am to 4.30 pm with extended hours in summer to 7 pm. In summer a ticket is $7 and includes the gardens, the greenhouses and the Insectarium. In the low season prices drop a couple of dollars. Also see the combination tickets available listed under the Biodome. The gardens are next to the Olympic Buildings in Parc Maisonneuve. The Métro stop is Pie IX (pee nerf). A shuttle bus runs to the Olympic Park.

## INSECTARIUM

Whether you love or hate the creepy crawlies, this collection (☎ 872-8753) of bugs from around the world will fascinate you. The Insectarium is a museum in the east end of the city at 4101 Rue Sherbrooke Est; take the Métro to Pie IX. It's open daily from 9 am to 7 pm in summer, winter opening hours are slightly shorter. Admission is $7 but check out the combination tickets available with the Botanical Gardens and the Biodome.

## INTERNATIONAL MUSEUM OF HUMOUR

The recently opened humour museum, 2111 Boulevard Saint Laurent, has closed due to major financial troubles – no joke. Plans are afoot to alter the displays, the costly admission charge and then try again. For those interested, call the tourist office for latest details.

## McGILL UNIVERSITY

On the corner of Rue University and Rue Sherbrooke, this is one of Canada's most prestigious universities. The campus is rather nice to stroll around, since it sits at the foot of the mountain. The **Redpath Museum** houses McGill's natural history collection, which includes animals, birds, fossils, rocks etc. It's free and open every day except Friday and Saturday. On Sunday, it's only open in the afternoon.

## PLACE DES ARTS

Place des Arts (☎ 844-1211) is Montreal's modern centre for the performing arts. There are three main theatres in the complex on Rue Sainte Catherine on the corner of Rue Jeanne Mance. The new contemporary art gallery is here, too. Free tours lasting about 45 minutes are given but call for details and schedule. There's not that much to see on a tour but it's a good place to catch a show or concert.

## COMPLEX DESJARDINS

Complex Desjardins is one of the city's modern, multi-use structures with offices, plenty of stores and a hotel (the Méridien) all connected to the vast underground network. It's several storeys high with a large open space in the centre for walking, watching and putting on shows. You can keep an eye on things from the Hôtel Méridien's café on the top floor.

The mall is open 24 hours a day and has lots of benches and places to sit. It is linked with Place des Arts across the street and the subway system.

Alexis Nihon Plaza on the corner of Rue Sainte Catherine and Avenue Atwater is much the same as is Place Bonaventure on the corner of Rue de la Gauchetière Ouest and Rue Mansfield.

## DOW PLANETARIUM

The planetarium (☎ 872-4530) is at 1000 Rue Saint Jacques Ouest near Windsor Station. It offers laser shows as well as regular star and solar-system programmes;

QUEBEC

the shows are usually good and interesting. Admission costs $4, laser shows $5.

## HABITAT 67

At Cité du Havre, a jutting piece of land between Old Montreal and Île Sainte Hélène connected with the island by the Pont de la Concorde, is a residential complex known as Habitat 67. It was constructed for the World's Fair as an example of a futuristic, more liveable apartment block. It has aged well, is still appealing with its block modular look, and has become a popular, but not cheap, place to live.

## PARC DES ÎLES (The Islands Park)

South of the city in the St Lawrence River largely in the area between the Jacques Cartier and the Victoria bridges are Sainte Héiène and Notre Dame islands (☎ 872-4537). They were the site of the immensely successful 1967 World's Fair, Man & His World. For the event Île Sainte Hélène was considerably enlarged and Île Notre Dame was completely created with landfill. They are now primarily parkland though a couple of vestiges remain of the fair and there are a number of other attractions of note.

### Île Sainte Hélène

At the extreme northern end of Île Sainte Hélène is **La Ronde**, the largest amusement park in the province with restaurants and bars as well as an assortment of games and rides. 'The Monster', a roller coaster, is ranked as one of the world's best – hold on to your stomach. The gentle mini-rail offers good views of the river and city. A variety of concerts and shows are held through the summer often including circus performances and excellent firework displays. A schedule is available.

Full admission to La Ronde including all the rides is $18. There is also a ticket to the grounds and shows at half the price which offers limited rides.

In May La Ronde is open only on weekends, from 11 am to 11 pm. Through the summer it's open daily from 11 am to midnight but stays open an hour later on the weekends.

There are also some portions of an old fort near La Ronde. Inside the remaining stone ramparts is the **David M Stewart Museum** (☎ 861-6701) with artefacts and tools from Canada's past. There are demonstrations by uniformed soldiers and others in period dress, and military parades are held daily in summer by the museum. Admission is $5.

There are walkways around the island past gardens and among the old pavilions from the world's fair.

There are a couple of different ways to get to the islands but all access is through Île Sainte Hélène. Two bridges lead to the island if you're driving: the Pont Jacques Cartier and Pont de la Concorde. Definitely consider taking the Métro to the Île Sainte Hélène stop rather than driving, as they hit you pretty hard for parking. From the Métro stop, where there is an information desk, there are bus trips around to the island's various attractions. Another possibility is to take the water shuttle (☎ 281-8000) across the river from the Old Port at Quai Jacques Cartier. The shuttle takes pedestrians and bikes for $2.75.

### Île Notre Dame

Île Notre Dame, largely parkland, has some attractions of its own. First among them is the new – and popular – **artificial sandy beach** (☎ 872-6093) with room for 5000 people. The water is filtered and treated with chemicals. There are picnic facilities and snack bars at the site. It's open every day from 24 June to Labour Day (at the beginning of September) from 10 am to 7 pm depending on the weather. Call to check if it's open – their idea of a bad day and hence not opening may not be the same as yours. A ticket is $6, less for children. To get there take the Métro to Île Sainte Hélène and from there a bus runs to the beach.

Also on Île Notre Dame is the **Outdoor & Nautical Centre** based around the former Olympic rowing basin. In summer you can rent windsurfers and paddle boats but perhaps it's more fun in winter when the area becomes a huge skating rink. There are lockers and a snack bar and you can rent skates – a lot of fun. There is also some cross-country (nordic) skiing; equipment can also be rented. The centre's open until 9 pm daily.

A new attraction here situated in the old Quebec pavilion is the **Dinosaurium** (☎ 861-3462). Exhibits, displays and models detail the life and times of the ancient beasts. A ticket is $9.

The **Casino de Montréal** (☎ 392-2746) opened in late 1993 and was so popular (and earning so much money) so quickly that expansion plans were underway almost instantly. It is open daily from 11 am to 3 pm and is busy pretty well continually. Weekend nights in particular can be hectic and long queues to get in are not uncommon. Entry is free and non-alcoholic drinks are available at no charge. Liquor is served at bar prices. There is also an upmarket restaurant. No jeans are permitted and in the evenings and nights, dress is formal. During the afternoon, it's more casual. Do not attempt to drive there as the free parking fills up quickly. I'd recommend taking the Métro to Île Sainte Hélène and from there catching the free casino shuttle bus.

Much of the surrounding grounds are parkland which you can stroll around for free. At the **Gilles Villeneuve race track** (named after a Quebec racing-car driver) the occasional Formula 1 Grand Prix race is held.

Buses run from Île Sainte Hélène to the various attractions around Île Notre Dame.

## MARKETS
Two fairly central markets are the **Atwater Market**, south on Avenue Atwater, below Rue Sainte Catherine at the Lachine Canal, and the **Marché de Maisonneuve** on the corner of Rue Ontario and Avenue Létourneaux in the east end of the city. These markets are open daily but Saturday is by far the best day to attend.

At Atwater Market, aside from all the usual stuff, maple syrup is available, often from farmers who produce it. They can

answer any questions about this traditional Quebec treat.

More ethnically varied is the happening **Jean Talon Market** in the middle of Little Italy on Jean Talon between Rue Henri Julien and Casgrain north of the Plateau district.

## MONTREAL EXCHANGE
Another market to visit is the stock exchange (☎ 871-2424), where tours are given for $5, daily during July and August. For details and times, ring the above number. The exchange is on the 4th floor at 800 Place Victoria.

## LACHINE
Out in Lachine, a suburban town south of Montreal, is a national historic park called the **Fur Trade in Lachine** (☎ 637-7433). It's at 1255 Boulevard Saint Joseph on the corner of 12th Avenue. The museum tells the story of the fur trade in Canada, which was so critical to the development of the country. Take the Métro to Lionel Groulx and then bus No 191. Admission is free. It's not well known and is about 10 km from the downtown area but has been recommended by a reader.

Nearby, on Boulevard Saint Joseph but down near 7th Avenue, free walking tours are given along the Lachine Canal which was built for trade purposes. The tours run from Wednesday to Sunday only.

## KAHNAWAKE INDIAN RESERVE
South of Lachine where the Mercier Bridge meets the south shore is the Kahnawake (pronounced 'con-a-wok-ee') Indian Reserve (☎ 632-7500) where some 5000 Mohawks live. This reserve, about 18 km from central Montreal, was the location of a major confrontation which lasted for months between the Mohawks and the Quebec and federal governments through the summer of 1990 which made headlines internationally. The residents' support of the Mohawks in Oka over their land dispute exploded into a symbolic stand against the continuing treatment of Native Indians across the country on any number of problems.

The **Museum** (☎ 632-1098) was shut at

the time of writing but was to possibly re-open. **Mission buildings** from the early 1700s can be seen. Also in the town is a church with its own small museum and some gift shops with crafts. It's free and is open daily from 10 am to noon and from 1 to 5 pm. Sunday mass at 11 am is sung in Mohawk.

Also on the site is a **Cultural Centre** with an extensive library relating to the Six Nations of the Iroquois Confederacy as well as exhibits dealing principally with this reserve and its history. Shows with traditional dancing were held before the events of summer 1990. Call the museum for current information.

Cheap cigarettes and alcohol may also be purchased on the reserve. Canada's national game, lacrosse, is still popular here and you may see some boys playing on the sports fields around town.

## ST LAWRENCE SEAWAY
The seaway system of locks, canals and dams opened in 1959 along the St Lawrence River and enables ocean-going vessels to sail 3200 km inland via the Great Lakes. Across Victoria Bridge from the city is an observation tower over the first locks of the system, the Saint Lambert Locks, where ships are raised five metres.

There are explanatory displays. The observation area is open from April to December between 9 am and 9.30 pm, free. In January, February and March the locks are closed – they're frozen like the river itself, until the spring thaw.

## CANADIAN RAILWAY MUSEUM
This museum (☎ 632-2410) is at 122A Rue Saint Pierre in Saint Constant, a district on the south shore near Châteauguay. The museum, with Canada's largest collection, has examples of early locomotives, steam engines and passenger cars.

Admission is $4.50 and it's open daily from May to early September. To get there, take Champlain Bridge from town to Hwy 15, then Hwy 137 at the Châteauguay cut-off to Hwy 209.

## ORGANISED TOURS
### Sightseeing Tours
Gray Line (☎ 934-1222), at the tourist office on Square Dorchester, operates 11 sightseeing tours. The basic city orientation tour takes 1½ hours, costs $17 and takes in some of the principal sights and residential districts. The deluxe trip is better value and costs $32.50 which includes admission into some of the attractions such as the Biodome. An eight-hour all-day trip is $39. Other bus trips are to the Laurentian Mountains north of Montreal and a sunset tour.

Another tour company is Murray Hill (☎ 871-4733) also at 1001 Rue du Square Dorchester in the Infotouriste centre. Tours aboard pseudo trolley buses leave from here. They offer a lot of flexibility and you can choose from a number of options to customise the tour. You can hop on and off the bus at different sights and take advantage of reduced admissions to some attractions. Like Gray Line, Murray Hill is a reputable company.

The Amphi Tour (☎ 849-5181) offers a surprise. A bus tools around the Old Port area for half an hour and then drives into the river! It then provides a port-area cruise for another half an hour. It operates daily from May to the end of October. The tour departs from Quai King Edward and reservations are essential.

### Jet-Boat Tours
A couple of companies offer boat trips through the nearby Lachine Rapids. Lachine Rapids Tours (☎ 284-9607), at 105 Esplanade de la Commune Ouest, have 90-minute trips leaving from Old Montreal, costing $45.

### Boat Trips
A couple of companies offer straight boat trips. Montreal Harbour Cruises Ltd (☎ 842-3871) has river tours from Quai Victoria also called the Clock Tower Pier (Quai de l'Horloge), the pier at the foot of Rue Berri in Old Montreal. The one-hour trips around the port are $12. Longer sunset trips and later weekend night cruises with disco-dancing and drinks are other options.

Tours aboard the comfortable *Le Bateau Mouche* (☎ 849-9952), a more deluxe, Parisian type vessel have been recommended. These tours depart Quai Jacques Cartier for the 90-minute narrated cruises. Call for details and reservations.

A third option is the various cruises aboard the *New Orleans* (☎ 842-7655), a Mississippi-style paddlewheeler.

## FESTIVALS
Some of the major festivals held in Montreal are:

January
  *Fête des Neiges* – This is a winter festival held at the end of January and based around the Old Port and Parc des Îles.
May-June
  *International Benson & Hedges fireworks* – Towards the end of May and into June on weekends the International Benson & Hedges fireworks competition lights the skies.
  *Montreal Jazz Festival* – The Montreal Jazz Festival held at the end of June and the beginning of July is a major event with both internationally-known and local players. Indoors and out, concerts are held at various places around town, and many shows are free. There's usually quite a few performances around the Saint Denis area. Accommodation may be tight at this time as this event is a big draw.
  *Fête Nationale* – Formerly known as St Jean Baptiste Day (or Johnny Baptiste to the English), held each year on 24 June is a major parade and holiday. Originally a religious holiday then transformed into a strident Québecois political demonstration it has recently become more of a feel-good, beginning-of-spring celebration with some optimistic Quebec nationalism thrown in.
July-September
  *Just for Laughs Comedy Festival* – The bilingual Just for Laughs comedy festival with both free and admission-charged performances is held in July. Over half a million attend with some 200 performers featured.
  *Montreal World Film Festival* – The Montreal World Film Festival is held in mid to late August and early September with screenings at cinemas around town.
  Several big cycling races are held through the summer including one around the island and one through the streets.

## PLACES TO STAY
Montreal, like Quebec City, is popular with tourists in summer, so rooms can be hard to find and cost slightly more than during the rest of the year.

### Camping
There's not too much camping close to town. There are some places including a *KOA* (Kampground of America) (☎ 763-5623) as you come from the west, before you actually get on the island of Montreal, on Hwy 138 in Coteau du Lac. It's just off the highway around Dorion, about a 45-minute drive to downtown.

A 45-minute drive west of Montreal will also get you to *Camping D'Aoust* (☎ 458-7301) on Hwy 342 in Hudson-Vaudreuil. Take exit 26 from Hwy 40 (the Trans Canada Hwy) then it's three km down the road on the right.

South of the city there is another *KOA* (☎ 659-8626) at 130 Boulevard Monette in St Phillippe and others can be found about 20 minutes from town south on Hwy 15.

### Hostels
The central HI *Auberge de Montreal* (☎ 843-3317) is well established at 3541 Rue Aylmer, with 275 beds in summer, less in winter. Members pay \$15, nonmembers \$19. It's open all year with check in from 9.30 am to 2 am. Rue Aylmer runs off Rue Sherbrooke, just to the east of McGill University; get off at the McGill Métro stop.

Most of the rooms accommodate four people each, some are co-ed. There is a maximum stay of seven nights and making reservations three weeks in advance is a good idea in summer. Actually reservations are suggested all year, although perhaps not so far in advance during the low season. It's small and does get crowded. The hostel has shared kitchen facilities and runs free walking tours of the city. It is also well situated right in the centre of the so-called McGill ghetto. This is an old area of three-storey row houses where many of the university's students live although it is becoming more expensive and upscale.

During the summer months a seasonal hostel (☎ 843-8890) with the same rates is operated at 1600 Rue St Hubert.

*Auberge Chez Jean* (☎ 843-8279), affiliated with Backpackers, runs a place halfway between a B&B and a hostel out of a private

QUEBEC

apartment home. The cost is $14 a night including breakfast. Depending on demand, visitors may have a room to themselves or may be sharing. It is open from mid-June to mid-November. The address is 4136 Rue Henri Julien, north of Rue Duluth, south of Rachel in the Plateau Mont Royal. Look for 'Jean' on the mailbox, it's the only sign. He is the owner and speaks quite good English.

The *YMCA* (☎ 849-8393) is at 1450 Rue Stanley. It's central too, and huge, with 350 beds. Singles/doubles are $33/48 and they take both sexes although couples are supposed to be married. The cheap cafeteria is open from 7 am to 7 pm weekdays, to 2 pm weekdays.

The *YWCA* (☎ 866-9941), for women only, is at 1355 Boulevard René Lévesque Ouest. Singles/doubles cost from $40/54 and there is a kitchen on every floor. There is also a cafeteria and a pool which guests can use. Get off at the Peel Métro stop.

Open all year and good value is the *Collége Francais* (☎ 495-2581 or if that doesn't work call ☎ 270-9260 at 5155 Rue de Gaspé where they have a range of cheap beds. Dorms go for as little as $9.50. There are good-value rooms with four beds and a toilet, shower and sink at $12.50 per person. A double room goes for $15.50 per person and there are good rates for a single room. Inexpensive breakfasts are offered at a nearby restaurant or there is a cafeteria. Parking is available too. The college is near the corner of Rue Laurier and Rue Saint Denis. The Métro stop is Laurier, 300 metres east of Rue de Gaspé. Although there are 120 beds it's busy in the summer months so call ahead to check availability.

The college also has another residence out of the centre in Longueuil (pronounced 'long guy') and perhaps of more interest, one in the Eastern Townships, where otherwise accommodation can be a little pricey.

*McGill University*, on the corner of Rue Sherbrooke and Rue University, opens its residences from 15 May to 15 August. The accommodation office (☎ 398-6367) is at 3935 Rue University. Singles (which is all

there is) cost $37, for students $27. There are cafeterias, laundry rooms, etc and some residences include breakfast but are more expensive. Rates go down with stays of more than one night and the weekly rates are good.

The central *Concordia University* (☎ 848-4756), at 7141 Rue Sherbrooke Ouest, is even cheaper but the residences aren't here. They are a Métro and then bus ride away in the western part of downtown. The student rate is $19 per person, single or double. Nonstudents pay $26/40 for singles/doubles.

Lastly, the French *Universitaire de Montréal* (☎ 343-6531), 2350 Rue Édouard-Monpetit west of the downtown area, offers rooms at $23/35 for students/nonstudents with good weekly rates available.

Pretty inexpensive rooms are also available at *St Joseph's Oratory* (☎ 733-8211). Singles/doubles cost $25/40. Go to Pavilion Jean 23rd at 4300 Queen Mary Rd.

### Tourist Homes & Small Hotels

Most standard hotels in the city are costly. Tourist homes are the alternative and there is a good, central assortment. Most of them are in the eastern portion of the downtown area. Nearly all are in older houses and buildings with 10 to 20 rooms. Quality ranges from the plain and functional to old-world-charm comfortable. Price is the best indicator of quality but sometimes just a few dollars can make quite a difference. All these places are OK, though. Practically all the smaller ones have a variety of rooms with price differences depending on what facilities the room has – whether it has a sink or toilet or a full bathroom. Air-con adds a few dollars too. Prices are highest from June to October.

My first choice of location would be the convenient Saint Denis bus station area. There are quite a few places here.

On Rue Saint Denis in the middle of the café district there's the *Castel Saint Denis* (☎ 842-9719) at No 2099, up the hill just south of Rue Sherbrooke. It's close to the bus station, has been renovated and redecorated a couple of times, and is good value. It's not fancy but it's clean and convenient. Singles range from $35 to $45, doubles from $40 to $50. Further south on Rue Saint Denis between Sherbrooke and Old Montreal plainer, cheaper rooms can be found at such places as the *Hôtel de la Couronne* (☎ 845-0901) at No 1029. A little nicer place, with a wider range of rooms and prices, is *Hôtel Saint Denis* (☎ 849-4526) at No 1254.

À *l'Américain* (☎ 849-0616), a small hotel at 1042 Rue Saint Denis, is good and European in style. It has 20 rooms at singles from $35 to $48 and doubles from $40 to $55. The rooms on the top floor are like those in tryst scenes in French movies but, as the manager has mentioned, there is nothing wrong with the other rooms! Montreal's gaytown is nearby and the hotel has become popular with out-of-towners who visit that part of the city but straights also find the location convenient.

East of Rue Saint Denis is *Le Breton* (☎ 524-7273), in an excellent location on a pleasant street. It's at 1609 Rue Saint Hubert, beside the bus station. Singles go from $30 to $45, doubles from $40 to $60; some rooms come with shower or bath, TV, etc. Further south, at 1001 Rue Saint Hubert on the corner of Avenue Viger, is the cheaper but good *Hôtel Viger Centre Ville* (☎ 845-6058). They have a wide variety of rooms from singles/doubles $30/45. The least expensive of the 22 rooms come with sink, colour TV and fan. A continental breakfast is included. Near Rue Sainte Catherine at 1216 Rue Saint Hubert is *Maison Kent* (☎ 845-9835) with singles from $29 to $48 and doubles from $35 to $58. If you don't need your own bathroom, you'll save quite a bit.

West of Rue Saint Denis there are a couple of places to stay on Rue Ontario. At No 307, *Maison de Tourist Villard* (☎ 845-9730) has good rooms with good prices for singles at $30 but the doubles aren't such a bargain at $44. Next door is the *Karukera Hotel* (☎ 845-7932) with prices about the same for a single but less for the doubles and with more of a range of rooms in both categories.

On Rue Sherbrooke Est at Hôtel de Ville, between Boulevard Saint Laurent and Rue Saint Denis, are three tourist homes next door to each other, all in old houses. *Hôtel Pierre* (☎ 288-8519) is at No 169. The *Hôtel Manoir Sherbrooke* at No 157 is now run by the same people as the *Armor Tourist Lodge* (☎ 285-0140) on the corner. The latter is a large place, lined with natural wood inside. Both are busy places with prices from $29/35 for singles/doubles with no room costing over $55.

At 264 Rue Sherbrooke Ouest, west of Rue Jeanne Mance, is the yellow-and-green *Maison Casa Bella* (☎ 849-2777). The price range at this central hotel is quite wide with singles from $40 to $60, doubles from $45 to $68 but these prices include breakfast and parking.

There are also places scattered about the downtown area. Several can be found along Rue Sainte Catherine near Boulevard Saint Laurent, where the men, painted ladies and some in-betweens appear at about 6 pm. They're *not* selling insurance but the area is not really tough. *Villa de France* (☎ 849-5043) at 57 Rue Sainte Catherine Est, is a well-kept, friendly place with a pair of antlers on the lobby wall. Without a bath, singles/doubles cost $30/35; with bath, add $5 or $10.

At 9 Rue Sainte Catherine Ouest is the *Hebergement l'Abri du Voyageur* (☎ 849-2922) which is nothing fancy. The rooms are simple but clean and if you're really on a budget, they're quite OK. Rates are $21/32 for singles/doubles. Other places nearby tend to be a little dubious.

Going west, the *Ambrose* (☎ 844-0342), at 3422 Rue Stanley, is nicer and in a better location but it costs more, of course, with singles from $30 all the way up to $75, and doubles from $55 to $75. Compared to the sterile international hotels, it's still a bargain and has 22 rooms.

Rooms in the city's lowest-priced luxury hotel can be found just six blocks from the centre of downtown, Peel and Sainte Catherine, at the small *Hôtel Chateau Napolean* (☎ 938-1500), 1030 Rue Mackay. A double is $60.

Lastly, next door on Rue Mackay south of Boul René Lévesque, the *Aux Berges*

(☎ 938-9393) at 1070 Rue Mackay has an unusual approach limiting itself to serving male homosexual visitors. It's central but on a quiet street and has rooms in the $35 to $40 range.

## B&Bs

Another alternative to the high-priced hotels are the B&Bs. Though a relatively new phenomenon in the province, these have caught on so much in Montreal that it's hard to keep up with all the various associations which organise rental rooms in people's homes. There are some individually operated places and some commercial establishments offering this style of accommodation but the majority, by far, are listed by agencies. If you're staying a while, it's worth asking about a weekly rate.

*B&B Downtown Network* (☎ 289-9749) is an agency run by Bob Finkelstein which has been operating successfully for years. He has checked over 50 private homes for quality, hospitality and uniqueness beyond minimum requirements. Hosts range from students to lawyers, the places from mansions with fireplaces in the bedrooms, to Victorian homes, to apartments filled with antiques. Rates are quite reasonable at $25 to $40 for singles, $35 to $55 for doubles and triples are available too. For information and reservations, call or write to 3458 Laval Avenue, Montreal, H2X 3C8. There is now a toll free number which may prove useful: ☎ 1-800-267-5180.

*B&B à Montreal* (☎ 738-9410) run by Marion Kahn, is a similar organisation with some higher-priced homes as well which offer something special. She also has some places in Quebec City which can be booked here.

A third organisation is *Montreal Oasis* (☎ 935-2312) run by Swedish Lena Blondel out of her own B&B place at 3000 Chemin de Breslay (off Avenue Atwater just north of Rue Sherbrooke). Almost all of her participant homes are in older houses in the central core and they pride themselves on the quality of their breakfasts. Ask about the places on quiet and particularly attractive Rue Souvenir which is perfectly located near Rue Sainte Catherine or about the historic home in Old Montreal. Prices range from $40 to $70 a single, $50 to $90 a double and, again, triples are available. Most of the places welcome children.

*Welcome B&B* (☎ 844-5897) is a smaller, less-expensive agency which specialises in turn-of-the-century places around the interesting French area of Rue Saint Denis and Carré Saint Louis. Call or write to 3950 Laval Avenue, Montreal H2W 2J2. Laval Avenue is one block west of Rue Saint Denis and the office is a couple of blocks north of Rue Sherbrooke, a short walk from the Sherbrooke Métro stop. The owners, Carole Sirois and Allard Coté, operate a B&B themselves at the above address which is a great location very close to the Prince Arthur restaurant district. There are several other organisations – the tourist office will have a complete list. Prices are generally quite moderate.

## Hotels & Efficiencies

If you really like a more conventional, modern hotel but not the prices accompanying the usual downtown luxury choices try the *Hôtel Europa* (☎ 866-6492) part of the Best Western chain. It will fill the bill with prices as reasonable as you're likely to find with doubles from $80. The Red Lobster restaurant in the hotel is not too bad for reasonably priced seafood either. The lunches are better value than the dinners. The central hotel is at 1240 Rue Drummond near Rue Sainte Catherine.

*Comfort Suites* (☎ 878-2711), at 1214 Rue Crescent, is $99 a night for two people.

Other middle-priced hotels include the *Hôtel Montréal Crescent* (☎ 938-9797), at 1366 Boulevard René Lévesque, with prices from $75 to $90.

*Le Riche Bourg* (☎ 935-9224) central at 2170 Avenue Lincoln has rooms with a double bed or two twins with a kitchenette for $65 a day and there are good weekly rates. Facilities include a swimming pool.

The following hotels are in the 'expensive' category. Despite the rather hefty prices, geared mainly to the business traveller, what irks the most in these places is being nickled and dimed outrageously for parking, telephone calls, drinks in the room fridge, and every other time you turn around. Some of the major hotels do have pretty good lower-priced weekend specials which may appeal to some for a splurge; prices are generally lower in summer when there is less commercial traffic.

*Le Château Champlain* (☎ 878-9000), Place du Canada, has rooms from $140 to $240. This hotel is right across the street from the Windsor train station. Ask for a room facing Square Dorchester and the view will be quite good. The top-floor bar also has windows overlooking the city. There's a restaurant and has Vegas-style revues are often presented.

Nearby is the *Bonaventure Hilton* (☎ 878-2332), Place Bonaventure, with rooms from $135 to $375.

The *Ritz Carlton Kempinski* (☎ 842-4212), 1228 Rue Sherbrooke Ouest, with rooms from $180 to $340, has long been a hotel of distinction and reputation. The penthouse suite here is the most expensive place to stay in Canada (and it's probably not too shabby either). This seems to be the hotel of choice for business, entertainment and, if it's not an oxymoron, political superstars.

**Motels**

There are two main motel districts in Montreal; other motels are scattered. All charge less in the low season (ie not in summer): the rates here are summer ones. The area closest to town is conveniently situated along Rue Saint Jacques. It's west of the downtown area, south and parallel to Rue Sherbrooke. Look around where Rue Cavendish runs into Rue Saint Jacques from Rue Sherbrooke. This area is about a 10-minute drive from the centre. Coming from the west (from places like Dorval Airport), Hwys 2 and 20 flow into Rue Saint Jacques.

The *Colibri* (☎ 486-1167), at 6960 Rue Saint Jacques Ouest, charges singles/doubles $39/45. It's the white place behind Harvey's hamburger restaurant.

The new *Motel Sunrise* (☎ 484-0048) at 6120 Rue Saint Jacques Ouest, just west of Boulevard Decarie, is good; singles/doubles cost $40/50.

The smallish *Aubin* (☎ 484-5198) with 20 rooms, at 6125 Rue Saint Jacques Ouest, has singles/doubles for $48/53.

The *Ideal Motel* (☎ 488-9561) at No 6951 charges a steep $79 single or double. Nearby at No 7455, *Motel Raphaël* (☎ 485-3344), is good value at $44.50 for doubles, with swimming pool and restaurant.

The second district for motels is on Boulevard Tashereau on the south shore, across the river on the mainland. The street is also known as Hwy 134 and stretches out of the city in both directions. Many of the motels are at the bridges – check at the Jacques Cartier (in Old Montreal) and Champlain in the west end. Victoria Bridge is between these two.

At 1277 Boulevard Tashereau is *La Parisienne* (☎ 674-6291). Singles/doubles cost $55.

The *Falcon Motel* (☎ 676-0215) is at 6225 Boulevard Tashereau, with singles/doubles from $35/45. Ask for the rooms with no extras, the rooms in the newer section are more costly.

There are several other places in the blocks around No 7000.

Two: *Le Paysan* (☎ 640-1415), at 12400 Rue Sherbrooke Est, where singles/doubles cost $51/56 and *Le Marquis* (☎ 256-1621), at No 6720, where it costs much less for singles but more for a double. Others in the area are more costly.

The *Motel Métro* (☎ 382-9780), at 9925 Rue Lajeunesse, is a good bargain with singles/doubles for $37/45, TVs and city maps included. From the Metropolitan East Hwy take exit 73 (Rue Saint Hubert), go to Sauvé and then you'll see Rue Lajeunesse. Or get off at the Sauvé Métro station.

Lastly, you may want to try *Chomedey Inn* (☎ 681-9251) at 590 Boulevard Labelle – it has adult movies, water beds and mirrors on the ceiling. There are reduced prices on – oh my God – Sunday.

QUEBEC

## PLACES TO EAT

The French have long been responsible for Montreal's excellent restaurant reputation, which various immigrant groups have only added to over the years. There is no shortage of restaurants here, some 5000 at last count, and you'll find good food in all price ranges. Many places have lunch specials – always the best bargains – and at dinner, a table d'hôte fixed-price complete dinner.

Many Montreal restaurants, generally in the lower and middle-price brackets, have a 'bring your own' wine policy. If you want to take advantage of this great idea and bring your own wine for a meal, you can get it in a *dépanneur* (convenience store) if there is no government outlet around or it's past closing time. In Quebec you can pick up a bottle of French wine, bottled in the province, for $7 to $9 at the liquor outlets, or from grocery stores where the price goes up a dollar or slightly more.

In Montreal, as in all of Quebec there was a long tradition of 'men only' drinking establishments known as taverns. These were generally small, grubby congenial places offering cheap beer and good inexpensive meals. These have now passed into lore many having become reincarnated as larger, brighter, cleaner establishments often known as brasseries. Many of these and the remaining unchanged older places have Bienvenue aux Dames signs outfront, a reminder of the time some 15 years ago or so when women slowly began sitting in to also enjoy the casual atmosphere and prices.

Many restaurants, particularly the better ones, don't start to get busy until around 8 pm and will stay that way for a couple of hours. If you're an early eater in this city, you may have the place to yourself.

A recent phenomenon to keep an eye, ear or nose out for are the so-called tam-tams. Translated directly, a tam-tam is a fuss, a bally hoo. There have been a series of these unexpected, semi-spontaneous large outdoor parties featuring Asian-style street food stalls, live music and illegal drinking and smoking. They've been taking place on Mont Royal, usually on a Sunday in the summer. The city authorities seem dead set against them (and all kerb-side food sellers) and make attempts to shut them down whenever found. Many people find these bashes a lot of fun and some vendors have vowed to continue.

### Central Area

On the corner of Boulevard de Maisonneuve and Rue Metcalfe, *Ben's* is an institution. Montreal is known far and wide for its smoked meat and the Ben's name is familiar across the country. It's an informal deli, full of office workers at lunch time. Sandwiches are served lean or fatty – you can ask for your preference – and they're around $4 or $7 with French fries, pickle and coffee.

The *Bar B Barn*, at 1201 Rue Guy, is too small – it's usually packed, with a queue out the front to boot – but they serve the best and biggest spareribs you've ever had. It's a comfortable, attractive place as well. The only other thing on the menu is chicken. This place is good value with meals costing from $11 to $16 and there's parking around the back.

Rue de la Montagne and Rue Crescent offer a range of places. *Aida's*, 2020 Rue Crescent on the corner of Boulevard de Maisonneuve, has felafels and other cheap light meals. At 2170 Rue de la Montagne *Katsura* is a popular Japanese place which is quite reasonably priced at lunch but more pricey for the evening meal. *O Blitz* at 1189 Rue de la Montagne is one of several good brasseries in the area. They're busy at noon because of the cheap beer and meals for $4.50 and up. On weekends they open at 4 pm.

Further east along Rue Sainte Catherine Ouest on the 3rd floor of the Eaton Centre is the *Magic Pan Crêperie*, with crêpes from $5.50 to $7.25. The address is actually 1500 Avenue McGill College.

The busy *Tramway* is in the centre of town at 1122 Rue Sainte Catherine Ouest. It's basically a brasserie, although spiffier, with standard meals and steaks. The low-priced lunch specials are a bargain. The *McLean's Pub*, formerly the males-only Rymark Tavern, around the corner and south of Rue Peel towards Windsor Station, is an old gem that's been around for a long time. Check out the wood panelling. They serve cheap beer with inexpensive, standard tavern fare. Across the square at 1243 Rue Metcalfe, just south of Rue Sainte Catherine is the lively *Dominion Pub* where a speciality is ham boiled in beer with baked beans, a tavern classic. Women will not feel out of place here.

*Chenoy's Deli* nearby at 1205 Rue Peel is mentioned for its cheap breakfasts.

Out of the beer parlours, for a splurge there is *Chez Pauzé*, another old-time place (it began in 1862) with a good name. It's on the north side of Rue Sainte Catherine Ouest at No 1657, towards the Forum on the corner of Avenue Atwater. Seafood is their speciality. Meal prices range from $12 to $25.

On Rue Metcalfe up from Rue Sainte Catherine is the well-known, long-established *Joe's* steak house. Good steak dinners range from $8 to $17; the meal includes a baked potato or French fries and an excellent all-you-can-eat salad bar. You can have just the salad bar to catch up on some greens for $7. All meals though are good value.

*Dunn's*, at 892 Rue Sainte Catherine Ouest near Rue Peel, is a deli open (and usually pretty busy) 24 hours a day. It's good for a late night snack or early morning breakfast.

There are several East Indian restaurants in this central area. At 1241 Rue Guy is the good but expensive *Woodlands New Indian Restaurant*. The South Indian vegetarian dishes are the best priced. The masala dosa, a crêpe filled with potatoes, onions and spices for $4.25, is good.

Next door the *Phaya Tai* at 1235 Rue Guy is a fancier place offering tasty Thai food. Vegetarian main dishes are $6, seafood and meat dishes range from $8 to $12. The *Curry House* over at 1433 Rue Bishop has dinner for three for a little over $40 and some interesting dishes available. There is also *Pique Assiette*, at 2051 Rue Sainte Catherine Ouest, one of the city's oldest Indian restaurants. Dinner for two costs about $25. This was the first of the international Bombay Palace chain of East Indian restaurants.

Very pricey but mentioned because this is Montreal and people here like to eat is *Chez*

*La Mere Michel*, a city institution at 1209 Rue Guy for fine French food. It's been around so long an entire generation knows it as Mother Michael's. Dinner for two will set you back roughly $120 including wine, tax and tip. The three-course lunches are top value at $13. The service, the food and the style – everything is 1st class. Note that it is closed on Sundays and there is no lunch on Saturdays.

For lingering over a coffee, there are numerous cafés in the Rue Crescent and Rue de la Montagne area. There are a couple of Parisian-style ones on Boulevard de Maisonneuve here. Less ostentatious is *Café Drummond* at 2005 Rue Drummond.

For making up your own meal, try shopping around *Le Fauberg* at 1616 Rue Sainte Catherine Ouest. The basement of this Parisian-style mall is devoted to food and is a sort of market, which includes a bakery and liquor store. Also see Markets at the end of the Things to See section earlier.

## Old Montreal

Old Montreal is a fine place to splurge. Menus with prices are generally posted outside. The charm of many of these places is in some measure the location and restaurant decor rather than purely gastronomic excellence. Also, because this is a major tourist area, prices tend to be a little high. Nonetheless, it is such a great area that a meal out should not be resisted too strongly.

For good French seafood, try *Le Fripon*, at 436 Place Jacques Cartier in front of the Hôtel de Ville, with dishes from $14 to $17. The Dover sole is good with lobster soup and *escargot* from the 'prix fixe' menu. If you need help with the French menu, the waiters will explain. The only drawback is the price of the wine.

Also good for lingering over a meal is French *La Sauvagine* at 115 Rue Saint Paul on the corner of Rue Saint Vincent. Lunch prices range from $5 to $8, dinners from $13 to $18. Both restaurants are comfortable and friendly.

A third possibility for a special meal is the long running, *Gibby's* (☎ 282-1837), popular with Montrealers as well as visitors, at 298 Place d'Youville in a 200-year-old converted stable. The speciality is steak and atmosphere and, though a dinner is about $30 per person, reservations are suggested, at least for a weekend evening.

There are inexpensive places in this busy part of town too. *Bistro du Vieux*, at 250 Rue Saint Paul on the corner of Place Jacques Cartier, is a real bargain. Lunches cost from $4.25, everything included. The food is good and this is a dining room, not a greasy spoon.

At 273 Rue Saint Paul Est is *L'Usine de Spaghetti Parisienne* where meals cost from $6 to $12, including all the bread and salad you can eat. At 48 Rue Notre Dame Est on the corner of Rue Saint Gabriel are two cafeteria-style restaurants in one location. One of them, *Restaurant Sultan*, serves up inexpensive Lebanese food.

The informal *Brasserie Lambert Closse*, at 435 B Rue Saint Vincent near Rue Thérèse, is also cheap. It's not far from Rue Notre Dame and the tourist office – around the back, down the alley. Tables are available outside in summer. They serve various lunch specials costing from $3.75 to $5.50 and cheap mugs of beer. Dinner, much the same, is served until 7 pm. On the corner of Rue Saint Paul and Boul Saint Laurent is the *Restaurant Le Coin du Vieux Montreal* with basics such as omelettes, hamburgers and pizza.

*Chez Delmo*, 211 Rue Notre Dame Ouest, is slightly away from the heavily touristed area and relies on locals for business as it has for many years. It's busy at lunch time serving its inexpensive seafood specialities; the daily specials are cheapest. It's open for lunch until 3 pm, then later for dinner. Lunches cost around $8 and are served at the long counters on both walls – a strange set-up. Dinners are more expensive at $16 for a main dish but the food is good. It's closed on Sunday but open Saturday evening from 6 to 11 pm. Every July it shuts down for holidays for two weeks at the end of the month.

There are lots of cafés set up around Place Jacques Cartier. In summer, they are great for sipping a coffee, resting the feet or contemplating life's mysteries at the outside tables. The *Restaurant des Gouverneurs* is the least expensive, although they all charge more at the outdoor tables.

The small *Café St Paul* at 143 Rue Saint Paul Ouest away from the crowds, is more reasonable with light lunches for $4. They serve croissants and espresso too.

## Rue Prince Arthur

Rue Prince Arthur is a small street which was converted into a pleasant eating area about a dozen years ago. The restaurant segment runs west from Place Saint Louis on Rue Saint Denis (just north of Rue Sherbrooke) to a block west of Boulevard Saint Laurent. Many small, mostly ethnic restaurants line the 'pedestrians only' street. Greek and Vietnamese restaurants are most prominent but there are also French and Polish places among others. Most of the restaurants here have a 'bring your own' wine policy. The Greek places specialise in a Montreal favourite, brochettes, known to many as kebabs. Generally the more traditional dishes such as moussaka are absent but vine leaves or spanokopita show up as appetisers and there is always Greek salad.

An excellent Greek dinner can be had at *La Casa Grèque*, at 200 Rue Prince Arthur Est, for about $20 for two – good value. I've also had a good lunch at *Cabane Grèque Restaurant*, another Greek place, this one at 102 Prince Arthur Est. For a bit of a splurge the *Akita*, a Japanese place at 166 Rue Prince Arthur Est, does everything well. Before 7.30 pm the set meal is good value.

## Saint Denis Area

The *Café Croissant de Lune* on the east side of Rue Saint Denis, downstairs just south of Rue Ontario, is a great place for breakfasts. *Café au lait* and one or two of the fresh sweet buns or croissants will hold you for a few hours.

On Rue Ontario just west of Rue Saint Denis, in the 300 block, there are several cheap cafés, mostly patronised by students and arty types, offering light meals. At 2115

Top Left: Alfresco dining area at the Forks Historic Site, Winnipeg, Manitoba (ML)
Top Right: Provincial Legislature, Winnipeg, Manitoba (ML)
Bottom: The *Blue Nose II* in Toronto Harbour, Toronto, Ontario (MA)

Top Left: Flora in the Valley of the 10 Peaks, Banff National Park, Alberta (ML)
Top Right: Alberta flora (TS)
Bottom Left: The Athabasca Glacier, off the Icefields Parkway, Alberta (ML)
Bottom Right: Flora in the Valley of the 10 Peaks, Banff National Park, Alberta (ML)

Rue Saint Denis, *Le Commensal*, open daily from 11 am to midnight, offering good self-serve vegetarian meals, salads and desserts priced by weight, is highly recommended. You can really heap it up and the cost won't be high. They also have outlets at 680 Sainte Catherine Ouest and one at 1204 Rue McGill College.

*Au Vieux Calife*, at 1633 Rue Saint Hubert, is a small, unpretentious place with offerings like vegetables with couscous and mint tea or coffee for $4.25. You can select other Tunisian meals as well.

A well-established, popular low-cost restaurant is *Da Giovanni* at 572 Rue Sainte Catherine Est. You can have a good, complete meal (from soup to dessert) featuring spaghetti for under $5. Other dishes such as fish or meat are available at not much higher prices. Arrive before 5.30 pm to avoid waiting in line. It closes at 8 pm.

### The Main & Avenue Duluth

Boulevard Saint Laurent, the major north-south street which divides the city streets east from west (the street numbers start in each direction here) has long had a reputation for its characters, varied ethnic groups, their businesses and restaurants. As I've said before, it's affectionately known as The Main.

Just south of Rue Sainte Catherine are several of the city's best known French fries/hot dog places – memorably good. The dogs are known as steamies because of the way they're cooked. If you ask for 'all dress', everyone will understand and you'll get the full Quebec treatment, complete with chopped cabbage.

Much further north is a must: *Schwartz's* at No 3895. It's a small, casual, friendly deli that's practically never closed. It is always packed and has absolutely the best smoked meat in town. They make it right on the premises and age it naturally without chemicals.

The section of Boulevard Saint Laurent around Rue Prince Arthur has numerous places in either direction, many of them reasonably priced. But anywhere along the street you could discover a new East Indian or African restaurant.

Avenue Duluth runs east-west off Boulevard Saint Laurent at about the No 4000 block. Much like Rue Prince Arthur it's a narrow old street, once a red-light district, that has been redone as a restaurant centre although it is not as busy as Rue Prince Arthur. From just east of Boulevard Saint Laurent, running east to Rue Saint Denis and beyond, there are numerous Greek, Italian and Vietnamese eateries.

Near Boulevard Saint Laurent at 65 Avenue Duluth Est, *L'Harmonie d'Asie* is a moderately priced Vietnamese place. At No 450 try *La Maison Grèque*, which is busy but large, with an outdoor area for good-value brochette dinners. There's a dépanneur nearby for grabbing a bottle of wine. Further east near Rue Saint Hubert, there are a couple of more expensive French restaurants.

### Chinatown

Montreal's Chinatown is a small but well-entrenched part of the city. Though its restaurants can't compare to those in Toronto's or Vancouver's Chinatowns, there are quite a few of them. As always, it's best to eat with three or more people so you can sample more dishes. The district is centred on Rue de la Gauchetière Ouest between Rue Saint Urbain and Boulevard Saint Laurent, east of Square Dorchester, north of Old Montreal. A portion of the street is closed to traffic. The food is mainly Cantonese although some spicier Sichuan dishes show up on more menus these days. Many places offer lunch specials from as low as $5 or $6.

Places both cheap and not so cheap can be found along Rue de la Gauchetière. At 43 de la Gauchetière Est is *Tong Por* on the corner of Saint Dominique. The vast menu has both Cantonese and Thai dishes. It's good and cheap, too.

On Boulevard Saint Laurent, the *Cristal de Saigon* at No 1068 has cheap but plain Vietnamese food, and the *Fung Lam* across the street at No 1071 is the same but has Cantonese food. *Bon Ble Riz* at 1437 Saint

Laurent is more costly but not expensive for Cantonese and Sichuan fare.

## Avenue du Parc

Avenue du Parc, running north up beyond the mountain, has numerous more traditional Greek restaurants (no kebabs or brochettes), many specialising in fish. Moderately priced (dinner for four at $90) and good is the casual *Milos* at 5357 Avenue du Parc. Fish makes up most of the menu and it is by far most economical if there are four of you because you order a whole fish and it is priced by the pound. There are also a few Portuguese places along here too.

## ENTERTAINMENT

Montreal nightlife is good, varied, and comes in two languages. Clubs serve alcohol until 3 am – the longest opening hours in Canada, that's civilisation. Many places don't get going until around 10 pm or later. Films, plays and shows are not censored here as in more puritan places, eg Ontario.

The *Mirror* is a free weekly entertainment newspaper which can be picked up around town. The Saturday *Montreal Gazette* also has club and entertainment listings.

The Montreal Info Line (☎ 685-4636) has information on shows, nightclubs and also sells tickets to concerts and performances.

## Live Music & Disco

Rue Crescent, Rue de la Montagne and Rue Bishop are lively at night, with mostly disco-type places (no jeans allowed) but more casual places, too. This is the area for the English nightlife, whereas the French tend to party on Saint Denis. The *Sir Winston Churchill Pub* at 1459 Rue Crescent is popular and has dancing. *L'Esprit*, at 1234 Rue de la Montagne below Rue Sainte Catherine, is in a former funeral parlour. It's sort of dressy and admission costs $7 on weekends.

*Thursdays* at 1449 Rue Crescent is a singles-style spot. Nearby, over on Rue Bishop, there are several pubs. It's fun just to wander around this area at night, maybe have a beer and people-watch. Most of the many bars don't start cooking until 10 or 11

pm and after that time there will be queues to get in.

The *Metropolis*, at 59 Rue Sainte Catherine Est, is the largest dance club in town, with bars spread over three floors and impressive sound and lighting systems. It's only open from Thursday to Sunday. For the business and professional crowd, the *Pacha* at 1215 Boulevard de Maisonneuve Ouest on the corner of Rue Drummond is popular.

The *Old Munich* is in the large, square building on Rue Saint Denis on the corner of Boulevard René Lévesque. Inside it's a vast, cavernous, pub-style place that's often full with people of all types and ages. The place has a real party atmosphere. In the centre, amidst the smoke and noise, a band encourages you to break from drinking and dance to German oompah Oktoberfest-type music. Cover charge is $3 or more, depending on the entertainment but Tuesday nights are free.

The *Salsathèque* at 1220 Rue Peel can be a fun place. It's a bright, busy, dressy place featuring large live Latin bands who pump out infectious Latin dance music. And if you like to see dancing, the patrons here will feast your eyes.

The *Yellow Door Coffee House* (☎ 392-6743), at 3625 Rue Aylmer, has survived from the '60s – US draft dodgers found refuge here. Folk music in a casual ambience is still presented but now only occasionally. Call for upcoming concerts. It is closed through the summer.

In Old Montreal at 104 Rue Saint Paul, *Les Deux Pierrots* is a huge, two-storey spot with local French singers and a casual atmosphere – and it's free.

New-wave music can be heard cheaply at *Les Foufounes Electriques*, 87 Rue Sainte Catherine Est.

Up in Plateau Mont Royal the *5116* at that address on Avenue du Parc has been recommended as has the *Café Campus* at 57 Rue Prince Arthur Est.

There are several good spots for jazz in town. *L'Air du Temps* (☎ 842-2002) is in Old Montreal at 191 Rue Saint Paul Ouest on the corner of Rue Saint François Xavier. Solo music starts at 5 pm, groups after 9.30 pm; performers are mostly local musicians. There's no cover charge and the atmosphere and decor are pleasant.

At *Biddles* (☎ 842-8656), at 2060 Rue Aylmer, you might get a standard trio, a swing band or a vocalist. You can eat here too; there's no cover charge. The *Grand Café*, at 1720 Rue Saint Denis, presents live jazz and blues at a modest price. Not far away on Rue Ontario, local musicians play at *Café Thélème* also with no cover charge.

### Cinema

There are several English-language repertory film theatres around town, usually offering double bills and midnight movies on weekends. These theatres are always cheaper than the chains showing first runs.

More central, but with a similar policy, is The *Paris Cinema* (☎ 875-7284) at 896 Rue Sainte Catherine Ouest. It presents two different films nightly. Most are of US origin but European films are regularly shown as well.

The McGill and Loyola campuses often run film series. There is an IMAX (☎ 496-4629) large-format theatre in the Vieux Port (Old Port) area of Montreal.

### Other Entertainment

For a view of the city, try the top floor bar in the luxury *Château Champlain* on Square Dorchester. Drinks are costly but the view is fine and worth the price of one drink any way.

The *Comedyworks* upstairs at 1230 Rue Bishop presents stand-up comics, usually several in a night. Admission is charged. For theatre, the *Centaur Theatre* (☎ 288-3161) at 453 Rue Saint François Xavier, generally has the best in English presentations. *Les Ballet Jazz de Montreal*, a Montreal modern dance troupe, has a good reputation and often performs in town. *Place des Arts* presents an array of concerts, the symphony, and dance.

The now internationally famed *Cirque de Soleil* animal-free circus is based in Montreal. If they are in town performing, a ticket is worth considering. The circus is based on acrobatics and a range of astounding acts of dexterity.

The Palais de la Civilisation is now housed in Old Montreal's impressive, restored Bonsecours Market Building at 330 Rue Saint Paul Est. The Palais mounts large, informative public exhibitions on historical and cultural themes. Several readers have written to say the shows are good.

### THINGS TO BUY

The Canadian Guild of Crafts, at 2025 Rue Peel, has a small and rather expensive collection of the work of Quebec artisans and other Canadiana, as well as Inuit prints and carvings. It's free to look around.

The Baffin Inuit Art Gallery (☎ 393-1999), at 4 Rue Saint Paul Est on the corner of Boulevard Saint Laurent, has a fine varied collection of stone carvings. You can buy as well as look, but the pieces here are real collectables and are not cheap.

### GETTING THERE & AWAY
### Air

There are two airports. Dorval, 20 km west of the centre of town, is used for domestic and North American flights. Mirabel Airport is just over 50 km north-west of the town's centre and handles all other international flights.

Many airlines serve Montreal, including the major Canadian ones. A selection of fares includes: Air Canada (☎ 393-3333), to Halifax $281, Toronto $213, and Winnipeg $457. Canadian Airlines (☎ 931-2233) has the same prices as Air Canada.

A good place for students to start looking for cheap fares is Voyages Campus (☎ 843-3851), 1613 Rue Saint Denis, which also has an office at the McGill University campus.

Montreal can also offer low fares to Florida, Mexico and parts of the Caribbean.

### Bus

The bus station (☎ 842-2281) is central on the corner of Boulevard de Maisonneuve and Rue Berri, near Rue Saint Denis. It's right beside the Berri-UQAM Métro stop. The station serves Voyageur lines, Orleans

Express, Greyhound from the USA, and also Vermont Transit, which runs between Montreal and Boston, about seven hours away, with a transfer in Burlington, Vermont. When dealing with Greyhound for US destinations, make sure you know which currency is being discussed. Orleans Express operates the buses in Quebec from Montreal eastwards.

Voyageur destinations and services include to Ottawa every hour for $25 and to Toronto about five services daily, more on weekends for $60.

Orleans Express connects Montreal to Quebec City with direct express runs and other slower trips which stop at smaller places along the way. A ticket for Quebec City is $35, or $49 return with 10 days notice as long as you don't travel on a Friday.

Murray Hill (☎ 871-4733) runs ski bus expresses in season. They make two runs into the Laurentians and two to Vermont destinations. Call for information on when and where the trips start.

### Train
There are two train stations right near each other in the central area. You can walk underground from one to the other in 10 minutes.

The CN-VIA Rail station, also called Central Station, below the Queen Elizabeth Hotel on the corner of Boulevard René Lévesque and Rue Mansfield, gets most VIA Rail (☎ 871-1331) passengers. Use the Bonaventure Métro station.

Windsor Station, the CP terminal, is on the corner of Rue Peel and Rue de la Gauchetière, a few blocks from the CN station. Use the same Métro stop. It's mainly local commuter trains which use this venerable old station now.

There are three trains a day to Ottawa most days and five trains a day to Toronto, starting at 7.30 am. Fares are: Ottawa $32, Toronto $75, and Quebec City $40.

For information about US destinations call Amtrak on ☎ 1-800-872-7245. Amtrak to New York costs $US69 one way, with cheap returns available. Fares vary depending on the month in which you travel.

Remember when inquiring about fares to US destinations to check whether prices are being given in US dollars. They probably are.

### Car
The Trans Canada Hwy runs right through the city and Hwy 15 leads south to US 87 heading for New York. Hwy 401 joins Montreal to Toronto and beyond westward.

**Car Rental** For car rentals, Budget (☎ 866-7675) with offices around town has one in Central Station downtown charges $40 per day with 100 free km, 14 cents per km over that for their economy cars. Tax is extra. Tilden (☎ 878-2771), at 1200 Rue Stanley, has similar rates as Budget but may be better for weekends.

For cheaper rates try Via Route (☎ 871-1166), at 1255 Rue Mackay or Mini-Prix (☎ 524-3009), at 2000 Rue Sainte Catherine Est. The latter has vans as well as cars. Getting a small group together could be quite economical.

There are many other companies and outlets all over town including at both airports. Prices tend not to vary a heck of a lot but differences can be found among the weekend specials and other multiple-day offers.

**Car Sharing** Allo Stop (☎ 985-3032), at 4317 Rue Saint Denis, is an agency that gets drivers and passengers together. Call a day ahead and tell them where you want to go or, if you're a driver, where you're going. Prices are good, considerably less than a bus ticket; it's $15 to Quebec City, for example. Allo Stop also goes to Toronto, New York and other cities. Passengers must pay a $6 membership fee, drivers a higher fee. Those with cars can have some of their expenses paid by taking along passengers. Allo Stop has offices in Toronto, Ottawa, Quebec City and many other points around Quebec such as the Saguenay and the Gaspé. This is an agency really worth checking out.

## GETTING AROUND
### To/From the Airport

The cheapest and quickest way to Dorval Airport is to take the Métro to Lionel-Groulx. Transfer to the No 211 bus outside. The first stop, about 15 to 25 minutes later, is the Dorval Bus Transfer Station. Switch here, with free transfer, to any No 204 bus which runs into the airport.

An alternative, at the same price, but slower unless you are near one of these bus lines is to take the Métro to Crémazie, then catch bus No 100 west towards the airport and ask the driver to let you off to catch bus No 209, which will take you right in. The total cost for either of these routes is $1.75.

From the airport, catch the 204 East (Est) to the Dorval Bus Transfer Station and switch to the 211 Est. This will take you to the Métro. There is a maximum wait time of half an hour between buses, through most of the day waiting time will be much less.

Bus Nos 204 and 211 run from 5 am to 1 am.

Autocar Connaisseur (☎ 934-1222) run by Grayline, runs buses between Dorval and downtown luxury hotels for $8.50. Autobus Aéro Plus (☎ 633-1100) runs buses between Mirabel Airport and Dorval Airport and Mirabel and downtown for $11.15. The latter trips take about 45 minutes. Between Dorval and downtown the ride takes a little under half an hour.

A taxi from downtown to Dorval is roughly $23, from downtown to Mirabel, a hefty $56.

### Bus & Métro

The city has a fairly widespread, convenient Métro – bus system (☎ 288-6287). The Métro is the name for the city's underground train system. The Métro runs until 1 am and some buses run even later. One ticket can get you anywhere in the city as it entitles you to a transfer to any connecting bus or subway

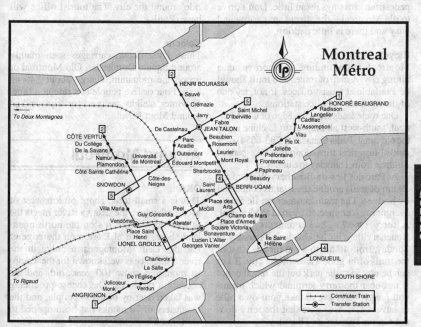

**Montreal Métro**

To Deux Montagnes

To Rigaud

- HENRI BOURASSA
- Sauvé
- Crémazie
- Jarry
- De Castelnau
- Saint Michel
- D'Iberville
- Fabre
- JEAN TALON
- Beaubien
- Rosemont
- Laurier
- Mont Royal
- Sherbrooke

CÔTE VERTU
- Du Collège
- De la Savane
- Namur
- Plamondon
- Côte Sainte Catherine
- Université de Montréal
- Parc
- Acadie
- Outremont
- Édouard Montpetit
- Côte-des-Neiges
- SNOWDON

- HONORÉ BEAUGRAND
- Radisson
- Langelier
- Cadillac
- L'Assomption
- Viau
- Pie IX
- Joliette
- Préfontaine
- Frontenac
- Papineau
- Beaudry
- BERRI-UQAM
- Saint Laurent

- Villa Maria
- Peel
- McGill
- Place des Arts
- Champ de Mars
- Guy Concordia
- Vendôme
- Atwater
- Place d'Armes
- Square Victoria
- Place Saint Henri
- Lucien L'Allier
- Georges Vanier
- Bonaventure
- LIONEL GROULX
- Île Saint Hélène

- Charlevoix
- La Salle
- De l'Église
- Jolicoeur
- Monk
- Verdun
- ANGRIGNON

LONGUEUIL

SOUTH SHORE

Commuter Train
Transfer Station

QUEBEC

train. On the buses, get a transfer from the driver and on the Métro from the machines past the turnstiles. A strip of six tickets is $7 or single tickets cost $1.75 each. Buses take tickets, transfers, or correct cash only. If you will be in town for a calendar month and plan to use public transit frequently consider the monthly pass. It can be shared as no picture is required.

Métro routes are shown on the tourist map and stops are indicated above ground by large blue signs with a white arrow pointing down. The system runs basically east-west with a north-south line intersecting at Berri-UQAM. It runs on rubber tyres and is safe, clean, fast and quiet. For information on how to get to any particular spot call the above number.

### Car

In town, most streets are one way and the drivers are aggressive. Watch the action at yellow lights. Pedestrians are fair game; pedestrian crossings mean little. Don't drive to old Montreal – the streets are narrow and busy and there is little parking.

### Bicycle

Montreal is continuing to improve as a biking city. A map of routes and trails should be available at tourist offices. If not, try one of the libraries or police stations.

One route leads from the edge of Old Montreal, south-west all the way to Lachine along the old canal. Parks Canada (☎ 283-6054) runs guided historical trips along this bike path in summer from Thursday to Sunday.

At Parc des Îles-de-Boucherville there are 22 km of trails around the islands connected by bridges. The main entrance on Île Sainte Marguerite is connected by road to Montreal. A ferry (☎ 873-2843) connects Quai de Boucherville with Île Grosbois Thursday to Sunday, from 10 am to 4 pm for $3. Most of the trails offer good views of the city. Bikes can be rented at the park but the rental depot is not near the ferry terminal which means you pretty well have to take your own bike or have a car. Also note that the ferry does not run on Tuesday or Thursday.

For rentals or repairs, Velo Aventure (☎ 847-0666) on Quai King Edward at the Old Port is recommended. They're open every day from May to October and have good bikes in good condition. Roller blades (in-line skates) with all the padding necessary for novices are also offered. Rentals are by the hour, half-day or full-day and there are kids and family rates. Child seats are available. Perhaps best of all, there is a major bike path going for miles from right at the door of the shop. Maps of the city's bicycle paths, one of which circles the entire island, are available from Velo.

Bicycles can also be rented at the Infotouriste office (☎ 393-1528) at Square Dorchester.

Bicycles can be taken on the Métro in the last two carriages of the train and on the water shuttles over to Park des Îles.

The light-hearted, good-time Tour des Îles on the first weekend in June is a major biking event for everyone with any kind of bicycle. Some riders wear wacky costumes in this ride around the city. The tourist office will have details.

### Calèche

These horse-drawn carriages seen mainly around Square Dorchester, Old Montreal or up on the mountain, charge about $40 an hour. Four or five people can ride at a time. In winter, sleighs are used for trips up and around Mont Royal.

# Around Montreal

### OKA

This is a small town about 60 km west of Montreal, where the Ottawa River meets the St Lawrence River. It's on the north mainland shore, north of Dorion on the edge of Lac des Deux Montagnes, a bulge in the river. The place is well known for the Trappist monastery, now 100 years old, and the cheeses it produces. The cheese-producing was taken over by business people, and the monastery of 70 monks has been opened to visitors. There are religious artworks, a mountain with the Stages of the Cross and several old stone buildings.

Oka became internationally known late in 1990 as the site of a major confrontation between Mohawk people and the federal and provincial governments. At first a local land squabble, this issue soon came to represent all the continuing problems such as land claims and self-government which Native Indians across the country would like to see properly resolved.

## ROUGE RIVER

Not far north-west of Montreal near the Ontario border, the Rouge River is well known for white-water rafting. Several companies offer day or weekend trips which most people reckon are a lot of fun. One to try is New World River Expeditions (☎ 1-800-567-6881) with an office in Montreal. They have an office in Calumet, Quebec on the river or you can call toll free. They have a lodge with pool and bar, so you're not roughing it in the bush the whole time. Another is Adventure Eau Vive (☎ 819-242-6084) which has operated for 10 years.

## SUCRERIE DE LA MONTAGNE

Situated in a maple forest, the sucrerie (☎ 451-0831) depicts a 1900-era Quebec sugar shack where sap is converted to maple syrup and sugar. A visit includes a tour and explanation of the process, a meal and entertainment. The lunch package is $30, the dinner, $40.

To get to the site 45 km from downtown, take the train to Rigaud and then it's about a $7 taxi ride.

## THE LAURENTIANS (LAURENTIDES)

Between 80 km and 150 km north of Montreal, this section of the ancient Laurentian Shield is a mountainous, rolling lake-sprinkled playground. The land proved a dismal failure for lumber and mining, but when skiing caught on, so did this area as a resortland. The district today is used not only for the best in eastern skiing but for camping, fishing and swimming in summer. The many picturesque French towns dominated by their church spires and the good scenery make it popular for just lazing and relaxing as well. Plentiful accommodation and restaurants provide a wide range of services, from elegant inns with fine dining rooms to modest motels.

The Laurentian Autoroute (Autoroute Laurentienne), also known as Hwy 15, is the fastest route north from Montreal and is the way the buses go. The old Hwy 117 north is slower but more pleasant. A second major route goes north-east of Montreal to Joliette and then smaller roads continue further north.

The better known towns and resorts are all clustered near the highways. Cottage country spreads out a little further east and west. In general terms the busy area ends at Mont Tremblant Provincial Park. The smaller villages on the upper areas of Hwy 117 are quiet and typically 'Laurentian'.

To find less-developed areas or to camp, you pretty much have to head for the big parks, as most of the region is privately owned. Many of the towns have tourist offices so you can ask about things as you go. Outside the parks, campgrounds are generally privately owned too, and tend to be small and busy. Motels are next up the economic scale; the lodges are generally (but not always) quite pricey. There is usually a traveller's hostel somewhere in the area, but locations change often, so ask in Montreal.

The busiest times in the Laurentians are July, August, around Christmas, February and March. At other times, prices tend to be reduced, like the crowds. Fall is a good season to visit, the hills are colourful and the cooler air is ideal for walking. The whole area (in all seasons) has a festive, relaxed atmosphere.

In ski season, special buses operate between Dorval Airport and various hills. They're a little more expensive than the usual bus fares; return tickets are cheapest.

Year-round tourist information offices with accommodation assistance can be found in the villages of Saint Adèle, Sainte

Agathe, Saint Jovite and at Mont Tremblant
(☎ 425-2434), 248 Rue du Couvent.

## Saint Sauveur des Monts
Saint Sauveur des Monts, known simply as
Saint Savueur, the first stop-off on the way
north, about 60 km from Montreal, is a small
pleasant resort town with four nearby ski
hills. Summer or winter, day or night, the
main street, Rue Principale, with its restaurants, cafés, bars and shops is busy. Saint
Savueur has B&B, hotel and motel accommodation.

## Mont Rolland
Mont Rolland is a recreation centre based at
Mont Gabriel. There's excellent skiing in
winter and in summer the mountain turns
into a huge slide complex, a trend which
many of the area's resorts have embraced.
This one differs in that it is not a water slide,
as such, but instead uses bobsleds sliding on
ball bearings. Hang on tight!

The Rolland Paper Company, one of the
oldest and most important paper makers in
the country, is based here.

The Auberge Mont Gabrie on top of the
mountain is one of the larger, more expensive lodges in the Laurentians.

## Sainte Adèle
Sainte Adèle is one of the nicer-looking
highway towns, with a popular recreation
area, Lac Rond.

A museum recreates a story by one of the
towns most illustrious sons, popular Quebec

---

## Skiing
The Laurentians are without doubt one of the prime ski regions in the country. The region has the
hills, the snow, the scenery, the experience and perhaps most of all, the relaxed, friendly sporting
atmosphere that adds immeasurably to a day at the slopes.

With over 20 ski centres within 2½ hours of Montreal offering runs for the novice and the expert
the alpine skiing is convenient and varied enough to offer something for everyone. Over a quarter
of the 350 ski runs are now lit for nightskiing – a wonderful experience, and often less busy than
the trails through the day.

Through a good winter, skiing can be enjoyed for four months with many lodges making artificial
snow to complement what the sky provides. Although renowned for its downhill slopes, the region
has plenty of good cross-country skiing as well and this can be tried and enjoyed for considerably
less money. Equipment can be rented at a couple of sport shops around Montreal (try the yellow
pages telephone book or the tourist office) and, more commonly, at the ski centres up north. Arrive
early in the day for the best selection and help in getting fitted out. Renting the whole package –
boots, skis and poles – runs to about $20 to $25 for a full day which isn't bad at all because the
equipment tends to be good.

Tow prices vary from centre to centre but range from $20 to $30 a day. Half-day tickets are
sold at many resorts and there is a separate night-ski pass available which is less money.
Children's tickets are also offered. Prices are lower during the week than on weekends and all
prices rise for the period around Christmas and New Year.

Less than an hour from Montreal there are some fine places such as Habitant and for beginners
or the rusty, Olympia with a good selection of wide, easy runs. Go for it!

As a rough guide, the further from Montreal, the more challenging the hills can become although
even resorts with deadly runs also offer some for novice or intermediate skiers so you don't have
to get in over your head.

The grandaddy of them all is Mont Tremblant with the highest vertical drop in the Laurentians
at 650 metres. The Mont Tremblant and Grey Rocks ski centres are huge offering multiple runs.
Travel down one side of the mountain in the morning and then, when the sun shifts, ski down the
other side. This resort, hoping to  lure visitors from far and wide, is undergoing a major overhaul
to bring all the facilities up to top rate international standards.

The Mont Tremblant area has some 150 km of mechanically set cross-country trails around
the provincial park, Saint Jovite, and around the village of Mont Tremblant, itself. Many of the
trails, even further south, say at Mont Rolland, are interconnected and some have warming huts
at intervals along the way. ■

author Claude-Henri Grignon. Another museum, Musée Village de Séraphin, is a small recreated European pioneer village.

**Places to Stay** Accommodation, mainly good hotels, tends to be expensive here; budgeters try the *Auberge aux Croissants* (☎ 229-3838) at 750 Chemin Sainte Marguerite.

### Sainte Agathe des Monts

With about 9000 people, this is the largest town in the Laurentians and a busy resort centre. With numerous bars, cafés and restaurants, as well as shops for replenishing supplies, there is always plenty of activity. The local bakery, on Rue Sainte Agathe, is known far and wide.

At the edge of Lac des Sables, more or less in town, there is room for a picnic, and cruises of the lake depart from the wharf. Around the lake are beaches and places to camp. One km north of town, Village du Mont Castor is a modern townhouse development created in turn-of-the-century Quebécois style using full-size logs.

**Places to Stay** B&Bs, inns (auberges) and motels all tend to be quite busy, especially on weekends, so planning ahead is advisable. Try the B&B *La Villa Verra* (☎ 326-0513) at 246 Saint Venant. At the end of July, watch for the annual music and dance festival.

### Val David

Close to Sainte Agathe but to the east off Hwy 15, Val David is a considerably smaller town that's become an arts & crafts centre. Studios and workshops can be visited, and stores sell a variety of handicrafts.

**Places to Stay** There is an HI hostel, *Le Chalet Beaumont* (☎ 322-1972), at 1451 Rue Beaumont, in a rustic log chalet perched on a hill with great views. If you call from Montreal a shuttle bus will meet the bus from Montreal and take you to the hostel. This is the only hostel in the region but it's in a good location.

### Saint Faustin

Saint Faustin has a population of about 1200 and a large nature interpretive centre on grounds containing 15 km of walking and hiking trails. It's free and maps are available at the centre where there is information on the flora & fauna of the area.

There is also a trout hatchery here in a nice setting which can be visited. The fish raised here are used to restock the rivers and lakes of the Laurentians.

### Saint Jovite

Heading further north, this smaller town is south of but near **Mont Tremblant** which lies just outside the provincial park of the same name. The mountain, with its 650-metre vertical drop, is the highest peak in the Laurentians. With over 20 runs, it's the most popular skiing spot, and marks the northernmost point of the easily accessible Laurentian destinations. Saint Jovite is a supply centre for the Mont Tremblant area with its many lakes. Along Rue Ouimet an array of restaurants can be found.

The Musée de la Faune at 65 Rue Limoge has a collection of indigenous animals.

At the foot of the mountain, 146 km from Montreal, is Mont Tremblant Village, an accommodation centre which has a chair lift to the peak in summer and winter.

In Weir, not far south of Saint Jovite, is the **Laurentides Satellite Earth Station**, an international telecommunications installation. There are free guided tours of the facilities and 10-storey-high antennae, as well as slide presentations. It's open daily from mid-June to Labour Day. Follow the signs from Weir.

### Saint Donat

North-east of Sainte Agathe, this little lakeside town is a supply centre for the main entrance to Mont Tremblant Provincial Park which lies just to the north.

There are beaches on **Lac Archambault** and, in summer, 90-minute cruises around the lake.

Accommodation of all types can be found

QUEBEC

in and around town. Bars and cafés along the main streets are lively at night.

## Mont Tremblant Provincial Park

Opened as early as 1894, this is a huge area – over 1500 sq km – of lakes, rivers, hills and woods. There are many campsites in the park – some with amenities but most are basic. The most developed area is north of Saint Donat. Roads are paved, canoes can be rented, and the campgrounds have showers, etc. Not too far from the entrance there are a couple of good walking paths with views and, a little further in, a fair-sized waterfall with nearby picnic tables.

Towards the interior, some campsites are accessible only by foot, canoe or unsurfaced roads some of which are rough old logging routes. The more off-the-track areas abound in wildlife.

In the far eastern section one September, we had whole lakes to ourselves, saw moose and heard nearby wolves howling as we sat around the fire. Nights were very cold so be prepared.

**Mark Lightbody**

## LANAUDIÈRE

Lanaudière refers to the region north-east of Montreal and, though it is essentially still 'up north' or 'the Laurentians', it has cultivated its own identity. Without the quality ski hills and fewer large towns it is, though still popular, a less visited region. There are plenty of parks with walking trails over mountains and along rivers to enjoy. The southern area has its own cowboys. And food and lodging is noticeably cheaper than in the places further west along the Autoroute. For any specific area information call the Lanaudière tourist office on ☎ 1-800-363-2788.

## Terrebonne

Believe it or not the Moulins region of south-west Lanaudière around the towns of Terrebonne and Mascouche and along the north shore of Rivière des Milles Îles is cowboy country. Here, about a 45-minute drive from downtown Montreal, there are about 30 ranches, thousands of horses and plenty of events for their fully Western-style riders to compete in. Throughout summer various horse shows, rodeos and gymkhanas are an almost weekly occurrence.

Pretty well every Saturday night at Tico-Smokey Ranch outside Terrebonne there is a competition of one sort or another. On Friday and Saturday nights, fans and riders meet for country music and dancing at the Chalet de la Vallée at 1231 Chemin Pincourt in Mascouche, but don't arrive too early – these cowboys don't have to get up before the sun.

Frequently throughout the summer there are major two-day rodeos with calf-roping, steer wrestling, bronco busting, the whole bit. For a schedule of events and locations call the Lanaudière tourist office. Many stables in the area offer horses and trail rides, some not ending until midnight.

When your legs have had enough, the Wild West can be left far behind with a visit to the village of Vieux Terrebonne along the Rivière des Milles Îles, opposite Île des Moulins. Here along the waterfront are numerous restaurants and cafés.

## Joliette

Joliette is a principal town and centre for the local tobacco-growing industry. You may notice that in some areas, the farmland is divided into long strips. These are known as *rangs* and were a traditional way of dividing up the land not seen outside the province.

There is also a lot of maple-syrup production in the area. In spring, many farmers allow visitors to the 'sugar shacks' for a look-see and a taste. Or you can see how it's done all year at Chez Madeleine in Mascouche, where they provide information and sell various maple goodies. I don't want to rush you, but it's said that, in time, acid rain could wipe out this traditional industry.

Joliette is the site of the annual Festival International de Lanaudière, a major international, classical-music festival, which draws crowds of thousands to the 50 or so concerts which take place throughout summer. Many events are held at the new outdoor amphitheatre which has a capacity of 10,000. Free half-hour tours of the facility are offered.

### Rawdon

Rawdon, the other main town, has **Moore Canadiana Village**, a re-created 1800s town, complete with workers in costume. Most of the buildings are authentic (the schoolhouse is from 1835). Other attractions include a museum and art gallery.

Lakeside Rawdon has long been a local beauty spot. Trails and observation points wind along the Ouareau River with the **Dorwin Falls**. Nearby there are other hilly, wooded areas good for walking. Ask at the tourist office.

There are numerous lakes in the region, many with inns, resorts or campgrounds.

### Berthierville

To the east of Joliette on the St Lawrence River is Berthierville, the birthplace of the late Gilles Villeneuve, the Formula 1 racing car driver. A museum details his exciting career on the Grand Prix circuit.

### EASTERN TOWNSHIPS (ESTRIE)

The Eastern Townships area (Les Cantons de l'Est), the 'Garden of Quebec', generally known as L'Estrie by the French, extends from Granby to the New Hampshire border. The area is appreciated for its rolling hills, green farmland, woods and lakes – an extension of the US Appalachian region.

It's a popular resort area, with fishing and swimming in the numerous lakes in summer and excellent skiing in winter. L'Estrie abounds in cottages and chalets both private and commercial, and inns. The region also has a reputation for its many fine but expensive dining rooms.

In spring, 'sugaring off' – the tapping of trees for maple syrup, and then boiling and preparing it – takes place throughout the region. In the fall, a good time to visit, colours are beautiful as the leaves change, and apple harvesting takes place with the attendant cider production. Skiing is a major winter activity with centres at Mont Orford and Sutton.

The Eastern Townships have a long history and, as evidenced by the place names, were until quite recently predominantly English. Though originally occupied by the Abenakis Indians much of the region was first developed by Loyalists fleeing the USA after the revolution of 1776. Later in the next century many Irish people arrived. Soon after, French settlers arrived to help with the expanding economy and that made up the mix of people which has continued to today.

Many of the towns and villages are

---

### Maple Syrup

Liquid, golden maple syrup is a traditional, all natural taste sensation. Quebec is the world's largest producer and Estrie with its abundance of sugar maple forests has long been the major focal point.

It is believed the Indians who had a spring date known as the sugar-making moon passed their knowledge onto to early pioneers. Production techniques now vary but essentially in spring, when the sap begins to run, the trees are tapped and buckets hung from them to collect, drop by drop, the nearly clear sap. The liquid is then collected into large kettles and boiled at the 'sugar shack' for days, driving off most of the water. As it thickens, the colour becomes more intense and the sugar content rises to 90% or so. It is then cooled, graded and bottled.

It is most often spread over vanilla ice cream or pancakes. A further refining results in maple sugar, a solidified version. The Montreal or regional Estrie tourist offices will be able to tell you where to see a demonstration of the process in early spring.

Acid rain has adversely affected the maple forests of Quebec and there is concern over the future of this small farm tradition. Eastern and central Ontario also produce maple syrup as does New Brunswick. ■

popular with antique-hunters; small craftshops and galleries line many a main street. Another lure is the area's growing reputation for its spas and health centres where the stressed-out can be treated like Hollywood actors for a couple of days. Around the countryside on the smaller roads keep an eye out for the remaining wooden covered bridges and the round barns.

There is a B&B programme in the region (the tourist office will have the latest guide) and dozens of campgrounds. This region of the province is the only one where B&Bs make up the bulk of the accommodation and prices can be reasonable. The more historic and deluxe choices offer supreme grace but prices rise accordingly.

The main L'Estrie tourist office (☎ 1-800-263-1068) is on the Autoroute (Hwy 10) south from Montreal at exit 68. It's open daily all year. Other offices can be found in Magog, Granby and Sherbrooke.

L'Estrie is one of the good cycling regions in the province and rentals are available in Magog, Orford, North Hatley and other places. Both cycling and B&B maps are for sale at the regional tourist offices. One major cycling trail begins at Granby and runs to Waterloo. The district also produces some wines and most notably, mead, an ancient nectar made from fermented honey. A self-guided wine tour can be followed through the region.

### Granby

This town is known far and wide for its **zoo**, even though it was never particularly good. I swear everybody in Quebec knows of it, if in fact they haven't seen it at one time or another. It seems it has been there forever.

Newer exhibits such as the insectarium containing 100,000 little creatures, the reptile displays and a dinosaur exhibit with moving beasts have improved the zoo considerably in recent years. Granby is also well endowed with highly respected restaurants and hosts a gastronomical festival every autumn.

### Knowlton (Lac Brome)

Nearby, south of Hwy 10 on Hwy 243, is Knowlton on Lac Brome. In fact nowadays the town is often called Lac Brome. Many of the main street's Victorian buildings have been restored and it's become a bit of a tourist town with craft and gift shops, etc. The good local history museum includes a tea room. A favourite meal in this area is Lac Brome duck and it shows up frequently on the better menus.

### Sutton

Further south, Sutton is synonymous with its important ski hill, one of the area's highest. In summer, there are hiking trails in Sutton Park. The area around Sutton and south of Cowansville near the village of Dunham supports Quebec's wine industry and some of the wineries can be visited. This is also an important apple-growing region where casual work can be found in the fall.

At the natural environment park there is the decidedly nonregional llama-breeding farm where rides upon the haughty creatures can be attempted.

The Sutton area, again, is well known for its comfortable country inns and the fine restaurants many of which specialise in using local produce.

A modest B&B is the *Willow House* (☎ 538-0035) at 30 Rue Western.

Near the village of Sutton Junction Rural Route (RR) 4 sits what was once the farm of Madame Benoît, Canada's best known cook. She appeared on national TV for many years and wrote a couple of dozen cookbooks.

### Lac Champlain

Although essentially a US lake, which divides Vermont from New York State, it does protrude into Quebec as well. Steeped in history, the area is now popular with Canadians and Americans as a summer vacation and cottage spot.

The lake is good for swimming and fishing and, in places, is scenic. At Plattsburgh, New York there is a good and busy beach, where on any weekend you'll find plenty of Quebeckers. The short ferry trip across part of the lake is quite pleasant and worth doing if you're travelling through the area.

## Magog

Magog, sitting right at the northern tip of large Lac Memphrémagog, is an attractive town with 15,000 residents. The main street, Rue Principale, has a resort flavour with its numerous cafés, bars, bistros and restaurants.

On this same street, but just west of town, the tourist office can help provide information about the area. Daily boat cruises lasting a little over two hours are offered around the lake in summer.

There are numerous places to stay in and around town, mostly motels in the singles/doubles $40/60 range. The 10 B&Bs around town charge about the same. Hotels tend to be rather pricey.

## Lac Memphrémagog

This is the largest and best known lake in the L'Estrie area. Most of the lakefront properties are privately owned. Halfway down the lake at Saint Benoît-du-Lac is a **Benedictine monastery** where monks continue the tradition of the ancient Gregorian chant. Visitors can attend services and there's a hostel for men and another nearby at a nunnery for women if you want to stay. One of Quebec's cheeses – L'Ermite, a blue – is made and sold here. Also try to taste the cider the monks make.

**Rock Island**, the busy border crossing to the USA, is at the southern end of the lake and contains four of the Eastern Townships' best French restaurants.

## Mont Orford Provincial Park

Just out of Magog, this is a good but relatively small park (though the largest in the Eastern Townships). Dominated by Mont Orford (792 metres), the park is a skiing centre in winter but fills up quickly with campers in summer as well. You can swim here, use the walking trails, and the chair lift operates throughout the summer.

Each summer, the Orford Art Centre pres-

ents the Jeunesses Musicales du Canada music and art festival.

## North Hatley

Just east of Magog, North Hatley sits at the north end of Lac Massawippi.

I nearly drowned here during a storm in my adolescence. I guess what they said about its long thin shape and surrounding hills contributing to waters which quickly turn rough is true.

**Mark Lightbody**

North Hatley was a popular second home for wealthy Americans who enjoyed the scenery but even more the lack of Prohibition during the 1920s. Many of these huge old places are now inns and B&Bs. Try the Massawippi dark beer at the Le Pilsen pub.

## Sherbrooke

Sherbrooke is the principal commercial centre of the region and a fair-sized city in its own right. It's a bilingual town with several small museums, a wide selection of restaurants and is a pleasant centre lying between the Magog and Saint Francois rivers.

The tourist office (☎ 564-8331) is at 48 Rue Depôt. The 18-km walking and cycling path along the Magog River known as *Réseau Riverain*, makes a pleasant stroll. It begins at the **Maison de l'Eau**, a museum on aquatic life, found at the edge of the Magog River at 755 Cabana St in Blanchard Park.

The **Musée des Beaux Arts** in the centre on Rue du Palais is a sizeable art gallery open every afternoon except Monday. The annual fall fair is a big local event held each August.

On the outskirts is the **Shrine of Beauvoir**, dating from 1920, a site of religious pilgrimages with good views over the city and the surrounding area. In **Lennox-ville**, there's Bishop's, an English university. Also in Lennoxville are a couple of cottage breweries and some antique and craft shops to browse through. On Hwy 216 toward Stokes is the **Centre d'Interpretation de l'Abeille**, the Honey Bee Interpretive Centre, a research facility open for visitors with dis-

**QUEBEC**

plays about the little buzzers and the honey they produce. Other nearby attractions include the Magog River Gorge and the Frontenac Hydro-Electric Plant.

**Places to Stay & Eat** Here, as elsewhere around the Eastern Townships, the motels, hotels and inns are not at all cheap. Alternative B&Bs can be found through the local tourist office although these, too, in Sherbrooke are not inexpensive. In summer, rooms are also available at low rates at the university. *Hotel-Motel La Réserve* (☎ 566-6464) at 4235 Rue King Ouest charges from $55 double.

Two well-established four-star eateries are *Au Petit Sabot* and *l'Élite*. For simpler fare there is the *Marie Antoinette* at 333 Rue King Ouest.

**Getting There & Away** There's a VIA Rail station in Sherbrooke and frequent bus services to Montreal. The train goes through town three times a week in each direction between Montreal and Saint John, New Brunswick. It passes through Maine, USA en route.

South-west of town, several of the smaller area highways join Hwy 55 which leads south to Rock Island, a small town which is the major entry point into the USA, close to the states of New York, Vermont, and New Hampshire. During the summer, particularly on weekends, there can be major waits (as in hours) at this border. This is especially true going into Quebec as vehicles are checked for how much stuff was bought in the USA and duty collected. If possible find a smaller entry point, perhaps south of Coaticook.

### East of Sherbrooke

East of Sherbrooke the rolling farmlands and historic cultured towns and villages give way to a much rougher, less-populated region of primary resource industry and untouched woodlands. In the northern section of this district is the large Frontenac Recreation Park for access into an unspoiled region.

Further east is the border with Maine, USA.

## MONTREAL TO QUEBEC CITY

Leaving Montreal behind, travelling east on Hwy 138, you begin to get a sense of what small-town Quebec is like. Stone houses with light blue trim and tin roofs, silver-spired churches, ubiquitous chip wagons called *cantines* and main streets with shops built right to the road, are some characteristics. The best section is from Trois Rivières onwards to the north-east.

A much quicker route is Hwy 40, a four-lane expressway that can get you from Montreal to Quebec City in 2½ to three hours. There are not many services along this route, so watch your fuel levels.

From Montreal there is also one fast and one slow route along the south shore to Quebec City and beyond. The old Hwy 132 edges along the river but isn't as nice as its north shore counterpart (Hwy 138), and the Trans Canada Hwy is fast but boring until Quebec City, where it runs a little closer to the water. At Trois Rivières, you can cross the river.

### Saint Antoine de Padoue Church

This is on the north side of the St Lawrence River in Louiseville. It would be hard to miss, but take a peek inside too; it's one of Canada's grandest churches – very impressive. Next door, the tourist booth is helpful.

### Odanak

Almost directly across the river from Louiseville is Odanak, a small Abénakis Indian village settled in the early 1600s. A museum right on Hwy 226 outlines their history and culture. Perhaps of even more interest is the annual powwow held in July.

### Trois Rivières

Trois Rivières, over 350 years old and the largest town between Quebec's two main cities, is a major pulp and paper centre.

The **old section** around Rue des Ursulines, with its reminders of a long history, is small but good for a stroll. There is a tourist office in the Manoir Boucher-de-Niverville, an historic house at 168 Rue Bonaventure near the corner of Rue Hart.

Another tourist office is found west of town on Hwy 138 by Laviolette Bridge through the summer months.

The bus station is at 1075 Rue Champflour.

On Rue des Ursulines are several **old houses** now open to the public as small free museums and examples of various architectural styles. The **Ursuline Museum** at No 734 displays materials relating to the Ursuline Order of nuns who were prominent in the town's development.

The **cathedral** at 362 Rue Bonaventure, built in 1858, is the only Westminster-style church on the continent and is open daily.

Two-hour **cruises** along the river aboard the MS *Jacques Cartier* depart from the dock in **Parc Portuaire** at the foot of Boulevard des Forges in the centre of the old town.

Also in the park is an exhibit with models and videos on the local pulp and paper industry but there are no tours of the plant itself. The exhibit is worth seeing.

Just north of town is the **Saint Maurice Ironworks National Park** which was the first major iron-ore operation in North America. Built in 1730, the forge ran sporadically, with a number of owners, until 1883. An information centre details the historic significance and also explains how the iron was produced and used.

Also out of the town centre at 2750 Boulevard des Forges is the **Archaeological Museum** with displays on fossils, early pottery discoveries and North American Indians. It is free and closed on Monday. This museum was closed for major renovations at the time of writing and it could take two years before it reopens. Check in town on its current state of repair.

There is an HI hostel in town, *Auberge la Flotille* (☎ 378-8010) which is at 497 Rue Radisson. Rooms cost members/nonmembers $13/15 and an inexpensive breakfast is available. There is also a communal kitchen and laundry facilities. It's about a 10-minute walk from the bus and train station.

Beyond the city, the road becomes hilly with gradients up to 17%. There are lots of camping places along the way as well as stands offering fruit, cider and wood sculpture – an old Quebec folk art. The old-style double wooden swings on many a front lawn are popular in Quebec but rarely seen in the rest of Canada.

### Shawinigan & Grand Mère

These medium-sized towns further north up the Saint Maurice River are rather grim, with little to hold the visitor. Both are industrial: pulp and paper has long been the backbone of the area. Both also have generating plants, at Shawinigan, you can visit the large hydroelectric power station. If you're heading for any of the northerly parks, stock up here because the food and supply selection doesn't get any better further north.

Between here and La Mauricie National Park, there isn't much in the way of accommodation, so you're pretty much stuck with one of the few ordinary motels in Grand Mère or Shawinigan. In both places a decent meal can be had before or after venturing out with the canoe.

### La Mauricie National Park

North from Trois Rivières, up past Shawinigan and Grand Mère, La Mauricie National Park (☎ 536-2638) is the only national park among the many large provincial wilderness parks north of the St Lawrence River.

The park covers 550 sq km, straddling northern evergreen forests and the more southerly hardwoods of the St Lawrence River Valley. The low, rounded Laurentian Mountains, probably the world's oldest, are part of the Canadian Shield that covers much of the province. Between these hills are many small lakes and valleys. Within the park, mammals include moose, fox, bear and beaver.

The park is excellent for canoeing. There are maps of five canoe routes, ranging in length from 14 km to 84 km, for beginners to experts. Canoes can be rented for about $15 a day at Lake Wapizagonke,

QUEBEC

itself scenic with sandy beaches, steep rocky cliffs and waterfalls. There's also fishing for trout and bass.

Hiking trails, guided nature walks and an interpretive centre are offered. The Route des Falaises hiking trail is a good one with fine scenery. Some of the trails go along or offer views of the Saint Maurice River, which is one of the last rivers in the province where logging companies still float down their timber to the mills. Along the edges of the river you can see the strays that get collected periodically.

There are serviced campgrounds available, at $11.50 a night, with free firewood.

Interior camping (camp sites accessible only by foot or canoe found in the park interior) is free but you do need to pre-plan your route and register. On holiday weekends in summer, calling ahead to check on availability is a good idea. No fires are permitted so take a stove. Supplies are available in Grand Mère, but the selection is minimal; it's better to bring most stuff with you.

The park is 220 km north-east of Montreal. Voyageur Bus Lines link Montreal to Shawinigan.

Two adjacent provincial parks also offer wilderness camping: one is to the north, one to the west, but road access is more difficult.

The English language is at a premium up here, so be prepared to communicate in French.

### La Domaine Joly de Lotbinière

This is a stately museum on the south shore of the St Lawrence River, between Lotbinière and Sainte Croix on the way to Quebec City from Trois Rivières. It was built for Henri Gustave Joly de Lotbinière (1849-1908), once the premier of Quebec. Not only is this one of the most impressive manors built during the seigneurial period of Quebec, it remains nearly as it was in the mid-1800s. It's now a government-operated museum containing period furniture and furnishings, and the grounds and outbuildings are a treat in themselves. Lunch and teas are served.

# Quebec City

Quebec City (Québec), rich in history, culture and beauty, is the heart of French Canada. If you're anywhere in the eastern part of the country, make the effort to visit.

The town is unique in several ways, most noticeably in its European appearance and atmosphere. It has the charm of an old world city. Montreal has this feel to some degree, as does the French Quarter in New Orleans, but nowhere in North America is the picture as complete. The entire old section of town, essentially a living museum, has been designated by UNESCO as a World Heritage Site.

As the seat of the provincial government and Laval Université, this is the centre of Québecois consciousness, in both its moderate and extreme manifestations. Quebec City has been the Canadian centre of French nationalist thought for hundreds of years and many of today's intellectuals and politicians speaking for independence are based here.

Although many people are bilingual, the overwhelming majority are French-speaking and 94% have French ancestors. But this is a tourist town, ranking with Banff and Victoria as one of the country's most visited destinations, so English is spoken around the attractions and in shops. However, if you can, speak French, this will make you more friends and enable you to feel more comfortable away from the busiest areas. Quebec City is a year-round tourist centre. In July and August it gets crowded.

The city is also an important port, lying where the Saint Charles River (Rivière Saint Charles) meets the St Lawrence River. It sits on top of and around a cliff, an excellent setting with views over the St Lawrence River and the town of Lévis (pronounced not as in jeans but 'lev-ee') across the river.

Much of Quebec City's past is still visible. Its many churches, old stone houses and narrow streets make it an architectural gem. The old port of Quebec remains the only walled city in North America.

The climate in Quebec City must be

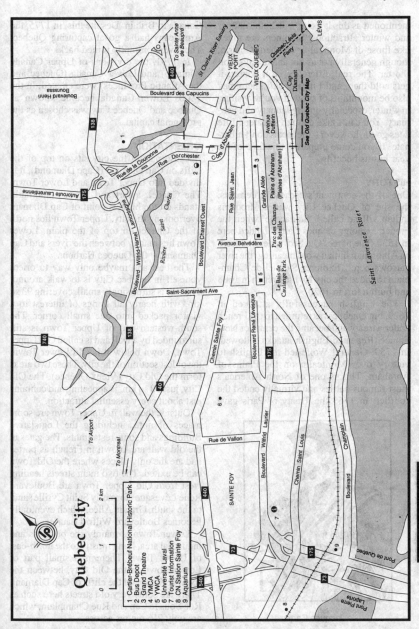

# Quebec City

1 Cartier-Brébeuf National Historic Park
2 Bus Depot
3 Grand Theatre
4 YMCA
5 YWCA
6 Université Laval
7 Tourist Information
8 CN Station Sainte Foy
9 Aquarium

0  1  2 km

To Sainte Anne de Beaupré

St Charles River Estuary

Quebec-Lévis Ferry

LÉVIS

VIEUX PORT

VIEUX QUEBEC

Cap Diamant

See Old Quebec City Map

Avenue Dufferin

Boulevard des Capucins

Boulevard Henri Bourassa

138

Rue de la Couronne

Rue Dorchester

Côte d'Abraham

Rue Saint Jean

Rivière Saint Charles

Boulevard Wilfrid-Hamel Lamontagne

Boulevard Charest Ouest

Grande Allée

Parc des Champs de Bataille
Plains of Abraham
(Plaines d'Abraham)

Avenue Belvédère

Le Bois de Coulonge Park

Saint-Sacrement Ave

Chemin Sainte Foy

Boulevard René Lévesque

Saint Laurence River

Autoroute Laurentienne

175

440

138

740

40

175

SAINTE FOY

Chemin Saint Louis

Boulevard Wilfrid Laurier

Rue de Vallon

To Airport

To Montreal

440

73

540

73

175

Pont de Québec

Pont Pierre Laporte

Chemin Saint Louis

Chemin Saint Louis

QUEBEC

mentioned as this is a city with both summer and winter attractions. Summers are much like those of Montreal or southern Ontario, though generally not as hot and always a bit shorter. The real difference is in winter: it gets cold then, and I mean *cold*. There may also be mountains of snow if you're visiting in winter, especially during January and February. You can't take enough sweaters. Life does go on, however – the locals don't hibernate. If you come prepared, this time of the year has its benefits.

## HISTORY

One of the continent's earliest settlements, the site of Quebec City was an Iroquois Indian village called 'Stadacone' when the French explorer Jacques Cartier landed here in 1534. The name 'Quebec' is derived from an Algonkian Indian word meaning 'the river narrows here'. Explorer Samuel de Champlain founded the city for the French in 1608 and built a fort in 1620.

The English successfully attacked in 1629, but Quebec was returned to the French under a treaty and became the centre of New France. Repeated English attacks followed. In 1759, General Wolfe led the English to victory over Montcalm on the Plains of Abraham. This is one of North America's most famous battles and virtually ended the conflict. In 1763 the Treaty of Paris gave Canada to Britain. Despite this, in 1775, the Americans had a go at capturing Quebec. They were promptly turned back.

In 1791, the divisions of Upper Canada (Ontario) and Lower Canada (Quebec and the Atlantic Provinces) were created. In the 1800s Lower Canada became known as Quebec and Quebec City was chosen as the provincial capital.

## ORIENTATION

Because part of the city sits on top of the cliffs on Cap Diamant (Cape Diamond), it is divided into Upper Town and Lower Town. The Citadel, a fort and famous landmark, stands on the highest point of Cap Diamant overlooking the city. Upper Town lies north of the Citadel on top of the plain. Lower Town lies mainly between the rivers and Cap Diamant by the Quebec Harbour.

The best and maybe only way to orient yourself in Quebec City is to walk around. The city is surprisingly small, covering 93 sq km, with nearly all things of interest to a visitor packed into one small corner. The south-western end of Upper Town is still surrounded by a wall and is called Old Upper Town. Down below it is Old Lower Town, the oldest section of the city. These two areas form the Old City (Vieux Québec). The Old City, just 10 sq km, is appealing and contains just about every essential attraction.

Outside the wall in Upper Town are some places of note, including the Legislative Buildings and some restaurants. The gates in the old wall are known in French as *portes* and are the only places where the Old Town can be exited. The two main streets heading west from Old Upper Town are Boulevard René Lévesque (formerly Saint Cyrille) and, to the south, Grande Allée, which eventually becomes Boulevard Wilfrid Laurier.

Lower Town is mainly the business and industrial area, lying mostly to the north-east of Upper Town. There is a small part of Lower Town in the Old City, between the river, harbour and the cliffs of Cap Diamant. There are some very old streets here such as Rue Sous le Cap and Rue Champlain, which are only 2½ metres across.

Jacques Cartier

QUEBEC

The focal point of this small area, at the south-eastern edge of Old Quebec, is Place Royale. From here, you can walk (it's not hard, nor far) or take the funicular railway (elevator) for 75 cents one way to the top of the cliff of Upper Town. The funicular terminal in Lower Town is on Rue Petit Champlain. The ferry, which plies across the river to Lévis, docks in Lower Town.

To the extreme west of the city you'll see signs for either Pont de Québec or Pont Pierre Laporte. Both these bridges lead to the south shore.

The area north of Boulevard René Lévesque is mainly residential. Then you'll encounter the cliff again – this time its northern edge. Beneath it, the section of Lower Town is of little interest and is residential or industrial.

Much further north in Lower Town are the highways leading east and west. In this section of the city you'll find some of the motels.

Back in the old, walled section of Upper Town, Rue Saint Jean is a main street with many bars and restaurants. Running south from it, Côte de la Fabrique is another main street. Further south, running into Côte de la Fabrique, is Rue Buade, another of the central streets. At the bottom of Rue Buade and a little to the east is the post office, in a huge old stone building. Across from it, with good views over the water, is the pleasant little Parc Montmorency.

A well-known landmark in Old Quebec is the copper-topped, castle-style Château Frontenac hotel dating from 1892. Behind the château, a large boardwalk edges along the cliff providing good views over the river. The boardwalk leads to the Promenade des Gouverneurs, a path which runs between the cliff's edge and the citadel. Beyond the citadel, outside the walls, is the huge park called Parc des Champs de Bataille. This is where the battles over Quebec took place. The park has several historical monuments and some sites within its boundaries.

The views are good from the boardwalk, called the Terrasse Dufferin, behind the Château Frontenac. There are always people strolling and often musicians and other street entertainers doing their numbers here. Here you will also find the statue of Monsieur de Champlain who started it all. At the other end is the wooden slide used during the winter carnival.

For a look from higher up, go to the government building called Edifice 'G' at 675 Boulevard René Lévesque. The observation deck with great views from the 31st floor is open from 9 am to 4 pm Monday to Friday, from March to October and is free. An alternative is the restaurant at the top of Loews Le Concorde Hôtel, 1225 Place Montcalm off Chemin Saint Louis, outside the wall.

## INFORMATION

There are several tourist offices where the staff are bilingual and well supplied with maps and other information.

The main office is at 60 Rue d'Auteuil (☎ 692-2471), just north of Grande Allée. It's in the Parc de l'Esplanade, near the Porte (Gate) Saint Louis. Usually they will help out with off-beat questions and will even make telephone calls for you and help with booking accommodation. Most of the workers are friendly, considering the crowds they get at peak times. In summer it is open from 8.30 am to 8 pm daily otherwise it closes at 5.30 pm.

A second tourist office (☎ 643-2280) is on Place d'Armes, to the east side of the Château Frontenac hotel. This one deals primarily with destinations elsewhere around the province.

Another tourist office is at 215 Rue de Marché-Finlay (☎ 643-6631) on the corner of Rue de l'Union in Lower Town. It's on a large square near the water, south of Place Royale and deals mainly with the Place Royale area.

There is a post office outlet in the walled section of Upper Town, at the bottom of Rue Buade, opposite Parc Montgomery. The main post office is at 300 Rue Saint-Paul near the corner of Ruelle des Bains.

## A Note on Quebec City
Nearly every second building in Old Quebec

QUEBEC

is of some interest; a list of all the sites in this area would fill a book. For a more complete guide, ask at the tourist office for the walking-tour booklet. Following are some of the most significant sites in the old section as well as some outside the walls.

Watch for a symbol in the shape of a key on buildings and businesses around town. It indicates something of historical note is on display. The tourist office has a guide to the 'key' locations as well.

Historic Old Upper Town not only has most of the city's interesting accommodation and restaurants but also many of the important sites and attractions.

## OLD UPPER TOWN
### Citadel
The French started to build here in 1750 when bastions were constructed for storing gunpowder. The fort (☎ 648-3563) was completed by the British and served as the eastern flank of the city's defence system. It was begun in 1820 and completed 30 years later. The irregularly sided structure sits on the plain over 100 metres up from the river at an appropriate vantage point.

Today the citadel is the home base of Canada's Royal 22s (known in bastardised French as the Van Doos), a French regiment that developed quite a reputation through WW I and II and the Korean War. There is a museum outlining their history and a more general military museum containing documents, uniforms and models situated in a few different buildings including the old prison at the south-east end.

The entrance fee of $4 includes admission to these museums and a guided tour. The Changing of the Guard ceremony takes place at 10 am daily in summer. The Beating of the Retreat which follows the last tour at 6 pm on Tuesdays, Thursdays, Saturdays and Sundays takes place during July and August. There are also cannon firings at noon and at 9.30 pm from the Prince of Wales Bastion. The citadel is still considered a working military site so wandering around on your own is not permitted.

### Parc des Champs de Bataille (Battlefields Park)
This is the huge park running south-west from the citadel. Its hills, gardens, monuments and trees make it pleasant now; however, the park was once a bloody battleground, the site of a conflict that may have determined the course of history in Canada. The part closest to the cliff is known as the Plains of Abraham and it was here in 1759 that the English finally defeated the French with both generals, Wolfe of the English and Montcalm of the French, dying in the process. In the park is the National Battlefields Park Interpretive Centre (☎ 648-4071) focusing on the dramatic history of the park. It is housed in the Musée du Québec (see below). The centre is open every day in summer but closed on Mondays during the rest of the year. There is also a Martello Tower (a small tower for coastal defence) in the park and a fountain with a lookout.

### Musée du Québec (Quebec Museum)
Towards the south-western end of the park at 1 Avenue Wolfe-Montcalm, is this museum/gallery (☎ 643-2150) with changing exhibits, mainly on Quebec's art. It shows both modern and more traditional art, ceramics and decorative works. It's small and not especially memorable, but it is free on Wednesdays when it is open from 10 am to 10 pm. On other days it is $4.75 and open from 10 am to 6 pm although out of the summer season it is closed on Mondays. The old prison nearby is now part of the gallery. Note that the museum also contains the Battlefields Park Interpretive Centre.

### Fortifications of Quebec National Historic Site
The largely restored old wall, now a protected national site (☎ 648-7016), can be visited for free. In fact, you can walk a complete circuit on top of the walls, 4.6 km, all around the Old City. In the old Powder Building beside Porte Saint Louis, an interpretive centre has been set up, which provides a little information on the wall's history. Along the circuit are two other infor-

mation booths, one on Terrasse Dufferin and one on the Promenade des Gouverneurs.

## Parc d'Artillerie

Beside the wall at Porte Saint Jean, Parc d'Artillerie (☎ 648-4205), a National Historic Site, has been used militarily for centuries. A munitions factory built cartridges for the Canadian Forces here until 1964. It's now an interpretive centre with a scale model of Quebec City the way it was in the early 1800s. In the Dauphine Redoubt, there are costumes and displays about the soldiers for whom it was built during the French regime. The Redoubt, built between 1712 and 1748, is a defence structure designed to protect a prominent point. In this case, the edge of the hill could be well guarded by the soldiers within. In the officers' quarters there's a history lesson for children. Admission is $2.60.

## Musée du Fort

This is a small museum (☎ 692-2175), at 10 Rue Sainte Anne near Place d'Armes, dealing with more provincial military history. With the aid of a large model of 18th-century Quebec City, six sieges and battles are retold using sound & light (son et lumière). The half-hour show isn't bad and costs $4.25.

## Musée Historique

Also facing Place d'Armes, the Musée Historique, a wax museum (☎ 692-2289), depicts historical events like Columbus's landing in America. Admission is $4, for students $3.50.

## Ursuline Convent & Museum

This convent (☎ 694-0694) on Rue des Jardins is the oldest girls' school on the continent. There are several buildings on the estate, some recently restored. The Ursuline Museum, which you enter at 12 Rue Donnacona, deals with the Ursulines and their lives in the 1600s and 1700s, and also displays paintings, crafts, furniture and other belongings of the early French settlers. A reader has written to say that the skull of

General Montcalm is now on display. Admission is $2.50, students $1.25. The convent, chapel and museum are open daily from 9.30 am to noon and 1.30 to 4.45 pm but closed on Sunday mornings.

Nearby, on the same street, is the Anglican **Cathedral of the Holy Trinity**, built in 1804, which is open in summer from 9 am to 8 pm Monday to Friday, 10 am to 8 pm Saturday and 11 am to 6 pm Sunday.

## Latin Quarter

The Latin Quarter refers to a section of Old Upper Town surrounding the large Quebec seminary complex. The seminary was originally the site of the Université Laval which outgrew the space here and was moved in the 1960s to Sainte Foy, west of the downtown area. Many students still live along the old, narrow streets which look particularly Parisian. To enter the seminary grounds, go to 9 Rue de l'Université. In the grounds are many stone and wooden buildings, a toy museum, the university's museum and several grassy, quiet quadrangles. For tours the entrance is at 2 Côte de la Fabrique.

## Parc de l'Esplanade

Just inside the Old City by Porte Saint Louis and Rue Saint Louis is this city park where many of the Quebec Winter Carnival's events are held. Calèches, the horse-drawn carts for sightseeing, line up for business along the edge of the park.

## Around Old Upper Town

In the 1700s Upper Town began to grow after Lower Town was destroyed once too often in battle.

**Place d'Armes** is the small square to the north of the Château Frontenac. It was once a military parade ground and is now a handy city orientation point.

**Rue du Tresor** is up, away from the water, off Place d'Armes. This narrow street, linking Rue Sainte Anne with Rue Buade, is jammed with painters and their wares – mostly kitsch stuff done for the tourists but some pretty good work too. At the end of Buade is the **Hôtel de Ville** (City Hall) dating from 1833. Next to the Hôtel de Ville, the park is used for shows and performances throughout the summer, especially during festival time.

On the corner of Rue Buade and Rue Sainte Famille is the **Basilica of Notre Dame**, dating from 1647. The interior is ornate and contains paintings and treasures from the early French regime.

## OLD LOWER TOWN

The oldest section of Quebec City, like the Upper Town, is well worth exploring. Get down to it by walking down Côte de la Montagne street by the post office. About halfway down on the right there is a shortcut – the break-neck staircase – that leads down to Rue Petit Champlain. A second method is to follow the sidewalk beside the Musée du Fort toward the river and Lower Town and the staircase will lead you down. Alternatively, you can take the funicular from Terrasse Dufferin down; it also goes to Rue Petit Champlain, to Louis Jolliet House. The house dates from 1683 and Jolliet lived in it when he wasn't off exploring the northern Mississippi. Rue Petit Champlain, a busy, attractive street, is said to be the narrowest in North America and is also one of the oldest.

### Place Royale

This is the central and principal square of the Lower Town area with 400 years of history behind it. The name is now often used to refer to the district in general. When de Champlain founded Quebec, it was this bit of shoreline which was first settled. For the past few years the entire area has been under renovation and restoration, and the good work is now nearly complete.

There are many houses and small museums to visit, some with period furniture and implements. The streets are full of visitors, people going to restaurants and cafés, and school children from around the province getting history lessons. It's not uncommon to see a bride coming down the church steps either. Other places are now galleries, craft shops and the like.

Also on the square are many buildings from the 1600s and 1700s, tourist shops (don't buy film here, it's too expensive!) and in the middle a statue of Louis XIV.

At 25 Rue Saint Pierre, near the square, is an interpretive centre which gives a free outline of the history of Lower Town and Quebec City. Right on the square at No 3A is another interpretive centre, the Centre of Trade in New France, with some exhibits and an audio-video show dealing with early French settlement. Again, this is free. See the Quebec City Information section earlier for details of the tourist office which specialises in this part of town. They can tell you of the many free events, concerts and shows which frequently take place in and around the Lower Town streets.

Right by the interpretive centre on the square, **The House of Wines** is a mouth-watering vintage wine store in a restored 1689 dwelling. It's free to visit and may include a sample drink. It's closed on Sundays and Mondays.

### Church of Notre Dame des Victoires

Dating from 1688, this house of worship on the square is the oldest stone church in the province. It's built on the spot where 80 years earlier de Champlain set up his 'Habitation', a small stockade. Hanging from the ceiling is a replica of a wooden ship, thought to be a good luck charm for the ocean crossing and early battles with the Iroquois.

### Royal Battery

This is at the foot of Rue Sous le Fort, where a dozen cannons were set up in 1691 to protect the growing town. The Lower Town information office is just off the park here.

The Canadian government has a coast-guard base near the ferry terminal across the street.

### VIEUX PORT (OLD PORT)

Built around the old harbour in Lower Town east of Place Royale, Vieux Port is a recently redeveloped multipurpose waterfront area. It's a large, spacious assortment of government buildings, shops, condominiums and recreational facilities with no real focal point but a few things of interest to the visitor.

Near Place Royale at the river's edge you'll see the MV *Louis Jolliet*, offering cruises downriver to the waterfalls Chute Montmorency and Île d'Orléans. You'll get good views of the city, but you can also get them from the cheap ferry plying the river between town and Lévis. Near the wharf is the Musée de la Civilisation.

Strolling along the waterfront leads to the Agora, a large outdoor concert bowl and site of many summer shows and presentations. A little further along is a warehouse-style building housing numerous boutiques.

A large Naval training centre was being built on the waterfront here. It is a controversial development with many local people decrying the ugly look of it not to mention the negative effect it will have on the riverside views. Its future has yet to be decided.

### Musée de la Civilisation

Opened in 1988 this large, striking waterfront museum (☎ 643-2158), 85 Rue Dalhousie, deals with both Quebec and broader historical and communication topics

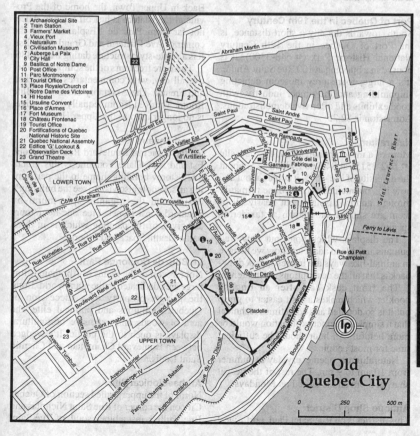

1 Archaeological Site
2 Train Station
3 Farmers' Market
4 Vieux Port
5 Naturalium
6 Civilisation Museum
7 Auberge La Paix
8 City Hall
9 Basilica of Notre Dame
10 Post Office
11 Parc Montmorency
12 Tourist Office
13 Place Royale/Church of Notre Dame des Victoires
14 Ursuline Convent
15 Place d'Armes
16 Fort Museum
17 Château Frontenac
18 Tourist Office
19 Fortifications of Quebec National Historic Site
20 Quebec National Assembly
21 Edifice 'G' Lookout & Observation Deck
23 Grand Theatre

Old Quebec City

0   250   500 m

QUEBEC

through permanent and changing exhibits. Human history and culture is explored through new and old artefacts and the creations of humankind.

It's spacious and well laid out. Aside from the static exhibits, it includes dance, music and other live performances.

It's definitely worth seeing and unlike many museums around the province there are English-speaking guides on hand. Admission costs $4.75 and it's open from 10 am to 7 pm daily from 24 June to 6 September. Note that on Tuesdays it's free. The rest of the year it closes at 5 pm and it is not open at all on Monday.

### Port of Quebec in the 19th Century
South, towards the city a short distance, is the Port of Quebec in the 19th Century National Historic Park (☎ 648-3300). It is housed in a building at 100 Rue Saint André. It's a large, four-storey museum depicting shipbuilding and the timber industry, with good exhibits and often live demonstrations. Admission is $2.25.

### Naturalium
More of a museum than a zoo, this new site (☎ 692-1515) at 84 Rue Dalhousie is about the diversity of life – how it comes about and how it is maintained. This is done primarily through animal displays, but nearly all of them are stuffed and shown as taxidermy specimens.

The displays which point out how well humans are able to adapt and how we behave in animal-like ways are interesting. A drawback is that all the descriptions are in French.

The front desk can offer an English booklet which makes a visit easier to grasp but it is so detailed and sometimes technical that a simple, succinct explanation would be more helpful. An hour should be sufficient time for most people.

Naturalium is open every day in summer from 10 am to 9 pm. The rest of the year it shuts at 5 pm and is closed on Mondays.

### Antique Shop District
This district is on Rue Saint Paul, north-west of the Place Royale and near the Port of Quebec in the 19th-Century museum. From Place Royale, take Rue Saint Pierre towards the harbour and then turn left at Rue Saint Paul. About a dozen shops here sell antiques, curiosities and old Québecois relics. There are also some good little cafés along this relatively quiet street. Right against the cliff on Côte de la Canoterie, you can walk up to Upper Town. Further along is the Farmers' Market on the right-hand side, and a little further on, the Gare du Palais train station.

## OUTSIDE THE WALLS
### National Assembly
Back in Upper Town, the home of the Provincial Legislature is just off Grande Allée, not far from Parc de l'Esplanade, on the corner of Ave Dufferin and Grand Allée Est. It is a castle-style structure dating from 1886.

There are free tours of the sumptuous interior all day, with commentaries in English and French. The Assembly sits in the Blue Room. The Red Room, equally impressive, is no longer used as the Upper House.

### Grand Theatre
On the corner of Boulevard René Lévesque Est and Rue Claire Fontaine is this grand, three-storey building, home to the performing arts. People also visit to see the building's design and the gigantic epic mural by Spaniard Jordi Bonet. Free one-hour tours are given of the painting which is in three parts: Death, Space and Liberty.

### Le Bois de Coulonge Park
Not far west of the Plains of Abraham is this large area dedicated to the plant world. Long the private property of a succession of Quebec's religious and political elite, the area of woods and extensive horticultural displays is open to the public. It's wedged between Boulevard Champlain and Chemin Saint Louis.

### Archaeological Site
North of the upper walled section of Quebec City on the corner of Rue Saint Nicholas and Rue Vaillier, just a block south of Rue Saint

Paul, a major street which runs into Boulevard Charest Est, is this interesting idea for an historic site. It's set up as a working dig of the first city intendant's house, actually a palace. Platforms lead over foundations, firepits and outlines of several buildings which local university students uncovered and explored. There's an interpretive centre to supply background information. From the beginning of May to the beginning of September it is open in the afternoons each day except Monday.

### Cartier-Brebeuf National Historic Park

On the Saint Charles River north of the central walled section of the city, this park (☎ 648-4038) marks where Cartier and his men were nursed through the winter of 1535 by the local Native Indians. Later the Jesuits established a settlement here. Displays provide more information on Cartier, his trips and the Jesuit missionaries.

There is a full-scale replica of Cartier's ship and one of a Native Indian longhouse in the park's green riverside setting. Throughout summer it is open every day, but on Mondays only in the afternoon. It is free. From the downtown area take Rue Dorchester north by car or go by bus to Rue Julien from where you can walk to the park.

### Aquarium

This is in the Sainte Foy district at 1675 Avenue des Hôtels (☎ 659-5264). They have about 250 species of fresh and saltwater fish. There's a cafeteria and, out on the grounds, picnic tables. It's open daily and costs $5 for adults and 75 cents for children.

### ORGANISED TOURS

There is no shortage of tour possibilities here. Some companies use minibuses for rather private tours, others offer a driver and you use your own car. Several companies offer bus tours of the city or full-day regional trips.

Gray Line (☎ 622-7420) runs numerous narrated tours from Place d'Armes. A 1½-hour trip around town costs $12.50 and a four-hour trip to Sainte Anne de Beaupré, the falls Chute Montmorency and a short visit to Île d'Orléans, is $28. Several other companies offer similar tours which may offer more time around Île d'Orléans or some other variation. Gray Line seems to have the lowest prices. The tourist office has promotional pamphlets on the various tours available; there is also a ticket booth on Terrasse Dufferin representing many of the tour companies.

Maple Leaf (☎ 649-9226), with an office at 240 3rd Avenue, has six different tours in and around Quebec City costing from $15 to $49. One of their trips is done partially by bus and partially by boat. Free pick-up from your (or any) hotel is available so you needn't ever go to the out-of-the-way office. Another service is a shuttle bus which goes around Old Quebec. For one fare of $3 you can hop on and off at will for the day. Pick up a copy of their schedule. This company also runs the airport shuttle service.

Under a different number (☎ 622-3677), Maple Leaf offers two-hour walking tours twice daily.

A worthwhile alternative is Quebec by Foot (☎ 658-4799), which provides a walking tour lasting around 2½ hours guided by history or architecture students. It's educational but not dry. Reservations may be made at the Musée du Fort on Place d'Armes. There are two walks a day. They cost $12.

The less established operators tend to charge a few dollars less or provide longer tours for the same money.

Sonores (☎ 692-1223) rents spoken tape cassettes which you can use for your own walking or driving tours. Rental costs $7.95. The cassettes are available at tourist booths but only during the summer months.

### River Cruises

A variety of boat tours is given on the big open-decked MV *Louis Jolliet*, which has an 800-passenger capacity. Tickets (☎ 692-1159) may be purchased at the kiosque, on the boardwalk behind the Château or at the booth along the waterfront near Place Royale.

QUEBEC

The basic one-our trip costs $13, but there is a longer trip further downriver to Île d'Orléans and Chute Montmorency and a three-hour evening trip with music and dancing for $21. All these cruises are popular so getting a ticket early is a good idea.

Another company with a smaller vessel, the *Saint André* (☎ 659-4804), does similar day-cruises around Quebec City and down the river at slightly cheaper rates. For information call or see them at quay No 22 along the Old Port dock opposite the Agora.

There are several other companies all offering variations on the theme.

Note that the ferry over to Lévis is, in a sense, a short cruise and provides a great view of the Château and costs next to nothing.

## FESTIVALS
Some of the major festivals and celebrations held in Quebec City are:

February
  *Winter Carnival* – This is a famous annual event unique to Quebec City. The festival lasts for about 10 days, always including two weekends, around the end of February. If you want to go, organise the trip early as the city gets packed out (and bring lots of warm clothes). Featured are parades, ice sculptures, a snow slide, boat races, dances, music and lots of drinking. The town goes berserk. If you take the train into Quebec City during Carnival, be prepared for a trip like no other.
  Many activities take place in Parc de l'Esplanade. The slide is on the Terrasse Dufferin behind the Château. Other events take place above the Gare Saint Rôche, between Pont Dorchester and the bridge of the Autoroute Dufferin.
  In recent years, some celebrants have become overly unruly to the point of being problematic at times. Those with families may wish to inquire about participating in particular night-time festivities.
July-August
  *Summer Festival* – Summer Festival held at the beginning and middle of July, consists basically of free shows and concerts throughout the town, including drama and dance. Ask about it at the tourist office. They should have a list of things going on indicating what, where and when. Most squares and parks in the Old City are the sites of some activity daily, especially the park beside Hôtel de Ville at noon and in the evening.

*Quebec City Provincial Exhibition* – The other major summer event is held around the end of August each year and features individual and commercial displays, handicrafts, a Black Jack parlour, horse racing and midway, the latter a large carnival with 65 rides and games of chance. The entrance fee is $10 which includes everything, even rides. Nearly three-quarters of a million people visit each year. Parc de l'Exposition (Exhibition Park) is north of the downtown area, off Route 175, Laurentienne.

## PLACES TO STAY
There are many, many places to stay in Quebec City and generally the competition keeps the prices down to a reasonable level. There are relatively few standard hotels – by far the bulk of the accommodation is in guesthouses, and small European-style hotels. As you'd expect in such a popular centre, the best cheap places are often full at night. Midsummer and Carnival time are the busiest times. If you can't find a place in the Old City, consider one of the motels slightly out of the centre or be prepared to stretch your budget.

Outside the peak periods, prices do drop. For accommodation assistance go to the tourist office on Rue d'Auteuil where they have lists of places and a phone you can use. Do not take their occupancy information as gospel, however. They may have a place down as 'full' when in fact a call will turn up a room, after everybody else has ignored it. The tourist accommodation guide also doesn't list all the places – a wander around will turn up others. Lastly, remember that morning is the best time to find a place and Friday and Saturday are often the worst.

### Camping
There are numerous campgrounds close to town. One is *Camping Municipal de Beauport* (☎ 666-2228) north of Quebec City. To get there, take Hwy 40 towards Montmorency and turn north on Hwy 369; the park is not too far, on the left. It costs $19. There are also a few places on Hwy 138 going east from Quebec City through the Sainte Anne de Beaupré area including *Parc du Mont Sainte Anne* (☎ 826-2323).

On the south shore just one km west from the Quebec bridge is *Camping du Pont de Quebec* (☎ 831-0777) with simple tent sites as well as electrical hook-ups.

There are many private campgrounds on this south shore road particularly west of Quebec City.

## Hostels

There are two well-established and busy hostels here. I like the one called *Auberge La Paix* (☎ 694-0735) at 31 Rue Couillard. It's open all year and has 40 beds. The hostel is marked with a peace sign on the white, European-style building. The cost is $15 with breakfast, and $2 extra if you need a sleeping sheet and blanket. The doors close at 2 am. The location is perfect; there is a grocery store, a bar and restaurant all minutes away. It's best to arrive early in the morning to assure yourself of a bed. It's walkable from the bus station (about 30 minutes), or the closer train station, but it's uphill all the way.

The other hostel, *Centre International de Séjour de Quebec* (☎ 694-0775) affiliated with the international organisation, is also well located at 19 Rue Sainte Ursule. Despite its great size, it's usually full in summer. It costs $15 for a standard bed and there are some double and some family rooms. The cafeteria offers all three meals. The hostel-run activities are worth looking into and include free walking tours and an excursion to Lévis across the river.

There are no rooms at the *YMCA* but the *YWCA* (☎ 683-2155) at 855 Avenue Holland takes couples and also single women. Singles/doubles cost $28/40 and they have a cafeteria and pool. The Y is often full, so reservations may be useful. Avenue Holland runs off Chemin Sainte Foy, which becomes Saint Jean in the old section. Bus No 7 along Chemin Sainte Foy goes past Avenue Holland. Walk south on Avenue Holland – it's not far.

The *Université Laval* (☎ 656-56322921), between Chemin Sainte Foy and Boulevard Wilfrid Laurier to the east of Autoroute du Vallon, rents rooms in the summer from May to 21 August. Rates are $25 for singles and

a few dollars less in a twin room. Student price is $14.50 or, again, less if sharing a room. Bus No 8 from the Old City will get you there; it's about halfway between the bridges and the walled area.

## Tourist Homes

Other than the hostels, the cheapest and best places to stay are these small, sometimes family-run hotels, often created out of old houses. There are literally dozens of them within the walls, which lets you stay in the centre of things and experience their individual characters.

Most of the cheaper ones are in one specific area. This area is roughly bounded by Rue d'Auteuil on the west, Rue Sainte Anne to the north, the Château Frontenac to the east and Avenue Saint Denis to the south. The two most fruitful streets as far as places to stay are concerned are Rue Sainte Ursule and Rue Saint Louis. Rue Sainte Anne and Rue Laporte are also good.

Many places are full by early evening in summer. Look for a room before 2 pm or phone ahead for a reservation. Prices at these places can be flexible, depending on the time of year and other factors such as on-going events. Consider bargaining if you're staying for more than a couple of days. Compared to the motels or larger downtown hotels here or in most cities, the places in this category still aren't bad value. Note too that most of the small places do have some parking available but it comes with an extra charge.

One of the best of the cheapies is *Auberge Saint Louis* (☎ 692-2424) and it is at 48 Rue Saint Louis. The 23 rooms start at a reasonable $38 a single or double but go up to twice this. Parking is available but costs extra.

Further down at 72 Rue Saint Louis is *Maison du Général* (☎ 694-1905). There are 12 rooms which range in price from singles/doubles $33/38, without bath. As in many of these places, it's cheaper without TV, showers, the view or the biggest room. The cheaper rooms are sometimes noisier as they're often on the street but despite these

QUEBEC

drawbacks they always seem to be the ones to go first.

Also on Rue Saint Louis at No 71 is *Hôtel Le Clos Saint Louis* (☎ 694-1311, 1-800-461-1311) with 15 rooms at $45 to $80 for singles or doubles when things are busy, and dropping to $35 to $65 at other times.

Running off Rue Saint Louis is Rue Sainte Ursule, a pleasant, much quieter street. There are several places worth checking here. *Le Manoir La Salle* (☎ 647-9361) is at 18 Rue Sainte Ursule and has become one of the best buys because it has held its prices while those at so many other places have jumped. They have nine rooms at $30 to $40 for singles, $40 to $55 for doubles. Some may prefer the upstairs rooms to avoid having to go through the lobby to the bathroom, as is the case from the ground floor rooms.

*La Maison Sainte Ursule* (☎ 694-9794) at No 40, looks and is more expensive, at $39 to $59 for singles and $48 to $89 for doubles. Kitchenettes are available – the only place offering this possibly big money-saving feature. They also have some rooms on the adjacent side street.

Across the street at No 43 is *Maison Acadienne* (☎ 694-0280, 1-800-463-0280). Singles/doubles cost from $41/45 singles/doubles to $80 depending on the number of people, size of room and facilities. It's a good place and if you're lucky and have a small car you may get one of the parking spots around the back. A continental breakfast served out on the patio is available for $2.

*La Maison Demers* (☎ 692-2487) at No 68, charges about the same rates for its eight rooms although the better doubles cost more and include a TV.

Further north-west off Rue Sainte Ursule is Rue Sainte Anne. *Maison Doyon* (☎ 694-1720) at No 9 has 20 rooms some of which have been spruced up. The plain, simple ones go for singles/doubles $35/45 and the prices go way up from there. Taking a washbasin rather than a shower saves at least $10.

There are numerous places on and just off the Jardin des Gouverneurs to the south of the Château Frontenac. *Manoir Sur le Cap* (☎ 694-1987), at 9 Avenue Sainte Geneviève, has 14 rooms carved out of the old house, some of them have views of the park, others of the river and Lévis. Singles/doubles cost from $40 to $75.

The *Manoir de la Terrasse* (☎ 694-1592) is at 4 Rue Laporte. Singles or doubles are the same price and range from $39 to $70.

On the corner of Rue Saint Louis and Rue d'Auteuil is *Manoir de L'Esplanade* (☎ 694-0834), a large old refurbished place where prices are a little steep. The 36 rooms cost between $60 and $90 and the corner rooms can be noisy.

### B&Bs

While certainly not a tradition in Quebec, a few places providing the morning meal are now showing up. An agency to try is *Bonjour Québec* (☎ 524-0524) at 450 Rue Champlain (postal code G1K 4J3) run by Michelle Pacquet. The places she lists are all quite central and priced at $42/60 for singles/doubles.

Also if you're first in Montreal, *B&B à Montreal* listed under that city can arrange something for you there.

### Motels

I don't think I've ever seen a city with more motels than Quebec City. Whether you have a car or not, they may be the answer if you find everything booked up downtown.

There are three major areas to look in for motels. All are out of the Old City, but not really far and not difficult to reach.

**Beauport** One area is Beauport, a section of Quebec City to the north of the downtown area. You pass by on the way to Sainte Anne de Beaupré or on a trip along the northern coast. The easiest way to reach it if driving from the downtown area is to head north up Rue Dorchester to Boulevard Hamel. Turn right (east); Boulevard Hamel becomes Rue 18 and then, further east, Boulevard Sainte Anne. This is Beauport. Look when the numbers are in the 1000s. Most of these motels are off the road with the river running behind them.

At 1062 Boulevard Sainte Anne is *Motel Chevalier* (☎ 661-3876). Rooms cost from $45 to $60 for singles/doubles.

*Motel de la Capitale* (☎ 663-0587) is at 1082 Boulevard Sainte Anne. The rate for singles/doubles is $55/60.

Nearby, there's the *Motel Olympic* (☎ 667-8716), at 1078 Boulevard Sainte Anne, where prices range from $40 to the outrageous $90. They have just 16 rooms here.

North-west of the centre at the intersection of Boulevard Henri IV and Hwy 138 up towards the airport is *Journey's End Motel* (☎ 872-5900). It is quite good value at singles/doubles $47/54. This Canada-wide budget chain is always reliable.

**Boulevard Wilfrid Laurier** The second major area for motels is along Boulevard Wilfrid Laurier, west of the city. The motel section runs just east of Boulevard Henri IV, which runs into the bridges from the south shore. Check around the 3000 numbers. Prices are generally quite a bit higher here, but it is closer to town.

The *Motel Fleur de Lys* (☎ 653-9321), at No 3145, has good prices with doubles from $65 all the way up to $95.

Further east after Boulevard Wilfrid Laurier turns into Grande Allée, there are a few smallish, reasonably priced places around the 600s addresses. The places closer to town are generally more deluxe and more expensive.

**Boulevard Wilfrid Hamel** The third area for motels is on Boulevard Wilfrid Hamel, marked only as 'Hamel' on street signs. To get to this area, head north up Boulevard Henri IV from the river or south from Hwy 40. It's about seven km from town. Start looking around the 5000 block, although the road is lined with motels. Some of these motels are in Sainte Foy.

*Motel Plaza* (☎ 872-1552) at 7155 Boulevard Hamel has singles/doubles from $32/45.

Other reasonable places are the *Motel Le Sabilier* (☎ 871-8916) at 3290 Boulevard

Hamel and the more expensive *Motel Pierre* (☎ 681-6191) at 1640 Boulevard Hamel with rooms from $60 to $80.

## PLACES TO EAT

There are dozens of restaurants in Quebec City and the food is quite good, but prices are generally high. Still, there are some reasonably priced exceptions, and the costlier restaurants do generally provide good service in an attractive setting.

Most restaurants post their menus outside on the door, which is helpful when you are shopping around. If you're here for any length of time you're likely to find a favourite.

At dinner the set menus include soup, a roll, dessert and coffee. Many of these same dining rooms offer midday specials which aren't bad value at all. Some serve lunch until 3 pm and one place recently seen was offering it until 6 pm! Prices for the complete lunch can be as low as half the dinner cost although often portions are a might smaller. More modest places have the usual cheap lunches of pizza, sandwiches and the like.

The ethnic restaurants, which aren't numerous in Quebec City, provide an alternative. The Upper Town restaurants, within the walls as a rule, offer the least price range and tend to be costly. Outside the wall or down in the quieter sections of Lower Town less expensive and more casual places are easier to find.

## Upper Old Town

If you're anything like me you can tolerate a pricey lunch and don't mind spending a little extra on dinner. But paying a lot for breakfast really grates. The morning meal has always been a bit of a problem here and now the one good, cheap bacon and eggs place has gone trendy and up-market and doesn't offer the morning meal.

So now, for eggs, a moderately priced (not cheap) restaurant which is always busy for any meal of the day is *l'Omelette*, at 66 Rue Saint Louis, specialising in – what else – omelettes. They have about a dozen varieties which are served with home-fried potatoes.

QUEBEC

Three breakfast specials are also offered which include juice, toast and coffee with a choice of cereal, eggs or croissants.

For a more French-style breakfast there is *Le Petit Coin Latin* at 8½ Rue Sainte Ursule near Rue Saint Jean. Open every day, this small café has croissants, muffins, eggs, café au lait, etc, with low-priced lunch specials which include a glass of wine. They now have an outdoor summer patio with a fixed-price dinner of $10 to $12. At 25 Rue Couillard, one block east of Rue Buade, *Chez Temporal* is a little café which serves coffee, croissants, salads, etc. It's perfect for snacks, breakfasts and light meals. The café feels very French – a good place to sit in the morning and plan the day.

One of the Old Town restaurants suitable for families is the *Café Buade* right in the middle of everything at 31 Rue Buade, just south of Rue des Jardins. In the downstairs section, simple, light breakfasts can be had for $2.95 to $3.50. The lunch and dinner fare is similarly straightforward and moderately priced.

Over on Rue Garneau opposite the Hôtel de Ville at No 48, *Croissant Plus* is busy day and night with snacks and light meals.

A cheap breakfast can always be had at the bus station, too.

The *Fleur du Lotus* at 38 Côte de la Farbrique is good for dinner with Thai, Cambodian and Vietnamese specials from $16.

Along Rue du Tresor from Rue Buade you'll find the Place d'Armes. In the *Hôtel du Tresor* is a dining room – pleasant, done in wood with ceiling fans and white tablecloths. The evening meal will set you back around $20, which is about the norm.

One of the main streets for restaurants is Rue Saint Jean. There are many places to eat as well as night spots scattered along here, both inside the wall and further out. Some places act as both. At 1136 Rue Saint Jean, near Côte du Palais, is *Casse Crêpe Breton*, a small restaurant specialising in crêpes of many kinds, starting as low as $2.90. It's a favourite because it has been here for years and hasn't been dressed up for the tourists at all. You sit right up at the counter and watch

them put the tasty crêpes together. *Café Mille Feuille* at 32 Rue Sainte Angèle, off Saint Jean, is a vegetarian restaurant with daily specials at $7 and an outside patio. At 1087 Rue Saint Jean is the busy *Saint Alexandre Pub* with 200 kinds of beer and an array of pub-type grub.

For making a meal yourself try *Marché Richelieu*, a grocery store at 1097 Rue Saint Jean which offers breads from the in-house bakery, fruits, cheeses and even bottles of wine with screw top lids.

For excellent South-East Asian fare, try *Apsara* at 71 Rue d'Auteuil. Dishes are about $9 or a complete dinner for two will cost around $34. A few doors down at No 23, there's a cheap Lebanese spot, *Restaurant Liban*.

Not far from Rue Saint Jean, at 48A Rue Sainte Ursule, is *Le Sainte Amour* with a $25 table d'hôte and a good reputation. The menu offers about six meat and six fish dishes daily. For a splurge you're probably better off in a place like this, on one of the quieter streets.

There are plenty of other places for a night out. One which has been around for years is *Le Biarritz*, at 136 Rue Sainte Anne, which has some pasta dishes for $14 and beef or seafood from $18. It's been recommended by local people and a reader has recently said the lunches from soup to coffee at under $7 are good value. It's on a quieter street, away from most of the tourist strolls.

*Café de la Paix*, at 44 Rue des Jardins, is very French in decor and atmosphere and offers a varied menu of seafood, fowl and meats. It's very well established and is recommended and, while not cheap, is not exorbitant either. *Restaurant au Parmesan*, nearby at 38 Rue Saint Louis, is always busy and festive. They have a large menu of mainly Italian fare with most dishes from $14 to $20. They also have a huge collection of about 2000 bottles and live music.

At 34 Rue Saint Louis is *Aux Anciens Canadiens* in Jacquet House, Quebec's City's oldest house, dating from 1677. Aside from the historical aspect it is noteworthy for its reliance on traditional dishes and typically Québécois specialities. It's not cheap, but costs no more than many of the upper-middle places and is one of the few with a distinctly different menu. Here one can sample such provincial fare as apple wine, pea soup, duck or trout followed by dessert of maple syrup pie. The special table d'hôte menu offered from 11 am to 6 pm is good value at $12.50.

### Place Royale (Old Lower Town)
At 46 Boul Champlain, with a pig on the sign, is Le Cochon Dingue. They serve meals but it's a good place for breakfast, with café au lait in a bowl (as it's served in parts of France) and croissants. At dinner French-style steak frîtes is a speciality.

Along Rue Saint Paul, an old quiet street away from the main tourist haunts, there are several inexpensive places although this area too, has recently been seeing some redevelopment. La Bouille Café at No 71 is good for light meals or a coffee. And at No 95 the Buffet de l'Antiquaine is a small simple place for things like sandwiches or hamburgers at nontourist prices. They even have a few tables out on the pavement.

At 77 Rue Sault au Matelot which runs perpendicular to Rue Saint Paul look for the Le Lotus Royal for Asian meals. This is one of the few places in town where there is a 'bring your own wine' policy. A little cheaper at $10 to $12, is the Asia at 91 Rue Sault au Matelot with Vietnamese and Thai meals.

Moving up-market, Le Vendome, at 36 Côte de la Montagne, is an expensive French restaurant which has had a European-style menu for 40 years.

Le Pape-Georges, a wine bar on Cul de Sac near the corner of Rue Notre Dame, sells the grape juice by the glass.

### Outside the Wall
Outside the city centre, things are a little quieter and not so densely packed. Rue Saint Jean, west beyond the gate, has numerous bars, cafés, taverns and restaurants. There is Vietnamese, Lebanese and Mexican food available. This is a far less-touristed area, and prices are correspondingly lower.

Walking and looking will turn up places all the way down to Ave Cartier.

At 780 Rue Saint Jean is Le Kismett, an East Indian place with a vegetarian lunch buffet for $7. On Rue Scott at No 821 south just around the corner from Rue Saint Jean is La Pailotte, a good, casual Vietnamese place. Le Commensal, 860 Rue Saint Jean, is a good-value/good-food, vegetarian restaurant with meals paid for by weight.

Further west, about six blocks, is Avenue Cartier which runs south down to Boulevard René Lévesque (formerly Boulevard Saint Cyrille Est). There are a few Chinese restaurants here if you feel like a change. There are also a few standard French ones. On the corner on Boulevard René Lévesque is Restaurant La Nouvelle Reserve, below which is a small delicatessen called Delices Cartier. They have superb croissants which have even been described as being the best anywhere outside France. There are also a range of pastries and tortiéres (Quebec meat pies).

West, along Grande Allée from Old Quebec, past the Quebec National Assembly and other government buildings, and just past Rue d'Artigny, is a popular and lively strip of over a dozen alfresco restaurants. They make a good spot for a beer or lunch if you're out near the Plains of Abraham. All have complete lunch specials for $6 to $9 (from soup to coffee) and at most places, dinners range from $10 to $20. Restaurant Patrimoine at 695 Grand Allée is one of the cheapest. At No 625, La Veille Maison du Spaghetti offers a variety of pasta dishes at below average cost.

### The Farmers' Market
The Farmers' Market is on Rue Saint André in Old Lower Town near Bassin Louise, not too far from Vieux Port (Old Port) or the train station. It's a covered open-air building where you'll find fresh bread, cheeses, fruit and vegetables. The best time to visit is busy Saturday morning.

### ENTERTAINMENT
Though Quebec City is quite a small city, it's

active after dark and there are plenty of nightspots although they change faster than editions of this book. Many of the cafés and restaurants – some mentioned under the eating section – have live music at night. Others are clubs open only at night. Most of the nightlife is in the Old City or just outside the walls. Brasseries – taverns for men and women – close at midnight while bars stay open until around 3 or 4 am.

Rue Saint Jean is alive at night – this is where people strut. There are good places for just sitting and watching, and places with music.

Folk clubs known as *boîtes à chanson* come and go along and around Rue Saint Jean and are generally cheap with a casual, relaxed atmosphere.

At *Bar Le d'Auteuil*, at 35 Rue d'Auteuil, there is often live blues.

Lastly, there are a couple of spots on Rue Saint Pierre in Place Royale. There are also lots of dance venues around town but they change quickly, so ask.

The *Grand Théâtre de Québec* (☎ 643-8131) is the city's main performing arts centre presenting classical concerts, dance and theatre among its shows.

*Théâtre Capitole* (☎ 694-4444) at 972 Rue Saint Jean is another performing arts centre.

### Cinema
*Cinema Le Clap* (☎ 650-2527), at 2360 Chemin Sainte Foy in Sainte Foy, shows English, French and other international films, many with sub-titles. There are two films nightly. Another cinema in town shows English movies. The *Cinema Sainte Foy* screens first-run American films out of the centre in Sainte Foy.

### Just Sitting
The restaurant with a bar on the top of the Lowes Hôtel on Grande Allée, on the corner of Rue Bethelot, is good for views. Away from the clubs, if you just want to sit, Terrasse Dufferin behind the Château is perfect. It's cool, with views over the river.

## GETTING THERE & AWAY
### Air
The airport is west of town, off Hwy 40, near where Hwy 73 intersects it on its way north. Air Canada (☎ 692-0770) flies to Montreal and Ottawa as well as most major Canadian cities further afield. Canadian Airlines (☎ 692-0912) also serves Montreal and Ottawa and has nearly all the same routes covered.

### Bus
Voyageur Colonial Ltd (commonly referred to simply as Voyageur) serves Quebec City. The station is Gare Centrale d'Autobus (☎ 524-4692) at 225 Boulevard Charest Est. This is quite a way west of the downtown area. Buses to Montreal run nearly every hour during the day and evening; the fare is $35. There are also regular services to Rivière-du-Loup and then on to Edmundston, New Brunswick. The fare to Edmundston is $45. Rivière du Loup is the connecting point with SMT bus lines for destinations in Atlantic Canada.

There are no direct buses to or from the USA. Most go via Montreal.

To get to town from the Voyageur bus station, take a No 3 or a No 8 city bus. Going to the station from downtown, take the bus to the corner of Avenue de la Canonne and Boulevard Charest. From there walk two blocks west along Boulevard Charest to the station.

### Train
Odd as it may seem, small Quebec City has three train stations (☎ 692-3940). They all use the same phone number. The recently renovated and absolutely beautiful old station complete with bar and café on Rue Saint Paul in Lower Town is central and convenient. It is used for trains going to and from Montreal and beyond Montreal westwards. The station in Sainte Foy, south-west of the downtown area, by the bridges over to the south shore, is used by the same trains and is simply more convenient for residents on that side of the city.

Also of interest to travellers is the third

Top: Loyalist graveyard, Saint John, New Brunswick (CK)
Bottom Left: Buskers' Festival, Saint John, New Brunswick (ML)
Bottom Right: Statue of businessmen, Stephens Ave Mall, Calgary, Alberta (TS)

Top Left: Old Montreal, Quebec (CK)
Top Right: Architecfure of Old Montreal, Quebec (CK)
  Bottom: Float-plane base, Latham Island, Yellowknife, Northwest Territories (TS)

station, the one across the river on the south shore in Lévis, right opposite Quebec City. The station is just up the hill from the ferry landing. VIA Rail ticket holders do not have to pay for the ferry. This station is used primarily for trains heading eastward to the Gaspé Peninsula or the Maritimes. Some Montreal trains also use the Lévis station.

To Moncton, New Brunswick there are three eastward trips a week, Wednesday, Friday and Sunday. It's an overnight trip, leaving at 10:30 pm and taking 12 hours. A ticket is $92.

For Montreal there are trips daily and the fare is $44.

### Car

For car rentals, Budget (☎ 692-3660) is at 29 Côte du Palais or there's an office at the airport. For sub-compact vehicles the rate is $45 a day with unlimited free km if you take it on a weekend. Rates are higher during the week. All rental agencies here suggest booking two days ahead.

**Car Sharing** Allo Stop (☎ 522-0056), at 467 Rue Saint Jean, is an agency that gets drivers and passengers together. Membership for passengers is $6, then you pay a portion of the ride cost to the agency three hours before the trip, and the rest goes to the driver. They offer good deals, such as to Montreal $15, Ottawa $29, Toronto $41, New York (from Montreal) $65, and Gaspé $35. There are even rides all the way to Vancouver – especially in May.

Allo Stop also has offices at the Saguenay River, Baie Comeau and Sept-Îles among others. If you'll be travelling around the province pick up a list of all their offices and phone numbers.

### Ferry

The ferry between Quebec City and Lévis runs constantly – all day and for most of the night. One-way fares are $1.25, less for kids and seniors; it's $2.85 extra for a car. You'll get good views of the river, cliffs, the Quebec skyline and Château Frontenac even if the cruise only lasts a few minutes. The terminal

in Quebec City is in Place Royale, Lower Town. In Lévis, the ferry terminal is right beside the VIA Rail station.

### GETTING AROUND

Transportation can be a problem in Quebec City. Driving in the old section (and worse, trying to park) is a headache. The airport is a fair distance out and the bus station is none too convenient either. But the situation is better than it used to be; the train station is central and there is an airport bus.

### To/From the Airport

A bus service operated by Maple Leaf Sightseeing Tours (☎ 649-9226) saves you from paying the $30 taxi fare. The fare is $7.50. The bus makes four trips a day during the week with a reduced service on weekends. It leaves from major hotels, but will make pickups around town if you call at least one hour before flight time.

Another bus service, Autobus La Québecoise (☎ 872-5525) runs to the Mirabel International Airport in Montreal.

### Bus

There is a good city bus system (☎ 627-2511) which costs $1.80 with transfer privileges. The buses even go out as far as Sainte Anne de Beaupré on the north shore. The terminal, Gare Centrale d'Autobus, is at 225 Boulevard Charest Est in Lower Town and will supply you with route maps and information or you can call the above telephone number. City bus No 15 goes from the downtown area to the train station in Sainte Foy and back regularly – all day until about midnight. You can catch it on Avenue Dufferin or in Place d'Youville near the National Assembly.

To the Beauport motels, take bus No 53 north from Rue Dorchester. Bus No 8 goes from downtown to Laval Université.

### Car

In Quebec City, driving isn't worth the trouble. You can walk just about everywhere; the streets are narrow and crowded, and

QUEBEC

parking is an exercise in frustration. Don't bother.

### Bicycle & Scooters

Vélo Didacte (☎ 648-6022) is at 463 Rue Saint Jean. Also central and within the Old City is Location Mobylettes & Vélos (☎ 692-2817), at 92 Rue Petit Champlain in Lower Town, which rents scooters and bikes. You may see bikes for rent along Rue Saint Louis near the Château, too. Ten-speed and mountain bikes are available. The Auberge la Paix at 31 Rue Couillard also has bikes for hire.

### Calèche

Horse-drawn carriages (calèches) cost $50 an hour.

# Around Quebec City

## NORTH SHORE

About 15 km north-west of the city is the small town of **Wendake** which makes an interesting day trip for those with an interest in the country's Native people. In the late 1600s, some Hurons, a group native to the lands of Ontario, came to this region of Quebec to escape European disease epidemics and tribal conflicts.

Things to see in town include the Notre Dame de Lorette Chapel of 1731 which contains some articles from the first Jesuit mission set up for the Hurons. The Musée Aroünne at 10 Rue Alexandre Duchesneau has a small collection of Native artefacts. It is open daily from the beginning of May to the end of September but only on afternoons on Sundays.

Of most interest is **Onhoüa Chetek8e** (this is not a spelling error!) (☎ 842-4308) a reconstructed Huron village. Craft demonstrations, a gift shop with books, tapes by Indian Indian musicians and a restaurant serving traditional Native foods such as caribou, corn soup and bannock are part of the site. It's open from May to October, daily from 9 am to 6 pm. It is at 575 Stanislas-

Kosca St. A visit is more worthwhile with the guided tour of the traditional house. Ask whether an English-speaking guide will be on hand.

### The Laurentians

As in Montreal, the Laurentians north of town are a summer/winter playground. **Lac Beauport** is one of the closest and most accessible resort lakes.

### Laurentides Wildlife Reserve Provincial Park

Further north up Hwy 175, about 40 km from Quebec City, is this huge wilderness park with its wooded hills and mountains, and scores of lakes and streams. You can hike and fish and there are campgrounds along the road through the park. The road continues to Chicoutimi.

In the southern portion, **Jacques Cartier Park** (☎ 848-3169) is ideal for a quick escape from the city. In less than an hour's drive you can be camping, hiking trails or canoeing along the Jacques Cartier River. Near the entrance, an information centre provides details on the park's activities and services. Camping equipment, canoes and bikes can all be rented. In some backcountry sections simple overnight cabins have been set up. In winter there is cross-country skiing with shelter huts along some of the routes.

### Île d'Orléans

East of Quebec, this 30-km-long, green island gives a picture of traditional rural Quebec life. It offers great scenery and views, and you'll see old wooden or stone houses and cottages, some in Normandy style. Some of the villages are over 300 years old. Then, as now, the prime activity was farming for the Quebec City market. Recently, city folks have been building homes here, at least at the western end. There's lots of fruit, especially apples and strawberries. A view tower stands at the eastern tip. There's a campsite in the middle of the south-side at Saint Jean. The island is linked to the mainland by a bridge at its north-west end.

## Chute Montmorency

About seven km east of Quebec City, along Hwy 138, just past the bridge for Île d'Orléans, are the pleasant Montmorency waterfalls, higher than those at Niagara but not nearly as impressive. They're set in the newly redeveloped Parc de la Chute Montmorency where there are good walking paths, stairs to the top of the falls, picnic grounds, an information centre with historical and geological displays but also, in a case of total overkill, cable cars and helicopter rides above the flowing water. The falls are accessible by city bus No 53 from Place Jacques Cartier in Quebec City.

## Sainte Anne de Beaupré

This gaudy little tourist town is justly renowned for its immaculate and mammoth church. From the mid-1600s the village has been the site of Québecois pilgrimages. An annual pilgrimage takes place here in late July, attracting thousands of people. The grounds become a huge camp. The beautiful basilica, now standing, replaced earlier chapels and was begun in the late 1920s. Note the many crutches inside the door.

There's good tile-work on the floor, and stained glass and ceiling mosaics.

Check the hotel across the street. It's designed like a chapel, stained glass included – yuk!

Also in town are a museum, a monastery with a seminary and a few other churches. There's a 360-degree painting of Jerusalem on the day Jesus died. Admission to see it costs $3.50.

City bus No 50 from Place Jacques Cartier in Quebec City runs to the town.

About three km north of town, towards Mont Sainte Anne, is *La Camarine*, a fine place for a splurge on a good French meal. It's run by a woman in an old Quebec-style house and offers complete dinners from $21 and up – not cheap but very nice.

## Chutes Sainte Anne

Six km east of Beaupré, in a deep chasm, are the 74-metre-high Sainte Anne waterfalls (☎ 827-4057). You can walk around and across them on a series of steps and a suspension bridge for $5. Though busy this is quite a pleasant spot – less developed and more dramatic than the falls at Montmorency. The

---

### Skiing

The excellent skiing is the main draw of the Québec City area through the winter.

Mont Sainte Anne (☎ 827-4561) at 800 metres with alpine runs down the north, south and west faces is the premier ski centre in the region, indeed in Eastern Canada. Despite the obvious downhill lure it also has a spectacular system of cross-country ski trails. Access to the cross-country area is eight km from the alpine centre on Route 360, in the village of Saint Ferreol les Neiges. For both types of skiing there are novice, intermediate and expert trails. The season runs from the end of November to the end of March. Numerous resorts, lodges and hotels can be found in and around the foot of the mountain. The tourist office has publications detailing winter vacation packages which include hotel and ski passes. Meals and the shuttle bus to the lifts may also be options.

The second major downhill centre is Stoneham (☎ 848-2411) in the village of the same name up Hwy 175 north of Québec City. With 26 alpine slopes, it is half the size of Mont Sainte Anne. Ticket prices here are about 25% less.

Smaller, less expensive alpine centres are Centre de Ski Le Relais at Lac Beaufort and Mont Saint Castin also at Lac Beauport. These, too, have snow-making and a range of lifts and slopes of varying degrees of difficulty.

All four resorts offer rentals, lessons, child care, night skiing (a magical experience) and lodging right on the hill. The latter is a luxury that must be paid for but there is plenty of accommodation near the centres. The week between Christmas and New Year's and the March school break should be booked well in advance. Aside from Mont Sainte Anne, there are other cross-country ski centres but a very good day can be had right in town in the Parc des Batailles. Where else can you ski on a battlefield that determined the future of a country? ■

water roars loudest in spring but fall is grand with the surrounding red and gold of the maple leaves. The site, with restaurant, is open from May to the end of October.

## Mont Sainte Anne Park

A little further east, 50 km from Quebec, Mont Sainte Anne Park is best known as a ski area – it's the number one hill near Quebec City and one of the top slopes in the province. There are about a dozen lifts. In summer, there is camping and a gondola to the mountain's summit. Or if you're up to it, bicycle and hiking trails wind to the top.

Buses depart from the centre of Quebec City.

A few km east are more waterfalls at **Les Sept Chutes**. There is defunct hydroelectric station here and a dam. Trails wind along the river past the various falls and through the woods and there is information about the old power-production facilities. There's a restaurant and picnic tables as well. Admission will set you back a few bucks.

## SOUTH SHORE
### Lévis

There's not much here for the visitor. It's a cross between a smallish town and a suburb of Quebec City. The ferry ride over makes a mini-cruise and the views of Quebec are good. Near the terminal is a train station (☎ 692-3940) for trips east and to Montreal. For more information about trains, see the Getting There & Away section of Quebec City.

Part of the way up the hill into town are the remains of a fort from where there are excellent views.

Between 1865 and 1872 the British built three forts on the south shore cliffs to protect Quebec. One, known as Pointe-Lévis Fort No 1 has been restored and operates as a national historic park, which has free guided tours. It's on the east side of Lévis in Lauzon.

### Eastward

Leaving Quebec City, the landscape is pretty flat but looking across the river you can see the mountains and hills; the large one with the ski runs is Mont Sainte Anne. Going along Hwy 132 through the little towns, Île d'Orl,ans lies just offshore. Without offering anything of particular note, **Saint Michel** strikes me as attractive and a quintessential example of small-town Quebec.

### Montmagny

About 60 km east of Lévis, offshore from Montmagny, is the first main point of interest, the Gross Île National Historic Site.

The town is also of note for being on the migration route of the snow goose. Each spring and fall thousands of these birds stopover on the shoreline around town. Bird watchers can feast their eyes and enjoy the festival initiated by the geese.

At 45 du Bassin Nord in town is a dual-purpose interpretive centre (☎ 248-9196) which illuminates the phenomenon of migration, both bird and human. The first portion is an exhibit on the Great White Goose. The second presents the history of Gross Île and the surrounding south shore through a sound & light show. Admission is charged for each or a double discount ticket is offered.

In and around Montmagny there are numerous places to stay including lodges, motels and campgrounds. About a dozen places to eat can be found in town including a pub at 186 Boulevard Taché Ouest.

### Gross Île National Historic Site

The government park here commemorates the significant role this small island has played in Canada's history. It lies just offshore from the town of Montmagny along Hwy 132. For 105 years, from 1832 until as late as 1937, Gross Île was the major Canadian quarantine station for immigrants coming to the new land from Europe.

Through the last century and into the middle of this one, four million people passed through Quebec City en route to points across North America. Isolated Gross Île was meant to screen out those amongst the thousands of people of varying nationalities with typhus, cholera and the like. In attempting to perform this service it became, in a sense, a city of woe.

There are over 100 buildings or remains of buildings still on the historic site including churches, a school, the 'hotel' residences and hospital. And, of course, the cemeteries.

There are half or full-day excursions but, in either case, reservations are required and can be made by calling ☎ 648-4168 in Quebec City or ☎ 248-9196 in Montmagny. Bilingual guides are available to lead visitors around the site which is open from May to October.

From Montmagny there are several different operators who run boats the short distance over to the park but these trips, some including a meal, can be pricey. For information on the various choices call the above numbers or try the main boat company at ☎ 622-2566. Asking around at the docks in Montmagny will turn something up.

Other day trips are run to Île-aux-Grues another small island in the archipelago where there are a couple of inns and a restaurant but they are even more expensive and are geared to those in need of a quick splurge escape from the rat race. There is, however, a campground on the island.

### Saint Jean-Port-Joli

This small but spread-out town, with the big two-spired church right in the middle, is a centre for the Quebec art of woodcarving. Good examples can be seen in the **Musée des Anciens Canadiens** where admission costs $3.50 The museum has work done by some of the best known local sculptors, past and present. There is a gift shop and snack bar here too. It's open every day from May to November.

More recent carvings in the same style and in a variety of other styles can be seen in the many workshops and stores in and around town. Some carvers specialise in figures, others in religious themes, and still others in boats and ornate murals. Courses in carving can be taken as well. Other crafts produced and sold here are ceramics and textiles but they are distant seconds to the number of works in wood.

On the east side of town, with the 1953 Constellation aircraft out the front, is the **Musée Les Rétrouvailles** with an assortment of farm and household articles from the past decades. There is a small admission fee. There is also a **maritime museum** in town for those with a special interest.

At 322 Rue de Gaspé Ouest is the **Maison Médard-Bourgault** the former home of a wood carver who left reminders of his work on the walls and in the furnishings of the old house.

The impressive **church** dates from 1890 and the priest's house next door was built even earlier in 1872.

Pretty well everything can be found along one street, Rue de Gaspé. In town you'll find a restaurant or two, including the *Dorian Casse Croûte* for topnotch fries and burgers. There are a few motels, a B&B and a campground. Right in the middle of town is a tourist office.

On the west side of town is a good picnic area with views over the river. Orleans Express bus lines stop right in the town centre.

Wood carving by Pier Cloutier

QUEBEC

# East along the St Lawrence River

East along the St Lawrence River from Quebec City are some of the most scenic landscapes in the province – the shoreline becomes more typical of that found in Eastern Canada. With neat small farms and little villages dominated by the church – usually topped by a silver spire – this is rural Quebec. With few changes, life has been pretty much the same here for well over a century. You won't hear English spoken in this part of the province, but you won't find any hostility either.

From Quebec City you can take either the north or south shore up towards the Gaspé. Just don't take the super Hwy 20 from which you'll see nothing.

There are ferries across the river at various points. The further east you go, the wider the river becomes and the more costly the ferry.

## NORTH SHORE & CHARLEVOIX

The north shore is hillier and more dramatic than the south shore as the northern mountains come down close to the river. It also has the more physical points of interest. Orleans Express buses serve the area stopping at many of the small as well as the larger towns.

Beyond Sainte Anne de Beaupré is the scenic coastal district known as Charlevoix. For 200 years this pastoral strip of hilly, flowery farmland counterbalanced with steep cliffs and woods wedged between northern wilderness and the river has been a summer retreat of the wealthy and privileged. Though vestiges of this remain and prices are on the high side it is now a more democratic destination. UNESCO has classed it as a biosphere or heritage cultural and environmental region and this has meant worthwhile restrictions on the types of permitted developments.

It's long been a popular district with artists, and numerous galleries and craft shops may be found in the towns and villages. Inns and less-expensive B&Bs abound

and there is no shortage of quality restaurants. Aside from the summer visitors, people from Quebec City enjoy Charlevoix as a place for a weekend break or a short holiday destination. Due to its popularity as well as upper-class tradition (and quality), prices for food and lodging are higher here than elsewhere up the St Lawrence but the terrain and parks make a short visit worthwhile even for those on tight budgets.

### Cap Tourmente

At Cap Tourmente is a **bird sanctuary and wildlife preserve.** Flocks of snow geese come here in spring and autumn. There are walking paths through the swampy land. The area is open every day from 9 am to 5 pm.

### Baie Saint Paul

Heading east along the St Lawrence River the first urban stop after Quebec City is Baie Saint Paul, with its old streets and big church. There are good views from the tourist chalet and a picnic area on the west side of town. The main street of this attractive town is lined with historic houses some of which have been converted into galleries and restaurants. Artists' studios and craft shops are scattered around the side streets.

A major gallery is the Exposition Centre at 23 Rue Ambroise-Faford. Another to have a peek at is the Art Centre at 4 Rue Ambroise-Fafard. At 58 Rue Saint Jean Baptiste is a house/museum where a local painter lived and worked and played host to some of the country's most prominent painters through the mid-1900s.

Down the street at 152 Rue Saint Jean Baptiste, the natural-history centre has displays on the geography, flora & fauna of the Charlevoix district. It's open from June to October. Remember that many of the exhibits are described in French.

Bicycles can be rented in town at several locations and an afternoon's cycle around the area should be considered.

For spending the night check the inexpensive *Maison Chez Laurent* (☎ 435-3895) where singles/doubles in motel units and chalets start at singles/doubles $35. The simple *Auberge La Grande Maison* (☎ 435-5575), at 160 Rue Saint Jean Baptiste, is also priced about the same, again with some costlier rooms as well. There is also good camping down towards the village of Saint Louis on Île aux Coudres 25 km from town. Ferries run to the island from Saint Joseph de la Rive. Once the base for whale hunting, the island has a number of small low-key historic sites, a windmill and is now mainly farmland. At the ferry terminal there is an information booth and bicycles can be rented for exploring the island. The difficulty is the bike rental place is five km from the dock! Turn left at the blinking light after leaving the boat and keep walking. The ferry trip takes 15 minutes and runs frequently, especially through the summer months.

Hwy 381, north from Baie Saint Paul, runs along the edge of Laurentide Park offering good scenery and steep hills.

Excellent hiking and rugged topography can be found north of Baie Saint Paul in **Grands Jardins Provincial Park** which encompasses an area of mountains and taiga (northern evergreen forest) and includes a caribou herd amongst the wildlife. There is camping in the park as well as bike and canoe rentals.

Going east along the Saint Lawrence, don't even consider taking Hwy 138 but take the coastal Hwy 362 which goes up and down hills beside the river. The scenery is superb around **Les Éboulements**, with farms running from the town's edge to the river. You may have to stop while a farmer leads cattle across the highway. Note the piles of wood used for the long winters and the many carving outlets. In the villages along the coast here, such as Saint Joseph de-la-Rive and Pointe-au-Pic, there are several small hotels with good food.

### Pointe-au-Pic

Seemingly a small, insignificant little village, Pic was a holiday destination for the wealthy from as far as New York at the turn-of-the-century. The scenery, the isolation and the trendiness had many building fine summer residences along the shore. One such resident was William-Howard Taft, former president of the USA. Some of these large, impressive 'cottages' along Chemin des Falaises have now been converted into comfortable inns.

A **museum** in town offers a good view and exhibits on the life and times of Charlevoix. A major part of the museum is the art gallery which has both a permanent display as well as changing shows which promote the works of local artists. The museum is open daily in summer from 10 am to 5 pm, with shortened hours at other times, and admission is $4, less for students. The address is 1 Chemin du Havre.

On Ave Richelieu is a small Protestant church.

Pointe-au-Pic has a considerable number of lodgings, least expensive of which are the motels. Also in this small town outside of La Malbaie is the *Manoir Richelieu* dating from 1928 – a huge, elegant, romantic hotel worth a look. They offer one, two and three-day packages including some meals and entertainment but we're talking serious dollars. One exception is that the cafeteria in the basement has a low-cost breakfast – a good excuse for checking it out.

### La Malbaie

About 44 km north of La Malbaie and Pointe-au-Pic is the impressive **Parc Hautes-Gorges** a geographically and scenically intriguing area of mountains cut through by the Malbaie River and its valley. The sheer cliffs along the river reach 700 metres high at places. Fine hiking trails crisscross much of the park. In Pointe-au-Pic cruises along the northern section of the river can be organised. The 1½-hour cruises cost $18. Organised hiking and bus excursions through the park with naturalist guides are offered out of Baie Saint Paul at the Natural History Centre, 152 Rue Saint Jean Baptiste. Most of these will be in French but some guides do speak English.

There are a couple of places for overnighters. If still operating, the old-fashioned *Hôtel Lapointe* in front of the church is a fine, cheap place to spend the night. See if

QUEBEC

you can get a peek at the mahogany cupboard in the old dining room. Rumours suggest the hotel is now closed.

In Cap-à-l'Aigle, the recommended *Auberge des Peupliers* has lunches at $10 and dinners costing $24.

### Saint Siméon

The ferry (☎ 862-5095) to Rivière-du-Loup on the south shore departs from Saint Siméon. At this point in the river, a crossing is 75 minutes. It's in this area that the river on its way to the Atlantic, begins to get salty. The ferry is comfortable with lounges, an information desk and a capacity of 100 vehicles. Whales may be seen if you're lucky. The trip takes 65 minutes. There are three or four trips a day during summer, spring and fall but the schedule varies according to the tides. Visitors with vehicles should be at the dock an hour before departure but for walk-ons this is not necessary. For prices see under the south shore.

The ferry terminal is in the centre of town.

### Baie Sainte Catherine & Saguenay River

Baie Sainte Catherine at the mouth of the Saguenay River marks the eastern end of the Charlevoix district and together with Tadoussac acts as a centre for exploring the majestic Saguenay and surrounding waters.

The Saguenay is the largest of Eastern Canada's few fjords – a spectacular saltwater inlet, edged in part by steep cliffs and running to a depth of 500 metres along a crack in the earth's crust. Ocean-going ships can ply the deep black waters as far as Chicoutimi and aboard smaller vessels, several different cruises are possible. The river can become stormy very quickly, take warm clothing. Trips upstream past the cliffs are interesting, as you lose your ability to judge size and distance against the rock walls. The river and the surrounding land is part of the Saguenay Provincial Park. A federal marine park covers the region where the Saguenay empties into the St Lawrence.

At the confluence of the Saguenay River and the St Lawrence shrimp and capelin abound, attracting beluga, finback, humpback, rorqual and even blue whales.

**Whale-watching** has become a major activity. Beluga whales which are suffering most from the regional pollution, live in and around the Saguenay River all year round. In June, minkes and finbacks arrive from the Gulf of St Lawrence and, later in the summer, the huge blue whale shows up to feed on the krill which is produced in copious amounts where the two rivers meet. August to October is the best whale-watching period.

There are several **boat cruise** operators working out of this small port, the biggest of which is Navimex Cruises (☎ 237-4274).

In July and August they run two cruises daily up the fjord. A ticket costs $40 and includes a meal. The return trip takes about 4½ hours. The ships used for these tours are large and offer bars and all the extras.

Whale-watching cruises run from the beginning of June until mid-October. A three-hour trip out on the river in search of the big mammals is $30. Four trips are offered daily in mid-summer.

Regardless of how warm a day it is in town, take warmer clothes with you on the boat. It is always breezy out on the river and the water temperature here is low, even in July. The trips using Zodiacs (small, motorised inflatable boats) have had good reviews.

Navimex cruise boats can be boarded here or in Tadoussac where several operators have offices.

Also visit the **Pointe Noire Coastal Station**. This whale-study post (☎ 237-4383) on the Saguenay River has an exhibit, a slide show and films, and an observation tower with a telescope for views over the mouth of the river. The centre is open from June to September.

Once numbering 6000, only 500 beluga whales still remain and the area around Pointe Noire has become their refuge. Other types frequent the area; in fact, minkes were seen just a few metres from shore on one visit. Entrance to the centre is $3 and recommended if you have a car. The station is west of town and not accessible without your own transportation. It is not worth a major effort to get to.

During the first week in August is the Cod Festival.

**Places to Stay** For accommodation in Baie Sainte Catherine you can stay at *Hôtel Saguenay et Cabines* (☎ 237-4271), on Hwy 294, for singles/doubles $30/40 or check out one of the several fairly priced B&Bs. For example, the *Gîtes du Saguenay* (☎ 237-4290) at No 294 on Route 138, the main street, is $30 for a double. Remember this can be a fairly busy place in midsummer so don't leave finding a bed too late.

Small, simple inexpensive eateries can be found along the highway here or over in Tadoussac.

**Getting There & Away** From 15 June to 15 September, a ferry runs across the river to Tadoussac every 20 minutes from 8 am to 8 pm, then every 40 minutes. The 10-minute trip is free. It is not uncommon to see a few whales from the ferry across the river.

### Tadoussac

Across the Saguenay, Tadoussac, with a population of just 832, is about three times the size of Baie Sainte Catherine and though still a small town, acts as the regional centre. It's an attractive place and nearly all the numerous points of interest are within walking distance of each other. It, too, acts as a centre for the whale-watching and river trips around the Saguenay waters. See under Baie Sainte Catherine earlier for information on the river and whales.

The tourist information office (☎ 235-4776) open from mid-June to the beginning of September is at 196 Rue des Pionniers in the middle of town. The hours are from 8 am to 8 pm. All the sites and boat trips operate seasonally and from the end of September to spring time, Tadoussac pretty much shuts up and visitors are few.

The quay and waterfront area along Rue du Bord de l'Eau facing out to Tadoussac

Bay has offices for the various boat trip operators.

There are some fine green areas around town for walking. From Pointe de l'Islet, a peninsular park at the southern edge of town, spying whales from the shore is possible. A walking trail beginning and ending from the Rue du Bord de l'Eau leads around the peninsula. Also great for views is the Parc du Saguenay. If driving, park in the lot across the street from the Fish Hatchery (Pisciculture) and walk to the information office. Walks from the information centre around the hill afford views over the confluence of the rivers. Longer trails running north begin across the street at the Pisciculture. Ask about them at the information office. The **Parc du Saguenay**, beginning in Tadoussac, is a huge park which runs along both sides of the Saguenay River virtually all the way to Chicoutimi. It includes the land all around Lac de l'Anse à l'Eau, the lake just north of town. One of the walking trails beginning at the Pisciculture leads along the edge of this lake.

Another walking trail leads six km northeast along the beach and waterfront from the downtown area to the dunes, a geographical site.

The headquarters for **The Saguenay Marine Park** (☎ 235-4703) is at 182 Rue de l'Eglise. The park's mandate is to protect and promote the Saguenay, its waters, surroundings and wildlife. Naturalists can answer questions. Affiliated interpretive centres are found at Pointe Noire in Baie Sainte Catherine and at Cap de Bon Désir near Grandes Bergerons 22 km north-east of Tadoussac up the St Lawrence. At both there are whale-viewing decks and displays on the mammals of the sea.

At 108 Rue de la Cale-Sèche is the **Marine Mammal Interpretive Centre** (CIMM). It's open daily from May to November and gives visitors some background information on the creatures found in local waters. Admission is $4.50 for adults.

**Maison Chauvin** at 157 Rue du Bord de l'Eau is a replica of Canada's first fur-trading post and offers some history on the first transactions between the Native Indians and Europeans. It, too, is open every day but through the warm months only.

**La Vielle Chapelle** built in 1747 by the Jesuits, is one of the oldest wooden churches in the country. It is also known as the Indian Chapel.

**The Pisciculture** or fish hatchery at 115 Rue du Bateau Passeur is passed as Tadoussac is entered from across the Saguenay. Run by the provincial government, the hatchery which can be toured at no charge, provides fish for the re-stocking of Quebec's salmon streams and rivers. Some

of the Parc du Saguenay's walking trails begin from behind the hatchery.

At 143 Rue du Bateau Passeur is the small specialised **Musée Molson Beattie** which through models, photographs and other artefacts outlines the history of shipping on the St Lawrence and the development of the seaway.

Also in town is the **Tadoussac Hôtel**, a seemingly out-of-place and huge old attractive resort. For a splurge, dinner prices are reasonable at $25 to $30 at the hotel and a walk through the lobby and around the grounds is certainly an experience. The hotel

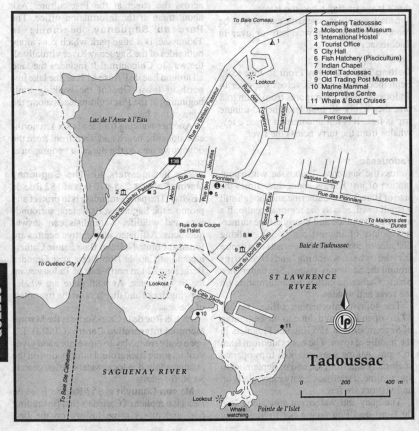

1 Camping Tadoussac
2 Molson Beattie Museum
3 International Hostel
4 Tourist Office
5 City Hall
6 Fish Hatchery (Pisciculture)
7 Indian Chapel
8 Hotel Tadoussac
9 Old Trading Post Museum
10 Marine Mammal Interpretive Centre
11 Whale & Boat Cruises

**Tadoussac**

was built in 1941 but was renovated in the mid-1980s.

Between five and six km north-east of town are the so-called dunes and the **Maison des Dunes Interpretive Centre** on Chemin du Moulin à Baude. The dunes are land forms sculptured by glaciers. The centre, part of the Parc du Saguenay, has information about their origins and is open daily from mid-June to the end of September. The beach trail from town leads to the dunes.

There is an HI hostel, *La Maison Majorique* (☎ 235-4372), at 154 Rue de Bateau-Passeur where a bed costs $12. One reader has said the atmosphere at the hostel was so congenial that it wasn't surprising that a number of visitors meeting there later married.

**Places to Stay** There's camping two km from the ferry on Hwy 138. Tadoussac also has a couple of B&B's. One to try is *Maison Gauthier* (☎ 235-4525) at 159 Rue du Bateau Passeur. A couple of motels offer alternative low-end accommodation. At 188 Rue des Pioneers is the *Maison Clauphi & Motel* (☎ 235-4303. Another is the *Motel Chantmarin* (☎ 235-4242) at 414 Rue du Bateau Passeur and with an inexpensive restaurant. Rates at both start at $40 but may be more in peak season.

### Up the Saguenay River

Just north-west of Tadoussac, Parc du Saguenay (Saguenay Park), which protects the river's edges almost all the way to Chicoutimi, begins. Visit the park information office (☎ 235-4238) off Rue du Bateau Passeur at the parking lot across from the entrance to Pisciculture at the eastern edge of Tadoussac. They can recommend walks and have information on some of the boat trips available. Some cruises of the fjord depart from the quay in Tadoussac. There is camping in the park and guesthouses in the nearby villages.

From the village of Sacré Coeurs, 10 km from Tadoussac on the east side of the river, a small road leads to L'Anse de Roche with a good view of the fjord.

One cruise departs from L'Anse Saint Jean in the middle of the park region on the west side of the Saguenay. Two trips run daily through the summer for $18. Another trip leaves from La Baie just south of Chicoutimi. There are several other trips to choose from, leaving from various places along the fjord.

### Chicoutimi

The roads along the Saguenay River up to Chicoutimi offer good views of the river. Chicoutimi lies not far from Lac Saint Jean, the source of the Saguenay. There are a couple of wilderness parks in the vicinity and from town you can take boat trips south down the river and fjord.

Despite being one of the province's largest northern towns, Chicoutimi is quite small with a population of 60,000. It's nestled between mountains with the Saguenay River flowing through. The large number of students in town (there is a university and a community college (CÉGEP) in town) makes this quite a lively place with a lot of nightlife. Rue Racine is the city's main street.

See the **House of Arthur Villeneuve** at 669 Rue Taché Ouest. In the late 1950s when Monsieur Villeneuve retired as a local barber, he began painting. His depictions of the town and landscape along the river attracted a lot of attention and are now sold and collected around the world. The house, he and his wife's former home, is now a museum known not so much for the paintings it contains but for the painting it is. The entire house has been painted inside and out like a series of canvases in Villeneuve's bright, naive folk style. It's open Tuesday to Friday from mid-May to mid-October, admission is $3.

At 534 Rue Jacques Cartier Est is the **Musée du Saguenay-Lac Saint Jean** with displays on the history of the area including some Native Indian and Inuit artefacts. It's open every day in summer but closed on weekends for the rest of the year. Admission is charged.

You can visit the large (although no-longer operating) pulp mill, once the world's biggest. If you want a free tour in English, call ahead for reservations on ☎ 698-3100. The mill is at 300 Rue Dubuc.

From the old harbour and market area, tour boats depart for trips down the Saguenay River.

North of Chicoutimi the highway continues on to Lac Saint Jean and then through northern timberland and a huge nature reserve to the town of Chibougamou. From there the roads start to peter out.

**Places to Stay** North of Chicoutimi near the town of Roberval is *Auberge Kukum* (☎ 275-0697), an HI hostel, situated on a Native Montagnais Indian Reserve. Ask about the excursions where you live in the forest with an Indian family for a week.

In Chicoutimi, there is low-budget accommodation in the community college (CÉGEP) from May to mid-August. There are very low weekly rates if you're staying awhile.

*Auberge Centre Ville* (☎ 543-0253) at 104 Rue Jacques Cartier, has been recommended as a good, cheap central place, at least for males. There is a choice of basic rooms or more costly ones which have their own bathrooms. Either way a TV is included.

Also good value is *Motel au Parasol* (☎ 543-7771), at 1287 Boulevard Saguenay Est, with moderately priced rooms and a great view.

There are many other hotels, motels and some fine auberges (inns) around the region.

**Places to Eat** Rue Saint Jacques has numerous places to eat. *La Forchette* near the Chez Gérard Hôtel is said to be good value.

At night the *Guiness Pub* on Rue Racine is good and has a wide selection of beers. Along Rue Racine are several other places for raising a glass or kicking up the heels.

### Jonquière
West from Chicoutimi along Hwy 170, Jonquière is about the same size but not as interesting as Chicoutimi but it's worth a look if you've come this far. It has an enor-

mous aluminium smelter and two paper mills.

The lookout at the **Shipshaw Dam** is a good stop. Turn right after crossing the Aluminium Bridge which is before downtown if you're arriving from Chicoutimi.

A puppet festival is held during the first week of July.

There are a number of cheap hotels and inexpensive summer accommodation at the community college at 2505 Rue Saint Hubert.

Rue Saint Dominique, the main street, has a number of bars and cafés which are very busy at night.

### Baie Comeau
Beyond Tadoussac on the north shore of the Saint Lawrence, the road continues northeast through hilly and less-populated areas to the newsprint town of Baie Comeau with a population of 27,000.

There isn't much to see here but in a small part of town known as the **Quartier Saint Amélie** there is another of the grand northshore hotels, Hôtel le Manoir. It's surrounded by a heritage district with much more modest houses dating from the 1930s.

For spending the night, not a fortune, the *Hotel Baie Comeau* (☎ 296-4977) in the centre of the upper town, not far from the highway at 48 Place Lasalle, has been recommended. A double is $40. For those with wheels there are several motels on Lasalle further west from the centre.

Baie Comeau is one of the semi-remote industrial centres which seem to proliferate in this part of the country. As well as the pulp mill, there is a huge aluminium smelter, **Reynold's**, which runs free guided tours throughout the summer, twice on weekday afternoons.

But most associate the town with hydropower because of the large projects along the Manicouagan River. Each of three 'ginormous' **dams** operated by Hydro-Quebec – Manic Deux, Trois and Cinq – can be visited free. The first dam is 50 km north of town and the last one 200 km north. The scope and scale of these projects will really boggle the eyes and mind.

From Baie Comeau, Hwy 389 runs north past the Manicouagan projects and then beyond to Wabush and Labrador City on the border of Quebec and Labrador, Newfoundland. For details of these similarly awesome towns and Labrador, see the Labrador section in the Newfoundland chapter. There is also some more information on travelling the road to Labrador in that section. About 120 km north-west of Manic Cinq are the **Groulx Mountains** which reach as high as 1000 metres. This is a fascinating far-north landscape with lake-filled barrens and tundra.

Baie Comeau is connected by ferry to Matane across the river. For ferry details see under Matane.

### Sept-Îles

Sept-Îles is the last town of any size along the north shore. It's a port city and international freighters make use of the docking facilities. In fact, despite the rather isolated location, this is Canada's second busiest port measured by tonnage.

Along the waterfront park a boardwalk fronts the shoreline and a tourist office. The tourist office (☎ 962-1238) is at 546 Ave Dequen and is open all year.

Vieux Poste is a reconstructed trading post where the French dealt with the Montagnais Indians whose land this traditionally was. There is also a small museum in town. The Native Cultural Centre has some traditional crafts for sale.

From Sept-Îles, you can go to **Île Grand Basque**, part of the Sept-Îles Archipelago. Here there is camping, hiking, beaches and a few other things to see. Nature trails cross the island. Camping costs $7. There are frequent ferries to Île Grand Basque which cost $5. Île du Corosol is a bird refuge.

Bicycles and kayaks can be rented in town at Location Rioux, 391 Ave Gamache.

You can also take cod-fishing trips from Sept-Îles out among the many islands for $15.

The train from Sept-Îles permits access to

part of Quebec's north and the western portions of Newfoundland's Labrador. See also the Labrador section of the Newfoundland chapter. The road continues eastward to Havre Saint Pierre.

**Places to Stay & Eat** For places to stay there is an HI hostel (☎ 962-8180) and half a dozen motels mostly in the expensive category. Further down the road in Havre Saint Pierre there is a campground. For something to eat, can you believe it, there is both a Chinese and Vietnamese restaurant? The *Restaurant Saigon* is about as far out of context as imaginable.

**Getting There & Away** Buses run between Baie Comeau and Havre Saint Pierre stopping at Sept-Îles en route. Call Autobus du Littoral on ☎ 962-2126 for the schedule. From Baie Comeau buses connect Quebec City.

The twice weekly train north from Sept-Îles to Labrador City, Labrador offers a fascinating trip through northern spruce forest and open tundra. The train crosses a 900-metre-long bridge, 50 metres over the Moisie River and past the 60-metre-high Tonkas Falls. The dome car is from the famous Wabush Cannonball train, a name often heard in American folk songs.

The route through the remote, rugged terrain was begun in 1950 and took 7000 workers four years to finish – a dirty job. These people had to be flown in, making the largest civilian airlift ever. For information in Sept-Îles call the Quebec and North Shore Railway on ☎ 418-968-7539. The station is at 100 Rue Retty. For more information see under Labrador City.

### Around Sept-Îles

A side trip from Sept-Îles (or Labrador City in Newfoundland) can be made to Fermont (Quebec), a mining town 27 km west of Labrador City, right on the provincial borders. Built in 1974, it has a unique design consisting of a 1.5-km-long, five-storey arched building which contains most of the town's commercial establishments. The housing is all built inside the windbreaking curve. Access is by the above-mentioned train which continues on to Schefferville, another mining town.

### Havre Saint Pierre

This is the end of the road and the jumping-off point for visits to the island national park just offshore. In town visit the park's reception and information centre. In the former Hudson Bay Company store at 957 Rue de la Berge, the Cultural & Interpretive Centre is a museum on local history and a place for visitors to pick up information on the area. There is also tourist information available at the government office at 1081 de la Digue.

On the eastern outskirts of town is the *Camping Municipal* (☎ 538-2415). Out of town, 15 km, there is an HI *Auberge de la Minganie A J* (☎ 252-3117). Reservations are suggested. The bus from Sept-Îles will let you off at the hostel on its way to Havre Saint Pierre. *Chez Louis* (☎ 538-2799) at 1045 Rue Boréal is a B&B.

For the adventurous, there are also ferries from town to Île d'Anticosti and along the coast to Labrador.

### Mingan Archipelago National Park

The park features some interesting 'flowerpots' and other odd erosion-shaped limestone formations along the shore. A variety of sea birds can be seen around the 40 islands and, in the water, there are seals and whales. Many visitors bring their own boats – kayaks are good, but commercial boat trips run from the mainland too. Some of the islands have hiking paths and free wilderness camping sites. There is a visitor centre (☎ 949-2126) open through the summer months at 30 Rue du Bord de la Mer in Longue Pointe de Mingan and park guides run interpretive programmes.

### To Labrador or Newfoundland

From Havre Saint Pierre, a ferry skips along the barren north shore servicing about 10 of the 15 little fishing villages. The people eking out a living sometimes without even running water are a mix of French and Montagnais Indian. In Harrington Harbour, lodging is often available in people's homes but it's a matter of asking around. The ferry stops at Blanc Sablon, two km from the 54th parallel and the border of Labrador. These ferries run from April to mid-January depending on the ice situation.

From Blanc Sablon another ferry can be caught over to Saint Barbe, Newfoundland. See Newfoundland for details. For more information on the Quebec ferry call Relais Nordik Inc in Sept-Îles on ☎ 968-4707 or in Havre Saint Pierre. The ferry costs are quite low as they are partially subsidised by the government.

### ÎLE D'ANTICOSTI

A large island at the mouth of the St Lawrence, halfway between the Gaspé Peninsula and the north shore, Anticosti was privately owned by different companies and individuals from 1680 to 1974. One of these was Henri Menier, a French chocolate whiz. The island is now a natural wildlife reserve. It's a remote, heavily wooded, cliff-edged island with waterfalls and good salmon rivers. Due to the population of 120,000 white-tailed deer, the island attracts hunters. Ones who don't like to have to look too hard, I presume.

There are about 300 residents, living mainly around Port Menier on the western tip, from where the island's lone road ventures to the interior.

Port Menier has a restaurant and lodging, rental cars, gas and groceries are available. There is a campground not far from Port Menier, towards West Point at the end of the island. Potential campers should be well equipped and prepared for poor weather when planning trips anywhere in this region of the province.

The one basic road leads along the north coast past a four-km-long canyon and a couple of simple camping areas.

The *Auberge Port Menier* (☎ 535-0122) with 25 rooms is the only game in town, other than full package resorts, and charges $70 double.

A ferry runs between the town here and Havre Saint Pierre on the north coast of the

Gulf of St Lawrence where the road eastward ends. It's operated by Relais Nordik (see the ferry for Blanc Sabon under To Labrador or Newfoundland section). A longer ferry runs to Port Menier from Sept-Îles. There are also flights into Anticosti.

## SOUTH SHORE

### Rivière-du-Loup

Rivière-du-Loup, on the south shore of the St Lawrence River, is a pleasant surprise for many people. Although a small, second-level city in the middle of nowhere, it's a lively and attractive town with an appealing and distinctively Quebécois atmosphere. The massive stone church, Saint Ludger, in the upper portion of town dominates the skyline.

Much of it is built along winding, hilly streets offering views of and across the river to the mountains beyond. The location also makes it quite a busy stopping-off point for those going either through the Maritimes or further east into the Gaspé region of Quebec. There is free parking all around the central area, look for the signs with the letter 'P' on them.

The main street, Rue Lafontaine, leads up the hill from Hwy 132 and Boulevard Hôtel

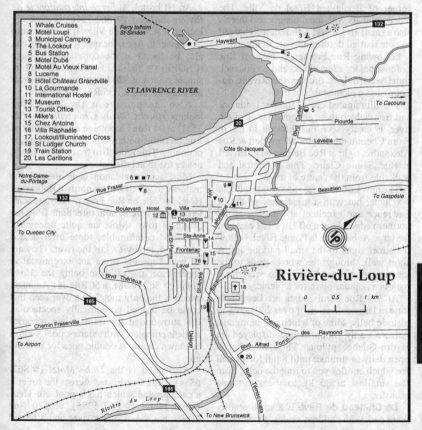

1  Whale Cruises
2  Motel Loupi
3  Municipal Camping
4  The Lookout
5  Bus Station
6  Motel Dubé
7  Motel Au Vieux Fanal
8  Lucerne
9  Hôtel Château Grandville
10  La Gourmande
11  International Hostel
12  Museum
13  Tourist Office
14  Mike's
15  Chez Antoine
16  Villa Raphaéle
17  Lookout/Illuminated Cross
18  St Ludger Church
19  Train Station
20  Les Carillons

ST LAWRENCE RIVER

Ferry to/from St-Siméon

Hayward

To Cacouna

Plourde

Léveillé

Côte St-Jacques

Notre-Dame-du-Portage

Rue Fraser

Beaubien

To Gaspésie

Boulevard Hotel de Ville

Desjardins

To Quebec City

Ste-Anne

Frontenac

Laval

Blvd Thériault

**Rivière-du-Loup**

0      0.5      1 km

To Airport

Chemin Fraserville

des Raymond

Blvd Alfred Fortin

To New Brunswick

Rivière du Loup

To New Brunswick

QUEBEC

de Ville. Many of the restaurants are found along it.

The tourist office (☎ 867-3051) is at 189 Rue Hôtel de Ville on the corner of Rue Hôtel de Ville and Rue Saint Pierre. It's open every day in summer and from Monday to Friday the rest of the year. You can't miss it coming into town. There is another office on Hwy 20 just west of the city.

**Things to See** Across the street from the central tourist office is the **Musée du Bas Saint Laurent** (Museum of the Lower St Lawrence) at 300 Rue Saint Pierre on the corner of Boulevard Hôtel de Ville. The museum deals with local history and there's also a small art gallery. Admission is charged so note that all descriptions are in French.

Following Rue Frontenac, east off Rue Lafontaine, for a few blocks and you'll reach some waterfalls, a drop in the Rivière-du-Loup, and a picnic table or two.

The illuminated cross, another landmark and from which there are good views of the river, is easily seen but difficult to reach. From Chemin des Raymond turn left at Rue Alexandre, right at Rue Bernier and then left at Rue Sainte Claire. This is central and walkable from the centre of town.

The new **Lookout**, less accessible without a vehicle, but with a great view of the St Lawrence and excellent at sunset is at the northern edge of town off Hwy 132 east past the large Auberge de la Pointe Hôtel. Follow the street signs to the small parking lot. A short walk through the woods leads to the viewing platform. Below, the waterfront park is a popular place for a picnic.

At 393 Rue Témiscouata are **Les Carillons**, a large collection of over 200 new and historic bells, some of which are enormous. All are oddly mounted and displayed on Hydro-Quebec pylons. This collection is open daily in summer until 8 pm for a small fee which entitles you to ring the bells, from the smallest at 35 kg to the two-tonne monster.

**Le Château de Rêve** is a small amusement park with children's rides, a swimming pool and farm animals among other things. It's off Hwy 20, east of the centre.

Ask at the tourist office about boat tours and whale-watching. Trips are made to several of the Lower St Lawrence islands which are protected nature sanctuaries. Lying just offshore, west from the city, the islands are good for walking and observing birds and seals. To the east, the river really begins to widen.

**Places to Stay** There is a convenient campground, *Camping Municipal* next to Ave Cartier beside the Auberge de la Pointe Hôtel on the north side of town.

An HI hostel, *Auberge Internationale de Rivière-du-Loup* (☎ 862-7566) is centrally located at 46 Hotel de Ville. It's closed from November to April. Inexpensive lodging can also be found at the community college (CÉGEP) (☎ 867-2733) which rents out its simple rooms at $20 per person throughout the summer. It's at 335 Rue Saint Pierre.

Also inexpensive is the interesting looking *Hôtel Château Grandville* (☎ 862-3551) at 94 Rue Lafontaine on the corner of Rue Iberville, with rooms from $35 a single or double. This is north of the centre of town, nearer the motel district.

Most accommodation is in motels, the majority of which are just north of Boulevard Hôtel de Ville on Rue Fraser. They are scattered along here in both directions from the centre of town. Most are quite pricey but large and comfortable; some offer heated pools and good views of the river. They are all well kept and some are exceptional in appearance, the ultimate being the *Motel Loupi* (☎ 862-6898), at 50 Rue de l'Ancrage, which is the only motel I've ever seen that could be termed eccentrically spectacular. It's surrounded by immaculate terraced gardens complete with aviaries, pool, swings and lawn chairs. A double goes for $65 and up.

Also good is the *Dubé Motel* (☎ 862-6354) at 182 Rue Fraser. Across the street is a campground which has a pool. *Au Vieux Fanal Motel* (☎ 862-5255), at 170 Rue Fraser, has views of the river and a heated swimming pool which is good for the typically cool evenings. A double costs $60.

Another fine place at the same price is the *Motel Bellevue* (☎ 862-5229) right beside the ferry terminal and overlooking the river. Some rooms have kitchenettes. *Journey's End* (☎ 867-4162) is somewhat (but not much) cheaper and seems pedestrian in relation to the settings offered by the others.

**Places to Eat** There is good eating in this town. Many restaurants can be found along Rue Lafontaine along with a smattering of drinking places. *Gina's* at No 362, near Rue Sainte Anne, is good value with a good table d'hôte for under $12 and a varied menu which includes Chinese food.

*Mike's* is a classy submarine-sandwich shop across the street which actually makes a pretty tasty and inexpensive meal. At No 433 *Chez Antoine* and, next door, the busier *Villa Raphaèle* are both attractive, enticing places with more expensive complete dinners. For breakfast head to *La Gourmande* at 120 Lafontaine. It's a café and bakery. More costly, *Madame Coucounette*, at No 274, has a number of vegetarian dishes as well as seafood and meat items. A tofu burger is $7.

The other major eating area is along Rue Fraser and serves the motel crowd. The *Lucerne* is a moderately priced place good for families as well as those without children.

**Getting There & Away** The ferry to Saint Siméon runs from early morning to early evening and the trip takes 1¼ hours. About seven services a day run in summer costing $23 per car and $9 per person. The first (7 am) and the last (8 pm) trips of the day are offered at half price. There is a restaurant and bar on board. Same-day return passenger-only fares, in other words a three-hour cruise, are reasonable. Boarding is on a first-come, first-served basis and hopeful passengers should be at the dock an hour before departure. This only applies to those with vehicles, walk-ons have no trouble arriving just before departure. The ferry, with a capacity of 100 vehicles, runs from April

to January. For pedestrians, there is no bus to the ferry terminal about six km from the centre of town. If you want a cab try Taxi Capitol (☎ 862-6333).

The bus station is at 83 Boulevard Cartier, a short walk from the centre. It's open 24 hours a day and has coin lockers.

VIA Rail (☎ 1-800-361-5390) connects to Quebec City and to Campbellton, New Brunswick via the Matapédia Valley.

I've heard of hitchhikers asking to have their ride requests broadcast over the PA system before docking and being surprised by having their announcement meet with success.

**Mark Lightbody**

**Towards New Brunswick**

Hwy 185 with its pulp and paper mills and forests interspersed with farms provides a foretaste of New Brunswick. A highlight is the privilege of passing through and being able to say you've been to Saint Louis du Ha! Ha! Also pleasant is the beautiful, green rolling landscape around **Lac Temiscouta**.

There is some camping and, most notably around Canso, a number of motels where, as is so typical of Quebec, the amenities include a bar.

In the heart of the Temiscouta region a recommended place to stay is the *L'Auberge Marie Blanc* (☎ 899-6747) in Notre Dame du Lac. The address is 1112 Rue Commerciale. Built in 1905 by a lawyer for his mistress, Marie Blanc, the house has been operated as an inn since the early 1960s. It's open from the beginning of April until the end of October and serves good food. Overnight rates are $55 double.

During the summer a ferry runs across the lake but this remains a largely undeveloped area.

**SOUTH-EAST ALONG THE ST LAWRENCE RIVER**

**Trois Pistoles**

The coast becomes more hilly and less populated as you head for the Gaspé Peninsula – it looks somewhat like the Scottish Highlands. To add to the comparison, people in

QUEBEC

the area, particularly between Saint Simon and Saint Fabien, cut and sell peat for garden fertiliser.

The town of Trois Pistoles is dominated by a massive church. There's a ferry (☎ 851-3099) here, going to Les Escoumins across the river on the north shore. The trip takes 1¼ hours and costs $15.50 per car, $8 per person. It runs from May to November, with three services a day in July and August. For campers, there are three campgrounds by Trois Pistoles.

Offshore, L'Île aux Basques was used by Basques whalers in the 16th century. The coast between Saint Fabien sur Mer and Bic is particularly scenic.

### Bic

Bic was a little village in a beautiful setting a few km from Rimouski but has now become a sort of suburb. There are some good coastal views in the area and a visit to **Parc Bic** is recommended. The village has a good picnic spot and the park offers camping.

Parc Bic protects an unusual landscape of irregular, lumpy, conical mountains that edge the rough, rocky shoreline here. Numerous bays, coves and islands link land and sea. The park is a vegetation transition zone which makes for an interesting mix of southern deciduous and northern Boreal forest. The diverse flora reflects these two influences. The park is also rich in wildlife. Of most interest are the varied sea birds and most of all, the colony of grey and harbour seals offshore.

Roads and walking trails (with a free map available in English) lead to mountain tops and beaches and cut through portions of forest. There is good camping in the park as well as picnic sites. Guided walks are offered. On one trip the guest book listed visitors from Holland, London, Paris, California – and none from English Canada. A visit is recommended, bring binoculars if you have them. The park is easily big enough to spend a couple of days exploring and day use is free. Note that it is officially closed

from September to May but people do set up camp nearby and walk in during the day.

Boat tours around the river side of the park are available but are not really worth the money.

### Rimouski

Rimouski is a fairly large, growing industrial and oil-distributing town. The main streets are Rue Saint Germain, which runs east and west from the square, Place des Veterans, where you will find a helpful tourist office (☎ 723-2322) at 50 Saint Germain Ouest, and Avenue Cathédrale.

Place des Veterans, in the centre of town, is right by the highway near the **regional museum** in the neo-Gothic **cathedral** from the 1850s. The museum, closed on Mondays, presents varied and changing exhibits including the works of Canadian artists.

About five km east of the tourist office, along Hwy 132, is **Maison Lamontagne**, an 18th-century house now an historic site, set in parkland. It's open daily throughout the summer and displays period furniture and other items and represents a now almost extinct style of construction.

Ten km east of town in **Pointe au Père**, past the ferry terminal, is a maritime museum and lighthouse with displays on a shipwreck and other marine matters. Admission is $3.75. The nature reserve here is a good place to look for coastal flora & fauna.

Late summer is a good time to be passing through as the months of August, September and October bring a different festival to the city.

**Places to Stay** *Auberge la Voile* (☎ 772-8002) is an HI hostel at 58 Saint Germain Est, a central and handy location.

*Gites du Centre Ville* (☎ 723-5289) is a central B&B at 84 Rue Saint Pierre with doubles at $45.

There are plenty of motels especially on Rue Saint Germain Ouest where there are also a couple of places with small, simple individual cabins for rent.

**Places to Eat** For eating, there is a pretty

good selection. *La Nature*, at 208 Rue Saint Germain Est, is an inexpensive vegetarian place where you can take your own wine. The well-established *Le Riverain*, at 38 Saint Germain Est, specialises in seafood. East of Avenue Cathédrale on Rue Saint Germain there are three or four popular restaurants and bars with outdoor tables and live music. Avenue Cathédrale also has a number of eateries and some more nightspots.

*Restaurant Marie Antoinette* on the highway is always reasonable with a selection of Canadian standards. Just east of town you'll see quite a few fish shops (*poissoneries*) where bargains can be had on sole, cod, Atlantic salmon, shrimps and the biggest lobsters I've seen outside a museum. Some 2½-kg brutes! Aside from fresh fish, many shops offer dried or smoked fish. Also in this area are some seafood restaurants.

**Getting There & Away** The bus station is at 186 Rue des Gouverneurs. Rimouski is on the VIA Rail line (☎ 1-800-61-5390) but this is about as far as it goes. At Mont Joli, the line heads for Campbellton, New Brunswick.

After leaving Rimouski the land becomes noticeably more wooded as you enter the Gaspé region.

A ferry (☎ 463-0680) departs from here for the 11-hour crossing to Sept-Îles on the north shore. This is not one of the regular daily crossing points such as those west at Trois Pistoles or east at Matane. It runs just once a week and goes way down river to Sept-Îles.

# Gaspé Peninsula

This is the rounded chunk of land that juts out north of New Brunswick into the Gulf of St Lawrence. To the people of Quebec it's 'the Gaspésie'. From west of Matane the characteristic features of the region really become evident: the trees and woods become forests, the towns become smaller and further apart, the weather becomes windier

and cooler. The landscape is hilly and rocky with excellent views along the rough coastline.

To my mind the area is at least as impressive as the better known Cape Breton Island of Nova Scotia, and it's much less crowded. There is less development and less organised tourism, which compensates for the fewer attractions and possible communication difficulties. At the eastern tip and around the south shore are a number of English communities so if French is a struggle, these will make a petit respite! The numerous parks are excellent for getting out into the rugged terrain or exploring the shoreline.

The Gaspé Peninsula is popular with cyclists, despite the hard climbs, and there are plenty of hostels, campgrounds and unoccupied woods to sleep in. All towns of any size have motels and there is a good number of guesthouses as well. Lots of seafood is available and the little trucks and chip wagons throughout the area make superb French fries and real meat hamburgers. You should expect cool evenings even in midsummer.

You may see some of these French signs so here's a quick run-down:

| | | |
|---|---|---|
| *pain de ménage* | – | homemade bread |
| *gîte du passant* | – | B&B |
| *à vendre* | – | for sale |
| *des vers* | – | worms (not a tasty snack) |
| *bière froide* | – | cold beer (available at most stores) |
| *crêtons* | – | a local pork paté |

Prices in the region are relatively low (except for gasoline) and a trip around this part of the country is highly recommended. A caution though, the region virtually shuts down visitor attractions between September and May – even Forillon National Park is open only seasonally. Parks can be visited for walking the trails but services will be nonexistent.

## SAINTE-FLAVIE/MONT JOLI
In Sainte-Flavie on Hwy 132 is a large, year-round information centre for the Gaspé Peninsula. From Mont Joli, Hwy 132 south

goes through the Matapédia Valley directly to New Brunswick, useful for those wishing to bypass the Gaspé Peninsula. See the end of the Gaspé Peninsula section for a description of this route.

In Sainte-Flavie the **Centre d'Art Marcel Gagnon** is worth a visit. It's an inn, restaurant and art school based around an exhibit of some 80 life-sized stone statues by sculptor and painter Marcel Gagnon. It's open daily from May to September and admission is free. There is other artwork on display. Aside from having a meal, you can just sit with a coffee.

Also in town is the **Atlantic Salmon Interpretative Centre** with various displays on this queen of fish, an aquarium, videos, a restaurant and walking trails. There is a rather high admission charge, though.

There are four motels in town with *Motel Rita* (☎ 775-7269) the most modestly priced.

### GRAND MÉTIS
On the west side of Grand Métis, the **Jardins de Métis** is an oddity worth looking at. It's an immaculately tended, Japanese-style garden with streams, flowers, bushes and trees – all labelled. In addition, there's a fantastic view over the coast by the old wooden mansion. The garden was started by a Mrs Reford, who inherited the land from her uncle, the first president of the Canadian Pacific railway. Begun in 1910, it is now looked after by the government. Admission is $4.25 per adult. In the house at the centre of the park is a museum and a restaurant with lunches from $6 to $10.

### MATANE
A small, typical French town, Matane makes a good stopover. There's an information office at the lighthouse off the highway and it's open daily in summer and weekdays all year. The small museum is also here. Avenue Saint Jérôme and Boulevard Saint Pierre are the main streets. The promenade along the waterfront makes for a pleasant stroll.

Matane is a fishing town with salmon and shrimp among the catch. In mid-June is the shrimp *(crevette)* festival: a time when you can feast on them.

Salmon go up the river here to spawn, beginning in June. The government has set up a monitoring system where you can see the fish heading upstream and learn something of this curious phenomenon. An information office is in the little building by the dam, adjacent to the Parc des Îles and near the Hôtel de Ville.

Salmon and other fish can be bought at the packing plant on Rue Saint Pierre, on the corner of Avenue Fraser. The shrimp processing plant at 1600 Matane Sur Mer can be visited free.

Behind the Hôtel de Ville is a large park with an open-air theatre for summer shows.

### Matane Wildlife Preserve
The preserve (☎ 562-3700) can be reached south of Matane off Hwy 195. It's a huge area with camping, canoeing, hiking, fishing, boat rentals and abundant moose. The road continues on to New Brunswick but don't follow it. Go around the rest of the Gaspé Peninsula.

### Places to Stay
The best places to stay are the motels strung out along the highway. Some are expensive though *Les Mouettes* (☎ 562-3345), at 298 Rue McKinnon, is one of the cheapest at $50 for a double room. Priced similarly is the *Motel Le Beach* (☎ 562-1350).

As alternatives there are the *Hôtel de Roy* at 74 Rue Saint Pierre, or the *Hôtel L'Ancre* at No 292. Both are primarily drinking establishments but both offer basic accommodation for $18 (single room) and neither can be recommended for women.

The modern-looking *Collège de Matane* (☎ 562-1240), on the outskirts of town at 616 Ave Saint Redempteur, offers its rooms to visitors at low rates through the summer months and is a better alternative for most people on a tight budget.

### Places to Eat
For the stomach, the *Le Moussallin* at 50 Avenue d'Amours is recommended. It offers

QUEBEC

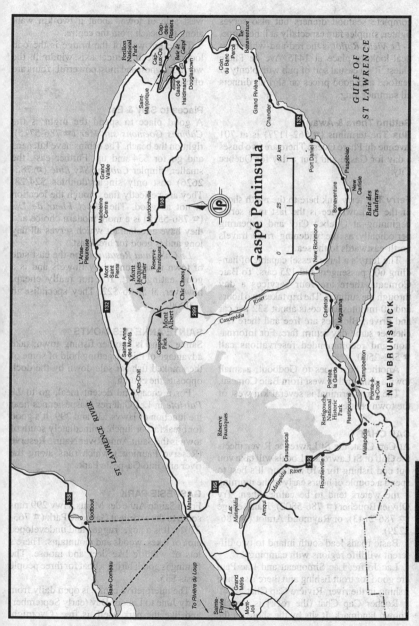

complete seafood dinners but also serves lighter, simpler fare especially at lunch time.

*Le Vieux Rafiot* is the red-and-white nautical-looking place at 1415 Ave de Phare Ouest. It's a casual sort of pub with plenty of seafood and good prices on shrimp dinners all summer long.

### Getting There & Away
**Bus** The terminus (☎ 562-1177) is at 701 Avenue du Phare Ouest. There are two buses a day for Gaspé and four a day for Quebec City.

**Ferry** The ferry link here to the north shore of the St Lawrence is the last in a series beginning at Quebec City and appearing periodically as the widening river travels north-eastwards to the sea.

The ferry's a large vessel capable of handling 600 passengers and 125 cars. To Baie Comeau, there are four services a day through the summer. The trip takes two hours and 20 minutes and costs about $32 per car and driver. Bicycles are free and there is a cheaper same-day return fare. For information and recommended reservations call ☎ 562-2500.

Another boat goes to Godbout, a small town a little further west from Baie Comeau.

The ferry terminal is several km west of the town centre.

### CAP CHAT
At Cap Chat, the St Lawrence River meets the Gulf of St Lawrence. Locals will take you out cod fishing for $10 an hour. It's best to spend a couple of hours early in the morning – the waters tend to be calmer then. Try Olivier Boucher (☎ 786-5802), Jean Lepage (☎ 786-2143), or Raymond Amiot (☎ 786-2229).

Basic roads lead south inland to two different wildlife regions with camping.

Lac Joffre, Lac Simoneau and Lac Paul are good for trout fishing and there's salmon fishing in the river, Rivière Cap Chat.

Rocher Cap Chat (the rock) is a well-known landmark. It sits by the shore on the west side of town, about a two-km walk along the beach from the centre.

Three km west of the bridge is the odd looking hi-tech vertical axis windmill, the world's highest and most powerful. Tours are offered.

### Places to Stay & Eat
A good place to spend the night is the *Cabines Goémons sur Mer* (☎ 786-5715), right on the beach. The cabins have kitchens and go for $34 and up. Further east, the smaller, simpler *Cabines Sky Line* (☎ 786-2626) cost only singles/doubles $24/28. They are perfectly fine, though the location is not as good. The *Motel Fleur de Lys* (☎ 786-5518) is a more modern choice and they have a restaurant which serves all day long and is good for breakfast.

*Le Cabillaud Restaurant* on the east side of town is surrounded by flowers and is a good eating spot. It's not really cheap, however, at $8 to $22. They specialise in seafood.

### SAINTE ANNE DES MONTS
Sainte Anne is another fishing town; take advantage of this by getting hold of some of the smoked fish for sale down by the dock opposite the church.

For a cheap and decent meal, go to *Le Patriote* in Les Galéries Gaspésiennes near the junction of Hwys 132 and 299. It's good for breakfast or lunch. Immediately south of town is the Saint Anne River Nature Reserve (Réserve Faunique) which runs along the river and into Gaspésie Park.

### GASPÉSIE PARK
From Sainte Anne des Monts, Hwy 299 runs south to the excellent Gaspésie Park (☎ 763-3301). It is a huge, rugged and undeveloped area of lakes, woods and mountains. There's lots of wildlife like deer and moose. The fishing is good; hiring a boat for three people costs $35.

The interpretive centre is open daily from early June to Labour Day (early September) and like the park itself, is free. Overnight camping does cost and is $12. Maps and information on the hiking trails are available.

At Gite du Mont Albert there is camping and a lodge (☎ 763-2288) with a highly praised restaurant. Singles/doubles can be reasonable; the range is great but they start at $38 and go way up. Bicycles can be rented but this didn't strike me as ideal cycling country.

The roads leading through the park are rough and will take you to various hiking trails – some overnighters – and lookouts over the lumpy Chic Choc Mountains (Monts Chic Choc).

**Mont Jacques Cartier**, at 1270 metres, is the highest peak in this part of the country. It rises above the tree line and epitomises the conditions of the Gaspé Peninsula: cold, windy and often wet at the peak too.

Hiking takes about 3½ hours for the return trip, and is well worthwhile – the alpine scenery and views are fantastic and it is fairly common to see some of the herd of woodland caribou near the top. These are the last of the caribou found this far south; they seem to find the barren lands quite fine and happily munch on lichen all day. The trail is now tightly regulated in order to protect the herd from being disturbed.

After driving to a designated parking area, a shuttle bus runs hikers six km to the beginning of the trail and charges $4 to do it. The first bus is at 10 am, the last leaves the trail at 4 pm and no one is permitted on the summit between the end of the afternoon and the next morning. At the peak naturalists are on hand to answer questions and talk about the caribou.

You can also climb **Mont Albert**, a steeper, more rigorous trail despite the mountain not reaching the same elevation as Cartier.

It is not uncommon to see moose in the early morning or evening feeding at Lac Paul.

You can enter the park at Sainte Anne des Monts and return to the coast highway at Mont Saint Pierre.

## MONT SAINT PIERRE

Not far from Sainte Anne des Monts on Hwy 132 is this little white village nestled in a short bay. The setting is spectacular with rocky outcrops on one side and a nearby crescent-shaped beach on the other. This small community, far from any big city, is famous for hang gliding. Indeed, it is considered one of the best spots for the sport in North America. Each year around the end of June is the two-week hang gliding festival (La Fête du Vol Libre). A rough road goes to the summit of Mont Saint Pierre where there are three take-off stations and excellent views from the summit. A 4WD vehicle is recommended if you're not hoofing it up.

The cliffs east of town are etched with interesting rock patterns. They continue like this for some distance out of town.

There is an HI hostel called *Auberge Les Vagues* (☎ 797-2851) at 84 Rue P Cloutier. The hostel also offers camping. Meals including seafood dinners are available at the hostel's own restaurant. Alternatively, there are several motel-hotels in town. The grocery store has hot chicken to takeout.

East of Mont Saint Pierre there are lots of good picnic areas with coastal views and great sunsets. There are also plenty of campgrounds, motels or cabins with cuisinettes (kitchenettes).

In and around town you'll see lots of signs here for *pain frais* or *pain chaud* (fresh or hot bread).

## CONTINUING EAST

At L'Anse Pleureuse, turn off to Murdochville for tours of its **copper mine**. Madeline Centre, a particularly beautiful village, has lots of baked goods for sale. At Pointe à la Frégate, the *Auberge*, in the old white house, has good food for $25 to $35. At Cloridorme, there is a good picnic site overlooking the Gulf of St Lawrence.

## FORILLON NATIONAL PARK

The park (☎ 368-5505) lies at the extreme north-eastern tip of the peninsula and is worth a stop. The northern coast consists of steep limestone cliffs – some as high as 200 metres – and long pebble beaches. See Cap Bon Ami for the best of this topography.

QUEBEC

There is a telescope for whale-watching – good from May to October. Sometimes you can hear the whales surface. Seals are common all year.

There are good trails through the park, some with overnight camping. Two trails are 16 km long and take about six hours each to walk but there are others that take from 30 minutes to three hours to travel.

The Parks Service naturalists offer information programmes and free guided tours. You can also use the information chalet. Boat trips to bird sanctuaries and seal colonies are possible. In the woods there are moose, deer, and an increasing population of black bears. The shoreline cliffs attract numbers of sea birds.

The south coast has more beaches – some sandy – and small coves. **Penouille Beach** is said to have the warmest waters. Petit Gaspé is the most popular organised campground as it is protected from sea breezes and it has hot showers too.

The hike along the southern shore to **Cap Gaspé** is easy and pleasant, with scenery that's good though not spectacular. The headlands, with a lighthouse, have viewing stations.

At **Grand Grave**, the Haymen & Sons store is an interesting place for a snoop around.

## CAP DES ROSIERS

This is a small, old and interesting little village on the north shore. The **graveyard**, right on the cliff, tells the town's history – how the English came from Guernsey and Jersey, how the Irish settlers were Kavanaghs, O'Connors, etc; and how both groups mingled with the French. Generations later, the same names live on.

The **lighthouse**, built in 1858, is one of the highest in the country at 37 metres and is now classed as an historic site. It can be visited for a small admission fee.

Saltwater sport-fishing trips depart from the wharf on the *Anna-Lucie*.

There are a couple of places to stay. The *Chalets Cap Cabins*, (☎ 892-5641) costing about $25, are pleasantly rustic with views over the bay. There's also a restaurant in town.

## CAP AUX OS

On the south side of Forillon National Park, Cape of Bones got its name because at one time whale bones often washed ashore here. Hostellers can use the village as a base for exploring the park, otherwise there is no reason to stop here. The HI hostel (☎ 892-5153) at 2095 Boulevard Forillon is good – it's one of the most established places in the province and has a fine view overlooking the bay. It's a fairly large three-storey place which can accommodate 56 people. (There are some rooms for families.) It's open 24 hours and breakfast and dinner are available. The bus stops at the hostel throughout the summer months. A drawback for those without vehicles is that it is a long way from any of the hiking trails although they do have bicycles for rent.

## SAINT MARJORIQUE

Past this village towards Gaspé look for *Marguerite's Mini Restaurant-Casse Croûte*, a little café that has been highly recommended for its inexpensive French food with an emphasis on fish.

## GASPÉ

After all the good scenery and attractive little villages, the town after which the entire peninsula takes its name seems pretty ordinary. It does, however, have all the amenities and services, gas stations and grocery stores, etc. A fair bit of English is spoken too. Perhaps surprisingly, from here around the head of the peninsula and down along the Baie des Chaleurs, there are quite a few historic English towns which have stuck it out.

The **Jacques Cartier monument** at the north side of town, is worth a look. It's different and well done. It was here that the explorer landed in 1534, met the Iroquois and claimed the area for the king of France. He took two sons of Chief Donnacona back to see Paris and later returned them. (They must have had a few stories to tell.) Beside the sculpture is a museum depicting the difficulties of those settling the Gaspé Peninsula, some maritime exhibits, crafts and a section on traditional foods. Admission costs $3.50. It's open daily but afternoons only on weekends.

The **Cathédrale de Gaspé** is interesting. It is the only wooden cathedral in North America. A fresco commemorates the fourth centennial of Cartier's landing. It's at the top of Rue Jacques Cartier about a 15-minute walk from the museum.

Continuing in a religious vein, the **Sanctuaire Notre Dame des Douleurs** is a church which has been a pilgrimage site since 1942. It's open daily from 7 am to 9 pm from early June to late October.

South of town there are beaches at Sandy Beach and Haldimand but the water is cool. There's camping by the Fort Ramsay Motel near the water.

For eating or sleeping most people will prefer to be in nearby Percé. A place worth checking is for a cheap bed through the summer is the central community college (☎ 368-2749), at 94 Rue Jacques Cartier, a regional college which rents its many residents' rooms through the summer at reasonable rates. Otherwise there are numerous motels. A cheap breakfast can be had at one of the motel dining rooms.

## DOUGLASTOWN

Like some of the other small English towns of the region, Douglastown was established by Loyalists. Their ancestors continue to fish and farm.

## PERCÉ

Named after the immense offshore rock with the hole pierced through it (one of Canada's best known landmarks), this town is the main tourist attraction of the Gaspé Peninsula. Despite this, it's a pleasant, pretty place and the **Rocher Percé** (Pierced Rock) is truly an impressive sight.

Percé is the only place on the peninsula that gets busy and, because of this, June or September make good visiting times. The weather is usually good. The tourist office is in the centre of town beside the dock for boats to Île Bonaventure.

Just north of town is the Pic de l'Aurore (Peak of Dawn), which dominates the north end of town. From the next hill you'll see Rocher Percé below and, further out, Île Bonaventure, an island bird sanctuary. Other good views of Rocher Percé are seen from the road, south of town.

You can also walk out to the rock at any time and it's even possible to walk around much of it at low tide.

For $13, a boat will take you to the green **Île Bonaventure** beyond Rocher Percé. There are free Wildlife Service-sponsored walks on the island and a gannet colony of 50,000 is among the number of shorebird species roosting on the cliffs. Over 200,000 birds can make some kind of noise! Some intriguing hardy plant life can also be seen.

The service also runs a **Wildlife Interpretive Centre** south of town on the Route d'Irlande, which is open from 10 am to 5.30 pm. There's a walking trail, film, aquariums and exhibits relating mainly to the seabirds. Naturalists are on hand to answer questions on the geology and flora & fauna of the area.

Behind the town are some interesting walks, for which the tourist office map is useful. Hike up to **Mont Sainte Anne** for a great view and to see the cave along the three-km path which begins behind the church.

Another area walking trail leads to the **Great Crevasse**, a deep crevice in the mountain behind the well-known Auberge de Gargantua Restaurant. This three-km trail begins behind the restaurant which is two km west of town. At the south end of town, the museum features artwork by local children.

In town there are lots of souvenir shops selling glasswork, pottery and some good quilts.

At nearby beaches, rock hounds can look for agate, which is abundant. There is also diving in the area and an underwater park; check the dive shop by the tourist office.

### Places to Stay

Much of the budget accommodation is in

guesthouses in and around town. The tourist office will help in locating one, even calling places for you including some inexpensive farmhouses not far from the centre of town.

There are a number of good value guesthouses which are centrally located. *Maison Avenue House* (☎ 782-2954) is on Rue de l'Église, which runs off the main street in the middle of town. Before the church, you'll see this fine house with five rooms of varnished wood at just $20 a single, and from $24 to $28 a double. There are sinks in the clean rooms. The guesthouse is in an excellent location and both English and French are spoken. The place next door also rents rooms.

A little more expensive is *Maison le Havre* (☎ 782-2374), formerly known as the Haven before the Quebec language laws kicked in making English signs difficult to live with. It's on the main street, Hwy (Route) 132 at No 114 with rooms from $25 to $40.

*Gite Maison Tommy* (☎ 782-5104) a B&B at 31 Route 132, has singles/doubles for $24/36. Another is *Gite Rendez-vous* (☎ 782-5152) at 84 Hwy 132. A double is $40.

Right in the centre of town, the green and white *Fleur de Lys* (☎ 782-2772) is a reasonably priced motel charging from $35 to $55. Unlike the guesthouses, where a price is a price, the motels' bills tend to fluctuate with the season, the weather and the traffic.

On the north edge of town at 104 Hwy 132, *Auberge Le Coin et Chalets* (☎ 645-2907) has rooms from $40 and a swimming pool.

South of town are a few bargains. The *Hotel-Motel aux Vagues Vertes* (☎ 782-2382) with 16 rooms charges from $30 to $60 a double depending on how busy they are.

There are many other places to stay, mostly motels. The lower-priced ones are generally out of the centre of town. There are also campgrounds with views on both sides of town.

## Places to Eat

*Biard's*, on the highway just north of the town centre, is a standard place with OK prices for such a town. It serves cheap breakfasts and offers daily lunch and dinner specials and is probably the spot for the town's best priced lobster.

*Les Fous de Basson* is a casual café slightly south of the centre of town and beside the art gallery. For coffee, vegetarian meals or breakfasts of yoghurt, granola, croissants and the like, this is the place. At dinner the prices rise sharply for the more substantial meals and seafood. Inexpensive meals are available all day at *Auberge La Table à Roland* at No 190 on the main street (Hwy 132).

There is a *brasserie* on Rue de l'Église. It's always good for a cheap feed and a couple of cold ones.

The *Pantagruel*, five km east of town, has complete dinners for $10.95. It has fresh cod, other seafoods and some regional dishes on the menu. It's open for dinner only.

Seafood is also a speciality at *Auberge au Pirate* in the centre of town on Bord de Mer along the water.

There's also a *bakery* north of town, on the left-hand side.

## Entertainment

At night there is often folk music or jazz at *Les Fous de Basson Café*.

## Getting There & Away

**Bus** Orléans Express (☎ 368-1888) buses link Percé to Matane, Rimouski and Quebec City. They also go to Edmundston and Campbellton, New Brunswick via Carleton and the south shore of the peninsula. The Petro Canada gas station on the main street is used for the bus station.

**Train** From Montreal, VIA Rail (☎ 368-4313) serves the south side of the St Lawrence River with main stops at Lévis, Rivière-du-Loup, Rimouski and as far as Matane. The train then goes south through the Matapédia Valley and along the Baie des Chaleurs and up and around past Percé to the town of Gaspé. Many of the smaller places (along the entire route) are serviced. The train runs three times a week from Montreal: on Mondays, Thursdays and Saturdays. The one-way fare from Lévis to Percé for the 11-hour ride is $78.

## THE BAY SIDE

The south shore of the Gaspé Peninsula along the Baie des Chaleurs is quite different from the north coast. The land is flatter and less rocky and the weather is warmer. Farming and various small industries are important here. Also, unlike on the north side, there are quite a few English towns. Much of the French population is descended from the original Acadian settlers.

### Chandler

For a long time a pulp and paper town, Chandler is still based on the huge Abitibi-Price newsprint mill which can be toured for free. Freighters carry the finished product to South America and Europe from the town's own port facilities. At least they try to, the wreck of the Peruvian ship visible from shore indicates they all don't make it.

### Port Daniel

Residents of this former Micmac settlement are of Scottish, Irish and Acadian backgrounds. Secondary roads from town lead to the wildlife reserves of Port Daniel and Rivière Port Daniel. Sitting halfway between Chandler and New Carlisle, Port Daniel is also mentioned for the attractive blue-and-white *Maison Enright B&B* (☎ 396-2062).

### Paspébiac

Descendants of Normans, Bretons and Basques live in this town. An historic site, open daily throughout summer, depicts the early life of the village as a fishing port. There are tours around the site which has a restaurant and craft shop.

### New Carlisle

One of the area's English towns, New Carlisle was founded by Loyalists and has some grand colonial homes. Hamilton House, on the north side of the road at the east end of town, is open for tours.

### Bonaventure

A small, pleasant Acadian town by the water, Bonaventure is the focal point for the area's farming community. Attractions include the Acadian museum, a wide sandy beach and a shop which sells various items made of fish-skin leather. It's soft, supple and attractive and, no, it doesn't smell.

The museum is open all year and unlike many Quebec museums bilingual guides are available to explain some of the Acadians' tragic yet fascinating history. For more on them see the New Brunswick chapter.

North of town, in **Saint Elzéar** (no public transportation will get you there) some of the oldest caves in the province were discovered in 1976. A visit to the site (☎ 534-4335) is recommended but you won't be able to afford eating for a few days. There is an information centre with displays and bones and a slide show but the guided tour of the cave (la grotte) is the only real attraction.

The four-hour trip, including safety equipment and a snack, is extensive and takes in the largest found variety of stalagmites and stalactites in Quebec. The cave is estimated to be 500,000 years old and it feels like it's never seen the sun. Warm clothing is essential or you'll freeze. Are you ready for the price now? It's $35 a ticket. Children aged 10 or more are admitted and their tickets are discounted. The museum is $2.50 and pictures show some of the cave. The cave is open from the beginning of June until the end of October, for some reason the museum opens a month later and closes a month earlier.

### New Richmond

Nestled in the bay near the mouths of two rivers New Richmond with a population of 4000 is another Loyalist centre. Just east at Duthie's Point in the **British Heritage Centre** there's a re-created Loyalist village of the late 1700s period which is open daily from mid-June to September. It consists of 14 buildings including an interpretive centre, houses, a general store and a lighthouse. The centre also covers the influence of later Irish and Scottish immigrants.

## Carleton

About half the size of New Richmond, Carleton has a pretty location on the water backed by rounded hills. The setting, the sandy beach and the relatively warm air and water of Chaleur Bay have made Carleton a mini-resort. This is where the people of the Gaspé come for a day at the beach and to hang out.

From the docks there are boat excursions for fishing or sightseeing. At the bird sanctuary herons, terns, plovers and other shore birds can be observed. Walking paths and a road lead behind the town to the top of Mont Saint Joseph which at 555 metres, provides fine views over the bay and across to New Brunswick. The oratory at the top can be visited and after the climb, the snack bar is a welcome sight.

Good food is available down near the water at *Café l'Independant*, specialising in fish. *Ciné Café* at 681 Boulevard Perron is a smaller, cheaper place which is good for breakfast. There is both a picnic site and campground near the centre of town.

If you want to spend the night, there are half a dozen motels which tend to be pricey. Most economical is the *Motel Shic Shoc* (☎ 364-3288) which is also the one furthest from the centre at 1746 Boulevard Perron.

## Miguasha

For those headed to Dalhousie, New Brunswick, a ferry runs from Miguasha making a short cut across the Baie de Chaleurs. See Dalhousie for details.

The small peninsula here is renowned for its fossils. The Parc de Miguasha and Information Centre is set up around the 365-million-year-old fossil site and is free to visit. Guided walks take visitors through the museum and along a trail to the beach and the fossil filled cliffs.

## Restigouche National Historic Park

A few km west of the bridge from Pointe à la Croix, the park (Parc Historique National La Bataille de la Restigouche) details the 1760 naval battle of Restigouche which pretty well put the kibosh on France's New World ambitions. An interpretive centre explains the battle's significance to the British and has articles salvaged from a sunken French frigate. It's open from the end of June until early September.

There's an excellent HI hostel (☎ 788-2048) in Pointe à la Garde at 155 Boulevard Perron. In addition to the hostel by the street, the manager has built a stunning wooden castle in the woods. Here there are double, triple and family rooms and a dining room, where, during the summer months, Jean, the host, offers banquet-style dinners. Breakfasts are offered daily and are included in the overnight price. The hostel is open all year. The bus through town will stop 100 metres from the door if you ask the driver.

## Restigouche

Restigouche has always been and remains a Micmac Indian community. These east coast Native Canadians have traditionally produced fine basket work. The best pieces are now seen in museums but modern versions can be viewed or purchased on the reserve here.

The small Micmac Interpretive Centre outlines some aspects of their culture and history and the gift shop sells crafts. The Micmacs are found all around the Atlantic Provinces although their numbers are not large.

## MATAPÉDIA VALLEY

From the village of Matapédia, Quebec, across the Restigouche River from the province of New Brunswick near Campbellton, the Matapédia Valley runs northward to Mont Joli on the St Lawrence River. This pretty valley is unlike any other portion of the Gaspé Peninsula. Alongside the Matapédia River and the railway line, traffic-free Hwy 132 passes through fertile farmland with a backdrop of green mountains for about 70 km. Aside from the good farming areas, the valley differs from much of the rocky, more sparsely vegetated peninsula by supporting broad-leafed maple and elm trees. The river is renowned for its salmon fishing. There are several smallish towns along the way, a few sites to see and, around Lac Matapédia, a couple of picnic sites as well as a campground.

### Routhierville

The first of many wooden bridges seen through the valley is in this small village. Some of them, known as settler's bridges, are covered, like the ones seen in greater abundance across New Brunswick. The picnic site here is about all there is. People fishing out in the river with waders and fly rods, are the main attraction.

### Sainte Florence

This larger town with a good-sized lumber mill is situated where the valley is broadening out and the landscape is more gentle. There's a place for gas and one *cantine* for burgers and fries.

### Causapscal

Say this name three times quickly. Causapscal is the best place for a stop on the trip through the valley. It's a pretty town with a traditional look, a beautiful stone church and many older houses with typical Québecois silver roofs.

The Causapscal and Matapédia rivers meet here. There are a couple of covered bridges south of town and, in the centre, a pedestrian-only suspension bridge across the Matapédia. Again, sawmills are the main

economic focus and the smell or smoke from the processing chimneys is ever present.

There is a tourist office near the interesting **Domaine Matamajaw** or Salmon Lodge Museum. The museum, in what was the lodge, the outbuildings and much of the riverfront property were all part of a private fishing estate built by Lord Mount Stephen of Canadian Pacific Railway fame in 1870. In the early part of the century a group of moneyed Canadian and US businesspeople bought the place and ran it as a private club for 60 years. Take a look in the lodge some of which remains much the way it was – some people know how to live. Other rooms are devoted to the Atlantic salmon, the impetus for all this. The site is open from 10 June to 10 September from 9 am to 9 pm daily and costs $3.50.

Across the street from the museum is a craft shop with some unique items – wallets, jewellery and more made of salmon and cod 'leather'. Other articles include tablecloths and rugs woven by local women and some homemade jams.

Fifteen km north are some waterfalls with riverside walking trails.

**Places to Stay & Eat** For spending the night or having dinner, there is the *Auberge La Coulée Douce* (☎ 756-5270) on the hill opposite the historic site. *Les Pignons Verts* (☎ 756-3754), at 100 Rue Morin, is a B&B

Snow goose

QUEBEC

with slightly less-expensive rooms with singles/doubles for $30/42. There are also a few cheaper rooms to let where the Orléans Express bus linking New Brunswick to the St Lawrence shore stops at 122 Rue Saint Jacques Sud. Also in town there are a couple of restaurants and the ubiquitous takeout cantines or chip wagons.

North of town is a campground and the *Motel Du Vallon* (☎ 756-3433) with doubles at $45, less out of season.

### Amqui

The largest town in the valley doesn't have much to recommend it. All the basic needs can be met, and north of town beyond the bridge is a campground. Towards the end of summer you may see people standing by the side of the road waving jars. They're selling locally picked wild hazelnuts *(noisettes)* which are not expensive. Around **Lac Matapédia** there are some viewpoints over the lake and picnic spots.

# The Gulf Islands

## MAGDALEN ISLANDS
## (ÎLES DE LA MADELEINE)

Out in the Gulf of St Lawrence, closer to the Atlantic Provinces than to Quebec, lies this lovely 100-km-long string of islands. There are about a dozen islands, 120 km north-east of Prince Edward Island, and most of them are linked by long sand spits. In fact, the islands are little more than spits themselves, so excellent sand beaches line the shores.

Because of their remoteness, the quiet life, the superb seashore scenery of carved red and grey cliffs and the great beaches, the islands have appeal and are becoming more popular with visitors. Quebeckers make up at least 90% of the tourists. Most people stay two to four days and this enables them to look around most of the islands. More time can easily be spent walking the trails and beaches and exploring in depth.

The local people make their living mainly from fishing as they have always done but now the two months of busy tourism, July and August, are supplementing many an income. Sealing used to be important, but the commercial hunt has all but disappeared under international pressure from those opposed to it. Some former hunters are now taking tourists out on the ice in early spring to see and photograph the baby seals. The Magdalens are considered the best place for this. Although expensive as a single purpose excursion, they are becoming the basis for popular brief trips to the islands.

Over 90% of the population of 14,000 speak various French dialects, but many Scottish and Irish descendants live on L'Île d'Entrée and La Grosse Île. The towns and the people too, are sophisticated despite the remote, isolated nature of the islands. Restaurants and living rooms could be transplanted from downtown Montreal. Unlike many fishing or farming regions, the islands seem quite prosperous and don't really have the old-time feel, of say, Prince Edward Island. Food and accommodation prices can, but need not, reflect these characteristics.

The main islands are Havre aux Maisons, which has an airport, and Cap aux Meules. At the town of Cap aux Meules, the ferry from Souris, Prince Edward Island, ties in and there is an information office (☎ 986-2245).

### Things to See & Do

Most of the islands' activities and sights revolve around the sea. Beach-strolling, and exploring lagoons, tidal pools and the cliff formations can take up days. More time can be spent searching out the best vistas, skirting around the secondary roads and poking around the fishing villages. The waters aren't tropical by any stretch of the imagination but are warmed (slightly) by the Gulf Stream. Swimming is possible in the open sea or, preferably, in some of the protected, shallow lagoons. Currents are strong and venturing far from shore is not advisable. With nearly constant breezes, windsurfing is good and several places offer boards and lessons.

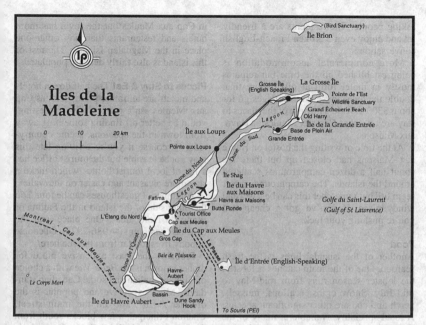

Îles de la Madeleine

Fishing expeditions can be arranged and diving on the reefs is possible.

There are also some historic points of interest such as the **old churches** and unusual **traditional buildings** such as the now-disappearing hay barns. Also around the countryside look for the old smoke houses (marked on the islands' map) now disused but once part of the important herring industry. Keep an eye out for the many fine and distinctive houses dotting the largely barren terrain.

In the evenings during the summer, you may be lucky to find a concert, a play, or an exhibition of some sort in one of the towns.

### Festivals
At Grande Entrée, a lobster festival is held during the first week in July. Also in July watch for the annual sandcastle-building contests along a two-km stretch of beach on Havre Aubert.

### Accommodation
From June to September the islands are busy and accommodation gets seriously scarce. If, upon arrival, you do not have a place booked (as most people appear to) go directly to the tourist office and have them find you something. After that first night and when settled a bit, you can always look around for something else. Before arrival, you could call the tourist office from Prince Edward Island and ask them to book a place in an area that appeals to you.

A good portion of the Magdalen Islands' accommodation is in people's homes or in cottages and trailers they rent out. These represent by far the most interesting and best value lodgings averaging $25 a single and from $30 to $40 a double. The tourist office has a sheet listing many of these places but it is far from complete. The tourist office will call and book the ones they know (including ones not on the list) for you, still others can be found by following roadside signs or just asking people. The residents are a friendly lot and enjoy even a broken French-English conversation.

More commercial accommodation is being established all the time but remains mostly in motel form at often more than double the guesthouse rate. Cottages go for about $300 a week. The bulk of the places to stay are on either Cap aux Meules or Havre aux Maisons.

At the time of writing the hostel on Havre aux Maisons had closed up but there are about half a dozen campgrounds scattered around the islands. The campgrounds never seem full but remember this can be a wet and windy place. If you've got a cheap tent you're pushing your luck.

### Food

Another of the islands' lures is the fresh seafood. One of the main catches is lobster; the lobster season runs from mid-May to mid-July. Snow crabs, scallops, mussels, perch and cod are other significant species. A local speciality available at many of the better restaurants is *pot-en-pot*, a dish of mixed fish and seafoods in a sauce baked in its own pie crust. The adventurous eater may want to try seal meat which is served a couple of ways.

All the major villages have some sort of a restaurant but out of Cap aux Meules choices are limited. Cantines with burgers, hot dogs and fries are seen here and there.

### Cap aux Meules

With the ferry depot and Cap aux Meules, the largest town of the islands, this is the commercial centre of the archipelago. It's quite busy and modern which can be a little disconcerting for those looking for something else. This first glimpse is, however, atypical of the rest of the towns, villages and landscapes around the islands. Supplies, banking and any necessary reservations should all be taken care of here.

The islands' tourist office is a short distance from the ferry landing on the left-hand side.

There really isn't anything of note to see in Cap aux Meules but the town has more hotels and restaurants than any other one place in the Magdalen Islands. The rest of this island is also fairly densely populated.

**Places to Stay & Eat** The half dozen hotels and motels are all rather pricey and, as Cap aux Meules isn't particularly interesting, you'd be better off finding something away from town in the spacious, scenic countryside. Of course if you're arriving late this may not be feasible but the tourist office has a list of local tourist homes which make a stay more pleasant and easier on the wallet.

A number of guesthouses can be found on the other side of the island in the Fatima or Étang du Nord areas. One place near the beach is *Cummings* (☎ 986-2978). Of course nobody lives too far from the sea here.

Probably the least expensive place for dinner in town is the *Belle-Vue* with a choice of Chinese, Italian and some Canadian standards. More expensive and popular is the dressier *Pizza Patio* on the main street, Chemin Principal, a few blocks south from the ferry terminal. *Casse Croûte Raymond* is good for breakfasts and fries and burgers. The *Alexandre* has seafood.

### La Belle Anse

The coast around La Belle Anse on the north-western side has some dramatic red cliffs and interesting coastal erosion features. There are some paths right along the cliffs offering excellent views. For a good and inexpensive meal go to the *Cooperative de Gros-Cap*, a lobster *(homard)* processing plant with a cafeteria-restaurant known as *La Factrie* upstairs with a large window overlooking the plant below. Just follow the road, Chemin de Gros Cap, north of the town of L'Étang du Nord. You needn't eat lobster, there is a selection of other seafoods with soups and salad all reasonably priced. It's open from noon to 9 pm daily, Sunday 3 to 9 pm. In Fatima, the small plain looking *Decker Boy Restaurant* is cheap and good. Try one of the chowders.

North of La Belle Anse at the good sandy beach at Anse de l'Hôpital is a small complex of tourist-oriented shops and a snack bar.

One afternoon, on a trip to the beach here for a quick picnic, strains of irresistible traditional fiddle were heard coming from the building complex. Showing no shame we edged through the drinking and laughing crowd on the porch and invited ourselves in to what was some kind of a reception with people clapping and jigging to the music of one guitar and the distinctive violin.

An old man I'd noticed outside because of his thick, pure white hair and bright red shirt with cheeks to match began slowly making his way across the dance floor to the lavatory. After gingerly hobbling halfway across he was mercilessly grabbed by a woman about half his age and forced to dance. For a moment he stood still and unsure and then his feet took on a life of their own. For a good five minutes using every trick in the book he brought whoops of approval and amazement as he mopped the floor with the rest of the dancers and egged on the musicians to quickening reels. And all the while he was slowly edging towards the bathroom into which on the appropriate beat he quickly slipped followed by his partner half a step behind.

The door shut to the applause of the spectators but before the uproar had a chance to diminish the door once again flew wide open framing the old man peeing in the toilet. The woman, hands on hips, was still beating hell out of the floorboards. Well, you can imagine the frenzied crescendo the crowd attained when confronted by this spectacle.

**Mark Lightbody**

## Île du Havre Aubert

South of Cap aux Meules, connected by long strings of sand at points barely wider than the road, is the archipelago's largest island.

The most lively area of the town of **Havre Aubert** is known as La Grave, an old section by the water at the south-eastern tip of the island. The main street is lined with small craft and gift shops, some restaurants and many old houses. There is a theatre here for summer productions in French only.

On any rainy day the interesting aquarium is packed with visitors disturbed from their seaside activities. A pool with various creatures which can be handled is a major attraction. The **Musée de la Mer** has displays on shipwrecks and various aspects of the islands' transportation and fishing history.

Both are open daily in summer and have low admission fees.

Near town is the **Centre Nautique de l'Istorlet** with sail boat and windsurfer courses and rentals. There is also a simple campground at the coastal property.

**Places to Stay & Eat** The *Auberge Chez Denis à François* (☎ 937-2371) is somewhere you could stay overnight. There are six rooms; singles/doubles cost $42/47 and meals are available in its restaurant which is open to nonguests.

In La Grave, the *Café de la Grave* is a good place for simple, inexpensive meals or a coffee and cake. *La Saline* open at lunch and dinner time only is a pricier seafood restaurant where the local speciality, pot-en-pot can be sampled.

## Havre aux Maisons

All-told, probably the most scenic of the Magdalen Islands, Havre aux Maisons has a bit of everything. Definitely take the south shore road (Chemin des Montants) from Pointe Basse up around Butte Ronde and into a beautiful little valley. Excellent views, some traditional-style houses, smoke houses and a lighthouse are all seen along this route. There are several restaurants along the main road across the island.

**Places to Stay & Eat** For a place to stay on Havre aux Maisons, the *Auberge Les Sillons* (☎ 969-2134) is friendly, has a good location, and is reasonably priced at $45 a double and meals are available. A guesthouse, on the main road across the island, is *Rina Arseneau's* (☎ 969-2579). It charges $30 a double and is a five-minute walk to the beach.

The coastal area around Dune du Sud is also attractive and there are some fine places to stay in the area including some little cottages right on the water by a beach with huge sandstone arches.

## Pointe aux Loups

On either side of this small community in the middle of the long sand spits connecting the

**QUEBEC**

north and south islands are stretches of sand beaches and dunes. For a quick dip, the water is warmer on the lagoon side.

### La Grosse Île

This, the principal English section of the Magdalen Islands, was settled by Scottish pioneers. As soon as you arrive, you'll notice all the signs are in English. Despite generations of isolation, many of the local people barely speak a word of French! La Grosse Île, East Cape and Old Harry are the main communities.

**Trinity Church**, known for its stained glass depicting Jesus the fisherman, is worth a look. Out through the windows the eye captures the graves, the piles of lobster traps, some solitary houses and then the sea: the island's world in microcosm.

There is a commercial **saltmine** just off the main road en route to Old Harry. No tours are given but there is an information office open in the afternoon. Begun in 1983 the mine is 223 metres deep.

About 16 km off La Grosse Île is **Île Brion**, an ecological reserve, once but no longer inhabited by humans. It remains home to 140 species of birds and much interesting vegetation. On days that are not too windy it can be visited. Even camping is possible, but for details, call the office of the Corporation for the Access to and Protection of Brion Island in Cap aux Meules on ☎ 986-6622.

**Places to Stay & Eat** Many of the people around La Grosse Île rent a room or two during the summer but are not listed in the guides.

For eating, the *Country Kitchen* is recommended for its wide selection, modest prices and simple, casual atmosphere. The house Bordeaux is a pleasant treat at lunch. It was on sale on last visit, so its future is uncertain.

### Île de l'Est

Linking La Grosse Île and Grande Entrée is this wild region which boasts the islands' most impressive beach: from Pointe Old Harry, **La Grande Échouerie Beach**

extends, a curving sweep of pale sand, about five km down Île de l'Est. A short road with parking areas and trails stretching down to the beach begins near the Old Harry harbour. From Hwy 199 (through Île de l'Est which, other than the beach is entirely a national wildlife refuge area) a few turn-offs lead to hiking paths.

### Île de la Grande Entreé

On this island is Old Harry, a fishing wharf with about 10 boats and some spectacular shoreline cliffs, portions of which have caves in them. Walruses once inhabited the area but they were slaughtered with little concern. Sea Cow Lane is the site of the walrus landing.

In the other direction from Old Harry don't miss **Saint Peter's by the Sea**, a beautiful, peaceful little church overlooking the sea and bounded by graves, belonging almost exclusively to members of the Clark and Clarke families. It's open to visitors and well worth a visit. On a breezy day the inside offers a quiet stillness broken only by the creaking rafters. It's all wood, including a richly carved door honouring a drowned fishermen.

Across the street is a fine area for watching the sea explode into sparkling bits up onto the rugged, rocky shoreline.

**Places to Stay & Eat** *Club Vacances 'Les Iles'* (☎ 985-2833) is a resort built around the island's nature and the activities it affords: walking, windsurfing, boat tours, bird-watching etc. Package deals include rooms, all meals and organised activities. The same package is offered to tenters at their on-grounds campsites for $45 per person per day. Very little English seems to be spoken. If you just want to put up a tent, the fee is $10 a night and you can use the cafeteria-style restaurant.

At the far tip of the island are more colourful fishing boats to check out along the docks and a couple of places to eat. Best is the *Restaurant du C E P I M* where lobster is cheap and other seafood is offered. The nearby *Café Spello* is also an attractive little place.

## Île d'Entrée

This is the one inhabited island not interconnected by land with the others. A ferry links it to the port at Cap aux Meules. The boat runs twice a day from Monday to Saturday: once early in the morning and once in mid-afternoon. Board in front of the coastguard building. The ferry crossing takes between 30 and 60 minutes. The virtually treeless island has an English-speaking population of around 175 and is primarily a fishing community. It's about four km long and less than one km wide with walking trails leading over much of it.

The gentler western section supports some farms before ending in high red cliffs. The eastern section is mountainous with the highest point, Big Hill, at 174 metres above sea level. A trail from Post Office Road leads up to the views from the top.

There is one *guesthouse* (☎ 986-5744) on the island but call before arriving if you wish to stay. Also on the island are a couple of grocery stores and one basic snack bar.

### Getting There & Away

**Air** Canadian Airlines flies in daily from Halifax; Air Alliance has two flights a day from Montreal, Quebec City, Sept-Îles, Gaspé and other points.

**Ferry** The cheapest and most common way to get to the Magdalen Islands is by ferry from Souris on Prince Edward Island. The boat leaves daily at 2 pm except Tuesdays. On Tuesdays the ship leaves at 2 am.

In midsummer arrive at least two hours ahead of time. I mean it, at least two hours. The boat, the MV *Lucy Maud Montgomery*, with a capacity of 90 vehicles and 300 passengers is always completely full and no reservations are taken. If, after waiting in line for hours, you do not get aboard they will give you a reservation for the very next ferry only. Sometimes at peak season there is another boat put into service but it leaves

Prince Edward Island at 2 am. Nonetheless, it too, will be packed.

For the return trip, reservations can be made. It's advisable to do this on arrival or not long after. You can book up to seven days in advance. In peak season there will be at least several days worth of returns choc-a-bloc as soon as you arrive. The return to Prince Edward Island departs at 8 am except on Tuesdays when it leaves at 8 am. Again, the supplementary trip is at night.

This is not a cheap trip. The cost is about $33 per person for the five-hour, 223-km cruise. It's the car fee that really kills you though. That's another $64. And these are both one-way fares only. Campers, trailers etc are still more costly. Bicycles can be taken for $8. Credit cards are accepted for payment.

The ship is well appointed, however, with a surprisingly inexpensive cafeteria. For those with a little extra money there is also a white-tablecloth dining room with meals in the $16 to $20 range and a full course (from soup to dessert) table d'hôte which is not bad value. The ship has some outdoor decks, various inner lounges and a bar with live entertainment.

Passenger boats operated by the same line, cruise to the islands down the St Lawrence River from Montreal, but are expensive. There is also a passenger and cargo ship once a week from Montreal, which is less costly but still over $325 one way. The CTMA *Voyageur* taking cargo and 12 passengers departs Montreal once a week for Cap aux Meules and returns four days later. In Montreal call ☎ 257-0323. Meals are included in the price of the ticket. In the off-peak tourist season the price drops by about one third.

### Getting Around

Five of the main islands are linked by road but distances are small and cycling is not uncommon. Bicycles can be rented at Le Pedallier in Cap aux Meules. The office is closed on Sunday.

There is a guided bus tour of the islands available out of Cap aux Meules and taxis will take you to specific parts of the island.

QUEBEC

Also cars and motorcycles can be rented in Cap aux Meules or at the airport.

A ferry connects Île d'Entrée with the two principal islands.

One boat tour operator, Excursion de Pêche Îles, offers day-trips to Île d'Entrée, fishing excursions and trips around the coast to see the cliffs.

# Ontario

Entered Confederation: 1 July 1867
Area: 1,068,587 sq km
Population: 10,084,885
National Capital: Ottawa
Provincial Capital: Toronto

The name 'Ontario' is derived from an Iroquois Indian word meaning 'rocks standing high near the water', probably referring to Niagara Falls.

Ontario, located smack in the middle of the country, is also the centre of Canadian politics and economics, and much of the arts as well.

It is traditionally conservative – politically and socially. The provincial social democratic party (NDP), now in power for the first time, couldn't have chosen a worse period to try their left-wing approach to economics and social policy, and has had to suffer a nosedive in popularity as the electorate tries to tough out the hard financial times.

Ontario has many excellent government parks for outdoor activities.

## HISTORY

When Europeans arrived in the region, they found it settled and occupied by numerous Indian Nations. The Algonquin and Huron first dominated the southern portion of the province, but by the time of White exploration and trade in the 1700s, the Iroquois Confederacy, also known as the Five Nations, dominated the area south of Georgian Bay and east to Quebec. In the north and west, the Ojibway covered the lands north of the Great Lakes and all the way west to the Cree territory of the prairies.

## CLIMATE

Within Ontario is the country's most southerly region, important when considering climatic factors. Around Niagara the summers are long and the winters mild. Lake Ontario keeps the bulk of the population from being too cold in winter. Summers can be hot and muggy. Temperatures drop progressively (and considerably) the further north you go.

## ECONOMY

It is by far the richest province, although the recession beginning in 1990 and still continuing has hit harder here than elsewhere.

Economically, the area around the western shore of Lake Ontario generates much of the provincial wealth. There is as much manufacturing in Ontario as in all the other provinces combined, and it is in this critical sector that the downturn has been felt most. Hamilton is Canada's iron and steel centre, while nearby cities such as Oshawa and Windsor make Ontario the national leader in car production.

Odd as it may seem, Ontario is also tops in farm income, although the area of excellent farmland (around the Great Lakes) shrinks each year as fields are lost to asphalt. Fruit is a major market crop, and (to an ever decreasing extent) tobacco. The Niagara Peninsula is a significant wine-producing region.

Further north are tremendous resources. Sudbury produces a quarter of the world's nickel; Elliot Lake sits on the largest uranium deposits known – and, of course, there are the forests. I guess you can see why Ontario is called one of the 'have' provinces.

Despite all this, there remains much uncluttered, wooded lakeland and large areas of quiet country towns surrounded by small market gardens. And within the northern regions, vast areas of wilderness still exist.

## POPULATION

The province is now Canada's most populous and ethnically diverse, with about a third of all Canadians living within its borders. Over 80% of Ontarians are urban dwellers, most living between Kingston and Windsor along the great waterways that make up the southern boundary.

## INFORMATION
### Provincial Symbols

The provincial flower is the trillium and the as yet unofficial bird is the loon.

### Telephone

The area code for Toronto and immediate vicinity is 416. The area surrounding Toronto (in all directions) is 905. This district includes Colborne to the east, up to Lake Simcoe to the north, and Bradford, Hamilton and Niagara to the east and south.

South-western Ontario and the Bruce Peninsula are covered by area code 519. Eastern

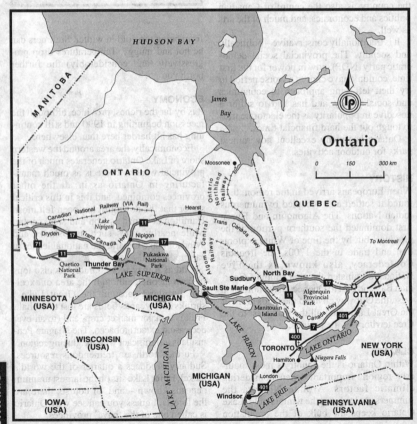

Ontario South

0   40   80 km

QUEBEC

Ottawa River

Ottawa Hwy

Trans Canada Hwy

Algonquin Provincial Park

Gatineau Park

Hull

OTTAWA

Morrisburg

Cornwall

Prescott

St Lawrence Islands National Park

Kingston

Belleville

Picton

Trenton

Tweed

Pembroke

Barry's Bay

Petroglyphs Provincial Park

Peterborough

North Bay

Lake Nipissing

Sundridge

Kearney

Huntsville

Parry Sound

Georgian Bay Islands National Park

Christian Island

Midland

Penetanguishene

Wasaga Beach

Orillia

Lake Simcoe

Barrie

Collingwood

Owen Sound

Port Elgin

Sudbury

Little Current

Manitoulin Island

South Baymouth

Meldrum Bay

Killarney Provincial Park

Killbear Provincial Park

Awenda Provincial Park

Bruce Peninsula National Park

Fathom Five National Marine Park

Tobermory

Bruce Peninsula

Trans Canada Hwy

LAKE HURON

MICHIGAN (USA)

Sarnia

Grand Bend

Woodstock

London

Stratford

Kitchener

Waterloo

Cambridge

Elora

Fergus

Guelph

Milton

Brantford

Hamilton

Mississauga

TORONTO

Oshawa

LAKE ONTARIO

St Catharine's

Niagara-on-the-Lake

Niagara Falls

Fort Erie

Buffalo

NEW YORK (USA)

Port Colborne

Port Dover

Simcoe

Long Point

LAKE ERIE

Point Pelee National Park

Kingsville

Windsor

Detroit

Lake St Clair

Georgian Bay

ONTARIO

Ontario (including Ottawa) is area 613. Northern Ontario (including Manitoulin Island and Sault Ste Marie) are in area 705. The north-western section of the province which includes Thunder Bay and west to Manitoba is area code 807.

For emergency service dial ☎ 911 anywhere in the province. If the 911 line is not active in your location, the call will be routed through the operator automatically.

### Time

Ontario is on Eastern time, except for the far western area, which is on Central Time (matching neighbouring Manitoba). Thunder Bay is on Eastern Time; Kenora is on Central Time.

### Tax

Ontario's provincial sales tax is 8%.

### Road Rules

As in the rest of Canada, motorists may turn right on red lights after having come to a full stop. In Toronto, all vehicles must stop for streetcars, behind the rear doors, while the streetcar is loading or unloading passengers. Once the streetcar doors are closed, other vehicles may proceed to pass. Stopping is also a must at all pedestrian crosswalks if someone is on or about to step onto the painted crossing. The pedestrian crosswalks are clearly marked above the street with a sign and lights.

Ontario is the first province to consider making the wearing of helmets mandatory for all cyclists. This law has not yet been passed but is on the agenda, so potential bike riders should ask to avoid any possible fine.

Radar detectors are illegal.

### HIGHLIGHTS

The country's largest city, Toronto, is here, as are Niagara Falls and Ottawa, Canada's capital. These three places alone make this region one of the most heavily visited in the country. Historic Kingston, in between Ottawa and Toronto, and some of the middle-sized towns to the west of Toronto, with their country flavour and varying attractions (such as the Shakespeare Theatre of Stratford and the German Oktoberfest of Kitchener), are also busy tourist centres.

Less travelled but equally representative of the province are areas such as the beaches of Lake Huron and Georgian Bay, with its shoreline made archetypally Canadian by the country's best known painters. Further north again, accessible wilderness parks offer respite from the densely populated southern regions and provide opportunities to see the northern transitional and Boreal forests. The resource-based cities of Sudbury, Sault Ste Marie and Thunder Bay, each with their own attractions, are also good starting points for trips around the more rugged areas of Ontario, from the Lake Superior shoreline to as far north as James Bay, where you'll find one of the province's oldest settlements, Moosonee.

# Ottawa

Ottawa, the capital of the country, arouses in all Canadians the mixed emotions worthy of a nation's capital. It sits attractively on the south bank of the Ottawa River at its confluence with the Rideau River. The gently rolling Gatineau Hills of Quebec are visible to the north.

The government is the largest employer, and the stately Gothic-style parliament buildings act as landmarks.

The city attracts four million tourists a year, many to see just what the heck the capital is like. The abundance of museums and cultural activities is another enticement. And then, of course, in summer you can see the traditionally garbed Royal Canadian Mounted Police (RCMP), also known as the Mounties.

You may be surprised by the amount of French you hear around town. Quebec is just a stone's throw away, but probably just as important is the fact that most federal government workers are now required to be bilingual.

Ottawa is not an exciting city but its streets, if not lively, are wide and clean; the

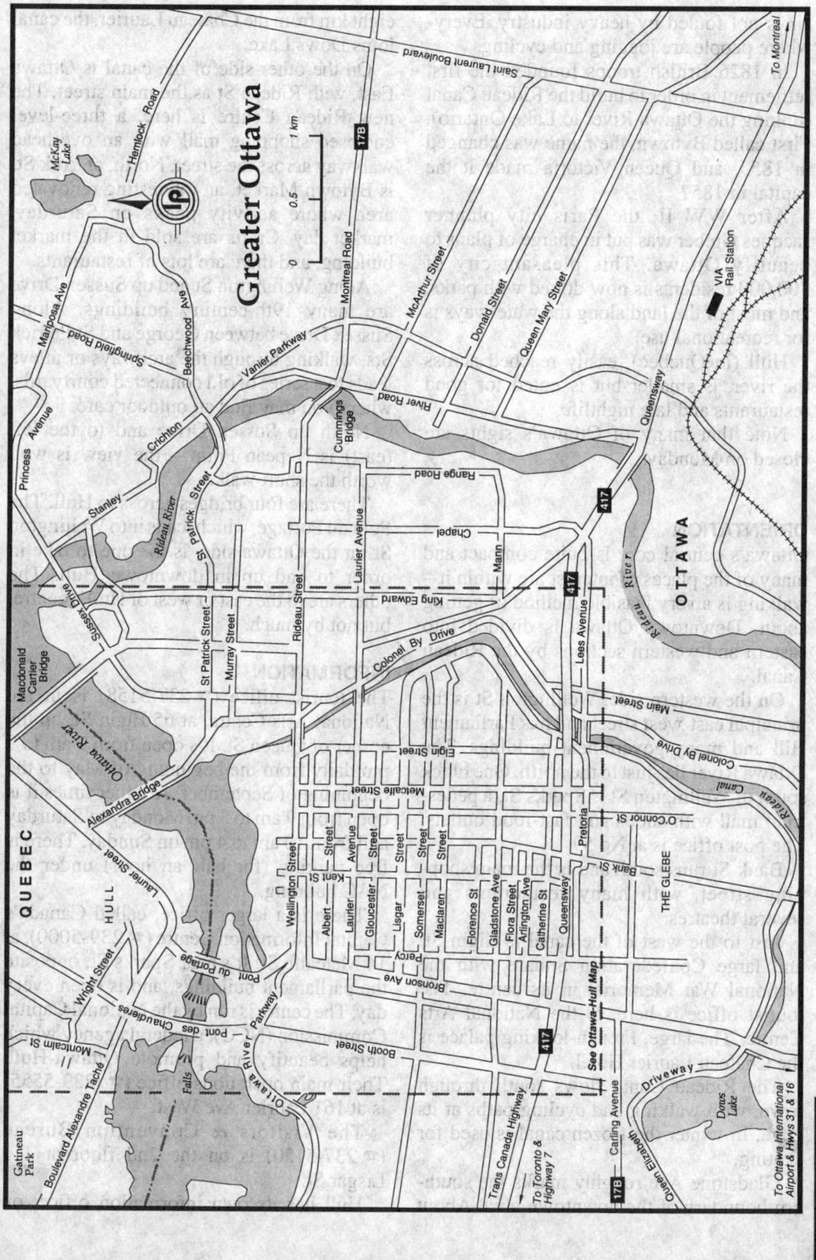

## Greater Ottawa

0    0.5    1 km

QUEBEC

OTTAWA

Gatineau Park

Hull

Ottawa River

Rideau River

Rideau Canal

McKay Lake

Dows Lake

VIA Rail Station

To Montreal

To Ottawa International Airport & Hwys 31 & 16

To Toronto & Highway 7

See Ottawa-Hull Map

THE GLEBE

Streets and labels:

Saint Laurent Boulevard, Hemlock Road, Montreal Road, McArthur Street, Donald Street, Queen Mary Street, Vanier Parkway, Beechwood Avenue, Springfield Road, Mariposa Ave, Princess Avenue, Crichton, Stanley, St Patrick Street, Cummings Bridge, Range Road, River Road, Chapel, Laurier Avenue, Mann, King Edward, Rideau Street, Murray Street, Colonel By Drive, Sussex Drive, Macdonald Cartier Bridge, Alexandra Bridge, Wellington Street, Laurier Street, Wright Street, Montcalm St, Pont du Portage, Pont des Chaudières, Falls, Ottawa River Parkway, Booth Street, Bronson Ave, Percy, Kent St, Bank St, O'Connor St, Elgin Street, Metcalfe Street, Pretoria, Albert, Lisgar, Somerset, Maclaren, Florence St, Gladstone Ave, Flora Street, Arlington Ave, Catherine St, Gloucester, Lees Avenue, Main Street, Colonel By Drive, Carling Avenue, Queensway, Queen Elizabeth Driveway, Trans Canada Highway, Boulevard Alexandra Taché

417, 178, 7, 31, 16

ONTARIO

air is not fouled by heavy industry. Everywhere people are jogging and cycling.

In 1826 British troops founded the first settlement in order to build the Rideau Canal (linking the Ottawa River to Lake Ontario). First called Bytown, the name was changed in 1855, and Queen Victoria made it the capital in 1857.

After WW II, the Paris city planner Jacques Greber was put in charge of plans to beautify Ottawa. This pleasant city of 300,000 residents is now dotted with parks, and most of the land along the waterways is for recreational use.

Hull (in Quebec), easily reached across the river, is smaller but is noted for good restaurants and late nightlife.

Note that many of Ottawa's sights are closed on Monday.

## ORIENTATION

Ottawa's central core is quite compact and many of the places of interest are within it – walking is a very feasible method of getting about. Downtown Ottawa is divided into eastern and western sections by the Rideau Canal.

On the western side, Wellington St is the principal east-west street and has Parliament Hill and many government buildings. The Ottawa River lies just to the north. One block south of Wellington St is Sparks St, a pedestrian mall with shops and fast-food outlets. The post office is at No 59.

Bank St runs south and is the main shopping street, with many restaurants and several theatres.

Just to the west of the canal is Elgin St, and large Confederation Square with the National War Memorial in its centre. The tourist office is here, in the National Arts Centre. The large, French-looking palace is the Château Laurier Hotel.

The Rideau Canal flows south through town, with walking and cycling paths at its edge. In winter the frozen canal is used for skating.

Gladstone Ave roughly marks the southern boundary of the downtown area. About

eight km from the Château Laurier, the canal joins Dows Lake.

On the other side of the canal is Ottawa East, with Rideau St as the main street. The new Rideau Centre is here, a three-level enclosed shopping mall with an overhead walkway across the street. North, at York St, is Bytown Market, an interesting renovated area where activity peaks on Saturday, market day. Crafts are sold in the market building, and there are lots of restaurants.

Along Wellington St and up Sussex Drive are many 19th-century buildings. Along Sussex Drive between George and St Patrick Sts, walking through the archways or alleys leads to a series of old connected courtyards, where you may find an outdoor café.

North up Sussex Drive and to the left (east) is Nepean Point – the view is well worth the short walk.

There are four bridges across to Hull. The Pont du Portage, which leads into Wellington St on the Ottawa side, is the one to take in order to end up in downtown Hull. The others are to the east or west of Hull's centre, but not by much.

## INFORMATION

The tourist office (☎ 237-5158) is in the National Arts Centre, at 65 Elgin St, on the corner of Queen St. It's open from 9 am to 9 pm daily from the beginning of May to the beginning of September. At other times it is open from 9 am to 5 pm Monday to Saturday and from 10 am to 4 pm on Sunday. There is free parking (for half an hour) under the NAC building.

There is a larger office, called Canada's Capital Information Centre (☎ 239-5000), at 14 Metcalfe St. It's near Sparks St, opposite the parliament buildings, and is open every day. The centre is run by the National Capital Commission (NCC), a federal agency which helps beautify and promote Ottawa-Hull. Their main operations office (☎ 239-5555) is at 161 Laurier Ave West.

The Visitors & Convention Bureau (☎ 237-5150) is on the 2nd floor at 111 Lisgar St.

Hull has its own information office, on

Rue Laurier at the corner of Boulevard Saint Laurent, near the Alexandra Bridge. There is another in City Hall, in downtown Hull.

The museums and attractions of Ottawa are in a state of flux and are frequently closed, either being renovated, repaired, upgraded or moved. If there is something you really wish to see, it is not a bad idea to call first to find out its current status. Also note that admission at many of them is free on Thursday.

Nearly all day and night, the market is a busy place. Late at night, however, it does get a bit of an edge to it, with some drug and prostitution traffic. Walking alone in the quieter areas in the wee hours should probably be avoided.

Lately the Promenade du Portage area has been pretty wild on occasion, with some nasty fights, rowdy drunkenness and worse. The city has put in video surveillance cameras to keep a lid on the bar strip, so exercise common sense if it looks as though the troublemakers are getting cranked up.

## VIEWS

For a good, free view of the Ottawa River area where it's met by the Rideau River, and across to Hull, go to the 8th floor observation deck and cafeteria at the Ottawa City Hall, 111 Sussex Drive. It sits on Green Island overlooking Rideau Falls, which are east of the Macdonald Cartier Bridge. At the time of writing, City Hall was undergoing substantial (and controversial) renovations and the observation deck was closed. I imagine the mayor's new handcrafted wooden desk will be quite impressive – at least the price of $40,000 is. There is also a park along the river beside City Hall.

A view of the downtown area can be had from the tower at the parliament buildings (see Parliament Hill for details).

## PARLIAMENT HILL

Federal government buildings dominate downtown Ottawa, especially those on Parliament Hill off Wellington St, near the canal.

The Parliament Building itself, with its Peace Tower and clock, is most striking.

Beside it are East and West blocks, also with the sharp, green, oxidised copper-topped roofing.

Inside the Parliament Building, the Commons and Senate sit and can be viewed in session. The interior is all hand-carved limestone and sandstone. See the beautiful library with its wood and wrought iron. Free tours (☎ 239-5000), about 20 minutes long, run frequently and include the Peace Tower Lookout. To go up the tower elevator you must be part of a tour, and for that there is often a queue. Reservations are required. In summer book the tour in the white tent out on the lawn. In winter there is a desk inside for making the reservation.

When parliament is in session, Question Period in the House of Commons is a major attraction. It occurs early every afternoon and at 11 am on Friday. It's free, but be prepared for some hassle – security has become very tight. For information and tickets call ☎ 992-4793.

At 10 am daily in summer, see the Changing of the Guard on the lawns – very colourful.

Pick up a free copy of the *Walking Tour of Parliament Hill*, which lists various details in and around the buildings. Free tours are also given in the External Affairs Building, 125 Sussex Drive.

At night during the summer, there is a free sound & light show on Parliament Hill – one version is in English and the other in French.

## NATIONAL GALLERY

The National Gallery (☎ 990-1985) is a must. As Canada's premier art gallery, it has a vast collection of North American and European works in various media, all housed in an impressive building in the centre of town, on Sussex Drive. It's just 15 minutes' walk from the Parliament Buildings.

Opened in 1988, the striking glass and pink granite gallery overlooking the Ottawa River was designed by Moshe Safdie, who also created Montreal's Habitat (a unique apartment complex) and Quebec City's Musée de la Civilisation. The numerous galleries, some arched and effectively coloured,

ONTARIO

display both classic and contemporary pieces, with the emphasis in general on Canadian artists. The US and European collections do, however, contain examples from nearly all the heavyweights. The gallery also presents changing exhibits and special shows.

The excellent, chronological display of Canadian painting and sculpture not only gives a history of Canadian art but also, in a real sense, provides an outline of the development of the country itself, beginning with the depictions of Native Indian life at the time the Europeans arrived.

For a recharging break, two pleasant courtyard-style areas offer the eyes a rest. Between them sits one of the gallery's most unusual and most appealing components, the beautifully restored 1888 **Rideau St Chapel**, which was saved from destruction a few blocks away.

On level 2, along with the contemporary and international work, is the **Inuit Gallery**, and one room for the display of some of the extensive and fine photography collection.

The complex is large; you'll need a few hours and still will tire before seeing all the exhibits, let alone the changing film and video presentations, lectures and concerts. There is a café and a restaurant. Underneath the gallery are two levels of parking. Admission is $5 ($3 for seniors) but is free for full-time students, and for all on Thursdays. Some of the special shows may have an additional entry fee. The gallery is open from 10 am to 6 pm daily in summer, except on Thursdays, when it's open until 8 pm. The rest of the year, it's open from 10 am to 5 pm but is closed on Mondays and holidays.

## CANADIAN MUSEUM OF NATURE

Formerly the Museum of Natural Sciences, the Museum of Nature (☎ 996-3102) is housed in the attractive old Victorian building on the corner of McLeod and Elgin Sts.

The four-storey building fostering an appreciation and understanding of nature includes a good section on the dinosaurs once found in Alberta. Also excellent are the realistic mammal and bird dioramas depicting Canadian wildlife. Major temporary exhibits on specific mammal, mineral or ecological subjects are a feature. One I saw was on all manner of crawling bugs – from cockroaches to earwigs and many other such fine creatures.

The new Viola MacMillan Mineral Gallery is excellent, with some of the largest gems and minerals you're ever likely to see. The reproduction mine comes complete with shaky elevator. The east-coast tidal zone recreation is also very realistic.

A separate section of the museum is geared to children.

The museum is open until 5 pm every day of the year, opening at 9.30 am in summer and at 10 am the rest of the year. On Thursday, hours are extended until 8 pm. Check for more extended hours during the summer. Admission is $4, with special rates for seniors, kids and families. On Thursdays, it is half-price from opening time to 5 pm and then free from 5 to 8 pm.

There is a restaurant and a cafeteria on the premises. From Confederation Square, take buses Nos 5, 6 or 14 down Elgin St. Walking from the Parliament Buildings takes about 20 minutes.

## SUPREME COURT OF CANADA

This rather intimidating structure (☎ 995-4330) is partially open to nonlitigants. Visitors can stroll around the grounds and lobby from 9 am to 5 pm. Construction of the home for the highest court of the land was begun in 1939 but not completed until 1946. The grand entrance hall, 12 metres high, is certainly impressive. During the summer a visit can include a free tour given by a law student. Call for the schedule. The court's on the corner of Wellington and Kent Sts.

## BYTOWN MUSEUM & THE OTTAWA LOCKS

Focusing on city history, Bytown Museum is in the oldest stone building in Ottawa. It's east of Parliament Hill, beside the canal – go down the stairs from Wellington St and head to the locks at the river. Used during construction of the canal for storing military equipment and money, it now contains arte-facts and documents pertaining to local history.

On the ground floor, Parks Canada runs an exhibit about the building of the canal, open mid-May to mid-October from 10 am to 4 pm on Monday to Saturday (closed Tuesday) and from 2 to 5 pm on Sunday. In spring and fall, it's open from Monday to Friday and there's a small admission fee. The series of locks at the edge of the Ottawa River in the Colonel By Valley between the Château Laurier and the Parliament Buildings marks the north end of the 198-km Rideau Canal, which runs to Kingston and the St Lawrence River. Colonel By, who was put in charge of constructing the canal, set up his headquarters right here in 1826. Though never fulfilling any military purpose, the canal was used commercially for a while and then fell into disuse. The locks are now maintained by the government as heritage parks.

## CANADIAN WAR MUSEUM

At 330 Sussex Drive, this museum (☎ 992-2774), with the country's largest war-related collection, contains all manner of things military and traces Canadian military history. The life-sized replica of a WW I trench is good. You'll also see large displays, with sound, showing the American invasion of 1775 and the Normandy D-Day landing. The museum also contains the country's largest collection of war art. A new exhibit focuses on Canada's navy in WW II.

The museum is open from 9.30 am to 5 pm daily (until 8 pm on Thursday). Admission is $2.50, $1.25 for students and seniors and free for veterans. It's free for everyone on Thursday.

## ROYAL CANADIAN MINT

Next door to the War Museum is the mint (☎ 993-8990). No longer producing day-to-day coinage, it now strikes special-edition coins, commemorative pieces, bullion investment coins and the like. Founded in 1908 and renovated in the mid-1980s, this imposing stone building has always been Canada's major refiner of gold. Tours are

given by appointment; call to arrange one and see the process – from sheets of metal to bags of coins. It's open (in summer only) from 8.30 to 11 am and 12.30 to 2.30 pm Monday to Friday. Admission is $2. Sorry, no free samples.

The main circulation-coin mint is now in Winnipeg, Manitoba.

## CURRENCY MUSEUM

For those who like to look at money, you can see lots more of it at the Currency Museum (☎ 782-8914) in the Bank of Canada at 245 Sparks St. In summer, it's open Monday to Friday and on Sunday afternoon. From September to May, it is also closed on Monday. Various displays tell the story of money through the ages, from whales' teeth to collectors' banknotes. The emphasis is on Canadian monies. Admission is $2 (free on Tuesday).

## NATIONAL AVIATION MUSEUM

This collection of over 100 aircraft is housed in a huge triangular building (about the size of four football fields) at Rockcliffe Airport (☎ 993-2010), not too far from the centre of town. See planes ranging from the Silver Dart of 1909 or the first turbo-powered Viscount passenger carrier right through to more recent jets. Peace and wartime planes are equally represented; included is the renowned Spitfire. The Cessna Crane is the very one my father (Alexander Lightbody) trained in for the RCAF.

Other exhibits include aviation-related video games and audiovisual presentations.

Admission is $5, less for seniors and kids, and again, it's free on Thursday. From May to September the museum is open daily from 9 am to 5 pm (until 9 pm on Thursday). In winter it's open until 8 pm on Thursday and is closed on Monday (unless it is a holiday). Call to check on opening hours, though, as they tend to vary according to attendance levels and the time of year.

The airport is off Saint Laurent Blvd north-east of the downtown area, near the river and the Canadian Forces base.

ONTARIO

## NATIONAL MUSEUM OF SCIENCE & TECHNOLOGY

At 1867 Saint Laurent Blvd, on the corner of Russell Rd, this museum (☎ 991-3044) has all kinds of participatory scientific learning exhibits. Try things out, test yourself, watch physical laws in action, see optical illusions. Also on display are farm machines, trains, model ships and stagecoaches. The bicycle and motorcycle collections are good. Higher-tech exhibits include computers and communication technologies. And don't miss the incubator, where you can see live chicks in various stages of hatching.

The large, new display on space technology is interesting, with lots of interactive exhibits and an assortment of Canadian space artefacts. An astronomy section has films and slides about the universe; on clear nights, take a peep through the large refracting telescope. Telephone reservations should be made for the stargazing.

While popular with all age groups, this place is great for kids. Those without children may wish to avoid weekends and the increased numbers of young ones.

Admission is $5 for adults, less for students, seniors and children, and is free on Thursday from 5 pm to 9 pm. In summer, opening hours are 9 am to 6 pm daily (until 9 pm on Thursday). After September it is closed on Monday. In winter it also closes earlier in the day. Free parking is supplied.

## CANADIAN SKI MUSEUM

The ski museum (☎ 233-5832) has a small, specialised exhibit at 457A Sussex Drive, near the market, with a collection of equipment and memorabilia outlining the 5000-year history of skiing. The museum is open Tuesday to Saturday, from 11 am to 4 pm in summer, from noon to 4 pm throughout the winter. The entry fee is $1.

## CANADIAN CENTRE FOR CARICATURE

At 136 St Patrick St, by the corner of Sussex Drive at the edge of the market, this unusual collection (☎ 995-3145) from the National Archives consists of 20,000 drawn cartoons

| | |
|---|---|
| 1 | Maison du Citoyen |
| 2 | Tourist Office |
| 3 | Canadian Museum of Civilisation |
| 4 | City Hall |
| 5 | Royal Canadian Mint |
| 6 | Canadian War Museum |
| 7 | National Gallery |
| 8 | Canadian Ski Museum |
| 9 | National Archives |
| 10 | Bytown Museum |
| 11 | Market |
| 12 | Château Laurier |
| 13 | Tourist Office |
| 14 | National Arts Centre & Tourist Offce |
| 15 | Nicholas St Jail Hostel |
| 16 | Bus Terminal |
| 17 | Canadian Museum of Nature |
| 18 | YM-YWCA |

and caricatures concerning Canadian history and people, culled from periodicals from the past two centuries, though the vast majority of the collection is from the past 30 years. If you like political cartoons and social satire, this is the place – otherwise it's a real yawner. It's free and is open every day. As far as I know, it's one of a kind.

## CANADIAN MUSEUM OF CONTEMPORARY PHOTOGRAPHY

Wedged in between the Château Laurier and the canal, in a reconstructed railway tunnel at 1 Rideau Canal, CMCP (☎ 990-8257) is the new photo museum. Originally part of the National Film Board, the still photography division has acquired its own space, where it houses the country's vast photographic archives and the photographic research departments. Unfortunately, gallery space is limited, so you may want to check what's on before visiting. Exhibits are not always of Canadians' work and may not be of interest to the casual viewer unacquainted with esoteric approaches to the photographic medium. Shows change quarterly.

The gallery is open from 1 May to October from 11 am to 5 pm daily (until 8 pm on Thursdays), except Wednesdays, when hours are just 4 to 8 pm. The rest of the year it is closed on Monday and Tuesday.

HULL

Ottawa-Hull

*0     250     500 m*

RIVER

Macdonald Cartier Bridge

Rideau River

Sussex Drive

Rue Laval
Rue Kent
Boulevard
Maisonnneuve
Rue Notre Dame
Rue Champlain
Rue Laurier
Rue Hotel de Ville

Promenade du Portage

Pont du Portage

Ottawa River Parkway

OTTAWA

Alexandra Bridge

Nepean Point

Ottawa Locks

Parliament Buildings

Mackenzie Ave

Wellington Street

Sparks St
Queen St
Albert St
Slater St

Bay St
Lyon St

Gloucester St

Lisgar St

Cooper St

CHINATOWN

Bronson Avenue
Percy St
Kent St

Somerset St

Maclaren St
Gilmour St
James St
Florence St
Gladstone Ave
McLeod St
Flora St
Arlington Ave
Catherine St

Sparks St Mall

DOWNTOWN

Laurier Avenue West

Nepean St

OTTAWA

Bank Street
O'Connor St
Metcalfe St
Elgin Street

Mackenzie King Bridge

Laurier Bridge

Laurier Avenue East

Queen Elizabeth Driveway

Colonel By Drive

Cartier Street
Macdonald St
Robert St

Rideau Canal

University Of Ottawa

Nicholas Street

Waller Street
Cumberland St
King Edward Avenue

Boteler Street
Bolton St
Cathcart St
Bruyer St
St Andrew St
Guigues St
St Patrick Street
Murray Street
York Street
Rideau Street

Trans Canada Hwy 417

Chamberlain Ave

Queensway

Isabella Street

To Airport

To VIA Rail Station

Main St

ONTARIO

Admission is $2.50, free to full-time students, and free to all on Thursdays.

## CATHEDRAL BASILICA OF NOTRE DAME

Built in 1839, this is one of the city's most impressive houses of worship. A pamphlet available at the door outlines the many features, including carvings, windows, the organ and the Gothic-style ceiling. It is on Guigues Ave, across from the art gallery, in the Byward Market area.

## CENTRAL EXPERIMENTAL FARM

This Agriculture Canada government farm (☎ 995-5222) on the corner of Queen Elizabeth Driveway and Carling Ave is about 500 hectares of flowers, trees, shrubs and gardens. The site is used for research on all aspects of farming and horticulture. There are tours, or you can go on your own walking tour. The farm also has livestock and showcase herds of cattle, an observatory, a tropical greenhouse and the arboretum. The latter is good for walking or having a picnic and is great in winter for tobogganing. The farm is linked to the rest of Ottawa's cycling routes. Admission is free and the farm is open every day. Call regarding shows and special displays.

## LAURIER HOUSE

This Victorian home at 335 Laurier Ave (☎ 992-8142), built in 1878, was the residence of two prime ministers: Laurier and the eccentric Mackenzie King. It's beautifully furnished throughout – don't miss the study on the top floor. Each of the two prime ministers is represented by mementoes and various possessions. It's free, and is open Tuesday to Saturday and on Sunday afternoon.

An early morning visit is suggested (that is, before the tour buses arrive) so you'll have the knowledgeable guides all to yourself.

## PRIME MINISTER'S & GOVERNOR GENERAL'S HOUSES

You can view the outside of the present prime minister's house, at 24 Sussex Drive, as well as Rideau Hall, the governor general's pad, around the corner and up from the river, at 1 Sussex Drive. Both houses are north-east of the market area. Rideau Hall is off Princess Drive, the eastern extension of Sussex Drive.

For security reasons, there is no strolling around the grounds of either place, but at the latter residence 45-minute walking tours are given, with stories of some of the goings-on over the years. Tours are offered through the day, in summer only.

The Governor General's house was built in the early 1900s. At the main gate there's the small Changing of the Guard ceremony, which happens on the hour through the day, from the end of June to the end of August.

## ROCKCLIFFE VILLAGE

East along Sussex Drive, this is one of the poshest, most prestigious areas in the country. Behind the mansion doors live some very prominent Canadian citizens and many foreign diplomats.

## PRINCE OF WALES FALLS

Where the Rideau River meets the canal south of town (at the junction of Colonel By St and Hog's Back Rd), there are falls, walking and cycling paths, and some historical plaques.

## RCMP STABLES & PRACTICE GROUND

Even the Mounties have to practise, and the RCMP Stables & Practice Ground (☎ 993-3751) is where the musical ride pageant is perfected. The public is welcome to watch the practice sessions and the other equestrian displays held from time to time.

Every evening for the week prior to Canada Day, there is a full musical ride with band. Otherwise the daily evening practices are without the band and colourful uniforms. Also note that the ride is sometimes away on tour. Call for details. Tours are given of the stables Monday to Friday from 9 to 11 am and 1.30 to 3.30 pm.

The grounds are out of the centre. If travelling by car, take Sussex Drive east to the

Rockcliffe Parkway. At Birch St, turn right to the grounds. No admission fee is charged.

## LOG FARM

A re-creation of a 19th-century farm (☎ 825-4352), complete with costumed workers, this site is 20 km west of Parliament Hill. Both here and at Jacques Cartier Park, there are historical exhibits and activities, some of which you can participate in. Sporadically through the year, special events are put on. The farm is open daily in summer but on Sunday only for the rest of the year. Admission is $4.50 per adult, less for seniors, and there is a family rate.

## ACTIVITIES

In summer you can rent a boat for trips along the canal. Canoe and rowing-boat rentals are at Dows Lake Marina (☎ 232-5278), or at the marina on Hog's Back Rd (☎ 736-9893). Hourly to weekly rentals are available.

Surrounding the city on the east, south and west and connecting with the Ottawa River on each side is a broad strip of connected parkland known as the Greenbelt. Within this area of woodlands, marsh and fields are nature trails, bicycle paths, boardwalks and picnic areas. In the western Greenbelt, 20 minutes by vehicle from the downtown area off Richmond Rd, the Stony Swamp Interpretive Centre has a staff naturalist, trails and displays about the area. It's open from Friday to Sunday. On the eastern side of the Greenbelt is another conservation area, Mer Bleue. The Greenbelt is not entirely a reserve: the airport lies within it, for example.

There are several outfits not far from Ottawa which run one or two-day whitewater rafting trips. No experience is needed and the locations are less than two hours from town. Two organisations to call, both in Foresters Falls, are Wilderness Tours (☎ 646-2241 in Quebec or ☎ 1-800-267-9166) and OWL Rafting (☎ 1-800-461-7238). The Ottawa and the Magnetawan are two rivers that are used. Book ahead for weekends, as the trips fill up. Considerable savings can be enjoyed by going on a weekday.

In winter there's skiing as close as 20 km from town, in the Gatineau Hills. Two resorts with variously graded hills are Camp Fortune and Mont Cascades. Tow passes are more expensive on weekends. Gatineau Park has excellent cross-country ski trails with lodges along the way for warming up in. In warm weather, the park is good for walking and picnicking.

Again in winter, the Rideau Canal is famous for the skating along five km of maintained ice. Rest spots on the way serve great doughnuts (known as beavertails) to go with the hot chocolate, although the beaver must be getting scarce to judge by the prices. Ask at the tourist office about skate rentals.

The city has an excellent parks system with a lot of inner-city green space. There are many walking, jogging and cycling trails as well as picnic areas. You'll even find some fishing. The tourist office has a sheet, with map, of all the parks and a description of each. Bicycle paths wind all over town; get a map of them. For rentals see the Getting Around section.

## ORGANISED TOURS

Gray Coach Line (☎ 748-4426) offers a 50-km, two-hour tour of the city. They operate daily from April to October. Tickets are available from the departure point, on Wellington St near the Château Laurier, on the north side of Confederation Square. They also do longer tours of the region.

A double-decker bus makes a similar, though shorter, trip. It operates only during summer and is run by Piccadiily Tours.

Capital City Trolley Tours (237-5158) uses a bus decorated to look like a trolley (?!) to run tours of the city, allowing passengers to get on and off at any of 14 stops along the way. A ticket is $15 and rides begin at Confederation Square.

Paul's Boat Lines (☎ 235-8409) runs cruises on the Ottawa River and the Rideau Canal. Each takes about 1½ hours and costs $9.50, less for kids. For tickets and information, there is a dock at the Rideau Canal, across from the National Arts Centre

The Ottawa Riverboat Company

(☎ 562-4888), at 173 Dalhousie St, does much the same thing but along the river only. Some trips include dinner and/or dancing.

Choo Choo (☎ 778-7246) runs a two-hour trip by steam engine up the Gatineau River area to Wakefield, daily from the end of May to the end of September and then less frequently through October. The Gatineau is a major north-south tributary of the Ottawa River. Call about ticket prices, as they vary a lot – a tip is that money will be saved if you go on a weekday. The lunches in the Railway Station Restaurant in Wakefield are very good.

Ottawa Valley Tours (☎ 725-3045) runs several day trips to attractions in Eastern Ontario, including the Thousand Islands, Upper Canada Village and Kingston.

## FESTIVALS
Some of the major events held here are:

January-February
> Winterlude – In late January and early February, the good and popular Winterlude is held. The three consecutive weekends of festivities centre mainly on or around frozen Dows Lake and the canal. The ice sculptures are really worth seeing.

May
> Canadian Tulip Festival – A big annual event is the Canadian Tulip Festival in May, when the city is decorated with 200 types of tulips, mainly from Holland. Festivities include parades, regattas, car rallies, dances, concerts and fireworks.

June
> Franco-Ontarien Festival – Held in June, this festival is good fun and an opportunity to see some of the country's French culture through music, crafts and more.

July-August
> Astrolabe – In July and August the outdoor stage in Major's Hill Park, known as Astrolabe, is used for concerts, dance, mime and other performances. It's open nightly and is free.
> International Jazz Festival – This event lasts for 10 days at the end of July, with venues in Ottawa and Hull.
> Central Canada Exhibition – An annual event held towards the end of August, it involves 10 days of displays, a carnival and entertainment. The exhibition is held at Lansdowne Park.

## PLACES TO STAY
### Camping
There is an excellent camping site practically right in the centre of town for $7.50 per night per person, with a stay limited to five nights. You'll find room for 200 tents on the corner of Fleet and Booth Sts. The site is called Camp Le Breton (☎ 943-0467), west along Wellington St past the Parliament Buildings. The camp, designed primarily for cyclists and hikers, has no electric or water hook-ups and is for tents only. It's open from mid-May to Labour Day (early in September). The city bus from the downtown area goes right to the campground, which is near the Ottawa River. Close to the campground are some rapids known as Chaudière Falls.

Camp Hither Hills (☎ 822-0509), 10 km south of the city limits on Hwy 31 (Bank St), charges $13 for a tent.

There are other places to camp both east and west of town on Hwy 17. The tourist office has lists of places in the Ottawa area, and there is camping in Gatineau Park, across the river in Quebec province.

### Hostels
The HI Ottawa Hostel (☎ 235-2595), at 75 Nicholas St, in the old Ottawa jail – see the gallows at the back – is one of the best known hostels in the country. It has a very good, central location near the Parliament Buildings. Nicholas St is just east of the Rideau Canal, off Rideau St. There are 150 beds in the restored building, some of them in old cells – wake up behind bars.

Prices are $14 for members, $18 for non-members. Facilities include kitchen and laundry, and there is a café in summer. This is another busy hostel, and though it is quite large, reservations are recommended in mid-summer, and in February when the Winterlude Festival is on. The hostel is open all year. Check-in is from 7 am to 2 am.

There is a new houseboat service which plies the Rideau Canal from here to the hostel in Kingston. For details see under Kingston.

The No 4 bus from the bus station at the corner of Arlington and Kent Sts goes within two blocks of the hostel. From the train station, the No 95 bus does the same thing.

The *YM-YWCA* (☎ 237-1320) is at 180 Argyle Ave on the corner of O'Connor St, in the southern downtown area. Singles for either sex are $40 with a shared bathroom; better value are doubles for $49. More expensive rooms with private bath are available. There's a cafeteria and a pool which guests can use.

The *University of Ottawa* (☎ 564-5400) has some of the cheapest dormitory space in Canada. The dorms are open for visitors from May to August. Rates for singles/doubles are $19/34 for students, $31/39 for non-students. They have laundry facilities, a swimming pool, parking, and a cafeteria with cheap meals. Reception is at 100 Hastey St. The university is an easy walk south-east of the Parliament Buildings. They also offer accommodation at Little White Fish Camp, in Gracefield, Quebec, where there are extensive sports facilities.

*Carleton University* (☎ 788-5609), pretty central but south of the downtown core, has a residence offering summer rooms at 1233 Colonel By Drive. The price is $29 per person with breakfast included. Athletic facilities and full meal service are available. Check at the Tour & Conference Centre in the Commons Building at the university. Families are welcome.

### Tourist Homes & B&Bs

Spending nights in this town can make a mess of a budget. While not necessarily the cheapest form of accommodation in Ottawa (motels and some hotels are about the same price), this category generally has the advantage of a central location, a bit of personality and breakfast. There are quite a few places, with a range of prices and facilities. Some are simply an extra room in a resident's house; others are commercial enterprises in the small European hotel tradition. Many fall somewhere between the two.

Ottawa B&B (☎ 563-0161) is an organisation listing, promoting and booking such places. There are city, suburban and country

locations and prices begin at $45/55 for singles/doubles.

Another such service is Capital B&B Reservation Service (☎ 737-4129), again with a variety of places and locations, and they can find places all year round. Prices vary. Some locations offer perks such as fireplaces or swimming pools and nearly all have free parking at least.

The tourist office also should have some information about tourist homes.

Generally, whether independent or under an agency, the places closer to the centre of town are more expensive than those further out. I've included mostly the central ones because of their added convenience to the city's sites and because they do not require a car for easy access. Many of them offer free parking, however. Almost all prices include breakfast, but this may vary from continental to full.

In the downtown area, just east over the canal and south of Rideau St, is a small pocket where many of the central guesthouses are found. Convenient Daly St has some good places but they are not among the cheapest. Smaller places with just a few rooms do not have to charge tax.

The Swiss-style *Gasthaus Switzerland Inn* (☎ 237-0335) has one of the best locations in town, at 89 Daly St, two blocks south of Rideau St and the market. Go south along Cumberland St to Daly St and it's near the north-east corner. The No 4 bus runs along Rideau St from the downtown area. The guesthouse has been created out of a large, old stone house and now has 17 rooms with varying amenities. Cheapest are the single rooms with shared bathroom, which go for $52 with a breakfast of muesli, bread, cheese and coffee. Singles/doubles with private bath are $68/78. Prices go down a few dollars through the winter. The managers, from Switzerland, speak an impressive array of languages, including German and French. Another plus is the laundry.

At 201 Daly St is the heritage *Maison-McFarlane House* (☎ 241-0095), with singles/doubles at $55/65. There are only three rooms but they include full bathroom and air-conditioning, and there is parking. The pricier suite has its own jacuzzi.

Also on Daly St, at No 185, *McGee's Inn* (☎ 237-6089) has 14 rooms in a restored Victorian mansion. Prices here are about the same, beginning at $62/68 and increasing with the number of features. Some rooms here have private bathrooms, which is not the norm in tourist homes, and a full breakfast is included.

Guesthouses of varying size and price seem to constantly open and close along Stewart St, one block south of Daly St. A stroll along the street may also turn up someone who has just opened a few rooms for the summer. There are certainly some fine houses in the neighbourhood. Recommended is *Ottawa House* (☎ 789-4433), at 264 Stewart St, run by the friendly Connie McElman. Three rooms with shared bath are available in this Victorian house, at $60/75 a single/double. A good breakfast is included.

Another good street to check is Marlborough St, south-east of Daly and Stewart Sts, south from Laurier Ave, west of the Rideau River. It is still quite central but a bit of a walk to the downtown area – it takes around half an hour to the parliament buildings. Prices here are quite a bit lower.

*Australis Guesthouse* (☎ 235-8461), with three rooms, is at 35 Marlborough St and is quite good value. Singles/doubles with shared bath cost $40/50 (including breakfast) and there are lower weekly rates.

Not far away, at 329 Laurier Ave East, the *Laurier Guesthouse* (☎ 238-5525) has three rooms from as low as $35/45. There is also a more deluxe suite with a fireplace. Breakfast is included in the room prices.

There are a couple of places to check in the convenient Bytown Market area north of Rideau St. The inviting, rural-looking *Foisy House* (☎ 562-1287), at 188 St Andrew St, has three rooms and charges $45 a single or double with breakfast. It has a pool, which can be a real plus. St Andrew St runs east-west through the market area a couple of blocks north of most of the action.

Another central place to try is *L'Auberge du Marché* (☎ 235-7697), at 87 Guigues

Ave. It's a renovated older house with three rooms ($45/55) and there is parking.

Closer to the downtown area but on the other side of the canal, *Beatrice Lyon* (☎ 236-3904) takes in guests all year long at her home at 479 Slater St (about four blocks west of Bank St, near the corner of Percy St). The three rooms are good, simple and some of the cheapest in town ($35/45 including breakfast). The owner will not only accept children as guests but will even look after them!

Also in this section of town is *Albert House* (☎ 236-4479), 478 Albert St, but this is more a real inn, with 17 rooms. It is more expensive than the small, modest guesthouses – from $59/69 a single/double – but it has a good location, is a heritage home and offers all the comforts.

If Ottawa seems booked up or you want to try staying across the river in Quebec, there are some guesthouses listed under Hull.

### Hotels – bottom end

There are few older or budget hotels in Ottawa. Most moderately priced accommodation is in motels away from the town centre, or in tourist homes.

One of the very few older no-star hotels left in town is the *Somerset House Hotel* (☎ 233-7762), at 352 Somerset St West. It has 35 rooms starting at $34/45 with shared bath, $50/62 with private facilities. Somerset St runs perpendicular to Bank St about 10 blocks from the Parliament Buildings.

The next two choices have little character but are not bad value. The *Townhouse Motor Hotel* (☎ 789-5555), at 319 Rideau St, charges $55/58. The *Parkway Motor Hotel* (☎ 789-3781), at 475 Rideau St, is also close to the downtown area. Singles/doubles cost $54/58, including breakfast in the inexpensive coffee shop.

The *Butler Motor Hotel* (☎ 746-4641) is comparable, at $50/58. The 95 rooms are large and it's just a five-minute drive to downtown. The hotel is at 112 Montreal Rd.

### Efficiencies

The central *Doral Inn* (☎ 230-8055), at 486 Albert St, is good value; there are 35 rooms at $59/69 a single/double, plus a few house-keeping units (kitchenettes). The inn has a coffee shop and a swimming pool.

The renovated *Capital Hill Motel & Suites* (☎ 235-1413), at 88 Albert St, is much larger, has kitchen facilities and can be a relative bargain. A room with two double beds, suitable for four people, goes for $59. Note that prices are slated to rise but only marginally. Relative to the high-priced downtown hotels, this is still a good deal.

### Hotels – middle & top end
In the middle range is the straightforward *Journey's End Hotel* (☎ 789-7511), at 290 Rideau St. Singles/doubles are $79/89.

The *Hotel Roxborough* (☎ 237-5171), 123 Metcalfe St, is one of the city's top hotels and is expensive, with rooms starting from $70, but look for some good weekend specials.

The classic *Château Laurier*, the castle-like place at 1 Rideau St, by the canal, is the city's best known hotel and a landmark in its own right. Rates are $100 to $150 and there is a large indoor swimming pool.

During the summer, when Parliament is in recess and business traffic is light, many of the corporate-oriented downtown hotels offer very good daily and weekend specials. For example, the *Aristocrat Hotel* (☎ 232-9471), at 131 Cooper St, rents its rooms at $55 for two people. The stately old *Lord Elgin* (☎ 235-3333), at 100 Elgin St (with free parking), has summer prices starting at $79. Even the Château Laurier offers discounts.

### Motels
There are two main motel strips, one on each side of the downtown area. On the east side, look along Montreal Rd, an extension of Rideau St, which leads east out of town. The motels are about six km from the downtown area.

The *Miss Ottawa* (☎ 745-1531), 2098 Montreal Rd, charges $45/55 a single/double and has a pool. The *Beacon Hill Motel* (☎ 745-6818), at 1668 Montreal Rd, is slightly more costly. It has a swimming pool too. The *Concorde Motel* (☎ 745-2112), at

333 Montreal Rd in Vanier, is simpler and less expensive, at $45 a double.

On the west side of town, check along Carling Ave, where there are numerous places to choose from about 10 km from downtown. The *Stardust* (☎ 828-2748), at 2965 Carling Ave, charges $42 a single or double for its 25 rooms. There are others closer to the centre but they tend to be more costly. *Webb's Motel* (☎ 728-1881), at 1705 Carling Ave, for example, is more expensive ($58) but has its own restaurant.

### PLACES TO EAT
Hull has the best restaurants but Ottawa has a pretty good range of places in the lower and mid-price brackets. I've grouped them by area.

#### Market
We'll start with the market – it's central, very popular and offers a good selection of places to eat. During the warm months, many of the eateries in the area have outdoor tables.

For breakfast try *Zak's Diner*, a 1950s-style eatery at 14 Byward St, which opens early and stays open late. It's usually busy and is cheap. For something a little quieter, the *Domus Café*, at 269 Dalhousie St (at the back of the Domus Kitchenware store), is recommended. It's open every day from 9 am (11 am on Sunday) for breakfast and lunch and the food is becoming well known.

The *Café Bohemian*, at 89 Clarence St, is good for lunch or dinner. It's a busy European-style place with meals like quiche, fish and the latest trendy foods for $5 to $8. Sunday brunch is good value, with desserts and coffee. Café au lait is good here, especially the large size served in a bowl.

Across the street, the inexpensive *Bagel Bagel* has all sorts of bagel toppings and sandwiches, as well as salads and other light meals and deli items. It's open daily and is also a good spot for breakfast.

The *William St Café*, at 47 William St, is pleasant, with one side for eating and one for drinking. The place is good for snacks or a meal ($4 to $9). Try the carrot cake. Across the street is another café, the *Heritage Café*, in the market building itself.

*La Crêpe de France* is at 76 Murray St, at the corner of Parent Ave. It specialises in crêpes and has a patio bar and glassed-in terrace. Similar, but a bit less casual and a little more expensive, is the *Crêperie*, on the corner of York and By Ward Sts, with salads and crêpes from $4.50 to $8.95.

For inexpensive pasta dishes there is *Oregano's*, on the corner of William and George Sts. There is a good-value, all-you-can-eat lunch ($5.95) or, for another dollar, an early-bird dinner (from 4.30 to 7 pm) of pasta, salad and soup. On Sunday the menu changes slightly and there is a brunch.

Another international choice is *Las Palmas*, at 111 Parent Ave, which has been recommended for its Mexican food. The fajitas especially are not to be missed.

Excellent Indian food is dished up at the *Haveli*, 87 George St. The tandoori chicken is highly recommended. Also in the market building, at the York St end, look for the stand selling 'beavertails' – hot, flat doughnuts which first became popular when sold to skaters along the canal in winter. There is a food fair in the Rideau Centre.

## Downtown

Along Bank St and its side streets are numerous restaurants.

*Suisha Gardens*, on Slater St near the corner of Bank St, is a highly recommended Japanese place. The food is excellent (though somewhat Westernised), the environment authentic and the service perfect. The best room is downstairs and to the left. It's inexpensive at lunch time; prices are higher after 6 pm.

There are several British-style pubs around; try the *Royal Oak*, 318 Bank St, for British beer and food. It's friendly and you can play darts. The *Duke of Somerset*, at 352 Somerset St West, is similar.

*Kamal's*, at 683 Bank St, has good Lebanese food ($3 to $9) and is licensed.

*Flippers*, upstairs on the corner of Bank St and Fourth Ave, is a reliable fish restaurant with main courses (entrées) from $10 to $16.

Further south, the *Glebe Café*, at 840 Bank St, is good. It offers a few Middle Eastern dishes, some vegetarian food and burgers. Try the lentil soup. Prices are $4 to $9. It's a casual place, with newspapers to read, local information and an entertainment noticeboard.

At 895 Bank St, *Mexicali Rosa's* is pleasantly decorated and has tasty, moderately priced Mexican food. There are three other locations around town.

Good, cheap, mainly vegetarian Indian food can be found at the simple and unlikely named *Roses Café*, at 523 Gladstone Ave, between Bay and Lyon Sts. It's closed on Sundays.

All through the downtown area and around the market, look for one of the numerous chip wagons, with names like *Chipsy Rose*. They're excellent for French fries and hamburgers.

## Chinatown

Ottawa has a small Chinatown, within walking distance west of the centre. It's based around the corner of Bronson St and Somerset St West. There are quite a few restaurants; for Cantonese food the *Yang Sheng*, right on the corner, is cheap and not bad.

*Ben Ben*, at 697 Somerset St, has been recommended for Sichuan and Cantonese food, as has the *Mekong*, at 637 Somerset St, good for Vietnamese food as well as for Chinese dishes.

There are also a few Chinese places on Rideau St.

For a splurge, *Chez Jean Pierre*, at 210 Somerset St West, is said to be good for French food. If you're out this way, why not go a little further to 200 Preston St (Preston St runs north-south), a few blocks west of Bronson St, and try the *Paticceria-Gelateria Italiana* for a dessert and coffee.

## Rideau St

Across the canal from Wellington St, this area also has a number of eateries. The difficult-to-find *Sitar*, at 417A Rideau St, is in the bottom of a high-rise building not far east from the canal. It's not cheap ($22 to $34 for two) but the Indian food is good.

*Nate's*, at No 316, is something of a local

institution. This Jewish delicatessen is known far and wide for its low prices on basic food. The popular breakfast special is the cheapest in the country ($1.75 for the works). Ask for the Rideau Rye – good bread for toast. The service is incredibly fast. They also serve things like blintzes and cream-cheese bagels. It's open and busy on Sunday.

### Elgin St
A stroll along Elgin St always turns up a couple of places to eat; it's popular for night-spots too. The *Ritz*, at 274 Elgin St, is very good for Italian food; in fact, there's usually a line of people waiting to get in. Prices range from $5 to $12. *Charlie's Party Palace*, known simply as the Party Palace, is at 252 Elgin St (with the neon sign jutting out over the sidewalk). This locally famous place has been around forever. It serves the usual low-cost Canadian standards well and quickly and is another place that's good for breakfast.

## ENTERTAINMENT
### Music
Check Friday's *Ottawa Citizen* for complete club and entertainment listings.

*Zaphod Beeblebrox*, at 27 York St, is a popular eclectic place for live punk, new-age rock, African, rhythm and blues, and other alternative bands. Saturday and Sunday matinees feature rockabilly and jazz respectively. They also have a good selection of small brewery beers.

*Barrymores*, on Bank St, has live rock and blues and is a busy spot. The *New Live Penguin Café*, at 292 Elgin St, brings in a very good assortment of jazz, blues and folk acts. There is a cover charge (which varies). Comfortable *Irene's Pub Restaurant*, at 885 Bank St, often has live Celtic and folk music to go with the great variety of imported beers.

*Patty's Place* is a cosy Irish pub with music from Thursday to Saturday and an outdoor patio in summer. It's on the corner of Bank and Euclid Sts. *Yuk Yuk's*, in the Beacon Arms Hotel, 88 Albert St, has live stand-up comedy from Thursday to Saturday – admission is not cheap, however. The

*Hotel Lafayette*, in Bytown Market on York St, is good for its cheap draught beer day or night. It's your basic dive, but its character and characters attract a wide cross-section of people.

For jazz, *Friends & Company*, at 221 Rideau St, has a live band on Saturday after-noons and Tuesday nights. There's folk music upstairs at night.

For details of other local entertainment, see the Hull section.

### Performing Arts
The *National Arts Centre*, known as the NAC, has theatres for drama and opera and is home to the symphony orchestra. It also presents a range of concerts and films. It's on the banks of the canal, in Confederation Square.

### Cinema
There are several repertory theatres around Ottawa, showing two films a night. The *Mayfair* (☎ 234-3403), at 1074 Bank St, charges $7 for nonmembers but has less expensive matinees. The *Bytown Cinema* (☎ 789-3456), at 325 Rideau St, between King Edward and Nelson Sts, is about the same price.

*Cinémathèque Canada* (☎ 232-6727), the Canadian Film Institute, also presents non-commercial alternative, classic and foreign films on a regular basis at the theatre in the Canadian Museum of Civilisation in Hull.

For details of film showings in the National Arts Centre, check the box office or newspaper.

## GETTING THERE & AWAY
### Air
The airport is 20 minutes south of the city and is surprisingly small. The main airlines serving the city are Canadian Airlines (☎ 237-1380) and Air Canada (☎ 237-5000). Canadian Airlines destinations include Toronto ($176), Halifax ($301) and Winnipeg ($399). Excursion fares (return) are much cheaper. Air Canada fares, promo-tional sales aside, are much the same.

ONTARIO

**Bus**
The bus station is at 265 Catherine St, near Bank St, about a dozen blocks south of the downtown area. The main bus lines are Voyageur which runs to Montreal and Greyhound which runs to Toronto. Both lines can be contacted on ☎ 238-5900. One-way fares include Toronto $50, Kingston $25, Montreal $24 and Sudbury $65. Students can get a third off the price for a book of tickets; ask about it.

There are about seven buses daily to Montreal and Toronto, some of which are express. There are frequent departures for Kingston, Belleville, Sudbury and other towns.

**Train**
The VIA Rail station (☎ 244-8289) is out of the centre, in a big building a long way south-east of the downtown area. It's at 200 Tremblay Rd, near the junction of Alta Vista Rd and Hwy 417, just east of the Rideau Canal.

There are four trains a day to Toronto and to Montreal.

One-way fares include Toronto $69, Kingston $29 and Montreal $32. Booking at least five days in advance can sometimes save up to 40% if you avoid peak days, eg Friday.

For trips west, say to Sudbury, there is no longer a direct line. Connections must be made in Toronto, so it's now a long trip.

**Car**
Tilden (☎ 232-3536) is at 199 Slater St and also at the airport. Their small-car rate is $29 per day (with 250 free km, and 10 cents per km after that) or – not bad value – $169 a week (with 1500 free km). Also ask about the unlimited km rates.

Budget and Hertz also have outlets, which aren't as central as the Tilden office.

**Ride Sharing**
Allo Stop (☎ 778-8877), a popular service in Montreal, Quebec City and Toronto which gets drivers together with passengers, now has an office in Ottawa. Call to see what they have going. It should not be difficult to get low-priced share rides to the cities mentioned above, or to Kingston.

Carleton University's radio station, CKCU (☎ 788-2898), also has a ride-sharing bulletin board – people call in with rides wanted/offered.

**Hitching**
Hitching is easy between Montreal and Ottawa but is convoluted if you're heading for Toronto. Going to Montreal, take the eastbound Montreal-Ogilvy bus on Rideau St; this leads to Hwy 17 East, where you can begin. For Toronto take Hwy 31 south to Hwy 401 near the town of Morrisburg. The busy Hwy 401 (probably the most travelled route in Canada) connects Toronto with Montreal and hitching is fairly common along the way. For a more rural trip, take Hwy 7 to Tweed and Hwy 37 to Belleville, then Hwy 401 from there.

## GETTING AROUND
### To/From the Airport
The cheapest way to get to the airport is by city bus. Take bus No 5 on Elgin St going south (away from the river) to Billings Bridge Mall and then transfer to the No 96 to the airport. Or simply catch the No 96 as it runs along Slater downtown.

There is also an airport bus, which leaves every half hour on the half hour from in front of the Château Laurier Hotel from 6.30 am to midnight. It costs $7 and takes about 25 minutes. The bus is not as frequent on weekends; ask about scheduling.

### Bus
Both Ottawa and Hull operate separate bus systems. A transfer is valid from one system to the other but may require an extra partial payment. The city bus system here is volatile, with frequent changes in routes and fares. There is a two-tier fare structure: during peak hours (6.30 to 8.30 am and 3 to 5.30 pm Monday to Friday), a ticket is $2; at any other time, the fare drops to $1.30. Using tickets is cheaper than cash, and these can be

purchased at many convenience or corner milk stores.

For Ottawa information call ☎ 741-4390 – they're very helpful. All Ottawa buses quit by around midnight, most earlier. Drop in at the office of OC Transport (which runs the city buses) and get a Tourpass, good for unlimited use for one day (beginning after 9.30 am). The office is central, at 294 Albert St. You can take the following buses from downtown to:

Bus station – No 4 south on Bank St or, more frequently, either the No 1 or No 7 stop within a block of the terminal
Train station – Transitway No 95 east on Slater St
Museum of Nature – No 14 on Elgin St is good but Nos 99, 1, 4 and 7 all go within a block or so
Aviation Museum – Transitway Nos 95 or 99 to Saint Laurent Blvd and transfer to No 198 to the museum
Hull – No 8 west on Wellington St, but only during the day; the Outaouais bus service runs to Rideau St from Hull and continues at night.

## Car & Motorbike
Visitors to the city can park free at many locations; get the details at any tourist information office.

## Bicycle
Ottawa is the best city in Canada for cyclists, with an extensive system of paths in and around town and through the parks. Get a bicycle route map from a tourist office.

For rentals try Cycle Tour Rent-A-Bike (☎ 233-0268), at the Château Laurier. They're open every day from May to September and rent three, five and 10-speed bikes. ID is required. They run tours, with discounts for HI hostel members, and have a repair shop as well. It's at the side of the hotel, near the entrance to the parking garage.

## HULL
Across the river, in Quebec, Hull is as much the other half of Ottawa as it is a separate city (that's why it's included in the Ontario chapter of this book). It warrants a visit for more than the Canadian Museum of Civilisation. Hull now has its share of government

offices, and workers cross the river in both directions each day, but the Hull side remains home to most of the area's French population. The architecture (at least the older stuff) is different, and you'll find the top restaurants here, as well as livelier, later nightlife.

Promenade du Portage, easily found from either Pont du Portage or Alexandra Bridge, is the main downtown street. Between the two bridges are numerous and varied eating spots, bars and discos, Place Aubry (a square), as well as a few places where people have to work.

The City Hall, known as Maison du Citoyen, is an attention-getting, dominating modern building with a 20-metre-high glass tower in the centre of town, at 25 Rue Laurier. It also contains an art gallery and a meditation centre (what English-speaking bureaucracy would do that?).

The tourist office for Hull, La Maison du Tourisme, is at the corner of Boulevard Saint Laurent and Rue Laurier, just over the Alexandra Bridge. There is also a tourist information desk in the Maison du Citoyen (☎ 778-2222); it covers the Outaouais region of western Quebec. The desk is open every day in summer, on weekdays only for the rest of the year.

A free two-hour walking tour of Hull begins at the tourist office in the Maison du Citoyen at 10 am Monday to Friday during July and August, taking in much of the history and green areas of central Hull. Call to confirm, as government cutbacks have threatened this programme.

In July, Hull is home to the Gatineau Clog, a weekend-long bluegrass festival. The tourist office has a list of other events based on this side of the river.

Hull is also the main city of the region of Quebec known as Outaouais (which is pronounced basically as though you were saying Ottawa with a French accent). The Quebec government has a booklet outlining the region's attractions and activities, mostly of the outdoor variety. Within a few hours' drive, there are some huge parks and reserves.

ONTARIO

## Canadian Museum of Civilisation

The Canadian Museum of Civilisation
(☎ 776-7000) is Ottawa/Hull's feature
museum. It's in the large, modern complex
with the copper domes at 100 Rue Laurier,
Hull, on the river bank opposite the Parliament Buildings. The museum is principally
concerned with the history of Canadians.
The permanent upper-level History Hall
presents displays and realistic re-creations
tracing the story of the European founding,
voyages of the country's explorers, settlement and historical developments through to
the 1880s. The Basque ship section, complete with the sound of creaking wood in the
living quarters, brings to life the voyages
undertaken to reach the New World. Also

Native Indian vase

particularly good are the Acadian farm
model and the replica of the early Quebec
town square.

The main level consists of three halls containing temporary exhibits on varying
aspects of human history, culture and art.

The Native Indian & Inuit Art Gallery
usually, but not always, offers various shows
by Native Canadian artists – painting, dance,
crafts and more. Don't miss the chance to see
the art of British Columbian Indians, especially that of the Haida, if there is any on
display.

You'll need roughly three hours for a reasonably thorough look at the above two
levels, as they're not laid out especially well
and you'll need some time to get oriented.

The Grand Hall of the lower level, with its
simulated forest and seashore, offers explanations of the huge totems and other coastal
Native Indian structures. In the entertaining
and educational Children's Museum section,
exhibits permit hands-on interaction.

Cineplus is a film theatre for IMAX and
OMNIMAX, realistic large-format film presentations. The always changing shows are
extremely popular, with waits of two to three
shows not uncommon, so arrive early for a
ticket.

There is a good cafeteria, which offers,
among other things, sandwiches and a salad
bar or economical full meals, all served
within view of the river and Parliament Hill.

There is also a bookstore and a gift shop,
which are worth a look.

From April to September the museum is
open every day; for the rest of the year it is
closed on Monday. On Thursday it stays
open until 8 pm; otherwise it closes at 6 pm
during the summer and an hour earlier the
rest of the year. Admission is $4.50, less for
seniors and kids. A cineplus ticket is extra;
prices vary depending on the show but tend
to be rather high. Again, it's less for kids and
seniors. Admission is free from 5 to 8 pm on
Thursday. Parking can be found under the
museum.

## Places to Stay

If you want to stay on this side of the river,

there are a number of accommodation choices.

The *Couette & Croissant* (☎ 771-2200), at 330 Champlain St, a short drive north-east, is a B&B in central Hull. Although a bit of a walk from Promenade du Portage, it's quite close to the Canadian Museum of Civilisation.

There are others, and prices tend to be a bit lower here than the Ottawa average. The tourist office also has information on B&Bs in the surrounding area, with places around Gatineau Park and Aylmer, Quebec, just up the Ottawa River. Motels can be found along Boulevard Taché, which runs beside the river to the west of downtown Hull after coming across the bridge from Ottawa.

There are also some large, typical business-oriented hotels in the central area.

### Places to Eat
For a bite, head for *Café Le Coquetier*, at 145 Promenade du Portage, an unpretentious, casual bistro with very good yet cheap food. *Le Bistro*, on Rue Aubry just off Promenade du Portage, is a bar/café serving light lunches for no more than $6 or $7, usually less. There's an outdoor patio in summer. A similar place is found at 44 Rue Laval.

The central *Brasserie Le Vieux Hull*, at 50 Rue Victoria, in the Place du Portage office complex, is an inexpensive tavern for a beer or two or a cheap meal, and there is a low-priced cafeteria geared to staff in the building, too.

Rues Papineau and Montcalm have several restaurants, including some of the expensive French ones for which the city has a reputation.

### Entertainment
Boulevard Saint Joseph has several popular, up-market discos. Also a bit out of the centre, but with live music in a large, friendly, typically Québecois brasserie, *Les Raftsmen* is at 60 Rue Saint Raymond, which runs east of Boulevard Saint Joseph. They also have a menu of standard beer-hall fare at good prices, served until 9 pm.

After 1 am, when the Ontario bars close, partygoers head across the river from Ottawa

to Hull, where things are open until 3 am and later. Promenade du Portage, in the middle of the downtown area, has numerous nightspots, some with live music, some dressy, some quiet and dark – there's a good range.

*Chez Henri*, on Promenade du Portage, is an up-market disco. *Le Bistro* attracts a more casual and younger crowd for loud dance music. It's on Rue Aubry, at the top of the hill, on the brick pedestrian mall off the Promenade. There are plenty of other places in the area. Local jazz groups play at the *Saint Jacques*, Rue Saint Jacques in Hull, every Friday and Saturday night.

### Getting There & Away
**Bus** The Outaouais Bus System (☎ 770-3242) has buses which run along Rideau and Wellington Sts in Ottawa. From downtown Ottawa, bus Nos 33, 35, 41 and 42 all go to Promenade du Portage. Within Hull, the bus Nos 37 or 60 go up to and along Boulevard Saint Joseph.

**Bicycle** A bicycle route over the Alexandra Bridge from Ottawa connects with a trail system which goes around much of the Hull centre and to Ruisseau de la Brasserie (Brewery Creek), a park area east of downtown Hull.

### AROUND OTTAWA-HULL
#### Gatineau Park
Gatineau Park is a deservedly popular 36,000-hectare area of woods and lakes in the Gatineau Hills of Quebec lying across the river from Ottawa, north-west of downtown Hull.

It's only a 20-minute drive from the parliament buildings in Ottawa. On weekends some roads may be closed to cars, and note that parking must be paid for at the more popular destinations such as Lac Meech and the King Estate.

The park has plenty of wildlife, including about 100 species of birds, as well as some 150 km of hiking trails. **Lac Meech, Lac Phillipe** and **Lac Lapêche** have beaches for swimming and so are the most popular. Many of the camping facilities are around

Lapêche and are accessible by canoe only. (Canoes can be rented.) You can fish in the lakes and streams, and the hiking trails are good for cross-country (nordic) skiing in winter. Small **Pink Lake** is pretty but is now off limits for swimming. A boardwalk rims the lake for strolling. The lake is best during the week, when there are fewer people around. The nude beach at Lac Meech is now a gay scene.

Also in the park is Kingsmere, the summer estate of William Lyon Mackenzie King, prime minister in the 1920s, late 1930s and early 1940s. Here he indulged his hobby of collecting ruins, both genuine and fake. In 1941, King had bits of London's House of Commons brought over after the German blitz. His home, **Moorside**, is now a museum. An astute politician, King was much interested in the occult and apparently talked to both his dead dog and deceased mother. There's a pleasant tea room at Moorside, with items such as cucumber sandwiches or blackforest ham on pumpernickel bread.

**Festivals** Occurring in September or October, **Fall Rhapsody** celebrates the brief but colourful season when the leaves change colour – a time when the maples and birches of the Gatineau Hills are having their last fling before winter. An arts festival is part of the affair, as are hot-air ballooning and various concerts and competitions. Events are held in the park, with a few around town as well. During Fall Rhapsody, there are cheap buses from Ottawa-Hull to various spots in Gatineau Park.

# Eastern Ontario

West from Ottawa there are two main routes through Ontario. Hwy 17, the Trans Canada Hwy, leads north-west to Pembroke, then continues to North Bay and on to Sudbury. This is the quickest way to western Canada.

From Pembroke, Hwy 60 leads west through the southern portion of Algonquin Park to Huntsville, where Hwy 11 runs north to North Bay and south to Toronto.

The southern route from Ottawa goes to the more populated southern region of Ontario, the St Lawrence River, the Great Lakes and Toronto. From Ottawa, Hwys 31 and 16 lead directly down to the 401, the expressway to Toronto. A prettier, though slower drive is to take Hwy 7 west out of Ottawa going through Perth and as far as Hwy 37. From here Hwy 37 leads south through Tweed before dropping down to Hwy 401. This route is a standard itinerary and is a compromise between speed and aesthetics. Taking Hwy 7 any further west really starts to add on the hours. By car between Ottawa and Toronto, is about five hours on the Hwys 7 and 37 route.

## EGANVILLE
North-west of Ottawa, this small town is worth a stop if you're going through for the nearby **Bonnechere Caves**, eight km southeast, but does not warrant a special trip. The caves and passages were the bottom of a tropical sea about 500 million years ago and contain fossils of animals from long before the dinosaur age. Pathways lead through parts of the extensive system, past fossil banks where you are likely to find fossils as well as stalactites. Tours are offered through the summer months at this privately developed and operated site.

## MERRICKVILLE
South-west of Ottawa, Merrickville is a small, pleasant late 18th-century town along the Rideau River/Canal route from Ottawa to Kingston. There are a couple of B&Bs in town, as well as some places to eat and a bakery along St Lawrence St. A few craft and antique shops can also be found in the central area.

Historic sites include the **locks** (dating from 1830) and the **blockhouse**, its metre-thick walls built by the British in 1832 to protect the canal in case of attack. The blockhouse is now a small museum.

## SMITHS FALLS

Midway along the Rideau Canal system, Smiths Falls is a small centre for the recreational boats that use the system. Unfortunately, there are no commercial ventures here for trips along the canal.

Smiths Falls has become known as much for the **Hershey Chocolate Factory** here as for its history or its canal location. A tour of the Canadian branch plant of this famous US chocolate company based in Hershey, Pennsylvania is recommended. Find out all about how chocolate bars are created and then start eating. It's open from Monday to Saturday and is on Hershey Drive off Hwy 43 East – just follow your nose. No tours are given on Saturdays.

Best of the three small historical museums is the **Rideau Canal Museum**, in a 19th-century mill at 34 Beckworth St South. Exhibits detail the history and operation of the canal.

## CORNWALL

Cornwall is the first city of any size in Ontario along the St Lawrence Valley and has the Seaway International Bridge to the USA. It was here in the 1870s that Thomas Edison, creator of the light bulb, helped set up the first factory lit by electricity.

Despite this corner of Ontario's having Scottish and Loyalist ancestry, there is a good-sized French population in Cornwall.

The Pitt St Mall, in the centre of town, is a pedestrian-only two-block section of stores and gardens.

There are a couple of **museums** in town, and the **R H Saunders Energy Information Centre** has displays on the big, important hydroelectric facility here. It's open daily in July and August, on weekdays only in June. Tours of the power facilities at the dam are available. The **Inverarden Regency Cottage Museum** represents Ontario's finest example of Regency Cottage architecture. Built in 1816 by a retiring fur trader who had evidently done quite well, it's on the corner of Hwy 2 and Boundary Rd and is open from April to November.

Just out of town, at the college on the Native Indian reserve on Cornwall Island, there is a **log cabin museum** focusing on the Cree, Iroquois and Ojibway Indians. It's not open on weekends. The big Native Indian powwow held at the reserve in July or August is worth catching, as it's one of the biggest in the province. Traditional crafts and souvenirs can be purchased.

The bridge over to Massena, New York makes Cornwall another busy port of entry for US visitors.

In **Maxville**, to the north, Scottish Highland Games held at the beginning of August commemorate the region's Scottish heritage. **St Raphael** has some interesting church ruins dating from 1815.

West of Cornwall, the **Long Sault Parkway** connects a series of parks and beaches along the river.

## MORRISBURG & UPPER CANADA VILLAGE

This small town lies west of Cornwall on the St Lawrence River. Despite its small size, it's known far and wide for its good historic site – Upper Canada Village (☎ 543-3704), the detailed re-creation of a country town of a century ago. About 40 buildings and costumed workers bring that past period to life. There's a blacksmith's shop, inn and sawmill as well as a working farm, and the setting is a fine one, on the river.

You'll need at least several hours to fully explore the site, which is open from 15 May to 15 October. Hours are 9.30 am to 5 pm. Admission is $9, less for kids.

Without transport, the village can be reached aboard buses running between Ottawa and Cornwall and on some buses which follow the Montreal to Toronto route. Many are direct, while others putt along, stopping at the smaller towns en route. Nearby **Crysler Battlefield Park** is a memorial to those who died fighting the Americans in 1812.

**Parks of the St Lawrence** (☎ 543-3704), a government agency based in Morrisburg, runs Upper Canada Village, the Upper Canada Migratory Bird Sanctuary and Old

ONTARIO

Fort Henry, as well as many of the campgrounds and parks along the river between Cornwall and Kingston.

Hwy 2 along the river is slower to travel on but provides a more scenic trip than Hwy 401. It's used by cyclists, including long-distance riders between Montreal and Toronto. There are numerous provincial parks along the way, especially east of town along the Long Sault Parkway. Going west there is a seaway-viewing platform at **Iroquois** and a good campground for cyclists.

There are about half a dozen motels in Morrisburg and four campgrounds. Among the latter is the *Upper Canada Migratory Bird Sanctuary Awareness Campsite* (☎ 543-3704). With that mouthful, just hope you don't have to tell too many people where you're staying. It's a little different from the average campground and is educational, too. Find it 14 km east of town along Hwy 2. They have about 50 tent sites but few creature comforts.

## PRESCOTT
Another 19th-century town, Prescott is the site of the International Bridge to Ogdensburg, New York. The harbour area has been overhauled and has a busy marina, but there isn't anything of note for the traveller passing through.

Just to the east of the downtown area and walkable from the centre is the **Fort Wellington National Historic Site** (☎ 925-2896). The original fort here was built during the War of 1812, fought against the Americans. It was rebuilt in 1838 and served militarily until the 1920s. Some original fortifications remain, as does a blockhouse and the officer's quarters from the 1830s. During the summer, guides in costume supplement the interpretive displays. In the third week of July, the fort hosts the country's largest military pageant, which includes mock battles in full regalia.

The fort is open daily from the end of May to the middle of October. Also here, outside the grounds, are a few picnic tables with views of the river.

## BROCKVILLE
A small community along the river, Brockville is a particularly attractive town, with its many old stone buildings and the classic-looking main street. The courthouse and jail in the centre of town date from 1842. During the summer, many of the finest buildings are lit up, accentuating the slight resort flavour of this casual river port by the Thousand Islands.

The historic museum in **Beecher House** provides a look at the area's history but there really is no reason to linger. The other principal attraction, the oldest train tunnel in the country, isn't worth the trouble.

For the Thousand Island Parkway area west of Brockville, see the Around Kingston section following the Kingston description.

## KINGSTON
Kingston (population 137,000) is a handsome town that retains much of its past through preservation of many historic buildings and defence structures. Built strategically where Lake Ontario flows into the St Lawrence River, it is a convenient stopping-off point almost exactly halfway between Montreal and Toronto, and it's not difficult to spend an interesting and enjoyable day or three in and around town.

Once a fur-trading depot, Kingston later became the principal British military post west of Quebec, and was the national capital for a while. The many 19th-century buildings of local grey limestone and the streets of Victorian red-brick houses give the downtown area a certain distinctive charm. The attractive waterfront is also pleasant.

There is a major university here, Queen's, and the city is also known across the country for its several prisons.

On Tuesday, Thursday and Saturday, a small open-air market takes place downtown, behind City Hall on King St.

### Orientation
The town lies a few km south of Hwy 401. Princess St, the main street, runs right down to the St Lawrence River, along which are

many fine old buildings. The whole city is low-rise, with few buildings higher than two or three storeys, and there aren't many modern structures either.

At the bottom of Princess St, Ontario St runs along the harbour by the start of the Rideau Canal to Ottawa. This is the old, much-restored area, with a tourist office, old military battery and Martello tower. There are views across the mouth of the canal to the military college. The market is on the corner of Brock St and King St East.

King St leads out along the lake's shore towards the university. Here you'll see many fine 19th-century houses and parkland. The impressive limestone County Courthouse is near the campus, facing a small park. Further out is Lake Ontario Park, with camping and a small beach.

### Information

The main downtown tourist office is the Kingston Tourist Information Office

(☎ 548-4415), at 209 Ontario St, across from City Hall in Confederation Park.

Away from the city core, the Old Fort Henry Information Centre (☎ 542-7388) is at the fort, at the junction of Hwys 2 and 15. It's open only from May to September.

### Old Fort Henry

The restored British fortification (☎ 542-7388) dating from 1832 dominates the town from its hilltop perch and is the city's prime attraction. It's a bit of a disappointment, though, as there is more space inside than anything else. But the beautiful structure is brought to life by colourfully uniformed guards trained in military drills, artillery exercises, and fife and drum music of the 1860s. Admission is $9, less for children, and includes a guided tour.

The soldiers put on their displays periodically throughout the day. They're best at 7 pm on Wednesday and Saturday, when there is a rifle-firing, cannon-blasting ceremonial

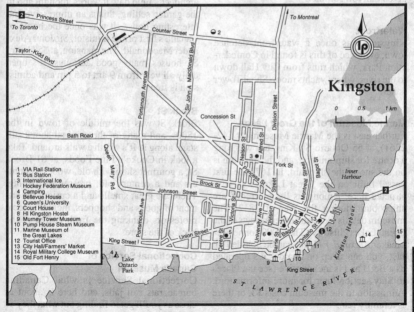

1  VIA Rail Station
2  Bus Station
3  International Ice
   Hockey Federation Museum
4  Camping
5  Bellevue House
6  Queen's University
7  Court House
8  HI Kingston Hostel
9  Murney Tower Museum
10 Pump House Steam Museum
11 Marine Museum of
   the Great Lakes
12 Tourist Office
13 City Hall/Farmers' Market
14 Royal Military College Museum
15 Old Fort Henry

**Kingston**

military retreat. Note this is held mid-season only. In addition, special events are held almost monthly. Inside the fort's rooms are artefacts, uniforms, weapons and more. The location provides good views. The fort is open daily through its season but is closed from 15 October to 15 May.

Without a car, the fort is a little difficult to reach, as there is no city bus. You can walk – it's not that far, over the causeway from town – but the last 500 metres or so is all uphill. Other than hoofing it, try to share a cab and maybe talk yourself into a ride back with a fellow visitor. Or if you have a few things to do around town, consider renting a bike for the day.

### City Hall
The grand City Hall, in the downtown area, is one of the country's finest classical buildings. Built of limestone, it dates from 1843, when Kingston was capital of the then United Provinces of Canada. Free tours are given daily in summer.

### Waterfront
Kingston was once a waterfront defence town; evidence of this is found in Confederation Park, which runs from City Hall down to the river, where yachts moor. Shoal Tower is here.

### Marine Museum of the Great Lakes
Further east is the Marine Museum (☎ 542-2261), at 55 Ontario St. Kingston was long a centre for shipbuilding, and the museum is on the site of the shipyard. In 1678 the first vessel built on the Great Lakes was constructed here. Among its list of credits are ships built during the War of 1812. The museum details these and other aspects of the Great Lakes' history. The 3000-tonne icebreaker *Alexander Henry* can be boarded. In fact, you can sleep on board – it's operated as a B&B and is inexpensive (see the Places to Stay section later for more information). Admission to the museum costs $3, or there is a family rate.

### Macdonald Park
On the corner of Barrie St and King St East is Macdonald Park, right along Lake Ontario. Just offshore, in 1812, the British ship *Royal George* battled with the USA's USS *Oneida*. At the western end of the park is the **Murney Martello Tower**, dating from 1846. This round defence structure was part of the early riverside fortifications and is now a museum housing local military and historical tidbits. There's a small admission fee. The museum is open daily from the end of May to the beginning of September. There are walking and bicycle paths along here and further west by the water's edge.

On the corner of King St East and West St is a big city park featuring a statue of Sir John Alexander Macdonald.

### Bellevue House
This National Historic Site (☎ 545-8666) is an immaculately maintained Tuscan-style mansion, which apparently means a very odd-shaped, balconied, brightly painted architect's field day. It works, though, and in the garden setting, this is an impressive and interesting house. It was once the home of Canada's first prime minister, Sir John Alexander Macdonald. The mansion, at 35 Centre St, houses many good antiques. It's open daily all year from 9 am to 5 pm and admission is free.

### Brock St
Brock St was the middle of town in the 1800s, and many of the original shops still stand along it. It's worth a walk around. Take a look in Cooke's Fine Foods, at 61 Brock St, a gourmet shop with old, wooden counters and a century-old, pressed-tin ceiling. There are great smells and a curious assortment of goods and shoppers, including local professors drinking the fresh coffee at the back of the store.

### Correctional Service of Canada Museum
Correctional Service is what Canadian bureaucrats call jails, and here is about as close as you'll get to finding out what they're

like without doing something nasty. Located at 555 King St West, in the administration building across from the main prison, the museum has a collection of articles ranging from confiscated weapons to tools used in escapes and all sorts of things from everyday prison life. Some of the history of Canadian penitentiaries is also outlined. It's open Monday to Friday from mid-May to August.

### Pump House Steam Museum
Here we have a one-of-a-kind, completely restored, steam-run pump station (☎ 542-7388). First used in 1849, it now contains several engines and some scale models, all run on steam. The address is 23 Ontario St. It's open from the start of May to Labour Day but is closed on Mondays.

Train buffs will also want to see the 20 model trains from around the world displayed in a special exhibit room.

### Royal Military College Museum
In the Fort Frederick Martello Tower on the grounds of the college (☎ 541-5010) is the Royal Military College Museum. This is the largest of the city's historic towers and has a collection on the history of the century-old military college. You have to wonder how or why, but also here lies the small arms collection of General Porfirio Diaz, president of Mexico from 1886 to 1912. The museum is just east of town, off Hwy 2, and is open daily in summer.

### International Ice Hockey Federation Museum
On the corner of Alfred and York Sts, this collection (☎ 544-2355) honours the history and stars of Canada's most loved sport. The displays include lots of memorabilia, photos and equipment. The museum is open daily from mid-June to mid-September, on weekend afternoons for the rest of the year. There's a small admission fee.

### Kingston Archaeological Centre
If you've been out along Hwy 401, you probably noticed the sedimentary rock outcrops, one of the few interesting things along

that highway's entire length from Montreal to Toronto. The Kingston Archaeological Centre, at 370 King St West, in the Tett Centre, has displays on the 8000-year human history of the area, featuring items dug from the surrounding landscape or found along the shoreline. It's open on weekdays and there is no charge to have a look around at the artefacts, photographs, etc.

### Kingston Mills Lockstation Blockhouse
Away from the centre, up Kingston Mills Rd just north of Hwy 401, this restored blockhouse (☎ 359-5377) dates from 1839. The purpose of the lock station and what it was like to run it are part of the explanatory exhibits. The blockhouse is open daily through the summer and is free.

### Other Museums
There are several other specialised museums in or near Kingston (see the Around Kingston section), including one on county schools, one at the military base detailing the history of military communications and electronics, and others on such things as geology and mineralogy and art. Ask at the tourist office for details about all these small museums.

### Wolfe Island
It is possible to have a free mini-cruise by taking the car ferry from Kingston to Wolfe Island. The 20-minute trip affords views of the city, the fort and a few of the Thousand Islands. Wolfe Island, the largest in the chain, lies halfway to the USA and is basically flat farmland, although many of its inhabitants now work in town.

There is not a lot to see on the island, but there is the *General Wolfe Hotel*, a short walk from the dock, with its three busy and highly regarded dining rooms. Prices are moderate to slightly expensive. There are also some moderately priced cabins on the island, and a campground. On the Kingston side, the ferry terminal is at the intersection of Ontario and Barrack Sts. The ferry runs continuously every hour or so from very early to very late each day, taking about 50 vehicles at a time.

**ONTARIO**

From Wolfe Island, another ferry links Cape Vincent, New York, but a toll is charged on this segment if you have a car.

### Activities

The Kingston Boardsailing Academy, a windsurfing school, has an office in Macdonald Park, at the foot of Emily St. Windsurfing equipment can be rented here.

For local swimming, head to Macdonald Park, on King St west of Princess St.

### Organised Tours

The tourist office has a pamphlet with map for a self-guided walking tour in the older historic part of town.

On summer days, a trackless mini-train departs regularly from the tourist office area for a tour of the central Kingston area.

St Lawrence Cruise Lines, 253 Ontario St, runs cruise ships out of Kingston to Quebec City, to the Saguenay River for whale-watching, and on other trips up the Ottawa River to Ottawa, aboard either the MV *Canadian Empress* or the replica steamship *Colonial Explorer*. Trips last two to five days and fares include all meals, entertainment and activities.

Several other local boat tours from Kingston go around the Thousand Islands; see the Around Kingston section for details of these.

### Places to Stay

Kingston doesn't have a lot of hotels – most accommodation is in motels and, more and more, in B&Bs.

**Camping** There are quite a few places to camp in the area. *Hi-Lo Hickory* (☎ 385-2430), on Wolfe Island, is reached by ferry from Kingston. There's a beach, and a bridge on the other side connects the island with New York state. The campground is about 12 km east of the Kingston ferry.

In town, only four km from the centre, you can camp at *Lake Ontario Park* (☎ 542-6574), which is operated by the city's parks department. It's west out along King St, and there's a beach too. A city bus runs from downtown right to the campground, from

Monday to Saturday until 7.30 pm and on Fridays until 10.30 pm. The park will almost always be able to fit in another tenter.

*KOA* (Kampgrounds of America, seen all over North America) has a branch 1.6 km north of Hwy 401 off Hwy 38. These places can be very plastic, having as little to do with camping as possible, and are also expensive, big and generally pretty busy. They cater mainly for trailers but have some tent sites here too.

**Hostels** The HI *Kingston Hostel* (☎ 546-7203), at 210 Bagot St, is conveniently central – buses (No 1 from the train, No 2 from the bus) will get you within a block or two. They have 30 beds in summer (about half that many in winter), a room for couples and some rooms for families. Continental breakfasts are available and there's also a complete kitchen. Rates are $11/17 for members/nonmembers. The hostel is closed from 15 December to 15 January.

Rooms are available in residences at *Queen's University* (☎ 547-2775) from mid-May to mid-August. Rooms cost $30 ($18 for students) and meals are available. The campus is on the corner of University and Union Sts.

*Waldron Tower* (☎ 544-6100) is a residential complex of the Kingston General Hospital. It's great if you can get in but is usually full, so call ahead. The price is $24 a day, with a good weekly rate, but there are only single rooms. They have a cafeteria, kitchens, all manner of facilities and a view over the river to boot. The tower is at 17 King St West, near Macdonald Park.

The *YM-YWCA* (☎ 546-2647), at 100 Wright Crescent, has beds for women only. There are kitchen facilities and a pool.

The *Salvation Army* (☎ 548-4411) is for men who are broke, or virtually so.

**B&Bs** Kingston & Area B&B Association (☎ 542-0214) runs a booking agency in Kingston. There are about 40 participating homes in and around town. Tell them where you want to be and what your interests are and you'll be matched up suitably. Rates start at $40/50 for singles/doubles with full breakfast included, plus $10 to $15 extra for children. Cheaper rates are available for extended stays.

In summer, you can stay at a unique B&B on a moored, retired 64-metre icebreaker, the *Alexander Henry* (☎ 542-2261), which is part of the downtown Marine Museum of the Great Lakes. Beds are in the former crew's quarters and a continental breakfast is served from the galley. You can wander all over the ship. It hasn't been gentrified at all – the vessel is plain, simple and functional and rooms are pretty much like those on a working ship. This partially explains the good prices, which start at $36 a double and go up to $65 if you want the captain's cabin.

*O'Brien House* (☎ 542-8660), at 39 Glenaire Mews, up near the train station and north-west of the downtown area, is a little less costly than the city norm. It's a B&B whose owner seems to particularly like overseas visitors. Singles/doubles cost $35/45, including a full breakfast and coffee or tea at any time. There are reduced rates for children.

**Hotels** A couple of the older downtown hotels have been overhauled and make pleasant, if a bit pricey, central places to stay.

Among the old cheapies, only the *Plaza Hotel*, 46 Montreal St, on the corner of Queen St, remains. It exists basically for the downstairs bar but is not badly kept, It's no family place and is not recommended for single women, but it is cheap – $26/32 a single/double with own bathroom.

Also inexpensive, but better, the *Donald Gordon Centre* (☎ 545-2221), at 421 Union St, is affiliated with (and very near) Queen's University. The centre rents their quiet, air-conditioned rooms for $38/45.

Moving up and offering more amenities, style and services is the *Queen's Inn* (☎ 546-0429), dating from 1839. It was completely renovated in 1987 and now offers modern facilities in 17 rooms in a central setting. It's one of the oldest continually running hotels in the country. Rooms vary from $65 to $95 in high season (April to November) and from $45 to $75 for the rest of the year.

The *Prince George Hotel* (☎ 549-5440) dates from 1809 and has been restored (with National Heritage recognition). Its comfortable rooms, with balconies overlooking the lake, come at splurge prices – $80 to $140.

**Motels** There are plenty of these. At 1454 Princess St is *Journey's End* (☎ 549-5550), a two-storey place. Rooms are a couple of dollars cheaper upstairs and cost $61 to $64 for singles or doubles.

A little cheaper is the *Hilltop* (☎ 542-3846), at 2287 Princess St, where singles/doubles are $40/46. There are many other motels on Princess St, and some along Hwy 2 on each side of town.

**Places to Eat**
Kingston has pretty good eating, especially considering its relatively small size.

The *Sunflower Restaurant*, serving good vegetarian food, is a bright spot with sturdy wooden tables and batiks on the walls. Meals start at around $5 and there are lots of desserts and snacks. It's at 20 Montreal St and is open until 9 pm daily (except Sunday).

The *Delightfully Different Café*, at 118 Sydenham St, is an unlikely looking place which turns out excellent fresh sandwiches, salads, bagels, etc for lunch and muffins and the like for breakfast. It's only open from 7 am to 4 pm Monday to Friday but is worth getting to for a light meal and is very inexpensive. It's between Brock and Johnson Sts.

At 34 Clarence St, the *Kingston Brewing Co* is a pub which brews its own ales and lagers and also has a good selection of non-house brands. There is also a good selection of inexpensive tavern-style things to munch on and, interestingly, a daily curry.

For a light lunch, snack, dessert or just a coffee, try the *Chinese Laundry Café*, at 291 Princess St. It has an outdoor courtyard patio and is open late.

*E P Murphey & Sons & Daughters*, at 70 Brock St, has been around for ages, and though the restaurant upstairs is closed, fish & chips are still offered in the store front. At 479 Princess St, you can get a good Indian meal at the *Darbar*. It serves the usual north-

ONTARIO

452 Ontario – Eastern Ontario

ern dishes, including tandooris, and is open daily for lunch (with five specials each day) or dinner.

For a more up-market place, try the *Canoe Club* in the Prince George Hotel, near the waterfront. It's across from Confederation Park and is a nice place, but moderate in price. Seafood is the speciality, but you can drop in for just a drink.

For a real splurge there's *Chez Piggy*, probably the city's best known restaurant, in a renovated early 19th-century building at 68 Princess St but really down a small alley off King St between Brock and Princess Sts. At lunch, from 11.30 am to 2 pm, soup and a sandwich or the good salads are not expensive. Dinners, starting at 6 pm, cost $9 to $17 for a main course, so the final bill can be quite high. The selection includes lamb, steaks and omelettes, with some interesting appetisers to start with.

There is also a Sunday brunch, with some items you don't see on a standard brunch menu (but again, it is not for the budget-conscious).

The restaurant is owned by a member of a successful (and tuneful) 1960s American pop band. No clues, but he likes it that way. It's open daily.

*Lino's*, on the corner of Division and Ontario Sts, is open 24 hours a day.

Division St towards Hwy 401 has a good cross-section of places representing the standard restaurant chains. At 2455 Division St, away from the centre a bit, the *Bonanza* offers very good value – steak and chicken with an all-you-can-eat salad bar.

### Entertainment

**Bars & Nightspots** The *Cocama*, at 178 Ontario St, is a huge dance bar down near the water. It's styled after the Limelight in New York City. *Dollar Bills*, in the Prince George Hotel, one of several student drinking spots, has videos and dancing. *AJ's Hangar*, at 393 Princess St, is a place to check out for live rock and blues bands on weekends (or for a drink the rest of the week).

Kingston has quite a few British-style

pubs. The *Toucan*, at 76 Princess St, near King St, often has live music.

On the corner of King St East and Brock St, near City Hall, the *Duke of Kingston Pub* serves British beers in British-style decor.

**Cinema** The *Princess Court Cinema* (☎ 546-FILM), at 394 Princess St, is a good repertory movie house presenting calibre American, European and Canadian films. Different films are run just about every night and prices are reduced on Tuesdays.

### Things to Buy

The Canadian Shop, at 219 Princess St, near Montreal St, sells handicrafts, including Cowichan sweaters from Vancouver Island for about the same price they are there. The shop also sells Inuit carvings and all kinds of books about Canada.

The Book Bin, at 225 Princess St, sells used books.

### Getting There & Away

**Bus** The Voyageur bus station (☎ 548-7738) is at 175 Counter St, a couple of km south of Hwy 401. Services going to Toronto are frequent throughout the day (at least eight trips); to Montreal, buses are slightly less frequent, but there are still plenty of them. To Ottawa, there are buses each morning, afternoon and evening. Services also go to some of the smaller centres, such as Pembroke and Cornwall. One-way fares include Montreal $37, Ottawa $25 and Toronto $32.

**Train** The VIA Rail station (☎ 544-5600) is a long way from the downtown area, but city bus No 1 stops at the corner of Princess and Counter Sts, just a short walk from the station. It's on Counter St near the corner of Princess St, north-west of town. There are six to eight train services to Montreal daily (morning, noon and night), costing $44. To Ottawa ($29) there are three trains a day (morning, afternoon and evening). To Toronto ($47) there are eight services daily. Discounts may be available on weekday trips if tickets are purchased five days or more in advance.

**Car** Tilden, at 2212 Princess St, offers daily, weekly and longer car rentals.

### Getting Around

**Bus** For information on buses, call Kingston Transit (☎ 544-5289). The city bus office is on the corner of Barrack and King Sts.

For getting into town, there is a city bus stop across the street from the bus station. Buses depart at a quarter to and a quarter past the hour.

**Bicycle** Bicycle rentals are available at Source For Sports, 121 Princess St. A second place to try is LaSalle Sports, at 574 Princess St. A bike may provide transport to the fort and a way of getting around a bit. The area is generally flat and both Hwys 2 and 5 have paved shoulders.

### AROUND KINGSTON
### Thousand Islands Parkway

East of Kingston between Gananoque (which is pronounced 'gan-an-ok-way') and Mallorytown Landing, a small road – the Thousand Islands Parkway – dips south of Hwy 401, runs along the river and then rejoins the highway. This can make for a scenic and recommended side trip when travelling Hwy 401 in either direction. The route offers picnic areas and good views out to many of the islands from the pastoral strip of shoreline. There is also a **bicycle path** over the fibre-optic telephone lines. Bicyles can be rented at the 1000 Islands Camping Resort (☎ 659-3058), eight km east of Gananoque. The St Lawrence Parks System maintains a series of recreational and historic places along this route and on Hwy 2 from Adolphustown to beyond Upper Canada Village at Morrisburg and all the way to Lancaster, near the Quebec border.

Boat cruises around the islands depart from Rockport and Gananoque.

Sixteen km east of Kingston, in a log house in Grass Creek Park, you'll find the **MacLachlan Woodworking Museum**. The museum uses an extensive collection of tools to outline the development of working in wood. There are displays on trees themselves and on some common wooden objects used for varying purposes, as well as a changing exhibit area (which had a show of decoys when I was there).

Close to the town of **Lansdowne** between Gananoque and Rockport is the busy bridge to New York State. The **Skydeck**, a 125-metre-high observation tower, is open every day from May to October. Its three decks (and binoculars) provide great views over the river area. Admission is reasonable and there is a restaurant on the premises.

At **Mallorytown Landing** is the headquarters for the **Thousand Islands National Park**, Canada's smallest national park, consisting of 17 islands together with the mainland location.

Along the parkway are privately run campgrounds, numerous motels, and some cottages to rent for longer stays. In Gananoque, at 279 King St West, the *Victoria & Rose Inn* (☎ 382-3368) is a fabulous-looking place dating from around 1870. The interior has been totally updated and guests will not lack for comforts. Prices reflect this and start at $65 a double.

There is a bit of an art colony in the area, and in the fall many of the local studios are open to the public. Ask the tourist office in Kingston for a list of the painters, sculptors, woodworkers, glass workers, weavers, etc.

**The Thousand Islands** This scenic area just east of Kingston actually has more than 1000 islands which dot the river between the two national mainlands. In spring the islands undulate with the white blooms of the trillium, the provincial flower.

Boat tours from Kingston will take you around some of the islands; a couple of companies run daily trips in summer. The short and straightforward one is aboard the *Island Princess* (☎ 549-5544), a 1½-hour trip around the interesting Kingston shoreline with a commentary on some of the noteworthy sites. Departing from the same place is the *Island Queen* showboat, providing live family entertainment or a three-hour evening cruise with a buffet dinner. Through the summer they offer two or three trips a day,

ONTARIO

leaving from the *Island Queen* dock, on Ontario St at the foot of Brock St.

Other tours leave from Rockport and Gananoque, two small towns east down the river a bit. Most tours last about 3½ hours, cost $15 per adult and include glimpses of such island curiosities as **Boldt Castle.** The Rockport Boat Line (☎ 659-3402) has two-hour trips out among the international islands for $10. Trips depart hourly in peak season, less frequently in spring and fall, from the dock three km east of the Thousand Islands International Bridge.

The Gananoque Boat Line (☎ 382-2144) does much the same thing but offers a 90-minute trip that goes through the Admiralty and Fleet groups of islands. They also have sunset cruises. At impressive-looking Boldt Castle, you can get off for a closer look and return to Gananoque on a later boat.

A new angle is to do it all yourself on a rented houseboat. This is gaining in popularity all over Ontario and can be a lot of fun, but tends to be a little pricey unless you get a few people together. If you want to look into it, check out Thousand Islands Houseboats in Kingston. They rent by the day, week or part of a week. Prices depend on when you go – at weekends it costs considerably more than midweek. The boats come with all kitchen necessities and sleep eight people.

Kingston is also home to the St Lawrence Cruise Lines (☎ 1-800-267-7868), which runs three, five and seven-day luxury cruises on replica steamboats down the St Lawrence River to Ottawa, Montreal, Quebec City and the Saguenay River.

**St Lawrence Islands National Park** Within the gentle, green archipelago, this park covers 17 islands scattered along 80 km of the river. At Mallorytown Landing, as well as the park interpretive and information centre, you'll find a 60-site campground but no camper or trailer hook-ups. There are some trails and a beach.

Many of the islands have picnicking and camping, with minimal facilities, and 13 islands offer primitive campsites accessible only by boat. Water-taxis and boat rentals are available from the park headquarters and from many of the small towns along the parkway. Tourist offices or park headquarters will have information on what's available. Park islands stretch from just off Mallorytown all the way down to Gananoque.

## West of Kingston

West of town along the coast, Hwy 33 has been designated the Loyalist Parkway. It retraces the steps of the Loyalists who settled this area some 200 years ago after fleeing the American Revolution. The parkway runs for 94 km from Kingston to Trenton, passing over Quinte's Isle.

Just west of Kingston, in Amherstview, **Fairfield Historical Park** runs along the shoreline. It includes **Fairfield House**, one of the province's oldest, built in 1793 by Loyalists from New England. North about 10 km, in Odessa, the historic **Babcock Mill** is a working water-powered mill which now again produces the baskets originally made here in the mid-1800s.

At **Adulphustown**, catch the continuously running short, free ferry ride over to Glenora (on Quinte's Isle) and continue on to Picton.

## North of Kingston

North of Kingston is the **Rideau Lakes** region, an area of small towns, cottages, lodges and marinas with opportunities for fishing and camping.

In a day's drive, or even in an afternoon, you can explore some of the smaller, rural Ontario villages.

**Wilton** has one of the many southern Ontario regional cheese factories with a retail outlet. In the little town of **Yarker**, straight up Hwy 6 from Hwy 401, the *Waterfall Tea Room* is right on the river, by a waterfall, and has been highly recommended.

**Camden East**, home of Harrowsmith Magazine, has an excellent bookstore on outdoor, nature, gardening, country living and related matters, as well as a range of 'how-to' books.

The region has attracted 'back-to-the-landers' and countercultural people. Their influences show up in the number of health-food stores, craft outlets and bakeries. In **Tamsworth**, where there is a big arts & crafts outlet, try the *Devon Tea House*. In nearby **Marlbank** there is *Phioloxia's Zoo, Bakery, B&B and Vegetarian Restaurant*. What, no disco?

**Frontenac Provincial Park** (☎ 376-3489) straddles both the lowlands of southern Ontario and the more northern Canadian Shield, so the flora, fauna and geology of the park are an admixture. The park is designed for overnight hikers and canoeists. There is no formal campground – rather, there are interior campsites scattered through the park, accessible only on foot or by water. Trails and canoe routes have been mapped out. Though the park is large, there aren't many designated camping sites; this has not yet been a big problem, as the park remains relatively unknown.

The entrance and the information centre are at **Otter Lake**, off Hwy 5A north of Sydenham. The swimming is excellent and I drink the water straight from the lakes, although it's probably not recommended that you do so without boiling it. There are no bears to worry about and the bass fishing is pretty good.

North-west from Kingston up Hwy 41 is **Bon Echo Provincial Park** (☎ 336-2228), also good for canoeing. Some of the lakes are quite shallow and get very warm. There are walk-in and canoe-in campsites or roadside campgrounds with facilities. At **Mazinaw Lake** there are Native Indian rock paintings on granite cliffs. This is one of the largest parks in eastern Ontario (generally speaking, the larger the park the better because you can lose your fellow humans for a spell and wildlife viewing is more likely).

**Rideau Canal** The 150-year-old, 200-km-long canal/river/lake system connects Kingston with Ottawa. The historical route is good for boating or canoeing trips, with parks, small towns, lakes and many places to stop en route. When travelling from one end to the other, boats must pass through 47 old lock systems. The old defence buildings along the way have been restored.

After the War of 1812 there was a fear that there could be yet another war with the Americans. The Duke of Wellington decided to link Ottawa and Kingston with a canal in order to have a reliable communications and supply route between the two military centres. Although the canal is just 200 km in length, its construction was a brutal affair, involving as many as 4000 men, battling malaria and the Canadian Shield, with some of the world's hardest rock. It climbs 84 metres from Ottawa over the Shield, then drops 49 metres to Lake Ontario. And guess what? Right! It never saw any military service.

It did prove somewhat useful later in the century for shipping goods around, and is now used for recreation and education.

Roads run parallel to much of the canal, so walking or cycling is also possible.

A houseboat shuttle service runs the length of the canal, connecting the Kingston International Hostel to its counterpart in Ottawa. It operates through July and August; for details call either one of the hostels. There may also be businesses along the canal which rent houseboats, allowing you to meander about at your own speed, but so far this area hasn't been developed like that along the Trent Canal System running from Georgian Bay to Lake Ontario. The tourist office in Kingston has information on history, times, lock fees (which are minimal) and boat rentals.

**Rideau Trail** The Rideau Trail is a 400-km-long hiking-trail system which links Kingston with Ottawa. It passes through Westport, Smiths Falls and many conservation areas, traversing forests, fields and marshes as well as some stretches of road along the way. There are some historic sites on the route, and you'll see the Rideau Canal. There are also 64 km of side loops. Most people use the route only for day trips, but longer trips and overnighting are possible. The main trail is marked by orange triangles, side trails by blue triangles. The Rideau Trail Association, which has an office in Kingston, prints a map kit for the entire route. Between Kingston and Smiths Falls are numerous camping spots. The rest of the way, there is not as much provision for camping but there is commercial accommodation. Camping on private land is possible; get the owner's permission first.

## BELLEVILLE & AROUND

There's not much for the visitor in Belleville, a town with 35,000 residents – it's more a departure point for Quinte's Isle to the south. In July, the Waterfront & Folklorama Festival is three days of events, music and shows.

Twenty-nine km east of town, in Deseronto, Native Renaissance II has a sizeable collection of Native Indian arts & crafts and a section where new ones are created. It's open every day and can be found on Hwy 49.

At Shannonville, in the same direction but just 12 km from Belleville, the Mosport Speedway is the site of motorcycle and drag racing periodically through the summer.

Mapledale Cheese is worth a visit to buy some of the excellent cheddar. It's north of Belleville up Hwy 37, roughly 10 km north of Hwy 401.

Hwy 37 continues north through old Tweed to Hwy 7, which is the main route to Toronto from Ottawa. It's a bit slow, with only two lanes, but the scenery is good. There are a couple of parks along the way and several places to eat.

## QUINTE'S ISLE

Irregularly shaped Quinte's Isle is a quiet and scenic, historic retreat from the bustle of much of southern Ontario. The rolling farmland is reminiscent of Prince Edward Island, and in fact Quinte's Isle is also known as Prince Edward County. Many of the little towns were settled in the 18th and 19th centuries. The cemeteries adjacent to the village churches reveal clues to these earlier times.

It's only been in the past few years that the island has been somewhat discovered and developed for visitors, but it still hasn't changed very much.

### Things to See & Do

Traffic is light on most of the island's roads, which lead past large old farmhouses and cultivated fields. The **St Lawrence River** is never far away and many routes offer good views. Fishing is quite good in the **Bay of Quinte** and the locals use the waters for sailing. The island is popular with cyclists – it's generally flat and some of the smaller roads are well shaded.

---

### The Loyalists

The issue of American independence from Britain divided the American colonies into two camps: the Patriots and the Loyalists. During the American Revolution of 1775-83, the Loyalists maintained their allegiance to the British Crown. About a third of the 13 Colonies' population remained loyal to Britain. Severe laws were passed against them, forcing some 200,000 to leave during and after the Revolution. Of those, between 50,000 and 60,000 fled to Canada, settling in the Maritimes, the Eastern Townships of Lower Canada (Quebec) and the St Lawrence-Lake Ontario region of Upper Canada (Ontario). Unknown to many today, not all were of British descent – they represented a mix of ethnic backgrounds. Regardless, their arrival strengthened Great Britain's hold on this part of the Empire. In Nova Scotia, for example, the migration meant that the French no longer made up the majority of the population.

In this region, the Loyalists' arrival essentially meant the formation of the province of Ontario. Both the British and local governments were generous in their support, offering clothing, rations, and various aid and land grants.

Soon the Loyalists in Canada were not only self-sustaining but prosperous and powerful. Today their descendants make up a significant and influential segment of the English population.

Loyalist sites can be seen in southern Quebec, the Gaspé and, in particular, Saint John, New Brunswick and Shelburne, Nova Scotia. ∎

The excellent strawberry-picking in late June draws many outsiders.

There are three provincial parks, including **North Beach** and the fine **Sandbanks**. Sandbanks (☎ 393-3319), the only one offering camping, is one of the most popular parks in the province. Book ahead – reservations are definitely required for weekends, when a fair bit of partying goes on. The park is divided into two sections: the Outlet (with an excellent strip of sandy beach) and Sandbanks itself (containing most of the area's sand dunes, some over three storeys high). There's a large undeveloped section at the end of the beach – good for walking and for exploring the dunes and backwaters.

On the other side of the island, **Lake on the Mountain**, the third park, is really nothing more than a picnic site but is worth a visit to see the unusual lake. It sits on one side of the road at a level actually higher than that of the road, while just across the street is a terrific view over Lake Ontario and some islands hundreds of metres below. Geologists are still speculating as to the lake's origins. The local Mohawk Indians have their own legends about the lake, which appears to have no source.

**Picton** This small town is the only town of any size on the island and has one of the six district museums. The tourist office has detailed maps of the island and some information on current accommodation. Pick up the walking-tour guide of Picton – the tour leads you past some of the fine historic buildings in town. Another guide lists various island attractions, including **Bird House City**, with dozens of painted birdhouses (including a fire station and courthouse).

**Tyendinaga Indian Reserve** This is just off Quinte's Isle and is also mainly farmland. In mid-May the original coming of the Mohawks is re-enacted in full tribal dress.

**Places to Stay**
The area is best known for its camping. There are several commercial campgrounds nearby which, if you can't get in at Sand-

banks, aren't quite as busy. The large one opposite the Outlet is geared mainly for recreational vehicles. There's also quite a nice one, good for tenting as well, out at the tip of Salmon Arm; it offers minimal facilities but great sunsets.

There are numerous resorts, cottages, motels and B&Bs covering a range of prices. For a day or two you're best off at a B&B, but for longer stays check into one of the simpler cabins or cottages. Some of the less costly places seem to be in the Cherry Valley area.

For B&B information, try *B&B Prince Edward County* (☎ 399-1299), at 76 Main St in Wellington, on the island.

*Isiah Tubbs Resort* (☎ 393-2090), the most expensive place on the island, is costly even by Toronto or Muskoka standards but the luxury facilities and very fine design keep visitors coming back for more.

If all the accommodation options are booked out, try the motels around Belleville's perimeter – it's not far to return to the island the following day.

## TRENTON
Small Trenton is known as the starting point of the Trent-Severn Waterway, which goes 386 km through 44 locks to Georgian Bay in Lake Huron. Yachties and sailors of every description follow this old Native Indian route each summer. **Presqu'Île Provincial Park** (☎ 475-2204) is west of town and south of Brighton. A popular feature is the immense beach – both long and wide – but bird-watchers make up a sizeable portion of the campers. The park has a large adjacent marsh, which is home to many species and represents a migration pit stop to many more in spring and fall. Boardwalks allow access to portions of the wetlands. The camping is good, too, with large, treed sites. At Beach 3, you can rent boats, sailboarding equipment and bicycles.

The Loyalist Parkway road route leads down onto Quinte's Isle and heads east.

## Trent-Severn Waterway
The Trent-Severn Waterway cuts diagonally

across southern Ontario cottage country, following rivers and lakes for 386 km from Trenton (on Lake Ontario) to Georgian Bay at the mouth of the Severn River (near Port Severn and Honey Harbour). It travels past, through or near many of the region's best known resort towns and areas, including the **Kawartha Lakes, Bobcaygeon, Fenelon Falls** and **Lake Simcoe.**

Used a century ago for commerce, the system is now strictly recreational and is operated by Parks Canada. The waterflow is regulated by a series of 125 dams along the route.pen the The canal is opened for use in mid-May and closes in mid-October. A cruise ship plies the route, taking seven days. Shorter, four-day trips are also available. These are not cheap, but ask in Peterborough for details. Perhaps of more interest is renting your own houseboat to explore the canal, an idea which has become amazingly popular in the past few years. Several companies at varying points along the route now rent boats by the weekend, by the week or for longer periods.

The houseboats come more or less fully equipped, some even including a barbecue, and can accommodate up to eight people (six adults), which makes for not only a good party but also a reasonably priced one. The trips are good for families, too, with separate sleeping rooms for the kids.

One organisation to try for a houseboat is Egan Houseboat Rentals (☎ (705) 799-5745), which is located at Egan Marine, RR4 in the village of Omemee, west of Peterborough on Route 7. They've been in business for 20 years, and the location, right by the Kawartha Lakes, gives you the option of hanging around the lakes or going all the way to Lake Simcoe. You get some brief training – anyone can operate the boats with little difficulty.

Rates vary quite a bit, depending on timing, but start at about $500 a weekend (or for several days mid-week) for the basic boat, up to about $1600 for a full week on the larger deluxe model during the peak season (July). Three and four-day rentals are also offered. On average, you will use about $100 worth of gas in a week, but of course the size of the boat is a determining factor.

Even if you're not on the water, there are things to see along the route, including all the locks.

## KAWARTHA LAKES

Many of the pretty towns in the Kawartha Lakes vacation region have a good restaurant or two and, usually, a couple of antique dealers – **Bobcaygeon** and **Fenelon Falls** are two that are worth dropping into if you're up this way. (The former also hosts a big fiddle contest each July.)

Nearby **Balsam Lake** is popular for swimming and fishing. In **Lindsay,** a more ordinary small town, don't miss the *Dutch Treat,* on Kent St, for excellent, cheap food – good homemade muffins and various treats. This town has a summer theatre programme.

At **Burleigh Falls,** who could resist a place called the *Lovesick café*? It's a typical country shop with food, souvenirs, fishing tackle, etc. The date squares are recommended.

The district has some interesting parks as well. **Petroglyphs Provincial Park** has probably the best collection of prehistoric rock carvings in the country. Rediscovered in 1954, there are reportedly 900 figures and shapes carved into the park's limestone ridges. The portions of the collection which are easy to view are much smaller than the figure 900 might suggest, and though interesting, it is not an overwhelming site. Recently, this relatively small, exposed section has had to be enclosed to protect the rock from acid rain, a serious problem over much of Ontario. The people in positions to do something about the situation continue to sit on their butts. The area and small lake within the park remain important spiritual sites for the local Native Indians.

**Serpent's Mound Provincial Park** is the site of an ancient Native Indian burial ground. The **Warsaw Caves Conservation Area** contains tunnels eroded into limestone; there are walking trails here.

## Peterborough

Peterborough is a middle-sized Ontario town more or less at the centre of the Kawartha Lakes region. The older downtown area has some fine buildings; it's all very green, although the city seems in some danger of becoming a Toronto suburb. Trent University is another feature of the town's character.

The Trent-Severn Waterway passes through the large hydraulic-lift lock, a major landmark in town. A visitor centre shows how the locks along the system operate, and there is a working model. You can go on a trip through the locks into the Otonabee River or, if you're hooked, on a three or five-day cruise through the locks and along part of the system.

Canoeing is a popular activity. From Peterborough, you can get to Serpent's Mound Provincial Park. Canoeing possibilities include easy trips on the canal or, in spring, tougher white-water trips on rivers in the area. Ask at the tourist office in town. The Ministry of Natural Resources publishes a map called *North Kawartha Canoe Routes*, which shows some possible trips and their portage distances.

In late July or early August, the Summer Festival is held, with various events and shows.

### Around Peterborough

**Century Village** South-east of Peterborough is Century Village, a pioneer village with costumed workers, demonstrations, and 20 buildings dating from 1820 to 1899.

**Lakefield** A few km north is Lakefield, a small town with a co-educational school (formerly a boys' only school to which Queen Elizabeth II sent Prince Andrew).

**Curve Lake Indian Reserve** About 900 Ojibway people live on this 400-hectare reserve roughly 34 km north of Peterborough. A trip to the reserve's Whetung Ojibway Arts & Crafts Gallery is worthwhile. The log building contains both new and old examples of Native Indian art and

the museum section has traditional pieces and valuable works from such artists as Norval Morrisseau, perhaps Canada's best known.

In the gallery area, newer articles created by Native Indian craftspeople from across the country are displayed. Many articles can be bought, including handmade jackets and baskets.

Lunch is available: you can sample a number of traditional Native Indian foods or try a buffalo burger. The reserve, established in 1825, is off Curve Lake Rd, which runs out of Hwy 507.

## NORTH OF KAWARTHA LAKES

Continuing north you come to a less-busy, less-populated, hilly region known as the Haliburton Highlands. Hwy 507, leading up from Bobcaygeon through Catchacoma and Gooderham (which has a small waterfall), is the narrowest, oldest-looking highway I've driven on anywhere in the province. It often looks more like a country lane.

### Bancroft

A district centre, Bancroft is well known for its minerals and for the big gem festival held each August. Examples of 80% of the minerals found in Canada can be dug up in this area.

### Combermere

Up Hwy 62 from Bancroft is the **Madonna House Pioneer Museum** (☎ 756-3713), 18 km south of Combermere. Run by a lay religious group operating a cooperative farm, the museum has displays on the area's early settlers. An adjoining gift shop sells a range of items, with the profits going to charity.

### Barry's Bay

The old lumber town is now a supply centre for the cottagers in the area on and around **Lake Kaminiskeg**. It's also pretty close to **Algonquin Park** and is on the main highway to Ottawa. Odd as it may seem, this is the centre for a sizeable Polish population, attracted to the hilly, green topography, which is much like that along the Baltic Sea in northern Poland. The town of **Wilno** in this area was the first Polish settlement in Canada. Nearby Killaloe, towards Ottawa, is a small centre for craftspeople and artisans.

The entire region has cottages for rent, and lakeside resorts, but advance reservations are a very good idea. **Pembroke**, east at the Quebec border, is the nearest town of any size.

# Toronto

Toronto (population 2.6 million) is the country's largest city, and it continues to grow, currently due mainly to its popularity with new immigrants, who arrive from an ever increasing number of disparate homelands. These new arrivals have helped stabilise the population numbers through a very grim three years of recession when many inhabitants have been forced to leave. The economic boom of the late 1980s saw Toronto become well entrenched as the nation's financial and business capital as well as being a primary focus for English Canadian arts and culture, and these legacies remain.

Two of the first things you'll notice about Toronto are the vibrancy and the cleanliness of the downtown area. These factors alone separate it from the bulk of large North American cities, but another great thing is that Toronto is safe. The streets are busy at night, with restaurants and entertainment places open and the downtown streetcars and subways generally used without hesitation. Of course, some prudence is always wise and women alone should take care after dark. There are some rougher parts of town, but these tend to be away from the centre and not where most visitors are likely to be.

There is a lot of central housing in the city, part of an urban planning scheme which has kept a balance of business and residence in the city, making it a more liveable place than many. Despite high costs, there are no areas of concentrated poverty. Toronto is one of the most expensive cities in North America in which to live, but fortunately this is not overly evident to visitors, for much of the cost is in real estate.

Throughout the city, various ethnic and immigrant groups have collected in fairly tight communities to form bustling, prosperous districts. These various neighbourhoods are one of the best and most distinctive aspects of the city and have helped to warm up what has been the rather stand-offish character of Toronto.

Toronto celebrated 150 years as a city in 1984 but has only recently attained its prominent stature and international attention. About 25 years ago, the city scored points in its traditional rivalry with Montreal by surpassing it in size. Since this largely symbolic achievement, Toronto has grown in every way. It is the busiest Canadian port on the Great Lakes and is a major centre for banking, manufacturing and publishing. The Toronto Stock Exchange is one of North America's most important and the city is the provincial capital.

As you will notice, Toronto is new and shiny. Much of the downtown area has been rebuilt during the past 15 to 20 years. Such embracing of progress and change was not always so, however.

## HISTORY

In the 1600s the Seneca Indians lived in this area. Étienne Brule, on a trip with Samuel de Champlain in 1615, was the first European to see the site. The Native Indians did not particularly relish the visit, and it wasn't until around 1720 that the French established a fur-trading post and mission in what's now the west end of the city.

After years of hostility with the French, the British took over. John Simcoe, lieutenant-governor of the new Upper Canada, chose Toronto as the capital in 1793 and it became known as York. Previously, Niagara-on-the-Lake had served as capital. In 1993, the city celebrated the 200th anniversary of the founding.

During the War of 1812, the Americans

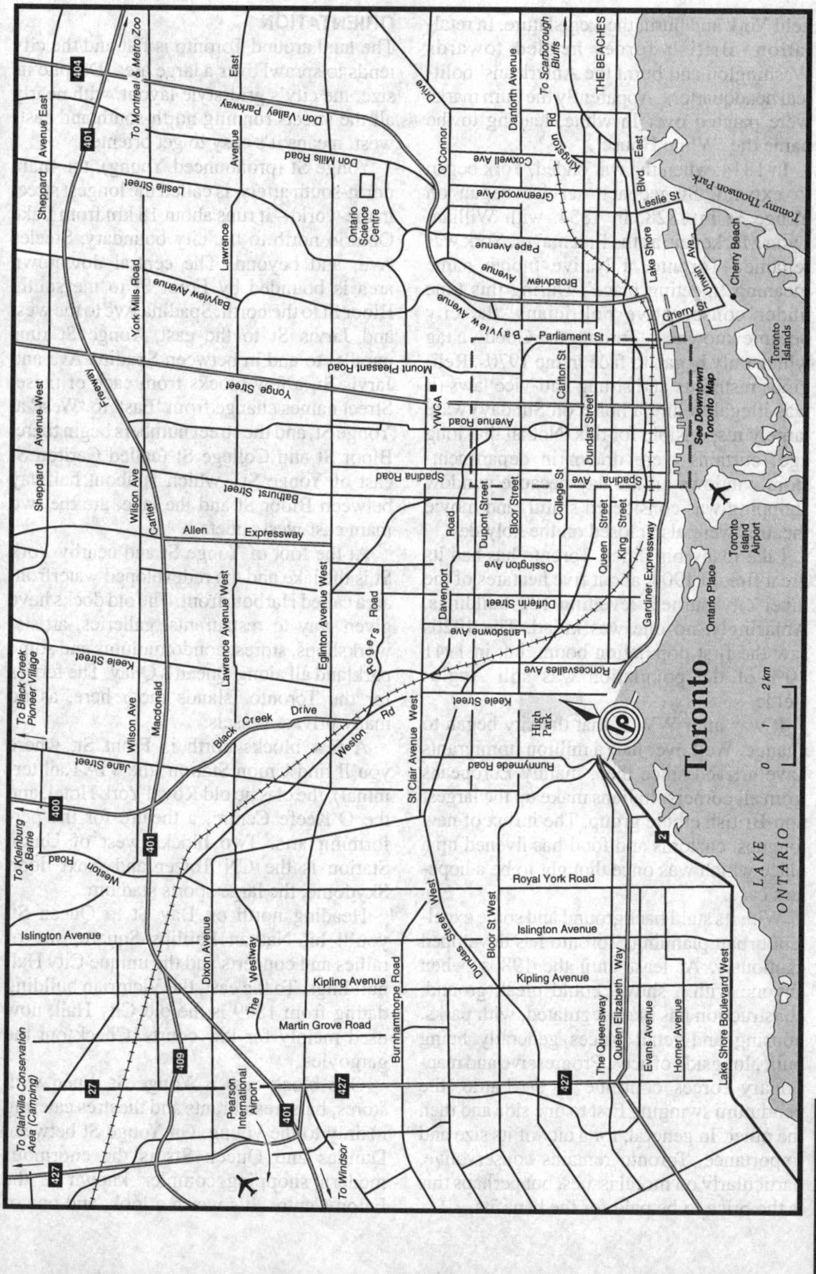
Toronto
LAKE ONTARIO
0 1 2 km
Toronto Islands
Cherry Beach
Tommy Thomson Park
THE BEACHES
To Scarborough Bluffs
See Downtown Toronto Map
Toronto Island Airport
Ontario Place
High Park
YWCA
Ontario Science Centre
Pearson International Airport
To Windsor
To Clairville Conservation Area (Camping)
To Kleinburg & Barrie
To Black Creek Pioneer Village
To Montreal & Metro Zoo
Don Valley Parkway
Don Mills Road
Leslie Street
Bayview Avenue
Mount Pleasant Road
Yonge Street
Avenue Road
Spadina Road
Bathurst Street
Allen Expressway
Eglinton Avenue West
Lawrence Avenue West
Sheppard Avenue West
Sheppard Avenue East
York Mills Road
Wilson Ave
Keele Street
Jane Street
Weston Rd
Black Creek Drive
Rogers Road
St Clair Avenue West
Davenport Road
Dupont Street
Bloor Street
College St
Dundas Street
Queen Street
King Street
Gardiner Expressway
Lake Shore Blvd East
Lake Shore Boulevard West
Parliament St
Carlton St
Broadview Avenue
Pape Avenue
Greenwood Ave
Coxwell Ave
Danforth Avenue
Kingston Rd
O'Connor Drive
Cherry St
Unwin Ave
Leslie St
Ossington Ave
Dufferin Street
Lansdowne Ave
Roncesvalles Ave
Runnymede Road
Royal York Road
Islington Avenue
Kipling Avenue
Martin Grove Road
Burnhamthorpe Road
The Westway
Dixon Avenue
Bloor St West
Dundas Street West
The Queensway
Queen Elizabeth Way
Evans Avenue
Horner Avenue
Macdonald Cartier Freeway
Weston Road
401
404
400
409
427
27
2

ONTARIO

held York and burnt the Legislature. In retaliation, British forces headed towards Washington and burnt the Americans' political headquarters. Apparently the burn marks were painted over in white, leading to the name the 'White House'.

In 1814, when the war ended, York began to expand. Stagecoach service began on Yonge St in 1828. In 1834, with William Lyon Mackenzie as the first mayor, York was renamed Toronto, a Native Indian name meaning 'meeting place'. During this time under conservative politicians, the city became known as 'Toronto the Good', a tag which only began to fade in the 1970s. Religious restraints and strong anti-vice laws (it was illegal to hire a horse on Sunday) were largely responsible for this. Not all that long ago, curtains were drawn in department-store windows on Sunday because window shopping was considered sinful, and movie theatres were also closed on the holy day.

Like many big cities, Toronto has had its great fire. In 1904, about five hectares of the inner city burned, levelling 122 buildings. Amazingly, no one was killed. The 1920s saw the first population boom, but in 1941 80% of the population was still Anglo-Celtic.

It was after WW II that the city began to change. Well over half a million immigrants have arrived since then, mainly Europeans from all corners. Italians make up the largest non-British ethnic group. The influx of new tongues, customs and food has livened up a place which was once thought to be a hopeless case.

With its staid background and some excellent urban planning, Toronto has developed cautiously. At least until the 1980s, when anyone with a shovel could break ground, construction has been regulated, with parks, housing and retail places generally being built alongside offices. Progressive and reactionary forces continue to do battle, the pendulum swinging first to one side and then the other. In general, for a city of its size and importance, Toronto remains conservative, particularly on moral issues, but perhaps this is the price to be paid for the benefits.

## ORIENTATION

The land around Toronto is flat and the city tends to sprawl over a large area. Despite its size, the city's grid-style layout, with nearly all the streets running north-south and east-west, means it's easy to get oriented.

Yonge St (pronounced Young), the main north-south artery, is called the longest street in the world – it runs about 18 km from Lake Ontario north to the city boundary, Steeles Ave, and beyond. The central downtown area is bounded by Front St to the south, Bloor St to the north, Spadina Ave to the west and Jarvis St to the east. Yonge St runs parallel to and in between Spadina Ave and Jarvis St, a few blocks from each of these. Street names change from 'East' to 'West' at Yonge St, and the street numbers begin there. Bloor St and College St (called Carlton St east of Yonge St), which is about halfway between Bloor St and the lake, are the two main east-west streets.

At the foot of Yonge St and nearby York St is the lake and the redeveloped waterfront area called Harbourfront. The old docks have given way to restaurants, galleries, artists' workshops, stores, condominiums and some parkland all along Queen's Quay. The ferries for the Toronto Islands moor here, as do many private vessels.

A few blocks north is Front St, where you'll find Union Station (the VIA Rail terminal), the classic old Royal York Hotel, and the O'Keefe Centre, a theatre for the performing arts. Two blocks west of Union Station is the CN Tower and, next door, Skydome, the large sports stadium.

Heading north on Bay St to Queen St, you'll hit Nathan Phillips Square, site of rallies and concerts and the unique City Hall buildings. To the east, the Victorian building dating from 1899 is the old City Hall, now used mainly for law courts. Check out the gargoyles.

One block east is Yonge St, lined with stores, bars, restaurants and theatres catering mainly to the young. On Yonge St between Dundas and Queen Sts is the enormous modern shopping complex known as the Eaton Centre. It's worth a look, and one of the tourist offices is here. Further east is an area known as Cabbagetown, a formerly run-down neighbourhood now renovated and trendy in sections but still retaining some of its earlier character.

On the west side of City Hall is Osgood Hall, home of the Law Society. Queen St West between University Ave and Spadina Ave and beyond to Bathurst St has seen a rebirth and is now busy with many restaurants (some cheap) and book, record and distinctive clothing shops. A lot of young people involved in and on the fringes of the arts live in the area.

University Ave, lined with offices and trees, is Toronto's widest street and the location of most major parades. The lit beacon atop the stately Canada Life Building on the corner of University Ave and Queen St is a guide to the weather. The light at the top is colour-coded: green means clear, red means cloudy, flashing red means rain and flashing white means snow. If the tower lights are ascending, the temperature will rise; if they're descending it will cool. Temperatures are stable if the lights are on and static.

Toronto's Chinatown lies west along Dundas St, from Bay St and continuing to Spadina Ave. Interesting old Spadina Ave, once a strictly Jewish area, now shares its remaining delis and textile shops with the burgeoning Oriental businesses. Dundas St and College St West are mainly Italian. University Ave leads north to Queen's Park at College St. Here are the provincial Parliament Buildings. To the west is the University of Toronto.

North of the park the street is called Queen's Park Ave; it leads to Bloor St, where you'll find the city's principal museum, the Royal Ontario Museum. Just north of Bloor St, between Avenue Rd (Queen's Park Ave) and Yonge St, Yorkville St was once the scene of the 1960s folk music and drug vanguard. Now it's been done over with expensive shops and restaurants. The city is served by expressways on all four sides.

Along the lake, the Gardiner Expressway runs west into the Queen Elizabeth Way (QEW). The QEW goes to Niagara Falls.

Just at the city's western border is Hwy 427, which runs north to the airport and Hwy 401. Hwy 401 runs east-west above the downtown area, east to Montreal and west to Windsor, Ontario, which is opposite Detroit, USA. On the eastern side of the city, the Don Valley Parkway connects Hwy 401 to the Gardiner Expressway at the southern edge of the city.

## INFORMATION
### Tourist Office
The Toronto Visitor Information Centre (☎ 203-2500) has an office in the Queen's Quay terminal, down at the lake at Harbourfront between Yonge and York Sts. It's open all year from 9 am to 5 pm Monday to Friday. On weekends and holidays, someone will answer telephone questions. To get to the office, take the elevator (midway down the mall) up to the Galleria offices on level 5.

For city information, there is also a year-round city information booth outside the Eaton Centre, on the south-west corner of Yonge and Dundas Sts.

Two other booths operate through the summer months. One is at Nathan Phillips Square, in front of City Hall (off Queen St west of Yonge St). The other can be found on the north-east corner of Yonge and Bloor Sts, in front of the Bay department store in the Hudson Bay Centre. These are open every day.

For information on other areas of Ontario as well as Toronto, the Ontario Travel Centre (☎ 314-0944) is conveniently located on the lower level of the Eaton Centre (which is at 220 Yonge St, on the corner of Dundas St). It's open the same hours as the shopping centre, currently 10 am to 9 pm on weekdays, 9.30 am to 6 pm on Saturday and noon to 6 pm on Sunday.

Hostelling International (HI) Canada has its regional Great Lakes office (☎ 363-0697), at 209 Church St, just a few doors from the Toronto hostel.

### Post
Mail can be picked up at General Delivery,

Toronto at 25 The Esplanade, Toronto M5W 1E0, from Monday to Friday.

## Library
The excellent Toronto Public Library is on Yonge St, about a block north of Bloor St on the east side.

## Books & Maps
For travel books, guides, maps and a range of books on nature, camping and outdoor activities, see Open Air (☎ 363-0719), 25 Toronto St, near the corner of Adelaide St East and Yonge St; the door is downstairs off Toronto St.

Also selling maps, including a wide selection of topos, is Canada Map (☎ 362-9297), on the lower level at 211 Yonge St.

## CN TOWER
The highest free-standing structure in the world, the CN Tower (☎ 360-8500) has become a symbol and landmark of Toronto. The tower is in the southern end of the city, near the lake, south of Front St West at John St. The top antenna was put in place in 1975 by helicopter, making the tower 533 metres high. Its primary function is communications – radio and TV signals – but up at the top there is a restaurant, a disco and two observation decks. The one outside is windy, naturally, and not for those easily subject to vertigo. On a good, clear day you can see for about 160 km, which easily includes US cities across the lake.

A glass elevator travels up the outside of the tower. The cost for a trip up and entry to the observation deck is $12 for adults. If you're eating either lunch or dinner at the Top of Toronto revolving restaurant (☎ 362-5411), the elevator ticket price is waived. Call for an idea of the latest menu prices. If you just want a drink in the bar, though, the elevator must be paid for.

The tower is open daily until 10 pm, an hour later on Saturday. The time and weather display at ground level is worth a look.

At the base of the tower is a separate attraction known as the Tour of the Universe. Entry includes a walking tour of a simulated

space port, a laser show, and a special-effects film which suggests a shuttle ride through space. Most people find it all quite good. Admission costs $8 for adults, $6 for children aged five to 12. The Tour is open from 10 am to 10 pm daily, with a 25-minute show commencing every half hour.

## OTHER VIEWS
For a pleasant and free view of the city, head to the rooftop bar of the Park Plaza Hotel. It's on the corner of Bloor St West and University Ave. You can sit under the sun at white wrought-iron tables and chairs and sip a cool one above the masses. Unfortunately, after many years, the bar here has been renovated, making the outdoor section smaller and introducing a dress code. Outside the summer months, men must sport a jacket and tie. Regulations are relaxed in summer, but you'll still get the once over and jeans will no longer be tolerated. It's open from 2.30 pm until 1 am.

The Aquarius Lounge, atop the Manulife Centre at 55 Bloor St West (on the corner of Bay St), is popular with a younger crowd. There is no admission charge and the pianist can be fun. Drinks are a little pricey but the view is terrific.

## SKYDOME
Beside the CN Tower, at 1 Blue Jay Way, this rounded-dome sports stadium was opened in 1989 and is best known for its fully retractable roof, the world's first such facility. The stadium is used primarily for professional baseball and football but also stages concerts, trade shows and various other presentations.

Although not particularly eye-catching from the outside, the interior is strikingly impressive. It can be seen on the tours which are offered every day, on the hour, until 5 pm, events permitting. The tour is not cheap ($8). It's a bit rushed but quite thorough, offering a look at one of the box suites, the view from the stands and press section, a locker room (without athletes), a walk on the field and all sorts of informative statistics and tidbits of information. Did you know that eight 747s would fit on the playing field and that the stadium uses enough electricity to light the province of Prince Edward Island?

Another way to see the place (and a game) is via one of the three restaurants at the stadium (see the Places to Eat section). For those with money (lots of it), rooms can be rented in the adjacent Skydome Hotel, with rooms overlooking the playing field.

The hotel became instantly notorious when, during one of the first ball games, a couple in one of the upper-field side rooms either forgetfully or rakishly became engaged in some sporting activity of their own with the lights on, much to the amusement of the crowd. Since then the hotel insists on signed waivers stipulating there will be no such free performances – party poopers.

**Mark Lightbody**

A cheap-seat ticket ($6) to a Blue Jays baseball game is easily the least expensive way to see the Dome. See the Spectator Sports section later for more information.

## ROYAL ONTARIO MUSEUM (ROM)

The multidiscipline museum (☎ 586-5551), on the corner of Queen's Park Ave and Bloor St West, is Canada's largest and has exhibits covering the natural sciences, the animal world, art and archaeology and, broadly, the history of humankind. For several years the museum has been undergoing extensive renovation and modernisation, a process which is finally in the last stages. The museum covers five floors, so a visit takes some time.

The collection of Chinese crafts, textiles and assorted arts is considered one of the best anywhere. The Egyptian, Greek, Roman and Etruscan civilisations are also represented. The newly designed dinosaur and mammalogy rooms are very good, with the latter containing a replica of part of an immense bat cave found in Jamaica. Another section outlines the history of trade between the East and West, from the ancient caravan routes through to more modern times. The recently added bird gallery, with a huge stuffed albatross and pull-out drawers to explore in the

numerous display cabinets containing such items as eggs, is very good.

A section opened in July 1993 is the S R Perron Gem & Gold Room (actually four octagonal rooms), displaying a dazzling collection of riches, including the 193-carat Star of Lanka Sapphire, a 776-carat behemoth opal from Australia and handfuls of rubies, diamonds and gold nuggets. They are made all the more appealing by the unique fibre-optic lighting system. There are even displays designed for children so parents can ogle in peace. In addition to these permanent exhibits, there are often in-depth touring exhibits – these are generally excellent but a surcharge is added to the admission fee.

The museum is open daily from 10 am to 6 pm and until 8 pm on Tuesday and Thursday. Admission is $7, less for seniors and students, and is free on Tuesday from 4.30 pm until closing time. Family rates are also offered. If you go to the planetarium the same day, discounts are available.

The subway is close by (Museum stop), but if you're driving, there is parking on Bedford St, west of Avenue Rd north of Bloor St.

An annex to the museum is the *Canadian Decorative Arts Department*, down the street in the Sigmund Samuel Building, at 14 Queen's Park Crescent West. The focus is on Canada's early artists and craftspeople. It's open Monday to Saturday from 10 am to 5 pm and from 1 to 5 pm on Sunday. Admission is free.

A ticket to the ROM also permits free entry to the Gardiner Museum (see below).

## GEORGE R GARDINER MUSEUM OF CERAMIC ART

At 111 Queen's Park Ave, this museum is part of the ROM just across the street. The collection is divided into four periods of ceramic history: pre-Columbian, Italian majolica from the 15th and 16th centuries, English delftware of the 17th century and English porcelain of the 18th century. (I particularly admire the pottery from Mexico through to Peru done before the arrival of

Europeans.) It's quite an extensive collection spread over two floors. Admission costs $4 and the opening hours are 10 am to 5 pm Tuesday to Sunday.

## ART GALLERY OF ONTARIO (AGO)

This is one of the top three art galleries in the country (☎ 979-6648), the others being in Ottawa and Montreal. Though not the Louvre, it is excellent, and unless you have a lot more stamina than I do, you'll need more than one trip to see it all. The gallery houses works (mainly paintings) from the 14th century to the present. There is also a Canadian section and rooms for changing exhibitions, which can sometimes be the highlight of a visit. The gallery is best known for its vast Henry Moore sculpture collection – one room holds about 20 of his major sculptures of the human form.

The gallery is at 317 Dundas St West, two blocks west of University Ave. There is a cafeteria if you need a break, and a good gift/book store. At the door, pick up a schedule of the films and lectures that go on in the gallery.

Hours are 10 am to 5.30 pm Wednesday to Sunday (until 10 pm on Wednesday and Friday). It's closed on Mondays and Tuesdays but opens on holiday Mondays.

Admission is a rather steep $7.50, students and seniors $4, but entry is free to all on Wednesday evenings.

The Ontario Art College is next door, on McCaul St.

### The Grange

The Grange (☎ 977-0414) is a restored Georgian house adjoining the AGO (from the Art Gallery, there is a door down in the basement, beside the cafeteria). Admission is included with the gallery ticket. Authentic 19th-century furniture and workers in period dress represent life in a 'gentleman's residence' of the time. The hours are noon to 4 pm Wednesday to Sunday and until 9 pm on Wednesday and Friday.

### CASA LOMA

This is a 98-room medieval-style castle-cum-mansion built between 1911 and 1914 by Sir Henry Pellat, a very wealthy and evidently eccentric man. The mansion (☎ 923-1171) has been a tourist site since 1937, when the cost of upkeep became too much for its owner. The interior is sumptuous, built with the finest materials imported from around the world. Note especially the conservatory. Pellat even brought in stonemasons from Scotland to build the walls around the estate.

Despite all this, it's not a great attraction, though there are fine views from the towers. Bring your camera. Kids seem to enjoy the castle and exploring such features as the tunnels leading out to the former stables (now used to house some antique automobile memorabilia).

In summer, the restored gardens behind the castle are definitely worth a visit. This area is open to the public (without the need to buy a ticket to the castle) on one Monday per month – call to check – and every Tuesday, from 4 pm to dusk.

At Christmas time, elaborate thematic indoor exhibits are put on, geared mainly to children.

Casa Loma is open every day from 10 am to 4 pm. A ticket costs $8 and parking at the site is pricey. If you're lucky, you may find

| 1 | Bay Department Store & Tourist Office |
|---|---|
| 2 | Royal Ontario Museum |
| 3 | McLaughlin Planetarium |
| 4 | Parliament Buildings |
| 5 | Kensington Market |
| 6 | Art Gallery of Ontario |
| 7 | Bus Station |
| 8 | Tourist Office |
| 9 | HI Hostel |
| 10 | City Hall, Information Centre & Nathan Phillips Square |
| 11 | Old City Hall |
| 12 | St James Cathedral |
| 13 | St Lawrence Market |
| 14 | O'Keefe Centre |
| 15 | VIA Rail Station |
| 16 | Skydome |
| 17 | CN Tower |
| 18 | Island Ferry Terminal |

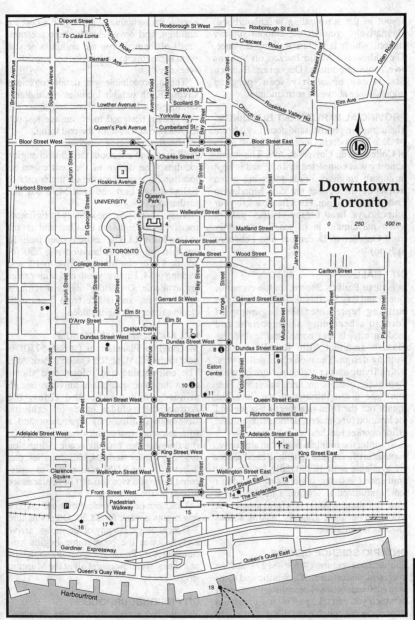

Downtown
Toronto

0    250    500 m

a spot in the surrounding neighbourhood; alternatively, consider the Dupont subway station, which is within walking distance. The address is 1 Austin Terrace, off Spadina Ave. From the corner of Dupont and Bathurst Sts, it can be clearly seen, perched impressively above its surroundings.

## PROVINCIAL PARLIAMENT BUILDINGS

The attractive pinkish sandstone Legislature (☎ 325-7500) sits in Queen's Park, just north of College St on University Ave. The stately building was completed in 1892 and is kept in superb condition. Free tours are given frequently throughout the day, Monday to Friday until 3.30 pm. For a flashback to your school days, head for the visitors' gallery when parliament is in session (roughly from October to December and February to June).

## CITY HALL

In Nathan Phillips Square, on the corner of Queen and Bay Sts, this distinctive three-part building represented the beginning of Toronto's becoming an important and modern city. It was completed in 1965 to Finnish architect Viljo Revell's award-winning design. The twin clamshell towers, with a flying saucer-style structure between them at the bottom, are unmistakeable. Free tours are given throughout the day. The square out the front is a meeting place and the location for concerts, demonstrations and office-worker lunches.

In winter the fountain pool is an attractive, popular artificial skating rink. Rental skates are available until 10 pm daily for this recommended activity. It's a lot of fun; don't feel intimidated if you are a novice – you won't be alone. Immigrants from around the world are out there gingerly making strides towards assimilation.

## ONTARIO SCIENCE CENTRE

The science centre (☎ 696-3127) has an interesting assortment of scientific and technological exhibits and demonstrations, most of which you can take part in. It's a museum where you can touch everything. You might

even learn something, although it's best for children, and on weekends there are hundreds of them. If you are childless or you want some time to look seriously, consider a weekday visit.

The approachable yet detail-conscious Living Earth exhibit includes a simulated rainforest, a limestone cave and an ocean eco-system designed to encourage respect, knowledge and awe for the real thing.

The fitness-testing machines are fun to challenge, and ask about the good changing exhibits. The design of the centre and its location, in a small ravine on the corner of Eglinton Ave East and Don Mills Rd, are further assets.

To get there, take the subway to Eglinton, transfer to the Eglinton East bus and get off at Don Mills Rd. The centre is open from 10 am to 6 pm daily. Admission is $7.50 for adults, $3 for children aged five to 10, and parking is $4. Family, youth and senior rates are available. On Friday nights it remains open to 9 pm and is free from 5 pm until closing time, parking included.

## MCLAUGHLIN PLANETARIUM

McLaughlin Planetarium (☎ 586-5750) is next to the ROM, at 100 Queen's Park Ave. The entertaining and informative shows about the solar system and universe last 45 minutes, and on the 2nd floor, the Astrocentre includes hands-on exhibits, slide shows, astronomy equipment and a solar telescope that enables viewers to watch sun flares as they actually occur. Admission is $5.50, less for students, kids, families, etc. A ticket for the ROM entitles you to a discount here (and vice versa) if both places are visited on the same day.

Laserium or laser rock shows are given a few nights a week for $8.50. Others feature 3-D technology. For any of the shows, arrive early – once the programme begins you cannot get in. Phone for programme details and times. By subway, get off at the Museum stop.

## CITY NEIGHBOURHOODS

Toronto has a very wide variety of ethnic

groups, some in large, concentrated numbers. Throughout the city, these neighbourhoods maintain the homeland cultures and offer outsiders glimpses of foreign countries. Such areas are good for restaurants, and several are mentioned in the Places to Eat section. All these neighbourhoods have changed considerably through the years, and continue to do so as other newer groups (such as Sri Lankans and Latin Americans) arrive in Canada. Other neighbourhoods are mixed areas that preserve a distinctive character. Descriptions of a few of the most prominent districts follow.

### Chinatown

Toronto has by far the largest (and growing) Chinese population in the country, and the principal Chinatown area is right in the centre of town. The original old area runs along Dundas St from Bay St, by the bus station, west to University Ave. There are many restaurants here, but this area has become rather touristy and isn't really where the local Chinese shop.

The bigger and more interesting segment of Chinatown is further west. Also on Dundas St West, it runs from Beverley St, near the Art Gallery, to Spadina Ave and a little beyond. Most of Spadina Ave, from south of Dundas St all the way north to College St and then east and west for a bit along College St, is now primarily Chinese.

The narrow residential side streets of the area are home to many Chinese people. Again there are lots of restaurants, but also variety and grocery stores, jobbers, herbalists, bakeries and places selling many things recognisable only to the initiated. In addition to all the businesses, vendors often set up along the sidewalks. The area gets packed on weekends, when it's sharp with sounds and smells and the restaurants do good business. There are a few Japanese and more and more Vietnamese places in the neighbourhood.

There is also a small group of Chinese merchants and restaurants around Gerrard St and Broadview Ave (in the city's east end) and many in the north-eastern suburb of

Scarborough. Neither of these areas is of particular interest to visitors, but they do indicate the size of Toronto's Chinese community.

### Elm Ave

One of the city's wealthiest areas is just north-east of the corner of Yonge and Bloor Sts. Driving or walking up Park Rd north of Bloor St leads to Elm Ave, where nearly every house on the north side is listed by the Historical Board as being of architectural or historical note. All the streets branching from Elm Ave contain some impressive domains, however. East along Elm Ave, Craigleigh Gardens is a fine, old park.

### Cabbagetown

Cabbagetown, east of Yonge St, is both a residential district (ranging from poor to comfortable) and a commercial district. As well as the differences between its denizens, the area is distinguished primarily by its 19th-century Victorian terrace houses: the area is said to have the richest concentration of fine Victorian architecture remaining in North America.

Cabbagetown is bounded roughly by Gerrard St East to the south, Wellesley St to the north, Parliament St to the west (which is the main business centre) and Sumach St to the east. The last couple of decades have seen considerable gentrification of the once run-down area, and there are certainly some attractive and interesting-looking houses. The new money has brought a certain uniformity to the neighbourhood, though the remaining unrenovated places add a little contrast. The necropolis off Sumach St at Winchester St is one of the city's oldest and most interesting cemeteries. Across the street is the Riverdale Farm, a popular place for families and kids. It's run as a real working farm, with two barns to wander through and a selection of waterfowl and animals, some of which may permit a pat or two. Also at the site, which is free, there may be an art or craft display or some other activity.

Riverdale Farm is a good place to start a

walking tour of the Cabbagetown side streets and houses.

## Danforth Ave

In the east end of town along Danforth Ave, roughly between Pape and Woodbine Aves, is a large Greek community. This has become one of the city's most popular dining areas, and warm summer nights in particular bring out serious crowds. There are many restaurants, a few smoky men's cafés, and also some big, busy, colourful fruit, vegetable and flower stores which stay open into the night.

## Little India

Also out this way is Little India, with numerous speciality stores, women in saris and the scent of spices in the air. It's along Gerrard St East, one block west of Coxwell Ave.

## St Clair Ave West

Italians, in number, are found in many parts of the city, but if there is one centre of the community it's probably on St Clair Ave West east and west of the Dufferin St intersection. Here you'll find Italian movies, clothing stores, espresso cafés and pool halls for the young men. The area went nuts when Italy won the World Cup Soccer Championship in 1982. I've heard that the crowd that gathered was the largest ever recorded in Toronto. Another significant Italian area is on College St between Manning and Ossington Sts.

Nearby is a Portuguese neighbourhood, based along Dundas St West between Ossington and Dufferin Sts.

## Yorkville

Once Toronto's small version of Greenwich Village or Haight-Ashbury, this old counter-cultural bastion has become the city's trendy boutique area. The district is central, just above Bloor St between Yonge St and Avenue Rd. It's centred around Cumberland Ave, Yorkville Ave and Hazelton Lane. Along the narrow, busy streets are many art galleries, cafés, restaurants, nightspots and expensive shops, while the shops of the

enclosed Hazelton Lane are some of the most expensive and exclusive in the country.

The whole area has been renovated and in summer can be pleasant for its outdoor cafés and people-watching. It's worth a stroll but the pretension and snobbery can grate. I mean, a boutique that sells only men's underwear?

Still, there are some intriguing shops and the galleries present a range of work, several displaying or selling Inuit pieces (for big dollars). The Inuit Gallery on Prince Arthur St specialises in Inuit art.

To linger, the Bellair Café has long maintained its position as the place to go. It's not too costly for either a drink or a coffee.

## Markham Village

As you approach the corner of Bloor and Markham Sts (one block west of Bathurst St), you'll see Toronto's most colourful, gaudy store: the zany Honest Ed's. Giant signs say things like 'Don't just stand there, buy something'. Hardly subtle but you won't believe the queues outside the door before opening time. Most patrons are from the nearby Italian and Portuguese districts. There are some good buys – cheap running shoes, T-shirts and various household necessities. With the money Eddie Mirvish has made, he has established quite a reputation and become a major patron of the arts. Markham St south from Bloor St, with its galleries, boutiques and bookshops, is mostly his or his son's doing.

There are some interesting little specialised import shops to browse in. The Mirvish bookshop has good sales on Sunday. Bloor St around this area is fun to stroll along, with numerous restaurants and bars, patronised mostly by a mix of students and immigrants.

## HARBOURFRONT

Harbourfront is a strip of lakefront land running from the foot of Bay St westward to roughly Bathurst St. Once a run-down district of old warehouses, factories and underused docklands, the area was originally slated for redevelopment, primarily as parkland but with people and arts-oriented halls, theatres, galleries and workshops, etc included. Although this has happened to some degree, it is now generally acknowledged that construction was allowed to run amok and too much of the waterfront has been blighted by ugly condos. My blood boils to think of what might have been.

For visitors, the centre of activity is the attractive York Quay, at 235 Queen's Quay, where there is an information office. Something goes on there nearly every night: a dance, a concert or who knows what. Some presentations are free. They may be held outdoors, or inside in the various theatres and galleries. For information on Harbourfront events call ☎ 973-3000. There are also a couple of nearby restaurants and a place or two for a drink. Boat tours depart from the shore here and many private boaters moor around the area.

Just to the east is the impressive-looking Queen's Quay terminal, with the green glass top. It's a refurbished 1927 warehouse now containing some interesting speciality and gift shops, restaurants and, up above, offices and apartments.

Contemporary art is displayed in the Power Plant, an old power station near Queen's Quay. Admission is $2.

On weekends the area is popular for a walk along the pier or a browse in the antique and junk market. Try the French fries from one of the many chip wagons. The Canoe School rents canoes, which can be used for an enjoyable paddle out to the harbour or near the shore either east or west.

To visit Harbourfront, first get to Union Station, the train station on Front St, a few blocks north of the lake. The subway will take you this far south. From here, either walk south on Yonge St or take the LRT streetcar which goes south, running along the harbourfront area on Queen's Quay to Spadina Ave and then returning the same way. Service is continuous through the day and evening. Parking in the area can be a headache and/or costly, so seriously consider public transport.

**TORONTO ISLANDS**

From the foot of Bay St near the Harbour Castle Hotel, you can take a 10-minute ferry ride out to the three Toronto Islands: Ward, Centre and Hanlan's Point. Once mainly residential, the islands are now largely public park and are very pleasant. Centre Island has the most facilities, many summer events and the most people. Boats can be rented, and there is a small animal farm and an amusement area for kids. Beaches line the southern and western shores, and there are two licensed restaurants and some snack bars.

Hanlan's, to the west, is the best beach. You may see some nude sunbathing at Hanlan's south-western end – it's popular with homosexuals – but this is illegal, even though the law is only sporadically enforced. Inland from the beach are picnic tables and some barbecue pits. Towards the city, on Hanlan's Point, is a small private-craft airport. Also at Hanlan's there is a trout pond.

Ward Island, the one on the east side, still has quite a few houses that are lived in all year. There is a small restaurant here for snacks and light lunches out on the lawn.

A ferry ride is as good as a harbour tour and offers good views of the city. Ferries to the islands run frequently in summer and cost $3 return, less for children and seniors. You can walk around the islands in under two hours. The cool breezes are great on a hot, sticky day, and it's pretty quiet during the week. Cycling along the islands' boardwalk on the southern shores isn't a bad way to spend some time. You can take bicycles on some of the ferries or rent them on Centre Island.

Because there is a year-round community living on Ward Island, the ferries run through the winter (though less frequently) and between September and May service only Ward. The other islands can be reached on foot, but note that pretty much everything else on the islands is shut tight. Good thing, too, because the winter wind over here is none too hospitable.

## ONTARIO PLACE

This 40-hectare recreation complex (☎ 314-9900) is built on three artificial islands offshore from the CNE grounds, 955 Lakeshore Blvd West. Entrance to the site is free but almost all activities and attractions must be paid for separately. The futuristic-style buildings and parkland contain about a dozen restaurants, beer gardens, an outdoor concert stage called the Forum, and an IMAX cinema (the Cinesphere), where 70-mm films are shown on a six-storey-high curved screen. Check what film is showing; the effects can be amazing. There is also a large, free, popular play area for kids where you can just let them go nuts. A water park with slides, a wading pool and other water activities has an admission fee. Or, for those at a loose end, there is a bungee jump.

In summer there are nightly concerts at the Forum, with everything from ballet to rock. Bring a sweater, even on a hot day: it gets cold at night down by the water. At the western end is another stage with a waterfall as a curtain, where amateurs or lesser names perform free concerts, shows, etc. Nearby is the 700-metre-long flume water slide with simulated rapids and tunnels. A ticket is $3.

Moored off one of the islands is the *Haida*, a destroyer, open to visitors. This also has an admission charge.

The park is open from mid-May to October from 10.30 am to 1 am (until midnight on Sundays). If there is a concert you really want to see or the act is a big name, arrive early (or even better, very early with a picnic dinner). The price of the concerts varies from $4 to $12. The IMAX prices are $5 to $9. If you are driving, parking is a whopping $9. Take a subway or streetcar to Bathurst St and then the streetcar south down Bathurst St to the CNE exhibition grounds. Over the summer months a shuttle bus runs from Union Station, to the gate of Ontario Place and back frequently through the day.

## HIGH PARK

The city's biggest park is popular for picnics, walking, cycling and jogging. There is a small children's zoo, a lake where people fish and a pool for swimming (which is free). Some parts of the park are well maintained garden; others are left as natural woods. No cars are allowed on summer weekends.

Also in the park is **Colborne Lodge**, built by one of Toronto's first architects and now run as an historical site with costumed workers. It's open daily. Not far from the swimming pool, on the main road through the park, is a restaurant which serves a vast selection of quite good homemade meals at low prices. The park is off Bloor St West at Parkside Drive and runs south down to Lakeshore Blvd, west of the CNE. The subway stop is either Keele or High Park.

## TOMMY THOMPSON PARK & THE PORT

Formerly called and often still known as the Leslie St Spit, this artificial landfill site is presided over by the Metro Toronto Conservation Authority (☎ 661-6600). It extends out into the lake and has unexpectedly become a phenomenal wildlife success. It was designed to improve and develop shipping facilities but within a few years became the second largest ring-billed seagull nesting place in the world. Terns and other bird species nest here too, and you may spot many more types which drop by.

The spit is now a sanctuary for ducks, geese, swans and sandpipers. Nearly 300 kinds of plants, some found nowhere else in Toronto, have also taken root here. Even mammals such as foxes, rabbits and mink are arriving – from where?

The area, a narrow five-km-long strip, is open to the public on weekends and holidays. It's still under construction and arguments over development continue. Marinas are being built on portions of it. During the week, heavy trucks continue the dumping of excavation waste. The park is south of the corner of Queen St East and Leslie St, actually on the corner of Unwin Ave and Leslie St.

In summer, from June to Labour Day, a free shuttle bus runs from the nearest bus stop, on Leslie St at Commissioners Rd (about three long blocks from the main gate), through the gate at the spit and down about halfway. It runs every half-hour from 9 am to 5 pm. At the far end (named Vicki Keith Point after a local long-distance swimmer), out by the eastern edges of the Toronto Islands, there is a lighthouse and views to the city. The park closes at 6 pm. No vehicles are permitted, but many people use bicycles – the Martin Goodman Recreational Trail runs by in both directions.

At the gate there is a map, a bird checklist and a snack wagon. Occasional portable toilets can be found along the main path. Although some small sections are wooded, note that there is very little shade, so be prepared in midsummer. Check the schedule at the gate for the free guided walks, which often have an ornothological (birding) or photography angle.

At the foot of industrial Cherry St, connected to Leslie St by Unwin St, the sandy, relatively quiet, poseur-free beach is popular with windsurfers and those seeking a cool breeze on hot days. There's a snack bar, a few barbecues among the trees and some walking paths along the shoreline.

The Port of Toronto is further north along Cherry St towards Lake Shore Blvd. Freighters can be seen moored along the docks, but you can't get very close and there is no public access or viewing station. Off Cherry St, there is a small park at the end of Poulson St from where there is a fine view of the harbour, the islands and the city skyline.

## THE BEACHES & THE BLUFFS

The Beaches is a rather wealthy, mainly professional neighbourhood along Queen St East at Woodbine Ave, down by the lakeshore. For those who are not local residents, The Beaches means the beach itself and the parkland along the lake – very popular in summer, even if the water has been condemned and is off limits. The sandy beaches are good for sunbathing and picnicking, and for strolling, a boardwalk edges the sand.

You can rent sailboards, with or without lessons. Beach Park is the centre of things, although there are adjacent parks. At the west end, in Woodbine Park, there is a public swimming pool.

About five km further east are the Scarborough Bluffs, limestone cliffs set in parkland at the lake edge. Erosion has created some odd shapes and has revealed layers of sediment that indicate five different glacial periods. There are paths here with good views over the lake. Below, in the lake itself, landfill has been used to form parkland, Bluffers Park, and boat-mooring space. To access Bluffers Park turn south off Kingston Rd at Brimley Rd.

If you want to be atop the cliffs (and you do), there are several parks which afford excellent views of the bluffs and panoramas of Lake Ontario. To reach one area worth visiting, for those with vehicles, turn south of Kingston Rd onto Scarboro Crescent and then Drake Crescent. Park here; the bluffs are within walking distance. Another excellent vantage point at the highest section of the bluffs (about 98 metres high) is at Cathedral Bluffs Park. Still further east along Kingston Rd, turn south at Cathedral Bluffs Drive. The bluffs are accessible by public transport from downtown – call the Toronto Transit Commission (TTC) for route directions (see Getting Around later).

Not far (by vehicle) east of the park is the Guild Inn, with its large lakefront grounds. From behind the inn there are good views along the shoreline to some bluffs. In the garden is a collection of statues and sculptures as well as many columns and gargoyles that were taken from old buildings being demolished. One nearly complete façade looks like something from the Parthenon. Tea is served on the patio in the afternoon. The Guild Inn (which does rent rooms) is on Guildwood Parkway, south from Kingston Rd at Livingstone Rd.

### OTHER PARKS

**Allan Gardens** is an often-mentioned, much-publicised park that's rather overrated. Most of it is nothing more than a city block of grass interspersed with a few trees and benches. The highlight, the large, old, round-domed greenhouse with its three arms, is a worthwhile site, though, particularly in winter or on any day the weather is depressing. It's open daily from 10 am to 5 pm and is free. Plants include many tropical specimens, among them huge palm and flowering trees from around the world. One room is devoted to cactuses. The greenhouses are at the western edge of the park, which is a few blocks east of Yonge St. It's bounded by Carlton, Jarvis and Gerrard Sts. After dark, the entire place is unsavoury enough for me not to recommend visiting or even taking a short cut through it.

Just around the corner from Yonge St, west a few doors at 40 Adelaide St West is an indoor, inner city park which provides a real sanctuary in the downtown centre. Built vertically rather than spread out over a wide area, it is a well designed green space with a range of vegetation including a tropical section and a waterfall. It's open through the day only.

Toronto does have some very fine largely natural parks in numerous ravines formed by rivers and streams running down to the lake. Start in **Edwards Gardens**, on the corner of Lawrence Ave East and Leslie St. It's a big, cultivated park with flower gardens, a pond and picnic sites. You can take a ravine walk from the gardens via **Wilket Creek Park**. The Science Centre backs onto the park here. Along Wilket Creek you can walk for hours all the way down to Victoria Park Ave, just north of Danforth Ave. Much of the way is through woodland.

From the corner of Yonge St and St Clair Ave, walk east to the bridge and the sign for the nature trail. This leads down into the **Don River Valley**, another good walk.

## MARKETS

The city's prime one, **Kensington Market** is a colourful and lively multicultural, old-style market squeezed along Baldwin St and Augusta Ave off Spadina Ave, just south of College St and east of Bathurst St. It's open every day but is wild on Saturday morning. The cheese shops are good, and there's all manner of fresh fruit and vegetables. You can bargain over prices. This was the heart of the

city's Jewish area, but as you'll see, people from many countries have changed that. There are a few small restaurants in the area, too. On Saturday, don't even think of driving down here.

The **St Lawrence Market** is at 92 Front St East (at Jarvis St) in what was Toronto's first City Hall, dating from 1844. Here nearly all the shoppers are of British ancestry and the atmosphere is closer to sedate – there are even classical musicians playing. Although it's best on Saturday, it is open every day but Monday. The range and quality of produce – from fish to more rice varieties than you knew existed – is excellent. On Sunday there is an antique and flea market here.

Just north of the old City Hall building is **St Lawrence Hall**, topped with its clock tower. It is one of the city's finest old buildings; used as a public meeting hall in the last century, it is now – among other things – the venue for National Ballet rehearsals.

The **Market Gallery** on the 2nd floor of the market building, is the city's exhibition hall and displays good, rotating shows (paintings, photographs, documents, artefacts) on Toronto's history. It's free, but is closed on Mondays, Tuesdays and holidays.

Two major health-food stores are the Big Carrot Natural Food Market, 348 Danforth Ave, and the more central but smaller Baldwin Natural Foods, at 20 1/2 Baldwin St.

## HISTORIC SITES

There isn't a lot for history buffs, as the city is so new, but the few small sites are well presented and the tourist office has a guide to the historic homes and sites. Many of these remaining old buildings stand where the old town of York was situated – in the southern portion of the city. Descriptions of some of the best sites follow. Also see The Grange, listed after the Art Gallery of Ontario earlier.

### Fort York

The fort (☎ 392-6907) was established by the British in 1793 to protect the town, which was then called York. It was largely destroyed at the end of the War of 1812 but was quickly rebuilt. Now restored, it has eight original log, stone and brick buildings. In summer, men decked out in 19th-century British military uniforms carry out marches and drills, and fire musket volleys. The fort is open every day, all year, from 9.30 am to 5 pm. Admission is $4.75 for adults, less for kids and seniors. Free tours are given on the hour, to 4 pm. It's on Garrison Rd, which runs off Fleet St West (which in turn is near the corner of Bathurst and Front Sts). Take the streetcar south on Bathurst St.

## Mackenzie House

Owned by William Lyon Mackenzie, the city's first mayor and the leader of a failed rebellion against the government, this mid-Victorian home (☎ 392-6915) is furnished with antiques dating from the 1800s. In the basement is an old print shop where (it's said) the machines can be heard mysteriously working some nights. The house is at 82 Bond St, a couple of blocks east of Yonge St, near Dundas St East. It's open daily (afternoons only on Sundays) and admission is $3.25.

## Spadina House

This was the gracious mansion (☎ 392-6910) of local businessman James Austin. Built in 1866, the impressive interior contains fine furnishings and art collected over three generations. About 10 of its 35 rooms are open to the public. The family gave the house to the historical board in 1982. The address is 285 Spadina Ave, just east of Casa Loma, and it's open daily (but only in the afternoon on Sundays and holidays). Admission is $4.75.

## Campbell House

Downtown on the corner of Queen St and University Ave, this house (☎ 597-0227) was once the residence of the chief justice of Upper Canada. It is a colonial-style brick mansion furnished in early 1800s fashion. The house is open daily in summer, Monday to Friday only from October to late June. There is a small admission charge.

## Colborne Lodge

Situated in High Park, the lodge (☎ 392-6916), built in 1836, is a Regency-style cottage and contains many original furnishings, including possibly the first indoor flush toilet in the province! Informative tours are offered by the costumed staff and may include baking or craft demonstrations. Admission is inexpensive and the site is quite popular.

## Gibson House

This Georgian-style house (☎ 225-0146) which belonged to a successful surveyor and politician offers a glimpse of daily life in the 1850s. Costumed workers demonstrate crafts and cooking and offer a tour around the house daily except Monday. Special activities are planned regularly through the year. On weekends it's only open in the afternoons. It's not far from the Sheppard subway stop in the far northern part of the city, at 5172 Yonge St north of Sheppard Ave. A small admission fee is charged.

## Churches

The Anglican **Church of the Holy Trinity** (☎ 598-4521), hidden right downtown in behind the Eaton Centre on Trinty Square, is one of a kind. It's a funky, welcoming cross between a house of worship and a drop-in centre – everything a community-oriented inner-city church should be. Opened in 1847, it was the first church in the city not to charge parishioners for pews. And it's been going its own way ever since. Don't miss the wonderful Christmas pageant tradition if you're in town in December. There is no charge (a donation is suggested) but tickets are required – call for information.

On the corner of King and Church Sts, the town's first church was built, in 1807. **St James' Cathedral**, built in 1853, now stands here, and is the country's tallest church. Nearby, on the corner of Queen and Parliament Sts, the first Catholic church was constructed, in 1822. On this site, a second **St Paul's Anglican Church** now stands, one of Toronto's most impressive Renaissance-style buildings.

## Montgomery's Inn

Built in 1832 by an Irish military captain of the same name, Montgomery's Inn (☎ 394-8113) is a fine example of Loyalist architecture and has been restored to the period from 1830 to 1855. Afternoon tea is served, and costumed staff answer questions, bake bread and demonstrate crafts. Open daily (afternoons only on weekends and holidays), it's at 4709 Dundas St West, near Islington Ave, in the city's far western end.

## Enoch Turner Schoolhouse

The school (☎ 863-0010) dates from 1848. It's a restored, simple, one-room schoolhouse where, quite often during the week, classes show kids what the good old days were like. It was opened as the first free school so that the children of poorer citizens could learn the three 'r's'. You can visit it, free, when classes or other special events are not being held – call ahead and check the schedule. Through the summer months, there shouldn't be much problem arranging a visit. The address is 106 Trinity St, which is near the corner of King and Parliament Sts.

## Post Office

Toronto's first post office, dating from the 1830s, is at 260 Adelaide St East. One of only two original city buildings remaining in its original location (the other is the Bank of Upper Canada), it has been designated a National Historic Site. Letters can still be sealed with wax by costumed employees and sent from here. It's open seven days a week.

## University of Toronto

The principal campus of the large, prestigious university is just west of the Queen's Park parliament buildings, off College St at University Ave. The attractive grounds feature a range of architectural styles, from the University College building of 1859 to the present. Free walking tours of the campus are given on weekdays through the summer months, departing from Hart House three times daily (weather permitting).

## Other Historic Sites

Todmorden Mills Historic Site, near the location of an important 1794 sawmill and gristmill on the Don River, preserves two houses, complete with period furnishings, and a brewery dating from around 1825. Also on the site is a train station moved from nearby (now a small railway museum) and a former paper mill (now used as a playhouse). The park is at 67 Pottery Rd and is open daily (except Monday) from May to December. A small admission fee is charged.

The large, red-brick houses found all over downtown Toronto were built around the 1920s. The taller, narrower ones, often with more ornately decorative features, are Victorian and mostly date from 1890 to 1900 – a few are older.

## BLACK CREEK PIONEER VILLAGE

A replica of an Ontario village a century ago, Black Creek Pioneer Village (☎ 736-1733) is the city's top historic attraction. It's about a half-hour drive from the downtown area, on the corner of Steeles Ave and Jane St in the north-west section of town, and is accessible on public transport.

Restored buildings and workers in authentic dress give a feeling of what rural life was like in the 19th century. Crafts and skills of the times are demonstrated, using the old tools and methods. One reader raved about the herb garden. You can buy the results of the cooking and baking. In one of the barns is a large toy museum and woodcarving collection. It's open from 10 am to 5 pm daily from April to December. Adult admission is $7. Special events are offered regularly through the season. There is parking, which is free – a rarity in Toronto, as you know by now.

## TORONTO ZOO

Opened in 1974, this huge zoo (☎ 392-5900) has gained an excellent reputation and, although still expanding, is one of the country's largest and best. There are over 4000 animals on the 283 hectares, some in natural-setting pens the size of football fields. Of course, with enclosures so large, it takes a lot of walking around. In fact, there's a small train that goes around the site, but walking is best. You need a full day to see it all.

The animals are in five areas, each covering a major world geographical zone. There are outdoor sections, as well as simulated climates in indoor pavilions. A good idea is the black-light area that enables you to observe nocturnal animals. Through the use of lights, the animals' days have been turned upside down so that we can see them at their active time. Other good exhibits include those which allow for underwater viewing of such animals as beavers, polar bears and seals. One area has displays especially geared to children, with some animals to touch and ponies to ride.

The zoo is on Meadowvale Rd, north of Hwy 401, at the eastern edge of the city. To get there using public transport, take the subway on the Bloor St line east to Kennedy, the last stop. From there get the No 86A Scarborough bus to the zoo. It's quite a trip – about 20 minutes on the subway from the centre of town and then about 40 minutes on the bus, plus waiting time.

Admission is $9.75, less for kids. Parking is $5. Opening hours are 9 am to 6.30 pm daily, with an extension of an hour or so during the summer months. Call for the current schedule.

You may want to take your lunch, as McDonald's has an exclusive food contract for the grounds.

## WONDERLAND

Away from the centre of town, Wonderland (☎ 832-2205) – a sort of Canadian Disneyland – opened in May 1981. The large-scale $120 million theme park has exhibits, games, animals, shows and, of course, rides, including some killer roller coasters, one going 80 km/h. There is a huge artificial mountain with a waterfall and areas made to look like scenes from fairy tales. Recently purchased by Paramount, the park is to undergo some major changes in the next couple of years.

Covering 150 hectares, the park can't all be seen in one day. Get a guidebook at the entrance and decide what you want to see the most. Prices vary but are not low. A one-day pass, good for all attractions and rides, is $27. Straight admission to the grounds is $17. Children's passes cost less. Parking is another $6. Top-name entertainers appear in summer at the Kingswood Theatre; tickets for these shows cost extra. Wonderland is open from approximately early June to early September, and on weekends a month before and after these dates. Opening hours are 10 am to 10 pm in peak season.

Wonderland is on Hwy 400, 10 minutes' drive north of Hwy 401. Exit at Rutherford Rd if you're travelling north, at Major Mackenzie Drive if you're going south. There are buses from Yorkdale and York Mills subway stations.

## WILDWATER KINGDOM

Open daily from June to September, this huge water park (☎ 369-9453) offers about half a dozen twisting water slides and a couple of steep, high, straight speed slides, along with a wave pool and huge whirlpools. There are picnic grounds and food concessions. An all-day ticket is $15, less for kids. The park is 1.6 km west of Hwy 427 on Finch Ave, north-west of the centre of Toronto. On the grounds is a sports complex, with a range of activities available on a pay-as-you-play basis.

## MUSEUM FOR TEXTILES

Obscurely situated with no walk-in traffic at all, this excellent museum (☎ 599-5321) is highly recommended for anyone with the slightest interest in textiles. It's the only museum in the country to exclusively collect and display handmade textiles and tapestries from around the world, and what a collection it is. There are pieces from Latin America, Africa, Europe, South-East Asia and India. The Tibetan collection is particularly fine, as is the one from Indonesia. Some pieces are on permanent display; others are incorporated into in-depth temporary exhibits.

In addition to the international and historic displays, there are changing shows of contemporary fibre works, weavings, rugs and all manner of cloth art.

The museum can be found (look hard, the door is tucked back from the street) at 55 Centre Ave (running south off Dundas St West in Chinatown between Bay St and University Ave), behind the Toronto City Hall. It's open Tuesday to Friday from 11 am to 5 pm, and from noon to 5 pm on weekends. Admission is $5.

## MARINE MUSEUM OF UPPER CANADA & HISTORIC RESTAURANT

In the officers' quarters of an 1841 army barracks at Exhibition Place, this museum (☎ 392-1765) shows the history of the city as a port. On exhibit are models and old ship relics, and in summer, there's a restored steam tugboat moored outside. Admission is $3.25, less for children. It's open Monday to Saturday from 9.30 am to 5 pm, and on Sunday from noon to 5 pm.

In the basement of the museum is the *Officer's 1893 Restaurant* (☎ 868-6077), which every Thursday to Saturday night recreates a dinner party held in 1893 to celebrate the naming of Stanley Barracks. Original recipes are used for the menu. The cost for the 12-course meal, including alcohol, is $75 per person, and it's usually sold out.

## HOCKEY HALL OF FAME

Housed in the beautiful old Bank of Montreal building (dating from 1885) at the north-west corner of Front and Yonge Sts, the Hockey Hall of Fame (☎ 360-7765) gives young and old fans all they could ask for, and more. And for visitors unfamiliar with the game, enough background and history is presented to perhaps help explain Canadians' passion for this, the fastest of sports. Included is a replica of hockey's biggest prize, the Stanley Cup, a re-creation of the Montreal Canadiens' dressing room and all manner of interactive exhibits and activities. Admission is $7.50 for adults, less for seniors and kids. It's open every day (afternoons only on Sundays), with extended evening hours on Thursdays and Fridays.

## POLICE MUSEUM

A new police museum is being developed in the impressive new headquarters building at 40 College St. It was due to open in late 1993 and will be open every day, free. The range of displays and equipment covers the period from 1834 to the present. Included in the collection are uniforms, vehicles, equipment and details of some noteworthy cases.

## MUSEUM OF THE HISTORY OF MEDICINE

New quarters are being sought for this museum, and at press time it was closed.

## REDPATH SUGAR MUSEUM

Along the waterfront, at 95 Queen's Quay West, a free museum (☎ 366-3561) is part of the large sugar mill. There is a film on the production of the sweet stuff, as well as exhibits of equipment. The museum is open on weekdays only, from 10 am to noon and 1 to 3.30 pm.

## TORONTO DOMINION GALLERY OF INUIT ART

Housed on the mezzanine floor of the AETNA Tower of the Toronto Dominion Centre, on Wellington St between Bay and York Sts, this gallery (☎ 982-8473) displays a top-rate collection of far northern art dating mainly from WW II to the present. It consists primarily of sculpture in stone and bone, which is the foremost form of Inuit art.

The gallery is free and is open daily. Hours are 8 am to 6 pm Monday to Friday, 10 am to 4 pm on weekends. Occasionally, you may find a rope across the door of the gallery. Just take it down and go in; the gallery is still open though there may well be no attendant. Free tours are given once a day on Tuesday and Thursday but can be arranged for any day – call and ask.

## TORONTO STOCK EXCHANGE

The city's exchange (☎ 947-4700) is Canada's largest and one of the most modern anywhere. Stock worth $100 million is bought and sold each day, so it's a fairly hectic place. A free 45-minute presentation on the exchange's history and operation is offered Tuesday to Friday at 2 pm sharp. The public viewing gallery is open on weekdays from 9 am to 4.30 pm. The stock exchange is at 130 King St West, on the north-east corner of King and York Sts, right in the centre of the city's financial district.

## URBAN ENVIRONMENT CENTRE
The Urban Environment Centre (☎ 461-9654), a 100-year-old demonstration house at 16 Howland Rd, has been renovated to show how any house can be adapted to reduce its impact on the environment. See and hear tips on energy conservation and efficient housing. It's open Tuesday, Wednesday, Thursday and Saturday afternoons. Admission is free.

## CHESS GAMES CORNER
Right in the heart of the city, at the corner of Yonge and Gould Sts, is the unofficial chess centre. Here through all kinds of weather, night and day, chess players and aficionados of every description gather to duel and bet. It all began with the late 'open highway' Joe Smolij in 1977, who can be found in the Guinness Book of Records as the world's fastest chess player.

## ACTIVITIES
### Cycling
For cyclists, the Martin Goodman Trail is a bicycle route along the waterfront which stretches from The Beaches in the east end, past Harbourfront and the downtown area, to the Humber River in the west end. From here, it connects with paths in parkland running northwards along the Humber. This section is a really fine ride. You can go as far at least as far as Eglinton, and that's quite a few km. Visit the tourist office for a free pamphlet detailing sights along the path.

The Toronto Bicycling Network (☎ 766-1985) organises short, medium and long weekend trips (some overnight) throughout the summer.

### Water Sports
Free swimming in public pools can be found

in High Park, the Gus Ryder Pool (formerly known as the Sunnyside Natatorium) south of the park at the lake on Lakeshore Drive, and in Woodbine Park at The Beaches in east-end Toronto, at the foot of Woodbine Ave. Many other city parks include pools but the three above are selected for their good locations, large size and popularity.

Sandy beaches, a boardwalk and, on any hot summer day (especially on weekends), lots of people can also be found around The Beaches. Kew Beach is the most popular section and the boardwalk goes through here. The same thing on a smaller, more low-key scale can be enjoyed at Sunnyside Beach in the west end, south of High Park. Both are fun, relaxed and relaxing (with everybody in bathing suits) but you can't go in the water – it's too polluted.

There is windsurfing at The Beaches too, rentals are available in the Ashbridges Bay area at the western end of the beach.

### Other Activities
In winter, there are good, free places to skate at City Hall and at Harbourfront, both with artificial ice. If it's been quite cold, there is also large Grenadier Pond in High Park. Skates can be rented at the City Hall rink.

For out-of-town outdoor activities, two of city's best known camping stores – Trail Head, at 40 Wellington St East, and Mountain Equipment Co-op, nearby at 35 Front St East – have information on adventure trips such as white-water canoeing and wilderness hiking.

The Balloonery (☎ 620-7500) provides the opportunity to go hot-air ballooning. It's big bucks – about $135 an hour or more. Flights go on summer weekends outside of the city, with champagne included in the price.

## ORGANISED TOURS
The reliable Gray Line (☎ 594-3310) runs a basic, two-hour, inner-city tour for $20, less for seniors and children. Various other, more specialised tours lasting from 2½ hours and up are offered, with stops at sites included. Another, an all-day affair, runs west to

Niagara Falls. They pick up passengers at downtown hotels and at the main bus terminal (610 Bay St). Tickets can be bought on the bus, or at the Gray Line desk in the Royal York Hotel, on York St across from the train station.

For a more specialised tour call Architectural Walks (☎ 922-7606). These 2½-hour guided walks begin at the front door of the old City Hall, 60 Queen St West, and take in the new and old of the downtown core. Tours cost $10 and run Tuesday to Saturday from June to September.

Another very interesting walking tour is a three to 3½-hour intensive look at Chinatown, with visits to shops, a herbalist and much more, plus a dim sum lunch at the guide's own restaurant. It's put on by David Ko (☎ 595-6855) and is offered every day, all year. The price ($48) includes pick-up from and return to your lodgings, and the meal.

The University of Toronto (☎ 978-5000) runs free guided tours of the campus through the summer, three times daily. This is the country's largest university and the campus has some fine buildings. Tours start from the map room in Hart House.

Several companies run boat tours in and around the harbour and the islands. Most depart from Harbourfront around Queen's Quay, John Quay and, especially, York Quay. For general information on boat tours ☎ 973-4094.

The main operator is Mariposa Cruise Lines (☎ 203-0178). The *Chippewa*, a retired Maid of the Mist from Niagara, is used for the one-hour, basic, narrated tour. A ticket is $12. Mariposa also offers trips on a sail boat and, more expensively, leisurely evening trips aboard the *Northern Spirit*, with buffet, cash bar and dancing. For all of the above, purchase tickets in advance at Queen's Quay Terminal Pier Six.

Some privately owned sailing ships and schooners offer trips of varying duration as far as Niagara-on-the-Lake. The *Challenge* (☎ 461-3866), a three-masted schooner, goes out beyond the islands on its cruises. Other boats are geared for fishing. Look around the dock area; you'll see signs advertising these and various charters.

The island ferry has good views of the city and is very cheap. If you're visiting the islands, remember to check the time of the last return trip. In summer the ferries run about every half-hour but not very late at night. See under Toronto Islands for more details.

## FESTIVALS

Some of the major events held here are:

June

*Caravan* – This is a nine-day event of cultural exchange during which ethnic groups offer music, dance and food native to their homelands. A passport ($14) entitles you to visit the 50 or so different ethnic pavilions set up around the city. Buses travel between the pavilions.

The event takes place during the last days of June. Ask at the tourist office for a complete list of events and things to see and do. The Japanese pavilion is always rated highly and has frequently taken first prize in recent years.

*Queen's Plate* – The year's major horse race and one of North America's oldest (held since 1859), the Queen's Plate is run at the Woodbine Track (☎ 675-6110) around the end of June. Get lucky and your trip will be paid for.

*Gay Pride Day Parade* – Now well into its second decade and continuing to get larger and more notorious, Gay Pride Day culminates in an outrageous downtown out-of-the-closet parade towards the end of June. People of all persuasions come to watch floats and the participants and to generally party, with recent crowds estimated as high as 100,000. Toronto has a large homosexual and lesbian community based around Church St between Carlton and Bloor Sts, and this is where the parade takes place.

June-July

*Jazz Festival* – The excellent and ever-growing annual du Maurier Downtown Jazz Festival is held throughout the central city in June and early July, with a week of concerts day and night. The jazz is varied, featuring local, US and European players. More gospel, blues and world beat influences have been creeping into the mix. In recent years, about a thousand musicians have performed annually. Workshops, films and even jazz cruises are part of the event. Shows range from freebies on the streets, to nightclub performances, to concert hall recitals. Prices vary considerably but for the most part are pretty reasonable.

Top Left: The Big Nickel, Sudbury, Ontario (ML)
Top Right: Cross-country skiing on the Bruce Trail, Ontario (MA)
Bottom: Niagara Falls from the top, Ontario (RE)

Top: Spring maple-syrup production, Southern Ontario (ML)
Bottom Left: Trillium, the provincial flower of Ontario (CK)
Bottom Right: Spanish aerocar, Niagara Falls, Ontario (ML)

*Soul & Blues Festival* – Also keep an ear open for the Soul and Blues Festival, held towards the end of July and based at Harbourfront.

*International Picnic* – At the beginning of July each year, to welcome summer, the huge International Picnic is held at the CNE grounds. Admission is free and there's music, dancing, contests and lots of food. It's very popular with the Italian community.

*The Molson Indy* – Toronto's only major car race, this has now become an annual tradition, held in early July. Well-known names from the international circuit compete in front of large crowds during the two days of practice and qualifying trials, with the big race on the last day of the three-day event. It's held in and around Exhibition Place and Lakeshore Blvd, in the south-central portion of the city.

*Fringe Theatre Festival* – With over 400 performances in six venues over 10 days, generally in July, the Fringe Festival has become a major theatrical hit. The participants are chosen by lottery, so the performances vary widely in style, format and quality. Expect the unexpected. Drama, comedy, musicals and cabaret-style shows are all part of the event. Ask at the tourist office for the year's details and a programme guide.

July-September

*Mariposa* – Begun in the early 1960s, Mariposa (☎ 778-9063) is a festival of mainly folk but also bluegrass and American Indian music. Having grown from just a three-day event, the festival now schedules concerts throughout the year at various venues around town.

The main annual event is held in either July or August in Toronto, often on one of the islands. Workshops, jam sessions and ethnic folk dancing are featured as well. For information on all the events and locations, call their office or inquire at the tourist office.

*Caribana* – An ever-growing annual West Indian Festival, Caribana (☎ 925-5435) celebrated its 25th year in 1991. Held on Centre Island around the beginning of August, it is primarily a weekend of reggae, steel drum, and calypso music and dance.

The main attraction, however, is the lengthy and colourful parade featuring fantastic and outrageous costumes à la carnival in Rio. This parade can have perhaps 6000 people in it and can take five hours or more to pass by! Other events and concerts are spread over the two weeks leading up to the island weekend. Phone for details of events and tickets.

*Canadian National Exhibition (CNE)* – The CNE claims to be the oldest (about 100 years old) and the largest annual exhibition in the world. It includes agricultural and technical exhibits, concerts, displays, crafts, parades, a good air show, a horse show, all manner of games and rides, and fireworks. The exhibition is held during the two weeks prior to, and including, the Labour Day Holiday, which falls in early September. The location is Exhibition Place, which is by the old CNE football stadium on Lakeshore Blvd West, at the lake.

*Film Festival* – The annual Festival of Festivals is now a prestigious and major international cinematic event. Usually held in September, it lasts about a week and a half and features films of all lengths and styles, as well as gala events and well-known stars.

Get more information from the tourist office or check the papers for special guides and reviews. You can obtain tickets for individual screenings or buy expensive, all-inclusive packages.

*Toronto Star Great Salmon Hunt* – This annual fishing derby, held in summer (July or August), attracts anglers to Lake Ontario from far and wide, hoping to catch some of the hundreds of thousands of dollars in prizes for landing the big one.

October

*International Festival of Author* – Held in the fall (usually October) at Harbourfront, this very engaging event presents well-known fiction writers from around the world reading from their work. Novelists, poets, short-story writers and more are featured. Each evening three or four writers are presented.

Readings are also held through the year on a weekly basis, generally featuring less prominent authors.

## PLACES TO STAY
### Camping

There are several camping/trailer grounds within 40 km of the city. The tourist office has a complete list.

One of the closest is *Indian Line Campground*, part of Clairville Conservation Area (☎ 678-1233). It's north up Indian Line Rd, which runs north-south on the east side of the airport. The campground is near Steeles Ave, which marks the northern edge of the city limits. This is probably the best place for tenters and has 224 sites.

Also close to the city is *Glen Rouge Park* (☎ 392-2541), on Kingston Rd (Hwy 2) at Altona Rd, near Sheppard Ave East. It's on the lakefront, at the border of Scarborough – part of metropolitan Toronto – and the town of Pickering at the eastern edge of the city. There are about 120 sites.

## Hostels

The hostel situation has improved since the last edition. The HI *Toronto Hostel* (☎ 368-0207) remains right downtown, at 223 Church St, just south of Dundas St East. The subway stop is Dundas. The location, three blocks east of the Eaton Centre on Yonge St, is excellent and central. The three-storey renovated brick building is open all year round and can accommodate 154 guests. During the summer, reservations are advised. Facilities include a kitchen and laundry. The hours are good (the hostel is open from 7 am to 2 am every day) and prices are low for the heart of the city – $14/20 for members/nonmembers. Semiprivate rooms for four are also available, at a slightly higher cost. If you don't have a sleeping sheet, one will be supplied.

Hostelling International (HI) Canada (☎ 368-6469), a few doors down at 209 Church St, is where memberships may be purchased.

A good alternative is the independent *Leslieville Hostel* (☎ 461-7258), four km from downtown at 185 Leslie St, in an east-end residential neighbourhood. From downtown, it's a 20-minute ride on the Queen St streetcar, with 24-hour service, to Leslie St, a short walk from the hostel. Go north on Leslie St from Queen St. The family-run hostel has 25 beds, mostly in small dormitories, but there are also a couple of private rooms. Rates are $15 for a dorm, which includes a good breakfast. It's open all day and has parking.

For this edition, the Leslieville generated more positive mail than any other lodging place in the country.

Nearby, the *Merry Mattress* (book through Leslieville) is a little cheaper if no breakfast is required, though the morning meal is offered. Again, it consists mainly of dorms but has one or two private rooms as an option. Neither place has cooking facilities for guest use.

The *Marigold International Hostel* (☎ 536-8824) is another independent place. Affiliated with Backpackers, this one is in the west end of town, at 2011 Dundas St West. It, too, is right on the streetcar line. Take either the College St or Dundas St cars from downtown for the roughly 20-minute ride. Avoid the Dundas car on weekends, as it goes through the heart of Chinatown – with the congestion then, a passenger could die of old age before reaching the hostel. An alternative is the subway to the Dundas West stop, from where the Dundas streetcar begins its route eastbound, going right by the hostel on the run into downtown.

The Marigold supplies complimentary coffee and doughnuts each morning but has no kitchen facilities. Check-in is from 7 to 11 pm. The dormitory beds are $17.50 per night ($19.50 if you check in after 11 pm). You cannot get in during the day, but if you have spent the night you do not need to leave by any particular time – the door locks behind you. There are 36 beds and one room for couples. It's open all year.

The *YWCA* (☎ 923-8454), for women only, is central, at 80 Woodlawn Ave, near Yonge St. There's an inexpensive cafeteria. The price for a single room is $42, less if you share a double, and a dormitory bed costs $17. A continental breakfast is included, and there are winter discounts for stays of a week or longer. The *YMCA* in town doesn't rent rooms.

## Colleges

The central *University of Toronto* (☎ 978-8735) rents rooms in various college residences. The campus is by the corner of University Ave and College St. Rooms are available from the middle of May until late August. Singles/doubles are $42/60, which includes breakfast and maid service, and there are very good weekly rates (but without the daily-rate perks). Rooms are also available at another campus, which is smaller and more suburban, and there are still more beds in other downtown residences such as Trinity College.

*York University* (☎ 736-5175) has a similar deal, renting rooms from May to the end of August. The trouble with accommodation here is that it's a long way from the downtown area, at the northern boundary of

ONTARIO

the city. The address is 4700 Keele St, near Steeles Ave. Singles/doubles are $30/50, less for students, and reservations are preferred.

*Neil Wycik College Hotel* (☎ 977-2320), a well-located, apartment-style student residence and hotel, is at 96 Gerrard St East, by Ryerson Polytechnic University. It's now affiliated with Backpackers Hostels. During the summer the residence's rooms are rented out (long term only, for four months). The hotel rooms, though, are rented by the day at the good-value rate of $29/36 a single/double. Inexpensive family rooms are also available. There is a student-run cafeteria for breakfasts (which are included in the price).

*Tartu College* (☎ 925-4747), at 310 Bloor St West, not far from Yonge St, rents rooms in the summer. A single is $30 a day or $130 per week.

## Tourist Homes

There aren't a lot of commercial guesthouses in town but the ones that do exist are generally central, pretty well established, fairly priced and good. For the most part, unlike the hotels, the guesthouses charge a constant price throughout the year.

*Karabanow Guesthouse* (☎ 923-4004) has a good location, at 9 Spadina Rd, just north of Bloor St West. The tariff includes parking, daily cleaning and cable TV. Singles start at $45 and doubles range from $50 to $60. For every night stayed over five, a $5 saving is offered.

Another recommended guesthouse is the *Beverley Place* (☎ 977-0077), at 235 Beverley St, a small north-south street running south from College St to Queen St West between University and Spadina Aves. The guesthouse is excellently situated near the corner of College St, very close to the university. Chinatown, Queen St West and even the CN Tower are all within walking distance. The house is a well-restored, three-storey Victorian place dating from 1877, with lots of original features and wonderfully high ceilings. The entire place is furnished and decorated with interesting antiques and collectables.

One of the most appealing attributes is the small, comfortable courtyard with a huge tree, off the kitchen. A full breakfast is included in the room prices, and guests are encouraged to enjoy eating it on the patio.

The prices are quite reasonable and vary depending on the room. Singles/doubles begin at $45/60. The 'Queen Room' (with an impressive bed) costs more, as does the 3rd-floor, self-contained apartment with its own balcony and city view. The busy season lasts from June to November, and during this period reservations are not a bad idea. This would be true of all the places listed in this section.

The owner, Bill Ricciuto, also runs a similar house across the street. Guests staying here come over to No 235 for breakfast.

Very convenient, just north of College St at 322 Palmerston Blvd, a quiet tree-lined avenue, is the *Burkin Guesthouse* (☎ 920-7842). It's a well-kept, large older house with eight guest rooms and a pleasant 2nd-storey balcony. Prices are a little higher than at the others – $45 to $55 for singles and $60 to $65 for doubles, depending on the size of the room – but a continental breakfast is included. Smoking is not permitted. Some free parking is available.

At 1233 King St West is the simpler *Candy Haven Tourist Home* (☎ 532-0651), right on the King St streetcar line; look for the bright paint job and sign. It's central and there are sinks in the rooms. Singles/doubles are $40/45.

Still further west, at 1546 King St, near Roncesvalles Ave, is the *Grayona Tourist Home* (☎ 535-5443). It's a renovated old house run by Marie Taylor, a friendly, enthusiastic Australian. Singles range from $35 to $45 and doubles are $45 to $55. Every room except the small single has a fridge and a TV. Marginally more expensive rooms which are good for families (there is even a cot) have cooking facilities. A new family room comes with bathroom and kitchen and goes for $75 a night.

The Grayona is about seven km from the centre of town, and although some of the visitors walk, there is a streetcar along King St which stops practically at the door. There are two other guesthouses within a few doors to the west towards Roncesvalles Ave.

In the east end, a few steps from the Greenwood subway stop and just around the corner from the Greek restaurant district, is the *Allenby* (☎ 461-7095), at 223 Strathmore Blvd. The top floors of this three-storey house contain very comfortable guest rooms, and there is a basic kitchen with a microwave for visitors to share. The room rates vary, mainly depending on size, with singles from $45 to $60 and doubles from $50 to $65. There are also self-contained apartment units available. Weekly rates are offered.

## B&Bs

This has become an increasingly popular form of accommodation and most participating homes seem to be quite busy, particularly in summer, although many guests are not vacationing but are on courses or a business trip.

There are several B&B associations in town which check, list and book rooms in the participating homes. Indicate where you'd like to be and any other preferences and attempts will be made to find a particularly suitable host. Prices are fairly standardised, at $45/55 a single/double, with some variation (mostly upward). Places in suburban areas cost $5 or so less than those downtown. There is generally no need to go to the agency – a telephone call should get things organised.

Metropolitan B&B Registry (☎ 964-2566) is the largest outfit, with members in and out of town. The office is at 615 Mount Pleasant Rd, Suite 269, Toronto M4S 3C5. They seem to have the lowest rates for singles (with rooms from $40), and doubles are $50 to $75. Foreign languages are spoken at some places and, as is the norm generally, smoking is not permitted in the homes.

Toronto B&B Inc (☎ 588-8800), at mailing address Box 269, 253 College St, Toronto M5T 1R5, has about 20 members.

Singles/doubles average $45/55. There's no office to visit; if you're in town, just call.

Thirdly, there is the Downtown Toronto Association of B&B Guesthouses (☎ 690-1724) at 153 Huron St (PO Box 190, Station B, Toronto, M5T 2W1). Their rooms are all downtown, mainly in renovated Victorian houses, and cost $45 to $65 for singles, $55 to $75 for doubles. The association's founder, Susan Oppenheim, rents rooms in her own house and serves breakfast in a kitchen that you won't forget.

Each of these associations produces a booklet listing the participating hosts and the type of places and features they offer. Send a stamped self-addressed envelope to receive one of the listing guides.

## Hotels – bottom end & middle

Toronto has an abundance of large, new, modern hotels, and more are being added continually. There are many downtown places, plenty around the city's edges and a good number out around the airport. Of course, they tend to be rather pricey and sterile. The city, unfortunately, lacks smaller, older hotels with character. There are a few exceptions, but most of these places fall into the middle-price ranges. Many hotels offer discount weekend packages and practically all have higher rates during summer.

The inner city still does have some older, cheaper hotels, and a good number of these are found in the Church, Jarvis and Sherbourne Sts area east of Yonge St. Sections of this part of town can be a little rough, with some hotels' rooms used for more than sleeping. Single women may not like walking in the area alone at night and may be asked their price. This is particularly the case around Church and Jarvis Sts near Isabella St and again down around Dundas St. The southern section of Jarvis St, say between Carlton and Queen Sts, and the streets nearby should probably be avoided late at night.

Despite these considerations, this is not a battle zone and there are perfectly safe places to stay. Best in the low-budget category, and good value, the *Selby* (☎ 921-3142) is at 592

Sherbourne St, north of Wellesley St. The turreted Victorian mansion, dating from 1882 and designated as a heritage site, has an interesting history. At one time it was a girls' school. Later, Ernest Hemingway lived here when he worked for the *Toronto Star* in his younger days, before heading to Paris.

Much of the hotel has been upgraded. Rooms cost $50 to $80 for either singles or doubles, depending on size, upgrades, features and whether there is an ensuite bathroom. This makes the less-expensive rooms quite a bargain for two people sharing. There is a slight discount through the slower winter months and a weekly rate is always in effect. A continental breakfast is included in the price. Reservations are recommended from May to October.

A separate bar and grill are popular with men from the local gay community but straights make up a good portion of the hotel clientele.

Further south is the *St Leonard* (☎ 924-4902), at 418 Sherbourne St. It's worn and perhaps a little less judicious in screening guests but is clean and friendly. There are 22 simple rooms, some with private bath and TV, with singles starting at $42 and rising to $50 for a room with all the extras. Doubles range from $49 to $59.

The *Whitehouse Hotel* (☎ 362-7491), at 76 Church St, is a narrow, unobtrusive place whose 35 rooms take up nine floors. It has been popular with out-of-towners, mostly Americans, but maintenance and service have slipped quite a bit in the past few years. A single is $65; the same room with one double bed is $75 for two people in high season. Ask to see the room before checking in. Nearly everything downtown is within walking distance.

For connoisseurs of classic dives there's the *Gladstone*, at 1214 Queen St West. It's a beautiful old building long past its hey day (although sandblasted), with plenty of 'rubbies' throwing 'em back in the bar downstairs. Rates are cheap – under $30 – but this place is not recommended for women.

The mid-range *Strathcona* (☎ 363-3321) is also an older place that has been over-

hauled and upgraded. It now has all the usual amenities and yet is, for the downtown area, moderately priced ($75 for singles up to $90 for the top doubles). The Strathcona has an excellent location, at 60 York St, very near the train station. There's a dining room, a coffee shop and a bar.

One of the best of the small, old downtown hotels is the *Victoria* (☎ 363-1666), at 56 Yonge St, near its southern end. Refurbished throughout, it maintains such older features as the fine lobby and it has a lot of history. Prices are now between $75 and $95. Also in the more European mode is the *Comfort Inn* (☎ 924-7381), at 15 Charles St. Prices are comparable.

The more standard high-rise *Bond Place* (☎ 362-6061) is busy with vacationers – there are often tour buses out the front. It has a great location near the Eaton Centre, at 65 Dundas St East. Prices range from $69 to $109 for singles and doubles.

More like a motel, but perfectly good, cheaper and with parking, is the *Executive Inn* (☎ 362-7441), at 621 King St West. The 75 rooms are priced at about $75 a double. It's central and the King St streetcar goes right by.

## Hotels – top end

The costliest rooms in town are found at the *Four Seasons* (☎ 964-0411) in Yorkville, at 21 Avenue Rd, where prices start at around $225 a night (less on weekends). Also well appointed, with a good reputation and a fine lobby area, the *Hilton International* (☎ 869-3456) is right in the centre, at 145 Richmond St West. Singles/doubles cost from $185/200.

The *Harbour Castle Westin* (☎ 869-1600) has a fine location right at the edge of the lake, opposite the Toronto Islands. The address is 1 Harbour Square, near the bottom of Yonge St. The revolving restaurant offers good views over the city and lake. Basic prices are about $20 less than at the Hilton. Others in this category are the comfortable *King Edward* and the *Skydome Hotel* at the downtown stadium.

The venerable *Royal York* (☎ 368-2511),

at 100 Front St, opposite the train station, deserves mention. Among the top-class hotels, it's the oldest and has served people from rock stars to royalty. There are several bars and places to get a bite to eat on the premises. You can grab a single here from just under $150, much less on weekends.

The airport strip features a number of upper-end hotels convenient for those who need to be near the runways. At the low end is the plain *Journey's End Hotel* (☎ 240-9090), at 2180 Islington Ave.

## Apartment Hotels

Numerous, fully furnished rooms with kitchen facilities have sprung up in apartment buildings, private homes and hotels in recent years. Although they can provide reasonable value, they are mostly in the luxury category, with all mod cons, and are geared to the corporate client and business executive. Many have a minimum stay, which ranges from three days to a month.

Very central is the new *Town Inn Hotel* (☎ 964-3311), at 620 Church St, two blocks south of Bloor St. For the price of one of the commercial hotel rooms, you can get a suite here with kitchen. There is also a pool and sauna. A double is $95 a day, including a small breakfast.

At the *Andrews Apartments* (☎ 267-1118), there is a three-week minimum stay in their private one to five-bedroom home units. They also have some housekeeping motel units on their premises at 2245 Kingston Rd, between Midland and Danforth Aves. One of these costs about $375 a week.

*Executive Travel Suites* (☎ 273-9641) has four such properties in the downtown area, with prices starting at about $100 a day (with a three-day minimum stay). Each unit has a separate bedroom and living room and each building offers one or more extras, such as a pool, balconies, roof deck or restaurant.

A lot of contract signing is required, including forms for damage liability. Make sure the contents are in good shape before you move in. Complaints have been received concerning some of the stipulations, the quality of the furnishings and, especially, the

service. Despite this, Executive has been around for quite a few years. It is primarily geared to the business traveller, and perhaps those visiting for pleasure are not as well cared for.

Another place is the *Cromwell* (☎ 962-5604), at 55 Isabella St. The minimum rental is for three days and rates average $55 a day. This location is central but is also in one of the downtown prostitution districts. It is not really a tough or dangerous area but women alone at night may well be mistaken for being 'on the game'.

The tourist office will know of other apartments for short-term rent.

## Motels

For such a large city, Toronto is rather short on motels, so in summer they are often full. There are two main districts for motels in the city and others scattered throughout and around the perimeter.

On the west side of town, a strip of motels (now threatened with redevelopment) can be found along the lake on Lake Shore Blvd West (formerly Hwy 2), informally known as The Lakeshore. Many are between the Humber River and Park Lawn Ave, just west of High Park. The area has become widely known for its prostitution and the attendant problems. Several of the motels are now short-time places, but some perfectly legitimate motels are suffering unnecessarily from a lack of business. Others are now boarded up.

This district isn't too far from the downtown area, about 12 km from Yonge St, and the streetcar lines run the whole way. To get there, take the Queen St or King St streetcar from downtown to Roncesvalles Ave and continue on the Queen St streetcar to the Humber River. Switch (for no charge) to the Humber streetcar, which goes along the lakeshore. The motels edge the shoreline, and several nearby parks on the waterfront offer cool breezes in summer and good views of the city and islands. There are about a dozen motels more or less side by side. The better ones are often full in summer.

Furthest west, with the yellow sign, the

*Beach Motel*, at 2183 Lake Shore Blvd West (☎ 259-3296), is good. It has 40 rooms (from $55) and is beside the entrance to a park.

A little cheaper is the *Silver Moon* (☎ 252-5051), at 2157 Lake Shore Blvd, with rooms from $45 to $65.

The *Hillcrest* (☎ 255-7711) is a little closer to town, at 2143 Lake Shore Blvd. It's also good, at about the same prices. The *North American* (☎ 255-1127), the bigger, greenish two-storey place at 2147 Lake Shore Blvd West, seems to be on the way down.

The large, modern, well-maintained *Seahorse* (☎ 255-4433), probably the most prosperous of the lot, features rooms for the amorous, with waterbeds, lots of mirrors, etc. And there is a swimming pool. Of course it is more expensive, but some of the simpler rooms aren't too badly priced.

Back closer to town, actually before the start of the motel strip itself, the *Inn on the Lake* (☎ 766-4392) is at 1926 Lake Shore Blvd West. It's popular with US visitors; a look in the parking lot reveals cars from all over the USA. Room prices are often posted on the motel's sign and start at around $69. The adjacent Golden Griddle pancake house is a good place for a buffet breakfast and packs them for brunch in at weekends for brunch.

Not too far away, but west on the Queensway, try the *Queensway Motel* (☎ 252-5281), at No 638. It's sort of away from the traffic, may have rooms when others are booked out and has considerably lower prices. Still further west, at No 1554, is the *Deluxe* (☎ 252-5205).

Motels dot Lake Shore Blvd sporadically all the way along its course to Hamilton (many years ago this was the main highway, and actually ran all the way from Montreal) but there is no real concentration like the one by the Humber River.

More motels, although not in great numbers, can be found along Dundas St West, west of Hwy 427 (which is in the suburb of Mississauga rather than Toronto proper). From Lakeshore Blvd, go north up Hwy 427 and turn left (west).

The other main motel district is on the east side of town, on Kingston Rd which branches off Queen St East east of Coxwell Ave and later turns into the old Hwy 2 to Montreal. Motels start just east of Brimley Rd. This district is further from the centre and away from much of Toronto's incoming traffic (particularly from the USA) and so tends to be less busy and less costly. On the other hand, access to it is slow and awkward. The Guildwood station of the GO train, a commuter service, is just east of the motel strip. It has parking and trains run frequently into downtown. Alternatively, the Toronto Transit Commission can get you into town but at a much slower rate. Again, there are good motels out this way and others that are best avoided.

The *Avon* (☎ 267-0339), at 2800 Kingston Rd, just past Bluffers Park, gets top billing and is quite an attractive-looking place. Rooms here cost $35 to $50 with TV and radio, and there is a heated pool.

Next door is the *Royal Motel* (☎ 264-4381), at 2746 Kingston Rd. It's also good, and has rooms from $38 to $55. Both are near Brimley Rd. Up Brimley Rd one block north at St Clair Ave, buses can be caught going to the subway system.

At 3126 Kingston Rd is the *Park* (☎ 261-7241), with prices about the same or slightly lower than those at the Royal or the Avon.

Still further out, east of Eglinton, the appealing *Idlewood Inn* (☎ 286-6861) is a large, modern motel with a well-treed property and a pool. It's often used by businesspeople. The address is 4212 Kingston Rd. Rates here are higher, ranging from $50 to $70.

There are quite a few other places along this strip, between the ones listed here.

## PLACES TO EAT

Toronto has a good selection of restaurants in all price categories and a wide variety to choose from, thanks to the many nationalities represented in the city. The following places are mostly central and accessible by public transport. They are listed according to area and cuisine categories.

ONTARIO

## Yonge St & Around

Yonge St itself, although busy night and day, is not one of the prime restaurant districts of the city. In the downtown centre, Yonge St has, in general, become swamped with fast-food franchises and cheap takeout counters. There are exceptions on and near Toronto's main street but some places tend to be geared more to lunch than to dinner.

South of the Eaton Centre, Yonge St has always been a bit of a backwater, so we'll start with the centre itself and work north to Bloor St. Among the many places to eat in the huge shopping mall are a couple of busy pubs. On the lower level, *Michel's Baguette* stands out in an inexpensive and otherwise undistinguished food fair, a collection of takeout places which share central tables. This little spot offers a tasty array of fresh goods baked on the premises, as well as salads, sandwiches and good coffee. *Aida's* cranks out quite decent and cheap felafels, tabouli and a limited number of other Lebanese basics.

At 362 Yonge St, *Swiss Chalet* is an outlet of the popular Canadian roast chicken & chips chain. The meals are economical and tasty.

The large, crowded, noisy cafeteria at *Ryerson Polytechnic University* serves up reasonable meals at student prices. Food is served (at meal times only) in the cafeteria in Jorgenson Hall, which is on the corner of Gerrard St East and Victoria St.

Most of the better places to munch at are between College and Bloor Sts. Between the Eaton Centre area and College St there isn't much, but north of there things pick up again and it's busy all the way to Bloor St and beyond. At the hole-in-the-wall *Papaya Hut*, at 513A Yonge St, the homemade vegetable soup, one of the sandwiches (such as avocado with tomato) and a papaya drink or smoothie provide an alternative to the nearby junk food. British-style pub grub and a variety of beers can be found at the *Artful Dodger*, with an outdoor patio. It's on Isabella St, a few doors east from Yonge St.

The cafeteria-style *Vegetarian Restaurant*, at 4 Dundonald St, just a few doors from Yonge St, is one of the few of its kind in the city and is recommended. The tasty and inexpensive fare includes daily specials, soups, salads, create-your-own sandwiches and good desserts. It's a very quiet, low-key place, open every day but closed on Sunday until late in the afternoon.

All along Yonge St, usually on corners, *Mr Submarine* outlets make good submarine sandwiches for $4 and up. A simple cheese sub, microwaved, is good. Also with a couple of outlets is *La Maison du Croissant*, which is a fine place for a quick breakfast or an afternoon snack. The place on the corner of Yonge and Maitland Sts is especially good. Another is at the corner of Yonge and Bloor Sts.

At 649 Yonge St, *Alfred's* has been serving up good fish (halibut) & chips for 20 years.

Church St, around Wellesley St, has quite a few cafés and restaurants and a range of nightspots. This area is Toronto's lively, busy and somewhat more up-market district, principally centred along Church St.

For a splurge on a good steak, try *Le Baron*, further south at 425 Church St, an established place in an area with many new restaurants. They've been doing it for over 30 years and steaks are the only main courses on the menu. The restaurant offers soft lights and attentive service but dress is casual.

Next door to Hostelling International (HI) – Canada is the very casual, cheap little *Passport Café* where you can get a meal, a coffee or a beer. The outdoor patio is pleasant during warm weather.

Down at 287 King St West at John St near the Skydome is the *Groaning Board*, a casual eatery recently moved but a mainstay for many years among Toronto restaurants. As well as the good soups and salads there are some vegetarian dishes available. It has long been known for its nightly showing of reels of international advertisements and commercials which can be food for thought or just plain funny. It's open every day from 8 am to midnight.

In ascending order of price and style, the three restaurants at the Skydome are the *Hard Rock Café*, *Café on the Green* and

*Windows*. Meal prices are higher when there is a game on. A hot and cold buffet at Windows is $30 at such times; the full meal offered at Café on the Green is slightly less. At the Hard Rock Café, reservations a month in advance are required for a table with a good view, and there is a minimum meal purchase if a ball game or other major event is on. The price of the meal is about a third less than at the other places. When no event is taking place, it more or less runs as the regular restaurant/pub that it is; you can simply go in for a hamburger and a coffee and have a look at the playing field. It's open every day from lunch until late. For restaurant information and reservations call ☎ 341-2424.

## Bloor St

Bloor St offers all sorts of eating along its considerable length. Around Yonge St, an area of expensive shops and fashion boutiques, there is a very good never-advertised spot: the *Café at Holt's*, on the 3rd floor of Holt Renfrew, a department store for the well-heeled, at 50 Bloor St West. It used to be a real bargain but price increases have made lunch too pricey. However, the afternoon tea with scones and Devon cream, served after 3 pm, is still an affordable little pleasure.

A cheap place, worth going to if you're in the area, is the *Masters' Restaurant*, at 310 Bloor St West. It's in the University Faculty of Education Building, just east of Spadina Ave. Mostly for students, it's open from 7 am to 7 pm Monday to Friday. Cafeteria-style meals like lamb, sole and shepherd's pie are served at rock-bottom prices. Complete breakfasts are also available. Bloor St West around Bathurst St is a lively student area, with many good and generally cheap restaurants, a few cafés, the *Brunswick Tavern* – an institution – and the popular Bloor St Cinema.

The *Continental*, a Hungarian place at 521 Bloor St West, is cosy, with the usual red and white checked tablecloths. About five meal choices are offered each day, including rice dishes and schnitzels, for an average of $10.

The name says it all for the *Kensington Natural Bakery Vegetarian Restaurant*, at 460 Bloor St West.

*By the Way Café*, with the former 'Lickin' Chicken' sign still in place, is a popular sitting and meeting place which also serves pretty decent Middle Eastern or vegetarian food and excellent desserts. There are some outdoor tables. The café is on the north-west corner of Bloor St and Brunswick Ave.

## Queen St West

Queen St West between Spadina and University Aves has seen something of a boom in restaurants in the midst of a general local revival. First claimed by the arts community and their followers, numerous shops and eateries sprang up, many to be replaced as the money moved in. Some of the places cater more to trend than to quality, but it's an interesting and varied area with some good and reasonably priced restaurants. One of the better and more stable eateries is the comfortable *Queen Mother*, at 208 Queen St West. It offers a good, varied menu for full meals and serves coffee and snacks all day.

*Barney's*, at 385 Queen St West, is definitely not a newcomer. More than 35 years old, this has become one of the small elite of classic local institutions that North American inner cities seem to produce. The few small tables and 13 stools are usually full at lunch time, and you'll be reminded that dawdling is *verboten*. The chilli, corned beef and breakfasts are highlights. The *Black Bull*, a licensed place with a busy outdoor patio, is at 298 Queen St West, on the corner of Soho St, right in the middle of the Queen St action.

Many of the area's younger residents and more impecunious artists have now moved further west to between Spadina Ave and Bathurst St or beyond. Along here you'll find various new, small restaurants and speciality stores, including quite a few bookshops. Definitely try the *Future Bakery*, at 739 Queen St West, a fine place for a light meal, snack or coffee at any time of day (or night). It's casual and comfortable and the smell of all the breads and pastries baked on the premises is irresistible.

ONTARIO

## Theatre District

Down on the corner of King and Simcoe Sts is Ed Mirvish's one-man development complex. Across from Roy Thompson Hall and centred around the Royal Alexander Theatre are his unmistakeable restaurants, which are famous for their garish exteriors, sumptuous interiors and straight, simple food served at low prices. The meats are good; the instant potato and frozen vegetables are just filler.

*Old Ed's* is a fairly casual place, with dinners costing $10 to $15 and lunches a few dollars less. Selections include lasagna, chicken, fish, ribs and veal. As in all Ed's restaurants, which run in a line linked by the white signs and lightbulbs, the main course comes with potato, salad and rolls. *Ed's Warehouse* (☎ 593-6676) is a bit more up-market. No jeans are allowed and jackets are required. At the door they usually have some jackets and ties to hand out to those without them. Call ahead to make sure, if you don't have one. Prices are $13 to $17 at dinner, a few dollars less at lunch. The menu offers a couple of selections of roast beef and steak only.

The main attraction of both these places is the decor – a wild, sense-stunning compilation of antiques and oddities lit by dozens of Tiffany lamps. Wedged in and around these two places are others specialising in either Italian, seafood or Chinese dishes. I'm telling you, this guy leaves no stone unturned. The restaurants are one block north of the CN Tower.

The *Rotterdam*, at 600 King St West (at Portland St), brews its own fine beer but can also sell you beer from around the world. The chicken satay dinner ($6) is a tasty, good-value meal.

Further east, by the O'Keefe Theatre and St Lawrence Market, is another busy eating, entertainment and nightclub area popular with both visitors and residents. Toronto, like many Canadian cities of any size, has its *Spaghetti Factory*. This one is at 54 The Esplanade, behind the O'Keefe Theatre, which is on Front St near the corner of Yonge St. The restaurant offers good value; meals

(from salad through to dessert) start at $7.50 and are served in an interesting eclectic, colourful atmosphere popular with everybody, including families and teenagers. The lunch menu is even cheaper. They make numerous spaghettis, and other Italian dishes such as lasagna and chicken cacciatore.

Nearby are several other places to eat, many with large outdoor sections. Church St has a number of places for dinner. At 12 Market St, across from the market building, the *Old Fish Market* has lots of nautical adornments and offers a variety of seafood ($15 to $22) at dinner or standard British fare like shepherd's pie ($7) at lunch. Two meals for the price of one are offered on Tuesdays.

## Chinatown

The city's large Chinatown is based around the corner of Spadina Ave and Dundas St West and is home to scores of restaurants. As the area developed, so did the tastes of restaurant patrons. As well as the standard Cantonese fare, the city now has Sichuan, Hunan and Mandarin places, and more. Browse around reading menus. The district extends along Dundas St West, especially to the east of Spadina Ave and north up Spadina Ave to College St.

For tasty, inexpensive Chinese food in a variety of styles, including some fine spicy dishes, *Peter's Chungking Restaurant*, at 281 College St, is recommended. As well as the superior food, the decor is a cut above the usual fluorescent and plastic, yet prices are no higher – around $25 to $35 for two. Longstanding *Lee Garden*, at 358 Spadina Ave, offers a consistently good and unusually varied Cantonese menu and is not expensive.

Until the 1970s, the Jewish community dominated Spadina Ave. Despite the Oriental influx, textile shops and jobbers remain. Much of the Jewish population has moved north with some of the former Spadina restaurants now way up on Steeles Ave West around Bathurst St at the edge of the city.

Once again, the area seems to be changing, with more and more Vietnamese restaurants opening as some Chinese people leave the central core for more suburban areas. A good, quick, little noodle shop is the *Swatow*, at 309 Spadina Ave. Excellent meals of soups and noodles cost $5 to $15. It's open for lunch and until late daily (except Wednesday, when it's closed).

Also for Vietnamese, the simple *Pho Hung*, at 374 Spadina Ave, is recommended. Despite the emergence of the Vietnamese restaurants on Spadina Ave and Dundas St, one of the best and oldest places is not in the neighbourhood, but on a small street a few steps from Yonge St, north of Bloor St. The *Saigon Star* is at 4 Collier St, right behind the massive Toronto Public Library. The menu includes soups, salads, seafood, curries and brochettes (kebabs), with main dishes ranging from $8 to $11, less at lunch.

An interesting street on the edge of Chinatown which not too many out-of-towners get to is Baldwin St running east off Spadina Ave about two blocks north of Dundas St. About three blocks from Spadina Ave towards the east end of Baldwin St, on the corner of McCaul St, is a small, low-key commercial and restaurant enclave. Long a blend of Chinese and Western counterculture, it's especially pleasant on summer evenings, when many of the varied restaurants have outdoor patios. One place to consider is the *Chinese Vegetarian House* at 39 Baldwin St, with an unusual, strictly vegetarian menu.

On the other side of Spadina Ave, the market area on Kensington Ave and particularly on Augusta Ave is busy during the day and has some small cheap cafés. Formerly here but now a little further north, the *Kensington Kitchen*, at 124 Harbord St, is a fine and comfortable Middle Eastern restaurant. They serve generous portions; try the soup with a felafel or grilled cheese and I'll bet you'll have found a favourite little lunch spot in Toronto. The appetisers are also definitely worth sampling – around $6 at lunch, $10 or a bit more at dinner.

For those in need of a smoked meat sandwich in a small, busy, Jewish-style deli check out *Zupas Deli* at 342 1/2 Adelaide St West, east of Spadina. You'd have to be an alligator to get your mouth around one of these mega-sandwiches.

## Little India

Little India, based on Gerrard St East just west of Coxwell Ave, has numerous inexpensive restaurants. The *Moti Mahal*, at No 1422, is plain (and bright!) but the food is good and ridiculously cheap. The *Bar-Be-Que Hut* (peculiarly named), at No 1455, is plusher than most; again, the food is good, though the portions are pretty small.

The *Madras Durbar*, a tiny, exclusively vegetarian place that serves South Indian dishes. The thali plate is good and makes a complete meal for only $5.50. The address is 1435 Gerrard St East. Best of the lot and not expensive is *Haandi*, at 1401 Gerrard St East. The menu offers a varied selection, from the numerous breads through to desserts, and the ambience is pleasantly more subtle than that offered by many of the competitors. After dinner, take a walk around the area and pop into one of the shops to ask for a paan made to order. With or without tobacco, this is a cheap, exotic taste experience.

A smaller, less visible Indian community has developed on Bloor St West around the Lansdowne and Dufferin Sts area. There are a number of small, modest Indian restaurants here but the overall atmosphere is not as interesting.

All on its own in a rather nondescript area but closer to the central core is the *Indian Rice Factory*, at 414 Dupont St, between Spadina Ave and Bathurst St. Quite unlike many of the Gerrard St choices, this is a sedate, tastefully decorated dining room. The food is excellent. This place is more expensive than many, but the only real drawback is the interminably slow service. It's open every day.

Also recommended is the tiny *Babur Restaurant*, 279 Dundas St West at the edge of Chinatown. It's inexpensive and very informal but the food is top rate. On one recent visit it was packed even though the streets were deserted all over town as it was the coldest night of the year. It's open seven days a week. Dinner without wine for two ranges from $30 to $50.

## Danforth Ave

The Greek area along Danforth Ave is also a good place to get a meal. Restaurants are mostly noisy, informal and suitable for children. Some are old-style places where you can check out the kitchen and tell the chef what you'd like, but these are disappearing. *Ellas*, at 702 Pape Ave, carries on the tradition of presenting most of the Greek standards. To find others means walking out of the busiest sections. *Zorba's*, at 713 Danforth Ave, is smaller and cheaper.

Kebab houses have become popular in the past few years and there are now quite a few in the neighbourhood. One that's good and cheap – just look for the queue – is *Omonia*, at 426 Danforth Ave. The outside tables are a little less hectic. Similar and just as busy is the *Astoria*, at 390 Danforth Ave, with several barbecue-style dishes to try. It's near the Chester subway stop.

Moving up-market, the popular *Ouzeri*, at 500A Danforth Ave, presents a range of more sophisticated main courses amid colourfully trendy surroundings and fellow diners. A full meal with appetisers and wine is roughly $50 for two. I've had the rabbit pie and thought it was tasty but the calimari salad was a bit leathery. At about the same price I'd recommend the *Kapilyo*, at 401 Danforth Ave. Good food, great service and a very agreeable taverna atmosphere make for a memorable night out.

Most of the restaurants along here get very busy on weekend nights, when there's quite a festive air to the street. Eating early or after 8.30 or 9 pm is recommended if you want to avoid the crowds.

## Other Restaurants

Also out in this Greek area is a good seafood restaurant, the *Round Window* (☎ 465-3892), at 729 Danforth Ave. Phone for reservations – it gets full. A meal with a glass or two of wine costs $35 to $55 for two. The food is always fresh and is cooked simply,

without much in the way of sauces or spices. The meals are always good value.

For as authentic a Mexican meal as you'll find, try *La Mexicana*, at 229 Carlton St, a few doors east of Parliament St. As well as enchiladas and the like, there are tamales, moles and a sort of Mexican lasagna. It's open for dinner every day, and on weekends begins filling up before 6 pm. Dinner for two with a couple of beers ranges from $30 to $40. After dinner, a stroll along Parliament St is interesting for the varied shops and for a small place for coffee and/or dessert.

An excellent and very cheap Thai meal can be had at the *Thai Shan Inn*, 2039 Eglinton Ave West – well worth the trip to this part of town. It's open every day and meals average $25 for two. Don't miss the kang ped, a hot, spicy beef dish with lemon grass. It's a very small place which fills up easily and quickly, so arrive early or late or be prepared to queue.

Another good Asian place is the *Ole Malacca*, a Malaysian restaurant at 828 St Clair Ave West. Satays (kebabs), which you cook at your table over a small barbecue grill, are good to start with. Meals cost $30 to $45 for two.

If you're down at Harbourfront, the *Water's Edge Café* at York Quay isn't bad, with a selection of fairly simple cafeteria-style food. When the weather is fine and the windows are all open, lunch with a beer can be pretty nice. There are also several more substantial restaurants nearby, in the Queen's Quay terminal. Or try the *More Glorious Food Café*, right on the water, at the foot of York St.

## ENTERTAINMENT

Toronto is busy after dark, with countless nightspots, concerts, films, lectures and the country's largest theatre scene.

Bar hours are 11 am to 1 am, as they are all over Ontario. Numerous clubs stay open until 3 or 4 am without serving any more alcohol, but who knows how many unofficial boozecans there are where pricey drinks can be had at all hours.

Beer can be bought retail at Brewers Retail

Stores, now often marked as the Beer Store, and liquor and wine at Liquor Control Board of Ontario (LCBO) outlets. Addresses for all outlets can be found in the phone book. There are plenty of shops around town, but hours vary and they are all closed on Sundays and holidays. The drinking age in the province is 19 years and drunken driving is a very serious offence.

All three daily newspapers provide weekly entertainment listings. Check either the *Thursday Star* or the *Friday Sun* for full listings or the *Saturday Globe* for film and theatre. The most complete entertainment guide is provided by *Now Magazine*, a good weekly tabloid-style paper available free around town. Find it at cinemas, restaurants, cafés, record stores and some street-corner newsboxes (where it must be paid for). It comes out every Thursday and offers detailed information on the arts, including concerts, theatre and general events as well as local news.

### Sipping Alfresco
In good weather, Ontario Place or Yorkville are good spots to sit outside for a drink. Ontario Place usually has nightly concerts. There are several bars here, and it's cool and festive on a summer night. Yorkville is one area where there is some concentration of outdoor cafés and restaurants, which until a few years ago, the city had sorely lacked. It's a place to be seen and is a bit pricey but it's still OK if you're in the right mood.

Queen St West east of Spadina Ave and Bloor St near Bathurst St have several places where you can enjoy a glass at an outside table.

### Live Music
The small, crowded *El Mocambo*, on Spadina Ave just south of College St, is one of the local institutions and the city's best known (if no longer so popular) bar. It has a long, celebrated history, and the Rolling Stones once played here. Shows feature live rock and blues. Admission varies with the band upstairs and can be a bit high; down-

stairs admission is free and there's cheaper drinking with a local band.

Just down the street, at 379 Spadina Ave, *Grossman's* is bright and grubby but one of the cheapest places in town. They sometimes have very good bands and there's usually an interesting, mixed crowd. Sunday afternoons and evenings are reserved for blues jams. Admission is free. Some of Toronto's best known musicians played the place in their very early days.

Further down Spadina Ave at King St is the *Cabana Room*, in the Spadina Hotel (☎ 368-2864). Entertainment includes live rock, art-school bands and new-wavish groups. Admission costs about $5 and the drinks are fairly cheap.

The *Bamboo*, at 312 Queen St, is very popular, with excellent music in the ska, reggae, African and similar genres. It's always busy, with a 30-ish crowd. In summer they have a rooftop patio to catch a breath, and in addition the kitchen serves tasty, spicy meals. Admission costs $5 to $10. Nearby is the *Horseshoe*, at 370 Queen St West, which presents good live folk, blues, rock and blends of all three.

The *St Louis*, at 2050 Yonge St, often has good R&B or blues bands with dancing; it's free to get in. The free *Island Club*, at the western end of Ontario Place, has great live Latin American music on summer Saturday nights. This place is a lot of fun and the many Latins now in town can show you a thing or two about dancing – the men especially will really wow you. If this stuff doesn't get your feet tapping, you're probably dead.

The *Brunswick*, at 481 Bloor St West, is a funky place, a bit like a pub and a bit like a frat house and often a lot of fun. It has good, well-known jazz or blues players upstairs in *Albert's Hall*. Downstairs, where there is never a cover, entertainment ranges from contests to bizarre amateur nights. The downstairs area is cheap, upstairs less so, but it varies. There's live folk music at the *Free Times Café*, at 320 College St.

For jazz, *C'est What*, at 67 Front St East, has a new act nearly every night. Another is the *Café des Copains*, at 48 Wellington St.

For more experimental music, the *Music Gallery* (no liquor served) is at 1087 Queen St West. *Meyer's Deli*, at 69 Yorkville St, has more conventional jazz.

### Disco

*RPM*, at 132 Queen's Quay, has DJ-dancing every night. It's open after hours, which means dancing but no drinking after 1 am. Another busy, popular place is the *Big Bop* at 651 Queen St West on the corner of Bathurst St. Expect line-ups on the weekend even though it is very large and has dancing on several floors.

### Cinema

There are several repertory film houses around town.

The *Bloor Cinema* (☎ 532-6677), at 506 Bloor St West, is popular with the many students in the area. A wide variety of films is shown – American, European, old and new. The *Revue* (☎ 531-9959), at 400 Roncesvalles Ave, in the west end, also features different films nearly every night.

Prices are a couple of dollars less than those at first-run theatres and are much lower for those with an inexpensive annual membership card. There are three or four similar theatres around town, and the *Art Gallery of Ontario* and *Cinémathèque Ontario* also screen noncommercial films. IMAX large-format movies can be seen at *Ontario Place*.

### Theatre

There is more theatre in Toronto than in any other Canadian city, and productions range from Broadway-type spectacles and musicals to Canadian contemporary dramas. Also big is dinner theatre. For current listings, check newspapers or the guides to Toronto available at hotels. The classified sections of the *Sun* and *Star* newspapers list tickets available for every sold-out event in town, from opera to Rolling Stones, hockey to baseball. For a price, any seat is yours.

Theatre costs vary widely. A dinner show costs $40 to $60 per person for a meal and show.

The city's longest-running play is Agatha Christie's *The Mousetrap*, which has played at the Toronto Truck Theatre for 16 years. A ticket is about $17. One of the more physically impressive theatres is the traditional Royal Alex, on King St West, which presents established plays and performers. Next door is the new, lavish *Princess of Wales Theatre*, with one of the largest stages in North America. The theatre was built to accommodate the musical *Miss Saigon*. The Mirvishes, who own the Alex and much of the block, are also responsible for this new venture.

The *Dream* in High Park is a great summer theatre presentation in which one Shakespearean play is put on each night through July and August, free. The Toronto Free Theatre's production and acting is top rate. For details, call their downtown theatre. Shows begin at 8 pm, but go very early with a blanket and picnic or you'll require binoculars. A donation is requested.

*Five Star Tickets* (☎ 596-8211) sells half-price theatre and dance tickets – leftover seats for shows the same day. They have a booth at the Eaton Centre, on the corner of Dundas and Yonge Sts (you can't place telephone orders). The booth is open from noon to 7.30 pm Tuesday to Saturday, and on Sunday from 11 am to 3 pm.

### Spectator Sports

The Toronto Blue Jays play major-league baseball at the *Skydome* against US teams of the American League. The home team has been very competitive for the past few years and won the World Series in 1992 and 1993. These wins represent the only times that baseball's top prize has been won by a non-US team. The Skydome has set attendance records for the major leagues and is generally sold out, despite a seating capacity of over 50,000.

If you'd like to take in a game, book as early as possible (☎ 341-1234 and use a credit card). Tickets are also available at the box office at gate 9 at the stadium or at Ticketmaster (a ticket agency with outlets around Ontario). There are four price brackets. The cheap tickets are a mere $6 but are a long way away and are high, to boot. Recommended are the $18 seats at the 500 level behind home plate. Try for somewhere between the 517s and the 530s, through gates 7, 8 or 9. The priciest seats go for $23 and rim the infield. Behind the home plate at this low level, beware of the protective net, which must be peered through. Kids under 15 are entitled to half-price tickets (except on the top-price seats) for Saturday games and all games with a 12.35 pm start.

Tickets are always available from scalpers at the stadium just prior to the game. After the game has started, it is often possible to get tickets for less than face value.

Note that food and drink, especially beer, is expensive and that bottles or cans cannot be taken into the dome. Take a jacket – things cool off down here at night if the roof is open, as it's fairly close to the water.

The Toronto Argonauts, of the professional Canadian Football League (CFL), also play in the 'Dome'.

For horse racing, *Woodbine Racetrack* (☎ 675-6110) features both the thoroughbreds and the standard-breds and is home to the prestigious Queen's Plate. It's north-west of the centre, at 555 Rexdale Blvd. By public transport, take the subway to Islington and then catch the direct 'Race' bus. Admission to the track is $3.50 and bets start at $2. Call for the racing schedule.

In winter, National League hockey is played at Maple Leaf Gardens (☎ 977-1641), downtown on the corner of Carlton and Church Sts, a couple of blocks from Yonge St. Tickets are hard to get at the box office, as every game is pretty well sold out, but they can be bought without difficulty from scalpers outside the door just before the game. Hockey tickets are costly, with the 'cheap' seats and standing room at $19!

At the end of 1993, Toronto was awarded a National Basketball Association (NBA) franchise, the first granted to a city outside the USA. The as-yet unnamed team is to begin play in the 1995-96 season. A new 20,000-seat stadium is to be built downtown, at the corner of Bay and Dundas Sts.

**Other Entertainment**

Toronto has several places for comics, called *Yuk Yuks*. A central club (☎ 967-6425) is at 1280 Bay St. Presentations are sometimes funny, sometimes gross, sometimes a joke. Admission ranges from $4 on some weekdays to $15 on weekend nights, when there are two of the two-hour shows. Dinner packages are also available. Second City (☎ 863-1111), at 110 Lombard St, has an excellent reputation for both its comedy shows and the people it develops.

The Toronto Symphony (☎ 598-3375) plays at the new *Roy Thompson Hall*, 60 Simcoe St, not far from the CN Tower. A range of other, mainly classical concerts are presented here. In early fall, the Canadian Opera Company performs at the *O'Keefe Centre* (☎ 393-7469), on Front St. The National Ballet of Canada is based in town and also performs at the O'Keefe.

The marvellous Recital Hall of the brand-new North York Performing Arts Centre (☎ 324-9333) presents classical concerts by the world's top musicians and vocalists. The centre is at 5100 Yonge St (on the corner of Sheppard Ave). The North York Centre subway station is nearby.

The dance, symphony and opera seasons start in October or November and run through the winter.

*Pantages*, a beautiful, restored, 1920s cinema, now presents Broadway-style shows such as *The Phantom of the Opera*. At 189 Yonge St are the refurbished historic *Elgin* and *Winter Garden* theatres (☎ 314-3580), worth checking for such varied productions as operas and lectures. If performances don't interest you, guided tours are available of the ornate theatres themselves.

For dance, look into what's happening at Harbourfront's *Premiere Dance Theatre*.

Those from Down Under may be interested to drop in at the TRANZAC (Toronto Australia New Zealand Club), at 292 Brunswick Ave, where there is a bar open to all.

**THINGS TO BUY**

ABC, at 552 Yonge St, south of Wellesley St, is a good place for camping gear, tents, sleep-

ONTARIO

ing bags, packs and footwear. It's not a trendy place at all, with no fashion wear, but it does have good-quality stuff at good prices and the staff is straightforward.

Europe Bound, at 2 McCaul St (off Queen St West, near the Art Gallery of Ontario) and now with two other locations, has a selection of camping and hiking clothing, gear and books. They will even rent you a tent or take a passport photo.

For the best in outdoor clothing, visit Tilley Endurables, a small Canadian company begun in 1980 which turns out some of the finest, toughest, low-maintenance threads imaginable. All their stuff looks good, needs no ironing and comes with the washing instruction 'Give 'em Hell'. Their clothes (pants, shirts, skirts and the well-known hats) have been used on various expeditions, from mountaineering to sailing. The shorts ($95) are guaranteed for life. Hats cost around $45. The main store is at 900 Don Mills Rd, and there is an outlet at the Queen's Quay terminal at Harbourfront.

For cyclists, quite a few bicycle shops can be found along a strip of Bloor St around Dufferin St, but there are others all over town.

## GETTING THERE & AWAY
### Air

The airport, Pearson International, is about 24 km north-west of the downtown area in a part of the city known as Malton. This is actually a separate city, but you wouldn't know it from the continuous urban landscape. The major Canadian airlines fly in and out of Toronto, as do many international companies. Pearson is by far the busiest airport in the country.

It has long been a congested and confusing place, but the third terminal, known as Trillium Terminal, added in early 1991, has alleviated much of the crowding, delays and annoyance. This is the first airport terminal in Canada to be developed, owned and operated by private interests rather than by the government. As well as the main hall, with its 15-metre-high, vaulted, glass ceiling offering natural lighting, the main distin-

guishing feature is the number of shops, including a Harrod's outlet, and restaurants. Late in 1993 the federal government was going ahead with plans to privatise the other two terminals, although opposing forces were rallying against the plan, complaining it was going to cost the public too dearly.

Food, drink and parking at the airport is costly, particularly at the Trillium Terminal.

When departing from the airport or picking someone up at arrivals, be sure to ask the terminal number. Signs on the roads into the airport direct you to each terminal and indicate which airlines they serve. Trillium is the main terminal for Canadian Airlines, American, British Airways, KLM, Lufthansa and Air France. Within the Trillium Terminal, Pier A handles domestic flights and Pier B handles international ones. Terminal 2 is home to Air Canada.

Some one-way fares on Air Canada (☎ 925-2311) are to Montreal $199, Halifax $367 and Calgary $624. Canadian Airlines (☎ 675-7587) has virtually the same prices, but they do vary during the numerous special promotions.

For the purchase of tickets around the country and out of Canada, Travel Cuts (Canadian University Travel Services) is recommended. They have six offices in town, the main one being central, at 187 College St (☎ 979-2406). They'll shop around for the best deal, and offer even better rates for young people (under age 26) and students. For the latter two groups, identification cards can be issued.

Alternatively, agencies such as the Last Minute Club (☎ 441-2582), which specialise in late sell-offs and the filling of flights and charters, may be worth a call. For flights to destinations such as Mexico or Florida, particularly during the Canadian winter, you could turn up a bargain.

The many large immigrant and ethnic parts of the city are good places to seek out travel agencies for charters and cheap flights to a particular homeland, be it Hong Kong, the Philippines or Poland.

The newspapers, especially the weekly

*Now Magazine,* also list tickets for sale – check the classifieds.

Small independent airlines which fly between Toronto and nearby destinations at very low cost come and go but never seem able to survive. Some of these upstart companies tend to use the small Toronto Islands Airport, on the lake at the foot of Bathurst St. The airport is used by such commuter-style airlines as well as being busy with private planes.

At the moment, Air Ontario (☎ 925-2311) is the only regularly scheduled company using the Toronto Islands Airport. The smaller aircraft get you to where you're going a lot quicker than the major carriers because you don't have to drag yourself all the way out to the airport, which costs time and money. Air Ontario serves mainly the business market, with flights to and from Montreal (Ottawa) and London (Ontario).

A shuttle bus (free for flight ticketholders) runs from the Royal York Hotel down to the two-minute ferry across to the airport. The Union subway stop is across the street from the Royal York. Otherwise there is TTC service close to the airport ferry – take the streetcar south on Bathurst St to Lake Shore Blvd (generally known as Lake Shore Road or The Lakeshore). From there the ferry is a two-block walk.

It is not uncommon for Canadians (and visitors) to skip over to Buffalo to take advantage of the periodically much cheaper US airfares. For example, a flight from Buffalo to Seattle could cost hundreds of dollars less than the fare from, say, Toronto to Vancouver. At either end, a short bus ride links the Canadian cities. Travel Cuts is up on the latest possibilities. Recently, the US fares have not been the bargains they were a few years ago, and with the expense of getting to Buffalo, flights out of Canada have been comparably priced.

### Bus

The revamped bus station for out-of-town destinations is central, on the corner of Bay and Dundas Sts, at the edge of Chinatown, one long block west of Yonge St. It's the depot for the numerous bus lines which cover Ontario from Toronto. For destinations in Eastern Ontario and north of Toronto ☎ 393-7911. This number covers Voyageur, PMCL (Penetang-Midland Coach Lines), Canar and Ontario Northland bus companies. Collectively these lines serve Barrie, Orillia, Huntsville, Parry Sound, North Bay, Montreal and their districts.

Gray Coach (now run by Greyhound) and Greyhound (☎ 594-3310) pretty much cover Ontario west of Toronto, including the Niagara region, Guelph, Kitchener, London, Windsor, Owen Sound, Sudbury and beyond, on to western Canadian cities such as Winnipeg and Vancouver. They also run to Detroit, New York and Boston. Greyhound now also operates the route to Ottawa and Peterborough. Smaller, local bus lines around Ontario connect to towns served by one or more of the above major carriers. Always ask about express buses.

Some routes have slow, milk-run trips (which stop frequently) and other express, direct trips (which can be hours quicker). Ask about return tickets – some bus lines offer these at reduced rates.

The station is also the depot for Gray Line (☎ 594-3310) sightseeing buses.

There are departures for Ottawa at 9.30 and 11.30 am and 2.30 and 5.30 pm. The five-hour trip costs $50 one way.

To Montreal, there are five or six buses a day, depending on the day of the week. One of them is an overnighter, which leaves at 12.15 am. Tickets for Montreal costs $57. Montreal and Ottawa are covered by Voyageur Bus Lines. Greyhound routes cover south-western Ontario, much of northern Ontario and US destinations. Four runs a day head to Niagara Falls ($22 one way, about two hours).

To Thunder Bay, buses depart at 1 and 5 pm and 1 am ($120 one way, about 20 hours). There are regular buses for Buffalo, New York and Detroit.

Lockers can be found on the lower level, and the upper floor has a restaurant. There's a bakery and café on the other side of Bay St. On the evening prior to a holiday or long

ONTARIO

weekend, expect crowds and arrive early to ensure getting a ticket before departure time.

Adjacent to the terminal, on the western side, is the bus depot for (among other runs) the GO (☎ 665-0022) buses, a government line which services many of the nearby surrounding towns, stopping frequently along the way. It's mainly used by commuters but goes a relatively long way (to Hamilton, for example) to the west of Toronto.

GO buses also go to the satellite communities of Barrie (to the north) and Oshawa (to the east), supplementing the regular bus service. Trips in these directions are not as frequent as the westbound ones and the downtown bus terminal is not used as the departure point. For Barrie, catch the GO bus at the Finch subway station during evening rush hour. For Oshawa, catch it at the York Mills subway, also during the end-of-day rush hour. In the mornings, the buses come into town.

### Train

Grand old Union Station, for VIA Rail (☎ 366-8411) trains, is conveniently situated. It's on Front St (which runs east-west) at the south end of the city, at the bottom of University Ave, York and Bay Sts. The subway goes right into the station; the stop is called Union.

Trains leave for Ottawa at 9 am and 1, 3 and 5 pm ($70, about six hours); others go to Kingston with bus connections for Ottawa. To Montreal, there are six trains daily ($80).

To Sudbury, there are three trips weekly, departing on Tuesdays, Thursdays and Saturdays at 12.45 pm ($50, 7½ hours). Note that for Sudbury, the train actually goes to Sudbury Junction, a station about 10 km from the centre of town.

Other cities which can be reached by train include Niagara Falls, London, Kingston and Montreal. Ontario Northland (☎ 314-3750) runs trains to northern Ontario destinations, including the Polar Bear Express to Moosonee.

Amtrak (☎ 800-872-7245) trains link Toronto with New York City, Buffalo or Chicago, with stops or other possible connections along the way. Amtrak offers good-value return fares. Reservations are needed for all trains.

The station has several restaurants, some fast-food outlets and a bar. Sometimes on the arrival level, just as you come out the gate from the train, a travellers' aid booth is in operation to help with basic directions and to answer questions.

GO trains also use the station; see the Getting Around section later.

### Car

If you're renting a car, be aware that many places require that you be at least 21 years old; for some places the minimum age is 23. There are countless rental agencies in the city. Surprisingly, it can be difficult to get a car on holiday weekends, so plan ahead.

The cheapest place to try is Rent-A-Wreck (☎ 961-7500), at 374 Dupont St, between Spadina Ave and Bathurst St; used cars cost $35 a day for a middle-sized vehicle, less for compacts. No km fee is charged for use in Ontario. There are weekly and monthly rates, too. Insurance is extra, as it is at all places, and goes up as the driver's age decreases. If you're going for a used car, check it out before proceeding too far – I haven't had much luck with them.

A place with a choice of new or used cars and with a good central location is Downtown Car & Truck Rental (☎ 585-7782), at 77 Nassau St, in Kensington Market off Spadina Ave. The used ones (best for using in or near the city) start at $10 a day plus km travelled and the new vehicles (for trips further afield) are priced competitively.

Tilden (☎ 364-4191), with an office in Union Station as well as several other downtown locations and one at the airport, is a more standard rental company and offers new cars. Their rate is $40 per day for the smallest economy cars, plus 15 cents per km after the first 200 km. They offer weekend specials; book early. Also available, and a good idea, are child seats and ski racks.

Avis (☎ 964-2051) is on the concourse level of the Hudson Bay Centre, on the corner of Yonge and Bloor Sts. Rates here are comparable to those at Tilden and elsewhere. Again, reservations are often required. Another major company is Budget.

**Car Sharing & Drive-Aways** Allo-Stop is a service based on a great idea – getting drivers and cars together with passengers. Their Toronto office (☎ 323-0874) is central, at 663 Yonge St. They mainly deal with trips to Montreal and Ottawa, but other things come up too, including rides to New York City and even to Florida. Give them a call a couple of days before you want to go and they may be able to line up a ride. Rates are very good.

A new service operating out of Toronto and Montreal takes passengers in vans between the two cities. The trips are frequent, the rates low and the operators friendly. Names, addresses and telephone numbers can be found under Travel in the classifieds of *Now Magazine* and *Eye*, both Toronto entertainment/alternative weeklies. These van shuttle services are not legal and so, names may change frequently. Trips can also be arranged to/from Kingston and Ottawa.

For long-distance trips, there are driveaway cars – about half a dozen places are listed in the yellow pages phone book. One company is Toronto Drive-Away Service (☎ 225-7754), with cars for Canadian and US destinations. Also check the business personal columns in either the *Toronto Sun* or the *Star* and the ads in the weekly *Now Magazine* entertainment tabloid. (See the notes in the introductory Getting Around chapter for more information on driveaways.)

**Hitching**
Thumbing is illegal on the expressways in the city. On city streets there's no problem but it's not commonly done, except by women offering their company for a price. You can hitch on Hwy 401 out of town or on the lead-in ramps in town.

If you're heading east for Montreal, the best bet is the city transit to roughly the corner of Port Union Rd and Hwy 401 in Scarborough, near the Metro Zoo. To get

there from downtown is a bit complicated and the fastest way takes about $1\frac{1}{2}$ hours. Take the subway east to Kennedy stop. From there catch the Scarborough LRT (light rail transit) to the Lawrence East Rt station. Transfer to the Lawrence East 54E bus. Go east to East Drive at Lawrence East. Transfer (free again) to the Rouge Hill No 13 bus to Hwy 401.

If you're going west, take the subway to Kipling. Transfer to the West Mall bus, Nos 112 or 112B, and go to the corner of Carlingview Drive and International Blvd almost at Hwy 401. This is just at the city limits, so you are OK on the highway, but it could be busy and difficult for cars to stop at rush hour. Public transit to this point takes about one hour from downtown.

If you're northbound, you're stuck. The best bet is to take the bus to Barrie and then hitch the rest of the way on Hwy 400 or Hwy 11, depending on your destination. The Trans Canada Hwy westbound can be picked up at Sudbury.

### GETTING AROUND
#### To/From the Airport
In Toronto, there are several ways to get to the airport. The cheapest is to take the subway to Kipling on the east-west line. From there, take the Kipling or Martingrove bus (Nos 45 or 46) north up to Dixon Rd. Transfer to the Malton No 58A bus, which goes west to the airport. Keep your transfer from the subway, but the second bus will cost $1.50 extra. Reverse the same route to get downtown from the airport.

Alternatively, take the subway to the Lawrence West stop on the north-south Spadina-University line and from there catch the Malton No 58A bus. Again, the bus costs an additional $1.50.

The next method is a little easier, a little quicker and a little more costly. Between the airport and the Islington subway stop (one before Kipling), at the far western end of the Bloor Line, there is a direct bus run by Pacific Western (☎ 672-0293). It leaves every 20 minutes or so, every day, takes half an hour and costs $6 one way. The bus also runs between the airport and the Yorkdale and York Mills subway stations. Each of these stops costs a bit more.

Pacific Western also operates buses every 20 minutes to and from the airport and half a dozen major hotels, such as the Royal York, the Sheraton, the Hilton Harbour Castle and the Holiday Inn, which is very near the bus terminal. The one-way fare is $10.75 and the trip takes about 80 minutes. These buses operate roughly between the hours of 4 am and 10.30 pm, depending on where you are and in which direction you're travelling.

The buses leave the airport terminals from outside the arrival levels.

Of course, there are taxis and, for a couple more bucks, limousines. The taxi fare from Yonge and Bloor Sts to the airport is $33.

### Toronto Transit Commission (TTC)
The city has a good subway, bus and streetcar system (see the following Toronto Subway map), called the TTC (☎ 393-4636). There is a 24-hour, recorded, route and fare information line, (☎ 393-8663). Fares are $2 cash, or five tickets, or tokens for $6.50. Tickets or tokens (small dime-like coins) are available in the subway or at some convenience and corner variety stores. Once one fare is paid, you can transfer to any other bus, subway or streetcar within one hour at no extra charge. One ticket can get you anywhere the system goes. Get a transfer from the driver, or in the subway from the machine inside the turnstiles where you pay the fare.

A day pass ($5) allows for unlimited travel after 9.30 am. On Sundays and holidays, the day pass is good for two adults and up to four children.

The subway system is clean, safe and fast. There is one east-west line, which goes along Bloor St and Danforth Ave, and two north-south lines, one up Yonge St and one along Spadina Ave, where some of the stops are decorated with the work of Canadian artists. The above-ground Scarborough RT train line connects the subway with the north-east part of the city, from the Victoria Park stop to the Scarborough Town Centre. The Harbourfront LRT (Light Rail Transit) car runs above

and below ground from Union Station (on Front St) to Harbourfront, along Queens's Quay West to Spadina Ave and back again.

The subway runs until about 1.30 am and begins at 6 am (except on Sunday, when it starts at 9 am). Bus hours vary; some run late but are infrequent.

The Toronto system connects with bus routes in surrounding suburban cities such as Mississauga, Markham and Vaughan.

### GO Train
GO trains, (☎ 665-0022), leaving from Union Station from 7 am to 11.30 pm daily, service the suburbs of Toronto east to Whitby and west to Hamilton. Ticket inspection is random and basically on an honour system. Service is fast and steady through the day and frequent during weekday rush hours.

### Streetcar
You may want to try the streetcars. Toronto is one of the few North American cities still using them and, in fact, has added some new models to the old yellow and red fleet. Find them on St Clair Ave and on College, Dundas, Queen and King Sts, all of which run east-west.

### Car
All over Ontario, you can turn right on a red light after first having made a full stop. In Toronto, parking is expensive – usually about $1.50 to $3.50 for the first half-hour, then slightly less. Most places have a flat rate after 6 pm. Look for the city of Toronto municipal lots, which are scattered around the downtown area and are marked by green signs. These are cheaper than the privately run lots.

Rush hours are impossible, so avoid them. And watch where you park during rush hours because the tow trucks show no mercy and getting your vehicle back will cost a bundle in cash and aggravation. Pedestrians use the painted crosswalks across the street and traffic must stop for them. If you're driving, keep an eye out for these. Hitting someone on a crosswalk in Toronto is a big no-no.

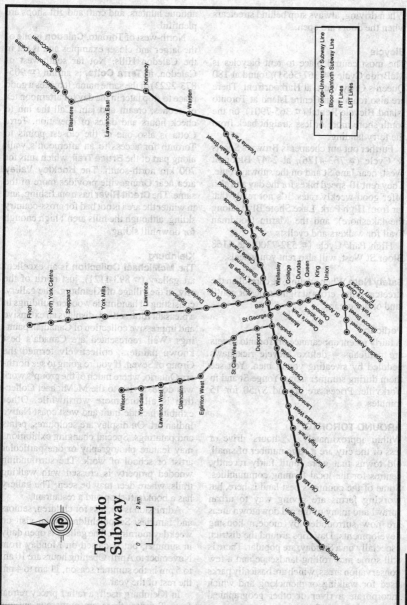

When driving, always stop behind streetcars when the doors are open.

## Bicycle

The most central place to rent bicycles is McBride Cycle (☎ 367-5651), found at 180 Queen's Quay West, at Harbourfront. There are also rentals on Centre Island at Toronto Island Bicycle Rental (☎ 365-7901), on the south shore more or less straight back from the ferry landing.

Further out but cheaper is Brown's Sports & Cycle (☎ 763-4176), at 2447 Bloor St West, near Jane St and on the subway route. They rent 10-speed bikes for the day and also offer good weekly rates. It's not really that far from High Park, Lake Shore Blvd (along the lakeshore), and the Martin Goodman Trail for walkers and cyclists.

High Park Cycle (☎ 532-7300), at 1168 Bloor St West, will also rent you wheels.

**Safety Note** When cycling, be careful on the streetcar rails – cross at right angles or you'll land on your ear.

## Pedicab

A fairly recent appearance on Toronto streets are pedicabs – deluxe bicycle rickshaws peddled by sweating young men. You see them during summer along Yonge St and in Yorkville. Prices are around $7.50 for 15 minutes.

## AROUND TORONTO

Within approximately 1½ hours' drive or less of the city are a large number of small, old towns that were, until fairly recently, centres for the local farming communities. Some of the country's best land is here, but working farms are giving way to urban sprawl and many of the old downtown areas are now surrounded by modern housing developments. Day trips around the district, especially on a Sunday, are popular. There is still some nice rolling landscape and a few conservation areas, which are basically parks used for walking or picnicking and which incorporate a river or other geographical feature. Quite a few of the towns attract

antique hunters, and craft and gift shops are plentiful.

North-west of Toronto, **Caledon** is one of the larger and closer examples and is set in the Caledon Hills. Not far south-west of Caledon, in **Terra Cotta**, is an inn (☎ 905-873-2223) of the same name. It makes a good place to stop later in the day for afternoon tea of scones, cream and jam. Call the inn to check hours and dates of operation. Terra Cotta is also one of the closest points to Toronto for access to an afternoon's walk along part of the **Bruce Trail**, which runs for 700 km north-south. The **Hockley Valley** area near Orangeville provides more of the same. The **Credit River** has trout fishing, and in winter the area is not bad for cross-country skiing, although the hills aren't high enough for downhill skiing.

## Kleinburg

The **McMichael Collection** is an excellent art gallery (☎ 893-1121), just north of the city, in the village of Kleinburg. The gallery, consisting of handmade wooden buildings in a pleasant rural setting, displays an extensive and impressive collection of Canadian paintings. Well represented are Canada's best known painters, collectively termed the Group of Seven. If you're going to see northern Ontario, where much of the group's work was done, a visit to the McMichael Collection is all the more worthwhile. Other exhibits include Inuit and west coast Native Indian art. On display are sculptures, prints and paintings. Special changing exhibitions may feature photography or one particular artist or school of work. The surrounding wooded property is crossed with walking trails, where deer may be seen. The gallery has a book/gift shop and a restaurant.

Admission is $6, less for children, seniors and families. Schoolchildren often visit on weekday mornings. The gallery is open daily in summer, but is closed on Monday from November to April. Opening hours are 10 am to 5 pm in the summer season, 11 am to 4 pm the rest of the year.

In Kleinburg itself, a rather pricey retreat from Toronto, there are numerous antique shops, small galleries, craft shops and places for a nosh.

**Getting There & Away** Kleinburg is 18 km north from the corner of Islington Ave and Hwy 401 in Toronto. To get there by car, go north up Hwy 427 to Hwy 27 and continue north. Turn right at Nashville Rd.

Public transportation is limited and a little awkward, but can be used. There is no service, though, on weekends or holidays. First, take the Toronto subway west to Islington on the east-west line. From there, catch the bus No 37 north for around 35 minutes to Steeles Ave. At the intersection of Steeles and Islington Aves, transfer to the No 3 Vaughan bus. The only one of these of any use for those wishing to visit the gallery is at 8.15 am, so you must make this connection. The bus will take you to the gallery gate in about 20 minutes, from where it is a 10-minute walk in. On the way back, the bus No 3 leaves at 5 and 6 pm. To check details, call Vaughan Transit (☎ 832-2281).

Evidently a new bus service may soon be operating which would make transit to the gallery much easier and quicker. The bus is to run between the gallery and the Yorkdale subway station in Toronto. Call the gallery for details.

**Dunlap Observatory**
Just north of the Toronto city limits, the Dunlap Observatory (☎ 884-2112) has what was once the world's second-largest telescope; it remains the biggest in Canada. From April to October, it is open to the public on Saturday evenings at 9.30 pm. A brief introductory talk is given to accompany a slide show, which is then followed by a bit of stargazing through the scope.

The programmes are free, but it is essential that you call ahead on a weekday for reservations. Every Tuesday at 10 am, tours of the grounds and buildings are offered. To reach the observatory, drive up Hwy 11 (the continuation of Yonge St) towards Richmond Hill; you'll see the white dome on the right. For public transportation, check with the TTC and their Vaughan Transit connections.

**Cathedral of the Transfiguration**
It seems nobody builds churches anymore, especially on the grand old scale. But north of Toronto, straight up Hwy 404 from the city, at 10350 Woodbine Ave in the village of Gormley (near the town of Markham), there is one heck of an exception. Opened in 1987, this Byzantine Catholic cathedral (☎ 887-5706) is one of the country's largest, standing 62.7 metres high to the tip of its copper-topped spire. Based on a smaller version found in Czechoslovakia, this is a 1000-seater church. One of the impressive features is the French-made main bell, ringing in at 16,650 kg, second in size only to the one in Sacré Coeur in Paris. Also, it is the first cathedral in the Western hemisphere to be blessed by a pope – John Paul II did the honours in 1984.

**Pickering Nuclear Plant**
About 40 km east of Toronto on the Lake Ontario shoreline is this nuclear power station (☎ 839-0465), which has portions open to the public. Whether you're pro or con nuclear plants, you could find out something you didn't know. Free films, displays and a drive around the site explain the operation. It's open from 9 am to 4 pm daily. Look for the signs on Hwy 401 – the plant is at the foot of Liverpool Rd. If your kids are born glowing in the dark, don't blame me.

**Cullen Gardens & Miniature Village**
About a 45-minute drive east from Toronto on Hwy 401, in the town of Whitby, is a 10-hectare site of carefully tended gardens interspersed with miniature models (☎ 294-7965). A path, which will take two or three hours to walk if you're looking at all the impressive detail, winds through the gardens. On the way are miniaturisations of a village, a modern suburban subdivision, a farm and a scene from cottage country. The buildings, people and activities portrayed offer, in a sense, a glimpse of life in southern Ontario. It's quite nifty the way small plants

have been sculpted to represent trees and other larger, full-sized flora. The floral aspect of the gardens, although colourful and quite extensive, should not be confused with botanical gardens but, rather, should be viewed as the setting for the various scenes. The park appeals to a variety of people but is particularly fascinating to children.

The gardens are on Taunton Rd West, off Hwy 12 about five km north along Hwy 401. It's open daily from the middle of April to the beginning of January. Admission is $9, less for children and seniors. When hunger strikes, there is a pleasant picnic and snack bar area (bring your own food) or a fairly pricey sit-down restaurant.

### Canadian Automotive Museum
Further east, near Oshawa (a centre for car assembly), this museum (☎ 905-576-1222 from Toronto) has a collection of over 50 cars. Included are a Redpath Runabout from 1890, a Model T (of course) and various automotive memorabilia. It's at 99 Simcoe St South and is open daily all year.

### Parkwood
Also in Oshawa, at 270 Simcoe St North, Parkwood (☎ 905-579-1311 from Toronto), is the estate of R S McLaughlin, who once ran the Canadian division of General Motors. The property consists of a 55-room mansion with antique furnishings, set amidst large gardens. Admission is $5. It's closed on Mondays (unless it's a holiday, when it remains open). Afternoon tea is served outside during summer and in the conservatory during winter.

### Local Conservation Areas
South-western Ontario is urban. To offset this somewhat, the government has designated many conservation areas – small nature parks for walking, picnicking and (sometimes) fishing, swimming and cross-country skiing. The quality and characteristics vary markedly. Some protect noteworthy geographic areas, others are more historic in emphasis. Generally, they are not wild areas by any means, and some are not even pretty, but they are close to major centres and do offer some relief from concrete. The tourist office has a list of those around Toronto and within a 160-km radius of town. The Metro Toronto Conservation Authority (☎ 661-6600) is responsible for their development and operation. The authority can help with information on conservation areas in and around the city and will be able to track down sources for more distant areas. Most areas are difficult to reach without a vehicle.

One place which makes a good, quick escape on a nice summer day is the large **Albion Hills Conservation Area**. It's primarily a quiet, wooded area with walking trails. In winter it allows for decent cross-country skiing. On the west side of town, take Indian Line (by the airport) north. It becomes Hwy 50, which leads to the park.

Also in this region, near Kleinburg, is the **Kortright Centre for Conservation.** There are trails here, too, but it's more of a museum, with displays and demonstrations on resources, wildlife, ecology, etc. It's open daily to 4 pm.

West of Toronto, near Milton, there are two conservation areas to consider visiting. **Crawford Lake** (☎ 905-854-0234) is one of the most interesting in the entire system. The deep, cool and pretty glacial lake set in the woods is surrounded by walking trails. Details on its formation and unique qualities are given in the well laid-out interpretive centre. Also on the site is a reconstructed 15th-century Iroquoian longhouse village.

Crawford Lake is open on weekends all year, and daily in July and August. It is five km south of Hwy 401 down a road called Guelph Line. There is a snack bar and some picnic tables at the site. The Bruce Trail, described elsewhere (see under Tobermory), also runs through the park.

In the same general area is the **Mountsberg Conservation Area** (☎ 905-854-2276). To reach it, exit south off Hwy 401 at Guelph Line and continue to the No 9 Sideroad. Travel west to Town Line and turn north for 3.2 km. It's 19 km west of the town of Milton. The centre provides a series of country-related educational programmes throughout the year. One of the best is the maple syrup/sugaring-off demonstration put on each spring; it explains in detail the history, collection and production of this Canadian speciality.

# South-Western Ontario

This designation covers everything south and west of Toronto to Lake Huron and Lake Erie, which border the USA. For the most part, the area is flat farmland – the only area in Ontario with little forest – and population density is high. With the warm climate and long growing season, this southern tip of Canada was settled early.

Arching around Lake Ontario is a continuous strip of urbanisation. This 'Golden Horseshoe' helps make the region one of the most industrialised and wealthy in the country.

Hamilton, the largest city in the area, is a major steel town. Niagara, with its famous falls, is an important fruit-growing and wine-producing district.

Further west, the soil becomes sandier and the main crop is tobacco, although this is changing as the Canadian cigarette market shrinks. Around Kitchener and London, the small towns are centres for the mixed farming of the region. Lake Erie and, especially, Lake Huron both have sandy beaches. In some of the older country towns, crafts and antiques are available.

Windsor – like Detroit, Michigan, its counterpart across the river – is an auto-manufacturing centre.

Because the area is heavily populated and the USA is close by, attractions and parks do get busy in summer. In general, this is an area for people-related activities and pastimes, not for nature or rugged landscapes.

## HAMILTON

Hamilton, sometimes referred to as Steeltown, is a heavily industrialised city with about 310,000 residents. It's halfway between Toronto and Niagara Falls. This is the centre of Canada's iron and steel industry, with two major companies here: Stelco and Dofasco. Because of this industry, the city has a bit of a reputation as a pollution centre.

Action has been taken to clean it up and work in this direction continues. Although the air cannot be compared to that of the far north (what can?), these days some of what one sees billowing from the many smokestacks is actually steam. While Hamilton is obviously not a tourist centre, there are nonetheless a few good things to see in and around town. As accommodation is reasonable here, it may be worth considering spending the night if you're planning a look around Niagara-on-the-Lake, which has high prices.

### Orientation

King St (a one-way street going west) and Main St (one way going east, parallel to and one block south of King St) are the two main streets. King St has most of the downtown shops and restaurants. King and John Sts are the core of the downtown area. Jackson Square, on King St between Bay and James Sts, is a large, shopping complex that includes restaurants, cinemas and even an indoor skating rink. The Convention Centre (with an art gallery) is on the corner of King and MacNab Sts. Just south across Main St is City Hall. The bus terminal is on Rebecca St, off John St, about three blocks from the centre of town.

### Information

The downtown central tourist office (☎ 522-7772) is at 127 King St East and operates seven days a week, all year. Other summer-only information centres are in busy visitor centres around the city, such as the Royal Botanical Gardens or the African Lion Safari.

### Royal Botanical Gardens

The Royal Botanical Gardens – nearly 1000 hectares of flowers, natural park and wildlife sanctuary – is probably the big attraction in the area. It is one of the largest of its kind in

ONTARIO

the country and only one of five in the world to be designated 'Royal'. The grounds are split into sections, with trails connecting some areas.

In July and August, the Trial Garden – the rock and herb gardens – and Hendrie Park are best. The arboretum has the world's largest lilac collection (what an olfactory treat), which is best in May. The sanctuary takes up nearly half of the grounds and consists of trails winding through marsh and wooded ravines – not what one normally finds at such manicured, formal gardens. There is also an interpretive centre and two restaurants at the gardens.

The site is between Hamilton and the suburban community of Burlington, on Plains Rd near the junction of Hwys 2 and 6, and is open daily all year. It's free, but donations are invited.

### Art Gallery of Hamilton

The art gallery (☎ 527-6610), the province's third largest, is spacious and has a good selection of Canadian and international paintings. They also run an interesting film series, with screenings mainly on weekends. Tours of the gallery are given, if requested in advance.

The gallery is open Tuesday to Saturday from 10 am to 5 pm (until 9 pm on Thursday) and on Sunday from 1 to 5 pm. It's closed on Mondays and holidays. Admission is $3, or $1.50 for students.

### Hamilton Place

In the same complex as the art gallery, this theatre-auditorium for the performing arts features shows of various types almost nightly, including regular performances by the Philharmonic and the Opera Company. Tours are available.

### Hess Village

Two blocks west of the Convention Centre on Hess St is this renovated area of old

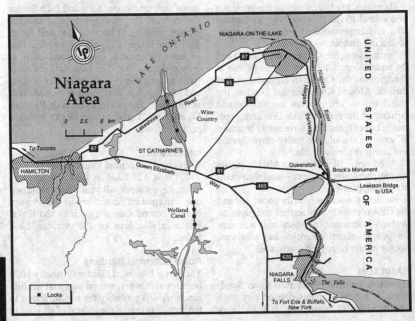

houses now containing boutiques, restaurants and cafés. It is well promoted, but small and not particularly interesting.

### Dundurn Castle

One man's castle, Dundurn (☎ 522-5313) is actually a 36-room mansion once belonging to Sir Allan Napier McNab, prime minister from 1854 to 1856 of what was then the United Provinces of Canada. It's furnished in mid-1800s style. The mansion is on York Blvd just out of town, about a 15-minute walk (or you can grab the York city bus). It's open daily all year, in the afternoons only from June to September.

Concerts and various shows are held on the grounds through the summer. Also at the site is a military museum, with weapons and uniforms dating from the War of 1812 to more modern times.

### Whitehern

At 41 Jackson St West, this elegant mansion (☎ 522-5664), lived in by the prominent McQuesten family from 1852 to 1968, contains original furnishings, art, etc and is surrounded by well-tended gardens. It offers a peek into both the Victorian era and the life of the well-to-do. Admission is charged.

### Canadian Warplane Heritage Museum

The museum (☎ 679-4183) has about 40 vintage planes, including that monster of the skies – a huge, restored Lancaster bomber from WW II. All are in flying condition. Many of the planes, together with newer ones from a variety of sources, are part of an excellent two-day air show held in mid-June, which attracts tens of thousands of people. The museum is in hangars 3 and 4 at the Hamilton Airport. There is a cafeteria and a gift shop. In 1993 the museum suffered a major fire and has lost some of its irreplaceable plane collection, including a Spitfire.

### Museum of Steam & Technology

The old pumphouse (☎ 549-5225), dating from 1860, was built to supply clean water when cholera and typhus menaced the city.

Now restored, these steam engines are among the largest in North America. Trimmed with mahogany and brass, they are quite attractive objects. Also featured are photographs and engine exhibits. Admission costs $2.50 and the museum, at 900 Woodward Ave, is open daily (but in the afternoons only from October to May).

### Confederation Park

Not far north of town on Centennial Parkway, this park contains Wild Waterworks, featuring a water slide and a swimming pool with waves. There is also a beach along Lake Ontario, and picnic and camping facilities.

### African Lion Safari

About 1000 animals and birds roam this vast, cageless park (☎ 623-2620). You drive through, sometimes getting very close to lions, tigers and other animals. Monkeys and others climb and grope all over the car, and for this reason those with particular pride in their vehicle are advised to use the park tour bus instead.

The park is not cheap ($13.50 for adults, $9.50 for children), but seeing the whole thing can take a full afternoon and most people feel it's worth the money, especially if you have children with you. Try to make time for the live demonstrations such as one on birds of prey.

African Lion Safari is open from April to October. The longest hours are in July and August, but even at that time of year it closes at 5.30 pm. The park is between Hamilton and Cambridge, on Hwy 8. For the daring, there is a campground at the site.

### Festivals

The Festival of Friends happens each August in Gage Park and features music, crafts and foods from many countries.

Each June, in the town of Stoney Creek (south of Hamilton), an interesting spectacle is the re-enactment of a War of 1812 battle between British and US soldiers. It's held at Stoney Creek Battlefield Park.

ONTARIO

## Places to Stay

**Camping** There are numerous local campgrounds, including one in Confederation Park, just north of town on Centennial Parkway.

**Hostels** For low-budget lodgings, the *YMCA* (☎ 529-7102), at 79 James St, has 171 rooms, for men only, at $25 a single. The *YWCA* (☎ 522-9922), at 75 McNab St, is comparable, although much smaller, with rooms at $30/44 for singles/doubles. Both have pools and inexpensive cafeterias.

**Tourist Homes** Try the *Cobblestone Lodge* (☎ 545-9735), a huge old place now a tourist home at 684 Main St East, on the corner of Holton Ave. It is often busy, and the owner, Aileen Harvey, prefers to see you rather than speak over the phone, but it's worth a try. Rooms cost $32 to $55 a double, depending on facilities.

**Hotels** Though many of the downtown hotels are new and large, there are some choices which are not too expensive. Accommodation is generally more reasonable here than in either Toronto or around the heavily touristed region of Niagara-on-the-Lake.

At 737 King St East, the *Budget Motor Inn* (☎ 527-2708) has singles/doubles at $40. Also central, the *Visitors Inn* (☎ 529-6979), at 649 Main St West, is more expensive but quite good value.

Further out and close to McMaster University, the *Mountainview Motel* (☎ 528-7521), at 1870 Main St West, costs $45 to $50 for two people. Out at the other end of Main St is the *City Motor Hotel* (☎ 549-1371), at 1620 Main East.

On the outskirts, either east or west, motels abound, and for the most part they are in the budget to moderate price categories, with rates much lower than those around Niagara-on-the-Lake.

## Places to Eat

The downtown area around King St has numerous restaurants, including various ethnic places. You can choose between Chinese, Greek and Italian food.

At Ferguson and King Sts, the *Black Forest Inn*, with a German and Austrian slant, is pleasant and reasonable for soups and sandwiches. The more expensive and extensive dinner menu features a variety of schnitzels.

*Le Ganges*, at 234 King St, is not really cheap but serves good Indian food.

In Hess Village, the *Gown & Gavel*, a British-style pub at 24 Hess St, serves light meals and beer under the umbrellas.

There are many low-priced places to eat in the Jackson Square shopping mall. Many others suiting a range of budgets can be found along King, Main and William Sts.

Don Cherry's *Grapevine* (owned by one of the country's best known hockey commentators, who is admired or vilified for his strong and vocal opinions), is a popular sports bar and watering hole, at 157 Main East.

## ST CATHARINE'S

Lying on Lake Ontario between Hamilton and the Niagara River, St Catharine's is the major town of the Niagara fruit and wine-growing district. To each side are farms and small towns with vineyards and wineries.

Port Dalhousie (pronounced 'dal-oo-zey') is an old harbour area of St Catharine's where the early canals opened into Lake Ontario. It is now a blend of the new and historic, with a reconstructed wooden lock, the oldest and smallest jail in the province and a lighthouse set alongside contemporary bars and restaurants.

In late September, the Niagara Grape & Wine Festival is held, with concerts, wine and cheese parties and a parade.

## WELLAND CANAL

The most noteworthy feature of the area is the historic Welland Canal, a bypass of Niagara Falls which connects Lake Ontario with Lake Erie. A series of locks along the 42-km-long canal overcomes the difference of about 100 metres in the lakes' water levels.

The canal was initiated in 1829 by local

businessmen to promote trade and commerce. Now in its fourth incarnation and part of the St Lawrence Seaway, it is a vital link in international freight service, allowing shipping into the industrial heart of North America from the Atlantic Ocean.

The three principal cargoes going through the canal are wheat, iron ore and coal. The average trip through the canal and its eight locks takes 12 hours.

Remnants of the first three canals (built in 1829, 1845 and 1887) can be seen at various points. The fourth version, still in use but with some modifications and additions, was built between 1914 and 1932.

At Lakeside Park, along the waterfront in Port Dalhousie, the early canals met Lake Ontario. Old locks, lighthouses and various structures from the last century can be viewed. At **Mountain View Park**, on the corner of Mountain and Bradley Sts, there are locks at the escarpment from the second canal, along with some other 19th-century buildings.

For a more up-to-date look, visit the **Welland Canal Viewing & Information Centre**, on Canal Rd also in St Catharine's. It's at lock 3 of the currently used canal, and includes a museum with exhibits on the canal and its construction, a viewing platform and audiovisual displays on many aspects of the waterway. Ships from around the world may be seen on their way to and from the centre of North America and the Atlantic Ocean. Fifty million tonnes of cargo are transported through the canal annually. Open daily all year, the centre is on Canal Rd, off Glendale Ave (which exits from the Queen Elizabeth Hwy). Follow the signs to the locks. You can also get a bite to eat and something to drink here while you watch the ships. A daily shipping schedule is posted.

The last lock, number eight, is at Port Colbourne (on Lake Erie).

Fortune Navigation (☎ 646-2234) is a company offering cruises of the canal, which depart from Port Dalhousie where the first canal began. The three-hour trip, costing $15, continues as far up the new canal at Port Wellar (on Lake Ontario) as possible, but passing through lock 1 depends on freight traffic, so trips will vary in distance covered. There are family and kids' rates.

The cruises depart at 2 pm and run from mid-May to October. Getting to the dock area is a little tricky. It's near Lakeside Park in Port Dalhousie. If driving, take the Ontario St exit off the Queen Elizabeth Way (QEW) and continue north to Lakeport Rd, where a left turn should be made. From there just keep going over the bridges and you should see a sign.

For hikers, there is the Merritt Trail, a walk which stretches from Port Dalhousie in St Catharine's to Port Colbourne, mainly following the Welland Canal. It is detailed in the Bruce Trail guidebook; see Tobermory later in this chapter. Local tourist offices will also have information about this trail.

## WELLAND

Despite the predominance of agriculture in the region, Welland is primarily a steel town. A portion of the canal cuts right through town, while a larger, newer, busy bypass channel is two km from the downtown area; from there, international freighters can be viewed.

The city has become known for its two dozen or so painted murals depicting scenes from the history of the area and the canal. Begun in 1988, they can be seen around town on the sides of buildings. The heaviest concentration of murals is along East Main St and the streets connecting it to parallel Division St, one block away. There are others along King and Niagara Sts. This interesting idea has been immensely successful in Chemainus on Vancouver Island in British Columbia, and a couple of the paintings here were done by a Chemainus artist. A pamphlet on the paintings can be picked up in an office upstairs at 800 Niagara St in the Seaway Mall, or at one of the local tourist offices. The Chamber of Commerce is at 32 Main St East.

The museum at 65 Hooker St offers more details on the canals.

In the Seaway Mall, a shopping centre at 800 Niagara St, the Seaway Serpentarium

ONTARIO

has a fairly extensive reptile collection of 300 species, including some endangered ones which are studied and bred here.

In early June, the two-week Rose Festival celebrates the queen of flowers. There are displays, contests, a parade and other events.

## PORT COLBORNE

Situated on Lake Erie at the southern end of the Welland Canal, Port Colborne has one of the largest water locks in the world. This lock (lock 8) can be seen from Fountain View Park. The summer tourist information booth is here, too. The quiet town doesn't really offer much to see or do. At 280 King St is a small pioneer heritage village. There are also some beaches in the area, and a number of cottage communities nearby along the shoreline.

## NIAGARA-ON-THE-LAKE

This small, pretty village (population 12,500) is about 20 km downstream from the falls, and with its up-market shops and restaurants, well-known George Bernard Shaw Festival and curbs on development, it acts as a sort of foil to the hype and flash of Niagara Falls. The surrounding vineyards and history-filled parkland add to its appeal. Originally a Native Indian site, it was settled by Loyalists from New York State after the American Revolution. In the 1790s it was made the first capital of Ontario, and it is considered one of the best preserved, 19th-century towns in North America.

The main street, Queen St, has many well-maintained shops from the 1800s. The lakeside location, tree-lined streets and old houses make Niagara-on-the-Lake a nice place to see before or after the falls. The village does get busy on good summer days, though generally only on the main street. Stroll down the side streets and you'll get a quiet taste of former times in a small, prosperous Ontario town. Decidedly atypical (sort of rural Japan in Canada) and worth a look is the house at the corner of Wellington and Byron Sts, not far from the tourist office.

### Information

The tourist office (☎ 468-4263) in the Chamber of Commerce, on the corner of King St and Prideaux/Byron Sts, is good, friendly and helpful and will book accommodation for you. From May to early September, the office is open every day; later in the year, the hours are shortened and it's closed on weekends. On the eastern side of the downtown area towards Niagara Falls, King St crosses Queen St at large Simcoe Park, on the east side of Queen St.

Ask for the *Historic Guide*, a free pamphlet outlining in brief the town's history and a self-guided walking tour. It lists many of the noteworthy structures around town and indicates them on a map.

Also ask about the Garden Tour put on by the Conservancy, which allows visitors a peek around some of the splendid gardens in town. The annual area B&B house tour gives you another chance to see behind the fences and doors of town.

---

### The Niagara Escarpment

An escarpment is a steep rock face, or cliff of great length. The Niagara Escarpment, so often referred to in southern Ontario, runs for 725 km, with a maximum height of 335 metres. Once the shore of an ancient sea centred in what is now Michigan, USA, the escarpment begins in Ontario, at the town of Queenston on the Niagara River. On its way north to Tobermory and Manitoulin Island, it passes through or beside Hamilton, Collingwood and Owen Sound. A major outcropping of the escarpment can clearly be seen from Hwy 401 west of Oakville, at Kelso Conservation Area.

The Niagara Escarpment Commission, through a series of parks and conservation areas, seeks to preserve the escarpment's natural beauty, flora & fauna. Now largely a recreation area, the escarpment is used for activities such as skiing and bird-watching but is best known for the hiking along the Bruce Trail. For more details on the trail, see under Tobermory. ■

Niagara-
on-the-Lake

## Queen St

The town's main street, Queen St, is the prime attraction. Restored and well-preserved wooden buildings and shops now contain antiques, bakeries, various specialities, Scottish souvenirs and restaurants. Note particularly the apothecary dating from 1866, now a museum, fitted with great old cabinets, remedies and jars. Also recommended is a jam sample from the Greaves store; the people here are fourth-generation jam-makers. There are a couple of fudge shops, too.

The renovated courthouse, on Queen St, is another impressive building.

Towards the falls but still in town, Queen St becomes Picton St.

## Museums

The **Historical Museum** at 43 Castlereagh St is the oldest local museum in the province. It opened in 1907 and has a vast collection of early 20th-century items relating to the town's past, ranging from Native Indian artefacts to Loyalist and War of 1812 collectables. Admission is $2. From March to December, it is open daily from 10 am to 6 pm. During January and February, it opens only on weekend afternoons.

**McFarland House** is a handsome Geor-

ONTARIO

gian-style place built around 1800 by John McFarland, a carpenter from Scotland. Restored in 1959, it is now furnished with pre-1840 articles. During the War of 1812 it was used as a hospital. The house is in McFarland Park, two km south of town on the Niagara Parkway, and is open daily during summer from 11 am to 5 pm. Tea is served.

Also in town is the **Fire Museum**, with firefighting equipment that dates from 1816 to 1976.

### Historic Military Sites

Just out of Niagara-on-the-Lake towards the falls, **Fort George**, dating from 1797, is one of several local historic military sites. It's open daily and admission is $2 for adults. The fort was the site of important battles during the War of 1812 and changed hands between the British and Americans a couple of times. Within the walls are the officers' quarters, a working kitchen, the powder magazine and storage houses. There isn't a lot to see, but the various costumed workers, particularly the soldiers performing different exercises, provide some atmosphere.

Tucked behind the fort is **Navy Hall**, at the water's edge. Only one building remains of what was a sizeable supply depot for British forts on the Great Lakes during the 1700s. It was destroyed during the War of 1812. The American Fort Niagara is across the river.

In a fine location on the west side of town, at the opposite end of Ricardo/Front St, are the minimal remains of **Fort Mississauga**. There are some plaques but no organised tours or facilities.

Also in town are **Butler's Barracks**, off John St at King St. Pedestrians can reach it either from Mary St or along a trail leading from Fort George. First used by the British at the end of the War of 1812 as a storage and barracks site, the location has since been used for a variety of purposes by the Canadian military. Troops trained here for both World Wars and for the Korean War. Some buildings remain from the various periods of use, and markers lead visitors around on a mini-Canadian military history tour.

### Organised Tours

Call Kiely House (☎ 468-4588) for guided bicycle tours, with the bikes provided. General tours are offered daily, with stops at a winery or two. Kiely House is also a B&B inn.

### Festivals

The Shaw Festival is an internationally respected theatre festival held annually (May to September). It features the plays of George Bernard Shaw and his contemporaries, played by top actors. There are three different theatres, within walking distance of the town centre, and the location has a bearing on ticket prices. Cheapest are the weekday matinees.

Tickets range from $20 up to $50 for the best seats in the house on Saturday night at Festival Theatre. Cheaper rush seats go on sale at 9.30 am on the day of performance but are not available for Saturday shows. There are brief lunch-time plays for $10.

The box office (☎ 468-2172) is open from 10 am to 9 pm every day from June to mid-October. If you're planning to take in a play ☎ 1-800-267-4759 from anywhere in Canada or 1-800-724-2934 from the USA, well in advance, and ask for the Shaw Festival guide. It will give you all the details, the year's performances and other useful information, as well as ticket order forms.

### Places to Stay

Accommodation is expensive. For many people, a few hours spent looking around will suffice before looking for cheaper lodging elsewhere. When the Shaw Festival is on, beginning in early June, the town can get booked right out on weekends, so plan accordingly.

The town has some fine inns and several good hotels. By far the bulk of the accommodation, though, is in the many less-expensive tourist homes and B&Bs. And though I said less expensive, this does not mean cheap, with rates at about $65 and up for a double. The tourist office has a free accommodation reservation service.

One of the least expensive of the tourist

Top: Brilliant fall display, Ontario (ML)
Bottom: Windswept shore of Ontario's Georgian Bay (ML)

Top: View of downtown Calgary (TS)
Bottom: Horseshoe Canyon, part of the badlands near Drumheller, Southern Alberta (T

homes is the central *Endicott's B&B*, at 331 William St. Prices are $50 to $60 and bicycles are available.

Similarly priced is *Rose Cottage*, also in the downtown area, at 308 Victoria St. There's just one room and it comes with a private bath. Both these places are booked through the Chamber of Commerce (☎ 468-4263).

Also with reasonable rates is *Amberlea Guest House* (☎ 468-5607), found at 285 John St. There are a couple of rooms at $55 and one with private bath at $75. All include a full breakfast.

A fourth possibility is the central *Saltbox* (☎ 468-5423), in an old house at 223 Gate St. Again, a full breakfast is provided and smoking is not permitted. It's open all year and charges around $65 for doubles.

A place definitely worth considering if there are four of you is *Nautical Cottage* (booked through ☎ 468-4263), at 515 Regent St, within walking distance of the town centre and the theatres. It has a double bed, two twin beds and a kitchen and goes for $100 a night.

*Mrs Lynda Kay Knapp* (☎ 468-3935) offers a separate, private unit (almost like a little apartment, with some cooking facilities and a fridge) at $75 for two people. It's not open in winter. Her house is close to the centre of town, at 390 Simcoe St. Couples, note that she may ask if you're married and not want to rent if you don't answer satisfactorily.

Among the pricier options is the *Angel Inn* (☎ 468-3411), dating from 1823, one block south from Queen St on Regent St. The slightly older *Kiely House Heritage Inn* (☎ 468-4588) is a 13-room B&B at 209 Queen St. The *Moffat Inn* (☎ 468-4116), an attractive white-and-green place at 60 Picton St, offers all the amenities at the relatively reasonable rate of about $90.

## Places to Eat

There are a number of good places to eat in town. At 45 Queen St, the *Stagecoach* is cheap and always busy. You can get a good-value breakfast before 11 am.

For a pub meal, try the *Buttery*, at 19 Queen St, with a pleasant patio. On Saturday nights, they put on Henry VIII-style feasts, with entertainment, drink and victuals aplenty.

The *Angel*, just off Queen St on Regent St and dating from 1823, is another British pub-type place with fish & chips, sandwiches and various beers. Prices range from $7 to $8 at lunch, about twice that at dinner.

*Fan's Court*, around the back at 135 Queen St, provides some fine ethnic diversion in this most Anglo of towns. It serves Chinese and Asian dishes, such as Singapore-style noodles with curry. Apart from the pleasant dining room, there are also a few tables outside in a small courtyard. Prices are moderate at lunch but the dinner menu has become a little pricey.

*McCray Hall Gifts*, a shop on the north side of Queen St, has a pleasant and quiet little tea room at the back and out on the patio; it makes a fine place for a short afternoon break. The *Prince of Wales Hotel* has a good dining room for finer, more costly eating. Most of the inns and hotels have their own dining rooms.

For a good cup of coffee try *Monika's*, at 126 Queen St.

A few blocks from Queen St, Queen's Royal Park makes a good place for a picnic along the water.

## Entertainment

In Simcoe Park, right in town, there are often free classical music concerts on summer Saturdays.

## Getting There & Away

**Bus** There is one bus each way between here and Toronto on Wednesdays, Fridays, Saturdays and Sundays, but only during the summer. The fare is $20.50 for the two-hour trip. Charterways Bus Lines runs between St Catharine's and Niagara-on-the-Lake three times a week – on these three days Gray Coach doesn't connect Toronto. And since Gray Coach (operated by Greyhound) runs to St Catharine's every day, you can get here from Toronto one way or another any day of the week. In town, the buses to and from St Catharine's stop at Simcoe Park.

It's hard to believe, but there is no public transport between here and Niagara Falls. However, there are ways around this peculiarity. Double Deck Tours out of Niagara Falls runs bus tours around the region, including a wine tour from Niagara-on-the-Lake. They end up running the buses back and forth between the two towns to link their tours, and these can be used as a regular bus service. There are three trips each way daily. Catch the bus across the street from the tourist office on King St, where you can find out the times as well.

**Taxi** Taxis to Niagara Falls charge a $23 flat rate.

### Getting Around
**Bicycle** Cycling is a fine way to explore the area, and bicycles can be rented by the hour, half-day or full day at 92A Picton St, past the Moffat Inn. They don't have much of a selection.

### AROUND NIAGARA-ON-THE-LAKE
#### Vineyards & Wine Tours
The triangle between St Catharine's, Niagara-on-the-Lake and Niagara Falls is, along with the Okanagan Valley in British Columbia, the country's most important wine-producing area. The Ontario region, though, produces about 80% of the grapes used in Canada's wine production. The moderate microclimate created by the escarpment and Lake Ontario is a big part of the area's success.

The ever-increasing number of wineries – there are now nearly 20 – are producing some pretty fine grape juice. In the past five years, the wine producers have grown from operating an essentially small cottage industry to being internationally recognised vintners capable of turning out calibre vintages. Many offer visitors a look around and a taste. A full day could be enjoyed touring the countryside and emptying glasses. Three of the principal wines are riesling, chardonnay and gewurztraminer. Whites tend to dominate

but reds are also produced. The expensive icewines have recently gained a lot of favourable attention. The wineries are open to the public from approximately the beginning of May to the end of October. Some of the commercial tour operators include a winery or two on their bus excursions. Most of these are operated out of Niagara Falls.

The eight premier wineries are known collectively as the Group of Seven Plus One. The following wineries are taken from this group. They tend to be clustered south of Niagara-on-the-Lake. The better wines have a Vinter's Quality Alliance (VQA) designation.

The Reif Estate Winery (☎ 468-7738) is south of Niagara-on-the-Lake, between Line 2 and Line 3 on the Niagara Parkway. The winery, with tastings, is open every day of the year, as is the shop. Call for tour times.

Inniskillin (☎ 468-3554) is practically next door, at Line 3. It's open from May to October. Inniskillin has developed a good reputation and is the leading award-winner of the region. A display outlines the process and history of wine making in Niagara.

Château des Charmes (☎ 262-4219) is in St David's, between the falls and Niagara-on-the-Lake. It's on Line 7 off Four Mile Creek Rd, not far from Hwy 55, and is open all day, every day. Again, although the store with tastings is virtually always open, call for tour times for a more in-depth look around the estate.

Others of the Group of Seven Plus One are Marynissen, Konzelmann, Stonechurch, Hillebrand and Pillitteri.

Another vintner, not part of this grouping, is Bright's (☎ 357-2400), Canada's oldest winery. It's at 4887 Dorchester Rd, Niagara Falls, north off Hwy 420. Call for specific directions; the best route depends on where you're starting from. Free one-hour tours with wine sampling are given at 10.30 am and 2 and 3.30 pm every day (except Sundays and holidays).

Area tourist offices will have complete lists of the wineries and their locations.

## NIAGARA PARKWAY & RECREATIONAL TRAIL

A slow, 20-km trip along the two-lane **Niagara Parkway** to Niagara Falls is most enjoyable. Along the way are parks, picnic areas, good views over the river and a couple of campgrounds, all of which make up part of the Niagara Parks Commission park system. It runs pretty well the entire length of the Niagara River, for 55 km, from Niagara-on-the-Lake past the falls to Fort Erie. A three-metre-wide recreational trail for cycling, jogging or walking runs the entire way, paralleling the parkway. It's excellent for either a short or long cycling excursion. The terrain is flat and the riverside scenery pleasant, and it's rarely very busy. It is also free. Historic and natural points of interest are marked with plaques. Perhaps best of all, in season, are the fresh-fruit stands with cold cherry ciders and juices.

In the small village of Queenston, just before the Lewiston Bridge to the USA, is the **Laura Secord Homestead**. Laura, one of Canada's best known heroes (partly because of the chocolate company which bears her name), lived here, on the corner of Queenston and Partition Sts, during the War of 1812. At one point during the war, she hiked nearly 30 km to warn the British soldiers of impending attack by the Americans. The house can be visited for a small fee, which includes a chocolate sample. There is also a small candy shop on the premises. The rose garden out front is said to have been planted by Laura herself.

At the juncture of the Niagara Parkway and Queenston St (the main street in Queenston), by the War Memorial, is the **Samuel Weir Collection & Library of Art**. Mr Wier had the house built as a live-in gallery and library in 1916 to house his remarkably extensive art, book and antique collection. He formed a foundation to administer the estate for public access, provided that he was buried on the front lawn. He was. It's free and is open from May to October, from Wednesday to Saturday and on Sunday afternoons.

In Mackenzie House, also in town, the **Mackenzie House Printery** has a collection highlighting printing and printing equipment as history. Displays detail historic newspapers, such as the *Colonial Advocate* edited by William Lyon Mackenzie, who later led the Upper Canada Rebellion.

Also in Queenston is the southern end of the Bruce Trail, which extends 700 km to Tobermory on Georgian Bay. There are numerous access points in the Niagara and Hamilton area. For more details on the trail, see the Tobermory section in this chapter.

A little further along the parkway is **Queenston Heights Park**, known for its large monument of Major General Brock. The winding inside stairwell will take you up 60 metres to a fabulous view. (You'll need the reward after that climb.) Also here is the Queenston Heights Restaurant, which itself has fine views of the river. Have a beer on the balcony here on a warm summer afternoon. This is not a bad place for a meal, either, although it's not in the low-budget category.

Near the restaurant is a monument to Laura Secord, and from here begins a 45-minute self-guided walking tour of the hillside, detailing the Battle of Queenston Heights. Pick up a copy of the good walking-tour booklet at any of the information offices. It explains some of the historical background, outlines the War of 1812 and describes how the British victory here was significant in Canada's not becoming part of the USA. Interpreters are on hand at the huge **Brock monument**, and the guidebook should be available there.

The Niagara Parkway continues through Niagara Falls and beyond, southbound. Attractions between Queenston and Niagara Falls, all of which can be reached on the Niagara Falls People Mover buses during the summer season, are covered in the Niagara Falls section; there is a Niagara Parkway section to cover the southern part of the route to Fort Erie.

## NIAGARA FALLS

The roaring falls make this town one of Canada's top tourist destinations. It's a busy spot – about 12 million people visit annually and you'll hear and see people from all over the world.

The falls themselves, spanning the Niagara River between Ontario and upper New York State, are impressive, particularly the Canadian Horseshoe Falls. They look good by day and by night, when colourful spotlights flicker across the misty foam. Even in winter, when the flow is partially hidden and the edges are frozen solid – like a stopped film – it's quite a spectacle. Very occasionally the falls stop altogether. The first recorded instance of this occurred on the morning of Easter Sunday 1848, and it caused some to speculate that the end of the world was nigh. An ice jam had completely cut off the flow of water. Some residents, obviously braver than I, took the opportunity to scavenge the river bed beneath the falls! It is said that Napoleon's brother rode from New Orleans in a stagecoach with his new bride to view the falls and that it has been a honeymoon attraction ever since. In fact, the town is sometimes humorously but disparagingly called a spot for newlyweds and nearly deads.

Supplementing the falls, the city now has an incredible array of artificial attractions which, together with the hotels, restaurants and flashing lights, produce an environment as close as Canada comes to the gloss and garishness of Las Vegas. It's a sight in itself.

Niagara Falls is approximately a two-hour drive from Toronto by the Queen Elizabeth Way (QEW), past Hamilton and St Catharine's. Public transportation between Toronto and Niagara Falls is frequent and quick.

### Orientation

The town of Niagara Falls is split into two main sections: the older commercial area, where the locals go about their business, and the other part around the falls, which has been developed for visitors. In the 'normal' part of town, known as downtown, Queen St and Victoria Ave are the main streets. The area around Bridge St, near the corner of Erie St, has both the train and bus stations and a couple of cheap hotels. The international hostel is in the downtown area, not far from the train station. Generally, however, there is little to see or do in this part of town.

About three km south along the river are the falls and all the trappings of the tourist trade – restaurants, motels, shops and attractions. In the vicinity of the falls, the main streets are the busy Clifton Hill, Falls Ave, Centre St and Victoria Ave. The latter has many places to stay, and some of the numerous restaurants which can be found on all the main streets.

Going the other way, north, along the river is scenic parkland, which runs from the falls downstream about 40 km to Niagara-on-the-Lake.

Many of the local tourist homes are also between the two sections of town.

### Information

**Tourist Offices** The most central place for tourist information is at Horseshoe Falls, in the building known as Table Rock Centre. The Niagara Parks Commission runs the good but busy desk here (☎ 314-0944). It's open daily from 10 am to 6 pm (until 10 pm in summer).

The area's main tourist office, though, is the Ontario Travel Information Centre (☎ 358-3221), which is out of the centre west on Hwy 420 from the Rainbow Bridge toward the Queen Elizabeth Way, at 5355 Stanley Ave. It's about halfway between the bridge and the highway. Ontario maps and information on destinations across the province can be picked up here. It's open until 8 pm through the summer.

There are also a couple of information offices about town run by the Visitors & Convention Bureau, which use the same central phone (☎ 356-6061). One of these offices is at 5433 Victoria Ave.

**Parking** A good, free parking lot about 15 minutes' walk from the falls is by the IMAX movie theatre, south of Murray St towards Robinson St, near the Skylon. After leaving your car, walk to the concrete bridge on the

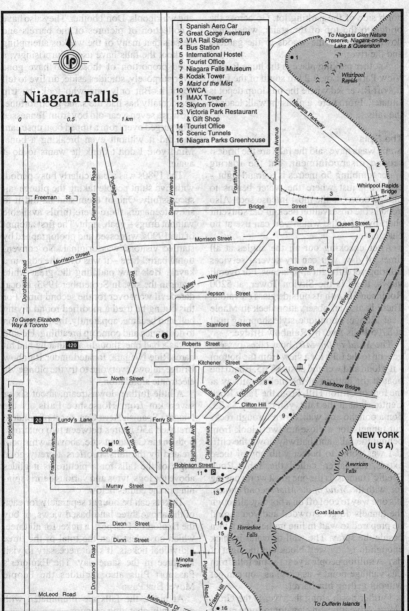

# Niagara Falls

1 Spanish Aero Car
2 Great Gorge Aventure
3 VIA Rail Station
4 Bus Station
5 International Hostel
6 Tourist Office
7 Niagara Falls Museum
8 Kodak Tower
9 Maid of the Mist
10 YWCA
11 IMAX Tower
12 Skylon Tower
13 Victoria Park Restaurant
   & Gift Shop
14 Tourist Office
15 Scenic Tunnels
16 Niagara Parks Greenhouse

0    0.5    1 km

To Niagara Glen Nature
Preserve, Niagara-on-the-
Lake & Queenston

Whirlpool
Rapids

Niagara Parkway

Whirlpool Rapids
Bridge

Victoria Avenue

Freeman    St

Portage    Road

Drummond    Road

Stanley Avenue

Fourth Ave

Bridge        Street

Queen Street

Morrison Street

Dorchester Road

Morrison Street

Valley    Way

Simcoe St

St Clair Rd

To Queen Elizabeth
Way & Toronto

Jepson    Street

Stamford    Street

Palmer    Ave

River    Road

Niagara River

420

Roberts    Street

Kitchener    Street

Centre St  Ellen  St

Victoria Avenue

Rainbow Bridge

North    Street

Clifton Hill

Brookfield Avenue

20        Lundy's    Lane

Ferry    St

NEW YORK
(U S A)

Franklin Avenue

Main Street

Avenue

Buchanan Ave

Clark Avenue

Niagara Parkway

American
Falls

10
Culp    St

Robinson Street

11        12

Murray    Street

13

Goat Island

Dixon    Street

Stanley

14

Dunn    Street

15

Horseshoe
Falls

Minolta
Tower

McLeod    Road

Drummond    Road

Portage    Road

Fraser  Hill

Marineland Dr

16

To Dufferin Islands

ONTARIO

north side of the parking lot. Go across the bridge to the top of the stairs, which lead down through some woods to the gardens and the river.

Another parking place is the huge Rapids View Parking Lot, 3.2 km south of the falls. It's off River Rd where the bus loop depot is situated. From here, a pleasant walk leads to the falls.

## The Falls

Some wags have said the falls are the brides' second disappointment, but the roaring water tumbling 56 metres is a grand sight – close up, just where the water begins to plunge down, is the most intense spot. Also good is the observation deck of the souvenir shop by the falls, which you can use at no charge.

After checking out all the angles at all times of day, you can try several services offering yet different approaches. For overall views, there is the Skylon Tower, at 5200 Robinson St, with its outside glass elevators. There is also an observation deck in Maple Leaf Village, a boutique-style shopping mall at 5705 Falls Ave, by Rainbow Bridge.

The *Maid of the Mist* boat takes passengers up to the falls for a view from the bottom – it's loud and wet and costs $8.65. Board the boat at the bottom of the incline railway at the foot of Clifton Hill. From the Table Rock Centre right at the falls, you can pay $5.25, don a poncho and walk down through rock-cut tunnels for a close-up (wet) look from behind the falls and halfway down the cliff. If I was going to bother with any of these extras, the latter, called the Table Rock Scenic Tunnels, is the one most worth paying for, with the *Maid of the Mist* second choice. It's one way to cool off on a hot day, although the tunnels do get crowded and you should be prepared to wait in line in them for a turn beside the spray. The wall of water is thick enough to pretty well block out the light of day. A million people a year see the falls from this vantage point – as close as you can get without getting in a barrel.

Further north along the river is the Great Gorge Adventure, an elevator to some rapids

and whirlpools. Don't bother. They also have a collection of pictures of the barrels and vessels that many of the wackos attempting to shoot the falls have used. Surprisingly, a good proportion of those who have gone over purposely, suicides aside, do live to tell about it. But only one who took the trip accidentally has had the same good fortune. He was a seven-year-old boy from Tennessee who surged over from a tipped boat upstream and did it without even breaking a bone. Mind you, I don't think he wants to do it again.

The 1980s was a particularly busy period, with five stunt people taking the plunge, all successfully. One of them said he did it to show teenagers there were thrills available without drugs – yeah, right. The first attempt of the 1990s, witnessed and photographed by startled visitors, was original. No conventional barrel here – it was over the edge in a kayak. He's now paddling the great white water in the sky. In September 1993, a local daredevil went over for the second time. For this outing he used a modified round diving bell, and became, apparently, the first person to do it twice and come up breathing. He said it was a bad one, though, and that he had hit hard. Ride Niagara, located under Rainbow Bridge, allows everyone to try the plunge via electronic simulation.

A little further downstream, about six or seven km from Horseshoe Falls, is the Niagara Spanish Aero Car, a sort of gondola stretched 550 metres between two outcrops, both on the Canadian side, above a whirlpool created by the falls. It offers a pretty good angle of the falls for a picture as it glides above the logs, tyres and various debris spinning in the eddies below.

Tickets can be bought separately for each of the above three land-based views, or buy the Explorer's Passport, a ticket for all three, which costs less than the total of the three individual tickets. It's not necessary to visit all three in the same day. The Explorer's Passport Plus also includes the People Mover Bus Pass.

At night, the falls are illuminated with constantly changing colours.

Brown bears

## Other Views

The Skylon Tower, at 5200 Robinson St, is the large, grey tower with yellow elevators running up the outside. There is an observation deck at about 250 metres, with both indoor and outdoor viewing. Aside from great views of the falls, both Toronto and Buffalo can be seen on clear days.

There are also a couple of dining rooms at the top, the more expensive of which revolves once per hour. The other one offers buffet-style breakfasts, lunches and dinners at more moderate (but not inexpensive) prices. In the revolving restaurant, the early-bird dinner special (4 to 5.30 pm) saves some money.

The Minolta Tower, at 6732 Oakes Drive, is close to the falls and virtually overlooks the lip. It has a restaurant with spectacular views and observation galleries. The food served here is not just an afterthought, and meals are well prepared, if straightforward. An incline railway leads from the base of the tower down the hillside close to the falls.

Views can also be had from the tower or ferris wheel at Maple Leaf Village, a shopping and eating complex at 5685 Falls Ave, near Rainbow Bridge.

## Bridges

Two bridges run over the river to New York State: the Whirlpool Rapids Bridge and, closer to the falls, Rainbow Bridge, which celebrated its 50th year in 1991. You can walk or drive across to explore the falls from the US side, but have your papers in order.

## Niagara Falls Museum

This is the original of the many 'daredevil collections' of objects in which people have gone over the falls. As well as telling the stunt stories, there are displays of curios and artefacts from around the world, including Egyptian mummies and a dinosaur exhibit. The address is 5651 River Rd and the museum is open all year.

## Lundy's Lane Historical Museum

Sitting on the site of the 1814 Battle of Lundy's Lane, the museum catalogues local pioneer and military history, notably the War of 1812.

## Clifton Hill

Clifton Hill is a street name but also refers more generally to the commercial part of the downtown area near the falls given over in sense-bombarding intensity to artificial attractions in Disney-like concentration. You name it – museums, galleries, displays such as Ripley's Believe It or Not, Tussaud's Wax Museum, Houdini's Museum, Criminal's

ONTARIO

Hall of Fame (you get the drift) – they're all here. Looking is fun, but in most cases paying the entrance fee will leave you feeling like a sucker. I know – I've done it. They don't live up to their own hype. Also in this bright, busy section are dozens of souvenir shops and restaurants.

## Marineland & Game Farm
Of the many commercial attractions, this is probably one of the best. Marineland (☎ 356-8250) is an aquarium with special family shows by dolphins, sea lions and killer whales. Admission includes the game farm, which has buffalo, bears, lions, deer and others in an outdoor park setting. There are also rides (including the world's largest steel roller coaster), all covered in the cost of admission. It's open from 9 am to 6 pm, and admission is $17 for adults. It's roughly two km from the falls, south on Portage Rd.

## IMAX Theatre
The large-format (the screen is six storeys high) IMAX cinema (☎ 374-IMAX), at 6170 Buchanan Ave, near the Skylon Tower, presents a 45-minute show about the falls, its history and some of the stunts that have been pulled in and over them. Shows run continually and cost $7.50. In the same complex is a museum, with artefacts from some of those who have run the falls.

## Niagara Parks Greenhouse
Flowers and gardens are plentiful in and around Niagara Falls, which has moderate temperatures. The greenhouse and conservatory just south of the Horseshoe Falls provide a year-round floral display and are free. A bonus is the tropical birds. The greenhouse is less than one km from the falls.

## The Old Scow
Across the street, rusting away in the river, the *Old Scow* is a steel barge which has been lodged on rocks waiting to be washed over the falls since 1918. So were the three men aboard when it broke free of the tug pulling it and drifted to within 750 metres of the brink, or is that drink. Without speed boats

or helicopters, rescuing the men was some feat. Red Hill Senior, a local daredevil, climbed out hand over hand along a line that had been shot out from the roof of the waterside power plant building, which still stands beside the shore. He was able to untangle the lines, allowing an attached buoy to reach the men, who climbed on and were pulled ashore.

## Botanical Gardens & School of Horticulture Gardens
Also free for browsing around are the fastidiously cared-for 40 hectares here. The school and gardens, which are open all year, are north along the Parkway towards Queenston, about nine km from Horsehoe Falls.

Further north 2½ km, is the **floral clock**, which is over 12 metres in diameter. Beside the floral clock, don't miss the Centennial Lilac Gardens, which are at their fragrant best in late May.

Notice, too, that across the road the gorge of the Niagara River is especially impressive.

Other flower gardens are at Queen Victoria Park (right beside the Canadian falls) and at Oakes Garden Theatre (opposite the Maid of the Mist Plaza, near the falls). Across the street from the American falls, Victoria Park also has varied and colourful floral displays through most of the year.

## Green Areas
Niagara Falls can be a fairly congested, urban experience, but there are some worthwhile quiet places to explore apart from the well-tended areas of plant life listed above.

**Niagara Glen Nature Preserve** Top of the list and highly recommended, this is the only place where a sense of what the area was like before the arrival of Europeans can be gained. There are seven different walking trails here covering four km, where the falls were situated 8000 years ago. The preserve is maintained by the Parks Commission (☎ 356-2241), who offer free guided walks four times a day through the summer (July to early September). But the trails are always open to public use at no charge. The paths wind down the gorge, past huge boulders, icy cold caves, wildflowers and woods. Some people fish at the bottom from the shore. The river trail runs north to Pebbly Beach and south to the whirlpool, site of the **Spanish Aero Car** attraction.

The whirlpool is an impressive sight from the Aero Car Terminal, but the size of the gorge itself isn't fully appreciated until seen from right down at the shoreline. As noted above, there seems to be a lot of garbage trapped in the currents, mainly wood and tyres, often from cottage docks and boathouses, but remember that everything which leaves Lake Erie has to pass into the whirlpool.

Officially, the excellent trails end here. Some people do clamber over the rocks along the water's edge – to be safe, a good dozen or more metres back from the water – upstream toward the falls. The area where the river flows (or rather shoots) into the whirlpool can be reached and is very dramatic. This is not easy walking: the rocks can be slippery and the river is dangerous.

A local resident has said that from here, a further arduous 30 minutes leads to another set of even more overwhelming (and more dangerous) rapids. Twenty minutes beyond is the boardwalk for the Great Gorge Adventure. At this stage you can turn around, carry on for another five hours to a point close to the falls, or hop the Great Gorge elevator up to street level. Tickets evidently are not checked at the bottom, only at the top, because there are so few misfits who would take the time and effort to get down there on their own!

Walkers should take a snack and something to drink, for despite all the water, the Niagara is one river from which you do not want to drink – this region is one of the industrial centres of America.

The Niagara Glen Nature Preserve is one km north of the Whirlpool Golf Course entrance on the Niagara Parkway (towards Niagara-on-the-Lake). The People Mover stops at the site, or in spring and fall at the Spanish Aero Car attraction, from where the glen is walkable (about three km).

**Dufferin Islands** This series of small, interconnected, artificial islands was created during the development of the hydro system. The area is green parkland, with walking paths and a short nature trail around the islands and through the woods. There are picnic tables, and a small area for swimming which is best for children (though anyone can be a kid if it's hot enough). The islands are located less than two km south of the falls, on the west side of the road, and entry is free.

Another 250 metres south is **King's Bridge Park** with more picnic facilities and another small beach.

### Organised Tours

Double Deck (☎ 374-7423) offers bus tours on British red double-decker buses. For $17, one of the tours includes admission to three of the city's major attractions and stops at other free sites. You can stay on or get off at will, even taking two days to complete the tour. A second, 50-km trip takes in many more of the things to see and travels further, taking about six hours. A third goes to Niagara-on-the-Lake and a winery.

A tour which sort of blends number one and number two above into an economical package is run by Honeymoon City Tours (☎ 357-4330), 4943 Clifton Hill.

More extravagant are the helicopter tours over the falls offered by Niagara Helicopters (☎ 357-5672), at 3731 Victoria Ave. However, helicopter trips seem to be in abeyance since a recent fatal crash called the entire concept into question.

### Festivals

The Blossom Festival is held in early or mid-May, when spring flowers bloom in the many parks. Featured are parades and ethnic dances.

The annual Niagara Grape & Wine Festival is held in late September. There are many events, including parades and tours of five major wineries. In addition, activities are planned throughout the region.

For winter visitors, the annual Festival of Lights is a season of day and night events stretching from the end of November to the middle of February. The highlight is a series of night lighting displays set up along a 36-km route.

## Places to Stay

Accommodation is plentiful and, overall, prices aren't too bad, what with all the competition from both sides of the border. Outside the peak summer season, costs drop, and through the winter there are some good bargains. At this time many of the hotels and motels offer two or three-day packages, often including some meals, discounts on attractions and maybe even a bottle of wine thrown in. Checking the travel section of weekend newspapers in town or in Toronto will turn up some deals. Since a room is a room, many places offer enticements such as waterbeds, saunas, heart-shaped jacuzzis, FM stereos, movies, etc for a 'dirty weekend' escape.

**Camping** There are campgrounds all around town. Three are on Lundy's Lane, leading out of Niagara Falls, and two are on Montrose Ave south-west of downtown. They are decidedly not primitive. *Niagara Glen View Campground* (☎ 374-7052), with tent and electrical sites, is at Victoria Ave and River Rd, north of town toward Queenston. There are others along the Niagara Parkway further north.

**Hostels** Best bet in town is the HI *Niagara Falls International Hostel* (☎ 357-0770), 4699 Zimmerman Ave, off River Rd near Queen St in the old town, near the train station. The hostel is in a Tudor-style house near the Niagara River and has good facilities. Members pay $12, nonmembers $16. There is room for 58 guests and the hostel is open all year and all day. They offer bicycle rentals, and discounts for some of the museums and the *Maid of the Mist*.

The *YWCA* (☎ 357-9922), at 6135 Culp St, has rooms ($20) for women only, but they are meant first for victims of abuse or other social misfortunes. The *YMCA* has no residence.

**Tourist Homes** The tourist homes represent the best value in commercial accommodation. They are often cheaper (but not always) than either motels or hotels and are usually more interesting. Many are central.

There are basically two kinds of tourist homes: the cheaper kind is a family home with a spare room or two to rent. Unfortunately this type of place seems to open and close frequently, so keeping track of them is difficult. Others, although small, are actually commercial establishments. Though costlier, these tend to be more permanent and reliable.

The season for many tourist homes, particularly the ones in people's houses, is from May to October, when they're all open. The tourist office might (but doesn't always) have a complete list. The Visitors & Convention Bureau is the best one of the tourist offices to try for accommodation assistance. A look around some of the streets mentioned here will turn up something, as many of the guesthouses put a sign out the front. Prices range from about $35 to $75, with the average being $45 for singles and $60 for doubles.

At 4407 John St (☎ 374-1845), opposite the Rainbow Bridge, the appropriately named *Rainbow View* has four rooms (from $40 to $75, with continental breakfast included). If you're a student or have a hostel card, it's worth asking about a lower rate – they have been known to knock a good bit off the price. And, of course, the rooms with shared bathroom are less costly. They also have reductions for stays of four days or longer. John St is a quiet residential street not far from the falls.

River Rd links the falls area with old Niagara Falls downtown, three km downriver. There are quite a few tourist homes along here, with good views of the river and a convenient location. The *White Knight Inn* (☎ 374-8767), at 4939 River Rd, is more like a small hotel, complete with baths, air-conditioning, full breakfasts and parking. There are doubles from $50 to $65, but also rooms for four people which, at $70 to $85, are not a bad deal. The *Butterfly*

*Manor* (☎ 358-8988), at 4917 River Rd, is $55 a double (kids under 12 free) but the price goes up $10 on weekends. If they're full, they'll probably help you find someone else with a room. Breakfast is included in the price.

Also with four rooms, and charging the same price, is the nearby *Glen Mhor Guesthouse* (☎ 354-2600), at 5381 River Rd. You can walk to the falls or bicycles are offered. Another is the *Eastwood Tourist Lodge* (☎ 354-8686), at 5359 River Rd, in a fine old home with balconies overlooking the river. Each room is large with ensuite bath, so prices are a bit higher. English, German and Spanish are spoken.

A look along either Robert St or Victoria Ave may turn up something. The other main area for guesthouses is along Lundy's Lane.

**B&Bs** From 4917 River Rd, itself a guesthouse, a B&B programme (☎ 358-8988) operates. The organisation has homes all around town; some include little extras like a swimming pool or air-conditioning. Note that not all of them necessarily include a breakfast. Prices range from $50 to $70 a double. The White Knight, mentioned above, does much the same thing.

**Hotels** There are few hotels in town; most accommodation is in motels or various styles of motor inn. True hotels tend to be new and expensive. A couple of basic, budget alternative hotels can be found away from the falls, near the train and bus stations. The better of the two is the *Europa* (☎ 374-3231), on the corner of Bridge St and Erie Ave, where a room can cost less than $30. Nearby, across from the train station, is the slightly tattered *Empire* (☎ 357-2550), on Erie Ave. These are not recommended for single women.

**Motels** There're millions of 'em. The cheapest ones seem to be along Lundy's Lane, which leads west out from the falls and later becomes Hwy 20. There are many other motels on Murray and Ferry Sts. The wide price ranges are partially because many places have honeymoon rooms with double

bathtubs, waterbeds and other price-bumping features. Rates vary dramatically by season but are most costly in July and August. Later, it's a buyer's market. You may be able to strike a deal if you're staying two, three or more nights.

Very near the lights of Clifton Hill and restaurants and under 30 minutes' walk to the falls is the central *AAA Royal Motel* (☎ 354-2632), at 5284 Ferry St. The rooms are plain but fine and there is a small pool. Meal vouchers are offered to guests for discounts at several nearby eateries. Rates range from $30 to $60, with a double just $35 in June, before the big crowds arrive. The *Thunderbird Motel* (☎ 356-0541), at 6019 Lundy's Lane, has rooms from $35 all the way up to $90. At 6267 Lundy's Lane is the *Bonanza* (☎ 356-5135), with 50 rooms. Prices range from as low as $30 up to $68, depending on the room and season. There is a heated pool.

The upgraded *Caravan Motel* (☎ 357-1104), at 8511 Lundy's Lane, has 37 rooms and is about the same price. Winter rates are about half the summer prices. Fridges are available.

At 7742 Lundy's Lane is the small *Alpine Motel* (☎ 356-7016). Their rates are $40 to $58 and they also have a pool. The *Melody Motel* (☎ 227-1023), at 13065 Lundy's Lane, charges $45 to $70 and has a pool. This street has literally dozens of other motels.

The modestly priced *USA Motel* (☎ 374-2621) is at 6541 Main St, near George's Parkway.

The always reliable *Travelodge* (☎ 357-1626) is at 5591 Victoria Ave, with rooms beginning at $50.

### Places to Eat

Finding food in Niagara Falls is no problem, and while the dining isn't great, it isn't bad either; most places provide pretty good value.

Down by the falls, around Clifton Hill and along Victoria or Stanley Aves, there are scores of restaurants. Japanese, German, Hungarian and, especially, ever-popular Italian eateries can all be found. Some offer breakfast and/or lunch specials – just look around. Taking a leaflet from one of the hustlers on the street can lead to a good bargain.

*Mama Mia's*, at 5719 Victoria Ave, has been serving up standard Italian fare at moderate prices for many years. Inexpensive meals can also be found at the *Victoria Park Cafeteria*, opposite the American falls, in the building complex in the park of the same name, run by the Parks Commission. On the 2nd floor is a more expensive restaurant and an outdoor beer patio. Good for breakfast is the *Niagara House of Pancakes*, at 7241 Lundy's Lane, but it is a long way out of the centre. At night, it offers a Chinese buffet.

Very good value ($7 to $10) is *Ponderosa*, a budget steak house where all meals are accompanied by a huge help-yourself salad bar. Chicken and pasta are also available. It's a couple of blocks from the falls, at 6519 Stanley Ave, by the corner of Main St south of Lundy's Lane.

In the northern, older section of town there's *Tony's Place*, a large, popular spot at 5467 Victoria Ave which specialises in ribs and chicken. Until 6.30 pm they offer an early-bird special ($9.75). Regular à la carte dishes range from $7 to $16 and there is a lower-priced children's menu.

Lundy's Lane also has many restaurants, and there are restaurants in both the Skylon and Minolta Towers (see under Views).

## Getting There & Away

**Bus** The bus station (☎ 357-2133) is in the older part of town and away from the falls area, across the street from the train station, on the corner of Bridge St and Erie Ave.

This is the depot for buses to other cities, but a shuttle to the falls and even bus tours also depart from here.

For Toronto, service is frequent, with a bus leaving about once an hour from early morning (around 7.30 am) to about 10.30 pm. The one-way fare is $22 and the trip takes about two hours. On weekends there are fewer runs. Buses also depart from here for the airport in Buffalo (New York state) and for Detroit (Michigan state).

The shuttle over to the falls is $3.50.

**Train** The station (☎ 357-2133) is in the older, nontourist part of town, on Bridge St close to this area's downtown section.

There are three runs a day to Toronto – two in the morning and one around dinner time ($21, about two hours). There is a special reduced fare if you go and return between Toronto and Niagara on the same day. There is one train daily west to London (Ontario) and one daily to New York City.

## Getting Around

Walking is best; most things to see are concentrated in a small area.

**Bus** For getting further afield, there is the economical and efficient Niagara Parks People Mover bus system, which operates from 1 May to mid-October. It runs in a straight line from upstream beyond the falls, past the Greenhouse and Horseshoe Falls, along River Rd past both the Rainbow and Whirlpool bridges, north to the Niagara Spanish Aero Car attraction and, depending on the time of the year, beyond to Queenston Heights Park. From there, it turns around and follows the same path nine km back. From the falls, it gets you close to either the bus or train station. One ticket is good for the whole day and you can get on and off as much as you like at any of the 12 stops. For a low extra charge, transfers can be made to the regular city bus system. Such a connection will get you right to the door of the train or bus station. The People Mover ticket is good value at $3 and can be purchased at any one of the stops. Throughout the summer, the bus runs daily from 9 am to 11 pm, but after 8 pm does not go further out than the Rainbow Bridge. In spring and fall the schedule is somewhat reduced, and in winter the system does not run at all.

Niagara Transit (☎ 356-1179) runs two similar shuttle services around town. One route, the Red Line Shuttle, goes around the downtown area by the bus and train stations and connects with the People Mover. The other, the Blue Line Shuttle, runs from the Rapids View depot (at the southern end of the People Mover route, by the falls) along

Portage Ave and up Lundy's Lane. This is a 30-minute trip and the bus runs half-hourly from 8.30 am to midnight. Free transfers can be made from these shuttles to any city bus. All-day shuttle passes are available and can be bought from the driver. Both these routes cover many of the more popular sites and may be worth considering.

**Car** Driving in and around the centre is nothing but a headache. Follow the signs to one of the several parking districts and stash the car for the day.

## AROUND NIAGARA FALLS

See Around Niagara-on-the-Lake for details about the area between Niagara Falls and Niagara-on-the-Lake.

South from Niagara Falls, the Niagara Parkway, which begins at Niagara-on-the-Lake continues to Fort Erie, edged by parkland. The land along this strip is much flatter, the river clearly in view as the falls have not yet cut a gorge out of the river bed. But they are coming this way. Come back again in a few thousand years. There is not as much of interest here, as the road runs through residential districts, but there are certainly plenty of places to stop for a picnic or to rest under the shade of a tree by the water.

### Fort Erie

The town of Fort Erie, situated where the Niagara River meets Lake Erie, across from Buffalo, New York state, is connected to the USA by the Peace Bridge. This is a major border-crossing point and buses from Toronto connecting with many eastern US cities use it. On summer weekends, expect queues. Some air travellers find it worthwhile to go by bus to Buffalo from Toronto and its vicinity to take advantage of sometimes cheaper US airfares. For example, a flight from Buffalo to Seattle may be less costly than one from Toronto to Vancouver, with only short bus trips at each end. At times (when the discrepancy in fares warrants the traffic), there are buses from Toronto direct to the Buffalo airport, and some connecting

with specific flights. This situation varies with airlines opening and folding and fares increasing and decreasing, but is worth remembering.

The town is best visited for the reconstruction of **Fort Erie**, first built in 1764 and which the Americans seized in 1814 before retreating home. At the fort, a museum, military drills and uniformed soldiers can be seen. Admission is $2.

On Central Ave is the **Historical Railroad Museum**, with articles and a locomotive relating to the steam era of train travel.

Fort Erie is also well known for its old, attractive horse-racing track. Races are held from May to October. The track is off the Queen Elizabeth Way at Bertie St.

Slightly south of town is **Crystal Beach**, a small beach-cottage resort with a sandy beach. At one time there was a huge amusement park here and the town had a busy, casual, summer atmosphere, with people coming from far and wide, including many Americans from across the bridge. Well, the park is no more, and the town is just about gone, too. Many of the old commercial buildings are boarded up and the area now has a tacky, has-been feel about it. Even the beach is nothing special and there's a fee to get on it.

What hasn't changed is that this is one of the warmest areas of the country, and the one with the longest summer.

## BRANTFORD

West of Hamilton and surrounded for the most part by farmland, Brantford is known for several things. It has long been associated with Native Indians – Chief Joseph Brant, based here, led the Six Nation Indians, who lived in an area stretching from the district to parts of upper New York State. The **Brant County Museum**, at 57 Charlotte St, has information and artefacts on Brant and his people. **Her Majesty's Chapel of the Mohawks**, three km from the centre of town on Mohawk St, is the oldest Protestant church in Ontario and the world's only Royal Indian Chapel. It's open every day from 1

July to Labour Day, and from Wednesday to Sunday the rest of the year.

The **Woodland Cultural Centre Museum**, at 84 Mohawk St, has displays on the various aboriginal peoples of eastern Canada and offers some history of the Six Nations Confederacy. The confederacy, made up of the Mohawk, Seneca, Cayuga, Oneida, Onendaga and Tuscarora tribes, was a unifying cultural and political association which helped settle disputes between bands.

Brantford was the home of Alexander Graham Bell, inventor of the telephone. The **Bell Homestead**, at 94 Tutela Heights, displays some of his other inventions and is furnished the way it was when he lived in it. It's closed on Mondays.

The town is also known for local son Wayne Gretzky, the greatest ice-hockey player the world has yet produced.

There are some additional attractions, such as **Myrtleville House**, dating from 1837, and the interesting eight-sided (what else?) **Octagon House**, now a restaurant.

## SIX NATIONS INDIAN RESERVE

To the east of Brantford, in Ohsweken, this Iroquois reserve is one of the best known in the country. Established in the late 1700s, it provides interested visitors with a glimpse of Native Indian culture. Through the week (and on weekends by appointment), tours are given of the reserve and its Band Council House, the seat of decision-making. Various events are held through the year, including the major Grand River Powwow, a summer theatre programme, and a handicrafts sale in November.

## ONTARIO AGRICULTURAL MUSEUM

With 30 buildings on 32 hectares of land, the museum brings to life the farming history of the area through demonstrations, displays, and costumed workers in historical settings. It's near Milton, 52 km south-west of Toronto, about a 45-minute drive. Leave Hwy 401 at exit 320 and follow the signs. The museum is on Townline (also called Tremaine Rd), and is open daily from the middle of May to October.

## GUELPH

West on Hwy 401 from Toronto, Guelph is an old, attractive, middle-sized university town that makes a nice place to live but doesn't have much of interest to a visitor. There are some fine houses along tree-lined streets, and the Speed River and downtown area is pleasantly overseen by the dominant **Church of Our Lady**.

The **Macdonald Stewart Art Centre**, at 358 Gordon St, often has good shows in its galleries, which specialise in Inuit and other Canadian art. It's open every afternoon except Monday, and is free.

**McRae House** is the birthplace of John McRae, the author of the antiwar poem *In Flanders Fields*, written during WW I, which every Canadian reads as a kid in school. The museum, at 108 Water St, is open every afternoon.

Through the summer, cheap accommodation can be found at the *University of Guelph* (☎ 824-4128). The campus is on Old Brock Rd (Hwy 6) at College Rd.

Near the main intersection of town (Wyndham and Quebec Sts), at 41 Quebec St, is the *Bookshelf Café*. The front area contains a good bookshop, while the back portion is an excellent restaurant, although not in the low-budget category. There is also an outdoor patio, a bar and, upstairs, a repertory cinema. Less expensive for a good meal is *Latino's*, at 51 Cork St East, which features Latin American food. Most menu items are in the $6 range.

## KORTRIGHT WATERFOWL PARK

This is a wildlife area and waterfowl research centre with 3000 birds representing close to 100 species. There is an observation tower, an interpretive centre and some nature trails. The park is open daily from March to October and admission is $4. The park is on the Speed River near Guelph, on Kortright Rd, two km west of the Hanlon Expressway.

## ROCKWOOD & THE CONSERVATION AREA

About 10 km east of Rockwood along Hwy

7, Rockwood Conservation Area makes a good destination for an afternoon outdoors. It's definitely one of the best conservation areas within the Toronto area. Admission is $5. The park offers swimming, canoeing and picnicking, but of most interest are the wooded landscape and natural features, which include cliffs, caves and glacial potholes, all of which can be explored on foot. Trails wind all through the park and canoes can be rented. There is also overnight camping available.

In the village of Rockwood, an hour or so can easily be spent strolling along the main street, with its antique and junk shops, craft boutiques and eateries of various types.

*Saunders Bakery* has been turning out baked goods for 75 years. Good, inexpensive food can be had at the *Out-to-Lunch* restaurant, open every day but Monday. The afternoon tea with fresh scones is good value. You'll find a B&B or two in town as well.

Nearby **Acton**, a larger town, is known for its leather-goods warehouse and its *Tannery* restaurant.

## KITCHENER-WATERLOO

These twin cities – amalgamated to form one – are about an hour west of Toronto, in the heart of rural southern Ontario. About 55% of the 210,000 inhabitants are of German origin. The city also acts as a centre for the

---

### The Mennonites

The Mennonites are one of Canada's best-known yet least understood religious minorities – everybody knows of them but few know about them. Most people will tell you that Mennonites wear black, ride in horse-drawn carriages and, eschewing modern life, work farms in a traditional manner. And while basically true, these characteristics are, of course, only part of the story.

The Mennonites originated in Switzerland in the early 1500s as a Protestant sect among the Anabaptists. Forced from country to country due to their religious disagreements with the state, they arrived in Holland and took their name from one of their early Dutch leaders, Menno Simons. To escape persecution in Europe and to develop communities in rural settings, they took up William Penn's promise of religious freedom and began arriving in North America around 1640, settling in south-eastern Pennsylvania, where they are still a significant group. Most of North America's 250,000 Mennonites still live in that state. In the early 1800s, lured by the undeveloped and cheaper land of southern Ontario, some moved northwards.

There are about a dozen Mennonite groups or branches in Ontario, each with slightly different approaches, practices and principles. The Mennonite Church is the middle ground, with the numerous other branches either more or less liberal. The majority of Mennonites are moderates. Most visible are the stricter or 'plain' groups, known for their simple clothes. The women wear bonnets and a long, plain dress; the men tend to wear black and grow beards. Automobiles, much machinery and other trappings of modern life are shunned. The Old Order Mennonites are the strictest in their adherence to the traditions.

The Amish, who took their name from Jacob Ammon, a native of Switzerland, are another Mennonite branch. They split from the main body, believing Mennonites to be too worldly. Traditional Amish are the plainest of the plain; they won't even wear buttons on their clothes, considering them a vanity. They don't worship in a church, but hold rotating services in houses in the community. Homes are very spartan, with no carpets, curtains or wall pictures.

Despite their day-to-day differences, all the groups agree on a number of fundamentals, which include the freedom of conscience, separation of church and state, adult baptism, refusal to take oaths, practical piety and education stressing the moral and practical. Science is rejected by many. The simple life is esteemed. Mennonite and Amish communities are largely self-sufficient and they do no proselytising. Less than 10% of their followers are not born into Mennonite families.

Mennonite sites can be visited in Kitchener-Waterloo, St Jacob's and Elmira. It is not uncommon to see their carriages rolling along local roads or, on Sundays, parked by their country churches.

Many local stores and farmers' markets feature Mennonite goods. Perhaps the best-known, most sought after of crafts are the beautiful, but pricey, bed quilts. The simple, well-made furniture is also highly regarded. More recently, their organic produce and meat has become of interest, and the very good baked goods and jams are inexpensive and readily available. ∎

528 Ontario – South-Western Ontario

surrounding Amish and Mennonite religious farming communities. It is these two factors that attract visitors and make the towns stand out from their neighbours. There is not a lot to see, and at a glance things here are much the same as in any other large town. However, it's worth a short visit, particularly if your timing is right and you arrive for Oktoberfest. The towns share two universities and therefore have a fair number of young people.

## Orientation

Kitchener is the southern portion of the twin cities and is nearly three times the size of Waterloo, but you can't really tell where one ends and the other begins. The downtown area refers to central Kitchener. King St is the main street and runs roughly north-south; at the northern end it runs to the two universities and beyond.

The farmers' market on the corner of King and Frederick Sts marks the centre of downtown. This area of town has the train and bus stations, hotels and restaurants. King St runs south to Hwy 8, which continues to Hwy 401, west for Windsor and east for Toronto.

Hwy 8 West, at the junction of King St, heads to Stratford.

## Information

Maps and information are available at the Kitchener-Waterloo Visitors & Convention Bureau (☎ 748-0800), south of the centre, at 2848 King St East. From June to the end of August, it's open from 9 am to 5 pm Monday to Wednesday, from 9 am to 7 pm on Thursday and Friday and from 10 am to 4 pm on weekends. The rest of the year, hours are 9 am to 5 pm Monday to Friday.

## Farmers' Market

One market is in a new building right downtown, on the corner of King St East and Frederick St. The market began in 1839 and features the products of the Amish and Mennonites – breads, jams, many cheeses and sausages, and handicrafts such as quilts, rugs, clothes and handmade toys.

Whether they like it or not, it is the farmers

themselves who are often the main attraction. Some of these religious people, whose ancestors were originally from Germany via Pennsylvania, live much as their grandparents did in the 19th century. They use horse-drawn buggies for transportation, and don't drink alcohol, vote or use the courts. Some do not use any modern machinery. The strict Old Order members are easily recognisable, with the bearded men in black suits and hats, and the women in bonnets and ankle-length skirts. There are also many merchants, including bakers, craftspeople and farmers, who aren't Mennonite. The market is held on Saturday from 5 am to 2 pm, and during summer on Wednesday too, from 7 am.

On Sunday, you may see the wagons rolling down the country roads and lining up outside the old wooden churches of the district.

Across the street, on the corner of King and Benton Sts, a 23-bell glockenspiel rings at noon and at 5 pm.

## Woodside National Historic Park

This park contains the 100-year-old mansion where former prime minister William Lyon Mackenzie King (Canada's 10th prime minister) once lived. It has been restored and refinished in upper-class 1890s style. The basement houses displays on the life of Mackenzie King. On weekends you can witness demonstrations of period crafts, music and cooking by guides in costume. The park is at 528 Wellington St North in Kitchener. It is open daily and admission is free.

## Universities of Waterloo & Wilfrid Laurier

In Waterloo, west off King St North on University Ave, these two universities sit right beside each other, and both have attractive, green campuses. The former is well regarded for its engineering; the latter specialises in economics. Waterloo has an art gallery, and the **Museum & Archive of Games**, which depicts the history of games around the world. The museum is open on weekdays. Waterloo offers inexpensive summer lodging.

## Doon Heritage Crossroads

The Doon Heritage Crossroads (☎ 748-1914), just south of Kitchener, is a re-creation of a pioneer settlement circa 1914. The 23 buildings include a general store, workshops and a sawmill. There is also a model of an original Russian Mennonite village and a replica of an 1856 railway. To get to the site, go down King St, turn right on Fairway, left at Manitou St and left again at Homer Watson Blvd. It's open from spring to fall. Admission is $4, less for students, seniors and families. It's open daily but is closed from 1 January to 1 May. Special events are often held on weekends.

## Joseph Schneider Haus

At 466 Queen St South, not far from the market, this Heritage Canada site (☎ 742-7752) is the restored house of a prosperous German Mennonite. It's a museum depicting life in the mid-1850s, with demonstrations of day-to-day chores and skills. Through the summer, it is open every day; the rest of the year it is closed on Mondays. Note that it is shut completely for the last week in December and for the first six weeks of the new year. There is a nominal admission fee.

## Seagram Museum

Set in a section of the original Seagram distillery in Waterloo, this neatly laid-out museum (☎ 885-1857) shows the history and technology of booze production. On display are 2000 artefacts from around the world and many different time periods, including some beautiful tools and equipment. Explanatory films are shown. Also on the premises are an elegant restaurant, a gift shop and a speciality liquor store. The address is 57 Erb St. The museum is open daily from May to December but is closed on Mondays during the rest of the year.

## The Centre in the Square

On the corner of Queen and Ellen Sts is this performing-arts complex, with an art gallery and a theatre.

## Homer Watson House & Gallery

One of Canada's first notable landscape painters is the subject of this small, specialised museum. Watson (1855-1936) once lived here, and there are various pieces relating to his life and work. The museum, at 1754 Old Mill Rd, is open every afternoon from April to December (closed on Mondays).

## Festivals

Some of the major events held here are:

May
*Mennonite Relief Sale* – It's is a large sale of homemade foods and crafts and also includes a quilt auction. It's held on the last Saturday in May in New Hamburg, 19 km west of Kitchener-Waterloo.

June
*Summer Music Festival* – This festival is four days of free or low-cost outdoor music concerts held at the end of June at venues around the downtown area.

August
*Busker Carnival* – An annual festival of street entertainers which takes place in late August. Some of these performers are very good and the whole thing is free.

October
*Oktoberfest* – The event of the year, Octoberfest, the biggest of its kind in North America, attracting 500,000 people annually. The nine-day festival starts in early to mid-October and includes 20 beer halls, German music and foods, and dancing. A huge parade wraps up the festivities on the last day.

For more information, ring K-W Oktoberfest Inc (☎ 576-0571). Upon arrival, visit one of the reception areas for a map, tickets, information and all the details on how to tie on your stein so you don't lose it. Reservations for accommodation during the festival should be made well in advance. For getting around, there is a free bus in addition to the usual city buses.

## Places to Stay

**Hostels** Backpackers' has a hostel here, the *Waterloo International Home Hostel* (☎ 752-5202), at 102B Albert St. The *YWCA* (☎ 744-0120) (for women only) is at Frederick and Weber Sts in Kitchener. It charges $28 per night, including breakfast, and offers weekly rates. The *YMCA* no longer has a residence. The *House of Friendship*, down the street from the YWCA, may have some rooms available (for men only), on or off the premises, but is not really geared to travellers.

The *University of Waterloo* (☎ 885-1211) has summer accommodation. Singles/doubles are $28/45. Meals are available on the campus at several outlets. Included is free use of the facilities (including a pool) and free parking.

At *Wilfrid Laurier University* (☎ 884-1970), contact the housing officer at 75 University Ave West. Singles/doubles are $25/35. Rooms are available from 1 May to 15 August but are generally used by those attending conferences. The dining room is open in the summer, too.

**B&Bs** Out of Millbank, a village to the west of Kitchener, a local B&B association (☎ (519) 595-4604) has the latest on guesthouses in Kitchener. The rates aren't bad, starting at $35/45 for singles/doubles. During Oktoberfest, many more local residents offer rooms.

**Hotels** For the dollar-conscious, a central hotel is not in the cards.

For those holding a different hand, the *Walper Terrace Hotel* (☎ 745-4321) is central, at 1 King St West. It's an old place that has been restored and won a heritage award. They have over 100 rooms, starting at $80, which is actually rather good value compared to the other top-end places in town. In between is the *Barons Motor Inn* (☎ 744-2215), at 901 Victoria St, with beds in the $45 to $60 range.

During Oktoberfest, many people rent out rooms. For information, call K-W Oktoberfest Inc (☎ 576-0571).

**Motels** Motels are numerous, good and clean. Most of them are on Victoria St, which runs east-west off King St, just north of downtown Kitchener. Two of the cheapest are the *Mayflower* (☎ 745-9493), at 1189 Victoria St, which costs $34/46 for singles/doubles, and the *Shamrock* (☎ 743-4361), situated at 1235 Victoria St, with singles/doubles at $35/45.

**Places to Eat**
There are many restaurants on or near King St in Kitchener. At 607 King West, casual *Koalaby's* has an Australian theme and is open every day for lunch and dinner. The Canadian basics, including breakfasts, are available at *Macarthur's*, at 103 King St West. For solid German fare try the *Concordia Club*, at 429 Ottawa St South, for lunch or dinner. Live entertainment is included on Friday and Saturday nights and the restaurant is closed on Sundays. Also serving German meals is the more up-market *Rathskeller*, at 151 Frederick St.

After the nose gets a whiff of the *Café Mozart*, at 53 Queen St, the mouth will soon be munching on pastries, cakes or something covered with chocolate. It's open until 10 pm (except Friday and Saturday nights, when it serves late-night snacks until midnight).

At 130 King St in Waterloo, the *Ali Baba* is a steak house which has been in business for nearly three decades.

**Entertainment**
**Nightclubs** Kitchener-Waterloo has two nightspots of particular note. *Pop the Gator* is a top-quality live blues bar at 44 Queen St South. It's open Thursday to Saturday. Known far and wide, *Lulu's* is an immense, popular disco-dancing bar located on Hwy 8 in Kitchener, with what is said to be the world's longest bar. On a weekend evening, buses arrive from as far away as Toronto.

**Entertainment Parks** Sportsworld (☎ 653-4442) is an entertainment park containing, among other diversions, a water slide, wave pool, go-kart track and snack bars and restaurants. Bingeman Park, (☎ 744-1555) at 1380 Victoria St North, on the Grand River, is bigger than Sportsworld and offers much the same thing; it has 600 campsites.

**Getting There & Away**
**Bus** The station (☎ 741-2600) is at 15 Charles St West in Kitchener, a five-minute walk from the centre. Gray Coach connects Toronto and Guelph with frequent service.

**Train** Kitchener is still served by VIA Rail (☎ 745-9911). From Toronto, there are two trains a day. The station is on the corner of Victoria and Weber Sts, an easy walk north of downtown Kitchener.

## AROUND KITCHENER-WATERLOO
### St Jacob's
Just north of town is St Jacob's, a small historic village with the **Meeting Place**, a little museum and interpretive centre on the Mennonites and their history, and numerous arts & crafts shops housed in original buildings dating from the 1800s. The museum, at 33 King St, is open daily through the summer (afternoons only on Sunday). Through the winter, it is closed on weekdays. Admission is by donation. The MCC Craft Shop sells Mennonite goods.

Also in town have a look at the **Maple Syrup Museum**, with exhibits on the production of this Canadian speciality. The museum is at 8 Spring Rd and is open daily all year, except for Mondays in January and February.

The **Waterloo Market** is another, more authentic version of the farmers' markets, with horse and buggy sheds still in place. It's near St Jacob's. It's open the same days as the market in Kitchener-Waterloo (Saturday and Wednesday), but doesn't begin as early in the morning.

If you want to stay, the town has an inn, *Benjamin's*, and a guesthouse, *Jakobstetta*, as well as a couple of restaurants. The St Jacob's B&B Association (☎ 664-2622) can fix you up with a less costly bed in the area. Singles/doubles average $40/55. Whether you spend the night or not, drop in to the bakery. The main street also has numerous craft shops to browse through.

### A Local Drive
Take Hwy 401 past Kitchener (going west) to the Doon exit and go to New Dundee. From there, travel north-west to Petersburg, where you'll find the Blue Moon Pub. Then on to St Agatha, with the church steeple, followed by St Clements and Lindwood – both are Mennonite towns with some inter-

esting stores. Drive back east to Hawkersville, where there is a blacksmith's shop, and take a gravel road with fine scenery to St Jacob's. Continue north up to Elmira and over to West Montrose, where there is a covered bridge – one of the few left in Ontario.

### The Pub Crawl
Just west of Kitchener-Waterloo, four fine historic, country taverns can be found in four neighbouring villages. Each one is at least 120 years old and offers atmosphere, good food and something to wash it down with. Begin in Petersburg, at the *Blue Moon* (☎ 634-8405), a Georgian-style inn dating from 1848. It's off Hwy 7 and 8 at Regional Rd 6 and 12.

Next stop to the west is *EJ's*, in Baden, again with some intriguing original decor, including hand-painted ceiling tiles. In fine weather there is a patio as well. Beer from around the world is offered on tap.

*Kennedy's Country Tavern* is back east and north (not far from stop one – remember to designate a nondrinking driver, it's getting confusing). Kennedy's, in the village of St Agatha, has a bit of an Irish slant, although much of the food shows a German influence.

Last stop is the *Heidelberg Restaurant & Brew Pub* in Heidelberg, north from St Agatha, at the junction of Hwys 15 and 16. Here, in the middle of Mennonite country, a German country-style meal can be enjoyed with Bavarian beer brewed on the premises. The Heidelberg was built in 1838.

Stops one and two are closed on Sundays. Call any one of them and ask about the bus tours which sometimes do the circuit.

### The Grand River
Beginning north on Georgian Bay, the Grand River winds its way south just to the east of Kitchener-Waterloo, eventually emptying into Lake Erie. The Grand River watershed is the largest inland river system in the southern portion of the province. Numerous parks and conservation areas are located along the river – the tourist office should have a guide to them. Canoeing is possible in some sec-

tions; at others there are swimming facilities and walking trails.

## CAMBRIDGE

South of Kitchener, Cambridge is an old mill town now grown large, set alongside the Speed and Grand rivers. There isn't much to see, but the redeveloped waterfront area known as Riverbank, with its many factories, is pleasant and attracts shoppers. Many of the businesses once drawn by the power from the mill now have factory outlets.

Cambridge has a Scottish background, and this is celebrated with the annual summer Highland Games.

## ELMIRA

Not far north of Kitchener-Waterloo and slightly west is Elmira, another Mennonite centre. In spring, there is a Maple Syrup Festival, with street activities and pancake breakfasts. The Sap Bucket is a store specialising in local crafts, including fine quilts, but these are not cheap. Brox's Old Towne Village is a shopping centre designed to look like it belongs to an earlier era. Brubacher's Country Store, in the complex, is a 19th-century general store. You'll also find antiques and restaurants in the centre.

You can visit the Elmira Mennonite Church, at 58 Church St West, and see a film on the congregation. The MCC Thrift Shop sells Mennonite products.

There are quite a few B&Bs in the area, many on farms and with owners who speak Pennsylvania Dutch or German. For information on who has a room available, call the local B&B Association (☎ 669-2379) in Elmira up until 5 pm. Rates are $45/65 for singles/doubles. One farm B&B is *Washa Farms* (☎ 846-9788), seven km north of town, at $55 for two (with breakfast). It's on an 88-hectare working farm where the house dates from 1877.

## ELORA

Not far from Kitchener-Waterloo, north-west up Hwy 6 from Guelph, is this small, heavily touristed town. Named after Elora in India, with its famous cave temples, this was

once a mill town using the falls on the Grand River, which runs through town. The falls, the old mill, the pleasant setting and the nearby gorge and park make the town a popular day trip for both out-of-province visitors and Ontarians.

The main streets are Metcalfe, Mill and Geddes Sts, all right by the mill and river.

There is a tourist office in the Village Common, a small shopping mew on Metcalfe St up the hill from Mill St.

### Things to See & Do

Not far from town, at the **Elora Gorge Conservation Area**, the river flows through a deep limestone canyon. Much of the area is park, and trails lead to cliff views and caves at the water's edge. Riding the water in a tyre tube is a fun way to spend a warm afternoon. There are also picnic areas in the park.

About a dozen blocks east of town along Mill St East is the Elora Quarry – worth a look and, better, a swim.

The Grand River is good for canoeing, and overnight trips are possible. You can actually paddle along the river all the way to Lake Erie. More information is available at the park.

### Festivals

The Elora Festival (☎ 846-0331), an annual music festival, is held during the last weeks of July and into the first two weeks of August. The music is primarily classical (with an emphasis on choral works) or folk. Some of the concerts are held at the quarry, with performers playing in the middle of the water on a floating stage. On a warm summer night with the stage lit up, it really is an impressive experience.

Other events include the annual summer **Antique Show & Sale** and, in May, the **Open House Tour**, when many of the older local houses are open to the public.

### Places to Stay

There is a large campground at the *Elora Gorge Conservation Area* (☎ 846-9742) which, though usually full on holiday weekends, has a number of sites that can be reserved one week in advance.

At 60 Mill St, right in the centre of the action, is *Naomi's B&B* (☎ 846-0822), with rooms for $60 per couple.

There are at least 12 other B&Bs in and around town. For information, ring ☎ 846-9841 or call at 82 Metcalfe St. Average price is $45 for two with breakfast. The *Gingerbread House* (at the same address, call ☎ 846-0521) has rooms, but the deluxe features, special breakfasts, fine furnishings and decor put it into a considerably higher price bracket.

One to try that's central and costs a little less than the rest is *Clark House* (☎ 846-0218), at 89 Water St, with singles/doubles at $30/40, including a pull-out bed for extra people or kids. A full breakfast is included.

The *Elora Mill Inn* (☎ 846-5356) is the prestige place to stay in town; it offers a convenient location, views of the river, fireplaces and a dining room but you may have to look in both pockets to pay the bill.

### Places to Eat

The town has several good eating spots near the mill. Top choice for a casual meal would be the *Wellington Fare*, at 163 Geddes St; it's a restaurant, bakery and delicatessen. *Tiffany's* is a fish & chips place at 146 Metcalfe St. At the back of *Leyanders*, a store at 40 Mill St, is a quiet tearoom, good for afternoon cream tea with a view of the river.

Other places along Mill St, and the dining room of the *Mill Inn*, offer more expensive menus, although simple *Jenny's* is a place to grab an ice cream.

The *Metcalfe Inn*, at the corner of Mill and Metcalfe Sts, has an outdoor patio where beer is served.

### Things to Buy

Plenty of small stores in Elora offer crafts, jewellery, paintings and pottery, etc much of it produced by the numerous local artisans.

### FERGUS

Fergus is Elora's neighbour and a quiet, farm-area town. As the name suggests, the heritage here is Scottish, and this is best appreciated at the annual Highland Games, held during the second week of August. Included are Scottish dancing, pipe bands, foods, and sports events such as the caber toss. It is one of the largest Scottish festivals and Highland Games held in North America.

The main street is St Andrew St. Many of the attractive buildings are made of limestone, again suggesting the old country, and a town oddity are the painted fire hydrants. The **Templin Gardens** are in the centre of town, along the Grand River. A farmers' market is held on weekends.

Between Fergus and Elora Sts is the **Wellington County Museum**, with artefacts relating to the history of the county.

Canoes can be rented in town at Templin Gardens for a paddle down the gorge to Elora.

The annual Old Time Fiddle & Step Dance Contest is held on the second weekend in July.

Like Elora, Fergus is quite busy, and accommodation is not overly abundant. For B&Bs, call or drop around to the *4 Eleven* (☎ 843-5107), at 411 St Andre St East, within walking distance of the downtown area. You can get a room here or they'll fix you up with someone else. Prices are from $35/45 for singles/doubles (in general, a little lower than in Elora).

For food try the *Honeycomb Café*, at 135 St David St North, which has homemade soups, breads and desserts.

### STRATFORD

With a population of 25,000, this commercial centre surrounded by farmland is a fairly typical slow-paced, rural Ontario town except that it's consciously prettier than most and is home to the now world-famous Shakespearean Festival. Many of the numerous older buildings in the attractive, architecturally interesting central area have been restored, and the layout along the river adds to the charm. Stratford's Avon River, with its swans and green lawns, together with the theatres help the town deliberately and successfully resemble Stratford-upon-Avon in England.

London (Ontario) is about 60 km or 45 minutes' drive south-west, and Toronto is about two hours' drive east.

## Orientation
Ontario St is the main street and everything is close to it. At the foot of Huron St is the Perth County Courthouse, one of the town's most distinctive and dominant landmarks.

## Information
There is a friendly, helpful and well-informed tourist office (☎ 273-3352) on the corner of York and Erie Sts, in the heart of town. You can see pictures of guesthouses and peruse menus from many of the town's restaurants.

On fine days, heritage walks depart from the tourist office at 9.30 am Monday to Saturday from 1 July to Labour Day (early September). Or, with one of the descriptive maps available, you could do your own walking tour. Another walking tour map, put out by the Local Architectural Conservation Advisory Committee, details some of the history and architecture of the downtown area.

Between November and May, information can be obtained from the tourist office in City Hall, at 1 Wellington St.

## The Gallery
This is a good art gallery in a fine old building near Confederation Park, at 54 Romeo St North. Featured are changing international shows of modern painting, with the emphasis on Canadian works. Three shows are presented at any given time. The gallery is closed on Mondays.

## Queen's Park
Down by the river, near the Festival Theatre, this park is good for a picnic or a walk. Footpaths from the theatre follow the river past Orr Dam and a 90-year-old stone bridge to the formal English flower garden.

## Shakespearean Gardens
Just north of the courthouse by the stone bridge dating from 1885, these gardens on the site of an old wool mill run along the waterfront. Near the bridge is the mill's chimney and a bust of Shakespeare. Here and there, picnic tables can be found.

## Shakespeareland
This is a miniature model of Stratford in England, in a park setting on Romeo St North. It's open daily from June to September and admission is $4, with a good discount for students.

## Stratford-Perth Museum
Articles collected around the region from the turn of the century are on view at this small museum (☎ 271-5311), at 182 King St. Admission is by donation. It's open from May to September from 10 am to 4 pm.

## Organised Tours
Festival Tours runs trips around town several times daily through the summer, using red British double-decker buses. The tour lasts one hour. Ask at the tourist information office for details.

Another outfit, Coach House Tours, has a similar trip, but also runs a longer one around Mennonite country. Again, get details at the tourist office, from where the bus tour departs.

Also near the tourist office is the hitching post for horse-drawn cart tours of the central area.

**Boat Trips** A small tour boat runs around the lake and beyond the Festival Building from behind the tourist office. The 35-minute trip costs $5 and the boat glides by parkland, houses, gardens and swans. Also at the dock, canoes and paddle boats can be rented.

## Shakespearean Festival
Begun humbly in a tent in 1953, the theatre now attracts international attention. The productions are first rate, as are the costumes, and respected actors are featured. The season runs from June to October each year. Tickets

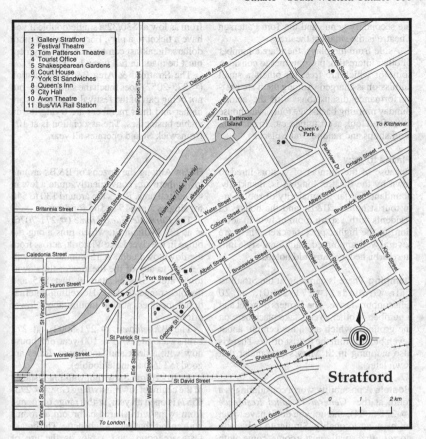

1 Gallery Stratford
2 Festival Theatre
3 Tom Patterson Theatre
4 Tourist Office
5 Shakespearean Gardens
6 Court House
7 York St Sandwiches
8 Queen's Inn
9 City Hall
10 Avon Theatre
11 Bus/VIA Rail Station

Stratford

for plays cost $18.75 to $49.50, depending on the day, seat and theatre, and go on sale from the first week of March. By show time, nearly every performance is sold out. A limited number of rush seats are available at good reductions, and for some performances, students and seniors are entitled to discounts. Less are tickets to the concerts, lectures (including a fine series with well-known writers) and other productions which are all part of the festival. Bargain-hunters note that the two-for-one Tuesday performances offer good value.

Write for the festival booklet, which gives all the details on the year's performances, dates, prices, etc. Also in the booklet is a request form for accommodation, so you can organise everything at once. Tickets are available from the box office at the Festival Theatre (☎ (519) 273-1600), or by mail (PO Box 520, Stratford, Ontario, N5A 6V2) or telephone.

There are three theatres – all in town – that feature contemporary and modern drama and music, operas and works by the Bard. Main productions take place at the Festival Theatre, with its round, protruding stage. The Avon Theatre, seating 1100 people, is

ONTARIO

the secondary venue and the Tom Patterson Theatre is the smallest theatre.

Aside from the plays, there are a number of other interesting programmes to consider, some of which are free; for others a small admission is charged. Among them are post-performance discussions with the actors, Sunday morning backstage tours, warehouse tours for a look at costumes, etc. In addition, workshops and readings take place.

## Places to Stay

Because of the number of visitors lured to town by the theatre, lodging is, thankfully, abundant. By far the majority of rooms are in tourist homes, B&Bs and the houses of residents with a spare room or two. In addition, in the higher price brackets, there are several well-appointed, traditional-style inns in refurbished, century-old hotels.

**Camping** There is camping at the Stratford Fair Grounds (☎ 271-5130), at 20 Glastonbury Drive. The farmers' market and a number of other events take place here on the grounds, which are quite central, about seven blocks from the tourist office. There is also camping in St Mary's (see under that town later).

**Hostels** A possibility worth considering is a room at the *General Hospital Residence* (☎ 271-5084), and no, you don't have to get hit by a car to qualify. Similar to university dorms, the small, neat rooms come with single or twin beds, a fridge and a sink. A single/twin is $29/35 and there are excellent weekly rates. There are laundry and cooking facilities, a cafeteria and an outdoor swimming pool – all in all, a pretty fair bargain. The address is 130 Yonge St.

See also the Burnside Guest Home, listed below.

**Tourist Homes** Apart from the above, by far the most economical method of finding a cheap bed is to book a place through the Stratford Festival Accommodation Department (☎ (519) 273-1600), at 55 Queen St. They will find a room in someone's home

from as low as $30/32 a single/double if you have a ticket to a play. For a couple of more dollars, breakfast can be included. Payment must be made in full when booking.

The Stratford & Area B&B Association (☎ 273-2052) does much the same thing, but not being part of the festival, their prices are higher and their members are trying to run viable businesses. The association is at 101 Brunswick St and operates all year.

**B&Bs** Among the dozens of B&Bs around town, there are, conveniently, quite a few in the central area. Rates are around $30 to $40 for singles and $45 to $65 for doubles.

The *Burnside Guest Home* (☎ 271-7076) is at 139 William St, which runs along the bulge in the river Lake Victoria, across from the downtown core. A 15-minute walk will get you to any of the theatres or the downtown area. Singles start at just $35 and doubles range to $60. Hostelling International members should inquire about lower prices.

The *Whitehaven* (☎ 271-5002), at 272 Brunswick St, is in a 100-year-old house now with a deck and small pool. Rates are good ($32/40 a single/double).

At 107 Huron St, within walking distance of the centre of town, *Anything Goes* (☎ 273-6557) is open all year, with a range of rooms, from twins with shared bathroom to rooms with ensuite bath and kitchenette. The breakfasts are good, and a plus is the use of bicycles during your stay. They are open all year.

Also central, at 220 Church St, the *Maples of Stratford* (☎ 273-0810) is in a large Victorian house. A double goes for $55 with a good continental breakfast included.

At 66 Bay St is *Acrylic Dreams* (☎ 271-7874), an updated cottage from 1879 which has some pleasant little touches for guests to set it apart.

Moving up in price, one to try is *Stratford Knights* (☎ 273-6089), at 66 Britannia St. It's away from the centre a bit, on the other side of the river, off Mornington St. This fine old house has a pool in the yard, which guests can use. Doubles start at $58, including a continental breakfast.

Close to the theatre is the *Heinbuck Tourist Haven*, at 411 Ontario St; it's open through the summer and may be slightly cheaper than many of the others.

**Hotels** The *Queen's Inn* (☎ 271-1400), at 161 Ontario St (near Waterloo St), is around 135 years old – the oldest hotel in town. Refurbished and reopened in 1988, it's a fine place to stay, though prices have risen sharply. A double will cost at least $85 in summer, but prices drop in the off season. The *Albert Place Hotel*, at 23 Albert St, is another updated old inn but with somewhat lower prices.

**Motels** Motels are generally expensive. Try the *Noretta* (☎ 271-6110), on Hwy 7 towards Kitchener. Rooms cost from $45 a double. The *Majers* (☎ 271-2010), a little further out, is slightly more expensive. There are other motels along here, including the *Rosecourt*, which is attractive but even more costly.

**Places to Eat**
At 11 York St, near the tourist office, is a small sandwich shop, which is literally a hole in the wall doing takeout orders only. They make good sandwiches, and picnic plates which might include a bit of smoked salmon or corn on the cob. The park by the river (right across the street) makes a good eating spot. The shop is closed on Mondays.

*Connie's*, at 159 Ontario St (near Waterloo St), covers the basics and has pizza and spaghetti. Away from the centre, over the bridge and down Huron St about two km, *Madelyn's Diner* is a fine, friendly little place for any meal. Breakfasts are served all day (from 7 am) and are good, as are the home-made pies. It's at 377 Huron St, and is closed on Sunday evening and all day Monday.

As befits an English-style town, there are quite a few pubs about. *Stratford's Olde English Parlour* has an outdoor patio; it's at 101 Patrick St (near Wellington St). The *Queen's Inn*, at 161 Ontario St, with several

different eating rooms, brews its own beer and the pub has an inexpensive and standard menu including a ploughman's lunch.

*Katsuri*, at 10 George St West, serves Indian food at mid-range prices.

Dining rooms in some of the inns, including the good one in the *Queen's Inn*, cater to the theatre crowd and have more expensive fare. Less costly and good value are the Queen's Sunday and Wednesday evening buffets. Expensive *Rundles*, at 9 Coburg St, has a good reputation.

*Let Them Eat Cake* is a dessert and coffee bar at 82 Wellington St. There are a few fast-food joints and a Chinese place on Ontario St heading out of town.

**Getting There & Away**
**Bus** Several small bus lines servicing the region operate out of the VIA Rail station, which is quite central at 101 Shakespeare St, off Downie St about eight blocks from Ontario St. Cha-Co Trails (☎ 271-7870) buses connect Stratford with Kitchener, from where you can go to Toronto. They also run buses to Goderich, London and Owen Sound, among other southern Ontario towns.

**Train** Train services depart from the VIA Rail station (☎ 273-3234). There are thrice-daily trains to Toronto, or you can go west to London or Sarnia, with connections there for Windsor.

**SHAKESPEARE**
Twelve km east of Stratford along Hwy 8, this village is geared to visitors, and the main street has numerous antique, furniture and craft shops. The *Shakespeare Inn* is a large, up-market hotel. At the west end of town is a moderately priced restaurant.

**ST MARY'S**
To the west of Stratford, St Mary's is a small Victorian crossroads with a former opera house and some fine stone homes as reminders of its good times last century.

The *Westover Inn*, down a side street, Thomas St, and surrounded by lawns and trees, is a quiet, five-star hotel with a dining room.

Several km from town, off Hwy 7 back towards Stratford, is the **Wildwood Conservation Area**. It isn't particularly attractive but you can camp or go for a quick swim. For better swimming, try the spring-fed limestone quarry just outside St Mary's. It costs a couple of dollars and there are change rooms and a snack bar. Apparently prime minister Trudeau took a dip here some years ago after fulfilling his official functions in Stratford.

### TILLSONBURG & DELHI

These two small towns are in the centre of a flat, sandy, tobacco-growing region. The number of smokers has been declining more rapidly in Canada than in other Western countries, so various crop alternatives are being sought to keep the area productive.

On Hwy 3 west of Delhi there is a **Tobacco Museum**, with displays on the history and production of tobacco. It's open daily through the summer, and on weekdays only the rest of the year.

For males, casual work picking tobacco starts in mid-August. Ask at the Canada Manpower offices in these towns. Jobs last roughly a month. It's hard work, but room and board are often thrown in with the wage and you can have a good time. Watch your valuables in the bunkhouse.

### LAKE ERIE SHORELINE WEST

The shallowest of the five Great Lakes, Erie suffered badly through the 1970s with extreme pollution. While not to be confused with a mountain stream, slow improvements in the past decade or so have brought the waters back from the brink of destruction. Scattered along the lake's Canadian northern shoreline, from Windsor to Fort Erie, there are government parks, some with camping, some for day use only. Most are busy on summer weekends.

Turkey Point and, even more so, **Long Point** are good and popular. Still, for swimming, the parks along the Lake Huron shoreline are superior.

Apart from these Lake Erie recreational areas, the region is mainly summer cottages, small towns and farmland.

**Port Dover** is a centre for commercial lake fishing, although some people (your author among them) are leery of eating any of the lower Great Lakes catch due to possible chemical contamination. There is a fishing museum in town and cruises along the lakes's edge are available.

At **Port Stanley**, a small resort village, a five-km portion of the old L&PS Railway still operates, running north to the village of Union. The trip takes about 45 minutes and there are three offered in early afternoon through the summer months.

Further west is **Point Pelee National Park**, on the southernmost point of mainland Canada. It's known primarily for the thousands of birds that show up in spring and fall on their migrations. Up to 342 have been observed here – about 60% of all the species known in Canada.

The region also contains some plants found nowhere else in the country, such as the prickly pear cactus.

There are numerous nature trails, a 1½-km boardwalk through the marsh and sandy beaches within the park. Both bicycles and canoes can be rented. No camping facilities exist, but there are privately run grounds in the vicinity.

**Hillman Marsh**, on the shoreline north of Point Pelee, offers good bird-watching as well and provides an observation tower and a boardwalk. Nearby, in the town of Wheatley, *Burton House* (☎ 825-4956) is a moderately priced B&B. Note that during bird migration periods, this is a relatively busy area. For B&B accommodation, call the local B&B association (☎ 326-7169).

Quite close to Windsor, about 40 km driving straight overland rather than around the lakeshore, are the lakeside towns of Leamington and Kingsville, from which ferries run to the largest island in the lake, **Pelee Island**. Pelee (pronounced 'pee-lee') is halfway across to Ohio, and ferries run across to the US side as well. Ferries run from March to the beginning of December.

For reservations and ticket prices call ☎ 1-800-661-2200. Children and seniors get discounts.

The island is known for its good beaches and small vineyards. Visit the ruins of Vin Villa Winery and the old lighthouse. Tours are offered of the current winery. There are a few restaurants on the island, an inn and one B&B.

## LONDON

London (population 316,000) is the most important town in the Lake Erie area and blends a fair bit of industry and manufacturing with its insurance company head offices and one of the country's largest universities. Despite the activity, the city preserves a quiet, conservative atmosphere, in part due to the tree-lined streets and fine old houses edging the central downtown area. Unfortunately, the core is suffering commercially as growth and development occur more and more around the expanding perimeters.

The city harks back to London, England; the Thames River flows through town, in the centre is Hyde Park and there are many streets, such as Oxford St, whose names parallel those of the English city.

There are a few things to see in and around town, and it might prove to be a convenient stopover, as it lies roughly halfway between the US-Canadian border at Detroit-Windsor and Toronto.

### Orientation

The main east-west street is Dundas St; Richmond St is the main north-south one. The central area is bounded by York St to the south, Talbot St to the west, Oxford St to the north and Waterloo St to the east.

### Information

There is a downtown tourist office (☎ 661-5000), on the main floor of City Hall, on Dufferin Ave at the corner of Wellington St. It's open from 8.30 am to 4.30 pm Monday to Friday.

A second office is on Wellington Rd between Hwy 401 and Commissioners Rd heading north into town from the highway.

It's open daily from 8 am to 8 pm and also has information on points all around Ontario.

### London Museum of Archaeology & Lawson Indian Village

Both an educational and a research facility affiliated with the university, the museum (☎ 473-1360) displays materials and artefacts spanning 11,000 years of Native peoples' history in Ontario. Adjacent to the museum building is an active dig of a Neutral Indian village of about 500 years ago. Parts of the village, including a longhouse, have been reconstructed.

Special events are scheduled through the year and some displays in the museum are changed regularly. A gift shop offers crafts such as baskets, quill boxes and pottery.

Well worth a visit, the museum is open daily from 10 am to 5 pm. The Indian village site is open in fine weather from May to November. An adult ticket is $3.50 and there are senior, student and family rates. The address is 1600 Attawandaron Rd, north-west of the university.

### Fanshawe Pioneer Village

On the eastern edge of the city, at the 22-building Pioneer Village (☎ 457-1296), staff in costume reveal skills and crafts and give a sense of village life of the European settlers in the 1800s. There is a tea room at the site, or you can bring your own picnic (tables supplied).

Tickets are $5 for adults, less for students and kids, and there is a family rate, too. The site is open from 1 May to 31 October daily from 10 am to 4.30 pm. The rest of the year, it's open afternoons only and is closed on Mondays and Tuesdays. The entrance is off Fanshawe Park Rd just east of Clark Rd.

The adjoining Fanshawe Park is a conservation and recreation area with swimming, walking, picnicking and the like.

### Royal Canadian Regiment Museum

Known as the RCR (☎ 660-5102), this is the oldest infantry regiment in Canada. The museum has displays on its involvement in the North-West Rebellion of 1885 right through both World Wars and Korea. As well as the various displays, exhibits and dioramas, there is a gift shop with a range of military items.

The museum is at Wolseley Hall National Historic Site, on the Canadian Forces Base on Oxford St East (at the corner of Elizabeth St). Admission is free. It's closed on Mondays.

### The University of Western Ontario

North of the downtown area, the beautiful university campus is pleasant to stroll around. Western is one of the country's larger universities and is known particularly for its business, medical and engineering faculties. The tourist office has a self-guided walking-tour pamphlet outlining some history and giving details which might make a walk more interesting.

### Eldon House

At 481 Rideout St North and dating from 1834, Eldon House is the city's oldest house and is now an historical museum, with period furnishings from the Victorian era. It's open afternoons only, from Tuesday to Sunday. On Tuesdays it's free; otherwise there is an admission charge of $3.

### Guy Lombardo Museum

At 205 Wonderland Rd South in Springbank Park, this museum (☎ 473-9003) honours the late musician and native son Lombardo, well known across the continent for his New Year's Eve concerts. The collection of articles and memorabilia outlines his career. Admission is $2. Note that the museum is open daily from May to September only, from 11 am to 5 pm.

### Springbank Park

Located by the Thames on the western side of the city, Springbank is a huge, well-tended park of lawns and gardens. Within it is Storybook Gardens, a children's play area with figures from fairy tales, a small zoo area and more. This area has a small admission charge but the park itself is free.

### Banting Museum

Situated in the house where Dr Sir Frederick Banting once lived and worked, the museum (☎ 673-1752) outlines the history of diabetes and the work of Nobel Prize winner Banting, the co-discover of insulin. Displays include a doctor's office from the 1920s and a WW I battlefield injury area.

The museum is at 442 Adelaide St North and is open Tuesday to Saturday from noon to 4.30 pm. A ticket costs $3 for an adult, less for students and seniors.

### Ska-Nah-Doht Indian Village

Thirty-two km west of the city, Ska-Nah-Doht (☎ 264-2420) is a re-creation of a small Iroquois longhouse community of 1000 years ago. Guided tours are available or you can wander about yourself. It's in the Longwoods Road Conservation Area off Hwy 2 and is open daily through the summer and in January and February. The rest of the year, it is closed on weekends. Admission is $6 per car.

### Children's Museum

Walkable from downtown, the Children's Museum (☎ 434-5726), at 21 Wharncliffe Rd South, provides a variety of hands-on exhibits for kids to play and learn with. Examples are digging for dinosaur fossils or entering caves. It's open every day from 10 am to 5 pm and admission is $3 per child, $3.50 per adult.

### Sifton Bog

This site is a little different – in fact, it's unique in southern Ontario. It's an acid bog which is home to a range of unusual plants and animals, including lemmings, shrews, the carnivorous sundew plant and nine varieties of orchids. Access to the bog can be gained off Oxford St between Hyde Park Rd and Sanatorium Rd. There is also a pedestrian gate into the bog from the Oakridge Shopping Mall parking lot.

### Westminster Ponds

Also for nature-seekers, this area of woods, bogs and ponds supports a variety of

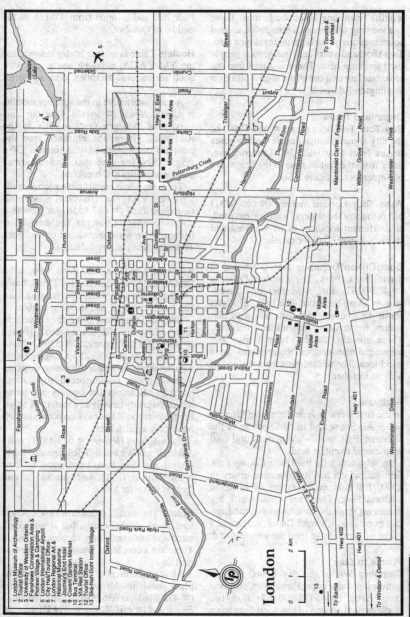

London

1  London Museum of Archaeology
2  Tourist Office
3  University of Western Ontario
4  Fanshawe Conservation Area &
   Pioneer Village & Camping
5  London International Airport
6  City Hall Tourist Office
7  London Regional Art &
   Historical Museums
8  Journey's End Hotel
9  Covent Garden Market
10 VIA Terminal
11 VIA Rail Station
12 Tourist Office
13 Ska-Nah-Doht Indian Village

wildlife, including foxes and herons. There is a viewing tower, and a boardwalk around some sections of the large undeveloped area. Two thousand years ago, indigenous people used to camp here. There is a trail into the area, heading east out of the tourist office on Wellington Rd South.

### Organised Tours
**Bus Tour** Two-hour tours (☎ 661-5000) of the city aboard British double-decker buses depart from City Hall, 300 Dufferin Ave, daily from the end of June to the beginning of September. A ticket is $6.

**Wine Tour** London Winery (☎ 686-8431) offers tours of the winery (with tastings) and, at a different location, of its vineyard and research centre. Call for details.

**Boat Cruise** Departing from a landing in Springbank Park, the *London Princess* (☎ 473-0363) does a number of different cruises along the river. The basic trip lasts about 45 minutes and costs $7, with discounts for seniors, students and children. There are also Sunday brunch trips and evening dinner cruises. Reservations are a good idea. The season runs from the end of May to October.

### Festivals
In the first week in June there is an International Air Show, and in mid-September the Western Fair, a 10-day agricultural and amusement event, is held.

In July, watch for the Home County Folk Festival, which had its 20th anniversary in 1993. It's held in the centre of town, in Victoria Park. There are some pretty big names on stage over the course of the four-day event, and it's free! Dance, crafts and a range of inexpensive food are also featured.

### Places to Stay
**Camping** Within the city limits, there is convenient camping at Fanshawe Conservation Area (☎ 451-2800). It's in the north-eastern section of town, off Fanshawe

Park Rd, and is open from 1 May to the middle of October.

**Hostels** There is no true hostel in town and the YM-YWCA, although active and with good recreational facilities, does not offer rooms.

A good alternative in the summer months is *Alumni House* (☎ 661-3814) at the University of Western Ontario. It's at the Richmond Gates, the entrance into the campus from Richmond St. A room is $30 a single ($24 for students), and the rates include a continental breakfast.

There are some comfortable rooms available at Victoria Hospital's *Victoria Gartshore Hall* (☎ 667-6556) for $29/38 a single/double. Lounges include TVs, fridges, microwave ovens and coffee pots. There are also laundry facilities.

**B&Bs** The London & Area B&B Association (☎ 471-6228), at 720 Headley Drive, has a list of places to stay, with prices ranging from $25 to $45 a single, $35 to $55 a double.

Betty & Doug Rose offer three rooms in their 115-year-old home, *Rose House* (☎ 433-9978). It's central, at 526 Dufferin Ave, and costs from $30/55 a single/double with breakfast. Note that there is no smoking – this is now a widespread stipulation. Smokers all across the country are being leaned on pretty heavily in a variety of ways. Pretty soon you'll have to step across the US border for a quick butt.

*John & Terry Herbert* (☎ 673-4598), at 87 Askin St, off Wharncliffe Rd, are also fairly central and they have two rooms in their house (built in 1871). Rates are $35/40 and there is room for kids.

**Hotels** The small, older downtown hotels tend to be alcoholic city, but if you don't mind the ambience they're cheap enough. There are a couple on Dundas St; otherwise read on.

Most economical in the central core is the plain, no-frills *National Traveller Hotel* (☎ 433-8161), at 636 York St. The *Journey's End Hotel* (☎ 661-0233), at 374 Dundas St, is central and has its own restaurant. Rooms here are in the $60 to $70 range.

Other hotels are primarily geared to the business trade.

**Motels** Most of the city's commercial accommodation is in motels. For many visitors, the most convenient area to look will be along Wellington Rd, which leads north up from Hwy 401 to the centre of town. Of course, prices are higher here.

Both *Days Inn* (☎ 681-1240), at 1100 Wellington Rd South, and *Econo Lodge* (☎ 681-1550), at No 1170, are clean, decent and reasonably priced. Prices at the former start at $50/60, marginally less than at the latter.

On the west side of town, the *Rainbow Motel* (☎ 685-3772), at 1100 Wharncliffe Rd South (Hwy 2 toward Windsor), is cheap – and you get what you pay for. It's seen better days but the beds are good and the location makes it quiet. Oh yeah, there may not be any hot water. Rooms start at $25, depending on the day and season, but bargaining is worthwhile if the quote is a lot higher. The nearby *Rossholme Motel* rents rooms not morals; give it a miss.

If you're sleepy on the east side of town, Dundas St East, a commercial strip, has a number of motels between the 1500 and 2300 street number addresses. Dundas St East becomes Hwy 2 East away from the centre of the city. Quality and prices here are somewhere in between the other two motel districts. One to try is the *White Village* (☎ 451-5840), at 1739 Dundas St East.

**Places to Eat**

A good place to whet and/or satisfy the appetite is at the excellent market known as *Covent Garden*, which is in the centre of downtown, hidden in behind the Bay department store at the corner of Richmond and Dundas Sts. There is plenty of fresh produce to buy, as well as cheeses and breads. A number of small counters also prepare food. The adjacent Covent Garden restaurant is fine for basic meals, especially the breakfasts.

While in the market, check out Mac the mackaw, in the pet shop. He's been there forever. Sometimes he talks, sometimes he bites, sometimes he just sits.

*Say Cheese*, at 246 Dundas St (near Clarence St), is both a speciality shop with fine breads and cheeses and a restaurant with good fresh food which can be washed down with featured wines. Lunch will set you back about $8.

Next door, *Shutters* is a cut above the usual lunch bar and is cheap. It's open from 7 am to 3 pm daily but is closed on Sundays.

On Dundas St at Wellington St is *The Scots Corner*, a British-style pub. *Under the Volcano*, named after Malcolm Lowry's great novel, is worth getting to for its Mexican food. Main dishes are about $10. It's open every day (but not for lunch on Sunday) and the location is 300 Colborne St.

Expensive, fine dining in a well-appointed, oak-lined room overlooking the Thames River can be found at *Michael's on the Thames* (☎ 672-2892), at 1 York St. Specialities are seafood and chateaubriand.

**Entertainment**

London has always been a bit of a blues town, and though bars come and go, there is usually at least one place to hear some bar classics. Try *Leadbelly's*, at 221 Dundas St.

The *Basement* is a place to look into for live folk. It's also central, at 331 Richmond St.

The *CEEPS* at 671 Richmond St (at Mill St), is a spot for drinking university students – and I mean drinking.

**Getting There & Away**

**Bus** The Greyhound Bus Depot (☎ 434-3245) is at 101 York St, at the corner of Talbot St, in central downtown. Buses run to Toronto every couple of hours and to Windsor about half a dozen times daily.

**Train** The VIA Rail station (☎ 667-1645) is nearby, on York St at the foot of Richmond St. It serves Toronto four times a day, one trip going via Stratford. In the other direction, the train goes to Chicago via Sarnia. Note that for Toronto, the train fare is nearly double the $22 bus fare.

## Getting Around
For fares and route information, the London Transit Commission (☎ 451-1347), the city bus service, has an office on Dundas St a couple of doors east of Richmond St.

## ST THOMAS
South of London, St Thomas is a small farm community centre made a little more interesting by the fine Victorian and other period architecture. In the downtown area, City Hall, the Court House and St Thomas Church are all worth a look.

Also for history buffs are the two small museums, one on pioneer life, the other on the military past in the vicinity.

The Guildhouse Building (dating from 1912), at 180 Talbot St, now houses a number of arts & crafts stores and galleries.

St Thomas has another, not-so-agreeable claim to fame: it was here in 1885 that Jumbo, that famous circus elephant, was hit and killed by a train. The life-sized statue at the west end of town pays tribute to this tragedy.

Eleven km west and three km south of St Thomas, near the village of Iona, are the earthwork remains of a double-walled Neutral Indian fort. There isn't much to see, but it is interesting in that North American Indians were not known for building such structures.

## WINDSOR
Windsor, with a population of 200,000, sits at the south-western tip of the province, across the Detroit River from Detroit, Michigan. It is not in any way a tourist city, but like its counterpoint over the river, it is a major international border crossing. From here it is about two hours' drive to London, 4½ hours to Toronto. From Detroit, there are routes to Chicago.

Like Detroit, Windsor is a car-making city, and this is by far its major economic activity. The inner cities, however, differ markedly.

Recent reports from across the river suggest that the core has just about been given up for dead. In contrast, the downtown area of Windsor is neat and clean, with an abundance of parks and gardens, especially along the river. The central area can be found around the junction of Riverside and Ouelette Sts, along the water. Pitt and Chatham Sts are also important. There are good views of the Detroit skyline, especially from the pleasant Dieppe Gardens, which run right along the waterfront from the corner of Ouelette and Riverside Sts. The Art Gallery of Windsor is nearby, at 445 Riverside St.

For information, there is a visitors bureau at 80 Chatham St, near the bus station.

In a bold move to bolster both the local economy and the provincial coffers, a controversial government-sanctioned gambling casino should be open by the time you read this.

The International Freedom Festival combines Canada's 1 July national holiday with America's 4 July celebrations for an event of parades, concerts and dances, with one of the continent's largest fireworks displays to end the affair.

## Places to Stay
If you arrive at night or wish to sleep over, most accommodation is in motels, and the place to look for moderately priced ones is in South Windsor, on Dougall St. For example, the *ABC* (☎ 969-5090), at 3048 Dougall St, charges $30 to $40 for either a single or double. Another to try is the *Star Economy* (☎ 969-8200), at about the same price. A little more expensive and with a better rating is the *Cadillac Motel* (☎ 969-9340), at 2498 Dougall St. Rooms here are $50.

Another area rich in motels is Huron Church Rd, and out by the airport, Division Rd has a number of places, such as the *Casa Don* (☎ 969-2475) at No 2130.

The tourist office has a listing of some local B&Bs, but these tend to be away from the centre.

## Black Settlement in Ontario

To the story of the Native peoples, the French and the English, who created so much of Canada's early history, this region of southern Ontario can add new plots and themes. Together Essex and Kent counties around Windsor and Chatham make up one of the two regions of early Black settlement in Canada. (The other is around Halifax, Nova Scotia.)

Windsor, as a terminal on the so-called Underground Railroad, was a gateway to freedom for thousands of former Black slaves in pre-Civil War (1861-65) America. The railway was really just a network of people ('conductors') who aided, directed and fed the fleeing slaves, as each night, they followed the north star to the next 'station'.

Aside from the museum in Amherstburg, there are several sites in the region relating directly to this saga.

The **John Freeman Walls Historic Site** is located 1.6 km north off Hwy 401 at exit 28 out of Windsor heading west. The site includes the log cabin built in 1876 by Walls, a fugitive slave from North Carolina. The Underground Railroad Museum is here.

Further west, visit the **Raleigh Township Centennial Museum** near Chatham, on County Rd 6 south of Hwy 401 after exiting at Bloomfield Rd. This museum concentrates on the lives of the Black settlers who turned the Elgin Settlement into a new home and welcoming centre for others following in their footsteps.

In the town of Dresden is **Uncle Tom's Cabin Historic Site**. Uncle Tom was a fictional character in the controversial novel of the same name written by Harriet Beecher in 1852. It was based on the life of Josiah Henson, another southern Black man. The site displays articles relating to the story and salient history.

Just how much the tales of the Underground Railway are engrained in the hearts of Black Americans was suggested a few years ago when the Toronto Argonaut football team outbid some American teams for the services of a new hot rookie, Raghib 'Rocket' Ismail, just out of college. A few days after he toured Toronto and sensed the racial tolerance, the deal was struck. After Rocket signed for some obscene amount of money, reporters at the obligatory news conference asked his mother what she thought of the agreement. Her reply was that they were going to ride that train north to freedom. ■

## Places to Eat

For a nosh, the *Himalaya*, at 841 Ouellette St, is said to be good for curry. *Cultures*, at 300 Ouelette St, makes inexpensive and fresh sandwiches and salads. The restaurant in the Art Gallery of Windsor, 445 Riverside St, is quite good, and inexpensive, too. A number of eateries can also be found along Pelissier St.

## Getting There & Away

The bus station is central, on Chatham St slightly east of Ouellette St. The VIA Rail station is about three km east of the downtown core, at the corner of Walker and Wyandotte Sts. Trains run to Toronto via London.

## AMHERSTBURG

Located south of Windsor, where the Detroit River flowing from Lake St Clair runs into Lake Erie, Amherstburg is a small, historic town.

Much of this history is outlined at the **Fort Malden National Historic Park**, along the river, at 100 Laird Ave. There are some remains of the British fort of 1840.

Beginning with the arrival of the fur traders, the area was the focal point for a lot of tension between the Native Indians, French and English and, later, the Americans. Here during the War of 1812 against the Americans, General Brock (together with ally Shawnee Chief Tecumseh) discussed plans to take Detroit.

The **North American Black Historical Museum** has displays on both Black history in North America in general and Black settlement of the Windsor area in particular. It's at 277 King St West and is open Wednesday to Sunday.

**Park House Museum**, the oldest house in town, wasn't built here – it was ferried across the river in 1799 and is now furnished in 1850s style. Located at 214 Dalhousie St, it's open daily in summer but is closed on Mondays and Saturdays the rest of the year.

Also from here, ferries run to Canadian **Boblo Island**, where there is a huge amusement park which has been here for nearly 100 years. Boats also connect the island to Detroit. Moonlit night cruises run in midsummer.

## LAKE HURON SHORELINE & AREA

North of Windsor, on the southern tip of Lake Huron, **Sarnia** is an industrial and oil-refining centre. Sarnia is the hub of 'Chemical Valley', a large, modern oil and chemical production complex of the surrounding area.

Across the Bluewater Bridge over the St Clair River is Port Huron, Michigan.

South-west of Sarnia on Hwy 21 is the **Oil Museum of Canada**, a National Historic Site and the location of the first commercial oil well on the continent. Producing wells can be seen in the area, and the search for more oil continues.

Along Lake Huron as far up as Tobermory on the Bruce Peninsula are numerous and popular parks, good sandy beaches, cottages and small summer resort towns. The water is warm and clean, the beaches broad and sandy.

At **Kettle Point**, about 40 km north-east of Sarnia, is a 350-million-year-old attraction. Along the shoreline are a series of spherical rocks called kettles (to geologists, concretions). Some of these calcite formations, which sit on beds of softer shale, are nearly one metre in diameter. The rare kettles are found in other countries but are often underground, and this collection is considered top rate. A little further up the coast, both Ipperwash Provincial Park **and the Pinery Provincial Park**, south of Grand Bend, have camping. The Pinery, a large park with 1000 sites, long had a reputation as a party spot but has been quietened down in recent years. The beach is 10 km long and trails wind through the wooded sections. Further north is Point Farms Park, about the size of Ipperwash.

**Grand Bend** is one of the Lake Huron resort towns, similar to Sauble Beach. It's a lively place in summer, with a few places for a drink along the shoreline.

Acting as the regional centre, **Goderich** is a small, green and attractive town with a distinctive circular main street. It bills itself as the prettiest town in Ontario. About a quarter of the town's area is park, so it is very green.

At dusk, view the 'world's best' sunsets from near the Governor's House & Historic Gaol Museum. It's set on a cliff on the town bluffs over the water. And these sunsets really are spectacular.

Also in town, on West St, is a Marine Museum (with displays on shipping and the lake) and the Huron County Pioneer Museum.

There is a good, small, rustic HI *hostel* (☎ 524-8428) 6½ km out of town on Rural Route 2. To get there, take a taxi. The hostel is in an old log cabin by the lake and has room for eight people. Call first for a reservation.

Goderich is also known for its expensive, resorty *Benmiller Inn* (☎ 524-2191).

The nearby village of **Blyth** is home to a major summer theatre festival which features primarily Canadian plays, both new and old. A unique B&B in town is the *Blyth Station House* (☎ 523-9826), in the converted train station. A double room goes for $50 (plus $10 each for one or two more people), and that includes brunch in the former waiting room.

Several restaurants can be found along Queen St, the main street.

See after Owen Sound under the Georgian Bay & Lakelands section following for details of the northern Lake Huron region as far as Manitoulin Island.

# Georgian Bay & Lakelands

North of Toronto, the lakes and woods, towns and resorts, beaches and cottages, all presided over by magnificent Georgian Bay and its varied shoreline, make up the playground of southern Ontario.

The mostly wooded hills, scores of lakes and rivers and numerous parks are scattered in and around prime farmland, making for fine summer fishing, swimming, camping and lazing – just what the doctor ordered. In winter the area is busy with winter recreation: skiing, snowmobiling and lots of ice fishing. In September and October, people tour the region to see nature's annual, brilliantly coloured tree show. Despite the emphasis on outdoor activities, this is generally a busy and developed area. For more space or wilderness, head further north, or to the larger government parks such as Algonquin.

The district around Barrie and Lake Simcoe to Orillia and north-west to Penetanguishene, and then around Georgian Bay west to Collingwood, is known collectively as **Huronia**.

The area north of Orillia (roughly between the towns of Gravenhurst and Huntsville along Hwy 11) and west to Georgian Bay is referred to as **Muskoka** or the Muskokas. The name is taken from one of the larger lakes of the region.

West from Collingwood along the south of Nottawasaga Bay, a smaller bay within Georgian Bay, is Owen Sound. Located at the southern entrance to the Bruce Peninsula, Owen Sound is the largest town in this area. The 'Bruce' is the narrow strip of land running north which divides Georgian Bay from the main body of huge Lake Huron. From the tip of the peninsula at Tobermory, ferries may be taken to Manitoulin Island, with connections to the mainland of northern Ontario.

The following text leads first from Barrie west and north to Manitoulin Island, around western Georgian Bay, and then from Barrie north and east through the Muskoka-Huronia region, around eastern Georgian Bay.

## BARRIE

About 1½ hours north of Toronto is the town of Barrie, which is more or less the unofficial gateway to the big city's northward cottage country. There is nothing of particular note in Barrie itself, although the popular beach at Centennial Park (on Kempenfelt Bay of large Lake Simcoe) is convenient and generally busy.

## Skiing

Though the region north of Toronto tends to have milder winters and the topography is considerably less dramatic than that found in either Quebec or out in the far west around the Rockies, skiing is still a major winter activity. There are three main alpine centres, all offering daily equipment rental.

Closest to Toronto (about a two-hour drive) is **Horseshoe Valley** (☎ 835-2790; 283-2988 in Toronto). Take Hwy 400 up past Barrie to Horseshoe Valley Rd. Turn off and the ski hill is six km east. This is the smallest and lowest in elevation of the three and so is ideal for kids, families, the inexperienced or the merely out of shape. It's open every day and has night skiing until 10 pm. Plenty of lifts (including a quad chair) mean the lines move quickly even on busy days. A plus here is that there is also a good system of nearly 40 km of groomed cross-country trails. The trails close at 4.30 pm.

**Mount St Louis Moonstone** (☎ 835-2112; 368-6900 in Toronto) is one of the province's top ski resort/complexes, and the largest (in terms of number of ski slopes) in southern Ontario. It is at the village of Coldwater, about 10 or 15 minutes north of Horseshoe Valley continuing on Hwy 400. Take exit 131 to the right. Features include snowmaking, two fully licensed lodges (no accommodation) and equipment rentals. There are 42 runs, ranging through easy to difficult, with a 160-metre vertical drop.

**Blue Mountain Resorts** (☎ 445-0231; 869-3799 in Toronto), at Collingwood, is considered the most challenging of southern Ontario's ski centres and, being relatively far north, tends to have more natural snow and a longer season. The vertical drop here is 216 metres, with the maximum run length 1200 metres. Lifts include one quad, three triple and eight double chairs, as well as two pomas and a rope tow.

Collingwood is about a 2½-hour drive from Toronto. The slopes are 13 km west of town on Blue Mountain Rd. There is daily bus service from Toronto.

Cross-country (nordic) skiing is considerably less expensive; entrance fees to most places are in the range of $7 to $10 for the day.

For cross-country skiing north of the city, there is the aforementioned Horseshoe Valley, or for a relatively wild, undisturbed winter wonderland, **Awenda Provincial Park** (☎ 549-2231) in Penetanguishene is recommended. Both are open daily.

Close to Toronto are two good places to consider for cross-country skiing. **Albion Hills Conservation Area** (☎ 661-6600) is eight km north of the town of Bolton, which is north-west of Toronto. They rent equipment and have 26 km of trails winding through the woods. A good day can end with a snack in the coffee shop.

A second choice is to ski the grounds of **Seneca College** (☎ 833-3333, ext 5024) at their King Campus, at 13990 Dufferin St, in King City. They offer 'old, used and abused' skis and boots for rent. Call for trail conditions. When there is a lot of snow, the trails are open every day, and they are good, winding through the woods. There is no public transportation to the campus.

For the ski conditions report (☎ 314-0988 (alpine) and (☎ 314-0960 (cross-country) in Toronto. ∎

## Information
On Hwy 400 northbound at Barrie is a large Ontario Travel Information Centre, with details on regional points of interest. It's open all year.

Smaller, more locally oriented tourist offices can be found in Barrie itself (at 17A Mulcaster St), in Collingwood (at 55 Hurontario St) and in Orillia (at 150 Front St South). Many other towns have small information offices and booths where you can pick up local information on sights, events, festivals and places of historic interest.

## Getting There & Away
**Bus** The bus station (☎ 739-1500) is central, at 24 Maple Ave. From here buses go in all directions.

**Car & Motorbike** From Toronto, Barrie is straight up Hwy 400. On Friday afternoons, especially holiday summer weekends, expect a lot of traffic, at least to Barrie and often beyond. Coming back into Toronto, the traffic is heavy on summer Sunday nights.

## WASAGA BEACH
Wasaga is the beach resort closest to Toronto. Around Wasaga Beach and the strip of beaches (about 14 km long) running up along the bay are hundreds of cottages, a provincial park and several private campgrounds. The centre of activity is the decidedly unsubtle town of Wasaga Beach and the excellent beach (with fine swimming) at Wasaga Beach Provincial Park.

A popular weekend spot, Wasaga Beach is nearly empty during the week. Some areas of the beach are more for families; others (like those around the snack bars) attract the younger crowd, although drinkers are now often fined on the spot. Water-slide complexes are one of Canada's fastest-growing diversions, and Wasaga Beach has two water slides, including one right on the shore in town. One slide is over 100 metres long.

## Places to Stay
The local Chamber of Commerce (☎ 429-

2247), with an office open all year at 35 Dunkerron St, should be able to help with finding accommodation.

There are many motels around the district, including several along Main St or Mosley St, and they range from $35 for singles to $75 for doubles. They're slightly cheaper for a two-night stay, more so by the week. Also check on Rural Route 1. Others places to stay are on the beach. Lots of cottages with housekeeping facilities are available as well, but these are generally for stays of a week or longer.

## Getting There & Away
Two buses run daily in both directions between Toronto and Wasaga Beach, one in the morning and one in the afternoon. It's a 2½-hour trip, with a change of buses in Barrie. In Wasaga Beach, the bus travels right down the main road.

## COLLINGWOOD
In the centre of the Blue Mountain ski area and right on the water, this little resort town has a reputation for being pretty, but really isn't. The surroundings are scenic enough, with the highest sections of the Niagara Escarpment nearby. The escarpment runs south, all the way to Niagara Falls. The caves along it near town are heavily and misleadingly promoted; they are not what you and I expect of that term, but are really more like overhangs. There is some good walking, however; the hour-long trail by the caves loops over interesting terrain and the offers excellent views. An admission fee is charged to the area around the caves, with an additional charge to actually see the caves.

A chairlift runs to the top of Blue Mountain, from where there is a choice of the chairlift or a slide ride down in summer.

The area is known for its 'blue' pottery, which is nice but not cheap. A bluegrass music festival is held here in summer.

## Places to Stay
Collingwood has an excellent Backpackers hostel. The *Blue Mountain Auberge* (☎ 445-1497) is open all year but is often booked out.

There are about 60 beds and a kitchen in a chalet-style building. The hostel also has a sauna. You'll find it on Rural Route 3, near the ski hills north of Craigleith – about 2½ hours from Toronto. Rates are $11 in summer, $15 in winter.

There are plenty of motels too. *Moore's Motel* (☎ 445-2478), on Rural Route 3, is a mid-size place with rooms from as low as $35 (but quite a bit more in season). Offering budget accommodation is the *Glen Lake Motel* (☎ 445-4676), on Rural Route 2, and the *Village Store* (☎ 444-286), on Rural Route 3, close to the Blue Mountain Slides. Of course, there are more expensive places in the area, including some resorts, lodges and inns with all the amenities.

## SHELBURNE

A rather nondescript small southern Ontario country town between Toronto and Owen Sound, Shelburne comes alive once a year for the old-time fiddlers' contest. It's held for two days in August, and has been for over 40 years. There's a parade and free music shows, and the contest finals are only $4. Saturday night grand finals are $8; those tickets must be reserved. For rooms in people's homes for the weekend call ☎ (519) 925-5535. For camping contact the Kinsmen Camp, Box 891, Shelburne.

## DURHAM

Slightly to the north and west of Shelburne, this little town is the location of the annual North American banjo contest.

## OWEN SOUND

Owen Sound, with a population of 20,000, is the largest centre in the region, and if you're going up the Bruce Peninsula or north to Manitoulin Island, you'll pass by it. It sits at the end of a deep bay, surrounded on three sides by the steepness of the Niagara Escarpment.

Although still a working port, it is not the shipping centre it was from the 1880s to the first years of this century. In those early days before the railway, the town rocked with brothels and bars, battled by the believers –

one intersection had a bar on each corner and was known as Damnation Corner; another had four churches and was called Salvation Corner. I guess the latter won out, because the churches are still there. In fact, for 66 long years from 1906 to 1972, you couldn't buy alcohol. There aren't too many merchant sailors on the waterfront now, but sections of it have been restored and it's an attractive setting for the marinas and restaurants.

## Orientation & Information

The Sydenham River drifts through town, dividing it between east and west; the main street is Second Ave. The Visitors & Convention Bureau (☎ 371-9833) is at 232 Second Ave East. A folder for a two-hour, self-guided historic walking tour of the city is available here or at City Hall. A Saturday market is held beside City Hall.

## Harrison Park

This large, green park is right in town, along the Sydenham River. It has picnic areas, trails, fishing and even camping.

## Tom Thomson Memorial Art Gallery

Thomson was a contemporary of Canada's Group of Seven and is one of the country's best known painters. He grew up here and many of his works were done in this part of the country. The gallery, at 840 First Ave West, also displays the work of some other Canadian painters. It's open daily in July and August but is closed on Sundays and Mondays in other months.

## County of Grey & Owen Sound Museum

Here you can see exhibits on the area's geology and human history. On display are a half-sized replica of an Ojibwa Indian village and an eight-metre birch-bark canoe. The museum is at 975 Sixth St East.

## Mill Dam & Fish Ladder

In spring and fall, it's interesting to see the struggle trout must go through to reach their preferred spawning areas – this dam and ladder were set up to help them on their swim upstream.

## Billy Bishop Heritage Museum

Home-town boy Billy Bishop, who became a flying ace in WW I, is honoured here. The museum is in the Bishop home, at 948 Third Ave West. Billy is buried in town, at the Greenwood Cemetery.

## Marine & Rail Heritage Centre

In the old train station at 1165 First Ave West, this museum details the transportation and ship-building history of Owen Sound.

## Kelso Beach

North of downtown is Kelso Beach, on Georgian Bay. Free concerts are held regularly here in summer.

## Inglis Falls

Six km south of town, off Hwy 6, the Sydenham River falls over the Niagara Escarpment. The falls, a 24-metre drop, are set in a conservation area which is linked to the Bruce Trail. The trail runs from Tobermory south to the Niagara River. See under Tobermory for details. The segment by Owen Sound offers good views and springs, as well as the Inglis, Jones and Indian falls. It makes a nice half-day walk.

## Festivals

The three-day Summerfolk music festival, held annually around the second or third weekend of August, is a major North American festival of its kind. The event is held in Kelso Park, right along the water, and attracts crowds of up to 10,000. Musicians come from around the continent. Tickets cost $18 a day – and each day is a full one. There's camping nearby.

## Places to Stay

**Camping** Very conveniently, there are campgrounds right in town. One is across the road from Kelso Beach, ideal for the music festival. Another is in Harrison Park (☎ 371-9734), which charges $12 per site (without electricity), and you can use the heated pool – Georgian Bay is known for its cold water.

**Hotels** The old downtown hotels such as the Seldon, at 1005 Second Ave East, which was built in 1887, are being converted to other uses but new, more expensive places are springing up around town and along the waterfront. An example is the 60-room *Inn on the Bay* (☎ 371-9200), at 1800 Second Ave East.

**Motels** Most of the accommodation here is provided by motels. There are several on Ninth St, including the low-priced *Travellers Motel* (☎ 376-2680). The *Key Motel* (☎ 794-2350), 11 km south of town on Hwys 6 and 10, is costlier but still in the moderate range, with rooms from $41 to $55.

## Places to Eat

There are a few places along the waterfront and most offer seafood. One, the *Jolly Rodger*, is on a boat moored off the harbour. *Belamy's*, at 865 Tenth St West, offers a bit of everything, from pasta to steak.

## PORT ELGIN

Port Elgin is a little resort town on Lake Huron, west of Owen Sound. There are sandy beaches, the warm waters of Lake Huron, cottages and camping. **MacGregor Provincial Park**, with campgrounds and some walking trails, is five km south.

Further south is the **Bruce Nuclear Plant**, which is controversial, of course, as are all nuclear plants in Canada. They offer free tours and a film on nuclear power.

The **Saugeen River** has been divided up into canoeing sections ranging from 20 km to 40 km. Half-day and longer trips have been mapped out, with camping at several points along the river. A shorter trip is along the **Rankin River**.

## SAUBLE BEACH

Sauble Beach is a summer resort with an excellent, sandy 11-km beach and warm shallow waters. The coast all along here is known for good sunsets. There are plenty of hotels, motels and cottages for rent, as well as entertainment diversions.

There are also many campgrounds in the area, all busy on summer weekends. Best is the *Sauble Falls Provincial Campground* (☎ 422-1952). Reservations are a good idea. Further north along the road are several commercial grounds – for example, *White Sands* (☎ 534-2781) in Oliphant. The sites at the back have trees and are quiet. Many of the private campgrounds tend to be noisy at night with young partyers – check out the neighbours if this is a concern! A walk around some of the side streets of the downtown area sometimes turns up a guesthouse sign or a seasonal B&B.

Cottages tend to be cheaper than motels. *Chilwell's Cottages* (☎ 422-1692), at 31 Third Ave North, has six small cottages and is one of the cheapest, at $30 to $40 for doubles. Prices generally range from $40 to $75.

## THE BRUCE PENINSULA

The Bruce, as it's known, is an 80-km-long limestone outcropping at the north end of the Niagara Escarpment. Jutting into Lake Huron, it forms the western edge of Georgian Bay, splitting it away from the main body of the lake. This relatively undeveloped area of the province offers some striking scenery, mixing rocky, rugged shorelines, sandy beaches, lakeside cliffs and green woodlands. The north end has two national parks. From Tobermory (at the tip of the peninsula), ferries depart for Manitoulin Island.

### Dyer's Bay

If you have a car, a good scenic drive can be made around Dyer's Bay, which is about 20 km south of Tobermory. From Hwy 6, take Dyer's side road into the village and then the road north-east along the coast. It's not long, but with Georgian Bay on one side and the limestone cliffs of the escarpment on the other, it is impressive. The road ends at the Cabot Head Lighthouse. Before arriving there, you'll pass by the ruins of an old log flume where logs were sent over the edge.

The road south of Dyer's Bay is also good, leading down to a 'flowerpot' formation known as the Devil's Monument. The so-called 'flowerpots' of the Bruce Peninsula are top-heavy standing rock formations

created by wave erosion. This secondary road continues to Lion's Head, where you can connect back with the main highway.

### Dorcas Bay

On Lake Huron about 11 km south of Tobermory, there is a preserve owned by the Federation of Ontario Naturalists. This undeveloped preserve attracts many walkers and photographers for its wildflowers – up to 50 species of orchids can be spotted. To reach the site, turn west from Hwy 11 towards Lake Huron. You're there when you reach the parking lot with a few picnic tables and a toilet.

### Bruce Peninsula National Park

This recently formed national park (☎ 596-2233) protects and makes accessible some of the best features on the entire peninsula. For hikers, campers and appreciators of nature, it is not to be missed.

The park has several unconnected components, with segments on both sides of the peninsula, including Cypress Lake, some of the Georgian Bay coastline, the Niagara Escarpment between Tobermory and Dyer's Bay, and a great section of the Bruce Trail. See under Bruce Trail later for more details. Cypress Lake, with the campground, swimming and some shorter walking trails, is the centre of most activity.

### Tobermory

This small, somewhat plain fishing and tourist town sits at the northern tip of the Bruce Peninsula, which protrudes into Lake Huron. On one side of the peninsula are the cold, clear waters of Georgian Bay, and on the other is the much warmer main body of Lake Huron. There is not much to see in town itself, but it is a busy spot in summer for several reasons. Firstly, the ferry to Manitoulin Island departs and arrives here. Many people driving across Ontario and further west take this route because it's quicker than driving around Georgian Bay. Manitoulin Island has its own charms as well.

In addition, Tobermory is the centre for several government parks and marks the end of the Bruce Trail. The town is also a diving centre; the crystal-clear waters offshore contain 50 known sunken ships.

Activity is focused in the centre of town, at the harbour area known as Big Tub and Little Tub. The visitor centre is here, with general area information or more detailed facts on diving at Fathom Five Park. Boats for tours of Flowerpot Island moor here as well.

To reach Tobermory from the north, see under Manitoulin Island later.

**Fathom Five National Marine Park** This is Ontario's first partially underwater park, developed to protect and make more accessible this intriguing offshore area. Nineteen wrecks lie in the park's waters, scattered between the many little islands. The visitors centre on Little Tub Harbour has displays and can offer information and advice on things to see and do.

Five km offshore from Tobermory, **Flowerpot Island** is the best known, most visited portion of the park and is more easily enjoyed than the underwater attractions! The island, with its unusual, precarious-looking rock columns formed through years of erosion, can be visited by boat from town.

There are various trails on the island, taking from a little over an hour for the shortest one to 2¼ hours for the more difficult. Look for the wild orchids. The island has cliffs, quite a few caves which can be explored (after registering), some picnic spots and just a few basic camping sites. Reservations are needed for camping, particularly on weekends, and you should take all supplies. Note that the mental image may not correspond with reality – there is little privacy, with boatloads of mainlanders constantly arriving to stroll by with inspecting eyes. So much for the isolated island adventure.

Various companies and tugboats offer boat trips to the island, where you can hop off if you wish and catch a later boat back. The cost is about $12; just ask around the harbour area. The glass-bottomed boat is the best known, but the waters are so clear that wrecks can be seen simply by peering over the side of any boat. The *True North* boat doesn't charge any extra to drop you at Flowerpot Island. The price also includes a cruise past some of the shipwrecks.

**Bruce Trail** Tobermory marks the northern end of this 700-km footpath, which runs from Queenston (on the Niagara River) to this point (on the tip of the Bruce Peninsula, on Georgian Bay) over private and public lands. You can hike for an hour, a day or a week. The trail edges along the Niagara Escarpment, providing good scenery, and much of it is inaccessible from the road.

The most northerly bit, from Dyer's Bay to Tobermory, is the most rugged and spectacular. A good day's walk within the park is possible. You may even get a glimpse of the rare Ontario rattlesnakes, though the chance of seeing one is slight and they tend to be timid, so don't let their existence deter you from a hike.

The Bruce Trail Association (☎ 529-6821 in Hamilton) puts out a detailed map of the entire route for about $20, less for members. The head office is at Raspberry House, PO Box 857, Hamilton, L8N 3N9. There is also an office in Toronto. The Grey-Bruce Tourist Association has a $2 map of the top portion of the trail. Other tourist offices can tell you where there are access points.

Some parts of the trail are heavily used on summer weekends. Near Hamilton, at the southern end, there is a popular day-walking area at Rattlesnake Point Conservation Area. Another southern one is at Terra Cotta, not far from Toronto. Yet another is at the forks of the Credit River.

There are designated areas for camping along the path, although in the gentler, busy southern sections, there are some huts where you can even take a shower.

In other sections there is accommodation in B&Bs or old inns. Either of the above trail offices can help with information about B&Bs along the trail. Prices are around $40/45 to $65 for singles/doubles.

Remember the insect repellent, don't drink the water along the trail, and bring good boots – much of the trail is wet and muddy.

**Diving** The waters here are excellent for scuba diving, with many wrecks, geological formations and clear water. The water is also cold, however. Programmes are available for beginners and more advanced divers. Equipment is available in Tobermoray. Snorkelling is possible in some areas, too. Again, a wet or dry suit will be required, but these do come with rental packages.

The Ontario government puts out a pamphlet listing dive sites with descriptions, depths and recommendations. It's available free at the tourist office.

In the summer of 1993, a large section of well-preserved, 8000-year-old underwater forest was officially discovered. University researchers had publicised their search for an ancient submerged block of land, and were rewarded when a local diver said he had explored the remnants of such a site off the east side of the peninsula, at Colpoys Bay. It is believed the forest became submerged hundreds of years after the retreat of the last ice age, when the lake levels rose.

**Other Activities** Swimming in Georgian Bay in August can be good and warm, but not around here. Shallow Cypress Lake, in the park, is definitely a more sane choice. Further south on the bay, at **Wasaga Beach** and **Penetanguishene**, the water is quite pleasant. The waters along the Lake Huron shoreline are also warm, even on the west side of the Bruce Peninsula.

**Places to Stay** There are many places to stay in and around Tobermory but prices are a little high in peak season. The *Grandview* (☎ 596-2220), right by the harbour, has a fine view and the meals are quite good. Nearby motels are less costly.

## MANITOULIN ISLAND
The world's largest freshwater island, Manitoulin Island is basically a rural region of small farms. About a third of the population is Native Indian. Recently, tourism has

become the island's main moneymaker, a growth trend which continues, and many southerners own summer cottages.

The island is about 140 km long and 40 km wide, with a scenic coastline, some sandy beaches, 100 lakes (including some large ones), lots of small towns and villages and numerous hiking trails. It has so far remained fairly undeveloped. Visitors will soon find out that part of the reason for this is the difficulty of getting to the island and, once there, in getting around. Transportation is minimal.

There are information offices in South Baymouth, Gore Bay and Little Current; the latter is the only one to remain open all year.

West of the ferry landing, at the village of **Providence Bay**, is the island's best beach. Beyond **Meldrum Bay**, at **Mississagi Point** on the far western tip of the island, an old lighthouse (dating from 1873) provides views over the strait. There is a campground here, as well as a restaurant and a museum. Meldrum Bay has an inn with a restaurant. Along the north side of the island from Meldrum Bay to Little Current is some of the best scenery.

**Gore Bay**, on the rocky north shore, has one of the island's many small museums, displaying articles relating to the island's early settlers. See the prisoners' dining-room table from the jail. From the eastern headland at the edge of town, the lookout offers fine views. On the other side of town, the headland has a lighthouse and a campground. One of the main beauty spots, **Bridal Veil Falls**, is 16 km east.

The largest community is **Little Current**, at the beginning of the causeway north to the mainland towards the town of Espanola. The main tourist office for the island is here and can help you find a B&B. Rates are not bad on the island, relative to the southern mainland. There are two viewpoints of note near town and one good walk. The Cup & Saucer Trail, 19 km east of town, leads to the highest point on the island (351 metres), which has good views over the North Channel. Closer to town is **McLeans Mountain**, four km west, and 16 km south on Hwy 6 is a lookout with views towards the village of **Killarney**, on the mainland.

### Activities
Two principal attractions of the island for many visitors are the fishing and boating. There are several fishing camps around the island. For cruising, the 225-km North Channel is superb. The scenery is great: one fjord, **Baie Finn**, is 15 km long, with pure white quartzite cliffs. And the water is clean enough to drink from the side of the boat.

### Organised Tours
From the ferry landing on the island at South Baymouth, four-hour sightseeing tours (☎ 282-2848 on the island) by bus operate Tuesday to Thursday during July and August. Tours depart early in the afternoon and include stops at some of the scenic spots as well as at Native Indian craft shops.

### Festivals
As mentioned, Manitoulin Island has a considerable Native Indian population. At the **Wikwemikong Reserve**, known as Wiky, the largest powwow (loosely translated as 'cultural festival') in the province is held on the first weekend in August, a three-day civic holiday. Native Indians from around the country participate. It's an all-inclusive event, with dancing and music, food and crafts. Wikwemikong is in the north-east part of Manitoulin Island.

### Getting There & Away
**Bus** Getting to the island is a little difficult, particularly without a car. From Toronto, buses run to Tobermory only in summer and are infrequent even then. Greyhound runs to Owen Sound. A transfer to a different bus line must be made in Owen Sound for the rest of the trip (which line that is varies from year to year). The complete trip takes almost the whole day. The schedule varies each year, so call for the latest information, but at last check, the bus ran – inconveniently – in both directions only on Friday, Saturday and Sunday. This means you either get at least a week or just a day at Manitoulin Island. It's

quite a long bus trip, and not cheap either. Furthermore, there is no train service up this way.

Greyhound goes all the way around Georgian Bay from Toronto to Espanola, and from there down to Little Current (on Manitoulin).

**Ferry** From Tobermory, two ferries run over to South Baymouth, on the southern edge of Manitoulin. The principal ship is the *Chi-Cheemaun*, and despite its being able to handle 600 passengers and 115 cars, it became so busy that a second ferry, the MS *Nindawayma*, has been added. It's still not uncommon to have to wait in line for a crossing.

The *Chi-Cheemaun* makes four crossings daily in midsummer, two in spring and fall. From Tobermory, departure times are 7 and 11.20 am and 3.40 and 8 pm. Tickets are $11 per adult, $23 for a car; it's slightly cheaper in spring and fall. The *Nindawayma* runs twice a day. There's a small charge for bicycles.

The ferry season is from early May to mid-October, and outside the prime season, the second ship does not operate. The 50-km trip takes about 1¾ hours and there are cafeterias on board. For reservations call ☎ 1-800-265-3163 toll free.

**Car & Motorbike** The island also makes a good short cut if you're heading to northern Ontario. Take the ferry from Tobermory, cross the island and then take the bridges to the north shore of Georgian Bay. The route can save you a few hours of driving around the bay and is pleasant, although more costly.

### Getting Around
AJ Bus Lines, a shoestring operation, runs buses between South Baymouth, Gore Bay and Little Current.

### MIDLAND
North of Barrie, on the eastern side of Georgian Bay, is the small commercial centre of Midland, the most interesting of the Huronia region's towns. The Huron Indians first

settled this area, and developed a confederacy to encourage cooperation among neighbouring Native peoples. The established Huron settlements attracted the French explorers and, more critically, the Jesuit missionaries.

Midland has a number of worthwhile things to see. Unfortunately, even though the town is quite small, getting to the cluster of sites out of the centre is difficult without your own vehicle.

### Information
For information, see the Chamber of Commerce (☎ 526-7884), at 208 King St.

### Huron Indian Village
Within the park, the Huron Indian village (☎ 526-2844) is a replica of what the Native Indian settlements were like until the early 1600s. Things changed not long after this date; in 1639 some French Jesuits arrived on a soul-saving drive. The **Huronia Museum**, adjacent to the village site, has a good collection of Native Indian and pioneer artefacts, as well as some paintings and sketches by members of the Group of Seven painters.

### Sainte Marie among the Hurons
Away from the centre of town, this historic site (☎ 526-7838) reconstructs the 17th-century Jesuit mission and tells the story of a rather dramatic chapter in the book of Native Indian/European clashes. Graphic depictions of missionaries' deaths by torture were forever etched in the brains of countless older Canadians by now-discarded school history texts. Six of the eight martyred missionaries in North America were based at the Sainte Marie mission. **Martyrs' Shrine**, opposite the Sainte Marie complex, is a monument to them and is the site of pilgrimages each year. Even the pope showed up in 1984. Sainte Marie is five km east of the town centre on Hwy 12. All four of the above attractions are open daily from mid-May to mid-October.

### Wye Marsh Wildlife Centre
Right next to the mission site, the centre (☎ 526-7809) provides boardwalks, trails and an observation deck over the marsh and its abundant birdlife. Most notable of the feathered features are the trumpeter swans, once virtually wiped out in the area and now being brought back. The first hatching in the wild as part of this programme took place in the spring of 1993. Displays offer information on the flora & fauna found in the area. Canoe trips through the marsh are also possible (at extra cost) and guided walks are offered free with admission ($6). The site also offers a pleasant picnic area set amid gardens of various indigenous plants. It's open daily and is beside the Sainte Marie historic site.

### Little Lake Park
At the south end of town, south of Yonge St, Little Lake Park is beside a small lake and has a sandy beach and 100-year-old trees – a good place for a picnic.

### Organised Tours
From the town dock, 2½-hour boat cruises depart aboard the *Miss Midland* (☎ 526-0161) for the inside passage to **Georgian Bay** and the islands around **Honey Harbour**. Cruises run from mid-May to the first week of October, with two trips daily during the summer months.

### Getting There & Away
Penetang & Midland Coach Lines, or PMCL (☎ 393-7911 in Toronto), departs from the main bus station in Toronto and serves Midland and Penetanguishene.

## PENETANGUISHENE
Slightly north of Midland, this town (pronounced 'pen-e-TANG-wish-een' but known simply as Penetang) is smaller but similarly historic. It has both a British and French population and past. Early French voyageurs, fur traders, set up around the British military posts, and both communities stayed.

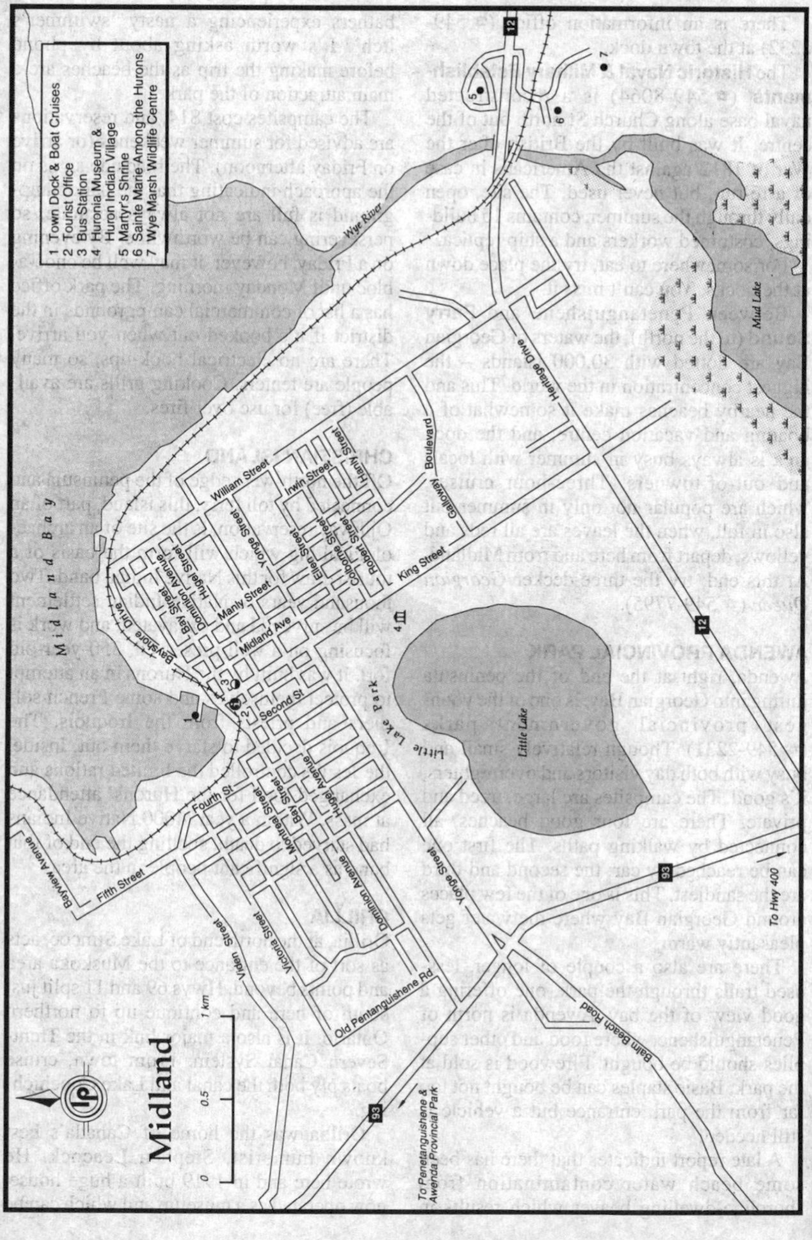

Midland
0
0.5
1 km
1 Town Dock & Boat Cruises
2 Tourist Office
3 Bus Station
4 Huronia Museum & Huron Indian Village
5 Martyr's Shrine
6 Sainte Marie Among the Hurons
7 Wye Marsh Wildlife Centre
Midland Bay
Wye River
Mud Lake
Little Lake
Little Lake Park
Heritage Drive
Galloway Boulevard
King Street
William Street
Irwin Street
Hanly Street
Yonge Street
Ellen Street
Robert Street
Colborne Street
Hugel Street
Dominion Avenue
Bay Street
Bayshore Drive
Manly Street
Midland Ave
Second St
Fourth St
Fifth Street
Bayview Avenue
Montreal Street
Hugel Avenue
Victoria Street
Vinden Street
Old Pentanguishene Rd
Balm Beach Road
To Hwy 400
To Penetanguishene & Awenda Provincial Park
12
93

ONTARIO

There is an information office (☎ 549-2232) at the town dock.

The **Historic Naval & Military Establishments** (☎ 549-8064) is a reconstructed naval base along Church St north out of the centre. It was built by the British after the War of 1812 against the Americans in case of a re-run, but never used. The site, open daily through the summer, contains 15 buildings, costumed workers and a ship replica.

For somewhere to eat, try the place down at the docks. You can't miss it.

Between Penetanguishene and **Parry Sound** (to the north), the waters of Georgian Bay are dotted with 30,000 islands – the highest concentration in the world. This and the nearby beaches make it somewhat of a boating and vacation centre, and the dock area is always busy in summer with locals and out-of-towners. Three-hour cruises, which are popular not only in summer but also in fall, when the leaves are all reds and yellows, depart from here and from Midland. At this end, try the three-decker *Georgian Queen* (☎ 549-7795).

## AWENDA PROVINCIAL PARK

Awenda, right at the end of the peninsula jutting into Georgian Bay, is one of the youngest provincial government parks (☎ 549-2231). Though relatively small and busy with both day visitors and overnighters, it's good. The campsites are large, treed and private. There are four good beaches, all connected by walking paths. The first one can be reached by car; the second and third are the sandiest. This is one of the few places around Georgian Bay where the water gets pleasantly warm.

There are also a couple of longer, less-used trails through the park, one offering a good view of the bay. Awenda is north of Penetanguishene, where food and other supplies should be bought. Firewood is sold at the park. Basic staples can be bought not too far from the park entrance but a vehicle is still needed.

A late report indicates that there has been some beach water contamination from shoreline-dwelling beaver which results in bathers experiencing a nasty 'swimmer's itch'. It's worth asking about by phone before making the trip as the beaches are a main attraction of the park.

The campsites cost $14, and reservations are advised for summer weekends (or arrive on Friday afternoon). The roadside signs on the approach indicating that the park campground is full are not always accurate, so persevering can be worthwhile. By evening on a Friday, however, it may well be choc-a-bloc until Monday morning. The park office has a list of commercial campgrounds in the district if it's booked out when you arrive. There are no electrical hook-ups, so many people are tenters. Cooking grills are available (free) for use over fires.

## CHRISTIAN ISLAND

Off the north-west edge of the peninsula and connected by toll ferry, this island, part of an Ojibway reservation, is the site of an archaeological dig which will form the basis of a tourist draw for this Native Indian band. Two thousand years of Native Indian settlement will be surveyed and excavated, and work is focusing on a well-preserved, 350-year-old fort. It was built by the Hurons in an attempt to protect themselves and some French soldiers and priests from the Iroquois. The Iroquois decided to starve them out. Inside, the Jesuits controlled the limited rations and exchanged food for the Hurons' attendance at mass. Within a year, 4000 Native Indians had starved to death, spelling the end of that band as a significant people in the area.

## ORILLIA

Orillia, at the north end of Lake Simcoe, acts as sort of the entrance to the Muskoka area and points beyond. Hwys 69 and 11 split just south of here and continue up to northern Ontario. It is also a major link in the Trent-Severn Canal System. From town, cruise boats ply both the canal and Lake Couchiching.

Orillia was the home of Canada's best known humorist, Stephen Leacock. He wrote here and in 1919 built a huge house, now operated as a museum and which can be visited all year. His *Sunshine Sketches of a Little Town*, based on Orillia, has been called the most Canadian book ever written.

Perhaps of most interest are the four and eight-day canoe trips of Algonquin Park offered from June to mid-September by the Orillia Home Hostel (☎ (705) 325-0970). All supplies are included, as is transportation to the lakes. The trips are always booked out, so call for details and reservations. The four-day excursion costs $150.

### Places to Stay

For spending the night, there are about a dozen standard motels and inns. The area around the north end of Lake Simcoe also has three provincial parks with camping. All are busy, easy-going, family-oriented places. None of them offers much to do or dramatic scenery but they are the closest places to Toronto. Bass Lake (☎ 326-7054) has a sandy beach, warm waters and a nature trail. There are also boat and canoe rentals, and fishing in the lake.

The HI *Orillia Home Hostel* (☎ (705) 325-0970), at 198 Borland St East, is close to the bus station. There are 20 beds and some family rooms and the hostel is open all year.

### Places to Eat

For drivers heading north and in need of a snack, stop at *Webber's*, a hamburger joint so popular that a pedestrian bridge had to be put up to enable patrons to cross the highway. It's on Hwy 11, south of the Severn River.

### GRAVENHURST, BRACEBRIDGE & HUNTSVILLE

These three towns, discussed from south to north, are the principal centres of the Muskokas. They supply this older, well-established and, in some sections, exclusive cottage country. None of them is especially attractive as a destination in itself but there are a few things of interest.

In Gravenhurst is the **Bethune Memorial House**, in honour of China's favourite Canadian, Dr Norman Bethune, who travelled throughout China in the 1930s as a surgeon

and educator and who died there in a small village. The house details this and other aspects of his career and life. Through the summer, professional theatre is performed at the Muskoka Festival, in the restored Opera House.

A restored 19th-century steamship, the *Segwun* (☎ 687-6667) is based in Gravenhurst and provides touring cruises around some of the more well-known Muskoka Lakes (including Lake Rosseau, with its 'millionaires' row' of summer retreats). The ship is the oldest operating steamship in North America and was used around the area before the days of the automobile. There is an office at Sagamo Park in Gravenhurst, at 820 Bay St.

Other boats tool around Lake Muskoka or Lake Joseph, including one departing from Bracebridge.

Huntsville is a commercial centre and the last major place for supplies for those going into Algonquin Park. It's also the shopping area for those with summer places around the large Lake of Bays.

All of these towns have numerous places to eat and many nearby motels and resorts.

### ALGONQUIN PROVINCIAL PARK

Algonquin is Ontario's largest park and one of Canada's best known. It is also the oldest park in the province, having celebrated its 100th birthday in 1993. About 300 km north of Toronto, it offers hundreds of lakes in approximately 7800 sq km of near wilderness. There are 1600 km of charted canoe routes to explore, many of them interconnected by portage paths. The one road through the park, Hwy 60, runs through the southern edge. Off it are lodges and nine campgrounds, as well as wilderness outfitters who rent canoes and just about everything else. Maps are available at the park.

If you want some peace and quiet and a bit of adventure, I highly recommend this park. Algonquin and the Temagami area represent the two wilderness regions closest to Toronto and southern Ontario and provide a good opportunity to experience what much of Canada is all about. There is a lot of wildlife

ONTARIO

in the park and not bad fishing either. Near the park gate is a logging museum. The park is open every day, all year.

## Information
Located 43 km from the west gate of the park on Hwy 60, overlooking Sunday Creek, is the good, new visitors centre. Various displays and dioramas illustrate the park's wildlife, history and geology. The centre also contains an excellent bookstore, which includes cheap trail-guide brochures. There is also a cafeteria. The centre is open every day from May to October, on weekends only the rest of the year.

On the reverse side of the canoe route maps, available for $3.50, there is camping advice and a lot of good information about the park. (It's handy reading material when you're inside the tent waiting for a storm to pass.)

## Canoeing
Summer weekends are a busy time for canoeing, so a system of admitting only a certain number of people at each canoe route access point has been established. Arrive early, or book at Algonquin Interiors (☎ 705-633-5538, 633-5725), PO Box 219, Whitney, Ontario, K0J 2M0.

At two canoe-route access points off Hwy 60 within the park – Canoe Lake and Opeongo Lake – there are outfitters for renting canoes (about $20 a day) and gear. This is where most people begin a canoe trip into the park interior. To begin an interior trip from any other access point means transporting the canoe to it. (The interior refers to all areas of the park accessible only on foot or by canoe.)

A good trip takes three to four days. I find the western access points – Nos 3, 4 and 5 on the Algonquin map – good, with fewer people, smaller lakes and plenty of moose. The further in you get by portaging, the more solitude you'll find. I've had a whole lake to myself. One of my favourite spots is the campsite on the island in Timberwolf Lake, which is accessible either from the south or

from the west. This is where my mind goes when I'm stuck in city traffic.

Most rental places have ropes and mounting pads to enable renters to carry the canoe on the roof of their vehicle. To be safe, it is a good idea to bring enough of your own rope to secure the canoe. If the small styrofoam pads are unavailable, the life jackets supplied can be used between the canoe and the metal of the car roof.

Different types of canoes are available. The heavy aluminium ones are the cheapest but their weight makes them unsuitable for portaging. They are also noisy and the seats get hot in the sun. For paddling around the main lakes, though, they are fine and virtually indestructible. If you want to get into the interior, where carrying weight becomes an issue, pay the extra to get a kevlar canoe (which weighs in at about 30 kg).

One of several outfitters outside the park boundaries is Rick Ward's (☎ 705-636-5956) in Kearney, north of Huntsville; he rents canoes for just $18 a day, including paddles and life jackets. Another outfitter which has been recommended is Algonquin Outfitters, in the village of Oxtongue, just outside the western edge of the park on Hwy 60.

The park runs its own wilderness canoe trips, which include all equipment – canoe, food, supplies and even sleeping bags – for about $40 per day (less for longer trips). For details call ☎ 633-5622 or visit the outfitting stores mentioned.

Also see under Orillia earlier for the good-value canoe trips organised by the HI Orillia Home Hostel.

## Hiking
There are some interesting hiking trails within the park, ranging from short half-hour jaunts around a marsh to treks of several days' duration. Most of the short trails and lookouts are just off or near Hwy 60 and so can be enjoyed as part of a day trip. Hwy 60 can be taken through the park at no charge, but if you want to stop and take in some of the accessible sites, a day fee of $6 is charged.

## Dog-Sled Trips

Algonquin Canoe Route Ltd (☎ 637-2699) in Whitney three km east of the east side gate of the park along Highway 60 offers dog sled trips in the winter. There are one day and weekend trips or longer excursions of up to a week long with overnight accommodation in rustic cabins. Despite potentially very cold, snowy weather, lack of creature comforts and difficulty in handling both the sleds and the dogs, the trips are fully booked months in advance. Some of the work and preparations must also be done by the guests. This is not a trip for those wishing to be pampered but some advice and training is offered with each outing. Many participants come from outside Canada.

## Places to Stay

Interior camping is $4 per person per night. At the campgrounds, where there are showers and real toilets, a site is $12 or more. Among the highway campgrounds, I would suggest Mew Lake. It has its own warm lake for swimming, some fairly attractive campsites by the far side of the lake away from the highway, some walking trails nearby, and a store within walking distance.

## Getting There & Away

**Bus** For those without vehicles, the park is accessible by bus during the summer months. Take the Ontario Northland (☎ 393-7911) bus from the central Toronto bus station to the town of Huntsville. Transfer in the station there to a Hammond Transportation (☎ 645-5431 in Huntsville) bus into the park along Hwy 60.

## SIX MILE LAKE PARK

Six Mile Lake (☎ 705-728-2900), another of the many provincial parks in the region, is on Hwy 69 just north of Port Severn, about halfway between Orillia and Parry Sound. There is nothing particularly special about this over many of the other parks, but it is in a convenient location right by the highway and so may be prove useful as a one-night stop-over point. There are 192 basic sites but

no showers or electricity. There is swimming in the lake and boat rentals nearby. The park has access to a canoe route.

## GEORGIAN BAY ISLANDS NATIONAL PARK

This park, consisting of some 50 islands in Georgian Bay, has two completely separate sections. The principal segment is not far from Six Mile Lake – take Hwy 400 from Toronto then Hwy 69 to Honey Harbour. Once there, water-taxis can be taken to the islands.

**Beausoleil Island** is the largest island and is the park centre, with campgrounds and an interpretive centre. Several of the other islands have primitive camping facilities, at just $5 a site. The islands are home to the (now quite rare) eastern Massasauga rattlesnake. You may like to know that it is rather small and timid – usually.

Recreation includes swimming, diving, snorkelling and fishing – the bay is great for bass and pike. Boating is also big in the area, what with all the islands and the Trent-Severn Canal system. Many boaters – and they range from those putting along in aluminium 14-footers (four-metre boats) to would-be kings in their floating palaces – tie up for a day or a night at the park islands, so they are fairly busy.

The park is really centred around the boating subculture and is otherwise not particularly interesting. For those seeking some sort of retreat, it is disappointingly busy and rather ostentatiously competitive. The water-taxis are not cheap and, while providing some flexibility in destinations and schedules, still offer only limited access.

For park information, there is an office (☎ 765-2415) in Honey Harbour, near the grocery store. In summer, a relatively inexpensive shuttle service runs over to Beausoleil.

Section two of the park, consisting of a number of smaller islands, is further north up the bay, about halfway to Parry Sound. This section, although quieter, is inaccessible to those without their own vessels.

## PARRY SOUND

Parry Sound sits about midway up Georgian Bay and is the largest of the small district supply towns between southern Georgian Bay and Sudbury. A large, new tourist office sits on the east side of Hwy 69 about 10 minutes' drive south of town. In town, there is a lookout tower with views over the bay.

The town bills itself as the home of Bobby Orr. For the uninitiated, he was a superb hockey defence player who changed that position forever with his offensive prowess. Economics being what they are, he played in Boston, USA.

Boat cruises of the 30,000 islands, on the *Island Queen*, push off from Government Wharf. The trips are about three hours long, departing in the early afternoon, and run from June to September.

The town is also known for its excellent and popular summer classical music festival called the Festival of the Sound. Quality live theatre is presented in July and August.

There are literally dozens of motels and cottages for rent in the area, some quite reasonably priced. The Parry Sound B&B Association (☎ 746-8372) lists such places available in and around town.

## KILLBEAR PROVINCIAL PARK

Lake Huron's Georgian Bay is huge, and grand enough to dwarf most of the world's waters. It's cool, deep, windy and majestic. The deeply indented, irregular shoreline along the eastern side, with its myriad islands, is trimmed by slabs of pink granite barely supporting wind-bent pine trees. This unique setting represents for many central Canadians the quintessential Canada. The works of the country's best known painters, the Group of Seven, have linked this landscape to the Canadian experience.

**Killbear Provincial Park** (☎ 342-5227) is one of the best places to see what it's all about. There is shoreline to explore, three short but good walking trails, numerous little hidden sandy beaches and camping. Of course it's popular; in July and August call ahead to determine camping vacancies. I was there in September, however, and it was less than half-full. Many of the visitors spent the day taking photographs and painting. May and June would also be less busy. The park is highly recommended, even if an afternoon is all you have.

From Parry Sound east to Burk's Falls is more lake and timberland with numerous cottages, both private and commercial. Out of the summer season, things are pretty quiet up here.

# Northern Ontario

Northern Ontario is a vast, thinly populated region of lakes and forest. How large an area it is will quickly become evident if you're motoring over Lake Superior to or from Manitoba.

Commercial activity up here is almost all involved with natural resources – forestry and mining and their spin-offs. Sudbury is one of the world's major mining centres. Way up north beyond Sudbury, on James Bay, is the little town of Moosonee, one of the province's oldest settlements, accessible by wilderness train. The big cities on the Great Lakes, Sault Ste Marie and Thunder Bay, are major ports and shipping centres. Outside the widely spaced towns, much of the land is wild, with clean waters and abundant wildlife. This is one of the best regions for really typically Canadian outdoor activities. Note, though, that summers are short.

## NORTH BAY

North Bay, with a population of a little over 50,000, sits at the eastern end of big Lake Nipissing. At about 350 km north of Toronto, it is the southernmost of the north's major towns.

The Trans Canada Hwy, which connects Sudbury to the west and Ottawa to the east, passes through town. North Bay is also an access point to the many mining towns above it which straddle the Quebec-Ontario border. There is also some fine wilderness in the area, which attracts outdoor enthusiasts, anglers, etc.

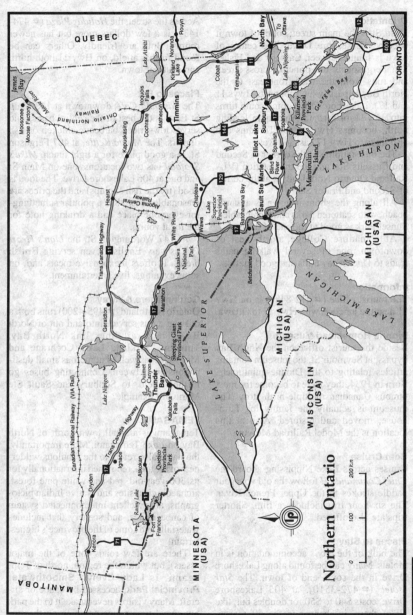

Northern Ontario

QUEBEC

James Bay

Moosonee
Moose Factory

Moose River

Ontario Northland Railway

Iroquois Falls

Kirkland Lake
Rouyn
Noranda

North Bay

To Ottawa

Cobalt
Temagami

Lake Nipissing

TORONTO

400

12

11

11

17

69

Matheson
Cochrane
Timmins

Kapuskasing

Hearst

101

Sudbury

Elliot Lake
Spanish
Blind River

Espanola

Killarney
Provincial
Park

Georgian Bay

6

17

144

Algoma Central Railway

Chapleau

129

Sault Ste Marie

Manitoulin
Island

LAKE HURON

MICHIGAN
(USA)

White River

Wawa

Batchawana Bay

Lake
Superior
Provincial
Park

17

Batchawana Bay

LAKE MICHIGAN

11

Trans Canada Highway

Geraldton

Marathon

Pukaskwa
National
Park

17

LAKE   SUPERIOR

MICHIGAN
(USA)

WISCONSIN
(USA)

Nipigon
Ouimet
Canyon
Provincial
Park

Thunder
Bay

Sleeping Giant
Provincial Park

Lake Nipigon

Kakabeka
Falls

Canadian National Railway  (VIA Rail)

Trans Canada Highway

17

Ignace

Dryden

Quetico
Provincial
Park

Atikokan

11

Rainy Lake

Kenora

Fort
Frances

17

MANITOBA

MINNESOTA
(USA)

0     100     200 km

ONTARIO

## Orientation

Main St is the main street; south of town it becomes Lakeshore Drive. The centre of town is found between Cassells and Fisher Sts. Ferguson is the principal cross-street, and runs from the waterfront east to the North Bay bypass (which connects Hwys 11 and 17). Lakeshore Drive going south turns into Hwy 11 for Toronto. Algonquin, leading north, becomes Hwy 11 for Timmins and also links to Hwy 17 east and west.

The bus station is at the corner of Second and Cassells Sts, and the train station (VIA Rail and Ontario Northland) is at the corner of Second and Fraser Sts.

All along the shore in town is a sandy beach, with scattered parks and picnic tables. Sunset Park is good at the end of the day.

At Canadore College, north-west of downtown, one of several walking paths leads to Duchesnay Falls and good views.

## Information

The tourist office (☎ 472-8480) is on Hwy 11 near the junction with Hwy 17 to Ottawa.

## Dionne Homestead Museum

Beside the tourist office on the North Bay bypass, at Seymour St, the museum contains articles relating to the Dionne quintuplets. Born in 1934, they were to become the most famous Canadian multiple-birth story. The museum is actually the family log farm-house, moved and restored. Also at this location is the Model Railroad Museum.

## Boat Cruise

Cruises across Lake Nippissing aboard the *Chief Commanda II* follow the old voyageur paddle strokes to the Upper French River. The six-hour trip includes a film. Shorter trips are also offered.

## Places to Stay

The bulk of the city's accommodation is in motels. Many can be found along Lakeshore Drive in the south end of town. The *Star Motel* (☎ 472-3510), at 405 Lakeshore Drive, costs $40 to $50 for doubles but, like all of them, is cheaper in the off season.

Across the street, the *Holiday Plaza* (☎ 474-1431) is a few dollars more but has newer rooms. Both are friendly. Others can be found further afield, on Hwy 11 both north and south of town.

## Places to Eat

The *Windmill Café*, downtown at 168 Main St East, is the best of the central basics and serves low-priced barbecue chicken or fish dinners. The *Magic Kettle*, at 407 Ferguson St, is a good place for a light lunch. *Mike's Seafood* has two locations: one on Main St and one at 406 Lakeshore Drive. The food is good (try the fish & chips) and the prices are reasonable. *Casey's* is a popular something-for-everyone place and a drinking hole for the local young.

At 147 Worthington St, the *Lion's Heart Pub* is very English, even serving British brews. It offers inexpensive meals and, on some evenings, live entertainment.

## Getting There & Away

Ontario Northland (☎ 495-4200) runs both a rail and a bus service into and out of North Bay. Their rail lines link North Bay, Timmins, Kirkland Lake, Cochrane and Moosonee, as well as numerous small destinations in between. Connecting buses go further afield, to Sudbury and Sault Ste Marie, for example.

## TEMAGAMI

Temagami is a small town north of North Bay on Lake Temagami. More importantly, the name also refers to the fabulous wilderness of the area, renowned internationally for its 300-year-old, red-and-white pine forest, archaeological sites and Native Indian pictographs, an excellent interconnected system of canoe routes, and scenery that includes waterfalls and some of the province's highest terrain.

There are few roads (one of the major assets), but within the region, north of Temagami, is **Lady Evelyn Smoothwater Provincial Park**, accessed by canoe or aircraft. Many visitors never make it to the park but spend time canoe camping on the sur-

ONTARIO

rounding Crown land. Maps are available, and there's no charge for camping in the region outside the park. The local canoe routes are suitable for all levels of expertise, and some routes begin right in town, on Lake Temagami.

The area is under some threat from logging interests, which are being opposed by local conservation groups as well as by the respected International Union for Conservation, based in Switzerland.

Just two km from the town of Temagami is **Finlayson Provincial Park**, which has a commemorative plaque for English author Grey Owl, who lived with the local Ojibway Indians for several years and then convinced the world, through his writing on nature and its preservation, that he was a Native Indian himself. For more information on him, see under Prince Albert in the Saskatchewan chapter.

The town of Temagami is the park supply centre, where canoes can be rented and trips into the park organised, and where there are motels and restaurants. There is also a local B&B association (☎ 569-3309).

The Shell gas station has a restaurant, good for breakfasts and light meals.

On Lakeshore, along the waterfront, the Welcome Centre is worth a visit for its background information on the area and for the collection of canoes. It's open daily in July and August.

For all your canoeing, fishing or camping needs or for organising trips into the region, visit the centre run by the Wilsons, Smoothwater Wilderness Outfitters (☎ 569-3539). It's a short distance from the town centre, off the main road. Hap Wilson literally wrote the book on the area, and Wilsons can suggest trips based on your skill and the amount of time available to you. They're highly recommended.

Ontario Northland runs trains from Toronto to Temagami almost daily.

## SUDBURY

Sudbury sits on the rocky Precambrian Shield and for over 100 years has been supplying the world with nickel. Inco Ltd, the world's largest nickel producer, is the town's biggest employer and was, until recently, its lifeblood. While still vitally important, Inco and its rival Falconbridge have seen their fortunes decline somewhat with the drop in international demand and price. But Sudbury, for the first time in its history, is diversifying from being a one-industry town. Provincial government decentralisation has meant the relocation to Sudbury of several major departments, such as Energy & Mines, and this has helped push things along in new directions.

The city has long had a reputation for ugliness. The naturally rough, rocky landscape was debased for years by indiscriminate felling of trees and by merciless pollution from the mining and smelting operations. The result was a bleak, moonscape-like setting.

Much to Sudbury's credit, the worst of these characteristics have been (and are continuing to be) reversed. Indeed, the city has earned honours in environmental improvement, and with the development of parks and the creation of Inco's superstack to scatter emissions, the difference from years ago is impossible to miss. Some bleak areas do remain. From up at the Big Nickel park, the views indicate how barren the terrain can be around the mines. The lack of vegetation is mainly due to industrial discharges, but the naturally thin soil covering the rocky Canadian Shield never helped.

Still, most of the town is no longer strikingly desert-like, and in fact Sudbury is surrounded by a vast area of forests, hills and lakes, making it a centre for outdoor and sporting activities. On the east side of town, away from the mining operations, the land is green and wild-looking. There are over a dozen lakes just outside town, including large, attractive Ramsey Lake, at the southeast edge of the city. And Sudbury gets more hours of sunshine than any other industrial city in Ontario.

The downtown core, however, lacks character and there really isn't much to see. Sudbury isn't a place worth making a major effort to get to, but if you're heading across country you'll probably pass through, and there are a few interesting things to see and do around the edges, mostly related to mining. Science North is a significant draw.

The city has a large French population and a Scandinavian community.

Note that in July and August, the Sudbury region tends to be sunny and can be hot. However, it is generally dry and nights can cool off sharply.

### Orientation

The main streets downtown are Elm St (running east-west) and Durham St (going north-south). The core runs along Elm St from Notre Dame Ave to Lorne St.

On Elm St is the City Centre shopping complex and the Holiday Inn. The post office is across the street. The local bus routes start nearby.

Elgin St, running south off Elm St, divides Elm St East from Elm St West; at its southern end is one of the two VIA Rail stations. As you head east on Elm St, at Notre Dame Ave you'll encounter the brown-bulbed Ukrainian church. Further east the street changes names several times. It passes a commercial strip of gas stations, fast-food spots, motels and the bus station, and eventually becomes Hwy 17 to Ottawa.

South of town, Regent St becomes Hwy 69 for Toronto. It also passes through a long commercial district.

Going west, Lorne St leads to Hwy 17, the Trans Canada Hwy. Along the way there are motels, the Big Nickel park, Inco Ltd, smelters and Copper Cliff.

Laurentian University lies on a hill on the far side of Ramsey Lake, south-east from downtown along Ramsey Rd – good views.

### Information

There is a central tourist desk (☎ 675-4346) at 199 Larch St, in the big, grey government complex, Civic Square, on the corner of Paris St. There is also an office upstairs (☎ 688-3035). They are open all year, Monday to Friday, except on holidays.

In addition, Ontario Travel Information has a large, new tourist office on Hwy 69

eight km south of town. The Chamber of Commerce (☎ 673-7133), at 100 Elm St, also has information.

### Science North

Opened in the mid-1980s, this large participatory science centre (☎ 522-3701) at the south-western end of Lake Ramsey has become a major regional attraction. The museum complex is conspicuously housed in two snowflake-shaped buildings built into a rocky outcrop at the lake's edge, beside Alex Baumann Park (named after an Olympic swimmer native to Sudbury). Bell Park runs adjacent to the north, back toward downtown.

Inside, after you enter by tunnel through the 2½-billion-year-old Canadian Shield, is a collection of exhibits and displays on subjects ranging from the universe to insects, communications to fitness, animal life to rocks. Visitors are welcome to get involved with the displays through the many computers, the hi-tech equipment and the helpful, knowledgeable staff, many of whom are from the university.

Some highlights are the white-quartz crystal displayed under a spotlight (looking like a lingam in an Eastern temple), the excellent insect section (how about patting a tarantula?) and lying on a bed of nails. The fitness test is fun but can be humbling. The 3-D film presented in the pitch black cave is also quite remarkable – just reach out and grab that image.

There are major changing exhibits, on topics such as the world's rainforests, and expansion continues. A recent addition is Shooting Star, a film and laser presentation on the formation of the Sudbury Basin. An IMAX theatre is to be added soon.

Also in the complex is an inexpensive cafeteria, a restaurant, and a science and book shop. At the swap shop, you can trade anything natural for anything else from nature's wonders.

From the dock at the centre, boats (☎ 673-7844) depart for one-hour cruises of Lake Ramsey. The dock is part of a boardwalk

# Sudbury

0    0.5    1 km

To Timmins
To Sault Ste Marie
To North Bay
To Toronto
To Sudbury Junction VIA Rail Station
To Airport

Bancroft Drive
Lasalle Boulevard
Barrydowne Road
Falconbridge Highway
Second Ave
Kingsway
Howey Drive
Notre Dame Avenue
Kathleen St
Lasalle Boulevard
Frood Rd
Regent Street
York St
Lorne St
Paris Street
Big Nickel Drive
Elm Street West
Lorne St
Balsam St
Godfrey Dr
Long Lake Rd
Regent Street
Southwest Bypass

Ramsey Lake
Bethel Lake
Lake Laurentian
Nepahwin Lake
Kelly Lake

See Inset

**Inset streets:**
Ste Anne Rd
Notre Dame Ave
Lloyd St
Elm St East
Cedar St
Larch St
Paris St
John St
Elm St West
Brady Street
Durham Street
Douglas St
Lorne St
Regent St
Elgin St
Shaughnessy St
York St
Regent St
Frood Rd
Ramsey Lake

1   New Sudbury Shopping Centre
2   Bus Station
3   Flour Mill Heritage Museum
4   City Centre Shopping Complex
5   President Hotel
6   Post Office
7   Lispar St Terminal (City Buses)
8   Memorial Park
9   Tourist Office & Civic Square
10  Sudbury Theatre Centre
11  Central VIA Rail Station
12  Senator Hotel
13  Laurentian University Museum & Art Centre
14  Inco Smelter
15  Copper Cliff Museum
16  Big Nickel Mine
17  Science North
18  Laurentian University
19  Tourist Office
20  Carol Campground
21  Mine Mill Campground

ONTARIO

which rims the edge of the centre around a portion of the lake.

Admission costs $8 at Science North, $6.50 at the Big Nickel, or you can buy a combined ticket ($12.50) covering both sites. Another ticket also includes a bus tour around town (see Path of Discovery later). For information on all three attractions, call Science North. Opening hours are 9 am to 6 pm daily in summer, till 5 pm in spring and fall; from October to May, they're open from 10 am to 4 pm but are closed on Mondays. Buses run from the centre of town to Science North every day; catch the No 500.

### Big Nickel Mine
Just west of town on Hwy 17 West, up on the hill, the Big Nickel is the symbol of Sudbury. The huge nickel, however, is actually made of stainless steel. You can go down a 20-metre mine shaft, view equipment and see an exhibit of mining science, technology and history. Also in the mine is a vegetable garden and the country's only underground post office. The mine is open every day from mid-May to mid-October and keeps the same hours as Science North. Entry is $6.50, and city bus No 940 will get you there. From up at the Big Nickel, there's a good view of the surrounding area. The nickel can be viewed and photographed without buying a ticket.

### Path of Discovery
Departing from the Big Nickel, this 2½-hour bus tour takes visitors on a geological tour around the city, on the rim of the Sudbury Basin, a 56-km-long, 27-km-wide depression or crater formed two billion years ago. The principal theories for the origin of the basin are volcanic activity or a crashing

meteorite. The trip includes the only public access to Inco Ltd and part of their mining operations just west of town. Visitors get a look at the deepest open-pit mine in the country, as well as the grinding mill, smelter and refinery. Also included is a close-up look at the superstack, the world's tallest smokestack. A ticket costs $11; other ticket options that combine various attractions provide a small saving. Details can be obtained from Science North (see above), which operates all three attractions. The Path of Discovery runs twice a day, at 10 am and 2 pm, through the summer months.

### Copper Cliff Museum
On Balsam St in Copper Cliff, where Inco has its operation, this pioneering log cabin (☎ 674-3141) with period furnishings and tools is open in June, July and August, from 11 am to 4 pm Tuesday to Sunday.

### Flour Mill Heritage Museum
This is a similar place – a pioneer house (☎ 674-2391) with period implements, artefacts and furnishings from the late 1800s. The museum is at 514 Notre Dame Ave and is named after the three flour silos on this street. It is open from 10 am to 4.30 pm Monday to Friday and on Saturday afternoons, from mid-June to September.

### Laurentian University Museum & Art Centre
The centre (☎ 674-3271) exhibits changing art shows, often the work of local artists. There is also a permanent display of articles relating to the region's history. The centre is open all year from Tuesday to Sunday (afternoons only) and is closed on all holidays.

---

### The Sudbury Basin
The town of Sudbury sits on the south rim of a ring of low hills outlining a unique and complex geological structure known as the Nickel Irruptive. The mines located around the outer rim of this boat-shaped crater produce most of the world's nickel, platinum, palladium and related metals, as well as large amounts of copper, gold, tellurium, selenium and sulphur. The inner basin area is roughly 60 km long and 30 km wide. Science North has a show offering possible explanations for its formation (which include a volcano or a giant meteor). ∎

Note that the centre is at the corner of John and Nelson Sts, not at the university campus.

## Slag Pouring

You may hear about the pouring of molten slag or see the impressive-looking postcards taken at night of the orange-coloured mining by-products being dumped, but sad to say, the spectacle no longer exists.

## Bell Park

After all the serious Sudbury sites, perhaps a bit of relaxation is in order, and Bell Park, walkable from downtown, fits the bill. This large green area with sandy beaches offers swimming practically in the centre of town. It runs off Paris St south of downtown. Walk or drive toward Lake Ramsey and turn east on Facer St, beside the hospital. Walking paths follow the shore of the lake south all the way to Science North, and others continue north from the hospital.

## Organised Tours

Free weekday tours are given of the Civic Square (Sudbury's government building), departing from the information desk. There are also tours of Laurentian University (☎ 675-1151), which has a planetarium, an arboretum and sporting facilities, which you can use (for a small fee).

## Festivals

The Northern Lights Festival is a good, successful annual music event which features unknowns and rising stars from around the country. It takes place in early July in Bell Park.

Other concerts and theatre are presented at Bell Park regularly through the summer, at the bandshell. It's on the corner of Paris and York Sts and overlooks Ramsey Lake.

Sudbury, with its rocky, sunny landscape is prime blueberry territory. A walk off the road anywhere in the region will probably turn up a few berries. Celebrating them is the annual Blueberry Festival, held in mid-July. There are lots of outdoor events, and public feedings such as pancake breakfasts.

## Places to Stay

Sudbury was never a city with an abundance of accommodation choices, and the selection has thinned further. Still, there are always the motels, and it's never so busy that finding one is a problem.

**Camping** Sudbury is surrounded by rugged, wooded, lake-filled land. There are quite a few government parks within about 50 km of town. The best bet is *Windy Lake Provincial Park* (☎ 966-2315), 26 km south of town. More commercial and designed for trailers and campers is *Carol Campsite* (☎ 522-5570), just eight km south of town on Hwy 69. Also here is *Mine Mill Campground* (☎ 522-5076), again mainly for campers, but with some tent sites. A little further out (about 90 km) is *Halfway Lake Provincial Park* (☎ 965-2702), on Hwy 144 north-west of town.

**Hostels** There is no longer a hostel in town, although HI does have one on a horse ranch north of town, *Rocky Mountain Horse Ranch* (☎ 897-4931). It's about 16 km (a 15-minute drive) from downtown. This multi-use place offers family-style outdoor activities, with riding, a petting zoo and various nature programmes. It is also the Northern Ontario Animal Hospital, a wildlife refuge centre and hospital tending to injured and abandoned animals.

The alternative is *Laurentian University* (☎ 675-4814), a Backpackers affiliate on Ramsey Lake Rd, which rents rooms from mid-May to mid-August. Features include a cafeteria (which is closed on weekends), vending machines and use of physical education facilities. The only problem is that the university is south-east of the downtown area, around the other side of Ramsey Lake. The views are good, though, and the area is pleasant and quiet. They charge $25/35 for singles/doubles (less for hostellers). The No 500 bus from downtown runs to the university.

The *YWCA* (☎ 673-4754), downtown at 348 Elm St, no longer has rooms for rent. The *YMCA*, at 185 Elm St, has no accommodation facilities either. There's a *Salvation Army Hostel* for men in trouble, on Elm St a few blocks from the corner of Notre Dame Ave.

**B&Bs**  The B&B situation in town has completely dried up, and there are no similar-type guesthouses.

**Hotels**  The bottom-end hotels are pretty minimal as well, with none that can be recommended. Down on Elgin St near the train station, on the strip belonging to the street people, there are a couple of basic cheapies. Surrounded by a lot of gritty urban life are the *Elgin*, at 196 Elgin St, and the *Ledo* (☎ 673-7123), opposite the old train station. The Ledo is reasonably clean and has 25 rooms, starting at $23/27 for singles/doubles. Ask in the bar about the rooms.

Better and acceptable, but not in the star-rated category, the central *President* (☎ 674-7517), at 117 Elm St West, has rooms priced around $60/80. Also central is the similar but better *Senator* (☎ 675-1273). It's on the other side of downtown, at 390 Elgin St.

**Motels**  The bulk of Sudbury's accommodation is in motels found around the edges of town.

Hwy 17 West is called Lorne St near town, and a few km from the centre there is a collection of motels along it. At 965 Lorne St is the *Canadiana* (☎ 674-7585), with a glassed porch and a black-and-white sign. Single and double rooms cost $40 and up. The *Imperial* (☎ 674-6459), at 1111 Lorne St, is a colourfully painted place that serves breakfast. Singles/doubles cost $45 to $60.

The better motels are found south of town on Hwy 69. The *Journey's End* (☎ 522-1101) is here, at 2171 Regent St South, with rooms at $60. The *Brockdan Motor Hotel* (☎ 522-5270) is five km south on Hwy 69. Rooms cost $47 to $57.

There are other motels along Hwy 69, or on Kingsway leading to Hwy 17 East. Along the latter are the *Sorrento* (☎ 566-1132) and

the *Ambassador* (☎ 566-3601), both in the $60 range.

**Places to Eat**
Like the accommodation and bars, many of the eating spots are not in the centre. The Friday or Saturday newspaper lists the weekend restaurant specials and Sunday brunches.

*Frank's*, a deli at 114 Durham St (near Larch St), is good and serves all three meals of the day. The cheap *Friendly*, on ragged Elgin St, serves the basics without elegance or pretension. It's friendly, open long hours and good for breakfast.

For good-value fresh seafood, *Seafoods North* is at 1543 Paris St, in a small shopping plaza. The front of the place is a seafood store; the restaurant, tucked at the back, offers good fish & chips or chowder at lunch and more complete meals at dinner. Unless you state otherwise, the fish is fried, but they will broil it and it comes accompanied by potato, a roll and coleslaw. It's just south of Walford St – too far to walk from downtown.

*Pat & Marios* is away from the centre, on the corner of Lasalle Blvd and Barrydowne Rd, near two big shopping malls. This fairly dressy eating place is popular for Italian and finger foods.

For a bit of a splurge, consider the comfortable *Snowflake Room*, at Science North. It overlooks Lake Ramsey. The menu is varied at lunch or dinner and a Sunday brunch is offered.

Regent St South (Hwy 69 to Toronto) is a commercial strip which has a few restaurants. Among the many offerings are *Marconi's*, at No 1620 (specialising in steaks and Italian fare and with an extensive salad bar) and *Smiley's* (where the pancake breakfast is good value).

At 1893 Lasalle Blvd is *Teklenburg's*, a good seafood house. Watch for the lighthouse.

*Casey's*, at the Cedar Point Plaza south of the town centre on Regent St, is a loud, popular restaurant with a varied menu. It's nothing great but has something to satisfy most people.

## Entertainment

Downtown, the lowbrow *Coulson Hotel*, on the corner of Durham and Larch Sts, draws a mixed crowd for live rock or country music. There is no admission charge and drink prices are good. During the winter months, there is a pub out at the university. *Mingles*, at 762 Notre Dame Ave, has dancing to a disc jockey.

The *Sudbury Star* on Fridays has complete club listings.

## Getting There & Away

**Air** The airport is at the north-east corner of the city. Companies flying here are Air Canada and Canadian Airlines.

**Bus** The Greyhound Bus Depot (☎ 524-9900) is about three km north of the downtown core, at 854 Notre Dame Ave. The station is also a depot for Northland Ontario buses (same phone number), which run north to Timmins and south to Toronto.

There are three eastbound buses a day for North Bay/Ottawa/Montreal, and four a day westbound for Sault Ste Marie/Winnipeg/Vancouver. There are several buses a day southbound for Toronto; ask for the express trip.

One-way fares are Ottawa $64, Sault Ste Marie $36 and Toronto $53.

**Train** There are two VIA Rail stations servicing Sudbury. The original (☎ 673-4771) is conveniently situated at the corner of Minto and Elgin Sts, about 10 minutes' walk from the centre of town. It's in the low, grey building that is mostly black roof.

Unfortunately, there is only one train which uses this station. The Budd car is the local nickname for the one-car train that makes the thrice-weekly trip from Sudbury through northern bush past Chapleau to White River, north of Lake Superior. It's an interesting eight-hour trip through sparsely populated forest and lakeland. For many villages and settlements – some nothing more than a few buildings and the odd tourist lodge – this is the only access. The train stops and starts as people along the way, often

wilderness seekers with their canoes and gear, flag it down. A moose or bear on the track also means an unscheduled stop. There's lots of birdlife, including hill cranes and great blue herons. You might even do a bit of fishing or berry picking if you're stuck waiting for a freight train to pass. The train doesn't make money, so there's regular talk of cancelling it.

The other trains, such as those for Toronto or westbound, use a less central station known as Sudbury Junction (☎ 524-1591), which is about 10 km from the old downtown station. It is on Lasalle Blvd past Falconbridge Hwy, in the north-east section of town. There is no city bus to the station.

There are three trips a week to Toronto: on Tuesday, Thursday and Sunday. The fare is $59 one way.

Going north and west, the route now heads straight up through basic wilderness to Geraldton, on to Sioux Lookout and eventually across the border to Winnipeg in Manitoba.

No direct route runs to Ottawa, so you must go via Toronto.

**Car** Renting a car may be useful in Sudbury. Tilden (☎ 560-1000) has the best rates and will pick you up. The address is 1150 Kingsway. Hertz (☎ 566-8110) is at 450 Second Ave North.

**Hitching** Hwy 17, which becomes Kingsway in town, goes east to Ottawa. Regent St runs south from town into Hwy 69 south to Toronto. If westbound, head out along Lorne St, which eventually becomes Hwy 17 West.

## Getting Around

**Bus** For transit information call ☎ 675-3333. The city buses collect on Lisgar St beside the post office, between Elm and Larch Sts, and this is a major transfer point. Outside the Eaton's store on Notre Dame Ave is the stop for regional buses to some of the surrounding small towns. Route 940 goes to the Copper Cliff Mine smelter site and the

Big Nickel site, at quarter to and quarter past each hour.

## AROUND SUDBURY

The area around and north of Sudbury is both one of the richest mining districts in the world and a destination for those seeking outdoor adventure and recreation. The fishing, camping and other activities attract visitors from the populated southern regions and the USA.

Some of the mines and smelters are open to the public, although the number of companies offering such tours seems to be decreasing. Ask at the tourist office for the *Mine Guide* of the area. For sportspeople, there are endless lodges, camps and guide services – usually fairly costly, especially the fly-in trips.

### French River

South of Sudbury, the French River is famous for its fishing. There is also white-water canoeing. One group which organises such trips here and elsewhere is Voyageur Canoeing (☎ 705-932-2131) in Millbrook, Ontario. There is also white-water rafting on the **Spanish River** near the town of Espanola.

### Killarney Provincial Park

Killarney (☎ 287-2368) is one of the provinces's most impressive parks, and a visit is highly recommended, even if only for a day's paddle. Members of Canada's Group of Seven artists worked in the park, and a provincial artists' association was instrumental in its establishment.

Because the lakes are relatively small, the maximum number of overnight campers is low. The park's beauty is outstanding, so it's popular and often full. Try to go midweek, and make reservations, including booking a canoe, before arriving – call as far in advance as you can. Getting in on holiday weekends is nearly impossible.

The park is a uniquely mountainous forested area about 80 km south-west of Sudbury, on the shores of Georgian Bay. It's one of Ontario's three wilderness parks and has few conveniences. Access around the park is by canoeing, hiking or skiing. There is excellent scenery, with birch and pine forest edged by the **La Cloche Mountains.** Some lakes are lined on one side by white quartz mountains and on the other side by more typical reddish granite.

The lakes themselves offer astoundingly clear water with remarkable visibility, but unfortunately this is in part due to acid rain. Indeed, some of the lakes are essentially dead, devoid of life.

Portaging from lake to lake is relatively easy, as the trails tend to be short, at least for the first few, most visited lakes. Two lakes could be explored from the dock at **Lake George**, making a fine day's outing for those without camping gear.

There is a campground at the park headquarters, on Lake George, and another at the village of **Killarney**, but to see more of the park, venture to the interior via portions of the 75 km worth of portages. There are places for pitching a tent at most of the interior lakes. Outfitters can be found at Killarney village and along the road between the park entrance and Killarney.

Also in Killarney village is a small, rustic but comfortable and reasonably priced lodge, the *Sportsman's Inn* (☎ 287-2411), with rooms from $45. Excellent fresh fish & chips can be had down at the dock area.

### Halfway Lake Provincial Park

This is one of the many small, relatively developed parks with camping that surround Sudbury (☎ 965-2702). Within this park are various hiking trails of four, 10 and 34 km in length, as well as several scenic lookouts. The park is about 90 km north-west of Sudbury on Hwy 144.

### Gogama

Continuing north up Hwy 144 about two-thirds of the way to Timmins, you reach the Arctic watershed, at Gogama, from where all rivers flow north to the Arctic Ocean. Did you notice it was getting a bit cool?

573 Ontario – Northern Ontario 573

## TIMMINS

Way up here in northern Ontario is Timmins, the largest city in Canada – in area that is. This notwithstanding, it's a small (population about 50,000) and particularly neat northern town. Originally the centre of the most productive gold-mining area in the western hemisphere, Timmins still acts in the same capacity, but the local mines now work copper, zinc, silver, iron ore and talc as well as gold. Kidd Creek Mines is the world's largest producer of silver and zinc and the main employer in town. One mine, now closed, was the country's deepest, going down nearly 2½ km! There are still over 2000 km of underground workings in the area.

Forestry products are also important in this rough, rugged, cold region of primary industry. There are hundreds of lakes within the designated city limits, as well as 45 registered trap lines – not a bad idea for New York City.

Sports are popular (winter sports, as there isn't really much of a summer), and the local arena has cranked out a number of top-rate figure skaters and hockey players. Also popular is drinking: a resident told me that this is because there is really little else to do. The combination of sports and hard drinking is a characteristic common to many northern towns.

The first White people to settle this area were East Europeans from Poland, Croatia and the Ukraine, and many of their progeny are still here. To them must be added numbers of Italians, Finns and Scots, all of whom came with the lure of gold in the 1920s.

As in much of north-eastern Ontario, there is a large French population in and around town, and Native Indians, the original inhabitants, are a significant ethnic group.

A multicultural festival is held in June.

### Orientation

Timmins is actually made up of a number of small communities, the more important of which, strung together running from west to east over a distance of about 10 km, are Timmins proper, Schumacher, South Porcupine and Porcupine.

Hwy 101 passes through the centre of town (where it is known as Algonquin Blvd) on its way west to Lake Superior and east to Quebec. In town, the main streets are Third St (which runs parallel to the highway), Pine St and Cedar St. The central core is marked by the brick streets and old-style lampposts.

### Information

The Chamber of Commerce (☎ 360-1900), east of town, on the main road in Schumacher, acts as the tourist office. In addition to the usual local information, it has details on numerous industrial tours of the Porcupine-Timmins area and sells the tickets for them. The address is 916 Algonquin Blvd East. Also ask whether the Ukrainian Museum has reopened. It had a good collection of artefacts relating to this important cultural group, many of whose members helped develop northern Ontario.

### Timmins Museum

In South Porcupine, at 70 Legion Drive (near Algonquin Blvd East), this small but good museum (☎ 235-5066) doubles as an art gallery and exhibition centre, presenting changing exhibits ranging from paintings to masks to performances, and more. In the museum section, see the prospector's cabin, which gives an idea of the life these people led. The history of the area is outlined. There is some old mining equipment outside on the grounds, too. The museum is open every day (in the afternoons on the weekend). It also closes at noon during the week for one hour. Admission is free.

### Other Sights

The disused **Daily Press building** in Timmins, now with a heritage designation, is worth a look and is considered one of the country's best examples of Moderne architecture, a variation on Art Deco.

**Deadman's Point**, on Porcupine Lake in South Porcupine, has the atmospheric cemetery where many of the town's people were buried after the great fire of 1911. There are good views over the lake.

The old storefronts of Schumacher, on First Ave between Pine St and Hollinger Lane, are being restored to the 1920s and 1930s period. This strip once had more bars per capita than anywhere else in the country.

## Organised Tours

**Gold Mine Tour** The tour of the old Hollinger gold mine (☎ 268-9211) is the city's prime attraction. The mine was discovered in 1909 and was at one time the biggest producer in the western hemisphere – hundreds of millions of dollars worth of gold was dug out of here. Tours began at the mine in 1990. The site has now been developed into a varied complex, with stores, a craft outlet, jewellery sales and a restaurant. The highlight remains the underground mine tour, which takes visitors down 50 metres in full mining gear and includes a rail ride and a simulated dynamite blast.

There are also some surface attractions worth seeing. Hollinger House is a relocated original worker's house; the company built these in numbers for the miners and their families. There are still a few in Timmins, a few blocks north of the highway. This one, though, holds artefacts and memorabilia of past eras. Large families were raised in these none-too-snug dwellings. There is also an open-pit mine to see, and some trails past rocky outcrops from which minerals could be extracted. You can even try panning for gold.

All in all it's an interesting site, but tickets are not cheap; indeed, for many they may be prohibitively costly. Tickets for the full tour cost $16, though there is a lower family rate. The full tour lasts about 1½ hours and includes both underground and surface portions. Tickets can be purchased for the above-ground attractions separately, at a rate of $6.

From May to October, tours run seven days a week and there are five a day. Tickets must be bought ahead of time at the Chamber of Commerce. Pants and flat shoes are essential, and take a warm sweater; other equipment is supplied. The mine is between Timmins and Schumacher on James Reid Rd, which is off the 'back road' from Timmins to South Porcupine.

**Kidd Creek Metallurgical Site & Buffalo Tour** Kidd Creek Mine runs tours of their concentrator (sometimes I wish there were home-use models) and zinc smelter. It's a walking tour which shows how the valuable minerals – zinc, silver, lead and cadmium – are separated from the waste and then how the zinc is processed into shippable ingots. The same dress regulations apply as at the gold-mine tour.

The tour, which lasts 2½ hours and costs $3, is only offered on Wednesdays and Fridays through July and August. Get information and tickets through the Chamber of Commerce. The site is 26 km east of the centre of Timmins on Hwy 101.

Also at the Kidd Site, the employees keep a herd of bison, which can often be seen from the road.

**McChesney Lumber Tour** A third industrial-site tour is the trip through the now fully automated sawmill by the Mattagami River, where it has been since the turn of the century. Follow the processing of a log to the cut lumber that consumers get at the store. The sawmill is central, just off Algonquin Blvd. Tickets here are also $3 and the tour is about one hour long. Reservations and tickets are through the Chamber of Commerce, who coordinate all the company tours.

On all the tours described, very young children are not permitted.

**Pulp Mill Tour** Tours are offered three times daily from Monday to Friday at the Abitibi-Price Pulp & Paper Mill in Iroquois Falls, north-east of Timmins. The mill is a major newsprint producer.

## Places to Stay

East of town 35 km and then north three km is the recommended *Kettle Lakes Provincial Park* (☎ 363-3511), good for camping but also recommended for a day trip to see the 20 or so small, round, glacial kettle lakes. You need a car to get here.

Accommodation in Timmins is limited but includes several motels on each side of town. The *Matagami Motor Hotel*, on the west side, is OK. It charges $45 for doubles, and there's a restaurant and a bar featuring adult entertainment. On the east side of town, in South Porcupine, the *Regal* (☎ 235-3393) is better and the same price but is further from central Timmins.

In town are a couple of basic hotels and the good *Venture Inn* (☎ 268-7171), at 730 Algonquin Blvd East, where a double sets you back $65.

### Places to Eat

There are plenty of places along the highway between towns and several around the central streets of Timmins.

*Bentley's*, at 36 Wilson Ave, is recommended for the soup-and-sandwich lunches.

In Schumacher, the *McIntyre Community Centre* (☎ 360-1758) also known as the arena, serves a good breakfast. Later, sandwiches and various East European dishes are offered. The homemade pies and butter tarts are noteworthy.

At the Italian *Porcupine Dante Club* (☎ 264-3185), 172 Cedar St South, you can get a satisfying, inexpensive Italian lunch or dinner – call to check the hours.

*Casey's*, east of town, is a popular chain restaurant and place to have a beer, mainly catering to the young.

For a more expensive dinner out, try the *Airport Hotel*, an historic lodge out by Porcupine Lake in South Porcupine. Out the window you can see the runway – the lake. At one time this was a busy float-plane landing strip, hence the hotel name, and the bush pilots ate and slept at the lodge. A speciality is the fresh pickerel (walleye). There is still a flying school next to the lodge, so you may well see some landings and take-offs. Also, if you wander over, there are pilots who will, for a price, take visitors for a spin around in their planes. Try to get back in time for dessert.

### Getting There & Away

**Bus** The train and bus stations (☎ 264-1377) are in the same building, at 1 Spruce Ave, not far from Algonquin Blvd. Ontario Northland has a daily bus service from Toronto. Sudbury and other northern points are connected to Timmins by bus. During the summer, a bus runs from Timmins to Cochrane for the Polar Bear Express.

**Train** There is no train service into Timmins itself, although Ontario Northland does get as close as the town of Matheson. From there a bus makes the one-hour trip into Timmins. A ticket on the train from, say, Toronto includes the bus transfer.

### THE POLAR BEAR EXPRESS

The *Polar Bear Express* is the best known line of the small Ontario Northland Railway service (☎ 1-800-268-9281, or 272-4428 in Cochrane). The *Polar Bear* heads north from Cochrane through northern wilderness to Moosonee, the oldest permanent settlement in the province, on the edge of James Bay (part of vast Hudson Bay). Three hundred years ago, this was the site of an important fur-trading centre.

Those taking the train have two choices. There is a one-day return trip or a slower two-day trip. The express runs primarily for tourists or those in a hurry. It leaves early in the morning and returns late the same day, taking 4½ hours each way and allowing for a look around Moosonee and Moose Factory. The slower local train, the *Little Bear*, caters to an odd mix of tourists, Native Indians, trappers and geologists.

The fare on both trains is $44 return, with reservations required. There are family, child and senior discounts. Trips can be booked from Ontario Northland Railway in Toronto, North Bay, Timmins or Cochrane. In Toronto, there is an information office in Union Station, the main train station, found on Front St.

Ontario Northland Railway also offers three and four-day all-inclusive tours (excluding most meals) out of North Bay and Toronto.

The *Polar Bear Express* runs daily (except Fridays) from 21 June to 1 September. The *Little Bear* operates beyond these dates but does not run every day. Simple lunches and snacks can be bought on the train but you're better off taking your own food for the trip. If you've driven to Cochrane, there is free parking beside the train station.

Visitors should know that despite the train's name, there are no polar bears in the region.

### Cochrane

Little Cochrane (population under 5000), roughly 100 km north of Timmins, is the departure point for the *Polar Bear Express*. The large polar bear statue at the entrance to Cochrane symbolises the importance of the train to the town.

Also in town is the **Railway & Pioneer Museum**, with some early railway, Native Indian and pioneer exhibits.

**Places to Stay** Cochrane has several motels and a provincial park campground to service the passengers. Drury Park, for camping, is close to the train station. Note that the half-dozen motels tend to fill up in midsummer, so arriving early in the day or calling ahead is not a bad idea. The *Northern Lites Motel* (☎ 272-4281), at $56 a double, has a handy restaurant on the premises. Another place to try is the slightly lower-priced *Country Haven B&B* (☎ 272-6802), on a huge property about 23 km from the train station. The morning meal is included.

**Getting There & Away** From Cochrane, Ontario Northland Railway connects south with Timmins (via Matheson and a bus ride), North Bay and other regional towns. There are also buses between these points. The Ontario Northland train runs between Toronto and Cochrane.

### Moosonee

Moosonee, which sits near the tundra line, is as far north as most people ever get in eastern Canada. There are no roads. Once there, see the historic sites and the museums and, best of all, get out on the water on one of the boat-tour options.

Ontario Northland can supply information on things to do and places to stay in Moosonee.

**Moose Factory Island**, out in Moose River, is the actual site of a Hudson's Bay Company trading post founded in 1672. It's two km and 15 minutes from town by boat. Moose Factory itself is a community of about 1500 people, mainly Cree, at the far end of the island. Things to see include some buildings at the historic site, a cemetery, an Anglican church dating from 1860 (with moosehide altar cloths and Cree prayer books) and one of the museums.

An inexpensive large 'freighter' canoe takes visitors to the island. More costly and extensive tours are available which include the trip to the island, a bus tour around it and other optional side trips (for example, to Ship Sands Island Bird Sanctuary, down the Moose River or out to James Bay).

On **Tidewater Island**, between the mainland and Moose Factory, is a provincial park. Trips here can be arranged and camping is possible.

Boat trips or the freighter canoes (for $17) also take people upstream to **Fossil Island**. Fossils over 300 million years old can be found.

Back in Moosonee, the other museum, **Revillon Frères Museum**, documents the Hudson's Bay Company's rival, the North West Company, which was based in Montreal. The James Bay Educational Centre has some crafts done by local Cree Indians.

Another attraction is the sometimes visible Aurora Borealis, also known as the northern lights.

**Places to Stay** If you're staying overnight in Moosonee, which is likely if you take the overnight train, there are a handful of places to stay, but they are not cheap.

Rooms at the *Polar Bear Lodge* (☎ 705-336-2345) or *Moosonee Lodge* (☎ 705-336-2351) go for $60/78 a single/double.

Reservations are pretty well a necessity wherever you stay.

## NORTHERN ROUTE

Hwy 11 runs west from Cochrane, eventually connecting with Thunder Bay. The province's most northerly major road, it cuts across rough, scrubby forest through several mining towns. There are campgrounds along the way.

The principal town along the route is **Kapuskasing**, with its circular downtown centre. In town, a river tour-boat runs upstream to **Beaver Falls** providing historical and geological commentary and allowing for glimpses of local wildlife like beaver and muskrat.

Hearst, as noted in the Sault Ste Marie section, is the northern terminal of the Algoma Central Railway.

## WEST OF SUDBURY

From Sudbury, Hwy 17 (the Trans Canada Hwy) runs 300 km along the north shore of Lake Huron. Driving straight through, the trip takes slightly under four hours. There are a few things to see along the way if you wish to dawdle, and several smaller highways lead to more northern points. South of Espanola, Hwy 6 leads across Lake Huron's North Channel to Manitoulin Island.

### Espanola

Espanola is the largest centre between Sudbury and Sault Ste Marie, and how it got its name is an interesting tale.

In about 1750, the Ojibway Indians of the district went on a raid down south, in what is now the USA but which at the time was under Spanish control. They brought back a captive woman, who later taught her children Spanish. When the French explorers arrived on the scene, I guess they were a little surprised to hear familiar Spanish being spoken. They called the settlement Espanole, which was subsequently anglicised to its present form.

Espanola is a pulp and paper town (E B Eddy, one of Canada's biggies, has a mill here) and acts as a gateway for the Manitoulin Island ferry. The island can be reached by road on this side but connects with southern Ontario by ferry (see Tobermory earlier).

In July and August, E B Eddy Forest Products Ltd (☎ 1-800-663-6342) offers three different tours of their operations. Call for details and reservations or visit their information centre in Espanola. One trip lasts all day (eight hours) out in the bush, learning how the forest is managed. Good walking shoes are required.

Each of the other two tours is three hours in duration. One is through the pulp mill to see the paper-making process; the other is through a sawmill – the biggest this side of the Rocky Mountains. These last two tours are not open to kids under the age of 12 and safety gear (supplied) must be worn. Not every tour is offered every day, so be sure to check the schedule. All the tours are offered free.

White-water rafting is offered on the Spanish River. In town are a couple of standard motels and a few places to grab a bite.

### Deer Trail

The Deer Trail refers to a driving route north from the highway at Serpent Lake through Elliot Lake, around a little-developed region along the Little White River and back south to Hwy 17 at Ironbridge.

Mississagi Provincial Park is about a third of the way around from Serpent Lake. At the park and at Flack Lake there are nature trails, the latter with good examples of fossils and a feature known as ripple rock. There are other areas of geological interest along the way, such as the tillite outcrops formed $1\frac{1}{2}$ million years ago and now found four km north of the Elliot Lake Uranium symbol.

Ask at the Blind River tourist office for information on other sites on the trail. There are over a dozen canoe routes in the district.

### Elliot Lake

North of the Trans Canada Hwy, Elliot Lake is a mining town based mainly on uranium. It's a relatively new town, having been founded in 1954 when the ore was discovered.

With the tough times the local mining industry has been suffering, Elliot Lake has been promoting itself as a fine retirement centre with a quiet, easy pace and especially low costs.

The **Mining & Nuclear Museum** (☎ 848-2287) features displays on the mining and applications of uranium but also has some area historical exhibits and a section on the wildlife of the region. The museum is open every day from 1 June to 1 September, on weekdays only the rest of the year.

Good views over the North Channel can be had from the Firetower Lookout, north of town five km up the Milliken Mine access road.

### Blind River

Blind River, sitting almost exactly halfway between Sudbury and Sault Ste Marie, is a good place to stop for a break. Though small, it's a neat and clean little town with a few good places to find a meal. On the east side of town is a large, helpful tourist office (☎ 356-2555), with information on the entire region as well as on Blind River.

Beside the information building is the **Timber Village Museum**, outlining the history of logging in the area. There are also some interesting items from the Mississagi people, the original Native Indian inhabitants.

The veneer mill south of town offers tours, and Huron Beach, 13 km from Blind River, is a nice, sandy spot for a swim.

A roving event to watch for (the location changes each year) is the annual **North Channel Fiddle Jamboree**, held in July.

**Places to Stay & Eat** Camping is available near town; ask at the information office. Blind River also has five motels, and it's not likely they'd all be full up unless Madonna and Tom Cruise both came to visit.

For food, *JR's* chip stand, beside the highway, has good burgers and fries, but there are several sit-down restaurants to choose from as well.

### Tallest Tree

North up Hwy 129 toward Chapleau is Kirkwood Forest, where the tallest tree in Ontario is said to grow.

### SAULT STE MARIE

'The Soo', as the city is called, sits strategically where Lake Huron and Lake Superior meet. Once a fur-trading outpost, the Soo is now an industrial town important as a shipping centre, for here, on St Mary's River, is a series of locks which enables ships to navigate the seaway system further west into vast Lake Superior.

Aside from the busy canal, the steel, pulp and paper, and lumber mills are major employers. The huge Algoma Steel mill, long one of the city's mainstays, has had to scale back considerably due to lost markets. Diversification has been assisted by the relocation of some provincial government offices from Toronto to the Soo.

The International Bridge connects the city with its twin in Michigan, USA. Going west to Winnipeg is slightly shorter via Michigan and Duluth than over the lake but is not as impressive.

With the bridge and the Trans Canada Hwy, the Soo is a convenient stopover and acts as a tourist supply centre. I find it the most appealing of the northern cities, and there are some fine outdoor possibilities within range to complement it. With a population of around 85,000, it's the last big town until Thunder Bay to the west. Sudbury is 300 km to the east, a drive of between three and four hours.

### Orientation

The approach to Sault Ste Marie from the east or west is a long row of eateries, gas stations and motels. Hwy 17 North becomes the Great Northern Rd and then Pim St in town. Hwy 17 East becomes Wellington St, which is the northern edge of the downtown core. If you're passing through, use the bypass to avoid traffic hassles.

For visitors this is a dream town in terms of convenience. The downtown area is quite small and pleasant, with pretty much every-

**Sault Ste Marie**

0    250    500 m

To Airport

Second Line West
Second Line East

550

To Trans Canada
Highway

Northern Avenue

Wellington St West
Conmee Ave
Saint George's Avenue
McNabb Street

Korah Road
Wellington St West
John Street
North Street
Martin St
Great Northern Road

Cathcart Street
Albert St West
Queen St West

Pim Street

Huron St
Canal Dr
Bay Street
Queen St East
Bruce Street
Albert St East
East Street

North Saint
Mary's Island

St Mary's River Dr
Boardwalk

Canal Dr

South Saint
Mary's Island

International Bridge

Whitefish Island

Wellington St East

Foster Dr
Bay Street

Queen St East

Government Dock

1 Tourist Office
2 St Mary's Paper Mill
3 Municipal Fish Hatchery
4 Lock Viewing & Canals
5 Bus Terminal
6 ACR Station (Tour Trains)
7 Station Shopping Mall
8 Holiday Inn
9 Boat Tours & Norgoma Museum
10 Sault Ste Marie Museum
11 Art Gallery
12 Bush Plane Museum
13 Old Stone House
14 Algonquin Hotel

thing of interest either on or near the long, upgraded Queen St. South from Queen St is the waterfront area, which has also undergone a fair bit of renovation in the past few years. This process continues, and the slow, thoughtful approach taken by the city is paying dividends in creating a central core popular with residents and visitors alike.

Many of the city's attractions, the bus station, the Station Mall (a large shopping centre) and several hotels are here, within walking distance of each other. Also in this general vicinity is the main tourist office.

A couple of buildings of particular note in town are the imposing courthouse in the middle of Queen St and the Precious Blood Cathedral, constructed of local red-grey limestone in 1875 and originally a Jesuit missionary. Queenstown refers to the renovated downtown core.

**Information**
There is a huge, modern tourist information centre, Ontario Travel Information (☎ 949-7912) in town, on the corner of Huron St and Queen St West, just near the International Bridge leading to the USA. Here you can get

maps, guides and advice and can change money. The office is open daily in summer.

The Chamber of Commerce (☎ 949-7152), at 360 Great Northern Rd (Hwy 17 North, near the large, white mushroom-like water tower), also has an information desk. It is, however, closed on the weekend. They also operate a couple of seasonal information booths. One is central, in the Bay St Caboose next to the Algoma Central Railway (ACR) station; the other is on Trunk Rd, beside a McDonald's restaurant.

### Locks & Canals

If Sudbury is rock city, the Soo is lock city. At the south-west corner of downtown, at the bottom of Huron St (by the International Bridge), are the locks linking Lake Superior to Lake Huron. Joining the two great lakes is the narrow St Mary's River, with its rapids. It is here that in 1895 the locks were built, enabling lake freighters to make the journey hundreds of extra km inland.

Lake Superior is about seven metres higher than Lake Huron. The often continuous lake traffic (about 80 freighters a day pass through in summer) can be watched from a viewing stand or from anywhere along the locks for no charge. There are four US locks, and one Canadian lock, found in the narrow channel between North St Mary's Island and South St Mary's Island. This Canadian lock is the oldest canal and lock system, built in 1895, and is now used only by small pleasure craft. In 1993, it was closed for maintenance work and a completion date was unavailable.

A visitors centre on North St Mary's Island, open daily in summer, provides more details and information. The Canadian Coast Guard is also here.

Walk over the locks to South St Mary's Island, on which there is a circular walking trail. The paths, winding through the woods and under the International Bridge, make a nice retreat, with views of the shorelines, rapids and ships. It's a good picnicking spot. Further south, out in the river a stone's throw but inaccessible without a boat, **Whitefish Island** has been designated a National His-

toric Site. For 2000 years the Ojibway Indians fished these plentiful waters. Fishing is still popular, and anglers can be seen all along the canal and around the islands.

Boat tours (☎ 253-9850) of the locks depart from the dock beside the Civic Centre, off Foster Drive, which is parallel to and south of Bay St in the centre of town. Two boats operate several times daily from June to October. The two-hour cruise, which includes passing through the Canadian lock, costs $14.50 for adults and for my money doesn't offer anything you can't see from shore. Still, being out on the water on a fine day can't be knocked. Longer dinner cruises are also offered.

### Sea Lamprey Control Centre

Down at the locks is this small research centre where you can view some lamprey and the fish they victimise and learn more about these giant leeches. It's open from Monday to Friday, in summer only, and is worth a look. At night when it's closed, you can still peek into the lighted building and the tanks, though there really isn't much to see.

### Municipal Fish Hatchery

Also down near the locks, follow Huron St south towards the canal; on the left, on Canal Drive, is the hatchery (☎ 759-5446). The hatchery raises chinook salmon, rainbow trout and brown trout and releases them into the river and surrounding waters to develop and maintain major sport fishing in the district. And it seems to be working. The region is getting a good reputation and sizeable fish are being taken right off the boardwalk in town.

Free tours of the facility are offered from 10 am to 4 pm, daily from June to Labour Day and on weekdays only the rest of the year. The 20-minute tour around the various tanks and the fish at different stages of growth is quite interesting, but take a sweater with you – it's kept cold in there!

### The Boardwalk

A boardwalk runs alongside the river off Bay St, behind the Station Shopping Mall, affording good views of the river and across to the USA. As well, there are places to fish and a number of city attractions to be found on or near the river. Near the Holiday Inn, the white tent-like structure is for concerts and various events. Further east, towards the edge of the downtown core, is the Art Gallery of Algoma (worth a visit) and the public library. Along the boardwalk, see the plaque on Anna Jameson (1794-1860).

In 1836, this woman from Ireland left Toronto, where she lived with Robert Jameson, the Attorney General. She took off unescorted to the Detroit area. From there she reached the Soo by boat, descended the rapids and attended a Native Indian assembly on Manitoulin Island. Through Georgian Bay and south to Lake Simcoe, she travelled back to Toronto and later home to Britain, where she published an account of the trip entitled *Winter Studies and Summer Rambles in Canada*. I'd say!

### MS Norgama

This ship, now a museum (☎ 942-6984), was the last one built for overnight passenger use on the Great Lakes. It's open daily from mid-June until the beginning of September. The *Norgama* is moored at the Norgama Marine Park dock beside the Holiday Inn, near the foot of Elgin St.

### St Mary's Paper Mill

The large paper mill (☎ 942-6070) on Huron St, at the south-western edge of downtown, offers free walking tours on Tuesday and Thursday afternoons. Register at the security gate.

### Sault Ste Marie Museum

Housed in an Ontario heritage building at 690 Queen St East, on the corner of East St, this small, but well-put-together museum (☎ 759-7248) has various displays representing the Native Canadians, exploration, fur trading, lumbering, geology and other aspects of the area. Another section, on the Inuit, is good. In the turn-of-the-century exhibits, the cigarettes recommended for asthma relief are a lark. The museum is open from 9 am to 4.30 pm Monday to Saturday

and on Sunday afternoons. Admission is by donation ($2 is suggested).

### Historical Museum

This museum (☎ 256-2566) has a small collection of artefacts and curios from the city's past. It's on the 2nd floor of the Pine St Armoury, on the corner of Macdonald Ave and Pine St. The museum is closed on Sundays, Mondays and holidays. Admission is free.

### Bellevue Park

On the water two km east of town along Queen St, near the university, this is the city's largest park. There is a small zoo, picnic areas, sports fields and a marina.

### Old Stone House

Also known as Ermatinger House (☎ 759-5443), this was built in 1814 by a British fur trader and his Ojibway wife. It's the oldest stone house west of Toronto and was where many explorers, including Simon Fraser and Alexander Mackenzie, put up for the night. Inside, the house has been restored and contains furnishings from the 1800s. Someone there will answer questions. It's open every day in summer, from Monday to Friday during other seasons, and admission is free. The museum is at 831 Queen St East, near the corner of Pim St.

### Bush Plane Museum & Forest Fire Education Centre

This two-in-one museum (☎ 945-6242) is in an old government hangar by the waterfront, at the corner of Bay and Pim Sts. The history of bush flying in Canada, a great story in itself, is tied closely to its role in forest-fire fighting. Many of the early small-plane pilots in the country were returning from the air force at the end of WW I. They also served in aerial mapping, surveying, medical assistance and rescuing. The museum has full-size planes on display, as well as some replicas, engines and parts. There are also maps, photographs and a tent set up as it would be in the bush.

The centre is open daily from May to

October, on weekends only the rest of the year. Admission is free and tours are offered.

## Ontario Forest Research Institute

The research centre (☎ 946-2981), at 1235 Queen St East, runs free tours at 10.30 am and 2 pm Monday to Friday. The work here, and therefore the tour, is mostly about forest pests. There is also an audiovisual presentation.

## Forest Ecology Trail

Also operated by the government forestry service is this 2½-km, self-guided nature trail out of the town centre off Hwy 565. There is an attendant to answer questions. Ask at the Ontario Forest Research Institute for details and directions.

## Kinsmen-Crystal Creek Conservation Area

Known locally as Hiawatha Park, this is about a 10-minute drive from Great Northern Rd, north-west of downtown Sault Ste Marie. Stop at the big Hiawatha Lodge, where there is a swimming pond and waterfalls in Crystal Creek and from where there are lots of walking trails, ranging in length from two km to 10 km. Admission is free.

## Gros Cap

About 20 km west on Hwy 550 is this ridge about 150 metres above Lake Superior and Blue Water Park. Hike up the cliffs for excellent views of Lake Superior, where there's usually a ship or two cruising by. Or take the Voyageur Trail (marked by white slashes), which winds up along the ridge edge providing views of St Mary's River and the lake. The trail will one day run all the way from Manitoulin Island to Thunder Bay, but so far stretches from Gros Cap 200 km east to Serpent River on Hwy 108 along the North Channel of Lake Huron.

Beside the park and parking lot is the *Blue Water Inn* (☎ 779-2530), a great place to eat, especially popular on the sporadic weekends when the Yugoslavian owner puts on big barbecues. The inn is open in summer only.

## Agawa Canyon & the Algoma Central Railway

Together, these two make up the best known and most visited attraction in the area. The Agawa Canyon is a rugged wilderness area accessible only by the ACR trains. The 500-km rail line due north from town to Hearst goes through a scenic area of mountains, waterfalls, valleys and forests. The route, constructed at the turn of the century, was originally built to bring raw materials into the plants of Sault Ste Marie. There are now several different options for passengers seeking access to the canyon and its surroundings. Note that the best views are from the seats on the left-hand side of the train.

The basic one-day visitor return trip to the canyon takes a full nine hours, with a two-hour stopover for a quick walk, fishing or lunch on the floor of the canyon. There is a dining car on board and snacks and drinks are also available. An adult ticket costs $44, with considerable reductions for children. The train departs at 8 am daily from June to October. This is the most popular trip, so booking a couple of days ahead is a good idea.

The trip is spectacular in the fall, when the leaves have changed colour and the forests are brilliant reds and yellows. Normally the colours are at their peak in the last two weeks of September and in early October. Yet another possibility is the winter snow and ice run, which is added (on weekends only) from January to March.

There are also trips that run the full length of the line to the town of **Hearst** (population 5000), about a nine-hour trip. Hearst, perhaps surprisingly, is essentially a French town, with under 15% of the population listing English as their mother tongue. The town remains primarily engaged in lumbering, although it has its own small university.

Beyond the canyon, the track travels over less impressive flat, forested lakelands, various bridges and northern muskeg. This is a two-day trip with an overnight stay at the northern terminal. Alternatively, it's possible to stay in Hearst as long as you wish and return when ready, or not return at all. There are motels and B&Bs in Hearst; ask about them at the tourist information centre in Sault Ste Marie. From Hearst, buses can be caught east or westbound.

Lastly, there is the passenger train used by anglers, trappers, hunters, lodge operators and various other local inhabitants. This train will stop anywhere you like or anywhere someone is standing and flagging it down, so obviously the going is slow, but some find the passengers a colourful lot and the train provides the only true access into the region.

The fare on this train is calculated by the mile – the current rate is 25 cents per mile.

Information on backpacking, canoeing, swimming, camping and fishing lodges in the canyon and beyond is available at the train station. All manner of supplies can be taken on board, including canoes, boats and a maximum of three cases of beer per person! In Sault Ste Marie, the station (☎ 946-7300) is on the corner of Bay and Gore Sts, by the Station Shopping Mall in the centre of town. There is free parking at the station.

### Hiking
The partially completed Voyageur Hiking Trail will one day run between Manitoulin Island and Thunder Bay. The longest completed segment goes east from the Soo (see under Gros Cap) to Serpent River, a small village south of Elliot Lake, a distance of about 200 km. This is not an easy strolling path; obtain complete information from the Voyageur Trail Association, which has an office in Sault Ste Marie.

### Organised Tours
**City Tour** Hiawathaland Sightseeing Tours (☎ 759-6200) has a ticket booth on the waterfront, next to the Holiday Inn, and runs four different bus tours in and around Sault Ste Marie. The double-decker bus city tour is a 1½-hour trip costing $8.75. Out-of-town trips stop at various beauty spots and sites. There is a night tour, and a trip out of town through some of the local forests. They also rent bicycles.

**Brewery Tour** Northern Breweries (☎ 254-7373), downtown at 503 Bay St, offers free 45-minute tours of the facility and a chance to sample some of the various brews. This is one of the country's oldest beer companies and has been operating in northern Ontario since 1876.

### Festivals
The annual Tugboat Race, held in the St Mary's River on the 1 July weekend, is bit of good, silly fun. Competitors from both sides of the river dress up their boats with flags and banners and putt for prizes and prestige.

### Places to Stay
**Camping** There are several campgrounds close to town, though they are not rustic. *Rock Shop Campground* is 12 km from town on Hwy 17 North (called the Great Northern Rd in town).

*KOA* (☎ 256-2806) tent & RV park is eight km north of town on Hwy 17. Turn west at the flashing amber light (Fifth Line). The park is on a river and is equipped with laundry, store and pool.

A little further is *Pointe des Chênes*, on St Mary's River; go 12 km west on Hwy 550 to Hwy 565, then 10 km south past the airport to the community park. There are 82 sites.

Each of these campgrounds charges between $8 and $12 for two people tenting. There are other places close to those listed here.

**Hostels** Hostelling International (HI) has an affiliate here in the *Algonquin Hotel* (☎ 253-2311), a fine budget hotel for those with or without hostel membership. The central location is superb, at 864 Queen St East (on the corner of Pim St), within walking distance of just about everything. The rooms are plain, with no extras, but they're clean and each has a least a sink. Singles/doubles are $19/21 with a hostel card, a dollar more without, plus tax. If four of you want to share a room, it's the same price as two. The hostel also has a basic restaurant and a popular bar – ask for a room on the upper floor if you don't want to listen to the music thumping until 1 am. The Algonquin is open all year.

**B&Bs** The city now has a small number of B&Bs, but whether they have any staying power remains to be seen. The most central and least expensive place is run by *Lil & Oscar Herzog* (☎ 253-8641), at 99 Retta St, east of downtown off Wellington St. Singles/doubles are $25/30.

More up-market, the *Top O' The Hill* (☎ 253-9041), at 40 Broos Rd, is in the north-eastern section of the city, about a 10-minute drive from downtown. Prices (including breakfast) are $45/55. Another possibility is the *Hillsview* (☎ 759-8819), where a double goes for $40.

**Hotels** See the Hostels section for details of the budget-priced Algonquin Hotel.

Also central and good is the *Days Inn* (☎ 759-8200), at 320 Bay St, right by the river. Singles/doubles here are $70/85. Facilities include a restaurant and a heated pool. Their Jolly Roger bar is the only brew pub in town.

**Motels** Sault Ste Marie's location means that a lot of people pass through, so it is one of those places with scores of motels. Most of them are on Hwy 17 either east or west of town, though some are downtown. Prices vary but average $35 to $40 for singles and $45 to $55 for doubles – generally, the closer to town, the more costly. Overall, these prices are quite good; they're lower than you'd find around Sudbury or southern Ontario, for example.

The *Shady Pines Motel* (☎ 759-0088), way out east at 1587 Hwy 17, is one of the cheapest around. Though ugly at the front, it's actually good. Big, modern rooms open onto a treed back yard with picnic tables and barbecues. Singles/doubles cost just $30/35.

The *Evergreen Motel* (☎ 759-2626), at 1447 Hwy 17 East, has singles/doubles for $32/35.

The white place at 859 Trunk Rd (part of Hwy 17 East) is the *Travellers Motel* (☎ 946-

4133). It has colour TV, and kitchenettes are available. Doubles cost $36 to $50.

The *Holiday* (☎ 759-8608), at 435 Trunk Rd, is a pleasant-looking place. Single or double rooms cost $35.

*Journey's End* (☎ 759-8000), at 333 Great Northern Rd, is good at $62 a double. It's neat and busy and is part of a Canadian hotel and motel chain. You can save a few bucks by taking a room on the 2nd floor. It's on Great Northern Rd north of Northern Ave.

Other places can be found along Great Northern Rd, which leads north to the Trans Canada Hwy westbound.

**Places to Eat**
Most of the restaurants, many of which are the ubiquitous franchises, line the highway. However, I've listed mainly local establishments found in the city centre. Queen St has a real assortment of good, atmospheric beaneries of the old lunch-counter type.

The *Coral Coffee Shop*, at 470 Queen St (near Spring St), is a basic classic. They have good prices for homemade soups, muffins, chilli and the like, and have cheap breakfasts and various specials. It's the only place I've ever seen with menus in braille.

Recommended for something a little different is *Garden of Eden*, at 21 King St, a health-food store and vegetarian restaurant serving excellent, inexpensive food without meat or dairy products. King is a small street, more like an alley, tucked in behind Queen St on the north side. Go through the walkway beside 344 Queen St East.

Tiny *Mike's*, with just half a dozen stools at 518 Queen St, has been serving its regular customers since 1932. Meals are under $5 at this friendly place caught in a time warp.

At 663 Queen St East, near the corner of East St, the old-fashioned *Mary's Lunch* serves a lot of homemade stuff, including bread. The cheapest breakfast in town can be found here. Germans missing a taste of home should try the *Lunch Box*, at 75 Elgin St, open on weekdays only.

Two town specialities are lake trout and whitefish, and both turn up on menus all over Sault Ste Marie. *Muio's*, on the corner at 685

Queen St East, is a cheap place to sample one of them. It also offers daily specials, such as a complete meal with cabbage rolls for $5.25. You can't beat that, and it's open on Sundays.

Moving up-market, Italian food is popular in town and *Suriano's* at 357 Trunk Rd is well patronised. The best restaurant in the Soo is *Arturo's* (☎ 949-0810), at 116 Spring Rd, which offers a continental menu presided over by a chef from a well-known (now closed) Toronto hotel.

*Barsanti Small Frye*, 23 Trunk Rd (Hwy 17 East), is recommended for its basic good food, low prices, friendly waiting staff and style. They've been in the business for 60 years and have got it right. Conveniently, it's open long hours: 6 am to midnight daily. If you're just passing through, this may be the place to eat and run.

On Wednesday and Saturday mornings, a farmers' market is held downtown, in the parking lot at Memorial Gardens Arena.

### Getting There & Away
**Air** There are regular Air Canada and Canadian Airlines flights to Sault Ste Marie.

**Bus** The bus station (☎ 949-4711), serving both Greyhound and Ontario Northland buses, is downtown at 33 Queen St East (on the corner of Tancred St).

There are four buses a day to Sudbury. From there, three buses daily depart for either Toronto or Ottawa. The through fare to Ottawa is $102, to Toronto $88. There are three buses daily to Winnipeg ($120). Ontario Northland goes to Wawa.

For buses to Detroit or Chicago, you must get to the city bus terminal. For details see Getting Around later.

**Train** There is no VIA Rail service in or out of Sault Ste Marie.

**Hitching** The Soo is a major drop-off point for those thumbing east and west. In summer, there are plenty of backpackers hanging around town. If you're going west, remember that it's a long way from Sault Ste Marie

to Winnipeg, with little to see in between. Nights are cold and rides can be scarce. Try to get a through ride to Thunder Bay (715 km) and then go on to Winnipeg from there.

### Getting Around
**To/From the Airport** The airport is 13 km west on Hwy 550, then seven km south on Hwy 565. There are airport buses between the airport and such major hotels as the Holiday Inn and the Empire Hotel.

**Bus** The city bus terminal (☎ 759-5438) is on the corner of Queen and Dennis Sts. The Riverside bus from downtown goes east to Algoma University, near Belvedere Park. A city bus leaves from the terminal and goes over the bridge into Michigan, USA. Taxis will also take you across the bridge.

### AROUND SAULT STE MARIE
### Batchawana Bay
A relaxing afternoon or a full day can be spent north of town along the shore of Lake Superior around Batchawana Bay and beyond. The scenery is good and Batchawana offers beaches, swimming (the water is cool) and numerous motels, resorts and rental cottages.

It's 45 minutes' drive to **Chippewa Falls**, called the centrepoint of Canada, and it probably is close to being this. From the city up to Agawa Indian Crafts, a well-known landmark, it's about 75 km. With two sets of waterfalls, a couple of provincial parks and the shoreline, an enjoyable afternoon can be spent poking around. And you can visit the Montreal River garbage dump, about 25 km north-west of Batchawana Bay; you can drive in and see the bears.

### St Joseph Island
St Joseph lies in the channel between Michigan and Ontario, 50 km east of Sault Ste Marie. It's a rural island visited for swimming and fishing and for **Fort St Joseph National Park**. The British fort ruins date from the turn of the 18th century and are staffed by workers in period costume. The reception centre displays Native Indian, mil-

itary and fur-trade artefacts. A large bird sanctuary surrounds the fort. The fort is open from the end of May to the middle of October. Check at the Soo tourist office for complete details.

Also on the island is the **Museum Village**, housing 4000 island articles exhibited in six historic buildings varying from an old general store to a log school. Another thing to keep an eye out for are the so-called pudding stones – red, black and brown speckled white rocks. The jasper conglomerates (to rockhounds) found around the shoreline were named by English settlers (obviously hungry) who felt they resembled suet and berry pudding.

St Joseph has several private campgrounds, a motel and a B&B. The island is reached by a toll-free bridge off Hwy 17.

## NORTH AROUND LAKE SUPERIOR

From Sault Ste Marie to Thunder Bay, the Trans Canada Hwy is one of the few roads cutting through the thinly populated northern Ontario wilds. This huge area is rough, lake-filled timberland. So far, development has been slow to penetrate and the abundant minerals and wildlife remain undisturbed. There are areas where there's logging, but these are rarely seen. You may see signs of forest fires, which are common each year.

This quiet and beautiful part of the country is presided over by awesome Lake Superior – once known as Gitche Gumee (Big Sea Water) to the Ojibway Indians. The largest of the five Great Lakes (and one of the world's largest lakes), it's sometimes pretty, sometimes brutal, but always worthy of respect and admiration: a symbol of nature itself. Even today, there are disastrous shipwrecks when the lake gets angry, and according to a Canadian folk song, Superior 'never gives up her dead'.

Several of the Canadian Group of Seven painters were inspired to work here, and descriptions reaching the poet Longfellow had the same effect on him. Along the highway are many provincial parks, which make good places to stay and get a feel for the lake and surrounding forest.

### Lake Superior Provincial Park

Hwy 17 runs for 80 km through this large natural park north of Sault Ste Marie, so (luckily) you can't miss it. It's a beautiful park, with a few things to see even if you don't stay. The rugged scenery is good, with rivers in the wooded interior and a shoreline featuring rocky headlands and sandy beaches. Several of the aforementioned Group of Seven painters worked in the park.

The park has three campgrounds, short and long hiking trails usually accessible from the highway, and seven canoe routes. Naturalists give talks and guided walks. The park also offers fishing. Various mammals live here, including the odd bear.

At **Agawa Bay**, see the Native Indian pictographs on the shoreline rocks, believed to commemorate a crossing of the lake. There is no charge. Note the crevices in the rocks along the path. Further along, stop at **Sand River** and walk down to the beach. Though the water is cold, the beautiful sandy beach, long and empty, looks as if it's been lifted from a Caribbean island.

For access to the less visited eastern side of the park where there is no road, inquire about the train which runs along the far eastern edge. It can be caught at Frater at the southern end of the park or at Hawk Junction. The latter is a small village outside of the northern boundary of the park east of the town of Wawa. The train line is part of the Algoma Central Railway. For more details see under Sault Ste Marie, Agawa Canyon.

Distance hikers and canoeists should cross their fingers for good weather – this is one of the wettest areas in Ontario. Trails are often enveloped in mist or fog, which lends a primeval, spooky air to the woods. As always, interior camping costs a few dollars less than using the campgrounds with facilities.

### Wawa

Marked by the huge steel goose at the edge of town, Wawa is a small iron-mining centre. The name is an Ojibway word, meaning 'wild goose', bestowed on the town because

Caribou

of the thousands of geese which stop over on Lake Wawa during migrations.

There is nothing much to see here but the town does have several motels and places for a bite. In the restaurants, look for the fish (such as trout) which are caught locally.

Wawa long had a big, bad reputation for hitchhiking. The story is told of one man who

got stuck here so long waiting for a lift that he finally had to get a job. He ended up meeting a woman and getting married – he still lives here. As traffic has picked up over the years and the locals have become less isolated, things aren't as bad they were, but if you are hitching, it's still better to get a ride right through. There is nothing down at the highway and it can be a cold place at night, even in midsummer. Actually, cyclists are a more common sight these days than thumbers.

Wawa is a supply centre for the surrounding parks.

## Chapleau

Chapleau is a small logging and outdoors centre inland from Wawa. There are numerous provincial parks in the area, three within 80 km. **Missinaibi Lake Park** is in the middle of **Chapleau Game Reserve**, the largest in the western hemisphere. The boreal forest is ideal for wilderness camping, canoeing or fishing.

The tourist offices around the area have a listing of canoe routes. There are 12 trips ranging from one to 14 days, with five to 47 portages. The longest one is a river and lake circle route going through part of the reserve; it's good for viewing moose.

Tourist offices can also help with information on the many lodges and fly-in camps which operate in the area.

## White River

Back on the Trans Canada Hwy, this is called the coldest place in Canada, with temperatures recorded as low as -50°C. Get your picture taken near the thermometer.

Another bit of trivia has this as the original home of the bear which inspired A A Milne's *Winnie the Pooh* books. Apparently a Canadian soldier got a bear cub here and called it Winnipeg, after his home town. During the war it ended up at England's London Zoo, where it became quite popular, and was subsequently immortalised in fiction.

White River has a couple of motels, moderately priced, for overnighters.

VIA Rail connects the town to Sudbury. The station is on Winnipeg Rd, a short walk from the highway.

## Pukaskwa National Park

Find out how tough you are. There is no road in this park (pronounced 'puk-a-saw') and access is by hiking or boat. From Heron Bay, off the Trans Canada Hwy near Marathon, is

a small road, Hwy 627, which goes to the edge of the park at Hatties Cove. There is a small (67-site) campground and a visitors information centre. For day use, there is a picnic area, and swimming in a protected bay. In the lake itself, the water is cold and swells can be hazardous even for good swimmers.

The main attraction is the old 68-km coastal hiking trail, with primitive camping spots along the way. The terrain is rough but beautiful and the weather is changeable, switching quickly from sun to storm. The trail is often wet and slippery, black flies and mosquitos are guaranteed and bears are often a bother. Even the mice can be aggressive, digging into unattended supplies. Good luck.

The interior offers some challenging canoeing, including runs down the Pukaskwa and the less difficult, more accessible White River.

The park is open from late May to the third weekend in September.

## Slate Islands Provincial Park

Situated offshore from the small town of **Terrace Bay** is this cluster of islands, home to the highest density of woodland caribou anywhere. The islands, without natural predators, support hundreds of caribou. At times, there are too many for their food stocks and winters can take a heavy toll. The herd is studied by researchers looking into preserving the herds of mainland Ontario. Ask around Terrace Bay or the nearby provincial parks about trips over to the islands to see or photograph the caribou.

## Nipigon

Nipigon sits at the mouth of the Nipigon River, where Hwy 11 meets Hwy 17, the Trans Canada. There really isn't anything here of note, but it is interesting that this was the first European settlement on Superior's north shore. White traders established a fur post here, in the middle of the traditional Ojibway lands.

East of town along Hwy 17, look for the Kama Lookout, with good views of the Lake Superior shore. This segment of the highway is also known as the Terry Fox Courage Hwy; for details, see the Thunder Bay section.

## Ouimet Canyon Provincial Nature Preserve

About 45 km west of Nipigon and 40 km east of Thunder Bay, north-east of the highway, this park features a great canyon three km long and 150 metres both wide and deep. The walls on either side of the chasm are virtually perpendicular. Fences and viewing stations have been built right at the sheer edges for good, heart-pounding views. The canyon was scoured out during the last ice age and the bottom is home to some rare flora generally found only in Arctic regions. The canyon is definitely worth a quick stop; most times you'll find yourself alone. Walking trails meander around the top and there are some interpretive displays. Officially, there's no camping. There is no public transport out here, but that does help to keep it clean and serene.

## THUNDER BAY

Known as 'the Lakehead', Thunder Bay (on the northern shores of Lake Superior) is an amalgamation of the towns of Fort William and Port Arthur. Despite being so far inland, Thunder Bay is one of Canada's major ports and is as far westward as ships using the St Lawrence Seaway get. The main cargo switching hands here is prairie wheat going to market. The docks make the city the world's largest grain handler.

The city, halfway between Sault Ste Marie and Winnipeg – 720 km to either one – is a good stopping-off point. The place itself may not hold you long, but the setting is scenic and it makes a handy centre for experiencing some of the things to see and do in northern Ontario's rugged timberland.

The first Europeans here were a couple of Frenchmen who reached the area in 1662. For hundreds of years, this was a fur-trading settlement. In 1869 the Dawson, the pioneer's road westward, was begun. In 1882, the Canadian Pacific railway arrived,

and soon the prairie's first shipment of wheat was heading east.

Coming into town from the east on the Trans Canada Hwy, you'll pass mountains and see the city at the edge of the bay. Along the shoreline are pulp mills and grain elevators. Out in the harbour, ships are moored, and beyond is a long rock formation and an island or two. The unusually shaped mass of rock offshore is important in Native Indian legend and is said to be the Great Spirit, Nana-bijou, who turned to stone after a promise made to him was broken. Today the formation is known as the Sleeping Giant.

### Orientation

Thunder Bay still has two distinct downtown areas, which are connected principally by Fort William Rd and Memorial Ave. The area between the two is pretty much a wasteland of fast-food outlets, the large Inter City Shopping Mall and little else.

Port Arthur (Thunder Bay North), closer to the lakeshore, appears more prosperous and is more modern and generally more attractive. The main streets are Red River Rd and Cumberland St. Port Arthur's Landing, off Water St, is a redeveloped waterfront area and includes parkland. The Pagoda tourist office is across the street. This half of Thunder Bay has a sizeable Finnish population, which supports several specialised restaurants on Bay St. Indeed, for a city its size, Thunder Bay has quite a large and varied ethnic population.

Though of equal age, Fort William (Thunder Bay South) looks older and is rather drab, without the activity of its cross-town counterpart. Main streets in this half of the city are May St and Victoria Ave. The Victoriaville shopping mall is at this corner and is where most of the Fort William action occurs. The tourist office is nearby.

On each side of Thunder Bay is a commercial motel/restaurant strip.

### Information

One tourist information office is east of town on Hwy 11/17, just before the turn-off to Lakeshore Drive and Port Arthur – about 40 km out. It's open in summer only. Another office east of town on Hwy 17 is in the parking lot of the Mackenzie Inn. These are temporary; locations change but there will always be something somewhere along the highway close to town.

Downtown there are several places to go for information. In Port Arthur, the main summer tourist office (☎ 345-6812) is central, in the 1910 Pagoda in the park on the corner of Red River Rd and Water St. It's open daily.

In Fort William, there's an office (☎ 623-7577) in central Paterson Park on the corner of May and Miles Sts. During the off season, you can obtain information from the Visitors & Convention Bureau, 520 Leith St.

There is also an information booth at Old Fort William.

The tourist offices have pamphlets outlining architectural walking tours for both sections of town.

North of Superior Tourism is at 1184 Roland St, for any additional information required on the region.

### Thunder Bay Museum
The small history museum (☎ 623-0801), at 219 May St South (on the corner of Donald St), is open daily in summer from 11 am to 5 pm. The rest of the year it's closed on Mondays. The museum contains Native Indian artefacts and a collection of odds & ends of local history. Topics covered include fur trading, mining and the early pioneers. Changing exhibits may include photography, furniture or archaeological displays. The museum is not extensive but displays are well presented. Admission is free.

### The Port
Thunder Bay Harbour is Canada's second-largest port according to tonnes handled, with the greatest complex of grain elevators in the world. Terminals, elevators and other storage and docking facilities stretch along 45 km of central waterfront. At the Port Arthur shipyards, the huge freighters are built and repaired.

In the middle of the waterfront is the

Keefer Complex (☎ 345-6812), a cargo-handling facility where ships from around the world come and go. The Keefer Terminal mainly handles resource materials and grains. The terminal is at the end of Main St off Fort William Rd.

Very visible are the numerous grain elevators operated by a variety of private companies, such as the Saskatchewan Wheat Pool Grain Elevator (☎ 623-7577).

Thunder Bay Terminals Ltd, a bulk entrepôt facility on McKellar Island, just offshore, handles coal, potash and agricultural products.

In between the city's two halves, notice the large, high railway trestle, CN High Dock. This was used until the mid-1980s for transferring iron ore and potash from train to ship.

There are no tours of the port operations but the *Welcome* cruise ship sails by the port area, getting quite close to some of the terminals, and the captain is able to answer many questions regarding the operation of the port and its facilities. See under Organised Tours.

### Prince Arthur's Landing
Located in Prince Arthur, by the lake opposite the Pagoda tourist office, the landing is a waterfront redevelopment zone. It contains the marina, the dock for the *Welcome* cruise ship and fishing charters, a small art gallery, and a restaurant in the old train station. Also in the train station, on the 2nd floor, is a large layout created by the model railroad club.

Still, the site is primarily parkland. There are some walking paths which meander around three piers. Best is the one out to Wilson St Headland, with views of the lake and dock areas.

### Parks
**Centennial Park** Centennial is a large, natural woodland park at the eastern edge of Port Arthur, near Hwy 17. It's alongside Current River, which flows into Boulevard Lake before entering Lake Superior. The park is over the Boulevard Lake Bridge just off Arundel St. Entry is free. There are nature

# Thunder Bay

To Winnipeg & Manitoba

To Sault Ste Marie & Longhouse International Hostel

Centennial Park

Boulevard Lake

Hodder Avenue

11  17  Highway

Terry Fox Courage

Red River Road

Cumberland Street

Algoma Street

PORT ARTHUR

Tourist Office

Welcome Ship Dock

Bay St

Cumberland St

Water St

Oliver Road

Oliver Road

Canada Games Complex

Fort William Road

17  11

Lakehead University

Harbour Expressway

Memorial Avenue

Bus Terminal

Keefer Terminal

Confederation College

Balmoral Street

Neebing -McIntyre Diversion

May Street

Simpson Street

Fort William Gardens, Tourist Office & Paterson Park

Kaministikwia River

To Kakabeka Falls

Victoria Avenue

Donald St

McKellar Island

11  17

Arthur Street

Museum

Waterloo Street

Brodie St FORT WILLIAM

McKellar River

61

Walsh Street

Kingsway Avenue

To Duluth, Minnesota (USA) & Old Fort William

108th Ave

Mission Island

Kaministikwia River

City Road

To Duluth & Minnesota (USA)

Paper Mill

LAKE SUPERIOR

Chippewa Park

Mission River

0    1    2 km

ONTARIO

trails along the river and through the woods. On the grounds is a simulated logging camp of 1910 – not much to see but the log cabins and buildings themselves are good. A small museum has a cross-cut section of a 250-year-old white pine tree on display. Various dates in history are marked at the corresponding growth rings. It's amazing to think what has gone on while this tree quietly kept growing. You'll find canoes and boats for rent here as well. Up the road from the park is the Bluffs Scenic Lookout, for a view of the lake and shore.

**International Friendship Gardens** This good-sized city park is off Victoria Ave near Waterloo St. Various local ethnic groups, such as the Finns and the Hungarians, have erected monuments and statues. There is a pond and some flowers but no extensive gardens. The park is west of downtown Fort William, on Victoria Ave.

**Waverley Park** Free summer concerts are held in the Rotary Thundershell on Wednesday evenings and Sunday afternoons in summer at this city park. It's on the corner of Red River Rd and High St in Port Arthur.

**Hillcrest Park** Just to the west of Waverley Park, also on High St, Hillcrest has a lookout point for views of the harbour and to the Sleeping Giant.

**Chippewa Park** At the edge of Lake Superior and just beyond the southern end of Fort William, at the foot of City Rd, Chippewa Park has a beach, picnic and camping sites, a small amusement park and a good indigenous wildlife exhibit where many of northern Ontario's mammals can be seen from overhead walkways.

**Sleeping Giant Provincial Park** Formerly called Sibley Park, this is a larger, more natural and scenic park (☎ 933-4332) further out and on the east side of the city. Part of the Sibley Peninsula, the park arcs 35 km into Lake Superior. The setting and landscape are excellent, with woods, hills, shoreline and great views from several vantage points. On one trip in, just after dark, we saw three foxes at the road's edge, and moose also live in the park.

Activities include swimming, fishing and camping, and there are some good walks, including one out along the top of the Sleeping Giant rock formation, from where there are fine views. One hike, taking a minimum of two days, cuts across most of the west coast of the peninsula.

An Ojibway legend tells the story of the formation of the Sleeping Giant. In one version, Nana-bijou, the spirit of the Deep Sea Water, showed the Ojibway a mine where silver could be found, as reward for their peaceful, spiritual way of life. But, he said, if ever they should tell the White people of the source of the silver, he would be forever turned to stone.

Upon seeing the fine articles and jewellery made of silver, the Sioux, the Ojibway's historical enemy, sought to discover the metal's origins. When even torture failed to reveal the secret, the Sioux decided to send a man in disguise to live as an Ojibway. Eventually he was led to the mine.

On his way back to his people with the great news, the Sioux stopped at a White man's encampment. They were enthralled upon seeing the silver sample he had with him. After plying him with alcohol, he agreed to take several of the men by canoe to the mine. A great storm came up, drowning everyone but the Sioux, whom the Ojibway later found floating around aimlessly. When the weather cleared, the open bay had been partially blocked by a huge rock formation, and the Ojibway knew that Nana-bijou's words had come to be.

The park makes a good stop if you don't want to go into town to sleep. Note that it is further in off the Trans Canada Hwy than it looks on the map. It's about six km to the edge of the park but about 30 km to the campground.

**Thunder Bay Art Gallery**
The gallery at Confederation College campus (☎ 577-6427) collects, preserves and displays contemporary art by Canadian Native Indians. Works include paintings, prints, masks, sculptures and more. There are displays from the permanent collection, as well as travelling exhibits, which usually feature non-Native Indian artists. Norval Morrisseau, perhaps Canada's best known

Native Indian painter, was born in Thunder Bay and some of his work is on view. The gallery is open from noon to 8 pm Tuesday to Thursday and from noon to 5 pm Friday to Sunday. Admission is free. The Northwood bus from Fort William goes to the campus door.

## Canada Games Complex

The Canada Games recreational complex, at 420 Winnipeg St, includes an Olympic-sized swimming pool, a large water slide, saunas, whirlpools and a restaurant. It's open daily.

## Biloski Site

This Native Indian archaeological site was discovered in 1984 when the Cherry Ridge subdivision was being developed for new houses. The site is just east of Hwy 11/17, by the shoreline. Many of the tools and weapons found here are on display, along with explanations, in the Thunder Bay Museum.

## Old Fort William

Some of Thunder Bay's best known attractions are some distance from downtown, as is Old Fort William (☎ 577-8461), perhaps the city's feature site.

The old fort settlement, with 42 historic buildings spread over 50 hectares west of town, not far past the airport and off Broadway Ave, is worth getting to.

From 1803 to 1821, Fort William was the headquarters of the North West Fur-Trading Company. Here the voyageurs and Native Indians did their trading, and settlers and explorers arrived from the east. In 1821, after much haggling and hassling, the company was absorbed by its chief rival, the Hudson's Bay Company, and Fort William declined.

The fort re-creates some aspects of the early, thriving fur-trading days through buildings, tools, artefacts and documents. Workers in period dress demonstrate skills and crafts, perform historical re-enactments and will answer questions. Interesting displays include the Native Indian camp and the woodwork of the canoe building. Animals can be seen at the separate farm section.

A thorough but relaxed visit can take half

a day or more. Each year, it seems, there are new expansions and ideas. In August, watch for the Ojibway Keeshihunan, a weekend festival of Native culture.

Good, cheap homemade food is available in the fort's canteen.

Entry is $7.25, with family rates available; watch for the free special-event days held regularly in summer. The fort is open all year. From the end of June to the beginning of September, opening hours are 10 am to 6 pm.

Although the site is a long way out, city buses go close to the fort, departing from the terminal in either Fort William or Port Arthur every hour; the last bus from the fort leaves at 5.45 pm, but check this time. For any other information, call the fort.

It is also possible to get to the fort via the *Welcome* cruise ship; see under Organised Tours.

## Kakabeka Falls

Set in a provincial park 25 km west of Thunder Bay off Hwy 17, the waterfalls, about 40 metres high, are worth a look. It's most impressive in spring, when the water in the river is at its highest, or after heavy rains. Towards the end of the wet summer of 1993, about which locals justifiably moaned to me, the falls were like a mini-Niagara and very impressive. Sometimes the water flow is small, as it's dammed off for power. Walkways lead around and across the falls. Plaques tell the Ojibway legend of martyr Princess Green Mantle, who saved her village from the attacking Sioux by leading them over the falls.

Most people go to take pictures at the falls, but the park itself isn't bad, with camping, swimming at small beaches, and picnicking. There is no charge to see the falls.

## Mt Mackay

Mt Mackay is the tallest mountain in the area's north-western mountain chain, rising to 350-odd metres and offering good views of Thunder Bay and environs. The lookout is on an Ojibway reserve and an admission of $4 per car is charged to use the winding road to the top. It's not really worth it – the view of the city is good, but for seeing the Sleeping Giant you're better off at the Terry Fox Lookout, off the Trans Canada Hwy.

Mt Mackay is south-west of Fort William. Take Edward St to City Rd, towards Chippewa Park, and follow the signs. The road to Mt Mackay cuts through a portion of the residential area of the reserve. At the top there is a snack bar and gift shop. A walking trail leads further up to the peak. Camping is permitted but facilities are minimal. No city bus gets close enough to make public transportation to the mountain a viable option.

Legend has it that the local Ojibway had taken to some farming and were growing wheat. One harvest time, the crop was demolished by incessant flocks of blackbirds. The hunters were unable to replace the crop, due to early and heavy snows. The water froze, making fishing difficult, especially with the meagre bait available, and soon even this was gone. In desperation the daughter of the chief cut strips of flesh from her legs to give the fishers for bait. Enough fish were caught to stave off mass starvation but the girl died. In her honour, a visiting priest had the men build the small chapel which still sits atop Mt Mackay. Each year at Thanksgiving, the chapel is visited and prayers are offered for next year's crop.

### Terry Fox Courage Hwy

A segment of the Trans Canada Hwy northwest of town has been named after the young Canadian who, in the early 1980s, while dying of cancer, attempted to run across Canada to raise money for cancer research. After having one leg amputated, he made it from Newfoundland to Thunder Bay, raising millions and becoming a national hero before finally succumbing. Each year, cities across the country and around the world hold Terry Fox Memorial Runs to raise further funds for his cause. A monument to him sits at a fine lookout east of town.

### Activities

**Canoeing** Wildwaters Nature Tours (☎ 767-2022), out of town on Dog Lake Rd, offers canoe expeditions of various lengths and costs. They include wildlife, photography and fishing trips, and a special trip for women only. Some white-water trips are offered as well.

**Fishing** Fishing charters into Lake Superior (for salmon) are available from the Thunder Bay Marina. Trout fishing is possible in nearby rivers and streams; the tourist office has a list of local fishing spots put out by the Ministry of Natural Resources.

From Thunder Bay to Kenora, near the Manitoba border, there are almost limitless fishing camps and lodges. Many people fly in to remote lakes. Tourist offices will have more information. I'm sure these are good trips, but ask me if I can afford them! There are also places to rent canoes.

**Amethyst Hounding** Amethyst (a variety of quartz) is a purple semiprecious stone that is found in several areas around Thunder Bay. There are many superstitions surrounding amethyst, including the early Greek one that it prevents drunkenness. The ever-practical Greeks therefore often fashioned wine cups from the stone. It is mined from veins which run on or near the earth's surface, so looking for the stone and digging it out are relatively easy.

Within about 50 km of the city are five sites where you can go looking for your own stones. Each site has some samples for sale if you should miss out on finding some. Shops in town sell jewellery and finished souvenir items made of the purple quartz. The tourist office has a list of all the mines and can direct you to stores around town which sell a range of stuff produced with the finished stone – mostly pretty tacky. The stone generally looks better raw.

Visits to all but one of the sites are free. You simply pay for the pieces you find and want to keep.

Thunder Bay Amethyst Mine Panorama is a huge property off East Loon Lake Rd, which is east of Hwy 587 South. The site is about seven km north of the Trans Canada Hwy, and the road in is rough and steep in places. Entry is $1.

Three of the mine sites, all much smaller, are on Rd No 5 North, a little further east than East Loon. Located four km to six km north up from the Trans Canada Hwy, the three mine entrances can't be missed. You are given a pail and shovel and pointed in the right direction, then you're on your own – see what you come up with. All the sites are open daily from May to October and each has a shop on the premises.

**Sauna** You can get a sauna at Kanga's (☎ 344-6761), 379 Oliver Rd. Finnish saunas are popular in the region. At Kanga's there are also some Finnish eats and good desserts. See also under Canada Games Complex earlier.

### Organised Tours

In the Pagoda tourist booth, pick up a folder on a self-guided architectural walking tour of Port Arthur. The fire hall, some churches, various houses of note and other buildings are located and described. There is a similar brochure for downtown Fort William.

Daily through the summer months, boat tours of the port area and city waterfront are offered aboard the *Welcome* cruise ship (☎ 344-2512). There is an afternoon and an evening trip, each two hours in duration and with a narration. The boat tours are really the only way to get much of a look at the harbour area. Another option is the Old Fort William cruise, which sails to the historic site, allows three hours to visit and then returns to town via a bus. This can be done in either direction. Call for details and a schedule.

### Festivals

The Jamboree, an annual sailing event, is held in the harbour, with festivities centred around the Marina at Prince Arthur's Landing, on the waterfront in Port Arthur.

Mid-August sees the one-day Festa Italia, featuring food (of course), games and entertainment. It's held in the north-end Italian section of town.

Ask about the First Nation Powwow, featuring Native dancers, held on Mt McKay around 1 July.

### Places to Stay

**Camping** Thunder Bay is one of those happy places where good camping can be found close to the city. On the west side of the city

is *Trowbridge Falls* (☎ 683-6661) off Hwy 11-17 about half a km north up Copenhagen Rd. It's run by the City of Thunder Bay, as is the adjacent Centennial Park.

Further west out of town off Hwy 17 (the Trans Canada), at the junction of Hwy 800, is a *KOA* campground. A site costs about $12. Look for the road to the Mt Baldy ski area: it's nearby on the opposite side of the road.

There is also municipal camping southwest of the city, at *Chippewa Park* (☎ 623-3912), a short drive from Old Fort William historic site. From the junction of Hwys 61 and 61B, go 3.2 km on Hwy 61B to City Rd and look for the signs. The park is right on the lake. There is a good wildlife collection at the park, with examples of most of the mammals found in the northern Ontario wilds.

There is also good camping further west at Kakabeka Falls Provincial Park.

**Hostels** The Backpackers' *Longhouse Village Hostel* (☎ 983-2042) is excellent and open all year. It's a fair distance from town – 22 km east, at 1594 Lakeshore Drive (Rural Route 13) – but is well worth the effort. The location is green and quiet, the atmosphere friendly and relaxed. The couple who run it, Lloyd and Willa Jones, spent six years as missionaries and Baptist teachers in Borneo (mementos can be seen all over the place) and are now active in refugee work. They are also the driving force behind Canada's link in the Backpackers chain of international hostels. Write to them (postal code P7B 5E4) for more information on this network.

The Joneses are knowledgeable about things to do around Thunder Bay – there is swimming and walking nearby, and ask about Mackenzie Point and the waterfall in the woods.

Basic food is available and guests can use the kitchen. Rooms and beds are scattered all over the property in a variety of units, including a trailer, cabins, the main house and even a bus. The price is $13, or a tent can be set up on the lawn for $9. Couples and families can be accommodated.

From the highway, head down Mackenzie Station Rd (easily walkable); the hostel is near the corner – the only hostel I've seen with an electric sign. Note that there are no city buses into town, but see the Getting Around section later for information on the Greyhound bus.

The *YM-YWCA* has no beds for rent.

There are places available in the *Lakehead University Residence* (☎ 345-2121) from 1 May to 20 August. Singles/doubles cost $28/38 ($20/30 for students). Breakfast is also available. The university is at 855 Oliver Rd, between the two downtown areas and slightly west. The cross-town city bus goes past the campus in both directions.

There's a *Salvation Army Hostel* (men only) at 545 Cumberland St North. It's free for a night or two if you're hard up.

**B&Bs** Also economical are the B&B places run from people's homes, which in Thunder Bay generally charge around $35 a single and $50 a double, with breakfast. Unfortunately, these change quickly and have never been abundant. Not being true commercial establishments, but only operating seasonally, their listings tend not to be printed in the general information available on the city. However, the tourist office should know of any current places worth checking out.

One well-established place, and a fine one for spending a night or two, is the *Unicorn Inn* (☎ 475-4200). Singles are a might steep at $47 but the doubles are a more standard $60. The rooms on the ground floor of an old farmhouse are comfortable and the breakfasts are worth waking up for. It's out of town about half an hour's drive, at Unicorn Road, Rural Route 1, South Gillies. See under Places to Eat later for directions. Call ahead to check availability.

**Hotels** Top of the list of the corporate hotels in town is the *Prince Arthur Hotel* (☎ 345-5411), on the corner of Cumberland St and Red River Rd, right by the Pagoda tourist office. It's large, has several places to eat or drink and costs about $70 a single or double. Some rooms look out over the lake.

Over in Fort William, which is more convenient for the airport, train and bus stations, a decent cheap place is the small *Intowner* (☎ 623-1565), on the corner of Arthur St East and Brodie St South. It's simple but clean. There is an adjoining restaurant and a popular bar with live music. This means noise in the rooms until 1 am. Singles cost $35.

Best of the skid-row specials is the *Hotel Empire* (☎ 622-2912), at 140 Simpson St, with singles/doubles at $18/24 (plus $2 for the key). There is a snack bar and a drinking bar downstairs. Similar places are found all along Simpson St but none is really recommended.

Moving back up-market, *Best Western Crossroads Motor Inn* (☎ 577-4241) is at 655 West Arthur St.

**Motels** Most of the moderately priced accommodation is in the newer motel strips. There are two areas of heavy motel concentration, one on each side of the city, as well as a few rather good places in between the two downtown areas, along Memorial Ave. The *Circle Inn* (☎ 344-5744) and the *Sleeping Giant Motor Hotel* (☎ 345-7316) are here, with 50 rooms each and prices in the range of $43 a double. More up-market is the nearby *Venture Inn* (☎ 345-2343).

The motel area in Port Arthur is on and around Cumberland St. It heads out to Hodder Ave, which then leads to the Expressway or Hwy 17 East. The motels are mainly found near the grain elevators along the lakefront. Cumberland St leads right into the downtown area of Port Arthur.

The *Strathcona* (☎ 683-8351), at 546 Hodder St, is a small, well-kept, blue-and-white place. Singles or doubles range from $45 to $55.

The *Hodder Avenue Motel* (☎ 683-8414), at 321 Hodder Ave, is a nice place. Singles/doubles are $32/36.

The *Lakeview* is the pale yellow place at 391 Cumberland St, on the left-hand side approaching town. Singles and doubles are $42 and have cable TV. There are other, lower-priced places along Cumberland St.

ONTARIO

The other motel district is along Arthur St, heading out of town from downtown Fort William past the airport. There are a few motels side by side on Kingsway Ave, off Arthur St, but these are priced higher than they're worth.

The *Ritz Motel* (☎ 622-4112), at 2600 Arthur St East, is good and has some kitchenettes. Rooms cost $44 to $60 in this red-brick building close to town. Less expensive is the *Paradise Motel*, at 221 Arthur St West. Even cheaper, but still fine, is *Bob's Motel* (☎ 475-4546), at 235 Arthur St West. Rooms here start at $39.

### Places to Eat
**Port Arthur** At 11 South Cumberland St, *Deli Greens Café* is recommended for good soups, salads and fresh sandwiches at tasty prices.

Nearby, south at 25 Cumberland St, the well-established *Prospector* is a steak-and-roast beef house serving meat from a local cattle ranch. Steaks cost $15 to $20. Also on the menu is another area speciality, walleye, one of Canada's best eating freshwater fish. The restaurant is on the corner of Cumberland St and Park Ave. It opens daily at 5 pm, closing at 9 pm Monday to Thursday, 10 pm on Fridays and Saturdays and 8 pm on Sundays. They have a kids' menu, too.

The *Hoito*, at 314 Bay St, is a Finnish place set up about 60 years ago. It is known for its homemade food served in plain surroundings. The large portions pack them in, even at lunch on the weekends. There are a couple of similar places in this Finnish neighbourhood, and around the corner, on Second St, is a Finnish bakery. At 189 South Algoma St, near Bay St, the *Expresso* serves espresso and cappuccino.

For something with a Far East accent, the *Cumberland*, at 45 South Cumberland St (across from the Keskus Mall), has cheap noodle lunches. Nearby, at 10 South Cumberland St, the *Subway* has inexpensive submarine sandwiches.

The shopping malls also have restaurants. The *Office*, in the Keskus Mall, Red River Rd, is a pub with inexpensive meals and live music – top 40 and often blues – at night.

Away from the central core, at 901 Red River Rd (at the corner of Junot Ave), is the popular *Port Arthur Brasserie*, a brew pub where, in addition to the usual meals, they have a Sunday brunch.

There are numerous spots offering hamburgers and similar fare on Memorial Ave, which links the two parts of the city. Best is *Bonanza*, at No 1075, where full meals are inexpensive and include an all-you-can-eat salad bar. Known for their cheap steaks, they also serve chicken and fish. Also on Memorial Ave are the Inter City Shopping Mall (which has a cheap food fair), and the casual *Casey's* (at No 450) or *East Side Mario's* (at No 1170), both geared to the young.

**Fort William** The *Columbia Grill & Tavern*, at 123 May St, is a friendly, basic, all-purpose restaurant used by the locals. It gained some infamy in the early 1990s as the place where Laurie 'Bambi' Bembenek, the popular protagonist in one of North America's most captivating criminal cases, worked while on the run from US authorities. The restaurant is open daily from 8 am for breakfast. Similar, the *Venice Grill*, at 636 Simpson St, is also a good, basic place. It's fine for a cheap breakfast and is open every day but Sunday.

The *Royal Canadian Legion, Polish Branch*, at 730 Simpson St, has a small coffee shop and bar where they serve up large, filling portions at low prices.

Victoria Mall, or the Victoria Centre, right in the centre of town, has a food fair. *Boston Pizza*, at 217 Arthur St West, serves pastas and ribs at moderate prices.

The *Williams Restaurant*, at 610 Arthur St West, has a menu of standard Canadian and some Mexican-style dishes. The food is good and the portions large, but it's not strictly low budget, with dinner costing $20. From Sunday to Wednesday, there is a good, economical dinner package with an all-you-can-eat salad bar.

The *Timbers*, at 1 Valhalla Inn Rd, in the Valhalla Inn, features Mexican meals on

Monday and Tuesday evenings, Italian dishes for the next two nights and Chinese food on Fridays and Saturdays.

About half an hour south-west of the city, the *Unicorn Inn*, in a turn-of-the-century farmhouse, is the best restaurant in northern Ontario and has been ranked among the best in the country. Take highway 61 south of the city 20.2 km from the airport and then turn right onto Hwy 608 for South Gillies. The restaurant is on Unicorn Rd. Reservations (☎ 475-4200) are required for dinner, and calling even a week ahead is not too soon. It's dressy, and pricey – the fixed-price meals, from appetiser to coffee, cost over $30 per person. Main courses of seafood, chicken, fowl and beef are all offered. Bon appétit.

A portion of the farmhouse also acts as a B&B.

### Entertainment

**Bars & Nightspots** The *Innplace* is a popular hotel bar. It's in the Intowner, on the corner of Arthur and Brodie Sts. Entertainment is live commercial pop-rock; shows change frequently, as does the cover charge.

The *Pacific Club*, at 201 Syndicate Ave, is a dance palace with recorded music.

The *Elephant & Castle*, in the Inter City Shopping Mall, is a pub-style place with a large dance floor. *Casey's*, at 450 Memorial Ave, is basically a restaurant but also serves as a casual place for an evening's drink accompanied by recorded pop music.

*Armani's*, a somewhat dressy restaurant in the centre of Fort William, at 513 East Victoria St, has a casual rooftop bar in summer; it's not a bad place for a quiet beer.

**Theatre** A summer theatre programme, Moonlight Melodrama (☎ 623-7838), is held in the theatre on the lower level in the Kekus Harbour Mall, 230 Park Ave, in Thunder Bay North.

### Getting There & Away

**Air** Thunder Bay Airport is about 15 minutes' drive south-west of town, at the junction of Hwy 11/17 (the Trans Canada Hwy) and Hwy 61 to Duluth, Minnesota and the USA.

Air Canada (☎ 623-3313) and Canadian Airlines (☎ 577-6461) offer flights to Winnipeg ($280) and to Toronto ($295).

Bearskin Airlines (☎ 475-0066) services the region and other northern parts of the province.

**Bus** The Greyhound Bus Depot (☎ 345-2194) is closer to Fort William but lies in between the two downtown areas, at 815 Fort William Rd (near the Inter City Shopping Mall). It's a long walk north from central Fort William; grab the city bus. The Mainline bus goes past the door as it runs between Fort William and Port Arthur.

For Winnipeg ($68) and points further west, there are three buses a day, beginning early in the morning and running until the wee hours.

For Sault Ste Marie ($73) and points east, such as Toronto, there are also about three trips daily, and again the schedule is evenly spaced out over the 24 hours (with some departures at rather ungodly hours).

For Sudbury ($89), there is just one trip a day, departing in the early evening.

The Grey Goose bus line runs to Fort Francis and via the USA to Manitoba.

**Train** The VIA Rail terminal is in the Canadian Pacific railway passenger station in Fort William. It's on Syndicate St just south of Arthur St, near the City Hall. All train services in and out of Thunder Bay have been cut. The train across Ontario now runs way north of Thunder Bay. It's hard to know why.

**Car** Avis (☎ 577-5766) is at 1475 Walsh St West. They charge $31.95 a day with 200 free km. Additional km are $0.15 each.

Budget Rent-a-Car (☎ 345-2425), at 899 Copper Crescent, has weekend specials which may be useful. There are several agencies with desks at the airport including Thrifty (with good weekend rates) and Tilden (which also has offices in town).

Thunder Bay is 720 km from Sault Ste Marie, 731 km from Winnipeg and 315 km from Duluth (in Michigan, USA). It's an eight-hour drive to Winnipeg.

A circular tour of northern Ontario can be made by car from Thunder Bay by back-tracking to Lake Nipigon and following Hwy 11 (the most northerly provincial route) through Geraldton and Kapuskasing, returning south via Timmins, Sudbury or North Bay. Provincial parks are found at regular intervals along Hwy 11. Towns are small.

**Hitching** Westbound travellers should head out to Arthur St; the airport bus will take you to a good spot. Alternatively, if you can get to Hwy 102 (Red River Rd-Dawson Rd) on the north edge of Port Arthur, you save a few miles along Hwy 11/17 before the turn-off to Winnipeg. If you're eastbound, anywhere on Hwy 17 is OK. For $4 the eastbound Greyhound bus will take you to the edge of town, but talk to the driver before reaching your stopping area.

### Getting Around
**To/From the Airport** An airport bus departs from the local city bus terminal, beside the Paterson Park tourist office (in Fort William, on the corner of May and Miles Sts) every 20 minutes until 6 pm, then every 40 minutes. The ride takes about 15 minutes.

A city bus, the 'Arthur' route, also goes from the Fort William side of town right to the door of the airport. It's much slower but costs less. Catch it anywhere on Arthur St.

**Bus** There is a good bus system which covers all areas of the city, and the drivers are some of the friendliest and most helpful in the country. Tell them I said so. For information call ☎ 344-9666.

In Fort William, the terminal for local buses is across the street from the tourist office, on the corner of May and Miles Sts. To get to the Port Arthur end of town, take the Memorial bus on May St or the Mainline bus along Fort William St (same thing going the opposite way).

In Port Arthur, the terminal is on the corner of Water and Camelot Sts (just down from

Cumberland St), by the waterfront. The Pagoda tourist office is next door.

The cross-town bus from either end of Thunder Bay goes to the university. The Neebing bus goes to Old Fort William from the Fort William terminal.

For the hostel, there are no city buses, so take the eastbound Greyhound bus from the terminal at 815 Fort William Rd. For $4 they'll take you along Lakeshore Drive to the hostel (or will at least let you off at Mackenzie Station Rd at the Trans Canada Hwy, from where it's a walk of one or two km straight to the hostel). Be sure to tell the driver beforehand that you want to get off at the hostel. There is a trip into town in the morning and one back in the evening, but ask about up-to-date scheduling.

City buses also go to and from the motel and fast-food strips on both sides of town.

### WEST OF THUNDER BAY
Beyond Kakabeka, the traffic thins appreciably. At Shabaqua, the highway forks, the south branch leading to Atikokan and Fort Frances and the north branch heading for Kenora and the Manitoba border. Along the Trans Canada Hwy from this point, moose are often seen, especially at night, so drive with caution and with your eyes frequently scanning the shoulders of the road. In the Upsala region, a sign indicates the Arctic watershed. From here, water flows north. Another marks the beginning of a new time zone – you save an hour going west. Also note that you won't get much on the radio until you pick up Ignace stations.

### Quetico Provincial Park
This huge wilderness park (☎ 597-2735), 100 km long by 60 km wide, is linked to another border park in Minnesota. Quetico is undeveloped for the most part but has one major organised campground. It offers excellent canoeing (1500 km of routes), primarily for those wanting peace and quiet. Portages tend to be short, averaging 400 metres. The use of motor boats is forbidden (except in a few areas by status Native

Indians) and you'll find no roads or logging within the park.

The park is a maze of lakes and rivers, with lots of wildlife and some Native Indian pictographs. Rocky shores and jack pines are typical of some parts, but there are large areas of bog in others and stands of red and white pine in yet others. The park can be accessed from several points, the principal one on the Canadian side being from the campground, Dawson Trail, off Hwy 11 where there is an information pavilion. There are outfitters (for canoes and equipment) and maps available in and around the park.

### Atikokan

This is the supply town for the park. It has two small museums, a number of motels and lodges to put up at and plenty of casual places to find a meal. Rockhounds may want to explore the interesting old mine sites of Steep Rock and Caland. Fifteen different types of minerals can be found at the closed pit mines and waste dumps. Get a map at the tourist office, as the roads around the mines are rough and confusing.

There is a lot of wilderness camping in the district but you really need topographic maps. Between here and Ignace lies **White Otter Lake**, site of **White Otter Castle**, a locally well-known oddity built in 1904 by a Scottish immigrant named Jimmy McOuat. He did it all by himself and nobody knows why: he was a bachelor, yet this is a huge timber place with a four-storey tower, now being restored and preserved. It's on the north-western arm of the lake, accessible only by canoe.

### Fort Frances

Situated on Rainy Lake opposite International Falls, Minnesota, this is a busy border-crossing point into the USA. Both sides are popular outdoor destinations, with countless lakes, cottages, fishing, camping, etc. In town you can visit a paper mill, the town's main business. A causeway across **Rainy Lake** towards Atikokan offers great views of the lake.

The **Fort Frances Museum** examines

Native Indian history and the fur trade, as well as more recent developments. The museum also operates **Fort Saint Pierre**, a replica fur-trading post and lookout tower at **Pither's Point Park**, on the eastern side of town.

North Hwy 71 connects with Kenora and Winnipeg.

### Ignace

Back on the Trans Canada Hwy is Ignace, with a number of motels and a couple of gas station restaurants. It also has a large tourist office (on the west side of town, beside the old fire tower), good for regional information and for details on fishing and canoe routes, including the White Otter Lake district.

In the evening, head over to the garbage dump on the east side of town, north up Hwy 599 just past the golf and country club on the right-hand side. It's a great place to see bears. Although generally pretty blasé about the presence of people, they are unpredictable, so this is not recommended for cyclists. Drivers, I don't suggest getting out of, or at least too far from, your vehicle. Bears may look clumsy but they can outdash any human – guaranteed.

### Dryden

Like so many of the towns in the region, Dryden is fishing crazy – I saw a gas station here offering free minnows with every tank of gas. If you don't hunt or fish, there isn't much here for a visitor. The paper mill, Dryden's major industry, offers interesting free tours on weekdays through the summer. On the radio, listen for the Sunday morning church sermon broadcast in Cree.

### Kenora

Kenora, a pulp and paper town about 200 km from Winnipeg, is the closest town of any size to the Manitoba border. It is a centre for much of the local tourist activity, which consists mainly of summer vacation cottages, fishing (the fish are all at least as big as the model by the highway on the western side of town) and hunting. The setting is attractive, on the convoluted shores of Lake of the Woods.

Tourist offices can be found on the Trans Canada Hwy on both sides of town, about five minutes' drive from the central core.

Main St and Front St along the water are the main centres of activity. The harbourfront area of downtown has been re-done to good effect; the marina is here, as are the docks for two-hour boat cruises out on the lake. Less expensive is the little shuttle over to **Coney Island** for an afternoon's swim at the best sandy beach near town. There are other nearby beaches, such as popular **Norman Beach**, about three km from downtown, at the junction of Parsons St and the Trans Canada Hwy.

On Main St South, in Memorial Park, the small but good **Lake of the Woods Museum** features local history, notably the period around the turn of the century, when Kenora changed rapidly. Tours can be taken of the Boise Cascade paper mill, at 504 Ninth St North.

There's an international sailing regatta in late July, held in and around the 14,000 islands in the lake. A folk festival takes place in early July each year.

Many Native Indians, Ojibway, live in the area (referred to as Treaty 3 Territory), and it is they who hand-pick the Canadian wild rice (manomin) which grows locally; it's $10 for half a kg in most places (natural-food stores) across the country and is delicious. Ask at the tourist office for a booklet on old Native Indian pictographs around the Kenora area. These paintings, done on rock using berry juices, tree gums and sap, depict history and legends, although the meaning of most is really unknown. Some of them are reasonably accessible. Visitors are able to take part in a number of Ojibway events, including regional powwows. Call the Treaty 3 Territory cultural tourism hotline (☎ 1-800-461-3786). Visits can be arranged by calling ahead to the weekly sweat lodge (☎ 543-2532) at Washagamis Bay. Some crafts can be purchased at the Ojibway Cultural Centre in Kenora.

There is camping just a few blocks from the centre of town, at Anicinabe Park on Sixth Ave South. It has showers, and there is a beach. Other provincial parks are nearby.

Motels can be found along the highway; there aren't any hotels in town to recommend. The *Whispering Pines* (☎ 548-4025), on the east side of town, has low price, a beach and also camping.

Places to eat can be found along Main St, and look for the chip wagons around town and by the waterfront.

### Sioux Narrows

About 80 km south of Kenora, on the eastern side of Lake of the Woods, Sioux Narrows is a local resort town.

In addition to the residents from around the region, many Americans and people from Winnipeg spend time here during the summer months. The town and its surroundings have a range of cottages, lodges, motels, campgrounds, and even houseboats for rent. Lake of the Woods fishing is renowned far and wide. Sioux Narrows Provincial Park has camping and contains some Native Indian pictographs.

# Manitoba

Entered Confederation: 15 July 1870
Area: 650,090 sq km
Population: 1,091,942
Provincial Capital: Winnipeg

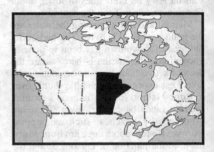

Manitoba, Canada's fifth province, probably gets its name from the Algonkian Indian languages – in Lake Manitoba there is a strait where the water hits the limestone edges, making an odd echoing sound; the Native Indians associated this sound with the 'great spirit' ('manito') and named the spot 'Manito Waba', which means Manito Strait. Manito Waba became Manitoba. The Assiniboine and Cree First Nations were the principal groups inhabiting the region upon the arrival of Europeans. The Chipewayen of the northern sections and around Hudson Bay soon became involved with the fur traders. The Ojibway, found mainly across Ontario, also moved as far west as the great lakes of Manitoba.

Winnipeg, the capital, has had a long and interesting history which influenced greatly the development of the west in general. The city has a variety of things to see and do, and many things are within walking distance of each other along architecturally diverse streets.

Winnipeg is a major cultural centre and offers plenty of choice in accommodation and eating out. Neighbouring St Boniface is the largest western French community in Canada. Scattered across the province are large parks, ideal for exploring the terrain.

## The Canadian Shield

The 'Shield' is one of Canada's most dominant physical characteristics. It surrounds Hudson Bay on the east, south and west in a vast U pattern, with a shield-like shape around the perimeter. In the north, it runs from the Atlantic Ocean on the coast of Labrador 3000 km west past Lake Winnipeg north-west to Lake Athabaska, to Great Slave Lake, Great Bear Lake and on to the Arctic Ocean. From the Hudson Bay areas, it stretches south from Lake Superior to the St Lawrence River around Kingston. And just what is it? A mass of ancient, stable rock, the first region of the continent raised permanently above the sea. The predominantly igneous, fossil-free, stratified rock from the archaeozoic period is among the world's oldest. The entire region was scraped and gouged by glaciers, resulting in an almost uniformly flat to undulating rocky surface very sparsely and intermittently covered with soil. Rarely across its expanse does it rise more than 500 metres above sea level. Many of the dips, dents, cracks and pits in the surface are filled with water – lakes, rivers and ponds of every shape and size. In several sections, as much as 40% of the surface is fresh water.

The southern sections tend to be forested, and in Manitoba, these boreal woodlands extend as far north as Churchill. Further north the trees begin to diminish, and eventually disappear altogether, leaving lichen and mosses as the principal vegetation.

The southern areas, bordering as they do much of the heavily populated regions of the country, have become part of the Canadian mental landscape. Synonymous with outdoor living, camping, cottages, hiking, fishing and wildlife, this generally inhospitable but wildly beautiful land is part of the quintessential Canada. ■

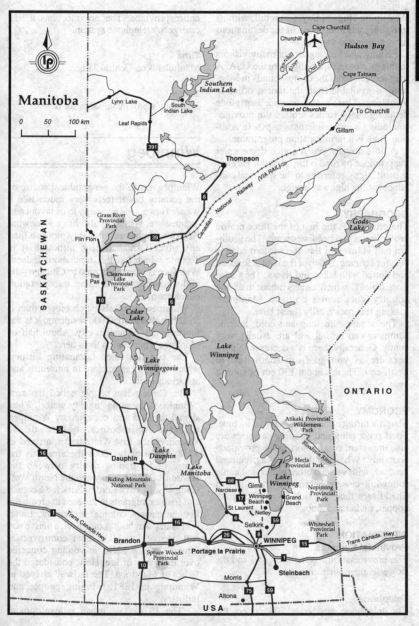

# Manitoba

0    50    100 km

SASKATCHEWAN

Lynn Lake

South Indian Lake

*Southern Indian Lake*

Leaf Rapids

391

Thompson

6

Gillam

*To Churchill*

**Inset of Churchill**

Cape Churchill

Churchill

*Churchill River*

*Owl River*

*Hudson Bay*

Cape Tatnam

Grass River Provincial Park

Flin Flon

39

Canadian National Railway (VIA RAIL)

*Gods Lake*

The Pas

Clearwater Lake Provincial Park

10

*Cedar Lake*

6

*Lake Winnipegosis*

*Lake Winnipeg*

**ONTARIO**

5

16

Dauphin

*Lake Dauphin*

*Lake Manitoba*

Riding Mountain National Park

68

Narcisse

17

Gimli

Winnipeg Beach

St Laurent

6

Netley

Grand Beach

59

Selkirk

Atikaki Provincial Wilderness Park

*Bloodvein River*

Hecla Provincial Park

Nopiming Provincial Park

Whiteshell Provincial Park

1

Trans Canada Hwy

Brandon

1

16

26

8

**WINNIPEG**

15

Trans Canada Hwy

Spruce Woods Provincial Park

Portage la Prairie

10

Morris

Steinbach

1

75

59

Altona

**USA**

Way up on Hudson Bay, Churchill, with its intriguing wildlife, is one of the destinations most alluring to visitors.

Fishing and hunting attract many visitors to this province, especially from the USA. A map indicating all the campgrounds in Manitoba is available from the tourist office in Winnipeg. There's also an excellent guide detailing canoe routes around the province (including some wilderness trips). In addition there is a farm vacation programme.

A little novelty you'll notice if you enter the province by road is the 'put your garbage in orbit' signs, referring to the spherical containers at the highway's edge.

## GEOGRAPHY

The province is the first of the three prairie provinces as you head westward. The southern half is low and flat; the western edge is best for farming. Much of the land is forested and dotted with lakes and rivers. The Canadian Shield, which covers about half the country, cuts across northern Manitoba, making this rocky, hilly forest land.

The winters are long and cold, but the summers can be hot and are usually very sunny. Generally there is a decrease in temperature as you go from south-west to north-east. There's about 130 cm of snow a year.

## ECONOMY

Manufacturing is the main source of income. Food processing and clothing factories are also important contributors to the provincial economy. Wheat is the major agricultural product, with various other grains and cattle following closely behind. In the northern Shield area there are rich deposits of gold, copper, nickel and zinc.

## INFORMATION
### Provincial Symbols

The provincial bird is the grey owl and the flower is the prairie crocus.

### Telephone

The telephone area code 204 covers the entire province. The province has a 911 emergency telephone system.

### Time

Manitoba is on Central Time.

### Tax

Manitoba's provincial sales tax is 7%.

# Winnipeg

Winnipeg sits in the geographical centre of the country but it feels very much like a western town. Due primarily to its layout and architecture, Winnipeg also has a somewhat American ambience, probably more so than any other Canadian city, although it is Toronto which has this reputation. Indeed, Winnipeg is often compared to Chicago – its mid-western, grain-handling, transportation counterpart.

Winnipeg also feels much bigger than it is, although with 650,000 residents, it is the fourth largest Canadian city. About half of Manitoba's population lives here.

The city has some fascinating history, which visitors can explore in museums and at various sites.

The Cree Indian people called the area 'Winnipee', meaning 'muddy water'. They shared the land now occupied by Winnipeg with the Assiniboines, before de la Vérendrye, the first White trader, arrived in 1738. In the early 1800s the area was the centre of fur-trading rivalry between the Hudson's Bay Company and the North West Company. In 1812 Lord Selkirk led Scottish and Irish immigrants to the area to create the first permanent colonial settlement. Later, Fort Garry was built. Louis Riel, a native son and one of Canada's most controversial figures, led the Métis in voicing concerns over their way of life. He is considered the father of Manitoba. The railway arrived in Winnipeg in 1881, bringing people and industry.

The 1970s saw urban redevelopment

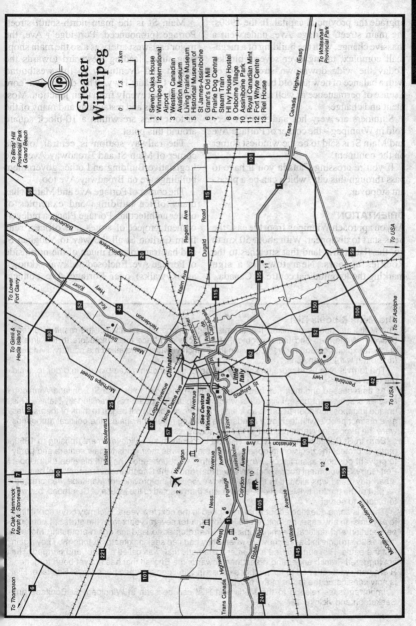

**Greater Winnipeg**

0    1.5    3 km

1  Seven Oaks House
2  Winnipeg International
   Airport
3  Western Canadian
   Aviation Museum
4  Living Prairie Museum
5  Historical Museum of
   St James-Assiniboine
6  Grant's Old Mill
7  Prairie Dog Central
   Steam Train
8  HI Ivy House Hostel
9  Osborne Village
10 Assiniboine Park
11 Royal Canadian Mint
12 Fort Whyte Centre
13 Riel House

To Birds' Hill
Provincial Park
& Grand Beach

Whiteshell
Provincial Park

Trans Canada Highway (East)

101

59

Regent Ave

Dugald Road

37

15

Lagimodière Boulevard

20

Nairn Ave

135

115

To Lower
Fort Garry

To Gimli &
Hecla Island

52

Red River

42

Henderson Hwy

100

To St Adolphe

150

59

180

101

Main Street

Chinatown

Provencher

Ave de la Cathédrale

46

1

62

13

To Oak Hammock
Marsh & Stonewall

7

90

McPhillips Street

Logan Avenue

Notre Dame Avenue

Ellice Avenue

See Central
Winnipeg Map

57

River

Little
Italy

Stafford St

9

Pembina Hwy

42

To USA

Inkster Boulevard

25

47

7

3

2

Wellington

Ness

Portage Avenue

Avenue

Assiniboine

Corydon

Kenaston

90

80

155

To USA

Avenue

10

12

105

Robin Blvd

Wilkes

Avenue

145

McGillivray Boulevard

6

5

4

11

8

Portage Avenue (West)

Trans Canada Highway

221

241

To Thompson

6

101

upgrade the provincial capital. In the 1980s, the main street, Portage Ave, underwent a massive change, with the building of a megamall complex, taking over several blocks. Today the wide downtown streets, edged with a balance of new and old buildings, give a sense of permanence as well as of development and change.

Summers are very hot and winters very cold in Winnipeg – the corner of Portage Ave and Main St is said to be the windiest corner on the continent.

If you're crossing Canada you'll have to pass through this city, which can be a pleasant stopover.

## ORIENTATION

As you approach Winnipeg from the east, the trees start to disappear. With about 50 km to go, the flat prairie land that stretches to the Rockies appears. Near town is a sign marking the longitudinal centre of Canada.

Main St is the main north-south street. Portage (pronounced 'Port-idge') Ave, the major east-west artery, is also the main shopping street, leading westward towards the airport and eventually to the westbound Trans Canada Hwy. The downtown core spreads out evenly from their junction. Most of the hotels and restaurants and many of the historic sites are within a 10-block square around this point.

The railway station is central, on the corner of Main St and Broadway Ave. The Legislative Building and other government buildings are on Broadway Ave too.

The corner of Portage Ave and Main St has many office buildings and examples of newer architecture. Portage Place, a redevelopment project of stores and offices, runs from Carlton St all the way to Vaughan St and has transformed much of the north side of Portage Ave. Enclosed walkways (known as skywalks) over Portage Ave connect

### The Métis & Louis Riel

The Métis are people of mixed Indian and French blood, almost always the result of unions between White men and Indian women. Many Métis can trace their ancestors to the time of western exploration and fur-trading, when the French voyageurs travelled the country, living like (and often with) the Indians.

The term is also used more loosely to include English-Indian mixed bloods, in order to avoid the term half-breed.

As time passed and their numbers grew, many Métis began to use the St Boniface/Winnipeg area as a settlement base, living a life which was part European, part traditionally Native. This unique juxtaposition soon became an identity, and those born into it began to think of themselves as a distinct people with their own needs. The ensuing rebellions against the political authorities were the almost inevitable product of this consciousness.

Born in St Boniface in 1844, Louis Riel led the Métis in an antigovernment uprising in 1869, partly to protest the decision to open up what they saw as their lands to new settlers and partly to prevent possible assimilation. When complaints went unheeded, he and his men took Upper Fort Garry. Government troops soon reversed that, and to the Canadian government, Riel became a bad guy. Land was allotted to the Métis, however, and the province of Manitoba was created. As part of the turning twists of Riel's fate, he was then elected to the House of Commons, but was forbidden to serve!

There is some question about what transpired in the next few years. Riel may have spent time in asylums. In any case, he took refuge in Montana for several years from the stress of personal persecution and political machinations. Later he returned to lead the again-protesting Métis in their 1885 struggle in Saskatchewan, where they had fled seeking greater autonomy. They again lost the battle. Riel surrendered and, after a dramatic trial, was called a traitor and hanged. The act triggered French anger and resentment towards the English that has not yet been forgotten. Riel's body was returned to his mother's house in Winnipeg and then buried in St Boniface. Riel is now considered the father of the province.

Important sites relating to the Métis and Riel can be seen in Winnipeg, St Boniface and Saskatoon and vicinity. ∎

Portage Place to major department stores on the south side. Many of the downtown side streets are one-way streets, which alternate in direction as a rule.

To the north-east of the city core is the old warehouse area known as the Exchange District. Nearby, north up Main St, the Centennial Centre is an art and cultural complex.

The small Chinatown is also in this area. The Chinese Cultural Building/Dynasty Building, at 180 King St, has a small oriental garden retreat. The Mandarin Building, on the corner of King St and James Ave, contains a replica of the Chinese Nine Imperial Dragon Mural and a statue of Buddha. The two buildings are linked by the China Gate, which runs above King St.

North of Rupert St on Main St is an area of cheap bars and dingy hotels, peopled by various down-and-outers, many of them, unfortunately, lost or alcoholic Native Canadians.

Further north on Main St, you'll find some evidence of the many ethnic groups, primarily Jews and Ukrainians, who once lived here in greater numbers.

South of the downtown area, across the Assiniboine River on Osborne St, is Osborne Village, a newish area with boutiques, stores and restaurants. Back across the bridge in the downtown area, the art gallery is on the corner of Memorial Blvd and Portage Ave and the bus station is nearby.

South of Osborne Village along Corydon Ave for a few blocks between Cockburn St North and Daly St North is a small Italian district which has become the centre of a little café and restaurant scene. It's particularly good for a stroll in summer, when many of the places have outdoor patios along the street.

## INFORMATION

The main tourist office (☎ 945-3777) is downtown, in the Legislative Building on Broadway Ave, near Osborne St. It's open from 8 am to 7 pm daily (in winter from 8 am to 4.30 pm Monday to Friday only). You

can also call Travel Manitoba on ☎ 1-800-665-0040, ext 35.

Another office is the Tourism Winnipeg branch (☎ 943-1970), on the 2nd floor of the Convention Centre on the corner of York Ave and Edmonton St, also downtown. It's open during business hours, daily in summer, on weekdays only from September to May.

For those flying in, there is a handy information desk (☎ 774-0031) at the airport, at the north end of the main level. This one is open year-round from 8.30 am to 10 pm.

Travel Manitoba (☎ 945-3777) has more detailed information on areas of the province outside Winnipeg. The office is on the 7th floor at 155 Carlton St.

There is also an office in City Hall, on Main St a few blocks north of Portage Ave.

Travel books and maps can be found at the Global Village bookshop in Osborne Village. Another good bookshop here is Mary Scorer.

The post office is at 266 Graham Ave. The general delivery window is open on Saturday mornings as well as during the regular weekday hours.

For a view of the city, go to the Observation Gallery of the Richardson Building, at 1 Lombard Place, on the corner of Portage Ave and Main St. Unfortunately it's only open on Wednesday, and then only for half an hour in the morning and half an hour in the afternoon. For information on visiting, call ☎ 956-0272. Advance notice is required (phoning on Wednesday morning is fine).

## WALKING TOUR

Free 'Historic Winnipeg' walking tours begin at the museum information booth. They take place Monday to Saturday at 11 am and 1.30 pm, Sunday at 1 and 3 pm, and Wednesday and Thursday evenings at 7 pm. The tour lasts one hour.

## CENTENNIAL ARTS CENTRE

On Main St, north of Portage Ave, the Arts Centre is a complex which houses several things to see. The all-inclusive ticket for admission to the three following museums is cheaper than paying the individual admission fees.

## Museum of Man & Nature

This very good museum (☎ 956-2830) has exhibits of history, culture, wildlife and geology. The dioramas of Native Indian life and animals are realistic, incorporating sights, sounds and even smells. There is an excellent recreation of a 1920s town, with barber shop, drug store and old cinema. One room has a full-sized replica of the *Nonsuch*, a 17th-century ketch that took the first load of Hudson's Bay Company furs to England. The museum is worth a few hours' visit. Admission costs $3.50. It's open every day from 10 am until 6 pm in summer. From September to June it's open from noon until 4 pm on weekdays and until 5 pm on weekends. It's closed on Monday.

## Planetarium

The planetarium (☎ 943-3142) has good programmes on space, the solar system and different aspects of the universe. There are also laser rock shows, fashion shows and other performances held in the planetarium, which utilise its unique equipment. The usual programmes are $4; the laser rock shows are more expensive. Ring for information and programme times.

## Touch the Universe

In the museum basement is a 'hands-on' science gallery with participatory displays designed to help reveal how our senses perceive the world. The staff put on demonstrations on a range of scientific topics. Admission is $3, less for kids.

## THE FORKS

Now the busiest people place in Winnipeg, The Forks has been a very successful redevelopment project. The fetching location at the forks of the Red and Assiniboine rivers, behind the VIA Rail station off Main St near Broadway Ave, has in one way or another been the site of pretty much all of Manitoba's history. A national historic site (☎ 983-2007) has been developed, with park staff on duty every day (find them at the round office structure). They can provide information on what's gone on through the years at this river

junction. Native Indians first used the area some 6000 years ago. The early explorers and fur traders stopped here, forts were built and destroyed, and Métis and Scottish pioneers later settled The Forks.

The site is essentially a riverside park. The Riverwalk is a path with historic notes written on plaques in English, French and Cree. Parts of the trail also provide views of the city along the way.

The public is invited to join archaeologists (☎ 942-6393) as they continue to excavate portions of the site. There is a small fee for this and reservations are required. If you don't want to dirty your hands, there are also free observational tours offered through the day.

The Forks is also a recreation area, with shops, restaurants, bars and events all centered around overhauled turn-of-the-century stables, warehouses and factory buildings. The Market Building contains craft shops, an art gallery, produce stalls (with such things as cheeses and breads) and a handful of restaurants, cafés and other food outlets. It's a fine place for a coffee and cinnamon bun breakfast with a newspaper. The Johnston Building is similar but also houses the Manitoba Sports Hall of Fame for sports or trivia buffs.

Future developments are to include a major Children's Museum, and a provincial tourist information centre to cover all of Manitoba's attractions.

Walking tours are offered from The Forks Pavilion and canoes can be rented at the site – a paddle along the historic river, perhaps past the Basilica over in St Boniface, is not a bad way to spend a couple of hours. A water bus runs back and forth across the river, too, or to Osborne Village with a stop at the dock behind the Legislature. Full-scale boat tours of the river depart from nearby. In winter, there is skating on the river or you can walk over the ice to the impressive-looking St Boniface Basilica. Cross-country ski trails are groomed along the river. Take a break and warm up beside the fire in the Pavilion.

City buses connect the downtown area to the site near the Market Building, but it is quite walkable. On weekdays the No 99 bus

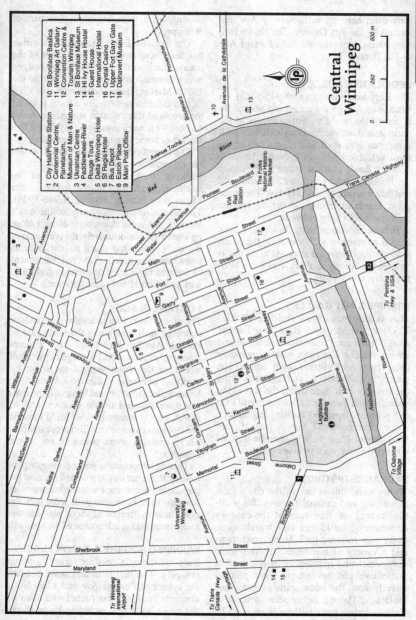

Central Winnipeg

1  City Hall/Police Station
2  Centennial Centre,
   Planetarium,
   Museum of Man & Nature
3  Ukrainian Centre
4  Paddlewheel-River
   Rouge Tours
5  Delta Winnipeg Hotel
6  St Regis Hotel
7  Bus Depot
8  Eaton Place
9  Main Post Office
10 St Boniface Basilica
11 Winnipeg Art Gallery
12 Convention Centre &
   Tourism Winnipeg
13 St Boniface Museum
14 HI Ivy House Hostel
15 Guest House
   International Hostel
16 Crystal Casino
17 Upper Fort Gary Gate
18 Dalnavert Museum

runs from here up to Broadway Ave and around by the Art Gallery. The No 96 bus, which runs on weekends, links Portage Ave to The Forks.

## LEGISLATIVE BUILDING

The Legislative Building (☎ 945-5813), on Broadway Ave on the corner of Osborne St, is one of the world's great examples of the neoclassical architectural style. It was built using rare limestone and is now one of the most valuable buildings in North America. 'Golden Boy', a bronze statue perched atop the building, is covered in 23½-carat gold and has become a city symbol. There are good, free tours throughout the day and the building has a cheap cafeteria.

Behind the Legislative Building, a park with a monument to Louis Riel, the Métis leader, runs beside the river. At night this is an area for commercial sex – as it has been for many, many years.

## WINNIPEG ART GALLERY

This is the pie-shaped building (☎ 775-7297) at 300 Memorial Blvd, near Portage Ave. It has a good collection of Inuit art and shows mainly Canadian works, including those by young, little-known artists. The gallery is well designed and laid out. During the summer it is open daily; the rest of the year it's open Tuesday to Sunday from 11 am to 5 pm (until 9 pm on Thursday and Friday). Admission costs $3 but is free all day Wednesday. There's a restaurant on the roof which you may want to investigate.

## EXCHANGE DISTRICT

To my mind this is one of the city's most interesting and unusual features. It's a 20-block area of fine turn-of-the-century commercial buildings and warehouses, many now restored for housing, restaurants and a variety of businesses. There's some very substantial architecture here, as well as distinctive old advertising signs painted directly onto the brick walls of numerous buildings. Though rarely seen in most of Canada today, such billboards seem to be undergoing a mini-revival in this part of Winnipeg.

The various Edwardian and Victorian buildings here arose to fill the needs of the many stock and commodity exchanges which boomed in the city from 1880 to the 1920s. Market Square, on the corner of King St and Bannantyne Ave, is a focal point of the area and there's often something going on here – on weekends, you may find a flea market or some live music, for example.

The tourist office has maps to follow for an informative walk in the district, or walking tours are offered daily in the summer, beginning in the foyer of the Museum of Man & Nature (☎ 986-5924). The area also contains many of the city's theatres and some clubs, so it doesn't close up after dark. Unfortunately, the recession of the early 1990s has taken its toll here, as elsewhere, and much of the redevelopment of the area has stalled or even slipped back, with many buildings partially vacant.

## PORTAGE PLACE

The city's downtown redevelopment indoor shopping mall runs along the north side of Portage Ave for three blocks. It's a three-storey affair, connected to large department stores on the south side of the street by enclosed overhead walkways. Aside from being a place to shop and hang out, the mall has three first-run movie theatres, and an IMAX movie theatre (☎ 780-SEAT) on the 3rd floor for large-format film presentations. There are also some places to eat in the complex.

This development is part of a major plan to keep the inner city viable and prevent the population becoming too suburbia oriented. It seems to be busy, and with some luck the other nearby streets and shops may be able to continue taking advantage of the spin-off.

## WINNIPEG SQUARE & EATON PLACE

Each of these is another large shopping complex. The first is underground beneath the corner of Portage Ave and Main St. It connects by skywalk or tunnel with many of the area's buildings, including Eaton Place, which lies between Portage Place and Winnipeg Square along Hargrave St.

If you'd spent a winter in Winnipeg, you'd know why these indoor, protected retail centres are so commonplace. There are food fairs in both, as well as several restaurants covering a variety of price ranges.

## MANITOBA CHILDREN'S MUSEUM
Hold onto your head: here's a museum (☎ 957-0005) set up for the kids themselves, especially those between the ages of three and 11 years. Hands-on exhibits encourage play and learning at the same time. In one section children can dress up in costumes and pretend they're in the circus. Another is a simulated spaceship cockpit. The museum is just off Main St, at 109 Pacific Ave, and admission is inexpensive. It's open daily, all day, but is closed on Sunday and holiday mornings until 11 am.

## WINNIPEG COMMODITY EXCHANGE
Canada's largest and oldest commodity futures market (☎ 949-0495) is here, with a visitors' gallery which overlooks the trading area. You can see grains and other crops being traded and prices fluctuating with the Chicago markets. Don't forget to find out how pork bellies are doing! Guides can explain some of this very different world to you at no charge. The exchange is open Monday to Friday from 9.30 am to 1.15 pm. It's in the Commodity Exchange Tower, 360 Main St.

## ST BONIFACE
Primarily a residential district, St Boniface, across the Red River on Boulevard Provencher, is one of the oldest French communities in Canada. There's not much to see, but the imposing facade of the **St Boniface Basilica**, dating from 1908, is worth a look. The rest of the church was destroyed by fire in 1968. Churches were built and rebuilt on this site from as early as 1818. In front, facing the river, is a cemetery used by the local French from the 1800s to the present. Louis Riel, the Métis leader, was born in St Boniface and is buried here.

The Métis people, of mixed North American Indian and French Canadian ancestry, founded a culturally and politically distinctive society in the late 19th century. In 1885 Riel led an unsuccessful rebellion against the British government of the east, and was later executed.

Next door, at 494 Rue Taché, is the **St Boniface Museum** (☎ 237-4500), in what was the nunnery around 1850. This is the oldest building in Winnipeg and evidently is the largest oak-log construction on the continent. It contains artefacts and relics pertaining to Riel and to other French, Métis and Native Indian settlers as well as to the Grey Nuns, who lived and worked here after arriving by birch-bark canoe from Montreal, a trip of nearly 3000 km.

There is also some information on Jean Baptiste Lagimodière, one of the best-known of the voyageurs (early French fur traders/explorers) who canoed between here and Montreal. There is a diorama of a Métis hunter's camp, with an example of the famous Red River Cart, which could be

Façade of St Boniface

floated across rivers by repositioning the wheels. Also in the museum are some articles that were saved from the destroyed basilica.

Admission is by donation. In summer, it's open from 9 am to 9 pm Monday to Friday, from 9 am to 5 pm on Saturday and from 10 am to 9 pm on Sunday and holidays. In winter it closes at 5 pm every day.

The St Boniface Historical Society offers walking tours of older parts of the area, including discussions of local history and culture. The tourist office has a booklet on St Boniface which includes a map and self-guided walking tour.

To get there from downtown, take the bus east along Portage Ave across the bridge and then walk along the river to the church and museum. Taché Promenade follows the Red River along Rue Taché, past much of St Boniface's history. A couple of plaques indicate the major points of interest and provide some details on the Grey Nuns.

**Gabrielle Roy House** was built in 1905 by Léon Roy, the father of Gabrielle, a well-known Canadian fiction writer who used the house as the setting for some of her works. The house is at 375 Rue Deschambault, where there is a small plaque but nothing much to see unless you're a literary fan.

At 340 Boulevard Provencher is the **French-Manitoban Cultural Centre** (☎ 233-8972). The centre is open daily and is responsible for organising, creating and promoting a variety of French cultural events around the city. A restaurant serves French Canadian food at lunch time.

## UKRAINIAN CENTRE
The Ukrainian Centre (☎ 942-0218), at 184 Alexander Ave, near the Museum of Man & Nature, contains a gallery and museum. Set up to preserve and present the culture of the Ukraine, the museum has costumes, textiles, ceramics and painted Easter eggs *(pysankas)*. The gallery displays both old and contemporary works. A specialised library holds 40,000 volumes relating to this important Canadian immigrant group.

The centre is open from noon to 7 pm daily in July and August and on weekends for the

same hours in May and June. Admission is free.

## HOLY TRINITY UKRAINIAN ORTHODOX CATHEDRAL
Within this church with the bulbous Byzantine domes is the provincial branch of the Ukrainian Museum of Canada (☎ 334-6531). Examples of traditional arts & crafts are displayed. The cathedral is at 1175 Main St. Call for opening times, as they vary seasonally and by day of the week.

## ROYAL CANADIAN MINT
The real money is made south-east of town, at 520 Lagimodière Boulevard, on the corner of the Trans Canada Hwy (☎ 257-3359). This ultramodern, glass, pyramid-shaped building contains some of the most modern minting machinery in the world. Free tours every half-hour show the procedures used in cranking out two billion coins a year. The mint produces Canada's coinage as well as coins for many other countries, especially in Asia. It's open Monday to Friday, 9 am to 3 pm, from May to September. (No free samples!)

## GAMBLING CENTRES
For hopeful gamblers, this entry is put after the information on the mint! Situated on the 7th floor of Hotel Fort Garry, 222 Broadway Ave, is the somewhat swish, up-market Crystal Casino (☎ 957-2600), featuring many of the classic games – roulette, blackjack, baccarat and, of course, the slots.

The casino is open from noon to 2 am Monday to Saturday and from 4 pm on Sundays. There is a rather restrictive, semiformal dress code in effect. Men should sport a jacket and tie, women the equivalent. Because the casino has proven so lucrative for the provincial government, they have now built two more casinos, or rather electronic bingo and slot-machine palaces, around town. The McPhillips Station, with an old-west train station motif, is in the city's north end. Aside from the many, varied slot machines, this casual, no-dress-code, no-alcohol monument to the one-armed bandit features a McDonald's! Club Regent, with a sort of Caribbean Island-paradise theme, is located in suburban Transcona.

Both are open daily from noon to 2 am, and they are busy.

The government is allocating $2.5 million this year to gambling-addiction programmes.

## WESTERN CANADIAN AVIATION MUSEUM

One of the country's largest aviation museums, the WCAM (☎ 786-5503) is still for plane buffs only. They have a good collection of 35 planes from over the years but only some of them are on display at any given time. There are a few particularly historic aircraft, including Canada's first helicopter. Other exhibits include uniforms, photographs, engines and various related artefacts. The museum is in hangar T-2 at the Winnipeg International Airport, 958 Ferry Rd, and is open every day (except Sunday and holiday mornings). Admission is inexpensive, and a tour is offered for a small additional fee. From the 'Flight Deck', traffic at the Winnipeg Airport can be watched coming and going.

## POLICE MUSEUM

At the Winnipeg Police Academy (☎ 986-3976), 130 Allard Ave, a small museum features uniforms, 'wanted' posters and various equipment. Highlights are the Harley Davidson and an original jail cell from 1911. It's free, but call about opening hours.

## RIEL HOUSE NATIONAL HISTORIC PARK

At 330 River Rd, in a residential area known as St Vital, quite a distance south of downtown, Riel House (☎ 257-1783) details Louis Riel's life here in the 1880s. Riel is an enduring figure in Canadian history whose story remains both fascinating and controversial.

The restored and furnished traditional French Canadian-style log farmhouse, built in 1881, belonged to Louis' parents. He was brought here to lie in state after his execution in Saskatchewan in 1885.

A staff interpreter offers information on the Riels and on the Métis in general.

To get there, take the No 16 bus from Portage Ave going west; after passing through Osborne Village, it'll take you nearly to the door. The site looks out of place beside the modern bungalows which surround it. Opening hours are 10 am to 6 pm, daily in summer, on weekends only in September (it's closed the rest of the year). Admission is free, but phone to be sure it is open before making the trip out here.

## MACDONALD HOUSE (DALNAVERT)

Near the Legislature, this beautiful Victorian house at 61 Carlton St is also called Dalnavert (☎ 943-2835). It was built in 1895 for the son of John A Macdonald, Canada's first prime minister, and is decorated with period pieces. It's closed on Monday and Friday. Admission is $3.50 and there's free parking around the back. From June to September the house is open all day; the rest of the year, it's open only in the afternoons.

## SEVEN OAKS HOUSE

The oldest habitable house in the province, Seven Oaks House (☎ 339-7429) was built (without nails) in 1851. It's about four km north of Portage Ave and Main St, on Rupertsland Ave. Seven Oaks House is open daily from mid-May to Labour Day (early in September) and on weekends in spring.

## GRANT'S OLD MILL

Grant's is a reconstruction of an 1829 water mill (☎ 837-5761), which is thought to be the first use of hydropower in the province. There's not really very much to see, although grist (grain) is ground every day and offered for sale. The mill is open from May to Labour Day from 10 am to 8 pm Monday to Saturday and from 2 pm to 8 pm on Sunday. It's on the corner of Booth Drive and Portage Ave West, near Sturgeon Creek.

## UPPER FORT GARRY GATE

In the small park on Main St, near Broadway

Ave and across from the railway station, is the old stone gate and some remaining wall (restored in 1982) of Fort Garry. Since 1738, four different forts have stood on this spot, or nearby. The gate dates from 1835 and was part of the Hudson's Bay Company's fort system. There are also some photographs and written descriptions.

## HISTORICAL MUSEUM OF ST JAMES-ASSINIBOINE

This small museum (☎ 888-8706) has a collection of Native Indian, Métis and pioneer artefacts from the area at the turn of the century. It's at 3180 Portage Ave and is open from 10 am to 5 pm daily, but is closed on weekends after Labour Day until the following spring. Admission costs $2. Next door is a 100-year-old log house with authentic furnishings.

## ROSS HOUSE

Ross House (☎ 943-3958), the first post office in the west, is an example of Red River log construction. It's open from mid-May to Labour Day, Wednesday to Sunday from 11 am, and is free. It can be found in Joe Zuken Heritage Park, on the west side of Mead St between Sutherland and Euclid Sts.

## NORTH POINT DOUGLAS & SELKIRK AVE

This section of the city, the North End, is the only area west of Montreal to be classified an historic area. Many of the houses are over 100 years old, and plaques and monuments commemorate various historical events.

It's north up Main St, just north and east of the junction of Hwy 42, which leads over the river and north out of town. Multiethnic Selkirk Ave has long been the commercial centre of the city's north end and first home of a range of immigrant groups. See Organised Tours later for details of free walking tours of the area.

## ASSINIBOINE PARK

Assiniboine is the largest city park and is open from 7 am until dark. Of course, it's free. The grounds hold an English garden,

and a 40-hectare zoo with animals from around the world. See the statue of Winnie the Bear, a bear purchased in White River, Ontario by a soldier from Winnipeg on his way to England to serve in WW I. The bear ended up at the London Zoo and is said to have been the inspiration for A A Milne's *Winnie the Pooh*.

Other features are the conservatory (with some tropical vegetation) and, nearby, the Leo Mol Sculpture Garden and a small art gallery. The sculpture garden displays a range of work by the internationally regarded Mol. There are also numerous playing fields. At the beginning of July, watch for the free evening outdoor Shakespearean performances.

The park is south of the Assiniboine River and just south-west off Portage Ave, about seven km west of the downtown area. Entrances are off Corydon Ave West (at Shaftesbury) or at the west end of Wellington Crescent.

## ASSINIBOINE FOREST

South of the Assiniboine Park, between Shaftsbury and Chalfont Aves, this largely undeveloped forest area is even larger than the park itself. In the middle is a pond with an observation area for bird-watching, and deer may be seen along the winding trails. No admission is charged.

## LIVING PRAIRIE MUSEUM

At 2793 Ness Ave, north of Grant's Mill, the Living Prairie Museum (☎ 832-0167) is really a park, or rather a preserve, where a 12-hectare area of now very scarce, original, unploughed tall prairie grass is protected and studied.

Within this small area, 200 native plants can be found, as well as a variety of animal and birdlife. The interpretive centre at the site is open on weekends (daily through the summer), and naturalists are on hand. Walking trails and guided walks are offered. Admission to the museum is free.

## FORT WHYTE CENTRE

The centre (☎ 989-8355), in a conservation

area with a marsh, lake and woods, is an environmental education facility. Walking trails, exhibits, demonstrations and slide shows on local wildlife are part of the programme. A freshwater aquarium depicts the province's different aquatic life. It's not a bad place to get a glimpse of some of the features of rural, undeveloped Manitoba as well as some of the province's fauna. Trails lead through replicas of various provincial wetland areas, where birds, waterfowl and even the odd mammal such as deer may be viewed. Outdoor activities are led, too. Admission is charged. It's open daily at 1961 McCreary Rd, about a 20-minute drive from downtown.

## OTHER PARKS

There are numerous parks in and around the city, some quite large. Aside from the ones mentioned above, there is Little Mountain Park, which has hiking trails and examples of local forest and prairie vegetation. It's two km east of Sturgeon Rd off Oak Point Hwy.

## ACTIVITIES
### Swimming

A couple of swimming pools in the city are open to the public. There's Central Outdoor Pool, administered by the City of Winnipeg Parks & Recreation Department, and the Pan-Am Pool (☎ 284-4031), 25 Poseidon Bay, which is one of the country's largest. Admission costs $2.

### Other

In summer the larger city parks are good for walking. In winter there is skating on the rivers, and for that perhaps the best spot is on the Red River near The Forks, in front of the St Boniface Basilica.

## ORGANISED TOURS

Gray Line together with Paddlewheel River Rouge (☎ 944-8000) have six boat and bus tours ranging in length and price. The basic downtown double-decker bus tour lasting 3½ hours is $17.

The lower-priced boat tours depart from a wharf down by The Forks Historic Site, at the foot of the Provencher Bridge on the corner of Water Ave and Gilroy St. The ticket office is also here.

There are straight along-the-river or more costly evening dinner-dance cruises on a replica paddlewheeler. Another travels down to Lower Fort Garry. The MS *River Rouge* also has dinner cruises, dance cruises and Sunday afternoon cruises.

There are walking tours (☎ 986-5924) of the Exchange District daily in July and August at a fee of $3 per adult. They depart from the Museum of Man & Nature and wander the old commercial centre, emphasising history and architecture.

Free one-hour walking tours (☎ 586-2720) of old Selkirk Ave begin from Main St westward to McKenzie in the city's historic north end. The latest schedule had two walks a day from Tuesday to Saturday. (See North Point Douglas earlier in this section.)

Beaten Trail (☎ 783-6735) offers three different walking tours, which may include The Forks, the Exchange District or the sites of St Boniface. Tours last one to two hours and are operate daily. Call for an updated schedule and the prices, which are not high.

## FESTIVALS

The following are some of the major festivals held in the province:

February
*Le Festival du Voyageur* – If you happen to be out here in the dead of winter, Le Festival du Voyageur, in mid-February, is a week-long event commemorating the early French voyageurs or fur traders with concerts, a parade, arts & crafts displays and lots of outdoor activities.

June-August
*Winnipeg Folk Festival* (☎ 231-0096 ) – This festival held annually is probably the country's biggest and best known. It takes place for three days in summer, usually early July, with about 100 performers, shows and workshops. The festival is held at Birds' Hill Park, 20 km north of downtown.
*The Red River Exhibition* – Held in late June at the Winnipeg Arena, this festival is a week-long carnival, with an amusement park and lots of games, rides and exhibits.
*Winnipeg Fringe Festival* – A nine-day event held in the Exchange District in July, features

theatre performances of every description.

*Black-O-Rama* – This is an annual summer festival of music, dance and poetry of West Indian origin.

*Folklorama* – This is the city's big, popular festival of nations. The tourist office will have up-to-date details on this August event, which celebrates the city's surprising number of ethnic groups through two weeks of music, dance, food, etc, with pavilions in and around downtown Winnipeg. It has become a considerable tourist attraction, and each year more Americans make the trek north to join in.

## PLACES TO STAY
### Camping

There are a few places to camp around town but most are a long way out, off the main highways or up at the beach areas around Lake Winnipeg.

*Jones Campground* (☎ 864-2721) is 13 km west on Hwy 1. Unserviced sites are $10. *KOA* (☎ 253-8168) has a site on the Trans Canada Hwy East at Murdock Rd, with rates from $11 to $18. Both campgrounds are open from May to mid-October.

### Hostels

The HI *Ivy House Hostel* (☎ 772-3022) is good and central. It's in an old turreted house at 210 Maryland St, near the corner of Broadway Ave and Sherbrook St, not far from the bus station. The hostel sleeps 38 and has kitchen facilities. It's closed during the day, opening at 5 pm. The rates are $12 for members, $16 for nonmembers. Nearby, over on Sherbrook St, is the hostelling regional office (for memberships, etc).

From the airport, catch the No 15 bus to the corner of Sargent and Maryland Sts. From there, take bus No 29 to the corner of Broadway Ave and Maryland St. From the train station, walk west along Broadway Ave, or take the No 29 bus to the corner of Broadway Ave and Sherbrook St and walk a block west.

Just a few doors away, at 168 Maryland St, in a large, comfortable three-storey house dating from 1912, is the principal alternative, the Backpackers *Guest House International* (☎ 772-1272), run by Bill Macdonald. It, too, can accommodate about 40 people in a

variety of rooms, including one for couples. The price here is $11 (no membership required), and it is open all day through the summer months. Both hostels can be full (or close to it) in July and August, so calling ahead is not a bad idea. Notification prior to arrival is necessary at Backpackers from November to March because the winter months are slow and Bill is not always at home.

There is no YM-YWCA accommodation in Winnipeg.

The *University of Manitoba* rents rooms from mid-May to mid-August. They're not cheap, at $28/40 a single/double, and are only available with a reservation and one night's deposit. For information, contact the conference coordinator (☎ 474-9942) at 26 MacLean Crescent, Pembina Hall.

### B&Bs

The provincial B&B Association (☎ 783-9797) is based in Winnipeg, and many of its members are also here. In addition there are independent operators in the city and around the province – the tourist office has a fairly extensive list. Prices aren't bad at all, with most in the range of $30/40 for singles/doubles. Breakfast may vary from a light continental breakfast to a complete hot meal.

In the central area near The Forks is the home of *Daisy Paully* (☎ 772-8828), at 141 Furby St. It's close to three bus routes and the price is good – $25/35. Nonsmokers only, please.

*Casa Antigua* (☎ 775-9708), at 209 Chestnut St, is in a pleasant old tree-lined residential area near Portage and Broadway Aves. A double here is $35, and again, it's no smoking. Dinners are offered and Spanish is spoken.

A third option is the more up-market *West Gate Manor* (☎ 772-9788), at 71 West Gate, in the historic well-to-do area of Armstrong Point, within walking distance of downtown. It's about a 20-minute walk south-east of the Art Gallery or bus station to this quiet, tree-lined neighbourhood. The tasteful, well-decorated rooms go for $35 to $45 a single, $45 to $55 a double.

Lastly, there is the place run by Mary and Walter Pederson (☎ 233-3218), at 476 St Mary's Rd. Here singles/doubles are $25/35, and they will pick up from the train station or airport for a small fee. English, Danish and Japanese are spoken. A full breakfast is included.

There are many other places, although some are not as central. You can also find hosts who speak French or German.

### Hotels – bottom end

Winnipeg has an abundance of small, older hotels in the downtown area. Unfortunately, most of these are basic and cater to locals on the skids, but they are cheap. With the exception of one (listed last), they are not recommended for women travelling alone. The low end of the middle price bracket offers better-calibre alternatives.

A few blocks up Main St towards Portage Ave from the railway station is the *Winnipeg Hotel* (☎ 942-7762), which is clean and friendly and the best of the very bottom-end places. Singles/doubles cost $16/18.

Many of the cheapies are clustered around the Exchange District near the intersection of Notre Dame Ave and Albert St. Two are the *Royal Albert Hotel* (☎ 943-8750) and the *Oxford Hotel* (☎ 942-6712), but neither is particularly good. The downstairs bars are the primary feature. Rooms start at about $15/18 for singles/doubles; rooms with a bath cost more.

The *Garrick* (☎ 943-7172), at 287 Garry St, on the other (south) side of Portage Ave, seems a little better. Singles/doubles cost $17/22. Avoid the *Windsor* (☎ 942-7528), down at 187 Garry St.

There are other, similar places in this area; all these types of hotels have very low weekly rates.

A cut above the shoestringers is found down in Osborne Village, the *Osborne Village Motor Inn* (☎ 452-9824). The 32 rooms are quite reasonably priced, at $32/34 a single/double. This is a better neighbourhood – in fact, it is quite a lively area with some good restaurants and stores. The hotel features live music, however, so be

prepared for some bass thumping in at least some of the rooms until last call.

### Hotels – middle

Winnipeg is also well served by moderately priced hotels with clean, safe rooms in a conveniently central location.

The *Balmoral* (☎ 943-1544), on the street of the same name, is on the corner of Notre Dame Ave and has singles/doubles at $38/48.

The *Gordon Downtowner Motor Hotel* (☎ 943-5581) is very central, at 330 Kennedy St, a few blocks from Portage Ave. It has a restaurant, a couple of bars and free parking. Singles/doubles are $47/52.

Similar is the *St Regis* (☎ 942-0171), at 285 Smith St, just south of Portage Ave, which has all the mod cons. Rooms cost $45/48.

Two other good-value places are the always reliable *Carlton Inn-Best Western* (☎ 942-0881) and the *Charterhouse* (☎ 782-0175). The Carlton Inn, at 220 Carlton St, has singles/doubles from $52/57. The Charterhouse, a middle-sized, middle-priced, right in the centre on the corner of York Ave and Hargrave St, charges $55/60, and each room has a balcony. The restaurant downstairs specialises in ribs.

### Hotels – top end

The *Delta Winnipeg* (☎ 956-1410), at 288 Portage Ave, has singles/doubles for $125/135. The *Westin* (☎ 957-1350), at 2 Lombard Place, has doubles from $140.

The attractive *Hotel Fort Garry* (☎ 942-8251), built in 1913, is the city's classic old hostelry. It's at 222 Broadway Ave, close to the railway station whose passengers it was meant to serve. The casino is here. A double costs $140, although weekend packages may provide good savings.

### Motels

The *Assiniboine Gorden Inn* (☎ 888-4806), at 1975 Portage Ave, on the park, has singles or doubles for $44 and a dining room offering food at good prices. *Down's Motor Inn* (☎ 837-5831), at 3740 Portage Ave, charges

$36/40. There are others along Portage Ave going away from the downtown area.

Pembina Hwy (Hwy 42) going south out of town has many motels. The *Capri* (☎ 269-6990), at 1819 Pembina Hwy, has singles/doubles for $35/45. The cheaper rooms are in one of the small, quiet cabins at the back and there is a swimming pool. Some of the units have cooking facilities. *Journey's End Motel* (☎ 269-7370), at 3109 Pembina Hwy, is immaculate, with singles/doubles for $42/49.

There are many other, more expensive places that are large, well appointed and well maintained. Generally, the larger the hotel, the more it costs.

## PLACES TO EAT

The cheapest place to eat in town is the *cafeteria* in the Administration Building, in the cluster of government offices between Main and King Sts on William Ave. Different lunches are served each day. The cafeteria is on the 2nd floor and opens from 8.30 am to 4.30 pm Monday to Friday. I don't know if you have to be an employee to eat here, but you shouldn't have any problems getting in unless you look like you've slept in the woods for a week.

The *cafeteria* in the Legislative Building is similar and is definitely open to the public.

Downtown on a Sunday you'll find most things closed, but there are several *Salisbury House* restaurants around town which tend to open early and close late every day. There's one at 212 Notre Dame Ave, another at 352 Portage Ave and one in the bus station. This local chain began in 1931 and has remained successful serving cheap, plain food in a cafeteria-style setting. They're good places for breakfast but their reputation has been built on their hamburgers, which are known as 'nips'.

West along Portage Ave away from the centre at No 1405 is *Ray and Jerry's*, a Winnipeg institution. This diner-style place has been serving up Canadian and American standards with panache for years and years. It seems every one in town knows of it.

The *Old Chocolate Shop Restaurant*, at

269 Portage Ave, is a likeable place for lunch, dinner, coffee and sweets or for the popular teacup and tarot card readings. It's moderately priced.

The *Old Swiss Inn*, at 207 Edmonton St, offers steaks, veal and seafood. The food is good, priced at $16 to $22. *Hy's*, at 216 Kennedy St, is a well-established steak house.

The popular *Grapes*, at 180 Main St, near the railway station, is a big bar/restaurant with lots of wood and plants. The menu offers a bit of everything at moderate prices. While certainly OK, the food's not great; it's more the place, the people and the drinks that make it work.

Down in the Exchange District are numerous eating spots. Around Market Square on Albert St, the *Old Market Café* is a small, comfortable place for an espresso.

Nearby, the *King's Head Tavern*, at 120 King St, is a busy British-style pub. One section of it is now the *Moti Mahal*, serving East Indian food. In summer, chip wagons set up all around the park. The very European *Chopin's Café*, on the corner of Albert St and McDermot Ave away from the park, is a little more expensive for its delicatessen-style sandwiches, among other things.

Winnipeg has an *Old Spaghetti Factory*, at 219 Bannantyne Ave, which is always reliable and good value, though it doesn't have stupendous food. It offers very reasonable, complete Italian meals at lunch or dinner in a well-designed space.

At 179 Bannantyne Ave, east of Main St, the *Ashdown Café* is open for lunch, and late at night on weekends for the after-theatre or show crowd. They have sandwiches, salads and plenty of dessert selections, including cheesecake.

At 180 King St is the new Chinese Dynasty Building, with the Heritage Gardens out the front and the adjacent Chinese gate over the street. Slightly beyond is the city's small Chinatown, on Rupert, Pacific and Alexander Aves. The restaurants are mainly on King St. *Marigold* is the biggest and poshest restaurant. The moderately priced *Foon Hai*, at 329 William Ave (at Adelaide), has both Cantonese and Sichuan dishes and is open late every day.

The Forks Historic Site is a pleasant place for a bite, and along with the food stalls and the small cafés of the Market Building, there is *Branigan's*, for a more substantial meal. Weekend brunches are offered. They also have a lounge which is open late. In the nearby Johnston Building, *Right On Billiards Café* is a place for coffee, desserts and perhaps a quick game of pool.

There are several worthwhile places in the area around Sherbrook St and Broadway Ave. At 106 Sherbrook St is the busy *Impressions Café*, which is licensed and open until midnight every day. It has a nice European atmosphere, with paintings and photographs on display, and sells sandwiches, bagels and omelettes, most priced at under $5. At breakfast, the freshly baked cinnamon buns with tea or coffee make life worth living.

*Bistro Dansk*, at 63 Sherbrook St, is a perennial Danish favourite, with well-prepared food, good lunches at $7 and pricier dinner specials. It's open from 11 am to 3 pm and 5 to 9.30 pm daily (closed Sunday). Specialities include frideller, salmon and, at lunch, various open-face sandwiches.

Down near the corner of Broadway Ave, at 226 Sherbrook St, the *Cork & Fork* is a more expensive but congenial spot for a dinner out. The speciality is fondue (try the bouillon fondue for $15), but there are other items on the menu as well.

Nearly next door, across from the gas station, *Champions* serves decent, basic Chinese and Vietnamese food. It's cheap and close to the two hostels.

Down at 576 Broadway Ave, the *Wheatsong Bakery & Café* has vegetarian meals at lunch and dinner and is now also open for breakfast. It's closed on Sunday.

Main St North, once a thriving Jewish, Ukrainian and other ethnic groups' area, now has its best days behind it. There are some remnants, such as *Kelekis*, at 1100 Main St. This locally famous semi-Jewish restaurant features the traditional photographs of stars and pseudostars on the walls. Though not especially good, it is still busy, partly for its nostalgic value (it's been here since 1931 – Mom and Dad probably came in for a snack when they were dating) and partly for its hot dogs.

At 911 Main St, the *Blue Boy Café* has Ukrainian food, but for similar fare, try a feed at *Alycia's*, north of the central area in the North End, at 559 Cathedral St. This casual local institution serves substantial meals at mid-range prices.

In Osborne Village there are many restaurants, and they're mostly quite good. Try the *Courtyard Deli*, at 100 Osborne St, for soups, salads and sandwiches or for just a coffee and a sweet. It's cheap but is only open until 6 pm daily. Larger and less casual is *Basil's Café*, at 117 Osborne St, with various speciality items and European snacks and sweets, as well as sandwiches and salads. They have a selection of teas and 12 different coffees.

*Messob*, at 106 Osborne St, serves very cheap Ethiopian fare from 5 to 10 pm daily. It's been here a few years now and is establishing itself as a unique alternative in the village.

Well established is *Carlos & Murphy's*, at 133 Osborne St, a Mexican place with an outdoor patio, a big menu and moderate prices. *Baked Expectations*, primarily for sweets, is open late and is not too pricey. *Pasquale's* has cheap pizza and spaghetti and other more expensive Italian dishes. It stays open until 2 am.

There are many other restaurants here, some a fair bit pricier than those just mentioned. The *Tea Cozy* is a posher place with highly rated food. The *Toad in the Hole*, a pub at 112 Osborne St, has recently become sort of the 'in' place for a beer.

Corydon Ave in the Italian area has some attractive places to eat, in particular the *Soffia Caffe*, at 635 Corydon, with a wonderful little summer courtyard outback and very reasonable prices for basic Italian fare. The *Bar Italia Caffe*, on the corner of Cockburn St, is good for sipping a latte or cappuccino.

The downtown shopping centres have food fairs, and the Convention Centre has a

MANITOBA

cheap cafeteria. Also, many of the better downtown hotels have Sunday brunches at noon, which are good value.

Out of the downtown area, St Boniface has several French restaurants. The *Café Jardin/Terasse Daniel Lavoie*, at 340 Boulevard Provencher, is a small place which offers low-priced French Canadian foods.

Pembina Hwy leading south out of town has numerous restaurants, including many of the familiar franchises.

## ENTERTAINMENT

To find out what's going on in the city, the *Winnipeg Free Press* has complete bar and entertainment listings on Friday, or look for the free entertainment monthly the *Interchange*.

### Casinos

Winnipeg which pioneered permanent legal gambling houses in Canada has three places at which to wager. The somewhat controversial *Crystal Casino* is on the 7th floor of the Hotel Fort Garry, at 222 Broadway Ave. It's open from 6 pm to 2 am Monday to Friday and from noon on Saturday. Try your luck at blackjack, baccarat, roulette or the slots. 'Proper attire' is required, which for men means a jacket and tie. There are two other casinos where you can call upon Lady Luck – for more information, see Gambling Centres earlier.

### Music

The *Spectrum*, at 176 Fort St, presents new and/or young alternative bands. The cover charge varies but is generally low. At 65 Rorie St is *Wise Guys*, a casual place for a simple meal and local bands. There is a jam on Sunday nights.

On the corner of Main St and St Mary Ave, close to the railway station, the inexpensive *Times Change Café* is good for jazz and blues. Live shows are on Friday, Saturday and Sunday nights. The nearby *Blue Note*, at 220 Main St, was long a Winnipeg institution and a place where the young Neil Young played; it has closed but may resurface, yet again.

There are several nightspots on McDermot Ave near Rorie St, such as the *Rollin' Stone* for rock or, on Monday nights, blues bands. The *Palladium* is out of the centre, at 2935 Pembina Hwy. This huge disco has lots of flashing lights, and a band on weekends.

The boat *River Rouge* has night cruises, with pop bands from Wednesday to Saturday and jazz music on Sunday and Monday nights.

The *West End Cultural Centre* (☎ 783-6918), at 586 Ellice Ave, often has cheap folk or classical concerts in a relaxed, casual atmosphere.

The *Centre Culturel Franco-Manitobain* (☎ 233-8972) presents all kinds of interesting shows, concerts and productions. It's in St Boniface; call for information. Some performances require a knowledge of French, some transcend language and still others use French and English.

The *Red Cactus*, at 695 Corydon Ave, is a cool place for hanging out with a beer in the middle of the summer patio scene in Little Italy, or there are a couple of nearby coffee bars to choose from.

On summer evenings there are often free outdoor concerts in parks around town. One place to ask about is the park off Preston Ave near the international hostels.

### Performing Arts

The *Royal Winnipeg Ballet* (☎ 956-0183) has an excellent international reputation. Their new home is on the corner of Graham Ave and Edmonton St, and they offer student rates on tickets.

The *Centennial Concert Hall* (☎ 942-7479), in Portage Place, is home to the Manitoba Opera.

The *Winnipeg Symphony Orchestra* (☎ 949-3999) plays the classics as well as pops; their season runs from November to May. Various plays and concerts are also presented at the symphony's home, the *Centennial Arts Centre*, at 555 Main St. Plays, dance, mime and more are presented at the *Gas Station Theatre* (☎ 284-2757), at 445 River Ave, in the centre of Osborne Village.

## Cinema

The *Cinema 3* (☎ 783-1097), on the corner of Ellice Ave and Sherbrook St, is a good, low-priced repertory cinema. The *Art Gallery Cinema*, in the Winnipeg Art Gallery, shows frequently changing foreign and alternative films. Prices are low here, too.

## Spectator Sports

The Winnipeg Jets play National League Hockey at the Winnipeg Arena about 40 times through the winter. In summer and fall, the Winnipeg Blue Bombers, representing the province, play professional football in the Canadian Football League (CFL). Games are played at the Winnipeg Stadium, on the corner of Portage Ave and King Edward St, west of the downtown core. The hockey arena is here as well.

## THINGS TO BUY
### Factory Outlets

Shoppers should know that Winnipeg has a surprising array of factory retail outlets. Canada's only Ralph Lauren factory store is here. Other such outlets include Arrow, Izod Lacoste and Woolrich.

## Aboriginal Art

Winnipeg, as a western city and a centre for the Hudson's Bay Company, has long been the site of trading and dealing with the sizeable Native Indian and Inuit populations of the region. Today it remains, with Churchill, a focal point for Native art. To see or perhaps purchase some contemporary Native work, check out the following stores/galleries: Northern Images, in Portage Place, for Inuit art & crafts; Upstairs Gallery, 266 Edmonton St, with one of the country's largest collections of serious Inuit art; Fourwinds Trading, at The Forks Market, for more popular, less expensive Native Indian crafts; and the similar Northern Bear, at 234 Donald St, with articles such as moccasins and jewellery.

## GETTING THERE & AWAY
### Air

The international airport is about 20 minutes north-west of the city centre. Several airlines serve Winnipeg, both for local trips and for destinations in the USA.

Canadian Airlines (☎ 786-4435) flies to Sault Sainte Marie twice daily. Air Canada (☎ 943-9361) also serves Winnipeg.

Canadian Airlines flies to Churchill four times a week but it ain't cheap. If you want to go, book at least two weeks in advance for the best deal. For more information about Churchill, see the relevant section at the end of this chapter.

### Bus

The station for both Greyhound and Grey Goose lines is the Mall Centre Bus Depot, at 487 Portage Ave. It's open from 6.30 am to midnight and there are left-luggage lockers and a restaurant in the station.

Greyhound (☎ 783-8840) covers all Ontario destinations (or at least to the required connecting point) and many western cities. There are three buses daily eastbound for Thunder Bay ($69) and beyond, three buses a day for Regina ($53) and two for Saskatoon. Be sure to ask which buses are express and which are the mail runs, because on a trip to Saskatoon, for example, the difference can be three hours.

The Greyhound desk also handles the small Beaver Bus Line, which serves Fort Garry, Selkirk and other points north of town. There's at least one bus an hour.

Grey Goose buses (☎ 784-4500) go to Regina, Thunder Bay and many of the small Manitoba towns in the area and further north.

### Train

The VIA Rail station (☎ 944-8780) is centrally located, where Broadway Ave meets Main St. In summer there's a tourist information booth in the station. Like everywhere else, train service has been greatly reduced here. The western route goes to Edmonton and Jasper and then down to Vancouver. The eastern route goes north, way over Lake Superior en route to Sudbury and the major cities of Ontario. There is no train at all to Regina.

For Edmonton the fare is $152 and the train departs on Sunday, Wednesday and Friday. There are three trains a week to Sudbury ($173).

There is also a train to Churchill – see the Churchill section of this chapter for more information.

### Car & Motorbike

Thrifty (☎ 949-7600) has a downtown office at 155 Fort St and another office at the airport. They offer weekend rates and free customer pick-up and return.

Budget (☎ 989-8505) is on the corner of Sherbrook St and Ellice Ave. Discount (☎ 949-3770), at 1380 Sargent St, offers weekend and holiday rates and has a student discount policy.

Dominion (☎ 943-4477), at 15 Marion St, by the Norwood Bridge in the Dominion Centre, offers good three-day specials and a half-day rate.

### Hitching

For hitching west out of town, take the express St Charles bus along Portage Ave. After 6 pm, take the Portage Ave-St Charles bus.

For hitching east on Hwy 1, catch the Osborne Hwy 1 bus or the Southdale bus on Osborne St South, on the corner of Broadway Ave.

### GETTING AROUND
### To/From the Airport

Very conveniently and economically, a city bus departs for the airport every 20 minutes from Vaughan St on the corner of Portage Ave. It's called the Sargent No 15 airport bus and costs $1.30, exact change.

A taxi from the airport to the centre of town is about $10 to $12. There is an airport limo, which runs from 9 am to nearly 1 am to and from the better hotels, but it costs more than a cab.

### Bus

All city buses cost $1.30, exact change. For

transit information, call ☎ 986-5700 (24 hours a day). Routes are extensive but you need a transfer, if you're changing buses. (A transfer is a numbered, dated slip of paper provided by the driver free upon request allowing the holder to change buses without further payment.)

### Bicycle

There are bicycle routes through town and some out of town. Ask at the tourist office for details. The hostels rent bicycles.

## AROUND WINNIPEG
### The Prairie Dog Central

The Prairie Dog is a 1900s-style steam train which takes passengers on a three-hour, 50-km trip north to Grosse Isle and back. From June to September the train makes two trips a week, on Sunday at 11 am and 3 pm. It costs $13, less for kids. The station (☎ 832-5259), which is a bit hard to find, is on Portage Ave West near Kenaston Blvd, just behind Manitoba Hydro and across from the Viscount Gort Motor Hotel. There is free parking at 1661 Portage Ave.

### Lower Fort Garry

Lower Fort Garry (☎ 785-6050), 32 km north of Winnipeg on the banks of the Red River, is a restored Hudson's Bay Company fort dating from 1830. It's the only stone fort from the fur-trading days that is still intact.

Although the fort was a failure as a fur-trading post, it remained in use as a police training centre, a penitentiary, a lunatic asylum, a Hudson's Bay Company residence and, later, a country club.

The buildings are historically furnished and the grounds are busy with costumed workers who'll answer questions. Go early in the day to avoid the crowds, and see the film at the entrance for the historical background – you should allow one or two hours for a visit. Admission to the fort costs $4. It's open from 10 am to 6 pm daily from mid-May to Labour Day (at the beginning of September). During the rest of September it's open on weekends only. There's a restaurant and a picnic area.

To get there, take the Beaver line bus from the main depot and tell the driver you're going to the fort – the fare is about $7 return.

## Selkirk

Beyond the fort, halfway to the lake from Winnipeg, is Selkirk, Catfish Capital of the World. The lunkers that are taken out of the Red River here would certainly turn heads in the American south, where the fish is considered prime eating. The Marine Museum of Manitoba is also here, with five high-and-dry ships, including a restored steamer and an icebreaker.

## Oak Hammock Marsh

Southern Manitoba has several very important, very large marshes. These critical wetlands are home to thousands of waterfowl and other birds and act as way stations along major migration routes for thousands more.

Oak Hammock Marsh is a swamp area north of the city, about halfway to Lake Winnipeg and eight km east of Stonewall, 15 km west of Selkirk. It's noted as one of the best bird sanctuaries on the continent; over 260 species can be seen. The bird-watching is excellent – you can amble about on viewing boardwalks or take out a canoe, and there is an information centre with interpretive displays. After a session here, head over to Stonewall and the May House Tea Room, at 391 Centre St, for afternoon tea and a sweet. Housed in a turn-of-the-century home, it is open daily (except Tuesday).

## East of Winnipeg

Dugald, not far east of Winnipeg along Route 15, is the home of the **Dugald Costume Museum**, a collection of 5000 items of dress and accessories dating from 1765 to the present. The various garments are displayed on mannequins to give a somewhat natural sense of how they appeared when worn. The costume museum is open daily from 10 am to 5 pm during summer; it's closed on Monday and Tuesday at other times of year. Admission is $3 and there is a tea room.

Also here is a restored pioneer home

dating from 1886, furnished as it would originally have been.

About 25 km east of town on the Trans Canada Hwy, the **Museum of Childhood** has a collection of furniture, toys, clothing and other articles which may remind visitors of their youth. Admission is $3.

## South of Winnipeg

South and slightly west of Winnipeg and bordered by North Dakota is an area known as the **Pembina Valley**. The Red River flows northward through this prime farming region.

**Morris** is the site of a major annual rodeo, second in size only to Calgary's. It takes place for five days at the beginning of August.

This is also sunflower country, and a festival to mark this is held in **Altona** on the last weekend in July. The Mennonites of the area supply some very fine homemade foods for the occasion.

East of the village of Tolstoi, three km down near the Minnesota border off Hwy 59, one of the best remaining examples of **tall grass prairie** in the region can be seen. The 130-hectare area was purchased by the Manitoba Naturalists' Society, making it the largest single protected acreage of this increasingly rare prairie plant life.

# Eastern Manitoba

The border region of Manitoba continues with the same rugged woodland terrain as is found in neighbouring Ontario. Toward Winnipeg this begins to give way to the flatter expanse more typical of the southern prairies. In the north-east, the sparsely populated timberlands continue through a series of gigantic government parks. The southern area of this side of the province is primarily farmland.

## MENNONITE HERITAGE VILLAGE

South-east of Winnipeg, about an hour's drive down through sunflower country, is the town of Steinbach. Two km north of the town on Hwy 12 is a museum featuring the Mennonites, a religious utopian group originating in Europe which reached Manitoba via Pennsylvania and Ontario. An information centre gives some of the history of the movement.

But the bulk of the site is a recreated late 19th-century Mennonite village with some century-old buildings. Various special events are held through the summer.

There's a restaurant on the grounds, which serves good, fresh traditional Mennonite food. The village is open from 1 May to 30 September. For more information on the Mennonites, see Kitchener in the Ontario chapter.

### LA BROQUERIE

Just out of Steinbach, this little village with a population descended from French and Belgian pioneers celebrates its Gaelic roots on 24 June (Fête Nationale, formerly known as St Jean Baptiste Day) and during the provincial Fête Franco-Manitobaine.

### WHITESHELL PROVINCIAL PARK

Due east of Winnipeg and lying along the Ontario border is this 2590-sq-km park. Though some parts are heavily commercialised (particularly around Falcon Lake), other areas, especially northward, are less developed. The park contains 200 lakes, and all kinds of outdoor activities are available, summer and winter. There are some good hiking trails – some short and others as long as 60 km. The park headquarters (☎ 369-5232), in the village of Rennie, on Hwy 44 in the south-west corner of the park, offers all the information a visitor could require, including recommendations for hiking, etc.

The park has 17 campgrounds, and there are moderately priced lodges which are rented by the day or week – a quarter of the province's fishing lodges are found within the park. More expensive, well-equipped resorts can be found at several locations.

Near the park headquarters in Rennie, the Alf Hole Goose Sanctuary is worth a visit,

particularly during the spring and fall migrations. There is a visitor centre, and an observation deck overlooking the small lake where a couple of hundred geese spend the summer.

At Bannock Point, not far north of Betula Lake, are centuries-old Native Indian petroforms: rock formations in the shapes of fish, snakes and birds.

### ATIKAKI PROVINCIAL WILDERNESS PARK

Heading north, the province quickly becomes rather wild. This wilderness park is best visited by canoe. In it, along the Bloodvein River, there are remnants of Native Indian cliff paintings thought to date back 6000 years. Access to canoe routes is through Wallace Lake, which can be reached by car along a rough road.

More accessible but still offering a taste of the true northern wilderness is Nopoming Provincial Park, north of Whiteshell. This park has a few campgrounds and at least a sketchy road system. The park also contains some woodland caribou, though you are unlikely to see them in the summer months.

# Lake Winnipeg

Canada's fifth largest lake, with its southern tip lying about 50 km north of Winnipeg, is far and away the dominant geographic feature of the province. It begins just beyond suburban Winnipeg and ends in virtually untouched northern wilderness.

The easily accessible southern region is where Manitobans play in summer. The two prime recreational features are the fine, sandy beaches, and the numerous parks and wetlands ideal for wildlife observation, most notably bird-watching. Oak Hammock Marsh is listed under Around Winnipeg, as it is very close to the city.

The eastern shoreline is lined with beaches, including the unofficial centre of summer fun, **Grand Beach**, which is very popular and a good place to relax. The excellent beach has light-coloured sand, and dunes as high as eight metres. The lagoon formed behind the dunes is home to literally hundreds of species of birds.

The other side of the lake is less accessible to visitors, as much of the land is privately owned; many people have cottages in the area. However, there are some good, popular public beaches, such as **Winnipeg Beach**. This is the resort centre for the west side of the lake. A provincial park protects the best strip of sandy beach for public use and there is good windsurfing out in the bay. In and around Winnipeg Beach is an abundance of camping areas, motels, restaurants and all other services. The government park is best for campers in tents.

At the southern end of the lake, Netley Marsh has high concentrations of waterfowl.

### ACCOMMODATION

There is camping at Grand Beach Provincial Park (☎ 754-2212) and further south at Patricia Beach. *Lakeshore Heights* (☎ 765-2791) is a B&B off Hwy 59 near Grand Beach, 90 km from the city. For detailed directions, call the above or call ☎ 475-8173 in Winnipeg. Most of the commercial services and motel accommodation are available just south of the park, in Grand Marais. The *Grand Marais Inn* (☎ 754-2141) is $60 a double.

### ORGANISED TOURS

North and east of the beach districts, a mini industrial tour circuit can be made. At Pine Falls, the Generating Plant (☎ 474-3233) is open for tours through the summer. Call for the schedule. Also here, the Abitibi-Price Paper Mill (☎ 367-2432) offers guided trips around the plant. South down Hwy 11 is the village of Lac du Bonnet and an underground research lab belonging to Whiteshell Laboratories (☎ 1-800-665-0436). Whiteshell also has an above-ground plant, at Pinawa, and is involved with nuclear research, among other things. At Pinewa, pregnant women and young children are not permitted on the tours, which might tell you all you want to know. Anyone can visit the underground site, however, for the 1½-hour tours of the labo-

ratory, which is built down in the rock of the Canadian Shield, below the water table.

### NETLEY MARSH

In the other direction, in more ways than one, is Netley Marsh, formed where the Red River drains into the southern end of Lake Winnipeg. This is one of the major waterfowl nesting areas on the continent, and hunters and watchers bring their conflicting points of view to enjoy the 18 species of duck and the flocks of geese. The fall is a particularly good time, as the birds collect in number, but this is also hunting season. The Breezy Point Observation Tower, within the Netley Creek Provincial Recreation Park, allows for views over a section of the marsh. Netley is 16 km north of Selkirk.

# Interlake

The region north of Winnipeg, wedged between massive Lake Winnipeg to the east and Lake Manitoba to the west, is known as the Interlake. The southern region of this area has been detailed in the Around Winnipeg section. In the northern Interlake region, to the east of Lake Winnipegosis, the population thins markedly, the cottage communities disappear and the real north begins.

### GIMLI

Ninety km north of Winnipeg, on the western shores of Lake Winnipeg and marked by the Viking statue, this fishing and farming community is made up largely of the descendants of Icelandic pioneers. Once known as the Republic of New Iceland, the area was settled by Icelanders around 1880. The **Gimli Historical Museum** outlines the history and possesses some artefacts of the local settlement, as well as items suggesting the influence of the Ukrainians, a major early immigrant group in the western provinces. Every summer, around the beginning of August, Islendingadagurinn (the Icelandic

Festival) is held, with three days of games, contests, parades and folk music.

The wide, sandy beaches of the south-western shore continue into the Gimli area.

Gimli has a couple of standard motels.

## HECLA PROVINCIAL PARK

Further north (Gimli is halfway from Winni-peg) and perhaps of more interest is Hecla, an island park jutting out and almost across Lake Winnipeg. A causeway leads to Hecla Island, the principal island, with its camp-grounds and villages. Hecla Village was the site of an Icelandic settlement in 1876. A museum and short walking trail detail some of the historical highlights.

The island is well populated with moose, although deer and smaller mammals are also commonly seen. The Grassy Narrows Marsh teems with waterfowl. Numerous hiking trails wind through the woods and along shorelines.

Another park adjacent, **Grindstone**, is still under development.

### Places to Stay

*Solmundson Gesta Hus* (☎ 279-2088) is a B&B in the village. A double goes for $55. At the northern tip of the island is Gull Harbour, where the campground is situated and where all supplies can be purchased.

## SNAKE PITS

Snake lovers, you're in luck. Here in Mani-toba is the world's largest population of red-sided garter snakes, concentrated in wig-gling mega-dens of up to 10,000 of the little funsters. Researchers, pet dealers and those with a taste for the macabre come from distant continents to view the snake pits, which are about six km north of Narcisse, off Hwy 17 due west of Gimli, in the middle of the Interlake region between Lake Winnipeg and Lake Manitoba.

In fact, the pressure of attention on them has resulted in a drastic decline in the numbers of snake dens, and harvesting reg-ulation is occurring. The mating ritual, when tens of thousands emerge from their lime-stone sinkhole lairs to form masses of entwined tangles, takes place around the last week of April and the first two weeks of May, or when the weather has warmed enough to perk up the slitherers. The greatest intensity of activity occurs when the snow has melted and the first hot, sunny days of spring have arrived. Fall is the other time of the year when viewing is good. Early in September, after a fancy-free summer, the snakes return to their dens, but remain at the doors until the cold autumn weather forces them to crawl inside for the winter. The snakes are not dangerous and can be picked up – no scream-ing please – but may not be removed from the site.

The **Narcisse Wildlife Management Area** protects one area of the snake pits and provides a walking trail and parking lot six km north of Narcisse – just follow Hwy 17. It is just under a two-hour drive from Winni-peg. Bring the camera and the kids, and make a day of it by visiting nearby **Komarno**, where there's a statue of the world's largest mosquito. Packing a lunch (or at least a snack) and something to drink is not a bad idea, as there isn't much around, although well water is available.

Other locations for snake pits are around Chatfield and Inwood.

## PEGUIS & FISHER RIVER

North of Narcisse, Hwy 17 leads to two fairly isolated Native Indian Reserves: Peguis and Fisher River. This is an undeveloped area, with few services and little in the way of tourist development. The Peguis Powwow is a five-day event featuring games, song, crafts and various activities, to which the Cree and Ojibway of the reserves invite the public. There is some camping in the area, and Hecla Provincial Park is just over 40 km to the east.

## LAKE MANITOBA SHORELINE

The area between the lakes is important for beef cattle, and some of the farms take in overnight guests.

Much less developed than Lake Winnipeg but with a series of small towns and some cottage communities, Lake Manitoba also has some fine, sandy beaches, particularly at Twin Lakes (in the south), around the town of Lundar and at Silver Bay (west of Ashern). St Laurent, a predominantly French and Métis community, is a regional supply town.

## NORTHERN WOODS & WATER ROUTE

This is a series of roads – now linked as one – which connects Winnipeg with British Columbia, running across northern portions of Saskatchewan and Alberta. Most of the roads are surfaced, though there are stretches of gravel. There are no cities, but many small communities, nine provincial parks and numerous campgrounds along the way. You'll find lots of lakes and woods up here, as well as fishing areas and wildlife. Nights are cool.

From Winnipeg, the route heads to The Pas (in the north-west of the province), continues to Prince Albert (in Saskatchewan, near the Prince Albert National Park) and on into Alberta, and ends up at Dawson Creek, British Columbia. The road is marked on signs as 'NWWR'.

# Northern Manitoba

Two-thirds of the province still lies northwards of The Pas, above the two big lakes at the 53rd parallel. Northern Manitoba is rugged, resource-based, lake-filled timberland which slowly evolves into the barren, treeless tundra of the far north. Flin Flon, The Pas and Thompson are important towns. Way up on Hudson Bay is Churchill, remote but one of the province's top draws.

## THE PAS

Once an important meeting site for Native Indians and British and French fur traders, The Pas is now a district centre and acts as a 'gateway to the north'. Although lumber is important, this is a rich agricultural area as well. During summer, days are long and sunny.

The small **Sam Waller Museum**, at 306

Fischer Ave, provides some historic background on the area.

**Christ Church** (☎ 623-2119), on Edwards Ave, was founded by Henry Budd, the first Native Indian ordained by the Anglican Church. On one wall, the Lord's Prayer and the 10 commandments can be seen written in Cree. Call and someone will arrange to let you visit.

Also of interest is Opasquiak Indian Days, an annual festival put on by The Pas Native Indian Band in mid-August. Included in the events are traditional contests and games and canoe races. A reserve lies just out of town across the river, and this is where almost all the non-White population lives. The early 1990s has seen some tension between the two groups, following a heavily publicised brutal crime committed against a Native woman by a group of Caucasian men.

Within the Clearwater Provincial Park, deep crevices and huge chunks of rock fallen from cliffs can be seen along the Caves Trail. It's Clearwater for a reason: the bottom can be seen from over 10 metres.

### Places to Stay

Camping is possible not far from town, in Clearwater Provincial Park. There are about half a dozen motels or hotels in town, and finding a vacancy should not be a problem.

### Getting There & Away

The Pas is connected to Winnipeg by air, Grey Goose buses and VIA Rail. Driving takes about eight hours if you take Route 327 and Hwy 6. The bus takes a longer route. VIA Rail continues on to Thompson and Churchill.

## FLIN FLON

Further north, right on the Saskatchewan border, Flin Flon is a copper and zinc-mining centre. The unusual name is taken, it's said, from the protagonist of a novel some prospectors found up here in 1915. A goofy statue of the character, Josiah Flintabbatey Flonatin, greets visitors at the edge of town.

Also here, on Hwy 10 as the town is entered, is a tourist office and campground run by the Chamber of Commerce. At the tourist office, have a look at the examples of birch-bark biting. This is an old Cree women's craft which has almost disappeared. Using their teeth, they etch patterns, often of animals, into the bark. I've also seen examples of this art in some of the better Native Indian craft outlets around Saskatchewan.

The town of about 8000 residents is built on the rocky Canadian Shield, meaning you'll be going up and down hills as you make your way around town.

The Hudson Bay Mining & Smelting Company surface mine in town can be toured in July and August. Copper, zinc, gold and silver are produced.

The city is surrounded by typical northern rocky, wooded lakeland. There are canoe and camping outfitters in town and the huge Grass River Provincial Park is not far east. The fishing is excellent. The Grass River system is ideal for canoeing, with about 150 lakes strung along the river. Woodland caribou, moose and deer are among the animals resident within the park. The river has been used for centuries by Native Indians and, later, European explorers and traders.

About halfway between Flin Flon and Grass River, south of town, is **Bakers Narrows Provincial Recreation Park**. It offers camping and canoeing and, with its beach and quiet, is also good for a relaxing day or afternoon.

Flin Flon has a couple of older hotels in the centre, on Main St, and a couple of motels around the edges. The *Victoria Inn* (☎ 687-7555) is more expensive and has a full range of facilities.

Buses run to The Pas and Winnipeg.

### THOMPSON

The last town northwards connected by road, Thompson (population 15,000) is a nickel-mining centre. There is virtually nothing but wilderness on the long road up here, whether you've come from The Pas or along Lake Winnipeg. And just out of town in any direction, civilisation disappears quickly. If driving, make sure you have the necessary supplies and fuel, as services are few to nil, especially on Hwy 6 north of Lake Winnipeg.

You can visit the Inco nickel mine but the tour does not descend into the earth; it shows instead all the surface operations. The Heritage North Museum, in an impressive log building, has exhibits and artefacts relating to natural history, the fur trade and early White settlement. The Thompson Folk Festival is held annually on the weekend closest to the summer solstice, usually around 22 June.

*Anna's B&B* (☎ 677-5075), at 204 Wolf St, is a good place to stay, and they will pick up guests from the airport or station. English and Dutch are spoken and a single goes for $35. There is a city-operated campground close to town.

VIA Rail, en route to Churchill, serves the city, as does Grey Goose Bus Lines.

### GILLAM

Situated about halfway to Churchill on the train line, Gillam exists because of its hydro-power development.

### CHURCHILL

If you've come this far, you've come for Churchill. Other than Winnipeg, this is the province's most interesting draw, especially for international travellers. It is one of Canada's few northern outposts that is relatively accessible, made so by the train line running all the way up from Winnipeg.

Despite its forbidding, remote location and extremes of weather – July and August are the only months without snow – Churchill has always been of importance. The area is one of the oldest, in terms of European exploration, in the country. The first Hudson's Bay Company outpost was set up here over 250 years ago and much of the exploration and settlement of the west came via this route. Explorers, traders and the military have all been here and it was once one of the largest grain-handling ports in the world. The railway was completed in 1929, giving the prairies an ocean port that is actually closer to Europe than Montreal. The town has had some tough years due to the decline in grain-handling. The population is now about 1000 and is relying more on its natural resources to draw business.

Tourism has become very important, and the town bills itself as the Polar Bear Capital of the World. It sits right in the middle of a polar bear migration route, which means the great white bears are often seen in and around town. Visitors are also taken out on the frozen tundra in large motorised buggies to see the huge and very dangerous bears.

Possibly of more economic significance will be the recently proposed communications satellite launching and monitoring station. It's said that if this project goes ahead, a population increase of several hundred or more might be expected. This would certainly give the town more than a shot in the arm.

The downtown area is quite small, with all hotels within walking distance of the train station. The large Town Centre Complex, at the north end of town, is a multipurpose structure housing everything from a high school to recreational facilities, which include a swimming pool.

## Natural Attractions

Churchill is a great spot for viewing a range of nature's pleasures. It is an excellent place for seeing the phenomenon known as the aurora borealis or northern lights (September to April) and is a prime location for observing wildlife, including polar bears (July to November, with the odds of sightings increasing each week to a peak in late October and November), beluga whales (mid-June to the last week in August), seals (mid-March to the end of August), caribou (July and August) and birds (mid-May to beginning of July, for migration and nesting). Fishing and flowers also attract visitors all summer.

Polar bears in number migrate through Churchill. Many spend summer south of

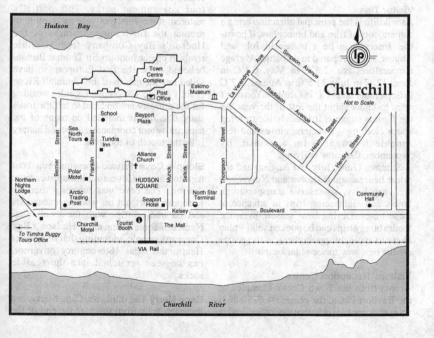

town and then, as the weather cools, head back north when the ice is beginning to form. They use the ice as a base for seal-hunting. Rather clumsy-looking on land, these mammoths (the females average 300 kg, the males 600 kg) are amazingly graceful in the water. They wander into town often enough that a polar bear alert system has been set up. You don't really want your child banging into one on the way to school! With no natural predators, the bears are fearless. For visitors, however, the tundra buggy tours are generally the best (and safest) way to see them. Check on the polar bear situation before going on any major walks around or out of town.

Migrating birds are another of the specialised attractions. In May and June, it is not difficult to see over 50 species, including nesting ducks, shore birds, various gulls and song birds. Serious birders spot many more and may see glimpses of such rarities as the Ross's Gull.

### Visitor Tips

As wildlife is the principal attraction bring a camera, lots of film and binoculars, if possible. Insects can be a bother in July and August, so be prepared to do battle. Average temperatures are -2.3°C in May, 6.1°C in June, 12°C in July, 11.5°C in August, 5.7°C in September and -1°C in October. You don't want to know about the rest of the year. As the figures suggest, it is advisable to bring warm clothing – sweaters, gloves and reasonable footwear – for any visit. By September, the snow is flying.

Summer (June, July and August) and the prime bear season (October and November) are very busy, so reserve transportation, hotels and sightseeing trips in advance at these times. During bear season, even the tundra buggy trips can be booked solid – plan ahead to avoid disappointment, as these trips are the best way to see polar bears.

### Visitors' Reception Centre

Across from the Town Centre Complex in the Bayport Plaza, the centre (☎ 675-8863) acts as a tourist information office and a

small, general museum. Films on the area, its history and the polar bears are shown. There are also some displays of furs and articles relating to the Hudson's Bay Company. The company is so widespread in area and influence that it's been said the initials HBC stand for 'Here Before Christ'.

### Eskimo Museum

The museum, on La Vrendrye Ave, has a good collection of Inuit artefacts and carvings, including kayaks from as early as 1700 BC. There are also displays about northern fauna. It's open Monday to Saturday, but only in the afternoons on Monday, and admission is free.

### National Historic Sites

**Fort Prince of Wales** Parks Canada administers four National Historic Sites in the Churchill area. Water-taxis run (tides and weather permitting) across the Churchill River from town to Eskimo Point and Fort Prince of Wales (not Whales!), one of the four government parks. This partially restored stone fort was originally built to protect the fur-trading business of the Hudson's Bay Company from possible rivals. A plaque honours Sir Thomas Button, believed to be the first European to have sailed into the mouth of the Churchill River. From 1 July to 1 September, guides working for the ministry are on hand to tell the fort's story. The fort is included on many of the trips run by tour companies. A second battery is by the mouth of the river.

**Sloop's Cove** Private operators run boat trips to Sloop's Cove, four km upriver from the fort. The cove was formerly used by European boats out on whaling excursions and on trading trips with the local Inuit. Names of some of the early Hudson's Bay Company people, including that of Samuel Hearn, the local 18th-century governor, can be seen scratched into the seaside rocks.

**Cape Merry** The third site, Cape Merry, is a three-km walk from town, at the end of the

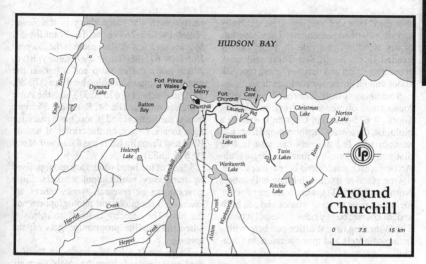

HUDSON BAY

Around Churchill

Cape Merry Centennial Parkway. Here you can see the remains of a stone battery built in 1746. Guides are on duty from 15 June to 15 September.

**York Factory** Much further afield (240 km), York Factory is a fur-trading post that operated for over 250 years. As it is accessible only by air or (for the very determined and experienced) by canoe, and as Churchill is not even the starting point for either possibility, the factory gets few visitors these days. In the 1700s and 1800s this was one of the Hudson's Bay Company's most significant trading posts. Part of the fort of 1832 is the oldest wooden structure still standing on Canadian permafrost. Also at the site are other ruins and a cemetery.

**Bird Cove**
Bird Cove, about 15 km east of town and accessible by vehicle (tours are available), is known for its abundant birdlife. Along the way (and with a short hike), you can see the wreck of a freighter which went down in a storm in 1961 at the western edge of the cove.

**Boreal Gardens**
About 1½ km east of town on Shore Rd, the gardens and greenhouses here produce some food for local consumption. Free tours are offered on Sunday afternoons from 2 to 4 pm during July and August.

**Organised Tours**
The list of companies offering tours in and around Churchill is astounding for a place of its size. Many are based in town, but several others work out of Winnipeg. Options include tours for viewing whales, birds, icebergs, historical sites or bears and even going on dog-team trips. If you're planning ahead, arrangements can also be made at travel agencies in Winnipeg. It may be worth calling to see if things are busy and whether reservations are required.

Sea North Tours (☎ 675-2198), in Churchill, specialises in boat and sea-life tours. North Star Tours (☎ 675-2629), also in town, has bus tours and tundra buggy trips. In general, the boat and bus tours are not exorbitantly priced, though the most popular tundra buggy trips to see the polar bears are not cheap. Tundra Buggy Tours (675-2121) is another company to try. The buggies are shortened buses of varying sizes, generally carrying 20 or so passengers. They have lots of big windows and ride on huge, deeply treaded tyres. North Star Tours will book accommodation and transportation, too. Ask about any all-inclusive package deals.

Something a little different are the year-round tours offered by Adventure Walking Tours (☎ 675-2826) in Churchill. Run by a biologist, these walking tours range from just an hour to a full day and can take in four distinct eco-zones – marine, taiga (sub-Arctic forest), tundra and boreal forest.

One place to try in Winnipeg is Frontiers North (☎ 663-1411), with a range of tours, including trips to view whales and sea birds and, of course, buggy rides to the polar bears. The Winnipeg tourist office can help with a listing of hotels and tour operators in Churchill.

### Festivals
The hardy may like to participate in the July Dip in the Bay event, part of which requires relay team members to jump into the balmy Arctic waters.

### Places to Stay & Eat
Churchill is not a cheap place to visit. However, there are about half a dozen places to stay and a few more places to eat. Accommodation costs are standardised (with one exception) at about $65 for singles and $70 to $80 for doubles. Reservations are recommended.

Best bargain and within walking distance of town is a *B&B* (☎ 675-2544) run by Vera Gould, at 108 Hearne St, A single in this modern bungalow is $30, with a very full breakfast (which often includes pancakes with Quebec maple syrup or toast with homemade jams). She has room for six people in three rooms and is very busy. Calling from Winnipeg is worthwhile.

The *Northern Lights Lodge* (☎ 675-2403), at 126 Kelsey Blvd and at No 101, across the street, charges $58/68 for singles/doubles. It's open from June to October only. Slightly more expensive for

pretty much the same thing is the *Polar Motel* (☎ 675-2647), at 16 Franklin St. Moving up a few dollars more is the *Seaport Hotel* (☎ 675-8807), at 299 Kelsey Blvd, which has a coffee shop and a bar on the premises. Singles/doubles here are $70/80. The *Tundra Inn* (☎ 675-8831), like the Polar Motel, is on Franklin St. Rates are $5 more than at the Seaport and it, too, has a place for light meals. Lastly, on the corner of Kelsey Blvd and Franklin St, is the *Churchill Motel* (☎ 675-8853).

Many of the hotel rooms are monopolised by temporary professional workers doing government or research work; others are taken by bush pilots and photographers and the like. The scarcity is likely to intensify when the satellite programme gets off the ground.

There aren't a lot of choices in town at feeding time. Aside from the hotels, there are a few restaurants and, in the Town Centre Complex, a cafeteria. Meals in Churchill cost $8 to $20. Consider bringing food of your own.

### Things to Buy
Various outlets sell contemporary Inuit arts & crafts. The Arctic Trading Company is one of several places where interesting souvenirs (such as carvings, and Inuit-style boots called *mukluks*) can be purchased. Also have a look in the Northern Store, formerly Hudson's Bay. The Eskimo Museum has some articles for sale, including jewellery.

### Getting There & Away
There is no road to Churchill; you must either fly in (Canadian Airlines has four flights a week from Winnipeg) or catch a train. The regular return airfare is $750, but savings of hundreds of dollars are offered on flights booked at least two weeks in advance. There are three trains a week from Winnipeg, departing at 9.55 pm on Sunday, Tuesday and Thursday. They arrive in Churchill two days later at 8.30 am. The straight return fare for the cheap coach seat is $351 for the 1½-day, 1600-km trip. If booked seven days

or more prior to departure, the fare drops to $209. Booking just seven days ahead shouldn't be a problem, as this train is rarely full, but be careful in midsummer.

# Western Manitoba

From Winnipeg westwards towards the Saskatchewan border, the flat prairie landscape dominates. Get used to it – it lasts until halfway through Alberta. The terrain is not totally barren or treeless, though, and there are a couple of government parks in this section of the province to consider visiting on the way by.

## WHITE HORSE LEGEND

Not far out of Winnipeg along the Trans Canada Hwy, where Hwy 26 runs north off the highway, is a statue of a white horse. Native Indian legend has it that a Cree rode this way on his white horse with his new bride, hotly pursued by his failed rival in love, a Sioux. Eventually overtaking the couple, the scorned man killed both bride and groom. The young woman's spirit entered the horse, which continued to roam the prairie for years, a living reminder of the tragic couple.

## PORTAGE LA PRAIRIE

Portage is a farm centre; on the way there, look for the crop identification markers indicating wheat, flax, mustard, etc. Other common crops include barley, sunflowers and rapeseed (sometimes known as canola these days, for political reasons). The latter two are grown for their oils, used in cooking and prepared-food production.

The main street in Portage is Saskatchewan Ave, East and West. There is a museum at Fort La Reine, built by explorer de la Vérendrye in 1738. Also at the fort is Pioneer Village Museum, which depicts life in a simple village of the 1800s. Exhibits include a replica of the famous Red River Cart, essentially the truck the pioneers used to travel across country from Quebec to

Manitoba's Red River Valley. It was an ox-drawn cart made entirely of wood. Because of the dust of the trails, the axles were not oiled, and it is said that the creaking and squeaking of a caravan of carts could be heard for miles. The site is open from May to September.

*Portage La Prairie Kampgrounds* (☎ 267-2228) is west of Winnipeg on Hwy 1 (the Trans Canada Hwy), 16 km east of Portage La Prairie; at $12 for a tent, it's good value. The site is grassy and quiet, with lots of trees. On the west side of town along the main road, there are a couple of places to eat, some motels and the Greyhound Bus Depot, but disembarking really can't be recommended.

North of town, along the southern shores of Lake Manitoba, is another of the provinces's essential wetlands. Eight km long, Delta Marsh is internationally known and is one of the most significant waterfowl staging marshes in North America. Public access to much of it is limited by research and wildlife management controls, but there is camping at the eastern edge, just north of the town of St Amboise.

The Trans Canada Hwy splits into two segments 11 km west of Portage. The Yellowhead Route runs north along the southern edge of Riding Mountain National Park and on to Edmonton, Alberta. The southern portion, the original, heads due west to Brandon and on to Calgary, Alberta.

## SPRUCE WOODS PROVINCIAL HERITAGE PARK

Within the park is a 25-sq-km area of desert-like sand dunes as high as 30 metres, which supports a number of snakes, lizards and even cactuses not found elsewhere in the province.

There are more hospitable areas in the park, too, with woods, lakes and camping areas. Walking trails lead to some of the more interesting sections of the park, including the dunes and underground-fed pools. Alternatively, horse-drawn carts can be taken from the information centre to these attractions.

## BRANDON

The second largest city in the province, with a population of 40,000, Brandon has little to attract the visitor, although it is considered a good place to live. Primarily a functional centre, it's situated four km south of the highway. Places to eat and sleep can be found along the highway.

Agriculture Canada, a federal government department, has a research centre here which investigates everything from cattle breeding to barley pasture weed control. In one form or another, this experimental farm has been operating since the mid-1880s. The town is also home of Brandon University and has a large railyard.

The main street is Rossen Ave, and the Assiniboine River flowing through town keeps it a fairly green-looking place. There is a tourist information booth on the Trans Canada Hwy.

The Greyhound Bus Depot is on the corner of Rossen Ave and Sixth St.

The Brandon Folk Music & Art Festival takes place each summer around the beginning of August.

### Commonwealth Air Training Plan Museum

At the airport is the Commonwealth Air Training Plan Museum, which tells the story of the thousands of recruits from around the British Commonwealth who were trained as pilots and navigators in Canada from 1939 to 1945 before heading over to Europe. There are 13 original training planes housed in the original Brandon hangar. Small training centres such as this one dotted the prairies.

Other displays include photographs, aircraft engines and other artefacts and memorabilia. It's open daily and there is a small admission charge.

### Places to Stay & Eat

There are plenty of motels and hotels, and a *YWCA* at 148 11th St, if you don't want to haul into Winnipeg.

Along 18th St is a variety of restaurants.

## CANADIAN FORCES BASE SHILO

South-east of Brandon on Route 340, there is a Canadian military base, in Shilo. On the base, for those with a special interest, is the Royal Regiment of Canadian Artillery Museum, with a vast collection of uniforms, guns, ammunition, vehicles and more, dating from 1796.

There are both indoor and outdoor exhibits. The museum is open daily through the summer, but only in the afternoons on weekends and holidays. The rest of the year it is closed on weekends.

## GRAND VALLEY PROVINCIAL RECREATION PARK

Just 10 km west of town is this privately operated park, campground, picnic area and waterslide. Perhaps of more interest is the Stott Site, within the park. A provincial heritage site, it was a Native Indian bison kill area dating back some 1200 years. Displays offer information on how it was used, and a Native Indian encampment has been recreated. There are also some live bison to send one's imagination to a time when the prairies saw herds of thousands. When they moved, the earth literally shook.

## NEEPAWA

Also north of Brandon, Neepawa was the childhood home of writer Margaret Laurence. Her home, at 312 First Ave, has now been set up as a type of Laurence museum and minicultural centre, with a gallery and space for artists.

## WEST TO THE BORDER

From Brandon west, there are a few small towns, such as Virden, of no real interest to the visitor. In some areas, derricks can be seen pumping oil. Remember that during the summer, clocks move back one hour at the Saskatchewan border because Saskatchewan, unlike the rest of the country, does not use daylight-savings time.

## RIDING MOUNTAIN NATIONAL PARK

North of Brandon, 300 km north-west of Winnipeg, Riding Mountain is the major attraction of western Manitoba. Covering nearly 3000 sq km, it is a huge island of a park rising from the surrounding plains. Much of it is highland, set on a forested escarpment that runs from North Dakota to Saskatchewan. Within the park are deciduous forests, lakes, rivers and meadows. Around **Clear Lake** is the developed area, but most of the park is wilderness. There are over 300 km of walking, cycling and horseback riding trails in the park, providing access to various sections of interest. At **Lake Audy** you might see a small herd of bison in an enclosed section of woods and meadow. Elk and moose are also plentiful in the park.

Canoe rentals are available. This is a good place to use the list of canoe routes in the province, which is available from the tourist office in Winnipeg. The park is patrolled by rangers on horseback, and a couple of companies run tours using this traditional method of exploring the region, which was always too rough for the pioneer's carts. These trips range from an afternoon's outing to three-day camping trips. Try Breezy Hill Horse Camp for short evening rides. For longer trips there is High Mountain Outfitters (☎ 967-2077), also in Kelwood. Note that the eastern section of the park is the highest, so the views are best. **Wasagaming**, on the south shore of Clear Lake, is a casual resort town with all the amenities. The park information centre is here. Also of note is the First Nation Celebration, held in early June, which provides an opportunity to see traditional dance, costume, games and crafts.

Camping is not expensive, with both serviced campgrounds or backcountry opportunities.

## The Bison

In the days before Whiteman's arrival in the west, huge herds of bison roamed from what is now Manitoba to the Rocky Mountains, from Texas to the shores of Great Slave Lake. On the wide-open grassy plains of the prairies, herds could number in the hundreds of thousands.

The name buffalo is very commonly, if not nearly always, used in relation to the North American bison, but this is incorrect. A buffalo is a type of heavy oxen found across Africa and Asia.

The bison is a large, shaggy form of wild cattle. An old bull can weigh as much as 900 kg and full-grown females average over 500 kg. To the western Indians, the bison were stores with legs, but were also beings with spirits, to be respected. Bison were the principle source of food. The hides and hair made clothes, tents and bedding. Horns were used in crafts and rituals, the bones as knives. Nothing went to waste – even the 'chips' (dried excrement) were burned as fuel.

Aside from eating the fresh meat, much was prepared and preserved during the summer for the long winters. It could be cut into strips, pounded with herbs and dried in the sun to create a type of jerky. I tried this once myself using beef, with great success, but had to endure the sideways glances of neighbours as I strung the strips out on my city clothesline. Native groups from more northern areas added currants and berries and boiled fat to the dried meat to form pemmican, a nutritious mix which kept many a fur-trader and explorer alive.

Bison would be hunted in a number of ways. Sneaking up on them, often disguised as an animal, and then firing arrows, was one simple method. Later, they were chased on horseback. (The horse, icon of the west, was unknown in North America before the arrival of the Spanish. Until then, Native Indians roamed the prairies on foot, aided only by domesticated dogs, who pulled materials and supplies.)

When possible, hunters made use of the lay of the land, such as at Head Smashed In, Alberta or the Stott Site (mentioned in Grand Valley Provincial Recreation Park). Animals would be herded and rushed over cliffs. While effective for the Indians' needs, none of these methods appreciably diminished the bison's numbers.

Through the late 1800s, Europeans with rifles and horses slaughtered the immense herds to near extinction, often for nothing more than amusement. For the Plains Indians, the demise of the bison led to starvation and meant the end of their way of life. In Canada, the largest remaining wild herd is found at Buffalo Woods National Park. Smaller groups and individual specimens can be seen at various parks and zoos around the country. ■

Aside from the camping possibilities, there are motels and cabins for hire in and around Wasagaming. A modest motel is the *Manigaming Motel* (☎ 848-2459), with doubles from $50.

## DAUPHIN

North of the park up Hwy 10, Dauphin is one of many Ukrainian centres found all across the prairie provinces. South-west of town is Selo Ukraina (Ukrainian Village), the location of the country's National Ukrainian Festival, held at the beginning of August each year. Dancing, traditional costumes and lots of food are part of the festivities.

# Saskatchewan

Entered Confederation: 1 September 1905
Area: 651,903 sq km
Population: 988,928
Provincial Capital: Regina

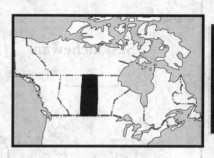

Saskatchewan is a Cree Indian word which refers to the Saskatchewan River and means 'river that turns around when it runs'.

Prior to the arrival of Europeans, first the fur traders and explorers, then the farmsteading settlers, the region was primarily Cree territory. They were a seminomadic people whose life was inextricably linked with the herds of buffalo (bison) who roamed the vast plains.

Tourism is not a major industry in Saskatchewan but many people do pass through. Each of the two major cities has some interesting things to consider on a stopover, and there are several good historical parks around the province which outline the Native Indian way of life. Prince Albert National Park is accessible Canadian timberland. The southern region has some intriguing landscapes and desert-like topography.

Many people find the scenery monotonous; the south of the province is mercilessly flat, often without a tree in sight. But such wide-open space is a scene much of the world cannot even imagine. And the sight of golden, ripening wheat rippling to the horizon in all directions can be beautiful. The sunsets, sunrises, cloud formations and night skies are all fantastic. There's a lot of space. You might hear people out this way say 'the Rocky Mountains are nice but they get in the way of the view'.

In the north of the province, 55 canoe routes have been mapped out, and there are canoe outfitters at Lac la Longe and in Flin Flon, just over the border in Manitoba. The northern half of Saskatchewan has over 100,000 lakes and few roads.

With so much farmland in this province, it's possible for visitors to stay on a farm, which can be a reasonably priced arrangement; the relevant tourist offices have more information.

Drivers should watch for the Mohawk gas stations, which sell an ethanol-blended gas made partly from wheat and said to cut undesirable emissions by as much as 40%.

## GEOGRAPHY

The far north of the province – part of the Canadian Shield – is rocky timberland and a wilderness of lakes and forests inhabited by few people. Of those who do live here, many are Métis.

Between this area and the bald, open prairie of the south is a transition zone stretching across the province, covering the lower middle section of Saskatchewan in rolling hills and cultivated farmland. This range, called the parklands, contains some large government parks and both the North and South Saskatchewan rivers.

## CLIMATE

The weather in Saskatchewan is changeable and extreme. Generally, winters arelong and cold: the temperature can get down to -50°C. Summers are warm and short, and maximum temperatures can reach 40°C. I've always found August and September warm, dry months, but even then the nights are cool. It's common to see signs of fronts moving across the sky, so you usually know what weather's coming.

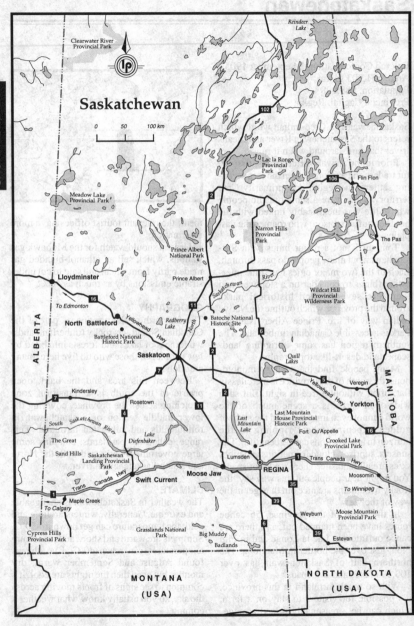

# Saskatchewan

0    50    100 km

Clearwater River
Provincial Park

Reindeer
Lake

Meadow Lake
Provincial Park

Lac la Ronge
Provincial
Park

Flin Flon

The Pas

Prince Albert
National Park

Narron Hills
Provincial
Park

Lloydminster

Prince Albert

Saskatchewan

River

Wildcat Hill
Provincial
Wilderness Park

To Edmonton

Yellowhead
Hwy

Redberry
Lake

North
Battleford

Batoche National
Historic Site

Battleford National
Historic Park

Saskatoon

Quill
Lakes

Veregin

Kindersley

Rosetown

Yellowhead Hwy

Yorkton

South
Saskatchewan
River

The Great
Sand Hills

Saskatchewan
Landing Provincial
Park

Lake
Diefenbaker

Last
Mountain
Lake

Last Mountain
House Provincial
Historic Park

Fort Qu'Appelle

Crooked Lake
Provincial Park

Trans Canada Hwy

Lumsden

REGINA

Moosomin

Moose Jaw

Swift Current

Trans Canada Hwy

Maple Creek

To Calgary

Cypress Hills
Provincial Park

To Winnipeg

Weyburn

Moose Mountain
Provincial Park

Grasslands National
Park

Big Muddy
Badlands

Estevan

ALBERTA

MANITOBA

MONTANA
(USA)

NORTH DAKOTA
(USA)

## ECONOMY

Saskatchewan and wheat are pretty much synonymous. The province is the greatest grower of wheat in North America and, with over a third of Canada's farmland, produces two-thirds of Canada's crop. Besides wheat, grains such as barley and rye are important, as are sunflowers and beef cattle.

In the past few years, oil has become increasingly important; you'll see the slowly cranking rigs in the fields. The province also has the richest potash deposits in the world. Along the Trans Canada Hwy, some of the soil is jet black – this is natural because the area was once totally submerged under water. Occasionally you'll see large patches of white stuff which looks like snow. This is sodium sulphate and occurs only in certain climatic conditions. It's used in various industries, like detergent preparation.

### Wheat

Since it's all you're looking at, I suppose a word about the golden grain is in order.

Wheat, brought to the New World by European settlers, was largely responsible for the development of the Canadian prairies. It is the primary crop across Manitoba, Saskatchewan and Alberta but by far the bulk of it is grown in Saskatchewan.

So productive are the fields here that Canada is the world's sixth largest producer after Russia, China, the USA, India and France. The majority of wheat is produced for the export market. Russia, despite its own massive wheat production, is one of Canada's most important clients. Canadian wheat is sought after for its quality and high protein content.

Because of the cold climate the principal variety grown is hard red spring wheat, a bread wheat which is planted in spring and then harvested in August and September. The other main type is durum wheat whose characteristics make it especially suitable for the production of pasta.

In late summer, when the ripened wheat is golden brown it is not uncommon to see the huge self-powered combines cutting and threshing through the fields at any hour of the night or day, often in teams. At night in particular, with the bright light beams skimming across the fields from the droning machines, it's quite a memorable sight.

The Canadian Wheat Board markets the crop. This organisation represents the farmers, the consumers and the government in buying, selling, setting quotas and regulating export. Needless to say, the Board's actions are hotly debated.

Farmers are paid when they deliver their bushels to the grain elevators, where the entire crop is pooled and then sold by the Board. Once that is accomplished the wheat is carried to ports by train and loaded onto freighters for destinations far and wide.

### Grain Elevators

The unique, striking, columnar red, green or grey grain elevators seen along rail lines across the province are the classic symbol of mid-western Canada. These vertical wheat warehouses have been called the 'castles of the New World' and to this day are the artificial structure most visible across the plains.

Very simple in design and material and built solely for function they have been described as Canada's most distinctive architectural form. Western painters, photographers and writers have taken them as objects of art, meditation and iconography.

Across much of the province they have represented the economic life of the town and district and indeed have topped in size, if not in importance, that other traditional landmark, the church.

The first grain elevators were built in the 1880s. While Canada was becoming the 'breadbasket of the world' at the turn of this century, the number of elevators mushroomed, reaching a peak of nearly 5800 in 1938. Through consolidation and changing conditions that number is now down to just under 2000. This decline has concerned many individuals and groups who hope to prevent (not just lament) any further major loss of elevators.

Formerly made all of wood, they are now built from materials such as steel and cement. The classic shape, about 10 metres square and 20 metres high, is being experimented with as well, in an attempt to improve efficiency.

The stark beauty of elevators catching the light or looming out of the horizon is certainly an unmistakable part of the prairie landscape. ∎

SASKATCHEWAN

## PEOPLE

The Cree remain the largest of the Saskatchewan First Nations. Other First Nations include the Dakota, Saulteaux, Nakota and Dene. The ethnic background of most of today's residents is either British or East European.

## INFORMATION
### Provincial Symbols

The provincial bird is the sharp-tailed grouse and the flower is the lily.

### Telephone

The area code is 306 which covers the entire province. For emergency calls, dial 911.

### Time

Saskatchewan is on Central Time and unlike the rest of the country, does not go on summer daylight-savings time.

### Tax

The provincial sales tax is 9%.

# Regina

Regina (population 180,000) is Saskatchewan's capital. It is the largest city and acts as the commercial, financial and industrial centre of the province, but it's still a relatively small, quiet town that pretty much closes down after dark.

The Cree Indians originally lived in this area, butchering buffalo and leaving the remains along the creek. It became known as Oscana, a Cree word meaning 'pile of bones'. Later, European settlers were prompted to dub the settlement 'Pile O'Bones'. In 1882 the city was made capital of the Northwest Territories and its name was changed to Regina in honour of Queen Victoria. The Northwest Mounted Police used the city as a base from the 1880s, and in 1905 it became the capital of the newly formed Saskatchewan.

In 1933, the Cooperative Commonwealth Federation (CCF), a socialist party, held its first national meeting in Regina and called for the end of capitalism. In 1944 it became the first socialist party to form a Canadian provincial government. The CCF merged with the New Democratic Party (NDP) in 1961, to form Canada's present left-wing party.

Wascana Creek and its parkland run through town, providing a change from the dry, golden wheat fields stretching in all directions.

Two interesting facts about the city: Regina is the sunniest capital in Canada and, oddly, every single tree you see here was planted by hand. It's not known as the bald prairie for nothing.

## ORIENTATION

The city's two main streets are Victoria Ave, running east-west, and Albert St, going north-south. Both streets are lined with fast-food places and gas stations.

East of the downtown area, Victoria St becomes Hwy 1 East (the Trans Canada Hwy) for Winnipeg. South of the downtown area, Albert St leads to both Hwy 6 (southbound) and Hwy 1 West. Albert St North leads into Hwy 11 for Saskatoon.

The downtown core is bounded by Albert St to the west, 13th Ave to the south, Osler St to the east and the railway tracks to the north.

Victoria Park sits in the middle of the downtown area. Scarth St and 12th Ave, which edge the park, are important shopping streets. Scarth St, between 11th and 12th Aves, has been converted into a small, pleasant pedestrian mall with trees and benches. On the north-east corner is the old City Hall, which houses a theatre, shops and a museum. With its pyramid shapes, the new Continental Bank building on the south corner is unusual and interesting. The large Cornwall Centre, a major shopping mall, is opposite the Scarth St mall on 11th Ave.

Wascana Centre, a 1000-hectare park, is the dominant feature of the city and, aside from its own natural appeal, contains many of Regina's primary attractions. It lies four

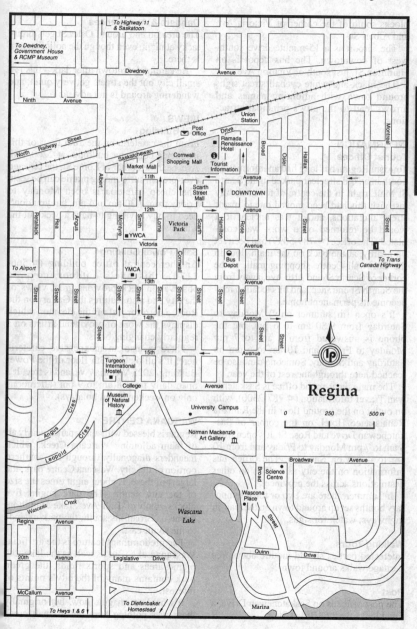

# Regina

0   250   500 m

blocks south of the corner of Victoria Ave and Albert St.

The airport is a 15-minute drive southwest of downtown. The bus depot is on Hamilton St, just south of Victoria Ave.

The black-and-white eyeball street signs around town with adjoining names and arrows lead to the city's principal attractions.

## INFORMATION
### Tourist Offices
Tourism Regina has long had an information booth in an old streetcar parked in the Scarth St Mall, right in the centre of town. On my last visit this had been moved due to major street alterations, and it was unclear if it would be returned once work was completed. The office (☎ 789-5099) had been set up nearby, at the back on the main floor in the Cornwall Centre shopping mall, at the corner of Scarth St and 11th Ave, away from the Scarth St entrance, and this location may become its permanent home.

It's open (in summer only) Monday to Saturday from 9.30 am to 6 pm, but the phone is answered from 8 am to 7 pm Monday to Friday and 10 am to 6 pm on Saturday and Sunday. Someone can also be reached here through the rest of the year.

The main, year-round office is Saskatchewan Travel Information (☎ 787-2300), with an outlet on the ground floor in the Ramada Renaissance Hotel, on the corner of Saskatchewan Drive and Rose St. It's open from 8 am to 7 pm Monday to Friday and from 10 am to 4 pm on Saturday. The office has information on the city as well as on other destinations across the province.

In summer, there are two or three temporary booths set up around town on the lead-in highways; watch for signs.

### Walking Tours
Interested parties should inquire about free heritage walks around town.

### Post
The post office is on Saskatchewan Drive, a few blocks west of Broad St.

### Dangers & Annoyances
The area on and around Osler St gets pretty tacky at night, even though the police station is there.

Be careful downtown after dark – this is a small city but the streets get very quiet, and wandering around is not advisable.

## VIEWS
### SGI Building
From the cafeteria on the 18th floor of this insurance company building, at 2260 11th Ave, near the corner of Lorne St, the city and ever-present surrounding prairie can be seen. The cheap cafeteria is open Monday to Friday from 7.30 am to 4 pm, but you don't need to buy anything to have a peek out the windows.

### Sask Power Building
Another central office building (☎ 566-3176), this one's outdoor, covered observation deck provides great views of the city and also features the Gallery on the Roof, a corridor just off the elevator, which displays the work of provincial artists on a regularly changing basis.

There is also an inexpensive cafeteria here. It's all on the 13th floor of the Power Building, 2025 Victoria Ave, and is free. It's open daily from 8 am to 9 pm (afternoons only on weekends and holidays).

## WASCANA CENTRE
Regina is blessed with many parks, nearly all of them adjoining Wascana Creek, which meanders diagonally through the southern portion of the city. Wascana Centre park, the largest of these, is about eight times the size of the city centre. The park begins five blocks south of 12th Ave. Take Hamilton, Lorne or Broad Sts south; the park extends to the south-east.

The predominant feature is the artificial Wascana Lake. But as well as the lake, the picnic areas and sports fields, the green park contains many of the city's points of interest.

It's hard to imagine now, but originally there was nothing here but a small creek called Pile O'Bones, surrounded by treeless prairie.

The headquarters of the park, Wascana Place (☎ 522-3661), is on Wascana Drive, west of Broad St, east of Wascana Lake and north of the marina. There's not really much of interest here, but there is an information office and a good view from the 4th level of the building.

A little ferry, which is cheap, runs to Willow Island on the lake, a good site for picnics. Catch it off Wascana Drive by the north end of the lake. Bikes, boats and roller skates can be rented beside the Wascana Pool building off College Ave. There is no swimming in the lake but the pool is open to all. There are flower gardens in the section north of the Legislative Building.

A waterfowl park off Lakeshore Drive, east of the Centre of the Arts,

has 60 species of birds and helpful identification displays. A boardwalk leads into the marsh, and naturalists are on duty through the week. The waterfowl park is open from 9 am to 9 pm from 1 May to 1 November.

The tourist office has a map of the Wascana Centre and a booklet detailing six walks through the park.

There is also a good, low-cost restaurant with an outdoor patio, The Bistro, at the Wascana Marina.

Free Sunday afternoon concerts are given at the Bandshell.

## Saskatchewan Science Centre

Also part of the park complex is the Saskatchewan Science Centre (☎ 791-7900), with its series of exhibits, hands-on participatory displays and demonstrations on the planet, its place in the solar system, physical laws and life.

The Science Centre is in the interesting, overhauled old Regina Power Plant (see the bank of old dials and meters in the lobby), on the north shore of the lake, east of Broad St near the corner of Wascana Drive and Winnipeg St. A bus up Broad St from downtown will get you to within a two-block walk of the door. The centre also houses a snack bar, a restaurant and a nifty little store.

A large-format **IMAX movie theatre** and the **Kalium Observatory** are other features of the centre, and have their own programmes. Stargazing nights at the observatory are well worthwhile and cost just a couple of dollars.

Entry to the centre is $7 per adult, with lower senior and family rates. IMAX shows are at additional cost (almost as much again), or you can purchase a money-saving combination ticket. From June to Labour Day (early September), the centre is open from 9 am to 6 pm Monday to Thursday, 9 am to 9 pm on Friday and Saturday and 10 am to 6 pm on Sunday. The rest of the year it closes at 5 pm daily, opens at noon on weekends and is closed on Mondays. It's worth calling to confirm hours, especially on holidays.

## Provincial Legislature

Just off Albert St, on the park's west side, this beautiful building was done in 1919 in loose English Renaissance style at a cost of $3 million. Inside, 34 kinds of marble were used. The building is open all day, every day, and there are free tours given on the hour (except at lunch time) from June to Labour Day. While at the Legislature, take a look at the **Native Heritage Foundation Gallery**, in the east wing on the main floor. The gallery exhibits and promotes Native Canadian art and is open daily.

## Museum of Natural History

Also in the park, the museum is just south of the corner of College Ave and Albert St (☎ 787-2815). Upstairs there are realistic displays of North American wildlife, particularly animals native to Saskatchewan, with good explanations accompanying the exhibits. Downstairs the displays outline the biology of insects, birds, fish and animals and attempt to explain their behaviour. Space is also given to palaeontology (fossils) and archaeology.

The First Nations Gallery, opened in the summer of 1993, presents thousands of years of Saskatchewan's Native Indian history. There are often films on a variety of topics.

The museum is open daily from the beginning of May to the beginning of September; call for the off-season schedule. Admission is free and a visit will take about one hour.

## Norman Mackenzie Art Gallery

Next door to the Museum of Natural History is the Norman Mackenzie Art Gallery, which specialises in Canadian painting, much of it by local artists. Exhibits change and may be historical or contemporary. The collection also contains works from US and European artists and good touring shows are staged. The gallery is free and is open every afternoon.

The art gallery is the venue for dramatic performances of *The Trial of Louis Riel*, which are held in summer; see the Entertainment section later for details.

## Diefenbaker Homestead

Although not in its original location, but on Lakeshore Drive west of Broad St in the park, this house is the boyhood home of former prime minister John Diefenbaker and is furnished with pioneer articles, some from the politician's family. It's open daily and admission is free.

## University Campus

The University of Regina is on the east side of the park.

## REGINA PLAINS MUSEUM

Yes, Virginia, there is life away from the park. The Regina Plains Museum (☎ 352-0844) is on the 4th floor of the old City Hall, on the corner of Scarth St and 11th Ave. There are several employees who will guide you around, lovingly telling stories about items from Saskatchewan's past. The museum deals with the various people in the city and province's life: the Native Indians, Métis and European settlers.

Through the summer, the small museum is open Monday to Friday from 11.30 am to 5 pm and on the weekend from 1 to 5 pm. The rest of the year it's closed on Monday and Tuesday. Admission is $2, less for seniors.

## GOVERNMENT HOUSE

Government House (☎ 787-5726) is the restored home of the lieutenant-governor of the Northwest Territories and Saskatchewan from 1891 to 1945. Indeed, Saskatchewan's current lieutenant-governor works (but doesn't live) in this house.

The Northwest territorial government was set up in 1870 to oversee the huge tract of land which was passing from the control of the fur-trading companies. You can imagine what a sight this building must have been in the dusty western village of Regina in the 1890s.

Government House contains period furnishings from the turn of the century, and interpreters are on hand to show visitors around.

The site is north-west of the centre, at 4607 Dewdney Ave, slightly west of Lewvan Drive. It's open Tuesday to Saturday from 1 to 4 pm, Sunday from 1 to 5 pm, and is closed on Monday. Through the winter it is also closed on Saturday. Admission is free.

## RCMP CENTENNIAL MUSEUM & DEPOT

This museum (☎ 780-5838) details the history of the Royal Canadian Mounted Police (Mounties) from 1874, when they first headed west to keep the peace. It was in this part of the country that their slogan 'we always get our man' became legend. On display are uniforms, articles, replicas and stories of some of the famous and/or notorious exploits of the force.

The training facilities and barracks, known as the depot, can also be seen. Mounties still police many of Canada's western and more remote towns and communities, as well as having various federal responsibilities, such as being part of the national security forces. Tours run almost hourly until 3.30 pm, Monday to Friday. In addition, a daily drill takes place each weekday at 12.45 pm.

Open every day, the museum is on Dewdney Ave West, beyond Government House, not far from the corner of McCarthy Rd.

Also at the depot you can see the popular Sunset Ceremony, a formal drill spectacle of drumming and marching surrounding the flag-lowering. It's a bit slow – call it a long hour – but the uniforms are colourfully impressive, and hey, the Mounties are one of Canada's best known symbols! The ceremony, like everything here, is free, but is held only once a week, at 6.45 pm, in July and August. Ask at the tourist office for details, or call the museum. Additional ceremonies take place at the Pile O' Bones Sunday event and on 1 August at the Legislature.

From downtown, city bus No 1 or 6 will get you close to the grounds.

## CITY HALL
Regina's seat of local government (☎ 777-7770), at 2476 Victoria St, is open on weekdays from 8 am to 4.30 pm, with free guided walks available. Call ahead to make arrangements.

## SPORTS MUSEUM & HALL OF FAME
In the former Land Titles building, a heritage site, this small provincial museum (☎ 780-9232) is at 2205 Victoria Ave, across from Victoria Park. It honours local athletes and teams, with Gordie Howe, a local boy made good and one of the greatest players in hockey history, one of the features. The museum is open daily (in the afternoons on weekends) and admission is free.

## HISTORICAL TELEPHONES
SaskTel, the provincial telephone company, has an historical display area on the main floor of their building at 2121 Saskatchewan Drive. It's free and is open all day, Monday to Friday.

## FIRE HALL
Displays of old firefighting equipment can be seen in this modern, working fire station (☎ 777-7830) at 1205 Ross Ave. It's open to the public on weekdays and is free.

## ANTIQUE MALL
For a mooch around on a rainy day or a Sunday when things are pretty quiet, try the Antique Mall, a grouping of 25 or so antique booths and dealers. It's open all year at 1175

Rose St, near Sixth St. Note that on Sundays, even this isn't up and running until after noon.

## FARMERS' MARKET
A smallish farmer's market is set up two days a week through the summer at the VIA Rail station on Saskatchewan Drive. Produce and baked goods (including jams and pies) as well as some crafts are offered for sale. Hours are 11.30 am to 4 pm on Wednesday and 8 am to 1 pm on Saturday.

## WILD SLIDES
About 1½ km east of town on Hwy 1, this water-slide park has snack bars and a picnic area. It's open daily from June to September.

## ACTIVITIES
A pass can be bought at the YMCA for use of their courts, gym or pool. The tourist office can give you information about swimming at public pools. There's one in Wascana Centre.

The Devonian Pathway is 11 km of paved bike routes through four city parks. It begins and ends at Rotary Park, off the Albert St bridge. Bicycle rentals are available in Wascana Centre park. The office, which is open only in the afternoons, is at the Wascana Pool, off College St.

The Regina Astronomical Society has a telescope set up on Broad St opposite the CBC building, by Wascana Centre, and is open on Wednesday nights in summer for public viewing. Also ask about the Kalium Observatory at the Science Centre.

Heritage Regina (☎ 584-4025) offers free guided walking tours on Sundays.

The Saskatchewan Wheat Pool (☎ 569-4411) can help you plan a visit to a grain elevator or a livestock saleyard.

## FESTIVALS
Some of the festivals held here are:

April
> *Saskatchewan Indian Federated College Powwow* – Should you be in town in April, consider the Saskatchewan Indian Federated

College Powwow, held in the Agridome of the Exhibition Grounds. It features dancers from around North America, as well as traditional crafts and foods.

**June**

*Mosaic* – It's a three-day multicultural event with ethnic foods, music and entertainment held in early June.

*Regina Folk Festival* – This three-day festival, based in Victoria Park but with concerts elsewhere around town, is also usually held in early June.

**July-August**

*Buffalo Days* – This 12-day celebration is a big annual event held towards the end of July or beginning of August. Stores put up special decor and some workers wear pioneer garb. A talent stage is set up to offer free entertainment and the days are filled with competitions, pancake breakfasts, a beard-growing contest and parades, peaking with a big concert/barbecue in Wascana Park on what is known as Pile O'Bones Sunday. The Midway exhibition features rides, music shows, a casino and various displays and exhibits. A fireworks display wraps up the festival.

**November**

*Agribition* – This is a five-day agricultural and livestock show held at the end of November.

## PLACES TO STAY
### Camping
As you approach Regina from the east on Hwy 1, there are a few campsites, which are geared mainly to trailers and recreational vehicles, not tenters. They might prove useful for a short stay but are definitely not rustic.

### Hostels
The HI *Turgeon Hostel* (☎ 791-8165), is in a fine old house once belonging to an Acadian French person from eastern Canada. It's at 2310 McIntyre St, not right downtown but quite central. McIntyre St is a residential street near Wascana Centre. The rates are $10 for members, $13 for nonmembers. They have 50 beds, as well as cooking facilities and a laundromat. It's closed during the day but remains open until midnight.

The men-only *YMCA* (☎ 757-9622), at 2400 13th Ave, rents small, quiet rooms for $17. There is a cheap cafeteria and pool you can use (see Activities earlier). Note that in summer it is not unusual for all the rooms to be booked out.

The *YWCA* (☎ 525-2141), at 1940 McIntyre St, for women only, is a little more expensive, at $27 plus a $2 returnable key deposit. They have a cafeteria, kitchen, pool and steam room.

For men in need there's the *Salvation Army*, on Osler St between 11th and 12th Aves. As in many cities, they'll offer free B&B. The place is neither especially pleasant nor designed for travellers, but they'll take you in.

### B&Bs
There are quite a few of these places around the province – mostly in small towns – and they are not expensive. In Regina there is *B & J's* (☎ 522-4575), at 2066 Ottawa St, only about three blocks from the downtown area and near the General Hospital. In this two-storey house on a residential street, there are four rooms, at $20/30 for singles/doubles, with evening coffee and breakfast; it's good value.

Another choice is *Eileen's* (☎ 586-1408) at 2943 Grant St, near the Plains Hospital.

### Hotels
The last of the basics that can be considered even half decent is the *Empire* (☎ 522-2544) 1718 McIntyre St, on the corner of Saskatchewan Drive. It's an easy walk north-west of the central downtown area. The clean, simple rooms have no toilet or bath but do have a sink. Singles/doubles are $19/26, but they can't be recommended for women alone. Any other cheap hotels around town are pretty grim.

A good budget hotel suitable for anyone is the central *Plains Motor Hotel* (☎ 757-8661), 1965 Albert St, at the corner of Victoria. Rooms cost $32 to $45 and each room has its own bath and colour TV. There is a restaurant and free parking. The neon tower atop the hotel sign indicates the weather forecast – blue means clear, green means precipitation and orange means unsettled weather. If the lights are running up, the temperature will rise, and vice versa.

Moving up-market, the *Relax Inn* (☎ 565-0455), 1110 Victoria Ave East, is good and has nearly 200 modern rooms. Rates are $40 to $58 for singles or doubles.

Other hotels in the downtown area are costlier. The *Regina Inn* (☎ 525-6767), at 1975 Broad St is right in the centre of town and is moderately priced, with rooms from $65. The totally upgraded old *Hotel Saskatchewan* (☎ 522-7691), on the corner of Scarth St and Victoria Ave, costs from $135.

The *Ramada Renaissance* (☎ 525-5255) features a three-storey-high indoor water slide, a swimming pool and whirlpools. Prices start at $65 for singles and go way up, but there are weekend specials. It's central, at 1919 Saskatchewan Drive.

## Motels

Most of the motels are on Hwy 1 east of town. Cheapest is the *Siesta* (☎ 522-0977), on the corner of Park St and Victoria Ave, by the Pump Bar, with rooms from $25 to $44.

The *North Star* (☎ 352-0723), a few km from town, is the last motel on the north side of the highway. It's pale blue and set back from the road. Rooms cost $30 to $50 for singles/doubles with air-conditioning.

The *Coachman Inn Motel* (☎ 522-8525) is closer to town. It's the orange place at 835 Victoria Ave. Rooms vary in price from $35 to $44.

The *Sunrise* (☎ 527-5447) is near the overpass on Hwy 1 East, just out of town. Rooms with TV and air-conditioning cost $35 to $60.

The *Inntowner* (☎ 525-3737), 1015 Albert St, has rooms from $37 to $53.

## PLACES TO EAT

There's a pretty decent range of places to eat in town, and a number of places offering international cuisine have recently added to the variety of restaurant fare. Most choices listed here are in the central area, many of them are closed on Sunday. The Saturday newspaper is full of ads for Sunday brunch buffets around town. Most of the eateries around the outskirts remain open on Sunday.

A basic friendly place for simple meals is the *Town & Country*, at 1825 Rose St. Open from 6.30 am to 8 pm daily, it's a good place for breakfast. The *Sandwich Tree*, at 1829 Hamilton St, is an office workers' kind of lunch place offering excellent sandwiches with such ingredients as avocado, shrimps and bean sprouts.

Downstairs at the 1928 Market Mall, a restored building on Lorne St near the corner of 11th Ave, *Olga's Deli & Desserts* has bagels, blintzes and coffees and pastries. It's open every day for breakfast and lunch and is inexpensive. Upstairs is the huge Italian restaurant, *Presutti's*, an inexpensive, casual place with an outdoor patio and wood-burning oven. Pizzas, pastas and the like are specialities.

For Chinese food, there's *Lang's Café*, at 1745 Broad St. It's open for lunch and closes late. The decor includes red-and-white table-cloths with vinyl chairs (what else?) but the food is cheap and not bad. A Vietnamese place, the *Mai Phuong*, at 1841 Broad St, has an inexpensive lunch buffet. Neither place is anything to write home about but, they get the job done adequately.

At 2425 11th Ave, near Smith St, *Café Ashani* is open for East Indian dinners nightly. It's not cheap but it's a nice place and the well-rounded menu is prepared carefully.

The *Copper Kettle*, at 1953 Scarth St, opposite the park, is open 24 hours and offers pizzas, other Italian food, Greek dishes and cheap breakfasts.

The *Elephant & Castle*, a British-style pub, is found in the Cornwall Centre, which you enter on the corner of 11th Ave and Scarth St. Part of the restaurant façade is from the bank building built on the site in 1911. Also in this shopping centre mall is a cheap food fair, found on the 2nd level.

The *Bistro* restaurant at the Wascana Marina, in the park near Broad St, is recommended. A small place with some pleasant outdoor tables, and run as a teaching restaurant by a youth organisation, it's good value. It's open every day but not for dinner on Sunday. Try a bison burger.

For a steak, there is the *Diplomat*, at 2032

Broad St, where they have been serving them up for over 10 years. It's open from 11 am to 2 pm and again from 4 pm to midnight (except Sundays).

The *Last Straw*, on the corner of Albert St and Sixth Ave North, is a brew pub and eatery.

Away from the centre, at 3926 Gordon Rd, the *Brown Derby* is a large, casual family place where you can't go wrong picking from the good, extensive and moderately priced menu, which includes steaks, roast beef and Greek main courses. It's open every day.

On Victoria Ave, on the corner of Lindsay St, *Robin's Donuts* is open 24 hours. It's a handy place to go if you're cold, tired or just need a break from the road.

## ENTERTAINMENT
### The Trial of Louis Riel
Held in the MacKenzie Art Gallery (☎ 522-4242), 3475 Albert St, the trial is a theatrical dramatisation of the 1885 court battle fought over this leader of the Métis (Canadians of French and Native Indian stock). One of Canada's most famous historical figures, Riel led two uprisings against the government. The re-creation of the trial highlights issues that are still important, as well as demonstrating the animosity between the country's French and British settlers.

It's worth catching, if your timing is right, and has become one of the longest-running shows in the country. There are shows three nights a week in July and August. Tickets ($9) are available at the tourist office or at the door.

### Spectator Sports
In summer and fall, the Saskatchewan Roughriders (☎ 525-2181) play professional football at Taylor Field as part of the Canadian Football League (CFL).

Curling is a major winter sport on the prairies, and the Curlodrome at Exhibition Park holds major competitions (known as bonspiels) through the snowy months.

### Other Entertainment
*Bart's*, on the corner of Broad St and 12th Ave, is a popular and nicely decorated restaurant/bar where the food prices are slightly more than low-budget. It's also a good place for just a beer, a snack and chat. No live music is offered.

*The Plains*, in the Plains Hotel, has live bands (often blues on weekends) and there is a late Saturday afternoon jam.

The *Copper Kettle* is a restaurant, though it's popular with students as a place for beer. No music is played here either.

The better hotels have lounges –some quiet, some with live music. *Applause Dinner Theatre* is a popular and successful dinner theatre which doesn't cost an arm and a leg. Two-act musical comedies are presented with dinner. It's in the Regina Inn, 1975 Broad St.

The *Saskatchewan Centre of the Arts* is in the Wascana Centre, at 200 Lakeshore Drive. It's the site of concerts and performances ranging through folk, musicals and rock to opera and the symphony orchestra.

Through the summer there are free Sunday performances during the Regina Folk Festival in the Bandshell in Wascana Centre.

## GETTING THERE & AWAY
### Air
Air Canada (☎ 525-4711), with an office at 2015 12th Ave, has flights east and west. Standard one-way fares include $319 to Vancouver and $349 to Thunder Bay. Canadian Airlines also serves Regina. Athabaska Airways flies to Saskatoon, Prince Albert and some of the smaller northern towns.

### Bus
The bus depot is downtown on Hamilton St, just south of Victoria Ave. There are left-luggage lockers and a quick-lunch counter. Three bus companies operate out of the depot.

Greyhound (☎ 787-3340), for daily interprovincial trips, runs west to Calgary and Vancouver and east to Winnipeg and Toronto.

The Saskatchewan Transportation Company (☎ 787-3340) covers the small towns in the province and runs to Saskatoon and Prince Albert. There are four trips a day to Saskatoon ($23). The 240-km trip takes three hours.

Moose Mountain Lines has one route into rural Saskatchewan.

## Train

Fine old Union Station sits boarded up on Saskatchewan Drive, at the foot of Broad St, in the northern portion of the downtown area. Train services in and out of the city have been cut completely.

## Car & Motorbike

Dollar Rent-A-Car (☎ 525-1000) is central, at 1975 Broad St, on the corner of 12th Ave. They also have an office at the airport. Other companies are Thrifty, Hertz and Avis.

## Hitching

For hitching east, take the No 4 bus from downtown.

## GETTING AROUND
### To/From the Airport

The airport is about a 15-minute drive from downtown, and the only way to get there is by taxi, which costs about $6 to $7. There are half a dozen car-rental agencies at the airport.

## Bus

Regina Transit (☎ 777-7433) operates the bus routes around the city. Buses run from 6 am to midnight Monday to Saturday and from 1.30 to 8.30 pm on Sundays. Call for route information.

## Bicycle

Rentals are available in Wascana Park, at the Wascana Pool building off College Ave, with discounts for Hostelling International (HI) members. The office opens at noon.

The Devonian Pathway is a system of 11 km of paved bike routes through four city parks.

## NORTH OF REGINA
### Lumsden

North of Regina, Lumsden sits nestled and protected in a convoluted, lumpy, hilly little valley on the main road (Route 11) to Saskatoon. The Franciscan monks here run the St Michael's retreat. The Heritage Museum outlines the history of the Qu'Appelle Valley.

### Qu'Appelle Valley

The Qu'Appelle Valley runs east-west from the town of Fort Qu'Appelle, north-east of Regina. Following the Qu'Appelle River and interspersed with lakes, this valley is one of the green and pretty playgrounds of Saskatchewan.

There are several provincial parks and historic sites along the glacially formed valley, both east and west of Regina. North of Lumsden, in Craven, the **Last Mountain House Provincial Historic Park**, is a fur-trading post dating from 1869 to 1871. Staff, displays and reconstructed buildings tell the story of the site.

It's open from the end of July to the beginning of September each afternoon from Thursday to Monday. The **Big Valley Jamboree**, held here annually in the middle of July, is one of the province's big country-music festivals, drawing acts from around the country and across the US border. Beer gardens, free camping and booths selling all manner of western garb are part of the three-day event.

Later in the summer, in August, another event worth catching (for those interested in western culture) is the **Craven Valley Stampede**. Chuck-wagon races, roping contests and country & western music are some of the features. There isn't much in Craven, but as it is only 37 km north-west of Regina, you can find accommodation in the city.

### Fort Qu'Appelle

Fort Qu'Appelle, a town of nearly 2000 people, lies north-east of Regina, by the Qu'Appelle River. The museum, at the corner of Bay Ave and Third St, has a collection of Native Indian artefacts, pioneer articles and some things from the old Hudson's Bay Company post (from 1864), which is adjacent to the museum. It's open every day through the summer. At Qu'Appele Crafts, 310 Broadway, Native Indian crafts produced for the commercial market can be seen or purchased. Each year in early or mid-August a large **Native Indian powwow**, takes place at the Standing Buffalo Reserve, nine km west of town. Dance competitors come from far and wide.

Also west of town is the **Echo Valley Provincial Park**, with swimming and trails around the valley.

## WEST OF REGINA
### Moose Jaw

Moose Jaw is a small, fairly typical farm-supply town but with some industry as well. Theories on the origins of the once-heard, never-forgotten name are numerous and neb-ulous; 'moosegaw' is a Cree word meaning 'warm breezes', so this possibility has some credence.

**Information** The tourist office (☎ 693-8097) is at 447 Main St. During the summer they also operate a booth out on the Trans Canada Hwy, beside the statue of the moose. Moose Jaw has long had a bad reputation as a place to get stuck hitchhiking. It ranks right up there with Ontario's Wawa and Nipigon.

**Things to See & Do** The downtown area has a number of heritage buildings from the town's boom days in the 1920s; the tourist office produces a pamphlet for a self-guided historical walking tour along Main St and nearby. Painted murals with a historical theme can be seen on 19 buildings in the core area. The Mural Centre, with more information on the project, is at 445 Main St. Situated halfway between the railway towns of Win-nipeg and Calgary, Moose Jaw was selected as a major Canadian Pacific railway terminal in the late 1800s.

There are four **Western Development Museums** around the province, each specialising in an aspect of provincial history. The one in Moose Jaw concentrates

on the development of transportation in the west, with old carts, cars and trains. Admis-sion costs $3.50.

Also here is **Wild Animal Park**, a zoo really, with mainly indigenous animals including bison. This was the site of Chief Sitting Bull's victory celebration after the famous 1876 Battle of the Bighorn (in what is now Montana, USA).

Curiosity-seekers might enjoy the **Sukanen Ship & Pioneer Village Museum**, 13 km out of town, with plenty of pioneer relics and remains and the ship built way out here for sailing on the sea. The odd collection also contains old cars and tractors. It's open in summer only.

The town also hosts a major **international band** (pipe, brass, marching, etc) and choral festival annually. There is an armed forces base in Moose Jaw, which is home to the famous Snowbirds, an aerial acrobatic squadron which performs at air shows across the continent. The **Saskatchewan Air Show**, largest on the prairies, is mounted here each July.

**Places to Stay** For camping, the *Besant Campground & Recreation Area* (☎ 756-2700) is a 20-minute drive west on the Trans Canada Hwy. There are both tent and trailer sections within the park, and a small pond for a swim.

There are about 10 motels and hotels in town and a B&B. The *Prairie Oasis Tourist Complex* (☎ 692-4894) is a family-oriented recreation centre (water slides, etc) with mobile homes which can be rented from $36 a night. It's at the corner of Ninth Ave North-East and Hwy 1.

# East Saskatchewan

## MOOSE MOUNTAIN PROVINCIAL PARK
Coming west from Manitoba along the Trans Canada Hwy, Moose Mountain (☎ 577-2144), south down Hwy 9, is a place to consider camping the night or stopping for a break from the unchanging pancake land-

scape. The park provides an oasis of woods on the highest plateau in this area of the province. It is a fairly developed area, however, with golf courses, water slides and the like available around the park's main gate. The central and western portions of the park are quieter, and walking trails can be found in these parts.

South of the park is **Cannington Manor Historic Park**. The park records an English settlement here between the years 1882 and 1900. It's open daily from 10 am to 6 pm.

There are a couple of motels in nearby Kenosee.

## CROOKED LAKE PROVINCIAL PARK
An alternative is Crooked Lake (☎ 728-7840), which is further west but not so far from the Trans Canada Hwy. The park is 30 km north of the highway, along the eastern stretches of the Qu'Appelle Valley and Qu'Appelle River. Again, there is camping.

## YORKTON
The onion-domed churches of Yorkton, due north of the Crooked Lake Provincial Park and a major town in eastern Saskatchewan, reflect the area's Ukrainian heritage. There's a branch of the provincial museum system here, depicting the various immigrant groups of the province, particularly the Ukrainians.

**St Mary's Church** is worth seeing, particularly the painted dome.

Nearby are two provincial parks: **Good Spirit Provincial Park**, with good swimming, and the larger **Duck Mountain Provincial Park**, on the border of Manitoba.

The *Corona Motor Inn* (☎ 783-6571), at 345 West Broadway Ave, has been recommended. It costs $46 for doubles and has good service, quiet rooms and a restaurant and bar.

## VEREGIN
Veregin is a small, essentially unknown town, more or less in the middle of nowhere, but it has a rather unexpected international and intriguing history. The town and its surrounding area were settled between 1898 and 1899 by the Doukhobours, a determined and somewhat extraordinary religious sect from Russia.

At the turn of the century, with help from writer Leo Tolstoy, a good many of these people left their homeland and the persecution there to come to Saskatchewan in search of religious freedom and seclusion. Here, under the leadership of Peter Veregin, they created a small but successful community.

Bliss was not to last, however, and soon the Doukhobours were in trouble with their neighbours and government again. They resisted all mainstream authority, be it church or state.

Partially based on fact, but somewhat exaggerated, are the well-known tales of nude demonstrations and arson which have, rightly or wrongly, come to be closely associated with the group.

After about 20 years here, many of the Doukhobours moved to British Columbia, where there's still a community. In the 1950s some of them returned to Russia, or headed to new lands once again, this time settling in Paraguay.

In town is the **Doukhobour Heritage**

Whitetail deer

**Village**, a series of mainly reconstructed buildings and homes which reveal aspects of the settlers' lives at the beginning of the 1900s.

Houses and the Prayer Home are decorated in typical traditional fashion and include some attractive textiles. The museum contains many other artefacts, as well as photographs. Bread baked in the old-style brick ovens can sometimes be purchased.

The village is open daily from mid-May to mid-September, on weekdays only through the winter. There is a small admission charge for visitors.

There is also a statue of author Leo Tolstoy, commemorated for his assistance in the Doukhobours' emigration.

Veregin lies near the provincial border with Manitoba. It is north of Yorkton, 265 km north-east of Regina.

# Southern Saskatchewan

Running across the southern section of the province is the Red Coat Trail, a highway route from Winnipeg to Lethbridge, Alberta. The trail is named after the Mounties and roughly parallels the route they took in coming to tame the west.

Tourist offices have a pamphlet which highlights the historical and geographical points of interest along the way. Here, as in much of the province, the towns themselves don't have much to interest visitors but the government parks do have areas of geographic, historic or cultural significance.

## ESTEVAN

Near the US border, Estevan (population 10,000) is one of the largest towns in southern Saskatchewan. It's a town with energy – it has the world's largest deposits of lignite coal, three electrical generating stations and some natural gas pockets and is surrounded by oilfields.

Local attractions include the sandstone rock formations at **La Roche Percée**, once a site of Native Indian religious observance,

and the **Estevan Brick Wildlife Park**, which has samples of most local species, including bison and antelope.

At the **Sanderson Buffalo Kill Site**, archaeologists are at work and visitors are welcome to watch or join in. The site is in the Souris River valley, about 10 km west-north-west of town.

Ask at the tourist office about rockhounding or visiting the dam and coal mines. There are about half a dozen standard motels.

South of town, in North Portal, gangster Al Capone used to hang out in the Cadillac Hotel – this was a big booze-smuggling area in Prohibition days (1920-33).

## WEYBURN

From Weyburn, a farming supply centre with nearly 10,000 residents, the so-called CANAM International Hwy leads northward to Regina and beyond and southward through North and South Dakota and Wyoming. A promotional pamphlet lists the attractions of a trip along the designated route.

There isn't a lot in Weyburn, but there is a park with camping facilities, a tourist office and a small museum, the Soo Line Historical Museum, which has some Native Indian artefacts and articles from the pioneer days.

Weyburn is the birthplace of Canadian author W O Mitchell and the setting for his best-known book, about a boy growing up, *Who Has Seen The Wind*.

## BIG MUDDY BADLANDS

Off Hwy 34 south of Regina and Moose Jaw, near the US border, this vast, hot area of sandstone formations, hills and valleys was once used by stagecoach robbers, cattle-rustlers and all the other bad-guy types you see in western movies. In fact, the outlaw Butch Cassidy used to ride here.

Food, accommodation and camping is available in the town of Bengough. There is another campground in Big Beaver, and guided tours of the badlands are available.

## ASSINIBOIA

South of this small centre at the junction of

Hwys 13 and 2 are two historic parks which may be of interest. At St Victor's are prehistoric Native Indian petroglyphs (carvings in rock). **Wood Mountain Post Provincial Historic Park** has more recent history, with displays on the North West Mounted Police and the Sioux people. There are some reconstructed buildings and tours are given. Note that the park is closed on Tuesday and Wednesday, and closes for the season at the beginning of September.

## GRASSLANDS NATIONAL PARK

Not yet completed, this park preserves noteworthy flora & fauna as well as remarkable geological and historical features. It's a two-section park lying between Val Marie and

Killdear, south of Swift Current and west of Assiniboia. The eastern block is west of Wood Mountain Post Provincial Park. Information on this section of the park can be found at the Rodeo Ranch Museum, in Wood Mountain. The western section of the park runs south-east from the town of Val Marie, at the junction of Hwys 4 and 18. Information and the latest details on the park are available at the Park Service Office and visitors' centre (☎ 298-2257) in Val Marie. Basic wilderness camping is permitted. As yet, there are no facilities in the park.

Surrounded by ranchland, the park protects a section of original, natural, short-grass prairie land. But this is not the only characteristic. Also protected in the

### The Royal Canadian Mounted Police

The 'Mounties', for better or worse, are one of Canada's two most enduring and clichéd symbols (the other is the beaver). No doubt the traditional scarlet uniforms are striking, particularly when worn by a handsome young man atop a fine chestnut steed. Alas, the opportunities for appreciating this sight are somewhat rare now, as the garb of lore is pretty much exclusively ceremonial and the horses have been largely replaced by gasoline-driven horsepower.

Still, this emblem of the west, much like the American cowboy, does have its origins in reality. Originally formed as the North West Mounted Police in 1873, the force was charged with bringing peace and order to the developing west, then known as the North West Territories. Their headquarters were set up in 1882 at a tiny settlement beside Pile O'Bones Creek, later to become Regina. Perhaps the best-known police force in the world, they developed a reputation for always 'getting their man'. What with the Native Indians caught in the middle of the rapidly changing west, the ever-increasing numbers of arriving pioneers and the coming of the railway, they had their hands full, and generally earned the respect of most. Canada did largely manage to avoid the full-scale Indian wars that plagued the American westward expansion.

Now involved in counterintelligence and thwarting international smuggling, terrorism and narcotics, the Mounties' actions are more controversial if less visible.

Traditionally attired Mounties can be seen in Regina at the RCMP Museum and, often, around the Parliament Buildings in Ottawa. Contrary to some international perceptions (and suggested by many a postcard), they are not seen on horseback in front of Niagara Falls, thief in hand, with beavers industriously gnawing away in the background. ■

park are the Killdear Badlands, 70-Mile Butte which is the second highest point in the province, cliffs and coulees (gulches, usually dry), a prairie-dog town and some historic Native Indian sites.

## SWIFT CURRENT

Though a fairly large town, Swift Current has little for the visitor. Still, a bed or a meal can be found without difficulty. Country music fans may want to check out the Canadian Country Music Hall of Fame (☎ 773-7854), off the Trans Canada Hwy, or the fiddle championships (held in September).

### GREAT SAND HILLS

Just west of Swift Current (or north of Gull Lake and Maple Creek) is a semidesert area with dunes and near-arid vegetation. The best viewing area is near the little village of **Sceptre**, in the north-western section of the hills near the town of Leader. Antelope and mule deer may be seen. There are farm B&Bs in the area; ask in Swift Current.

### SASKATCHEWAN LANDING PROVINCIAL PARK

Straight north up Hwy 4 from Swift Current, the section of the Saskatchewan River here was used as a crossing point by the early European explorers and, later, the White settlers. The Interpretive Centre, a stone house built by the North West Mounted Police, provides some details on this and on the Native Indian sites within the park. There is also camping.

### CYPRESS HILLS PROVINCIAL PARK

This is a small region on the border of southern Saskatchewan and Alberta which offers geographical respite from the prairies. It's a pretty area of small lakes, streams and green hills up to 1400 metres high. Much of the land is a park which stretches across the provincial border. There's organised camping on the Alberta side, around the lakes; tenting costs $10, but it gets crowded in summer.

A dirt road links this area to Fort Walsh, where there's a national historic park. The

fort, built in the late 1870s as a North West Mounted Police base, is a remnant of the district's rich but sad history.

The hills, always a sanctuary for animals, were at one time also a welcoming retreat for the Plains Indians. Information at the old fort tells the story of the time when 'a man's life was worth a horse and a horse was worth a pint of whisky'.

## MAPLE CREEK

At the northern edge of Cypress Hills, Maple Hills is worth a look for its old western main street. Many of the storefronts in this ranching district town are heritage vintage. The Oldtimer's Museum, at 218 Jasper St, is the oldest in the province. It has yet more artefacts on the RCMP and some on the Native Indian and pioneer communities.

If you're around here in late summer, ask about the weekend-long Cowboy Poetry Gathering & Western Art Show. Begun in 1989, the weekend poetry event has become a surprise success attracting, talkers and singers who carry on the tradition of cowboy (and cowgirl) narrative. The art show allows visitors a look at the work of artisans such as saddlemakers and silversmiths. On Saturday night there is a big western dance.

There are a couple of motels in and around town, and the *Willow Bend Trailer Court*, a campground geared to those with campers or recreational vehicles (RVs).

# Saskatoon

Saskatoon, a small, quiet city, sits smack in the middle of the Canadian prairies. The clean, wide streets, low skyline and flat surroundings give the city a western flavour. The South Saskatchewan River meandering through green parkland helps create the atmosphere of a peaceful, easy-paced community. The largest employer in town is the university, and Saskatoon has pretty much become the provincial cultural centre, with an active arts community.

As the second city of the province,

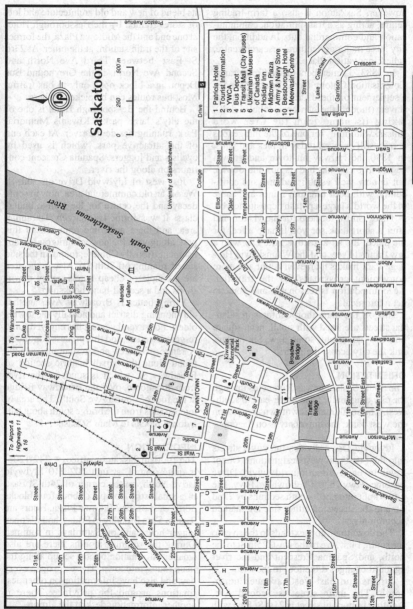

Saskatoon

1 Patricia Hotel
2 Tourist Information
3 YWCA
4 Bus Depot
5 Transit Mall (City Buses)
6 Ukrainian Museum of Canada
7 Holiday Inn
8 Midtown Plaza
9 Army & Navy Store
10 Bessborough Hotel
11 Meewasin Centre

0    250    500 m

South Saskatchewan River

University of Saskatchewan

Mendel Art Gallery

Kiwanis Memorial Park

DOWNTOWN

Broadway Bridge

Traffic Bridge

To Wanuskewin

To Airport & Highways 11 & 16

however, Saskatoon is also a farm-trading centre, acting as a transportation, communication and commercial hub. In addition, the city has a major agricultural research centre, called Innovation Place.

In 1883, 35 members of the Temperance Colonisation Colony from Ontario founded a settlement on these Cree lands. The town stayed (though the ban on alcohol didn't), taking its name from the Cree word 'misaskwatomin', for one of the indigenous berries still enjoyed today in pies and jams. In 1890 the railway hit town and growth began. The city has had its ups and downs, but is now well established and sits confidently, with both uranium mines and some of the world's largest potash deposits nearby.

There isn't a lot here for the visitor, and after a short look-see you'll have a feel for the place. It's an attractive little city with a few things to see, and the Wanuskewin Heritage Park makes it an even better and more convenient crossroads for the traveller. Accommodation is reasonable and you can get a fair meal.

Just off the main thoroughfares, residential streets are lined with small, neat, square houses – some old, some new. Six bridges link the city across the river.

## ORIENTATION
The South Saskatchewan River cuts through the city diagonally from north-east to south-west. The small main downtown area lies on the west bank; the university is on the opposite side.

Idylwyld Drive divides the city's streets into their east and west designations. Out of town in each direction, Idylwyld Drive becomes Hwy 16, the Yellowhead Hwy. The city is split into north-south sections by 22nd St, and the streets on either side are marked accordingly.

The downtown core extends to the river to the south, First Ave to the west, 25th St to the north, and Spadina Crescent and the river again (it changes direction) to the east.

Streets run east-west, avenues north-south. The main street is Second Ave. Another important street is 21st St East with

its blend of new and old architecture and lots of stores framed by the Bessborough Hotel at one end and the Midtown Plaza, the former site of the train station, at the other. At 23rd St East between Third Ave North and Second Ave North, is the Greyhound Bus Depot, in a block open only to bus traffic. Most bus routes can be picked up here.

Behind the Bessborough Hotel is one of the city's large parks, Kiwanis Memorial Park, running beside the river. At each end of the attractive park, which is used by cyclists and joggers, Spadina Crescent continues on along the river.

Just west of Idylwyld Drive on 20th St West is an old commercial area, now in some decay and the centre for the Native underclass. It was formerly a largely Ukrainian area, and there are some remnants of this past, along with the newer immigrant establishments (mostly Chinese, found on the side streets running off 20th St). Also in the area are a couple of cheap hotels, many pawnshops and a second-hand bookshop.

Faring better is Broadway Ave, another old shopping district and actually the town's oldest. For several years it has enjoyed some re-gentrification, and this process continues. A range of stores and restaurants can be found along this small historic section of Broadway St, which is south of the river from downtown, over the Broadway Bridge at the foot of Fourth Ave South. The area of interest runs from the bridge south about half a dozen blocks to Main St East.

## INFORMATION
The Tourism Saskatoon office (☎ 242-1206) is quite central, at unit 102 310 Idylwyld Drive North, on the corner of 24th St East, in a small strip complex about four blocks north-west of the Midtown Plaza. Hours are 9 am to 5 pm Monday to Friday, and it's open longer hours and on Saturdays in summer. During the summer months there are also smaller information booths set up along the main routes into town. These are open every day, and also have information on other destinations around the province. There is another information desk at the airport.

## WANUSKEWIN HERITAGE PARK

North of the city alongside the South Saskatchewan River, this is the premiere attraction in the Saskatoon area and, indeed, the entire province. The 100-hectare site (☎ 931-6767) around the remarkably attractive and diverse Opamihaw Valley presents and interprets the area's rich archaeology, prehistory and the Northern Plains Indian culture. Wanuskewin (wah-nus-KAY-win, Cree for 'seeking peace of mind') is a fascinating cultural, historical and geographical centre all in one. Two dozen prehistoric archaeological sites have been unearthed, attracting attention from researchers internationally. It's now known that hunters and gatherers lived in the area at least 5000 years ago. Active digs can be visited and there is an archaeological lab on site.

The visitor centre, developed in conjunction with provincial Native Indian groups, tells the story of the regional Native peoples and their way of life on the once buffalo-filled prairies. Displays also outline more

recent history and Native Indian life as it is now. Most of the site workers are Native.

Best of all is the land itself, left untouched to reveal why so many people over so many years found it a sacred place. Virtually invisible from the surrounding prairie, four trails lead the visitor down and around the valley amid wildflowers, songbirds and such park highlights as the old buffalo trail, a buffalo jump, the mysterious medicine wheel and tipi rings. The site harbours a concentration of flora & fauna, including a small herd of deer.

A suggestion for visitors is to arrive early in the morning –the earlier, the better. There will be few people, if any, and a walk around the trail system at this time is sure to be quiet and peaceful – the way the Native people would have found it. Also, if it is midsummer, the air will be fresh and cool and the odds of seeing some of the wildlife markedly increased. When it gets busy after lunch, the visitor centre can be viewed.

For the trails, wear flat comfortable shoes,

Native Canadian woman

and in high summer take a juice or water bottle because it can be extremely hot and there are, thankfully, no refreshment stands along the way.

To thoroughly see the site and walk the trails, watch a performance and take a break for lunch, allow around six hours.

The restaurant provides the opportunity of trying Native foods such as buffalo, wild rice and Saskatoon berry desserts. The buff stew with bannock, an unleavened bread, is inexpensive and good.

Getting to the site presents some difficulties for those without a car. It is listed as being five km from the city, but these must be Saskatchewan km – it is a lot further than that. It may technically be that distance from the northern city limit, which is a long way north of the downtown core. There is no public transportation and no tour buses or equivalent. Taxis by the meter cost about $18 one way, although a flat rate of $15 should be negotiable.

From the downtown transit terminal, the No 13 express bus runs towards the park. Tell the driver you're walking to Wanuskewin, and after he tells you you're crazy, he'll let you off at the best spot. This will be near Adilman Drive and Rowles Rd. The shortest route is to get off by the golf course and cut across it, then walk along the road from there. This is still a good three or four-km hike, however, and remember there is quite a bit of walking to be done at the site itself.

Perhaps best is to rent a bicycle in town, this is not really cheap either – $20 for the full day. Bikes can be rented at several outlets, including Joe's Cycle, Bike & Blade, the Ramada Renaissance Hotel and the Bessborough Hotel.

Taking one (with lock) from the Ramada Renaissance is not a bad idea, as it can be picked up at 9 am and doesn't need to be returned until 9 pm. Riding steadily at a good clip (but not racing), the trip took me exactly an hour one way. It's not an unpleasant ride: there isn't a lot of traffic, the terrain is flat and, once out of the city, cultivated fields edge the road. I thought it made a good

introduction to the park – an oasis surrounded by vast, open prairie.

Follow Warman Rd out of the centre (just keep going and going) and then look for signs with the park symbol (a buffalo in a circle). These signs are also seen if you're driving north out of the city along Idylwyld Drive, which becomes Hwy 11. For those with more time and a map, the pleasant Meewasin cycling trail can be used for part of the trip.

The site is open daily from 9 am to 8 pm from the end of May to Labour Day (at the beginning of September) and from 9 am to 5 pm daily for the rest of the year. Admission is $5 for adults, less for seniors and children, and there is a family rate. These costs were under review at the time of writing and may have increased.

## WESTERN DEVELOPMENT MUSEUM

You open the door of this museum (☎ 931-1910) and suddenly you're looking down Main St, circa 1910. It looks like a movie set, with stores, workshops, a hotel, a printing shop and other establishments. The general store is good. Don't miss the model of men playing chess. There are all manner of goods, tins, relics and supplies on display, as well as old wagons, cars and farm machinery.

The museum is at 2610 Lorne Ave, quite a way south of town. To get there, take a No 1 Exhibition bus from Second Ave downtown. When leaving the museum, get on the bus going the same way as when you arrived. It loops around, then goes back a different way. The museum is open daily. Admission costs $3.50, less for seniors and kids; it may be worth showing a HI hostel card too. There is a restaurant at the site.

## UKRAINIAN MUSEUM OF CANADA

This museum (☎ 244-3800), at 910 Spadina Crescent East, preserves and presents a Ukrainian heritage through articles donated by Ukrainian immigrants. The highlight is the collection of fantastic textiles used in formal and everyday dress and for other household purposes. In style, colour and design, they rival South American textiles.

Also interesting is the exhibit on symbolic, festival or special-occasion breads (such as wedding breads). Other items are the painted eggs (pysanka) and a brief history of the pioneers' arrival.

A visit is worthwhile, at only $2. The museum is near the downtown area, along the river. It's open Monday to Saturday from 10 am to 5 pm and on Sunday and holidays from 1 to 5 pm.

There are branches of this museum in other Canadian cities, such as Winnipeg and Edmonton, but this is the main one.

## UKRAINE MUSEUM

A small museum (☎ 244-4212) at 202 Avenue M South, this one has examples of Ukrainian crafts and dress, and through the exhibits portrays aspects of Ukrainian culture from prehistoric times to the mid-20th century. It's open daily in summer, on the weekend in winter, and there is a small admission fee.

The adjacent Byzantine-style Ukrainian cathedral can be visited; ask at the museum.

## MARR RESIDENCE

Just a block from the river, at 326 11th St East, sits the oldest building (☎ 975-8199) in Saskatoon still in its original location. Built in 1884, it was used as a hospital the following year, during the North West Rebellion. Admission is free; call for opening times.

## MEEWASIN VALLEY & CENTRE

The pretty, green Meewasin Valley follows the South Saskatchewan River down the middle of the city. (Meewasin is a Cree word meaning 'beautiful valley'.) From behind the Bessborough Hotel, the valley park runs in both directions and on both sides of the river for a total of 17 km.

There are good views of the river. The **Meewasin Valley Trail** is good for walking and cycling, and picnic tables are scattered among the trees, where black-and-white magpies flit. Bridges span the river at several places and the trail follows the banks on both sides. Many of the city's attractions and

events are along the river. The university lies along the east shore.

The **Meewasin Centre** (☎ 665-6888), 402 Third Ave South, is at the bottom of Third Ave South, on the corner of 19th St East. It's really a museum about the river and the city's history, with some good displays.

Although it's hard to imagine, the river is melted glacier ice from the Rockies far to the west near Lethbridge, Alberta. It flows north from Saskatoon, joining the Assiniboine River on its way to Winnipeg. The Meewasin Centre is open daily, and has good maps of the trail with its various parks. Admission is free.

## BEAVER CREEK CONSERVATION AREA

About 13 km south of the Meewasin Valley (from the Freeway Bridge) is the Beaver Creek Conservation Area, a large park protecting some of the river valley and its wildlife. Walking trails run through the area and the information centre provides geographical and historical background. The park contains some of the little remaining uncultivated prairie in the province. Beaver Creek is open daily and admission is free.

## MENDEL ART GALLERY & CONSERVATORY

These are at 950 Spadina Crescent East, a short walk along the river from the downtown area. The gallery has three rooms of changing exhibits, usually featuring Canadian works. One of the three galleries shows historical works, while the other two display contemporary art. The small conservatory has a few palms, amongst other plants. Admission is free and the centre is open daily from 10 am to 9 pm. There is a coffee shop and gift store on the premises.

## FORESTRY FARM PARK & ZOO

This park (☎ 975-3382) is eight km northeast of the downtown area, across the river and along Attridge Drive and then Forest Drive. The zoo inside the park has 300 animals, mostly those found in Saskatchewan and other parts of Canada: wolves, lynx, caribou and bison. There are also some gardens and picnic sites. In winter the park has a ski trail. There is also a restaurant. The park is over University Bridge; for specific details of how to get there, ask at the tourist office or call the park, but there are signs to follow along Attridge Drive. There is a vehicle charge of $2 and tickets are then required separately for the zoo section. It's open 365 days a year, until 9 pm through the summer months.

## UNIVERSITY OF SASKATCHEWAN

There are a few things to look at on the campus (☎ 966-8385), which is on a huge tract of land along the river. There's a small biology museum, an observatory for stargazing, an art gallery and other small faculty museums. For opening hours and information on free tours of the campus and many of the points of interest, call during office hours.

Also on campus is the **Diefenbaker Centre**, detailing aspects of former prime minister's Diefenbaker's life. It has changing exhibits on Diefenbaker, as well as other historical and craft exhibits. The centre is open daily, but afternoons only on weekends and holidays. His grave site is next to the centre.

The **Little Stone School**, dating from 1905, is the oldest public building in the city. It can be visited every day from May to September, opening all day on weekdays, in the afternoons only on weekends and holidays. A costumed interpreter provides information. It's free, as are all the university sights. The Natural Sciences Museum has some life-sized replicas of dinosaurs.

If you're going to stroll around the campus, pick up a copy of the architectural pamphlet *Building the University*, which offers details of the various structures and their dates of construction.

## SASKATCHEWAN RAILWAY MUSEUM

The province's railway history is here (☎ 382-9855), spread over 2½ hectares. There are engines, cabooses, even transplanted railway buildings. Smaller artefacts have also been collected from around Saskatchewan. It's open on weekends only and admission is free, although donations are

appreciated. The site is four km south-west of town via Hwys 7 and 60. Call for detailed instructions.

## THE BERRY BARN

Located on a working farm 11 km south-west of town, the Berry Barn (☎ 382-7036) sells a range of foods made with the Saskatoon berry. Light meals are also offered. In season, you can go into the fields and pick your own. Call for hours (they vary), information on the harvesting time and directions.

## ACTIVITIES

There are numerous city-operated swimming pools around town; the tourist office will help locate a convenient one. In winter there is a skating rink on the parkland beside the Bessborough Hotel.

## ORGANISED TOURS

Northcote River Cruises (☎ 665-1818) offer one-hour boat tours with historical narration, leaving from the lookout behind the Mendel Art Gallery. They run on the hour through the afternoon and early evening daily in June, July and August. There are weekend trips only in May and September. The cruise costs $6.50, less for kids. Guided walks of the university and some of its attractions are offered on Monday and Friday from June to August; call ☎ 966-8384 for information.

Borealis Outdoor Adventures (☎ 343-6399) runs weekend and longer bicycle trips around the province.

## FESTIVALS

Some of the major events held are:

June-August
  *Shakespeare on the Saskatchewan* – This is a successful and popular summer-long theatre programme, held in a tent near the river by the Mendal Art Gallery. Each year, one play by the Bard is presented for the season. Performances are in the evening and advance tickets are advised; call ☎ 653-2300 for bookings.
  *Saskatchewan Jazz Festival* – At the end of June or beginning of July is the annual Saskatchewan Jazz Festival (☎ 652-1421), held at various locations around town. Most of the concerts and performances are free. Emphasis is on conven-

tional jazz, but bands range from Dixieland to free form.

*The Exhibition* – This is a five-day event in mid-July, with livestock competitions, exhibits, concerts, rides and parades.

*Fringe Theatre Festival* – At the end of July, look for the week-long Fringe Theatre Festival, showcasing varied, experimental and inexpensive theatre, including drama, mime, comedy and dance.

*Louis Riel Day* – This is a one-day event held in the first week of July, with various outdoor activities and contests taking place by the Bessborough Hotel.

August-September

*Folkfest* – Folkfest (☎ 931-0100) is a three-day festival that takes place in late August or early September. The fee of $10 or so gets you into 25 multicultural pavilions set up around the city presenting food, crafts, music and dances. A free shuttle bus does the circuit around the various pavilions.

## PLACES TO STAY
### Camping

Quite close to the centre is the *Gordon Howe Campsite* (☎ 975-3328), on Ave P south of 11th St. Operated by the City Parks Department, it's quite green, although it is geared to those with trailers and campers, and is open from April to October. There is a small store for basic supplies. Tenters will have to go further afield to *Yellowhead Campground* (☎ 993-3343), about a 15-minute drive from the city, off Hwy 16. Call for directions and to check availability at this small campground.

### Hostels

A year-round HI *hostel* (☎ 242-8861) is set up in the good, central Patricia Hotel, on Second Ave North near 25th St East and the Greyhound Bus Depot. Some of the many rooms have been converted to dormitories with bunk beds. A bed costs $10 with a card or $12 without membership, plus taxes.

The hostel rooms are above the bar but there isn't live music every night. The bar is quite inexpensive, as is the restaurant in the basement, where there is lots to look at while you eat the good, cheap food. The hotel lobby has a TV lounge area.

The *YWCA* (☎ 244-0944), on the northwest side of 25th St East at Fifth Ave North,

rents rooms all year round to women ($38 a single). Look for the blue sign near Third Ave. They have a pool and a small kitchen.

Males in need can stay at the institutional *Salvation Army Hotel* (☎ 244-6260), on the corner of 19th St and Ave C, in south Saskatoon. If you arrive after 10.30 pm, you'll need a slip from the police station before they'll let you in. Meals and a dormitory bed are free, but you can only stay a few days.

### B&Bs

A fairly central B&B is the *House of Aird* (☎ 668-6198), at 1005 Aird St, near the corner of Clarence Ave, about three blocks from downtown. Built in 1920, the house now has three rooms for visitors ($32/40 a single/double, which includes a good continental breakfast).

### Hotels – middle

The *Patricia Hotel* (☎ 242-8861), 345 Second Ave North, near 25th St East, is the best and cleanest of the cheap places. In fact, this is one of the best budget hotels in the country – central, friendly and well run.

It's good value, with singles/doubles ranging from $25 to $34, depending on the facilities. The sports bar and restaurant on the premises are both good and inexpensive. Note that some rooms can be a little noisy on weekends if they are above the bar and a live band is on hand. Acting in part as an international travellers' hostel, the 'Pat' attracts visitors from around the world.

The *Senator* (☎ 244-6141) is right in the centre of town, on the corner of Third Ave South and 21st St East. It's old but has been renovated. The rooms are good and cost $32 for singles. It has a beautiful pub-style bar (though some of the patrons look like they've enjoyed it a few too many times) and a rooftop eating area.

There are a couple of cheapies on Second Ave at 20th St, but neither is really recommended. And I'd stay away from the ones on 20th St West.

Moving up the scale, there are several moderately priced places. The *Westgate Inn*

(☎ 382-3722) is at 2501 22nd St West, with rooms from $36 to $45.

On the corner of Second Ave and 20th St is the *Capri Motor Hotel* (☎ 244-6104). This was undergoing a major overhaul on my last visit, so the new incarnation has yet to be seen.

The *King George* (☎ 244-6133), at 157 Second Ave North, is large, one block from the bus depot, and costs $35 to $45.

### Hotels – top end

There are quite a few expensive hotels out around the airport, as well as these two, more central ones.

Firstly, the *Holiday Inn* (☎ 244-2311), at 90 22nd St East, has rooms from $66 to $100.

The classic *Delta Bessborough* (☎ 244-5521), a city landmark at 601 Spadina Crescent East, is a better choice at nearly the same price ($69 to $100). It's a large, chateau-like place at the bottom of 21st St, by the river. Built in 1932, it was run by Canadian National but is now operated by Delta Hotels.

### Motels

The *Travelodge Motel* (☎ 242-8881), near the airport at 106 Circle Drive West, on the corner of Idylwyld Drive, is like the others in the chain. Look for the pale yellow place with an orange name sign. The motel section has rooms from $60 to $99.

The following motels are all quite close to town.

The *Colonial Square Motel* (☎ 373-1676) is at 1301 Eighth St East, near the university. Rooms cost $40 to $45.

*Journey's End* (☎ 934-1122), at 2155 Northridge Drive, is near the airport. It offers good value, with rooms from $45 to $54.

The *Circle Drive Suites* (☎ 665-8121), 102 Cardinal Crescent, at the corner of Airport Drive, has singles/doubles for $35 to $55. It's clean and some of the rooms offer simple kitchens. They also offer a day rate: $25 for a room from 8 am to 5 pm.

### PLACES TO EAT

The *Cage*, at 120 Second Ave North, is a basic, all-purpose restaurant but it has a varied menu and the decor and furniture are a cut above the usual. Breakfasts are good value and will hold you long past lunch. The homemade fries are excellent. A range of dinner specials is offered daily for under $10. The Cage stays open 24 hours (except Sunday, when it's closed all day).

Next door is the *Gotta Hava Java*, a good place for a caffeine fix and a piece of cake.

*Smitty's*, a pancake house, is an admirable place for breakfasts. It's at the corner of Idylwyld Drive and 20th St West.

The *Adonis*, on Third Ave at the corner of 22nd St, is recommended for lunch. It serves excellent soups, salads, sandwiches, vegetarian offerings and some Middle-Eastern items, which are all fresh and inexpensive. There are outside tables too. It's open from 9 am to 7 pm every day (closed Sunday) and is busy at lunch time.

Johnny's Inn, on Third Ave just north of the corner of 22nd St East, is a small cafeteria popular with workers for its good hamburgers, homemade chili and large sandwiches.

The best meal in town, and suitable for any budget, can be had at the downtown *Saskatoon Asian*, a small, nondescript-looking place at 145 Third Ave South. The menu offers mainly Vietnamese dishes, but there are also some Thai-influenced items and Chinese plates to round out the options. For just $5, the rice noodle stir-fried chicken with Vietnamese rolls and a complimentary pot of tea makes a tasty dinner. The soups are also recommended. It's open every day from lunch to 10 pm.

The *Artful Dodger*, at 119 Fourth Ave South, is an English-style pub with typically British meals for around $6. Similar, but perhaps a bit pricier, the *Elephant & Castle* is in the Midtown Plaza (an enclosed mall on the corner of 21st St East and First Ave South, flanked by Eaton's department store at one end and Sears at the other). Or you can eat cheaply at the Food Court on the 1st floor.

For Greek food, *Cousin Nik's* is recommended; it's a little out of the centre, at 1100 Grosvenor Ave, about half a block from Eighth St East, south of the downtown area. It's open every day for dinner, with various daily specials and a full range of Greek dishes. The food is good, the atmosphere is congenial and the prices are in the middle range.

For a splurge on steak, try *John's Prime Rib*, at 401 21st St East. Also more expensive but good is *Dreen's* (☎ 931-8880), at 718 Broadway Ave, which serves a mix of continental and nouvelle cuisine and includes some vegetarian dishes on the menu. Blackboard specials change daily. It's open every day, but only for lunch on Sundays. Reservations are suggested for dinner.

There are a number of restaurants along 20th St West, an area once mainly Ukrainian but now with a small Chinatown among the hard-luck segment of the Native Canadian population. The better Chinese places can be found on or near Ave C, a few blocks from Idylwyld Drive. The large *Golden Dragon*, at 334 Ave C South, has been around for years. The *Wah Quo*, at 402 Ave C South, offers weekend dim sum lunches. The *Yummy Yummy* is a more modest place.

Around the outskirts, and for those with wheels, Eighth St East and 22nd St West both offer abundant choices. The Saskatoon Brewing Company sells the beer made on the premises in the casual *Cheers Pub & Restaurant*, at 2105 Eighth St East. They have an outdoor patio. For prime rib of beef and a good atmosphere, the *Granary*, at 2806 Eighth St East, is a good choice, with meals around $15. Steak and seafood are also on the menu. The (East) *Indian Restaurant*, at 3120 Laurier Drive, is said to be very good. It's only open for dinner and is closed on Monday.

Out of town, *Taunte Maria's Mennonite Restaurant* (☎ 931-3212), on the corner of Faithful Ave and 51st St, offers basic, healthy farm food for any meal of the day.

## ENTERTAINMENT

*Bud's*, at 817 Broadway Ave, has live rhythm and blues nightly and a Saturday afternoon jam. *Amigo's*, at 632 10th St East, has fairly well-known local and regional bands.

The *Artful Dodger* has free entertainment, and the *North 40 Inn*, on the corner of 20th Ave West and Sixth St, has live country music. Admission is a few dollars. A hot scene in town is bars with country music and volleyball courts! Ask around as to which place is wailin' (most popular).

For jazz, check out the *Bassment*, at 245 Third Ave South. They bring in some good acts and it's not expensive. Tuesday night is the free jam session.

The Saskatoon Symphony plays the *Centennial Auditorium* and other venues regularly from October to April. Large-scale theatrical productions and dance performances are held at the *Saskatchewan Centre of the Arts* (☎ 565-4500).

## THINGS TO BUY

A store that might be worth checking out is the large old Army & Navy, on the corner of 21st St East and Third Ave South. This is one of Canada's oldest discount department stores and is a real classic, with three floors of cheap goods, including clothes and some camping supplies. The elevator to get you up and down is still operated by a woman who shuts the metal gate and calls out the floors – one of the few such operators in the country still with a job.

Another place to have a peek at is the Trading Post, 226 Second Ave South. They specialise in crafts and souvenirs, with an emphasis on Native Canadian goods. There is some junk, but also some good stuff, including fine, wool Cowichan-style sweaters, Inuit prints and sculptures (ranging in price up to $1000, but it's interesting for we browsers to see and compare the various styles), some jewellery, woodcarvings and British Columbian jade. Other eye-catching articles are moccasins, mukluks (Inuit boots), teas, spices and wild rice.

Trading Post outlets can also be found in other locations around the province.

## GETTING THERE & AWAY
### Air

The airport is eight km from the centre, in the north-east of the city, off Idylwyld Drive. Air Canada (☎ 652-4181) and Canadian Airlines (☎ 665-7688) both fly in and out of Saskatoon. It's about a two-hour flight to either

Winnipeg, Calgary or Edmonton. Athabasca Airways serves Prince Albert and various small northern towns from Saskatoon and Regina.

## Bus

The big Greyhound Bus Depot (☎ 933-8000), for destinations all over Saskatchewan, is on the corner of 23rd St East and Ontario Ave. The latter is only a small street; the main corner of the bus depot is 23rd St and First Ave North, up a short block from Ontario Ave. The depot has a cafeteria and small store. The washrooms even have showers, which people with tickets can use.

Services include to Regina (daily at 8 am and 1.30, 5.30 and 8 pm, for $23), Winnipeg (two a day, one in the morning and one in the evening, for $78) and Edmonton (three a day, including one late at night, for $56). There are also two buses a day to Prince Albert.

## Train

You won't be too happy with this station's location – it's way out, a long way west from downtown on Chappell Drive. The taxi fare is about $12, but a city bus runs to town at a quarter to and quarter past each hour, from Elevator Rd (behind the curling rink, which is across from the station). It doesn't run very late at night, however. For train information call ☎ 1-800-561-8630.

You'll be even less happy with the Saskatoon timetable.

Trains run to Edmonton ($71) and on to Jasper and Vancouver three times a week, on Monday, Thursday and Saturday at 2.25 am. To Winnipeg ($101) and on to Toronto, trains also run three times a week, but on Monday, Wednesday and Saturday at 3.10 am!

There is no longer a train service to Regina.

## Car

For car rentals, Budget (☎ 244-7925) is at 234 First Ave South. There are other local and well-known companies around town and at the airport. Two are Dollar and Thrifty.

## GETTING AROUND
### To/From the Airport

A taxi to the airport is about $10. Alternatively, catch the No 21 bus from beside the Bay store on 23rd St downtown. A 20-minute ride will get you to within an easy four-block walk of the terminal. Ask the driver for the airport stop. There is a bus every half-hour through the day.

### Bus

All routes and schedules can be accessed through city bus information (☎ 975-3100), although most things of interest to the visitor are within walking distance of the centre of town. Many of the bus routes begin at the Transit Terminal, a section of 23rd St East between Third Ave North and Second Ave North blocked off to all traffic but the buses. At the depot area here, sometimes referred to as Transit Mall, there are signs for all the bus routes, benches to sit on and lots of people milling about waiting. One of the drivers will be able to help you with any destination questions.

For the train station, which bus you catch will depend on the time of day, so ask. None goes right into the station, but they do go within two blocks or so.

### Bicycle

Bicycles can be rented at Joe's Cycle (☎ 244-7332), 220 20th St West, and at Bike and Blade (☎ 665-2453), 205 Idlywyld Drive. The Bessborough Hotel and the Ramada Renaissance, both central downtown luxury hotels, also rent bikes. The rate is the same but a day's rental is longer, because the staff don't have to close up and go home.

## AROUND SASKATOON
### Potash Mine

If you're able to plan a month or so ahead, you can tour a potash mine. A trip involves descending 1000 metres underground and then travelling through tunnels to where machines dig out the potash. You can also see the stuff refined and prepared for shipping.

For details call ☎ 933-8500 or write to 'Tours', Public Affairs Department, Potash

Corporation of Saskatchewan, 500-122 First Ave South, Saskatoon, Saskatchewan. None of the four mines which can be visited is in or near Saskatoon city limits – rather, they are scattered around the province; perhaps your travels will take you near one. The one closest to Saskatoon is about a 45-minute drive from the city.

### Manitou Springs

Near the town of **Watrous** on Lake Manitou, about 120 km south-east of Saskatoon, is the **Manitou Springs Mineral Spa**, one of the oldest spa areas on the prairies. It's open all year for bathing or swimming. There are two modest motels in Watrous, and a luxury hotel, the *Manitou Springs Resort* connected to the spa and with all mod cons.

### Batoche National Historic Site

North-east of Saskatoon, 80 km up Hwy 11 and then along Route 225 off Hwy 312 from the town of Rosthern, is the site of the 1885 Battle of Batoche (more of an encounter really, although with tragic results), fought between the government and the rebellious Métis (led by Louis Riel).

The visitor centre tells the story of the battle, and includes an audiovisual display on the Métis from the 1860s to the present. Also here are the few remains of the village of Batoche, including the church and some of the trenches dug for military purposes. The site is open every day from mid-May to mid-October.

Batoche was the centre of a Métis settlement and its provisional government in the late 1800s; many of these people had left Manitoba after running into difficulties over land there.

Batoche is about halfway between Saskatoon and Prince Albert. Just north of Batoche on Hwy 11, **Duck Lake** is worth a stop. Throughout the town, which has been revamped with antique street lamps and brick sidewalks, painted murals tell some of the area's cultural and historical stories. One outlines the tale of a Cree, Almighty Voice, and how he and a White policeman ended up dying over the killing of a cow. The Duck

Lake Regional Interpretive Centre, at the north end of town off Hwy 11, has an artefact collection relating to the pioneers, Native Indians and Métis of the region. Further west, **Fort Carlton Historic Park** provides more information on the fur trade, the treaties signed with the Plains Indians and the Riel rebellion, in all of which the fort had a role.

# Northern Saskatchewan

The area north of Saskatoon seems like the northern portion of the province and I refer to it that way, but really this is central Saskatchewan. Geographically, Prince Albert National Park isn't even halfway to the northern border, so technically north begins somewhere beyond that point.

From Saskatoon, the Yellowhead Hwy, a branch of the Trans Canada, which comes from Winnipeg, runs north-west through North Battleford on its way to Edmonton and British Columbia. Pick up a copy of the Yellowhead map and pamphlet, which has some historical background, from the tourist office.

Between Saskatoon and Prince Albert is a farm belt which runs the width of the province. Prince Albert seems a long way north, and indeed, the growing season is short, even if it is in the middle of the province. At Prince Albert the land begins to change, and the big national park just north of town marks the start of the vast boreal (northern) forest which takes up the northern half of Saskatchewan.

Saskatchewan has over 100,000 lakes, and a good percentage of these are in the wilderness regions north of Prince Albert. This rugged region of the province is much like the north of the country everywhere from Newfoundland westward. It forms part of the rough, rocky Canadian Shield.

The national park and several others in the region are about as far north as most visitors (or residents) get.

Ask at a provincial tourist office for the

booklet titled *Heart of Canada's Old North-west*, which provides a more detailed look at the region north and west of Saskatoon, including historical information and sites and other things to see and do.

## PRINCE ALBERT

Prince Albert (population 34,000) is the most northerly town of any size in the province. Forests lie to the north, the flat grain fields to the south. It also sits right in the middle between Alberta and Manitoba. Known as PA, it acts as the jumping-off point for trips into the huge Prince Albert National Park. In 1776 a fur-trading post was built here among the Cree. The town was founded in 1866 by a churchman who came to set up a mission, and was named after Queen Victoria's husband.

A tourist information office is situated south of town on Hwy 2. The Tourism & Convention Bureau (☎ 953-4385) has an information office at 3700 Second Ave West.

In Prince Albert itself, there are a couple of minor attractions. The **Historical Museum** (☎ 764-2992) in the old firehall has displays on the city's past. The museum tea room overlooks the North Saskatchewan River, which flows through town to be joined, not far east, by the South Saskatchewan River.

Walking tours of the town begin at the museum, for those interested in more historical detail, but call the museum and make arrangements prior to showing up.

Prince Albert is the location of a major maximum security prison. The **Rotary Museum of Police & Corrections**, beside the tourist office out on Hwy 2, at the corner of Marquis Rd, outlines related history.

### Places to Stay

Most of the town's accommodation is in motels, and there is also a campground, less than two km north of town beside Hwy 2. *Aurora's B&B* (☎ 764-8997), at 619 Fourth Ave East, is an alternative. With a full breakfast, the rate is $25 per person. Motels cost about the same: $50 a double (but without

the breakfast). *Journey's End* (☎ 763-4466), at 3863 Second Ave West, is plain but clean and reliable.

## AROUND PRINCE ALBERT

East of town, 18 km out on Hwy 55, the **Weyhaeuser Pulp & Paper Mill** (☎ 764-1521) can be visited. The free two-hour tour showing the pulping, bleaching, drying and more is definitely an industrial tour, not a stroll in the park. Wear suitable clothes and footwear and be prepared for some noise.

On the other side of Prince Albert, 12 km out on Hwy 3, the **Satellite Communications Station** (☎ 764-3636) can be toured; phone for details.

In 1988, De Beers, the diamond company from South Africa, staked a claim on some land 40 km or so from Prince Albert. Since then, with obvious respect for De Beers' expertise, millions of hectares nearby have been staked for diamond searching and processing of ore has begun at some of the sites.

The area north of town is known as the lake district, a relatively undeveloped area of woods, bush, lakes and cottages. Aside from those found within the national park, other mega-lakes of the region are **Candle Lake** and **Montreal Lake**.

Still further north are three other immense parks: **Nipawin** to the north-east, **Meadow Lake** to the north-west and **Lac la Ronge** directly north. The latter provincial park completely surrounds enormous, island-filled Lac la Ronge, which has the reputation of being one of the most attractive lakes in the province. Beyond these areas is pretty much untouched wilderness.

## PRINCE ALBERT NATIONAL PARK

The national park (☎ 663-5322) is a huge, primarily wilderness tract of softly rolling terrain where the prairie of the south turns to the woodland of the north. Among the geographic features are huge cool lakes, spruce bogs and forested uplands. There are trails of greatly varying lengths, and good canoeing routes provide access to much of the park – the system of interconnected rivers and lakes is well suited to paddlers. There's fishing, a range of camping possibilities and, in winter, cross-country ski trails.

Other highlights are **Lavallee Lake** (with the second largest white pelican colony in the country), the herd of wild bison in the south-western grassland portion of the park and the cabin occupied for seven years by the controversial conservationist **Grey Owl**.

The park's southern border is about 50 km north of Prince Albert.

### Information

The park's service centre, where you'll find lodgings, groceries, gas, canoe rentals and swimming, is the village of Wakesiu, on the huge lake of the same name. The park information office (☎ 663-5322) is also here.

### Places to Stay

There are many campgrounds in the park, but it is a popular place and fills up on any midsummer weekend, especially holiday weekends. It's best to arrive as early as possible on a Friday.

One campground is geared to RVs, the rest to tenters. The smaller campgrounds are simple and quiet, or there is backcountry camping for canoeists and hikers.

The HI *Waskesiu Hostel* (☎ 663-5450) is on the accessible eastern side of the park, directly north of Prince Albert. Members pay $10, nonmembers $13, and there is a family rate available. Meals can be provided (with advance notice), and there are cooking and laundry facilities. The hostel accommodates up to 60 people and is within walking distance of the park facilities. It's open from the beginning of May to the middle of October but, as is often the case, is closed through the day.

### LAC LA RONGE PROVINCIAL PARK

La Ronge is Saskatchewan's largest provincial park. Aside from the main lake, it contains about 100 more, and a portion of the Churchill River known for its falls and rapids. Boat tours take visitors along the river and to some of the more impressive sights, or you can rent a canoe – some of the 55 provincial canoe routes are here. Campgrounds can be found along the western side of the lake and at the northern edge, at Otter Lake.

---

### Grey Owl

Naturalist Grey Owl was somewhat of a legend through the 1930s for his writings and lectures on conservation and for his love of the wilderness. He toured widely across North America and the United Kingdom, encouraging preservation and appreciation of the environment.

His first book, *The Men of the Last Frontier*, was published in 1931. *Tales of an Empty Cabin*, published in 1936, is possibly the best-known work, but in between there were several others.

Upon his death, in 1938 in Prince Albert, it was discovered that his identity and lifestyle as a Canadian Indian had been assumed and that in fact he was Archibald Stansfield Belaney of Hastings, England – this only enhanced the legend surrounding him. He had emigrated to Canada, become a trapper and guide, married an Iroquois woman and been adopted as a brother by the Ojibway tribe.

His wife, Anahereo, who died in 1986, was awarded the Order of Canada for her work in conservation. Her ashes are buried by the graves of Grey Owl and their only daughter, beside the cabin where they lived and worked in Prince Albert National Park. Much of his research was done in the park.

The small, simple, one-room cabin on Ajawaan Lake has become a pilgrimage site of sorts. From the cabin (known as Beaver Lodge), the couple worked to restore the nearly obliterated beaver population. It sits right on a beaver lodge by the lake's edge.

It is still a fairly inaccessible spot, which can be reached one of two ways. First is the Grey Owl Trail, a 20-km hike along Kingsmere Lake. Alternatively, you can canoe from the end of the road, on Kingsmere River upstream to Kingsmere Lake. From there, paddle across the lake to the north end, where there is a choice of either a three-km walking trail or a one-km portage to Ajawaan Lake, from where the cabin can be reached by paddling. ∎

On the west side of the park is the village of La Ronge, now a small resort centre for the park. Free tours are given of the La Ronge Wild Rice Corporation, which processes the rice gathered by local producers. It's open from mid-August to mid-October. If you are not familiar with Canadian wild rice, don't miss giving it a taste. Long used by Native peoples, it is black-hulled and has a mild, nutty flavour. Also here, the **Mistasinihk Place Interpretive Centre**, on La Ronge Ave, has displays on the life, crafts and history of the people of the north. It's not open on weekends. Among the four or five motels is the *Drifters Motel* (☎ 425-2224), on Hwy 2 on the way into town.

### FLIN FLON

Just over the border in Manitoba, Flin Flon has several canoe outfitters for canoeing the northern lakes.

### MEADOW LAKE PROVINCIAL PARK

Similar to Prince Albert National Park, this one (☎ 236-3382) runs along a chain of lakes by the Alberta border. Nature trails and a series of longer hiking trails allow for wildlife viewing. There is a lot of fauna in the park, and good beaches on many of the lakes. Aside from campgrounds, visitors can stay in simple, privately operated rental cabins.

The park is north of Meadow Lake off Hwy 55, and is part of the Northern Woods & Water Route, a road system that begins in Manitoba and ends in British Columbia.

# West Saskatchewan

### REDBERRY LAKE

Redberry Lake, about an hour's drive northwest of Saskatoon, is a prime bird-watching location. The lake and its islands are all protected as a federal bird sanctuary. Of most interest are the large, white pelicans and the small, scarcer piping plover, but there are many others. Bird-watching tours can be taken and boats and canoes or windsurfers

can be rented. The town of **Hafford** has all the conveniences.

Thirteen km east of town on Hwy 40 is the sanctuary interpretive centre. From here, displays on the white pelicans and closed circuit TV of their nesting sites can be seen, and then guided boat tours taken out on the lake. The centre is open daily.

### FORT BATTLEFORD NATIONAL HISTORIC PARK

This historic site is five km from the town of North Battleford, about 140 km north-west of Saskatoon off the Yellowhead Hwy. The North West Mounted Police built the fort in 1876 to help settle the area and police the Native Indians, traders and White settlers. Inside the walls are five buildings you can visit to see police and Native Indian artefacts, tools and memorabilia. The barracks contain an information display and there are guides in costume around the park. The Fort Battleford National Historic Park is open daily from 1 May to 10 October and entry is free.

In North Battleford, across the North Saskatchewan River, the Western Development Museum deals with agricultural history.

There is some interesting landscape around the Battlefords, with a little more topographic variety than you'll find in much of this region of Saskatchewan. Good camping can be found at Battlefords Provincial Park, north of North Battleford.

From the Battleford area, Hwy 16, the Yellowhead, runs north-west to Lloydminster (on the border) and then on to Edmonton, Alberta. A short stop can be made at **Cut Knife**, 50 km west from the Battlefords on Hwy 40, which was the site of a battle between the government authorities and the Native people in early summer 1885. About 15 km north of town through the Poundmaker Reserve, plaques mark the site of Chief Poundmaker's grave and outline the story of the skirmish. In Cut Knife itself, you can't miss the huge eight-ton tomahawk. A small campground is adjacent.

# Alberta

Entered Confederation: 1 September 1905
Area: 661,185 sq km
Population: 2,500,000 (fourth largest)
Provincial Capital: Edmonton

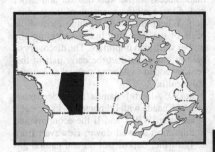

Not so long ago Alberta was a vast, sparsely inhabited wilderness. Today it has two of the largest cities in Canada – Edmonton and Calgary. Its huge wheat farms, cattle ranches and rich deposits of minerals and fossil fuels are the basis of its wealth. For the visitor, Alberta's main attractions are its wildlife, diverse scenery and the wide range of recreational pursuits it offers.

Alberta, the most westerly of the prairie provinces, is bordered in the north by the Northwest Territories; in the east by Saskatchewan; in the south by Montana; and in the west by British Columbia.

Although Edmonton is the most northerly of Alberta's major cities it is still geographically in the southern half of the province. It's connected with Calgary by Hwy 2; south from Calgary the highway goes to Montana in the USA. North-west from Edmonton Hwy 2 heads through Peace River to Dawson Creek in British Columbia, where the Alaska Hwy begins. North from Peace River, Hwy 35, the Mackenzie Hwy, takes you to the Northwest Territories.

The Yellowhead Hwy goes east from Lloydminster on the Saskatchewan border, through Edmonton to Jasper in the Rockies and on to Prince George in British Columbia. The Trans Canada Hwy goes north-west from Medicine Hat through Calgary to Banff and Lake Louise in the Rockies and on to Revelstoke.

Also from Medicine Hat the Crowsnest Hwy (Hwy 3) heads south-west to Lethbridge, Alberta's third largest city.

## HISTORY

Beginning around 9500 to 5500 BC, Alberta – particularly the southern portion – was occupied by the Plains Indians. For millen-

nia they lived a nomadic life walking great distances hunting the vast herds of bison which they used for food, clothing and shelter.

From our cinema and TV screens many of us have an image of these people pursuing the herds on horseback. This period in fact only lasted from about 1750 when the horse was introduced, to the end of the 19th century when most of the bison had been destroyed – and therefore so had the Plains Indians traditional way of life.

The Plains Indians included the Blackfoot, Blood, Peigan, Atsina (also called Gros Ventre), Cree, Sarcee and Assiniboine. The Sioux came from the south in the late 1800s.

The first Europeans in Alberta were fur traders who arrived around the middle of the 17th century. They were followed in the 18th century by the Hudson's Bay Company and its main rival the Northwest Company; both set up trading posts throughout the region. The two companies amalgamated in 1821 and the Hudson's Bay Company administered the area until 1870 when the territory became part of the Dominion of Canada. Settlers were then encouraged to migrate by the government's offers of cheap land.

The 1870s saw the establishment of the Northwest Mounted Police as a response to the lawlessness caused by the whisky trade

ALBERTA

in which the Plains Indians had been given cheap alcohol in exchange for bison hides.

The coming of the railway in the 1880s made access to the west quicker and easier and led to a rapid expansion of the population. Wheat and cattle farming formed the basis of the economy but coal mining and timber were also important. The discovery of natural gas and oil in the early part of this century added to Alberta's actual and potential wealth.

In 1905 Alberta became a fully fledged province of Canada with Edmonton as its capital.

Between WW I and II the economy and immigration slowed down. However, from 1947 further deposits of oil and natural gas were discovered. Then, with the oil crisis of the early '70s things began to change rapidly. For over a decade, people and money poured in from all parts of the country. Edmonton and Calgary became booming, modern cities – the fifth and sixth largest in the country.

In the mid-80s things took a new turn. With the fall in the price of oil and grains the boom ended and hard times came quickly to many people. Some Albertans left the province but most of those departing went back east to the homes they'd left in the middle of the Alberta boom.

The economic recession has continued into the '90s; the province is heavily in debt, unemployment is high and there have been many cutbacks in government services. Still, there is a lot of potential and the province now has more political clout. Development continues, although at a much reduced rate and, of course, things can change quickly depending on the world oil markets and commodity prices.

### The Naming of Alberta
The province of Alberta was named after the fourth daughter of Queen Victoria, Princess Louise Caroline Alberta (1848-1939), who was married to Canada's fourth governor general, the Marquis of Lorne. ∎

Alberta's strongly independent, individualistic rancher mentality remains intact.

## GEOGRAPHY & CLIMATE
Alberta has the most varied topography of any province. The east is a continuation of the Canadian prairies. The northern area is filled with rivers, lakes and forests; it's a rugged and largely inaccessible region especially in the north-east. The southwestern edge of the province rises from foothills into the Rocky Mountains; while much of the rest of the south is dry and flat with badlands (barren, arid land) in some areas.

Alberta has about 2000 hours of sunshine per year – more than any other province. In winter the weather is dry, sunny and cold. However, in the south the harshness of the cold is reduced by the chinooks: warm, dry winds from the west which can quickly raise temperatures by as much as 20°C. Alberta's summers are warm. The average annual rainfall is about 450 mm, a good part of which falls between June and early August. In the mountains summers are short and it's always cool at night.

The weather in August and September makes it a particularly good time for travelling.

### Chinook
The chinook is a warm, dry, south-westerly, winter wind which blows off the eastern slopes of the Rocky Mountains. These winds can change the snowy streets of Calgary, for example, to slush and puddles within hours. The name is derived from the Chinook Indians who lived along the north-west Pacific coast, mainly in what is now Washington state. In the days of the fur trade a language developed which mixed Chinook and other Native Indian words with French and English and was known as Chinook jargon.

In British Columbia (as well as Oregon and Washington states) chinook is also the name given to a Pacific salmon (elsewhere called spring, quinnat, king or tyee salmon). ∎

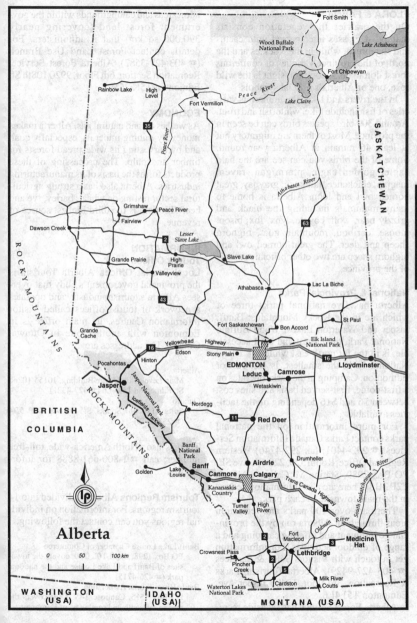

**ALBERTA**

**FLORA & FAUNA**

On the prairies the vegetation consists mainly of grasses interspersed with cactus and sagebrush, while in the Rockies and the north of the province varieties of coniferous forest dominate. A common sight is the wild rose, one of Alberta's official symbols.

In the rivers and lakes the numerous varieties of fish include pike, whitefish and trout. Around 300 bird species birds can be seen in the province. Most of them are migratory but at least 46 remain in Alberta year round. Some of the birds you can see are the bald eagle, golden eagle, ptarmigan, raven, magpie, chickadee, nuthatch, gray jay, great horned owl and loon. Alberta is home to many mammals including the black and grizzly bear, wolf, coyote, lynx, fox, bison, moose, caribou, mountain goat, bighorn sheep and deer. The great horned owl and bighorn sheep are two other official symbols of the province.

**National & Provincial Parks**

Alberta has five national parks three of which are in the Rocky Mountains: Banff, Jasper and Waterton Lakes. Wood Buffalo National Park, the largest and least accessible, is in the far north-east while Elk Island National Park, the smallest, is just east of Edmonton. Camping in the parks operates on a first-come, first-served basis and sites cost between $6 and $16 depending on the facilities available.

For more information on the national parks contact Parks Canada Information Services (☎ 292-4401; fax 292-4746) Western Regional Office, Room 520, 220 4th Ave SE, PO Box 2989, Station M, Calgary, Alberta T2P 3H8. There are also information centres in the main townsite in each park.

There are over 100 parks and recreation areas throughout Alberta run by the provincial government and offering camping and a range of outdoor activities. For information get in touch with Visitors Sales & Services (☎ 403-427-9429), Alberta Tourism, Parks & Recreation, 3rd floor, 10405 Jasper Ave, Edmonton T5J 4L6.

Alberta Forest Service has set aside recreation areas and campgrounds within the government forest land (covering nearly 390,000 sq km) that it administers. For details contact Forest Land Use Branch (☎ 403-427-3582), Alberta Forest Service, Recreation Section, 6th Floor, 9920 108th St, Edmonton T5K 2C9.

**ECONOMY**

As well as oil and natural gas, Alberta makes money by mining minerals, especially coal, and by harvesting its widespread forests for timber and pulp. The processing of these products forms the basis of its manufacturing industries. Alberta also has a strong agricultural sector resting on wheat, barley, rye and beef. Tourism is the third highest source of revenue.

**INFORMATION**
**Tourist Offices**
**Local Tourist Offices** Alberta Tourism is the provincial government's body that oversees Alberta's tourism industry and operates a network of tourist offices called Visitor Information Centres. Its main office is in Edmonton with another one in Ottawa, Ontario. The addresses are:

Alberta
    Main Level, City Centre Building, 10155 102nd St, Edmonton T5J 4L6 (☎ 427-4321)
Ontario
    Suite 1110, 90 Sparks St, Ottawa K1P 5B4 (☎ 237-2615)

There is also a North America-wide, toll-free number; call ☎ 1-800-661-8888 for information.

**Tourism Regions** Alberta is divided into 14 tourism regions. For information on individual regions you can contact the following:

Banff/Lake Louise Chamber of Commerce
    PO Box 1298, Banff T0L 0C0; covers the townsites of Banff and Lake Louise and the national park (☎ 426-4715)
Battle River Tourist Association
    PO Box 1515, Camrose T4V 1X4; covers the area to the south and south-east of Edmonton

Big Country Tourist Association
170 Centre St, PO Box 2308, Drumheller T0J 0Y0; covers the region east of Calgary (☎ 823-5885)

Calgary Convention & Visitors Bureau
237 8th Ave SE, Calgary T2G 0K8 (☎ 263-8510)

Chinook Country Tourist Association
2805 Scenic Drive, Lethbridge T1K 5B7; covers the south-west corner of the province (☎ 320-1222, 1-800-661-1222)

David Thompson Country Tourist Council
Old Court House, 4836 Ross St, Red Deer T4N 5E8; covers most of the area between Calgary and Edmonton (☎ 342-2032)

Edmonton Convention & Tourism Authority
104 9797 Jasper Ave, Edmonton T51 1N9 (☎ 426-4715)

Evergreen Country Tourist Council
PO Box 6007, Edson T7E 1T6; covers the area west of Edmonton (☎ 723-711)

Game Country Tourist Association
9932 111 Ave, Grande Prairie T8V 4C3; covers the area north-west of Edmonton and south off the Land of the Mighty Peace (☎ 539-4300)

Jasper Park Chamber of Commerce
PO Box 98, Jasper T0E 1E0; covers the townsite and national park (☎ 852-858)

Lakeland & Tourist Association
PO Box 874, St Paul T0A 3A0; covers the north-east of the province from the Northwest Territories border southward to the east of Edmonton (☎ 645-2913)

Land of the Mighty Peace Tourist Association
PO Box 6627, Peace River T8S 1S4; covers the north-west corner of the province (☎ 645-2913)

Midnight Twilight Tourist Association
1 Sturgeon Rd, St Albert T8N 0E8; covers the region to the north of Edmonton (☎ 458-5600)

South-East Alberta Travel & Convention Association
PO Box 605, Medicine Hat T1A 7G5; covers the south-east corner of the province (☎ 527-6422)

**Tourist Offices Abroad** Alberta Tourism also has four offices abroad:

Hong Kong
Room 1003-4, Admiralty Centre, Tower 2, Harcourt Rd, Central Hong Kong (☎ 5-284-729)

Japan
Place Canada 3F, 3-37 Akasaka, 7-chome, MinatoKu, Tokyo 107 (☎ 3-475-1171)

UK
1 Mount St, Berkeley Square, London W1Y 5AA (☎ 71-491-3430)

USA
27th Floor, General Motors Building, 767 5th Ave, New York City, New York 10153 (☎ 212-759-2222)

## Money
Visitors can take advantage of the lowest gasoline prices in Canada and the lack of any provincial consumer sales tax.

## Provincial Symbols
Alberta's provincial flower is the wild rose, while the lodgepole pine is the province's official tree. The great horned owl is Alberta's provincial bird, and the big horned sheep is its official mammal.

## Telephone
The telephone area code for Alberta is 403; in an emergency call ☎ 911.

## Time
Alberta is on Mountain Standard Time, one hour behind Saskatchewan and Manitoba.

## Tax
There is no provincial consumer sales tax. There is, however, a 5% tax on accommodation.

## ACTIVITIES
With its mountains, rivers, lakes and forested wilderness areas Alberta provides plenty of opportunities for independent or guided outdoor recreational activities. Tourism Alberta's free brochure, *Accommodation & Visitors' Guide*, lists companies offering fishing, horse riding, cycling, canoeing, white-water rafting, hiking, rock climbing and mountaineering. It's available from any Visitor Information Centre. *Outdoor Activities in Alberta's Heartland* (Whitecap Books, Vancouver/Toronto, 1993, $14.95) by Bill Corbett, describes some of the better places in Southern Alberta to pursue outdoor activities.

## Hiking & Cycling
There are lots of hiking and cycling trails in the national and provincial parks and in other recreation areas such as Kananaskis Country. Two of the more spectacular cycling routes are the Icefields Parkway between Banff and Jasper, and the Bow Valley Parkway between Banff and Lake Louise. *Backcountry Biking*

ALBERTA

*in the Canadian Rockies* (Rocky Mountain Books, Calgary, 1987) by Gerhardt Lapp is a useful book to have. Edmonton and Calgary have also set aside trails within their city boundaries for hiking and cycling.

## Canoeing & Kayaking

Some of the more popular places for canoeing are the lakes and rivers in Banff, Jasper, Waterton Lakes and Wood Buffalo national parks and Writing-on-Stone Provincial Park. In Jasper National Park there is white-water kayaking and rafting on the Athabasca, Maligne and Sunwapta rivers. The two major universities offer canoeing information in their respective areas as well as rentals:

Campus Outdoor Centre
    P153 Van Vliet Centre, University of Alberta, Edmonton T6G 2H9 (☎ 492-2767)
Outdoor Recreation Centre
    University of Calgary, 2500 University Drive NW, Calgary T2N 1N4 (☎ 220-5038)

To find out more about white-water rivers contact Alberta White-Water Association Division (☎ 453-8585/6; fax 453-8553), Percy Page Centre, 11759 Groat Rd, Edmonton T5M 3K6.

Hydrological and topographical maps are available from Maps Alberta (☎ 427-3520), 2nd Floor, 108th St, Edmonton.

## Skiing

The best downhill skiing areas are Nakiska in Kananaskis Country, Mt Norquay and Sunshine Village in Banff National Park and Marmot Basin in Jasper National Park. Many of the hiking trails in the national and provincial parks become cross-country ski trails in winter.

## Rock Climbing & Mountaineering

The Rocky Mountains provide plenty of challenges for the climber, from beginners to advanced. Mt Rundle near Lake Louise is a popular destination. Organisations based in Banff, Calgary, Canmore and Jasper offer instruction and guided climbing.

Banff Alpine Guides
    PO Box 1025, Banff T0L 0C0 (☎ 678-6091)
Canadian School of Mountaineering
    629 10th St, Canmore T0L 0M0 (☎ 678-4134)
Jasper Climbing Schools & Guide
    PO Box 452, Jasper T0E 1E0 (☎ 852-3964)
Lac des Arts Climbing School
    1116 19th Ave NW, Calgary T2M 0Z99 (☎ 289-6795)
Yamnuska
    PO Box 1920, Canmore T0L 0M0 (☎ 678-4450)

## ACCOMMODATION

Campers should get a copy of *Campgrounds in Alberta*, a free brochure available at Visitor Information Centres. It gives an alphabetical listing of places and the campgrounds, both government and private, in those locations. In national parks sites range from $6 to $16, in provincial parks from $5.50 to $17.25, and in private campgrounds from $5 to $22 depending on facilities. Also available is the *Alberta Accommodation & Visitors' Guide* which lists hotels and motels in the province. Both are published annually.

Hostelling International (HI) has 18 hostels in Alberta. For information about HI hostels in southern Alberta contact Hostelling International Southern Alberta (☎ 283-5551), 203 1414 Kensington Rd NW, Calgary T2N 3P9. For northern Alberta contact Hostelling Association Northern Alberta (☎ 439-3089), 10926 88th Ave, Edmonton T6G 0Z1.

A number of B&B agencies operate a booking service in the province. These are:

Affiliated Holiday Home Agencies
    10808 54th Ave, Edmonton T6H 0T9; has places throughout the province as well as other parts of Canada (☎ 436-0649/4196)
Alberta's Gem B&B
    Mrs Betty Mitchell, 11216 48th Ave, Edmonton T6H 0C7; has B&Bs throughout the province and other areas of Western Canada (☎ 434-6098)
Big Country B&B
    Jim & Marj Patterson, PO Box 1027, Drumheller T0J 0Y0; has places in the Drumheller region (☎ 533-2203)
Edmonton B&B
    Pat & Dave Yearwood, 13824 110A Ave, Edmonton T5M 2M9; offers accommodation in Banff, Calgary, Canmore, Drumheller, Edmonton, Hinton, Jasper and other locations (☎ 445-2297)

High Country B&B Association
    PO Box 61, Millarville T5M 2M9; offers accom-
    modation in the south-west of the province
    (☎ 931-3514)

One agency operates out of Vancouver:
Alberta B&B (☎ 604-944-1793), MPO Box
15477, Vancouver, British Columbia V6B
5B2.

# Edmonton

Edmonton, like Calgary and the west in
general, is in a period of reassessment after
a series of fluctuating fortunes. Once known
as 'The Gateway to the North' its title
changed to 'Oil Capital of Canada' in the
1970s when the entire province boomed.
Calgary had the head offices and oil management but Edmonton had the technicians, the
scientists and the wells – some 7000 of them
within a 160-km radius.

They were heady days. Edmonton,
Alberta's largest city, experienced explosive
growth; the downtown area was totally transformed and modernised. Towards the end of
the 1980s there was a dramatic downturn in
the oil business and the two main cities consequently eased up on development and
began to forge new identities in a less hectic
atmosphere.

The city averages over six hours of sun per
day. Summers are short, generally dry and
warm with daytime temperatures averaging
22°C. In January, the coldest month, the
average daytime high is -11°C.

## HISTORY

Until the arrival of White explorers and fur
traders in the late 18th century the area was
populated by the Cree and Blackfoot nations
for over 5000 years.

In 1795 the Hudson's Bay Company built
Fort Edmonton, which grew as a fur-trading
centre until about 1870, when the Canadian
government bought the land from the
company and opened up the area for pioneers. By 1891 the railway had arrived from

Calgary and in 1892 Edmonton was officially incorporated as a town, then in 1904 as
a city. In 1905, with the creation of Alberta,
Edmonton – then with 8000 residents –
became the capital.

With the discovery of gold in the Yukon
in 1897, Edmonton was the last outpost of
civilisation for many gold seekers coming
overland on their way north to the Klondike.
In 1938, North America's first mosque was
built here by 34 Muslims. WW II brought a
large influx of people, mainly to work on the
Alaska Hwy.

It was in the late 1940s and '50s that real
development in Edmonton began, when
wells started hitting oil with great regularity.
The rise in oil prices in the early '70s gave a
further boost to development and brought a
dramatic change in the city skyline.

The rapid changes to the city caused some
problems that still continue. Many of the
city's 25,000 Native Indians have little education or job training and the changes made
life harder for them in particular. However,
the establishment of educational programmes has meant more of these people are
completing high school and going on to trade
school or college. Despite the lack of much
physical evidence around town, the city does
have a fairly long history and the indigenous
people played a major part in it.

Greater Edmonton now has a population
of nearly 800,000 and many of the newcomers, from many different cultures, consider
themselves Edmontonians. The steep prices
of the '70s and early '80s have levelled off
and the cultural life of the city has grown
noticeably.

## ORIENTATION

From Edmonton the Rocky Mountains are
about 300 km to the west, the lake country
and Alaska Hwy are to the north, Lloydminster in Saskatchewan is to the east and Calgary
to the south. The North Saskatchewan River,
which starts in the Columbia Icefield in the
Rocky Mountains, drifts through the centre
of town.

All avenues go east-west; streets run
north-south.

## North of the River

Edmonton's main thoroughfare, Jasper Ave (101st Ave), is very long and has mainly stores and restaurants. Both Jasper Ave and 102nd Ave go west from downtown through a middle-class residential area. They then lead into Stony Plain Rd, a commercial strip which becomes the Yellowhead Hwy to Jasper. The strip includes motels and lots of fast-food restaurants.

North-west of the downtown area, off Kingsway Ave, is the municipal airport. The northern boundary of the airport is the Yellowhead Trail, which joins the Yellowhead Hwy east to Saskatoon and west to Jasper.

Though the city is spread out, the downtown centre with the Greyhound Bus Depot VIA Rail station, restaurants and hotels is quite small. The central area of town is bounded by 104th Ave to the north and 100th Ave to the south. The western edge is marked by 109th St, the eastern side by 95th St. The area is easily walkable.

The main intersection is Jasper Ave and 101st St. On 99th St, two blocks north of Jasper Ave, is the civic centre with several municipal buildings. Opposite the civic centre is Sir Winston Churchill Square, one block north of which is the new City Hall with its glass pyramid. To the east are the art gallery and law courts.

Another block north to 104th Ave will bring you to the main post office and the VIA Rail station below the CN Tower. To the west, covering four blocks between 105th St and 109th Sts, is the huge new City Centre Campus of the Grant MacEwan Community College. It will accommodate around 27,000 part and full-time students by the year 2000 and should help liven downtown Edmonton's nightlife.

The downtown area consists of many mirrored, 1970s-design, high-rise buildings. The southern end of 100th St is the office section. Many of Canada's banks have buildings in the area. This is also the theatre and shopping district, with the Eaton Centre and the large Edmonton Centre housing all types of stores.

Beneath the downtown area are underground pedestrian walkways called 'pedways' which connect shopping malls, hotels, restaurants and the VIA Rail station.

The eastward redevelopment of the city centre during the '70s and '80s stopped at 97th St (though this is now beginning to change) and for a few blocks east some of the streets are sleazy, especially 96th St. The bars and hotels here aren't recommended. Along the eastern side of 97th St are pawnshops, cash-for-goods stores, and a number of other inexpensive places which may or may not prove useful for the odd item or two. A few blocks further will take you to the HI Edmonton Hostel. Also in this area is a small Chinatown centred on 102nd Ave. The old part of downtown extends north as far as 103A Ave.

West a few blocks from Sir Winston Churchill Square are a number of hotels in all price ranges, and the Greyhound Bus Depot. West of the downtown centre, 124th St between 102nd and 109th Aves is an expensive shopping district, with fashion boutiques, art galleries and a few bistros and restaurants. From behind the Hotel Macdonald at 100th St and McDougall Hill, there is a good view of the river and southern side of Edmonton.

## South of the River

Across the river, 82nd Ave, also called Whyte Ave, is the main street. On 82nd Ave around 104th St there's a mini-downtown area with many stores and restaurants, including numerous Chinese ones.

To the east is Old Strathcona, a district with many old buildings that date from when this area was distinct from Edmonton itself. The area underwent some low-key redevelopment and is a very agreeable part of Edmonton with a good selection of restaurants and shops.

At the western end of 82nd Ave is the University of Alberta, and following the river south-west, Fort Edmonton, where the town began. Most of the southern side is residential.

Heading south, 104th St joins the Calgary

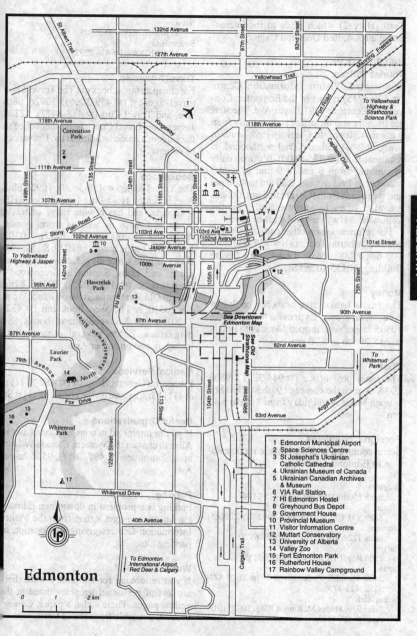

**ALBERTA**

1 Edmonton Municipal Airport
2 Space Sciences Centre
3 St Josephat's Ukrainian
   Catholic Cathedral
4 Ukrainian Museum of Canada
5 Ukrainian Canadian Archives
   & Museum
6 VIA Rail Station
7 HI Edmonton Hostel
8 Greyhound Bus Depot
9 Government House
10 Provincial Museum
11 Visitor Information Centre
12 Muttart Conservatory
13 University of Alberta
14 Valley Zoo
15 Fort Edmonton Park
16 Rutherford House
17 Rainbow Valley Campground

**Edmonton**

0    1    2 km

Trail (Hwy 2) which leads to the international airport, Red Deer and Calgary.

## INFORMATION
### Tourist Offices
The central Visitor Information Centre (☎ 426-4715) is part of the Edmonton Convention Centre at 9797 Jasper Ave. The staff are friendly and the office is open daily from 9 am to 4.30 pm. In Gateway Park south of town, at 2404 Calgary Trail northbound, is another office (☎ 496-8400). It's open daily in summer from 8 am to 9 pm; in winter Monday to Friday from 8.30 am to 4.30 pm and weekends from 9.30 am to 5 pm. Offices are also open in summer only, on the Yellowhead Hwy east and west of town.

For information on other parts of Alberta, contact Alberta Tourism (☎ 427-4321; 1-800-661-8888), Main Level, City Centre Building, 10155 102nd St.

### Money
The major banks have branches on Jasper Ave. American Express (☎ 421-0608), 10305 Jasper Ave, is open Monday to Friday from 8.30 am to 5.30 pm.

### Post
The main post office (☎ 944-3271), 9808 103A Ave on the corner of 99th St (Hull St), is open Monday to Friday from 8 am to 5.45 pm.

### Foreign Consulates
Some countries with diplomatic representation in Edmonton are:

Belgium
    Suite 1500 10250 101 St (☎ 425-0184)
France
    Suite 300, 10010 106 St (☎ 428-0232, 425-0665)
Germany
    Suite 1220, 10180 101 St (☎ 422-6175)
Italy
    1900 Royal Trust Tower (☎ 423-5153)
Japan
    2480 Manulife Place, 10180 101st St (☎ 422-3752, 423-4750)
Netherlands
    Suite 930, Phipps McKinnon Bldg, 10020 101A Ave (☎ 428-7513)
Norway
    2310 80 Ave (☎ 440-2292)
Switzerland
    11207 103 Ave (☎ 426-2292)

### Travel Agencies
For cheap airfares check out The Travel Shop travel agency (☎ 439-3096), 10926 88th Ave, and Travel Cuts (☎ 488-8477), 12304 Jasper Ave. Travel Cuts has another office in the student's union building at the University of Alberta.

### Bookshops
The Travel Shop (☎ 439-3809), 10926 88th Ave, is run by Hostelling International (HI – Canada and has a wide range of travel books and maps as well as travel goods. Audrey's Books (☎ 423-3487), 10702 Jasper Ave on the corner of 107th St, has two floors of books including Canadiana, travel guides and maps. Similar is Greenwood's Bookshoppe (☎ 439-2005), 10355 82nd Ave, in Old Strathcona. Also on 82nd Ave at No 10310 is The Wee Book Inn (☎ 432-7320) which has secondhand books and magazines. It has several other outlets including one on Jasper Ave.

### Medical Services
Edmonton General Hospital (☎ 482-8111) is at 11111 Jasper Ave on the corner of 111st St.

### Useful Organisations
If you're interested in conservation issues in Alberta contact the Western Canada Wilderness Committee (☎ 497-7617), 9526 Jasper Ave.

### Parking
Parking is a problem in downtown Edmonton but you can get a map from the Visitor Information Centres giving the location of parking lots.

### Work
If you're looking for temporary work there are lots of personnel agencies listed in the yellow pages. There's also a paper, *Career & Jobs*, available free around town.

## WALKING TOURS
To explore the city on foot get a copy of the free booklet the *Greater Edmonton Visitor Guide* from the Visitor Information Centre. It has four walking tours of the city including one of Old Strathcona. For a more detailed look at Old Strathcona get a copy of the booklet *A Walk Through Old Strathcona* which has descriptions of many of the buildings in the area.

## PARKS
On each side of the North Saskatchewan River, which flows in a north-easterly direction through the centre of the city, is parkland. This appears to be one long park, though it's actually a series of small parks joined together. You can walk, jog or cycle all day along the system using the many trails and bridges. In some, like **Whitemud Park**, south-west of downtown, and **Strathcona Science Provincial Park** north-east of town, the paths become cross-country ski trails in winter. Whitemud Park also has a hang-gliding area. One of the easiest ways to get there from town is to head south on 75th street and then turn right (west) along Whitemud Drive.

The 61-hectare **Hawrelak Park**, Edmonton's largest, is south-west of downtown on the southern banks of the North Saskatchewan River off Groat Rd. It has a lake for boating and fishing in summer, and for ice-skating in winter. The annual Edmonton Heritage Festival is held in the park at the end of July. Throughout the parkland are dozens of picnic spots. Many of the city's other sights are in this green belt area.

## PROVINCIAL MUSEUM
This excellent museum (☎ 427-1786), 12845 102nd Ave west of downtown, is well laid out with exhibits artistically displayed. The natural history section describes the natural forces which have shaped Alberta and the life forms, such as dinosaurs, that lived in the region millions of years ago. It has a large display of fossils and minerals. The habitat section shows animals and birds living in Alberta today in incredibly realistic settings.

The anthropology section covers the Native Indians of Alberta, their way of life and relationship with nature. There are drawings, photos and examples of various plants and how they used them for medicine, spice, tea and smoking; and of how feathers, animal hide and bark were used to decorate clothing and dwellings. Other displays include amulets incorporating the wearer's umbilical cord and many artefacts and crafts.

The history area covers the pioneer days and settlement of Alberta.

The museum also has frequent cultural shows and dancing, and free film programmes. To get there, take bus Nos 1 or 2 west along Jasper Ave. It's open daily from 9 am to 8 pm and admission is $3.25 (free on Tuesday).

## GOVERNMENT HOUSE
This is the large and impressive structure beside the museum, used for government conferences. It can be visited on Sundays between 1 and 4.30 pm if there are no government functions taking place. For information call ☎ 427-7362.

## ALBERTA LEGISLATURE
The Alberta Legislature (☎ 427-7362), on the corner of 97th Ave and 108th St, is built on the site of the original Fort Edmonton. A beautiful Edwardian building from 1912, it is surrounded by fountains and manicured lawns overlooking the river. Its dome has remained one of the permanent landmarks of Edmonton. Free tours are given daily, offering interesting details about the building and the government. The tours start from an Italianate lobby with marble walls and columns and last about half an hour. On weekdays they are available between 9 am and 8 pm, on weekends between 9 am and 4.30 pm. To get there catch bus No 43 west along 100th Ave.

## FORT EDMONTON PARK
On the southern side of the river over the Quesnell Bridge off Fox Drive, in Fort

Edmonton Park (☎ 496-8787), is a reconstruction of the old Hudson's Bay Company fort and the surrounding town, circa 1885. The fort contains the entire post of 1846 which was built to promote the fur trade (not as a military fort), and was presided over by Chief Factor John Rowland, head of Saskatchewan District from 1828 to 1854. It lacks some authentic feel but the carpentry, meant to re-create the times through furniture, tools and constructions, is excellent.

Outside the fort is a street re-creating downtown Edmonton between 1871 and 1891, when the railway arrived. It's quite interesting, with good explanations of the buildings, though hard to visualise the early Jasper Ave. Along the wooden sidewalks are examples of the various merchants and their goods. A newspaper office and a schoolhouse are represented. Check all the cabinets, bottles and vials in the chemist's. Rides on the train and horse-trailer are included in tickets, which cost $6.25 and $3 for children.

From the middle of May to the end of June Fort Edmonton is open Monday to Friday from 9.30 am to 4.30 pm, weekends from 10 am to 6 pm; July to early September it's open daily from 10 am to 6 pm; till early October on Sundays and holidays it's open from 11 am to 5 pm. It's closed in winter.

To get there take bus Nos 32 or 132 west along 102A Ave or south on 101st St.

On the grounds beside the fort is the **John Janzen Nature Centre** (☎ 428-7900) where you'll find a few examples of both living and dead local animals, insects and reptiles. You'll see educational exhibits in simulated natural environments – best is the live bee display. In summer the centre's open daily from 10 am to 6 pm. Admission is free.

## VALLEY ZOO

North-east of Fort Edmonton Park, this zoo (☎ 496-6911) in Laurier Park at the southern end of Buena Vista Rd has about 500 animals and birds, but it's mainly a children's zoo with models of storybook characters. It's open daily in summer from 10 am to 6 pm and admission is $4.75, children $2.50.

### PLACES TO STAY

| | |
|---|---|
| 4 | Hilton International |
| 5 | YMCA |
| 7 | Grand Hotel |
| 12 | Mayfair Hotel |
| 13 | Inn on 7th |
| 15 | Ambassador Motor Inn |
| 16 | Hotel Cecil |
| 19 | Alberta Place Hotel |
| 27 | Westin Hotel |
| 29 | Hotel Macdonald |
| 31 | Holiday Inn |
| 32 | YWCA |

### PLACES TO EAT

| | |
|---|---|
| 8 | Boardwalk Market |
| 10 | Michael's Deli & Bar |
| 18 | Russian Tea Room |
| 20 | Silk Hat |
| 21 | Bistro Praha |
| 22 | Mongolian Food Experience |
| 23 | Sherlock Holmes |

### OTHER

| | |
|---|---|
| 1 | VIA Rail Station |
| 2 | Main Post Office |
| 3 | Greyhound Bus Depot |
| 6 | Edmonton Art Gallery |
| 9 | Edmonton General Hospital |
| 11 | Audrey's Books |
| 14 | Jekyll & Hyde Pub |
| 17 | Red Arrow Office |
| 24 | Sir Winston Churchill Square |
| 25 | Citadel Theatre |
| 26 | Edmonton Transit Information Centre |
| 28 | Visitor Information Centre |
| 30 | AGT Tower |
| 33 | Alberta Legislature |
| 34 | John Walter Historic Site |

## MUTTART CONSERVATORY

South of the river off James Macdonald Bridge, the Muttart Conservatory (☎ 496-8755), 9626 96A St, is comprised of four glass pyramids, three large and one small. Each contains a different climate and the plants that go with it; one is desert, one temperate, one tropical while the fourth has regularly changing exhibitions to mark the changing seasons. If you walk up the hills

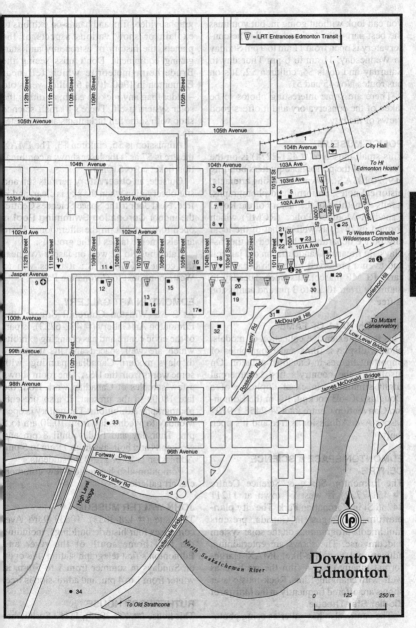

**ALBERTA**

= LRT Entrances Edmonton Transit

**Downtown Edmonton**

0    125    250 m

To Old Strathcona

North Saskatchewan River

High Level Bridge

River Valley Rd

Fortway  Drive

Waterdale Bridge

James McDonald Bridge

Low Level Bridge

Rossdale  Rd

Bellamy  Rd

McDougall Hill

Grierson Hill

To Muttart
Conservatory

To Western Canada
Wilderness Committee

To HI
Edmonton Hostel

City Hall

105th Avenue

104th Avenue

103rd Avenue

102nd Ave

Jasper Avenue

100th Avenue

99th Avenue

98th Avenue

97th Ave

97th Avenue

96th Avenue

104th Avenue

103rd Avenue

102nd Avenue

105th Avenue

104th Avenue

103A Ave

103rd Ave

102A Ave

101A Ave

100A St

101st Avenue

you can look without going in, but you miss the best part – the feel and smell. The conservatory is open from 11 am to 9 pm Sunday to Wednesday, 11 am to 6 pm Thursday to Saturday and costs $4, children $2. It's on bus routes Nos 45 and 51.

There are some interesting photos to be taken of the conservatory and it offers good views of the city.

## POLICE MUSEUM
This small museum (☎ 421-2274) is on the 3rd floor of the police headquarters building at 9620 103A St, downtown. Using artefacts, historical notes, uniforms and photographs, it tells something of the history of the Royal Canadian Mounted Police (RCMP) which formed in 1873, as well as that of the local city police department. Included in the displays are firearms, handcuffs, an old jail cell and even a preserved rat which became an early RCMP mascot. It's open Tuesday to Saturday from 10 am to 3 pm and admission is free.

## AVIATION HALL OF FAME
This is a an extensive collection of models, photos, displays, films and biographies of important figures in Canadian aviation. On display is the country's first commercial flight simulator, an exact duplicate of a Douglas DC-6B cockpit. It's in the Edmonton Convention Centre (☎ 424-2458 ), 9797 Jasper Ave. Admission is free and it's open daily.

## EDMONTON SPACE & SCIENCE CENTRE
The Edmonton Space & Science Centre (☎ 451-7722) is west of town at 11211 142nd St in Coronation Park. The city **planetarium**, the largest in Canada, presents multimedia programmes on the solar system and universe. The shows are entertaining, educational and life-like. IMAX (large-format cinema) has a film theatre here as well, with changing films. Rock-music laser shows are offered frequently in the **Margaret Ziedler Star Theatre**.

The centre also has galleries using photo-

graphs, video, film and hands-on exhibits to explain or show various aspects of the planets, the history of astronomy and stargazing equipment. Don't miss seeing the Bruderheim meteorite which fell near Edmonton in 1960. It's 4.6 billion years old – older than any rock on earth; as old as the solar system itself. There's a small science shop with some fun little items and a cafeteria.

Admission is $5, children $3. The IMAX theatre is $7 as is the laser show; a combination ticket costs $10.25.

Outside, an **observatory** permits sun and star observation when the sky is clear, and is free. Next door to the Space Sciences Centre, the indoor **Coronation Swimming Pool** is open to the public in the afternoons. There are also picnic tables in the grounds.

Catch bus No 22 west on Jasper Ave near the corner of 103rd St; it takes you to Westmount next to Coronation Park.

## EDMONTON ART GALLERY
At 2 Sir Winston Churchill Square, the Edmonton Art Gallery (☎ 422-6223), is part of the civic centre and has changing exhibits which are well spaced and lit. It mainly displays modern Canadian painting, with some works from the USA. One room shows a few samples of Canadian work from the late 1800s to the present. It also presents photography exhibitions. The gallery is open Monday to Wednesday from 10.30 am to 5 pm, Thursday and Friday until 8 pm and weekends and holidays from 11 am to 5 pm. Admission is $3 or $1.50 for students.

Edmonton also has quite a few commercial art galleries.

## JOHN WALTER MUSEUM
This site (☎ 428-3033), 10633 93rd Ave, comprises four historic buildings, including the first home south of the river and Edmonton's first telegraph station. It's open on Sundays in summer from 1 to 5 pm, in winter from 1 to 4 pm, and admission is free.

## RUTHERFORD HOUSE
This house (☎ 427-3995), 11153 Saskatche-

wan Drive, was built by Alexander Ruther-ford, the first premier of Alberta. Completed in 1911, the mansion is said to symbolise the end of the pioneer architectural style. The building has been restored and contains many antiques. Admission is free and it's open daily in summer from 10 am to 6 pm, in winter from noon to 5 pm. Several buses service the campus including Nos 32 and 35.

## ST JOSEPHAT'S UKRAINIAN CATHOLIC CATHEDRAL

This church, on 97th St on the corner of 108th Ave, one of a number of Ukrainian churches in the Edmonton area, is worth a visit. With its rounded domes outside, it'll remind you of Turkey, whether you've been there or not. Inside the Byzantine structure, pastel paintings cover the walls. Check the figure on the ceiling in front of the altar. There's a lot of gilt-work here, including the large screen in front of the altar.

## UKRAINIAN MUSEUMS

The **Ukrainian Museum of Canada** (☎ 483-5932), 10611 110th Ave, has a small collection of costumes, Easter eggs, dolls and very fine tapestries. In summer it's open daily from 9 am to 5 pm. Catch bus Nos 41 or 42 north on 101st St. Close by, the **Ukrainian Canadian Archives & Museum** (☎ 424-7580), 9543 110th Ave, has a library, archives and artefacts of Ukrainian culture. It's open Tuesday to Saturday from 10 am to 5 pm. Admission is free at both museums although they will accept donations.

## WEST EDMONTON MALL

If you thought a shopping centre as a sight to visit had no place in this guidebook, think again. The West Edmonton Mall (☎ 444-5300), 8770 170th St on the corner of 87th Ave, is really something else; it's so over-whelming it's worth taking a look. More than just the world's largest shopping mall and largest indoor water park, it's a self-con-tained city complete with roof. You could live inside for years.

There are over 800 stores, a hotel, an amusement park, a water park with beach, an ice rink, a mini-golf course, cinemas, subma-rines in simulated oceans, restaurants galore and lots more, plus thousands of people. A few highlights are the Drop of Doom, a ride in Fantasyland guaranteed to put your stomach in your mouth (and that's just watching!), the pool complex with slides and waves, the ice rink with skate rentals and the ersatz New Orleans Bourbon St, complete with statues of prostitutes.

If you get too tired to make it around everything you can rent yourself a little powered scooter.

To get there take bus No 10 west on Jasper Ave downtown; the journey time is about 25 minutes.

## WILD WATERS AQUATIC PARK

This water-slide complex (☎ 447-4476) is at 21515 103rd Ave (Yellowhead Hwy west). It's open daily in summer from 11 am to 7 pm. Admission is $13, children $10.

## CITY FARMERS' MARKET

This city food market is in downtown Edmonton on the corner of 102nd Ave and 97th St. It's open daily but is best on Satur-day.

## OLD STRATHCONA

The area south of the river, by 82nd Ave and 106th St, was once the town of Strathcona. It amalgamated with Edmonton in 1912. Though now absorbed into the city, this area is rich in historical buildings dating from 1891. There are about 75 houses built prior to 1926 in the residential district and about 40 buildings of note in what was the com-mercial core.

You can pick up a walking-tour map of the district at the Visitor Information Centre downtown, the Tourist Information Centre (in the Old Strathcona Caboose) on the corner of 82nd Ave and 103rd St, or the Old Strathcona Foundation Office (☎ 433-5866) at 8331 104th St. The tour will take you past the old CPR station, the Strathcona Hotel, Princess Theatre, Knox Church and many other gems. The area along 82nd Ave from 103rd St to 105th St has been spruced up

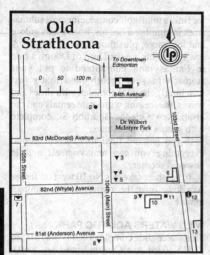

## Old Strathcona

To Downtown
Edmonton

0    50    100 m

84th Avenue

2

Dr Wilbert
McIntyre Park

83rd (McDonald) Avenue

82nd (Whyte) Avenue

81st (Anderson) Avenue

1  Knox Church
2  Old Strathcona Foundation Office
3  Johann Strauss Coffee House
4  New York Bagel Café
5  Uncle Albert's
6  Strathcona Hotel
7  Post Office
8  Bamboo Palace
9  Veggies
10  Princess Theatre
11  Commercial Hotel
12  Tourist Information Centre
    (Old Strathcona Caboose)
13  CPR Station

with brick sidewalks, old-style lampposts, etc. It's an area with numerous cafés, restaurants, buskers, street vendors and several bookshops. It is a pleasant change from the high-rise buildings of the downtown area.

## ACTIVITIES

For information on park and recreation facilities like outdoor swimming pools, skating and skiing areas or bicycle paths, call Edmonton Parks & Recreation (☎ 496-8703). (See also Parks earlier.)

The Kinsmen Sports Centre (☎ 428-

7970), 9100 Walterdale Hill, has public swimming and other programmes. Admission is $3.60. It's open Monday to Friday from 5.30 am to 10 pm, weekends 7 am to 10 pm. Mill Woods Recreation Centre (☎ 428-2888), 7207 28th Ave, has a wave pool, saunas, ball courts and other facilities. It's open weekdays from 5.30 am to 9 pm, Saturday 6 am to 9 pm, Sunday from 8 am to 9 pm. A swim in the wave pool costs $4.90. The Commonwealth Stadium Recreation Centre (☎ 428-5555), 11000 Stadium Rd, has a gym and ball courts.

Edmonton has an extensive network of bicycle routes and the best area to cycle is on the paths by the river. A map showing these routes is available from the Visitor Information Centre.

You can go horse riding in Whitemud Park; contact the Whitemud Equine Centre (☎ 435-3597) for details. Edmonton has four golf courses, the most central being the Victoria Golf Course (☎ 428-8022), 12130 River Rd, in Victoria Park west of downtown. You can also go hot-air ballooning up to 300 metres – every day if the weather is fine – with Windship Aviation (☎ 438-0111), 5615 103A St.

## ORGANISED TOURS

Royal Tours (☎ 488-9040), 203 10441 124th St, offers three tours of Edmonton. The 3½-hour, historical tour of the city visits the Alberta Legislature, the university and Old Strathcona and costs $23.50. The 2½-hour ecological tour which looks at the city's parkland and goes out to the Provincial Museum costs $20. The day tour combines the two and costs $28. On summer Sundays and holidays Edmonton Transit operates the Fort Edmonton-Valley Zoo shuttle between the zoo and the University of Alberta, for the basic fare. This route takes a circular tour of Edmonton, passing many of the city's sights. It leaves the university every hour on the hour from 11 am to 5 pm, and leaves the zoo hourly on the half hour from 11.30 am to 5.30 pm.

The North Saskatchewan Riverboat Company (☎ 424-2628), 9797 Jasper Ave, offers cruises of the river in an old sternwheeler. Tickets cost between $7 and $31. The boat leaves from the dock below the Edmonton Convention Centre.

Nite Tours (☎ 453-2134) does tours of the city in a British double-decker bus experiencing the city's nightlife. Tickets cost $18.50.

The HI Edmonton Hostel (☎ 429-0140) organises group outings on an ad hoc basis.

## FESTIVALS

Edmonton has many festivals throughout the year; the following are some of the bigger ones.

June

*Comedy Festival* – Local, national and international comics perform at this five-day event held in early June in different venues around town. Call ☎ 431-1763 for details.

July

*The Klondike Days* – This, Edmonton's biggest festival held towards the end of July, celebrates a less than honourable period in Edmonton's history. In the gold-rush days of 1898, unscrupulous entrepreneurs lured gold seekers to the city with tales of a trail, the Klondike Trail, from Edmonton to Dawson City in the Yukon, which didn't really exist. Many people didn't make it through and some returned to settle in Edmonton.

During the festival, locals dress up the streets, the stores and themselves in period style; stages dot the road and are alive with singers and dancers; parades run through the streets; the Northlands Coliseum presents nightly entertainment of rock, pop or country & western music; a Klondike village, with old-time stores and a gambling saloon, is set up in Northlands Park; and the Citadel Theatre puts on 'heroes & villains' melodramas. The street festivities last five days; the Northlands Park exhibition goes on for another five. Contact the Edmonton Klondike Days Association (☎ 426-4055), 1660 10020 101A Ave, for information.

July/August

*Edmonton Heritage Festival* – This three-day festival, held late July, early August in Hawrelak Park, celebrates the city's ethnic diversity. Call ☎ 433-3378.

August

*Folk Music Festival* – In early August the city holds a Folk Music Festival in Gallagher Park with blues, jazz, country & western and bluegrass as well as traditional folk music. Ask at the Visitor Information Centre or call ☎ 429-1899.

*Fringe Theatre Event* – Well worth catching is the Fringe Theatre Event (also called Rex the Wonder Fringe), a 10-day programme that brings all kinds of live alternative theatre to the public with over 800 performances of 150 productions in 14 theatres, in the parks and on the streets. Many of the performances are free and no theatre ticket costs over $8; there's no booking, you choose a theatre and stand in line. The festival takes place in Old Strathcona around the middle of August. For information contact Chinook Theatre (☎ 448-9000), 10329 83rd Ave, or ask at the Visitor Information Centre.

*Dreamspeakers* – Held at Sir Winston Churchill Square in late August, this is an aboriginal cultural and artistic festival which includes poetry, storytelling, dancing, live musical performances plus traditional food and craftwork. Films made by aboriginal filmmakers are also shown. For information call ☎ 439-3456.

## PLACES TO STAY
### Camping

Several camping areas, some run by the Alberta government, are close to town. *Ardrossan Campground* (☎ 922-3293), 18 km east of Edmonton on the Yellowhead Hwy, has 24 campsites for $5.50. There are firepits but nothing else, and no water. Similar is *Bretona Campground* (☎ 922-3293), 18 km south-east of Edmonton near Sherwood Park on Hwy 14 at the junction of Hwy 21, with 28 campsites.

The privately owned *Half Moon Lake Resort* (☎ 922-3045) 21524 Twp Rd, Sherwood Park, charges $12 for a site but has every convenience including showers and laundromat. The resort is very large and there is swimming on the lake. It's 29 km southeast of Edmonton; follow 82nd Ave east to Wye Rd, then head south. Closer to town is *Rainbow Valley Campground* (☎ 434-1621), 14240 56th Ave off Whitemud Drive in Whitemud Park. It has a laundromat and showers and sites for $12.

### Hostels

HI *Edmonton Hostel* (☎ 429-0140), 10422 91st St, is within walking distance of the centre of town. It has a well-equipped kitchen, a view across the river to the southern side of Edmonton and a pub nearby. It sells a few basic staples and issues daily

ALBERTA

transit passes for Edmonton's public transport system. There's a midnight curfew, but it's not strictly enforced, especially when the Folk Music Festival and Fringe Theatre Event are on. The phone is open 24 hours but only ring after midnight if you're stranded. You can pit your wits at Trivial Pursuit with the staff! They might even be able to tell you where to find work. A dorm bed costs $12 for members, $17 for nonmembers.

The hostel has discounts to many of the sights, restaurants, sports and recreation centres, retail outlets and pubs; also on car rental. It sells half-price tickets to the Edmonton Trappers home baseball games and rents out bikes for $12 a day including helmet. To get there from downtown, walk east on Jasper Ave or 103rd Ave (which eventually turns into Jasper Ave anyway) to 91st St, just before the bridge. The hostel is down a few doors on the left. Between the downtown area and the hostel are a couple of run-down blocks which are not great at night, especially for women alone.

The central YMCA (☎ 421-9622), 10030 102A Ave opposite the Edmonton Centre and next to the Hilton Hotel, is close to the Greyhound Bus Depot and VIA Rail station and takes in men and women. Singles/doubles cost from $25/36 and dormitory accommodation $20 with a maximum of three nights. It also has a TV room, swimming pool and a very cheap cafeteria which is open from 6 am.

The YWCA (☎ 423-4922), 10305 100th Ave on the corner of 103rd St, is also central. It takes women only and charges $12.50 in a dorm, $27.50 for a single or, with a private bath, $33.75. Doubles with private bath are $42.50. Sheets are supplied in all the rooms. There's a good, cheap cafeteria that anyone can use.

The University of Alberta, in south-west Edmonton, rents out rooms in the summer in Lister Hall opposite the Jubilee Auditorium. It has good facilities and cheap cafeterias. The rates are $26.80/35.70 (including tax) a single/double, cheaper if you're a student and weekly/monthly rates are available. Contact Guest Services (☎ 492-4281), 44

Lister Hall on the corner of 87th Ave and 116th St. On the university campus St Joseph's College (☎ 492-7681), on the corner of 89th Ave and 114th St, also rents out rooms for singles/doubles $20.75/31.50 (including tax).

### B&Bs
The Visitor Information Centre has details of B&Bs in Edmonton. See also the agencies, through which you can make bookings, listed under Accommodation at the start of this chapter.

Norma's Place (☎ 434-6832), 5220 104A St in south Edmonton is reasonably central and has singles/doubles for $30/40. Also central but north of downtown is Edmonton B&B (☎ 455-2297), 18603 68th Ave which has rooms singles/doubles for $35/55. These places only have a few rooms so it's worth ringing beforehand.

### Hotels – bottom end
Edmonton is not blessed with a great selection of cheap central hotels. But there are a few basic places that survived the downtown's redevelopment which may fit your bill.

The Grand Hotel (☎ 422-6365), 10266 103rd St on the corner of 103rd Ave right beside the bus depot, is probably the best of the downtown cheapies. For singles/doubles with bath you'll pay $26/34. The hotel is very clean and all rooms have colour TV. There's a bar downstairs with snacks and a TV. Hotel Cecil (☎ 428-7001), 10406 Jasper Ave, is a little rougher, especially in the bar. It's old and worn but clean, and the rooms are fine. Some have a bath; all have sinks and are comfortable. Singles/doubles are $32/48 (including tax). Downstairs there's a friendly, cheap restaurant. There are a few more in the old part of downtown east of 97th St, but they're not recommended.

West of town at the Klondiker Hotel (☎ 489-1906), 15326 Stony Plain Rd on the corner of 153rd St, the lobby has a gold-rush feel and a mural symbolising that period. Rooms with a bathroom cost $32.48/37.70 (including tax) plus $10 key deposit, and are alright. There are three bars downstairs so you won't go thirsty. The hotel is popular and features live music at night.

In south Edmonton a cheapie to try is the *Strathcona Hotel* (☎ 439-1992), 10302 82nd Ave on the corner of 103rd St, which has singles/doubles for $20/26. Rooms have no TV or telephone. It's a great old timbered building dating from 1891 and is registered as an Alberta Historic Resource. The *Commercial Hotel* (☎ 439-3981), 10329 82nd Ave, has live music in the bar downstairs and singles/doubles cost $25/28.

### Hotels – middle

*Mayfair Hotel* (☎ 423-1650), 10815 Jasper Ave, has apartments as well as rooms available. A free continental breakfast is included in the price of $59 for singles or doubles. The *Quality Inn Downtown* (☎ 428-6442), 10209 100th Ave, also offers a free breakfast with singles/doubles from $54/65.

More expensive is *Alberta Place Hotel* (☎ 423-1565), 10049 103rd St, where singles and doubles cost from $75. It has a sundeck, exercise room and indoor parking.

### Hotels – top end

Good value is the *Inn on 7th* (☎ 429-2861), 10001 107th St which has a licensed restaurant and rooms for $99. *Holiday Inn Crowne Plaza* (☎ 428-6611), 10111 Bellamy Hill on the corner of 101st St close to the centre of town, has singles/doubles from $99/114, and has a revolving restaurant. A couple of blocks north-east next to the Citadel Theatre is the *Westin Hotel* (☎ 426-3636), 10135 100th St on the corner of 101A Ave, with singles and doubles from $99.

One of Edmonton's older and more elegant hotels the *Hotel Macdonald* (☎ 424-5181), 10065 100th St, has been refurbished and has rooms from $129. *Hilton International* (☎ 428-7111), 10235 101st St near the corner of 102A Ave, has singles from $129 to $189 and doubles from $149 to $209. Pedways connect the hotel with the Edmonton Centre and Eaton Centre.

### Motels

The bulk of the city's mid-price range accommodation is in motels. Most motels have plug-ins (electric sockets for engine heaters) for your car – a good thing for Edmonton winter mornings. There are two areas near town where most motels are located.

One area is along Stony Plain Rd and the Yellowhead Hwy, west of downtown. To get to this area head out along Jasper Ave or 104th Ave which turns into Stony Plain Rd; further west, Stony Plain Rd becomes the Yellowhead Hwy. The other area is along the Calgary Trail south of the city with most of the motels there reasonably priced.

*Royal Scot Motel* (☎ 447-3088) is at 20904 Stony Plain Rd, about 1.5 km from Edmonton. It has singles/doubles from $36/40 or $5 extra for a kitchen. *Rest E-Z Inn* (☎ 447-4455), 21640 Stony Plain Rd, is a little over three km from town. It has 40 units with colour TV, priced at singles/doubles $35/38.

Closer to town *Comfort Inn West Edmonton* (☎ 484-1136), 18245 Stony Plain Rd, includes breakfast in its rates of singles/doubles $45/55 to singles/doubles $60/85. South of town try the *Derrick Motel* (☎ 434-1402), 3925 Calgary Trail North, which has singles/doubles for $32/38. Kitchenette and waterbeds are available. *Chateau Motel* (☎ 988-6661), 1414 Calgary Trail South-West, has 40 units with colour TV and telephone; a kitchenette is extra. Singles/doubles cost $35/40.

There are a couple of other motels worth mentioning. *Beverly Motel* (☎ 479-3923), 4403 118th Ave, is small with just 12 rooms but cheap at $30/32. *Ambassador Motor Inn* (☎ 423-1925), 10041 106th St, on the other hand, is more up-market with full facilities including cable TV, air-con, restaurant, cocktail lounge and pub. Singles/doubles cost $40.

There are many other motels besides these.

### PLACES TO EAT – BOTTOM END

The *cafeteria* in the Alberta Legislature

serves plain, decent food at the best prices in town. It's open Monday to Friday from 7 am to 4 pm, with lunches from 11.30 am to 1.30 pm. *Sarah's Café* in the YWCA is open daily to both men and women, resident or not. There's not a lot of choice but prices are good: breakfast specials are $2.25, omelettes $3.50. *Always Claudia's* in the YMCA, open Monday to Friday from 7 am to 6.30 pm is similar. The *Boardwalk Market*, on the corner of 103rd St and 102nd Ave, a renovated old building also containing offices and stores, has a food court with stalls selling all kinds of food including Chinese and East Indian.

The *Silk Hat*, 10251 Jasper Ave, opened in 1940 and was one of Edmonton's first restaurants. It still has the old, small wall jukeboxes at the booths and movie posters on the walls and is a hang-out for a lot of local characters. It has good prices: three pancakes for $4 and burgers $4.25. It's open Monday to Friday from 6.30 am to 8 pm, Saturday from 8 am to noon and Sunday from 10 am to 8 pm.

*Michael's Deli & Bar*, on the corner of 111th St and Jasper Ave, is a bit more up-market. It has outdoor tables and umbrellas and is busy at lunch serving sandwiches and burgers. Pancakes are $3.95 and burgers start from $4. It's open Monday to Friday from 7 am to 9 pm, Saturday from 9 am to 11 pm and Sunday from 9 am to 9 pm.

Across the river in Old Strathcona on the corner of 104th St and 82nd Ave, *Uncle Albert's* is popular. It has pancakes for $5 and fish & chips from $6.25. In Strathcona Market Square along 82nd Ave at 105th St, the *Basement* is a food mart with a bakery and various other food shops. The *Bamboo Palace*, 8032 104th St on the corner of 81st Ave, is a Chinese restaurant with smorgasbord lunches for $5.

## PLACES TO EAT – MIDDLE

The *Russian Tea Room*, 10312 Jasper Ave, is ideal for a late afternoon pick-me-up, especially for teas, coffees, sandwiches ($4 to $6) and cakes ($4). It's open daily.

Where 101A Ave and 100A St meet, right in the centre of town, a small restaurant district and people-place sanctuary sits amidst all the office towers. Trees have been planted and there are benches for lingering. Most of the restaurants have outdoor sections. The *Mongolian Food Experience* is pretty good and is open daily; it has seafood dishes from $9 to $13 and vegetarian meals for around $8. Close by, the *Bistro Praha*, 10168 100A St, is a European-style spot good for coffees, cakes and pastries. Main meals are about $12 and salads $4. It also serves wine by the glass. During nonmeal hours it's pleasant for a coffee and a flip through a newspaper.

Nearby at 10012 101A Ave and dwarfed by the tower blocks around it, is the *Sherlock Holmes*, a British-model pub good for both food and British and locally brewed beers. A ploughman's lunch is $5.95 and fish & chips $7.95. It's open daily. Similar is the *Elephant & Castle Pub & Restaurant*, on the 3rd level of the Eaton Centre.

A collection of mid-range eateries can be found in the Boardwalk Market. The *Old Spaghetti Factory* is a combined bar and restaurant with decent food at moderate prices in an interesting environment: lots of plants, Tiffany lamps and an old streetcar (tram). Spaghettis cost from $8 to $10 which includes bread, salad and coffee or tea. It's open Sunday to Thursday from 4 to 10 pm, Friday and Saturday from 4 pm to midnight. Next door is *Bones* for ribs (from $9 to $15), open Monday to Friday from 11.30 am to 4 pm; and a few doors down, *La Crêperie* which offers a range of crepes for $8 to $13. There are other places here both more and less expensive. Walk through the building and have a look.

In Old Strathcona there are quite a few good eating places on and around 82nd Ave. The *New York Bagel Café*, 8209 104th St next to Uncle Albert's, is recommended. This is a small, comfortable little spot serving espresso coffee, possibly the best cappuccinos in Canada and light foods, with tables on the sidewalk. About 30 metres along from there on 104th St is another busy and similar place, the *Johann Strauss Coffee*

*House. Veggies*, 10331 82nd Ave, is a vegetarian restaurant (in fact most of the dishes are vegan), which is good for lunch and dinner. Felafels are $4.25, vegetarian burgers $5.75.

One of the best eating buys in Edmonton is at one of the places with a lunch buffet or Sunday brunch. Some of the larger hotels put on big spreads at reasonable prices. Check the weekend newspapers for places and times. The *Inn on 7th* (☎ 429-2861), 10001 107th St, and *Mayfair Hotel* (☎ 423-1650), 1018 Jasper Ave, have lunch buffets every weekday. A good feed at one of these could last you till the next day's breakfast. Put for about $8 you can eat from a choice of hot and cold buffets. Lunch is from 11 am to 2 pm.

One traveller has recommended the *Steak & Ale Restaurant*, 14203 Stony Plain Rd, for its good food and choice of 90 Canadian and imported beers.

## PLACES TO EAT – TOP END

For dinner *The Harvest Room* in the Hotel Macdonald has main meals ranging in cost between $16 and $22. For a great view while you eat try *La Ronde* (☎ 428-6611), the revolving restaurant at the top of Holiday Inn Crowne Plaza Hotel. A three-course meal here costs about $40. In Old Strathcona at 9602 82nd Ave, *Unheardof*, which serves steak, chicken and seafood is similarly priced. *La Bohème*, 6427 112 Ave, offers good French food and wine. Main dishes are between $10 and $20.

## ENTERTAINMENT

*See*, *Pique* and *Culture Shock* are local art and entertainment papers free around town. *Nightlife*, also free, is a broadsheet listing the latest in drama, comedy and concerts. For daily listings see the entertainment section of the *Edmonton Journal*.

### Theatre & Nightlife

Edmonton offers a wide selection of live theatre. The *Citadel Theatre* (☎ 425-1820), 9828 101A Ave, Edmonton's foremost playhouse, is actually a complex of theatres showing mainstream drama, comedy, exper-

imental productions, concerts, lectures and films. Its season is from September to May. Depending on the production, theatre tickets cost from around $18 to $36. The *Chinook Theatre* (☎ 448-9000/9011), 10329 83rd Ave, puts on experimental plays and organises the annual Fringe Theatre Event.

*Northlands Coliseum* (☎ 471-7345), 7428 118th Ave on the corner of 73rd St part of the Edmonton Northlands complex, and *Jubilee Auditorium* (☎ 427-2760, 433-7741), 11455 87th Ave, show name acts on a regular basis. Tickets cost from around $33 for performances that range from rock music to ballet. The Jubilee Auditorium is the venue for the Edmonton Opera and the Edmonton Symphony Orchestra (one of Canada's best).

*Yuk Yuk's* (☎ 466-2131), 7103 78th Ave, has off-beat, stand-up comedy from Wednesday to Saturday. The *Stage West* (☎ 483-4051) theatre restaurant in the Mayfield Inn, 16615 109 Ave, puts on big musical productions. Laser-light concerts are held at the *Space & Science Centre* (see earlier for details).

*City Stage* in City Hall puts on a variety of performances during the day. There are lots of venues around town catering to different musical tastes. In Old Strathcona the *Commercial Hotel* (☎ 439-3981), 10329 82nd Ave, features live blues music as does the *Sidetrack Café* (☎ 421-1326), 10333 112 St. *El Zorro Loco Café* (☎ 428-6002), 9533 Jasper Ave, features blues and rock artists. The *Yardbird Suite* (☎ 432-0428), 10203 86th Ave, is the jazz bar in town. Admission is $5 to $9. A few British-style pub/restaurants, like the *Jekyll & Hyde* (☎ 426-5381), 10610 100th Ave, offer singalong sessions.

### Cinema

There are many commercial cinemas around town. The *Paramount Cinema* (☎ 428-1307), 10233 Jasper Ave, shows matinees for $4.25.

The *Princess Repertory Theatre* (☎ 433-5785/0979), 10337 82nd Ave near 104th St, is Edmonton's main outlet for good, varying films. It charges nonmembers $5 or $7 depending on the film. On Saturdays it shows matinees but the films are mostly for kids. The cinema itself is a historic site – it was the first marble-fronted building west of Winnipeg and at one time showed first-runs of Mary Pickford films.

The *Edmonton Film Society* (☎ 488-4335 after 4 pm), 6243 112A St, regularly shows classic films in the Provincial Museum auditorium (☎ 453-9100). Tickets are $4, children $2. The *Edmonton Art Gallery* shows commercial and classic films, borrowed from the National Film Theatre, for the price of admission to the gallery.

### Spectator Sports
If you're here during the ice-hockey season, from October to April, try to see a home game of the Edmonton Oilers at Northlands Coliseum (☎ 471-2791), 7428 118th Ave on the corner of 73rd St. Tickets are $12 to $40. Alternatively, you could see the Edmonton Eskimos play football, from July to October, at the Commonwealth Stadium (☎ 448-3757), 11000 Stadium Rd. Tickets are $18 to $28. The local baseball team, the Edmonton Trappers, play their home games at John Dulcey Park (☎ 429-2934), 10233 96th Ave, from April to August. Admission is $6.75.

### GETTING THERE & AWAY
#### Air
Edmonton International Airport is around 30 km south of the city along the Calgary Trail, about a 45-minute drive from the centre of town. This airport handles most flights, although it is losing some of its business to the municipal airport. Edmonton Municipal Airport, three km north of downtown off 97th St near 118th Ave, is generally used for smaller planes and therefore shorter flights, particularly within Alberta. City buses run between there and town.

Edmonton is well served by airlines. Canadian Airlines (☎ 421-1414), Main Floor, 10060 Jasper Ave, and Air Canada (☎ 423-1222) fly to the Yukon, Vancouver and major cities in eastern Canada. Time Air (☎ 421-1414), in partnership with Canadian Airlines, is Alberta's commuter airline. It has daily services to Grand Prairie, Calgary,

Lethbridge, Medicine Hat, Red Deer and other destinations in Western Canada. Delta Air Lines (☎ 426-5990), 10135 100th St, connects Edmonton with Alaska and many points in mainland USA. Northwest Airlines (☎ 1-800-225-2525), 10024 Jasper Ave, flies to Winnipeg and destinations in mainland USA.

Air Canada operates a 40-minute commuter service to Calgary with flights all day long. If you're not on business you'll probably find the regular one-way fare a bit pricey at $154.96 (including tax) but there are cheaper flights available in off-peak times. Standard, one-way fares (including tax) to other cities are: Inuvik $704, Vancouver $332, Yellowknife $420, Toronto $697, Winnipeg $401 and Ottawa $732.

### Bus
The large Greyhound Bus Depot (☎ 421-4211), 10324 103rd St on the corner of 103rd Ave close to the VIA Rail station, is very central. It's open from 5 am to midnight and has left-luggage lockers ($1.50) and a fast-food restaurant. Bus fares are usually cheaper than taking the train. Greyhound goes east to Winnipeg twice a day; the one-way fare is $125.19. Greyhound also goes to: Jasper $41.46, Calgary $21.96, Vancouver $107, Prince George $123.05, Yellowknife $171.15 and Whitehorse $222.40. From Whitehorse you can catch a bus with Gray Line of Alaska to Fairbanks, Alaska.

Another bus line serving Calgary is Red Arrow (☎ 424-3339, 425-0820), with its office in the Radisson Hotel, 10014 104th St. The office is open Monday to Saturday from 7 am to 9.30 pm, and Sunday from 10 am to 9.45 pm. It has four buses a day leaving from outside the hotel; the one-way fare is $31 (including tax). You travel on deluxe buses with kitchenette.

### Train
Entry to the VIA Rail station (☎ 422-6032 for arrival/departure information; ☎ 1-800-665-8630 for fares and reservations), at 10004 104th Ave on the corner of 100th St is through the CN Tower entrance and down

the stairs. The station is open Monday, Thursday, Saturday from 7 am to 3.30 pm; Tuesday and Friday from 8.30 am to 9 pm; Wednesday from 8.30 am to 4 pm; and Sunday from 10.30 am to 9 pm. There's a small shop and left-luggage lockers ($1).

Trains depart three times a week eastward to Saskatoon, Winnipeg, Toronto, Ottawa and Montreal and westward to Jasper, Prince George and Prince Rupert. At Prince George you can connect with BC Rail to Vancouver. The one-way fare (including tax) to Jasper is $78.11, to Prince George $123.05 and to Vancouver $186.18.

### Car
The downtown addresses of some of the car-rental companies operating in Edmonton are:

Avis
    Hilton Hotel, 10235 101st St (☎ 448-0066)
Budget
    10016 106th St (☎ 448-2000)
Rent-A-Wreck
    11225 107 Ave (☎ 448-1234)
Thrifty
    10036 102nd St (☎ 428-8555)
Tilden
    10131 100A St (☎ 422-6097)

Rent-A-Wreck is the cheapest charging $27 a day plus 10 cents a km after the first 200 km. Budget charges $40 a day plus 10 cents a km after the first 100 km. Thrifty charges $38 a day with unlimited km. These prices don't include tax or insurance which can raise the cost quite a bit. The companies often have special deals so ring around.

## GETTING AROUND
### To/From the Airports
City buses don't go as far south as the international airport, but you can take the Grey Goose Airporter Bus (☎ 463-7520). It leaves from the Hotel Macdonald every half hour from 5.15 am to 12.15 am for a one-way fare of $11 or $18 return. It also picks up and drops off at other top hotels and the Greyhound Bus Depot. A taxi from downtown to the international airport costs about $35.

City buses run to and from the municipal airport. Take bus Nos 41 or 42 north along 101st St to Kingsway then change to bus No 23. A taxi from downtown costs about $8.

A shuttle bus connects the two airports.

### Bus & LRT
Edmonton Transit (☎ 421-4636 for information about fares, routes and schedules) operates city buses and Canada's smallest subway system, the Light Rail Transit (LRT). The LRT has 10 stops running northeast from the university, east along Jasper Ave, north along 99th St then north-east all the way to 139th Ave in Clareview. Between Clareview Station and Stadium Station the LRT travels overground, from Churchill Station to Grandin Station it runs beneath the surface.

A single one-way fare is $1.35/1.60 offpeak/peak on the LRT or buses. You can transfer from one to the other but you must get a transfer receipt when you pay your fare and use it within 90 minutes of it being issued. You can also buy a day pass for $4.25. From 9 am to 3 pm Monday to Friday and from 9 am to 6 pm Saturday, the five subway LRT stations, Churchill to Grandin, form a free zone.

There is an information centre (open weekdays from 9.30 am to 5.30 pm) at Central Station on the corner of Jasper Ave and 100A St. Churchill Station, on the corner of 102nd Ave and 99th St, also has an information centre (open weekdays from 8.30 am to 4.30 pm) and you can buy passes and ticket books there.

Buses cover all parts of the city but not all routes operate on Sundays and holidays. Bus No 46 goes from downtown to the university and back. Bus No 12 goes from downtown south-west to the Valley Zoo in Laurier Park.

### Taxi
There are several cab companies in Edmonton. Two of them are Yellow Cab (☎ 462-3456), 10135 31st Ave, and Alberta Co-Op Taxi (☎ 425-8310), 105440 110st St. The fare with Alberta Co-Op Taxi from downtown to the West Edmonton Mall is

about $12. The flagfall (drop) is $2, then it's 10 cents for every 100 metres.

### Bicycle
River Valley Cycle & Sports (☎ 465-3863), 9124 82nd Ave, rents out bikes for $7 an hour or $21 per day. It also does guided history tours by bike. HI Edmonton Hostel also rents out bikes (see Places to Stay earlier).

## AROUND EDMONTON
### Alberta Pioneer Railway Museum
This museum (☎ 472-6229) has a collection of steam and diesel locomotives and rolling stock depicting the railways from 1877 to 1950. There is also an artefact exhibit. Admission is $3, children $1 and it's open in summer Thursday to Monday from 10 am to 6 pm. A ride on the train is an extra $1. To get there, drive north on 97th St (Hwy 28) to Namao then turn east onto Hwy 37 for seven km, then south onto 34th St for about two km.

### Elk Island National Park
In the northern Beaver Hills, 45 km east of Edmonton on the Yellowhead Hwy is this 194-sq-km reserve of original forest that is actually a wildlife sanctuary. There are free-roaming herds of elk and plains bison and a small herd of endangered wood bison. Bison can sometimes be seen from the road. About 35 other mammals also inhabit the park. It's a popular weekend spot with camping, hiking, trail cycling, canoeing and swimming in summer and cross-country skiing in winter. Parts of the park close for the season by October and re-open in spring. For information contact the Superintendent (☎ 992-6392), Elk Island National Park, RR 1, Site 4, Fort Saskatchewan T8L 2N7.

### Ukrainian Cultural Heritage Village
This village (☎ 662-3640/1), 50 km east of Edmonton on the Yellowhead Hwy, pays homage to Ukrainian immigrants. There is a replica pioneer home and other exhibitions of the first settlers in the area. From mid-May to the end of August it's open daily from 10 am to 6 pm. Admission is $5.

### Vegreville
The Ukrainian community in this town (120 km east of Edmonton on the Yellowhead Hwy) has constructed the world's biggest *pysanka* or painted Easter egg. Built of aluminium, the egg sits, over seven metres tall and 5.5 metres wide, just off the highway on the eastern side of town. The Ukrainian Pysanka Festival takes place in early July.

### Polar Park
Polar Park (☎ 922-3401), 22 km south-east of town on Hwy 14, specialises in animals of the north: snow leopards, polar bears and caribou are some of the 100 species. There are good walking and cross-country ski trails. It's open daily all year from 8 am till dark and admission is $4, children $2.

### Red Deer
Halfway to Calgary, this large town is in the centre of grain and cattle country. An international folk festival is held here every July and an international air show every August.

Travellers to either Calgary or Edmonton may find Red Deer a useful stopping-off point. During either Calgary's stampede or Edmonton's Klondike Days it might be worth considering Red Deer as a base. Accommodation will not be as tight and is not likely to be as expensive either. Either city is about an hour and a half away on the two-lane highway.

### Edmonton to Jasper
Jasper is 370 km from Edmonton along the Yellowhead Hwy. On the way there are commercial and government campgrounds as well as numerous motels, lodges and guest ranches.

About 30 km west of Edmonton is **Stony Plain** where the Multicultural Heritage Centre (☎ 963-2777), 5411 51st St, has displays on different pioneer groups and their crafts; you can even try some traditional food. It also has an art gallery.

For about 100 years, since prayers at **Lac Sainte Anne** by the Roman Catholic Mission to end a drought were answered, it has been believed that the waters of this lake have God-given curative powers. Here, 50 km west of Edmonton (about 25 km north off the Yellowhead Hwy), an annual pilgrimage takes place in July drawing about 10,000 people from around the province and across North America. It's a five-day event.

**Edson**, a small gas, oil, farming and forestry community, sits about mid-way along the highway. Another 85 km west brings you to **Hinton**, home of the Athabasca Nordic Lookout Centre, reputedly one of the best cross-country ski centres in North America. It has night-time skiing and a luge run. For more information, contact the Alberta Forest Service (☎ 865-2400), Hinton Ranger Station, 227 Kelly Rd, Hinton T7V 1H2.

# Northern Alberta

The land north of Edmonton is a vast, sparsely populated region of farms, forests, wilderness areas, lakes, open prairies and oilfields. The Cree, Slavey and Dene were the first peoples to inhabit the region and many of them still depend on fishing, hunting and trapping. The north-east has virtually no roads and is dominated by Wood Buffalo National Park, the Athabasca River and Lake Athabasca. From its headwaters in British Columbia, the mighty Peace River makes its way to Lake Athabasca in the north-east of the province. The north-west is more accessible with a network of highways that connect Alberta with northern British Columbia and the Northwest Territories.

## PEACE RIVER & AROUND

From Edmonton, Hwy 43 heads north-westward to connect with Hwy 34 then Hwy 2 to Dawson Creek (a distance of 590 km), the official starting point of the Alaska Hwy. Numerous campgrounds and several provincial parks line the route. The scenery is generally flat or gently undulating with dairy and cereal farms, and with grain silos in nearly every town. **Grande Prairie**, a large sprawling community, is an administrative, commercial and agricultural centre. Most of

the accommodation is centred on 100th St and 100th Ave.

Hwy 2 heading north directly out of Edmonton is a more interesting route as it follows the southern shore of **Lesser Slave Lake** part of the way. Just north of McLennan, **Lake Kimiwan** and its surrounding marshland is a special place for bird-watchers. It's in the middle of three migratory routes and nearly 300,000 birds pass through each year. The interpretive centre, next to Hwy 2, is open May to September, and a boardwalk takes you through the bird habitats. For information call ☎ 324-2004.

The Peace River is so called because the warring Cree and Beaver First Nations made peace along its banks. The town of **Peace River**, sits at the confluence of the Heart, Peace and Smoky rivers. The Visitor Information Centre, on Hwy 2, is open July to September daily from 9 am to 9 pm. The town has several motels and two campgrounds. Greyhound buses leave daily for the Yukon and Northwest Territories. West out of town Hwy 2 leads to the Mackenzie Hwy.

## MACKENZIE HIGHWAY

The small town of **Grimshaw** is the official starting point (though you might bypass it if you come via Peace River) of the Mackenzie Hwy (Hwy 35) north to the Northwest Territories. The road is paved all the way, though there are stretches of loose gravel or earth where the road is being reconstructed. Because it's relatively flat and straight the maximum speed limit is 100 km/h (in northern British Columbia it's 90 km/h).

The landscape, mainly agricultural between Grimshaw and Manning, gives way to endless stretches of spruce and pine forest. Come prepared, as this is frontier territory and services become fewer (and more expensive) as the road cuts north through the wilderness. **High Level**, the last settlement of any size before the border, is a centre for the timber industry and workers often stay in the motels in town during the week. Between High Level and Enterprise in the Northwest

Territories the only gas station is at Indian Cabins.

## LAKE DISTRICT

From St Paul, over 200 km north-east of Edmonton, to the Northwest Territories border lies Alberta's immense lake district. Fishing is popular (even in winter when there is ice-fishing) but many of the lakes, especially further north, have no road access and you have to fly in. **St Paul**, gateway to the lake district, is a trading centre. In the town is the only flying-saucer landing pad in the world. It's still waiting for its first customer. The region around St Paul has lots of provincial parks and campgrounds along the various roads.

Hwy 63, is the main route into Alberta's north-eastern wilderness interior. The highway, with a few small settlements and mainly government campgrounds along the way, leads to **Fort McMurray**. Originally a fur-trading outpost, it is now home to one of the world's largest oil fields. The Visitor Information Centre (☎ 791-4336), 400 Sakitawaw Trail, organises guided tours of the oil-processing plants.

## WOOD BUFFALO NATIONAL PARK

Established in 1922 and nearly 28,000 sq km in size, Wood Buffalo (☎ 872-2349) is Canada's largest national park and one of the world's largest parks. A world heritage site, it is bigger than Switzerland, and lies two-thirds in Alberta and one-third in the Northwest Territories. Vegetation in the park ranges from boreal forest to plains, bogs and marshes.

This wilderness park has the world's largest free-roaming bison herd – about 3000 – and is the only nesting ground of the rare whooping crane. Though few in number and endangered, conservation efforts have resulted in their population stabilising. Moose, caribou, bears and wolves abound as well as many smaller animals, and over a million ducks, geese and swans pass by in autumn and spring on their migratory routes. Also out of Fort Smith are the Slave River rapids where rare white pelicans nest.

On the shore of Lake Athabasca, **Fort Chipewyan** is the oldest settlement in Alberta.

Most of the scenic areas in the park are not visible from the roads and the roads themselves are not always open. For travel information contact the Park Superintendent (☎ 872-2349), Box 750, Fort Smith, Northwest Territories XOE 0P0. If you want to get a glimpse of what the early fur traders overcame, this is a good place to look.

### Activities

You can go swimming at **Pine Lake**, hike on the marked trails, or explore the deltas of the **Athabasca** and **Peace rivers** by canoe. The park staff run field trips and overnight camping trips or buffalo-watching hikes. In winter there are cross-country ski trails.

Northern Visions (☎ 872-3430), PO Box 1086, Fort Smith, NWT X0E 0P0, offers tours into the park.

### Places to Stay

There are few comforts in Wood Buffalo National Park. The small *Pine Lake Campground* (☎ 872-2349 in Fort Smith), 56 km south of Fort Smith, has 36 sites at $6.50 and pump water. In addition there are a couple of campgrounds just outside the park's border: one 17 km north-east of Fort Chipewyan at Dore Lake operated by the Alberta Forestry Service and the other near Fort Smith (see also Fort Smith & Wood Buffalo National Park in the Northwest Territories chapter). Within the park there are numerous designated basic campsites for individual campers which offer some primitive facilities such as an outhouse and sometimes a firepit. The more adventurous may set off on their own and camp anywhere they find agreeable.

### Getting There & Away

**Air** Northwestern Air Lease (☎ 872-2216 in Fort Smith) has a scheduled air service between Fort Smith, Fort Chipewyan and Edmonton.

**Road** Wood Buffalo National Park is not easily accessible by road. To get there, you go up the Mackenzie Hwy north-west of Edmonton to the Northwest Territories where Hwy 1 then Hwy 2 lead to Hay River on the southern shore of Great Slave Lake. South of Hay River, Hwy 5 heads east to Fort Smith. From Fort Smith roads head south into the park as far as Fort Chipewyan. North of 60 Bus Lines (☎ 874-6411) runs buses between Hay River and Fort Smith.

# Calgary

The name Calgary, meaning 'clear, running water' in Gaelic, comes from Calgary Bay on the Isle of Mull in Scotland. The area was initially home to the Blackfoot but they were joined in the 18th century by the Sarcee and the Stoney. In the 1800s there was war between them and trouble with White trappers and traders, so the Northwest Mounted Police were sent to cool things down.

They established Fort Calgary in 1875. The Canadian Pacific railway came this far in 1883. Settlers were offered free land and the population jumped to 4000 by 1891. Soon, cattle herders from the USA were pushing north looking for better grazing. Calgary became a major meat-packing centre and cowboy metropolis. It's now a major transportation-distribution point and is still the leading cattle centre.

During the last three decades the city has had to deal with some dramatic ups and downs, exploding from a fair-sized cow town to a brand-new city of steel and glass in under 20 years.

The reason for Calgary's changeable fortunes is simple: oil. Oil had originally been discovered as far back as 1914, but it wasn't until the late 1960s that the black gold was found in vast quantities across the province. Coupled with the energy crisis of the 1970s which bumped prices up sharply, the industry boomed. The city took off, becoming one of the fastest growing cities in the country. It became the headquarters of 450 oil companies and home to more Americans than any place outside of the USA.

The population mushroomed to 640,000 and the city centre was transformed. For years it looked like a construction site as buildings seemed to rise with the morning sun.

After a brief breath-catching period, the cultural side of the city began to develop as well. However, during the 1980s things became tough. With the bottom falling out of the oil market and 70% of the workforce relying on it, things turned sour quickly. Just when the city was struggling, attempting to maintain what it had become, Calgary's fortunes and reputation were boosted when it hosted the Winter Olympics in 1988. And by 1993 there was an upturn in the fortunes of the oil and gas industries.

Calgary has been labelled everything from a rootless boom town to a major new urban centre to a depressed area. But through it all, it continues to develop and remains quite a phenomenon.

The city's climate is dry and sunny. It gets hot in summer but remains amazingly cool in the shade. In winter the warm chinook wind blows off the mountains, raising temperatures – at least temporarily.

One of Alberta's greatest assets, Banff National Park, is just 120 km to the west. Edmonton is 294 km to the north.

## ORIENTATION

Calgary, like the plains around it, lies on flat ground. It began at the confluence of the Bow and Elbow rivers and has spread equally in all directions, but the downtown area is still bounded by the Bow River to the north. The Elbow River cuts through the southern portions of the city.

The person who dreamt up the street-numbering system must have thought it great, but it's a jumble and will take you a few days to get a grip of. The city is divided into four geographical segments: north-west (NW), north-east (NE), south-west (SW) and south-east (SE). These abbreviations are important as they're marked on street signs and included in addresses.

The Bow River and Memorial Drive divide the city between north and south,

ALBERTA

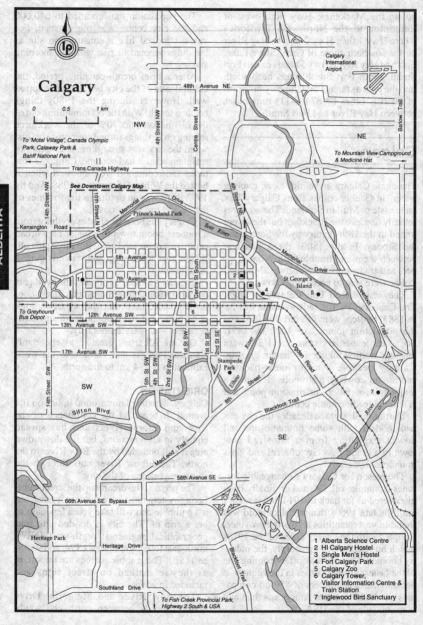

# Calgary

0    0.5    1 km

NW

To 'Motel Village', Canada Olympic
Park, Calaway Park &
Banff National Park

To Mountain View Campground
& Medicine Hat

NE

Calgary
International
Airport

48th Avenue NE

Barlow Trail

4th Street NW

Centre Street N

Trans Canada Highway

**See Downtown Calgary Map**

10th Street NW

Memorial          Drive

Prince's Island Park

Kensington          Road

14th Street NW

Bow River

4th Street NE

Memorial          Drive

Deerfoot Trail

5th Avenue
7th Avenue
9th Avenue

Centre St South

St George's
Island

2

3    4

5

To Greyhound
Bus Depot

12th Avenue SW
13th Avenue SW

6

1st St SW
1st St SE
2nd St SE

17th Avenue SW

14th Street SW

SW

5th St SW
4th St SW
2nd St SW

Stampede
Park

Elbow          River

Ogden          Road

Blackfoot Trail

7

Bow          River

Sifton Blvd

8th          Street          SE

MacLeod Trail

58th Avenue SE

66th Avenue SE Bypass

Heritage Park

Heritage Drive

SE

Southland Drive

Blackfoot Trail

To Fish Creek Provincial Park,
Highway 2 South & USA

1  Alberta Science Centre
2  HI Calgary Hostel
3  Single Men's Hostel
4  Fort Calgary Park
5  Calgary Zoo
6  Calgary Tower,
   Visitor Information Centre &
   Train Station
7  Inglewood Bird Sanctuary

ALBERTA

approximately. Centre St divides the northern part of the city and downtown between east and west; Macleod Trail divides the southern part of the city between east and west.

All city streets run north and south, all avenues run east and west. The downtown streets are all one way except for 7th Ave. Here all cars go west to east but there's one bus and taxi lane which goes the opposite way. The Light Rail Transit (LRT – known as the C-Train) also runs along 7th Ave.

## Downtown

Around the downtown centre the 'Plus 15 Walking System' refers to pedestrian bridges and over-the-street walkways (enclosed sidewalks) which are at least five metres above the ground. Various buildings and shops are connected in this way.

The Calgary Tower, right in the centre of town on 9th Ave at Centre St, is a good orientation point. If you look across the street up Centre St, you're looking north towards the downtown area. Ninth Ave is lined with modern offices, expensive hotels, banks and parking lots as well as the train station, Calgary Convention Centre and Glenbow Museum & Art Gallery complex.

Eighth Ave between 3rd St SW and 1st St SE is a very long pedestrian mall – Stephens Ave Mall, also called 8th Ave Mall. It's lined with trees, benches, shops including the large department stores, restaurants and fast-food places. There are also a lot of vendors selling crafts, odds & ends and souvenirs. At its western end Stephens Ave Mall connects with Barclay Mall (3rd St SW) which heads north towards the YMCA, Eau Claire Market and Prince's Island Park.

Around Centre St, before it heads north over the river, between 1st St SW and 1st St SE, is the small, vibrant Chinatown with grocery stores and video shops as well as restaurants.

The western downtown area is mainly offices and businesses. The eastern section was the last to undergo redevelopment. It used to be the saviour of the impecunious with its cheap bars and tatty hotels of which

a few vestiges remain but generally it's pretty cleaned up. The Single Men's Hostel and a couple of old hotels remain; the HI Calgary Hostel is down this way as well. Among the older buildings, a couple of fine ones are the City Council building dating from 1907 on 7th Ave SE and the Anglican church dating from 1904 on 7th Ave SE at 1st St SE. The latter replaced a temporary cathedral built in 1884. One of the newer complexes is the large Centre for the Performing Arts on the corner of 9th Ave and 1st St SE with the park nearby.

Stone lions on each side mark the Centre St Bridge over the Bow River, which has the greyish-green colour of Rocky Mountain waters. The river marks the northern edge of the downtown area. To the west of the bridge is Prince's Island, a park. Over the bridge, on the northern side, are stairs on both sides leading up to the cliff. There's a footpath along the cliff and good views of the city, especially if you take the stairs on the western side. If you're driving, turn left on 8th Ave NW, then head back towards the river.

Note that most places in the downtown area are within walking distance of each other.

## North

The city north of the river is primarily residential. The Trans Canada Hwy cuts east-west across here along 16th Ave NE and 16th Ave NW. In the north-west the University of Calgary is off Crowchild Trail (Hwy 1A). To the north-east, off Barlow Trail is the international airport. Just north-west over the river, off Memorial Drive, is the district of Kensington which has restaurants, cafes and some nightclubs.

## South

South of Calgary Tower, over the railway tracks, is another section of the city – a sort of mini-downtown. It's between 10th Ave SW and 17th Ave SW and on 4th St SW running north-south. There are quite a few restaurants in this area. Five blocks to the east is Stampede Park.

Heading west from Stampede Park is 17th Ave SW. It's lined with a wide range of restaurants as well as a variety of other businesses including many antique shops. Fourth St SW, south of 17th Ave SW, has boutiques, a few galleries and yet more eating places and night spots.

Further south is Macleod Trail (Hwy 2) which eventually heads to the USA. The best section of Calgary is east of Macleod Trail around the Bow River.

## INFORMATION
### Tourist Offices
The Visitor Information Centre (☎ 263-8510, 1-800-661-1678), is on the ground floor of Calgary Tower at the junction of 9th Ave SW and Centre St. It's run by the Calgary Convention & Visitors Bureau, has maps of the city and pamphlets on things to do and will help you find a place to stay. It's open Monday to Friday from 8.30 am to 5 pm. Seasonal offices are north-west in Canada Olympic Park at the junction of the 16th Ave NW (Trans Canada Hwy) and Bowfort Rd NW; and on the arrivals level of the international airport.

### Money
There are several banks on Stephens Ave, but the Hong Kong Bank of Canada in the Good Fortune Plaza on 3rd Ave SE in Chinatown is open on Saturdays. American Express (☎ 269-3757) is at 200 8th Ave SW.

### Post
The main post office (☎ 292-5512), 220 4th Ave SE, is open Monday to Friday from 8 am to 5.45 pm.

### Foreign Consulates
Consulates in Calgary include the following:

Austria
    1131 Kensington Rd NW (☎ 283-6526)
Belgium
    908 18th Ave SW (☎ 244-1478)
Denmark
    1235 11th Ave SW (☎ 245-5755)
Germany
    1970 700 4th Ave SW (☎ 269-5900)

Italy (Vice Consulate)
    416 1st Ave NE (☎ 237-6603)
Mexico
    3107 Vercheres St SW (☎ 245-0303)
Netherlands
    2103 421 7th Ave SW (☎ 266-2710)
Norway
    1753 707 8th Ave SW (☎ 263-2270)
Sweden
    420 47th Ave SW (☎ 243-1093)
Switzerland
    700 Sunlife Plaza N Tower (☎ 233-8919)

## Bookshops
The Hostel Shop (☎ 283-8311), 1414 Kensington Rd NW, open daily, has travel and outdoor-activity guides and maps, as well as travel goods. Map Town (☎ 266-2241), 6040 6th Ave SW, has travel guides and a wide range of maps. Topographical maps are available from Maps Alberta (☎ 297-7389), 703 6th Ave SW, plus some publications on the province's flora & fauna. A good second-hand bookshop is the Elephant's Knee, 1227 9th SE next to the Garry Theatre in Inglewood. It has a small café as well which is good for desserts.

## Medical Services
Calgary General Hospital (☎ 268-9111) is north-east of the downtown area over the river in the Bow Valley Centre, at 841 Centre Ave NE; take bus No 3.

## CALGARY TOWER
This building (☎ 266-7171), 101 9th Ave SW, at the foot of Centre St downtown, acts as a landmark and symbol of the city. It may not dominate the skyline but can be seen from far away. The 191-metre tower houses a revolving restaurant, an observation gallery and, at the very top, a cocktail lounge. While the elevator (for $4.25) takes just 48 seconds, walking the 762 emergency steps takes a bit longer.

The observation gallery is open from 7.30 am to midnight daily in summer, from 8.30 am the rest of the year.

## GLENBOW MUSEUM & ART GALLERY
The Glenbow Museum & Art Gallery

ALBERTA

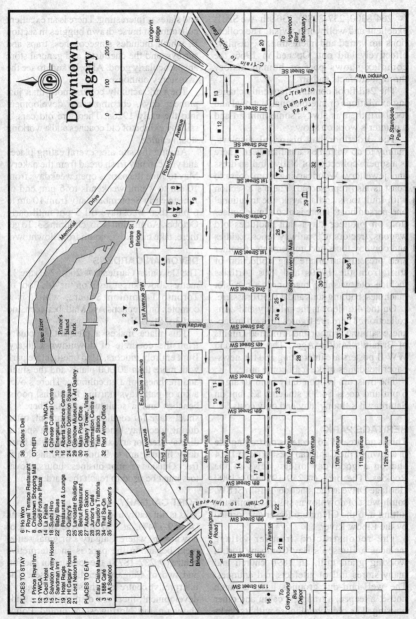

Downtown Calgary

0  100  200 m

PLACES TO STAY
11  Prince Royal Inn
12  YWCA
13  Cecil Hotel
15  Salvation Army Hostel
17  Sandman Inn
19  Hotel Regis
20  HI Calgary Hostel
21  Lord Nelson Inn

PLACES TO EAT
2  Eau Claire Market
3  1886 Café
5  AA Seafood
6  Ho Won
7  Royal Terrace Restaurant
8  Chinatown Shopping Mall
9  Good Fortune Plaza
14  La Paella
18  Sushi Hiro
22  Bibby Blues
Restaurant & Lounge
23  Quincy's
26  Beirut Restaurant
27  Lancaster Building
28  Auburn Saloon
29  Joop's Café
33  Claudio's Trattoria
34  Thai Sa-On
35  Mother Tucker's
36  Cedars Deli

OTHER
1  Eau Claire YMCA
4  Chinese Cultural Centre
10  Emergency
16  Alberta Science Centre
24  Toronto Dominion Square
29  Glenbow Museum & Art Gallery
30  Main Post Office
31  Calgary Tower, Visitor
Information Centre &
Train Station
32  Red Arrow Office

(☎ 264-8300, 237-8988), 130 9th Ave SE, is excellent and well worth a visit. The collections are varied and interesting, the displays effectively laid out. Opened in 1966, the complex shows part of human history through artefacts and art.

The 2nd floor contains frequently changing exhibitions of international, national and local art; there is always some Inuit art and a painter's work on show.

The 3rd floor has historical displays, mainly to do with the Canadian west. There is a superb collection of Native Indian dress and jewellery. Woodcarving from coast to coast is also represented. There's a section with Inuit tools and a kayak, the traditional one-person boat. There is also a huge collection on pioneer days that includes old wagons, tractors, CP railway relics, saddles and cowboy tools and implements. Another area presents an interesting collection of stuff from the 1920s and '30s. Articles include old washing machines, a car, slot machines, bathing suits and a 1930 brassiere.

On the 4th floor is the military and arms collection. There are figures dressed in Japanese samurai armour and armoured knights of Britain's Middle Ages. The WW I and WW II posters are interesting and the newspaper headlines make it all come alive.

The museum is open daily from 10 am to 6 pm and costs $4.50, students $3; but on Saturday it's 'loony' day and only costs $1.

## HERITAGE PARK

This is an area of 26 hectares portraying life in a town of the Canadian west prior to 1914 and on a good day offers views of the Rockies. The park (☎ 259-1954/00), 1900 Heritage Drive at the junction of 14th St SW, south-west of downtown, sits on a peninsula jutting into the Glenmore Reservoir formed by the Elbow River.

The reconstructed frontier village includes a Hudson's Bay Company fort, a working grain mill, an 1896 church and many stores full of artefacts and antiques. The well-laid-out grounds have a ranch house, a teepee, a trapper's cabin and other housing. The old schoolhouse with its desks

and slates is interesting. There is an excellent collection of horse-drawn buggies in section E, which includes stagecoaches, traps and surreys, and the chemist's and general store are particularly good. Also, be sure to see the two-storey outhouse.

The park actually covers more than just pioneer days, encompassing development into the early 1920s. There are old cars, a railway exhibit of old coaches and a working steam engine.

Around the site are several eating places and you can buy fresh bread from the bakery. May to June the park is open weekdays from 10 am to 4 pm, weekends to 6 pm; end of June to early September daily from 10 am to 6 pm; then weekdays till 5 pm until early October. Admission is $6, children $3. To get there, take bus No 53 south from downtown.

## DEVONIAN GARDENS

The Devonian Gardens (☎ 268-5207) are 15 metres above street level on the 4th floor of Toronto Dominion Square, which is a complex on Stephens Ave Mall, between 2nd and 3rd Sts SW.

This place makes a pleasant sanctuary from the concrete of downtown Calgary. Built entirely indoors, it's a one-hectare park with more than 20,000 plants and the smell and freshness of a greenhouse. There's over a km of pathways skirting fountains, pools, benches and a sculpture court. There's a small stage for regular entertainment, often during weekday lunch hours, and a special display area for art exhibitions. They're open daily from 9 am to 9 pm and admission is free. Outside regular business hours, elevators must be used to reach the gardens.

## FORT CALGARY

This is not really a fort but a 16-hectare park (☎ 269-7747), at 750 9th Ave SE, east of downtown, where Calgary's original settlement began. In the park is an interpretive centre (☎ 232-1875), the remains of the fort and two of Calgary's earliest houses. The interpretive centre tells the story of Calgary's development; there are displays and a slide show on the Northwest Mounted Police every 30 minutes in the theatre. The centre is open daily from 9 am to 5 pm and admission is $2, except Tuesday when it's free.

Here in 1875, where the Bow River meets the Elbow River, the first detachment of the Northwest Mounted Police arrived. They built a fort and called the developing settlement the 'Elbow'. Later it became Fort Calgary and remained a police post until 1914, when it was sold to the Grand Trunk Railway. All that remains of the fort are a few foundations. Plaques give some of the history.

The fort site is pleasant and has good views. You can follow paths down to the river and walk across the footbridge to St Patrick's Island and on to Calgary Zoo. The park is open every day and is free.

To the east, across the Elbow River, is **Hunt House**, probably the oldest building on its original site in the Calgary area. It was built by the Hudson's Bay Company in 1876 for one of its employees. Next door the larger **Deane House**, was built in 1906 for the commanding officer of Fort Calgary and is now a restaurant.

### ENERGEUM

The Energeum (☎ 297-4293), on the main floor of the Energy Resources Building at 640 5th Ave SW, outlines the development and uses of Alberta's energy resources. Models and charts depict the formation, discovery and exploitation of coal, oil and natural gas, and include a good explanation of the province's valuable yet problematic oil sands. Some interactive computers supply further details, as does a film. A gorgeous pink 1958 Buick is on display. The Energeum is open from 10.30 am to 4.30 pm Monday to Friday (plus Sunday from June to August) and admission is free.

### NATURAL GAS, LIGHT, HEAT & POWER MUSEUM

That's quite a mouthful (and it's not even the complete title). It's a lot of name for a fairly superficial display in the Canadian Western Natural Gas Company's lobby on the corner of 11th Ave SW and 8th St SW. The gas stove

from 1912 is quite a sight but beyond that, the few home appliances and old photographs don't amount to much. It's open Monday to Friday from 8 am to 4 pm and admission is free. Take bus Nos 2 or 13 west on 6th Ave.

### CHINESE CULTURAL CENTRE

This centre, straddling 2nd Ave at the junction with 1st SW, was completed in 1993 at a cost of $7 million. Skilled artisans were flown in from China to help build it. The centre houses a small museum (open daily from 11 am to 5 pm, admission $2) and you can watch people playing chess in the main hall.

### PRINCE'S ISLAND PARK

This is a pretty park on an island in the Bow River north of the downtown area, connected to both sides of the river by pedestrian bridges. It's a cool, quiet spot with lots of trees and flowers, picnic tables and jogging and cycling paths. This is a good antidote to a hot summer's day in Calgary. As the signs say, the water in the Bow River is dangerous for swimming: it moves fast and is cold. The bridge to the island from downtown is at the top (northern end) of 3rd St SW.

### ALBERTA SCIENCE CENTRE

The entertaining and educational Alberta Science Centre (☎ 221-3700), 701 11th St SW, is just west of downtown in Mewata Park at the junction of 7th Ave SW. The main attraction is the **Centennial Planetarium** with its ever changing one-hour show about different phenomena in our universe.

Weekend nights are given over to laser rock-music shows. Also on the premises is a small observatory with telescopes focused on the moon, the planets and star clusters. This is open on clear nights. There's also a new display area, **Discovery Hall**, which has changing exhibits with varying themes. The **Pleiades Theatre** (☎ 221-3707) puts on holiday variety shows and mystery plays four times a year.

The centre is open daily in the summer from 10 am to 8 pm. Admission to the science centre is $5.50, to the planetarium $5.50; a combined ticket is $6.50.

## CALGARY ZOO

The zoo (☎ 232-9372), one of Canada's largest and best, is east of downtown on St George's Island and the northern bank of the Bow River. It brings together 1100 species of mammals, birds, amphibians and reptiles, many in enclosures simulating the animals' natural habitats. Underwater viewing areas allow you to see polar bears, seals and other creatures as they behave beneath the water. Special blacked-out rooms enable you to see nocturnal animals. There is a section on Australian animals and pens for large, exotic mammals like tigers, giraffes and Himalayan cats. Hundreds of tropical birds are kept in greenhouses full of plants and flowers of warmer climes. Picnic areas dot the zoo and island and there is a café at the site.

The **Botanical Garden** in the zoo has changing garden displays, a tropical rainforest and a butterfly enclosure. The three-hectare **Prehistoric Dinosaur Park**, an extension of the zoo, contains fossil displays and life-size replicas of dinosaurs in natural settings.

The zoo is open year-round and charges $7.50, $3.75 for children under 16. In summer it's open from 9 am to 7 pm, in winter 9 am to 5 pm. Catch the C-Train east along 7th Ave to Zoo Station.

## INGLEWOOD BIRD SANCTUARY

This 32-hectare sanctuary (☎ 269-6688, 237-8811) is south-east of downtown at the end of 9th Ave, on a forested section of the Bow River flats. The area is home to many birds and a resting spot for those on the migratory trail. Trails lead through the sanctuary which is open daily from 7 am to 9 pm and admission is free. Bus No 14 goes within a few blocks of the sanctuary (Monday to Friday only).

## CALGARY STOCKYARDS

The stockyards (☎ 234-7429), 100 2635 Portland St SE, are one of the centres for western livestock dealing. If you want to see what's going on, there are cattle auctions on weekdays. Take bus No 24 from downtown.

## MUSEUM OF THE REGIMENTS

The Museum of the Regiments (☎ 240-7674) is at the Canadian Forces base, Currie Barracks, 4520 Crowchild Trail SW between 33rd Ave SW and 50th Ave SW. It pays homage to Calgary's home regiments: Lord Strathcona's Horse, Princess Patricia's Light Infantry, the Calgary Highlanders and the King's Own Calgary regiment. There are

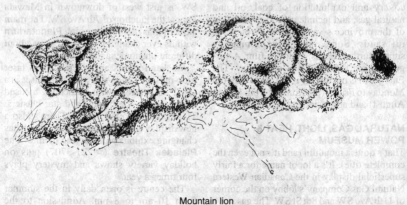

Mountain lion

collections of uniforms, weapons, badges, toys and memorabilia from both the 19th and 20th centuries.

Entry is free and it's open daily, except Wednesday, from 10 am to 4 pm. As it's on the base, you may be asked for identification – calling ahead is a good idea. To get there take bus Nos 18, 108, 111 or 112 from downtown.

## FISH CREEK PROVINCIAL PARK
On the south-western edge of Calgary, quite a way from downtown, is this huge tract of land more than eight-sq-km in size, running along Fish Creek, which flows into the Bow River. It acts as a shelter for many animals and birds as well as people on weekends. Park interpreters present slide shows and walking tours to explain some of the local ecology.

For details drop into the administration office or call Calgary Parks & Recreation (☎ 221-3950/99). To get there from downtown head south on the Macleod Trail.

## CALAWAY PARK
This large amusement park (☎ 240-3822/24), about 10 km west of town on the Trans Canada Hwy, features over 20 rides, a cinema with a 180° screen, restaurants and entertainment events. It costs $8.95 to get in to see the shows, or $14.95 including rides.

## WINTER OLYMPICS SITE
Calgary hosted the 15th Winter Olympics in 1988, a first for Canada. Some of the locations and facilities were already in place, others were specially built for the Olympics, but they all remain in use.

A 15-minute drive west of town on the Trans Canada Hwy, **Canada Olympic Park** (☎ 247-5403) is interesting to visit. There you can see the 70 and 90-metre ski jumps – from the top you realise how crazy those guys were – and the bobsled and luge runs built of concrete. If you don't want to try the real thing yourself there are simulators that recreate the sensation of bobsledding or skiing. Guided tours of the park cost $8. There's an **Olympic Hall of Fame** (☎ 247-

5452), open daily from 10 am to 5 pm and admission is $3.75, as well as the facilities now used as an Olympic training centre. The adjacent downhill ski area is open to the public in winter.

But the real alpine skiing took place 55 km west of town in Kananaskis Country (see that section later).

## BOW RIVER
The Bow River begins as clean, clear barely melted ice in Bow Lake in the Rockies not far from Banff, and flows swiftly through Calgary. From Calgary it slows and warms and eventually reaches Medicine Hat near the Saskatchewan border. There it melds with other meandering rivers, changes name and eventually slips into Hudson Bay.

The Bow River in its middle section – the 60 km from Calgary east to Carseland – is considered one of the best trout-fishing rivers in North America and the best dry fly-fishing river in the world. The fish, mainly brown and rainbow trout, are numerous and big, too. And the river will just float you along with no effort required. It sounds good even for those who don't fish. Swimming is out, though – the water here is still far too cool.

A good access point is just at the southern edge of Calgary's city limits under the Hwy 22X bridge. There are numerous fishing-guide services in town as well as sporting-goods stores for fishing tackle and information. One place to try that combines the two is Country Pleasures (☎ 271-1016), 570 10816 Macleod Trail South.

## IMAX THEATRE
Calgary's new IMAX Theatre, 132 200 Barclay Parade SW, is in the Eau Claire Market just south of the Bow River. These specially designed theatres show films up to 10 times the size of a normal 35 mm movie. Call ☎ 263-4629 for information.

## ACTIVITIES
Calgary has 180 km of bicycle and hiking trails, many in the parks and nature areas. Maps and information are available from

ALBERTA

Parks & Recreation (☎ 268-2300, 221-3999). Budget (☎ 263-0505), 140 6th Ave SE, rents bikes for $5/15 per hour/day.

Two leisure centres run by Parks & Recreation have giant wave pools, year-round skating, racquet courts and hot tubs. They are: Family Leisure Centre (☎ 278-7542), 11150 Bonaventure Drive SE and Southland Leisure Centre (☎ 251-3505), 2000 Southland Drive SW near the corner of 19th St SW. Downtown, the Eau Claire YMCA (☎ 269-6701), 101 3rd St SW, has the latest in keep-fit facilities. Admission is $9 in peak periods.

Bungee jumping is catching on and, at Canada Olympic Park, you can dive 37.5 metres into a specially designed 3.6-metre-deep pool for $79. Call Bungee Canada (☎ 286-4334) for details.

Horse riding, including lessons, is available in Fish Creek Provincial Park with Happy Trails (☎ 251-3344) riding stable. A one-hour trail ride costs $13.

## ORGANISED TOURS

The cheapest bus tour of town is to take the No 10 bus from along 6th Ave. For $1.25 this city bus goes on its 2½-hour circular route past old and new areas, the highest point of the city with views to the foothills, the university and some wealthy districts in the north-west.

Brewster's Gray Line (☎ 221-8242), 808 Centre St SE, runs tours of Calgary and various Rocky Mountain locations from Calgary. The tour of Calgary takes about four hours, covers about 50 km and costs $32. It includes Fort Calgary, Canada Olympic Park and the downtown area, with admissions included in the ticket. A history of the city is given. White Stetson Tours (☎ 274-2281), 6312 Travois Crescent NW, does a similar city tour for $28. Other tours offered by Brewster's Gray Line and White Stetson go to the Columbia Icefield, Banff, or some of the mountain lakes. The Brewster's Gray Line tour to Banff takes nine hours and costs $39 including a ride on the gondola up Sulphur Mountain. White Stetson does a similar tour, taking in Lake Louise as well, for $45.

Pacific Western Transportation (☎ 243-4990), 419 34th Ave SE, also runs bus tours. Tours can also be arranged through HI Calgary Hostel, including hikes, mountain-bike tours and a six-day wilderness bus tour of the Rockies and Edmonton for $135 plus accommodation at the hostels along the way.

The Old Town Calgary Society (☎ 265-4171), 1 917 9th Ave SE, runs 1½-hour walking tours of the historic buildings of Inglewood. The tours leave from the Firehall Restaurant, 1030 9th Ave SE, at 2 pm and cost $3.

White-water rafting on either the Kananaskis or Red Deer rivers is available through Rainbow Riders Adventure Tours (☎ 270-7678), 3312 3rd Ave NW. The cost is $42 for about 2½ hours. Calgary Helicopters (☎ 291-0017), 575 Palmer Rd NE, offer tours of the city for $80 per person and of the Rocky Mountains for $295.

## FESTIVALS

The following are some of Calgary's major festivals.

July

*The Calgary Stampede* – Dating from 1912, this is a wild 10-day festival that starts with a huge parade in the second week of July each year. Most organised events take place in Stampede Park south-east of the downtown area, but many of the streets are full of activity too. Stampede Park comes alive with concerts, shows, exhibitions, dancing and eating. There is also an amusement area with rides, a gambling hall and lots of contests.

Highlights are the chuck wagon race and the rodeo, which is said to be the biggest and roughest in North America. Events include rides on bucking broncos and bulls, and calf-roping and branding. At night the Stampede Stage Show takes over, with singers, bands, clowns and dancing girls.

Tickets for the main events go early and range in price from about $16 to $42. Prices all over town go up, so beware. And the town and nearby countryside are packed for the duration of the celebrations, so if you plan to be here at this time, it's a good idea to book ahead for somewhere to stay or arrive early.

For more information or tickets call or write to Calgary Exhibition & Stampede (☎ 269-9822;

1-800-661-1260), Box 1060, Station M, Calgary T2P 2K8.

*Calgary Folk Festival* – During this festival in late July there are free weekday lunch time performances in Stephens Ave Mall, Century Park Garden and Olympic Plaza. In the evenings there are performances in venues around town including Kensington Delicafé and King Edward Hotel. It includes local, national and international artists. For details call ☎ 225-5256.

August

*International Native Arts Festival* – This takes place in the middle of August and includes traditional dancing, music and arts & crafts by the indigenous peoples of North America and around the world.

## PLACES TO STAY

The prices quoted in this section are the regular ones but in some places they do rise when some special events are on, particularly the Calgary Stampede.

### Camping

There are several campgrounds near the city for both RVs and tents. They all have good facilities and are cheaper than other accommodation but are very developed and organised.

*Whispering Spruce Campground* (☎ 226-0097) is in Balzac along Hwy 2 about 15 minutes north of the city. It has complete facilities, including a small grocery shop, is open from mid-May to the end of October and has sites for $10. *Mountain View Campground* (☎ 249-7372), on a farm three km east of Calgary on the Trans Canada Hwy, is open all year. It has showers, laundromat, barbecue, even a small zoo and sites for $12. *Calaway Park* (☎ 249-7372), 10 km west of Calgary on the Trans Canada Hwy, has full facilities including showers and laundromat, and sites for $12.

South of Calgary, five km east of Okotoks on Railway St, is *Okotoks Wilderness Campground* (☎ 938-6036). Sites cost $11 and there are showers and hiking trails. To get there go south on Hwy 2 take the Okotoks turn off, then turn left at the lights and travel for about a km; the campground is just past the car wash.

### Hostels

The HI *Calgary Hostel* (☎ 269-8239), 520 7th Ave SE just east of downtown not far from Fort Calgary, is open 24 hours. It is a large hostel complete with laundromat, kitchen and snack bar; it also operates a shuttle bus to hostels out of town and operates trips to the Rockies. The hostel can get very crowded in summer and the rates are $13 for members, $18 for nonmembers.

A little further east on the opposite side of the street from the HI Hostel is the Salvation Army-run hostel for the needy, the *Single Men's Hostel* (☎ 262-6188), 631 7th Ave SE on the corner of 6th St SE. You can stay here and get a breakfast, too, for nothing, but the atmosphere can be quite grim. Check in after 4 pm. The *Salvation Army Hostel* (☎ 262-2756), 515 1st St SE, is much the same thing; a bed is $7.

The central *YWCA* (☎ 263-1550), 320 5th Ave SE, is for women only. The single rooms are $25/30 without/with bath, doubles are $30/40 without/with bath. A dormitory bed is $15. The rooms are clean, you can use the pool or gym and there's a cafeteria which is open every day.

The *University of Calgary* rents rooms in the residences from early May to the end of August. For details and information contact the University Housing Office (☎ 220-3210/03), Room 18, Dining Centre, University of Calgary, 2500 University Drive NW, Calgary T2N 1N4. Dormitory accommodation starts at $18. There are two sizes of apartments: in the smaller ones it's $35/22 unshared/shared, and in the larger apartments it's $46/28 unshared/shared. There are good facilities on campus, including a gym and a cheap cafeteria. The university is serviced by the C-Train.

### B&Bs

The Visitor Information Centre keeps a list of B&B places and will make a booking for you. An association which checks and lists houses offering B&B in the city is the Calgary B&B Association (☎ 284-0010), 1633 7A St NW, Calgary. See also the agencies listed under Accommodation at the start

ALBERTA

of this chapter. The *Accommodation & Visitors' Guide* also has a list of about 30 B&Bs in Calgary. The rates generally start from singles/doubles $30/50.

## Hotels

Central Calgary doesn't have an abundance of lodgings in any price range and many of the hotels are around the edges of the city. Downtown, the south-east section, once a rough and tumble area, was the centre for cheap hotels but as the area was cleaned up most of the small, older places disappeared. There are still a few hanging on though.

The *Cecil Hotel* (☎ 266-2982), on the corner of 4th Ave SE and 3rd St SE, is a low-budget place that's been around for a long time, but it can be noisy and some of the patrons are prone to a couple of drinks too many. Rooms are $27.40/36.35 for singles/doubles with no TV, no phone and no bath, but a sink in each room. At the bar downstairs you can get simple food.

The *St Louis Hotel* (☎ 262-6341), 430 8th Ave SE, is another basic place, but shoestringers will find it cheap at $24.65/30.25 for singles/doubles with bath and TV. There's a busy blues bar and simple restaurant downstairs. Neither of these places is recommended for women.

Better is the *Hotel Regis* (☎ 262-4641), 124 7th Ave SE, where singles/doubles cost $26/46 or $41/56 with bathroom. South-east, in walking distance of downtown and Stampede Park in the district of Inglewood, is the *Shamrock Hotel* (☎ 290-0084) which has very clean rooms with TV and telephone and costs $35/45 for singles/doubles. Don't be put off by the industrial landscape close by.

Going up in price, the *Lord Nelson Inn* (☎ 269-8262), 1020 8th Ave SW, is very central and has full facilities, including a fridge in each room. Rooms are $65/70. *Prince Royal Inn* (☎ 263-0520), 618 5th Ave SW, is a modern all-suite hotel. There's a laundry service and rooms have a kitchenette, fridge, telephones and cable TV. Rates

are $80 for a single or $90 to $110 for a double but this includes breakfast, and at weekends you can get special rates of singles/doubles $45. You can also rent by the week or month.

The *Sandman Inn* (☎ 237-8626), 888 7th Ave SW, is similar with rooms at $78/82. It has full facilities including gym, swimming pool, licensed restaurant and bar.

*Westward Inn* (☎ 266-4611), 119 12 Ave SW, is within walking distance of Stampede Park and has rooms for singles/doubles $79/86.

## Motels

Much of the cheaper and more moderate accommodation is found outside the centre of town. Calgary has dozens of motels in all parts of the city, but there are some areas of very heavy concentration, making it easy to shop around. One of these is along Macleod Trail south of the city. Macleod Trail is a commercial strip with service stations, fast-food restaurants, motels and furniture shops.

*Cedar Ridge Motel* (☎ 258-1064), 9030 Macleod Trail South, is reasonably priced. Singles/doubles cost $43/52. *Flamingo Motor Hotel* (☎ 252-4401), 7505 Macleod Trail South near the corner of 75th Ave SW, is marked by – you guessed it – a large pink flamingo. Rooms cost from $48/56 with a TV in each room, a laundry, pool and a sauna. The surrounding grounds are pleasant and have lots of trees and there are also restaurants nearby.

*Travelodge Calgary South Gate* (☎ 253-7070), 9206 Macleod Trail South near 90th Ave SE, is a two-storey building containing a pool, whirlpool and sauna. Rooms have air-con, cable TV and telephones and cost $68/78.

Another motel area is in the north-western section of the city on and just off 16th Ave (the Trans Canada Hwy). South-east of the University of Calgary, 16th Ave meets Crowchild Trail; linking the two on a diagonal, forming a triangle, is Banff Trail (also called Hwy 1A). Because of the many motels in and around this triangle, the area is called 'Motel Village'. It's a fair way from downtown but it is linked by the C-Train and city buses.

One of the cheapest motels is *Circle Inn Motel* (☎ 289-0295), 2373 Banff Trail NW. It has 30 rooms most of them at singles/doubles $36/38; those with kitchenettes cost $5 extra. There's a restaurant and a pub. The *Avondale Motel* (☎ 289-1921), 2231 Banff Trail NW, has a licensed restaurant, swimming pool and laundromat. Rooms are singles/doubles $53/63. *Budget Host Motor Inn* (☎ 288-7115), 4420 16th Ave NW, is simple but fine and has free coffee. Rooms are $59/64. *Panama Motor Inn* (☎ 289-2561), 2440 16th Ave NW, has a Latin American look about it. Some of its 55 rooms have kitchenettes but there's no extra charge. Singles/doubles cost from $45/48.

## PLACES TO EAT

The Saturday edition of the *Calgary Herald* has ads for breakfast and lunch buffets. The growing number of Calgary's different ethnic groups is reflected in the variety of food available.

### Downtown

Two cheap places are the cafeteria in the *YMCA* on Eau Claire Ave, and the restaurants in the Bay department store, on the corner of 1st St SW and Stephens Ave Mall.

For lunch or dinner, check out the 2nd floor of the Lancaster Building at 304 Stephens Ave Mall on the corner of 2nd St SW. There are 17 food kiosks serving cheap Chinese, Mexican, Indian, deli and other foods. Curry dishes or tacos are around $4. You get street views, too. Two other similar places are the food court (next to the Devonian Gardens) at Eaton's, 510 8th Ave SW, and the main floor of the new and much-touted Eau Claire Market off 1st Ave SW.

Also in the Lancaster Building but downstairs, is the agreeable *Unicorn Pub* with an Anglo-Irish flavour. It's a busy, friendly place which serves moderately priced food like fish & chips for $6 and steak & kidney

pie for $7.50, and the locally brewed Warthog Ale. It's open Monday to Saturday from 11 am to 1 am. *Beirut Restaurant*, 112 Stephens Ave Mall, offers the usual sandwiches plus Lebanese dishes, with starters for $3 to $5 and felafel for $8. Stephens Ave Mall has numerous other places, some that set up tables in the mall in fair weather.

*Junior's Café*, 507 8th Ave SW, is somewhat plastic, but is open every day for standard breakfasts and lunch-time specials; meals are from $3.50 to $8. There are good pizzas for $8 to $18 at *Baby Blues Restaurant & Lounge*, 937 7th Ave SW. Try the one with the spinach. It also has live music at night.

*1886 Café*, on the corner of 3rd St SW and 1st Ave SW, is an interesting little place in the old Calgary Water Power Company building, established in 1886. It's a worn, white wooden building away from the downtown area, by the river near the walking bridge for Prince's Island. At one time it stood out on its own surrounded by parking lots, but the YMCA recreation centre and the Eau Claire Market have helped revive the area and attract a lot of people. Despite competition from the market the café is still extremely popular and is recommended – if you can get in. It's open for breakfast and lunch daily from 7 am to 3 pm and serves mainly omelettes for around $5; or try the breakfast sundae ($5.50), consisting of muesli, yoghurt and three types of fruit.

For dinners downtown, the *Auburn Saloon*, on the corner of 7th Ave SE and 1st St SE, offers good pastas for $5.50 to $9 and salads for $5.50. It has subdued lighting, a bar and magazines. More up-market, *Quincy's*, 609 7th Ave SW, is a pleasant restaurant and bar that serves steak ($17 to $40) and seafood ($14 to $19) dishes. *Sushi Hiro*, near the corner of 7th St SW at 727 5th Ave SW, is a Japanese restaurant serving sushi appetisers for $5 to $7 and main dishes from $8 to $15. It's open in the evening Monday to Saturday from 5 to 11 pm, but is also open for lunch from 11.30 am to 2 pm. *La Paella*, on the corner of 6th Ave SW and

ALBERTA

7th St SW, serves Spanish food; soups are $2 to $7 and main dishes around $7 to $10. It's open Monday to Friday from 11.30 am to 11.30 pm, Saturday from 5 to 11 pm.

There is a small Chinatown on 2nd and 3rd Aves at Centre St. *Ho Won* and *AA Seafood* on Centre St offer dim sum lunches for around $5 or $6. *Chinatown Shopping Mall* on the corner of 3rd Ave SE and 1st St SE is fun on a Sunday around noon when the whole area is packed and lots of fresh pastries are on offer. There are also a couple of cheap Vietnamese restaurants inside. *Diamond Bakery*, downstairs in the Good Fortune Plaza on 3rd Ave SE, is a tiny place offering tasty Chinese and Western treats and sweets from around 70 cents. The *Royal Terrace Restaurant*, upstairs on the corner of Centre St and 3rd Ave SE, serves four-course lunch specials for $5.50 and is also good for dinners.

### South of Downtown

South across the train tracks below 9th Ave *Cedars Deli* on the right side, just after the underpass on 1st Ave SW, is worth the short walk for good, cheap Lebanese food in a green and white setting. It has good starters for around $3 to $4 and a felafel plate for $5.

*Thai Sa-On*, 351 10th Ave SW, is a good Thai restaurant with lunch-time specials for $5. It's open Monday to Saturday for lunch and dinner. Nearby at *Mother Tucker's*, 347 10th Ave SW, you can get huge sandwiches and salads for $6.50 to $8 and seafood dishes for $13 to $18. It's a very popular place and has music at night. On the corner of 10th Ave SW and 4th St SW is the up-market *Claudio's Trattoria*, which serves Italian food in elegant surroundings at a reasonable price and has live music. Main dishes are $9 to $11.

Further south are a couple of good areas for food searching. There's a variety of places along 17th Ave SW from 4th St SW westward for about 10 blocks. *Nellie's Kitchen*, 738 17th Ave SW near 7th St SW, is a small, pleasant café with good sandwiches for about $2.50 to $6 and has a patio out the back. Similarly priced, *Bagels &* *Buns* across the street at 807 17th Ave SW, is also good for informal breakfasts and lunches and is very popular. Fourth St SW itself, between 17th and 25th Aves SW, has lots of restaurants – Greek, French, Indian, delis, etc. Just take a wander.

### Other Areas

North of the river within walking distance of downtown, Kensington, a district based on Kensington Rd and 10th St NW, is an old city neighbourhood with plenty of restaurants and is well worth checking out.

Outside the central area, the commercial strips along Macleod Trail south and the Trans Canada Hwy east-west across the north of the city have many familiar food chains.

## ENTERTAINMENT

For complete entertainment guides pick up a copy of *Tonite* or *Cityscope* available free around town and read the local newspapers. The Friday edition of the *Calgary Herald* has a lift-out section called *What's Up* which tells you what's happening on the weekend and beyond.

### Theatre

The city has several live theatre venues. The *Lunchbox Theatre* (☎ 265-4292), in the Bow Valley Square on the corner of 6th Ave and 1st St SW, is a professional performing arts stage catering to downtown shoppers, workers and passers-by at lunch hours during the week. Shows vary from comedy to drama to musicals, and change regularly. They start around noon, usually with an additional afternoon programme each week. Admission is $7.

The *Calgary Centre for the Performing Arts* (☎ 294-7444), known as The Centre, is on Stephens Ave Mall on the corner of 1st St SE. It has performances by Alberta Theatre Projects (☎ 266-8888); it also has ballet, the Calgary Philharmonic Orchestra and more. The *Garry Theatre* (☎ 233-9100), 1229 9th Ave SE in Inglewood just east of the downtown area, puts on comedy and drama old and new. *Pumphouse Theatre* (☎ 263-0079),

2140 9th Ave SW, puts on experimental plays. The *Alberta Science Centre* has laser shows and the Pleiades Theatre there puts on variety shows and mystery plays (see Alberta Science Centre section earlier). *Stage West* (☎ 243-6642), 727 42 Ave SE, is a theatre restaurant that showcases well-known stars from south of the border.

## Music
In summer the Calgary Philharmonic Orchestra has a series of free community concerts at various locations around the city. There are also free concerts by various musicians in McDougall Centre Park, 455 6th Ave SE. Big-name concerts are held in the Olympic Saddledome in Stampede Park and in the Jubilee Auditorium, 1415 14 Ave SW; tickets cost from around $35.

Downtown, the *Old Scotch* (☎ 269-7440), 820 10th St SW on the corner of 9th Ave SW, brings in good country, folk and jazz bands. There are jam sessions on Sunday nights. For rock, there's the *Cecil Hotel* on the corner of 4th Ave SE and 3rd Ave SE, *T Jay's* on 7th Ave SW, and north of downtown *Frankie & Johnny's* in the North Centre Inn, 1621 Centre St N on the corner of 16th Ave. The *King Edward Hotel*, on the corner of 9th Ave SE and 4th St SE, has live blues bands and the *Unicorn Pub* has Irish music.

*Morgan's Pub*, 1324 17th Ave SW near 4th St SW, is a good spot for blues and jazz. There are other places along the street, some with dancing. On 11th Ave SW, between 4th and 6th Sts SW, there are some pubs and clubs. North over the river *Kensington's Delicafé*, 1414 Kensington Rd NW in Recreation Square next to the Hostel Shop, is a good restaurant and nightspot. It has cheap food, a relaxed atmosphere, live music and an outdoor patio. It's open daily. Nearby is *Pancho's* for rock 'n' roll and blues.

South of town the *Lake Bonavista Inn*, 747 Bonavista Drive SE, with views of the lake and mountains, is a more up-market place for a drink.

## Cinema
Calgary has many commercial cinemas all over town; see the local papers for listings. The film and video department (☎ 260-2781) of *Calgary Public Library*, 616 Macleod Trail SE, sometimes screens free films. The *Plaza Theatre* (☎ 283-3636), 1113 Kensington Rd NW, has two different shows a night plus midnight performances on Friday and Saturday. It presents off-beat US and foreign films. Tickets are $5.50. The *University of Calgary* often has films, mainly foreign, in either the 148 Science Theatre or the Boris Roubakine Recital Hall.

## Spectator Sports
The Calgary Flames (☎ 261-0475), arch rivals of the Edmonton Oilers, play ice hockey from October to April in the Olympic Saddledome. Tickets cost from $9.75 to $44. The Calgary 88's who play in the World Basketball League also use the Olympic Saddledome as a home base. The Calgary Stampeders (☎ 289-0205) play Canadian-style professional football from July to September in McMahon Stadium in north-west Calgary off Crowchild Trail. Tickets range from $15 to $28. The Calgary Cannons (☎ 284-1111), play their baseball home games at the Foothills Baseball Stadium from April to September.

## GETTING THERE & AWAY
### Air
Calgary International Airport is about 15 km north-east of the centre of town off Barlow Trail, a 25-minute drive.

Air Canada (☎ 265-9555), 100 5th Ave SW, and Canadian Airlines (☎ 235-1161), 407 2nd St SW, fly to many Canadian and US cities. Alaska Airlines (☎ 1-800-426-0333), American Airlines (☎ 1-800-433-7300) and Delta Airlines (☎ 263-0177), 905 530 8th Ave SW, connect Calgary with points in Alaska and mainland USA. Northwest Airlines (☎ 1-800-225-2525) flies to Winnipeg and destinations in mainland USA. United Airlines (☎ 1800-241-6522) has an office at the airport.

Air Canada operates a 40-minute commuter service to Edmonton with flights all day long. The regular one-way fare is a bit pricey at $154.96 (including tax) but there are cheaper flights available in off-peak times. Return fares (including tax) to some other cities are: Toronto $456, Winnipeg $370, Montreal $513 and Halifax $767.

Discount fares are advertised in the travel section of Saturday's *Calgary Herald*.

### Bus
The Greyhound Bus Depot (☎ 265-9111), 850 16th St SW at the junction with 9th Ave SW, is a bit away from the centre. It's walkable but most people opt for the free city shuttle bus which goes to the door. It has a small shop, cafeteria and left-luggage lockers ($1.50) and is open daily from 5 am to 1 am. There are frequent Greyhound buses to Edmonton for $29.96, Vancouver via the Okanagan or Fraser Canyon for $93.09; Banff, $14.28; Drumheller, $16.21; Lethbridge, $24.82; Winnipeg, $125.19; and Toronto, $232.16. Fares include tax.

Red Arrow Express (☎ 531-0350) offers four luxury buses a day to Edmonton from its Calgary depot at Westward Inn, 119 12th Ave SW. The fare is $31 one way.

### Train
Despite the closure of VIA Rail's southern route it is still possible to travel by train from Calgary to Vancouver via Banff and Jasper on the privately owned 'Rocky Mountaineer'. But it isn't cheap: direct to Vancouver the one-way fare costs $574 (which includes food and an overnight stop in a hotel in Kamloops). The service runs between the end of May and early October. For information contact a travel agent or the Great Canadian Railtour Company (☎ 604-984-3131; 1-800-665-7245), 104 340 Brooksbank Ave, North Vancouver

The train station is conveniently located in the Calgary Tower.

### GETTING AROUND
### To/From the Airport
The best way to and from the airport is the Airporter Bus (☎ 531-3909), which runs from 5.30 am to 11.30 pm between all major downtown hotels and the airport and costs

$7.50. One departs every 20 minutes from the Westin Hotel at 320 4th Ave SW. Alternatively you could take the C-Train north-east to Whitehorn then catch bus No 57 to the airport. A taxi to the airport costs about $20.

### Bus & LRT
Calgary Transit (☎ 262-1000), 240 7th Ave SW, operates the bus and Light Rapid Transit (LRT) rail system. The office has route maps, information and tickets and is open Monday to Friday from 8.30 am to 5 pm. The Calgary LRT train is known as the C-Train. One fare entitles you to transfer to other buses or the C-Train. The C-Train, is free in the downtown area along 7th Ave between 10th St SW and 3rd St SE. If you're going further or need a transfer, buy your ticket from a machine on the C-Train platform. A single one-way ticket costs $1.50 but you can get a day pass for $4.50.

The C-Train goes north-west to the university, north-east to the airport and south to Macleod Trail. Bus Nos 3, 17 and 53 go north-south along Centre St between the northern areas of the city and downtown. Bus No 19 runs east-west along 16th Ave (the Trans Canada Hwy). Bus No 10 goes south along the Macleod Trail.

### Taxi
Calgary has quite a few cab companies including Alberta South Co-Op Taxi Lines (☎ 531-8294), 2016 25th Ave NE, and Yellow Cab (☎ 250-8311), 3501 23rd St NE. The fare is $2.05 for the first 225 metres then 20 cents for every 225 metres thereafter.

### Car
Various rental outlets can be found around town. Rent-A-Wreck (☎ 237-6880) with the lowest overall rates, charges $29.95 per day plus 13 cents for every km over 150 km. Thrifty Car Rental (☎ 262-4400), at 117 5th Ave SE, requires $49 a day with unlimited km. Budget (☎ 263-0505), 140 6th Ave SE, charges a flat $49.99 per day. These are weekday rates.

## Hitching

Thumbing within the Calgary city limits is illegal and subject to very heavy fines. The law's enforced, so forget hitching here. If you're heading west to Banff take bus No 105 from downtown and ask the driver if there's a connecting bus going further. If not, walk to the city boundary before attempting to hitch.

# Southern Alberta

Southern Alberta is cattle-ranching country, although wheat is very important, too. Here you can visit the badlands with their unusual rock formations and vestiges of prehistoric beasts around Drumheller and Dinosaur Provincial Park, or see Head-Smashed-In Buffalo Jump where the Blackfoot used to kill the herds for food, etc. In the south-east corner rising out of the prairies is Cypress Hills Provincial Park. In Writing-on-Stone Provincial Park you can see hoodoos and ancient petroglyphs. To the west are the spectacular Alberta Rockies.

## LETHBRIDGE

Lethbridge, on the Crowsnest Hwy, is the largest town in southern Alberta, the third largest in the province, and a centre for the local agricultural communities. When you walk around town you'll see some people dressed in early 19th-century clothing. These are Hutterites, members of a Protestant sect who live on collective farms and eschew many aspects of modern society.

## Information

The Visitor Information Centre (☎ 320-1222) is on Brewery Hill at the western end of 1st Ave South. For information about the south-western region of Alberta visit the Chinook Country Tourist Association (☎ 329-6777), 2805 Scenic Drive South at the junction with Mayor Magrath Drive South. The main post office (☎ 320-7133) is at 704 4th Ave South on the corner of 7th St South. The Toronto Dominion Bank on the corner of 4th Ave South and 5th Ave South is open on Saturday from 9 am to 4 pm.

If you're interested in learning about Native Indian culture contact the Sik-Ooh-Kotok Friendship Society (☎ 328-2414, 327-0087), 10 535 13th St North.

## Things to See

The **Nikka Yuko Japanese Gardens** (☎ 328-3511), on the corner of 7th Ave South and Mayor Magrath Drive South, were built to symbolise Japanese-Canadian friendship. These authentic gardens consist of ponds, rocks and shrubs but no flowers. The buildings and bridges were built in Japan and reassembled here. Young women in traditional Japanese costume greet you at the entrance and recite their oft-repeated descriptions. The gardens are open from mid-May to early October and admission is $3, students $2.

On the western side of the city beside Oldman River is **Indian Battle Park**, named after a battle between the Blackfoot and the Cree, the last battle in North America between Native Indians. Within the park is **Fort Whoop-Up** (☎ 329-0444), a replica of Alberta's first and most notorious illegal whisky trading post.

Around 25 of these outposts were set up in the province between 1869 and 1874 for the purpose of trading whisky, guns, ammunition and blankets for buffalo hides, furs etc from the Native Indians. The existence of these trading posts led directly to the formation of the North-West Mounted Police who arrived in 1874 at Fort Macleod to bring law and order to the Canadian West.

Fort Whoop-Up is open Monday to Saturday from 10 am to 6 pm, Sunday from noon to 8 pm and admission is $2. Also in the park, the small **Sir Alexander Galt Museum** (☎ 320-3898), at the western end of 5th Ave South, displays artefacts from Lethbridge history. It's open daily from 10 am to 4 pm and is free.

The **Birds of Prey Centre** (☎ 345-4262), about 10 km east of Lethbridge off the Crowsnest Hwy in Coaldale, is a rehabilitation centre for injured predatory birds such

ALBERTA

as owls, hawks and bald eagles. The admission fee of $4 goes to help wildlife conservation.

### Places to Stay & Eat
The two closest campgrounds to downtown are *Bridgeview Campground* (☎ 381-2357), 910 4th Ave South off the Crowsnest Hwy north-west of town, and *Henderson Lake Campground* (☎ 328-5452), in Henderson Park off Parkside Drive (7th Ave South). Both have showers and laundromats, charge $11 for a tent site and are closed over winter. The *YWCA* (☎ 329-0088), 604 8th St South, is for women only, has a laundromat and gym and charges $22/40 for a single/double.

The *University of Lethbridge*, south-west of downtown over Oldman River, offers accommodation between May and August, with new, fully appointed apartments costing $30/43 or rooms with shared facilities for singles/doubles $24.50/39. For details contact Housing Services (☎ 329-2793), University of Lethbridge, C420, 4401 University Drive, Lethbridge T1K 3M4.

Lots of motels line Mayor Magrath Drive. For good fish & chips, try *Bill's Fish Market*, 543 13th St, on the corner of 6th Ave.

### Getting There & Around
The Greyhound Bus Depot (☎ 327-1551), 411 5th St South, is open daily from 9 am to 7 pm. Some sample one-way fares (including tax) are: Calgary $24.82, Banff $39.11 and Vancouver $101.70. For information about local buses call the Transit Infoline (☎ 320-3885).

### FORT MACLEOD
On Oldman River about 50 km west of Lethbridge, two hours south of Calgary, is the town of Fort Macleod. **Fort Macleod Museum** (☎ 553-4703), 219 25th St, is a replica of the North-West Mounted Police fort of 1874, the first in the region. The fort is patrolled by Mounties wearing traditional red uniforms, four times daily in July and August. Inside there is a small local history collection. Admission is $3.50.

For trivia enthusiasts Fort Macleod is the home town of Joni Mitchell, the popular singer/songwriter of the 1960s, '70s and early '80s whose most famous songs include Big Yellow Taxi, Both Sides Now and Woodstock.

### HEAD-SMASHED-IN BUFFALO JUMP
About 18 km north-west of Fort Macleod, Head-Smashed-In Buffalo Jump (☎ 553-2731), on Spring Point Rd off Hwy 2, is a UN World Heritage Site. It's the oldest, biggest and best preserved bison jump site in North America. For thousands of years Blackfoot used it to run buffalo, their 'living department stores', through drive lanes over the edge of the cliff. They then used the meat, hide, bone, horns and nearly everything else for their supplies and materials. Head-Smashed-In was one of a series of communal kill sites and was last used for this purpose in the early 19th century. According to legend a young brave wanted to view a killing from beneath the cliff but became trapped and was crushed by the falling bison, hence the name Head-Smashed-In.

The interpretive centre, which is built into the hillside, provides explanations of the site and how the Blackfoot's work was achieved. There are nearly two km of outdoor trails. A 10-minute film, a dramatised re-enactment of the buffalo hunt, is shown regularly during the day and sometimes Native Indians perform traditional music. The centre is open daily from 9 am to 8 pm and admission is $5.50, except Tuesday when it's free. There's a shuttle bus up from the parking lot to the centre.

### CROWSNEST PASS
West of Fort Macleod the Crowsnest Hwy heads through the prairies and into the Rocky Mountains to the Crowsnest Pass and the British Columbia border. At the turn of the century this was a rich coal-producing region which gave rise to a series of small mining towns. In 1903 one of these, Frank, was virtually destroyed when part of nearby Turtle Mountain collapsed and buried most of the town killing around 70 people. This and a number of other mining disasters plus

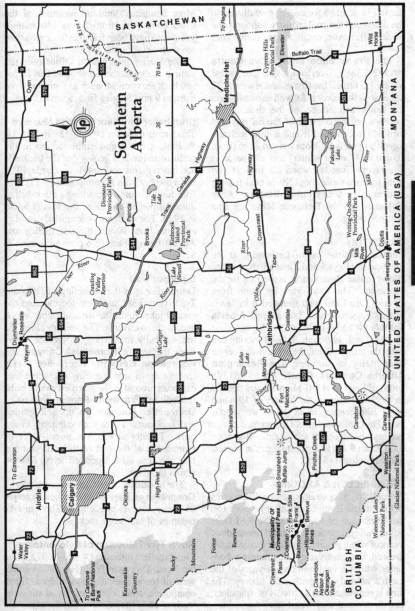

the fall in demand for coal eventually led to the demise of the coal industry although one mine, at Bellevue, continued to operate until 1961.

The **Frank Slide Interpretive Centre** (☎ 562-7388), overlooks the Crowsnest Valley 1.5 km off the Crowsnest Hwy and 27 km east of the border. As well as displays on the cause and effects of the slide, it has exhibits on the coming of the railway and turn-of-the-century life and mining technology. It's open daily from 9 am to 8 pm (from 10 am to 4 pm in winter) and admission is $3, except Tuesday when it's free. If you want to learn more about life in coal-mining communities **Leitch Collieries** near Coleman and the **Bellevue Mine** are also worth visiting.

## CARDSTON

Cardston, south-west of Lethbridge at the junction of Hwys 5 and 2 and adjacent to the Blood Indian Reservation, is a centre for the Mormons. The town gets its name from Charles Ora Card who founded it in 1887. The huge, renovated, box-shaped **Alberta Temple** (☎ 653-4142), 348 3rd St, was built in 1923 and, although only Mormons can enter the temple itself, there's a visitor centre open daily in summer. The **Remington Alberta Carriage Centre** (☎ 653-5139), south of Lee Creek off Main St, was opened in 1993 and records the history of 19th and early 20th-century horse-drawn transportation. The centre includes a museum, carriage factory, blacksmith and stable. It's open daily from 9 am to 8 pm (to 5 pm in winter) and admission is $5.50.

## DRUMHELLER & AROUND

A small city in a strange setting 122 metres below prairie level, Drumheller is about 150 km north-east of Calgary in the Red Deer River Valley dinosaur country. Thousands of years of wind, glacier and water erosion have created the captivating surrounding badlands which reveal millions of years of the earth's animal and geological history. The area is renowned for its fossils of dinosaurs, petrified wood and weird land formations.

More complete dinosaur skeletons of the Cretaceous Age (from 64 to 140 million years ago) have been found in the region than anywhere else on the planet.

The Visitor Information Office is in the same building as the Greyhound Bus Depot and both are open Monday to Saturday from 6 am to 9 pm, Sunday from 9 am to 9 pm.

### Drumheller Dinosaur & Fossil Museum

This small museum (☎ 823-2593), 335 1st St East, gives a good introduction to the prehistoric life and geology of the badlands and has remains and fossils on display. The main display is an Edmontosaurus, a four to five-tonne, nine-metre-long, duck-billed dinosaur pieced together from fossils found in 1923. The museum is open daily in May and June from 10 am to 5 pm, in July and August from 10 am to 6 pm. Admission is $2.

### Dinosaur Trail

Drumheller is at the beginning of Dinosaur Trail (Hwy 838), a 48-km loop around the area. It takes in all the attractions but you'll need a car to cover it. The scenery along the trail is really interesting, as are the views from the top of **Horsethief Canyon** and **Horseshoe Canyon**. There are trails leading down into the canyons where you can poke around in the petrified oyster beds. In **Midland Provincial Park** north-west of Drumheller you can go on self-guided walking tours. There's no camping in the park. Twenty-seven km north-west of Drumheller at the end of the trail you can take the free cable-operated ferry, *Bleriot*, across the river.

The **hoodoos**, about 18 km south-east of Drumheller on Hwy 10, are the best example of these weird, eroded, mushroom-like columns of sandstone rock.

### Royal Tyrell Museum of Palaeontology

This excellent museum (☎ 823-7707), along the North Dinosaur Trail (Hwy 838) north-west of town, uses displays, videos, films, computers, fibre optics etc to outline the study of early life on earth. Fossils of ancient creatures including flying reptiles, prehistoric mammals and amphibious animals help trace the story of evolution; best of all is the extensive display of over 30 complete dinosaur skeletons. It's open daily from 9 am to 9 pm in summer while the rest of the year it's open Tuesday to Sunday from 10 am to 5 pm. Admission is $5.50, except Tuesday when it's free.

### Places to Stay
A few km south of Drumheller the small communities of Rosedale and Wayne each have a small campground; they're free but have no facilities. The *Bleriot Ferry Campground* (☎ 823-1749) has pump water and sites for $5. In town the *Shady Grove Campground* (☎ 823-2576), 25 Poplar St on the northern side of the river, is open year round, has most facilities including showers and charges $10 for a site. A little further north the *Dinosaur Trailer Park* (☎ 823-3291), near the corner of Dinosaur Trail and Hwy 9, has tent sites for $14 and showers.

HI *Alexandra Hostel* (☎ 823-6337), 30 Railway Ave, holds 55 people and has showers, laundromat and kitchen. It costs $10.50 for members, $14.50 for nonmembers.

Drumheller has several hotels on and around Railway Ave, but one of the better value places is the *Badlands Motel* (☎ 823-5155) just north of town on the Dinosaur Trail. It has log cabins with singles/doubles from $39/42.

### Things to Buy
The Fossil Shop, 61 Bridge St immediately north of the bridge, is worth visiting for a look around and perhaps a purchase of a 75 million-year-old souvenir. There are all kinds of bones and dinosaur fragments to examine and the staff are very knowledgeable. Perhaps unexpectedly, some of the findings offered for sale are not at all expensive.

## DINOSAUR PROVINCIAL PARK
No, this isn't Jurassic Park but it's the next best thing. The six-sq-km Dinosaur Provin-

cial Park is a 76.5-million-year-old dinosaur graveyard and is a must if you're passing by. It's 48 km north-east of Brooks, roughly halfway between Calgary and Medicine Hat, off Hwy 544. Entry to the park is free.

The badlands of the park are a dry, convoluted lunar landscape, but they weren't always like this: at one time the area was a tropical rainforest on the shores of an inland sea and dinosaurs thrived there. Their remains and fossils lie buried all over the valley. The **Tyrell Museum Field Station** (☎ 378-4342) has four display areas where nearly complete skeletons have been uncovered, dusted off and encased in glass, just the way they were found.

More than 300 complete skeletons have been found, and many have been sent to museums around the world. Access is restricted but there are guided walks through the strange, eroded landscape, or in summer you can go on a 90-minute bus tour for $4.50. Good photographs are easy; the hoodoos especially, make a good subject. Take plenty of water along in summer (walking in the valley can be as hot as hell), a hat and sunscreen. And the mosquitoes can be unrelenting so make sure you have some insect repellent.

There is a pretty good campground in the park, by a river, making a small, green oasis in this stark place. A site costs $7.

## KINBROOK ISLAND PROVINCIAL PARK
This is a good camping spot on the way to or from Calgary. It's off the Trans Canada Hwy, 13 km south of Brooks then two km east off the secondary road 873 beside Lake Newell. This is an artificial lake home to many species of waterfowl including Canada geese, blue herons, cormorants and pelicans. You can swim and fish, or simply escape the very flat, totally treeless stretch of highway between here and Medicine Hat. The campground (☎ 362-2962/4525) has 167 sites and running water.

## WRITING-ON-STONE PROVINCIAL PARK
This park is south-east of Lethbridge close

ALBERTA

to the US border; the Sweetgrass Hills of northern Montana are visible to the south. To get to the park take Hwy 501 east off Hwy 4 from the town of Milk River, a distance of 42 km. The park gets its name from the carvings and paintings (North America's largest collection of rock art) made by the Plains Indians over 3000 years on the sandstone cliffs along the banks of **Milk River**.

You can see some of these petroglyphs and pictographs for yourself if you follow the two-km hoodoo trail along the north of the valley, but the best are to be found in a restricted area (to protect them from vandalism) which you can only visit on a guided tour (free) with the park ranger. In the valley is a police outpost dating from 1887 which has been restored to its original condition.

The river is used for canoeing and swimming, there's even a small beach beside the

Dall ram

river, and in winter there's cross-country skiing. The park also provides a wide variety of habitats for wildlife, which includes more than 160 species of birds, 30 kinds of mammals, four kinds of amphibians and three kinds of reptiles, not to mention the fish in the river. You can obtain details on all of these from the information office in the park or by contacting Writing-On-Stone Provincial Park (☎ 647-2364), PO Box 297, Milk River T0K 1M0.

The campground by the river has sites for $11 with running water and gets busy at weekends.

## MEDICINE HAT

This city, on the banks of the South Saskatchewan River at the junction of the Trans Canada and Crowsnest highways, was formed in 1883 when the Canadian Pacific railway, drilling for water, hit natural gas. Enough of it was subsequently found to prompt Rudyard Kipling to label it 'the city with all hell for a basement'. Even today the downtown street lamps are lit by gas.

The Visitor Information Centre (☎ 527-6422), 8 Gehring Rd SW south of downtown off the westbound side of the Trans Canada Hwy, is open daily throughout the year: summer hours are 8 am to 9 pm, winter 9 am to 5 pm. The Greyhound Bus Depot (☎ 527-4418), downtown at 557 2nd St SE, is open daily from 5 am to 11 pm. It has left-luggage lockers and a cafeteria. Most of the accommodation is along the Trans Canada Hwy.

From the Visitor Information Centre or from the highway you can see the **'world's tallest teepee'**. It's actually made of metal and was used at the opening and closing ceremonies of the 1988 Olympic games in Calgary; it now resides at Medicine Hat as a permanent tribute to Native Canadians. Medicine Hat is also notable for its parks and walking trails some of which line the South Saskatchewan River, and downtown has some fine old red-brick buildings. If you miss Calgary's Stampede, there's one here during the last week of July at the Exhibition & Stampede Grounds (☎ 527-1234), five km south-east of downtown off 21st Ave SE.

**CYPRESS HILLS PROVINCIAL PARK**
This park, an oasis of forest surrounded by seemingly endless prairie, straddles the Saskatchewan border. It is described in the Saskatchewan chapter.

# The Alberta Rockies

Much of the Rocky Mountain area of Alberta, running along the British Columbia border, is contained and protected within two huge, adjacent national parks Banff to the south and Jasper to the north. The Icefields Parkway links the two, though there is no real boundary. Adjoining the southern boundary of Banff National Park is Kananaskis Country an outdoor recreational area. To the south on the US border is the less-visited Waterton Lakes National Park.

The entire area is one of spectacular beauty with some of the best scenery, climbing, hiking and skiing to be found anywhere in the world. The national parks offer jagged, snow-capped mountains, peaceful valleys, rushing rivers, natural hot springs and alpine forests. The emerald-green colour of many Rocky Mountain lakes will have you doubting your eyes. The parks also have modern conveniences or backcountry trails to choose from and wildlife abounds, particularly in Jasper National Park.

Banff National Park was Canada's first national park and is the best known and most popular, attracting three million visitors annually. It covers an area of 6641 sq km and contains 25 mountains of 3000 metres or more in height. The skiing and climbing are world famous. Jasper National Park is larger, wilder and less explored but, like Banff National Park, offers excellent hiking trails. Waterton Lakes National Park, the smallest of the national parks, contains wildlife, scenery and activities to match its northern neighbours.

In order to preserve the region, the Canada Parks Service controls visitors' impact by designating specific park areas as campgrounds, picnic sites, fireplaces, service centres and townsites. Please stick to these areas and read the section in the *Backcountry Visitors' Guide* on how to minimise your effect on the parks' environment.

The small townsites of Banff, Lake Louise, Jasper, Canmore and Waterton Lakes act as focal points for orientation, supplies and information. In Banff National Park, accommodation during the summer is expensive and hard to find. So it's worth booking ahead or staying in one of the towns outside the park: Canmore, Field, Golden, Radium Hot Springs, Windermere or Invermere in British Columbia, then returning to the park during the day.

## PRECAUTIONS
When in the backcountry it's recommended that water be boiled for at least 10 minutes before drinking it, due to the risk of catching 'beaver fever' or giardiasis. This is caused by an intestinal parasite *(Giardia lamblia)* which is spread by animal waste.

If you're heading into wilderness regions, read the pamphlet *You are in Bear Country* which gives advice on how to steer clear of dangerous encounters with bears and what to do if this becomes unavoidable. You can get a copy from Visitor Information Centres.

The trails heavily used by horse trips are a real mess; long-distance hikers will want to avoid them. Ask at the park warden offices or the Visitor Information Centres which trails are used most by the horses.

Tenters should note that pretty well all the campgrounds in and around the Rockies are covered in pebbles or stones which are rather lumpy for sleeping on the ground! A sleeping pad or foam mattress of some description is more or less essential. Also, you can expect to bend or snap a few tent pegs.

## BANFF & AROUND
Banff, 138 km west of Calgary, is Canada's No 1 resort town in both winter and summer with seven million visitors a year, and as such is really the centre of the Rockies. Despite that, it's very small, consisting of one main street, so it can get crowded. The heaviest months are July and August.

ALBERTA

Although this can cause problems, the many vacationers generally create a relaxed and festive atmosphere. Many of the workers in and around town are newcomers, 'gorbies' (tourists) or long-term visitors themselves.

The town is clean and pleasant, the surroundings unbeatable. It makes a good R&R spot after travelling awhile, or hiking. Stores sell or rent skiing, hiking and camping equipment and supplies. You can do many good day trips and hikes from Banff.

### Orientation

Banff Ave, the main street, runs north-south

through the whole length of town. It heads off north to meet the Trans Canada Hwy. The street is lined with hotels, stores, restaurants and souvenir shops, many of which cater to the heavy Japanese trade. Over the bridge at Banff Ave's southern end is the Parks Administration building. This is a good place for a view and a photo of the town. Behind the building are flower gardens with a stream, ponds and a few benches.

To the left, over the bridge, Mountain Ave leads to Sulphur Mountain and the hot springs, while Spray Ave leads to the Banff Springs Hotel, the town's most famous land-

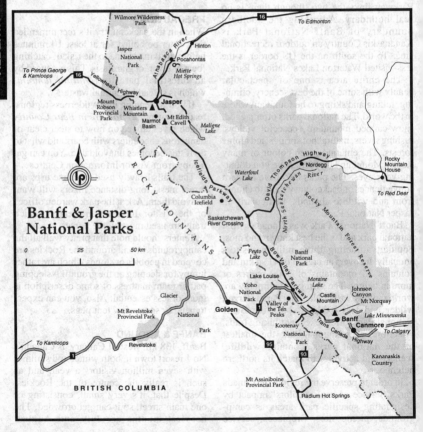

**Banff & Jasper National Parks**

mark. To the right, Cave Ave goes to the Cave & Basin Hot Springs; these were the first springs found in the area and led to the creation of the national park.

The side streets in town are mainly residential but the central ones also have eating spots and a few shops.

Banff Ave Mall is no longer a mall though it has retained the name.

### Information

**Tourist Offices** The Park Information Office and the Chamber of Commerce both have counters in the Visitor Information Centre (☎ 762-1550), 224 Banff Ave near the corner of Wolf St in the centre of town. Before doing any hiking, check in here: there are detailed maps and the staff will tell you about specific trail conditions and hazards. Anybody hiking overnight must sign in. The office also has the leaflet, *You are in Bear Country*. Free naturalist programmes and guided hikes happen regularly. The centre is open daily from 8 am to 8 pm in summer.

**Money** If you need to change money the Foreign Currency Exchange (☎ 762-4698) in the Clock Tower Village Mall is open daily from 9 am to 11 pm. The Bank of Montreal, 107 Banff Ave, opens Saturday from 9 am to 3 pm.

**Post** The main post office (☎ 762-2586), 204 Buffalo St on the corner of Bear St, at the southern end of downtown, is open Monday to Friday from 9 am to 5.30 pm.

**Bookshops & Library** The Book & Art Den (☎ 762-3919), 110 Banff Ave, is an excellent bookshop with all manner of guides and books on the mountains, hiking, canoeing and the history of the area.

The public library (☎ 762-2661) is at 101 Bear St opposite the post office.

**Medical Services** Mineral Springs Hospital (☎ 762-2222) is on Bow Ave near the corner of Wolf St.

**Emergency** The Banff Warden Office

(☎ 762-1470; in emergencies ☎ 762-4506), is open 24 hours daily year round.

**Work** Work is usually easy to come by in and around Banff in the hotels, bars, restaurants and ski areas. However, recent reports indicate that working without a permit has become more difficult for non-Canadians and many establishments are now having to ask for proper documentation. If you want to be absolutely sure of being able to earn some money, inquiring at home for the correct visa is advisable.

Some employers offer accommodation, but don't expect great pay. At some of the hotels accommodation may be included or offered at modest rates. Look for classified advertisements in the local newspaper *Crag & Canyon* and signs in the windows.

**Laundromat** Cascade Coin Laundry, 317 Banff Ave, is open daily in the summer from 7.30 am to 10 pm.

**Warning** Police are very strict in Banff and after 1 am, cars are often checked for drunk drivers and drugs. The fines are heavy. Drinking on the street or even carrying an open beer can or bottle is illegal. Hitchhikers should be aware they may often be thoroughly checked out. Cars are frequently broken into so don't leave valuables in them, especially at night.

Lastly, a warning from a reader about the elk in Banff:

The elk in Banff seem tame and, yes, they do stand in people's gardens munching away at the flowers, but they are still wild animals and will charge if they feel threatened.

I cringed every time a tourist stopped and tried to stand next to these animals for a photograph. People have been attacked by elk and it's advisable to stay 100 metres away particularly during the rutting and calving seasons.

Linda Broschofsky

### Museums

**Banff Park Museum** The park museum (☎ 762-1558), 93 Banff Ave by the Bow River Bridge at the southern end of town, is

| PLACES TO STAY | | OTHER | |
|---|---|---|---|
| 2 | Tunnel Mountain | 29 | Rose & Crown |
| | Village Campground | 31 | The Balkan Restaurant |
| 4 | HI Banff Hostel | 35 | Le Beaujolais |
| 6 | Spruce Grove Motel | | |
| 7 | Irwin's Motor Inn | | OTHER |
| 8 | Red Carpet Inn | | |
| 9 | High Country Inn | 1 | Buffalo Paddock |
| 10 | Mrs McHardy B&B | 3 | Banff Warden Office |
| 12 | Holiday Inn Lodge | 13 | Train Station |
| 14 | Mrs C Riva B&B | 17 | Banff Centre |
| 15 | Mr & Mrs Harnack B&B | 18 | RCMP |
| 16 | Mrs J Cowan B&B | 20 | Visitor Information Centre |
| 23 | Banff Park Lodge | 26 | Sundance Mall |
| 30 | Mt Royal Hotel | 32 | Bank of Montreal |
| 44 | YWCA | 33 | Barbary Coast |
| 46 | Banff Springs Hotel | 34 | Silver City |
| | | 36 | Clock Tower Village Mall |
| PLACES TO EAT | | 37 | Main Post Office |
| | | 38 | Whyte Museum |
| 5 | Bumper's Beef House | 39 | Public Library |
| 11 | Gus's Family Restaurant | 40 | Banff Park Museum |
| 19 | Rundle Restaurant | 41 | Mineral Springs Hospital |
| 21 | Rocky Mountain Ground | 42 | Bus Depot |
| 22 | Smitty's Family Restaurant | 43 | Canoe Dock |
| 24 | Melissa's Restaurant | 45 | Luxton Museum |
| 25 | Joe Btfsplk's Diner | 47 | Martin Stables |
| 27 | Grizzly House | 48 | Middle Springs |
| 28 | Magpie & Stump | 49 | Upper Hot Springs |
| | | 50 | Cave & Basin |
| | | | Centennial Centre |

housed in an old wooden building dating from 1903. The museum has been declared a National Historic Site and contains a collection of animals, birds and plants found in Banff National Park. Included are two small stuffed grizzlies and a black bear so you can study the difference. There's also an 1841 graffiti-carved tree. The museum is open daily from 10 am to 6 pm in summer (from 1 to 5 pm the rest of the year) and admission is free; at 4 pm daily there is a free half-hour tour.

**Natural History Museum** This museum (☎ 762-4747), on the 2nd floor of the Clock Tower Village Mall at 112 Banff Ave, has displays on early life forms, including Canadian dinosaurs. It has video and slide presentations and features a model of the notorious Sasquatch, the abominable snowman of the Rockies. The Sasquatch of Western Canada, is said to be about three metres tall and to have been spotted over 500 times. You can also read descriptions of Castleguard Cave, one of Canada's biggest at 12 km long, which is in the north of Banff National Park. The museum is open daily in summer from 10 am to 10 pm and admission is $2.

**Luxton Museum** Luxton Museum (☎ 762-2388), 1 Birch Ave in the fort-like wooden building to the right as you head south over the bridge, is worth a visit. It deals mainly with the Native Indians of the Northern Plains and the Rockies but also covers indigenous groups from all over Alberta. The museum has displays, models and re-creations depicting aspects of their traditional cultures including clothing, weapons and

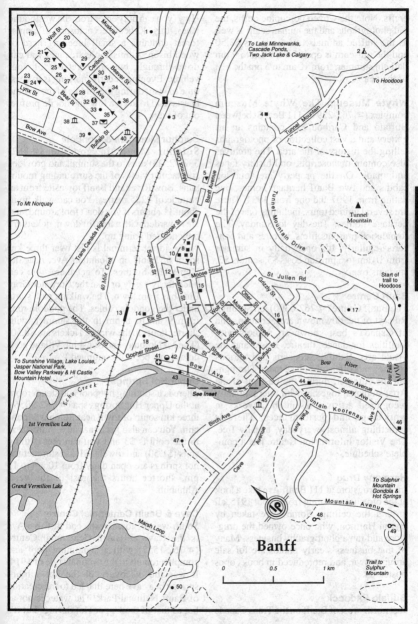

ALBERTA

**To Lake Minnewanka,
Cascade Ponds,
Two Jack Lake & Calgary**

To Hoodoos

Tunnel Mountain

To Mt Norquay

Tunnel
Mountain

Tunnel Mountain Drive

Start of
trail to
Hoodoos

St Julien Rd

Grizzly St

Cougar St

Marmot Cres

Banff Avenue

Moose Street

Squirrel St

Marten St

Wolf St
Otter St
Muskrat St
Beaver St
Banff Caribou St
Avenue
Street

Buffalo St

Elk St

To Sunshine Village, Lake Louise,
Jasper National Park,
Bow Valley Parkway & HI Castle
Mountain Hotel

Gopher Street

Bear Street
Lynx St

Bow
Ave

Bow     River

Glen Avenue

Spray Ave

Bow Falls

Mount Norquay Rd

Echo Creek

40 Mile Creek

Trans Canada Highway

1st Vermilion Lake

Grand Vermilion Lake

Birch Ave

Cave     Avenue

Park Ave

Mountain    Kootenay    Ave

To Sulphur
Mountain Gondola &
Hot Springs

Mountain Avenue

Marsh Loop

**Banff**

Trail to
Sulphur
Mountain

0        0.5        1 km

*Inset (top left):*

Wolf St
Muskrat
Beaver St
Caribou St
Banff Ave
Bear St
Lynx St
Bow Ave
Buffalo St

19    20
21    29
22    25    30    31    34
26    27    28    32    36
23    24    33    35
38    37
39    40

*Map labels:*

1
2
3
4
5
6
7   8   9
10   11
12
13   14
15
16
17
18
41   42
43
44
45
46
47
48
49
50

See Inset

crafts. Note the woven porcupine quills, the old photographs and the human scalp as well as the stuffed animals. Admission is $3.50 and the museum is open from 9 am to 9 pm daily in summer, from 10 am to 5 pm the rest of the year.

**Whyte Museum** The Whyte Museum complex (☎ 762-2291), 111 Bear St between Buffalo and Caribou Sts, contains an art gallery and a vast collection of photographs telling the history of the area. The archives also contain manuscripts, oral history tapes and maps. On the property are four log cabins and two Banff heritage homes, one dating from 1907 and one from 1931. There are several guided tours, including one of the heritage homes, Tuesday to Sunday. The foundation presents films, lectures and concerts regularly. It's open daily in summer from 10 am to 6 pm and costs $3, seniors $2, students free.

**Banff Centre**
The Banff Centre (☎ 762-6300), on St Julien Rd east of the downtown area, contains one of Canada's best known art schools with facilities for dance, theatre, music and the visual arts. Exhibits, concerts and various other events often take place there. Throughout the summer, during the Festival of the Arts, students, together with internationally recognised artists, present their works in workshops and performances. There is something almost every day, usually free. The Visitor Information Centre has a complete schedule.

**Harmony Drug**
In this drugstore at 111 Banff Ave take a look at the old photos, dating from about 1915, all around the ceiling. Some were taken by Byron Harmon, who once owned the drugstore and ran a photography business. Many of that business's early photos are for sale around town, and reproduced in books or as postcards.

**Buffalo Paddock**
Just north-west of Banff on the Trans Canada

Hwy (you can only enter from the westbound lane), this 40-hectare enclosure of poplar forest contains a small breeding herd of wood bison. Admission is free and you can drive through, but *don't* get out of your vehicle. Evening or early morning is the best time to visit; during the middle of the day the beasts tend to keep a low and docile profile, out of view.

**Sulphur Mountain & Gondola**
Sulphur Mountain gondola (☎ 762-3324/2523) runs to the summit and provides spectacular views of the surrounding mountains, Bow River and Banff townsite from an altitude of 2285 metres. You can walk up in about 1¼ hours if you don't fool around, and are rewarded with a free lift down: tickets are only needed going up.

The lower terminal is just over three km south of Banff on Mountain Ave, near the Upper Hot Springs. To get there, you can hitch fairly easily or take the Brewster Gray Line bus from town. The walking path starts under the gondola cables. The gondola runs from 9 am to 8 pm in the summer, with shorter hours in the winter. Tickets are $8.50. (The Mt Norquay and Sunshine Village gondolas have been discontinued.)

**Upper Hot Springs**
There is a soothing hot pool and steam room at the Upper Hot Springs spa (☎ 762-2056), three km south of town near Sulphur Mountain. You can also get a massage. Admission to the pool is $3 and you can rent bathing suits ($1.50) and towels ($1). In summer the hot springs are open daily from 10 am to 11 pm; shorter hours the rest of the year. Ahhhhhh.

**Cave & Basin Centennial Centre**
South-west of town at the end of Cave Ave is the Cave & Basin Centennial Centre (☎ 762-1557) with a swimming pool and complex rebuilt to the original style of 1914. It was the discovery of the hot sulphur springs in a cave here that led to the creation of Banff National Park. The water is not as hot as that of the Upper Hot Springs but it's

still comfortably warm. At the time of writing the pool was closed for repairs. The site also has several pleasant short walks: the 400-metre **Discovery Trail**; the 2.7-km **Marsh Loop** and the 3.7-km **Sundance Trail**. The centre has exhibits, films and a coffee shop. It's open daily from 9 am to 7 pm between the end of May and early September (from 9.30 am to 5 pm the rest of the year) and admission is free.

### Lake Minnewanka

Lake Minnewanka, the largest lake in the park, 11 km east of Banff townsite, is a scenic recreational area surrounded by forests and mountains with hiking, swimming, sailing, boating and fishing available. Lake Minnewanka Boat Tours (☎ 762-3473; 762-6767 for bus pick up) has a two-hour cruise on the lake to Devil's Gap for $20.

### Activities

**Hiking** There are many good short hikes and day walks around the Banff area. From the Visitor Information Centre get a copy of *Drives & Walks* which describes trails in and around Banff. For longer, more remote hiking, the leaflet *Backcountry Visitors' Guide* has a map showing trails in the whole park. Some good walks begin more or less right in town, like the ones to Tunnel Mountain and the hoodoos; others begin a little further out.

You can take a pleasant, quiet stroll by **Bow River** just three blocks west of Banff Ave beside Bow Ave. The trail runs from the corner of Wolf St, along the river under the Bow River Bridge and ends shortly thereafter on Buffalo St. If you cross the bridge, you can continue left through the woods along a trail to **Bow Falls** it's not far.

For a good short climb to break in the legs and to view the town and area, walk up stubby **Tunnel Mountain** east of the downtown area. There's a trail leading up from St Julien Rd; you can drive here, but it's not a long walk from downtown to the start of the path. From the southern end of Buffalo St a trail between Bow River and Tunnel Mountain heads north to the **hoodoos**.

Just west of downtown off Mt Norquay Rd is the two-km **Fenland Trail** loop which goes through marsh and forest and connects the town with First Vermilion Lake. If you follow Banff Ave north from town towards Lake Minnewanka for about five km you come to **Cascade Ponds**, just past the Trans Canada Hwy. There you can follow the trail north to join the **Bankhead Interpretive Trail** or climb up beside the waterfall for good views.

One good hike, that's not difficult, begins at **Johnston Canyon**. This is 25 km northwest of Banff on the **Bow Valley Parkway** (Hwy 1A), that branches off, then later rejoins, the Trans Canada Hwy en route to Lake Louise. The 12-km trail goes by many waterfalls, including two large ones, to some underground-fed crystal-clear, blue-green pools known as the Ink Pots. Here in the meadow is an ideal picnic spot. Along the Bow Valley Parkway watch for impressive **Castle Mountain**, also called Eisenhower Mountain: it's a huge piece of rock that catches the late afternoon light. From Castle Mountain you can follow the **Rockbound Lake Trail**, which is 18 km return, takes about six to seven hours and has some strenuous patches. The trailhead is opposite HI Castel Mountain Hostel.

At **Sunshine Village** you'll find long and short trails. On one of the trails you can walk across the boundary into British Columbia. A popular trail is the overnight trip to nearby **Egypt Lake**. From Sunshine Village it's a long, steady climb with great scenery over **Healy Pass**, including views to Mt Assiniboine (3618 metres) in British Columbia. You'll see lots of butterflies and flowers in the alpine meadows. You can take hikes to the higher lakes and fish for cutthroat trout. At the lakes is a basic hut that sleeps about 10 people, but you should register in Banff before you go because it may be booked out. There's tenting around the hut so a place inside is not essential. **Mt Norquay** offers good hiking trails.

**Skiing** Two of the finest ski centres in Canada are Mt Norquay and Sunshine

Village. At Mt Norquay, nine km north of Banff along Mt Norquay Rd, the ski season is from November to April. A day pass is $30. For information contact Mt Norquay (☎ 762-4421), PO Box 1258, Banff T0L 0C0. For a snow report call ☎ 221-8259. Sunshine Village, 22 km north-west of Banff, has the longer ski season lasting about seven months from mid-November to mid-June. It has 62 downhill runs the longest of which is eight km. A day pass is $35. For information (and snow report), call or write to Sunshine Village (☎ 762-6500) PO Box 1510, Banff T0L 0C0.

Many of the hiking trails become cross-country ski trails in winter.

Several companies offer heliskiing, where a helicopter flies you to a mountain and you ski out. Banff Helisports (☎ 678-4888), PO Box 2326, Banff T0L 0C0, has daily flights including guide and equipment for around $130.

**Climbing** Quite a few companies offer climbing courses and organised tours into the mountains. Beginners can start by using the climbing wall Monday, Tuesday or Thursday from 7 am to 9 pm at Mountain Magic Equipment (☎ 762-2591), 224 Bear St. It has classes ($15) each evening from Monday to Friday but will also give private lessons. Experienced climbers can use the wall free of charge. The Canadian School of Mountaineering (☎ 678-4134) is just outside the park in Canmore at 629 9th St. A weekend of rock climbing costs $130 for beginners or $188 for those at the intermediate level; it also has snow and ice climbing. Most fees include dormitory accommodation, breakfast, equipment and instruction. Banff Alpine Guides (☎ 670-6091) offer climbing instruction and guided climbs from $220 a day. The Alpine Club of Canada (☎ 678-2222) in Canmore can provide information and/or a guide.

**Canoeing & Rafting** You can go canoeing on **Two Jack Lake** north-east of Banff, the **Vermilion Lakes** (which have lots of wildlife) west of town, **Echo Creek, 40 Mile**

**Creek** and **Bow River**. Rocky Mountain Raft Tours (☎ 762-3632), rents canoes for $10/30 per hour/day from Canoe Dock by the river on the corner of Bow Ave and Wolf St. It also offers a one-hour rafting tour on the Bow River from Bow Falls to the hoodoos for $18 and three-hour trips for $33. For white-water rafting Kootenay River Runners (☎ 762-5385), on the corner of Banff Ave and Caribou St, has half-day and full-day trips.

**Cycling** You can cycle on the highways and on some of the trails in the park. Contact the Visitor Information Centre for trail conditions and permits. Excursions for a few hours, a day or several days with overnight stops at campgrounds, hostels or lodges are all possible. No cycling is allowed off the trails. Two good, short cycling routes close to Banff are along **Vermilion Lakes Drive** and **Tunnel Mountain Drive**. For a longer trip the scenic, 24-km **Bow Valley Parkway** connecting Banff and Lake Louise is very popular.

Banff Mountain Bike Tours (☎ 762-5459) has a 1½-hour tour for $10 and a half-day tour for $45; destinations include Tunnel Mountain, the Bow Falls and Vermilion Lakes. Mountain Coasters (☎ 678-6770) has cycling tours along the Icefield and Bow Valley parkways for $75. For bicycle rentals see the Getting Around section later.

**Horse Riding** In Banff the most popular routes are south of Bow River on the trail beside **Spray River**, the **Marsh Loop**, the **Sundance Trail**, the trail alongside **Cave Ave** and the one to **Middle Springs**. Warner Guiding & Outfitting (☎ 762-4551), 132 Banff Ave, offers horse-riding trips from one hour to one week in length. Martin's Stables (☎ 762-2832), on Birch Ave, and Banff Springs Hotel (☎ 762-2848) offer one to three-hour trips. Rates start at $18 per hour.

**Organised Tours**
Brewster Gray Line (☎ 672-6700) does a three-hour tour of Banff for $29.50. The bus goes to the hoodoos, Bow Falls, Tunnel

Mountain Drive, Buffalo Paddock and Sulphur Mountain.

Brewster Gray Line also runs tours to Lake Louise, the Columbia Icefield and Jasper. The tour to Lake Louise goes via the Vermilion Lakes and Bow Valley Parkway stopping at Johnston Canyon and Castle Mountain. The round trip takes four hours and costs $35. The tour to the Columbia Icefield in Jasper National Park takes approximately 9½ hours one way and costs $59.50. Rates are cheaper in the off-peak season. The return trip to Jasper takes two days and requires an overnight stay there; you travel to Lake Louise along the Icefields Parkway stopping at the Columbia Icefield with time allowed for a ride on the Athabasca Glacier, though that's not included in the price. The return fare is $83 and accommodation is extra. The rates are cheaper outside the peak season.

Tours in a helicopter offering spectacular views of the park are also available. Some popular sights are Mt Rundle, Mt Assiniboine, Bow River Valley, the Goat and Sundance mountain ranges, Spray Lakes, Hidden Glacier and the Three Sisters. Rates start at $75 for a 20-minute flight. Operators include Mountain Wings (☎ 678-6465), Canmore Helicopters (☎ 678-4802), Canadian Helicopters (☎ 678-2207) and Brewster Gray Line (☎ 672-6700).

If you're driving, you can hire or buy ($19.95) a self-guiding auto cassette tape that describes the journey between Banff and Jasper via Lake Louise and the Columbia Icefield. It's available at the Thunderbird Gift Shop (☎ 762-4661), 215 Banff Ave, or Miles High Image Centre at No 119.

## Places to Stay

Generally, accommodation here is fairly costly. The numerous motels are usually moderately priced, but the hotels are expensive. If you're not camping or hostelling, B&Bs and private tourist homes can be a reasonable alternative in many cases and are often interesting places to stay as well as good sources of local information.

As an alternative to finding accommodation in Banff, some people watching their wallets stay in the town of Canmore just outside the park, where the rates are lower; they then enter the park on a day basis.

**Camping** There are many campgrounds in the area around Banff. Most are only open between May or June and September. Note that they are all busy in July and August, and availability is on a first-come, first-served basis so book in by noon or you may well be turned away.

Tunnel Mountain Village is not bad. Tunnel Mountain is close to town and has three sites, two for RVs only and one for tents at $15.50 per site plus shower. At night you may hear coyotes yelping and howling. At Two Jack Lake there are a couple of campgrounds. Two Jack Lakeside, 12 km north-east of Banff on Lake Minnewanka Rd, is open from July to early September and costs $13 per site. One km north, Two Jack Lake Main has 381 sites at $10.50 each. Both campgrounds have running water but no showers. Along the Bow Valley Parkway there is a campground at Johnston Canyon, about 26 km west of Banff, and at Castle Mountain two km north of Castle Junction. Sites at both cost $13.

Alternatively, there are those who unfold sleeping bags anywhere in the woods surrounding Banff, including just up the road towards Sulphur Mountain. If you do this *don't* ever light a fire or use the food bag for a pillow. Who knows what animal is on the prowl?

**Hostels** HI *Banff Hostel* (☎ 762-4122), on Tunnel Mountain Rd three km from the downtown area, has 154 beds in small rooms, a cafeteria, laundromat and a common room with a fireplace. Members pay $16, nonmembers $21. The *YWCA* (☎ 762-3560), 102 Spray Ave, is more central but the facilities aren't as good. It takes men and women, can hold up to 60 people and has a cafeteria but no cooking facilities. Dorm beds are $17, and rooms are singles/doubles $47/51 without/with bath.

HI *Castle Mountain Hostel* on the Bow

ALBERTA

Valley Parkway, holds up to 36 people, has pit toilets, hot showers and volleyball courts. For members a dorm bed is $10, for non-members $15. It's closed on Wednesday nights.

**B&Bs & Tourist Homes** The Chamber of Commerce desk in the Visitor Information Centre gives a list of people offering B&B and tourist-home accommodation. Two B&B reservation agencies are: Rocky Mountain B&B (☎ 762-4811), 223 Otter St, and Banff B&B Bureau (☎ 762-5070), PO Box 369, Banff T0L 0C0. Some places rent out rooms in their houses, others in small separate cabins.

The prices for B&Bs and tourist homes vary, depending on their size and facilities, your duration of stay and the season, but are generally in the $25 to $80 range for a single or double. Banff has quite a few but you should telephone around first. Some prefer at least a week's stay, some prefer not to take young people or may ask if you're married. They get busy on weekends, so calling saves legwork.

*Mrs J Cowan* (☎ 762-3696), 118 Otter St, has eight rooms which she rents all year. Rooms without/with bathroom cost $20/45 with a continental breakfast. *Mr & Mrs Harnack* (☎ 762-3619), 338 Banff Ave, have six rooms at $25/45 a single/double. They also have two larger self-contained cabins out the back. *Mrs C Riva* (☎ 762-3431), 328 Elk St, has one room ($40) and one cabin ($50) with accommodation for up to eight people.

Marten St has several tourist homes. *Holiday Inn Lodge* (☎ 762-3648), 311 Marten St, run by George Baptist, is one of the nicest in town. George is a good source of information about Banff and cooks a great breakfast. Out the back, George also has two cabins with cooking facilities which hold four people. Rooms cost between $35 and $75. *Mrs McHardy* (☎ 762-2176), 412 Marten St, offers cabins with hot plates for $40 a double.

**Hotels** Banff has no cheap hotels anymore.

Downtown, *Rundle Manor Apartment Hotel* (☎ 762-5544), 348 Marten St, has rooms with kitchens for $108 a single or double. Children under 16 years of age can stay in their parents' room for free. The *Mt Royal Hotel* (☎ 762-3331), 138 Banff Ave, has absorbed the Cascade Inn; facilities include a sauna and hot tub. Rooms are $148/158 a single/double. The historic *Banff Springs Hotel* (☎ 762-2211), on Spray Ave south of downtown, has everything including golf course, tennis courts, riding stables, bars and restaurants. Singles or doubles cost from $165 to $337.

**Motels** Most accommodation is in motels many of which are on Banff Ave north of Elk St; they are not cheap either but are not as costly as the hotels. There are many places geared for skiers, which offer kitchens and can be good value if there are four of you or more. Of course, there are many deluxe places too if you're looking to really splurge.

*Spruce Grove Motel* (☎ 762-2112), 545 Banff Ave, has standard rooms with colour TV and charges singles from $39 to $65. *Red Carpet Inn* (☎ 762-4184), 425 Banff Ave, is close to town and charges singles/doubles $75/85. It has a licensed restaurant and spa and is usually full in summer. Close by, *Irwin's Motor Inn*, 429 Banff Ave, has covered parking and charges $65/80.

*High Country Inn* (☎ 762-2236), 419 Banff Ave, has air-con and heated parking and rooms for $80/95. If you don't want to stay in town *Johnston Canyon Resort* (☎ 762-2971) is one of the cheaper motels but it's 26 km west on the Bow Valley Parkway. Singles or doubles cost from $51 to $72; rooms with a kitchen cost extra. Groceries are available. The resort is open mid-May to the end of September.

**Places to Eat**
Like any resort town, Banff has plenty of restaurants. It's a good place to catch up on a meal or two if you've been in the back-country. There are plenty of places to choose from but prices tend to be a bit high.

**Places to Eat – bottom end** For reasonably priced meals try *Café Alpenglow* in the HI Banff Hostel and the *cafeteria* in the YWCA. Their breakfast specials cost around $4. If you make an early start you can have the breakfast special in the *Summit Restaurant* atop Sulphur Mountain for $3.95 between 8.30 and 9.30 am.

There are several places opposite the Visitor Information Centre. *Joe Btfsplk's Diner* (pronounced 'bi-tif-splik'), 221 Banff Ave, is a busy US-style diner, with juke boxes on the walls, open daily from 8 am to 10 pm. It has breakfast specials of two eggs, bacon and toast for $4, burgers from $6.25. *Smitty's Family Restaurant*, 227 Banff Ave, is always reliable if not great. The best value are the five pancakes with syrup for $4.75 and the $3.95 breakfast special. Smitty's is open daily from 6.30 am to 10 pm.

North along the street, *Rundle Restaurant*, 319 Banff Ave, is one of the few steady long-term places that doesn't even try to be trendy. It's straightforward, reasonable and a good spot for breakfast. Pancakes are $3.75 and omelettes start from $4. It also serves Chinese food. Nearby, *Rocky Mountain Ground*, in Banff Ave Mall, is a café selling gourmet coffee and snacks. For those of you who would rather be eating chocolate, go to *The Fudgery* in the Sundance Mall on Banff Ave or *Welch's Chocolate Shop* at No 126. It's great for on the trails, and besides, you're burning off calories, right?

**Places to Eat – middle** For something a bit tastier try the popular *Magpie & Stump*, 203 Caribou St on the corner of Bear St. Built like an old-style saloon with cosy brown colours inside, it serves mainly Mexican (including vegetarian) food like tacos, enchiladas and burritos from $10. It also serves steaks and is open from noon till midnight. Meals are cheaper at lunch time.

Also up the ladder a rung is *Melissa's Restaurant*, 217 Lynx St near the corner of Caribou St, looking sort of like a wood cabin inside and sort of like an English cottage outside. The menu includes pizza, steaks and seafood with main dishes between $8 to $20.

It has a bar and is open daily from 7 am to 10 pm.

The *Balkan Restaurant*, 120 Banff Ave, is a moderately priced Greek-style restaurant with a very good reputation, open daily from 11 am to 11 pm. It offers Greek dishes like moussaka and souvlaki plus pastas and seafood. Dinner including side dishes and salad costs between $7 and $17. *Michael's Café*, 415 Banff Ave next to High Country Inn, is good for soups, sandwiches, salads and burgers. Much of the food is organically grown and the menu includes vegetarian dishes. Breakfast costs from $4 to $8 and dinner up to $18.

**Places to Eat – top end** For a splurge, try *Grizzly House*, 207 Banff Ave, open daily from 11.30 am to midnight. It's basically a fondue place with prices for main courses starting from $17. It serves a variety of food including beef, seafood and escargots. Appetisers like onion soup are $4.95 while rattlesnake fondue, at the top of the price list, is $56!

There are several other places for splurges serving steaks, seafood, Italian or French food. *Le Beaujolais*, 212 Buffalo St on the corner of Banff Ave, is expensive but highly rated. Main dishes of steak, fish or poultry cost between $18 and $35. The restaurant is open daily from 6 to 11 pm. *Bumper's Beef House*, 603 Banff Ave north of downtown behind a service station, serves beef for around $18, and has a salad bar and casual atmosphere.

The *Terrace Lounge*, in the Banff Park Lodge at 222 Lynx St, serves mainly seafood. Main meals cost between $11 and $18. Also in the Banff Park Lodge, the *Chinook Family Restaurant* serves a good-value Sunday brunch. The excellent desserts and pastries are made here fresh daily.

### Entertainment

Banff is the social and cultural focus of the Rockies. You can find current listings in the free *Bow Valley This Week* newspaper.

The *Banff Centre* (☎ 762-6100), St Julien Rd, presents movies, theatre and concerts

**ALBERTA**

throughout the year, but especially from June to late August during the Festival of the Arts, when it puts on over 80 performances.

The *Lux Cinema Centre* (☎ 762-8595), 229 Bear St on the corner of Wolf St, is a four-screen commercial cinema. *Rundle United Church*, 104 Banff Ave on the corner of Buffalo St, shows the one-hour movie *Challenge*, at 4, 7 and 9 pm daily in summer. (For a description see Entertainment under Jasper later.) For information call ☎ 7624214.

The *Rose & Crown*, 202 Banff Ave on the corner of Caribou St, is a British-style pub and restaurant which has live rock music and one room where you can play darts. At *Grizzly House* there's live jazz and recorded music nightly from 9 pm to 1 am. *Bumper's Beef House* has live music till 1 am. *Silver City*, 110 Banff Ave, is a bar with live music at weekends; it's open from 4 pm to 2 am. *Barbary Coast*, upstairs at 119 Banff Ave, has live music, including blues, most nights.

Many of the larger hotels and motels provide their own live entertainment.

### Getting There & Away
**Bus** Greyhound (☎ 762-6767) buses run from the Brewster Transportation Depot, 100 Gopher St, near the police station. Greyhound no longer goes to Jasper. There are five buses daily to Calgary and Vancouver. All Vancouver buses stop at Lake Louise, some also stop in Kelowna or Kamloops.

One bus makes the journey via Radium Hot Springs. You can stop off at Lake Louise for free with a ticket on to Vancouver provided you let the company know beforehand. The one-way fare including tax to Lake Louise is $6.63 and to Calgary $14.28. Note that some buses to Calgary go downtown, others go straight to the international airport.

Brewster Transportation (☎ 762-6767) has one bus a day to Jasper; it takes about 4½ hours and the one-way fare is $37. It also operates a bus daily between Calgary's international airport and Banff for $26 one way; Pacific Western (☎ 762-4558) runs a similar service. These fares include tax.

**Train** VIA Rail no longer goes through Banff. However, the privately owned 'Rocky Mountaineer' travels via Banff between Calgary and Vancouver. The one-way fare from Banff to Vancouver is $529 which includes meals and an overnight stop in a hotel in Kamloops. The service runs between the end of May and early October, and leaves Banff Tuesday, Thursday and Sunday for Vancouver at 9.20 am. For information contact a travel agent or the Great Canadian Railtour Company (☎ 604-984-3131; 1-800-665-7245), 104 340 Brooksbank Ave, North Vancouver.

The train station is the ochre building at the northern end of Lynx St past the police station, close to the downtown area.

**Car** The major car-rental companies have offices in Banff. Their addresses are:

Avis
    Cascade Plaza, Wolf St (☎ 762-3222, 1-800-879-2847)
Budget
    204 Wolf St (☎ 762-4565)
Hertz
    Banff Springs Hotel, Spray Ave (☎ 762-2027, 1-800-263-0600)
Tilden
    Corner of Lynx St & Caribou Ave (☎ 762-2688, 1-800-387-4747)

Tilden is about the cheapest charging $23 plus 16 cents per km for the smallest cars; by the week it's $138 plus the km charge. Insurance is $11. Hertz charges $32.95 per day with the first 200 km free and 12 cents per km after that. Insurance is $12.95 per day. Rates vary all the time so ring around. During the busy summer months the weekends especially can be booked out, so reserving in advance is a good idea.

### Getting Around
**Bus** Banff Explorer Transit Service operates two bus routes through town. One goes along Banff and Spray Aves between Banff Springs Hotel and the RV parking lot north of town; the other goes from the Luxton Museum along Banff Ave, Wolf St, Otter St and

Tunnel Mountain Rd to Tunnel Mountain Village One Campground. Buses go every half hour and cost $1.

Brewster Transportation has a bus departing the Banff Springs Hotel for Sulphur Mountain hourly between 9.40 am and 4.40 pm. It only goes as far as the Upper Hot Springs; if you're going to the gondola it's a short walk from there to the lower terminal. The one-way fare is $4. The bus also acts a shuttle between the hotel and downtown.

**Bicycle** Park n' Pedal (☎ 762-3191), 226 Bear St near the corner of Wolf St, rents bicycles and is open from 9 am to 8 pm. Most bikes cost $6/24 per hour/day. Peak Experience (☎ 762-0581), 209 Bear St, rents mountain bikes for $7/24 while Performance Ski & Sports (☎ 762-8222), 208 Bear St, charges $6/26. Bactrax Bike Rental (☎ 762-8177) at the Ptarmigan Inn, 339 Banff Ave, charges $5/20; it's open from 8 am to 8 pm.

**Hitching** Hitchhiking is common in and around town.

## LAKE LOUISE

About 57 km north-west of Banff is Lake Louise, the jewel of the Rockies. There isn't much in the village of Lake Louise but don't let that put you off; carry on to the lake itself, five km away. It's a much-visited but gorgeous lake sitting in a small glacial valley, surrounded by green, snow-capped mountains. A visit to the lake is best early in the morning when it's less crowded, and there are better reflections in the water. There are also some good nearby walks and hikes.

### Information

The Visitor Information Centre (☎ 522-3833) in the village is open daily during the summer from 8 am to 8 pm (from 9 am to 5 pm in winter). It has an exhibition on the geological and natural history of the Rocky Mountains. In Samson Mall nearby you can buy basic grocery supplies and hire camping equipment; the laundromat offers showers. Woodruff & Blum bookshop (☎ 522-3842) has general guides to the Canadian Rockies,

as well as hiking, cycling and climbing guides and maps.

### Things to See & Do

**Mt Whitehorn** East of the village along Lake Louise Drive is Mt Whitehorn. A gondola (☎ 522-3555) takes you to the top from which there are hiking trails and views of Lake Louise and Victoria Glacier. The gondola ride costs $9 for the round trip. Mt Whitehorn is an important ski centre in winter.

**Hiking** For a short stroll, there's a path on the southern banks of Lake Louise beginning by the boathouse which goes through spruce forest and offers excellent views of the lake and the Chateau Lake Louise Hotel.

One trail follows the northern banks of the lake westward to the **Plain of Six Glaciers**. On the way, between the lake and the lookout at the end of the trail, is a teahouse. For a more rigorous venture take the switchbacks up to **Mirror Lake**. There's another teahouse here and good views from **Little Beehive** or **Big Beehive** (not real beehives, but mountains shaped like them). From there you can climb still higher to **Lake Agnes**, then around the long way to join the Plain of Six Glaciers trail and back along Lake Louise to the hotel. These are both a good day's walk.

Another option is to drive from Lake Louise 15 km south to **Moraine Lake**. From there the roughly 20-km return hike through the **Valley of the 10 Peaks** is highly recommended. Take a quick detour to **Larch Valley** where there's a stream and superb scenery. Before Larch Valley a trail heads west past **Eiffel Lake** into Yoho National Park. Better still, hike to Moraine Lake from Lake Louise via **Paradise Creek** and **Sentinel Pass**. This is a full day's hike with some steep parts but is an excellent route, with great scenery. You can do it the other way round but that's doing it the easy way! Getting up through Sentinel Pass is a long, scree-filled trek but well worth it. At the top, 2600 metres high, it's cool and breezy. Once at Moraine Lake you can hitch back to Lake Louise along Moraine Lake Rd.

ALBERTA

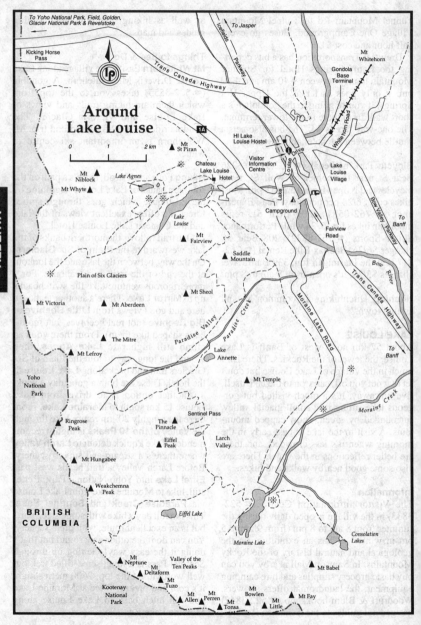

To Yoho National Park, Field, Golden,
Glacier National Park & Revelstoke

Kicking Horse
Pass

Trans Canada Highway

To Jasper

Icefields Parkway

Mt
Whitehorn

Gondola
Base
Terminal

Whitehorn Road

# Around
# Lake Louise

0        1        2 km

1

1A

HI Lake
Louise Hostel

Chateau
Lake Louise
Hotel

Visitor
Information
Centre

Lake Louise Drive

Lake Louise
Village

Mt
St Piran

Mt
Niblock

Lake Agnes

Mt Whyte

Campground

Fairview
Road

To
Banff

Bow Valley Parkway

Lake
Louise

Mt
Fairview

Saddle
Mountain

Bow River

Trans Canada Highway

Plain of Six Glaciers

Mt Sheol

Paradise Valley

Moraine Lake Road

Mt Victoria

Mt Aberdeen

Paradise Creek

Lake
Annette

To
Banff

Moraine Creek

The Mitre

Mt Lefroy

Yoho
National
Park

Mt Temple

Sentinel Pass

The
Pinnacle

Larch
Valley

Ringrose
Peak

Eiffel
Peak

Mt Hungabee

Weakchemna
Peak

BRITISH
COLUMBIA

Eiffel Lake

Moraine Lake

Consolation
Lakes

Mt Neptune

Mt
Deltaform

Valley of the
Ten Peaks

Mt
Tuzo

Kootenay
National
Park

Mt
Allen

Mt
Perren

Mt
Tonsa

Mt
Bowlen

Mt
Little

Mt Fay

Mt Babel

ALBERTA

There are other trails in the area as well: the brochure *Drives & Walks* lists and describes them.

It is common to see pikas (plump, furry animals also called conies) and the larger, more timid marmot along these trails. You often hear ice rumbling on the slopes, too.

After your hikes, back at the Chateau Lake Louise Hotel, the cafeteria in the basement has reasonably priced snacks.

**Climbing** Rock climbing on the **Back of the Lake**, a backwater crag, is popular. Access is easy and there are lots of different routes with interesting names like Wicked Gravity and Chocolate Bunnies from Hell. Other places to climb, of varying degrees of difficulty, are **Mt Fairview, Mt Bell, Mt Niblock, Eiffel Peak, Mt Temple** and **Mt Whyte**.

### Places to Stay
**Camping** The two campgrounds in Lake Louise are run by the Canadian Parks Service and are both on the Trans Canada Hwy. The tenting campground, off Moraine Lake Rd, is open year round with sites for $12; the RV campground is open mid-May to early September with sites for $14. Both have flush toilets but no showers.

**Hostel** The HI *Lake Louise Hostel* (☎ 522-2200), on Village Rd north of Samson Mall, has eased pressure on accommodation in the townsite in summer. There's room for 105 people and it has a kitchen, showers and laundromat. Dorm beds cost $15 for members, $20 for nonmembers. It also has private rooms.

**Hotels** Of the hotels in the area *Lake Louise Inn* (☎ 522-3791; 1-800-661-9237), 210 Village Rd, offers the best value with full facilities including a gym. Rooms start from $70. For something more rustic try *Baker Creek Chalets* (☎ 522-3761), 12 km east of Lake Louise Village on the Bow Valley Parkway, which has log cabins with fireplaces, also starting at $70.

### Getting There & Around
The bus to Jasper leaves from Lake Louise Inn and costs $32. No buses run from the village to the lake but hitching is fairly easy; taxis do the trip for about $7 one way.

## ICEFIELDS PARKWAY
This is the 230-km road (Hwy 93) opened in 1940 which links Lake Louise with Jasper. The highway follows a lake-lined valley between two chains of the Eastern Main Ranges which make up the Continental Divide. The watershed rivers from the Continental Divide flow eastward towards the Atlantic Ocean and westward towards the Pacific Ocean. The mountains here are the highest, most rugged and maybe the most scenic in all the Rockies. The highway is good but slow, as animals such as goats, bighorn sheep and elk are often beside or on it.

You can drive the route in a couple of hours but stopping at the many viewpoints, picnic spots and sights or hiking on one of the many trails can easily make it a full day or longer. Visitor Information Centres will have trail details. Cycling the Icefields Parkway is very popular, but because of the terrain it's much easier going from Banff to Jasper than vice versa.

On the way see **Peyto Lake**, one of the world's most beautiful glacial lakes; again, early in the morning is the best viewing time. Further north, around **Waterfowl Lake**, moose are plentiful.

About halfway between Lake Louise and Jasper is the **Athabasca Glacier**, a tongue of the vast **Columbia Icefield**. The icefield itself covers an area of 325 sq km and parts of it are over 900 metres thick. Its meltwaters flow into the Mackenzie, Saskatchewan and Columbia rivers. Brewster's Gray Line (☎ 762-6700), PO Box 1140, Banff T0L 0C0, can take you on a 1½-hour ride out on the ice for $18.50. Athabasca Glacier Walks (☎ 762-5385; or ☎ 852-5665 in Jasper), 304 Caribou St, Banff, has a three-hour walk of the Athabasca Glacier for $20 and a five-hour one to various destinations for $24. You can buy tickets at the parking lot next to the glacier.

The Columbia Icefield Visitor Information Centre across the highway from the glacier has a display and film on glaciers for free. In summer the centre is open May to September daily from 10 am to 5 pm (except between mid-June and late August when it's open till 7 pm).

Other points of interest are **Sunwapta Falls** and **Athabasca Falls**, closer to Jasper.

### Places to Stay

The route is lined with a good batch of rustic HI hostels charging $10 for members, $15 for nonmembers. Most are quite close to the highway in scenic locations, small and without showers but usually there's a 'refreshing' stream nearby. HI *Mosquito Creek Hostel*, on the Icefields Parkway about 27 km north of Lake Louise, is excellent, with a sauna, cooking facilities and friendly wardens. HI *Hilda Creek Hostel* (☎ 762-4122), seven km south of the Visitor Information Centre, has 21 beds and a kitchen. HI *Athabasca Falls Hostel* (☎ 439-3089) is about 30 km south of Jasper and has 40 beds.

You can also find campgrounds and moderately priced motels along the way.

### JASPER & AROUND

Jasper, 369 km west of Edmonton, is Banff's northern counterpart. It's smaller with fewer things to see and do and its setting is less grand, but some people prefer its quieter streets and less full-scale pandering to tourists. It's a good connecting point, with the Yellowhead Hwy and VIA Rail running east to Edmonton; west to Prince George; and the Icefields Parkway going south to Lake Louise. The town is a good supply centre for trips around Jasper National Park, which is teeming with wildlife and has excellent backcountry trails of various lengths.

### Orientation

The main street, Connaught Drive, has virtually everything including the bus depot, train station, banks, restaurants and souvenir shops. Outside the toy-like train station is a 21-metre totem pole carved by a Haida artisan from British Columbia's Queen Charlotte Islands. Nearby is an old CN steam engine. On Patricia St, parallel to Connaught Drive, traffic runs one way north of Hazel Ave.

Off the main street, the town is made up of small wooden houses, many with flowered gardens befitting this alpine setting.

### Information

**Tourist Offices** Right in the centre of town at 500 Connaught Drive is Jasper's Visitor Information Centre (☎ 852-6176), easily one of Canada's most eye-pleasing tourist offices. It's a stone building covered in flowers and plants and with a large lawn out the front. The lawn is a popular meeting place and often has people and backpacks lying all over the place.

The centre has information on trails in the park and will offer suggestions to fit your specifications. It has two good publications on hiking in the area: *Day Hikes in Jasper National Park* and *Backcountry Users' Guide* and a list of tourist homes in town. The booklet *Profiles* has details of park regulations, wildlife, campgrounds etc. In summer the centre is open daily from 8 am to 8 pm, in winter from 9 am to 5 pm.

South at 632 Connaught Drive, the Chamber of Commerce (☎ 852-3858) gives information on Jasper townsite and is open daily from 8 am to 8 pm. In the same building Alberta Tourism has maps and information on other parts of the province.

**Post** The main post office (☎ 852-3041), 502 Patricia St, near the corner of Elm Ave, is open Monday to Friday from 9 am to 5 pm.

**Medical Services** The local hospital (☎ 852-3344) is at 518 Robson St.

**Laundromat** Beside the post office at Jasper Laundromat you can wash clothes and sleeping bags; it's open daily from 9 am to 10 pm and there's a café next door. At Coin-Op Laundry, further south on Patricia St opposite the Toronto Dominion Bank, you can

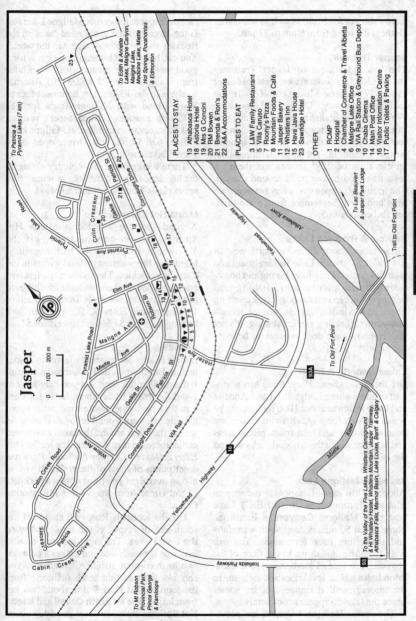

# Jasper

0    100    200 m

**To Patricia & Pyramid Lakes (7 km)**

**To Edith & Annette Lakes, Maligne Canyon, Maligne Lake, Medicine Lake, Miette Hot Springs, Pocahontas & Edmonton**

Pyramid Lake Road

Pyramid Lake Road

Patricia St

Connaught Drive

Colin Crescent

Geikie St

Pyramid Ave

Elm Ave

Miette Ave

Maligne Ave

Robson St

Willow Ave

Cabin Creek Road

Contraught Drive

Patricia St

Geikie St

Hazel Ave

VIA Rail

Cabin Creek Drive

Patricia St

Crescent

**To Mt Robson Provincial Park, Prince George & Kamloops**

Yellowhead Highway

Icefields Parkway

Athabasca River

Yellowhead Highway

93A

Miette River

93A

**To Old Fort Point**

**To Lac Beauvert & Jasper Park Lodge**

**Trail to Old Fort Point**

**To the Valley of the Five Lakes, Whistlers Campground & HI Whistlers Hostel, Whistlers Mountain Jasper Tramway, Athabasca Falls, Marmot Basin, Lake Louise, Banff & Calgary**

16

16

93

**ALBERTA**

### PLACES TO STAY
13  Athabasca Hotel
18  Astoria Hotel
19  Mrs G Concini
20  RM Bowen
21  Brenda & Ron's
22  A&A Accommodations

### PLACES TO EAT
3   L&W Family Restaurant
5   Villa Caruso
7   Roony's Pizza
8   Mountain Foods & Café
11  Jasper Bakery
12  Whistlers Inn
15  Hava Java House
23  Sawridge Hotel

### OTHER
1   RCMP
2   Hospital
4   Chamber of Commerce & Travel Alberta
6   Maligne Lake Office
9   VIA Rail Station & Greyhound Bus Depot
10  Chaba Cinema
14  Main Post Office
16  Visitor Information Centre
17  Public Toilets & Parking

have a shower for $1.50 as well as wash your clothes; it's open from 8 am to 11 pm.

## Jasper Tramway

The lower terminal of Jasper Tramway (☎ 852-3093) is about six km south of Jasper along Whistlers Mountain Rd off the Icefields Parkway. The gondola goes up Whistlers Mountain in seven minutes and offers views 75 km south to the Columbia Icefield and 100 km west to Mt Robson in British Columbia. The upper terminal is at an elevation of 2285 metres and there's a restaurant and hiking trails around the top. The tramway is open every day between late May and early September from 8 am to 10 pm and costs $9.65.

## Patricia & Pyramid Lakes

These lakes, about seven km north-west of town along Pyramid Lake Rd, are small and relatively quiet. They have hiking and horse-riding trails, picnic sites, fishing and beaches; you can rent canoes, kayaks, sailing boats and windsurfers. In winter there's cross-country skiing and ice skating. It's not uncommon to see deer, coyotes or bears in the vicinity.

## Lakes Annette & Edith

Off the Yellowhead Hwy, three km north-east of town along Lodge Rd, Lake Annette and Lake Edith, at about 1000 metres, can be warm enough for a quick swim. There are beaches, hiking and bike trails, picnic areas and boat rentals in the wooded parks around the lakes.

## Jasper to Maligne Lake

About 11 km east of Jasper on the way to Maligne (pronounced 'ma-LEEN') Lake you pass **Maligne Canyon**, a limestone gorge about 50 metres deep, with waterfalls and interesting rock formations. You can walk from the café down to the floor of the canyon. A further 21 km brings you to **Medicine Lake** whose level rises and falls due to the underground drainage system; sometimes the lake disappears completely.

The scenic **Maligne Lake**, 48 km south-

east of Jasper at the end of Maligne Lake Rd, is the largest of the glacier-fed lakes in the Rockies and the second largest in the world. You can hike or go horse riding near it for a good view, or hire a canoe for $7 an hour from Maligne Tours (☎ 852-3370). Alternatively, take the 40-km, 1½-hour boat tour to Spirit Island with Maligne Tours for $27 ($45 with transfers to/from Jasper): you can make a reservation in Jasper at Maligne Lake Office, 626 Connaught Drive, open daily from 8.30 am to 9 pm.

There's excellent cross-country skiing in the highlands around the lake in winter (the season lasts from November to May).

## Miette Hot Springs

A good spot for a bathe is Miette Hot Springs, 61 km east of Jasper off the Yellowhead Hwy near the park boundary. Miette has the warmest mineral waters in the Canadian Rockies. The modern spa has two pools, one deep and one suitable for children. It's open in summer daily from 8.30 am to 10.30 pm and costs $2.50; you can hire bathing suits for $1.50 and towels for $1.

## Activities

**Hiking** Hikers are generally fewer in Jasper than in Banff and wildlife is more plentiful. If the weather has been wet you may want to avoid the lower trails where horse trips are run; they make the path a mud bath. Topographic maps are available for all routes. As well as the hikes around the lakes mentioned earlier there are many others. The leaflet *Day Hikers' Guide to Jasper National Park* has descriptions of most of the walks. If you're hiking overnight you must obtain a park-use permit (free) from the Visitor Information Centre.

Off the Icefields Parkway, about 10 km south-east of Jasper, is the small **Valley of the Five Lakes**. The eight-km loop around the lakes is mostly flat and makes a pleasant two to three-hour stroll. Alternatively, you can take the trail that heads off north from the loop to **Old Fort Point** about two km from Jasper. The **Mt Edith Cavell** and **Miette Hot Springs** areas also have good day hikes.

There are quite a few two and three-day hikes in the park. One is the 45-km **Skyline Trail** which starts at the north-western end of Maligne Lake and finishes on Maligne Lake Rd about 13 km from Jasper. Approximately 26 km of the trail is at or above the tree line and has great scenery. The trail has plenty of wildlife too; watch out for grizzlies.

There are also a few four, seven and 10-day hikes.

**Cycling** As in Banff National Park you can cycle on the highways and on some of the trails in the park. No cycling is allowed off the trails. Journeys of a few hours, a day or several days with overnight stops at campgrounds, hostels or lodges are all possible. For more information get a copy of *Trail Bicycling Guide, Jasper National Park* from the Visitor Information Centre.

A good route close to town is along **Maligne Lake Rd** to Maligne Canyon or further to Medicine Lake. A popular, scenic but fairly tough trail ride is through the Valley of the Five Lakes to Old Fort Point a distance of about 23½ km. For bicycle rentals see the Getting Around section later.

**Climbing** Jasper Climbing School & Guide Service (☎ 852-3964) PO Box 452, Jasper T0E 1E0, is run by Helen & Hans Schwartz and has two to five-day, beginner-to-advanced climbing schools. These run from May to September; in winter you can go waterfall ice climbing or ski mountaineering. It also has one-day guided tours ($200) to Mt Morro, Messner Ridge, Mt Athabasca, Mt Andromeda and Mt Edith Cavell.

**White-Water Rafting** Great white-water rafting can be found on the **Athabasca River** near Athabasca Falls, **Maligne River** and **Sunwapta River**. Maligne River Adventures (☎ 852-3370) does a 13-km trip on the Maligne River for $42.05 per person; you can book a ticket from Maligne Lake Office, 626 Connaught Drive. Letter writers have described it as exciting. Whitewater Rafting Ltd (☎ 852-4386/7238), PO Box 362, Jasper T0E 1E0, has 3½-hour trips to Athabasca

Falls and four-hour rides on the Maligne or Sunwapta rivers. Prices start from $35.

**Skiing**
Jasper National Park's main skiing area is **Marmot Basin** which lies 19 km south-west of town off Hwy 93A. It has good downhill runs for both beginners and experts, and plenty of scenic cross-country trails. Call ☎ 852-3816 for information or ☎ 488-5909 for a snow report. A day pass costs $33. Near Maligne Lake the **Moose Lake Loop** (eight-km) and the trail in the **Bald Hills** (11-km) are an easy introduction to cross-country skiing in the park as well as offering great scenery. The skiing season goes from December to May. For more information contact the Visitor Information Centre.

**Organised Tours**
Jasper Travel Agency (☎ 852-4400), in the Via Rail station, coordinates and sells tickets for various tours, river trips, sight-seeing tours and adventures. Brewster's Gray Line (☎ 852-3332) has a three-hour drive to some of the local sights including Jasper Tramway, Whistlers Mountain, Pyramid and Patricia lakes and Maligne Canyon. The trip costs $29.50. Its Maligne Lake cruise takes five hours and costs $45. It also has tours along the Icefields Parkway to Lake Louise for $53.50 one way, taking 7½ hours. Two other companies with tours of the park's sights are Jasper Heritage Tours (☎ 852-5254) and Mountain Meadow Tours (☎ 852-5595).

Jasper Raft Tours (☎ 852-3332/3613), 614 Connaught Drive, offers one and two-hour tours on the Athabasca River from $30.50, with descriptions of the natural and human history of the region. The cost includes the bus trip.

If you're driving, there are self-guiding auto-cassette tapes that describe the journey between Jasper and Banff via the Columbia Icefield and Lake Louise. Produced by Rocky Mountain Auto Tours, these can be rented, or purchased for $19.95 from Exposures, 612 Connaught Drive.

ALBERTA

## Places to Stay

In general, prices here are better than those in Banff, but hotel and motel prices are still fairly steep. The B&Bs and tourist homes are the best bet after the campgrounds or hostels.

**Camping** Jasper National Park has 10 campgrounds all operated by the Canadian Parks Service. Closest to town is *Whistlers Campground* about three km south off the Icefields Parkway on Whistlers Rd. It's quite good, with electricity, showers and flush toilets but, though large (it has 781 sites), it does get crowded. In summer, films and talks are presented nightly. Sites cost from $12 to $16.50.

A herd of wapiti (American elk) lives in the campground at certain times of the year. In the autumn a male looks after a large number of females – the harem – and his bawling instructions are heard far and wide.

Two km further south on the Icefields Parkway, *Wapiti Campground*, beside the Athabasca River, is the only campground in the park open during the winter. It has sites for $12 to $14. Two other campgrounds reasonably close to town are *Wabasso Campground* 17 km south on Hwy 93A, with sites for $9.25, and *Snaring River Campground*, 17 km north on the Yellowhead Hwy, with sites for $7.25.

**Hostels** HI *Whistlers Hostel* (☎ 852-3215) is about seven km south of Jasper on Skytram Rd towards the Jasper Tramway; the last two km are uphill. The hostel is one of the few big modern ones in the Rockies and has showers, a laundromat and a large kitchen. It opens at 5 pm and closes at midnight and you're woken up at 7 am. Members pay $14, nonmembers $18. We have had some complaints from travellers about the hostel guests being local workers or for whatever reason staying more or less fulltime. Call ahead to see if there are any beds available.

HI *Maligne Canyon Hostel* (☎ 852-3584), 11 km north-east of town on Maligne

Canyon Rd, is small but good with members paying $10, nonmembers $14. HI *Mt Edith Cavell Hostel* (☎ 439-3089) is south of Jasper on Mt Edith Cavell Rd, 11 km from the junction with Hwy 93A. It's open from mid-June to early September and charges $10 for members, $14 for nonmembers.

**B&Bs & Tourist Homes** The Visitor Information Centre has a list of over 50 tourist homes, all clean, most in or close to town, most charging similar prices, most open year round and some offering B&B. In July and August many of these places fill up early, so it's a good idea to book ahead. Most places charge from $35/40 for a single/double, but offer lower rates in the off season.

The cheapest of the lot is *RM Bowen* (☎ 852-4532), 228 Colin Crescent, with a couple of rooms with TV for $25 each. *Mrs G Concini* (☎ 852-3744), 312 Patricia St, has two rooms available for $35 each with shared bathroom. *Brenda & Ron's* (☎ 852-3822), 200 Patricia St, has one double room available for $40, also with shared bathroom. *A&A Accommodations* (☎ 852-5260), 110 Connaught Drive, offers two rooms at $50 with TV, private bathroom and complimentary coffee.

**Hotels, Motels & Bungalows** In town the *Athabasca Hotel* (☎ 852-3386), 510 Patricia St, has basic singles/doubles for $51/54 and more deluxe rooms for $91/95. The *Astoria Hotel* (☎ 852-4955), 404 Connaught Drive, has singles/doubles with telephone and $89/92. Both hotels have a pub and restaurant and provide entertainment. *Jasper Park Lodge* (☎ 852-3301), beside Lac Beauvert north-east of town, is Jasper's answer to the Banff Springs Hotel. It has everything including a world-class golf course. Singles/doubles start from $267, suites from $612.

In Jasper many of the motels are north along Connaught Drive. Out of town some places offer motel-type rooms and bungalows (usually wooden cabins).

*Patricia Lake Bungalows* (☎ 852-3560), on Patricia Lake Rd about five km north of town, is reasonable with singles/doubles from $45. A little further north along the road *Pyramid Lake Resort Bungalows* (☎ 852-3536) has singles/doubles from $50 to $110. It's beside the lake and has a licensed dining room. *Tekkara Lodge* (☎ 852-3058) is one km south of Jasper off Hwy 93A at the confluence of the Miette and Athabasca rivers. You can either stay in the lodge or in one of the cabins. Rooms cost from $65. It has a licensed restaurant and is open May to the end of September.

## Places to Eat

**Connaught Drive** *Mountain Foods & Café*, on Connaught Drive opposite the train station, is a good health-food café and shop. It serves soups, salads from $2.50, sandwiches from $3.45 and has good desserts. The shop also sells granola, nuts and other foods for hiking. It's open daily from 8 am to 10 pm. *Roony's Pizza*, 618 Connaught Drive, has pizzas from $6.50 and fish & chips and Middle Eastern food for around $7. *Villa Caruso*, 628 Connaught Drive, is a popular up-market restaurant serving seafood, pasta, pizza and steaks, the latter you can see being cooked in the window. It's open daily from 11 am and main meals average around $10 to $20.

Many of the hotels have restaurants. *Whistlers Garden Restaurant* in the Whistlers Inn, 105 Miette Ave on the corner of Connaught Drive, is a basic place ideal for breakfasts. Omelettes, burgers and pancakes cost from around $4.50. *Sunrise Coffee Shop* in the Sawridge Hotel, 82 Connaught Drive, is also good for breakfast which costs about $5. It's open daily from 6.30 am to 10.30 pm. *Papa George's* in the Astoria Hotel also has good-value breakfasts for around $5 as well as pastas and vegetarian dishes.

**Patricia St** *L&W Family Restaurant*, on the corner of Patricia St and Hazel Ave, is plastic-looking but has decent pizza, spaghetti or lasagne for about $9 to $14.50 and the service is fast. *Hava Java House*, 407 Patricia St, serves breakfasts for $4.50 and loaves of various breads for $2.25. The

coffee's good, you can sit out the front in fine weather and it's a good spot to meet other travellers. *Jasper Bakery*, 601 Patricia St on the corner of Miette Ave, has good bread, sandwiches and cakes.

## Entertainment

*Chaba Cinema* (☎ 852-4749), 604 Connaught Drive opposite the VIA Rail station, shows the one-hour movie *Challenge* at 4 pm daily in summer. Shot largely on the Columbia Icefield and narrated by Peter Ustinov, the film chronicles white-water kayaking, heli-skiing, ice-climbing and other activities in the Rockies well enough to have been shown at the Cannes Film Festival. It was produced by Wendy Wacko who lives in Jasper. The cinema also shows commercial movies. Admission costs $6.50.

The *nightclub* in the Athabasca Hotel regularly has live rock bands and dancing. For disco music head to *Champs* in the Sawridge Hotel; it's open nightly. The *Astoria Bar* in the Astoria Hotel is famous for its imported draught beers.

## Getting There & Away

**Bus** The Greyhound Bus Depot (☎ 852-3962) is situated in the VIA Rail station on Connaught Drive. Four buses go to Kamloops, Vancouver and Edmonton daily. The one-way fares (including tax) are: Kamloops $44.78; Vancouver $82.50; and Edmonton $41.46. Greyhound doesn't run buses between Jasper and Banff.

Brewster Transportation (☎ 852-3332), in the VIA Rail station, has one bus a day to Banff; it takes about 4½ hours and costs $37 one way. It also goes to Calgary for $49.50 one way. These fares include tax.

**Train** The ticket office (☎ 852-4102) in the VIA Rail station is open Monday and Saturday from 8.30 am to 4 pm; Tuesday and Thursday from noon to 4 pm; Wednesday from 8.30 am to noon and from 4.30 to 8.15 pm; and Friday and Sunday from noon to 8 pm. From here trains go west to Prince George and Prince Rupert, south-west through Kamloops to Vancouver and east

through Edmonton to Saskatoon, Winnipeg
and beyond. The train to Vancouver leaves
Monday, Thursday and Saturday at 3.30 pm;
to Winnipeg Tuesday, Friday and Sunday at
2.55 pm; and to Prince Rupert Wednesday,
Friday and Sunday at 8.10 pm. Some sample
one-way fares (including tax) are: Kamloops
$84.53; Edmonton $78.11; Winnipeg $214;
and Vancouver $134.82.

The 'Rocky Mountaineer' train takes you
via Jasper (or Banff) between Calgary and
Vancouver. The train leaves Tuesday, Thursday
and Sunday daily at 9 am and the
one-way fare to Vancouver is $529. See the
Banff Getting There & Away section earlier
for further details.

**Car** Car rental in Jasper is available through
the following:

Avis
      Petro Canada, 300 Connaught Drive (☎ 852-
      3970)
Budget
      Shell, 638 Connaught Drive (☎ 852-3222)
Hertz
      Avalanche Esso, 702 Connaught Drive (☎ 852-
      3888)
Tilden
      Via Rail Station, 607 Connaught Drive (☎ 852-
      4972)

Tilden rents small cars for $45 a day with 100
km free, plus 20 cents for each extra km.
Budget's rates are $44 a day with 100 km
free, plus 20 cents for each extra km.

### Getting Around
**Bus** Although Jasper doesn't have a public
transport system, small 24-seater buses, run
by Maligne Tours (☎ 852-3370), do go from
outside the Maligne Lake Office, 626 Connaught
Drive, to various places around
Jasper National Park. Some destinations and
one-way fares are: Jasper Tramway $5;
Maligne Canyon $6; Whistlers Campground
and HI Hostel $3; Maligne Lake $10; and
Skyline Trail (southern trailhead) $10.

Hikers' Wheels (☎ 852-2188) offers
transport to anywhere in Jasper National
Park and the Mt Robson Provincial Park in

British Columbia for under $20. Buses leave
from outside Hava Java House, 407 Patricia
St; pick-ups from campgrounds and hostels
can be arranged.

**Bicycle** Jasper has lots of places with bicycles
for hire. Mountain bikes can be rented
at Beyond Bikes (☎ 852-5922), 4 Cedar Ave,
for $4 an hour, $12 per day and $16 for 24
hours. Freewheel Cycle (☎ 852-3898), 600
Patricia St, rents mountain bikes for $5 an
hour, $12 for a half-day or $18 a day. Some
other places that rent bikes are Sports Shop
(☎ 852-3654), 416 Connaught Drive beside
the CIBC Bank, and Saito Sports & Hardware
(☎ 852-5555), 625 Patricia St. Rentals
are also available at Jasper Park Lodge and
the Sawridge Hotel.

### KANANASKIS COUNTRY
Adjacent to the south-western corner of
Banff National Park and 90 km west of
Calgary, Kananaskis Country has been set
aside as an outdoor recreational area. The
4000-sq-km region offers facilities for
skiing, climbing, cycling, hiking, horse
riding, boating, camping and picnicking.
Kananaskis Country is most notable for the
downhill skiing at **Nakiska** on Mt Allan
(☎ 591-7777), off Hwy 40, where the 1988
Olympic Winter Games were held. Skiers
today can use the slopes there when no competitions
are being held. Cross-country
skiing is also good with trails throughout
Kananaskis Country.

The fast-growing town of **Canmore**, off
the Trans Canada Hwy and squeezed
between Banff National Park and
Kananaskis Country, is the main focus for
the area. As well as campgrounds, hotels and
motels it has tour companies offering
outdoor activities throughout the Rockies.

The main access road to Kananaskis
Country is Hwy 40 which does a loop
through the area. It runs south of the Trans
Canada Hwy through Peter Lougheed Provincial
Park to link with Hwy 541, then Hwy
22. At the junction of Hwys 541 and 22 you
can either head north to Calgary or south to
the Crowsnest Hwy. The other main route

into Kananaskis is Hwy 66 from south-eastern Calgary.

## WATERTON LAKES NATIONAL PARK

This 525-sq-km national park in the far south-western corner of Alberta, 130 km from Lethbridge, was opened in 1895. It is joined with the Glacier National Park of Montana to form the Waterton Glacier International Peace Park. Each park is operated separately, however, and entry to one does not entitle you to entry to the other. The park entry fee to Waterton Lakes is not valid for Glacier; and to get to the latter you have to leave Waterton Lakes, head south on Hwy 6 (Chief Mountain Hwy) and go through customs and immigration at the border.

The land here rises from the prairie into rugged, beautiful alpine scenery with many lakes, waterfalls and valleys. The whole park has fewer visitors than its two more northerly sisters, Banff and Jasper. Partly because of this, spotting wildlife here is more common and there are more than 800 species of wildflowers. Waterton Lake is the deepest in the Rockies and the town of Waterton is smaller and much more low-key than Banff. The park information office (☎ 859-2224), on the highway just before you get to Waterton, is open daily May to September from 8 am to 8.30 pm.

The park has 255 km of hiking trails some of which are also good for cycling and horse riding, while in winter many become cross-country skiing trails. On Upper Waterton Lake sailing, windsurfing and scuba diving are popular. Waterton Inter-Nation Shoreline

Cruises (☎ 859-2362 in summer, 285-2180 in winter), PO Box 126, Waterton T0K 2M0, operates cruises on Upper Waterton Lake with boats holding up to 200 passengers. A limited operation begins in May with no stops in the USA; the full schedule operates between 1 July and 30 August with most cruises stopping at Goat Haunt in Montana. The fare is $14.

In the north-east of the park you can visit **Bison Paddock** containing a small herd of plains bison. The **Akamina Parkway** provides a scenic 16-km route west from Waterton along the Cameron Valley to Cameron Lake, while the 15-km **Red Rock Parkway** follows the Blakiston Valley to Red Rock Canyon.

### Places to Stay

The park has three government campgrounds. The *Waterton Townsite Campground*, on Hwy 5 at the southern end of town, is the largest with full facilities and sites for $13. There are also a few privately owned campgrounds just outside the park. Waterton has a number of lodges and hotels.

*Northland Lodge* (☎ 859-2353), on Evergreen Ave and open mid-May to the end of September, is the cheapest. Single rooms without/with bathroom are $46/52, doubles $55. *El Cortez Motel* (☎ 859-2366), on Mountview Rd, is clean and reasonably priced with rooms for $55. The town's showpiece accommodation is the *Prince of Wales Hotel* (☎ 859-2231), overlooking the lake. Even if you can't afford the $113 rooms it's worth a wander round.

# British Columbia

Entered Confederation: 20 July 1871
Area: 948,596 sq km
Population: 3,213,200
Provincial Capital: Victoria

British Columbia, known simply as BC, is probably the most beautiful province in the country and contains some of the most spectacular scenery in the world. The Rocky Mountains are in the east, the northern interior is full of mountain ranges, hills, forests and lakes. The southern interior has a small desert, while the lush Pacific coastal area has many inlets and islands. In short, there is a wide variety of landscapes providing a range of habitats for wildlife and opportunities for outdoor activities to suit every taste.

The general atmosphere in BC, particularly on the south-west coast, is slightly different from the rest of Canada. The culture, more permissive and lifestyle-conscious than that found in the east, partially reflects the influence of California.

These factors combine to make tourism – in a province with many lucrative industries – the second largest money-maker.

As in California, much of the early settlement was due to gold fever here around the 1850s. More than half the population lives in the south-west around Vancouver and Victoria so there is a lot of sparsely populated space, particularly to the north. Inaccessible areas of the province, however, continue to be developed. The bulk of the population is of British ancestry, although Vancouver has a large Chinese community.

BC is Canada's most westerly province bordered in the north by the Yukon and the Northwest Territories; in the east by Alberta; in the south by the three US states of Montana, Idaho and Washington; in the north-west by Alaska; and in the west by the Pacific Ocean.

Victoria, the province's capital, is at the southern tip of Vancouver Island, which lies

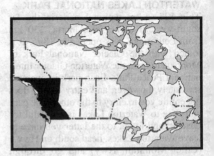

south-west of the mainland. The city of Vancouver, the province's business centre and by far BC's largest city, is in the south-western corner of the province near the mouth of the Fraser River.

The Trans Canada Hwy (Hwy 1) is the major route connecting Vancouver and southern BC with the rest of southern Canada. The busiest section is between Hope and Vancouver, where the road follows the Fraser River. The Yellowhead Hwy (mainly Hwy 16, but also including part of Hwys 37 and 5) links Prince Rupert in BC's north-west with Prince George in the east, Jasper and Edmonton in Alberta, then Saskatoon and Winnipeg.

The Cassiar Hwy (Hwy 37; also called the Stewart-Cassiar Hwy) links the north-west of the province with the Yukon, meeting the Alaska Hwy near Upper Liard, just north of the BC/Yukon border.

Hwy 97 from Washington state in the USA connects south-central BC with the north via Kamloops, Prince George and Dawson Creek. From Dawson Creek, Hwy 97 is also known as the Alaska (or Alcan) Hwy; it connects northern BC with Fairbanks in Alaska via Whitehorse in the Yukon.

## HISTORY

The earliest known inhabitants of BC are believed to have arrived from Asia between

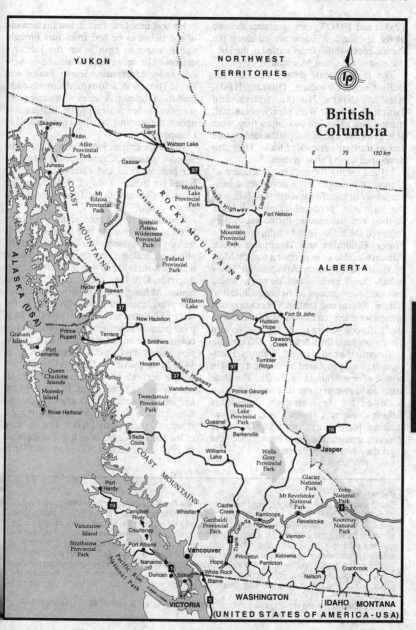

YUKON

NORTHWEST
TERRITORIES

British
Columbia

0    75    150 km

Skagway

Atlin

Atlin
Provincial
Park

Juneau

Upper
Liard

Watson Lake

Cassiar

97

Muncho
Lake
Provincial
Park

Fort Nelson

Liard Highway

Alaska Highway

Mt
Edziza
Provincial
Park

Stone
Mountain
Provincial
Park

Cassiar Mountains

Spatsizi
Plateau
Wilderness
Provincial Park

ROCKY MOUNTAINS

Tatlatui
Provincial
Park

ALBERTA

Hyder

Stewart

37

Williston
Lake

Hudson
Hope

Fort St John

COAST MOUNTAINS

ALASKA (USA)

New Hazelton

Terrace

Smithers

Kitimat

Houston

Yellowhead Highway

37

Dawson
Creek

Graham
Island

Prince
Rupert

Port
Clements

Queen
Charlotte
Islands

Moresby
Island

Rose Harbour

Vanderhoof

Tumbler
Ridge

97

Prince George

Tweedsmuir
Provincial
Park

Bella
Coola

Quesnel

Bowron
Lake
Provincial
Park

Barkerville

Williams
Lake

Wells
Gray
Provincial
Park

16

Jasper

Port
Hardy

19

Campbell
River

Courtenay

Vancouver
Island

Strathcona
Provincial
Park

Port Alberni

Nanaimo

Duncan

Sidney

VICTORIA

5

Whistler

Garibaldi
Provincial
Park

Cache
Creek

Trans Canada Highway

1

Kamloops

Revelstoke

Glacier
National
Park

Mt Revelstoke
National
Park

Yoho
National
Park

1

Kootenay
National
Park

Vancouver

Hope

Princeton

Kelowna

Penticton

Vernon

Nelson

Cranbrook

White Rock

Blaine

Pacific
Rim
National
Park

WASHINGTON

IDAHO    MONTANA

(UNITED STATES OF AMERICA - USA)

BRITISH COLUMBIA

12,000 and 10,000 years ago, after the end of the last ice age. Some settled along the Pacific coast while others settled in the interior east of the Coast Mountains.

The Pacific coast people included the Bella Coola, Cowichan, Gitskan, Haida, Kwakiutl, Niska, Nootka, Salish and Tsimshian groups. With plenty of animal, marine and plant life available, they were able to evolve a highly sophisticated culture and an intricate network of trade. They also developed a rigid class system.

Inland, with its greater extremes of climate, the people led a nomadic, subsistence way of life. To the north they followed the migratory herds of animals like the caribou and the moose; to the south they followed the bison. In the south, around the Fraser, Columbia and Thompson rivers, salmon was also an important resource. Most of these people were Athapaskans (now called Dene, pronounced de-nay), which included such groups as Beaver, Chilcotin, Carrier, Sekani and Tahltan. Other important groups were the Interior Salish (divided into the Lillooet, Okanagan, Shuswap and Thompson) and the Kootenay (or Kootenai).

Towards the end of the 18th century, European explorers appeared off the west coast in search of new sources of wealth. The Russians and Spanish came first and were soon followed by the seemingly ubiquitous British explorer Captain Cook, who was looking for a water route across North America from the Pacific to the Atlantic – the legendary Northwest Passage.

He was unable to find it, but his account of the riches to be had from furs brought traders eager to cash in on the lucrative market. The most famous of these were Alexander Mackenzie, Simon Fraser and David Thompson, who explored routes overland from the east. A series of trading posts was established which by the 1820s came under the control of the Hudson's Bay Company.

In the meantime, initially to counter the Spanish presence, Captain George Vancouver had explored and claimed Vancouver Island for Britain. Then in 1849, following years of dispute with the USA, it became a crown colony.

The discovery of gold along the Fraser River in 1858 brought in a flood of people seeking their fortune and led to mainland BC also being declared a crown colony. A second wave of fortune hunters came when gold was discovered further north in the Cariboo region. Although the gold rush only lasted a few years, many of those who came in the wake of the miners remained behind to form more permanent settlements. In 1866 the two colonies were united and, after much discussion, joined the Canadian Confederation in 1871 as the province of British Columbia.

The arrival of the trans-continental railway in 1885 opened up BC to the east; and the settlement of the prairies around this time created demand for the province's resources, particularly timber. The building of the Panama Canal, which was completed in 1914, meant easier access to markets in

---

**Potlatch**

The potlatch (a Chinook jargon word derived from the Nootka word *patschmatl* meaning 'to give' or 'gift') was a feast or ceremony common among the Native Indians of the Pacific North-West coast, especially the Kwakiutl. Its main purpose was to validate the status of the chief or clan, although individuals also used it to try to enhance their social ranking. The potlatch involved the public exchange of gifts and destruction of property in a competitive display of affluence. A significant social event such as a wedding or funeral was used as an occasion for a potlatch.

The potlatch was prohibited by the federal government in 1884, when the Kwakiutl, at the cost of their own impoverishment, used it to shame and humble their former enemies. However, the practice continued in secret; the ban was lifted in 1951 and small-scale potlatches again take place.

Nowadays the word is often used to mean a 'spree' or 'raucous party'. ∎

Europe and along North America's east coast. This brought about a boom for the BC economy.

Following WW I, however, there was an economic downturn which led to industrial unrest and unemployment. After a brief recovery, the Wall St crash of 1929 brought severe depression and hardship. Prosperity only returned with the advent of WW II and was sustained after the war with the discovery of new resources and the development of a manufacturing base.

The two major Canadian political parties, the Liberals and the Conservatives, have made little headway in this province. The Social Credit Party, ostensibly the party of small business, was in power for much of the 1970s and 1980s. In 1991, its main opposition, the New Democrat Party, which advocates a form of limited socialism, came to power.

BC politics are the most volatile in the country. The unions are strong and active and the electorate very opinionated.

## GEOGRAPHY

The north-eastern corner of British Columbia around Peace River occupies part of the geographical region known as the Interior Plains. The bulk of the province, however, is mountainous lying inside the Western Cordillera, which runs roughly north-west to south-east. Within the cordillera there are three major mountain ranges – the Rocky Mountains to the east, the Cassiar (north) and Columbia (south) Mountains in the centre and the Coast Mountains to the west.

The province contains scores of freshwater lakes and fast-flowing rivers and streams plus several plateaus, the largest of which is the Fraser Plateau in the south-west. The coastline is rugged, with numerous fjords and islands, including Vancouver Island. In the south of the Okanagan Valley near Osoyoos is a small desert.

## CLIMATE & WHEN TO GO

BC's climate is varied, influenced as it is by latitude, distance from the moderating effects of the Pacific Ocean and by the mountainous terrain. On the coast it is mild with warm, mostly dry summers and cool, very wet winters. The interior is much drier, particularly in the south along the Okanagan Valley; summers are hot and the winters cold. In the mountains summers are short, the nights cool. Winter snowfalls are heavy.

Unless you're coming for the winter activities like skiing, the best time to visit is from around mid-June to mid-September. During this period there is little rain, temperatures are warm, daylight hours are long and the transport routes are open.

## FLORA & FAUNA
### Flora

Estimates vary, but about 60% of BC is covered by forest, consisting mainly of varieties of coniferous trees – western red cedar and Douglas fir which occur in the moist coastal regions while pine, hemlock and spruce are more often found in the drier, higher interior. Other important types of trees are maple, birch, poplar and willow. Grasslands are found in drier areas of low elevation, while in the higher, tundra regions only the hardiest of plants, such as the saxifrage and phlox, can survive.

Wildflowers abound in BC; some have interesting names like old man's whiskers and nodding onion. One of the most common flowers is fireweed, which can be seen along roadsides and in fields.

### Fauna

In the straits off the west coast are sea lions, seals, porpoises, different kinds of whales (killer, gray, sperm, humpback, minke and blue) and even sharks. The waters are rich in fish, particularly salmon, which lives most of its life in the ocean, but then heads upstream far inland to spawn and die. Freshwater fish include whitefish, bass, goldeye, burbot and various species of trout. The waters off Vancouver Island are home to the world's largest octopuses. Crab is a BC culinary delicacy.

On land the most common animals are varieties of deer (white-tail, black-tail, mule), moose, caribou, cougars, wolves, marmots, squirrels, mountain goats, bighorn sheep and black, brown and grizzly bears.

BC also has a diverse birdlife, with over 440 different species. The bald eagle is widespread and can usually be seen near rivers and lakes; the golden eagle, on the other hand, is an endangered species but can still be seen along the coast and in the Rocky Mountains. There are waterbirds such as herons, swans, geese, ducks, grebes and loons. Other common varieties of birds are sparrow, swallow, thrush, warbler, owl, grouse, hawk, flycatcher and jay. The steller's jay is a provincial symbol for BC.

With so many lakes and rivers the warmer weather brings out dozens of insects. Some of these, like mosquitoes, horse flies, and no-see-ums, will become very familiar to you if you're camping or hiking. (See the Dangers & Annoyances section in the Facts for the Visitor chapter.)

### National & Provincial Parks

BC has six national parks and more than 340 provincial parks covering 5% of the prov-

ince, an area larger than Switzerland. The *Road Map & Parks Guide*, produced by Tourism BC and available free at Travel Infocentres, lists them all with their location and facilities. There are also publications and maps on individual parks which you can get by visiting or writing to the following:

BC Parks
   Parliament Buildings, Victoria, BC V8V 1X4
Ministry of Environment, Lands & Parks
   Visitor Services, 4000 Seymour Place, Victoria V8V 1X5 (☎ 387-5002; fax 387-5757)
Outdoor Recreation Council of BC
   Suite 334, 1367 West Broadway, Vancouver, BC V6H 4A9 (☎ 737-3000/58; fax 738-7175)
Parks Canada Information Services
   Western Regional Office, Room 520, 220 4th Ave SE, PO Box 2989, Station M, Calgary, Alberta T2P 3H8 (☎ (403) 292-4401; fax (403) 292-4746)

Four of the national parks are close to each other in the south-east – Yoho, Kootenay, Glacier and Mt Revelstoke. Yoho and Kootenay adjoin Alberta's Banff National Park in the Rocky Mountains while Glacier

Loon

and Mt Revelstoke are to the east in the Columbia Mountains. The Trans Canada Hwy passes through all four.

Pacific Rim National Park stretches along Vancouver Island's west coast and is divided in two by Barkley Sound. Hwy 4 gives you access to the northern half, while the southern section can be reached either by gravel road from Port Alberni or along Hwy 14 from Victoria. The park also includes the Broken Group Islands. South Moresby Gwaii Haanas National Park is on Moresby Island in the Queen Charlotte Islands and is only accessible by boat or by hiking from Moresby Camp.

Provincial parks occur throughout BC. They vary enormously in size from, for example, the 6568 sq km of Spatsizi Plateau Wilderness Park in the north-west to the one hectare of Ballingall Islets between southern Vancouver Island and the mainland. Most of them can be reached on sealed or gravel roads in conventional vehicles, while for some you will need a 4WD. Some parks have no road access at all and you'll have to hike in. You can take a ferry to a few of them.

Some of the national and provincial parks are open all year, but the majority are closed during winter and only open from April or May to September or October. Many have vehicle (RV) and tent campsites, picnic areas and toilets and offer activities such as hiking, swimming, boating and fishing. At most of them a camping fee, between $6 and $15.50, is charged during the peak visiting season. Near the more popular parks there are motels and privately run campgrounds.

Some places considered historically significant have also been set aside as parks. Examples of these are Barkerville east of Quesnel, Fort Rodd Hill near Victoria and Fort Steele in the south-east near Cranbrook.

The Ministry of Forests (☎ 387-6656; in Vancouver ☎ 660-7500), Integrated Resource Branch – Recreation Section, 1450 Government St, Victoria, V8W 3E7, has also allocated areas for camping and recreation. You can get information about these areas from the above address or from offices around the province.

## ECONOMY

BC enjoys a high standard of living based on its major industries of forestry, tourism, mining, agriculture and fishing. Casual work is often available in these industries. Despite problems BC's economy is growing at a faster rate than other provinces as the country struggles to recover from the recession of the late 1980s and early 90s. Forestry is BC's largest industry employing 18% of the workforce either directly or indirectly. More than five million tourists visit BC each year and tourism contributes around $4½ billion dollars to the provincial economy. Mining contributes about $4 billion dollars and the most important minerals are coal, copper, zinc, gold and silver.

Unemployment continues to be high in this, Canada's most unionised (more than 37%) workforce.

BC has some serious problems with environmental degradation and pollution to which it has begun to seek solutions. In 1990 Vancouver hosted Globe 90, till that time the largest ever international conference on industrial and environmental issues. The provincial government has established a Commission on Resources & Environment to protect plant and animal species while allowing people to earn a living from sustainable natural resources. It also plans to increase the protected parks and wilderness areas to 12% of the province. Nevertheless, there is still deep division within the community as the dispute in the middle of 1993 over the logging of old-growth forest in Clayoquot Sound on Vancouver Island demonstrated.

The BC economy has become more and more linked with the so-called Pacific Rim countries and much of its growth has come through these increasing ties to the economies of Japan and the rest of Asia.

## POPULATION & PEOPLE

With well over three million people, BC is Canada's third most populous province, and its fastest growing. Vancouver is Canada's third largest city with a population of more than 1.6 million. The overwhelming majority of people live in the south of the province mainly in the small area in and around Vancouver in the south-west corner of the mainland and Victoria on the southern tip of Vancouver Island. The north is virtually empty in comparison.

Britain and Ireland are the ancestral homelands of most British Columbians. However, successive waves of migrants, especially since WW II, have produced a multiracial society with people coming from dozens of different ethnic backgrounds. There are large groups whose origins are Ukrainian, German, Scandinavian, Dutch, Italian, Chinese, Japanese, East Indian or Indochinese, and many other smaller groups. In more recent years most migrants have come from other parts of Canada rather than from abroad, while Vancouver has also had a large influx of Hong Kong Chinese.

Twenty-eight First Nations live within the province and they have become more assertive over historical land claims and the right

to govern themselves. The decline in their numbers has been reversed by the introduction of better health provisions, but problems of poverty, unemployment and alcoholism remain.

## INFORMATION
### Tourist Offices
**Local Tourist Offices** Tourism BC is the name of the body which operates the province's comprehensive tourism infrastructure and produces a mountain of literature covering just about everything the visitor needs to know. It oversees a broad network of well-signposted tourist offices – called Travel Infocentres – throughout BC, many of which operate as an arm of or in conjunction with the local Chamber of Commerce. Some are open year-round (mainly those in towns) but the majority are seasonal, only opening their doors between April or May and the first weekend in September. For information on travel in BC contact Tourism BC (☎ 685-0032 or 1-800-663-6000 in North America; fax 387-1590), Parliament Buildings, Victoria V8V 1X4.

**Tourism Regions** BC is divided into nine tourism regions. For information on individual regions contact:

Cariboo Chilcotin Tourist Association
    190 Yorkston Ave, PO Box 4900, Williams Lake, V2G 2V8; covers the region west of Wells Gray Provincial Park to the coast (☎ 392-2226; fax 392-2838)
High Country Tourism Association
    2 1490 Pearson Place, Kamloops, V1S 1J9; covers the area north-east of Merritt to the Alberta border (☎ 372-7770; fax 828-4656)
Kootenay Country Tourist Association
    610 Railway St, Nelson, V1L 1H4; covers the area around the Kootenay and Arrow lakes (☎ 352-6033; fax 352-1656)
North by North-West Tourism Association of BC
    3840 Alfred Ave, PO Box 1030, Smithers, V0J 2N0; covers a huge area west of northern Jasper National Park on the Alberta border to the Alaska and Yukon borders, and includes the Queen Charlotte Islands (☎ 8475227; fax 847-7585)

Okanagan Similkameen Tourist Association
104 515 Hwy 97 South, Kelowna, V1Z 3J2; covers the area around Okanagan Lake and Similkameen River (☎ 769-5959; fax 861-7493)

Peace River Alaska Hwy Tourist Association
10631 100th St, PO Box 6850, Fort St John, V1J 4J3; covers the north-eastern corner of the province (☎ 785-2544; fax 785-4424)

Rocky Mountain Visitors Association
495 Wallinger Ave, PO Box 10, Kimberley, V1A 2Y5; covers the south-eastern corner of the province (☎ 427-4838; fax 427-3344)

Tourism Association of South-Western BC
Suite 204, 1755 West Broadway, Vancouver, V6J 4S5; covers the south-western corner of the mainland (☎ 739-9011; fax 739-0153)

Tourism Association of Vancouver Island
302 45 Bastion Square, Victoria, V8W 1J1; this region includes part of the mainland from Bute Inlet to just north of Rivers Inlet (☎ 382-3551; fax 382-3523)

**Tourist Offices Abroad** Tourism BC has offices in the UK and the USA. The addresses are:

UK
1 Regent St, London SW1Y 4NS, UK (☎ 071-930-6857; fax 071-930-2012)

USA
PO Box 34971, Seattle, Washington 98124-1971 (☎ 206-623-5937)

## Money

The major credit cards are accepted in BC but Visa and MasterCard are more widely accepted than American Express. US currency is accepted many heavily touristed areas, but the rate of exchange can vary.

There is a general provincial sales tax of 6%. Beer, wine and spirits have a tax of 10% while accommodation tax varies between 8% and 10%. There is no provincial tax on food bought in restaurants, or on books.

## Provincial Symbols

British Columbia's official bird is the blue-black stellar's jay *(Cyanacitta stelleri)*. The provincial flower is the Pacific dogwood *(Cornus nuttalli)* which blossoms in April and May, while the western red cedar *(Thuja plicata donn)* is the province's official tree. Jade is BC's mineral emblem.

## Telephone

The area code for BC is 604; the fire/ambulance/police emergency number is 911. If, in your travels, you notice a forest fire, telephone the operator (☎ 0) and ask for Zenith 5555, the province-wide number for information on such emergencies.

## Time

Most of BC is on Pacific Standard Time, three hours behind Eastern Standard Time. Two areas bordering Alberta, however, are on Mountain Standard Time: one is in the north-east around the Peace River; the other, in the south-east, covers the Rocky Mountains north from the Montana border to Vermount.

## ACTIVITIES

For general information about activities in the province contact the Ministry of Municipal Affairs (☎ 356-1185, in Vancouver 660-3352), Recreation & Culture, Sports & Recreation Division, 333 Quebec St, Victoria BC V8V 1X4. See also the addresses listed earlier under National & Provincial Parks and Tourist Offices. The Outdoor Recreation Council of BC produces detailed information on activities in its map series *Outdoor Recreation*.

## Skiing

BC's climate and mountainous terrain provide great conditions for downhill and cross-country (nordic) skiing in the many skiing resorts and provincial and national parks. Most of the downhill ski resorts are equipped with chair lifts which serve vertical rises that range between 400 and 700 metres plus a few around the 1100-metre mark. The cross-country resorts offer about 1500 km of prepared trails with thousands more km of unmarked trails. Many of the ski resorts have hotel accommodation either on the mountain or nearby. It's also possible to go heli-skiing or skitouring to the remoter parts of the province. Pick up a copy of Tourism BC's brochure *British Columbia Skiing* (free from any Travel Infocentre), which lists all the major downhill and cross-country skiing centres in the province. Most of these centres are in the south from Vancouver Island eastward to the Rocky Mountains.

Near Vancouver to the north are Blackcomb, Whistler and Grouse mountains and the Cypress Bowl and Seymour Ski Country resorts; Hemlock Valley and Manning Provincial Park resorts are to the east. On Vancouver Island you can ski on Cain, Washington and Arrowsmith mountains and Forbidden Plateau. In the Okanagan Valley region the ski resorts include Apex Alpine, Silver Star, Big White Mountain and Baldy Mountain.

In the Rocky Mountains area in the southeast of the province the main ski resorts are at Fernie Snow Valley, Kimberley, Panorama, Fairmont Hot Springs and Whitetooth. Where there are no roads to ski areas helicopters provide access – weather permitting.

In the centre of BC along the Yellowhead Hwy between Prince Rupert and the Alberta border there is access to a number of ski areas, including Hudson Bay Mountain near Smithers, and Tabor and Purden mountains near Prince George. These are less crowded and accommodation is cheaper than the resorts to the south.

### Hiking
Almost any kind of hiking experience is possible in BC: from short walks of a few hours along well-marked, easily accessible trails to treks of one or two weeks in remote terrain where you have to take your own food and equipment and be flown in by helicopter. There are well over 2000 km of maintained trails in the national and provincial parks giving you access to many of the province's most outstanding scenic features.

Close to Vancouver there are many good walks: in the Coast Mountains, Garibaldi Provincial Park and around Whistler to the north; and in the Cascade Mountains to the east. From Manning Provincial Park the Pacific Crest Trail goes all the way to Mexico! On Vancouver Island the trails in the Pacific Rim National Park and

Strathcona Provincial Park offer opportunities to see both marine and land wildlife, as do those in South Moresby Gwaii Haanas National Park Reserve in the Queen Charlotte Islands.

In the south-east of the province there is a host of walks (varying in degree of difficulty) in the provincial and national parks in and around the Rocky, Columbia and Cariboo mountains. Finally, to the north, for the adventurous, there is Tweedsmuir Provincial Park and in the far north Spatsizi Plateau and Kwadachi wilderness parks.

Many of these areas are also very good for rock-climbing or mountaineering.

### Canoeing
With the Pacific Ocean to the west and so many inlets, lakes and rivers there are plenty of opportunities to go canoeing on BC's waters. Some of the more popular spots are Bowron, Wells Gray, Slocan and Okanagan lakes inland; and for ocean canoeing around Vancouver, Gulf and Queen Charlotte islands. There are dozens of destinations for white-water canoeing (some are listed in the following section). Write to the Recreational Canoeing Association of BC (☎ 275-6651), 1200 Hornby St, Vancouver, V6Z 2E2, for details of canoe routes, etc.

### White-Water Rafting
BC's topography means that there are many rivers throughout the province suitable for this increasingly popular sport. Check with the local Travel Infocentre for details of where to go and which companies to use. You don't need to be experienced, either, as many of these companies will show you what you have to do. Commercial rafting is regulated by the provincial government and operators are allowed only on rivers that have been checked over by experts, guides must meet certain qualifications and companies must provide equipment that meets government requirements. Trips can last from three hours up to a couple of weeks. Wilderness rafting averages about $200 per

day for everything, while day trips start from around about $90.

The more favoured rivers are the Fraser, Thompson and Chilliwack close to Vancouver; to the east in the High Country near Kamloops the Adams and Clearwater rivers; in the Rockies the Kootenay, Kicking Horse and Illecillewaet rivers; the Chilko and Chilcotin rivers in the Cariboo region west of Williams Lake; and in the north the Skeena, Spatsizi, Stikine, Alsek and Tatshenshini rivers.

## Cycling

You can either go cycling on your own or in organised group tours. Many places in BC have bicycles for rent. The leaflet *Trail Bicycling in National Parks in Alberta & British Columbia* lists trails where cycling is allowed.

In Vancouver one of the most popular spots for cycling is along the 10-km road in Stanley Park. Around BC other favourite areas are the Rocky and Kootenay mountains for mountain-biking; the Fraser River Valley; the Gulf Islands; and along Vancouver Island's east coast. For information and maps contact the Bicycling Association of BC (☎ 737-3034), 1367 West Broadway, Vancouver V6H 4H9.

## Fishing

Fishing, both saltwater and freshwater, is one of BC's major tourist attractions. Particularly popular are the waters around Vancouver Island (where several places claim the title 'salmon capital of the world') and Queen Charlotte Islands; the Fraser, Thompson, Nass, Skeena, Kettle, Peace and Liard rivers; and the lakes of the High Country, Cariboo, Chilcotin and Okanagan Similkameen regions. Commercial operators offer boat rentals or charters or there are all-inclusive packages which include transport and accommodation.

Fishing is controlled by law and you will have to obtain a licence. For further information write to the tourism associations listed earlier under Tourism Regions or to:

Department of Fisheries & Oceans
  Communications Branch, 1090 West Pender St, Vancouver, V6E 2P1 (☎ 666-2074/0383)
Ministry of Environment, Lands & Parks
  Recreational Fisheries Branch, 780 Blanshard St, Victoria, BC V8V 1X5 (☎ 387-1161, in Vancouver 584-8822)

## Scuba Diving

The rich and varied marine life in the waters along BC's 7000 km Pacific coast make scuba diving a very rewarding activity. The best time to go is winter when the plankton has decreased and visibility often exceeds 20 metres. The water temperature drops to about 7°C to 10°C in winter while in summer it reaches 15°C. At depths of more than 15 metres, though, visibility is good throughout the year and temperatures rarely rise above 10°C.

The best places to dive are in the waters off the Pacific Rim National Park on Vancouver Island's west coast; in Georgia Strait between Vancouver Island's east coast and the mainland's Sunshine Coast north of Vancouver; and in Queen Charlotte Strait off Vancouver Island's north-east coast.

## Sailing

Sailing is another popular form of recreation and, though the best time is from mid-April to mid-October, in the sheltered waters of BC's Pacific coast it's possible almost year-round. Coastal marine parks provide safe all-weather anchorage and offer boat hire. Inland some of the more favoured places include Harrison, Okanagan, Arrow and Kootenay lakes in the south and Williston Lake in the north.

## Surfing

In Pacific Rim National Park on Vancouver Island, Long Beach reputedly has the best surfing in BC.

## Hang Gliding

British Columbia's rugged mountains offer some of the best terrain for hang gliding to be found anywhere. Backcountry roads take you to launch sites throughout the province. There is usually reliable weather, particularly in summer, and a well-organised group of hang-glider pilots to tell you about local conditions. Mt Seven, south-east of Golden, has been the site of several world and Canadian hang-gliding records. Some of the best sites for hang gliding are the south-east of Vancouver Island, Salt Spring Island, the Fraser Valley, the Kamloops area, the Okanagan Valley the Kootenay Mountains and in the north around Dawson Creek.

For more information contact the Darryl Staples, Hang Gliding & Paragliding Association of BC (☎ 734-3377), 1846 Vine St, Vancouver, V6K 3J7. The *Western Canada Hang Gliding Site Guide* describes launch sites and landing zones in detail.

### Whale-Watching

Killer whales inhabit the waters off the west coast around Vancouver Island. They frequent Johnstone Strait, and one area, Robson Bight, has been made into an ecological reserve: the whales must not be disturbed by humans. Pacific grey whales migrate between Baja California and Alaska, travelling north in spring and south in the autumn. You can go from Ucluelet and Tofino to see them.

### Caving

Exploring caves may not be everybody's idea of fun, but there are two major areas where you can do it. These the Cody Caves in the south-east north of Nelson and the Horne Lake Caves on Vancouver Island. Gold River, also on Vancouver Island, offers caving opportunities.

### ACCOMMODATION

*Super Camping* is a free guide available at Travel Infocentres. It gives region by region lists of private and government-owned campgrounds and their facilities, opening periods and prices. There is a fee for camping in most provincial and national parks during the summer season.

Hostelling International now has five hostels in BC – Kamloops, Penticton, Vancouver, Victoria and Whistler – as well as a number of associate ones. For information

contact Hostelling International, BC Region (☎ 604-684-7111; fax 604-684-7181), Suite 402, 134 Abbott St, Vancouver, V6B 2K4.

Also, available from Travel Infocentres is the free brochure *Accommodations*, published annually, which lists places to stay approved by Tourism BC. Most of the hotels and motels listed begin in the moderate price range. It also includes YM-YWCAs, some campgrounds and some B&Bs. Near the back of the brochure is a listing of regional B&B agencies to contact.

For further information on B&Bs throughout the province get in touch with British Columbia B&B Association (☎ 276-8616), PO Box 593, 810 West Broadway, Vancouver, V5Z 4E2. It's also worthwhile obtaining a copy of the *British Columbia B&B Directory*, which is a free booklet listing B&Bs across the province. It's available at Travel Infocentres, but is very popular, so not all offices may have a spare copy. If it's not on display, ask.

# Vancouver

Vancouver lies nestled between sea and mountains in the extreme south-western corner of British Columbia. Its physical setting and features make it easily one of the most attractive cities in Canada. The hilly terrain it's built on and the many bridges offer beautiful views of the ocean, sheltered bays and of the city itself.

The parks are numerous and large. One – Stanley Park – is the size of the downtown business area. Sandy beaches dot the shoreline and, like the towering mountains just out of the city, can be used for sports and recreation. Few cities can match Vancouver for its number and variety of interesting sights.

The port, the busiest on North America's west coast, operates all year round in the beautiful and practical natural harbour. It handles nearly all of Canada's trade with Japan and the East.

The US border is just 40 km to the south.

Aside from the city's physical resemblance to San Francisco, the attitudes and lifestyles of Vancouverites are more Californian than anywhere else in the country. The climate further extends the comparison with California, and attracts many eastern Canadians. The average January temperature is 2°C, the July average 17°C. It rarely snows and is not often oppressively hot. The only drawback is the rain – particularly in winter, when it rarely stops. Even in summer a rainy spell can last for weeks. But when the sun shines and the mountains reappear, most people here seem to forget all the soakings they've had.

## HISTORY

The Vancouver area was first inhabited by Salish Indians. The first European to see the region was the Spanish explorer Don Jos Maria Narvaez in 1791. There wasn't a real settlement until 1865, when Hastings Timber Mill was built. In 1867 a town sprang up around 'Gassy' Jack Deighton's bar. Gastown, as it became known, was the centre around which Vancouver grew.

In 1884 the Canadian Pacific railway (CPR) chose Vancouver for the western terminal of the newly built national railway. Soon after the town became incorporated, taking its name from Captain George Vancouver, a British explorer, who had sailed right into Burrard Inlet in 1792. On 13 June 1886 a fire almost completely destroyed the city in less than an hour, killing 21 people. Reconstruction began immediately and by 1889, with the CPR's work done, the population jumped to 8000. The city became the port for trade to the Orient, and the population rose to 42,000 by 1901.

In the next 10 years, the city boomed with the development of the fishing and wood-processing industries. Immigrants poured in. The completion of the Panama Canal increased Vancouver's significance as a port.

WW II catapulted the city into the modern era, and from then on it changed rapidly. The western end became the high-rise apartment centre it now is. In 1974 Granville St became a mall. Redevelopment included housing as

well as office buildings and this set the basis for the modern, liveable city Vancouver is today.

In 1986 the city hosted a very successful World's Fair (Expo 86); a few prominent structures remain, while the rest of the area where it took place is now being redeveloped. In April 1993 its international reputation was enhanced when it hosted the summit meeting between Boris Yeltsin and Bill Clinton.

## ORIENTATION

Vancouver proper is built on a strip of land bounded on the north by Burrard Inlet and on the south by the Fraser River. The city, however, spreads south and east to include suburbs like Richmond, Burnaby, New Westminster, Surrey, Coquitlam and Langley. To the north of Burrard Inlet lie West Vancouver and North Vancouver. The many bays, inlets and river branches, as well as the Pacific coastline, are a major feature of the city.

Generally, the avenues in Greater Vancouver run east-west; the streets go north and south. Some of the streets in the downtown area and many of the avenues in the Greater Vancouver area are given east or west designations depending on which side of Main St they are. So Hastings St, for example, is divided into West Hastings St and East Hastings St.

### Downtown

The real downtown area, in the north-western section of the city, is actually a peninsula, cut off from the southern portion of the city by False Creek. Robson Square, a three-block complex of offices, restaurants, shops and theatres, is pretty well the centre of downtown. It lies on the corner of Robson and Howe Sts. Robson St and, a block or so north, Georgia St, are the two principal north-west/south-east streets. Both run into Stanley Park, Georgia St continuing through the park to Lions Gate Bridge which spans Burrard Inlet, joining it to the separate municipality of North Vancouver.

The main north-east/south-west streets

are, from west to east: Burrard, Howe, Granville and Seymour. North of Georgia St, bordered by Howe and Burrard Sts, is the office, banking and financial district. Robson St is an interesting area with a blend of many ethnic shops and restaurants.

The area south of Robson St and west of Howe St all the way to Sunset Beach on English Bay is primarily residential in the form of rather expensive high-rise apartments.

This high-density area to the west of the downtown shopping area is known as the West End – *not* to be confused with West Vancouver on the North Shore, or the West Side, which is that part of Vancouver south of False Creek and west of Main St. Davie St, between Robson St and the beach, is a secondary commercial and shopping street.

On and around Granville and Seymour Sts, which run north-east from False Creek all the way to West Hastings St, are some of the cheaper hotels.

Much of Granville St, from Nelson St north to West Hastings St, is closed to cars. It's not a true mall as trucks and buses are still permitted and it has never worked very well as a central showcase. It's fairly drab and quiet during the day, but at night it's a lively focal point for some of the city's street scene. Musicians and various buskers line the street, teenagers by the dozen parade, various eccentrics and misfits appear and street kids beg for money. The southern end towards the bridge is something of a red-light area, with sex shops and bars advertising 'exotic' dancers. A couple of large legitimate cinemas also draw crowds to the area, so it's quite a mix.

Also on Granville St are the two main department stores, Eaton's and the Bay. Below these, towards Burrard Inlet, is the modern underground shopping mall called the Pacific Centre.

Georgia St near Granville St is the area with some of the city's top hotels. At the northern end of Granville and Seymour Sts is West Hastings St – the east designations begin at Main St.

Further north, at the bottom of Granville

St near Burrard Inlet, is Granville Place and Harbour Centre. Here you'll find modern shopping complexes with views of the harbour. At the water's edge at the foot of Howe St is Canada Place, an impressive Expo 86 leftover with jagged white 'sails'.

Hastings St has some cheap hotels, bars, restaurants, pawnshops and army surplus-type shops, but for a couple of blocks either side of Main St it is skid row, with many down-and-outs (see Dangers & Annoyances later). Gastown is north of West Hastings St between Columbia and Richards Sts. This is the interesting, tourist-oriented, restored area of old Vancouver.

Chinatown is very close by to the south, in the area around Pender, Gore and Carrall Sts.

The Pacific National Exhibition (PNE) stadium and exhibition grounds are further east on East Hastings St, near the Second Narrows Bridge.

**Greater Vancouver**

To the south of the West End and downtown, over False Creek, lies most of Vancouver – this vast area is primarily residential.

**West** Heading west after crossing Burrard Bridge or Granville Bridge is the area of Kitsilano, no longer a cheap area but still very popular with young people, students as well as professionals. When a kid from BC's interior moves to the city, this is where he or she wants to be. The main artery through the area is West 4th Ave. It's lined with shops, restaurants and cafés, few of which are pricey. The other important thoroughfare is West Broadway, south of West 4th Ave.

There are beaches all along English Bay, from Kitsilano past Jericho Beach and Spanish Banks Beach to the University of British Columbia (UBC) campus. Just before the campus is one of the expensive areas of town, with good views of the city. UBC is at the far western end of the 'hump' sticking out into the Strait of Georgia. You can walk around the coast all the way to Wreck Beach, south of the university (but wait until the tide is out).

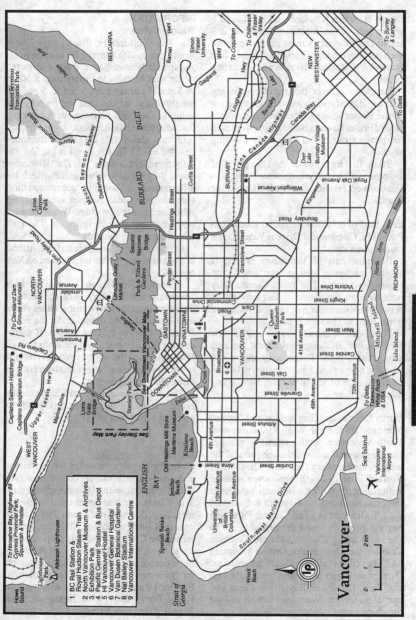

BRITISH COLUMBIA

Vancouver

1  BC Rail Station &
   Royal Hudson Steam Train
2  North Vancouver Museum & Archives
3  Exhibition Park
4  Pacific Central Station & Bus Depot
5  HI Vancouver Hostel
6  Vancouver General Hospital
7  Van Dusen Botanical Gardens
8  Nat Bailey Stadium
9  Vancouver International Centre

0    1    2 km

**South** Between Kitsilano and Sea Island – where Vancouver International Airport is – are some of the city's most exclusive areas, such as Shaughnessy Heights. Estates line South-West Marine Drive, facing out to Sea Island.

Further south is the rapidly growing municipality of Richmond, built on a portion of the Fraser River Delta. On the southern side of Fraser River is Burns Bog; this is used for peat extraction so very little building goes on.

Still further south is the port of Tsawwassen, where you can catch a ferry to Vancouver Island, the Gulf Islands or Seattle.

**East** East of downtown running south from Powell St, Commercial Drive is Vancouver's main Italian street.

Burnaby, east of Vancouver proper, is another residential area and contains Simon Fraser University. The Trans Canada Hwy runs through the centre of Burnaby on its way from Vancouver east to Chilliwack and north-west to Horseshoe Bay.

South-east of Burnaby is the city of New Westminster, BC's original capital, an area along the Fraser River with many old wooden houses and lots of industry. On the southern side of the river from New Westminster is Surrey.

**North** Over Lions Gate Bridge and Second Narrows Bridge lie West Vancouver and North Vancouver, both essentially middle-class residential areas, although parts of the western area are very exclusive. The shore of Burrard Inlet in North Vancouver is lined with commercial docks. In North Vancouver the principal north-south street is Lonsdale Ave. To the east is Lynn Canyon Park, and beyond is Mt Seymour Provincial Park. To the north along Capilano Rd are Capilano Canyon, the Lions Peaks, Grouse Mountain and the edges of the Coast Mountains. Further west and north lie Cypress Provincial Park, Horseshoe Bay (from where you can take a ferry to Vancouver Island) and the Sunshine Coast.

## INFORMATION
### Tourist Office
The Travel Infocentre, Plaza Level, Waterfront Centre, 200 Burrard St, is open in the summer daily from 8 am to 6 pm, and the rest of the year Monday to Friday from 8.30 am to 5 pm, Saturday from 9 am to 5 pm. It's usually busy, but the staff are friendly and helpful. They will help you with bookings for accommodation, tours, transport and activities. Call ☎ 683-2000 for information or ☎ 683-2772 for bookings. At the infocentre get a copy of *The Vancouver Book*, the official visitors' guide, which has information on shopping, accommodation, entertainment, local transport, etc and is free. Also useful is the brochure *Where Vancouver*, available around town for 75 cents, which comes out monthly.

On the corner of Georgia and Granville Sts is a booth giving visitor information on Vancouver.

Travel information is available in Tsawwassen at the ferry dock for Victoria. There are information booths at either end of the George Massey Tunnel under the Fraser River on the way to Tsawwassen. If you're coming from the east along the Trans Canada Hwy you'll see the signs as you get closer to town. Another infocentre is south on Hwy 99 just inside the US border.

The HI Vancouver Hostel has a notice board that lists rides, plane tickets, goods for sale and sometimes job offers.

### Money
Changing foreign currency or travellers' cheques is no problem. If you need to do any banking outside normal business hours quite a few banks around town open Saturdays including: downtown, Canada Trust, on the corner of East Pender and Main Sts, serving mostly the Chinese community, open from 9 am to 5 pm; Royal Bank, 269 East Pender St, open from 9 am to 3 pm; Toronto Dominion, on the corner of East Pender and Columbia Sts, open 9 am to 4 pm; and in Kitsilano, the Royal Bank, 2907 West Broadway, open from 9.30 am to 3.30 pm.

Thomas Cook has a number of offices in Vancouver including one (☎ 687-6111) at 1016 West Georgia St and another at 130 999 Canada Place. American Express (☎ 669-2813) is close by at 1040 West Georgia St. They're open on Saturday too.

You can also find currency-exchange offices, usually in the heavily touristed areas and often open every day. Downtown, the International Foreign Exchange (☎ 683-9666), 1169 Robson St, is open Monday to Thursday from 9 am to 7 pm, Friday and Saturday from 9 am to 9 pm and Sunday from 10 am to 7 pm.

Vancouver Airport provides banking and money-changing facilities too (see Getting There & Away later).

## Post
The main post office (☎ 662-5725), 349 West Georgia St between Homer and Hamilton Sts, is open Monday to Friday from 8.30 am to 5.30 pm. It has no separate poste-restante counter: you just join the queue, show some identification and the person behind the counter will look for your mail. The post office also has a good philatelic desk and a photocopier.

The American Express office, 1040 West Georgia St, will keep a card-holder's mail for a month.

## Foreign Consulates
The following countries have diplomatic representation in Vancouver:

Australia
    Suite 602, World Trade Centre, 999 Canada Place, V6C 3E1 (☎ 684-1177)
Austria
    716 525 Seymour St, V6B 3H9 (☎ 687-3338)
Belgium
    Suite 2900, 595 Burrard St, V6Z 2C7 (☎ 691-7566)
Brazil
    Suite 1300, 1140 West Pender St, V6E 4G1 (☎ 687-4589; fax 681-6534)
China (People's Republic of)
    3380 Granville St, V6H 3K3 (☎ 736-5910)
Denmark
    Suite 102, 475 Howe St, V6C 2B3 (☎ 684-5171)

Fiji
    1840 Clark Drive (☎ 254-5544)
Finland
    1120 1188 West Georgia St, V6E 4A2 (☎ 688-4483)
France
    Suite 1201, 736 Granville St, V6Z 1H9 (☎ 681-2301)
Germany
    Suite 704, 999 Canada Place, V6C 3E1 (☎ 684-4258)
Greece
    Suite 501, 1200 Burrard St, V6Z 2C7 (☎ 681-1381)
Hungary
    1650 West 2nd Ave (☎ 734-6644)
India
    2nd Floor, 325 Howe St, V6C 1Z7 (☎ 662-8811)
Indonesia
    1455 West Georgia St (☎ 682-8855)
Italy
    Suite 705, 1200 Burrard St, V6Z 2C7 (☎ 684-7288)
Japan
    900 Board of Trade Tower, 1177 West Hastings St, V6E 2K9 (☎ 684-5868)
Malaysia
    925 West Georgia St (☎ 685-9550)
Mexico
    Suite 810, 1130 West Pender St (☎ 684-3547)
Netherlands
    Suite 721, Crown Trust Building, 475 Howe St, V6C 2B3 (☎ 684-6448)
New Zealand
    Suite 1200, 888 Dunsmuir St (☎ 684-7388)
Norway
    200 Burrard St (☎ 682-7977)
Poland
    Suite 1600, 1177 West Hastings St (☎ 688-3530)
Portugal
    Suite 904, 700 West Pender St (☎ 688-6514)
Singapore
    Suite 405, 4603 Kingsway, Burnaby (☎ 439-3340)
Spain
    3736 Parker St, Burnaby (☎ 299-7760)
Sweden
    Suite 1106, 1177 West Hastings St, V6E 2K3 (☎ 683-5838)
Switzerland
    Suite 790, World Trade Centre, 999 Canada Place V6C 3E1 (☎ 684-2231)
Thailand
    736 Granville St (☎ 687-1143)
UK
    Suite 800, 1111 Melville St, V6E 3V6 (☎ 683-4421; fax 581-0693)
USA
    1075 West Pender St, V6E 2M6 (☎ 685-4311)

BRITISH COLUMBIA

## Travel Agencies

Travel CUTS, the student travel organisation, has four offices in Vancouver: one at 501 602 West Hastings St (☎ 681-9136), another at 1516 Duranleau St, Granville Island (☎ 687-6033) and one on the campus of each university, UBC and Simon Fraser.

## Bookshops

Vancouver has a number of very good bookshops. Duthie Books (☎ 684-4496), 919 Robson St, on the corner of Hornby St, has a range of books including a travel and Canadiana section. It has several other branches including one at UBC. Book Warehouse (☎ 685-5711), 1150 Robson St, has good-quality books, many at bargain prices. It's open seven days a week from 10 am to 10 pm and gives its customers free coffee. World Wide Books & Maps (☎ 687-3320), 736A Granville St, down a flight of stairs, has a variety of travel guides, atlases and maps for Canada and abroad. Another good bookshop is Blackberry Books (☎ 685-6188/4113), 1663 Duranleau St on Granville Island. It's open daily from 9 am to 9 pm and has two more outlets in Kitsilano. Also in Kitsilano at 2667 West Broadway, the Travel Bug (☎ 737-1122) has travel guides and maps plus language tapes and accessories.

Smith Books and Cole's are general chainstore bookshops: they both have a branch downtown in the Pacific Centre Mall.

## Library

Vancouver Public Library (☎ 665-2287), 750 Burrard St, next to Hotel Vancouver, at the junction with Robson St, is open Monday to Thursday from 10 am to 9 pm, Friday and Saturday from 10 am to 6 pm. In winter (October to March) it's open on Sundays from 1 to 5 pm. Visitors can obtain a library card for $20.

## Medical Services

Vancouver General Hospital is at 855 West 12th Ave. The emergency number is ☎ 875-4995; call ☎ 875-4000 for patient information.

## Emergency

Other important local emergency phone numbers are:

AIDS Hotline (☎ 687-2437)
Vancouver Crisis Centre (☎ 733-4111) – open 24 hours
Rape Relief Centre (☎ 872-8212) – open 24 hours

## Dangers & Annoyances

Hastings St for a couple of blocks either side of Main St is not a good area at night, particularly at weekends when there's been some heavy drinking. After dark it's advisable to stay out of the side streets. By day it's safe and has a few places you may want to look at.

If you're driving, traffic congestion and finding a place to park can be a problem (see Car under Getting Around later).

## Useful Organisations

The Western Canada Wilderness Committee (☎ 687-8224), 20 Water St in Gastown, has information and maps on hiking trails in wilderness areas and books on environmental awareness issues relating mainly to Western Canada. It helped to open up walking trails in old-growth forest areas such as the Carmanah and Clayoquot valleys and Meares Island. It also has a nature walking guide to Stanley Park.

The British Columbia Automobile Association (BCAA) (☎ 732-3911), 999 West Broadway, has a 24-hour breakdown service for its own members and those of other automobile associations. If you're interested in finding out about Native Indian culture contact the Native Heritage Centre (☎ 746-8119). Disabled persons can call the Handicapped Resource Line (☎ 1-800-465-4911).

## DOWNTOWN
### Gastown

The name is taken from 'Gassy' Jack Deighton, an English sailor who forsook the sea to open a bar servicing the developing timber mills. When a village sprang up around his establishment it was called Gassy's Town. The name stuck and Vancouver was on its way. The Gastown area today is bounded by Columbia and Richards Sts, with Water St the main thoroughfare. Burrard Inlet is just to the north. A statue of Gassy Jack has been erected in Maple St Square, where Cordova and Water Sts meet.

The whole Gastown area gradually became a skid row, but in the 1970s it was restored and renovated, pushing Vancouver's seedier characters a little south to Hastings St. The old Victorian buildings now house restaurants, bars, boutiques and galleries. The brick streets have been lined with old lamps. Street vendors and buskers add to the holiday feel of the area. The historic flavour is only a little marred by the parking lot several storeys high in Water St.

At the western end of Water St is the world's first clock run by steam. You can see it work through the side glass panels and will hear it toot every 15 minutes.

## Chinatown

About 35,000 people of Chinese descent live in the area around West Pender St, roughly bordered by Abbott and Gore Sts. For the most part it's genuine, serving the locals. Even some of the young people don't speak English. The streets are full of people going in and out of stores of hanging ducks and chickens: there are lots of restaurants and little grocery shops. The colours, signs and occasional old Chinese-style balcony can make you believe for a second that you're in the East, especially when you see the Chinese characters on signs for banks and Hertz Rent-a-Car. There are tourist and souvenir shops interspersed with the community businesses.

**World's Thinnest Office Building** Called the Sam Kee, this building at 8 West Pender St, near the corner of Carrall St, has made it into Ripley's *Believe It Or Not* and the *Guinness Book of Records*. It's easy to miss because it looks like the front of the larger building behind, to which it is attached.

**Dr Sun Yat-Sen Classical Chinese Garden** This is the only full-scale classical Chinese garden (☎ 689-7133) found outside China. Its design is subtle but exquisite in execution and effect. Modelled after the Ming Dynasty gardens, best represented in the city of Suzhou, it makes a real sanctuary in the centre of the city. The Taoist principles of Yin and Yang are incorporated in numerous ways throughout the garden.

The guided tours are included in the admission and are well worthwhile. If possible, go during the week when it won't be too busy. It's at 578 Carrall St behind the Chinese Cultural Centre in Chinatown. It opens daily from 10 am to 8 pm and admission is $3.50, concession $2.50. The adjacent park, built by local artisans using Chinese materials, is similar in design and has free entry.

**Robsonstrasse**

Robsonstrasse is the local name given to the section of Robson St between Howe and Broughton Sts. At one time mainly German, the area is now known for its many ethnic restaurants and shops. There are Italian, French, Japanese, Vietnamese and Danish places among them. For more detailed information on restaurants, see the Places to Eat section. The bottom of the street, down

### Gassy Jack
In the mid-19th century the men working in the sawmills along the shores of Burrard Inlet weren't allowed to drink alcohol on mill property. They had to travel a long way into town, New Westminster, to find somewhere to imbibe. An enterprising former riverboat captain, John Deighton, saw his opportunity and landed in his canoe close to the mill area with his wife, a few animals and a small barrel of whisky. He began selling the whisky immediately and soon became a huge success. He was called 'Gassy Jack' because he talked so much; the community that developed around his saloon, became known as Gassy's Town then Gastown. ∎

Downtown Vancouver

PLACES TO STAY

8   English Bay Hotel
10  Riviera Motor Inn
11  Robsonstrasse City Motor Inn
12  Barclay Hotel
16  Cecil Hotel
17  Travelodge
18  Austin Motor Hotel
19  Century Plaza Hotel
20  YMCA
26  Hotel Vancouver
27  Royal Centre & Hyatt Regency
29  YWCA
31  Day's Inn
36  Delta Place Hotel
38  Hotel Georgia
41  Pacific Centre
43  St Regis Hotel
46  Dufferin Hotel
48  Georgian Court Hotel
49  Kingston Hotel
50  Salvation Army House for Men
53  Marble Arch Hotel
54  Niagara Hotel
63  Dominion Hotel
64  Downtown Vancouver Hostel
69  Spinning Wheel Inn
72  Patricia Hotel
73  Harbourfront Inn
81  Backpackers' Vincent's Hostel

PLACES TO EAT

1   El Mariachi
2   Musashi Japanese Restaurant
3   Café Slavia
4   Jumpstarts
5   Crumble's
6   Bud's Halibut & Chips
7   Ciao!
9   Saigon
21  Pepita's
22  Heidelberg House
23  White Spot
30  Jolly Taxpayer Hotel & Pub
42  Elephant & Castle
45  India Gate
56  Kilimanjaro
58  Water St Café

59  India Village
60  Maharajah
61  Old Spaghetti Factory
62  Brother's Restaurant
68  Only Seafoods Café
70  Bodai Vegetarian Restaurant
71  Miu Jay Garden Vegetarian
    Restaurant
74  Lu Zuan
75  Max King Bakery & Restaurant
76  Maxim's Bakery & Café
77  On On Tea Gardens
78  Hon's Wun Tun House
79  Punjab Restaurant
80  Mom's Kitchen

THINGS TO SEE & DO

13  Vancouver Aquatic Centre
14  HR MacMillan Planetarium &
    Vancouver Museum
33  Canada Place
37  Pendulum
39  Vancouver Art Gallery
47  BC Place Stadium
55  Harbour Centre
57  Steam Clock
65  World's Thinnest Office Building
67  Dr Sun Yat Sen Chinese Classical
    Garden
82  Science World

OTHER

15  Granville Island Public Market
24  Duthie Books
25  Vancouver Public Library
28  Burrard Station
32  Travel Infocentre
34  Granville Square
35  Waterfront Station
40  Robson Square
44  Granville Station
51  Main Post Office
52  Queen Elizabeth Theatre &
    Vancouver Playhouse
66  Stadium Station
83  Main Street Station
84  Pacific Central Station & Bus Depot

BRITISH COLUMBIA

towards Stanley Park, has some of the newer, better restaurants.

**Stanley Park**
The city's main green area, a 400-hectare park, is one of the best in the country. With its wooded hills, parkland, trails, sports fields, swimming pools and beaches, there's something for everyone. The 10-km sea wall that encircles the park makes a good walk or

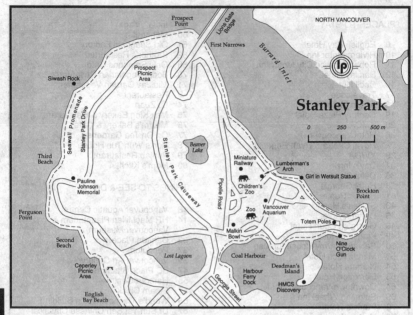

bicycle ride even if you don't go all the way round. From various points there are good views of downtown Vancouver, the North Shore and out to sea towards the islands.

Along the western side are several sandy beaches; Lions Gate Bridge extends from the northern tip and the road through the park to the bridge is usually busy. Just to the west of Lions Gate Bridge is **Prospect Point**, a popular point for views of the Narrows and passing ships. There's a restaurant here as well: it's a nice spot for a coffee on the terrace. Near **Brockton Point** there is a good collection of totem poles. There is a small, free zoo near Brockton Oval. Off the southern side, near the yacht club, is **Deadman's Island**, once used, it's said, by a northern Native Indian tribe as a camp for women captured in raids. Later it became a burial ground for Chinese people and Native Indians.

**Vancouver Aquarium** Within the park is the

Vancouver Aquarium (☎ 682-1118), Canada's largest, with 9000 sea creatures. Most popular are the dolphins and killer whales that put on shows several times a day. There is also a special tank for beluga whales. Other exhibits include octopuses, crocodiles, eels, piranhas and a wide variety of local sea life and freshwater fish. The aquarium is also used for research. It's open every day from 9.30 am to 8 pm July to early September, from 10 am to 5.30 pm the rest of the year and admission is $8.50.

### Vancouver Art Gallery

The city's art gallery (☎ 682-5621), 750 Hornby St, is right at the centre of things. It has a large collection of work by Emily Carr, a one-time resident of the area and one of Canada's best-known painters.

There's also a survey collection of other Canadians and some US and British paintings. The gallery is open daily from 9.30 am to 8 pm in summer; the rest of the year from

10 am to 5 pm Monday to Wednesday and Saturday, from 10 am to 9 pm on Thursday and Friday, from noon to 5 pm on Sunday. Admission costs $4.75.

## Pendulum
Worth a look (duck your head) is the swaying 26-metre sculptural piece called Pendulum in the Hong Kong Bank of Canada. It's on West Georgia St opposite the Vancouver Art Gallery.

## Canada Place
Canada Place, one of the few prominent buildings remaining from Expo 86, juts into the harbour at the foot of Howe St. It resembles an ocean liner with tent-like sails and has become a major city landmark. At the northern end are the promenade shops and restaurants, and outside, good views across Burrard Inlet. The complex contains the World Trade Centre, BC Convention Centre and Pan Pacific Hotel, and is a terminal for cruise ships. Also here is the CN IMAX Theatre (☎ 682-4629/6422) with a five-storey-high screen showing films made exclusively for such theatres. Canada Place is very close to Waterfront Station.

## BC Place
This name refers to both a large tract of city land being totally redeveloped and the stadium which kicked off the entire project. The land runs along the waterfront at False Creek at the southern end of Robson St, near Cambie Bridge. Formerly an area of disused railway lines and warehouses, it will contain apartments, parks, a theatre and museums as part of a 25-year plan.

BC Place Stadium (☎ 669-2300 for general information, ☎ 661-7373 for events), 777 Pacific Blvd South, was opened in 1983, and is a large sports arena covered by a translucent dome-shaped roof. The roof is 'air-supported', which means it is inflated by huge fans and kept in place by criss-crossed steel wires, hence its quilted appearance.

Concerts, trade shows, sports events and other large-scale gatherings are held during the year in this 60,000-capacity stadium which is also the home ground of the BC Lions football team.

To get to the stadium catch either bus No 15 or No 17, or take the SkyTrain to Stadium Station.

## Science World
Another structure that remains from Expo 86 is the geodesic dome just off Quebec St near Main St Station. It now houses Science World (☎ 687-7832), a museum where you can get involved through touching and testing the displays. Aimed primarily at children, hands-on exhibits and experiments help explain scientific and physical phenomena. One of the main features is the OMNIMAX film theatre (☎ 875-6664). Science World is open every day from 10 am to 5 pm except Saturday when it's open till 9 pm. The admission fee is $7 and the OMNIMAX theatre costs $9; a combined ticket is $11.

## Views
One of the best views of the city and surroundings is from the top of the **Sheraton Landmark Hotel**, 1400 Robson St, in the revolving restaurant. If you're eating there the elevator up is free. The hotel is one of the city's highest buildings. A second spot is the more-advertised observation deck (☎ 689-0421) and restaurant atop the **Harbour Centre** at 555 West Hastings St. The deck is open from 8.30 am to 10.30 pm (summer) and is reached by an external glass-walled elevator, which takes 50 seconds. The cost is $5.50, students $3.75; the ticket is valid all day so you can come and go. If you're going to eat in the restaurant, the ride up is free. Take a SkyTrain to Waterfront St or bus Nos 10, 14, 16, 20 heading towards the harbour on Granville Mall.

The commercial harbour area stretches along Burrard Inlet from Stanley Park to the Second Narrows Bridge. The plaza at Granville Square beside the SeaBus terminal, or Canada Place's observation deck, offer a view where you watch the many types of vessels moving in and out of the harbour.

**WEST SIDE**
**Granville Island**

On the southern side of False Creek, under the Granville Bridge, this formerly industrial little island has been redeveloped into a busy blend of businesses, restaurants, arts and entertainment. The Granville Island Information Centre (☎ 666-5784), 1592 Johnston St, is open daily from 9 am to 6 pm.

Major attractions include two important performing-arts centres, numerous theatre companies, and, on the north-western tip, the popular Public Market, open daily 9 am to 6 pm, with fresh fruit, vegetables and fish. A few prepared-food counters sell small meals and snacks.

There are several shops where local painters, jewellery makers and weavers make and display their crafts. Prices are fairly reasonable. You can also view the art galleries in the Emily Carr College of Art & Design (☎ 844-3800), 1299 Johnston St. The Granville Island Brewing Co (☎ 688-9927), 1441 Cartwright St, is a small company producing naturally brewed beer (ie without chemicals), and gives free tours at 1 and 3 pm with a sample at the end.

On the north-eastern edge of the island it's interesting to have a look at the attractive, pricey, floating houses. Note that much of the island's activity is shut down on Monday.

To get to the island from either Water St in Gastown or Granville St downtown, catch the No 50 False Creek bus. The bus stops near the information centre. Alternatively, you can take the False Creek miniferry (see Getting Around).

**Vanier Park**

Vanier Park, on English Bay south of False Creek and below Burrard Bridge, is home to the Vancouver Museum, HR MacMillan Planetarium and the Vancouver Maritime Museum. Also in the park are the Vancouver Archives, Academy of Music, Canadian Coast Guard and Burrard Civic Marina. The park is a popular recreational area and when the weather's fine you'll see people strolling, jogging, power walking, cycling, flying kites, walking their dogs or simply sitting

and watching the ships moving between English Bay and False Creek.

**Vancouver Museum** This museum (☎ 736-4431), 1100 Chestnut St, just west of Burrard Bridge and also called the Vancouver Centennial Museum, specialises in local history. On display are old photos of BC and sections on the archaeology of the area, concentrating on the Salish Indians and ethnology. There are a few examples of most Native Indian crafts. The basketry is impressive, especially the baskets made of cedar and pine roots. The part of the museum showing the European exploration and settlement of Vancouver is interesting. The last of the Hudson's Bay Company forts – Fort Victoria – was here.

The museum is open daily May to September from 10 am to 9 pm; from October to April it's open Tuesday to Sunday from 10 am to 5 pm. Admission costs $5, or $2.50 concession. Or you can buy a combination ticket for $7 which gives access to the Vancouver Maritime Museum as well. To get there (and to the Vancouver Maritime Museum close by) take bus No 22 from Burrard St downtown.

**HR MacMillan Planetarium** This planetarium (☎ 736-3656), part of the Vancouver Museum complex, has regularly changing, entertaining and educational shows which are projected onto a 20-metre dome. The shows are very popular, so make reservations early.

Admission is $5.50. There are also music-laser shows for $7.50 at 8.30 pm Sunday to Thursday and at 9.30 pm Friday and Saturday. The planetarium is closed on Monday during the winter, but open daily in the summer months. On Friday, Saturday and Sunday afternoons when the sky is clear the **Gordon Southam Observatory** (☎ 738-2855) is also open to the public and is free.

**Vancouver Maritime Museum** This museum (☎ 737-2211/2), 1905 Ogden Ave at the foot of Cypress St, is a five-minute walk from the Vancouver Museum. It is divided into two sections. The museum itself is strictly for boat buffs – lots of wooden models and some old rowboats on display. It's open daily May to September from 10 am to 5 pm and admission is $5, $2.50 concession.

The other section, designated a National Historic Site (☎ 666-3201), is good, and free. On display is the *St Roch*, a 1928 RCMP Arctic patrol sailing ship which was the first to navigate the legendary Northwest Passage in both an easterly and westerly direction. There are interesting free guided tours on the ship every half-hour or so. From the museum wharf you can take a ferry to Granville Island.

## Old Hastings Mill Store

Built in 1865, this was the first store on Burrard Inlet. It survived the Great Fire of 1886 and was moved in 1930 to where it stands today at 1575 Alma St on the corner of Point Grey Rd at the eastern end of Jericho Beach. It's the large, off-white, barn-like building with brown trim. It houses a small collection of Native Indian artefacts and some local memorabilia and is open daily in summer from 11 am to 4 pm, weekends the rest of the year from 1 to 4 pm. Admission is free. Call ☎ 228-1213 for information.

## University of British Columbia

The University of British Columbia (☎ 822-3131), often just called UBC, is at the most westerly point of Vancouver, on the spit jutting out into Georgia Strait. The huge campus serving 30,000 students is spread over 400 wooded hectares. Bus Nos 4, 10 and 14 heading south on Granville St run up to the university every 10 minutes or so; the journey takes about 30 minutes.

As well as the attractive grounds, there are several points of interest.

**UBC Museum of Anthropology** This museum (☎ 822-5087) is excellent. The exhibits include art and artefacts from cultures around the world. Asia, Africa and the Pacific are all well represented but the emphasis is on the work of BC's Coastal Indians, which includes a terrific totem pole collection – both indoors and out. The collection has some fine sculptures and carvings. Many of the items are stored in glass filing cabinets. Everything is numbered and catalogued, so you can look up details and cross-references yourself. The museum is open daily in summer from 11 am to 5 pm, till 9 pm Tuesday. It's closed Monday, between early September and the end of June. Admission is $5.

**Nitobe Memorial Gardens** These beautiful Japanese-style gardens (☎ 822-4208) are near the museum. Designed by a leading Japanese landscape architect, they're a perfect display of this symbolic Eastern art form. Get a guide at the gate when you buy a ticket. The gardens are open daily from 10 am to 6 pm in summer, Monday to Friday 11 am to 3 pm. Admission is $2.

Near the gardens, **Totem Park** has carvings and buildings representing part of a Haida Indian village. Admission is free.

**Wreck Beach** Along South-West Marine Drive, heading south past the Rose Garden and the Museum of Anthropology, are markers for trails into the woods. Follow trail No 3 or 4 down the steep steps to Wreck Beach, a pleasant and quiet – if notorious – nude beach.

**Aquatic Centre** If you don't fancy that, try the UBC Aquatic Centre (☎ 822-4521) back on the campus, off University Blvd, which has pools, saunas and exercise areas, and is open to the public.

**Queen Elizabeth Park**
This 52-hectare park, between Cambie and Ontario Sts and near 33rd Ave, is the city's second largest park. Up the hill to the Bloedel Conservatory there are great views of the city in nearly every direction. There's a well-designed sunken garden surrounded by small cliffs which has some fantastic plants, one with leaves a metre across.

Next to the parking lot is an unusual, Oriental-looking garden consisting of many pools and fountains. The garden is mostly cement, but is dotted with wooden frames holding plants and flowers. There is a restaurant and a cheaper coffee shop for snacks or tea. Catch bus No 15 heading south-east on Robson St to get there.

**Bloedel Conservatory** The conservatory (☎ 872-5513) has three climate zones including desert and tropical beneath its plastic dome. For the admission prices of $3 or $1.50 for students, however, you may consider it's not really worth it with all the flowers and gardens around for free. It's open weekdays from 9 am to 8 pm, weekends from 10 am to 9 pm.

**Vandusen Botanical Gardens**
These 22-hectare gardens (☎ 266-7194), 5251 Oak St between 33rd and 37th Aves, are not far from Queen Elizabeth Park. The gardens contain a small lake and a large collection of ornamental plants from around the world. They're open daily from 10 am to 8 pm in summer. The admission price is $4.50, students $2.25. Take bus No 17 south on Burrard St from downtown.

## NORTH SHORE
### Lonsdale Quay Market
Major redevelopment transformed the area by the SeaBus terminal on the North Shore. Foremost among the changes, which include a water's edge park, offices and residential complexes, is the Lonsdale Quay Market (☎ 985-6261). The 1st floor is devoted to fresh and cooked food; the 2nd floor is mainly speciality shops but has a restaurant with good views. As you leave the ferry, there's an information booth to offer guidance on the North Shore's attractions. The local bus depot is here as well.

The market is open daily 9.30 am to 6.30 pm except Friday when it stays open to 9 pm. To get there catch the SeaBus from the downtown terminal at Waterfront Station.

### North Vancouver Museum & Archives
The small museum (☎ 987-5618), 333 Chesterfield Ave, offers rather good changing exhibits on a wide range of subjects such as transport, antiques and Native Indian crafts. Admission is by donation and it's open Wednesday and Friday to Sunday from noon to 5 pm; Thursday it stays open till 9 pm.

### Capilano Suspension Bridge
This bridge (☎ 985-7474), 3735 Capilano Rd on the left-hand side going north, spans the Capilano River for almost 140 metres at a height of 70 metres. Open daily in summer from 8 am till dusk, it's very tourist oriented and, with little else in the small park, is really not worth the $6 (students $4) admission.

To get there from downtown take bus No 246, marked 'Highlands', going west on West Georgia St or bus No 236 from Lonsdale Quay to Edgemont Village; you then change to bus No 232. (This bus also goes to Capilano Salmon Hatchery and Cleveland Dam; in summer No 236 also goes all the way to Grouse Mountain.) If you're driving, head north over Lions Gate Bridge to Marine Drive then turn left (north) at Capilano Rd.

### Capilano Salmon Hatchery
The hatchery is a fish farm (☎ 666-17?) by the government to help stop the de? of valuable salmon stocks. Althoug? can't see the holding pools, there are e? with good explanations of the whole pr? Salmon in various stages of growth are on display in tanks, and you can see how they are channelled from the river into the hatchery when they head upstream to spawn. Admission is free. It's in Capilano River Regional Park, off Capilano Rd not far north of the suspension bridge.

### Cleveland Dam
The dam (☎ 987-1411) blocks Capilano Lake, which supplies much of Vancouver's drinking water. You'll get good views of the Lions, two peaks of the Coast Mountains. There are picnic areas and trails and it's free. The dam is slightly further north of the salmon hatchery, up Capilano Rd which becomes Nancy Greene Way.

## Grouse Mountain

Grouse Mountain (☎ 984-0661), 6400 Nancy Greene Way (the northern extension of Capilano Rd), is famous for its Swiss-built Superskyride cable car which operates weekdays in summer from 9 am to 10 pm, weekends from 8 am; the rest of the year it's 11 am to 5 pm weekdays, till 7 pm weekends. From the top – 1110 metres – you can see all of Vancouver, the coast, part of Vancouver Island and northward over the mountains. It's an expensive ride at $14.50. There are restaurants at the top and bottom of the mountain.

If you take the Superskyride, make sure it's a clear day. If it's raining, foggy or at all hazy with low clouds, forget it: by the time you reach the top you won't see a thing. Go in late afternoon; then you can see the city by day and night. (See Capilano Suspension Bridge earlier for details on how to get there.)

In winter there is day and night skiing (see the Activities section later).

## Lynn Canyon Park

Set in thick woods, this park gives a good glimpse of the rainforest vegetation so different from that found in eastern Canada. There are many hiking trails, and you can find your own picnic and swimming spots. Over Lynn Canyon is a suspension bridge; although not as big as Capilano, it's much the same and is free. The **Lynn Canyon Park Ecology Centre** (☎ 987-5922), 3663 Park Rd, has displays, films and slide shows about the biology of the area. It's open daily from 10 am to 5 pm.

To get to the park take bus Nos 228 or 229 from Lonsdale Quay. If you're driving go over Second Narrows Bridge, take Lynn Valley Rd then go right (east) on Peters Rd, where you'll see signs that lead you into the park.

## Park & Tilford Gardens

These 1.2 hectares of flower gardens, at 1200 Cotton Drive south-west of Lynn Canyon Park, were developed by the distillery of the same name. There are some unusual tree specimens, tropical birds and lots of flowers. Although free, these gardens are not highly recommended; they're used mainly by wedding photographers. They're open daily from 9.30 am till dusk.

To get there take bus No 239 from Lonsdale Quay to Phibbs Exchange, then change to No 232 heading east to Brooksbank, where the gardens are.

## Royal Hudson Steam Train

This 1930s steam engine pulls restored coaches on a 5½-hour return excursion to Squamish. The route follows the coast northward along the shore of Howe Sound through some beautiful scenery. The cost is $26.17 return. The train leaves from BC Rail's station, 1311 West 1st St at the southern end of Pemberton Ave, North Vancouver. For details of fares and the rather complicated schedule contact First Tours (☎ 688-7246; 1-800-663-1500), near the foot of Denman St. A variation is to take the train one way and cruise back on the MV *Britannia*; the fare is $54 return. (See Organised Tours in the Activities section later.)

## Lighthouse Park

Here in a stand of original forest are some of the largest trees in the Vancouver area. Trails lead to the lighthouse (☎ 922-1211) and bluffs, with views of the Georgia Strait. The park is at Point Atkinson in West Vancouver, eight km to the left (west) on Marine Drive after going over Lions Gate Bridge. Catch bus No 250 going west on West Georgia St.

## EAST VANCOUVER
## Simon Fraser University

The university sits atop Burnaby Mountain in Burnaby, about 20 km east of downtown. Its intriguing modern architecture and excellent vistas make it a worthwhile place to visit. The design, incorporating unusual use of space and perspective, was – and remains – controversial. There are huge courtyard-like quadrants and many fountains, including one on a roof. Some areas of the complex are reminiscent of Mayan ruin sites in Mexico. For information on tours around the university, call ☎ 291-3111. To get there, catch bus Nos 10 or 14 on East Hastings St then change near Boundary Rd to bus No 135, which will take you to the university.

**Museum of Archaeology & Ethnology** On the campus, this museum (☎ 291-3325) features a collection of Pacific Coast Indian artefacts and has a cheap cafeteria. The museum is open Monday to Friday from 10 am to 4 pm and admission is by donation.

**Burnaby Village Museum**
Located at 6501 Deer Lake Ave, beside Deer Lake, this museum (☎ 293-6501) is in Burnaby's Century Park, close to the Trans Canada Hwy. It's a replica of a village community which attempts to preserve both the artefacts and atmosphere of a south-western BC town in the years 1890 to 1925. There's an old schoolhouse, printing shop, drugstore and other establishments; a large, working steam train model is next to the village. Friendly, informed workers are in period dress. It's open daily from 10 am to 4.30 pm during summer, shorter hours the rest of the year. Admission is $5.25, $3.50 for students. Catch bus No 120 on East Hastings St.

**Teleglobe Canada**
The displays and exhibits here focus on videos, satellite and undersea international communications, telecommunications artefacts and related electronic equipment. The gallery, open Monday to Friday from 8 am to 4 pm, is in the **Vancouver International Centre**, 3033 Beta Ave, Burnaby, off Canada Way, 13 km from downtown. Call ☎ 293-4200 for details. To get there, go south of the Trans Canada Hwy on Willingdon Ave and turn left onto Canada Way; Beta Ave is the second turning on the left. Alternatively, take the SkyTrain to Nanaimo Station then catch bus No 25.

**ACTIVITIES**
**Swimming & Water Sports**
You can swim at a number of city beaches,

for example Second and Third beaches in Stanley Park, English Bay and Sunset beaches downtown, or at Kitsilano and Jericho beaches on the southern side of English Bay. Kitsilano Beach is the largest and most popular and where the beach culture scene is at its peak. On a hot summer day as many as 10,000 hit the sands. The prime spot to see and be seen is apparently around the lifeguard section; other areas attract those who prefer a little more material used in the construction of their bathing suits. For swimming, the saltwater Kitsilano Pool is generally busier than the waters of English Bay. (At one portion of the beach you might catch one of the semi-pro or professional volleyball tournaments which occur regularly through the summer months.)

The Vancouver Aquatic Centre (☎ 665-3424), 1050 Beach Ave near Sunset Beach, has an indoor heated swimming pool, whirlpool, diving tank, gym and sauna. It's open from 6.30 am and admission is $3. There's another aquatic centre at UBC (see earlier) and one (☎ 926-8585) in West Vancouver at 776 22nd St. Kitsilano Beach has an outdoor heated saltwater pool (☎ 731-0011). It's open in summer Monday to Friday from 8.45 am to 8.45 pm, on Saturday and Sunday from 10 am to 8.45 pm. Admission is $3.

If you've got the energy for canoeing or kayaking the Fraser and Chilliwack rivers offer plenty of opportunities for the beginner to the experienced. At Granville Island you can hire canoes. Ecomarine Ocean Kayak Centre (☎ 689-7575), 1668 Duranleau St hires out solo kayaks for $17 for two hours or $37 a day. It has another outlet at the Jericho Sailing Centre at Jericho Beach in Kitsilano near the HI Hostel and also does educational tours of the islands (see Organised Tours later).

In North Vancouver, on Indian Arm, Deep Cove Canoe & Kayak (☎ 929-2268), 2156 Banbury Rd, has rentals and will teach you how to use a canoe. At Deer Lake east of town in Burnaby you can rent solo canoes for $10 an hour from Deer Lake Boat Rentals (☎ 255-0081).

For the yachting enthusiast Duranleau St has a few places where you can hire boats: there's Corcovado Yacht Charters (☎ 669-7907), 104 1676 Duranleau St, and Blue Ocean Yacht Services (☎ 682-8354) at 106A 1650 Duranleau St.

Windsure Windsurfing School (☎ 224-7245), 1300 Discovery St at the Jericho Sailing Centre, gives lessons and rents boards. English Bay is a popular area for salmon fishing, for which the west coast is famous. Boats and equipment are for hire and there are expensive guided charters. Corcovado Yacht Charters and Blue Ocean Yacht Services are two companies offering these facilities. For details on good fishing locations call the Department of Fisheries & Oceans (☎ 666-3545/3271).

Scuba diving is popular north-west of the city off Lighthouse Park and at Porteau Cove 24 km north of Horseshoe Bay, both in Howe Sound; and at Indian Arm at the eastern end of Burrard Inlet. A number of outfits offer equipment, training and trips including AB Divers World (☎ 732-1344), 1817 West 4th Ave, and Diving Locker (☎ 736-2681), 2745 West 4th Ave, both in Kitsilano.

### Skiing
Vancouver has some great downhill and cross-country skiing a short distance away. Just north of the city there are major resorts at **Grouse, Whistler** and **Blackcomb mountains**; the latter two, further from town, are very close to each other but are operated separately.

Grouse Mountain (☎ 984-0661) is the nearest to the city and is notable for its night-time skiing, when most of the downhill runs are illuminated and open till 10.30 pm. The day pass for an adult is $25.

For information on Whistler and Blackcomb mountains see the Around Vancouver section later.

Other nearby ski resorts include Cypress Bowl (also with night-time skiing) and Hollyburn (☎ 926-5612 for either resort) both in **Cypress Provincial Park** on Vancouver's North Shore. Cypress Bowl has four lifts and a rope-tow that take you up to the two peaks but is best known for its cross-country trails. **Mt Seymour** (☎ 986-2261), in North Vancouver, is a semi-wilderness provincial park only 16 km from downtown. The park's 3.5 sq km contain downhill runs, groomed cross-country trails and a tobogganing slope. It also has night-time skiing. Garibaldi Provincial Park (☎ 929-1291) has cross-country skiing only (see Around Vancouver later).

Further out, Hemlock Valley (☎ 797-4411) is a two-hour drive east along the Fraser Valley on Hwy 7; and Manning Park (☎ 840-8822) in Manning Provincial Park, is a 2½-hour drive east on the Trans Canada Hwy to Hope, then the Crowsnest Hwy into the park (see that section later).

### Hiking
Hiking is available in many of the provincial parks around Vancouver. Cypress Provincial Park is the closest, just eight km north of West Vancouver off Hwy 99. It has eight hiking trails including the Baden-Powell, Yew Lake and Howe Sound Crest trails. Mt Seymour Provincial Park, 15 km north-east of downtown, has 10 trails varying in diffi-

Snowboarding on Mt Seymour

culty and length. On clear days both parks offer magnificent views. At both parks you should be prepared for continually changing mountain weather conditions.

There's hiking in Garibaldi Provincial Park (see Around Vancouver later).

Golden Ears Provincial Park is 48 km east of Vancouver. Take Hwy 7 as far as Haney, then turn left (north) and follow the 13-km road to Alouette Lake. The park has 11 hiking trails, and camping and picnic areas.

### Cycling

A good way to get around town and Vancouver's numerous parks and beach areas is by bicycle. Some areas with designated bicycle paths are the 10-km sea-wall promenade in Stanley Park; the route from Granville Island, through Vanier Park to Kitsilano Beach; and if you want to keep going west you could take Point Grey Rd to Jericho Beach Park then follow the shoreline to Spanish Banks Beach. (See also Getting Around later.)

### Strolling

In the heart of the city, Sunset Beach at sunset is beautiful and busy and there are cafés near the corner of Denman St. A stroll is highly recommended. The sea-wall promenades in Stanley Park, Vanier Park and Jericho Beach Park are also worth a leisurely walk.

### ORGANISED TOURS

The Gray Line Bus Company (☎ 879-3363) offers a wide selection of tours, ranging from ones of Vancouver or its immediate surroundings, to a 10-day tour of the Rockies. Most tours begin at the Hotel Vancouver, and all major hotels sell tickets. The most complete tour of Vancouver is the Deluxe Grand City Tour: it costs $29.50, lasts 3½ hours, will acquaint you with varying districts within Vancouver and stops at a few attractions. The same tour is offered in a choice of five languages – Cantonese, French, German, Japanese and Spanish – for $35. A two-hour tour on a British double-decker bus lasts two hours and costs $17. Another takes

you to the sights of North Vancouver and includes a ride up Grouse Mountain. This one lasts four hours and costs $45. For $79.50 you can go on a day trip to Victoria.

Another company with local area tours is Town Tours (☎ 879-5852). A tour of Vancouver including Stanley Park and Gastown costs $27 and lasts for 3½ hours; of similar duration is the tour to the North Shore sights and Grouse Mountain for $40. Town Tours also does a full-day tour to Victoria for $75.

The best-value bus tour is operated by Trolley Tours (☎ 451-5581). The full trip costs $15 and lasts two hours but you can get on and get off at one of 17 stops along the way.

Pacific Coach Lines (☎ 662-3222), at Pacific Central Station, operates a number of one-day excursions for about the same price as a normal bus ticket. Some destinations are Vancouver Island, the Sunshine Coast and Fort Langley.

Dominion Tours (☎ 325-5522) has a four-hour night tour that takes you to Grouse Mountain and includes a salmon barbecue in the price of $56.

Harbour Ferries' subsidiary, First Tours (☎ 688-7246; 1-800-663-1500), near the foot of Denman St, offers a sight-seeing tour by boat and train. The seven-hour trip past good scenery goes up Howe Sound to Squamish. You can travel to Squamish on the MV *Britannia* and return by the Royal Hudson Steam Train, or vice versa. The cost is $54, $45 for students. You can go both ways by train for $26.17 return. These tours are available between the start of June and the middle of September.

On Granville Island several places offer cruises of False Creek, English Bay and Burrard Inlet. Seaquest Harbour Tours (☎ 683-0545), 1808 Boatlift Lane, has a 1½-hour cruise for $15. Ecomarine Ocean Kayak Centre (☎ 689-7575), 1668 Duranleau St, Granville Island, has educational tours of the islands in Georgia Strait and in Clayoquot Sound on the west coast of Vancouver Island. The one to the central Gulf Islands lasts three days and costs $380.

Top: Little barn on the prairie, Saskatchewan (DS)
Bottom Left: Native Indian dancer in Saskatchewan (ML)
Bottom Right: Native Indian teepee at the Wanuskewin Heritage Site, Saskatchewan (ML)

Top: Museum of Anthropology, University of British Columbia, Vancouver (PBC)
Bottom Left: Detail of totem pole, Victoria, British Columbia (TS)
Bottom Right: Musicians performing on Inner Harbour with the Parliament Buildings in the
background, Victoria, British Columbia (PBC)

If you have the cash a number of companies provide helicopter tours. Vancouver Helicopters (☎ 270-1484) will show you Greater Vancouver for $80 per person or take you up to Grouse Mountain and back for $170 per person.

## FESTIVALS

Following is a list of some of the major events in Vancouver during the year. *The Vancouver Book*, available from the Travel Infocentre, has an up-to-date list of current events.

January

*Polar Bear Swim* – This popular, chilly affair has been taking place on English Bay Beach annually on 1 January since 1819. If you can't handle the water, watching is allowed.

February

*Chinese New Year* – In mid-February Chinatown provides the setting for one of Vancouver's most colourful events, with dancers, music, fireworks and food.

June

*International Dragon Boat Festival* – Originally staged as part of Expo 86, this annual event takes place in False Creek over three days in late June. It attracts nearly 2000 competitors from around the world and about 150,000 spectators. As well as the boat races there's music, theatre and international cuisine.

July

*Vancouver Folk Festival* – Held on 1 July, this is the province's largest multicultural festival. The main events take place in Gastown, Robson Square and the Orpheum Theatre – all free. There is music, dance, performances and, of course, traditional costumes and foods.

*Vancouver Sea Festival* – During this festival in mid-July there are concerts, parades, fireworks and salmon barbecues, which take place on the shores of English Bay. For details and times call ☎ 684-3378.

*Vancouver Folk Music Festival* – Also in mid-July, the Folk Music Festival is three days of music, including concerts and workshops, from some of the best North American folk musicians. It attracts about 30,000 visitors and most of the action takes place at Jericho Beach Park near the HI Hostel and UBC. For information about tickets call ☎ 873- 9949.

August

*Carnival* – From 1 to 3 August Carnival celebrates various ethnic cultures with pavilions scattered around town offering music, dance, foods, etc.

*Abbotsford International Air Show* – Known as Canada's National Air Show, the Abbotsford has been voted the world's best. The three-day event, held in early August, has everything that flies, from fighters to the Concorde. It's held 56 km south-east of Vancouver in Abbotsford near the US border.

*Festival of the Written Arts* – Held in early to mid-August in Sechelt, north up the Sunshine Coast beyond Horseshoe Bay, this event, which has been held annually since 1982, features writers from across Canada speaking to and meeting those attending.

August-September

*Pacific National Exhibition* – Known as the PNE (☎ 253-2311), this big fair, the second largest in Canada (Toronto's CNE is the biggest) features a little bit of everything – sports, competitions, international exhibits, concerts and shows, as well as amusement park rides. It starts off each year with a two-hour parade. The exhibition lasts about two weeks, from late August to Labour Day. The PNE takes place in Exhibition Park on East Hastings St near the Second Narrows Bridge. Catch bus Nos 14 or 16 from downtown.

September

*Vancouver Fringe Festival* – This is an increasingly popular theatre event with offerings in drama, musical theatre, comedy and dance from around the world. It takes place over two weeks from early to mid-September in various theatres around Main St, between East 6th and East 17th Aves in the Mount Pleasant area. Call ☎ 873-3646 for information.

October

*Oktoberfest* – The German-based Oktoberfest takes place in the Commodore Ballroom, 870 Granville St, over three weekends from early to mid-October. There's the usual oompah and Tyrolean music, Bavarian dancers, beer and more beer. It usually lasts until 2 am.

## PLACES TO STAY
### Camping

There are no government-run campgrounds in the Vancouver area and the trailer (RV) parks right in Vancouver do not allow tenting. The closest camping areas that do are south of the city, on or near Hwy 99, which runs to the US border. There are also a couple near the ferry terminal for Vancouver Island in Tsawwassen.

*Timberland Motel & Campground* (☎ 531-1033) at 3418 King George Hwy (Hwy 99A), Surrey, has sites for tents and trailers. A site costs $12 and there's a laundry and showers. The campground is a half-hour drive from Vancouver, six km from the US border. *Bayside Campground* (☎ 531-6563), 16565 Beach Rd, Surrey, has campsites for $15. Showers are available and the campground is close to the beach.

South of the middle arm of Fraser River, *Richmond RV Park* (☎ 270-7878), 6200 River Rd, Richmond, near Hollybridge Way is one of the closest to town. It's open from April to October and has sites from $15 for two people; it's $2 per extra person. *ParkCanada RV Inns* (☎ 943-5811), 4799 Hwy 17, Delta, is north-east of the Tsawwassen ferry terminal. It has free showers and sites from $13.

On the eastern side of town is the *Four Acres Trailer Court* (☎ 936-3273), 675 Lougheed Hwy, Coquitlam, which has some places for tents at $6. It has showers and a laundry and is about 25 km from the city centre. (The Lougheed Hwy is also called Hwy 7.)

## Hostels

Although the HI *Vancouver Hostel* (☎ 224-3208; fax 224-4852), 1515 Discovery St, Kitsilano, is away from the centre of town, its location is great. It's close to the beach in Jericho Beach Park on English Bay, about 20 minutes from downtown by bus. The hostel is open 24 hours, although there is a 'quiet time' between 11 pm and 7 am, and has well over 300 beds, making it the largest in Canada. Other facilities include kitchens, cafeteria, laundry room, notice board, TV lounge, parking and fax service. The rates are $13.50 for members, $18.50 for Canadian nonmembers and $18.78 for international nonmembers. Ask about the places in town where the hostel card will get you reductions. From downtown take bus No 4 south on Granville St, it continues south over False Creek, runs west along West 4th Ave then turns onto Marine Drive. Turn right (north) onto Discovery St and you'll come to it – it's the big white building on the left.

The Globetrotter's Inn in North Vancouver no longer offers accommodation to travellers, but two private hostels have opened up to help fill the gap. The more central of the two, *Downtown Vancouver Hostel* (☎ 669-8832), 144 West Hastings St, has dorm beds for $10 and single/double rooms for $20/25; a small breakfast and coffee is included in the price. All rooms have their own kitchen and bathroom. The 5th floor is being completely renovated and when it's finished may provide female-only rooms. Further east, the smaller *Harbourfront Inn* (☎ 254-0733), 209 Heatley Ave, has dorm beds for $15 and double rooms for $35. It only holds a maximum of 25 people, so call ahead. If it's full you can sleep on the patio at the back for $5. The rooms are clean, there are two shared bathrooms and kitchen and no curfew.

Backpackers' *Vincent's Hostel* (☎ 682-2441), 927 Main St, next to the Cobalt Motor Hotel, is not in the best of areas but is within walking distance of downtown and not too far from Main St Station, Science World and

---

**Greenpeace**

Originally called the Don't Make a Wave Committee, Greenpeace was founded in Vancouver in the early 1970s. Stressing the need for a balance between economic development and environmental conservation, it first drew attention when members hired a fishing boat to go to Amchitka Island in Alaska to protest against a hydrogen bomb test. In the mid-1980s, it was the focus of world attention when its ship the *Rainbow Warrior* was blown up in New Zealand by French agents attempting to end Greenpeace's activities against nuclear testing in the South Pacific.

Today, Greenpeace is a global organisation with 59 offices in 31 countries. It continues to campaign on such diverse environmental issues as commercial whaling, the proliferation of nuclear power, the logging of temperate and tropical rainforests and the dumping of radioactive and other waste. In British Columbia its office (☎ 388-4325) is at 10A 634 Humboldt Ave, Victoria. ∎

Pacific Central Station. The office is open 9 am to 11 pm, there's no curfew and the rates are $10/20/22/25 a dormitory/single/double/twin. It also offers weekly rates. The entrance is under the sign which says 'The Source'.

The *Salvation Army House for Men*, on Dunsmuir St between Seymour and Richards Sts, is for men on skid row. Male travellers who are low on cash can get a dorm bed there for $9, with a maximum stay of five nights.

The *YMCA* (☎ 681-0221) is right downtown at 955 Burrard St. Depending on whether you'd like a TV or not, singles are $31.90 or $34.10, doubles are $51.70 or $53.90. Single rooms can also be rented by the week for $165/172 without/with TV. These rates include tax. Women and couples are allowed and quite a few travellers stay here. There are gym and pool facilities and a small inexpensive restaurant serving good-value breakfasts and sandwiches.

The *YWCA* (☎ 662-8188), 580 Burrard St, further down towards Canada Place and not far from the Travel Infocentre, is really like a hotel. Singles are $45 to $53, twins $57 to $67, doubles $65 to $70 and rooms for four $60 to $64. Single men are allowed to stay, but the fitness centre is for females only. There are TV lounges and kitchen areas (you must supply your own cooking utensils). Provision is made for child care but not on the YWCA premises. The YWCA is scheduled to move, but not before 1995.

The *University of British Columbia* rents rooms from about the first week in May to the end of August. Singles/doubles with shared bath are $18/36 or you can get self-contained apartments for $80. Contact the Conference Centre (☎ 822-1010), Gage Towers, 5961 Student Union Blvd, UBC Campus, Vancouver. The pleasant campus has a cafeteria, some cafés, laundromat, pub and sports facilities. *Simon Fraser University* also rents out rooms from May to August. They're all fully furnished and bathrooms are shared; singles cost from $18 to $27, doubles $37. Contact Housing & Con-

ference Services (☎ 291-4503), Room 212, McTaggart-Cowan Hall, Burnaby, V5A 1S6.

## B&Bs

B&B accommodation has really mushroomed across the country, perhaps more so in BC than anywhere. The Travel Infocentre has information on agencies who select, inspect and book individual houses. The *Accommodations* guide also has a list of over a dozen agencies operating in Vancouver.

A couple to try are *AAA B&B* (☎ 875-8888), 650 East 29th Ave, Vancouver V5V 2R9, which has singles/doubles from $35/45 and *Old English B&B Registry* (☎ 986-5069), 1226 Silverwood Crescent, North Vancouver V7L 4L3, with rooms for $45/60. *Town & Country B&B.* in BC (☎ 731-5942), 2803 West 4th Ave, Vancouver V6K 1K2, offers a reservation service for the Vancouver area as well as publishing its home accommodation guide.

Other operators run independently and many have advertisements at the Travel Infocentre. Some are very central but nearly all have only two or three rooms, so you may have to call several to get a room.

One place which is recommended is *Paul's Guest House* (☎ 872-4753), south of the downtown area at 345 West 14th Ave between Cambie and Alberta Sts. It's popular with travellers and is in a quiet residential area. Paul himself speaks 11 languages and will pick you up from the airport and cook your breakfast. The rooms are clean, and there's a laundry service, TV lounge and free coffee or tea during the day. Singles are $30 to $35 and doubles $40.

## Hotels – bottom end

Many people find the HI hostel or universities too far from the centre and prefer one of the older, cheap central hotels. Vancouver, despite its rapid growth, has a great number of them, right in the downtown core. Many are well kept and offer good value, but Vancouver is one of Canada's biggest tourist towns so rooms in summer may be rather scarce. In winter you may get places a little cheaper, and if you're staying a week it's worth asking for a reduction any time of the year.

There are also numerous hotels serving the downtrodden and the fringe – Vancouver has more than any other Canadian city.

There are more cheapies than you can shake a stick at in Gastown, Chinatown and Hastings St; Cordova and Abbot Sts have several too; a few of these are all right for shoestringers. Rooms are rented by the day, week or month.

In central Gastown with a great location is the *Spinning Wheel Inn* (☎ 681-1627/2814), 210 Carrall St. Unfortunately, it's not the bargain it was but is still cheap enough with singles or doubles costing $35 or $45 depending on facilities. The old *Dominion Hotel* (☎ 681-6666), 210 Abbot St on the corner of Water St in Gastown, dates from 1899. The rooms go for $45 with shared bath or $57 with private bath. There are many others in the area but most are bottom-of-the-line.

Hastings St for a couple of blocks either side of Main St is a less-than-wholesome part of town (especially at night), but the *Patricia Hotel* (☎ 255-4301), 403 East Hastings St, is a reasonable place to stay. It's large, clean, well kept and good value with rooms from $32/39.

The downtown area has a better selection of hotels, ranging from basic ones through moderate to expensive.

At 435 West Pender St on the corner of Richards St is the *Niagara Hotel* (☎ 688-7574) with a sign depicting Niagara Falls tumbling four floors. It's old but good, with singles/doubles at $47/52 for rooms with TV and private bath. Nearby, the central *Piccadilly Hotel* (☎ 669-1556), 620 West Pender St, has 45 small simple rooms. Singles/doubles cost $30/40, but it's often full so call ahead.

The *Marble Arch* (☎ 681-5435), 518 Richards St near the corner of West Pender St, offers rooms for $41.15/48.15. Also in the area is the recommended *Kingston Hotel* (☎ 684-9024) at 757 Richards St. It was the city's first B&B hotel and still offers the morning meal. Prices depend on your room

and facilities: singles cost from $35 to $50, doubles from $45 to $65. It's a good, older hotel with a sauna and guests' laundry.

The southern end of Granville St, past Nelson St towards the bridge has a number of hotels. It's a seedy area and a few hotels are OK but are not recommended for female travellers.

The *Austin Motor Hotel* (☎ 685-7235) at 1221 Granville St, is fine and big with singles/doubles for $42/50. Rooms include bath, telephone and TV and there's free parking. The *Cecil Hotel* (☎ 683-8505), 1336 Granville St near the bridge, has simple rooms which aren't bad at $39/45 for singles/doubles. There's a popular bar downstairs with 'exotic' dancers working to loud rock music.

### Hotels – middle

At the *St Regis Hotel* (☎ 681-1135), 602 Dunsmuir St on the corner of Seymour St, all rooms come with bath and there is a bar and restaurant. Rooms are from $60/65.

The *Dufferin Hotel* (☎ 683-4251), 900 Seymour St, has self-contained rooms some of which include a kitchen. Room prices begin at $60/65. There's a good dining room and free parking, which is a plus. There's also a *Travelodge* (☎ 682-2767) at 1304 Howe St near Granville Bridge and not far from Sunset Beach. It has a dining room and heated outdoor pool. Singles/doubles cost $79/89.

Down Robson St towards Stanley Park are several good, moderately priced hotels. The *Barclay Hotel* (☎ 688-8850), 1348 Robson St, has air-con, TVs and a licensed lounge. Singles/doubles cost $65/85. The *Robsonstrasse City Motor Inn* (☎ 687-1674), 1394 Robson St, has rooms from $60 a night and offers weekly and monthly rates as well. It has underground parking. Across the street at 1431 Robson St, the *Riviera Motor Inn* (☎ 685-1301) has apartments with fully equipped kitchens. From some of the apartments you get a good view of the North Shore. Rooms cost from $78/88.

Two other apartment hotels worth considering are the *English Bay Hotel*

(☎ 685-2231), 1150 Denman St, and the *Shato Inn Hotel* (☎ 681-8920), a couple of blocks from Stanley Park and English Bay Beach, at 1825 Comox St off Denman St. The English Bay Hotel has good views over the bay and charges $70. You can also rent by the week or month. The Shato Inn Hotel charges from $55/65; apartments with a kitchen are $10 extra.

## Hotels – top end

The old Abbotsford Hotel has been transformed into the *Day's Inn* (☎ 681-4335), 921 West Pender St, and gone up-market. It's central and has a bar, restaurant and free parking. Singles/doubles cost from $95/105.

One of the older, more elegant hotels with its wooden panelling and chandeliers is the *Hotel Georgia* (☎ 682-5566), 801 West Georgia St. It has air-con rooms with TV, movies and a minibar. Singles cost from $130 to $160 and doubles from $140 to $170. Just downhill (north) from the Hotel Georgia is the modern *Delta Place Hotel* (☎ 687-1122) at 654 Howe St. It offers full facilities including racquet-ball courts, a library and business centre. Room prices start from $155/175.

The *Four Seasons Hotel* (☎ 689-9333), 791 West Georgia St, is in the Pacific Centre building. To get to reception you take the escalator left of the statue of the Buddha. Prices depend on the size of the bed as well as the number of people! Singles/doubles start from $200/225.

The largest hotel in Vancouver is the *Hyatt Regency* (☎ 683-1234), 655 Burrard St, where singles/doubles cost $195/220. At the *Century Plaza Hotel* (☎ 687-0575), 1015 Burrard St, the rooms include a kitchen and satellite TV. Singles cost from $99 to $160 and doubles from $114 to $175.

Despite the rising skyline the *Hotel Vancouver* (☎ 684-3131), 900 West Georgia St, remains a city landmark recognisable by its green copper roof. It's one of the largest hotels in Vancouver and has just about everything including a pool, saunas and three restaurants. Its rates are $160/185. Not far from BC Place is the elegantly furnished

*Georgian Court Hotel* (☎ 682-5555; 1-800-663-1155) at 773 Beatty St. Singles/doubles here cost from $125/145.

## Motels

There are three distinct areas where you'll find motels around Vancouver. They're all outside the downtown area but not a great distance away, and with a car they're very accessible. Some of the cheaper ones follow.

The closest strip to downtown is along East Hastings St around Exhibition Park and east into Burnaby. This is a convenient area, close to Second Narrows Bridge leading over Burrard Inlet to North Vancouver. The *Exhibition Park Best Western* (☎ 294-4751), 3475 East Hastings St on the corner of Cassiar St, has rooms from $80/85.

The second motel area is along Kingsway, a major road which branches off Main St south of 7th Ave. It is the former highway and runs south-east out of downtown through Burnaby, New Westminster and across the Fraser River. It's also called Hwy 1A and is south of the Trans Canada Hwy. One of the closest motels to town is the *Biltmore Motor Hotel* (☎ 872-5252) at 395 Kingsway. It has air-con, TV, licensed restaurant and coffee shop. Rooms are from $59/65.

The other motel area is on the North Shore, over Lions Gate Bridge. Look along Marine Drive and north up Capilano Rd. There are also a couple of spots on the Esplanade, which runs east-west along the North Shore, past the SeaBus terminal. *Avalon Motor Hotel* (☎ 985-4181) is at 1025 Marine Drive, North Vancouver, about five minutes' drive east of the bridge. Singles cost from $65 to $89, doubles from $70 to $89.

The good-value *Canyon Court Motel* (☎ 988-3181) is at 1748 Capilano Rd, North Vancouver. Singles range from $75 to $85, doubles from $75 to $85 and use of a TV or kitchen is $10 extra. All rooms are cheaper after 1 October. There's a laundry, free coffee and a swimming pool. The motel is close to Lions Gate, Stanley Park and Grouse Mountain.

One of the more central motels is *City*

BRITISH COLUMBIA

*Centre Motel*, 2111 Main St, a 10-minute walk south of Main St Station. It has singles/doubles for $55/60 and offers free coffee. If you're staying a week or more you might be able to negotiate a reduction.

## PLACES TO EAT

With its continuing increase in population and sophistication Vancouver's reputation as a good town for eating is true now more than ever. As in many places known for good restaurants, the quality and variety filters down through all budget levels. Coffee shops, selling a variety of gourmet coffees and snacks have sprung up all over town. The following is a sample of what you can expect to find.

### Downtown

We should start with the *White Spot*, a BC chain of family restaurants begun in 1928, serving good food at reasonable prices, and open every day. There are numerous White Spots in Vancouver. In the central area there's one at 1616 West Georgia St on the corner of Cardero St, one at 580 West Georgia St on the corner of Seymour St, and another on the corner of Burrard and Robson Sts. A sandwich with fries or salad is a meal in itself and costs from around $6, omelettes are $5.

For lunch or a snack you could try one of the eateries in the food court on the ground floor of the Royal Centre Mall on the corner of Burrard and Dunsmuir Sts, downstairs at the Pacific Centre Mall, or the Harbour Centre on West Hastings St, also downstairs. They have Chinese, Italian, Mexican, Japanese etc places, at reasonable rates.

A couple of places with interesting names are the *Jolly Taxpayer Hotel & Pub*, 828 West Hastings St near Howe St, and the *Elephant & Castle*, 700 Dunsmuir St, on the corner of Granville St. Both are British-style restaurants-cum-pubs serving dishes like bangers & mash or fish & chips for $7. (The name Elephant & Castle, one of a cross-Canada chain, is derived from a district of London, UK.)

A few doors from Vincent's Backpackers Hostel in Main St is the basic but friendly *Mom's Kitchen* which is open 24 hours a day, seven days a week. Breakfasts with coffee cost around $4; burgers are $4 too.

For a minor splurge try the *Punjab Restaurant*, 796 Main St on the corner of Union St a few blocks south of Chinatown. It serves good Indian food at reasonable rates: starters are around $3, vegetarian main meals around $9, non-vegetarian around $10. It's small, quiet and popular.

Another splurge can be had at the *Ferguson Point Tea House* in Stanley Park. With its wicker furniture, hanging plants, large windows and a view over English Bay, the atmosphere is right out of *The Great Gatsby*. The best prices are at lunch time, from 11.30 am to 2 pm Monday to Friday. Dinner is served from 5.30 pm to 10 pm seven days a week. The mostly seafood main meals cost between $9 and $15. Also in Stanley Park, near Lions Gate Bridge, *Prospect Point Café* has a varied menu, again mostly seafood. Main meals cost between $11 and $21; fish & chips are around $9. The food's a little overpriced, but the café is in a great spot with an outdoor patio and views across Burrard Inlet.

Open daily, on Granville Island a good restaurant to try for snacks, reasonably priced lunches or full meals is *Isadora's Co-operative Restaurant*, 1540 Old Bridge St. It has a small play area for children and some of the money you spend on food goes to help community organisations. Fish burgers cost around $6.50, sandwiches from $6.25 and main dishes $9 to $14.

**Robson St** This is one of the main eating areas of Vancouver and has a cosmopolitan collection of restaurants including Mexican, Indian, French, Greek, German, Chinese and Thai, plus a growing number of coffee shops.

*Robson Public Market*, 1610 Robson St, has a bakery, cheese shop, fruit stalls, delicatessens etc.

Open daily till 11 pm or 12 midnight, *Pepita's*, 1170 Robson St, offers very good Mexican and Spanish meals. Quesadillas are from $5 and main dishes like enchiladas are $11. You also get complimentary corn chips and salsa. For good, inexpensive meals, the *Saigon*, 1500 Robson St on the corner of Nicola St, is a very popular Vietnamese place. Its menu includes curries and seafood, and it has lunch specials for $6.

*Heidelberg House*, 1164 Robson St, has been serving various German specialities for years. The moderately priced menu includes goulashes, schnitzels and a variety of sandwiches. Bavarian sausage is $8.50. A long-time favourite is the *India Gate*, 616 Robson St, between Granville and Seymour Sts. It has an extensive menu of East Indian vegetarian and meat dishes. Starters and vegetarian main meals are between $6 and $9.

Robson St also has lots of coffee shops. *Starbuck's*, at No 1100, is popular, and has other outlets all over town. *Grabbajabba* is similar.

**Denman St** Denman St, near Stanley Park, is a lively, pleasant street to visit around evening meal time. There's a good selection of eateries, particularly towards the Georgia St end, and lots of people strolling and menu-reading. The choice includes Mexican, French and Greek food, and the following is a selection of what's available.

*Musashi Japanese Restaurant*, 780 Denman St between Robson and Alberni Sts, is cosy, casual and cheap. It's closed Monday. Diagonally opposite is *El Mariachi*, a busy Mexican restaurant with starters from $4 and main meals from $10 to $14. It's open in the evenings from 5 to 11 pm. *Café Slavia*, 815 Denman St, is a small, friendly, inexpensive place with a Slavic slant; it serves food like goulash and perogies (dumplings) for around $7. A few doors up from Café Slavia, at No 825, is *Jumpstarts*, a reasonably priced vegetarian restaurant; vegetarian lasagne is $4.75. *Bud's Halibut & Chips*, 1007 Denman St, is a good place for fish & chips ($5 to $7). It's open daily from 11.30 am to 9 pm and is often packed.

Close to Bud's, on the corner of Denman and Nelson Sts, *Crumble's* sells coffee plus an assortment of pastries and cakes for $2.25. *Ciao!* at No 1074 is a small Italian-style café with sandwiches for $3, cakes like pecan pie for around $4 and a variety of coffees including espresso ($1.20) and cappuccino ($2). For something a bit more healthy, close by at No 1110 *Arms Akimbo* is a vegetarian, fruit-and-juice bar.

**Gastown Area** The *Only Seafoods Café*, on Hastings St near the corner of Carrall St, is a Vancouver institution – it's been going since 1912 and has hardly changed. There's no toilet, no liquor licence and seating for only 25, mostly on stools. About 500 people eat here daily and over 200 litres of chowder are served every day. The people create the atmosphere: there are all types, including tourists on every kind of budget, and no shortage of drunks. The fare consists of large portions of seafood fresh from the docks which is served quickly by the Chinese waiting staff. A full meal of clams is $6.25 or cod $8.25. The café will also boil, steam or fry whatever fish you choose. It's open Monday to Thursday from 11.30 am to 9.30 pm, Friday and Saturday from 11 am to 10 pm; it's closed on Sundays.

For soup-and-sandwich lunches, try the *Cottage Deli*, 131 Water St, which has views of Burrard Inlet; or the corner of Carrall St near the statue of Gassy Jack, where there are several good-value cafés.

At *Brother's Restaurant*, 1 Water St, the decor has a monastic theme and the waiting staff are dressed in monks' habits. It serves seafood, pasta and poultry and includes items like 'Monastery burger'; starters are $5 to $9 and main meals $7 to $16. It's open daily from 11.30 am to 11 pm.

The *Old Spaghetti Factory*, 53 Water St, is good value. This is a branch of the popular Canada-wide chain. The decor is interesting; it's lined with all types of old machinery, stained-glass Tiffany lamps and even a 1910 Vancouver streetcar (tram). Starters cost between $2.35 and $4.50 and main meals go for $7 to $12. It's open Monday to Saturday from 11.30 am to 10 pm, Sunday until 9 pm.

*Water St Café*, 300 Water St opposite the steam clock, is very busy and has a large sidewalk seating area. This was once the Regina Hotel, built in 1875 and the only major building to escape the Great Fire of 1886. The food's good with lunch-time main dishes of pasta and fish for $9.

If you like East Indian food, Water St offers several choices. *Kilimanjaro*, at 332 Water St in the Le Magasin shopping complex, serves African dishes based on Indian cuisine. There's a restaurant upstairs and a bistro downstairs. It's a very attractive place with quality food; main meals cost $7 to $13. *Maharajah*, 137A Water St, has tables outside and is a good spot to do some people-watching. It offers good, mild to hot curries such as malai kofta; starters cost from $4 to $8, main meals from $9 to $14. *India Village*, next to the Water St Café, is similarly priced.

The *Bodai Vegetarian Restaurant*, 337 East Hastings St, and the *Miu Jay Garden Vegetarian Restaurant* close by at No 367, both serve lots of appetising, filling soups and dishes, some of which include simulated meat. Lunch-time dim sum specials at the latter go for $4.95.

**Chinatown** *Ming's*, 147 East Pender St, has excellent dim sum between 11 am and 2 pm daily. A wide variety of dishes, each priced at about $4, are served from a cart whirled around by the waiting staff. Arrive early for the best selection. *On On Tea Gardens*, 214 East Keefer St, is small, inconspicuous and cheap, and has good Cantonese food. It's open from 11 am to 9 pm Tuesday to Sunday, closed Monday. Close by is *Hon's Wun Tun House*, a Chinese fast-food place selling bowls of noodles from $3.75; it's also famous for its 'pot-stickers' – quick-fried dumplings. It's very popular and is open Monday to Saturday from 8.30 am to 1 am, Sunday from 8.30 am to 8 pm.

A few places combine as bakeries and restaurants. *Maxim's Bakery & Café*, 257 East Keefer St, and *Max King Bakery & Restaurant*, 277 East Pender St, both have tasty pastries and cakes starting from 80 cents. Try the lotus seed cream cake for $3.75.

Vietnamese restaurants have begun to appear in Chinatown. The reasonably priced *Lu Zuan*, 207A East Pender St, serves traditional Vietnamese beef or seafood soups for $4.50; main dishes are $5.50.

### Kitsilano

This is an area of students, alternative lifestylers, cafés and second-hand stores. It's also become very desirable real estate, attracting more professionals. Between Burrard and Alma Sts, West 4th Ave has a large, varying selection of eating spots with many nationalities represented. West Broadway also has numerous spots for stomach satisfaction.

At 1754 West 4th Ave near the corner of Burrard St is the *Heaven & Earth Curry House*. It serves meat or vegetarian dishes, priced at about $8 to $10. It looks a little run down on the outside but the place is established and good and is open only in the evenings for dinner. At No 1938, *Sophie's Cosmic Café*, 2095 West 4th Ave on the corner of Arbutus St, gets very busy at meal times with queues sometimes out on the street. The walls are covered in all sorts of memorabilia including an old billiard-table top. It sells a range of burgers, including vegetarian felafel burgers, from $6, or steak sandwiches for $8. It also does salads and enchiladas.

*Ristorante Simpatico*, 2222 West 4th Ave, is a very attractive, Greek-style taverna, also offering – as its name suggests – Italian food. Further west is the open-fronted *Maria's Taverna* at 2324 West 4th Ave. There you can have spinach pie or hummus with bread for $3.50; or moussaka for $9. The restaurant also serves some Italian dishes.

*Naam Restaurant*, 2724 West 4th Ave near the corner of MacDonald St, is a good, inexpensive 'new age', vegetarian and health-food restaurant. It's very casual, has live folk music every night and is open 24 hours. Main meals are around $6 to $9, or you could have a tofu hot dog for $2.75. It also has good cakes and pies for $3.50. *Topanga Café*, 2904 West 4th Ave, is a good place offering the standard Westernised

Mexican fare including Mexican pizza for $9.25 and tacos from $8. It's closed Sunday.

*Nyala Café*, 2930 West 4th Ave, provides Ethiopian food to be eaten without the use of cutlery: you use bread instead. Main dishes of lamb, poultry, beef and seafood are $9 to $11, vegetarian main meals are $7 to $9. Saturday night between 10 pm and 2 am there's African or Caribbean music and dancing.

Over on West Broadway in the 3000 block the ethnic mix includes the moderately priced Greek *Ouzeri*, at No 3189 on the corner of Trutch St. It's open till the wee small hours and offers starters like tsatsiki for $3.25 and calamari main dishes for $6. *Andale's*, 3211 West Broadway, serves a variety of tasty Mexican and Spanish dishes. Enchiladas start from $7 and paella $11. The restaurant is brightly decorated and even the lamps are wearing sombreros. For a caffeine fix try *Yoka's* at No 3171, which sells over 20 varieties of home-roasted coffee.

Good for lunch and snacks, *Greens & Gourmet*, 2681 West Broadway, is a cheap vegetarian and health-food restaurant. Its appetisers start from $1, salads from $1.50 and main courses from $3. Closer to Main St, the *Sitar*, 564 West Broadway, is a good East Indian tandoori restaurant. Starters are $3 to $6 and main dishes from $8 to $12 and it has a good selection of beers.

### Little India

The Vancouver area has the largest East Indian community in the country and the majority are Sikhs from the Punjab. The focal point of the population is the Punjabi Market south on Main St between 48th and 51st Aves. Here you'll find East Indian groceries, and shops selling saris, spices and East Indian records and tapes.

*Bombay Sweets*, 6556 Main St, is a simple place offering cheap, tasty lunch and dinner buffets, including half a dozen or so curries, lentil dishes and various breads. Lunch-time buffets are $5, dinner ones are $7 and you can buy a bag of mixed Indian sweets from $4.50. Along the street are other places specialising in Indian sweets. *Zeenaz Res-*

*taurant*, 6460 Main St, offers East African-style East Indian food – the spices used are more delicate. Lunch or dinner buffets are $9.95.

*Pabla's Trade Centre*, 6587 Main St opposite Bombay Sweets, is a market with a restaurant and shops.

### Commercial Drive

There are several interesting neighbourhood restaurants and cafés along a portion of Commercial Drive, between East 6th Ave and Parker St, popular with the mix of artists, professionals and various alternative types who live in the area. *Joe's Café*, 1120 Commercial Drive, long popular for snacks and conversation with an array of characters from punks to media personalities, is one with a measure of notoriety. There are several other nearby inexpensive eateries and coffee houses including *Fettucini's Café*, 1210 Commercial Drive, opposite Joe's Café; and *La Quena* at No 1111, which presents an array of political, social and musical evenings.

### North Vancouver

Lonsdale Quay Market has lots of places to munch at or buy food to take away. The British-style *Cheshire Cheese Inn* on level 2, sells traditional British food like steak & kidney pudding and shepherd's pie, for $7.45.

Several restaurants are concentrated near the corner of Lonsdale Ave and Esplanade. *Corsi Trattoria*, 1 Lonsdale Ave, is an Italian place where everything is made on the premises, including the pasta and bread. Appetisers are from $4.25 and spinach fettucini $12.25. It's open Monday to Friday for lunch from noon to 2 pm, and daily for dinner from 5 pm to midnight. Nearby *Anotoli's* sells Greek dinners for $11.

*Frankie's Inn*, 59 Lonsdale Ave, is a basic eatery with the usual Western food, but there's a Vancouver twist: Japanese dishes like sukiyaki, tempura and teriyaki are available, served with chopsticks. Breakfast specials are $3.25. This spot is popular with workers from the nearby docks. It's open

Monday to Friday from 9 am to 8 pm, Saturday from 9 am to 3.30 pm.

At 69 Lonsdale Ave, the *Jägerhof* specialises in schnitzels and also serves deer and moose meat. On the walls it has old framed photographs and prints and mounted animals' heads. Meat platters with soup or salad cost $15. North up the hill at 1352 Lonsdale Ave, *Cazba* is a moderately priced, casual Greek-Persian place. Kebabs cost $10 and souvlaki $7. Opposite at No 1445, *Tanoor* is a Greek-Italian place serving filling pasta dishes for $7.95 or spinach pie for the same price.

## ENTERTAINMENT
The best source of information on entertainment in Vancouver is the *Georgia Straight*, which comes out every Friday. The weekly *WestEnder* and the monthly *Playboard* give reviews and dates of events in the visual and performing arts. These are all free around town. The daily newspapers also have complete entertainment listings, including theatre, dance and concerts. The Travel Infocentre will also be able to help you.

### Theatre
The theatre, from mainstream to fringe, is flourishing in Vancouver. Next to the main post office, in Hamilton St, the *Queen Elizabeth Theatre* (☎ 665-3050) puts on major international productions; the *Vancouver Playhouse* and the *Orpheum* are part of the same complex. The *Metro Theatre* (☎ 266-7191), 1370 South-West Marine Drive, and *Firehall Arts Centre* (☎ 689-0926), 280 East Cordova St, put on plays by Canadian and foreign playwrights. The *Arts Club* (☎ 687-1644) has more experimental productions with three locations in town – two in Johnston St on Granville Island, and the other at 1181 Seymour St on the corner of Smithe St. Also on Granville Island, the *Waterfront Theatre* (☎ 685-6217), 1405 Anderson St, is the venue for a number of local theatre companies.

For spontaneous comedy visit the *Back Alley Theatre* (☎ 688-7013), 1161 Melville St, to see the competitors in the Vancouver

TheatreSports League perform. Tickets are from $8. *Punchlines Comedy Theatre* (☎ 684-3015), 15 Water St, has stand-up comedy shows at 9 pm Tuesday to Sunday, with an extra show on Friday and Saturday at 11 pm. Another place offering offbeat comedy is *Yuk Yuk's Comedy Club* (☎ 687-5233) at 750 Pacific Blvd near Cambie Bridge. It has one show on Wednesday (amateur night) and Thursday at 9 pm; two on Friday and Saturday at 9 pm and 11.30 pm. The entry price varies depending on the performer.

Several fringe theatres worth checking out are the *Vancouver East Cultural Centre* (☎ 254-9578), 1895 Venables St (east along Prior Street), *Vancouver Little Theatre* (☎ 876-4165), 3102 Main St, and *Station St Arts Centre* (☎ 688-3312), 930 Station St.

The two universities have theatrical events during the year which give drama students the chance to practise their craft. The universities also put on professional productions. Call Simon Fraser University (☎ 291-3514) and UBC (☎ 822-2678) for details.

For theatre tickets check the little booth on ground level in Robson Galleria, 1025 Robson St. It sells tickets for local shows at half price, usually close to showtime. It's open from noon to 1 pm and from 4.30 to 6 pm Monday to Saturday. Otherwise you can call the Vancouver Ticket Centre (☎ 280-4444) for normal-priced tickets.

### Cinema
Vancouver has plenty of mainstream, multi-screen cinemas playing the best (and worst) of the latest releases. Downtown these include: *Capitol 6* (☎ 669-8000), 820 Granville St; *Granville Seven Cinemas* (☎ 684-4000), 855 Granville St; and *Vancouver Centre* (☎ 669-4442), 650 West Georgia St.

At 919 Granville St the *Paradise* cinema (☎ 681-1732) shows commercial films at half price ($2.50) every day and the *Denman Place Discount Cinema* (☎ 663-2201), 1737 Comox St, shows three films for $1.75 on Tuesdays.

Vancouver also has a selection of repertory theatres which show a mix of North American and overseas films. *Hollywood Theatre* (☎ 738-3211) is at 3123 West Broadway; tickets are $3.25 from Tuesday to Sunday, $2.25 on Monday. *Ridge Theatre* (☎ 738-6311), 3131 Arbutus St on the corner of 16th Ave, charges $4. Other theatres include: *Pacific Cinémathèque* (☎ 688-3456), 1131 Howe St; *Starlight* (☎ 689-0096), 935 Denman St on the corner of Barclay St; and *Caprice Showcase Theatre* (☎ 683-6099), 965 Granville St.

## Music
In summer, every Friday at noon, there are concerts at the *Orpheum Theatre* (☎ 665-3050) at 884 Granville St. The programme varies each day but you might hear folk, blues, jazz or classical music. The Vancouver Symphony Orchestra often performs here.

There is a fair bit of nightlife in the Gastown area. The inexpensive *Savoy*, 6 Powell St, is a long-standing casual bar with live rock and reggae. The *Spinning Wheel*, 210 Carrall St, is small but comfortable with mainly rhythm & blues bands on Friday and Saturday nights; the rest of week it's karaoke. Nearby the *Town Pump* (☎ 683-6695), 66 Water St, has rock, jazz or reggae bands. One club playing current pop music as well as golden oldies is *Notorious* (☎ 684-1968) at 364 Water St. The cover charge is around $6. The *Lamplighter's Pub*, in the Dominion Hotel on the corner of Water and Abbott Sts, has live rhythm & blues music all week.

The *Railway Club* (☎ 681-1625), 579 Dunsmuir St on the corner of Seymour St, is a pub-like place with live music seven nights a week and good-quality, often original jazz sessions on Saturday afternoons between 3 and 7 pm. Nearby, Granville St is interesting after dark with lots of street activity. The *Commodore Ballroom* (☎ 681-7838), 870 Granville St, can accommodate over 1000 people and plays everything from punk to Lambada. At 1300 Granville St, on the corner of Drake St, the *Yale* (☎ 681-9253) is

one of the best blues bars in the country. It's open with live music seven nights a week from 9.30 pm to 1.30 am.

*Richard's on Richards* (☎ 687-6794), 1036 Richards St, is a popular, dressy singles bar. The entry charge is around $9. In the same street at No 818 is the *Shaggy Horse* (☎ 688-2923), a gay club. A gay bar that's been around for a long time and has music most nights is the *Royal Hotel* (☎ 685-5335), 1025 Granville St.

There's live, mostly traditional jazz at the *Hot Jazz Club* (☎ 873-4131), 2120 Main St. Admission is $10, less for students. The *Landmark Jazz Bar* in the Sheraton Landmark Hotel, 1400 Robson St on the corner of Nicola St, has shows that range from standards and bebop to New Orleans, but the emphasis is moving more to rhythm & blues.

Most clubs close at around 2 am, and pubs around midnight or 1 am.

## Spectator Sports
The BC Lions (☎ 583-7747) play Canadian-style professional football from July to September in BC Place Stadium. Tickets are from $15 to $48. The Vancouver Canadians (☎ 872-5232), the local baseball team, play their home games at Nat Bailey Stadium, 4601 Ontario St next to Queen Elizabeth Park. Admission is $5.50. If you're here during the ice-hockey season, October to April, try to see a home game of the Vancouver Canucks (☎ 254-5141) at the Pacific Coliseum in Exhibition Park. Tickets to their games cost between $27.75 and $45.75.

For tickets and information about games call ☎ 280-4400/44.

## THINGS TO BUY
Several shops in Vancouver sell Native Indian wares, but most have fairly poor-quality stuff. One store that has only good quality is Hill's Indian Crafts at 165 Water St. It's open seven days a week from 9 am to 9 pm and has a good selection of carvings, prints, masks and the excellent Cowichan sweaters for about $180. These sweaters are hand-knitted and 100% wool. Originally

BRITISH COLUMBIA

from the Lake Cowichan area on Vancouver Island, they are now made in many places.

The Inuit Gallery, opposite Le Magasin in Water St, sells Inuit sculptures, drawings and tapestries and Northwest Coast Native Indian masks, carvings and jewellery. It's open Monday to Saturday from 10 am to 6 pm, Sunday from noon to 5 pm. The art is free to look at, big bucks to buy. Images for a Canadian Heritage, 146 Water St, and the Marion Scott Gallery, 671 Howe St, are similar.

There are a number of good places selling camping and outdoor equipment, guidebooks and maps. Downtown there's Gulliver's at 757 West Hastings St and Wanderlust at 1244 Davie St. In the Kitsilano area are the Travel Bug at 2667 West Broadway and Coast Mountains Sports at 1828 West 4th Ave. All these shops give a discount to people staying at the HI Vancouver Hostel.

Mountain Equipment Co-operative (☎ 872-7859), 428 West 8th St, sells climbing and camping equipment at reasonable rates.

For general shopping Vancouver has a number of large indoor malls. Downtown these are in the Pacific Centre, 700 West Georgia St which connects with the Vancouver Centre Mall and Eaton's and the Bay department stores; the Royal Centre in the same building as the Hyatt Regency Hotel, at 665 Burrard St; and the Harbour Centre, 555 West Hastings St. Granville Mall, Robsonstrasse and Denman St have lots of shops.

In North Vancouver the Lonsdale Quay Market has a shop or stall for just about everything.

As well as art galleries and restaurants Granville Island has many speciality shops.

## GETTING THERE & AWAY
### Air
Vancouver International Airport is about 10 km south of the city on Sea Island – between Vancouver and the municipality of Richmond.

On arrival, when you leave the baggage-claim area, to the right there is a Royal Bank foreign-exchange office and an information desk through which you can book accommodation and organise transport. Ahead of you are the car-rental counters. The departure area has a bookshop, newsagent and small post office (open Monday to Friday from 9 am to 12 pm and 1 to 5 pm). There's also a Royal Bank, 24-hour automatic-teller machine (ATM) which will change the notes of all major currencies, and an ATM for American Express card holders.

When leaving Vancouver you have to pay an airport improvement fee (AIF): $5 if you're flying within Canada, $10 to the USA and $15 to the rest of the world.

Major Canadian airlines fly to Vancouver, as do many US and Asian airlines. Some Canadian and foreign airlines with offices in Vancouver are:

Air Canada (and Air BC)
1040 West Georgia St (☎ 688-5515)
Air China
1040 West Georgia St (☎ 685-0921)
Air India
6 601 West Broadway (☎ 879-0271)
Air New Zealand
1250 888 Dunsmuir (☎ 640-6400)
British Airways
1200 1188 West Georgia St (☎ 222-2508; 1-800-668-1080)
Canadian Airlines International
205 601 West Cordova St (☎ 279-6611)
Cathay Pacific
605 West Georgia St (☎ 682-9747, 661-2907)
Delta Air Lines
1030 West Georgia St (☎ 682-5933)
Garuda
930 1040 West Georgia St (☎ 681-3699)
Hawaiian Airlines
660C Leg-in-Boot Square (☎ 879-4858)
KLM Royal Dutch Airlines
305 1030 West Georgia St (☎ 682-4606, 278-3485)
Korean Air
1010 1030 West Georgia St (☎ 689-2000)
Lufthansa
1401 1030 West Georgia St (☎ 683-1313, 270-3611; 1-800-563-5954)
Pacific Coastal Airlines
4440 Cowley Crescent, Richmond (☎ 273-8666)
Singapore Airlines
1111 1030 West Georgia St (☎ 689-1730/1233)

Fares can be cheaper if notice is given and

may vary with the day of the week. Those given in this section are all full economy fares. Some one-way fares (including tax) with Canadian Airlines are:

| Destination | Fare (One-Way) |
|---|---|
| Toronto | $842.09 |
| Edmonton | $332 |
| Seattle | $128.62 |
| Yellowknife | $682.66 |
| Whitehorse | $532 |

A US$5 inspection tax is added to the Seattle flight; you go through US customs and immigration in Vancouver, not on arrival in Seattle. Air Canada prices are virtually the same as those for Canadian Airlines. Air BC is a local airline run by Air Canada, serving Vancouver Island, some points in the interior and Seattle. The pre-tax fare from Vancouver to Victoria is $88 one way.

You can also fly to Seattle on United Airlines (☎ 1-800-241-6522). The flight time is about 45 minutes and some flights carry on to San Francisco or various US connections from either point.

Many people going across the continent find it cheaper to go, say, Seattle to Buffalo rather than Vancouver to Toronto. You may want to do this to get a flight to New York – it's likely to be cheaper from Seattle than from a Canadian point. Bus connections can be made between the Canadian and US airports at either end. Flights to Asia also may be cheaper from US west coast cities than from Vancouver.

Northwest Airlines (☎ 1-800-225-2525) and Alaska Airlines (☎ 1-800-426-0333) fly to Alaska. American Airlines (☎ 1-800-433-7300) and Horizon Air (☎ 1-800-547-9308) fly to many destinations in the western states of the USA.

See the introductory Getting There & Away chapter for information about flights from Australia, New Zealand and Asia into Vancouver.

**Bus**
The bus depot is now beside Pacific Central Station (see the Train section following).

Greyhound (☎ 662-3222), Maverick Coach Lines (☎ 662-8051, 255-1171), Pacific Coach Lines (☎ 662-8074) and Cascade Coach Lines (☎ 795-7443) all stop here. Some examples of one-way fares with Greyhound (including tax) are: Banff (six daily) – $88.33; Kelowna (two daily) – $42.91; Calgary (eight daily) – $93.09.

Maverick Coach Lines operates eight buses daily to Nanaimo for $17.30 one way (including ferry); the trip takes 3½ hours. It also has buses to Powell River, Squamish, Whistler and Pemberton. Pacific Coach Lines has eight buses daily to Victoria, leaving the bus depot every two hours at 10 minutes to the hour from 5.50 am to 7.50 pm. The one-way fare is $21.25 including ferry and the journey takes about three hours. Cascade Charter Service (☎ 662-7953) goes to destinations along the Fraser Valley such as Abbotsford, Chilliwack, Harrison and Agassiz.

If you're heading for the USA, Quick Coach Lines (☎ 591-3571) operates a daily bus shuttle to downtown Seattle for $26, Seattle's Sea Tac Airport for $33 and Bellingham Airport for $15. Buses leave downtown Vancouver from outside the Sandman Inn, 180 West Georgia St, but also pick up from other major hotels.

You can also catch a city bus to White Rock close to the US border. Take bus Nos 351, 352 or 354 south on Granville St.

**Train**
**VIA Rail** Vancouver is the western terminal for VIA Rail. Pacific Central Station is off Main St at 1150 Station St between National and Terminal Aves. The closest main intersection is the corner of Main and Prior Sts. The station is marked 'Canadian National' and has a small park in front of it. It's a magnificent building inside, having been renovated in 1985, and was underused until the main bus depot was made part of the complex in April 1993. Now there's a McDonald's, a small shop and a car-rental outlet and it continues to be upgraded.

For 24-hour information on fares and reservations call the toll-free number

☎ 1-800-561-8630. The ticket office is only open restricted hours: Monday and Thursday from 8 am to 8 pm; Tuesday, Wednesday and Friday from 8 am to 3.30 pm; Saturday from 12.30 to 8 pm; and Sunday from 8 am to 1.30 pm. Left luggage is open from 8 am to 10 pm (closed between 3.30 and 4 pm).

The route east goes through Kamloops ($63.13), Jasper ($134.82), Edmonton ($186.18) and Saskatoon ($232.19) to Winnipeg ($300.67). Fares include tax. Trains leave Monday, Thursday and Saturday at 8 pm. Stopovers are permitted but you must re-reserve.

The southern leg of VIA Rail's trans-Canada route between Vancouver, Banff, Calgary (see the Rocky Mountaineer section later), Regina and Winnipeg no longer operates. VIA Rail does, however, provide a bus service between the towns of the southern and former northern routes: Kamloops to Penticton, Edmonton to Calgary and Saskatoon to Regina.

There is no rail connection with Seattle.

**Rocky Mountaineer** Despite the closure of VIA Rail's southern route it is still possible to travel by train from Vancouver to Calgary and Banff (and Jasper) on the privately owned 'Rocky Mountaineer'. But it isn't cheap: one way direct to Calgary costs $574, to Banff or Jasper is $529 (both fares include food and an overnight stop in a hotel in Kamloops). The service runs between the end of May and early October; the train leaves VIA Rail's Pacific Central Station every Sunday at 7.45 am. For information contact a travel agent or the Great Canadian Railtour Company (☎ 984-3131; 1-800-665-7245), 104 340 Brooksbank Ave, North Vancouver.

**BC Rail** British Columbia has its own railway system which heads north from Vancouver to Squamish, Whistler, Lillooet, 100 Mile House, Williams Lake, Quesnel and Prince George, where it connects with VIA Rail (from Prince George you can go west to Prince Rupert or east to Jasper). The train to Prince George operates daily in summer and

three days a week (Monday, Thursday, Saturday) the rest of the year. It leaves North Vancouver at 7 am and arrives in Prince George at 8.30 pm. The one-way/return economy (called 'coach') fare is $91/164. The train to Whistler leaves daily at 7 am arriving at 9.34 am and the fare is $14/26. Trains leave from BC Rail's station, 1311 West 1st St at the southern end of Pemberton Ave, North Vancouver. Call ☎ 984-5246 for information. To get to the station take bus No 239 west from the SeaBus terminal at Lonsdale Quay.

**Car**
If you're coming from the USA (Washington state), you'll be on Hwy 5 until the border town of Blaine. At the border is the Peace Arch Provincial and State Park. The first town in British Columbia is White Rock. Hwy 99 veers west, then north to Vancouver. Close to the city, it passes over two arms of the Fraser River and eventually turns into Granville St, one of the main thoroughfares of downtown Vancouver. In the centre of town Granville St becomes a pedestrian mall, and ordinary traffic is forbidden. Remember there is a network of one-way streets around here too.

If you're coming from the east, you'll almost certainly be on the Trans Canada Hwy, which takes the Port Mann Bridge over the Fraser River and snakes through the eastern end of the city, eventually meeting with Hastings St before going over the Second Narrows Bridge to North Vancouver. If you want to go downtown, turn left when you reach Hastings St.

If you're coming from Horseshoe Bay in the north the Trans Canada Hwy heads through West Vancouver and North Vancouver before going over the Second Narrows Bridge into Burnaby. If you're heading downtown leave the highway at the Taylor Way exit before you get to Second Narrows Bridge; from there Hwy 99 takes you over Lions Gate Bridge into Stanley Park.

**Car Rentals** There are many car-rental companies in Vancouver; the larger ones have several offices around town and some also have offices at the international airport. Some have discount coupons which are available at various outlets including the Travel Infocentre. Check the yellow pages for a thorough listing of car-rental companies and their agencies' addresses. Following is a list of a few companies and their central address:

ABC
   1133 West Hastings St (☎ 681-8555)
Avis
   757 Hornby St (☎ 682-1621)
Budget
   450 West Georgia St (☎ 668-7000)
Hertz
   1128 Seymour St (☎ 688-2411)
Lo-Cost
   1105 Granville St (☎ 689-9664)
Rent-A-Wreck
   1085 Kingsway (☎ 688-0001)
Thrifty
   1400 Robson St (☎ 688-2207)
Tilden
   1140 Alberni St (☎ 685-6111)

Lo-Cost and Rent-a-Wreck are two of the cheapest. Lo-Cost charges from $27.95 a day with unlimited km plus insurance and tax, while Rent-A-Wreck charges $39.95 a day, plus 15 cents a km over 200 km. Rates vary depending on the size and type of car, when you rent (rates are usually lower at weekends) and how long you intend to rent for.

**Car Sharing** Check the newspaper classifieds or the yellow pages for car drive-aways. Also check the notice boards at the hostels for opportunities to share car rides.

### Ferry

**BC Ferries** The main route between Vancouver and Vancouver Island is from Tsawwassen to Swartz Bay which is just north of Sidney. There are about 15 ferries in each direction daily in summer leaving every hour on the hour between 7 am and 10 pm. Sunday afternoons, Friday evenings and holiday Mondays are the busiest times and if you have a car there is often a one or two-ferry wait. To avoid long delays it's worth planning your crossing for other periods if you can.

Ferries also operate to Nanaimo from Tsawwassen and Horseshoe Bay. The one-way fare on all routes is $6 per adult, $2.50 for a bicycle and $22.50 per small car. Call ☎ 227-0277 for information.

To get to Tsawwassen by city bus catch the southbound bus No 601 from the corner of Granville St and West 4th Ave to the Ladner Exchange. From the exchange take bus No 640 to the ferry terminal. The fare is $1.50, or $3 if you travel in peak traffic time. From Swartz Bay you can take bus No 70 into Victoria. For Horseshoe Bay from Vancouver take bus Nos 250 or 257 northbound on Georgia St.

**Royal Sealink Express** This company operates a fast ferry service from Waterfront Station in Vancouver to Victoria and Nanaimo in high-speed, 39-metre, passenger-only catamarans. To Victoria takes about 2½ hours (the one-way fare is $40), to Nanaimo about 1¼ hours. For information and bookings call ☎ 687-6925.

### Hitching

Hitching on the Trans Canada Hwy is illegal until 40 km out past the city limits. One possibility is to take bus No 9 along East Broadway to Boundary Rd, then walk south to Grandview Hwy (which connects with the Trans Canada Hwy) and stick your thumb out. Alternatively, take the SkyTrain to Scott Rd Station then bus No 502 to Langley along the Fraser Hwy before getting onto the main route.

### GETTING AROUND

BC Transit produces two publications which have useful information on getting around the city. One is the *Transit Guide*, a map of Greater Vancouver showing the bus, train and ferry routes. It costs $1.25 and can be bought at newsagents and bookshops. *Discover Vancouver on Transit* lists many of the city's attractions and how to get there (and includes Victoria). It's free and is available

BRITISH COLUMBIA

at the Travel Infocentre; if it's not on display ask for a copy from one of the staff.

## To/From the Airport

There are two ways of getting to the airport by bus, but the quickest is to take one of the Airport Express buses from the bus depot beside Pacific Central Station for $8.25 ($14 return with no time limit). It also goes to top hotels. The bus leaves every 30 minutes starting at 6.15 am and takes about 30 minutes. Buses for the downtown hotels leave the airport from level 2, the last one departing about 12.15 am; for the bus depot buses leave from bay 9 on level 1. For information about the fare and schedules contact Perimeter Transportation (☎ 273-9023).

To get to the airport by city bus, take No 20 south on Granville St to 70th Ave. From there transfer to bus No 100 which will take you to the airport. The total travel time is one hour and the fare is $1.50 ($3 during peak traffic time). Call ☎ 261-5100 for information.

A taxi between downtown Vancouver and the airport takes about 25 minutes and costs around $24.

## Bus, SkyTrain & SeaBus

Vancouver doesn't have a subway, but does have an integrated bus network, light-rapid-transit (LRT) system using the SkyTrain, and ferry links using the SeaBus. For local transit information call ☎ 261-5100 or get a copy of the *Transit Guide* ($1.25) from the Travel Infocentre, bookshops or newsagents. Try to avoid buses at rush hour as the traffic jams are unbelievable.

The transport system is divided into three zones: the inner zone covers central Vancouver; the next zone includes the suburbs of Richmond, Burnaby, New Westminster, North Vancouver, West Vancouver and Sea Island; the outer zone covers Ladner, Tsawwassen, Delta, Surrey, White Rock, Langley, Port Moody and Coquitlam.

During off-peak times (between 9.30 am and 3 pm and after 6.30 pm Monday to Friday, and weekends and public holidays) you pay a flat $1.50 for a single journey good

for bus, SkyTrain or SeaBus. In peak times it depends on how many zones you travel across: $1.50 for one zone, $2.25 for two, $3 for three. All-day transit passes are $4.50 (good for unlimited rides on the bus/Sky-Train/SeaBus after 9.30 am). Buy passes at the SeaBus or SkyTrain stations or from shops displaying the 'FareDealer' sign.

**SkyTrain** The SkyTrain was introduced for Expo 86 and connects downtown Vancouver with Burnaby, New Westminster and Whalley in Surrey. The trains are fully computerised (ie there's no driver!) and travel mostly above ground along a specially designed track. From downtown they operate between 5.50 am and 1.17 am during the week, between 6.15 am and 1.17 am on Saturday, and 8.47 and 12.17 am on Sunday. The trains are scheduled to connect with buses. They leave from Waterfront Station.

**SeaBus** These super-modern catamarans zip back and forth across Burrard Inlet between Waterfront Station downtown and Lonsdale Quay in North Vancouver. They leave every 15 minutes on weekdays, every half hour at other times. The trip lasts only 12 minutes but gives good views of the harbour and city skyline. Try to avoid rush hours when many commuters go aboard. Waterfront Station, originally the western terminal for the Canadian Pacific railway, is a beautiful building that has been tastefully renovated.

## Car

If you're driving, you'll notice the city doesn't have any expressways: everyone must travel through the city. Congestion is a big problem, especially along Lions Gate Bridge (probably best avoided altogether), Second Narrows Bridge and right downtown. On a wet or snowy day it's worse: try to avoid rush hours. It's also costly to park and/or very difficult to find a parking spot in the inner city. You're better off parking the car out a bit and catching a bus or SkyTrain into the centre; it'll probably be quicker too.

## False Creek Miniferries

Two companies operate miniferry shuttles across False Creek. From 10 am to 8 pm daily Granville Island Ferries (☎ 684-7781) runs between the Vancouver Aquatic Centre on Sunset Beach at English Bay, Granville Island and the Vancouver Maritime Museum on Kitsilano Point. Other stops are at the eastern end of False Creek, including one by BC Place Stadium. From the aquatic centre to the maritime museum costs $1.50 one way. Aquabus (☎ 874-9930) travels between the Arts Club Theatre on Granville Island and Hornby St.

## Taxi

Unless you're staying at a big hotel, if you want to take a taxi somewhere your best bet is to phone for one; trying to hail one in the streets is likely to prove unsuccessful. Three of the companies are Black Top (☎ 681-2181, 683-4567), MacLure's (☎ 731-9211, 683-6666) and Yellow Cab (☎ 681-3311/1111). For a complete list check the yellow pages. The starting rate is $2.10 and $1.18 for every km thereafter.

## Bicycle

Cycling is a good way to get around town, though riding on the sidewalk is illegal and bikes are not allowed on the SeaBus. Get a copy of the Bicycling Association of BC's cycling map of the city (see the Activities section at the start of the chapter). One of the most popular routes is along the 10-km road in Stanley Park, which has a number of rental places close by, including:

Action Rentals
    1791 Robson St (☎ 683-5648)
Bayshore Bicycles
    745 Denman St (☎ 688-2453, 689-5071)
Kitzco Beachwear & Rentals
    1168 Denman St (☎ 684-6269)
Spokes Bicycle Rental & Coffee Bar
    1798 West Georgia St (☎ 688-5141)
Stanley Park Rentals
    676 Chilco St (☎ 681-5581)

There are others so check the yellow pages.

Rates start at $5 an hour, $15 for four hours or $20 a day.

# Around Vancouver

## NORTH OF VANCOUVER
### Mt Seymour Provincial Park

This park, 13 km north-east from downtown, is a quick, close escape from the city. There is a road up most of the way and a chair lift goes to the peak. The park has several hiking trails and the views of Vancouver's surroundings are beautiful. Some areas are very rugged, so visitors going on overnight trips should register. There's also skiing here in winter.

There are parking lots for RVs but no real tent campground; you can pitch a tent along the many alpine trails. From Lonsdale Quay take bus Nos 229 or 239 to Phibbs Exchange then No 215. If you're driving head over the Second Narrows Bridge and turn right (east) onto Mt Seymour Parkway.

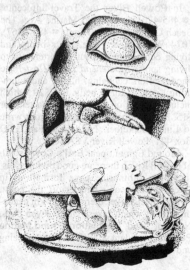

'The Raven and the first Men' carved by Haida artist, Bill Reid

**Sunshine Coast**

The name refers to the coastal area north of Vancouver from Horseshoe Bay to Lund, 23 km north of Powell River. The scenery is excellent: hills, mountains, forests, inlets, harbours and beaches. Hwy 101 along the coast is broken at two separate points where you'll need to take a ferry – from Horseshoe Bay to Langdale and from Earl's Cove to Saltery Bay. The highway ends completely at Lund. At Powell River there is a ferry over to Comox on Vancouver Island; the ferry to Nanaimo leaves from Horseshoe Bay. The ferries are rather expensive if you take your car; for information about the ferries, call BC Ferries (☎ 277-0277) or pick up a copy of their schedules from one of the Travel Infocentres.

**Horseshoe Bay** is a pretty spot, but commercial and expensive. From Horseshoe Bay you can either head further north up the Sunshine Coast by catching the ferry to Langdale, or take Hwy 99 north-east to Squamish, Garibaldi Provincial Park and Whistler.

In **Powell River** the Travel Infocentre (☎ 485-4701) is at 4690 Marine Ave. The Beach Gardens Resort Hotel (☎ 485-6267), 7074 Westminster Ave, rents boats and diving equipment and runs charters out to diving spots. *Fiddlehead Farm Hostel* (no phone) offers canoeing, hiking and swimming; it has dorm beds for $20 which includes meals or you can pitch a tent for $15. For information and reservations write to Linda Schreiber, Fiddlehead Farm, PO Box 421, Powell River V8A 5C2.

Around Egmont near **Earl's Cove**, south of Powell River, there are good diving spots, including submarine cave formations in Okeover Inlet, and wrecks off the coast. From Powell River there is a 65-km canoeing circuit which takes five to seven days. North of Lund, **Desolation Sound Marine Park** has abundant wildlife, diving, canoeing and wilderness camping.

**Horseshoe Bay to Whistler**

Squamish is the main town in this resort area. The Travel Infocentre (☎ 892-9244), 37950 Cleveland Ave, is open year round. Nearby there is great wind-surfing in Squamish Spit and rock-climbing on Stawamus Chief. Squamish is the destination for the Royal Hudson Steam Train (see Organised Tours under Vancouver earlier).

**Shannon Falls Provincial Park** South of Squamish, the Shannon Falls tumble over a 335-metre cliff just off the road. There's hiking, rock climbing and camping in summer, skiing in winter.

**Garibaldi Provincial Park** This park is a 195-sq-km mountain wilderness, 64 km north of Vancouver. Most of the park is undeveloped and it's a full-day's hike from the parking lot off Hwy 99 to the campground. There's some good hiking and cross-country ski trails. For more information and a map of the park, stop at one of the Travel Infocentres in Squamish or Whistler.

Garibaldi Provincial Park has five hiking areas – Diamond Head, Garibaldi Lake, Cheakamus Lake, Singing Pass and Wedgemount Lake – covered by more than 60 km of developed trails. Garibaldi is a wilderness park so you should take your own supplies and equipment, especially if you intend to go far from developed areas.

**Brandywine Falls Provincial Park** About 10 km south of Whistler (look for the sign) is a waterfall with some interesting pioneer lore. Evidently, they threw bottles of brandywine into the falls – mesmerised by the fine view? It's quite a scenic little place with hiking trails and a campground.

**Whistler Mountain**

Just outside the northern end of Garibaldi Provincial Park is this major resort area geared mainly for skiing, which is available all year round. In summer you can go hiking, cycling, canoeing, take the cable car up the mountain or visit an aquatic park. Ask about the 'singing tunnels', an old mine site, which you can visit. Whistler Village offers hotels, lodges, restaurants and bars.

The Whistler ski district has three centres,

Whistler Village, Blackcomb and Whistler's South Side. The latter is the least expensive while the village has the most action and socialising – with the larger hotels it is also more costly. Together the three areas make up Canada's largest ski resort. Blackcomb Mountain (☎ 932-3141; in Vancouver ☎ 687-1032) has the largest downhill ski area in North America, offering 1600 metres of continuous skiing. Whistler Mountain is a close second with 1530 metres. The usually reliable snow, the vertical drop and mild Pacific air combine to provide some of the most pleasant skiing to be found anywhere, from novice slopes to glacier skiing. The latter is available pretty well all year, providing the country's only summer skiing. Heli-skiing companies based in Whistler Village offer services to more than a 100 other runs on glaciers near the resort. There are cross-country trails as well.

On Blackcomb Mountain the day pass for an adult is $40. For a snow report call ☎ 932-4211. On Whistler Mountain (☎ 932-3434; in Vancouver ☎ 685-1007) the skiing and facilities (including the base station at Whistler Village and the 10-passenger, high-speed, enclosed cable car) make it one of the best resorts in the world. The day pass for an adult is $40. For a snow report call ☎ 932-4191; in Vancouver call ☎ 687-6761.

**Places to Stay** HI *Whistler Hostel* (☎ 932-5492) is in a beautiful setting on Alta Lake (West) Rd about five km from Hwy 99 and about 12 km from Whistler Village. It costs $13.50 for members, $17.50 for nonmembers and is open all year from 8 to 10 am and from 4 to 10 pm, with room for 35 people. During the ski season it's a good idea to book ahead. Facilities include kitchen, wood stove and ski waxing. The BC Rail train will stop at the hostel upon request.

*Whistler Backpackers Guest House* (☎ 932-1177), 2124 Lake Placid Rd in Whistler, is close to the centre of things. Private and shared rooms start from $16 a day in winter, $13 in summer.

**Getting There & Away** Maverick Coach

Lines (☎ 255-1171) has six buses daily to Whistler from the bus depot at Pacific Central Station in Vancouver. It's about a two-hour drive from Vancouver, along the edge of scenic Howe Sound and into the Coast Mountains from Squamish. The fare is $13/25 one way/return. Once in Whistler you don't need transport to get about.

On BC Rail the return fare to Whistler is $30.50 (see the Vancouver Getting There & Away section for more details).

## SOUTH OF VANCOUVER
### Reifel Bird Sanctuary
The 340-hectare bird sanctuary (☎ 946-6980) is on Westham Island, 10 km west of Ladner, south of Richmond. Each year, over 240 bird species pass through, including herons, eagles, falcons and swans. There are about three km of pathways and an observation tower. The sanctuary is open daily from 9 am to 6 pm in summer, to 4 pm in winter. Admission is $3.25. There's no public transport to the sanctuary. If you're driving, head south on Hwy 99 then after passing through the George Massey Tunnel head right on (south-west) on River Rd and follow it till you come to Westham Island Rd.

### Buddhist Temple
More than simply a temple, this Chinese Buddhist centre (☎ 274-2822), in Richmond at 9160 Steveston Hwy, consists of a temple, garden, small museum and library. You may also catch an art show or tea ceremony. The temple is ornate and has some fine work, but compared to the temples of the East it may seem a little clean, modern and sterile. The centre is free and open daily from 10 am to 5 pm. It's accessible by bus from the city: No 403 on Howe St.

### Steveston
This little town, in Richmond on the coast near the Buddhist Temple, is heavily promoted as a quaint fishing village. There's certainly nothing overly wrong with the place and you can get some reasonable fish & chips, but a quaint fishing village it ain't. There's a wharf where some of the fishing

fleet moors and a place to buy fresh seafood. It has lots of historical buildings and the Steveston Museum (☎ 271-6868), which dates from 1905, is open Monday to Saturday from 9.30 am to 5 pm and is free. To get to Steveston catch bus Nos 401, 402, 406 or 407.

### White Rock

Still further south, on Semiahmoo Bay south of Surrey and about two km from the US border, is the suburb of White Rock so-named because of the large white rock on its beach. All summer long the beach, with expanses of sand and warm waters, is quite a scene; strut your stuff if you've done your sit-ups. Unfortunately, the annual summer sand castle competition was cancelled a few years back: apparently participants got a little too rowdy.

Take the SkyTrain to 22nd St Station then catch bus No 353 to the beach, or catch bus No 354 heading south on Granville St.

### Fort Langley Historic Park

The 19th-century fort (☎ 888-4424) is at 23433 Mavis St, Fort Langley, 48 km east of Vancouver along the Trans Canada Hwy. It was erected in 1827 and served as a Hudson's Bay Company post until 1858, long before Victoria or Vancouver were established. It was here in 1858 that BC was proclaimed a crown colony. Most of the buildings were restored in 1956 and you can see the old palisades, furnishings and utensils. The park is open in summer from 10 am to 6 pm and admission is $2.25.

Take the SkyTrain to Scott Rd Station, catch bus No 501 to the Exhibition Centre in Fort Langley, then bus No 507 to the park.

### Vancouver Game Farm

The 48-hectare site (☎ 856-6825), off 264 St in Aldergrove about 12 km south-east of the fort, has 60 different kinds of animals in large, open pens, including tigers, lions, elephants and buffalo. It's open daily from 8 am till dusk and admission is $9.

# Vancouver Island

The attractions of Vancouver Island, the largest island off the west coast of the Americas, range from its rugged wilderness to the grand rooms of its provincial legislature.

The island is 450 km long and has a population of over 500,000 people, most of whom live along the south-eastern coast.

The geography is scenically varied. A mountain range runs down the centre of the island, its snow-capped peaks setting off the woods and many lakes and streams. The coast can be either rocky and tempestuous or sandy and calm.

South of the island, across the Juan de Fuca Strait, the sea is backed by the substantial Olympic Mountains of Washington state, the most evident being snowy Mt Baker.

Across Georgia Strait, which runs along the island's eastern shore, the mainland's Coast Mountains form the skyline. The open west coast is fully exposed to the Pacific. The waters around the island are filled with marine life, much of which is commonly seen and some, like the salmon, eaten.

The central north-south mountain chain divides the island into two distinct halves. The sparsely populated west coast is rugged, hilly, forested and cut by deep inlets. The more gentle eastern side is suitable for farming. The island's industries – forestry, mining and fishing – and nearly all of the principal towns are found along this side of the ridge. Up the east coast the resort towns and villages have plenty of camping grounds and motels, hotels and guesthouses. However, don't imagine the entire east coast to be urban sprawl: it's still quite undeveloped in places, especially north of Campbell River.

The island has the mildest climate in the country. It's particularly moderate at the southern end, where the northerly arm of Washington state protects it from the ocean. There is substantially less rain in Victoria than in Vancouver, and August and Septem-

Vancouver Island

ber, when the sky is usually blue, are excellent months during which to visit.

Vancouver Island is a popular tourist destination and Victoria especially can get crowded in mid-summer. For those seeking quieter spots, a little effort will be rewarded.

## VICTORIA

Victoria, the second largest city in the province and the provincial capital, lies at the south-eastern end of Vancouver Island, 90 km south-west of Vancouver. Although bounded on three sides by water, it is sheltered from the Pacific Ocean by the Olympic Peninsula across the Juan de Fuca Strait in Washington state. It is a gentle and genteel town-like city.

Both visitors and residents alike seem to indulge the British and resort flavour that has arisen. With the mildest climate in the country, its neat, clean streets, the interesting – and in many cases, visible – history, and its flowers to attract people, it's not surprising that two million tourists visit Victoria annually. This quiet, easy-paced traditional seat of – dare we say it – civilisation was once described by Rudyard Kipling as 'Brighton Pavilion with the Himalayas for a backdrop'.

PLACES TO STAY

3   Paul's Motor Inn
4   Imperial Inn
11  Fairfield Hotel
17  Hotel Douglas
19  Salvation Army Centre
22  Victoria Regent Hotel
23  HI Victoria Hostel
30  Dominion Hotel
35  Ritz Hotel
40  Strathcona Hotel
47  Green Gables Hotel
50  Empress Hotel
60  Crystal Court Motel
62  YM-YWCA
66  Backpackers' Victoria Hostel
72  Helm's Inn & T-Bird Motel
73  Beaconsfield Inn
74  Shamrock Motel
75  James Bay Inn

PLACES TO EAT

5   Herald St Caffé
6   Don Mee
7   Hunan Village
8   Foo Hong
9   Taj Mahal
16  Café Mexico
18  Chandler's Seafood Restaurant
21  Rising Star Bakery
24  Day & Night
25  Periklis
29  Eugene's Restaurant & Snack Bar
32  Koto Japanese Restaurant
34  Murchie's
36  Dion's Restaurant
37  La Petite Colombe
38  Pagliacci's
41  Sticky Wicket Pub
44  Sam's Deli
45  Chauney's Restaurant
46  Smitty's Family Restaurant
48  Millos Restaurant

63  Blue Fox Restaurant
64  Da Tandoor
68  Barb's Place
71  French Connection

THINGS TO SEE

2   Point Ellice House
14  Market Square
27  Bastion Square
31  Emily Carr Gallery
49  Classic Car Museum
51  Miniature World
52  Victoria Conference Centre
53  Royal London Wax Museum
54  Parliament Buildings
55  Royal BC Museum
56  Helmcken House & St Anne's
    Pioneer Schoolhouse
57  Thunderbird Park
59  Crystal Garden
67  Art Gallery of Greater Victoria
69  Fisherman's Wharf

OTHER

1   Spinnaker's
10  The Bay
12  Swans Hotel
13  McPherson Playhouse
15  E&N Railiner Station
20  Crown Publications
26  Victoria Express &
    Victoria Star Ferry Terminal
28  Main Post Office
33  Munro's Books
39  Victoria Eaton Centre
42  Victoria Clipper Ferry Terminal
43  Travel Infocentre
58  Bus Depot
61  Royal Theatre
65  BC Ferries
70  Black Ball Ferry Terminal
76  'Mile O' Trans Canada Highway

Although it is the provincial capital and home to an important university and naval base, Victoria is not an industrial city. About 30% of its 300,000 or so residents work in tourist and service-oriented businesses, while another 20% work in the public sector. The island is also a major retirement centre, with retirees making up around 20% of the population. Along with Vancouver, it is one of the faster-growing cities in the country.

**History**
The first residents were the Salish Indians. Although Captain Cook landed on Nootka

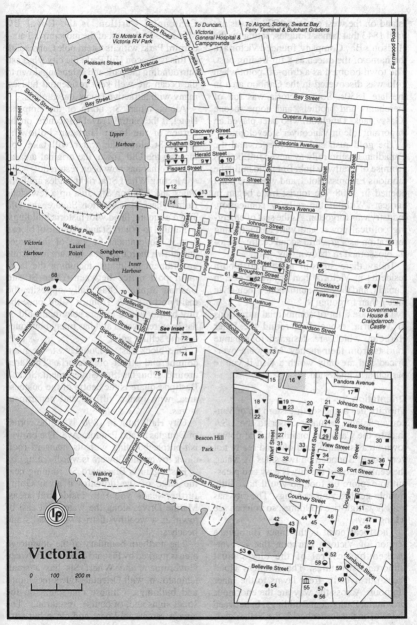

## Victoria

0    100    200 m

Island on the west coast in 1778, it was not until 1843 that James Douglas, acting for the Hudson's Bay Company, founded Victoria in the name of the queen as a fur-trading post. The town boomed as a drop-off point when gold was discovered in the Cariboo area in the late 1850s. Soon Victoria was full of merchants and brothels, and home to one 'Gassy Jack' Deighton, who later played an important role in Vancouver's development.

The gold rush ended, however, and the Canadian Pacific railway never fulfilled its promise of a railway link. But it did build the fabulous Empress Hotel, and when the hotel opened in 1908, the tourist trade began in earnest. Without the railway connection, industry was forgotten. As the seat of emerging political power and with an increasing reputation as a graceful social centre, Victoria blossomed in its own way.

Today there are still more British-born residents in Victoria than anywhere else in Canada, and they have entrenched their style rather than forgotten it.

There are a lot of commercial attractions in Victoria, especially around the Inner Harbour, which are designed to separate tourists from their money. Many are over-priced and are only worth a visit if you're particularly interested.

### Orientation

The city lies at the south-eastern tip of Vancouver Island, actually closer to the USA than to the Canadian mainland. The downtown area is simply laid out and really not very large. Bounded on two sides by water, the central area of the city is easy and pleasant to explore on foot, so you'll have little trouble getting your bearings. The city has very few high-rise buildings, so you can see a long way.

The focal point is the Inner Harbour, a section of Victoria Harbour, that is overlooked by several of the city's most important structures. The Empress Hotel faces out over its front lawns to the Inner Harbour. Across the way are the enormous provincial Parliament Buildings. In between the two, on the corner beside the Netherlands Centennial Carillon, is the Royal BC Museum. To the east of the museum is Thunderbird Park, with its totem poles, and south of this is Beacon Hill Park, the city's largest. Surrounding the park and extending down to the ocean are well-kept residential houses, many with attractive lawns and gardens.

Along Wharf St, north of the Empress Hotel, is the central Travel Infocentre, on the corner of the Inner Harbour. Following Wharf St along the water will take you through the Old Town, the original area of Victoria that has now been restored.

Meeting Wharf St at right angles are Fort, Yates and Johnson Sts. Just up a few steps from Wharf St is Bastion Square, the Old Town's square, lined with historic buildings.

Parallel to Wharf St and a couple of blocks east is Government St, one of the major downtown thoroughfares. In it are numerous government buildings, including the large main post office between Yates St and Bastion Square. Diagonally opposite the main post office is Trounce Alley, once the tiny byway where miners sold their gold. It has been renovated and has many boutiques – some selling gold.

One block east is Douglas St, the main commercial street of Victoria. The area around Douglas St, Government St and Bastion Square is the centre of the business area, with banks, offices and department stores.

City Hall, built in 1890, is on the corner of Douglas St and Pandora Ave. The brownish-purple building with its mansard roof, clock tower and flowers is worth noting.

East again is Blanshard St, running near the edge of the downtown area. Going further leads you into residential areas. Marine Drive, along the waterfront east of town, is a wealthy district with parks and beaches.

The northern boundary of the downtown area is marked by Fisgard St, which, between Government and Wharf Sts, has a small Chinatown, with Oriental-style street lamps and buildings, Chinese characters on the street signs and, of course, restaurants. The area is remarkably neat and clean but very colourful due mainly to the colour schemes of the buildings. Fan Tan Alley, halfway along, has a few small shops and connects Fisgard St with Pandora Ave; the alley is locked at night. About 130 years ago, when this, Canada's first Chinatown, was in its heyday and much bigger, the alley was lined with opium dens and gambling houses – it's a lot quieter now with no evidence of these early vice-filled days.

Both Douglas and Blanshard Sts lead north out of the city: the former to the Trans Canada Hwy and Nanaimo, the latter to Hwy 17 (Patricia Bay Hwy), Sidney and the Swartz Bay ferry terminal. To the north-west is Gorge Rd, an area of heavy motel concentration. It forms part of Island Hwy 1A, which cuts across both Douglas and Blanshard Sts, runs along the northern side of the gorge and meets up further west with Craigflower Rd and the Trans Canada Hwy.

Victoria International Airport is in Sidney, about 20 km north of Victoria on Hwy 17. The bus depot is at 700 Douglas St, on the corner of Belleville St and opposite Crystal Garden.

## Information

**Tourist Offices** The Travel Infocentre (☎ 382-2127), 812 Wharf St, is by the water at the Inner Harbour, across the road from the Empress Hotel. It has dozens of pamphlets, maps and information on shopping, sightseeing, transport, where to stay and where to eat. It's open daily from 9 am to 9 pm. There is also an office two km south of the Swartz Bay ferry terminal on Patricia Bay Hwy, and another in Sidney.

If you'd like to find out more about Victoria before you arrive contact Tourism Victoria (☎ 382-2127), 710 1175 Douglas St, Victoria V8W 2E1.

**Money** The major banks have branches along Douglas St. The Royal Bank has a branch on the corner of Douglas and Fort Sts; the Toronto Dominion Bank, 1070-1080 Douglas St, is open on Saturday from 9.30 am to 4.30 pm. You can change money at Money Mart, 1720 Douglas St, opposite the

Bay department store, and at Currency Exchange (open seven days a week from 7 am to 10 pm), 724 Douglas St opposite the Budget car-rental office. You can also change money at the American Express office on the corner of View and Douglas Sts. US currency is accepted in many establishments.

**Post** The main post office, 1230 Government St, on the corner of Yates St, is open Monday to Friday from 8.30 am to 5 pm.

**Bookshops** Crown Publications (☎ 386-4636), 546 Yates St, is a provincial-government bookshop selling maps and federal and provincial publications on Canadiana, Native Indian culture, and flora & fauna. It's open Monday to Friday from 8.30 am to 5 pm and Saturday from 9.30 to 5 pm. Maps BC (☎ 387-1441), 1802 Douglas St, is another government office with maps and atlases of the province. Earth Quest Books (☎ 361-4533), 1286 Broad St, has a good selection of travel books, guides and maps.

Munro's Books (☎ 382-2464), 1108 Government St, is in a beautiful old building originally built for the Royal Bank and restored in 1984. It is now classified as a heritage building; the atmosphere inside is almost ecclesiastical. It sells a whole range of books and has a good Canadiana section. In summer it's open Monday to Friday from 9 am to 9 pm, Saturday from 9 am to 6 pm and Sunday from 11 am to 6 pm.

There are also a number of second-hand bookshops along Fort St, including Renaissance Books next to Da Tandoor restaurant.

**Medical Services** The Royal Jubilee Hospital (☎ 595-9200; 595-9212 in an emergency) is at 1900 Fort St. Victoria General Hospital (☎ 727-4212; 727-4181 in an emergency) is at 35 Helmcken Rd, north-west of the downtown area, off the Trans Canada Hwy.

**Useful Organisations** Greenpeace (☎ 388-4325), 10A 634 Humboldt St, has details of environmental issues and helps organise information nights. Friendly by Nature

(☎ 388-9292) in Bastion Square, has information on environmental issues in BC and sells T-shirts etc.

**Left Luggage** Left-luggage lockers beside the bus depot cost $2; tokens are obtained from inside the depot.

**Dangers & Annoyances** At night, Broad St between Yates and Johnston Sts, is often occupied by hookers and drunks. Some drunks also hang out on the corner of Yates and Douglas Sts.

**Walking Tours**
Ask about walking tours at the Travel Infocentre or buy a copy of the booklet *Victoria on Foot* (Terrapin, Victoria, 1989), by Barrie Lee, which gives details of walking tours around the Old Town.

**Inner Harbour**
**Royal BC Museum** This excellent museum (☎ 387-3701), 675 Belleville St, is a must, even for people who normally avoid such places. The wide variety of displays is artistically arranged, beautifully lit and accompanied by informative, succinct explanations. There are sections on geology, vegetation, wildlife and ethnology. Many of the models and exhibits are incredibly realistic.

In the areas devoted to the BC Native Indians, see the detailed models of villages, the documentary 1914 film *In the Land of the War Canoes* on the Kwakiutl people, and the rock on which a man 'fell from the sky'. Also look at the Haida craftwork in argillate, a dense black carbon shale. The pipes represent some of the best Native Indian art anywhere.

There's a town made up of 19th century and early 20th-century buildings and goods, including a Model T Ford. Chaplin movies are shown in the old movie theatre. The museum also has an interesting collection of artefacts from the 1920s through to the 1970s. Outside, there is a garden of BC's native wildflowers.

Admission is $5, or $3 for students;

between 1 October and 30 April, Mondays are free. The museum provides free tours and is open daily from 9.30 am to 7 pm in summer and from 10 am to 5.30 pm in winter.

**Helmcken House** This house, in Eliot Square beside the Royal BC Museum, is the oldest in BC to have remained unchanged. The rooms are shown much the way they would have appeared in the early 1850s. John Helmcken, a doctor and politician, was very active in the local community. The house contains much period furniture and examples of decorations and implements. Staff members are friendly and helpful. It's open daily in summer from 11 am to 5 pm and admission is $3.25.

**St Anne's Pioneer Schoolhouse** Also in Eliot Square, this schoolhouse, operated as part of the Royal BC Museum, is one of the oldest buildings in Victoria still in use. Built sometime between 1840 and 1860, it was moved to its present site in 1974 from the grounds of St Anne's Academy.

**Thunderbird Park** This small but interesting strip of grass beside the Royal BC Museum has a collection of both plain and painted wooden totem poles, some of which are labelled. In the Thunderbird Park Carving Studio you can watch Native Indian artists at work and talk to them too. The studio is run on a volunteer basis with help from the Royal BC Museum.

**Parliament Buildings** The multi-turreted Parliament Buildings (☎ 387-6121), 501 Belleville St facing the Inner Harbour, were designed by Francis Rattenbury and finished in 1898. On top of the main dome is a figure of Captain George Vancouver, the first British navigator to circle Vancouver Island. Rattenbury also designed the Empress Hotel and the Parthenon-like Royal London Wax Museum, which was once a CP ticket office. The buildings are open Monday to Friday from 8.30 am to 5 pm, but the free guided tours only take place on weekends and public holidays between 9 am and 5 pm. The tours last about 30 minutes and are worthwhile.

The paintings in the lower rotunda depict scenes from Canadian history. Around the upper rotunda are paintings of four of BC's main industries. The Legislative Chamber is where all the laws of BC are made (there is no Senate in the provincial parliament). You can view the debates from the public gallery when the session is in. In the Legislative Library is the dagger used to kill Captain Cook in Hawaii, while on the lawn are a statue of Queen Victoria and a sequoia tree from California planted in the 1860s. The buildings are lit spectacularly at night, by more than 3000 lightbulbs.

**Royal London Wax Museum** This museum (☎ 388-4461), 470 Belleville St, in front of the Parliament Buildings, contains more than 200 wax models of historical and contemporary figures. It's open daily from 9 am to 9 pm and admission is $6.50.

**Miniature World** At Miniature World (☎ 385-9731), 649 Humboldt St, beside the Empress Hotel, you'll find numerous layouts depicting in exact detail various themes, such as the world of Dickens. The highlight is a large model train representing the development of the Canadian Pacific railway from 1885 to 1915. Miniature World is open daily from 9 am to 8 pm and admission is $6.50.

### Douglas St
**Beacon Hill Park** Just south-east of the downtown area, along Douglas St, this 62-hectare park is Victoria's largest. Bus No 5 will take you there. The park is a very well-cared-for oasis of trees, flowers, ponds and pathways. Trees of this size you don't see anywhere but on the west coast. Also in the park is the 'world's tallest totem'; and a cricket pitch (told you it was British here). The southern edge overlooks the ocean and offers good views of the coastline. At the lookout above Dallas Rd is a marker indicating the direction of places such as Seattle, and noting the elevations of mountains. At the south-western corner of the park, the path

along the water meets the **'Mile 0' marker**, the Pacific terminal of the Trans Canada Hwy.

**Crystal Garden** This garden (☎ 381-1213), 713 Douglas St, seems to be one of the more popular commercial attractions, but at $5 for admission, it's not really cheap. Designed by (who else?) Francis Rattenbury, it was fashioned after London's Crystal Palace and built in 1925. Once a focal point for the social elite, it was restored in 1977 as a visitor attraction, but remains a venue for splashy events. The principal draw is the indoor tea room overlooking a tropical-like garden complete with wildlife. It's open daily from 10 am to 9 pm in July and August; the rest of the year it closes at 5.30 pm.

**Victoria Conference Centre** The centre (☎ 361-1000), 720 Douglas St, near Crystal Garden, was opened in 1989. It has the capacity to hold 1500 people and has an indoor waterfall and totem pole. A covered walkway connects it with the rear of the Empress Hotel.

**Classic Car Museum** This museum (☎ 382-7118), 813 Douglas St, has over 40 beauties on display for auto lovers, ranging from the 1904 Olds to the 1967 Lincoln Limo. It's open daily from 9 am to 6 pm and admission is $5.

### Old Town
The original Victoria was centred along Wharf St and Bastion Square. This was where the first fur-trading ships moored. Wharf St was once busy with miners, merchants and all those heading for the Klondike.

**Bastion Square** was where Fort Victoria was situated and held the courthouse, jail, gallows and brothel. The whole area has been restored and redeveloped. The square is pleasant for strolling around or sitting in and people-watching. Many of the old buildings are now restaurants, boutiques, galleries or offices. The same is true of those in Wharf St.

Further north along Wharf St you'll come to **Market Square**, a former warehouse on the corner of Johnson St, dating from the 1890s. Renovated in 1975, this compact, attractive area now has two floors of over 40 shops and restaurants, built around a courtyard shaded by trees.

**Emily Carr Gallery** At 1107 Wharf St, this gallery (☎ 387-3130) pays homage to one of Canada's best-known and liked painters, a native of Victoria. Many of her paintings incorporated subject matter drawn from the culture of the west coast Native Indians, particularly the totem poles. The gallery shows changing exhibits and daily free films about the life and career of Emily Carr. It's open Monday to Saturday from 10 am to 4.30 pm and admission is free. Prints from originals are sold.

**Maritime Museum** This collection of artefacts, models, photographs and naval memorabilia is for nautical buffs only. The museum (☎ 385-4222), 28 Bastion Square near Government St, is open daily from 9.30 am to 6.30 pm and admission is $5, $3 for students.

**Victoria Eaton Centre** Although this is a shopping centre, it's worth a visit just to wander round. The whole complex has been modernised incorporating the facades of original buildings. As well as shops and eateries, it has fountains, pools and a rooftop garden. It occupies two blocks between Government and Douglas Sts.

**Rockland Area**
**Art Gallery of Greater Victoria** The gallery (☎ 384-4101), in a Victorian mansion at 1040 Moss St, 1.5 km east of the downtown area, just off Fort St, is best known for its excellent Asian art, including the Japanese and Chinese collections. It also has artworks from other parts of the world and from widely varying periods of history including pre-Columbian Latin American objects through to contemporary Canadian paintings. There are some good Inuit pieces. Take

bus Nos 10, 11 or 14 from the downtown area. It's open Monday to Saturday from 10 am to 5 pm, Thursday from 10 am to 9 pm and Sunday from 1 to 5 pm. Admission is $4, $2 for students. It has a restaurant too.

**Government House** This is the official residence (☎ 387-2080) of the province's lieutenant-governor. The impressive grounds are open to the public except when British royalty is in residence. The building is not far from the Art Gallery of Greater Victoria, away from the downtown area, at 1401 Rockland Ave. Take bus No 1 from downtown.

**Craigdarroch Castle** Near Government House, but off Fort St, 1050 Joan Crescent, this rather impressive home (☎ 592-5323) was built in the mid-1880s by Robert Dunsmuir, a coal millionaire, for himself and his wife. The interior remains decorated in the manner of that time. It's now a museum and has been restored. Admission is $5.50 (students $4.50) and it's open daily in summer from 9 am to 7 pm, the rest of the year from 10 am to 4.30 pm. To get there take bus Nos 11 or 14.

**Butchart Gardens**
If you're coming from the east, you'll probably notice the signs for this attraction beginning in Banff. They are without a doubt the most publicised of all Victoria's sights. No doubt the gardens are beautiful and extensive, but admission is costly at $11 (students $5.75). Whether it's worth it depends on you and your budget.

Parts of the gardens are sectioned into specialities like the English Rose Garden and the Japanese Garden. There are hundreds of species of trees, bushes and flowers. You can walk through in about 1½ hours, but linger as long as you wish. In the evenings from June to September the gardens are illuminated. There are also concerts and puppet shows around dusk. On Saturday night in July and August there is a spectacular fireworks display set to music – there's no extra charge to watch it.

Open daily year round from 9 am till dusk, the gardens (☎ 652-4422), 800 Benvenuto Ave, are about 21 km north-west of downtown in Brentwood Bay. City bus Nos 74 and 75 go within one km during the week and three km on Sunday.

## Dominion Astrophysical Observatory

On the way to the Butchart Gardens you could visit this observatory (☎ 388-0012), where you can peer out to space through a 183-cm telescope. There is a museum and equipment used to record earthquakes. The observatory is open Monday to Friday from 9.15 am to 4.30 pm and admission is free. It's north-west of the centre, at 5071 West Saanich Rd, on Little Saanich Mountain.

## English Village

This gimmicky but effective re-creation of some English Tudor-style buildings is in Lampson St, across Victoria Harbour from the Empress Hotel. The highlights are the replicas of Shakespeare's birthplace and the thatched cottage of his wife, Anne Hathaway. The cottage (☎ 388-4353), 429 Lampson St, and the rest of the 'village' are furnished with authentic 16th-century antiques. It is open daily from 9 am to 10 pm in summer, and from 9 am to 5 pm in winter. Admission is $6. Take bus No 24 from the downtown area.

## Point Ellice House

This beautifully kept house (☎ 387-4697), built in 1861, was sold in 1868 to Peter O'Reilly, a member of government and a successful businessman. Many of the house's immaculate furnishings now on display belonged to him and his wife. Admission is $3.25 and it's open mid-June to the end of September, Thursday to Monday from 11 am to 5 pm. It's north of the downtown area, at 2616 Pleasant St, off Bay St, at Point Ellice Bridge. Take bus No 14 from downtown.

## Craigflower Farmhouse

The farmhouse (☎ 387-4697) was built by Kenneth McKenzie in 1856. It was the central home in the first farming community on Vancouver Island and its construction heralded Victoria's change from a fur-trading settlement to a permanent one. Built to remind McKenzie of Scotland, the house was decorated with the many furnishings he had brought from his homeland. Because the family entertained frequently, the house became a social centre for Fort Victoria and the Esquimalt Naval Base.

The farmhouse is open Sundays only from 10 am to 5 pm and admission is $3.25. It's a little north-west of town, on the corner of Craigflower and Admiral's Rds, near Gorge Water. To get there catch bus No 14 from town.

## Fort Rodd Hill National Historic Park

This scenic 18-hectare park (☎ 363-4662) overlooking Esquimalt Harbour contains some historical points of interest. There are the remnants of three turn-of-the-century gun batteries. These artillery installations were built to protect the naval base in the bay and, until 1956, when such a defence system was deemed obsolete, were regularly upgraded. There are information signs around the park, as well as guides. The park is open daily from 10 am to 5.30 pm and admission is free.

Also in the park is **Fisgard Lighthouse**, which still works and has been in continuous use since 1860. It was the first lighthouse to shine its beam across the water in Western Canada.

The park is at 603 Fort Rodd Hill Rd, off Ocean Blvd, about 12 km north-west of downtown , on the western side of Esquimalt Harbour. To get there catch bus No 50 which takes you to within one km of the park.

## Fisherman's Wharf

The wharf area is on Victoria Harbour, west around the bay from the Inner Harbour, along Belleville St past Laurel Point, and is worth a look. It's a busy spot, with fishing boats and pleasure craft coming and going. You can sometimes buy fresh seafood from the boats or the little shed, and near to it is Barb's Place selling fish & chips (see Places to Eat later). Houseboats are moored at one end of the dock – a couple of them wouldn't be bad to call home.

### Scenic Marine Drive

Starting either from Fisherman's Wharf or Beacon Hill Park, the Scenic Marine Drive, with great views out over the sea, skirts the coast along Dallas Rd and Beach Drive. The road heads north past some of Victoria's wealthiest neighbourhoods and the retirement community of Oak Bay where you could stop for afternoon tea at the Blethering Place (see Places to Eat later).

You'll see several parks and beaches along the way, though access to the shore for much of the way is restricted because of private housing right on the coastline. The Gray Line double-decker buses include Marine Drive in their tours.

### Lookouts

At the northern end of Shelbourne St, **Mt Douglas Park Lookout** provides views of the Saanich Peninsula, the Georgia Strait and the islands in it and Washington state of the USA. There are good views at **Mt Tolmie Park Lookout**, off Cedar Hill Cross Rd; it is near the University of Victoria.

### Activities

**Swimming** One of the best swimming places is the **Sooke Potholes**, about an hour's drive west of Victoria on Hwy 14, by the town of Sooke, on the southern shore. Watch for signs at Milne's Landing. You can find your own swimming hole but the water ain't balmy. There's good picnicking and some walking trails too. Don't get caught drinking alcohol: the fines are heavy.

Also popular is **Thetis Lake Municipal Park**, not too far north-west of town (about 20 minutes), off the Trans Canada Hwy. It's very busy at the main beach but if you hike around the lake you'll find a quiet spot.

**Scuba Diving** The Georgia Strait provides opportunities for world-class diving. The undersea life is tremendously varied and has been featured in *National Geographic*. Several excellent shore dive sites are found near Victoria, including Saanitch Inlet, Saxe Point Park, the Ogden Point Breakwater, 10-Mile Point and Willis Point for deep diving. Race Rocks, 18 km south-west of Victoria Harbour, offers superb scenery both above and below the water. There are diving charters and dive shops in Victoria provide equipment sales, service, rentals and instruction. Poseidon Diving Systems (☎ 386-9191) is reasonably central at 2519 Douglas St.

**Fishing** The waters around Victoria are renowned as a place for deep-sea fishing with salmon being the top prize. The Travel Infocentre can supply you with information and you should also check the yellow pages. There are freshwater lakes and streams within an hour or two of Victoria as well as up-island that are good for trout and/or salmon fishing. Saanich Inlet has one of the highest concentrations of salmon in the world.

Scores of charter companies offer deep-sea fishing trips of varying lengths. Most supply all equipment, bait and even coffee. Discovery Fishing Adventures (☎ 386-4191), 183 Bushby St, is run by Allan Crow who offers four-hour trips for $175.

**Other Activities** Windsurfing is popular, especially in Cadboro Bay near the university, and at Willow's Beach in Oak Bay. Rentals are available at both for around $13; some places offer lessons too. Oak Bay is also a popular canoeing spot. Ocean River Sports (☎ 381-4233), 1437 Store St, rents canoes and kayaks, sells equipment and runs courses. Sports Rent (☎ 385-7368), 3084 Blanshard St, hires canoes and kayaks from $30 per day.

A few people offer horseback trips in the nearby highlands and lake areas. Some include overnight camping. Ask at the Travel Infocentre. Lakeshore Trailrides (☎ 479-6853), 482 Sparton Rd, has one-hour rides for $20.

The Crystal Pool & Fitness Centre (☎ 380-4686), 2275 Quadra St, on the corner of Wark St – an easy walk from the downtown area – has a pool, a sauna, a whirlpool and locker rooms. Entry to the pool is $3.

Scenic Marine Drive makes a good bike trip.

## Organised Tours

Some companies offer a variety of tours, from bus rides around downtown Victoria to quick trips around the island. Other companies only do one kind of tour, such as day and evening harbour boat trips, tours by horse-drawn carriage, self-drive tours using recorded tapes or tours up-island to view wildlife or hiking trips. It's best to find out what's available, decide what you want then shop around a little: again, the Travel Infocentre is a good place to start.

Gray Line (☎ 388-5248), 700 Douglas St, offers a variety of tours here, as they do in so many North American cities. Its city bus tour costs $12.50 for 1½ hours and takes in some of the major historical and scenic sights. Many of its bus tours include admission to attractions like the Butchart Gardens. You can buy tickets, and buses depart, from in front of the Empress Hotel. Heritage Tours (☎ 474-4332), 713 Bexhill St, offers more personalised city tours in limousines seating six people for $62 for 1¼ hours, or $82 for two hours.

Tallyho Sightseeing (☎ 479-1113) gives you a one-hour tour of the city in a horse-drawn carriage for $9.50 per person. More expensive is Black Beauty Line (☎ 479-1113) which has horse-drawn tours along James Bay for $20 for 10 to 15 minutes. Both leave from the corner of Belleville and Menzies Sts.

Seagull Expeditions (☎ 744-4268), 247 East Sunningdale Rd, Qualicum Beach V9K IL3, offers six-day tours of the island for budget travellers. The itinerary includes the Pacific Rim National Park and Strathcona Provincial Park, with opportunities for hiking in the rainforest. The bus carries 24 people and leaves from 1905 Store St near the Victoria HI Hostel, Mondays at 8.30 am.

The cost is $130. Freedom Adventure Tours (☎ 480-9409), Box 8606, Victoria V8W 3S2, has camping and hiking trips to the Clayoquot and Carmanah valleys and to the Sooke Potholes.

## Festivals

**May**

*Victoria Day Festival* – Held during the fourth week of May to celebrate Queen Victoria's birthday, features a parade, performances by the town's ethnic groups, stage shows and many sporting events. Many of the townspeople dress in 19th-century-style clothes, and some shopkeepers dress their windows in period manner. Call ☎ 382-3111 for information. The Swiftsure Lightship Classic, a sailing race, ends the event. Call ☎ 592-2441 for information. The last weekend can get pretty wild – a real street party.

**June**

*Jazz Festival* – In late June the Victoria Jazz Society (☎ 388-4423) puts on its annual jazz festival at various locations around town.

**June/July**

*Folkfest* – Held at the end of June and beginning of July this celebrates Canada's cultural diversity. Dance and musical performances take place in front of the Royal BC Museum.

**June/August**

*Victoria International Festival* – This festival, offering classical music performed by Canadian and foreign musicians, lasts through the summer till mid-August. For information and schedules contact the McPherson Playhouse (☎ 386-6121) or call ☎ 736 2119.

**August**

*First Peoples' Festival* – This takes place in August beside the Royal BC Museum and along Inner Harbour. It lasts three days and includes traditional craftwork, dancing, a potlatch and war-canoe rides. For information call ☎ 383-2663.

**August/September**

*Fringe Theatre Festival* – Featuring more than 50 performances in various locations around town, the festival includes drama, comedy, acrobatics, jugglers and street performers. It takes place in late August and early September. For details call ☎ 383-2663.

**September**

*Classic Boat Festival* – During this festival, held on the first weekend in September each year, vintage wooden boats powered by sail or engine compete in various categories. The competition is held on the Inner Harbour. Free entertainment is provided on the quayside for the spectators. For information call ☎ 385-7766.

**Places to Stay**

**Camping** Closest to town is *Fort Victoria RV Park* (☎ 479-8112), 340 Island Hwy, off Island Hwy 1A, 6½ km from the city centre. Take bus No 14 or 15 from the downtown area; there's a bus stop at the gate. The park caters mainly to RVs. It does have a few tent sites but there are no trees, and open fires are not allowed. It has full facilities including free showers and charges $19 for two for a powered site.

A little further out, *Thetis Lake Campground* (☎ 478-3845), 1938 Trans Canada Hwy, on Rural Route 6, is about a 15-minute drive north-west of the city centre. All facilities are available, including a laundry and shower. There's a store, and you can swim in the nearby lake. A site for two people is $13.91 including tax; electricity is $2 extra. The campground is open all year.

There's a government-run campground in *Goldstream Provincial Park* (☎ 387-4363), on the Trans Canada Hwy, about 20 km north-west of Victoria. A tent site costs $15.50 for one to four people and you can go swimming, fishing or hiking. Take bus No 50 from Douglas St. South of Goldstream Provincial Park, about 3½ km off the Trans Canada Hwy, at 2960 Irwin Rd, on Rural Route 6, is *Humpback Valley Campground* (☎ 478-6960). It's part of a nature sanctuary and is open from early June to the end of September. It has full facilities, canoe and kayak rentals, and charges $15 for two people.

The Travel Infocentre can tell you of other campgrounds not too far from town.

**Hostels** The HI *Victoria Hostel* (☎ 385-4511), 516 Yates St, is in the old part of town just up from Wharf St. It has room for over 100 people, family rooms, a larger common area, kitchen, laundry and good notice board. Memberships are available. A bed costs $13.50 for members and $18.50 for non-members.

The hostel is open Sunday to Thursday from 7.30 am to 2.30 am but the office closes at midnight. During the busy summer months it's advisable to book in before 4 pm.

In the peak season preference is given to HI members, and nonmembers may be asked to wait till 8 pm to check in. If the hostel is full there is a list of alternative accommodation on the notice board. You can find out, too, about the good mini-hostels around the island, some of which are in relatively remote places while others are more conveniently located.

*Selkirk Guest House* (☎ 389-12130), 934 Selkirk Ave in Esquimalt over the Johnson St Bridge, is affiliated with Hostelling International. For members a dorm bed costs $13.50, while for nonmembers it's $17.50; private rooms cost $30. There are showers and a laundry.

The *Backpackers Victoria Hostel* (☎ 386-4471), 1418 Fernwood Rd, has doubles for $30 or dormitory beds for $10. It has weekly and monthly rates too. There's a $10 deposit for the key. The hostel, on a hill overlooking the town, has no curfew and is close to shops and restaurants. Buses east along Fort St will take you there; the Haultain bus goes right past the door.

The *YM-YWCA* (☎ 386-7511) are both in the same building at 880 Courtney St, but the residence is only for women. There are 31 beds in single and double rooms with shared bathrooms. Singles/doubles are $31/46. It has a cafeteria that anyone can use and a heated swimming pool.

The *University of Victoria* rents rooms from the start of May to the end of August. Singles/doubles are $30/42, including breakfast and free parking. You can make use of the university's facilities and there are several licensed cafeterias on campus. Contact Housing & Conference Services (☎ 721-8396) at the University of Victoria, PO Box 1700, Victoria V8W 2Y2. Catch bus No 14 on Douglas St to the campus: it takes about 20 minutes.

The *Salvation Army Centre* (☎ 384-3396) is in a modern building at 525 Johnston St, on the corner of Wharf St, and is for men only. A bed in a dormitory costs $15, while a private room is $19. Meals are extra.

**B&Bs** This form of accommodation is very

Top Left: View of downtown Vancouver from Stanley Park, British Columbia (TS)
Top Right: The Steam Clock, Gastown, Vancouver, British Columbia (TS)
Bottom: Kamloops with the dry hills around, British Columbia (TS)

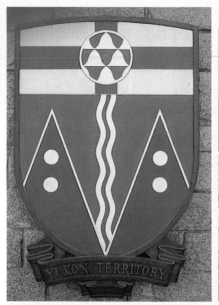

Top Left: Yukon's official shield (TS)
Top Right: Aerial view of Whitehorse, Yukon (TS)
   Bottom: Kluane National Park in the fall, Yukon (DS)

big in town and makes a good alternative to standard hotels and motels. There are several B&B associations that approve members, list them and make reservations at one central office. Check the listings of B&B agencies in the *Accommodations* brochure. Prices are between $35 and $75 for singles and between $45 and $120 for most doubles, though some go up to as much as $190.

A couple of associations to try are *All Seasons B&B Agency* (☎ 655-7133), PO Box 5511, Station B, Victoria V8R 6S4; and *Victoria Vacationer B&B* (☎ 382-9469), 1143 Leonard St. Many B&Bs advertise independently: see the pamphlets at the Travel Infocentre. A few of them are listed here.

North-east of the centre, *Renouf House* (☎ 595-4774) is a 1912 heritage home at 2010 Stanley Ave. It can cater to people with special diets and has homebaked bread. A single/double costs $35/45. *Battery St Guest House* (☎ 385-4632) is south of the centre, near Beacon Hill Park, at 670 Battery St. It's an old house dating from 1898 which now is run by a Dutch woman. Rooms are from $35/55. *Breland B&B* (☎ 383-0972), also south of the centre at 544 Toronto St, is close to the shops and sights. A single/double costs from $39/54 and parking is available. *Craigmyle Guest House* (☎ 595-5411), 1037 Craigdarroch Rd, about 1½ km east of the downtown area, is next to Craigdarroch Castle. Rooms are $55/70. One traveller has recommended *Marion Simms B&B* (☎ 592-3070), 1730 Taylor St, about a 10-minute bus ride from downtown. Singles/doubles are $35/50, the breakfasts are enormous and the owners are friendly and helpful.

**Hotels – bottom end** There are a few reasonable places right in the downtown area. The city really fills up in summer and room prices rise; after 1 October many are lower.

Some of the older hotels like the *Fairfield Hotel* (☎ 386-1621), 710 Cormorant St on the corner of Douglas St, and *Ritz Hotel* (☎ 383-1021), 710 Fort St, are cheap but not really geared for short-term visitors though

if there's a vacancy they will let the rooms out for about $35.

*Hotel Douglas* (☎ 383-4157), centrally located at 1450 Douglas St, on the corner of Pandora Ave, has singles/doubles from $50/55. It shares its lobby with an art gallery and has a restaurant and bar downstairs.

First opened in 1897, *Cherry Bank Hotel* (☎ 385-5380), 825 Burdett Ave, is east of the downtown area, up the hill a few blocks, opposite the law courts. It's simple but reasonable value and has singles/doubles for $45/51 with a shared bathroom, or $65/71 with a private bathroom. Prices include breakfast but rooms have no TV or telephone. A bar and restaurant are on the premises.

Good value, is the *James Bay Inn* (☎ 384-7151). It's the big old place with bay windows at 270 Government St, a few blocks south of the downtown area, in a residential area of small, attractive houses. Rooms with a shared bathroom are $62, while those with a private bathroom cost from $75. It has a TV room, bar, restaurant and food machines downstairs.

**Hotels – middle** At the *Strathcona Hotel* (☎ 383-7137), 919 Douglas St, a couple of blocks north of the Inner Harbour, you can get singles/doubles from $45/50 to $104/114. All the rooms have private bathroom, telephone and TV. It has free parking, several bars and a restaurant. At the *Dominion Hotel* (☎ 384-4136), 759 Yates St, singles/doubles start from $94/114. It has free parking and a restaurant. The *Green Gables Hotel* (☎ 385-6787), 850 Blanshard St, is close to the Inner Harbour and has an indoor pool, as well as a sauna and restaurant. Singles/doubles cost from $99 to $142.

**Hotels – top end** *Beaconsfield Inn* (☎ 384-4044), 998 Humboldt St, is a few blocks east of the downtown area and a couple north of Beacon Hill Park. It's in an Edwardian mansion and the rates include breakfast. Rates start from $120 for a single or double.

The *Empress Hotel* (☎ 348-8111), 721 Government St, looks out over the Inner

Harbour and is the focal point of Victoria. As you face the building, the reception area is to the left of the main entrance. Even if you're not staying here, the Empress Hotel is worth a visit. Singles/doubles are priced from $195/220 to $275/300.

*Victoria Regent Hotel* (☎ 386-2211), 1234 Wharf St, near the corner of Yates St, specialises in suites. Rates start from $155 for single or doubles. There's underground parking and the staff is friendly and helpful.

*Oak Bay Beach Hotel* (☎ 598-4556), 1175 Beach Drive, is a seaside hotel east of the downtown area, overlooking Oak Bay. It provides a shuttle service into the centre and lunch-time cruises. All rooms range from $116 to $236. *Laurel Point Inn* (☎ 386-8721), 680 Montreal St, west of the downtown area, near Laurel Point, is generally considered the best of all and is one of the most expensive. Singles/doubles start from $155 and go up to $495.

**Motels** Douglas St, being one of the main roads into Victoria, has a lot of motels, many of them just to the north of town.

The *Doric Motel* (☎ 386-2481), 3025 Douglas St, is a five-minute drive north of the downtown area. It has TV, laundry and free coffee. Singles/doubles are $47/58; a kitchen is $5 extra. *Paul's Motor Inn* (☎ 382-9231), 1900 Douglas St, has a 24-hour restaurant. Singles/doubles are priced from $77/82. The *Imperial Inn* (☎ 382-2111), 1961 Douglas St, costs $65/75 for singles/doubles and has a restaurant and bar.

*Crystal Court Motel* (☎ 384-0551) is at 701 Belleville St, on the corner of Douglas St, across the road from the Greyhound Bus Depot and Crystal Garden. Singles/doubles are $63/66, and a kitchen costs just $2 more. It's clean and the rooms have a TV, radio and telephone. The staff are friendly and helpful but note that you have to pay with cash or travellers' cheques. The motel is white, blue and gold.

Although the *T-Bird Motel* (☎ 385-5767), 600 Douglas St, and *Helm's Inn* (☎ 385-5767), 668 Superior St, have separate addresses, they adjoin each other and share

the same reception area and phone number. Singles/doubles at both start from $85 and all rooms have a kitchen. Opposite is the *Shamrock Motel* (☎ 385-8768), 675 Superior St, where singles/doubles are $89/99.

A good area for motels not far north-west of the downtown area is along Gorge Rd, which forms a section of Island Hwy 1A. From Gorge Rd it's about a five-minute drive to town.

At the *Capri Motel* (☎ 384-0521), 21 Gorge Rd East, singles/doubles are $50/52. At the *Friendship Inn* (☎ 386-8335), 39 Gorge Rd East, rooms start from $40/50; those with a kitchen cost $5 to $10 extra. *Budget Host Maple Leaf Inn* (☎ 388-9901), 120 Gorge Rd East, has a sauna, heated pool and laundromat. Rooms start from $58/62; those with a kitchen cost $10 extra. The *Royal Victorian Inn* (☎ 385-5771), at No 230, charges $35 to $39 for singles and $50 to $56 for doubles. There's a heated outdoor pool, laundromat and complimentary coffee or tea.

### Places to Eat

Though a small city, Victoria has a varied array of restaurants, due in part to its many visitors, and prices are generally good. As befits a tourist town, especially one with British roots, there are numerous cafés and tea shops. Some dining rooms offer good lunch specials but are fairly pricey in the evenings. The pubs in town are also good for reasonably priced meals.

**Places to Eat – bottom end** The *Public Cafeteria* in City Hall, on the corner of Douglas St and Pandora Ave, is clean and has daily specials for $4.50 or you could try the *cafeteria*, which has a wider selection, in the Bay department store. The modest and casual *Day & Night*, 622 Yates St, is good for any meal, with good-value plain food, including one of the cheapest breakfasts in town. Sandwiches are $4 and pasta dishes start from $4. *Smitty's Family Restaurant*, 850 Douglas St, is an old standby and best for cheap pancake breakfasts for around $6 or $7 including coffee. It's open from 6 am to 1 am.

*Scott's Restaurant*, 605 Yates St, is open 24 hours a day. It's clean and offers burgers and sandwiches for $5, grilled meats for about $7 and desserts such as cheesecake for $2.50. *Dion's Restaurant*, 772 Fort St between Douglas and Blanshard Sts, decorated with green plants, is open between 8.30 am and 10 pm. It has soup for $3.50, sandwiches from $3 and salads from $4.25 to $7.25 as well as other dishes. The *Rising Star Bakery*, on Broad St between Yates and Johnson Sts, offers croissant and coffee for $2.50. It also sells a variety of breads from $1.50 to $2.50.

The fish & chips are excellent in Victoria and there are several outlets for them. *Barb's Place*, 310 St Lawrence St, at Fisherman's Wharf, is a wooden shack sitting on a pontoon out over the water. Chips ($1.85) are served in newspaper. At *Cook St Fish & Chips*, 252 Cook St near Beacon Hill Park, fish & chips with coleslaw costs $4.95. The *Sticky Wicket Pub*, on the corner of Douglas and Courtney Sts, has fish & chips for $4.50 as well as other dishes such as nachos ($5.45) and pizza (from $5.65) and a variety of Canadian, US and UK beers. It's open from 11.30 am to 11 pm.

Another cheap but good place is the busy *Eugene's Restaurant & Snack Bar*, 1280 Broad St. Simple, basic Greek foods at about $3.50 to $7 are served cafeteria-style. It's open Monday to Friday from 8 am to 10 pm and Saturday from 10 am to 9 pm, but closed on Sunday. In Bastion Square, opposite Harpo's nightclub, is *C'est Bon*, a small French-style café which has lunch-time specials of soup, croissant and coffee for $4.35. Mel Gibson once ate here when shooting a film close by.

Market Square, 560 Johnson St, has several places to munch at: try *Café Bistingo* for sandwiches (from $4.25), and the *Bavarian Bakery* for good bread (around $2). *Café Mexico* has quick Mexican items such as tacos from $6; it's a pleasant little place, is licensed and has a patio overlooking the courtyard.

*Sam's Deli*, under the maroon awnings at 805 Government St, on the corner of Wharf St and diagonally opposite the main Travel Infocentre, is a perfect spot to have an espresso and write a postcard. There are a dozen tables outside on the sidewalk and more inside, where the walls are covered in 1920s and 1930s posters. This is a popular place with a European flavour. It serves good-value soups (from $3), salads ($4) and sandwiches ($3).

**Places to Eat – middle** For dinners the *Spare Rib House*, in the Cherry Bank Hotel, 825 Burdett Ave, is good. It serves rib dinners (from $12), steaks and seafood. There's a children's menu ($3.95) and the restaurant features live sing-along entertainment.

*Pagliacci's*, 1011 Broad St, between Fort and Broughton Sts, is mainly Italian. It costs $8 for salads and from $16 for main dishes and the food is good. It has live music most nights and is one of the 'in' spots in town, so it's best to book for the evenings, as there are often queues outside then.

*Taj Mahal* is an East Indian restaurant at 679 Herald St, just north-east of Chinatown. It has a good selection, including Tandoori and vegetarian, and food is spiced as hot as you like, but it's not cheap: starters are $3 to $8 and main meals $8 to $17. It's open for lunch Monday to Friday from 11.30 am to 2 pm and Saturday from noon to 2 pm, and for dinner every day from 5.30 pm. Also with a good selection and similarly priced is *Da Tandoor*, 1010 Fort St. It's open for lunch Thursday and Friday from 11.30 am to 2 pm and for dinner daily from 5 to 10.30 pm.

*Periklis*, 531 Yates St, is a Greek place opposite the HI Hostel. Starters are $2 to $6 and main courses between $10 and $24. It's open for lunch Monday to Friday from 11.30 am to 3 pm, and daily in the evenings from 5.30 pm till late. *Millos Restaurant*, 716 Burdett Ave, east off Douglas St behind the Classic Car Museum, is housed in a blue and white 'windmill'. It has starters from $5 to $6.50 and main Greek meals from $12; it also serves pastas.

Chinatown, marked by the Gate of Harmonious Interest over Fisgard St, has its share of eating spots. *Foo Hong*, 564 Fisgard St, is small and basic yet has good, simple Cantonese food. Starters cost around $4 and main dishes $7. *Don Mee*, 538 Fisgard St, serves Cantonese food. Combination plates are good value at lunch time. Spring rolls cost $2.50 and other starters cost up to $5; seafood, beef, pork or vegetable main courses cost from $5 to $12. *Hunan Village*, 548 Fisgard St opposite Fan Tan Alley, serves Cantonese and Sichuan food but is a little pricier than the Don Mee: starters cost from $3 to $9, main dishes from $9.50 to $12.50.

For afternoon tea try the *Blue Fox Restaurant*, 919 Fort St, which is away from the crowds and somewhat formal in style and decor. It serves an all-day breakfast for $4.50 and a variety of salads and sandwiches. *Murchie's*, at 1110 Government St, between View and Fort Sts, is a west coast, tea and coffee merchant with some of the best teas and coffees available and a decadent assortment of pastries and chocolates. Scones with strawberry jam and Devonshire cream cost $2.50. The tea room at the Royal BC Museum is cafeteria style and has sandwiches for $3.

A popular place with the locals is the *Blethering Place*, 2250 Oak Bay Ave, away from the centre of town. It has Devonshire teas for $7 to $9 and is open every day from 8 am to 10 pm.

*Milestone's*, 812 Wharf St, right on the harbour, below the Travel Infocentre, has a few tables outside and is also a good spot for an afternoon brew and view. It has burgers for $6, sandwiches for $8 and some vegetarian dishes (vegetarian fettucini is $10).

*Herald St Caffé*, 546 Herald St, is a small Italian restaurant serving delicious pastas for around $12 to $15. It also has vegetarian dishes, great desserts and a wine bar and gets busy after 10 pm.

**Places to Eat – top end** The *Empress Room* in the Empress Hotel has very good starters, including soups from $6.25, salads from $7.75, meat and seafood main courses from $23 to $30, and an array of desserts. The *Bengal Lounge*, also in the hotel, is a real treat. It serves seafood and poultry and every day a different curry for $12.50 (other daily specials are cheaper). The service and the style make it well worth the price. There is a tiger skin on the wall and it's all very colonially British. The *Crystal Room* has similar fare and prices but is often booked out by tour groups, while downstairs in the *Garden Café* lunch is cheaper. Finally, the tradition of afternoon tea is upheld in the lobby of the hotel, but you have to be suitably attired – a 'dress code is in effect'. There are regular sittings between 11 am and 5 pm.

*La Petite Colombe*, 604 Broughton St, near the corner of Government St, serves good crêpes, but the main fare is French-style seafood. Starters begin at $5 and main meals are between $10 and $21. The restaurant is small and quiet and has a good reputation. The best seafood house in town is *Chauney's Restaurant*, 614 Humboldt St, opposite the Empress Hotel. Soup and seafood starters cost from around $4 and Dover sole is $21.95. The restaurant also serves steak and poultry dishes and has live classical music six nights a week.

In Bastion Square opposite C'est Bon, on the corner of Wharf St, is the elegant *Rebecca's*. It serves mainly seafood with, starters from $3 to $7 and main meals between $8 and $15. *Chandler's Seafood Restaurant* near the Victorian Regent Hotel and the corner of Yates and Wharf Sts has starters from $5 to $10 and main dishes between $11 and $25. It also has a bar.

*Koto Japanese Restaurant*, 510 Fort St, just up from Wharf St, serves mainly seafood and has a sushi and salad bar; main courses cost from $12 to $26. There's a detailed, colourful display in the window of the kinds of dishes available in the restaurant. It's open for lunch Monday to Saturday from 11.30 am to 2 pm and for dinner daily from 5 pm.

You can get good food at the *French Connection*, 512 Simcoe St, a couple of blocks south of the Parliament Buildings. Main meals cost between $13 and $19.

## Entertainment

*Monday Magazine*, the free weekly entertainment paper, has extensive coverage of what's available in town. You can pick up a copy around town. The Travel Infocentre also has information on what's current.

**Theatre** Victoria has a number of live theatres that provide venues for plays, concerts, comedies, ballets and operas. The *MacPherson Playhouse* (☎ 386-6121), 3 Centennial Square, on the corner of Pandora Ave and Government St, regularly puts on plays and comedies. The box office is open Monday to Saturday from 9.30 am to 5.30 pm. The *Royal Theatre* (☎ 386-6121), 805 Broughton St, between Blanshard and Quadra Sts, currently being renovated, hosts a range of performances, including the likes Leonard Cohen and the Neville Brothers. You can get tickets and information for the Royal Theatre from the MacPherson Playhouse. Other theatres worth checking out are the *Belfry* (☎ 385-6815), 1291 Gladstone Ave, north-east of the downtown area, and the *Phoenix Theatre* (☎ 721-8000), on the University of Victoria campus.

*Open Space Gallery*, 510 Fort St, presents young poets, dancers and musicians.

**Music** One of the most popular nightclubs is *Harpo's* (☎ 385-5333), 15 Bastion Square on the corner of Wharf St, above Rebecca's. It has live bands playing a variety of music, including rock, celtic rock, ska, reggae and blues. The cover charge is generally about $5, but may be higher depending on who's performing. It's open Monday to Saturday from 9 pm to 2 am.

In the same building as the Strathcona Hotel there are several clubs that feature live music – including the *Forge* and *Big Bad John's* – charging about $4 or $5 admission and open until 2 am. The Forge is a long-standing nigl tclub and plays mostly live rock and blues music. Big Bad John's is more for country & western fans.

*Merlin's Nightclub* (☎ 381-2331), 1208 Wharf St, is on the Inner Harbour, down the stone staircase, opposite Bastion Square provides a different form of entertainment each night, including a Ladies' Night every Wednesday. Merlin's is open Monday to Wednesday from 8 pm to 2 am and Thursday to Saturday from 7 pm to 2 am.

*Pagliacci's* is popular not only for its food but also for the entertainment it provides. It's the centre for jazz in Victoria but varies this with comedy sessions. For information about jazz around town call ☎ 658-5255.

**Pubs** If you like a beer then Victoria's pub scene should please you. The city has a number of 'brew pubs' – pubs that brew their own beer – and although they're admittedly a bit trendy, the beer is good.

*Spinnaker's*, opened in 1984, was Canada's first brew pub. It's at 308 Catherine St, right on the water of Victoria Harbour, off Esquimalt Rd, west of the downtown area. It has a variety of excellent beers made in-house and starting from $3. To get there, cross Johnson Bridge into Esquimalt Rd, then turn left into a pathway that follows the shoreline round to the pub. There are good views back towards town. *Swans Hotel*, opposite Johnson Bridge, on the corner of Pandora Ave and Store St, has a variety of homemade beers; a half-pint glass of stout is $2.90. Two other brew pubs are the *Garrick's Head*, 69 Bastion Square, and the *Sticky Wicket Pub*.

**Cinema** There are several commercial cinemas around town. The *Cineplex Odeon*, 780 Yates St opposite the Dominion Hotel, has three screens. Sessions cost $8 except Tuesdays when it's reduced to $4.25.

## Things to Buy

There are a number of craft shops along Douglas and Government Sts selling Native Indian art and craftwork such as sweaters, moccasins, carvings and prints. Be careful: the good stuff is expensive. There are lots of imitations and lots of junk.

Canadian Impressions (☎ 383-2641), 811 Government St, has some quality items and Native Indian crafts. Check the prints upstairs, some of which cost between $25 and $170. Canadian Impressions has another shop at the airport.

Sasquatch Trading Company (☎ 386-9033), 1233 Government St, opposite the main post office, has a good selection of Cowichan sweaters. These hand-spun, hand-knitted sweaters average between $130 and $180 but are warm and should last a decade or more. No dyes are used. The store is open daily from 8.30 am to 9 pm. Other stores selling quality sweaters are Cowichan Trading (☎ 383-0321), 1328 Government St, Indian Craft Shoppe (☎ 382-3643), 905 Government St, and Hills Indian Crafts (☎ 385- 3911), 1008 Government St.

In Fort St, between Blanshard and Quadra Sts, there are a number of antique and bric-a-brac shops.

For chocolate lovers, Roger's Chocolates, 913 Government St, dating from 1885, offers a treat to both nose and tongue. Try one (or more) of the Victoria creams – chocolate-covered discs in over 20 flavours at $1.60. Everything on sale here is made on the premises. It's open Monday to Friday from 9.30 am to 8 pm, Saturday from 9.30 am to 5.30 pm and Sunday from 11 am to 5 pm.

For general shopping try the Victoria Eaton Centre, which covers two blocks and has over 140 shops and eateries on four levels. It's open seven days a week and the main entrance is on the corner of Government and Fort Sts. The Bay department store, 1701 Douglas St, is open on Monday, Tuesday and Saturday between 9.30 am and 5.30 pm, and from Wednesday to Friday between 9.30 am and 9 pm and on Sunday between noon and 5 pm.

Market Square, on the corner of Johnson and Wharf Sts, has two storeys of shops and restaurants. If you'd like (or you need?) to add some colour to your (safe) sex life then The Rubber Rainbow store here, which sells a huge variety of condoms including ones that glow in the dark, may be what you're looking for.

### Getting There & Away
**Air** Two airlines with offices in Victoria are: Air Canada (☎ 360-9074), 20 Centennial Square; and Canadian Airlines (☎ 382-6111) 901 Gordon St. Air Canada and Canadian Airlines connect the airports of Vancouver and Victoria. The normal, one-way, pre-tax economy fare is $88, but Air Canada has weekend return specials for the same price, and Canadian Airlines has a cheaper flight with conditions attached. The one-way fare to Seattle on Canadian Airlines is $280 plus tax.

If you're flying to Vancouver and beyond, the cost of a ticket from Victoria is just a few dollars more than one from Vancouver itself, so it's not worth paying the ferry price to catch a flight directly from Vancouver.

Several airlines operate out of Seattle. Horizon Air (☎ 206-762-3646 in Seattle; 1-800-547-9308), in conjunction with Alaska Airlines, has regular flights to destinations in Alaska and mainland USA. Lake Union Air (☎ 1-800-826-1890) connects Victoria with Tofino, Nootka Sound and Campbell River in central Vancouver Island, the San Juan Islands and Seattle. Kenmore Air (☎ 206-486-1257; 1-800-543-9595) flies between Victoria and Seattle by seaplane.

**Bus** Although Greyhound has no service on the island or to the mainland it does have an office (☎ 385-5248), in the bus depot at 700 Douglas St where you can get information and purchase tickets. The one-way fare (including tax) on Greyhound to Calgary is $114.34 and to Edmonton $128.25. There are reductions on some fares if you book in advance.

Pacific Coach Lines (PCL) (☎ 385-4411) and Island Coach Lines (☎ 385-4411) also operate out of the same depot. Pacific Coach Lines covers Vancouver Island and some of the southern BC mainland and also runs to Seattle. There's a bus to Vancouver every hour between 6 am and 9 pm; the one-way fare, which includes the cost of the ferry, is $21.25/38.25 one-way/return. It's the same price to Vancouver Airport; it connects with the airport shuttle bus at Delta Pacific Resort. The bus to Seattle, via Sidney and Anacortes, leaves at 10 am and gets there at 5 pm. The one-way fare, including the cost of the ferry, is $28.60.

Island Coach Lines covers Vancouver Island. There are eight buses a day to Nanaimo and northern Vancouver Island. The one-way fares are: to Duncan $8.80, Nanaimo $15.40, Port Alberni $26.40 and Port Hardy $74.05.

**Train** The Esquimalt & Nanaimo Railiner (or E&N Railiner), operated by VIA Rail (☎ 383-4324; 1-800561-8630), connects Victoria with Nanaimo, Parksville and Courtenay. There is one train in each direction per day – northbound from Victoria at 8.15 am, southbound from Courtenay at 1.15 pm. The journey, through some beautiful scenery, takes about 3½ hours. Some one-way fares are to Nanaimo $17.12, Parksville $22.47 and Courtenay $32.10.

For the full schedule, get a copy of the E&N Railiner pamphlet from the station, a travel agency or the Travel Infocentre. The station, 405 Pandora Ave, is close to town, right at Johnson Bridge, near the corner of Johnson and Wharf Sts. It's open from 7.30 am to noon and from 1 to 3 pm. The name of the train is *Malahat* and reservations are often required.

**Ferry** BC Ferries (☎ 656-0757, 24 hours), 1112 Fort St, on the corner of Cook St, runs frequent trips from Swartz Bay to Tsawwassen, on the mainland. The 38-km crossing takes about one hour 40 minutes. There are between 10 and 15 sailings per day: the schedule varies according to the season. The walk-on fare is $5.50, while for driver and car it's $25.50. Bus No 70 from the downtown area to the ferry terminal costs $1.25.

BC Ferries also operates between Swartz Bay and five of the southern Gulf Islands: Galiano, Mayne, Saturna, Salt Spring and Pender. There are about three or four services a day. The fare to the southern Gulf Islands is $4 per person, $1.50 for a bicycle and $13.50 for a car.

BC Ferries also links other more northerly islands in the Georgia Strait to towns along the coast up-island. For ferries north to Prince Rupert see Port Hardy at the end of the Vancouver Island section.

Royal Sealink (☎ 382-5465) has an express service to Vancouver costing $40 one way (see the Vancouver Getting There & Away section for more details).

The *Victoria Clipper* and *Victoria Clipper II*, run by Clipper Navigation (☎ 382-8100), 1000 Wharf St, sail between Seattle and Victoria. The clippers are water-jet-propelled catamarans and don't take cars. The journey lasts about 2¾ hours and the fare one way in summer is US$52; it's a little cheaper the rest of the year.

The ferry MV *Coho*, operated by Black Ball Transport (☎ 386-2202), 430 Belleville St, is much cheaper. It sails between the Inner Harbour and Port Angeles just across the Juan de Fuca Strait. It costs US$8 per person or US$32 with a car. It's a 1½-hour trip, and there are four a day in each direction during the summer months. From Victoria the ferry leaves at 6.20 and 10.30 am and 3 and 7.30 pm.

*Victoria Express* (☎ 361-9144) also goes to Port Angeles. The journey time is one hour and the return fare is $20. The *Victoria Star*, operated by Gray Line Cruises (☎ 1-800 443 4552) who are based in Bellingham, goes once a day to Bellingham in Washington state. The ferry leaves from Wharf St down from Bastion Square and the one-way fare is $33.60.

Lastly, Washington State Ferries (☎ 656-1531; ☎ 381-1551 in Victoria), 2499 Ocean Ave in Sidney, has a ferry service from Swartz Bay through the San Juan Islands to Anacortes on the Washington mainland. One way it costs US$6.05 or US$31.25 with a car. It's a very scenic trip and you can have stopovers on the islands (see San Juan Islands later for more details).

### Getting Around
**To/From the Airport** PBM Transport (☎ 383-7311), 2nd Floor, 3297 Douglas St, operates the airport bus to Victoria International Airport. It leaves every half hour from

outside Executive House Hotel at 777 Douglas St; the 25 km or so trip costs $13.

City bus No 70 passes within 1½ km of the airport, while a taxi to the airport from the downtown area costs about $28 to $35.

**Bus** For local transit information call Busline (☎ 382-6161) or get a copy of BC Transit's guide from the Travel Infocentre listing bus routes and fares. The city buses cover a wide area and run quite frequently: every 10 to 30 minutes. The normal one-way fare is $1.25; it's $1.75 if you wish to travel out to suburbs such as Callwood or Sidney. Have the exact change ready. You can get an all-day pass for $4 for as many rides as you want, starting as early as you like. These all-day passes are not sold on buses but are available from various outlets such as convenience stores around town.

Bus No 70 goes to the ferry terminal in Swartz Bay; bus No 2 goes to Oak Bay.

**Car** For rentals, it's best to shop around before parting with your money as prices can vary.

One of the cheapest places is ADA Rent A Used Car (☎ 388-6230), 892 Goldstream Ave, which rents older cars by the day for $13.95 and the newer ones for $19.95; add 10 cents per km and $7 insurance for both. Another is Rent-A-Wreck (☎ 384-5343), 2634 Douglas St, where you can rent a car from $18.95 a day plus 10 cents per km and $4.95 insurance.

The major companies and more are represented in and around the downtown area. Three are on or close to Douglas St:

Avis
    843 Douglas St (☎ 386-8468)
Budget
    727 Courtney St (☎ 388-7874)
Tilden
    767 Douglas St (☎ 381-1115)

Budget offers a daily rate of $35 with unlimited km plus $12 insurance. Avis has a daily rate of $49 with unlimited km plus $12.95 insurance.

**Taxi** There are several taxi companies in town. Two to try are Victoria Taxi (☎ 383-7111) and Blue Bird Cabs (☎ 382-4235). You can also hire three-wheeled bicycle taxis called pedicabs – a more leisurely way of getting around.

**Bicycle** Downtown you can hire bikes from Harbour Scooters (☎ 384-2133), 843 Douglas St, adjacent to the Avis car-rental office. They cost $5 per hour or $19 for 24 hours; you must also pay $2 insurance. Biker Bills (☎ 361-0091), 634 Humboldt Ave opposite the Empress Hotel, charges $5 per hour and $19.95 for 24 hours. The bike can be delivered to your hotel. The HI Hostel also hires out bikes.

**Ferry** Victoria Harbour Ferry runs an enjoyable, albeit short, ferry trip of about half an hour return from Inner Harbour to Songhees Park (in front of the Ocean Pointe Hotel), Fisherman's Wharf and Westbay Marina. The boat takes just a dozen people per trip and costs $2.

## AROUND VICTORIA
### Western Shore
West of Victoria, Hwy 14 takes you from the city's manicured parks and gardens to the pristine wilderness of the west coast. The highway runs through Sooke then along the coast overlooking the Juan de Fuca Strait to Port Renfrew at the southern end of the West Coast Trail (see Pacific Rim National Park later). There are parks and beaches along the way for walking, beachcombing, picnicking, etc.

Before you reach Sooke follow the signs from Milnes Landing to the **Sooke Potholes** where you can go swimming, picnicking and hiking. Sooke's Travel Infocentre (☎ 642-6351) and local museum are housed in the same building at 2070 Phillip's Rd. Victoria's bus network extends to Sooke: take bus No 50 to the Western Exchange then change to No 61.

Further along Hwy 14, the windswept **French Beach** and **China Beach** provincial parks have swimming, camping and walking trails.

At **Port Renfrew**, often the destination for a day trip from town, the main attraction is Botanical Beach, a sandstone shelf, which at low tide is dotted with tidal pools containing all manner of small marine life: starfish, anemones, etc. To return to Victoria without retracing your tracks, take the logging road across the island to Lake Cowichan, from where better roads connect with Duncan and Hwy 19. (See Getting Around under Duncan for more information on the logging roads.)

### San Juan Islands (USA)

Lying north-east off the coast of Victoria are the San Juan Islands, just beyond the US border, making them a part of Washington state. The big three of the grouping, San Juan Island, Orcas Island and Lopez Island, form a rough circle about halfway between Vancouver Island and the US mainland.

Washington State Ferries connects Swartz Bay in Sidney with Anacortes on the Washington mainland via the islands, making it a very scenic route between these ports. Stops are made at Orcas, Shaw, Lopez and San Juan. The ferries take cars, bicycles and kayaks and from Anacortes buses connect with Seattle. For information about buses contact Gray Line (☎ 206-624-5077) at the Greyhound Bus Depot on the corner of 8th Ave and Stewart St in Seattle.

The islands are good for cycling around and hitchhiking is accepted. The ferries sell a good road map indicating the topography, and there are numerous campgrounds and guesthouses on the principal islands. Note that you must pass through customs. Also, foot passengers may travel free between the main islands in either direction.

### Southern Gulf Islands

Lying north-east of Victoria, off Sidney really, at the northern end of the Saanich Peninsula, this string of nearly 200 islands is squeezed between the mainland and southern Vancouver Island. The ferry from Tsawwassen edges between a handful of them on its route into Sidney.

With a few important exceptions, most are small and nearly all of them virtually uninhabited, but this island-littered channel is a boater's dream. Vessels of all descriptions cruise in and out of bays, harbours and marinas much of the year. The fishing is varied and excellent: several species of prized salmon can be caught in season. BC Ferries connects with some of the larger islands, so you don't need your own boat to visit them. The fare from Tsawwassen is $7.50; from Swartz Bay and between the islands it's $4 return. Before heading to the islands check at the Travel Infocentre in Victoria about activities, accommodation and transport. Pick up a copy of the free newspaper *The Gulf Islander* which also has details of these.

Due to the mild climate, abundant flora & fauna, relative isolation and natural beauty, the islands are one of Canada's escapist-dream destinations. Indeed, many of the inhabitants are retired people, artists or counter-culture types of one sort or another.

There are cycling routes on the islands: contact the Bicycling Association of BC for details.

**Salt Spring Island** Salt Spring Island is the largest island in both size (29 km by 14 km) and population; its usual population of over 8500 swells to three times that size in summer. Artists, entertainers and crafts people have chosen to live here. As a consequence, there are craft fairs and art galleries with national reputations. The island has a long, interesting Native Indian history followed by settlement not by White people but by pioneering US Blacks. Seeking escape from prejudice and social tensions, a small group of settlers formed a community at Vesuvius Bay. Unfortunately, the Native Indians didn't care for them any more than they cared for the British in the area. Still, the Blacks stuck it out, began farms and set up schools. Later, immigrants came from Britain and Ireland.

There are three ferry terminals: Long Harbour serves Vancouver, Swartz Bay, the other Southern Gulf Islands and the US mainland; Fulford Harbour and Vesuvius Bay are for ferries plying back and forth to Vancouver Island: the former to Swartz Bay, the latter to Crofton.

**Ganges**, not far from the Long Harbour landing, is the principal village. It has the most accommodation and has a summer arts & crafts fair, a few tourist-oriented shops and a Saturday morning market. Artists welcome visitors to their studios – the Travel Infocentre (☎ 537-5252), 121 Lower Ganges Rd, has a list. **Mouat Provincial Park** is nearby and has 15 campsites.

South of Ganges, **Mt Maxwell Provincial Park** offers excellent views, fishing and picnic areas. In **Ruckle Provincial Park**, a former homestead 10 km east of Fulford Harbour ferry terminal, you can enjoy hiking through forest and along the shoreline, plus fishing and wilderness camping.

***Places to Stay*** At HI *Cusheon Creek Hostel* (☎ 537-4149), 640 Ocean Lake Rd, you can sleep either in a dorm or in a Native Indian teepee. The cost is $13 for members, $16 for nonmembers. The hostel is a short walk from the lake or ocean beach. There are quite a few B&Bs, some of which will have someone pick you up at the ferry terminal. Scattered around the island are resorts – usually with cottages for rent and maybe with some camping, a beach, boat rentals, etc. The cottages range in price from about $45/50 a single/double. Near the ferry terminals there are also a few motels with rooms for about $50/60.

***Getting Around*** Salt Spring Island Bus (☎ 537-2311) runs between Ganges and the ferry terminals. Cycling is possible but this is a fair-sized island and the terrain is hilly.

**North & South Pender Islands** Together these two islands, joined by a small bridge across the narrow channel that separates them, have nearly 1600 people. Again, there are art & craft studios to visit and the ever-present golf course. For beaches, try **Hamilton** in Browning Harbour on North Pender and **Mortimer Spit** on South Pender

(just after crossing the bridge). You might well see some of the more-or-less tame deer around the islands. You can hike and camp at **Prior Centennial Provincial Park** on North Pender, close to **Medicine Beach** at Bedwell Harbour. On South Pender there are good views from the summit of the 260-metre **Mt Norman**.

***Places to Stay*** Accommodation is mainly in B&Bs and cottages. If you want to splurge you can try the heritage farmhouse *Corbett House* (☎ 629-6305), in Corbett Rd, one km from the ferry terminal. It has singles/doubles for $60/80 including breakfast.

**Saturna Island** At Saturna Point by the ferry terminal in Lyall Harbour there's a store and pub. **Winter Cove Marine Park** has a good sandy beach from where you can go swimming, fishing, boating and hiking. At the top of **Mt Warburton Pike** is a wildlife reserve with wild goats and fine views. There are also good views of the Washington Mountains from the road on the island's leeward side. Just north of Saturna Island is **Cabbage Island Marine Park**, with swimming, fishing and wilderness camping.

***Places to Stay*** Accommodation is mostly in B&Bs. *Boot Cove Lodge* (☎ 539-2254), less than two km from the ferry terminal, has doubles for $90 including breakfast. It offers boat and bicycle rentals as well as other meals.

**Mayne Island** The ferry between Tsawwassen and Swartz Bay squeezes through Active Pass, which separates Mayne and Galiano islands. Village Bay, on the southern side of Mayne Island, is the ferry terminal, although there are docking facilities for boaters at other points. There are some late 19th-century buildings at **Miners Bay**, including the museum, which was formerly the jail. There are only a few places to stay, mostly B&Bs, so it's best to book ahead.

**Galiano Island** Galiano is a good island to visit. Despite its relatively large size, it has only 900 residents stretched along its long, narrow land mass. About 75% of the island is forest and bush. There's a Travel Infocentre (☎ 539-2233) at the ferry terminal in Sturdies Bay. Again, local artists and artisans invite visitors to their studios.

You can hike almost the length of the east coast and climb either **Mt Sutil** (323 metres) or **Mt Galiano** (342 metres), from both of which you can see the Olympic Mountains about 90 km away. If you're willing to tackle the hills, you can go cycling, while Porlia Pass and Active Pass are popular places for diving and fishing. The coast is lined with cliffs and small bays, and canoeing along the western shoreline is possible in the calmer waters. On the north-eastern tip of the island is the rugged **Dionisio Point Provincial Park** with swimming, fishing, hiking and wilderness camping.

**Places to Stay** You can camp at *Montague Harbour Marine Park* and around the island there are B&Bs and several places with cottage rentals. *Sutil Lodge* (☎ 539-2930) dates from the 1920s and is on the beach at Montague Harbour. It has singles/doubles from $40/65 and offers free use of canoes.

From Sturdies Bay there are two ferries daily to Tsawwassen and Swartz Bay.

## DUNCAN & COWICHAN VALLEY

About 60 km north of Victoria along the Trans Canada Hwy is the small town of Duncan. It marks the beginning of the Cowichan Valley running westward and contains the large Lake Cowichan. The turning for Lake Cowichan is eight km north of Duncan, left (east) of the Trans Canada Hwy; from the turn-off it's another 22 km. This is the land of the Cowichan people, who comprise BC's largest Native Indian group. Despite some problems they still maintain aspects of their unique culture.

A good day trip from Victoria is to head up to Chemainus, back to Duncan, then over to Lake Cowichan, across to Port Renfrew and down the west coast back to town. It's a

lot of driving but if you're in no hurry and can stop a lot it makes an interesting, full day.

The Travel Infocentre (☎ 746-4421) in Duncan, on the corner of the Trans Canada Hwy and Coronation St, is open daily from 9 am to 5 pm. In Lake Cowichan township the Travel Infocentre (☎ 749-4141) is open Sunday to Thursday from 9 am to 5 pm and Friday and Saturday from 8.30 am to 8 pm. It has lots of information on the area and Pacific Rim National Park.

There really isn't much in Duncan (although the old part of town is worth a look round) or the township of Lake Cowichan, but the valley and lake are good for camping, hiking, swimming, fishing and canoeing. The turn-off for Lake Cowichan is about four km north of Duncan.

Since 1985, Duncan, the 'City of Totems', has developed a project with the Cowichans to have totem poles carved and displayed in the town area. There are now more than 20 examples of this west coast art form.

Duncan is also home to the 'world's largest hockey stick'.

### Native Heritage Centre

Coming to Duncan from the south along the highway take the first turn left after crossing the bridge, into Cowichan Way. The centre (☎ 746-8119), 200 Cowichan Way, is 150 metres along on the left. It has exhibits of Cowichan craftwork and carvings which you can see being made. There's a gift shop and the admission price of $6 includes a 20-minute movie about the centre. It's open daily from 9.30 am to 5.30 pm.

### Cowichan Valley Museum

Located in the railway station on Canada Ave, this locally oriented museum (☎ 746-6612) is open in summer Monday to Saturday from 11 am to 4 pm.

### BC Forest Museum

This is about three km north of Duncan, offering on its 40 hectares both indoor and outdoor features. There's a stand of original forest of Douglas firs, 55 metres tall, that were present before Captain Cook arrived in

1778. Included in the price is a ride around the site in a small steam train. You can visit a bird sanctuary or view a replica of an old logging camp and logging equipment. There are also indoor displays and movies of logging that took place years ago. The museum (☎ 748-9389) is open daily in summer from 9.30 am to 6 pm and admission is $6.

### Sawmill Tours
The valley is a logging centre, worked by several companies. Some of them offer free tours of their mills. They are: MacMillan Bloedel (☎ 746-1611), at Chemainus Mill (☎ 246-3221); Doman Industries (☎ 748-3711); and Fletcher Challenge (☎ 246-3241). The tours run Monday to Friday in summer. At **Youbou**, west of Lake Cowichan township, there's a working sawmill: call ☎ 749-3244 about tours.

### Activities
There are many hiking trails around Cowichan River and Lake Cowichan. One is the **Cowichan River Footpath**. It's about 18 km long and there is a good variety of scenery along the way. You can do it in a day or camp on the way. The path goes to Skutz Falls; from there you can head back to Duncan or keep going up the river. Maps of the trail are available at sporting stores. The lake gets warm enough to swim in. You can also go fishing and canoeing in the lake and river.

### Places to Stay & Eat
There are plenty of hotels and motels, especially along the Trans Canada Hwy in Duncan and in the small townships along the river and lake. One of the cheapest is *Duncan Motel* (☎ 748-2177), 2552 Alexander St, Duncan; it has singles/doubles from $34/36.

Camping is best, however, and there is a wide variety offered. *Lakeview Park Municipal Campground* (☎ 749-3350) is on the southern shore of Lake Cowichan about three km west of the town. It has showers, toilets and free firewood. A tent site costs $10. Further west along the lake there is a government-operated campground at

*Gordon Bay Provincial Park* with 130 sites for trailers and tents. The fee is $14.50. For more remote camping, some of the forestry companies have set up unsupervised sites mainly between Lake Cowichan and the west coast of Vancouver Island. The Travel Infocentres or the logging companies have more information on these.

In Duncan most of the eating places are along the Trans Canada Hwy but there are a few small places in the old part of town. *Good Rock Café*, is a 1950s-style diner on the corner of Government and Jubilee Sts, complete with juke box (and old 45s hanging from the ceiling). It's good for breakfasts; French toast with coffee is $4. Also, nearby at 195 Kenneth St is the *Arbutus Café*.

### Getting There & Away
Island Coach Line buses travel between Duncan and Victoria for $8.80 including tax, one way. The 70-minute train trip on the E&N Railiner costs $9.63 including tax; there is one a day in each direction.

### Getting Around
The area around Lake Cowichan is full of logging roads, some of which you can use, though they're often rough; for some advice and rules, ask at the Travel Infocentres. The well-used logging road from Lake Cowichan to Port Renfrew is gravelled and in good shape; with a basic map, you shouldn't have any difficulty. The detailed maps showing all the logging roads look like a dog's breakfast so are more difficult to follow.

Hitching here and all over the island is common and accepted.

### DUNCAN TO NANAIMO
#### Crofton
About 16 km north of Duncan on Hwy 1A is the small town of Crofton, from where you can catch ferries to Vesuvius Bay in the north of Salt Spring Island (see Southern Gulf Islands earlier).

#### Chemainus
Chemainus, 10 km north of Crofton, had a novel and interesting way of putting itself on

the tourist map. In 1983 the town sawmill shut down, and to counter the inevitable slow death, a tremendously successful concept was nursed to fruition: murals. An artist was commissioned to paint a large outdoor mural relating to the town's history. People took notice, more murals were painted and now there are over 30 of them. A bustling and prosperous community developed and the sawmill re-opened.

The brightly painted Chemainus Theatre has been restored and is the most striking building in town. There are now lots of craft shops and restaurants, all making a short visit a worthwhile proposition.

The Travel Infocentre (☎ 246-3944) is in an old railway carriage on Mill St. Off the coast of Chemainus are **Thetis** and **Kuper islands**. Kuper Island is a Native Indian reserve.

The ferries for these islands leave from Oak St and the ticket office is opposite the Harborside Café; the fare is $4, or $8 for a car. The ferry to each island takes about 30 minutes from Chemainus. Thetis Island is primarily geared to boaters and has two marinas. There is a pub, however, at Quinn's Marina: turn left when you get off the ferry then left again into Harbour Drive where you see the anchor sign. There's one restaurant, the Pump House, which you can see to the left as the ferry pulls in. At Pilkey Point there are sandstone formations along the beach.

### Ladysmith

Ladysmith, a small town about 26 km north of Duncan, on the Trans Canada Hwy, sits on the 49th Parallel which on the mainland divides Canada from the USA. Originally built as a coal-shipping port by the industrialist James Dunsmuir, he named it after the South African town of the same name when the latter was rescued in 1901 from the Boers by the British general, Buller, during the Boer War.

The Travel Infocentre (☎ 245-8544) and the **Black Nugget Museum**, in Gatacre Ave, are in the same building, constructed in 1896 as a hotel. Many of the turn-of-the-century buildings have been restored. The warmest

sea waters north of San Francisco are said to flow at **Transfer Beach Park**; it's right in town and you can camp there. About 13 km north of town, off the highway, on Yellow Point Rd (follow the signs), pub aficionados will find the **Crow & Gate**, the oldest British-style pub in the province and the most authentic-looking. It's in a very peaceful setting.

### Petroglyph Provincial Park

About three km south of Nanaimo on the Trans Canada Hwy, this small park features some ancient Native Indian carvings in sandstone. As well as the original petroglyphs there are castings from which you can make rubbings.

### NANAIMO

Nanaimo is Vancouver Island's second major city, with a population of over 66,000. A number of Native Indian bands once shared the area, which was called Sne-Ny-Mos, a Salish word meaning 'meeting place'. Coal was discovered there in 1852 and for the next 100 years coal mining was the main industry in the town. Coal has declined in importance, but the city is now the centre of a forest-products industry as well as being a major deep-sea fishing port and a terminal for BC Ferries. Tourism is also important.

Nanaimo is the jumping-off point for Gabriola and Newcastle islands, but there are a few points of interest in town as well as some in the immediate vicinity.

### Orientation & Information

Nanaimo, about 110 km north of Victoria, is a convenient stopover and a departure point to Vancouver and the islands just off Nanaimo Harbour.

Behind the harbour is the central core. Most of the restaurants and shops are in Commercial and Chapel Sts and Terminal Ave, which run more or less parallel to the harbour. To the south, Nicol St, the southern extension of Terminal Ave, leads to the Trans Canada Hwy. To the north, Terminal Ave forks: the right fork becomes Stewart Ave and leads to the BC Ferries terminal in Departure Bay; the left fork becomes Hwy 19, which heads north up-island to Courtney, Campbell River and Port Hardy.

The Travel Infocentre (☎ 754-8474), 266 Bryden St, just north of the downtown area, has a walking guide of the town's historic area around the harbour. Many of the original buildings have been destroyed and are now marked only by plaques. If you're interested in seeing the ones that are left, get a copy of *Step Into History*, a booklet giving a walking tour of Nanaimo's historic buildings.

The main post office, 66 Front St, is open Monday to Friday from 8.30 am to 5 pm. Nanaimo Regional General Hospital (☎ 754-2121) is at 1200 Dufferin Crescent, north-west of the downtown area. The bus depot is north of the town centre behind the Tally Ho Island Inn at 1 Terminal Ave, while the railway station is east at 321 Selby Rd.

### Nanaimo Centennial Museum

The small museum (☎ 753-1821), 100 Cameron Rd, displays items of significance in the growth of Nanaimo. Included are Native Indian, Hudson's Bay Company and coal-mining artefacts. It's open Monday to Friday from 9 am to 6 pm and Saturday and Sunday from 10 am to 6 pm. Admission is $2.

Down the steps is Fisherman's Wharf.

### The Bastion

The Bastion, in Front St, on the corner of Bastion St, is the highlight of Nanaimo's old buildings. Built by the Hudson's Bay Company in 1853 for protection from Native Indians, it was never used. It's now a museum and is open daily from 9 to 11.30 am and from noon to 5 pm. Admission is free. From Wednesday to Sunday at noon the cannons are fired over the water.

### Parks

There are many parks in and around Nanaimo. The promenade, which takes in a number of the downtown ones, begins at the seaplane terminal and heads north to **Georgia Park**, where there are a few totem

poles, a display of Native Indian canoes including a large war canoe and a fine view of Nanaimo Harbour. It then continues to Swy-A-Lana Lagoon (good for children to splash in) and **Maffeo-Sutton Park**, from where ferries leave to Newcastle Island.

### Newcastle Island Marine Park

Just offshore of the downtown area is Newcastle Island, which offers cycling, hiking and beaches. It's also a good place for a picnic or overnight camping. Cars are not allowed. The island was once dotted with mine shafts and sandstone quarries but later became a quiet resort. In summer a small ferry travels between the island and the mainland every hour.

### Gabriola Island

Further out into the strait is Gabriola Island, the most northerly of the Southern Gulf Islands. It has several beaches and three provincial parks offering swimming, fishing and hiking. At **Malaspina Galleries** are some unusual sandstone caves carved out by the wind and tides. There is a ferry from Nanaimo (see Getting There & Away later).

### Activities

In August 1990 Nanaimo became the first place in North America to have bungy jumping. If you fancy diving 42 metres off a bridge into the Nanaimo River secured only by a rubber band then call ☎ 753-5867 for details. The specially designed Saunders Bridge is 13 km south of Nanaimo and a jump costs $95.

Off the coast scuba diving is possible among the northern Gulf Islands in excellent dive sites like Dodd Narrows, Gabriola Passage, Porlier Pass and Northumberland Channel. Three nearby spots where you can go hiking or canoeing are **Nanaimo Lakes**, **Nanaimo River** and **Green Mountain**. Hikes from **Colliery Dam Park** lead to Harewood and Overton lakes.

Nanaimo also has three good spots for bird-watching: **Buttertubs Marsh Sanctuary**, **Morrell Sanctuary** (take Comox Rd left (east) off Terminal Ave to both) and **Piper's**

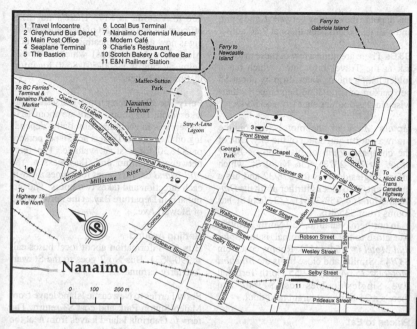

1  Travel Infocentre
2  Greyhound Bus Depot
3  Main Post Office
4  Seaplane Terminal
5  The Bastion
6  Local Bus Terminal
7  Nanaimo Centennial Museum
8  Modern Café
9  Charlie's Restaurant
10 Scotch Bakery & Coffee Bar
11 E&N Railiner Station

**Lagoon Park** off Hammond Bay north of the city.

### Festivals

The top annual event is the Nanaimo Bathtub Race to Vancouver, held each mid-July as part of the Marine Festival. Hundreds of fibreglass tubs start out, about 100 sinking in the first five minutes.

Through June and July the Nanaimo Festival, which used to be called Shakespeare Plus, presents both classic and modern plays at the Malaspina College south of town. For information call ☎ 754-7587.

### Places to Stay

**Camping** The best places to stay are not in Nanaimo itself but on the islands just off the coast. At *Newcastle Island Marine Park* there are 18 tent sites. Further out is the much larger *Gabriola Island*; there's no camping in the provincial parks but there are private campsites.

North of town are several campgrounds. *Jingle Pot Campsite & RV Park* (☎ 758-1614), 4012 Jingle Pot Rd, is eight km north of Nanaimo off Hwy 19. It has showers, laundry and tent sites for $11. The closest to town is *Beban Park Campground* (☎ 758-1177), 2300 Bowen Rd, about 1½ km west of Hwy 19, which has sites for $8. *Brannen Lake Campsites* (☎ 756-0404), 4228 Briggs Rd, is on a working farm; sites are $11.

**Hostels** Nanaimo has two mini-hostels affiliated with HI. The closest is *Nicol St Hostel* (☎ 753-1188), 65 Nicol St, several km south of the downtown area. Beds are $13 for members or $15 for nonmembers. Check in between 4 and 11 pm. *Thomson Hostel* (☎ 722-2251), 1660 Cedar Hwy, is about 10 km south of town. Bus No 11 stops right outside. It offers use of the kitchen and canoes and charges $12 per night; or you can camp on the lawn for $5 per person. The congenial owner will pick up travellers at the bus depot in the evening between 6 and 9 pm, and will take them back there at 9.30 am.

**B&Bs** There are quite a few of these in town: ask at the Travel Infocentre, which has a folder listing them. Rates drop by about $5 per person outside June-September; otherwise singles/doubles start from $35/$45.

**Motels** Many of the motels are on the highway north and south of the city. One of the cheapest, south of Nanaimo, is *Big 7 Motel* (☎ 754-2328), 736 Nicol St, which offers singles/doubles for $28/32 and has a restaurant. Two blocks further north the *Diplomat Motel* (☎ 753-3261), 333 Nicol St, has rooms from $35/40.

In northern Nanaimo, 950 North Terminal Ave close to the ferry terminal, is the *Colonial Motel* (☎ 754-4415). Rooms cost from $37/43. Similar and close by, is the *Bluebird Motel* (☎ 753-4151) at 955 North Terminal Ave. Singles/doubles cost $43/49, and there's a 24-hour restaurant next door.

### Places to Eat
Next to the ferry terminal in Stewart Ave, at the *Nanaimo Public Market* is a restaurant (which has lunch specials for $6) and a pub. The market is presently closed for renovations.

In Commercial St, *Modern Café* has soups and salads from $5.50. *Scotch Bakery & Coffee Bar*, 87 Commercial St, has great cakes priced from around 70 cents and bread. On the same side and up the hill is *Charlie's Restaurant*, a large spacious restaurant with sandwiches priced from $5.25, including fries or salad, and burgers for $8.

### Things to Buy
Hill's Indian Crafts, 20 Commercial St, sells the famous Cowichan sweaters.

### Getting There & Away
**Bus & Train** Island Coach Lines (☎ 753-4371) connects Nanaimo with points north and south; the one-way fare to Victoria is $15.40. The E&N Railiner passes through once a day in each direction; the one-way

fare to Victoria is $17. There's no ticket office at the station (part of the station building is now used as a meeting place for local Alcoholics Anonymous) which is at 321 Selby St; ring ☎ 1-800-561-8630 for information and tickets.

**Ferry** The 39-km ferry trip to Horseshoe Bay takes about 1½ hours. There are about 12 to 15 services in each direction daily, depending on the season. Tickets are $6 per person, or $22.50 for a small vehicle. The ferry between Nanaimo and Tsawwassen, the *Mid-Island Express*, goes four times a day in each direction and takes two hours. The terminal is in Departure Bay, at the northern end of Stewart Ave.

### Getting Around
**Bus** For information about local buses call ☎ 390-4531. Bus No 2 goes to the Stewart Ave ferry terminal.

**Ferry** Ferries to Newcastle Island leave from Mafeo-Sutton Park and cost $3 return. The ferry to Gabriola Island leaves from near the Harbour Square Mall and takes cars for $8.25, but only charges $3 if you're walking. After 2 pm you're stuck on the island until the next morning when the ferry returns. The ferry trip takes about 20 minutes.

### NANAIMO TO CAMPBELL RIVER
#### Parksville & Qualicum Beach
These towns and the coast towards Comox are known for long stretches of sandy beach. You can stop by the road, tone up the tan and have a quick swim in the nippy water. There is camping at **Rathtrevor Beach Provincial Park**, three km south-east of Parksville.

#### Parksville to Port Alberni
South of Parksville is Hwy 4, the road to Port Alberni and the west coast. You can also connect with Hwy 4 from Qualicum Beach via Hwy 4A. At Coombs check out the goats grazing on the roof of the general store! From Parksville to Port Alberni is some very fine scenery, with several provincial parks where you can stop a while.

**Englishman River Falls Provincial Park**, 13 km south-west of Parksville at the end of Errington Rd, is impressive with its waterfalls, hiking, swimming and camping. **Little Qualicum Falls Provincial Park** is another good park with hiking, fishing and camping. Both areas are forested and scenic. South-west of here, **Mt Arrowsmith** has skiing in winter, hiking trails in summer.

**MacMillan Provincial Park**, is at the western end of Cameron Lake. Right by the road, **Cathedral Grove**, regarded by Native Indians as a sacred place, is a grove of virgin forest with huge Douglas firs and red cedars some dating back 800 years. A series of trails lead through the grove which is a delicate, ancient ecosystem, so please respect the sign asking you not to touch the trees or plants. This half-hour stop is a must, but it can get busy with visitors.

There is a campground by Cameron Lake.

**Port Alberni**

Halfway across the island is this town (population 18,000) built on forestry and fishing. Over 300 commercial fishing boats work out of the area, most catching salmon. At Harbour Quay, at the bottom of Argyle St, there's an observation tower. Also here is the Forestry Visitor Centre, open daily from 10 am to 8 pm. Visitors can tour both the paper mill and the sawmill: for information call ☎ 724-7890.

Hikers can reach Dalla Falls (see Strathcona Provincial Park later) by an alternative route: canoeing the length of Great Central Lake from Port Alberni and taking the trail up from there.

At **Stamp Falls Provincial Park**, nine km north of Port Alberni, salmon can sometimes be seen jumping on their way up the river and there are petroglyphs at nearby **Sproat Lake**.

Perhaps the most noteworthy feature of Port Alberni are the MVs *Lady Rose* and *Frances Barkley*, which sail out of Harbour Quay to the west coast of the island. They're operated by Alberni Marine Transportation (☎ 723-8313). The freighters, which take mail and cargo as well as passengers, ply between Kildonan on Alberni Inlet, Bamfield at the end of the West Coast Trail, the Broken Islands and Ucluelet. Those planning to canoe or kayak around the Broken Islands can take their boats on board. The ferry company is one place that rents canoes and kayaks.

Fares to Bamfield are $16/32 one way/return. Fares to Ucluelet are $18/36.

BRITISH COLUMBIA

---

**Clayoquot Sound and its disappearing old-growth forests**

Clayoquot (pronounced 'clak-wot') Sound, on Vancouver Island's west coast 200 km north-west of Victoria, is the latest scene and symbol, in the continuing struggle between the forestry industry and those who seek to preserve Canada's old-growth forests. The Clayoquot Sound region contains fjords, islands, mountains and forests with trees as old as 1000 years and as high as 75 metres. The forestry industry says that their reforestation and improved environmental practices have been successful. Enviromentalists, on the other hand, argue that old trees are being removed carelessly and that a regenerated forest will not support the same biodiversity or even the same number of forestry jobs.

The debate had been building for a decade and came to a head in April 1993 when the BC government, after buying $50 million worth of shares in MacMillan Bloedel and so becoming the forestry company's biggest shareholder, legislated to allow logging by that company in some parts of Clayoquot Sound. Although the provincial government was cleared of any wrongdoing by the British Columbia Appeal Court, it lost what diminishing trust the environmentalists had had in it.

From early July, each morning demonstrators blockaded the Kennedy River bridge to prevent logging trucks crossing. Many of the demonstrators were arrested. The protesters set up a permanent camp just off the highway 30 km south of Tofino. The conflict has polarised the two communities of Tofino and Ucluelet: the former depends on tourism for jobs, the latter on logging.

The issue is further complicated by the land claims of the region's approximately 3000 Native Indians. They're not opposed to logging, but say they would do so with more environmental sensitivity. ∎

One-day return trips allow passengers some free time at Bamfield and Ucluelet for exploring. On summer Sundays a longer stay in Bamfield is possible.

The freighters depart Port Alberni for Bamfield on Tuesday, Thursday and Saturday all year, and for Ucluelet and the Broken Islands on Monday, Wednesday and Friday from 1 June to 30 September. In midsummer there are Sunday cruises to Bamfield only. Regardless of the weather, take a sweater and/or raincoat.

Orient Stage Lines (☎ 723-6924), 4541 Margaret St, runs buses daily to Tofino and Ucluelet. Western Bus Lines (☎ 723-3341), 4521 10th Ave, has buses Monday, Wednesday and Friday to Bamfield.

## Pacific Rim National Park

Of the many parks in the area, this is the granddaddy! A rough, rugged, inhospitable yet beautiful coastal area, the park is a long, thin strip of land divided into three distinct sections. Each is separated by land and water and is reached by a different route.

Whale-watching trips can be a highlight of a visit to the west coast. From mid-February to June Pacific grey whales migrate up the coast from Mexico to the Arctic Ocean; the peak time to catch them heading north is mid-April. In late fall they head back south. At these times you have a good chance of seeing one.

**Long Beach** The most northerly third of the park is Long Beach. It is the easiest to get to and the most developed. Hwy 4 leads from Port Alberni through the magnificent scenery (some heavily logged areas notwithstanding) of the Mackenzie Ranges at the southern edge of Clayoquot (pronounced klak-WOT) Sound into this section of the park. Long Beach is exactly that – about 20 km of wide, log-strewn surf and windswept, sandy beach. At other parts, the waves pound into a craggy, rocky shoreline.

In summer there are interpretive programmes and guided walks run by the Wickaninnish Centre next to the beach. At each end of Long Beach is a small fishing and tourist village – Tofino in the north, Ucluelet in the south.

There are eight short hiking trails in the park; the Park Information Office (☎ 726-4212) will have a description of them. The South Beach Trail leads to an area good for watching and hearing the huge waves roar in. Half Moon Bay Trail leads to a calm, sandy bay. Radar Hill is good for views and has trails leading down to some small, secluded beaches.

Another activity is looking for and maybe watching some of the local marine life. Seals, sea lions and porpoises are common, killer and Pacific grey whales a possibility depending on the time of year. Good viewing spots are Schooner Cove, Quistis Point, Radar Hill with its telescope, and Combers Beach near Sea Lion Rocks.

Hundreds of thousands of geese and ducks fly overhead in spring and fall. Also, the pools left behind by the tides are often filled with interesting life forms: starfish, anemones, sponges, fish, snails and many other small creatures.

Long Beach reputedly has the best surfing in BC. Note that the weather is generally poor here. Most days are cold, windy and rainy. A warm, sunny day about a km or so from the coast can disappear into mist and fog at Long Beach. A sweater or raincoat is protection not only against the weather but also against the mosquitoes. The water, too, is cold – those doing any water sports should use wetsuits or drysuits.

**Places to Stay** In Long Beach there are two campgrounds. The more primitive one is *Schooner Campground*, near the northern end; camping costs $6. *Green Point Campground* (☎ 726-4245) has washrooms with hot water and flush toilets and costs $13. Both grounds are often full in summer: arrive early in the morning to get a place. In Tofino and Ucluelet are private campgrounds and some motels.

**Tofino** At the northern end of Long Beach, just outside the park boundary, is the picturesque fishing village of Tofino, with a winter population of about 1100 and a summer population of nearly twice that. The Travel Infocentre (☎ 725-3414), 380 Campbell St, is open daily from 9 am to 7.30 pm. Also on Campbell St is the office of the Friends of Clayoquot Sound (☎ 725-4218); the postal address is PO Box 489, Tofino, V0R 2Z0. The Forestry Visitor Centre, 316 Main St, is open from 10 am to 6 pm.

***Things to See & Do*** The **Eagle Aerie Gallery** on Campbell St, houses the paintings of Roy Henry Vickers, a Native Indian artist based in Tofino.

There are charters of several types in town. For fishing, check at Smiley's on the 1st St wharf. For sightseeing charters, try Seaforth Charter (☎ 725-4252), 448 Campbell St in the laundromat or at Mackenzie Beach Resort (☎ 725-3439) two km south of Tofino.

For around $35 several companies offer boat trips to see Pacific grey whales which frequent the area in spring and summer. Clayoquot Whaler will take you out and also fill you in on the history and Native Indian culture of the area. For information and tickets get in touch with Clayoquot Sound Charters (☎ 725-3195, 1-800-665-WHALES), 320 Main St. Zodiac Adventures (☎ 725-3330) will also take you to see the whales and other wildlife and the to the hot springs; the boat leaves from Meares Landing.

Tofino Sea Kayaking Co (☎ 725-4222), also at 320 Main St, offers paddling tours to the nearby islands from $45 for four hours.

Tofino Airlines (☎ 725-4454) has scenic flights of the islands and whales for $100 for 20 minutes for three people. The seaplanes leave from the wharf at the bottom of 1st St.

A good trip is to **Hot Springs Cove** where a 20-minute hike will lead you to the hot springs (the only ones on Vancouver Island) overlooking the ocean. There are several pools, which become progressively cooler down the hillside to the sea. You can hire a boat or seaplane to the cove: contact Zodiac Adventures or Seaforth Charters. Overnight camping is possible.

Highly recommended is a trip to **Meares Island**, a 15-minute cruise past the Harbour Islands. This is a magical place of virgin rainforest with trees of mind-boggling age and stature: one is over 1000 years old and nearly 19 metres in diameter. Many are large enough to accommodate a tunnel that cars can pass through. Species include cedar, yew and varieties of spruce.

You can arrange trips out to the island at Weigh West Marine Resort (☎ 725-3277), 634 Campbell St, for $15. One dollar of that goes towards fighting logging plans for Meares. There are several rugged but well-marked trails on the island; the basic loop takes about 2½ hours. Before going on to the island find out about the condition of the trails, some of which have been seriously eroded by hikers; damage is greatest in wet conditions. The notice board in the Common Loaf Bake Shop may have some details.

***Places to Stay*** As well as the campgrounds in Long Beach there are several private campgrounds around Tofino. On Mackenzie Beach *Bella Pacifica Resort & Campground* (☎ 725-3400) has full facilities and sites from $18.50. *Crystal Cove Beach Resort* (☎ 725-4213), 1165 Cedarwood Place, has sites from $15. It also has housekeeping log cottages from $100.

Several other places offer housekeeping cottages for rent, and there are quite a few B&Bs. In town *Backpackers' Hostel* (☎ 725-2288), 241 Campbell St, has dorm beds for $10 and double rooms for $35. It offers bikes for rent and a weekly discount. One of the cheapest motels is *Dolphin Motel* (☎ 725-3377), 1190 Pacific Rim Hwy three km south of Tofino, with singles/doubles from $38/42.

***Places to Eat*** There are several places to eat at, and the *Common Loaf Bake Shop*, 180 1st St, is recommended. It has just a few tables but a large selection of excellent, delicious homemade muffins, cookies, breads and cakes from around 70 cents. In the morning try the bran muffins or the still-warm cinnamon buns. The shop's open daily from 8 am to 9.30 pm. *Organic Matters*, on Campbell

St near 4th St, sells organic food and has vegetarian soup and salad lunches for $5.50.

**Ucluelet** Ucluelet (the name is a Nootka word meaning 'people with a safe landing place'), with a population of around 1500, is not as attractive as Tofino. The Travel Infocentre (☎ 726-4641), 1629 Peninsula Rd, is open daily in summer from 9 am to 6 pm.

You might like to walk to the lighthouse at **Amphitrite Point**, at the foot of Peninsula Rd, or take one of the trails at **Terrace Beach** north of town. Subtidal Adventures, on the right as you head into town just after Ucluelet Campground, is an outfit offering Pacific grey whale-watching trips, from $34 for two hours, in March and April only. It also runs tours around the Broken Group Islands, will drop off people wishing to camp on an island and scuba-diving cruises. Ocean Kayak Tours (☎ 726-2868), as its name suggests, offers kayaking tours for $30 for 2½ hours.

***Places to Stay*** *Ucluelet Campground* (☎ 726-4355), 260 Seaplane Base Rd overlooking the harbour, with hot showers and flush toilets, has sites from $14. There are several motels, mostly on Peninsula Rd, and a couple of simple cheaper hotels. *Ucluelet Hotel* (☎ 726-4324), in Main St, has singles/doubles for $25/35. Near Long Beach, at 1755 Peninsula Rd the *Pacific Rim Motel* (☎ 726-7728) has rooms for $36/45.

**Broken Group Islands** The middle section of Pacific Rim National Park, called the Broken Group Islands, is made up of about 100 islands at the entrance to **Barkley Sound**, famous for its variety of rockfish.

This area is popular with canoeists, is good for wildlife and offers some of the best scuba diving in Canada. You can view wrecks in shallow waters and the abundant sea life found around all the islands. The waters can be dangerous and you should prepare for a trip using *Marine Chart 3670*, available from the Canadian Hydrographic Service, Chart Sales, Institute of Ocean Sci-

ences, 9860 Saanich Rd, PO Box 6000, Sidney V8L 4B2.

The only way to reach this section is by boat from Bamfield, Ucluelet or Port Alberni. There are some primitive campgrounds on the islands.

**West Coast Trail** The third and most southerly section of the park is called the West Coast Trail. It's a 77-km stretch between Port Renfrew and Bamfield. Either end can be reached by road, but to reach one from the other you've got to walk – and that's a challenge along this rugged, often rain-soaked path. To protect the environment and to keep hiker traffic to safe manageable limits, a quota system restricts the number of hikers using the trail. You can either book (which costs $25) in advance for a permit (call ☎ 728-1282) or turn up at the trailhead and put your name on the waiting list, but you may have to wait several days.

The trail is clogged with trees, and the camping areas are wherever you can find them. Passing cliffs, beaches and rainforests, the trail takes between five and eight days to travel. You've got to take all your food. The southernmost part is the most rough and difficult, but you get to see some spectacular scenery and a chance to test your stamina. Near the centre of the trail you pass close to the Carmanah Valley, an area of old-growth forest threatened by logging. The trail was historically used as a life-saving route for shipwreck survivors. The trail is open between 1 May and 1 October, with July and August being the driest and best months. This is one only for the experienced hiker.

**Bamfield**, the village at the northern head of the West Coast Trail, has a Marine Biological Station, a life-saving station and not much else. The West Coast Trail Information Centre (☎ 728-3234) is five km south-east of the village on **Pachena Bay**.

There are only a few places to stay. There are two campgrounds. The nearest is eight km east of town and is run by the Ohiaht people. The other is 20 km north of town. *Sea Beam Resort* (☎ 728-3286) has singles/doubles for $20/40 and camping for $18. For a B&B try *Barbara's* (☎ 728-1228) on Pan-chena Rd.

Bamfield can be reached by boat from Ucluelet and Port Alberni; the one-way fare on the MV *Lady Rose* or *Frances Barkley* from Port Alberni is $16. There is also 100 km of gravel road from Port Alberni. Western Bus Lines (☎ 728-3491, 723-3341 in Port Alberni) operates the Pachena Bay Express, which connects Pachena Bay and Bamfield with Port Alberni on Monday, Wednesday and Friday. From Victoria West Coast Trail Express (☎ 380-0580) runs a daily 11-person shuttle van to Bamfield and Panchena Bay for $45.

At the southern end of the trail is **Port Renfrew**, which can be reached by dirt road from Lake Cowichan or by the mainly paved Hwy 14 along the coast from Victoria. There is a seasonal trail information centre (☎ 647-5434) in the village. To reach the start of the trail you must charter a boat to take you across the narrow San Juan River. Because of the difficult terrain, getting out of the bay here is, well, let's say, one of the less enjoyable segments of the trail northbound. You can camp along the beach in Port Renfrew or there is a hotel with a pub and a couple of B&Bs. There is also a small store, but supplies are limited. (See also Around Victoria earlier.)

### Horne Lake Provincial Park
North of Qualicum Beach, 16 km off Hwy 19, spelunking (caving) enthusiasts can explore limestone caves at Horne Lake Provincial Park. The caves are undeveloped and the road to it is an active logging road, so be careful. Riverbend Cave has a total of 383 metres of mapped passages and you must take a guide. Cave tours of varying lengths and difficulty occur daily in July and August, and at weekends in June and September. At Main and Lower Main caves you can explore independently. Bring some warm clothing and a good pair of shoes.

### Denman & Hornby Islands
Further up the east coast are two lesser known Gulf Islands – Denman and Hornby.

There's good bird-watching on Hornby Island. The ferry for Denman Island leaves from Buckley Bay, about 20 km south of Courtenay, and takes 10 minutes. For Hornby Island you take another ferry from Gravely Bay on Denman Island. The fare for each is $2.50 per person, or $6.75 with a small car.

Each island has provincial parks, hiking, swimming, fishing, scuba diving and beaches, but only **Fillongley Provincial Park** on Denman Island allows camping. There are several private campgrounds and quite a few guesthouses and B&Bs.

### Courtenay & Comox
Basically commercial centres for the local farming, logging and fishing industries, these two towns with a collective population of just over 22,000, are also important as supply hubs for Mt Washington 32 km west of Courtenay, and Forbidden Plateau just outside Strathcona Provincial Park (see that section later), two major summer and winter recreation areas. Courtenay is the larger of these two essentially adjacent towns. The Travel Infocentre (☎ 334-3234), 2040 Cliffe Ave, in Courtenay serves both towns and is open daily from 8 am to 8 pm.

In Courtenay there is a small museum (☎ 334-3234), 360 Cliffe Ave, and not far out is the Puntledge River Fish Hatchery which farms salmon. At the Canadian Air Force base in Comox an international air show takes place each August in even-numbered years.

There is good hiking in the area, from afternoon walks to overnight climbs. **Miracle Beach Provincial Park** (☎ 755-2483), north of Comox, has hiking trails, a campground and a long, sandy beach. **Comox Glacier** is a good two-day hike, as is **Mt Albert Edward**, which offers excellent views. Ask at the Travel Infocentre for more information. You must register if you're going on an overnighter.

A good circular tour is to take the ferry from Tsawwassen to Victoria on Vancouver Island, travel up the island to Courtenay, go back across to the mainland by ferry from

Little River near Comox to Powell River and then down to Vancouver along the Sunshine Coast.

**Places to Stay** Six km out of Courtenay, at 4787 Lake Trail Rd is the *North Comox Lake Mini-Hostel* (☎ 338-1914), which charges $12. Meals are available and someone can pick you up at the bus or railway station. It's open all year and in summer there is extra sleeping space in a teepee.

If you prefer to stay in a B&B, contact Courtenay North B&B Homes (☎ 338-1328), 825 Nikoliasen St, Courtenay V9N 6C9. It offers a reservation service and covers Courtenay, Comox, Campbell River and Quadra Island. Prices average from $25 to $40 for singles and from $35 to $65 for doubles. In both towns you'll find numerous motels, and near Comox are several places renting cottages by the beach. One of the cheapest motels is *Economy Inn* (☎ 334-4491), 2605 Cliffe Ave (the name of the highway through town) in Courtenay. It has a pool and sauna and singles/doubles from $39/44.

## NORTH VANCOUVER ISLAND

North of Campbell River, Hwy 19 heads inland and much of the urbanisation that characterises the eastern coastline to the south disappears. It's a less-populated, less-visited, rugged area with lots of opportunities for outdoor activities. Many of the travellers you meet will be heading north to Port Hardy to catch the ferry to Prince Rupert.

### Campbell River

Campbell River, with a population of just under 26,000 is a major centre for salmon fishing, and marks the beginning of the northern part of the island. Campbell River is also the departure point for Strathcona Provincial Park. The Travel Infocentre (☎ 287-4636), 1235 Shoppers Row, is open daily from 10 am to 8 pm. In the same building is the Campbell River Museum, open daily from 10 am to 4 pm. The main

post office is in Beech St but there's another one in Tyee Plaza.

Most visitors come here to fish, but other activities in the parks and lakes around the town include hiking, swimming, canoeing, sailing and cycling. Off the coast in **Discovery Passage**, scuba diving is excellent at such dive sites as Row & Be Damned, Whisky Point, Copper Cliffs and Steep Island. On **Quadra Island** just offshore you can see marine and birdlife or the ancient petroglyphs of the Kwakiutl people at Cape Mudge in the south. Some petroglyphs are in the Kwakiutl Museum along with tribal costumes, ceremonial masks and potlatch artefacts. The island also has hiking trails including one up Chinese Mountain. **Cortes Island**, east of Quadra Island, has plenty of deserted beaches and lots of wildlife.

**Places to Stay** North and west of Campbell River there are government-run campgrounds in *Elk Falls Provincial Park*, on Hwy 28, in *Loveland Bay Recreation Area*, at Campbell Lake, and *Morton Lake Provincial Park*, 16 km from the Hwy 19 turn-off. Sites are $9.50, $6 and $7 respectively. There are also several private campgrounds. RV parks and numerous motels line the highway south of the downtown area. For B&Bs contact Courtenay North B&B Homes (see earlier) or get a copy of the leaflet listing places and prices from the Travel Infocentre.

On Quadra Island is a backpackers' hostel, the *Beach House* (☎ 287-9232, 285-3798). It only takes four or five people at a time so call ahead.

**Entertainment** For some down-home country & western music visit the Quinsam Hotel, on the highway north of downtown.

**Getting There & Around** Island Coach Lines (☎ 287-7151), on the corner of 13th Ave and Cedar St, runs one bus north daily to Port Hardy ($38.85 one way) and four buses south to Victoria. For information about local buses call ☎ 287-RIDE.

Ferries leave regularly from Discovery Crescent across from Tyee Plaza for

Quathiaski Cove on Quadra Island; the return fare is $2.50. Another ferry departs Heriot Bay on Quadra Island for Whaletown on Cortes Island; the return fare is $3.50.

## Strathcona Provincial Park

This is the largest park on the island and is basically a wilderness area. Campbell River is the main access point. However Mt Washington, just out of the park, and Forbidden Plateau are reached from Courtenay. Hwy 28 between Campbell River and Gold River cuts across the park and provides access to campgrounds and some developed trails.

At **Forbidden Plateau**, to the east of the park, the ski lift runs in summer and there's a restaurant at the top. There are lots of hiking trails, as well as trout fishing in the lakes on the plateau. In winter it's a major ski area, the island's original. **Mt Washington** ski resort has five lifts and 41 major marked runs, plus 35 km of cross-country (nordic) ski trails. In summer there's hiking, horse riding and mountain biking.

Two well-known hikes are the **Elk River Trail** and the **Flower Ridge Trail**. Both lead to very fine alpine scenery. Like other developed trails, these two are suitable for all age groups. Other less-developed trails demand more preparation and lead to remote areas.

There are many excellent backcountry hiking trails within the park. In the south of the park the **Della Falls Trail**, for example, is a tough two or three-day walk but is great for scenery and ends at the highest falls (440 metres) in North America. You need a good map. Other good walks are those in the **Beauty Lake** area and one crossing the **Big Interior Massif** up to Nine Peaks. From the highest peaks, such as Golden Hinde (at 2200 metres the highest on the island), Colonel Foster and others in the 650-metre range, you can see both the ocean to the west and Georgia Strait to the east. One thing you won't have to look at is a grizzly bear: there aren't any on Vancouver Island.

**Places to Stay** The park has two serviced *campgrounds* with running water and toilets: one at Buttle Lake (north) near the entrance to the park and the other at Ralph River, at the southern end of the lake on its eastern shore. Campsites are $12 and $9.50 respectively. You can also go wilderness camping within the park.

*Strathcona Park Lodge* (☎ 286-8206/3122), a resort outside the park on Upper Campbell Lake, has a range of accommodation. You can camp near the beach for $15 with the use of facilities. Camping equipment can also be rented. Alternatively, you can bed down in a HI-affiliated hostel (☎ 286-2008) for $15 with use of a communal kitchen. There are also lakefront cottages and apartments priced from $55 to $125.

You can rent canoes, kayaks and bicycles, or go rock climbing, windsurfing, hiking, sailing and swimming. Or you can take organised day trips if you wish. The lodge has an education centre which offers courses in the various outdoor activities.

### Gold River

In the centre of the island, west of Strathcona Provincial Park, Gold River, accessed by Hwy 28, is the last stop on surfaced roads. The little town is a caving capital and is the headquarters of BC's Speleological Association. Visitors can join spelunking trips to **Upana Caves** and also to **Quatsino Cave**, the deepest vertical cave in North America. Kayakers can try their luck on the whitewater section of the river known as the **Big Drop**. For more information, ask at the Travel Infocentre (☎ 283-2418) in Village Square Plaza.

Summer cruises go to **Friendly Cove**, where Captain Cook first met the west coast Native Indians in 1778. The freighter, *Uchuk III*, a converted WW II mine-sweeper, makes year-round trips to some of the remote villages in **Nootka Sound** and **Kyuquot Sound**.

### Valley of 1000 Faces

Worth a visit is The Valley of 1000 Faces west off Hwy 19 at Sayward Junction, north of Campbell River. Along this woodland trail are over 1400 figures painted on slabs of cedar, the work of a Dutch-born artist, Hetty Frederickson. The natural wood grain is used as a base for the image and the slabs are then nailed to trees. Facial portraits, with their wide variety, are best. It's open daily 15 May to 1 September from 10 am to 5 pm and admission is $2.50 to the trail and gallery.

Nearby, **Sayward** is a logging port, and there are whale-watching tours from the terminal.

### Telegraph Cove
East off Hwy 19, about eight km south of Port McNeill, this small community is one of the best of the west coast's so-called boardwalk villages – villages in which most of the buildings are built over the water on wooden pilings. Formerly a sawmill village, it's a good place to go fishing, but its main attraction is the killer whale boat tour to Robson Bight, an ecological reserve south of Telegraph Cove in Johnstone Strait, from June to October. The tour, run by Stubbs Island Charters (☎ 928-3185/17), might seem a bit pricey at $60, but you are out for five hours and it includes lunch. It's a good

idea to book ahead and to take warm clothing and a camera.

### Port McNeill
Three major logging companies have regional offices in this town of over 2600 people. The Travel Infocentre (☎ 956-3131) is next to the terminal. You can go scuba diving, book fishing charters or go on killer-whale tours from here. Port McNeill is the departure point for Cormorant and Malcolm islands and there are several campgrounds, including one near the ferry terminal, and hotels.

Ferries (taking 45 minutes and costing $3.50) run to **Alert Bay** on Cormorant Island where the Alert Bay Museum and U'Mista Cultural Centre show examples of Kwakiutl art. There are also a few minor historical sites. Gator Gardens Ecological Park, with its giant cedars and wildlife is also worth a look. Like some other places in BC, Alert Bay once claimed to have the world's tallest totem pole. *Pacific Hostelry* (☎ 974-2026/5363) in Alert Bay is an associate-HI hostel, open year round and with room for only 26, people so call ahead. It costs $13 for members, $15 for nonmembers.

### Killer Whales
Using sonar to track the fish, sixteen pods of killer whales (each pod containing about 20 members) come to Johnstone Strait in summer to feed on the migrating salmon. In Robson Bight, along one of its beaches, many of the whales go to swim, rubbing their sides and stomachs on the pebbles and rocks that have been smoothed and rounded by the action of the water. No-one knows quite why they do this, but the whales obviously get a lot of pleasure from it and maybe that's reason enough.

The Johnstone Strait killer whales feature in David Attenborough's documentary, *Wolves of the Sea*. ■

## Port Hardy

This small town at the northern end of Vancouver Island is best known as the departure point for the ferry trip aboard the *Queen of the North* through the famed Inside Passage to Prince Rupert. The terminal is three km south of town at Bear Cove, which is one of two sites where evidence of the earliest human occupation of the central and northern coastal areas of BC – around 8000 to 10,000 years ago – was found. The other site is Nanamu, now a canning town on the eastern shore of Fitzhugh Sound.

The Travel Infocentre (☎ 949-7622), open daily in the summer from 9 am to 8 pm, is at 7250 Market St and there's a laundromat up the hill on the same side.

There's little in the town itself except a small museum at 1110 Market St, open Monday to Saturday from 10 am to 5 pm, but the area around Port Hardy has good salmon fishing and scuba diving. North Island Diving & Water Sports (☎ 949-2664), on the corner of Market and Hastings Sts, rents and sells equipment and runs courses. You can also rent canoes and kayaks from the end of the jetty: call ☎ 949-7707 for details.

**Places to Stay** In and around town there are campgrounds, hotels, motels and about 20 B&Bs. Check the *Accommodations* guide or ask at the Travel Infocentre. Several of the campgrounds are near the ferry terminal. One of the closest is *Wildwoods Campsite* (☎ 949-6793) which is on the ferry terminal road and has sites for $10. Others are *Sunny Sanctuary Campground* (☎ 949-8111), 8080 Goodspeed Rd, and *Quatse River Campground* (☎ 949-2395), 5050 Hardy Bay Rd. One of the cheaper hotel options is the central *Seagate Hotel* (☎ 949-6348), 8600 Granville St, with rooms from $40.

Remember that the town fills up the night before a ferry is due to depart so it's worth booking ahead.

**Getting There & Away** Island Coach Lines (☎ 949-7532), on the corner of Market and Hastings Sts, has one bus a day to Victoria for $72.45. North Island Transportation, operating out of the same office, runs a shuttle bus to/from the ferry terminal for $4.30 one way. The bus will pick you up and drop you off wherever you're staying.

*Ferry – The Inside Passage* BC Ferries run the 15-hour, 440-km trip along the coast, around islands and past some of the province's best scenery. The ferry leaves every second day at 7.30 am (check in by 6.30 am, if you have already booked a place) and arrives in Prince Rupert at 10.30 pm. (In winter the ferry leaves once a week.) There's a short stop at Bella Bella, about a third of the way up, which is mostly for the locals but also to drop off kayakers. The one-way fare is $90, going up to $275 for a car and $408 for motorhomes. Outside the summer peak period (late May to the end of September) the fares are less.

If you're taking a vehicle in summer you should reserve well in advance. However, it's possible to go standby and if you do you should put your name on the waiting list as early as possible and be at the ferry terminal by 5.30 am at the latest on the day of departure. Binoculars are useful as you're often close to land and the wildlife viewing is good: the possibilities include bald eagles, porpoises, sea lions, and humpback and killer whales.

Once in Prince Rupert you can continue on Alaska State Ferries further north to Juneau and Skagway; catch BC Ferries to the Queen Charlotte Islands; or go by land into the BC interior and up to the Yukon and Alaska.

## Cape Scott Provincial Park

About 60 km west of Port Hardy over gravel road, this park has swimming off the pristine beaches in San Josef Bay, hiking trails and wilderness camping. Note that the west coast of this northern tip of the island is known for strong winds, strong tides and heavy rain. You'll need to take all supplies and equipment if you're camping.

# South-Western British Columbia

At the small town of Hope, 150 km from Vancouver, the road east splits. The Trans Canada Hwy follows the Goldrush Trail (the route the old wagon trail took to the Cariboo gold rush) north up the Fraser River Valley towards Cache Creek. As the road follows the river, which winds and twists through the canyon, there are many points of interest and viewing areas. The further north you go, the drier the land becomes and the fewer trees there are, until around Cache Creek the landscape resembles that of a cowboy movie.

North-east of Hope the Coquihalla Hwy heads to Kamloops. It's a wide, straight express route with a $10 toll. Service stations are few, so leave with a full tank. The scenery along the way is pleasant and there are plenty of places to stop and view it. Further west,

between Chilliwack and Vancouver, the road is uninterestingly flat and straight. It's more or less an expressway right into the city. There's no point trying to hitch along this stretch, as it's illegal for cars to stop for you.

The Crowsnest Hwy (Hwy 3) east of Hope heads first southward through Manning Provincial Park and then into the Okanagan Valley – the dry, beautiful fruit-growing region of BC. The green hills of the Hope area fade to brown as the road heads towards Osoyoos.

## HOPE

There's not much in Hope itself but it's a good access point for the Fraser River Canyon and southern BC. Several lakes and more than a dozen provincial parks are close by. South-east of town, on the Crowsnest Hwy, are the remains of the infamous 'Hope slide': in 1965 four people were killed when a small earthquake caused part of a mountain to crumble.

The Travel Infocentre (☎ 869-7322), 919 Water Ave near the river, is a good place from which to collect information. There's plenty of camping in the area; in Hope, motels are on the Old Princeton to Hope Rd as well as downtown, with singles or doubles starting from $35. The cafeteria occupies most of the Greyhound Bus Depot (☎ 869-5522), at 833 3rd Ave on the corner of Fort St. A bus leaves daily for Yale and Lytton at 10.15 am; the one-way fare (before tax) to Lytton is $10.60, to Vancouver $15.55.

## FRASER RIVER CANYON

Fraser River connects Vancouver with central BC; the Thompson River is a major tributary. A trip along the steep-sided canyon offers some of the most spectacular scenery in the province.

White-water rafting is a popular activity down the Fraser and its tributaries' fast-flowing rapids, and a number of companies offer raft trips. Fraser Rafting Expeditions (☎ 863-2336), in **Yale**, 32 km north of Hope, has river trips from one day ($75) and going up to 10 days; food is provided. Kumsheen (☎ 455-2296), in **Lytton**, north of Yale, does

South-Western British Columbia

trips of from three hours ($62) to three days ($298).

About 25 km north of Yale is the **Hell's Gate Airtram**, a widely advertised cable-car system that goes down to the rushing Fraser River. Look it over before buying the hype and $8 ticket.

There are several provincial parks along the canyon. **Emory Creek Provincial Park**, just north of Hope, has camping, fishing and hiking. Fishing, swimming and picnicking is available in **Alexander Bridge Provincial Park** one km north of Spuzzum. The suspension bridge, built in 1926, spans the Fraser River. You can also camp at Skihist and Goldpan provincial parks north of Lytton.

## MANNING PROVINCIAL PARK

This 66,000-hectare park in the Cascade Mountains, close to the border with the USA is about a two-hour drive east from Vancouver: take the Trans Canada Hwy to Hope then follow the Crowsnest Hwy south-east. The Crowsnest Hwy goes through the park. The park is noted for the variety of its wildlife which includes more than 206 species of birds plus mammal species such as marmots, beaver, chipmunks, black bear, mule deer and coyote. The park offers year-round outdoor activities. In the summer there's swimming, fishing, canoeing, sailing, hiking and wilderness camping. In the winter there's downhill and cross-country skiing (with nearly 80 km of trails), and snowmobiling. The **Pacific Crest Hiking Trail** begins in this park and goes south all the way to Mexico. See you, good luck!

The park has four fully serviced *campgrounds* with sites for $9.50 and $15.50 or at *Manning Park Resort*, on the highway, you could try one of the cabins which start at $59/64 a single/double.

## KAMLOOPS

Sitting at the point where the North Thompson, South Thompson and Thompson rivers meet, Kamloops has always been a service and transport crossroads. In fact the town was once called 'Kahmoloops', a Shuswap word meaning 'meeting of waters'. Today,

the Trans Canada Hwy cuts east-west through town; the Yellowhead Hwy (Hwy 5) heads north, Hwy 5A heads south and the Coquihalla Hwy heads south-west to Vancouver. With this strategic location, the city has grown rapidly since the late 1960s and is the major service and industrial centre in the district.

The city is not all business, though. It is surrounded by some 200 lakes, making it a good watersports area. The dry, rolling hills make interesting scenery and excellent ranching territory. This can be a very hot spot in the summer.

Kamloops, with a population of over 68,000 is spread over a very wide area. There are many motels, restaurants and other services in both directions along the Trans Canada Hwy. The core itself is quiet, clean and pleasant. Because it sits at a transport crossroads, accommodation is more expensive than might be expected.

Vancouver lies 356 km to the south-west, Calgary 619 km to the east.

### Orientation & Information

Train tracks separate the Thompson River's edge from the downtown area. Next to the tracks, running east-west, is Lansdowne St, one of the main streets. The other principal streets are Victoria and Seymour, both parallel to and south of Lansdowne. The Trans Canada Hwy is a few blocks further south. On the north-western corner of the city, along Lorne St, is Riverside Park, a pleasant spot for picnicking and swimming. The North Thompson River meets the Thompson River across from the park's shoreline. Some great sunsets can be seen over the Overlander Bridge from this point.

The Travel Infocentre (☎ 374-3377; 1-800-667-0143 within BC) is in a trailer on Notre Dame Drive opposite the main entrance to Aberdeen Mall; it's open daily from 8 am to 8 pm in summer. The main post office (☎ 374-2444), 301 Seymour St near the corner of 3rd Ave, is open Monday to Friday from 8.30 am to 5 pm. The Royal Inland Hospital (☎ 374-5111) is at 311

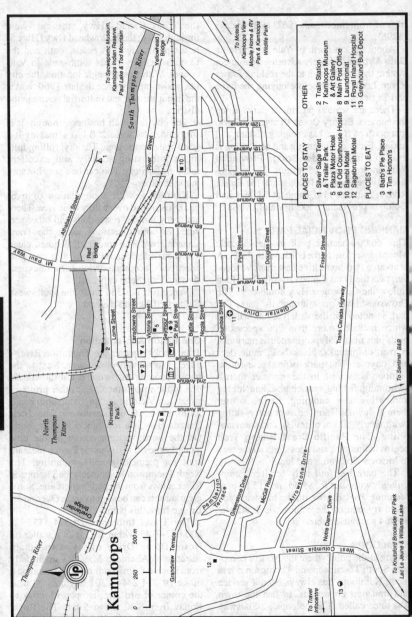

# Kamloops

0   250   500 m

**PLACES TO STAY**

1  Silver Sage Tent
   & Trailer Park
5  Plaza Motor Hotel
6  HI Old Courthouse Hostel
10  Bambi Motel
12  Sagebrush Motel

**PLACES TO EAT**

3  Barb's Pie Place
4  Tim Horton's

**OTHER**

2  Train Station
7  Kamloops Museum
   & Art Gallery
8  Main Post Office
9  Laundromat
11  Royal Inland Hospital
13  Greyhound Bus Depot

Columbia St. There's a laundromat on Seymour St, between 4th and 5th Aves.

## Things to See & Do

The **Kamloops Museum & Art Gallery** (☎ 828-3576) are in the same building at 207 Seymour St on the corner of 2nd Ave. On display are pioneer implements and Salish tools and ornaments. It's open daily from 9 am to 8 pm and admission is by donation. The **Secwepemc Museum**, 345 Yellowhead Hwy north of town, open Monday to Friday from 9 am to 8 pm, has displays on the history and culture of the Shuswap people. Entry is $2. Nearby is the **Chief Louis Centre** (☎ 828-9801) on the Kamloops Indian Reserve.

**Kamloops Wildlife Park** (☎ 573-3242) is 18 km east on the Trans Canada Hwy. Open year round (from 8 am to 8 pm in summer, to 5 pm the rest of the year), it has many animals found in Canada's west as well as camels, jaguars, monkeys and other animals from foreign lands. Admission is $5.50.

You can fish for salmon, trout and steelhead; as a general rule, the bigger the lake, the bigger the trout. **Adams River** is said to have very large sockeye salmon. There is even a Kamloops trout. The lakes and rivers also provide plenty of opportunities for swimming, canoeing, sailing, windsurfing, water skiing and scuba diving.

In winter there's downhill and cross-country skiing. **Tod Mountain**, 53 km north-east of Kamloops, off the Yellowhead Hwy, is the best spot for downhill, with 47 long, dry, powder-snow runs. It's currently undergoing a $50 million expansion. It also has 24 km of cross-country trails. Call ☎ 578-7232 for snow information. Better cross-country skiing can be found at **Lac Le Jeune**, 25 km south of town.

## Places to Stay

**Camping** *Silver Sage Tent & Trailer Park* (☎ 828-2077), north-east over the river at 771 East Athabasca St, is the closest to town. It has sites from $12 and a laundromat and showers. *Knutsford Brookside RV Park* (☎ 372-5380) is 12 km south-west of town,

on Hwy 5A (the Kamloops to Princeton Hwy), about six km south off the Trans Canada Hwy. All facilities are available, including showers and a laundromat; a site for two people costs from $11.50. *Kamloops View Mobile Home & RV Park* (☎ 573-3255) is about eight km east of town, on the Trans Canada Hwy. It has all facilities plus a swimming pool and fishing. A tent site for two people is $14.

You can also camp in two nearby provincial parks. *Paul Lake Provincial Park*, 24 km north-east of Kamloops, has sites for $9.50, as does *Lac Le Jeune Provincial Park*, 37 km south-west of town. Check in before 11 pm.

**Hostel** The HI *Old Courthouse Hostel* (☎ 828-7991), 7 West Seymour St on the corner of 1st Ave, is in a beautiful old building close to downtown. It has a kitchen, laundry, TV room, lounge and dining room (the latter two contain some of the original courthouse furnishings). The office is open from 8 to 11 am and from 5 to 11.30 pm. Beds cost $13.50 for members, $18.50 for non-members. From the Greyhound Bus Depot take local bus No 3 to the corner of Seymour St and 3rd Ave, then walk two blocks west.

The YM-YWCA has no rooms but does offer showers ($1.50) to travellers.

**B&Bs** The Travel Infocentre has a folder listing B&Bs in and around Kamloops. You could also try the Kamloops & Area B&B Registry (☎ 374-0668, 372-1297), 311 Columbia St, which provides a reservation service for B&Bs in the region with singles/doubles from $35/40. Some of the cheaper ones are *Mather's B&B* (☎ 376-3801), 821 Schubert Drive, north-west of the downtown area, which has singles/doubles for $25/35; *Sentinel House* (☎ 374-0841), 492 Sentinel Court with rooms for $30/40; and *Mr & Mrs McKay* (☎ 372-0533), 2034 High Country Blvd south-east of the downtown area, with rooms for $30/60.

**Motels** There are two main areas for motels: in Columbia St, west of the downtown area, and on the Trans Canada Hwy, east of town.

*Monte Vista* (☎ 372-3033), 2349 Trans Canada Hwy, is an old motel with singles/doubles for $30/33. There are no telephones in the rooms but it serves free coffee. *Kamloops Thrift Inn* (☎ 374-2488), at No 2459 Trans Canada Hwy, has a heated swimming pool and rooms for $33/35. Rooms have air-con and colour TV. Motels in Columbia St are pricier. One of the cheapest is the *Sagebrush Motel* (☎ 372-3151), 660 West Columbia St, which has rooms for $40/45, or $55/60 with private bath.

Another reasonably priced place is *Bambi Motel* (☎ 372-7626), 1084 Battle St, which runs east-west just south of the downtown core. Rooms cost from $36/38. The central *Plaza Motor Hotel* (☎ 372-7121), 405 Victoria St, has singles/doubles for $46/53.50 (including tax) and a café and bar downstairs.

### Places to Eat

Along and around Victoria St there are several places in which to eat. *Tim Horton's*, 336 Victoria St, is a fast- food place open 24 hours a day serving sandwiches (from $2.65) and donuts (70 cents each). The *Plaza Café* in the Plaza Motor Hotel serves breakfasts and has soup-and-sandwich lunch specials for $3.95. It's open from 6 am to 8 pm. *Barb's Pie Place* at 222 Victoria St has tables outside and serves breakfasts and snacks for $4 and delicious fruit pies for $2.75.

### Getting There & Away

**Bus** The Greyhound Bus Depot (☎ 374-1212), 725 Notre Dame Drive south-west of the downtown area off West Columbia St, has a cafeteria and left-luggage lockers. There are regular buses daily to Vancouver, Calgary, Jasper, Edmonton, Prince George, Prince Rupert and Penticton. Some sample fares (including tax) are:

| Destination | Fare |
| --- | --- |
| Jasper | $44.78 |
| Edmonton | $86.24 |
| Calgary | $69.12 |
| Vancouver | $37.72 |
| Prince George | $55.43 |

**Train** VIA Rail doesn't operate a passenger service through Kamloops, but you can take a tour on the privately operated Rocky Mountaineer which stops overnight here (see Getting There & Away in Vancouver for details).

**Hitching** Hitching is not allowed within the city limits.

### Getting Around

For information about local bus routes call Kamloops Transit Service (☎ 376-1216). A one-way fare is $1 and a day pass costs $2.50. For a taxi call Yellow Cabs (☎ 374-3333).

### KAMLOOPS TO WILLIAMS LAKE

West of Kamloops, the Trans Canada Hwy heads to **Cache Creek**, north of which Hwy 97 (the Cariboo Hwy) follows the Goldrush Trail to Barkerville east of Quesnel. The dry scrub-covered hills around Cache Creek give way to endless forest as you head north. From 100 Mile House (named after the roadhouse located at this distance from the start of the original Cariboo Wagon Rd) you can travel to Mahood Lake in Wells Gray Provincial Park (see that section later).

**Williams Lake** is mainly a transport centre most famous for the Williams Lake Stampede which takes place at the beginning of July. It's BC's answer to the Calgary Stampede and is a wild time lasting four days. It includes athletics and other sports as well as the rodeo. Accommodation prices go up a little while it's on.

North of Williams Lake is **McLeese Lake**, a small lakeside resort with log cabins.

# Okanagan Valley

The Okanagan, a beautiful and unique area of Canada, is a series of valleys running about 180 km north-south in south-central BC. To the east are the Monashee Mountains to the west the Cascade Mountains. The valleys were carved out by glaciers and are

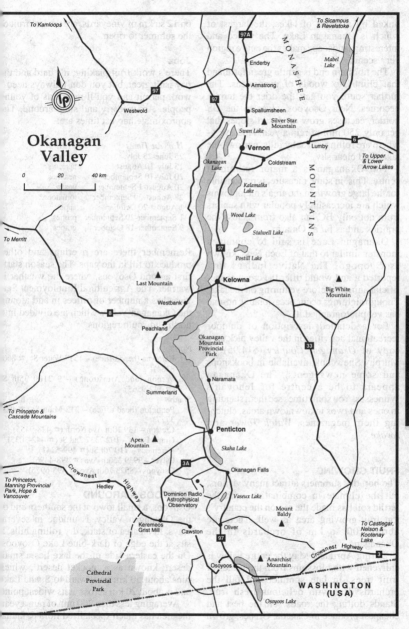

# Okanagan
# Valley

0    20    40 km

To Kamloops

To Sicamous
& Revelstoke

97A

Enderby

Armstrong

Spallumcheen

97

Westwold

Swan Lake

Silver Star
Mountain

Vernon

Okanagan
Lake

Coldstream

Lumby

6

To Upper
& Lower
Arrow Lakes

Kalamalka
Lake

MONASHEE

Mabel
Lake

MOUNTAINS

To Merritt

Wood Lake

Stalwell Lake

Postill Lake

97

Last Mountain

Kelowna

Westbank

Big White
Mountain

8

Peachland

33

Okanagan
Mountain
Provincial
Park

Naramata

Summerland

To Princeton &
Cascade Mountains

Penticton

Apex
Mountain

Skaha Lake

3A

To Princeton,
Manning Provincial
Park, Hope &
Vancouver

Crowsnest

Hedley

Highway

Okanagan Falls

Dominion Radio
Astrophysical
Observatory

Vaseux Lake

Mount
Baldy

To Castlegar,
Nelson &
Kootenay
Lake

Keremeos
Grist Mill

Cawston

Oliver

97

Anarchist
Mountain

Crowsnest    Highway

3

Cathedral
Provincial
Park

Osoyoos

WASHINGTON
(USA)

Osoyoos Lake

linked by a series of lakes, the largest of which is Okanagan Lake. The varied and interesting landscape makes the entire region very scenic.

The northern end is gentle green farmland that climbs to woods of evergreens. The further south you get, the drier the terrain becomes. Near Osoyoos, close to the US border, cactuses grow on desert slopes that get only 250 mm of rain a year. And everywhere are rolling, scrubby hills, narrow blue lakes and clear sky.

The Okanagan is a major retirement centre. This, in some measure, is responsible for the large growth of the area's major towns which are increasingly popular with seniors from not only BC but also from across the prairies and as far as Ontario.

Okanagan Lake is said to contain a monster similar to that of Loch Ness, known as Ogopogo. The Native Indians first reported it and would offer the creature sacrificial animals before venturing on the lake. Though sightings occur occasionally, no-one has yet photographed it.

For a detailed description of outdoor recreational activities in the valley pick up a copy of *Okanagan Country* ($14.95) by Murphy Shewchuk, available in bookshops and some newsagents. The Okanagan appears to be a centre for Jehovah's Witnesses. You sometimes see them standing in ones and twos in downtown areas, clutching their magazines, *Watch Tower* and *Awake*.

## FRUIT GROWING

The hot, dry summers attract many visitors, but the climate in combination with the fertile soil has made the region the country's top fruit-growing area as well. There are about 100 sq km of orchards in the Okanagan.

During April and May the entire valley is enlivened with blossoms from thousands of fruit trees. In late summer and fall the orchards drip with delicious fresh fruit. Stands dotting the roads sell the best and cheapest produce in Canada. Grapes, grown

on 12 sq km of vineyards, are the last fruit of the summer to ripen.

### Jobs

There's work fruit picking; it's hard and the pay isn't great, but you don't always need a work permit and you'll meet lots of young people. Arrive early and shop around. The approximate harvest times are:

| Harvest Times | Fruit |
|---|---|
| 25 June-25 July | cherries |
| 15 July-10 August | apricots |
| 20 July-10 September | peaches |
| 20 August-1 September | pears |
| 28 August-30 September | tomatoes |
| 1 August-20 October | apples |
| 1 September-20 September | prunes |
| 9 September-18 October | grapes |

Remember there are overlaps and other produce to fill in the gaps. The season starts first around Osoyoos, where the weather is warmer. The Agricultural Employment Services has a number of offices in and around the Okanagan Valley which are divided into north and south regions.

North
Kelowna (head office) – 1517 Water St (☎ 860-8384)
Vernon (and Armstrong) – 9 3100 35th St (☎ 542-9565)
South
Penticton (head office) – 212 Main St (☎ 493-3727)
Creston – 139 10th Ave North (☎ 428-9455)
Grand Forks – 102 7337 2nd St (☎ 442-3035)
Keremeos – 710 7th St (☎ 499-5341)
Oliver – 9939 350th Ave (☎ 498-4496)
Osoyoos – 8523 76th Ave (☎ 495-6925)

## OSOYOOS & AROUND

Osoyoos, a small town at the southern end of the Okanagan Valley, is unique in several ways. In an area of stark, dry rolling hills, it sits at the edge of dark-blue Lake Osoyoos. On the eastern side of the lake lies a small desert, known as a 'pocket desert', which runs about 50 km northward to Skaha Lake and is about 20 km across at its widest point.

Averaging less than 200 mm of rain a year the area has much specialised flora & fauna including the calliope hummingbird (the smallest bird in Canada), rattlesnakes, painted turtles, numerous species of mice and coyotes and various cactuses, desert brushes and grasses. The area is actually an extension of the northern Mexican desert and the life found here is remarkably similar to that at the 600 metres level in the Mexican portion.

In 1975, in cooperation with the provincial government, the locals adopted a theme to beautify the town. Because of the climate, topography and agriculture, a Spanish motif was chosen. Today many businesses and houses have taken on a Spanish look. With its warm, dry weather, the Osoyoos region produces the earliest and most varied fruit and vegetable crops in Canada. Look for roadside stands selling cherries, apricots, peaches, apples and other fruit. There are also many vineyards in the area.

### Orientation & Information
Osoyoos is at the crossroads of Hwy 97 heading north to Penticton (past several provincial parks where you can camp) and the Crowsnest Hwy running east to the Kootenay region and west to Hope.

The US border, cutting through Lake Osoyoos, is just five km to the south. To the west of Osoyoos is Cathedral Provincial Park.

The Travel Infocentre (☎ 495-7142) is slightly north-west of town, on the corner where the Crowsnest Hwy branches off westward from Hwy 97, next to the Husky gas station. The office of the Agricultural Employment Services, 8523 Main St, is open Monday to Friday from 7 am to 3.30 pm. The Greyhound Bus Depot (☎ 495-7252) is in the Pay 'n' Save gas station on the Crowsnest Hwy east of downtown.

### Things to See & Do
The small **Osoyoos Museum** (☎ 495-6723), at the bottom of Main St by the lake, has displays on natural history, the Inkameep people, orchards and irrigation. It's open daily between May and the beginning of September from 10 am to 4.30 pm and

admission is $2. The climate makes **Lake Osoyoos** the warmest in the country, and the warm water and sandy beaches make it good for swimming.

Less than a km east of downtown, over the bridge, is **Dutch Windmill** (☎ 495-7318), a replica of one built in Holland in 1816. In summer you can tour the windmill, see grain being ground and buy the delicious bread and cakes baked there. At 700 metres, east of Osoyoos, on the Crowsnest Hwy, the **Anarchist Mountain Lookout** offers a superb view of the town, valley, desert, lake and US border. You need a car or a ride to get there.

The **pocket desert**, off Black Sage Rd, is on the Inkameep people's reservation, but you can visit the desert by first asking permission from their office on the reservation. If you follow Black Sage Rd north from there to Oliver you'll pass several **wineries**. From Oliver, Camp McKinney Rd goes east to the **Mt Baldy** ski area (☎ 498-2262) which has cross-country trails and 11 downhill runs with a vertical drop of 420 metres.

At **Haynes Point Provincial Park**, which sits on a spit jutting into the lake two km south of town, you can go swimming, hiking and fishing.

West of Osoyoos is **Cathedral Provincial Park**, a 33-sq-km mountain wilderness area characterised by unusual rock formations. Mule deer, mountain goat and California bighorn sheep are some of the animals often seen by visitors. It's accessed by a gravel road off the Crowsnest Hwy three km west of Keremeos. Surrounded by orchards **Keremeos** is most noted for its fruit and wines. Fruit stands dot the highway as it passes through the town and valley.

### Places to Stay
**Camping** *Haynes Point Provincial Park* (☎ 494-0321) has showers; a tent site costs $14.50. At *Cathedral Provincial Park* (☎ 494-0321) there's no charge for camping. The area is chock full of private campgrounds, though they're often crowded and not very natural. *Cabana Beach Campground* (☎ 495-7705), 2231 East Lakeshore Drive, on Rural Route 1, three km south-east

of town, has small cabins, as well as tent and trailer space. Two people tenting costs from $16 to $22. *Brookvale Holiday Resort* (☎ 495-7514), 1219 45th St also along Rural Route 1, offers similar facilities; a tent site costs from $13 to $18.

**Hostel** A new hostel, *Osoyoos Backpackers Guesthouse* (☎ 495-2518/5288), 6902 62nd Ave, has opened up serving budget travellers and fruit-pickers. It has dorm beds for $10, double rooms for $30 and a kitchen, TV lounge and parking area.

**Hotels & Motels** The good-value *Rialto Hotel* (☎ 495-6922) is downtown near the lake. It has colour TV, air-con, restaurant and a pub downstairs. Singles/doubles cost $25/35. *Boundary Motel* (☎ 495-6050) is on Rural Route 2, close to the border with the USA. Singles/doubles cost $34/36. There are many more motels along 83rd St (Crowsnest Hwy) east of the downtown area over the bridge, and some along 89th St.

## PENTICTON

Penticton, the southernmost of the three Okanagan sister cities, sits between Okanagan Lake and Skaha Lake which are connected by Okanagan River. The sun shines for an average of 600 hours in July and August – about 10 hours a day – and that's more than it shines in Honolulu! It's not surprising, then, that the number-one industry is tourism.

To the Salish, Pen-Tak-Tin means 'place to stay forever', an idea that many White people took to heart. Between 1975 and 1985 the population rose from 13,000 to 25,000 and is now about 28,500. Penticton became a townsite in 1892, when several nearby mine claims were being developed. The Canadian Pacific railway made it a freight terminal and fruit companies started buying up land in early 1900. The industries grew and by the 1930s Penticton's location and climate was gaining a reputation. It soon became a vacation destination. The downtown core is undergoing something of a revival, particularly along the small Front St.

There is not a lot to do here, but this land of peaches and beaches is a good spot in which to cool your heels for a day or two.

### Orientation
The downtown area lies just south of Okanagan Lake. Most of the land along the lake is park. Lakeshore Drive runs west through this land from the downtown area to Riverside Drive and Hwy 97. The main street is Main St, running north-south; at the southern end it forks: to the left (east) it becomes South Main St, to the right (west) it becomes Skaha Lake Rd, which then turns into Hwy 97.

The downtown area extends for about 10 blocks southward from the lake. Martin St to the west and parallel to Main St is also important. Traffic on Main St is one way northbound, while on Martin St from Westminster Ave it's one way southbound. Running west-east, Westminster, Nanaimo and Wade Aves are the principal thoroughfares. Most of the restaurants and bars are in this area. This central area is small and easy to get around.

### Information
The Travel Infocentre (☎ 492-4103), in the Jubilee Pavilion of the Chamber of Commerce at 185 Lakeshore Drive, is open Monday to Friday from 9 am to 5 pm, weekends from 10 am to 4 pm. There's another on the corner of Westminster and Eckhardt Aves and one on Hwy 97 south of town. The main post office (☎ 492-5717) is south of downtown over Ellis Creek at 56 Industrial Ave West. In the centre, however, there is a postal outlet (☎ 492-8394) at Gallop's Flowers, 187 Westminster Ave, on the corner of Winnipeg St. The Toronto Dominion Bank, on the corner of Nanaimo Ave and Martin St is open on Saturday from 9.30 to 4 pm. Penticton Regional Hospital (☎ 492-4000) is south of downtown at 550 Carmi Ave. The Bookshop on Main St has a huge collection of second-hand books.

### Things to See & Do
Close to the downtown area, **Okanagan**

Beach is about 1300 metres long. It's sandy and the water temperature is about 22°C. You can visit the SS *Sicamous*, an old sternwheeler, which sits dry-docked at the western end of the beach. This section of the Okanagan Lake has some of the best windsurfing conditions in the Okanagan Valley. California Connection (☎ 493-0244) rents windsurfing boards and catamarans from $12 to $35 per hour. At the southern end of town **Skaha Beach** is about 1½ km long and has sand, trees and picnic areas and there's windsurfing here too. At the marina you can hire boats from $22 to $40 an hour from Skaha Boat Rentals (☎ 492-2024).

You can also go parasailing on both lakes: you start on the beach and a speedboat pulls you up 50 metres into the air. It costs $37.50 for a 10-minute ride, but people say the feeling and the views are worth the money. Call ☎ 492-2242 for details.

Penticton has two **wineries** in town: Cartier Wines (☎ 492-0621), 2210 Main St near the turn-off for Skaha Lake Rd, and Hillside Cellars (☎ 493-4424), 1350 Naramata Rd north-east of downtown. Both offer free tours that include taste samples.

On 2.25 sq km of dry land overlooking Skaha Lake, the **Okanagan Game Farm** (☎ 497-5405) has about 650 animals of 130 species, including Canadian and more exotic animals. It's eight km south of Penticton, on Hwy 97, and is open all year from 8 am to dusk. Admission is $8, or $6 for students.

North of Skaha Lake you'll find adults' and children's waterslides at **Wonderful Waterworld** (☎ 493-8121), at 225 Yorkton Ave. Full-day tickets cost $1.50. It's open in summer from 10 am to 8 pm daily.

### Festivals

The city's premier event is the Peach Festival, a week-long event that has taken place around the beginning of August since 1948. There are sports activities, novelty events, music and dance, nightly entertainment, and a major parade held on Saturday. The week following the festival is the Annual British Columbia Square Dance Jamboree. It goes on for six nights from 8 to 11 pm, and about

3500 dancers take part. There's an enormous dance floor in Kings Park. There are also street dances, dances held at both lakes – in the water! – pancake breakfasts and other activities.

At the end of August athletes are put through their paces in the Ironman Canada Triathlon. In early October for 11 days the Okanagan Wine Festival, centred in Penticton, takes place throughout the valley.

### Places to Stay

The beach closes at midnight and stays that way until 6 am. If you try to sleep on it you'll probably be rudely awakened by the police. Until the arrival of the HI hostel budget travellers were stuck with the usual alternatives.

**Camping** There are many tent and trailer parks, especially south of town, around Skaha Lake. Many are just off Hwy 97. Most are about $15 to $20 for two people in a tent. This is in no way wilderness camping, but is a cheap place to stay. The Travel Infocentre has a complete list.

**Hostel** The HI *Penticton Hostel* (☎ 492-3992), 464 Ellis St, is right downtown just south of the Greyhound Bus Depot. Facilities include private rooms, kitchen, laundry, lounge, patio, bike rental and discounts in town. It also has details about finding fruit-picking work. The office is open daily from 7 am to 12.30 pm and from 4 pm to midnight. Rates in a dorm are $13.50/18.50 for members/nonmembers.

**B&Bs** The Travel Infocentre also has a list of local B&Bs. One that's been going a long time is *Apex Alpine Guest Ranch* (☎ 492-2454) in Green Mountain Rd, 22 km west of Penticton. Rooms cost $40. It's near the ski resort and offers horseback riding and hiking. Close to downtown, *Budget B&B* (☎ 492-6743), 230 Farrell St, is open all year and has reasonable rates at $35/45 a single/double.

**Hotels** There aren't many hotels in Penticton

and they're not cheap. *Three Gables Hotel* (☎ 492-3933), 353 Main St, is the most reasonable one, with singles/doubles from $42/50. It's in the centre of town, three blocks south of Okanagan Lake, and has a good pub downstairs. Right on the shore of Okanagan Lake, at 21 Lakeshore Drive West, is *Coast Lakeside Resort* (☎ 493-8221), one of the top places in town. It's expensive, however, with singles and doubles costing from $85 to $172.

**Motels** Penticton is chock full of motels with Lakeshore Drive/Riverside Drive and South Main St/Skaha Lake Rd being the two main areas. *Club Paradise Motel* (☎ 493-8400), 1000 Lakeshore Drive, is a motel fronting Okanagan Lake. It has free coffee and aircon with singles and doubles costing from $40 to $60. Also fronting the lake but closer to the downtown area is the more expensive *Slumber Lodge Penticton* (☎ 492-4008), 274 Lakeshore Drive, where singles/doubles start at $60/65.

At the southern end of town *Holiday House Motel* (☎ 492-8422), 3355 Skaha Lake Rd, has singles/doubles from $45/49. *Paradise Valley Motel* (☎ 492-2756), at No 3118, has rooms from $35/40. Both have air-con and are close to Skaha Lake Beach.

### Places to Eat

Nearly all the downtown restaurants are on or near Main St, and the revival of the downtown core has brought an increase in choice. Many of the chain-store restaurants are also on Main St, south of Duncan Ave.

The *Elite*, 340 Main St (the restaurant with the 1950s Las Vegas-type sign outside) serves standard fare. Eggs with hash browns and toast cost $5.50 and it has lunch-time soup and salad specials for $4. *Grandma Lee's*, a cheap, cafeteria-style café diagonally opposite the Three Gables Hotel, offers soup and salad lunches for $4.25. At *Ortiz's Restaurante*, 452 Main St, the Mexican food is reasonable and filling. Main courses are around $8. More up-market, *Tumbleweed Grill*, 314 Main St near the corner of Nanaimo Ave, serves Mexican as well as

Spanish food. Further south *Turtle Island Café*, 718 Main St, is a popular local spot with a patio at the back. It has sandwiches and burgers from $3.50. *Edible Dried Goods*, 407 Main St, sells fruit leather, which is a blend of fruit purees dried into thin sheets and pressed together. It's great for backpacking and hiking. The store also sells spices, nuts and grains and is open every day.

### Entertainment

*Tiffany's*, 535 Main St, is the rock-music place in town, bringing in bands from Vancouver. There's usually a cover charge of around $5. Nearby is *Down Under Nite Club*, which has rock & roll and opens at 8.30 pm. *Nite Moves* is a disco next to the Three Gables Hotel. *Chaparal's*, 218 Martin St near the corner of Westminster Ave, has country music and dancing. A quieter spot at night or during the day is the large pub-like bar open from 10.30 am in the *Three Gables Hotel*. Further south, the British-style *Barley Mill Pub*, 2460 Skaha Lake Rd, is good for a quiet beer and a game of darts.

### Getting There & Away

The Greyhound Bus Depot (☎ 493-4101), 307 Ellis St on the corner of Nanaimo Ave one block east of Main St, is open daily from 6 am to 7 pm and has a cafeteria and left-luggage lockers. Buses depart daily for Vancouver ($40.98), Kelowna ($6.90), Vernon ($12.63) and Kamloops ($25.20). The fares include tax.

### Getting Around

For local bus information contact Penticton Transit (☎ 492-5602), or visit the Travel Infocentre and pick up a copy of the leaflet *Penticton Rider's Guide*, which lists routes and fares. The one-way fare is $1 and a day pass is $2.50. City buses go from town to both beaches. Bus No 202 from the corner of Wade Ave and Martin St goes down South Main St to Skaha Lake. There are no buses on Sundays or holidays, except for the summer lake-to-lake shuttle.

## AROUND PENTICTON
### Dominion Radio Astrophysical Observatory

Seen many of these lately? The observatory, about 20 km south-west of Penticton, contains radio telescopes that receive radio waves from the Milky Way and other galaxies. The waves are then amplified and analysed to provide information that conventional equipment cannot. Tours are given on Sunday between 2 and 5 pm in July and August. At other times you can see the equipment, hear a recorded explanation and visit the interpretive centre. The observatory is on White Lake Rd, about a 15-minute drive from the first turn south of Kaledan Junction on Hwy 97.

### Summerland

Summerland is a small lakeside resort town north of Penticton. From **Giant's Head Mountain**, an extinct volcano south of the downtown area, there are great views of Okanagan Lake. In town there are some fine 19th-century heritage buildings.

**Agricultural Research Station** This centre, 11 km north of Penticton on Hwy 97, was designed for the study of fruit trees, their growth, diseases and production. There is an ornamental garden displaying a variety of plants and trees, as well as picnic grounds. Tours are available, in the summer only, at 1 pm Monday to Friday but the grounds are open from 7.30 to 8.30 pm, to 5.30 pm the rest of the year.

**Summerland Trout Hatchery** You can tour the hatchery (☎ 494-3346), 13405 Lakeshore Drive, from 8.30 to 11.30 am and from 1.30 to 4.30 pm all year for free. This is one of three BC hatcheries used to stock lakes; here they concentrate on rainbow, eastern brook and kokanee trout.

### Apex Alpine Ski Resort

For skiing enthusiasts, Apex Alpine Ski Resort (☎ 292-8222), 37 km west of Penticton, off Green Mountain Rd, has more than 40 downhill runs which cater for all levels of ability, plus cross-country trails.

## KELOWNA

Kelowna sits halfway down Okanagan Lake, midway between Vernon and Penticton. All around are the rounded, scrubby hills typical of the valley. Closer to town they become greener, with terraced orchards lining their slopes and, unusually, the greenest area is the town itself, with its many parks and gardens. Beneath skies that are almost always clear, sandy beaches rim the dark blue water of the lake.

The city's name is a Salish word meaning 'grizzly bear'. A number of Oblate missionaries arrived in 1858. One of them – Father Pandosy – established a mission and planted the area's first apple trees. He has become Canada's lesser known equivalent of the USA's Johnny Appleseed. It was the success of his work that led to the first full-scale planting of apples, which was done in 1890. In 1892 the townsite of Kelowna was drawn up and today it is in the centre of Canada's largest fruit-growing district.

There are nearly 2000 hours of sunshine here each year. Summer days are usually hot but the nights are pleasantly cool. Winters are not harsh either. The combination of excellent weather and a good water supply makes Kelowna an ideal fruit and wine-producing area as well as a popular tourist destination. The dry, mild climate attracts both young and retired people.

Kelowna is the largest city in the Okanagan, with 80,500 people. As the hub of the fruit-growing area, and with an important lumber and wine industry, it is a valuable economic centre. Tourism is important too and the town has a distinct resort feel.

### Orientation

The large City Park on the lake's edge forms the western boundary of town. Starting from the big white modern sculpture 'Sails' and the model of Ogopogo at the edge of City Park, Bernard Ave runs east and is the city's main drag. Other important thoroughfares are Water, Pandosy and Ellis Sts, all running north-south. South of town Pandosy St becomes Lakeshore Rd. Hwy 97, called Harvey Ave in town, is the southern edge of the downtown area; it heads westward over the bridge towards Penticton.

Eastward, along roughly a 15-km stretch, Harvey Ave is an ugly, sprawling commercial strip lined with gas stations, junk-food spots and motels.

At the northern end of Pandosy St, where it meets Queensway Ave, is the town clock tower, standing in a fountain that marks the new civic centre. Beside the fountain, surrounded by flowers, is the museum and art gallery contained within the National Exhibition Centre.

There are 65 parks in the city area, including seven along the shore of the lake. Several parks are south-west of town, on the other side of the bridge. The beach continues a long way in this direction.

### Information
The Travel Infocentre (☎ 861-1515), 544 Harvey Ave (Hwy 97), near the corner of Ellis St, is open Monday to Friday from 9 am to 5 pm, weekends from 10 am to 4 pm. Another is on the western side of the lake, near Okanagan Lake Bridge, and there's a third on Hwy 97, about 10 km north of town, near the airport. Both of these only operate between May and September.

Most of the banks are on Bernard Ave, between Water and Ellis Sts. The Toronto Dominion Bank, on the corner of Bernard Ave and Pandosy St, is open on Saturday from 9 am to 4 pm.

If you're having mail delivered to Kelowna then you can pick it up from the Kelowna Mail Processing Plant (☎ 762-2118), 530 Gaston Ave north of downtown. However, to buy stamps etc you'll have to go to one of the retail outlets around town; there's one in the Towne Centre Mall on Bernard Ave.

Mosaic Books (☎ 763-4418), 1420 St Paul St, sells maps (including topographic ones), atlases, travel and activity guides and has a section on Native Canadian history and culture. Ted's Paperbacks & Comics ☎ 763-1258), 269 Leon Ave one block up from City Park, is a used-bookstore that will trade.

Kelowna General Hospital (☎ 762-4000) is south of Harvey Ave, at 2268 Pandosy St, on the corner of Royal Ave.

### City Park & Promenade
It's an excellent park, with sandy beaches, lots of shady trees, and water just slightly cooler than the summer air at 23°C. There are flower gardens and tennis courts; with the view across the lake, it's no wonder would-be fruit pickers are sitting around picking only guitars. Frisbees fill the air, boys toss girls in the lake, some people strut, some work overtime on the tan and the odd waterskier flies by in a foamy wake.

The beach runs from the marina to **Okanagan Lake Bridge** west of City Park. This is Canada's longest floating bridge; it's supported by 12 pontoons and has a lift span in the middle so boats up to 18 metres high can pass through.

From Bernard Ave, the lakeside promenade extends north past the marina, lock and artificial lagoon to the new condominium complex, a blend of Canadian and Spanish architectural styles. The promenade is good for a stroll or jog in the evenings.

### Fintry Queen
At the foot of Bernard Ave, behind the model of Ogopogo, the old ferry boat *Fintry Queen* (☎ 763-2780) is moored in the lake. Now converted into a restaurant, it also provides lake cruises. The two-hour cruise alone costs $9. Lunch only is $11, dinner only is $18.50.

### National Exhibition Centre
Housing the **Kelowna Centennial Museum** (☎ 763-2417) and **Kelowna Art Gallery** (☎ 762-2226), this is part of the civic centre complex, at 470 Queensway Ave, on the corner of Pandosy St. It features a reconstructed Salish underground winter home. Other exhibits include models of some of the town's first buildings and stores, stocked with goods and relics. The art gallery has a small permanent collection, mainly of the

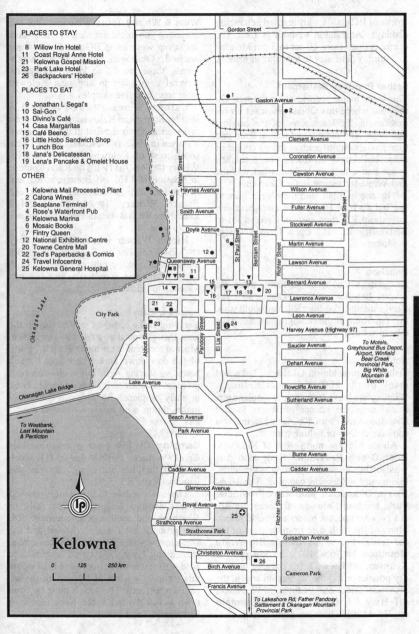

PLACES TO STAY

8   Willow Inn Hotel
11   Coast Royal Anne Hotel
21   Kelowna Gospel Mission
23   Park Lake Hotel
26   Backpackers' Hostel

PLACES TO EAT

9   Jonathan L Segal's
10   Sai-Gon
13   Divino's Café
14   Casa Margaritas
15   Café Beeno
16   Little Hobo Sandwich Shop
17   Lunch Box
18   Jana's Delicatessan
19   Lena's Pancake & Omelet House

OTHER

1   Kelowna Mail Processing Plant
2   Calona Wines
3   Seaplane Terminal
4   Rose's Waterfront Pub
5   Kelowna Marina
6   Mosaic Books
7   Fintry Queen
12   National Exhibition Centre
20   Towne Centre Mall
22   Ted's Paperbacks & Comics
24   Travel Infocentre
25   Kelowna General Hospital

Gordon Street

Gaston Avenue

Clement Avenue

Coronation Avenue

Cawston Avenue

Wilson Avenue

Fuller Avenue

Stockwell Avenue

Martin Avenue

Lawson Avenue

Bernard Avenue

Lawrence Avenue

Leon Avenue

Harvey Avenue (Highway 97)

Saucier Avenue

Dehart Avenue

Rowcliffe Avenue

Sutherland Avenue

Burne Avenue

Cadder Avenue

Glenwood Avenue

Guisachan Avenue

Christleton Avenue

Cameron Park

Water Street

Haynes Avenue

Smith Avenue

Doyle Avenue

Queensway Avenue

St Paul Street

Bertram Street

Richter Street

Ethel Street

Abbott Street

Pandosy Street

Ellis Street

To Motels,
Greyhound Bus Depot,
Airport, Winfield
Bear Creek
Provincial Park,
Big White
Mountain &
Vernon

Okanagan Lake

City Park

Okanagan Lake Bridge

To Westbank,
Last Mountain
& Penticton

Beach Avenue

Park Avenue

Cadder Avenue

Glenwood Avenue

Royal Avenue

Strathcona Avenue

Strathcona Park

Birch Avenue

Francis Avenue

Lake Avenue

To Lakeshore Rd, Father Pandosy
Settlement & Okanagan Mountain
Provincial Park

Kelowna

0    125    250 km

BRITISH COLUMBIA

works of BC artists, plus regularly changing displays. Admission to both is free. The centre is open from 10 am to 5 pm Monday to Saturday (Tuesday to Saturday in winter).

### Father Pandosy Settlement

This is the major historic site in the area. On the spot where this Oblate priest set up his mission in 1859 are some of the original buildings. The church and school from that time have been restored, as have a couple of other buildings: the barn, one furnished house and a few sheds from what was the first White settlement in the Okanagan.

The site is small, and there's not a lot to see, but it's free. To get there, go south along Lakeshore Rd, then east on Casorso Rd to Benvoulin Rd. It's open from 8 am to sundown.

### Beaches

As well as the beach in town, there are several beaches south of Okanagan Lake Bridge along Lakeshore Rd. You could walk this far. Some of the campgrounds along the lake also have beaches.

### Activities

Fishing is possible on Okanagan Lake and many of the 200 lakes near Kelowna. Windsurfers leave from the old seaplane terminal near the corner of Water St and Cawston Ave. From Kelowna Marina you can take cruises or fishing trips.

About 8½ km north-west of Kelowna, **Bear Creek Provincial Park** also has windsurfing as well as fishing, swimming, hiking and wilderness camping. The 10½-sq-km **Okanagan Mountain Provincial Park**, south of Kelowna off Lakeshore Rd, is a popular spot for hikers and horse riders. Many of the trails date from the days of the fur trade. For skiers there's **Big White Mountain** (☎ 765-3101), 55 km east of Kelowna, off Hwy 33. It's covered in deep dry powder and is the highest ski area in the province. South-east of town, in Westbank, off Hwy 97, there's **Crystal Mountain** (☎ 768-5189), which has night skiing.

**Wine & Whisky Tours** Wine tours are one attraction you might not want to miss. There are seven wineries in BC and five of them are in the Okanagan. From Kelowna southwards, there are 12 sq km of vineyards. Several companies in and near Kelowna offer tours and free samples.

Calona Wines (☎ 762-9144), 1125 Richter St, right in Kelowna, is BC's largest producer and was the first in the Okanagan: it started in 1932. In Westbank, about 13 km south-west of Kelowna, is Mission Hill Winery (☎ 768-7611). It's on Rural Route 1, in Mission Hill Rd, off Boucherie Rd, and has tours, tastings and sales. Cedarcreek Estate Winery (☎ 764-8866), 5445 Lakeshore Rd, has won international awards for its wine.

Hiram Walker Okanagan Distillery (☎ 763-4922), 899 Jim Bailey Rd, Winfield, north of Kelowna, produces Canadian Club whisky and has free tours and tastings Monday to Friday.

### Places to Stay

Camping is the cheapest way to stay in the area, though you'll be a fair way from town. Most of the motels are along Hwy 97, north of the downtown area. There aren't many hotels so staying right in the city can be a problem in summer. It's a good idea to book in early as places fill up fast. The hostel makes things a bit easier for budget travellers.

**Camping** The best place to camp is *Bear Creek Provincial Park* (☎ 494-0321), which has full facilities including showers and laundry. A site is $15.50.

There are numerous privately owned places around Kelowna, especially in Westbank and south along Lakeshore Rd. The grounds are usually crowded and the sites close together. To get to Westbank, head west along Hwy 97 over Okanagan Lake Bridge then turn off at Boucherie Rd. Follow this for quite a while and you'll hit the so-called resort area. This area is quite far from town – you'll need a car. Sites here cost between $10 and $19.

About six km south of the city is *Tiny Town Tent & Trailer Park* (☎ 762-6302), 3327 Lakeshore Rd. It's on the beach and has showers and bike rentals; sites are $13. Also on the beach, further south, is *Hiawatha RV Park* (☎ 861-4837), 3787 Lakeshore Rd. It's open from mid-May to mid-September and has tent sites for two people at $22.

**Hostels** The *Kelowna Gospel Mission* (☎ 763-3737), 251 Leon Ave, is a good, clean and free hostel. It's not really set up for travellers but rather offers a helping hand to those in need. The *Backpackers Hostel* (☎ 763-6024) is on the corner of Christleton Ave at 2343 Pandosy St just south of the general hospital – a short walk from the beach. It costs $10 for a dormitory bed. Breakfast is extra and coffee's free, there are showers, a kitchen, balcony and no curfew.

**B&Bs** Contact Okanagan B&B Association (☎ 764-2124), PO Box 5135, Station A, Kelowna, V1Y 8T9, for information about staying in B&Bs, or ask at the Travel Infocentre. Most places have singles for $30 to $40 and doubles for $45 to $55.

**Hotels** There are no cheap hotels in Kelowna. Downtown, the *Willow Inn Hotel* (☎ 762-2122), 235 Queensway Ave, on the corner of Abbott St, is right by City Park and the lake. It has a restaurant and bar on the premises, but is not recommended for female travellers. Singles/doubles cost from $55/60 with breakfast included in the price.

Close by and more up-market is *Park Lake Hotel* (☎ 860-7900), 1675 Abbott St, which has air-con rooms with TV, free movies and minibars priced from $79/89. *Coast Royal Anne Hotel* (☎ 860-7200), 348 Bernard Ave, has similar facilities and rates from $85/95.

**Motels** There are some good choices north along Hwy 97, not far past the Hwy 33 junction. *Western Budget Motel* (☎ 763-2484), 2679 Hwy 97 North, is the cheapest, with singles/doubles priced from $30/33. The *Town & Country Motel* (☎ 860-7121),

2629 Hwy 97 North near the junction with Hwy 33, has singles/doubles from $39/42 with air-con and TV. It also has a pool and sauna. Closer in, *Ponderosa Motel* (☎ 860-2218), 1864 Hwy 97 North, is reasonable, with singles/doubles including kitchen priced from $41/46.

**Places to Eat**

Many of the eateries are in Bernard Ave. *Lena's Pancake & Omelet House* is open every day and has all types of pancakes and omelettes from $4.75. Next door, *Jana's Delicatessen* sells European sausages and cheeses and serves soup-and-sandwich lunches for $3.75.

Between Pandosy and Ellis Sts, the *Café Beeno*, 467 Bernard Ave, serves good food at reasonable rates. Sandwiches which come with soup or salad cost from $4.25 and pastas from $6.75. At the *Lunch Box*, in Bernard Ave, near the corner of Ellis St, you can sit outside and take your choice of sandwiches for $4.50 and pies such as chicken and asparagus for $3. Between Water and Mills Sts there's a cluster of restaurants in the middle-range price bracket. *Casa Margaritas* serves Mexican food; tacos cost $5.50 and main dishes are priced from $9 to $15. The Vietnamese *Sai-Gon* has spring rolls for $5.55 and main meals from $8. At *Jonathan L Segal's* you can eat on the roof, from where you get a good view of the lake. The restaurant serves sandwiches and burgers from $5.50 and is licensed.

East along Bernard Ave, on the corner of Bertram St, and a little more up-market is *Divino's Café*, which serves delicious Italian food. Pasta dishes are priced from $9 to $12. The food is good and the restaurant offers a range of local wines.

The *Little Hobo Sandwich Shop*, 438 Lawrence Ave, specialises in sandwiches of all kinds and is popular with office workers. It's open from 7.30 am to 2 pm every day except Sunday. There's another at 1626 Richter St. If you're after something a little more spicy then try *Shalimar's*, 538 Leon Ave, an East Indian restaurant, or *Mon Thong*, 1530 Water St, for Thai food. If you need a fast-food fix head for Harvey Ave south and east of downtown where you'll find all the regular outlets.

### Entertainment

The Sunshine Theatre Company (☎ 763-1025) puts on a range of productions during the summer at the *Kelowna Community Theatre*, on the corner of Water St and Doyle Ave. Every summer Sunday afternoon there are free music concerts in City Park.

The Coast Royal Anne Hotel, though an expensive place to stay at, contains a popular pub-type bar, *Sergeant O'Flaherty's*. It's frequented by all types: visitors, workers and locals and entry is from the rear of the hotel in Queensway Ave. *Rose's Waterfront Pub*, off Water St, is good for a beer and view of the promenade and lake. *Flashbacks Nite Club* (☎ 763-1199), 1268 Ellis St, has classic rock & roll music, while *Iggyz* (☎ 868-2886), 229 Bernard Ave, has live rock music.

### Getting There & Away

**Air** The airport is about 20 km north of town, on Hwy 97. Air BC, Air Canada, Canadian Airlines, Central Mountain Air, Shuswap Air, Time Air and Trans-Provincial Air all fly into Kelowna. There are daily flights to and from Vancouver, Calgary and Edmonton; the regular one-way fares (including tax) are $191.59, $248.84 and $363.33 respectively.

**Bus** The Greyhound Bus Depot (☎ 860-3835) is north of the downtown area, at 2366 Leckie Rd, off Hwy 97. To get there, take city bus No 110 from the corner of Bernard Ave and Ellis St. It goes back and forth roughly every half hour from 6.30 am to 9.30 pm. The depot is open from 6.30 am to 10.30 pm daily, and the ticket office from 7 am to 7 pm.

There are five buses to Penticton and Vancouver daily, three to Osoyoos, two to Vernon and Kamloops, three to Prince George, Prince Rupert, Dawson Creek, Revelstoke and Calgary. Some sample one-way fares (including tax) are to Calgary $67.89, Prince George $73.67, Prince Rupert $150.50 and Vancouver $42.91.

**Hitching** If you're hitching south, walk over Okanagan Lake Bridge and start; northbound on Hwy 97, begin west of the commercial strip.

### Getting Around

**To/From the Airport** The Kelowna Airporter bus (☎ 764-8519, 888-8755), 765 Turner Rd, shuttles between town and the airport Sunday to Friday. It takes about 15 minutes and is available for each incoming flight. The one-way fare is $7 and the bus stops at the larger hotels as well as at other places on request. The one-way fare in a taxi is about $20.

**Bus** For information about local buses call Kelowna Transit Systems (☎ 860-8121) or pick up a copy of *Kelowna Regional Rider's Guide* from the Travel Infocentre; there are three zones and the one-way fare in the central zone is $1. A day pass for all three zones costs $3.50.

**Car** Kelowna has all the major rental companies.

Avis
    1310 Water St (☎ 762-5500)
Budget
    1553 Harvey Ave (☎ 860-2464)
Rent-a-Wreck
    2702 Hwy 97 North (☎ 763-6632)
Tilden Rent-A-Car
    1140 Harvey Ave (☎ 861-5242)
Thrifty Car Rentals
    1980 Springfield Rd (☎ 862-9091)

Hertz has a desk at the airport. Both Budget and Thrifty rent cars from $38 per day, with 100 free km then 15 cents per subsequent km. They all offer free pick-ups and drop-offs.

**Taxi** Kelowna has several taxi companies. Try Kelowna Cabs (☎ 762-4444/2222/1433), 1943 Kirschner Rd, or Checkmate Cabs (☎ 861-4445), 1145 Gordon Drive.

### VERNON & AROUND

Vernon, the most northerly of the

Okanagan's 'Big Three', lies in a scenic valley encircled by three lakes: the Okanagan, Kalamalka and Swan. The town developed because of its location. First there were the fur traders, then the gold prospectors streaming up the valley to the Cariboo district. Later, cattle were brought in, and in 1891 the railway made it. But it was in 1908, with the introduction of large-scale irrigation, that the town took on an importance that was more than transitory. Soon the area was covered in the orchards and farms present today.

Vernon's population of 23,500 is surprisingly cosmopolitan, with good numbers of Germans, Chinese and Native Indians. The Native Indians have a reservation to the west of town. Vernon itself doesn't have many attractions but accommodation is cheaper than in Kelowna or Penticton.

### Orientation
Surrounded by rolling hills, downtown Vernon is a clean, neat, quiet place. Main St, also called 30th Ave, is lined with trees and benches. To the north of 30th Ave, 32nd Ave is an important thoroughfare, as is 25th Ave to the south. At 25th Ave Hwy 6 leading south-east to Nelson and Nakusp, meets Hwy 97 which runs north-south becoming 32nd St in Vernon and bisecting the city. On 32nd St north of 30th Ave is a commercial strip with gas stations, motels and fast-food outlets. The other major north-south street is 27th St which eventually joins Hwy 97 north of town.

On 27th St is the provincial courthouse, the city's most impressive structure. All the downtown sights are within easy walking distance of each other.

### Information
The Travel Infocentre (☎ 542-1415) is about five km north of town on Hwy 97 (on the south-bound side) near the south-eastern shore of Swan Lake, so it's a bit of a hike to get to if you don't have your own transport. It's open Monday to Friday from 9.30 am to 4.30 pm. Another Travel Infocentre is only 2½ km south of the downtown area, on Hwy

97, towards Kelowna, near the army camp. It operates between May and September. If all you need is a map and visitor's guide to Vernon you can get them from the Chamber of Commerce (☎ 545-0771), downtown at 3700 33rd St.

The Bank of British Columbia, on the corner of 30th Ave and 34th St, is open on Saturday from 10 am to 3 pm. The main post office (☎ 545-8239), 3101 32nd Ave on the corner of 31st St opposite the civic centre, is open Monday to Friday from 8.30 am to 5 pm.

Bookland (☎ 545-1885), 3401 30th Ave, between 33rd and 34th Sts, has topographical maps of the region plus travel guides and books on activities in the Okanagan and BC.

The Vernon Jubilee Hospital (☎ 545-2211) is at 2101 32nd St.

### Polson Park
Polson Park, off 25th Ave and next to 32nd St, is very pleasant, with lots of flowers and shade and the small Vernon Creek running through it. If it's hot this is a good rest spot, especially if you're hitching or cycling. The Japanese and Chinese influence is evident in the gardens and open cabana-like structures dotting the park, at one end of which is a floral clock.

### Provincial Courthouse
Built entirely of local granite, the courthouse (☎ 549-5422) sits majestically at the eastern end of the downtown area, on the corner of 30th Ave and 27th St. In front of it across the road is a rather bizarre garden with a waterfall over a log platform which is supported by concrete sculptures.

### Greater Vernon Museum & Archives
This museum (☎ 542-3142) is in the civic centre, on the corner of 32nd Ave and 31st St, behind the glockenspiel-like clock tower. On display are historical artefacts from the area, including old carriages and clothes. It has a good antique telephone collection and lots of photographs of the area and the local people. It's open daily except Sunday from

10 am to 5 pm and admission is free. There's an art gallery here too.

## O'Keefe Historic Ranch

Twelve km north of Vernon, this old ranch (☎ 542-7868), on Hwy 97, was founded and lived on by the O'Keefe family from 1867 to 1977. Most of the buildings and artefacts were the property of this family. Among other things you'll see the original log cabin, a general store and St Ann's, the oldest Roman Catholic church in the province. The ranch is open daily spring to fall from 9 am to 5 pm. Admission is $5.

## Beaches

On blue-green Kalamalka Lake, about four km south of town, is **Kalamalka Beach** with a campground nearby. To get there take Kalamalka Rd south off Hwy 6. There's also **Kin Beach** on Okanagan Lake, which is about seven km west of downtown. Head west along 25th Ave which becomes Okanagan Landing Rd, then turn right onto Tronson Rd which leads to the beach. It has a campground, too.

## Provincial Parks

The 8.9-sq-km **Kalamalka Lake Provincial Park**, south of town and on the eastern side of Kalamalka Lake, provides swimming, fishing, hiking and picnic areas. **Ellison Provincial Park**, 25 km south-west of Vernon on Okanagan Lake, is the only freshwater marine park in Western Canada. Scuba diving is a popular activity here.

**Silver Star Provincial Park** is 22 km north-east of Vernon. Take 48th Ave off Hwy 97. The park offers good walking in summer, with views possible all the way west to the Coast Mountains. In winter it has 50 km of cross-country skiing on **Silver Star Mountain** and downhill ski runs plus trails for snowmobiles. In Lumby, **Mabel Lake Provincial Park**, 76 km north-east, off Hwy 6, has beaches, swimming, sailing and fishing.

## Places to Stay

Vernon has a wide range of campgrounds, B&Bs, hotels and, especially, motels. Down-town accommodation is cheaper here than in Kelowna and Penticton, but camping is the only real option for budget travellers since there are no hostels.

**Camping** By far the best campground is *Ellison Provincial Park* (☎ 494-0321); it has only 54 campsites and is often full, so call ahead. A site costs $12. *Mable Lake Provincial Park* (☎ 494-0321), at $9.50, has more sites.

There are lots of privately owned campgrounds, some close to town at Okanagan and Kalamalka lakes. These, too, get crowded. At *Seymour Marina* (☎ 542-6466), 7673 Okanagan Landing, you can camp right next to Okanagan Lake; a site costs $15 for two people. Follow 25th Ave west from Hwy 97. One of the closest campgrounds to town is *Swan Lake RV Park* (☎ 545-2300), 7255 Old Kamloops Rd, five km north of Vernon, which has tent sites for $10 plus tax. Head west along 43rd Ave then turn right (north) onto Old Kamloops Rd.

**B&Bs** Vernon has lots of B&Bs. For information contact the Travel Infocentre or Okanagan High Country B&B (☎ 542-4593), Rural Route 8, Site 10, Comp 12, which has singles/doubles priced from $30/40. Within walking distance of the downtown area, *Lawton House Gallery* (☎ 545-6497), 2906 26th St, has one double room ($60) in an artist's studio. In a rural setting *Coldstream Cottage* (☎ 545-2450), 266 Cypress Drive, has rooms with private bath and TV for $45.

**Hotels** The *National Hotel* (☎ 545-0731), 2922 30th Ave on the corner of 30th St, is a reasonably kept downtown hotel with the usual working-class bar downstairs. Single rooms without/with bath cost $20/24. Rooms include TV and air-con; a sauna is available and there's an old-style barber shop downstairs. *Kalamalka Hotel* (☎ 549-1011) opposite is similar. Further north *Coast Vernon Lodge* (☎ 545-3385), 3914 32nd St on the corner of 39th Ave, is more expensive. Singles/doubles cost from $64/72. The hotel has an indoor tropical garden, disco and nightclub.

**Motels** There are many, many motels in and around Vernon especially along 32nd St (Hwy 97). Two of the more central ones are *Polson Park Motel* (☎ 549-2231), 3201 24th Ave on the corner of 32nd St and opposite the park, and *Schell Motel* (☎ 545-1351), 2810 35th St, on the corner of 30th Ave. Polson Park Motel is good value and offers free coffee, a heated pool, bath, air-con and TV movies. Singles/doubles are $33/42, and a kitchen is $5 extra. Schell Motel has a heated pool, sauna, TV, and air-con. Rooms cost $33/42, or $8 extra with a kitchen.

**Places to Eat**

For a small town, Vernon has lots of places in which to eat – particularly little coffee shops and sandwich places. It seems to keep the quality up and the prices reasonable.

Downstairs at 3313 30th Ave near the corner of 34th St, is *Jackie's Coffee Shop*, popular with the locals. The food is the usual, the prices normal and the decor plain, so who can tell why? Sandwiches with soup or salad cost $4.75. *Sheila's Soup & Sandwich*, 2908 32nd St, between 29th and 30th Aves, is cafeteria style and does good-value breakfast and lunch specials at similar prices.

The cafeteria in the *Greyhound Bus Depot* has sandwiches for $3 and lunch specials for $4. It's basic but clean. Opposite the bus depot is *Paddington Station*, 2921 31st Ave, which has halibut and chips for $7 and salads for $3. It has an old-fashioned street lamp-post in the dining room. *RJ's* is in part of what used to be the railway station, at 3131 29th St. It has chicken dishes from $4.25 and salads for $3.75, chicken tacos for $2.75 and burgers priced from $2.25.

The Asian people here not only worked on the gardens in the park but also set up several Chinese restaurants. One is *Hong Kong Village* in 33rd St near 29th Ave which serves filling main courses for $6.50 to $9.

For a splurge, try *Kelly O'Bryan's*, 2905 29th St, near 30th Ave, which serves pasta, seafood, beef and vegetarian dishes. Fettu-

cini costs from $8. The restaurant has subdued lighting, stained-glass windows and an Irish theme. *Boa Thong*, 3210 30th Ave, is a Thai restaurant with starters for $6 and main dishes from $7.

**Entertainment**

The *Wildhouse Saloon*, on the corner of 30th Ave and 29th St next to Kelly O'Bryan's, features live country music or country rock nightly Wednesday to Saturday from 8 pm to 2 am. On the corner of 30th St and 30th Ave *Cloud 9*, has rock music. *Nite Magic*, 2900 29th Ave, has karaoke and comedy nights.

**Getting There & Away**

The Greyhound Bus Depot (☎ 545-0527), is on the corner of 31st Ave and 30th St. The ticket office is open from 5.30 am to 9 pm, but it closes between 1 and 2 pm and between 5.15 and 6.15 pm. Buses depart regularly for Vancouver, Kelowna, Penticton, Calgary, Jasper and Prince George. Some sample fares including tax are to Vancouver $45.58, Calgary $62.22 and Prince George $68.05.

**Getting Around**

For information about local buses contact KIA Transit (☎ 545-7221), 4210 24th Ave, or get a copy of the leaflet *Vernon Regional Rider's Guide*, which gives details of fares and routes, from the Travel Infocentre. The one-way fare is $1 and a day pass costs $2.50. For Kalamalka Lake catch bus No 1 south on 33rd St; for Okanagan Lake take bus No 7 west on 30th Ave.

For a taxi, try City Cabs (☎ 549-2227), at 2906 32nd St.

**NORTH OF VERNON**

At Sicamous there's a major highway junction where Hwy 97A meets the Trans Canada Hwy. From there the Trans Canada Hwy heads east past Shuswap Lake to Salmon Arm and Kamloops; west the highway goes to Revelstoke then through Mt Revelstoke, Glacier and Yoho national parks to Lake Louise in Alberta.

### The Shuswap Region

The district around **Shuswap** and **Mara** lakes is picturesque, with green, wooded hills and farms. The grazing cattle and lush, cultivated land make a pleasant change of scenery no matter where you're coming from. There are many provincial parks in the region, three of which you can camp at: Shuswap Lake, Herald and Yard Creek.

**Salmon Arm**, at the northern end of the Okanagan Valley on the southern tip of one of Shuswap Lake's 'arms', is mainly a resort town, although timber and fruit-growing are also important. If you're here in October head north to Adams River in **Roderick Haig-Brown Provincial Park** where you'll see between 25,000 and 2½ million sockeye salmon migrating upriver to spawn.

One way to explore the Shuswap and Mara lakes is by houseboat, which can be hired from **Sicamous**, the self-styled 'houseboat capital of Canada'. You can also rent them from Salmon Arm.

# South-Eastern British Columbia

The south-eastern part of BC is dominated by the Rocky, Selkirk, Purcell, Monashee, Cariboo and Columbia mountain ranges. This is an area for outdoor activities: camping, hiking and climbing in summer, and some of North America's best skiing in winter. Nestled between the parallel mountain chains is a series of populated valleys. There are national and provincial parks throughout the area. Summers are short in the mountains: it's not unusual to have snow in the Rockies at the end of August.

The south-eastern corner of this region is on Mountain Standard Time, while most of the rest of the province is on Pacific Standard Time, a difference of an hour.

## WELLS GRAY PROVINCIAL PARK

In the Cariboo Mountains about halfway between Kamloops and Jasper, off the Yellowhead Hwy (Hwy 5), is this huge, undeveloped, relatively little-visited, 520,000-hectare wilderness park. In **Clearwater**, the Travel Infocentre (☎ 674-2646), on the corner of the Yellowhead Hwy and Clearwater Valley Rd, has lots of useful information and maps on the park.

You can hike along more than 20 trails of varying lengths, go mountain biking, canoeing on the lakes and rivers, white-water rafting on Clearwater River, mountain climbing, downhill or cross-country skiing, and horse riding. Canoeing often provides the only access to hiking trails and only experienced, fully equipped mountaineers should attempt climbing or venture onto the snowfields and glaciers. Wildlife is plentiful. Of the many waterfalls in the park **Helmcken Falls**, where the Murtle River plunges 137 metres, is the most spectacular.

### Places to Stay

Wells Gray has four designated *campgrounds* (Dawson Falls, Clearwater Lake, Falls Creek and Mahood Lake) with sites costing $7 or $9.50, plus plenty of wilderness camping along the shores of the larger lakes.

### Getting There & Away

There are three access points to the park. From Clearwater to the south, the Clearwater Valley Rd enters the park at Hemp Creek; from Blue River a 24-km gravel road and 2-½-km track lead to Murtle Lake in the south-east; and from 100 Mile House off Hwy 97 it's 88 km on paved road to Mahood Lake in the south-west.

## MT ROBSON PROVINCIAL PARK

Skirting the Fraser River, the Yellowhead Hwy and VIA Rail line run along the valley of this 217,000-hectare park which adjoins Alberta's Jasper National Park. At the western end of the park, Mt Robson (3954 metres) is the highest point in the Canadian Rockies and, when the clouds are not hugging it, is visible from the highway. At the base of the mountain the visitor centre

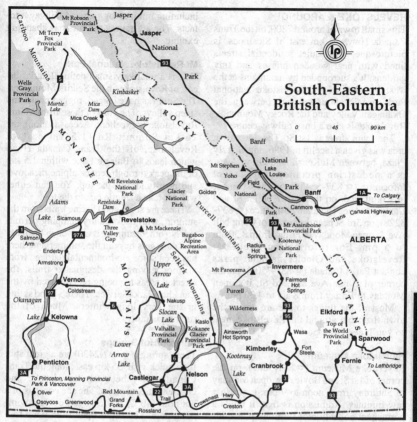

## South-Eastern British Columbia

has information on the park and runs interpretive programmes during the summer. The park has hiking trails, swimming, fishing, mountain and glacier climbing (only for the experienced and properly equipped), canoeing, rafting and horse riding. For the less-active visitor there are many picnic areas and lookout points. There is plenty of wildlife including more than 170 bird species. In August and September you can see salmon spawning on the river at Rearguard Falls.

Adjoining the western end of the park is the tiny **Mt Terry Fox Provincial Park**, named after the runner who lost a leg to cancer, then attempted to run across the country to raise money for cancer research.

### Places to Stay

Mt Robson Provincial Park has three *campgrounds*: two are near the visitor centre at Robson Meadows and Robson River with sites for $14.50; the third is at Lucerne on the southern shore of the Yellowhead Lake 10 km west of the Alberta border, with sites for $9.50. There is also wilderness camping in the park and commercial facilities at its western edge.

## REVELSTOKE & AROUND

This small town of around 7800, on the Trans Canada Hwy, 70 km east of Sicamous, is picturesque, with quiet residential streets lined with neat wooden houses and tidy gardens. It's surrounded by mountains at the western edge of Mt Revelstoke National Park and is about halfway between the Okanagan Valley and the Rocky Mountains. Revelstoke is also a busy railway centre.

The main street is 1st St. The downtown area was given a facelift in 1986, and Grizzly Plaza, between McKenzie and Orton Aves, is a pedestrian precinct. The Travel Infocentre (☎ 837-5345) is in the Chamber of Commerce, on the corner of 1st St and Campbell Ave. The main post office (☎ 837-3228), on 3rd St near the corner of Campbell Ave, is open Monday to Friday from 8.30 am to 5 pm. For information about Mt Revelstoke and Glacier national parks contact Parks Canada (☎ 837-7500), on the corner of Boyle Ave and 3rd St; it's open Monday to Friday from 8 am to 4.30 pm.

Most of the things to see are not in the town itself but around the Revelstoke area, so you'll need transport.

### Revelstoke Museum

Revelstoke Museum (☎ 837-3067), on the corner of 1st St and Boyle Ave, open Monday to Saturday from noon to 9 pm, is worth a few minutes. Admission is free. It holds a permanent collection of furniture plus odds and ends of historical interest from the area including mining, logging and railway arte-facts. The art gallery upstairs has changing exhibits.

### Mt Revelstoke National Park

This is a relatively small national park, just east of Revelstoke, in the Selkirk Mountains. The Selkirks have jagged, rugged peaks and steep valleys. The view of these from Mount Revelstoke is excellent. Access is along the 26-km Summit Rd (1.5 km east of Revelstoke, off the Trans Canada Hwy) which leads to Balsam Lake within 1.5 km of the peak through cedars, alpine meadows and near-tundra at the top. You can either walk or take a shuttle bus to the top.

There are some good hiking trails from the summit, with backcountry camping permit-ted. No other camping is allowed in the park. The park gets busy in the summer and there has been some environmental damage from visitors leaving the designated trails; the affected areas are being rehabilitated by the Canadian Parks Service. There's good skiing in the very long winters. Much of the summer is rainy.

### Canyon Hot Springs

These springs (☎ 837-2420) are a great spot for a quick visit, 35 km east along the Trans Canada Hwy between Revelstoke and Glacier national parks. The site consists of a hot pool (40°C) and a larger, cooler swim-ming pool. The site is open from 9 am to 9 pm and early in the morning you can have

---

**Terry Fox**

Terry Fox from Port Coquitlam in BC, discovered at the age of 18, when he was a student and athlete at Simon Fraser University, that he had cancer and had to have his right leg amputated. Four years later he attempted to run from the east to the west coast in order to raise money for cancer research. He started what he called the Marathon of Hope in St John's, Newfoundland, on 12 April 1980. As he headed west toward Port Renfrew in BC many people lined the route, while others followed his progress on the daily TV news bulletins. With a third of the marathon left to go and having run for 143 days he had to stop, at Thunder Bay, Ontario. The cancer had spread to his lungs and the following year on 28 June 1981, a month before his 23rd birthday, he died. His run had raised over $24 million for the Canadian Cancer Society.

Every year since then, in September on the second Sunday after Labour Day, Terry Fox Runs have been held throughout the country and indeed around the world. The money raised goes towards cancer research. ■

the place to yourself. Admission is $4.50 and that includes a locker and shower; a day pass is $6.50. You can rent a bathing suit and towel for $1.50 each.

## Three Valley Gap

On the Trans Canada Hwy, 19 km west of Revelstoke, is this re-creation of a pioneer community. It has more than 20 buildings; there's a saloon, an old hotel, a barber shop a blacksmith's and a theatre amongst others. Nearby is the site of Three Valley, a mining town which blossomed and died in the late 1880s. Admission is $6.50. There's a live performance in the theatre nightly; entry is $7. The site has a motel too, with an 850-year-old tree at the front.

## Dams

BC Hydro (☎ 837-6211) runs free tours of the 175-metre **Revelstoke Dam** on the Columbia River, four km north of town, off Hwy 23 and adjacent to Columbia View Provincial Park. It also runs tours of the **Mica Dam**, 149 km north of Revelstoke, in a bend of the Columbia River, at the end of Hwy 23.

## Mt Mackenzie

Five km south-east of Revelstoke, this is a major downhill and cross-country skiing area. Call ☎ 837-5268 for information.

## Places to Stay

South of Revelstoke, on Hwy 23, you can camp at *Blanket Creek Provincial Park* (☎ 825-4421). It has running water but no showers and a site costs $7. There are many private campgrounds east and west of Revelstoke along the Trans Canada Hwy. *Canyon Hot Springs* (☎ 837-2420) has full facilities including showers, toilets and a grocery store. Sites cost $15.

*Piano Keep* (☎ 837-2120), 815 Mackenzie Ave, is a 1905 heritage home B&B with a single room for $55 and doubles for $65 to $75. Vern Enyedy, the owner, collects pianos from all over the world (he now has about 60) and keeps them all in working order.

In town, *King Edward Hotel* (☎ 837-5104), on the corner of 2nd St and Orton Ave,

is a good, low-budget place. Singles cost $25.30/31.05 (including tax) without/with bath; doubles with bath are $44.85. *Peaks Lodge* (☎ 837-2176), five km west of town, on the Trans Canada Hwy, charges $58/68 for a single/double, with TV and includes breakfast. There are many other places, mostly motels, along the highway.

## Getting There & Away

The Greyhound Bus Depot (☎ 837-5874) is west of town, at 1899 Fraser Drive, off the Trans Canada Hwy. Greyhound makes four trips east and west daily. The fare (including tax) to Vancouver is $56.60, to Calgary $46.01. The Rocky Mountaineer train comes through on Tuesday and Thursday (see Getting There & Away in Vancouver).

## GLACIER NATIONAL PARK

In the Columbia Mountains, about halfway between Revelstoke and Golden lies this 1350-sq-km park. There are more than 420 glaciers here and it snows nearly every day in winter. The annual snowfall can be as much as 23 metres. Because of the sheer mountain slopes, this is one of the world's most active avalanche areas. For this reason skiing, caving and mountaineering are closely regulated; you must register with the park warden. Around Rogers Pass you'll notice the many snowsheds protecting the highway. With the narrow road twisting at up to 1330 metres, this is a dangerous area, sometimes called Death Strip – an unexpected avalanche can wipe a car right off the road. Still, the area is carefully controlled, and sometimes snows are brought tumbling down with artillery before they fall by themselves.

At Rogers Pass there's an information centre, open daily from 8 am to 8 pm in summer, and a park warden office (☎ 837-6274 for both), open 24 hours a day. The centre has films on the park and in the summer organises guided walks.

Not far from here are the park's only two *campgrounds*: at Illecillewaet River and Loop Brook; both have running water and flush toilets. *Glacier Park Lodge*

(☎ 837-2126), at Rogers Pass, has singles/doubles from $92/97. There's a 24-hour cafeteria and a service station close by.

## GOLDEN

As you travel along the Trans Canada Hwy from Alberta, this town of 3800 people is the first of any size in BC. It's also at the junction with Hwy 95 which connects the town with Radium Hot Springs and Invermere to the south. Despite what the tourist brochures say and what its name might suggest, Golden is not much more than a commercial strip of motels, fast-food restaurants and gas stations. Golden is the town to which workers in the area come for a bite to eat and a booze-up – something you might want to do yourself if you've been a while in the backcountry.

The Travel Infocentre (☎ 344-7125), 500 10th Ave, is open year round Monday to Friday from 9.30 am to 12.30 pm, 1 to 4.30 pm. There's another (seasonal) one on the highway next to the Husky gas station. *Golden Municipal Campground* (☎ 344-5412), 1407 South 9th St, has most facilities including showers (but no laundry) and sites costing $8 to $12.

### Heli-Skiing

South of Golden, in the Purcell Mountains, is the world's centre for helicopter skiing – in districts such as the Gothics, Caribous and, perhaps best known, the Bugaboos. The latter is a region of 1500 sq km of rugged, remote mountains accessible only by helicopter during the winter months. This dangerous, thrilling sport attracts rich visitors from around the world each winter and spring. The Bugaboos has been a favourite area for two decades.

The skiing is superb but a portion of the appeal is the danger. Avalanches are not uncommon, tumbling snows claim lives on a regular, though not frequent, basis – just often enough to give the run down that extra kick.

Canadian Mountain Holidays (☎ 403-762-4531; 1-800-6610-0252), 217 Bear St, Banff, Alberta T0L 0C0, is one of the oldest, most established operators providing visitors with transportation, comfortable lodges and helicopter lifts to pristine mountain tops of spectacular scenery and fine powder snows. ABC Wilderness Adventures (☎ 344-2639), PO Box 1829, Golden, offers a similar service. A week-long ski holiday can cost $4000.

During the summer months you can visit some of the lodges and enjoy hiking. Mountaineers too come from around the world to test their skills on the sheer rock faces in Bugaboo Glacier Provincial Park.

## YOHO NATIONAL PARK

Yoho National Park, in the BC Rockies, adjacent to the Alberta border and Banff National Park to the east and Kootenay National Park to the south, offers mountain peaks, river valleys, glacial lakes and beautiful meadows – a bit of everything. Yoho is more accessible and the weather is better than at Glacier. The name is a Cree word expressing astonishment or wonder. The rushing Kicking Horse River flows through the park.

### Field

The small town of **Field**, lying in the middle of the park, is the first town in BC as you head west along the Trans-Canada Hwy (which follows the Kicking Horse River). Field has a lot of old buildings dating from the early days of the railways. There's a grocery store – closed on Sunday – which is a good place to get supplies if you're going to stay in the park. It's cheaper than the store near Takakkaw Falls. Field also has a post office, a gas station, the park information centre (open from 8 am to 8 pm in summer, to 4.30 pm the rest of the year) and the warden office (☎ 343-6324 for the latter two). BC Tourism and Alberta Tourism both have a desk in the park information centre.

Near Field is the turn-off for and **Takakkaw Falls** – at 254 metres, one of the highest waterfalls in Canada. Also near Field are the famous **spiral tunnels**, the feats of engineering that enable the Canadian Pacific trains to navigate the challenging Kicking Horse Pass.

## Hiking

In the Yoho Valley the trail from Takakkaw Falls to **Twin Falls** makes a good day hike. The trail is mostly flat, with views of lots of rapids and waterfalls. There's camping on the way. The beautiful green **Emerald Lake** has a circular walking trail with other trails radiating from it and the water in the lake is warm enough in late summer for a quick swim. **Lake O'Hara** is another beauty spot with lots of excellent trails. You can hike the 13 km in along the Cataract Brook Trail, or take the bus (see Getting There & Around later), but the area gets busy.

## Places to Stay

Yoho has five *campgrounds* and they fill up quickly. Only the Kicking Horse River campground has showers with sites costing $13, and you need to reserve your place at Lake O'Hara (☎ 343-6433), where sites are $7.25. Other campgrounds are at Chancellor Peak ($7.25), Hoodoo Creek ($10.50) and Takakkaw Falls ($7.25).

The HI *Whiskey Jack Hostel* (☎ 283-5551), just before the Takakkaw Falls campground, is open mid-June to mid-September and has 27 beds. Nearby and highly recommended are the pleasantly rustic, good-value *Cathedral Mountain Chalets* (☎ 343-6442), at the base of Cathedral Mountain. From here, Mel Reasoner, a commercial guide, provides guided tours of Burgess Shale. The postal address for the chalets is: PO Box 40, Field, BC, V0A 1G0.

## Getting There & Around

The Greyhound bus stops at Field. The only transport within the park is the bus to Lake O'Hara but preference is given to those who've reserved a place at the campground or Lake O'Hara Lodge. To book a seat on the bus call ☎ 343-6433 between 8 am and 4 pm daily.

Hitching is OK.

## KOOTENAY NATIONAL PARK

Kootenay National Park is solely in BC but is adjacent to Banff National Park and runs south from Yoho National Park. Hwy 93 (the Banff-Windermere Parkway) runs down the centre and is really the only road in the park. From the northern entrance at Vermillion Pass to Radium Hot Springs at the park's southern end there are campgrounds, points of interest, hiking trails and views of the valley along the Kootenay River.

Kootenay has a more moderate climate than the other Rocky Mountain parks and in the southern regions especially, summers can be hot and dry. In fact it's the only national park in Canada to contain both glaciers and cactuses.

The Marble Canyon Information Centre

### Burgess Shale

The Burgess Shale fossil site, near Field in Yoho National Park, BC, was discovered accidentally in 1909 by Charles D Walcott from the Smithsonian Institute, Washington DC, when he was out horse riding. The Cambrian-age fossil beds on Mt Field and Mt Stephen contain the fossilised remains of marine animals that lived around 530 million years ago. The site is remarkable for its number, variety and detailed preservation of fossils of soft-bodied creatures such as worms and sponges, and of hard-bodied creatures (with their soft-body parts) such as molluscs. One major reason for their preservation was their burial in deep water where the oxygen level, and therefore the rate of organic decay, was low. In recognition of its importance to our understanding of evolution, Burgess Shale was declared a World Heritage Site by UNESCO.

Faced with the dilemma of preserving the site while allowing visitors the chance to see and learn about it, Yoho National Park restricts the amount of public access. Visitors can go on guided walks (which have to be booked in advance and are limited to 15 people) either with park interpreters or licensed commercial guides. If you don't get onto a guided walk or don't fancy the long, steep hike to Mt Field or Mt Stephen there are exhibitions on Burgess Shale in the park information centre near Field, at the Kicking Horse River campground and at the Lake Louise Visitor Information Centre in Banff National Park, Alberta. ■

(no phone), eight km south of Vermillion Pass, is open between June and September, Monday to Thursday from 8.30 am to 4 pm and Friday to Sunday from 8 am to 8 pm. The West Gate Information Centre (☎ 347-9505), at the southern entrance, is open daily from 9 am to 9 pm June to early September, then weekends only till early October.

Stop at **Marble Canyon** for the 30-minute walk – it is a real adrenalin-rush. The trail follows the rushing Tokumm Creek, criss-crossing it frequently on small wooden bridges with longer and longer drops below as you head up to the waterfall. Two km further south there is a short, easy trail through forest to ochre pools known as the **Paint Pots**. For years, first the Kootenay people and then European settlers collected this orange and red-coloured earth to use as a colouring agent. Now artificial dyes are used.

The park has lots more trails. You can also try white-water canoeing or rafting on the Kootenay River, or mountain biking in the Golden Triangle.

At the southern edge of the park where Hwy 93 joins Hwy 95, is **Radium Hot Springs**, a rather plain little town. The hot springs, two km north of the town, are always worth a visit, though they can be busy in summer when they're open daily from 9 am to 9 pm. Admission is $2.75.

### Places to Stay

The *Marble Canyon Campground*, across the road from the information centre, is good, but basic with no electricity or showers; it does have toilets and cold running water. *McLeod Meadows Campground*, in the park's south, is similar. *Redstreak Campground*, near the West Gate Information Centre, is fully serviced including showers. All three have sites for $10.50. If you're looking for a roof over your head, Radium Hot Springs has lots of motels.

### MT ASSINIBOINE PROVINCIAL PARK

Between Kootenay and Banff national parks is this lesser-known, 39-sq-km provincial park, a World Heritage Site. The craggy summits of Mt Assiniboine (3618 metres) and its near neighbours are a magnet for climbers. The park also offers hiking, horse riding on some of the trails, mountain biking on the Assiniboine Pass Trail, cross-country skiing and fishing.

Access is from Hwy 93: two hiking trails start from near the highway at Vermillion Crossing in Kootenay National Park. From Banff National Park in Alberta a gravel road takes you close to the park through the ski resort of Sunshine Village. Another road leads from Spray Reservoir south of Canmore to the trailhead near Shark Mountain. The trails all meet at Lake Magog where there is the park headquarters, a campground, some cabins and the commercially operated Mt Assiniboine Lodge (☎ 403-678-2883 in Banff). There's wilderness camping in other parts of the park.

### RADIUM HOT SPRINGS TO CRANBROOK

South from Radium Hot Springs, Hwy 93/5 follows the Columbia River between the Purcell and Rocky mountains until the road splits shortly before Wasa. From there Hwy 95 heads south-west to Kimberley and Cranbrook, while Hwy 93 goes south-east to Fort Steele.

**Invermere**, 14 km south of Radium, is a resort town, offering a variety of outdoor recreational activities, on the shores of Windermere Lake. The Travel Infocentre (☎ 342-6316), on the corner of 5A St and 7th Ave, is open daily May to September. **Mt Panorama**, in the Purcell Mountains 18 km south-west of Invermere, is BC's second world-class ski resort (after Whistler/Blackcomb). Mt Panorama has a spectacular setting and almost two-thirds of the downhill runs are ranked intermediate. **Fairmont Hot Springs** is another resort town, with the hot springs as its focus. A single swim costs $4.50 or a day pass $6; bring your own swimsuit. It gets very crowded on weekends and public holidays. There's horse-back riding here too. At Skookumchuk, shortly before Wasa, a gravel road provides access eastward to **Top of the World Provincial**

**Park**, where there are hiking trails and wilderness camping.

At 1117 metres, **Kimberley** is the highest city in Canada. Before 1973, Kimberley looked like what it is – a small mountain mining town. But as one of BC's 'theme' towns, it was made to look like a Bavarian alpine village. Most of the downtown section was transformed and with enough detail to make it interesting.

Kimberley is now home to the world's largest functioning **cuckoo clock**. In winter the skiing on nearby **North Star Mountain** is excellent. To the north-west, **Purcell Wilderness Conservancy** has hiking trails, fishing and wilderness camping; access is by a gravel road off Hwy 95A. The Julyfest in Kimberley is a week of dancing, parades and lots of beer.

The heritage park of **Fort Steele**, 20 km south-east of Wasa on Hwy 93, is a re-creation of an East Kootenay town in the late 1800s. Fort Steele arose as a commercial, social and administrative centre of the East Kootenays when major silver and lead discoveries were made in 1892. Its fortunes turned when, in 1898, the BC Southern Railway bypassed it in favour of Cranbrook. Now, Fort Steele has more than 60 restored and reconstructed homes and buildings. It's open daily from 9.30 am to 8 pm and admission is $5.50.

## CRANBROOK

Sitting at the base of the Rocky Mountains, Cranbrook, with a population of just under 17,000, is about 30 km south-east of Kimberley, on the Crowsnest Hwy. The Travel Infocentre (☎ 426-5914), 2279 Cranbrook St North, is open year round. There's not a lot to see in the town itself, but it is located where you can enjoy many outdoor activities.

You can go hiking or horse-riding along the mountain trails or go swimming, fishing, sailing, windsurfing, etc on any of the dozens of lakes. There's a municipal campground with full facilities, but you'll find pleasanter surroundings at **Jim Smith Lake** and **Moyie Lake** provincial parks

south-west of town; there's running water but no showers. Many motels line the highway at the northern end of town, and there are a few hotels downtown.

## NAKUSP & AROUND

Nakusp, sitting on Upper Arrow Lake, is the main town in the valley south of Revelstoke, east of the Okanagan Valley. The dry, picturesque valley follows a chain of lakes between the Monashee and Selkirk mountain ranges. This is a very attractive portion of the province which benefits from not having the high profile and hence major attention of some of the more famous districts. South-west of Nakusp, Hwy 6 heads to Vernon in the Okanagan Valley, going over the 1189-metre Monashee Pass. Near Vernon, the road goes through beautiful country scenery of small farms and wooded hills. There are campgrounds and a few small provincial parks along this route.

South-east of Nakusp, Hwy 6 heads to Castlegar and Nelson, past Slocan Lake and Valhalla Provincial Park, which has hiking trails and wilderness camping. The area has remnants of Japanese internment camps and Doukhobor settlements. Slocan Lake provides excellent canoeing and Slocan River, from the town of Slocan south to the Kootenay River, has Grade 3 rapids in its upper sections for the white-water canoeist and less-demanding water further down.

About 12 km north-east of Nakusp, off Hwy 23, are the pleasant Nakusp Hot Springs, open year round; there's a busy campground close by with full facilities including showers and sites for $8.50.

## CASTLEGAR

Castlegar, a town of just over 6000, sits on the Kootenay River at the southern end of Lower Arrow Lake, at the junction of the Crowsnest Hwy and Hwy 22. The Travel Infocentre (☎ 365-6313), 1995 6th Ave, is open year round. The post office (☎ 365-7237) is at 1011 4th St, and Greyhound Bus Depot (☎ 365-7744) at 365 Columbia Ave.

This is an area where many members of the Russian Christian pacifist sect – the

Doukhobors – settled at the beginning of the century. There is a reconstructed **Doukhobor village** to visit and a museum with a restaurant next door serving Doukhobor specialities. Seventeen km north-west of Castlegar, on Lower Arrow Lake, is 2¼-sq-km **Syringa Creek Provincial Park**, open from April to October. It has hiking, fishing, swimming, sailing and beaches. The campground is open May to October with sites for $12.

## TRAIL

Trail is an industrial town 27 km south-west of Castlegar, at the junction of the Crowsnest Hwy and Hwy 3A. It's home to Cominco, the world's largest smelter of silver, zinc and lead, whose buildings dominate the skyline. The Travel Infocentre (☎ 368-3144), 843 Rossland Ave, is open year round. The post office (☎ 364-2585), is at 805 Spokane St and the Greyhound Bus Depot (☎ 368-8400), at 1355 Bay St.

There are free tours of the **Cominco mine** which can be booked through the Travel Infocentre. You can also visit the **Italian Community Archives** (☎ 368-3144) in Columbo Lodge, 584 Rossland Ave, which records the history of Italian migrants who came here at the end of the last century to work in the mines. Off Hwy 3B, about four km north-west of Trail via Rossland, is the **Red Mountain Ski Resort** (☎ 362-7384 in Rossland) which has 30 downhill runs with a vertical drop of 850 metres and cross-country trails.

There are several provincial parks close by. Try **Nancy Greene Provincial Park**, north of Red Mountain; or **Champion Lakes Provincial Park**, north-west of Trail, off Hwy 23. Both have hiking, swimming, fishing and campsites. Nancy Greene, a former Canadian Olympic medal winner, remains one of the country's best known ski heroes.

## NELSON & AROUND

Nelson, 43 km north-west of Castlegar, at the junction of Hwy 6 and Hwy 3A, is beautifully situated on the shore of Kootenay Lake

surrounded by the Selkirk Mountains. The very picturesque town, nestled in the hillside, with over 350 carefully preserved and restored turn-of-the-century buildings, was chosen as the location of Steve Martin's 1986 film *Roxanne*. A large artists' colony lives here so there are lots of arts & crafts available.

Baker and Vernon Sts are the two main downtown thoroughfares. Baker St has many shops and restaurants, while Vernon St has government buildings including city hall, the courthouse and the post office. In summer the Travel Infocentre (☎ 352-3433), 8 Hall St, is open Monday to Friday from 8.30 am to 6 pm, Saturday and Sunday from 9 am to 5 pm; it closes on weekends the rest of the year. The post office (☎ 352-3538), 514 Vernon St, is open Monday to Friday from 9 am to 4.30 pm. The Greyhound Bus Depot (☎ 352-3939), 1112 Lakeside Drive, is in the Chacko Mika Mall.

In town there's a walking trail through **Lakeside Park**, or, using the *Heritage Walking Tour* leaflet from the Travel Infocentre, you can take a look round the town's historical buildings. There are good views from the top of **Gyro Park**. **Tram No 23**, one of the town's original trams, has been restored and now follows a track beside the lake from the bridge near Lakeside Park to the wharf at the bottom of Hall St.

One of the main attractions of this area is skiing. You can go downhill skiing at **Morning Mountain**, north-west of town, off Hwy 3A; or at **Whitewater Ski Area**, 19 km south-east, off Hwy 6. The latter also has well-developed cross-country skiing; for wilderness skiing head for **Kokanee Glacier Provincial Park**, to the north-west, off Hwy 31.

Other attractions in the region include swimming, hiking, fishing and camping at **Kokanee Creek Provincial Park**; visiting the old sternwheeler SS *Moyie* in **Kaslo** on Kootenay Lake; hiking, boating, swimming, fishing and backcountry camping in **Valhalla Provincial Park**; visiting the ghost town at **Sandon** near Silverton; taking the free ferry ride between Balfour and

Kootenay Bay on Kootenay Lake; and swimming at **Ainsworth Hot Springs** on Hwy 31, or exploring the **Cody Caves** four km further north.

### Places to Stay

*Allen Hotel* (☎ 352-7573), 171 Baker St, is an associate-HI hostel with 10 air-con rooms some with a kitchen (you must provide your own utensils). It also has a laundry and, because of its small size, it's best to book ahead. It costs $13 for members and $15 for nonmembers. For B&Bs check the leaflets at the Travel Infocentre or contact Lake City B&B Registry (☎ 352-5253), 624 Baker St, which has rooms starting at $35/45. There are many motels along the highway at the northern end of town, and some hotels downtown. One of cheapest is the *Lord Nelson Hotel* (☎ 352-7211), 616 Vernon St, with singles/doubles from $49/54. Rooms are clean and have TVs and telephones and there's a bar and coffee shop.

# North-Eastern British Columbia

North-Eastern BC is a largely undeveloped, sparsely populated region dominated by the Rocky Mountains to the west and south and by the Interior Plain to the north and east. Much of it is inaccessible except by aeroplane.

Two major highways connect this region with other parts of the country: east-west the Yellowhead Hwy runs between the Alberta border and Prince Rupert in the Pacific North-West; Hwy 97 connects the south of the province with Dawson Creek where it becomes part of the Alaska Hwy and heads north-west toward the Yukon. The two highways meet at Prince George, the largest town in the region. Hwy 29 connects the major settlements circling Dawson Creek. The VIA Rail line follows the Yellowhead Hwy.

Like the south-eastern corner of the prov-

ince the area around Dawson Creek is on Mountain Standard Time.

### PRINCE GEORGE

Prince George, 'The Gateway to the North', is not an interesting town but does serve as a useful crossroads point. BC Rail and VIA Rail meet here, as do the Fraser and Nechako rivers, the Yellowhead Hwy and Hwy 97. The town of nearly 70,000 people sprawls over a large area. To serve the through traffic there are dozens of motels and several hotels. Pulp and paper is an important industry. The prices are high in this area – you'll notice it most in the restaurants.

### Orientation & Information

Hwy 97 from Cache Creek cuts through the centre of town on its way north to Dawson Creek and the Alaska Hwy. Hwy 97 between Cache Creek and Prince George is also known as the Cariboo Hwy and is part of the Goldrush Trail, which begins north of Hope. The Yellowhead Hwy (Hwy 16) runs east-west through town: westward is the long, winding route to Prince Rupert on the coast; eastward, it goes through Jasper to Edmonton. From Prince George, it's 377 km to Jasper, 734 km to Prince Rupert and 781 km to Vancouver.

The downtown area is small, with little character. The main roads running east-west are 2nd, 3rd and 4th Aves, parallel to the train tracks. The main north-south thoroughfare is Victoria St, which forms part of the Yellowhead Hwy; Patricia Blvd, which becomes 15th Ave, is also a main street.

The Travel Infocentre (☎ 562-3700), 1198 Victoria St on the corner of Patricia Blvd, is temporarily closed while a new office is being built, but it should be open by the time you read this. There's another infocentre (☎ 563-5493) south of the downtown area, on the corner of Hwy 97 and the Yellowhead Hwy. It operates during summer, when it is open daily from 9 am to 8 pm. The main post office (☎ 561-5184), 1323 5th Ave, on the corner of Quebec St, is open Monday to Friday from 8.30 am to 5 pm.

Mosquito Books (☎ 563-6495), 1209 5th Ave on the corner of Dominion St, has a good selection of travel guides and maps. There's a laundromat on George St near the corner of 2nd Ave.

## Things to See & Do

At **Fort George Regional Museum** (☎ 562-1612), in Fort George Park, south-east of the downtown area, on the corner of 20th Ave and Queensway, you can see a number of stuffed animals, some Carrier, Cree and Kwakiutl artefacts and a few pioneer left-overs. It's open daily from 9 am to 5 pm and admission is by donation. There are many parks in Prince George. One close to the downtown area is **Cottonwood Island Nature Park**, north between the railway tracks and the river. Prince George Pulp & Paper Mills (☎ 563-0161) runs tours for which you can register at the Travel Infocentre.

Around Prince George there are dozens of lakes and rivers with good fishing. Some have camping sites; most have boats for hire. **Hart Highlands** (☎ 962-8006), Winslow Drive, is the closest downhill ski area being within the city limits. There's also good downhill skiing (including at night) at **Mt Tabor** (☎ 963-7542), about 25 km east of town and at **Purden Lake Provincial Park** (☎ 565-7777), 50 km east on the Yellowhead Hwy. Cross-country skiing is available close to downtown on **Cottonwood Island** or further out at **Eskers Provincial Park** north-west of town. Many of the cross-country trails become good hiking trails in summer; pick up the booklet *Prince George & Area Hiking Guide* from the Travel Infocentre for details of some of these.

## Places to Stay

*Prince George Municipal Campground* (☎ 563-8131), 4188 18th Ave, opposite Exhibition Park, south-west of the downtown area, is open May to early September. It has hot showers, and a site for two people is $11.25. *Purden Lake Provincial Park* (☎ 565-6340) has sites for $9.50. There are a few private campgrounds. *Spruceland*

*KOA* (☎ 964-7272) is about six km south-west of town, off the Yellowhead Hwy. It has full facilities and sites from $15 for two people. *Bee Lazee Campground* (☎ 963-7623), on Hwy 97 south of Prince George, has full facilities including free hot showers and laundry, with sites from $10.

**B&Bs** The Travel Infocentre has lists of B&Bs. *Adrienne's B&B* (☎ 561-2086), 1467 Fraser Crescent off 15th Ave, is reasonably close to the downtown area. Singles/doubles are $35/45.

**Hotels** Many of the cheaper hotels are in or around George St. The *National Hotel* (☎ 564-7010), 1201 1st Ave, on the corner of Dominion St, one block from the VIA Rail station, is alright for a low-budget place. Singles/doubles are $30/32.50. On the ground floor is a popular restaurant and a bar with live country music at night. *Prince George Hotel* (☎ 564-7211), 487 George St, is better. Singles/doubles cost $35.65/38; all rooms have a TV. There's music in the bar at night. The *Simon Fraser Inn* (☎ 562-3181), 600 Quebec St, has air-con rooms with TV for $60, which includes breakfast. It has a bar downstairs and free parking.

**Motels** One of the cheapest is the *Hi-Way Motel* (☎ 564-6869), 1737 20th Ave, with rooms starting at $30/36; for ones with air-con it's $38/40. *Downtown Motel* (☎ 563-9241), 650 Dominion St, has air-con and TV and singles/doubles from $34/38. The *Slumber Lodge* (☎ 563-1267), 910 Victoria St, is clean and has a laundry as well as the usual features. Breakfast is included in the room price of $55/60.

## Places to Eat

There aren't many places to eat at in the downtown area, though the older hotel bars usually serve a decent cheap meal that goes well with a beer.

Recommended is *Java Jigga Mocha*, on the corner of George St and 3rd Ave, which serves fruit juices, varieties of coffee from $1 and soups from $2.60 as well as delicious

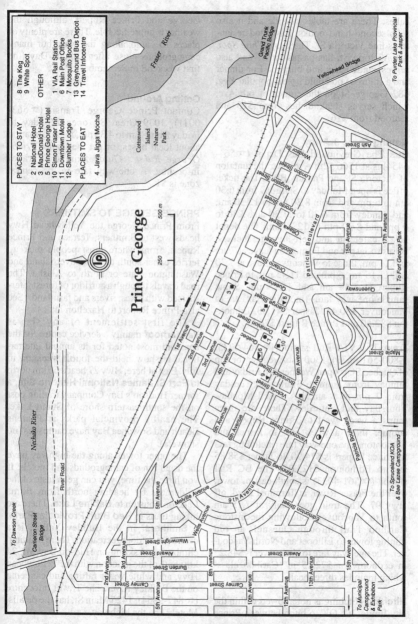

## Prince George

**PLACES TO STAY**
2  National Hotel
3  MacDonald Hotel
5  Prince George Hotel
10  Simon Fraser Inn
11  Downtown Motel
12  Slumber Lodge

**PLACES TO EAT**
4  Java Jigga Mocha

8  The Keg
9  White Spot

**OTHER**
1  VIA Rail Station
6  Main Post Office
7  Mosquito Books
13  Greyhound Bus Depot
14  Travel Infocentre

cakes. There are tables outside and it also sells second-hand books. Fast-food restaurants line Victoria St. The busy *White Spot*, 820 Victoria St, has pastas for $7 and also serves sandwiches and burgers. For dinner and a splurge you could try the popular *Keg*, 582 George St on the corner of 6th Ave, which serves steak dishes from $15 and seafood from $16.

### Getting There & Away
**Bus** The Greyhound Bus Depot (☎ 564-5454) is at 1566 12th Ave, near the junction of Victoria St and Patricia Blvd. The ticket office is open Monday to Saturday from 6.30 am to 6 pm and from 8.30 pm to 12.30 am; and Sunday from 6.30 to 11.30 am, 3.30 to 6 pm and 8.30 pm to 12.30 am. The depot has a cafeteria and left-luggage lockers. Buses to Jasper and Edmonton leave at 7 am and 11 pm; those to Vancouver leave at 7.30 am, 11.15 am, 6 pm and 11.45 pm; to Prince Rupert at 8.45 am and 11.15 pm. Some sample one-way fares (including tax) are to Vancouver $80.41, Jasper $41.03, Edmonton $82.50 and Prince Rupert $76.83.

**Train** The VIA Rail station (☎ 564-5233, 1-800-561-8630), 1300 1st Ave near the top of Quebec St, is open Wednesday, Friday and Sunday from 7 pm to 3 am, and Tuesday from 7 pm to 1 am; it's closed Monday, Thursday and Saturday. There are three trains a week west to Prince Rupert and another three a week east to Jasper and Edmonton. The one-way fare (including tax) to Prince Rupert is $74.90, to Jasper $58.85 and to Edmonton $123.05. The BC Rail station (☎ 561-4033) is south-east of town, over the Fraser River, at Terminal Blvd, off Hwy 97. The train goes daily at 7.15 am south to Vancouver, following the historic Cariboo Trail through Quesnel, an old mining town, to Lillooet and North Vancouver. The one-way fare to Vancouver is $48.25 in economy or $72.25 in 'Cariboo class' which includes three meals.

**Hitching** Hitching is not allowed within the city limits. It's OK to hitch between Prince George and Prince Rupert, although the weather is unpredictable. There are plenty of places to camp along the way, but many campgrounds close after Labour Day (the first weekend in September).

### Getting Around
Contact Prince George Transit (☎ 563-0011), 1039 Great St, open Monday to Friday from 8 am to 4.30 pm, for information about local buses; or get the leaflet *Prince George Rider's Guide* from the Travel Infocentre. A one-way fare in the central zone is $1.

### PRINCE GEORGE TO SMITHERS
From Prince George the Yellowhead Hwy heads west to Smithers, Terrace and Prince Rupert, from where most people pick up ferries either south to Vancouver Island and Washington state or north to Alaska. The road travels through a corridor of forest interspersed with lakes, rivers and farmland. (See also Prince Rupert to Hazelton later.)

The first settlement of any size is **Vanderhoof** mainly a service centre for the area and most noted for its annual international airshow held the fourth weekend in July. East of here, Hwy 27 heads 66 km north to **Fort St James National Historic Site**, a former Hudson's Bay Company trading post on the south-eastern shore of Stuart Lake. The nearby provincial parks at Paarens Beach and Sowchea Bay have campsites (no showers).

The other towns along the highway have the usual run of campgrounds and motels. If you have the time, you can get a taste of the wilderness by heading north from Burns Lake or Houston to **Babine Lake**. There are hiking trails in **Red Bluff Provincial Park**.

**Smithers**, in the Bulkley Valley, is a centre for outdoor recreation. There's hiking, climbing and skiing on Hudson Bay Mt, 24 km south of the junction with the Yellowhead Hwy, and white-water rafting and canoeing on the Bulkley River. The Travel Infocentre (☎ 847-9854), 1425 Main St, has the details. Motels line the highway.

## PRINCE GEORGE TO DAWSON CREEK

As you travel north from Prince George the mountains and forests give way to gentle rolling hills and farmland, until near Dawson Creek the landscape resembles more the prairies of Alberta. For the first 150 km the road passes **Summit, Bear** and **MacLeod** lakes with provincial parks and camping along the way. North of MacLeod Lake, Hwy 39 heads north to Mackenzie which sits on the southern shores of the immense **Williston Lake**. Nearby there is skiing at **Powder King Ski Resort** (☎ 997-6323) on Azu Mountain.

From **Chetwynd** you can take Hwy 29 north past Hudson's Hope (a 20-minute drive from the eastern arm of Williston Lake) to join the Alaska Hwy north of Fort St John.

## DAWSON CREEK

Dawson Creek, a city of just under 11,000 people 412 km north of Prince George, on Hwy 97, is most notable as the starting point – 'Mile 0' – for the Alaska or Alcan (short for Alaska-Canada) Hwy. The Alaska Hwy from Dawson Creek goes via Watson Lake and Whitehorse in the Yukon all the way to Fairbanks in Alaska. The Dawson Creek Travel Infocentre (☎ 782-9595), 900 Alaska Ave, can give you the details. It's open daily in summer from 8 am to 8 pm; in winter Monday to Friday from 9 am to 5 pm. The best place to eat is the *Alaska Café & Pub*, 10209 10th St downtown near the 'Mile 0' marker. Pasta dishes start at $5.25. It also has accommodation with singles/doubles from $35/40. One traveller has recommended the *Dawson Creek Bakery*, 1019 102nd Ave, for its donuts and coffee.

## DAWSON CREEK TO YUKON

Heading north-westward from Dawson Creek, the landscape again changes as the prairies are left behind and the Alaska Hwy crosses the Peace River on its way into the foothills of the Rocky Mountains. Except for Fort St John and Fort Nelson, most of the towns on the highway usually have little more than one or two gas stations, camp-grounds or lodgings.

Fort St John's main function is as a service centre for the oil and gas industries and the surrounding farms. Big Bam Ski Hill (☎ 785-7544) north-west of town has day and night downhill skiing. The Travel Infocentre (☎ 785-6037) and the Fort St John-North Peace Museum are together at 9323 100th St, the town's main street. **Fort Nelson** has one museum at the western end of town, and shops, restaurants and motels strung out along the highway. At **Mile 244** (393 km from Dawson Creek), past Fort Nelson, the Liard Hwy (Hwy 77) heads north to the Northwest Territories.

At **Stone Mountain Provincial Park** there are hiking trails with wilderness camping and a campground with sites for $9.50. The moose in the park can often be seen eating nonchalantly by the side of road. The 'stone mountain' in question is Mt St Paul (2127 metres).

**Muncho Lake Provincial Park** has several lodging and camping areas plus wild-life (mainly goats), swimming in the emerald-green lake and hiking trails. 'Muncho' means 'big lake' in the Tagish language and at 12 km long it's one of the largest natural lakes in the Rockies. This park is part of the northernmost section of the Rockies, which, ending at Liard River 60 km north-west, do not continue northward into Yukon and Alaska. The mountains which do extend northward, the Mackenzies, are geo-logically different.

## SOUTH OF PRINCE GEORGE

South of Prince George, Hwy 97 follows the Goldrush Trail through the northern reaches of the goldrush district known as Cariboo country.

### Quesnel

Quesnel's setting at the confluence of the Fraser and Quesnel rivers, and the carefully cultivated flowers in the streets can't dis-guise the fact that this is first and foremost a logging town. The pulp mills dominate the townscape and the smells coming from them permeate the air. However, it's worth stop-ping at the Travel Infocentre (☎ 992-8716),

---

**Cariboo Trail**
Between 1858 and 1861 the Cariboo Trail, now Hwy 97, was pushed north from Kamloops to Quesnel. It was lined with hastily built towns and gold prospectors came from around the world. In 1862, a Cornishman, Billy Barker, hit the jackpot, making $1000 in the first two days of his claim. Soon Barkerville sprang up, to become the largest city west of Chicago and north of San Francisco. The big boom was instrumental in British Columbia's becoming a crown colony in 1858. ■

---

703 Carson Ave, to get the lowdown on the area's main attractions, Barkerville Historic Park, Bowron Lake Provincial Park and Alexander Mackenzie Trail.

### Barkerville Historic Park
This restored goldrush town is 89 km east of Quesnel at the end of Hwy 26.

Today, you can see Barkerville as it was, with its general store, hotel, shops and, of course, saloon. In the Theatre Royal, dancing shows are staged in the manner the miners once whistled at. There is also a museum that gives some of the background story and displays artefacts. It's open daily in summer from 8 am to 8 pm. Try your luck panning for gold at the site and maybe you'll have a town named after you. Admission to the park is $5.50.

There are two campgrounds with sites for $12, and facilities include showers. Or you could stay at Wells, eight km west of Barkerville, which has a commercial campground and several motels. There's no bus to Barkerville so you'll have to hitch if you don't have a car.

### Bowron Lake Provincial Park
There is an excellent circular canoe route in Bowron Lake Provincial Park, near Barkerville. A number of lakes, separated by rapids and portages, form a connecting route around the perimeter of the park. The 116-km route takes an average of seven days to complete, no more than 50 individuals are allowed to start the route each day and canoeists must register at the park registration centre before heading out. Canoe rentals are available. Mountains in and around the park are about 2000 metres high. Access to the park is along a gravel road that leaves Hwy

26 just before you get to Barkerville. There are tent sites for $9.50.

### Alexander Mackenzie Trail
Heading north-west from Quesnel, this refurbished route follows ancient trails from the Fraser River west to Bella Coola, on the Pacific Ocean. Mackenzie made the first recorded crossing of continental North America on this route in 1793 in his search for a supply route to the Pacific Ocean. His graffiti can still be seen carved in a rock near Bella Coola. This 420-km trail winds its way through forest and mountains and is a tough 16-day walk. At least one food drop is required. You can do some of the more accessible segments for a few days: for example, the section through the southern end of Tweedsmuir Provincial Park. For detailed trail guides contact Alexander Mackenzie Trail Association, PO Box 425, Station A, Kelowna, V1Y 7P1.

# Pacific North-West

North-West BC is a huge, little-developed, scarcely populated region whose remoteness is one of its main attractions. It's dominated by forest, several mountain ranges and scores of lakes and rivers. The Yellowhead Hwy runs east to Prince George; the mostly-gravel Cassiar Hwy heads north to the Yukon.

### PRINCE RUPERT
After Vancouver, Rupert, as it's called, is the largest city on the BC coast. Originally built in the early 1900s as the western terminal of the Grand Trunk Pacific Railway, it's now

the fishing centre for the Pacific North-West, but its port also handles timber, minerals and grain. Once known as the world's halibut capital, it has adopted a new title, the 'City of Rainbows', which is one way of saying that it rains a lot. Despite this, the town's setting can look magnificent and when it's not raining, misty, foggy or under heavy cloud you'll appreciate it. Surrounded by mountains, sitting at the mouth of the Skeena River, looking out at the fjord-like coastline, the area is ruggedly beautiful.

Prince Rupert is a good starting point for trips to Alaska and the Queen Charlotte Islands. Many people, mainly young, arrive here in summer looking for work; and this town with around 17,000 inhabitants fills its needs quickly. Remember, too, that with the influx of tourists, accommodation in July and August can be difficult to find.

## Orientation & Information

Prince Rupert is on Kaien Island and is connected to the mainland by a bridge. The Yellowhead Hwy passes right through the downtown area, becoming McBride St then 2nd Ave which, along with 3rd Ave, forms the downtown core. McBride St divides the city between east and west. The ferry terminal is in Fairview Bay, two km south-west of town.

The Travel Infocentre (☎ 624-5637), open Monday to Saturday from 9 am to 9 pm and Sunday 9 am to 5 pm, is in the same building as the Museum of Northern BC, on the corner of 1st Ave and McBride St. There's another one at Park Ave Campground, which is south of town, about one km from the ferry terminal; it's open till midnight on nights when the ferry arrives/departs.

The Bank of Montreal (☎ 624-9191), 180-309 2nd Ave West, only charges $2 for cashing as many travellers' cheques as you wish. The post office (☎ 627-3085) is in the Rupert Square Shopping Mall on 2nd Ave West. If you need to clean some laundry try King Koin laundromat, 745 2nd Ave West on the corner of 7th St; it also has a small coffee bar. The general hospital (☎ 624-2171) is

south-west of the downtown area, in Roosevelt Park.

## Things to See & Do

The **Museum of Northern BC** (☎ 624-3207) has a good collection of Tsimshian art and craftwork, including masks, carvings and beadwork. It also has an art gallery and a room showing films on a TV screen of the history of the area. It's open the same hours as the Travel Infocentre and admission is free. The museum also organises tours to archaeological sites in the harbour. The gondola that used to take you up the 732-metre **Mt Hays** has closed and it's not known when or if it will reopen. However, there is a walking trail up to the mountain that begins at the parking lot on the Yellowhead Hwy three km from town. On a clear day you can see local islands, the Queen Charlotte Islands and even Alaska. Trails from the parking lot also go to **Mt Oldfield, Grassy Bay** and **Butze Rapids**.

Along Wantage Rd (take the turning after the civic centre), you can visit the **Oldfield Creek Hatchery** (☎ 624-6733) a small salmon hatchery. It's open daily in summer from 8 am to 4 pm and there are tours.

About 16 km east of town **Diana Lake** and **Prudhomme Lake** are two provincial parks where you can picnic, swim, fish, hike or take out a canoe. About 20 km south of Prince Rupert, **North Pacific Cannery** (☎ 628-3538), 1889 Skeena Drive, Port Edward, gives a history of fishing and canning along the Skeena River. It's open in summer daily from 10 am to 5 pm and admission is $5. Try not to say 'something smells fishy around here'.

## Places to Stay

**Camping** You can camp beside the lake at *Prudhomme Lake Provincial Park* (☎ 847-7320), open April to November, for $9.50. *Park Ave Campground* (☎ 624-5861), near the ferry terminal, has 87 sites, hot showers, laundry and flush toilets. A tent site for two people costs $10; in summer on ferry nights it's best to book ahead.

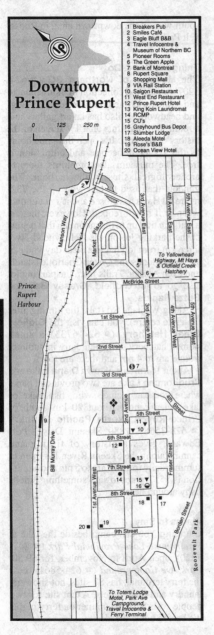

**Downtown Prince Rupert**

0    125    250 m

1 Breakers Pub
2 Smiles Café
3 Eagle Bluff B&B
4 Travel Infocentre & Museum of Northern BC
5 Pioneer Rooms
6 The Green Apple
7 Bank of Montreal
8 Rupert Square Shopping Mall
9 VIA Rail Station
10 Saigon Restaurant
11 West End Restaurant
12 Prince Rupert Hotel
13 King Koin Laundromat
14 RCMP
15 CU's
16 Greyhound Bus Depot
17 Slumber Lodge
18 Aleeda Motel
19 Rose's B&B
20 Ocean View Hotel

Manson Way

Market Place

3rd Avenue East

4th Avenue East

5th Avenue East

To Yellowhead Highway, Mt Hays & Oldfield Creek Hatchery

McBride Street

Prince Rupert Harbour

1st Street

3rd Avenue West

4th Avenue West

5th Avenue West

2nd Street

3rd Street

Bill Murray Drive

2nd Avenue

5th Street

6th Street

7th Street

8th Street

9th Street

1st Avenue West

4th Street

Fraser Street

Borden Street

Roosevelt Park

To Totem Lodge Motel, Park Ave Campground, Travel Infocentre & Ferry Terminal

BRITISH COLUMBIA

**B&Bs** There are several B&Bs in Prince Rupert: ask at the Travel Infocentre for an up-to-date list. One with a good location is *Eagle Bluff B&B* (☎ 627-4955), 100 Cow Bay Rd down by the marina. It has five rooms beginning at $40 for a single room with shared bath going up to a suite for $65 which can accommodate six people. The central *Rose's B&B* (☎ 624-5539), 943 1st Ave West, has singles/doubles for $40/50. Rose speaks French.

**Hotels** The cheapest place in town is *Pioneer Rooms* (☎ 624-2334), 167 3rd Ave East, and is the nearest thing in Prince Rupert to a travellers' hostel. Prices range from $15 to $35 for a single, double or twin room. There's a cooking area in the lobby, bathrooms are shared and it has a small café. The basic but friendly *Ocean View Hotel* (☎ 624-6259/9950), opposite Rose's B&B at 950 1st Ave West, has singles/doubles for $30/35. The shower and toilet are shared. *Prince Rupert Hotel* (☎ 624-6711), on the corner of 2nd Ave and 6th St, has air-con rooms for $66/76, a licensed restaurant and free parking.

**Motels** *Aleeda Motel* (☎ 627-1367), 900 3rd Ave West, has singles/doubles for $40/52 with free parking underneath. The *Slumber Lodge*, close by at 909 3rd Ave West, offers free breakfasts in its price of $55/60. *Totem Lodge Motel* (☎ 624-6761), 1335 Park Ave, is good but because it's close to the ferry terminal gets booked out early. Singles/doubles cost from $56/60.

### Places to Eat

Not many places open in the morning before 10 or 11 am, so those that do can get busy for breakfast. *West End Restaurant*, 610 3rd Ave West, opens early and is one of several restaurants in the same street offering Chinese as well as Western food. Cereal is $2.20 and omelettes cost from $4.20. *Charlie's* in the Prince Rupert Hotel, opens at 6 am and has continental breakfasts for $3.40.

With fishing a major local industry it's not surprising to find seafood on just about every menu. *CU's*, 816 3rd Ave West, has sandwiches and burgers starting around $5 and fish & chips for $6. Another good place for fish & chips at the same price is the *Green Apple* at 310 McBride St near the Pioneer Rooms. *Smiles Café*, 113 George Hills Way, on the waterfront, serves good steak and seafood: a main course of halibut costs $14. (Have a look in the window at the 1945 menu: hamburgers then were 25 cents.) *Saigon Restaurant*, on the corner of 2nd Ave and 6th St, adds a Vietnamese flavour to the fish on offer; soups start from $5. Two good neighbourhood pubs worth trying for a meal and a beer are *Breakers*, a busy place close to Smiles Café, and *Solly's*, at 2209 Seal Cove Rd, about four km north of the downtown area.

### Getting There & Away

**Air** Air BC (☎ 624-4554), 112 6th St, is near the Prince Rupert Hotel. Canadian Airlines (☎ 624-9181) is at 200 500 2nd Ave. With Air BC the standard one-way fare to Vancouver including tax is $322.11.

**Bus** The Greyhound Bus Depot (☎ 624-5090), in 3rd Ave between 7th and 8th Sts, is open Monday to Friday from 8.30 am to 8.30 pm, and weekends from 9 to 11 am and 6 to 8.30 pm. It has left-luggage lockers. Buses head west twice a day, at 11.15 am and 8.30 pm, buses arrive in Prince Rupert at 9.55 am and 7.25 pm. The fare, including tax, to Prince George is $76.83, while to Vancouver it's $157.240. Far West Bus Lines (☎ 624-6400), 225 2nd Ave West, has buses heading north to Cassiar.

**Train** The VIA Rail station (☎ 1-800-561-8630) is at 1150 Station St, by the harbour. The office is open Monday, Thursday and Saturday from 10 am to 4.30 pm and Tuesday, Friday and Sunday from 9 am to 12.30 pm. The inbound train arrives Monday, Thursday and Saturday at 3.40 pm; the outbound one leaves Tuesday, Friday and Sunday at 11.30 am. The standard, one-way fare to Prince George is $74.90, but if you

book seven days in advance you can get a 40% reduction.

**Ferry** From Prince Rupert, Alaska State Ferries head north through the Alaskan Panhandle. First stop is Ketchikan, but you can go north past Wrangell, Petersburg and Juneau to Skagway, where the Klondike Hwy comes south from Whitehorse in the Yukon. Various commercial cruise lines do the route as well, but they're all costly. The ferry systems are much cheaper and you'll see pretty much the same things.

Alaska State Ferries (☎ 624-1744), also called Alaska Marine Hwy, has its office – open from 7 am to 2 pm (or later if there's a delay in loading the ferry) – at the ferry terminal. The one-way fare to Skagway is $118, or $278 with a car. If you're travelling by car or RV you should book well ahead. You can go standby of course but you may not get on; if that happens your name goes on the waiting list for the next boat. If you do get on they warn you that local (that is Alaskan) traffic has precedence and they may put you off ('bump you') temporarily at one of the stops along the way. At the time of writing a new ferry terminal was being built.

The route between the Alaskan Panhandle and Washington state is known as the Inside Passage. It's a long, expensive trip but offers beautiful scenery past many bays, inlets, islands and small Native Indian settlements. It's not uncommon to see seals, herds of sea lions or pods of killer whales. You can take just part of the trip rather than the whole voyage.

BC Ferries (☎ 624-9627) run the MV *Queen of the North* from Rupert to Vancouver Island. Reservations are a good idea, especially if you're taking a vehicle. (See Getting There & Away under Port Hardy for more details.)

If you're coming from Port Hardy and you intend to continue north to Alaska by ferry then you should remember that the schedules of BC Ferries and Alaska State Ferries do not coincide and that you will have to spend at least one night in Prince Rupert.

**BRITISH COLUMBIA**

BC Ferries also operates between Prince Rupert and Skidegate in the Queen Charlotte Islands; there are five ferries a week in each direction. The one-way fare is $18, or $69 with a small car.

## Getting Around

For information about local buses contact Coastal Bus Lines (☎ 624-3343), 225 2nd Ave West. You can catch the bus from there to the ferry terminal. The one-way fare on buses is $1 and a day pass costs $2.50.

## QUEEN CHARLOTTE ISLANDS

The Queen Charlotte Islands, sometimes known as the Canadian Galapagos, are an archipelago of some 154 islands lying 80 km off the BC coast and about 50 km from the southern tip of Alaska. As the only part of Canada that escaped the last ice age, the islands are rich in flora & fauna markedly different from those of the mainland. Essentially still a wilderness area, the Queen Charlottes are warmed by an ocean current from Japan and hit with 127 cm of rain annually. All these factors combine to create a landscape of 1000-year-old spruce and cedar rainforests, abundant animal life and waters teeming with marine life.

The islands have been inhabited continuously for 10,000 years and are the traditional homeland of the Haida nation, generally

### Totem Poles

Totem is an Ojibway word meaning 'guardian spirit' or 'mark of my family'. The word refers to an object, plant, animal or natural occurrence – or its representation – believed to have some connection with a tribe, clan or family group. Originally, totem poles were house corner posts and beams with designs of these totems carved on them. Eventually the totem poles came to signify the chief's prestige which was emphasised by the poles' height and detail. Totem pole carving reached its peak in the second half of the 19th century when Native Indians were able to use the metal tools bartered from Europeans. The practice of building totem poles was most common among Native Indian peoples along the north-west Pacific coast.

Anthony Island in the Queen Charlotte Islands has the largest, original group of totem poles in the world. Until 1994, the world's tallest totem pole, at 52.7 metres, stood in Alert Bay on Cormorant Island off Vancouver Island's north-east coast. In August of that year a taller one was raised in Victoria for the opening of the Commonwealth Games. Made from a 250-year-old red cedar from the Nimpkish Valley on Vancouver Island, the 54.8-metre totem pole was given the name Spirit of Lekwammen (Lekwammen means 'land of the winds') and symbolises the speed of the athletes. The totem pole is divided into eight sections and each section was designed and carved by a different coastal Native Indian nation. The carvers from Alert Bay created the top section. ■

acknowledged as the prime culture in the country at the time of the arrival of Europeans. The arts of the Haida people – notably their totem poles and carvings in argillate (a black, glass-like stone) – are world renowned. They were also fearsome warriors who dominated the west coast.

Today the Haida are still proud, defiant people. In the 1980s they led an internationally publicised fight to preserve the islands from further logging. A bitter debate raged, but finally the federal government decided to save South Moresby and create a national park. The full name of the park is now South Moresby Gwaii Haanas National Park. Logging still goes on of course in other parts of the Queen Charlottes.

### Graham Island

About 80% of the population lives on Graham Island, the only island with any real road system. The principal towns are **Skidegate** and **Queen Charlotte**, on the south-eastern shore, and **Masset**, on the northern shore. The Travel Infocentre (☎ 559-4742) in Queen Charlotte town is open year round and has lots of information on the islands.

Near the ferry terminal in Skidegate is the Queen Charlotte Islands Museum (☎ 559-4643) with good displays on the area's history, including an excellent collection of Haida works. The Yellowhead Hwy heads 110 km north from Queen Charlotte past Tlell and Port Clements (famous for its golden spruce tree on the banks of the Yakoun River) to Masset, where you can go birdwatching at the **Delkatla Wildlife Sanctuary**, off Tow Rd, north of town.

The north-eastern corner of the island is taken up by **Naikoon Provincial Park** which has hiking, swimming and wilderness camping; most of the park's 60-km coastline is sandy beach. Scuba diving and ocean kayaking are other popular activities.

There are several commercial campgrounds on the island, and one at *Naikoon Provincial Park*, which has two campgrounds with sites for $9.50. They have toilets, water and firewood and are open all

year. The towns also have their share of B&Bs, lodges and motels but it's wise to book ahead in summer.

### Moresby Island

Most of Moresby and its neighbouring islands are accessible only by plane, boat or foot. **Sandspit**, a mainly logging town on the north coast, is the island's only permanent settlement. The Canada Parks office (☎ 637-5362), on Beach Rd, can give you information on South Moresby Gwaii Haanas National Park. There's free camping on the beach in Sandspit and a couple of B&Bs and hotels.

Tiny **Anthony Island**, near the southern end of the chain, is a provincial park and UN World Heritage Site. It protects an old Haida village, Ninstints, called the most impressive coastal Indian site in the Pacific North-West. There are 32 totem poles and remains of 10 longhouses.

### Getting There & Away

The ferry from Prince Rupert to Skidegate, the MV *Queen of Prince Rupert*, makes five trips a week, each taking 6½ hours and costing $18, or $69 with a small car. Some crossings are day trips and some overnight. Another ferry goes between Skidegate and Alliford Bay on Moresby Island; the return fare is $2.50, or $7 with a car.

## PRINCE RUPERT TO NEW HAZELTON

Prince Rupert sits near the mouth of the **Skeena River** and east out of town the Yellowhead Hwy follows the river, with some magnificent scenery of lakes, forests and mountains, and camping in provincial parks along the way. There are rest areas where you can stop for a while and take it all in.

**Terrace**, 147 km east of Prince Rupert, sitting in a valley surrounded by mountains, is a logging, service and transport centre. Hwy 16 becomes Keith Ave through town. The Travel Infocentre (☎ 635-4689/2063), 4511 Keith Ave just south and east of downtown, is open daily in summer from 9 am to 8 pm and has lots of information on the region. The Greyhound Bus Depot (☎ 635-7676) is nearby at No 4620.

About 35 km west of Terrace there is downhill and cross-country skiing at **Shames Mountain**. In **Kitimat**, south of Terrace, at the end of Hwy 37, there are free tours of the Alcan Aluminium Smelter and Eurocan Pulp & Paper Mill. At **Nisga'a Memorial Lava Bed Provincial Park**, north of Terrace, you can go fishing or hiking, but there's no camping.

North of New Hazelton, off the Yellowhead Hwy, is **K'san**, a restored village of the Gitksan people who are known for their craftworks in gold, silver and hardwood. There are longhouses, totem poles and examples of their tools, and K'san dancers perform traditional dances.

## CASSIAR HWY

Between Terrace and New Hazelton, the Yellowhead Hwy's northern tributary, Hwy 37, goes to Meziadin Junction and Stewart. The part of Hwy 37 extending north from Meziadin Junction is known as the Cassiar Hwy (also called the Stewart-Cassiar Hwy) and meets the Alaska Hwy in the Yukon.

The Cassiar is a mostly gravel road and passes through some beautiful countryside at places like **Spatsizi Plateau Wilderness Park** and **Dease Lake**. The highway is about 750 km long and there aren't many service stations along the way, so if you're driving, make sure the vehicle is in good working condition and take spare parts and extra gasoline. Flying gravel can crack the windscreen or headlights and dust can severely restrict your vision so treat approaching vehicles with caution especially logging trucks.

### Stewart & Hyder

From Meziadin Junction it's 67 km west to Stewart on the Alaskan border. On the way you pass **Bear Glacier**, 49 km from Stewart; there's a rest area where you can view the glacier. From Stewart the road goes straight through to Hyder in Alaska: there are no immigration or customs and Hyder accepts Canadian money except in the post office. At

**Fish Creek**, about three km past Hyder, between late July and September you can see salmon swimming upstream to spawn and bears coming to feed on them.

In Stewart *Stewart Lions Campground* (☎ 636-2537) on 8th Ave has sites for $10. There are only two motels and one hotel, all with similar prices; book for all three at the *King Edward Hotel* (☎ 636-2244), on 5th Ave. Singles/doubles cost from $51/58. In Hyder you can stay at the *Grizzly Bear Lodge*.

*Seaport Limousine Service* (☎ 636-2622), PO Box 217, Stewart, operates a bus to Terrace. There's one a day in each direction Monday to Friday; the trip takes four hours and costs $26.75.

## Spatsizi Plateau Wilderness Park

In this vast wilderness which includes the Spatsizi Uplands, the Stikine Plateau and the headwaters of the Stikine River, you can hike, canoe, raft or go horse riding. In the park **Gladys Lake Ecological Reserve** is home to Stone's sheep, mountain goats, moose, grizzly and black bears, caribou and wolves.

## Mt Edziza Provincial Park

This park has a volcanic landscape featuring lava flows, cinder cones and fields and an extinct shield volcano. It's accessed by gravel road from Dease Lake to Telegraph Creek and has hiking trails and wilderness camping.

## Stikine River

The Stikine River, which cuts through the glacier-capped Coast Mountains to Alaska and the Pacific Ocean, is one of the best rivers for wilderness white-water canoeing. In the upper reaches some rapids are Grade 5. The section west of the Cassiar Hwy as far as Telegraph Creek is considered unnavigable and you must pre-arrange to be picked up when you reach the Pacific Ocean.

## ATLIN

This small, remote town in the north-western corner of the province is reached by road via the Yukon. Take Hwy 7 south off the Alaska Hwy; from the junction of the two highways it's 60 km to the town. It sits at the edge of Atlin Lake, the largest body of freshwater in

BC which is surrounded by the huge icefields and glaciers of the Northern Coast Mountains. Atlin Provincial Park is to the south.

**BRITISH COLUMBIA**

# The Yukon & Northwest Territories

Canada's northern territories make up a vast tract of land stretching from the northern boundaries of the provinces to within 800 km of the North Pole and from the Atlantic Ocean to the Pacific Ocean. A third ocean, the Arctic, links Alaska and Greenland across the many islands of the far north.

For the most part, this land of the midnight sun is as reputation has it: a barren, treeless tundra that's nearly always frozen. But it is definitely not all this way. There are mountains and forests, abundant wildlife and warm summer days with 20 hours of light. In general, the development of the far north has occurred where conditions are most hospitable and the land most varied and scenic. Fortunately, these places are still the most accessible and tourism increases each year.

The designation of the Yukon and Northwest as territories rather than provinces is a political one. Because they have relatively small populations, the territories have not been given full status in parliament.

## Yukon Territory

Area: 483,450 sq km
Population: 31,500
Territorial Capital: Whitehorse

Some say God was tired when He made it;
Some say it's a fine land to shun;
Maybe; but there's some as would trade it
For no land on Earth – and I'm one.
**From *The Spell of the Yukon* by Robert Service**

The Yukon is a triangular slice of northern Canada wedged between the Northwest Territories and Alaska. To the south is British Columbia; the north is bounded by the Beaufort Sea in the Arctic Ocean. It's a sub-Arctic region about one-third the size of Alaska. Mountain ranges, including some that continue from the Rockies, almost entirely cover the Yukon. Forests, wooded hills, lakes and streams flow and grow amidst the mountains.

Most of the population lives in towns, about two-thirds in the Whitehorse region. The bulk of the rest live in and around mining camps. By far the majority of the people are White. The Dene (pronounced 'de-NAY' and meaning 'person'), or Athapaskans, number around 3000. They and the Inuit are

---

**The North Pole**
The North Pole, the imaginary point at the northern tip of the Earth's axis and about 800 km north of Ellesmere Island, lies in neutral territory – an area of permanently frozen water without national jurisdiction. However, the Magnetic North Pole, the direction to which a compass needle points at an angle to true north, is in Canada. Although it wanders around from year to year, the Magnetic North Pole is currently just north of Bathurst Island west of Cornwallis Island at about 100° longitude. In 1966 it was south of the island, in 1979 it was on the island and now it is just beyond the northern end of the island. At some point it will begin to shift southward again if history is indeed repeated. ■

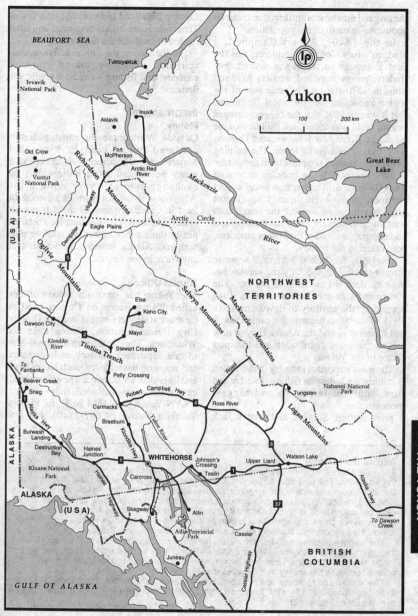

Yukon

0    100    200 km

BEAUFORT SEA

Tuktoyaktuk

Ivvavik
National Park

Inuvik

Aklavik

Old Crow

Fort
McPherson

Arctic Red
River

Richardson

Vuntut
National Park

Mountains

Mackenzie

Great Bear
Lake

(U S A)

Ogilvie

Mountains

Dempster

Eagle Plains

Arctic   Circle

River

NORTHWEST
TERRITORIES

Elsa
Keno City

Mayo

Highway

Dawson City

Klondike
River

Tintina Trench

Stewart Crossing

Selwyn Mountains

Mackenzie

Mountains

To
Fairbanks

Beaver Creek

Snag

Pelly Crossing

Robert   Campbell   Hwy

Carol   Road

Nahanni National
Park

Tungsten

Carmacks

Braeburn

Ross River

Logan Mountains

ALASKA

Burwash
Landing

Destruction
Bay

Haines
Junction

Klondike Hwy

Yukon River

WHITEHORSE

Johnson's
Crossing

Upper Liard

Watson Lake

Alaska Hwy

Kluane National
Park

Carcross

Teslin

ALASKA

(U S A)

Haines

Highway

Skagway

Atlin

Atlin Provincial
Park

Cassiar

To Dawson
Creek

Juneau

Cassiar Highway

BRITISH
COLUMBIA

GULF OF ALASKA

THE YUKON

the original inhabitants and together make up about one-seventh of the population.

In the 1840s, Robert Campbell, a Hudson's Bay Company explorer, was the first European to travel the district. Fur traders, prospectors and whalers followed him. In 1870 the area became part of the region known as the Northwest Territories. But it was in 1896 that the biggest changes began. Gold was found in a tributary of the Klondike River near what became Dawson City and all hell broke loose. The ensuing gold rush attracted hopefuls from around the world. The population boomed to around 38,000 – quite a bit higher than today's – and transport routes were opened up. Towns grew overnight to support the rough-and-ready wealth-seekers, but it was the suppliers and entertainers, rather than the prospectors, who raked in the money.

In 1898, the Yukon became a separate territory with Dawson City the capital, but the city declined as the gold ran out. The construction of the Alaska Hwy in 1942 opened up the territory to development. In 1953 Whitehorse became the capital, for it had the railway and the Alaska Hwy; it now acts as the main distribution and transport centre of the Yukon.

The most important industry in the Yukon is mining, and, despite fishing, forestry and furs, tourism is the second-biggest moneymaker.

Poet Robert Service and writer Jack London both lived and worked in the Yukon. Their words are highly respected and often recited throughout the territory.

For the visitor, the Yukon offers outdoor activities – camping, hiking, climbing, canoeing and fishing – amidst a scenic wilderness.

## INFORMATION
### Money
Outside Whitehorse the most generally accepted credit card is Visa, then MasterCard. US currency is accepted at many hotels and retail outlets, but the exchange rate can vary quite a bit. Whitehorse is the last town going north (at least in Canada) where the food is not too pricey. At Inuvik, for example, costs are nearly three times higher, so take supplies with you. Alaska, however, is cheaper than anywhere in the Yukon.

### Tourist Offices
The Yukon has six main tourist offices, called Visitor Reception Centres (VRCs): these are at Beaver Creek, Carcross, Dawson City, Haines Junction, Watson Lake and Whitehorse. They're all open from mid-May to mid-September. As well as information and maps on the territory, each has exhibits and laser-disc TV displays. They even broadcast their own combined radio service, CKYN Yukon Gold (FM 96.1), for visitors. Tourism Yukon (☎ 667-5340), PO Box

### Aurora Borealis
The aurora borealis can be seen from the Yukon, the Northwest Territories and in the far north of the provinces. The best time to see it is around March and April and from late August to late October. It appears in many forms – pillars, streaks, wisps, haloes of vibrating light and sometimes looks like the rippling folds of a curtain. Most often, the aurora borealis glows faintly green or pale rose, but during periods of extreme activity it can flare into bright yellows and crimsons.

The aurora borealis is commonly known as the northern lights, while in the southern hemisphere the phenomenon is known as the aurora australis or southern lights.

The visible aurora is created by solar winds (streams of charged particles from the sun) flowing through the earth's magnetic field in the polar regions. These winds are drawn earthward where the particles collide with electrons and ions in the ionosphere about 160 km above the earth. This collision releases the energy which creates the visible aurora.

The Inuit and other groups attach a spiritual significance to the aurora. Some consider it to be a gift from the dead to light the long polar nights, while others believe it to be a storehouse of events past and future. ■

2073, Whitehorse Y1A 2C6, sends out free information on the territory. Particularly useful is its free brochure *Canada's Yukon*, published annually, which has information on activities, events, accommodation and travel.

### Telephone
The telephone code for the territory is the same as Alberta's – 403.

### Time
The Yukon is on Pacific Standard Time.

### Maps
Topographical maps of the territory are available in Whitehorse from:

Jim's Toy & Gift
    208 Main St, Whitehorse Y1A 2A9 (☎ 667-2606)
Northern Affairs Program
    Geological Services, 200 Range Rd, Whitehorse Y1A 3V1 (☎ 667-3100)
Tourism Industry Association of the Yukon
    Suite 102, 302 Steele St, Whitehorse Y1A 2C5 (☎ 668-3331)
Yukon Gallery
    2093 2nd Ave, Whitehorse Y1A 2C6 (☎ 667-2391)

You can also get them from Canada Map Office (☎ 613-952-7000), 130 Bentley Ave, Nepean, Ontario K2E 629.

### Health Warning
If you're drinking water from lakes or streams boil it for at least 10 minutes. The lakes and streams may contain the intestinal parasite *Giardia lamblia* which causes giardiasis. If you're camping take some insect repellent with you.

### ACTIVITIES
The Yukon VRCs can supply you with general descriptions and specific information on hiking, canoeing, rockhounding, gold prospecting, climbing, skiing, fishing and various adventure tours. There are outfitters and tour companies to cover all these activities. Adventure trips range from white-water rafting to backpacking to do-it-yourselfers which provide no more than advice or drop-off and pick-up. There are places where you can rent canoes or boats in various parts of the territory. You don't need an organised trip and don't need to be wealthy to enjoy camping, hiking or canoeing in the Yukon.

For hiking, the most well-known trail is the Chilkoot Trail and there are other good ones in Kluane and Ivvavik national parks. Canoeists can travel the fast-flowing waters of the Yukon River and its tributaries, or face the challenge of white-water rivers like the Tsatshenini.

### ACCOMMODATION
If you rent or buy a recreational vehicle (RV), you've not only got a means of transport, but a place to stay as well. The Yukon government's series of campgrounds is good, with many along the highways; most have drinking water. There are also numerous private grounds which offer hook-ups, showers and laundry facilities; some of these campgrounds are geared strictly to the RV market.

### GETTING AROUND
The major towns in the Yukon are connected by air and bus (see the Getting There & Away sections for Whitehorse and Dawson City for details).

### Road
Driving your own vehicle is the best way to get around, and there are car and RV rental outlets in Whitehorse.

The road system in the Yukon is fairly extensive, if rough. Remember that most roads are gravel, apart from the Alaska and Klondike highways which are paved. The main highways in the Yukon are the Klondike, the Dempster and the Alaska. The Yukon VRCs have information on the highways, what there is to see from them and road conditions. Roads connect most southern towns. To the north the Dempster Hwy connects Dawson City with Inuvik in the

THE YUKON

Northwest Territories (see the Dempster Hwy section later).

A good circular trip is to travel the Klondike Hwy from Whitehorse to Dawson City, then take the Top of the World Hwy to the Alaska border. From the border, take the Taylor Hwy south to Tetlin Junction in Alaska and then follow the Alaska Hwy north-west to Fairbanks. On the way back take the Alaska Hwy south-east past Beaver Creek, Kluane National Park and Haines Junction to Whitehorse.

There are campgrounds along most of the highway routes. Keep your headlights on at all times.

**Gasoline** Gasoline prices along the highways are pretty outrageous so it's worth filling up at cheaper places even if you don't need to. It's a good idea always to have some spare too. Generally, along the main routes, there's a service station every 50 km, but in some areas there may be no competition for 150 km or more. Prices are lower in the main towns than they are out on the stretches, but they can vary considerably for no apparent reason.

Three places where gasoline is not so expensive are Dawson Creek in British Columbia, Whitehorse and Dawson City. Gasoline is very expensive in Inuvik.

## WHITEHORSE

Whitehorse, on the banks of the Yukon River, is by far the largest town in the territory. In fact its official city limits cover 421 sq km, making it one of the largest urban-designated areas in Canada, although the town itself is quite small. Whitehorse is on the Alaska Hwy about halfway between Dawson Creek in British Columbia, where the highway starts, and Fairbanks in Alaska. The city has a population of around 24,000 and the people are condescendingly known as 'southerners' by those living in the more northerly areas of the territory. Despite its growth Whitehorse still has something of a frontier feel about it.

### Orientation

Whitehorse stretches for several km along the banks of the Yukon River. The Alaska Hwy passes through the city although it bypasses the city centre which is reached by South Access Rd or Two-Mile Hill Rd. Downtown is designed on a grid system and

PLACES TO STAY

1   Sourdough City RV Park
2   Family Hotel
5   Fort Yukon Hotel
9   98 Hotel
10  Regina Hotel
11  Westmark Whitehorse Hotel
21  Gold Rush Inn
22  Town & Mountain Hotel
32  Fourth Ave Residence

PLACES TO EAT

3   Qwanlin Mall
7   Mom's Kitchen
8   China Garden
15  No Pop Sandwich Shop
17  Talisman Café
19  Sam 'n' Andy's
28  The Deli

OTHER

4   Greyhound Bus Depot
6   Prospect Yukon
12  MacBride Museum
13  MV *Youcon Kat*
14  Donnenworth House
16  City Information Centre
18  WP&YR Train Station
20  Northern Outdoors
23  Mac's Fireweed Books
24  Main Post Office
25  Old Log Church Museum
26  Log Skyscrapers
27  Klondyke Medical Building
29  Yukon Conservation Society
30  Yukon Transportation Museum
31  Visitor Reception Centre
33  Whitehorse General Hospital
34  SS *Klondike*

THE YUKON

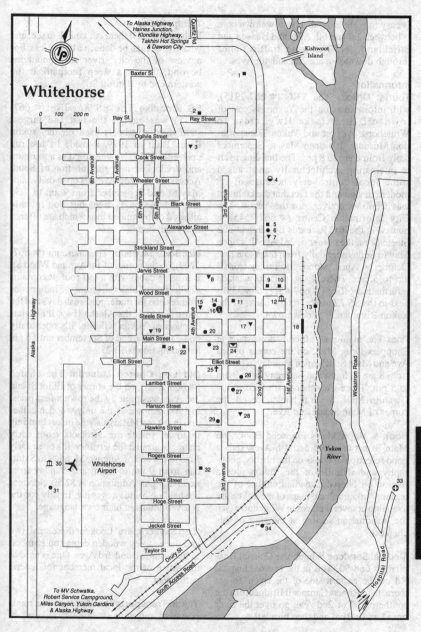

# Whitehorse

0    100    200 m

is easy to walk around. The downtown core is between 1st and 6th Aves and Hanson and Strickland Sts. The main traffic routes through downtown are 2nd and 4th Aves.

## Information
**Tourist Offices** The VRC (☎ 667-2915), with information on the Yukon, is east of town off the Alaska Hwy, close to Whitehorse Airport and Yukon Transportation Museum. It's open May to September daily from 8 am to 8 pm. The building itself is interesting architecturally and caused some local controversy because of its modern design and the fact that the architect was from Vancouver, not the Yukon. The City Information Centre (☎ 667-7545) is housed in the T C Richards Building at 302 Steele St on the corner of 3rd Ave. It's open May to September daily from 8 am to 8 pm; October to April, Monday to Friday from 9 am to 5 pm. There's also a Parks Canada information office (☎ 667-4511, 668-3398) next to the SS *Klondike*, on the banks of the Yukon River south of downtown.

**Post** The main post office is downstairs at Shoppers Drug Mart, on the corner of 3rd Ave and Main St. It's open Monday to Friday from 8 am to 6 pm and Saturday from 9 am to 5 pm. There's another post office in the Qwanlin Mall. Several banks are on the corner of Main St and 2nd Ave.

**Book & Maps** Mac's Fireweed Books, on Main St between 3rd and 4th Aves, sells a good selection of books on the history, geography and wildlife of the Yukon plus a section on Native Canadian culture of the region. Topographical maps of the Yukon are available at several places in Whitehorse (see the Information section at the start of this chapter).

**Medical Services** Whitehorse General Hospital (☎ 668-9333) is at the end of Hospital Rd on the eastern side of the river. To get there, take Robert Campbell Bridge from the southern end of 2nd Ave, go over the river onto Lewes Blvd and then turn left.

## Things to See
In the town itself there isn't much to see, and what there is can be done in a day or less. For a view of the city, river and mountains beyond, there's a steep footpath at the western end of Hanson St.

**SS Klondike** The SS *Klondike* (☎ 667-4511) was one of the last and largest sternwheel riverboats used on the Yukon River. Built in 1929, it made its last run upriver in 1955. Now restored as a museum and drydocked near the junction of South Access Rd and 2nd Ave, it's open daily mid-May to mid-September from 9 am to 7.30 pm. Admission is free, but you're only allowed on by guided tour which are offered every half hour.

**MacBride Museum** This museum (☎ 667-2709), on the corner of 1st Ave and Wood St, is in a log cabin with a turf roof. It contains a collection of materials from the indigenous cultures, the fur trade, gold-rush days and the construction of the Alaska Hwy. It also has displays of Yukon wildlife. It's open daily mid-May to the end of September until 6 pm and admission is $3.25.

**Old Log Church Museum** The church (☎ 668-2555), on the corner of Elliot St and 3rd Ave, was built by the town's first priest in 1900. Known as the only wooden cathedral in the world, it is also the oldest building in town. Inside are artefacts from early churches around the territory. It's open early June to the end of August, Monday to Saturday from 9 am to 8 pm and Sunday from noon to 4 pm. Admission is $2.50. Services are held on Sunday evening, mostly for the Native Indians in their own language.

**'Log Skyscrapers'** Look for these small two and three-storey wooden cabins on Lambert St between 2nd and 3rd Aves. One is used as the office of the local member for federal parliament.

**Yukon Transportation Museum** The transportation museum (☎ 668-4191), east of town at Whitehorse Airport, features the history of transport in the territory. It's open daily July to the end of August from 10 am to 7 pm. Entry is $2.

**Yukon Gardens** The Yukon Gardens (☎ 668-7972) are on South Access Rd close to the Alaska Hwy, about three km south-west of town. The gardens, covering almost nine hectares, have large displays of wild plants and flowers that can only be found in the north, plus vegetables and fruit trees. The gardens are open daily mid-May to mid-September from 9 am to 9 pm and admission is $5.

**Takhini Hot Springs** These hot springs (☎ 633-2706) are about 27½ km north-west of town on the Klondike Hwy. You can rent bathing suits and towels for 50 cents each. The springs are open daily all year, from 8 am to 10 pm. Admission is $3.50.

### Activities

In the area around Whitehorse you can go hiking and cycling, particularly at **Mt McIntyre Recreation Centre** and at **Grey Mountain** east of town and **Miles Canyon** south of town. The hiking trails become cross-country ski trails in winter.

Northern Outdoors (☎ 667-4074), 208A Main St, sells outdoor equipment and has a noticeboard with details of outdoor activities offered in the region.

### Organised Tours

The Yukon Historical & Museums Association (☎ 667-4704) at Donnenworth House, 3126 3rd Ave between Wood and Steele Sts, conducts free guided walking tours daily of the downtown area.

The Yukon Conservation Society (☎ 668-5678), 302 Hawkins St, offers free nature walks in the area on weekdays during July and August.

From early June to mid-September there are two-hour boat trips on the MV *Schwatka* down through Miles Canyon from Schwatka Lake south of town. The fare, including bus transfer to the lake, is $22. Contact Gray Line

Yukon (☎ 668-3225), in the Westmark Whitehorse Hotel for bookings. Gray Line Yukon also has two bus tours of the Whitehorse area. The four-hour, grand city tour which takes you around the city and out to the Yukon Wildlife Preserve costs $26.50. (You can only visit the preserve as part of an organised tour.) Atlas Tours (☎ 668-3161) also in the Westmark Whitehorse Hotel does a similar tour for $30 lasting 3½ hours. The MV *Youcon Kat* (☎ 668-2927) does a 2½-hour trip on the Yukon River for $15. It leaves from opposite the MacBride Museum.

If you'd like to do something more adventurous then there are plenty of opportunities. Atlas Tours can take you on a six-hour, hands-on, rafting trip of the Blanchard and Tsatshenini rivers for $100. Sportslodge (☎ 668-6848), in the Hougen Centre on Main St, offers kayaking and canoeing courses from beginners to advanced on Chadburn Lake and the Yukon and Wheaton rivers. A beginner's course starts at $80 for one day. Cloudberry (☎ 668-3890) offers similar courses.

Prospect Yukon (☎ 667-4837), 2159 2nd Ave next to Mom's Kitchen, offers guided wilderness canoe trips starting at $99 for one day and going up to 12 days.

### Places to Stay

**Camping** *Robert Service Campground* (☎ 668-8325) is one km south of town on South Access Rd. It's open late May to early September and has toilets, showers and firepits. The campground is closed between midnight and 7 am. A tent site, of which there are 40, costs $8. *Sourdough City RV Park* (☎ 668-7938), at the northern end of 2nd Ave, past the Greyhound Bus Depot, has a laundry and free showers. It's mainly for RVs but you can put up a tent on the patches of grass behind the office for $10. *Pioneer RV Park* (☎ 668-5944), eight km south of Whitehorse on the Alaska Hwy, has drinking water, laundry and showers and tent sites for $8.

You can camp at *Takhini Hot Springs* (☎ 633-2706), about 27½ km north-west of town on the Klondike Hwy, for $7 (plus $2 for power), and have the benefit of having the hot springs close by. South of Whitehorse there is a Yukon-government campground at Wolf Creek (16 km) and one at Marsh Lake (50 km); sites cost $8.

**B&Bs** The City Information Centre keeps brochures of B&Bs in and around Whitehorse. *Barb's B&B* (☎ 667-4104), 64 Boswell Crescent, south of downtown on the eastern side of the river, has two rooms with private bathroom. A single/double costs $55/60 and includes a complimentary evening snack. *International House B&B* (☎ 633-5490), 17 14th Ave in Porter Creek, north of downtown, has the same facilities and prices.

**Hotels & Motels** For a smallish town, Whitehorse has plenty of hotels and motels but most of them are not cheap. About $60 to $75 a single is average. Generally speaking, the smaller places cost less. *Fourth Ave Residence* (☎ 667-4471), 4051 4th Ave, is a hotel that offers hostel-type accommodation and a 10% discount if you're a member of HI. A bed in a shared room is $18 while a single costs $38/46 without/with bath. The hotel is in the process of being renovated.

*98 Hotel* (☎ 667-2641), 110 Wood St, is basic but central and cheap, with a single room for $35 with shared bath, or others for $45 with bathroom. The hotel has a bar which closes at 11 pm. *Fort Yukon Hotel* (☎ 667-2594), 2163 2nd Ave, is another relatively inexpensive place, with singles from $40 to $59 depending on facilities. The cheaper ones are the noisiest (because of the traffic and the bar next door) while the more expensive rooms have been refurbished.

The *Family Hotel* (☎ 668-5558), on Ray St, has singles for $60 with private bathroom and TV. There's a laundromat and 24-hour restaurant attached. Close to 98 Hotel is the more up-market *Regina Hotel* (☎ 667-4243), 102 Wood St, with a licensed restaurant and heated underground parking. All rooms have private baths, and singles/doubles cost from $62/76. *Town &*

*Mountain Hotel* (☎ 668-7644), 401 Main St, has 30 rooms, with singles/doubles at $90/95. There's a licensed restaurant and a piano bar. The top hotel in town is the *Westmark Whitehorse Hotel* (☎ 668-4700), on the corner of 2nd Ave and Wood St, which has 181 rooms and is home to the Frantic Follies revue.

**Places to Eat**
Food is more costly here than it is further south but not greatly so. There are several fast-food outlets and Chinese restaurants and most of the hotels have restaurants or dining rooms.

*Mom's Kitchen*, in a log cabin at 2157 2nd Ave near Fort Yukon Hotel, is good for breakfast. Sandwiches and omelettes with toast and hash browns cost from $6; three-course Chinese lunches are available for $7.50. It's open daily from 6.30 am. Paintings line the wall of the clean, popular *Talisman Café*, 2112 2nd Ave, between Steele and Main Sts. French toast is $5.95 and sandwiches start from $5.50.

*The Deli*, 203 Hanson St, is reasonably priced at around $3 to $5 for light meals of soups, salads or homemade sausages. It's closed on Sunday. The *No Pop Sandwich Shop*, 312 Steele St, serves good food. The sandwiches have interesting names like Beltch, Roman or Tel Aviv and cost around $4; vegetarian burgers are $4.25. It has a patio out the back. The *Alpine Bakery* next door serves great bread.

*Sam 'n' Andy's*, 506 Main St, is a licensed restaurant serving good Mexican food, with a garden in the front. Nachos cost $7.25 and main dishes are from $7.50 to $15.

Twenty-four varieties of pizza are available at *G&P Pizza House* in the Kopper King complex next to the Petro Canada gas station on the Alaska Hwy. The pizzas aren't cheap with most small ones costing between $10 and $12, but on the other hand one small one is probably big enough to feed two people. It has another outlet at 95 Lewes Blvd in the southern suburb of Riverdale. *China Garden*, 309 Jarvis St, has chicken and seafood dishes from $10, chow mein from

$8 and special lunch-time buffets. It's closed on Sunday.

## Entertainment

Strictly for the tourists is The Frantic Follies, an 1890s-style revue with comedy skits, dancing girls and the poetry of Robert Service. The show is held nightly in the *Westmark Whitehorse Hotel* through the summer and tickets cost $17.50. You book through Gray Line Yukon in the hotel.

*Robert Service Campground* has regular poetry readings.

If you want a taste of what the locals do for entertainment head for the *Roadhouse Saloon* next to the Fort Yukon Hotel. It has country & western musicians playing most nights.

## Things to Buy

Northern Images (☎ 668-5739), on 4th Ave between Jarvis and Wood Sts, is owned and run by Native Canadians and sells crafts made by the Inuit and Native Indians.

## Getting There & Away

**Air** Whitehorse Airport is east of town off the Alaska Hwy. Canadian Airlines (☎ 668-3535) has a daily service to Calgary, Edmonton and Vancouver. The standard one-way fare including taxes to Edmonton is $812; to Vancouver it's $532. Cheaper advance-purchase fares are sometimes available.

Air North (☎ 668-2228) connects Whitehorse with Dawson City and Old Crow, and the Alaskan towns of Fairbanks, Anchorage and Juneau. The one-way fare to Dawson City is $290. Alkan Air (☎ 668-6616; 1-800-661-0432) goes to places within the Yukon and to Inuvik in the Northwest Territories; the standard return fare to Inuvik is $780 plus tax but there are weekend excursion return rates of $585 plus tax.

**Bus** The Greyhound Bus Depot (☎ 667-2223/2772), 2191 2nd Ave, is open Monday from 8 am to 5.30 pm, Tuesday to Friday from 5 am to 5.30 pm, Saturday from 5 am to noon and Sunday from 5 to 9 am. Greyhound buses leave daily to Edmonton and Vancouver; the one-way fare to Edmonton is $222.40, to Vancouver $280. Cheaper tickets are available if you book seven days in advance.

Norline Coaches (☎ 668-3355) runs one bus daily in the summer (twice a week in winter) to Dawson City from the Greyhound Bus Depot for $72.76 (including tax) one way. Northwest Stage Line (☎ 668-6975) has buses to Kluane National Park, Beaver Creek, Faro, Ross River in the Yukon and to Skagway and Anchorage in Alaska. Gray Line of Alaska (☎ 667-3225; 1-800-544-2206) operates Alaskon Express buses to Skagway, Tok, Anchorage, Fairbanks and Haines in Alaska and other communities along the way. The one-way fare to Fairbanks is US$149, to Anchorage US$179. Some journeys involve an overnight stop so you'll need to add the cost of accommodation to the fare.

Alaska Direct Busline (☎ 668-4833; 1-800-288-1305 after hours) has buses to Anchorage, Skagway, Fairbanks and points in between.

**Train** There is a privately owned, 177-km, narrow-gauge railway line called the White Pass & Yukon Route (WP&YR) that connects Whitehorse with Skagway, Alaska. The trip is an interesting one over rough terrain. It has a good historical angle, too: the line opened in 1900 to feed the gold rush.

The train relied heavily on fees raised from transporting ore from mines, but with the fall in world metal prices the line was closed from 1982 until 1988. Currently the line only operates between Skagway and Fraser in northern British Columbia, from where a connecting bus takes you to Whitehorse. The train departs daily from Skagway at 12.45 pm and arrives in Whitehorse at 6.30 pm; from Whitehorse the bus leaves at 8.15 am, and the train arrives in Skagway at 12 noon. The one-way fare is US$92 (about $120 Canadian).

For information and bookings contact

THE YUKON

Whitehorse Travel (☎ 668-5598) in the Klondyke Medical & Dental Building on the corner of 3rd Ave and Lambert St; or Atlas Tours (☎ 668-3161) in the Westmark Whitehorse Mall.

**Car** Whitehorse is connected with Watson Lake in the east and Haines Junction and Beaver Creek in the west by the Alaska Hwy. The Klondike Hwy (Hwy 2) heads south to Carcross then to Skagway in Alaska; north of Whitehorse the Klondike Hwy connects the city with Stewart Crossing and Dawson City.

Cars can be rented from the following rental companies:

Budget
    4178 4th Ave (☎ 667-6200; 1-800-268-8900)
Hertz
    4158 4th Ave (☎ 667-2505; 1-800-263-0600)
Tilden
    2089 2nd Ave (☎ 668-6872)
Norcan
    Mile 917.4, Alaska Hwy (☎ 668-2137; 1-800-268-8900)

### The Alaska Highway

The construction in 1942 of the Alaska Hwy is one of the major engineering feats of the 20th century. Canada and the USA had originally agreed to build an all-weather highway to Fairbanks from the south as early as 1930, but nothing serious was done about it until WW II. Japan's attack on Pearl Harbor, then its bombing of Dutch Harbor in the Aleutians and occupation of the Aleutian islands of Attu and Kiska increased Alaska's strategic importance. Japan's military successes gave it near military control of the Pacific and made a full-scale invasion of North America's west coast seem likely. The US army was told to prepare for the highway's construction a month before Canada's prime minister signed the agreement granting the USA permission to do so.

The route chosen for the highway followed a series of existing airfields – Fort St John, Fort Nelson, Watson Lake and Whitehorse – known as the Northwest Staging Route. This route was used by US pilots as part of the Lend-Lease programme to ferry aircraft north to Fairbanks where the aircraft were then picked up by Soviet crews who flew them to Siberia.

Thousands of US soldiers and Canadians, including Native peoples, built the gravel 2450-km highway between Dawson Creek in British Columbia and Fairbanks in Alaska. They began work on 9 March 1942 and completed it before falling temperatures (in what was to be one of the worst winters in recorded history) could halt the work. Conditions were harsh: sheets of ice rammed the timber pilings; floods during the spring thaw tore down bridges; bogs swallowed trucks, tractors and other heavy machinery; in the cold months the road crews suffered frostbite while in the summer they were preyed on by mosquitoes, blackflies and other biting insects.

In spite of these hardships the single-lane pioneer road was completed at the remarkable average rate of 12 km a day, the road crews meeting, a little over eight months after construction began, at Contact Creek close to the British Columbia and Yukon border.

The Alaska Hwy was officially opened on 20 November at Soldiers' Summit (Mile 1061) overlooking Kluane Lake in the south-west corner of the Yukon. Five US soldiers and eight Royal Canadian Mounted Police constables all dressed in uniform lined up facing a red, white and blue ribbon stretched across the road. The ribbon was cut by US congressman E L Bartlett and Ian MacKenzie, a member of Canada's federal parliament. The following year the Canadian Public Roads Authority made it an all-weather road.

Several reasons were put forward to explain why the original road had so many curves and slopes. One is that they were constructed deliberately to prevent Japanese pilots from landing their aircraft. But it's more likely, with speed so essential and with the bulldozers right behind them, that surveyors didn't have time to pick the best route.

In April 1946 the Canadian part of the road (1965 km) was officially handed over to Canada. In the meantime private contractors, under the control of the Public Roads Authority, were busy widening, gravelling and straightening the highway; levelling its steep grades; and replacing temporary bridges with permanent steel ones. In 1949 the Alaska Hwy was opened to full-time civilian travel. For the first time year-round overland travel to Alaska from the south of the

The daily rate with Tilden starts from $38, with the first 100 km free and 14 cents for each subsequent km.

**Taxi** Whitehorse has four cab companies and the two most central are: 5th Ave Taxi (☎ 667-4111), 102 3211 3rd Ave, and Yellow Cab (☎ 668-4811), 2160 2nd Ave.

**Getting Around**
**Bus** Whitehorse Transit (☎ 668-8381), 110 Tlingit St, operates buses Monday to Satur-

day; there are no buses on Sundays or public holidays. The one-way fare is $1.25 but a day pass for $3 allows unlimited travel. If you're going to the airport take the Hillcrest bus from Qwanlin Mall. For schedules and routes, get a copy of the city bus guide from the City Information Centre.

## ALASKA HIGHWAY
The Alaska Hwy (also called the Alcan Hwy), the main road in the Yukon, is about 2400 km long and starts in Dawson Creek,

continent was possible. The completion of the highway opened the north-west to exploitation of its natural resources, changed settlement patterns and altered the Native way of life forever.

The name of the highway has gone through several incarnations. In its time it has been called the Alaskan International Hwy, the Alaska Military Hwy and the Alcan (short for Alaska-Canadian) Hwy. More irreverently, in the early days it was also known as the Oil Can Hwy and the Road to Tokyo. Officially, it is now called the Alaska Hwy but many people still affectionately refer to it simply as the Alcan.

The Alaska Hwy begins at the Mile Zero cairn in Dawson Creek in north-eastern British Columbia. It then heads north-west through Whitehorse the capital of the Yukon to Fairbanks in Alaska.   Actually the highway officially ends at Delta Junction (Mile 1422) about 155 km south-east of Fairbanks (Mile 1523). Between the two you follow the Richardson Hwy which comes north from Valdez in Prince William Sound.

Milepost signs were set up in the 1940s to help drivers calculate how far they had travelled along the road. Since then improvements and straightening of the road mean that its length has been shortened and the mileposts can't be used literally. On the Canadian side the distance markers have been written in km since the 1970s when that country went metric. Mileposts are still much in evidence in Alaska, and communities on both sides of the border still use the original mileposts for postal addresses and as reference points.

Until the mid 1970s conditions along the highway were extremely difficult. Traffic had to face loose gravel (which could puncture petrol tanks or crack windscreens and headlights) and dust stirred up by other vehicles, and sparsely strung-out services. Travellers also had to take plentiful supplies of food, clothing, gasoline and spare parts for their vehicle. Today the highway is almost completely surfaced except for stretches where road crews are doing maintenance work on potholes and frost heaves (raised sections of bitumen caused by water freezing below the road), and there are services every 50 km or so. Millions of dollars are spent annually maintaining and upgrading the road.

Although it's possible to travel the highway year round most visitors go between May and September when the weather is warmer and road conditions less hazardous. All the attractions, services and accommodation are open then too. During this time the traffic noticeably increases, particularly the number of RVs. In winter the number of vehicles dwindles and the road is left mostly to logging, oil and mining trucks, other commercial traffic and to military transports transferring personnel between postings.

As you travel the highway you see some magnificent scenery. North-west from Dawson Creek you pass through flat, rich, agricultural land growing, cereal and canola (a hybrid of rapeseed). Toward Fort Nelson then beyond to Watson Lake and Whitehorse in the Yukon the scenery gives way to coniferous forests, tundra, lakes, icefields and mountains as you cross the Rocky, Cassiar and Coast ranges. Between Whitehorse and Fairbanks the highway skirts the St Elias, Wrangell and Alaska mountain ranges. From the road you can catch sight of many forms of wildlife including black and grizzly bears, coyotes, moose, eagles and, if you're lucky, snowy owls. ■

THE YUKON

British Columbia. It enters the Yukon in the south-east and passes through Watson Lake, Whitehorse, Haines Junction and Beaver Creek en route to Fairbanks, Alaska. A joint project between the USA and Canada, it was built in 1942 as part of the war effort and was originally known as the Alaska-Canada Military Hwy. Now, each summer, it's very busy (some even say clogged) with visitors, mainly driving RVs. At times there are 10 of these homes-on-wheels for every car or truck. Services for gasoline, food and lodging occur at regular intervals along the highway.

The highway is nearly all paved except for a few stretches where road construction is taking place. On these stretches the biggest problems are dust and flying stones from other vehicles: slow down and keep well to the right. Potholes too can be a problem. A bug and gravel screen is recommended, as are covers for your gasoline tank and lights, a spare tyre, fan belt and hose.

Hitching on the highway is good, especially in summer when there are more vehicles. However, be prepared for the occasional long wait – it's a good idea to carry a tent, some food, water and warm clothing.

### Watson Lake

Originally named after Frank Watson, a British trapper, and now billed as the 'Gateway to the Yukon', Watson Lake is the first town in the territory as you head north-west on the Alaska Hwy from British Columbia. The town stretches out along the highway. The VRC (☎ 536-7469), at the junction of the Alaska and Robert Campbell highways, has an excellent video show on the history of the territory and the Alaska Hwy. The centre is open mid-May to mid-September daily from 8 am to 8 pm.

The town is most famous for its **Signpost Forest** just outside the VRC. The original signpost of 'Danville, Illinois' was put up in 1942 by the homesick Carl Lindlay, a US soldier working on the construction of the Alaska Hwy. Other people added their own signs and now there are around 20,000. As part of the celebrations of the 50th anniver-

sary of the Alaska Hwy, Carl Lindlay returned to Watson Lake in 1992 for the first time since the war. Now you can have your own sign made on the spot.

The Canteen Show, a recreation of a 1940s US army show, takes place in the military tent next to the Signpost Forest; call ☎ 536-7782 for information.

Twenty-six km west of Watson Lake is the junction with the Cassiar Hwy which heads south into British Columbia.

### Teslin

Teslin, on the Nisutlin River about 280 km west of Watson Lake, began as a trading post in 1903 set up to serve the Tlingit people. The George Johnston Museum (☎ 390-2550) has photographs, displays and artefacts on the Tlingit people and from the gold-rush days. It's open May to September daily from 10 am to 8 pm, and admission is $2. There's canoeing and camping at nearby Teslin Lake.

### Johnson's Crossing & Canol Rd

About 53 km north of Teslin, is Johnson's Crossing at the junction of the Alaska Hwy and Canol Rd. During WW II, the US army built the Canol pipeline at the same time as the Alaska Hwy, to pump oil from Norman Wells in the Northwest Territories to Whitehorse. The only services on Canol Rd are in Ross River at the intersection with the Robert Campbell Hwy. The road ends near the Northwest Territories' border; to go any further you have to hike the Canol Heritage Trail (see the Northwest Territories section later).

### Haines Junction

Haines Junction, just outside Kluane National Park, is reached by the Alaska Hwy from Whitehorse or by the Haines Hwy (Hwy 3, also called Haines Rd) from Haines in Alaska. The VRC (☎ 634-2345), on Logan St, has information about the park including an audiovisual display, and organises guided walks into the park. It's open mid-May to mid-September daily from 9 am to 9 pm. There's also a visitor centre (☎ 841-5161) at Sheep Mountain north-west of Haines Junction. The village has a post office, service stations, two campgrounds and several motels and lodges. The *Village Bakery & Deli*, opposite the VRC, is a good place to eat and keeps the same hours as the centre in summer.

## Kluane National Park

Kluane National Park is a rugged wilderness area covering 22,015 sq km that sits in the extreme south-western corner of the Yukon adjacent to Alaska's Wrangell-St Elias National Park. Kluane means 'many fish' and is pronounced 'klu-AH-nee'.

The park is very mountainous: Mt Logan, part of the St Elias Range, is, at 5950 metres, Canada's highest mountain; Mt St Elias, at 5488 metres, is Canada's second highest. Within the park there are valleys, lakes, alpine forest and tundra plus the world's largest non-polar icefields, remnants of the last ice age. Winters are long and harsh while summers are short; generally temperatures are comfortable from mid-June to mid-September, which makes that the best time to visit.

Fishing is good and wildlife abounds, including moose and thousands of Dall sheep which can be seen on Sheep Mountain even from the road. There are also grizzly bears, a small herd of caribou and 150 varieties of birds, among them the rare peregrine falcon and eagles.

The scenery makes for excellent hiking. There are several good trails, some following old mining roads, others traditional Native Indian paths. There's a hiking trail leading to **Kaskawulsh Glacier** – one of the few that can be reached by foot. The leaflet *Hiking in Kluane National Park* has a map and lists the trails with distances and starting points. You can buy topographical maps at the VRC. Hikers should take precautions to avoid attack from bears (for details see Dangers & Annoyances in the Facts for the Visitor chapter).

The St Elias Range provides excellent climbing and mountaineering.

The only campground within the park is at Kathleen Lake, 24 km south of Haines Junction off the Haines Hwy. It's open from mid-June to mid-September and costs $8 for an unserviced site. There are several other campgrounds just outside the park. Of course, you can try backcountry tenting along overnight trails.

## Soldiers' Summit

Near the Sheep Mountain Visitor Centre, from the parking lot off the highway, a path leads up to Soldiers' Summit, site of the official opening of the Alaska Hwy, on 20 November 1942. From the site there are good views overlooking Kluane Lake.

## Destruction Bay

This small village of about 50 people sits on the shore of Kluane Lake about 108 km north of Haines Junction. Like Burwash Landing and Beaver Creek, it started off as a camp and supply depot during the construction of the Alaska Hwy. It was given its present name after a storm tore through the camp. You can go boating or fishing on the lake and the village has a gas station, campground and motel.

## Burwash Landing

Sixteen km north of Destruction Bay, Burwash Landing is most noted for the **Kluane Museum** (☎ 841-5561), which has displays on natural history and the Southern Tutchone people or Dan as they call themselves (they are part of the family of Dene, or Athapaskan peoples). It also has tourist information. The museum is open mid-May to early September daily from 9 am to 9 pm and admission is $3.

## Beaver Creek

Beaver Creek, Canada's westernmost town, is on the Alaska Hwy 457 km north-west of Whitehorse close to the Alaska border. The VRC (☎ 862-7321), open mid-May to mid-September daily from 9 am to 9 pm, has information on the Yukon and Alaska. The Canadian customs checkpoint is just north of the town; the US customs checkpoint is about 30 km further west.

THE YUKON

## ATLIN (British Columbia)

The small, remote town of Atlin, 182 km south-east of Whitehorse in British Columbia, is reached by road via the Yukon – take Hwy 7 south off the Alaska Hwy. The scenery is great, with forests in Atlin Provincial Park and snowcapped mountains around Atlin Lake. (See also the British Columbia chapter.)

## ROBERT CAMPBELL HIGHWAY

From Watson Lake, this gravel road is an alternative route north to Dawson City meeting the Klondike Hwy near Carmacks. Named after Robert Campbell, a 19th-century explorer and trader employed by the Hudson's Bay Company, it is a scenic and less-travelled road with few services. **Ross River**, 362 km from Watson Lake at the junction with the Canol Rd, is home to the Kaska people and supply centre for the local mining industry. It has a campground and a couple of motels. There's also a small government campground 13 km further west at Lapie Canyon.

Near the mining town of **Faro**, 10 km off the Robert Campbell Hwy, you can tour the Anvil Dynasty Mine (the largest in the Yukon), which produces copper, lead and zinc. Contact Curragh Resources (☎ 994-2600) for details. (The mine was closed temporarily in 1993 and may have reopened again by the time you read this.) The road between Faro and the Klondike Hwy can be busy with trucks from the mine.

## KLONDIKE HIGHWAY

The 716-km Klondike Hwy from Skagway in Alaska, through the north-western corner of British Columbia to Whitehorse and Dawson City, more or less traces the trail some 40,000 gold seekers took in 1898. The highway, open year round, is paved most of the way but there are some long stretches of gravel where construction is taking place.

### Skagway (Alaska)

Skagway is at the southern end of the Klondike Hwy, which heads north through Whitehorse to Dawson City. The drive between Skagway and Whitehorse takes about three hours, passing lakes, mountains and meadows. A narrow-gauge railway line over White Pass, called the White Pass & Yukon Route (WP&YR), which was completed in 1900, connects the towns. (For more information on the train, see the Whitehorse Getting There & Away section.)

Skagway is the northern terminal for ferries and cruise ships plying the continental west coast. Beginning in San Francisco, Bellingham (Washington state), Vancouver, Vancouver Island and Prince Rupert, these ships edge along the coastline to Skagway. For details of ferries going south contact Alaska State Ferries (☎ 907-983-2229; 907-465-3941 in Juneau). The Alaska State Ferries company is commonly referred to as the Alaska Marine Hwy.

BC Ferries handles most of the traffic south of Prince Rupert along the Inside Passage (see the Getting There & Away sections of Prince Rupert and Port Hardy in the British Columbia chapter for more information).

### Chilkoot Trail

Skagway was the landing point for many in the gold-rush days. From there began the long, slow, arduous and sometimes deadly haul to the Klondike gold area near Dawson City. One of the old routes, the Chilkoot Trail over the Chilkoot Pass, is used today by hikers. For information packages on the trail contact the National Park Service Visitor Centre (☎ 907-983-2921), on the corner of Broadway St and 2nd Ave in Skagway; or the Parks Canada information office (☎ 667-4511, 668-3398) in Whitehorse. Before starting the hike you have to clear Canadian customs which you can do by calling ☎ 403-821-4111.

The well-marked, 53-km trail begins near Dyea, 13 km north-west of Skagway, then heads north-eastwards following the Taiya River to Bennett in British Columbia, and takes three to five days to hike. You must be in good physical condition to attempt it and come fully equipped. Weather conditions are unpredictable: take a few layers of clothes

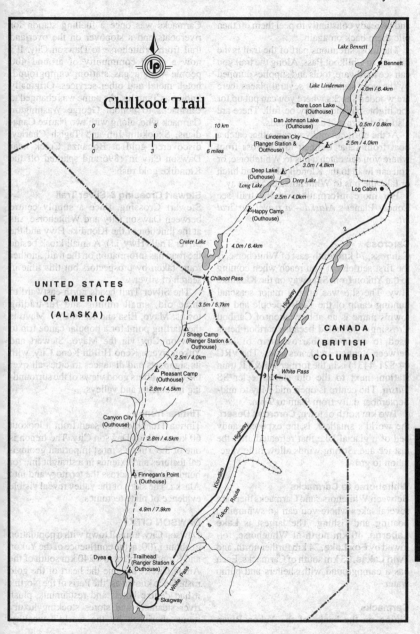

## Chilkoot Trail

0   5   10 km

0   3   6 miles

Lake Bennett

Bennett

Lake Lindeman

4.0m / 6.4km

Bare Loon Lake
(Outhouse)

0.5m / 0.8km

Dan Johnson Lake
(Outhouse)

Lindeman City
(Ranger Station &
Outhouse)

2.5m / 4.0km

3.0m / 4.8km

Log Cabin

Deep Lake
(Outhouse)

Deep Lake

Long Lake

2.5m / 4.0km

Happy Camp
(Outhouse)

Crater Lake

4.0m / 6.4km

Chilkoot Pass

UNITED STATES
OF AMERICA
(ALASKA)

3.5m / 5.7km

Sheep Camp
(Ranger Station &
Outhouse)

2.5m / 4.0km

CANADA
(BRITISH
COLUMBIA)

Pleasant Camp
(Outhouse)

2.8m / 4.5km

White Pass

Canyon City
(Outhouse)

2.8m / 4.5km

Finnegan's Point
(Outhouse)

4.9m / 7.9km

Kiondike

Yukon Route

Dyea

Trailhead
(Ranger Station &
Outhouse)

White Pass

Skagway

THE YUKON

and be ready constantly to peel them off then pile them back on again.

The most strenuous part of the trail is the hike up to Chilkoot Pass. Along the trail you can see hardware, tools and supplies dumped by the gold seekers. At several places there are wooden shacks where you can put up for the night, but these may be full. There are also 10 designated campgrounds.

At the northern end you can either catch a boat from Lake Bennett to Carcross from where you can catch a bus to Whitehorse; or you can head to the Klondike Hwy and hitch or take the bus to Whitehorse or Skagway.

For more information on the trail see Lonely Planet's *Alaska – a travel survival kit.*

### Carcross

Carcross, 74 km south-east of Whitehorse, is the first settlement you reach when coming to the Yukon from Skagway on the Klondike Hwy. The site was once a major seasonal hunting camp of the Tagish people and the town's name is an abbreviation of Caribou Crossing – so called because caribou herds used to cross the narrow strip of land between Bennett and Lares lakes. The VRC (☎ 821-4431) is in the former WP&YR train station, next to the old sternwheeler SS *Tutshi*. The centre is open mid-May to mid-September daily from 9 am to 9 pm.

Two km north of town, **Carcross Desert**, the world's smallest, is the exposed sandy bed of a glacial lake that retreated after the last ice age. Strong winds allow little vegetation to grow.

### Whitehorse to Carmacks

Between Whitehorse and Carmacks there are several lakes where you can go swimming, boating and fishing. The largest is **Lake Laberge**, 40 km north of Whitehorse, followed by **Fox Lake**, 24 km further north, and **Twin Lakes**, 23 km south of Carmacks. Each has a campground with shelters and pump water.

### Carmacks

Sitting on the banks of the Yukon River,

Carmacks was once a fuelling station for riverboats and a stopover on the overland trail from Whitehorse to Dawson City. It's now a small community of around 400 people with a gas station, campground, hotel, motel and other services. Originally known as Tantalus, the name was changed to Carmacks to honour George Washington Carmack who, along with two Native Canadians, Skookum Jim and Tagish Charley, discovered gold at Bonanza Creek near Dawson City in 1896 and sparked off the Klondike gold rush.

### Stewart Crossing & Silver Trail

Stewart Crossing, once a supply centre between Dawson City and Whitehorse, sits at the junction of the Klondike Hwy and the Silver Trail (Hwy 11). A small kiosk beside the road has information on the trail, another route taken by prospectors but this time in search of silver.

The Silver Trail heads north-eastward to three old, small mining and fur-trading towns: Mayo, Elsa and Keno City. Mayo is the starting point for a popular canoe trip to Dawson City via the Mayo, Stewart and Yukon rivers. Keno Hill in Keno City, with its signposts and distances to cities all over the world, offers good views of the surrounding mountains and valleys.

### Tintina Trench

Tintina Trench can be seen from a lookout 60 km south of Dawson City. The trench is one of the Yukon's most important geological features and extends in a straight line for hundreds of km across the territory and into Alaska. The sides of the valley reveal visible evidence of plate tectonics.

### DAWSON CITY

Dawson City, a small town with a population of about 1700, at the confluence of the Yukon and Klondike rivers just 240 km south of the Arctic Circle, became the heart of the gold rush. Once known as 'the Paris of the North', it had deluxe hotels and restaurants, plush river steamers and stores stocking luxury items cherished by the world's wealthy.

Today it is the most interesting of the Yukon towns, with many attractions remaining from its fleeting but vibrant fling with world fame and infamy. Many of the original buildings are still standing and Parks Canada is involved in restoring or preserving those considered historically significant. Regulations ensure that new buildings are built in sympathy with the old.

As many as 100 companies, employing 500 people, are still mining for gold in the region around Dawson City. In 1992 gold to the value of $33 million was found. One entrepreneur once offered to pay compensation for the complete removal of the town and the inconvenience it would cause, mine the land beneath it, then replace the town just as it was. The residents refused.

## Orientation & Information
Dawson City is small enough to walk around in a few hours. The Klondike Hwy leads into Front St (also called 1st Ave) beside the Yukon River.

On the corner of Front and King Sts is the VRC (☎ 993-5566), housed in a large wooden building. It's open daily from mid-May to mid-September between 9 am and 9 pm. Staff are dressed in turn-of-the-century costumes. Worth a look are the Klondike-era films on mining, the gold rush and other subjects shown continually in the centre. Opposite the VRC is the Northwest Territories Visitor Centre (☎ 993-5175), open daily June to August from 9 am to 9 pm, which has maps and information on the territories and Dempster Hwy.

The main post office (☎ 993-5342), on 5th Ave between Princess and Harper Sts, is open Monday to Friday from 8.30 am to 5.30 pm. If you're having any mail delivered, this is where you pick it up. The original post office still operates and is on the corner of King St and 3rd Ave. It's open from noon to 6 pm every day during the summer.

The Chief Isaac Memorial Centre, on the corner of Front and York Sts, a community centre operated by the Han people, has a laundromat and showers. The centre is open Monday to Friday from 9 am to 7 pm and at weekends from 10 am to 6 pm, but the laundromat stays open till 11 pm.

## Things to See & Do
### Diamond Tooth Gertie's Gambling Hall
This hall, on the corner of Queen St and 4th Ave, is a re-creation of an 1898 saloon, complete with gambling, honky-tonk piano and dancing girls. It's open May to September daily including most Sundays from 7 pm to 2 am and admission is $4.75.

**Palace Grand Theatre** The large, flamboyant opera house/dance hall, on the corner of 3rd Ave and King St, was built in 1899 by 'Arizona Charlie' Meadows. Like other restored buildings in town, it has a western movie-type front. There are free guided tours of the theatre.

In the theatre the Gaslight Follies presents stage shows – musicals or melodramas with villains in black and Mounties to the rescue. The shows are on every night (except Tuesday) at 8 pm from the end of May to early September and cost $11.50 or $13.50 in the balcony.

**Dawson City Museum** The museum (☎ 993-5291), on 5th Ave, houses a collection of 25,000 gold rush artefacts and displays on the district's people. Admission is $3.25 and it's open daily June to early September from 10 am to 6 pm.

**SS Keno** The SS *Keno*, one of the area's last riverboats, is on display as a National Historic Site beside the Yukon River. Admission is free.

**Midnight Dome** To the north the quarried face of this hill overlooks the town, but to get to the top you have to travel eight km outside Dawson City off the Klondike Hwy. The Midnight Dome, at 880 metres above sea level, offers good views of the Ogilvie Mountains, Klondike Valley, Yukon River and Dawson City. The hill gets its name from the fact that on 21 June the midnight sun barely sinks below the Ogilvie Mountains to the north before rising again.

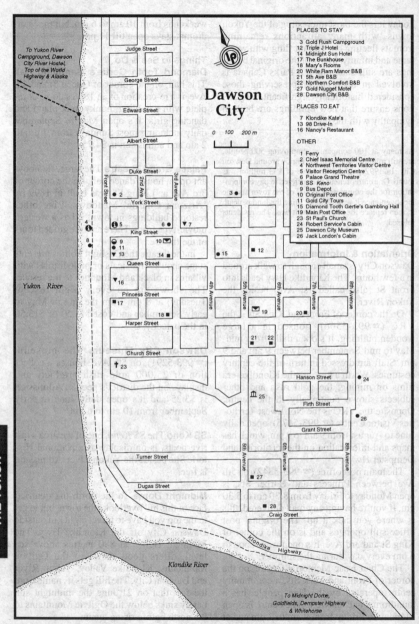

**Dawson City**

To Yukon River
Campground, Dawson
City River Hostel,
Top of the World
Highway & Alaska

Judge Street

George Street

Edward Street

Albert Street

Duke Street

York Street

King Street

Queen Street

Princess Street

Harper Street

Church Street

Hanson Street

Firth Street

Grant Street

Turner Street

Dugas Street

Craig Street

Front Street

2nd Ave

3rd Avenue

4th Avenue

5th Avenue

6th Avenue

7th Avenue

8th Avenue

5th Avenue

6th Avenue

8th Avenue

Yukon River

Klondike River

0  100  200 m

To Midnight Dome,
Goldfields, Dempster Highway
& Whitehorse

Klondike
Highway

PLACES TO STAY
3  Gold Rush Campground
12  Triple J Hotel
14  Midnight Sun Hotel
17  The Bunkhouse
18  Mary's Rooms
20  White Ram Manor B&B
21  5th Ave B&B
22  Northern Comfort B&B
27  Gold Nugget Motel
28  Dawson City B&B

PLACES TO EAT
7  Klondike Kate's
13  98 Drive-In
16  Nancy's Restaurant

OTHER
1  Ferry
2  Chief Isaac Memorial Centre
4  Northwest Territories Visitor Centre
5  Visitor Reception Centre
6  Palace Grand Theatre
8  SS Keno
9  Bus Depot
10  Original Post Office
11  Gold City Tours
15  Diamond Tooth Gertie's Gambling Hall
19  Main Post Office
23  St Paul's Church
24  Robert Service's Cabin
25  Dawson City Museum
26  Jack London's Cabin

THE YUKON

**Readings** Of literary interest are professional recitals at 10 am and 3 pm of Robert Service's poems by Tom Byrne in front of the log cabin on 8th Ave, where the former lived from 1909 to 1912. Robert Service's poems sing the praises of and hardships associated with life in the developing wilderness. Parts of 'Songs of a Rolling Stone' were written here.

In 1898, Jack London lived in the Yukon and wrote many of his popular animal stories. He is best known for *Call of the Wild* and *White Fang*. In the cabin on 8th Ave you can hear recitals from and talks about his works daily at 1 pm. Admission is free.

**Gold Panning** You can try panning for gold in nearby creeks. If you want to go on a tour contact Gold City Tours (☎ 993-5175) on Front St opposite the SS *Keno*, or Guggie Ville RV Park (☎ 993-5008) about two km south of town on Bonanza Creek Rd. Tours cost $5.75 and you're almost guaranteed to find some gold. Alternatively, you can go by car to one of the historic mining sites. Many other claims in the area are private, so pick your spot carefully. People have been killed for less!

**Organised Tours** The VRC has walking tours of the city four times daily. Gold City Tours (☎ 993-5175) has bus tours of the city, gold fields and Midnight Dome. Dawson Trading Post (☎ 993-5316) rents out canoes and offers wilderness camping trips.

**Festivals**
Events to look for include the Midnight Dome Race and the three-day Dawson City Music Festival in late July. In mid-August, there's Discovery Days, a three-day event commemorating the discovery of gold in the Klondike in 1896, featuring parades, music, dances and canoe races. In early September is the three-km Great Klondike International Outhouse Race (on wheels) – four people propel the outhouse through town while one sits on the seat!

**Places to Stay**
The growing competition to supply accommodation for Dawson City's visitors has kept prices stable.

**Camping** *Yukon River Campground* on the western side of the river has toilets, drinking water and shaded sites for $8. It's about 250 metres up the road to the left after you get off the ferry. You can also pitch a tent at the hostel – see the next section. In town, *Gold Rush Campground* (☎ 993-5247), on the corner of York St and 5th Ave, is for RVs only and has sites for $10 or $15 with electricity.

**Hostel** A new hostel has opened up, the HI-affiliated *Dawson City River Hostel* (no telephone). It operates between mid-May and early September, has cabins for two to four people, spaces for tents and cooking facilities. It also rents out bicycles and canoes. There's no electricity and you have to pay cash. It's $5 for a tent and $12.50/15 members/nonmembers for a cabin bed. Take the ferry over the river and head left up one of the two paths through the trees.

**B&Bs** The VRC keeps a folder listing the B&Bs in the Dawson City area.

*White Ram Manor B&B* (☎ 993-5772), on the corner of Harper St and 7th Ave, is a friendly, easy-going place with a laundry, kitchen and hot tub to easy those aching muscles. They'll also pick you up from the airport. Singles/doubles cost $60/70 with shared bath. *Dawson City B&B* (☎ 993-5849), 451 Craig St at the southern end of town, has singles/doubles for $59/69; lunch, dinner and transport to and from the airport are also provided. Others worth trying are *Northern Comfort B&B* (☎ 993-5271) and *5th Ave B&B* (☎ 993-5941).

**Hotels & Motels** One of the cheapest places to stay is *Mary's Rooms* (☎ 993-6013), on the corner of Harper St and 3rd Ave, which has singles/doubles with a communal bathroom for $43/53. It doesn't accept credit cards. Nor does the *Gold Nugget Motel* (☎ 993-5445), on the corner of Dugas St and

5th Ave, which is basic but cheap with rooms from $43. A better option would be *The Bunkhouse* (☎ 993-6164) on Princess St near the corner of Front St. Only opened in 1993 it has rooms for $45/50 or $75/80 with private bathroom.

More up-market is the *Midnight Sun Hotel* (☎ 993-5495), on the corner of Queen St and 3rd Ave. It has a licensed restaurant, a bar and singles/doubles for $83/93. The *Triple J Hotel* (☎ 993-5323), on the corner of Queen St and 5th Ave, occupies the whole block and has hotel rooms or log cabins (with kitchenettes) from $65.

## Places to Eat

There isn't a lot of choice in town. Many of the hotels have their own dining rooms.

There are several places along Front St. *River West* in the Chief Isaac Memorial Centre is a good place for a coffee and a sandwich ($4.50) and to catch up on some post cards. It also sells health foods. *98 Drive-In*, near the bus depot has hot dogs for $3 and fish & chips for $7.25. *Nancy's Restaurant* has outdoor tables and reasonably priced soups, salads, sandwiches and pastries from $4 to $7. It's open daily May to September from 6 am to 9 pm.

*Klondike Kate's*, next to the motel of the same name on the corner of King St and 3rd Ave, does good breakfast specials for around $4. The *China Village* restaurant in the Midnight Sun Hotel has all-you-can-eat, lunch-time buffets for $9.75.

The Han First Nation regularly puts on a salmon barbecue for $17.50 which includes an arts & crafts display. For details call ☎ 993-538 Monday to Friday.

### Getting There & Around

**Air** There is an airport 19 km east of town off the Klondike Hwy, with daily flights to Whitehorse and twice weekly ones to Inuvik in the Northwest Territories. One way to Whitehorse with Air North (☎ 993-5110) is $233.96 including tax. The flight to Inuvik with Alkan Airways (☎ 993-5440) costs $290 one way or $460 return. The flights are on Monday and Thursday; they return the following day to Dawson City. For tickets contact Gold City Tours who can also arrange transport to the airport.

**Bus** From the bus depot on the corner of Front and King Sts, Gold City Tours (☎ 993-5175) has two buses a week to Inuvik. The Arctic Tour Company (☎ 979-4100 in Inuvik) has three buses a week in each direction for $198 one way plus tax. Norline Coaches (☎ 668-3355 in Whitehorse) runs buses to Inuvik, Fairbanks and Whitehorse; the one-way fare to Whitehorse is $72.76 (including tax).

**Car** Three highways connect Dawson City with the rest of the continent: the Top of the World Hwy (Hwy 9) to Alaska; the Dempster Hwy to the Northwest Territories; and the Klondike Hwy to the southern Yukon. (See the relevant sections for details.)

### DEMPSTER HIGHWAY

The Dempster Hwy (Hwy 5 in the Yukon, Hwy 8 in the Northwest Territories) starts 40 km south-east of Dawson City off the Klondike Hwy. It heads north over the Ogilvie and Richardson mountains beyond the Arctic Circle and down to Inuvik in the Northwest

Territories near the shores of the Beaufort Sea.

The highway is named after Corporal Dempster of the Royal Northwest Mounted Police. In the winter of 1910-11, one of the coldest on record, four officers en route to Dawson City lost their way amid the Ogilvie Mountains. Dempster was sent to search for the lost patrol and he found them frozen to death near Fort McPherson, a little over 40 km from where they had begun their journey.

The highway, opened in 1979, makes road travel along the full length of North America possible. Inuvik is a long way from Dawson City – along 741 km of gravel road – but the scenery is beautiful: mountains, valleys, rivers and vast open tundra. The highway is open all year but the best time to travel is between June and September when the ferries over the Peel and Mackenzie rivers are able to operate. In winter ice forms a natural bridge over the rivers.

Accommodation and vehicle services along the route are few (at Eagle Plains in the Yukon and Fort McPherson and Arctic Red River in the Northwest Territories) so go well prepared and carry extra gasoline. The Yukon government has three basic campgrounds – at Tombstone Mountain (also called Campbell Mountain), Engineer Creek and Rock River; and there's a Northwest Territories' government campground three km south of Fort McPherson. For maps and information on road conditions ask at the Northwest Territories Visitor Centre (☎ 993-5175) in Dawson City.

### TOP OF THE WORLD HIGHWAY

At the northern end of Front St in Dawson City a free ferry crosses the Yukon River to the start of the scenic Top of the World Hwy (Hwy 9). Open only in summer, it's a gravel road which extends 108 km to the Alaska border. The small customs & immigration checkpoint is open between June and mid-September daily from 9 am to 9 pm; you can't cross outside these times. From the border, the Taylor Hwy runs south through Alaska to meet the Alaska Hwy at Tetlin Junction.

THE YUKON

## VUNTUT NATIONAL PARK

Vuntut, a Gwithch'in word meaning 'old crow flats', was declared a national park in 1993. It is south of the village of Old Crow, the most northerly settlement in the Yukon. Each spring a Porcupine caribou herd of 200,000 still follows its migration route north across the plain to calving grounds near the Beaufort Sea. In Canada these calving grounds are protected within Ivvavik National Park, but the grounds extend into Alaska where there is lobbying by oil companies to open them up for exploration.

With its many lakes and ponds Vuntut National Park is visited by around 500,000 waterbirds each autumn. Archaeological sites contain fossils of ancient animals like the mammoth, plus evidence of early human occupation.

The only access to the 4400-sq-km park is by aeroplane or foot.

## IVVAVIK NATIONAL PARK

Formerly the Northern Yukon National Park, Ivvavik, situated along the Beaufort Sea and adjoining Alaska, covers 10,170 sq km. The park is dominated by the British Mountains and its vegetation is mainly tundra. It's on the migration route of the Porcupine caribou (see above) and is also a major waterfowl habitat. Its facilities are minimal and, though there's no road access, flights on one of the small regional airlines will get you there.

Off the coast is **Herschel Island**, the Yukon's first territorial park. A former whaling station, it is rich in bird and other wildlife.

# Northwest Territories

Area: 3,426,320 sq km
Population: 57,700
Territorial Capital: Yellowknife

Stretching 3200 km from the Yukon in the west to Greenland in the east, the Northwest Territories cover an enormous area, about a third of Canada. The territories have a population density of around one person per 60 sq km. That's a lot of breathing room. Nearly half the region is north of the Arctic Circle and includes many islands in the Arctic Ocean.

The territories are divided into three districts: Mackenzie, Franklin and Keewatin. The District of Mackenzie in the west is the only one accessible by road and is the most developed, containing the territories' largest towns of Yellowknife, the capital, and Inuvik. The District of Franklin to the north and east includes the huge islands of Baffin and Ellesmere. The District of Keewatin is bordered in the south by the provinces of Manitoba and eastern Saskatchewan and in the east by Hudson Bay.

Given the ever fluctuating fortunes in natural resources, the territories are relying more each year on tourism as a money-earner. Increased accessibility, together with the lure of pristine wilderness, means a continuing rise in the number of visitors to the territories. Other sources of income include fish, fur and handicrafts.

## HISTORY

The earliest known inhabitants of the Northwest Territories, the Dene, or Athapaskans, came to the region from Asia somewhere between 10,000 and 40,000 years ago. The Inuit are thought to have arrived between 4000 and 8000 years ago.

The Vikings were the first Europeans to see the Northwest Territories, arriving in about 1000 AD. Later the search began for the legendary Northwest Passage – a sea passage from the Atlantic Ocean to the Pacific Ocean and the shortest route to China and its riches. Canada was thought of as merely a stopping-off point on the way to Asia. From 1524, British, French and Dutch adventurers all joined the search for a waterway through the continent. Many died but the north was mapped out in the process.

The first successful navigation was made in 1906 by Roald Amundsen. Since then, several others have done it, mostly in

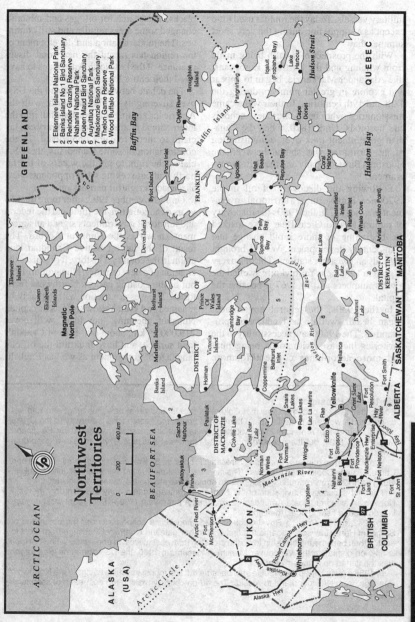

Northwest Territories

1 Ellesmere Island National Park
2 Banks Island No 1 Bird Sanctuary
3 Reindeer Grazing Reserve
4 Nahanni National Park
5 Queen Maud Bird Sanctuary
6 Auyuittuq National Park
7 Mackenzie Bison Sanctuary
8 Thelon Game Reserve
9 Wood Buffalo National Park

military vessels. Today the route is used little except as a supply line during the very short summer thaw.

With the prospect of wealth being made from whaling and the fur trade, Europeans, like Alexander Mackenzie, began to appear and explore in greater numbers during the 18th and 19th centuries. In their wake came missionaries who built churches, schools and hospitals. Until 1870, when the Canadian government took over, administration of the territories was shared between the Hudson's Bay Company and the British government.

Following the discovery of oil in the 1920s near Fort Norman, a territorial government was set up. In the 1930s the discovery of radium around Great Bear Lake marked the beginning of more rapid change and 20th-century development. WW II brought airfields and weather stations. The discovery of gold in 1934 near Yellowknife swelled the town's numbers and in 1967 it became the capital.

In the 1950s, the federal government began health, welfare and education programmes. The 1960s saw accessibility to the territories increase, with roads being built and more aeroplanes connecting more places. The search for oil, gas and minerals changed some areas rapidly and still continues. The modernisation and development of the region has meant the near-total disappearance of the last North Americans to have lived their entire lives out of doors.

The debate between Canada and the USA over sovereignty of the far north, with the Americans arguing that portions fall into the international realm so no one country can lay claim to them, remains unresolved. To the consternation of some Canadians, the USA claims the right to ply the waters of the far north without seeking what opponents view as Canada's rightful permission.

On 12 November 1992, after more than 15 years of negotiation, the Inuit and the federal and territorial governments signed an agreement known as the Nunavut Accord. The result of the largest Native Canadian land claim in the country's history, it promises the creation of a new territory, Nunavut, in 1999 out of the existing eastern Northwest Territories. The western section will probably be renamed and keep Yellowknife as its capital. Nunavut, meaning 'our land', will cover 219,000 sq km, about one-fifth of Canada's land surface, and have Inuktitut the official language of government as well as English.

## Northwest Passage

Soon after 1492 it became clear that Columbus had landed on a 'new' continent and had not discovered a westerly route to Asia. Others then began the search for a waterway to the Orient sailing around the Americas. The southern route was successfully navigated by Ferdinand Magellan in 1521, but the northern route – the Northwest Passage – was to take a good deal longer.

Many famous explorers – including Sir Martin Frobisher, Sir Francis Drake, Henry Hudson and Captain James Cook – tried but failed. The most tragic failure was in 1845 when Sir John Franklin, along with 128 crew members, disappeared somewhere among the islands of the Arctic.

The first successful navigation of the Northwest Passage came early this century when the Norwegian explorer, Roald Amundsen, completed a three-year (1903-1906), east-west voyage in a converted fishing boat, the *Gjöa*.

In 1942, the *St Roch*, a Royal Canadian Mounted Police schooner under the command of Sargeant Henry Lawson, became the first ship to navigate the Northwest Passage from west to east. It then became the first ship to do the crossing from east to west in one season. The *St Roch* is now on display in the Vancouver Maritime Museum. In 1960, the US submarine *Seadragon* was the first to do it under water.

In 1988 a New York-based cruise ship became the first tourist vessel to navigate the Northwest Passage, from Newfoundland to Alaska. The 40-day history-making trip cost each passenger a tidy $20,000. ■

## GEOGRAPHY & CLIMATE

The Northwest Territories can be separated into two geographical regions – the sub-Arctic and the Arctic. The dividing line runs more or less obliquely from the Yukon coast to the south-eastern corner of the District of Keewatin on the shores of Hudson Bay. To the south of this line the land is characterised by short coniferous forests which spread westward to the Mackenzie Mountains straddling the Yukon border. To the north lie the flat, treeless plains of the tundra.

The glacial action of the last ice age left hundreds of lakes and rivers and a permanently frozen layer of subsoil called permafrost.

Winters are long and extremely cold, but summers in the south are surprisingly warm, with temperatures reaching 30°C, which, coupled with the long daylight hours, makes travelling very pleasant. The climate is dry, the average annual rain/snowfall being less than 30 cm.

## FLORA & FAUNA

Survival in the north is hard for any form of life, but despite the harsh conditions there is a greater variety than commonly imagined. The Northwest Territories has more than 800 plant species, from the mosses, lichens, ferns and grasses of the Arctic tundra to the spruce, larch and white-birch trees of the sub-Arctic region.

There are 80 land and sea mammals and 60 species of fish. Whales, walruses and seals can be seen along the northern coast-lines and in the waters around the northern islands in summer. In the rivers and lakes the varieties of fish include char, pike, trout, pickerel (walleye), whitefish and inconnu (a relative of the whitefish whose name is French for 'unknown'). On land there are black, grizzly and polar bears. Other animals include the bison, Dall sheep, musk ox, fox, wolf, moose, caribou, beaver, porcupine and otter.

The Northwest Territories has at least 290 bird species including the Arctic tern, eagle, falcon, gull, hawk, ptarmigan, raven, snowy owl, snow goose and auk.

## National & Territorial Parks

The Northwest Territories have five national parks. Auyuittuq National Park is on Baffin Island to the east. Ellesmere Island National Park is on the north of Ellesmere Island, just across Robeson Channel from north-western Greenland. Nahanni National Park is in the Mackenzie Mountains in the far south-west. On the north of Banks Island, Aulavik National Park is the newest of the territories' national parks. Wood Buffalo National Park, south of Great Slave Lake, is the only one accessible by road.

There are three historic parks: Kekerten Island and Qaummaarviit, both off the east coast of Baffin Island; and Northwest Passage at Gjoa Haven on King William Island.

There are also more than 30 parks run by the territorial government for recreation, and a number of wildlife sanctuaries. Most parks and their campgrounds are open from mid-May to mid-September.

## PEOPLE

Around Mackenzie River and Great Slave

An Inukshuk

Lake the people call themselves the Dene, or Athapaskans. Together with the Inuit, who live mainly along the northern coast and on the Arctic islands, they are the original northern peoples. The word Inuit refers in general to an Eskimo in Canada, as opposed to the Eskimo of Asia or the Aleutian Islands (Alaska). The term Eskimo is not appreciated by the Inuit and is being used less and less. The term Inuit simply means 'people'.

The Inuit number about 21,600 and the Dene 9700; the rest are mainly Métis (of mixed race, 4000) and non-Native (22,400).

## INFORMATION
### Official Symbols
The territorial tree is the jack pine and the official floral emblem is the mountain avens, a member of the rose family. A logo featuring the polar bear appears on many government publications and all vehicle licence plates are shaped like one. The gyrfalcon, the largest of the falcon species, is the territorial bird.

### Tourist Offices
For information on all parts of the territories contact the Department of Economic Development & Tourism (☎ 403-873-7200; fax 403-873-0294), Yellowknife, NWT, X1A 2L9. It also operates the toll free 1-800-661-0788 number for visitor information. The free brochure *Explorers' Guide* is published annually and contains much useful information on travel and accommodation in the Northwest Territories.

The territories have been divided into eight different travel zones and the regional offices to contact are:

Arctic Coast Tourism Association
  Department EG, PO Box 91, Cambridge Bay X0E 0C0; covers the central Arctic coast and North-West Passage (☎ 403-983-2224; fax 403-983-2302)
Baffin Tourism Association
  PO Box 1450, Iqaluit X0A 0H0; covers Baffin and Arctic islands and north-eastern Arctic (☎ 819-979-6551; fax 819-979-1261)
Big River Tourism Association
  Department EG, PO Box 185, Hay River X0E 0R0; covers the area south of Great Slave Lake (☎ 403-874-2422; fax 403-874-6020)

---

> **Longest Word**
> The following is the longest word in the language of the Inuvialuktun Inuit (are you ready?):
>
> *Tuktusiuriagatigitqingnapinngitkyptinnga.*
>
> It means, 'You'll never go caribou hunting with me again'. So there. ■

---

Nahanni-Ram Tourism Association
  Department EG, PO Box 177, Fort Simpson X0E 0N0; covers the south-west corner (☎ & fax 403-695-3182)
Northern Frontier Visitors Association
  Department EG, PO Box 1107, Yellowknife X1A 2N8; covers the northern Great Slave Lake area (☎ 403-873-3131; fax 403-873-3654)
Sahtu Tourism Association
  Department EG, PO Box 115, Norman Wells X0E 0V0; covers Great Bear Lake and central Mackenzie River area (☎ 403-587-2054; fax 403-587-2935)
Travel Keewatin
  Department EG, PO Box 328, Rankin Inlet X0C 0G0; covers the south-east corner of the territories along the western shore of Hudson Bay (☎ 819-645-2618; fax 819-645 2320)
Western Arctic Tourism Association
  Department EG, PO Box 2600, Inuvik X0E 0T0; covers the Beaufort Sea and western Arctic coast area (☎ 403-979-4321; fax 403-979-2434)

VRCs can be found in Yellowknife, Inuvik, Fort Smith, Fort MacPherson, Rae-Edzo and Hay River. There's also one on the border with Yukon (Dempster Hwy) and Alberta (Mackenzie Hwy at the 60th parallel) and they are open from May to September.

### Telephone
The telephone code for places within the District of Mackenzie is the same as that for Alberta and the Yukon – 403. In Franklin and Keewatin it's 819.

### Time
The Northwest Territories cover four time zones. From west to east these are Mountain, Central, Eastern and Atlantic standard time. So when it's noon in Yellowknife it's 2 pm in Iqaluit at the eastern end of Baffin Island.

## Maps

Detailed topographical maps are available in Yellowknife, from Energy, Mines & Resources (☎ 403-920-8299), 8th floor, Precambrian Building, 4920 52nd St. The office is open for sales in the summer Monday to Friday from 8.30 to 11.30 am and 12.30 to 4.30 pm. The Canada Map Office (☎ 613-952-7000), 130 Bentley Ave, Nepean, Ontario K2E 629, has all types of detailed maps of the territories, including small-scale topographical ones which are good for hikers. The office will send you an index and you'll have to pick the map numbers you need from that. Maps in Yellowknife are in short supply, so getting one beforehand is not a bad idea.

## Holidays

As well as the national holidays, the first Monday in August is a public holiday.

## ACTIVITIES

For a lot of visitors, a trip to the Northwest Territories means hiking, rock and ice climbing, canoeing, fishing and camping in the national and territorial parks during the short summer season. For others it's to observe the wildlife. These activities permit the visitor to see the area's uniqueness and rugged beauty. There is every manner of tour and guided trip for visitors to pursue these outdoor activities, but – in the District of Mackenzie at least – most things can also be done on your own, which is much cheaper.

## ORGANISED TOURS

For many the best way to see the more inaccessible parts of the Northwest Territories, especially the districts of Franklin and Keewatin, is on an organised tour. These can be either general or highly specialised trips. They are, however, usually quite expensive. The *Explorers' Guide* has lists of companies, their addresses and the types of tours they offer. For further information contact the Department of Economic Development & Tourism or the relevant travel zone listed earlier.

## GETTING THERE & AROUND

### Air

Canadian Airlines flies from Edmonton, Winnipeg, Montreal and Whitehorse to Yellowknife, Inuvik, Fort Simpson, Iqaluit and other places. The one-way fare between Edmonton and Yellowknife is $420 including tax. Canadian North (☎ 403-873-5533/4484 in Yellowknife), a division of Canadian Airlines, flies to destinations within the Northwest Territories and to Quebec and northern Manitoba. Air Canada flies from Edmonton and Calgary to Yellowknife, with connecting flights on NWT Air (☎ 403-920-2500; 1-800-661-0789 toll free) to Inuvik, Cambridge Bay, Fort Simpson and Coppermine. NWT Air also flies between Winnipeg and Rankin Inlet, and between Yellowknife and Iqaluit.

From Whitehorse, Alkan Air (☎ 403-668-6616 in Whitehorse) has flights four times a week to Inuvik. First Air (☎ 403-920-2680; 1-800-267-1247), 4917 48th St, Yellowknife, flies from most provincial capitals and other major Canadian cities plus Chicago (USA) and Nuuk (Greenland) to Yellowknife, Pangnirtung, Broughton Island, Rankin Inlet and other destinations. Air Inuit (☎ 514-636-9445 in Dorval, Quebec) connects northern Quebec with communities in the District of Keewatin including Cape Dorset and Baffin Island.

About 10 small companies have scheduled flights between points within the territories. Many more operate on a charter basis, using floats (on lakes) or wheels to land in summer, skis in winter. The *Explorers' Guide* lists many of these companies under each region. Charter fares can sometimes be figured by finding out the price per distance rate – say $1.75 per km as a rough guide.

### Bus

Greyhound Bus Lines has a service Sunday to Friday from Edmonton in Alberta, to Hay River for $104.80 one way. Connections for points further north are available Monday to Saturday with Arctic Frontier (☎ 873-4892), 328 Old Airport Rd, Yellowknife. If you're coming from Edmonton and you don't want to go to Hay River you can change buses in Enterprise and continue via Fort Providence and Edzo to Yellowknife. Fares and schedules are available through Greyhound Bus Lines. The one-way fare between Edmonton and Yellowknife is $171.15 and the bus arrives in town at 10.50 pm. Arctic Frontier runs buses between Yellowknife and Fort Smith.

North of 60 Bus Lines (☎ 872-2031 in Fort Smith) has a service Tuesday to Saturday between Fort Smith, Hay River and Fort Resolution. The one-way fare between Fort Smith and Hay River is $46.51.

These prices include tax.

### Car
Only the District of Mackenzie in the west, north of Alberta, is accessible by car, and most of the highways are gravel. The Mackenzie Hwy north from Edmonton is almost completely paved as far as the junction with Hwy 3 north of Enterprise. A combination of paved and gravel roads connect Hay River, Wood Buffalo National Park, Yellowknife and Fort Simpson. The Mackenzie Hwy is the name for the section linking northern Alberta with Fort Simpson and Fort Smith.

The Liard Hwy, which heads north off the Alaska Hwy near Fort Nelson, is also gravel and links northern British Columbia with Fort Liard in the Northwest Territories. It then goes on to meet the Mackenzie Hwy (Hwy 1) south of Fort Simpson. From there the Mackenzie Hwy heads eastward to Enterprise.

The first part of the road from Fort Providence north to Yellowknife runs along the edge of the Mackenzie Bison Sanctuary and it's not uncommon to see bison on the road. Sandhill cranes and ptarmigans from the bird world are also fairly common. The ponds you'll notice by the side of the road are due to holes dug for sand and gravel needed for the road's construction.

In the northern part of the District of Mackenzie, the Dempster Hwy connects the Yukon with Inuvik. This route passes through excellent mountain scenery much of

the way to the Mackenzie River Delta, nipping into a portion of the huge Reindeer Grazing Reserve before ending up at Inuvik.

There are vehicle-rental outlets in Inuvik, Hay River, Fort Smith, Yellowknife, Norman Wells, Inuvik, Tuktoyaktuk and Iqaliut.

For information about conditions and ferry crossings on the Dempster Hwy the numbers to call are ☎ 1-800-661-0752 toll free or ☎ 979-2678 (Inuvik). For other highways call ☎ 1-800-661-0750 toll free or ☎ 874-2208 (Hay River). For information about ferries call ☎ 1-800-661-0751 toll free or within Yellowknife ring ☎ 873-7799.

**Warning** During a six-week period in the late fall and early spring, when river freeze-ups and ice break-ups occur, ferries cannot run over the rivers. Therefore there is no road access or bus service for this period. This includes to Yellowknife.

**Precautions** There can be long distances between service stations, so take extra gasoline, spare parts, water and food with you. Because most of the roads in the Northwest Territories are not paved it's a good idea to protect your gasoline tank, lights and windscreen with coverings.

### DISTRICT OF MACKENZIE
The District of Mackenzie is the most accessible area, being the only district with any roads, and is where most visitors go. It borders the Yukon in the west and Alberta in the south. This is the only area of the territories with a forestry business, and it has most of the fishing as well.

The Mackenzie Mountains, with peaks of 2700 metres, straddle the Yukon border. The Mackenzie River, the longest waterway in Canada, runs north-west along the Mackenzie Valley from Great Slave Lake to the Beaufort Sea in the Arctic Ocean. Most of the population lives around Great Slave Lake and Great Bear Lake, which has many mines. The two national parks in the District of Mackenzie are Nahanni in the south-west,

Husky puppies

and Wood Buffalo, which spreads south across the Alberta border.

The District of Mackenzie has fairly warm, dry summers with an average temperature of 13°C.

RV or tent camping is really the only way to see this part of the country at a reasonable price. Long-distance travelling, food and accommodation in the towns are expensive with a capital E. To keep costs down you'll have to work at it, which probably means going without some comforts and conveniences.

Both camping and canoeing are possible along the district's highway system. Several communities rent boats or canoes. From roadside campgrounds, trips can be taken around the lakes, and away from the roads you can pick your own camping spot. It is not hard to have a lake to yourself; inquire at one of the Visitor Information Centres for more information. Remember that the water is cold enough to kill you in 15 minutes, so keep close to shore in a canoe.

Along the highway system the fee for a site at a government campground is $10. Permits are required: get them from Visitor Information Centres, from park information

offices or from officers when they visit the campground. Campgrounds have firewood and are open from 15 May to 15 September. Don't forget to bring insect repellent.

## Yellowknife

Rising out of the wilderness in a region once occupied by the Slavey people, the city gets its name from the copper-bladed knives they used. Although gold was first found here in 1898 by Klondike-bound prospectors, it wasn't until the discovery of richer veins first in 1934 and again in 1945 that Europeans were attracted to the area in large numbers.

Today Yellowknife has a population of around 15,000 and is by far the largest town in the territories, of which it is the capital (at least until 1999). A modern, fast-growing settlement on the northern shores of Great Slave Lake, 341 km from Fort Smith by road, Yellowknife is essentially a government town. It also acts as the commercial and service centre for the region and people from all over Canada now live and work there. Visitors use Yellowknife as a base for camping and fishing trips as well as for exploring the rocky landscape and nearby lakes.

**Orientation** Yellowknife sits on the northern shores of Great Slave Lake and is connected with the south by the Mackenzie Hwy. The city is divided into the new (south) and old (north) parts of town, which are connected by Franklin Ave (50th Ave), the main thoroughfare. Coming from the south into the city, the highway leads you past the airport, along 48th St and into Franklin Ave.

**Information** The Visitor Information Centre (☎ 873-3131) is at 2 4807 49th St near the Prince of Wales Northern Heritage Centre. The Visitor Information Centre is also the home of the Northern Frontier Visitors Association. You can get maps, canoe routes and a guide to settlements across the territories, and also special fishing, canoeing and motoring guides. The centre is open daily from 8 am to 8 pm.

The main post office, on the corner of Franklin Ave and 49th St, is open Monday to Friday from 9 am to 5.30 pm. The Bank of Montreal in the Centre Square Mall is open on Saturday from 10 am to 3 pm. The Book Cellar, in Panda II Mall, has a good selection of books on Native culture and history of the Northwest Territories. If you're staying at the YWCA you can use the laundry on the 6th floor; alternatively, try Arctic Laundromat at 4310 50th Ave.

**Walking Tours** The Visitor Information Centre has a booklet detailing short walking tours of four areas in the Old Town: Latham Island, The Rock, Peace River Flats and Willow Flats.

**Prince of Wales Northern Heritage Centre** This museum (☎ 873-7551), beside Frame Lake off 49th St, is a good introduction to the Northwest Territories with diorama displays on the lifestyles of the Dene and Inuit, and natural sciences. It also has a gallery on the history of aviation in the Northwest Territories and a cafeteria. It's open daily in the summer from 10.30 am to 5.30 pm and admission is free.

**Eskimo Dog Research Foundation** Here,

at Bowspringer Kennels (☎ 873-4252), 101 Kam Lake Rd at the south-western end of town, you can see a project which has successfully preserved the *kingmik*, a rare Inuit dog. There are over 100 at the kennel, which is also a veterinary clinic.

**Bush Pilot's Monument** For a good view of the town, walk north up Franklin Ave to the Bush Pilot's Monument in Old Town. You can see over the lake and the town's odd assortment of housing.

**Ndilo Cultural Village** At the northern end of Latham Island, Ndilo (pronounced 'di-lo' and meaning 'end of the road') offers visitors the chance to see the Dogrib Dene taking part in traditional activities such as tanning hides and preparing food. Visitors also get the chance to have a go at making traditional crafts. The village (☎ 873-2869) is open Monday to Friday from 10 am to 5 pm and there are guided interpretive tours.

**Dettah** This is a small Dogrib Dene village south-east of town across Yellowknife Bay where you can get a look at the traditional way of life of these people. There are no tourist facilities. You can either hire a boat or take the 11 km road off the Ingraham Trail north-east of Yellowknife.

**Ingraham Trail** Starting from the junction with the Mackenzie Hwy, the 72-km Ingraham Trail (Hwy 4) leads to areas good for fishing, hiking, canoeing, camping and picnicking – but you'll need a vehicle. The road is paved as far as the turn-off to Prelude Lake. **Yellowknife River** is used for fishing and both short and long canoe trips. At **Madeline Lake** there is a 3.2-km hiking trail. **Prelude Lake Park**, 30 km east of Yellowknife, is a pretty spot with good fishing, hiking and camping.

Further east beginning at **Bailey Bridge**, which spans Cameron River, there is a trail to a small waterfall where the local people swim, though these waters ain't Miami Beach. You can also canoe in the river. At **Reid Lake**, 60 km from Yellowknife, you

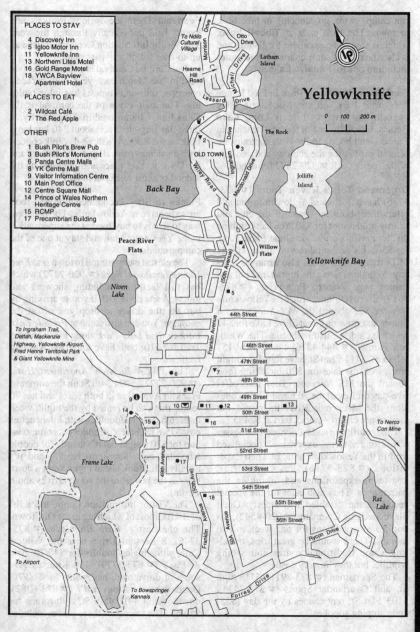

# Yellowknife

PLACES TO STAY
4  Discovery Inn
5  Igloo Motor Inn
11  Yellowknife Inn
13  Northern Lites Motel
16  Gold Range Motel
18  YWCA Bayview
    Apartment Hotel

PLACES TO EAT
2  Wildcat Café
7  The Red Apple

OTHER
1  Bush Pilot's Brew Pub
3  Bush Pilot's Monument
6  Panda Centre Malls
8  YK Centre Mall
9  Visitor Information Centre
10  Main Post Office
12  Centre Square Mall
14  Prince of Wales Northern
    Heritage Centre
15  RCMP
17  Precambrian Building

0   100   200 m

To Ndilo
Cultural
Village

Morrison Drive
Otto Drive
Michell Drive
Hearne Hill Road
Latham Island
Lessard Drive
Ingraham Drive
The Rock
OLD TOWN
Wiley Road
Macdonald Drive
Jolliffe Island

Back Bay

Peace River Flats

Niven Lake

Willow Flats

Yellowknife Bay

To Ingraham Trail,
Dettah, Mackenzie
Highway, Yellowknife Airport,
Fred Henne Territorial Park
& Giant Yellowknife Mine

44th Street
46th Street
47th Street
48th Street
49th Street
50th Street
51st Street
52nd Street
53rd Street
54th Street
55th Street
56th Street

Franklin Avenue
50th Avenue
49th (50th) Ave
Franklin Avenue
50A Avenue
54th Avenue

To Nerco
Con Mine

Frame Lake

Rat Lake

To Airport

To Bowspringer
Kennels

Rycon Drive
Forrest Drive

NORTHWEST TERRITORIES

can camp, swim, go canoeing or hike back to town. The road ends at **Tibbett Lake**, which is said to be excellent for fishing and is also the start of some charted canoe routes including one to **Pensive Lake**.

**Fred Henne Territorial Park** In Fred Henne Territorial Park, off the Mackenzie Hwy opposite the airport, there is **Long Lake Beach**, reputedly one of the best beaches in Canada, and hiking trails. Walking tours are offered explaining the ecology and geology of the region: call ☎ 920-2472 for details.

**Organised Tours** Raven Tours (☎ 873-4776) has its office in Yellowknife Inn and offers three-hour bus tours of the city and nearby gold mines for $30. You can combine this tour with a cruise on Great Slave Lake for $50; this cruise takes you to the village of Dettah. Raven Tours also arranges half-day excursions along the Ingraham Trail and fishing trips. Naocha Enterprises (☎ 873-8019) offer a two-hour cruise on Yellowknife Bay for $23 aboard the MV *Naocha*, or a four-hour cruise on Great Slave Lake for $47 which includes a fish barbecue. The Whitlock Family (☎ 444-4876; 1-800-663-9157 toll free), 5414 52nd St, have four-hour night cruises on the lake for $20 including food aboard the MS *Norweta*. They also offer five-day cruises of the lake and 10-day ones along the Mackenzie River to Inuvik, but they're not cheap – prices start at $2495.

Other outfitting and wilderness businesses offer longer-term, expensive specialised trips in the Yellowknife area. Et-Then Expeditions (☎ 873-8716), has canoe trips, dog-team expeditions and hiking in the barrenlands. They also cater for the special needs of the disabled and elderly. Great Slave Sledging Company (☎ 920-4542), has dog-team expeditions for one week to two months. These would be great trips, travelling some traditional routes and seeing wildlife, but they're very costly.

The Sportsman (☎ 873-2911), 5118 50th St, and Overlander Sports (☎ 873-2474), 5103 51st St, rent canoes by the day ($25) and camping supplies.

**Festivals** There are various festivals and events held periodically through the year. The Visitor Information Centre will have an up-to-date list of activities planned.

The Caribou Carnival is an annual festival held in late March each year, with parades, concerts, skits and contests like igloo building. The main event of the carnival is the Canadian Championship Dog Derby, a three-day dog-sled race about 240 km long. Folk on the Rocks is a three-day folk concert with musicians from all over the country and the USA. It takes place at Long Lake on the second or third weekend in July.

**Places to Stay** Accommodation and food are expensive in Yellowknife. The cheapest way to live is to buy food at the supermarket in the YK Centre Mall and stay at one of the campgrounds.

The closest campground to town is at *Fred Henne Territorial Park* (☎ 920-2472) which has full facilities including showers and toilets. A site costs $10. If you're arriving by bus ask the driver to drop you off at the entrance. You can also camp at *Prelude Lake Park* or *Reid Lake Park* along the Ingraham Trail for $10; both have toilet and washing facilities.

The *YWCA Bayview Apartment Hotel* (☎ 920-2777), 5004 54th St on the corner of Franklin Ave, takes in both sexes and has 70 rooms that can be rented by the night, week or month. Singles/doubles with kitchenettes cost $75/85. There's dormitory accommodation for $20 a night but it's mainly for people who stay on a long-term basis – and it's usually full. Book ahead if you want a dorm bed (as the bus from the south arrives about 11 pm).

The Visitor Information Centre has a list of B&Bs, most of which are in the Old Town. The cheapest is *Barb Bromley's* (☎ 873-3746), 8 Lessard Drive near the Wildcat Café, with singles/doubles for $40/70. *Eric & Eva's* (☎ 873-5779), 114 Knutsen Ave south of downtown, has rooms for $60/70. Good value is *Broussard's* (☎ 873-6382), downtown at 4910 45th St, with rooms for $50/65. The prices for these places includes tax. They are open all year but don't have a lot of space, so it's a good idea to phone before going.

In the hotel category, *Gold Range Hotel* (☎ 873-4441), 5010 50th St, is one of the cheapest, with singles/doubles from $65/75. It has a bar downstairs which can get a bit noisy and a café. *Northernlites Motel* (☎ 873-6023), on the corner of 50th St and 51st Ave, has rooms for $85/95. *Igloo Inn* (☎ 873-8511), 4115 Franklin Ave halfway between downtown and the Old Town, is a friendly place and charges $94/99 for singles/doubles. At the *Discovery Inn* (☎ 873-4151), 4701 Franklin Ave, rooms are $105/120. *Yellowknife Inn* (☎ 873-2601), on Franklin Ave between 49th and 50th Sts, has rooms for $125 single or double.

**Places to Eat** The eateries in Yellowknife are also a bit pricey, but there are some fast-food places in the shopping malls. The cafeteria-style *Lunch Box* in YK Centre Mall

Native Indians wearing goat wool blankets

has sandwiches and burgers from $4.50. *Ryan's Family Restaurant*, on the main floor of Panda II Mall, has pancakes from $3.75 or omelettes with hash browns and toast for $8. The *Red Apple*, on the corner of Franklin Ave and 47th St, serves Western and Chinese food and has a bar. Sandwiches cost from $3.75, fish & chips $7.75 and chop suey $7.50.

For a treat head for the *Wildcat Café* on the corner of Wiley Rd and Doombos Lane in the Old Town. Set in a log cabin reminiscent of Yellowknife's early days, the Wildcat Café is acknowledged as one of Canada's top 100 restaurants. It serves salads for $5 or main dishes like caribou bourgignon for around $20 and is open daily. It's very popular, particularly in the evening.

**Entertainment** There are a number of pubs on and around Franklin Ave, most offering live music. If you want to taste some locally brewed beer head for the *Bush Pilot's Brew Pub*, 3502 Wiley Rd in the Old Town, more or less opposite the Wildcat Café. You get a free basket of peanuts with your drink and you just throw the shells on the floor.

**Things to Buy** Yellowknife is the distribution centre and major retailer of craft items from around the territories. Of course, prices are lower in more remote areas but also higher in southern Canada. Whether artistic or purely functional, the goods are not cheap but are authentic and usually well made. Northern Images (☎ 873-5944) in YK Centre Mall has various Dene and Inuit works.

**Getting There & Away** Long-distance buses leave from outside the Yellowknife Inn. Bus tickets for other parts of Northwest Territories and south can be bought from the shop in the lobby, which is the agent for Frontier Coachlines/Arctic Frontier. See also the introductory Getting There & Around section.

**Getting Around** Arctic Frontier (☎ 873-4437/8) runs a bus service from Latham

Island along Franklin Ave to the southern suburbs. The one-way fare is $2. The two local taxi companies are City Cab (☎ 873-4444) and Gold Cabs (☎ 873-8888); the flag fall is $2.15 plus 10 cents for every km. Avis, Budget and Tilden car-rental companies have representatives in Yellowknife. One of the cheapest though, is Rent a Relic (☎ 873-3400), on the corner of 41st St and Franklin Ave, which has vehicles starting from $29 a day.

### Alberta Border to Yellowknife

The first stretch of the Mackenzie Hwy follows the Hay River which flows north into Great Slave Lake. At the border with Alberta the Visitor Information Centre is open daily in summer from 8 am to 8 pm. As well as road and travel information it has a display of arts & crafts and free coffee. Nearby is a campground with a kitchen shelter and running water.

About 72 km north of the border are the 33-metre **Alexandra Falls**, named after Princess Alexandra of Britain. A short trail leads to a platform overlooking the falls. A further two km north are the 15-metre **Louise Falls** where there are a couple of walking trails and overnight camping.

**Enterprise**, with a population of about 60, is the first settlement in the Northwest Territories that you come to. There's a small information office in the Esso gas station and a motel. From Enterprise the Mackenzie Hwy is paved most of the way as far as the junction with Hwy 3 which leads to the Mackenzie River ferry at Fort Providence. (North-east out of Enterprise, Hwy 2 takes you to Hay River.)

The Mackenzie River ferry, the MV *Merv Hardie* operates well into winter until the ice-bridge is thick enough to carry large trucks. It runs daily between 6 am and mid-night, takes about 10 minutes to cross and is free.

**Fort Providence**, a Slavey community of 700, lies on the banks of the Mackenzie River, 312 km south of Yellowknife. The site was settled in 1861 when a Roman Catholic mission was established there, followed

soon after by a Hudson's Bay Company trading post. About two km before town is a campground by the river; it has pit toilets and drinking water. In town itself are a couple of motels. *Big River Motel* (☎ 699-4301) has a service station, dining room, general store and rooms from $60. The larger *Snowshoe Inn* (☎ 699-3511) charges $70/90 a single/double.

North out of Fort Providence, Hwy 3 follows the western boundary of the **Mackenzie Bison Sanctuary** for nearly 100 km. The sanctuary holds the largest herd of free-ranging pure wood bison in the world, some of which can occasionally be seen by the side of the road.

From the twin Dogrib community of **Rae-Edzo** northwards to Yellowknife you see the rounded, copper-coloured rock outcrops that form part of the Canadian Shield.

### Hay River

The town of Hay River, with a population of 3200, sits on the southern shore of Great Slave Lake, 38 km north of Enterprise. It's a major distribution centre where barges load up for trips to settlements along the Mackenzie River and on the Arctic coast. Fish packing is done here too. The Visitor Information Centre (☎ 874-3180) is on the corner of Mackenzie Hwy and McBryan Drive.

**Places to Stay** The *Hay River Campground* is on Vale Island near the old part of town with sites for $10; facilities include hot showers and a barbecue area. There are several hotels and motels in town. *Cedar Rest Motel* (☎ 874-37632) is near the bus depot and has rooms from $37. *Migrator Motel* (☎ 874-6792) is also close to the bus depot and has furnished apartments with kitchenettes for $60/65 a single/double.

**Getting There & Away** As well as the bus (see Getting There & Around earlier) several airlines service Hay River: Canadian Airlines (☎ 874-2434) flies to Inuvik, Yellowknife and points south; Buffalo Airways (☎ 874-3333) flies to Yellowknife; Air Providence (☎ 699-3551 in Fort Providence) connects with Fort Providence; and Ptarmigan Airways (☎ 873-4461 in Yellowknife) flies to Yellowknife, Fort Simpson and other communities on Great Slave Lake.

## Fort Smith & Wood Buffalo National Park

Fort Smith, a town of 2500, is on the Alberta border at Mile 0 of the Northwest Territories highway system. It was once a fur-trading post in the north-western network of depots. Nearby is the entrance to Wood Buffalo National Park, for which the town acts as a supply centre. Get your food in town: there is nowhere to buy it in the park. For details on the park see the Alberta chapter.

There is a campground at Queen Elizabeth Park on the banks of Slave River close to town. In Fort Smith the *Pinecrest Hotel* (☎ 872-2320) is quite reasonable, at $45/50 for single/doubles without bath. *Pelican Rapids Inn* (☎ 872-2789) has singles/doubles with kitchenettes for $70/75.

## Nahanni National Park

This is a wilderness park in the south-western corner of the District of Mackenzie, close to the Yukon border. Nahanni National Park is designated as a World Heritage Site by UNESCO because of its spectacular, pristine nature. The park has plenty of wildlife, with good hiking, climbing and photographic opportunities. It is visited mainly by canoeists wishing to challenge the white waters (considered amongst the best on the continent) of the 322-km South Nahanni River. Canoeists should know that runs rushing through the three huge canyons are only for the experienced.

Also in the park are sulphur hot springs at **Rabbitkettle** and **Wildmint** and waterfalls, particularly **Virginia Falls**, which at 96 metres is about twice the height of Niagara Falls. For camping, there are seven primitive areas set aside with tables and fireplaces.

The main park access point is **Fort Simpson**, about 360 km west of Yellowknife, at the confluence of the Liard and Mackenzie rivers. The park is 145 km west

of Fort Simpson. The town has a park information office, camping facilities and several hotels.

**Organised Tours** From Fort Simpson there are boat, raft and canoe trips into the park. The park information office can supply details. Simpson Air (☎ 695-2505) in Fort Simpson and Deh Cho Air (☎ 770-4103) in Fort Liard are two companies offering tours of the park.

Other companies offer extended, but expensive tours into the park. Black Feather Wilderness Adventures (☎ 613-722-9717), 1341 Wellington St West, Ottawa, Ontario K1Y 3B8, runs canoe and hiking trips; a three-week canoeing trip along the South Nahanni River will set you back $3395. Whitewolf Adventures (☎ 604-736-0664), 2565 West 2nd Ave, Vancouver, British Columbia V6K 1J7, also has rafting and canoe tours.

For details of other organised tours see the Nahanni-Ram section of the *Explorers' Guide*.

**Getting There & Away** The park is not easy – or cheap – to get to. Access is by air or river. From Fort Simpson, Fort Liard, Fort Nelson in British Columbia or from Watson Lake in the Yukon, you can fly in by charter. There is no road access but the Liard Hwy, which connects Fort Liard with Fort Simpson following the eastern side of the Liard River, may make Nahanni more accessible. The highway passes within 30 km of Nahanni Butte and offers access to the river at Blackstone Territorial Park. As yet no bridge has been constructed, but when this is done, getting to the park will be a lot less hassle and considerably cheaper.

## Mackenzie River

The 1800-km Mackenzie River is Canada's longest river and the 13th longest in the world. The river was travelled by Native Canadians for thousands of years. Although its present official name honours the Scotsman, Alexander Mackenzie, who canoed and mapped the river in 1789, it is known locally as Deh Cho which simply means 'big river'. It's an important transport route, linking Fort Providence on Great Slave Lake with Inuvik and the Beaufort Sea in the north. Because of the extreme cold, however, it is only navigable for about four months of the year.

### Norman Wells

On the northern shore of the Mackenzie River halfway between Fort Simpson and Inuvik, this town of 800, has long been (and remains) an oil town. There's a campground in town and several hotels. Air service is available from Edmonton, Yellowknife and Inuvik. Canadian Airlines (☎ 587-2361) has an office in Norman Wells and North-Wright Air (☎ 587-2288) flies to Yellowknife and Inuvik.

Of more interest is the **Canol Heritage Trail**, a hiking trail designated a National Historic Site which leads 372 km south-west to the Yukon border. From there, a road leads to Ross River and the Yukon highway system. Originally intended as an oil-supply route to Whitehorse during WW II, the trail has the remains of army camps and abandoned equipment, as well as peaks, canyons, barrens and lots of wildlife. There are no facilities along this trail.

### Inuvik

Inuvik, with a population of 3500, is the territories' second largest town, although it was only founded as late as 1955 as a supply centre. It lies on the East Channel of the Mackenzie River about 90 km south of the Arctic coast. For nearly two months each year, from the end of May, it has 24 hours of daylight every day. The population is roughly one-third Inuit, one-third Dene and one-third European. Note that the first snow falls sometime around the end of August. Crafts, including locally made parkas, are for sale. The Visitor Information Centre is on Mackenzie Rd, Inuvik's main thoroughfare.

**Things to See & Do** The two main attractions in town are the igloo-shaped **Our Lady**

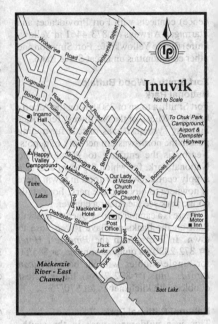

of Victory Church and **Ingamo Hall**, a three-storey community centre built of logs. There are several short walking trails beginning from Loucheux Rd. Walking, bus, boat and wildlife-viewing tours are available. Arctic Tour Company (☎ 979-4100), 181 Mackenzie Rd, offers a 1½-hour bus tour of the town and surrounding tundra for $20. (See also Around Inuvik later.)

**Festivals** The Arctic Northern Games, the biggest northern games of their kind, are often held in Inuvik in July, but the location and dates change, so ask where and when somewhere further south. The games feature traditional Dene and Inuit sports, contests, dancing, music, crafts and the 'Good Woman' contest, during which women display various household skills such as animal skinning.

Delta Daze is a smaller celebration held on Thanksgiving weekend (October) before the long winter sets in.

**Places to Stay** *Chuk Park Campground*, about 3½ km before town on the Dempster Hwy, is open from June to October and provides hot showers and firewood; the office is open 24 hours a day for the duration. The Dene operate the campground, charge $10 a site and put on various activities. The campground has a good view of the delta and the breeze keeps the mosquitoes down a bit. In town, *Happy Valley Campground* has similar facilities and also charges $10 a site.

*Outlook B&B* (☎ 979-3789), 78 Boot Lake Rd south of downtown, has great views of the Richardson Mountains and Mackenzie Delta. It has two rooms for $65/80 a single/double. In town try *Robertson's B&B* (☎ 979-3111), 41 Mackenzie Rd, which has laundry and kitchen facilities and rents out bikes and canoes. Both are open year round but you should book ahead in summer.

There are three hotels in Inuvik, all charging about the same price. Cheapest is the *Mackenzie Hotel* (☎ 979-2861), which has rooms from $100. *Finto Motel Inn* (☎ 979-2647), on the corner of Mackenzie Rd and Marine Bypass, has singles/doubles for $115/125.

**Places to Eat** Inuvik doesn't offer a lot of choice. If you're driving, consider bringing in your food (especially from Alaska) and you'll save a few bucks. The *Roost*, a sandwich and burger take-out, is one of the cheapest in town. The hotels have restaurants but the meals aren't cheap. On the menu at the *Green Briar Restaurant* in the Mackenzie Hotel is musk ox stew, something you won't see down south.

**Getting There & Around** There are scheduled air services from Edmonton, Yellowknife and Whitehorse. (See also the introductory Getting There & Around section.) Aklak Air (☎ 979-3555/777) flies to places within the region including Tuktoyaktuk, Aklavik and Fort MacPherson. Arctic Wings & Rotors (☎ 979-2220) flies to Aklavik and Tuktoyaktuk. North-Wright Air (☎ 587-2288 in Norman Wells) connects Inuvik with Norman Wells. These airlines also offer charter services.

Several companies run buses along the Dempster Hwy between Dawson City and Inuvik. Arctic Tour Company (☎ 979-4100) has three buses a week in each direction; Gold City Tours (☎ 993-5175 in Dawson City) has two a week. The Arctic Tour Company charges $198 one way plus tax. Norline Coaches (☎ 668-3355 in Whitehorse) runs buses from Whitehorse.

### Around Inuvik

Inuvik lies in the **Mackenzie Delta** which, covering an area of over 12,000 sq km, is the largest river delta in Canada and one of the world's great wildlife regions. It's home to many fur-bearing animals and hundreds of species of bird use it for summer nesting.

A number of companies offer a variety of trips on the Mackenzie River. Arctic Tour Company (☎ 979-4100) has two-hour cruises along the East Channel of the river and delta for $29. It also has four-hour, midnight-sun cruises through the delta to Tuktoyaktuk for $120. Midnight Express Tours (☎ 979-2104) offers similar cruises. Western Arctic Nature Tours (☎ 979-3300), next to the igloo church, specialises in ecotourism and has trips to Tuktoyaktuk to view beluga whales and to Herschel Island in the Yukon to watch birds and other wildlife.

### Tuktoyaktuk

About 137 km north-east of Inuvik in Kugmallit Bay on the Arctic coast is Tuktoyaktuk, commonly known as Tuk. Originally the home of the whale-hunting Karngmalit or Mackenzie Inuit, it's a land base for some of the Beaufort Sea oil and gas explorations. Pods of beluga whales can be seen from there in July and August. In the land around Tuk are **pingos** – huge mounds made of earth and ice caused by frost heaves.

### Aklavik

Aklavik, 113 km north of the Arctic Circle and about 50 km west of Inuvik, is home to the Inavaluit and the Gwich'in who, over the centuries, have traded and sometimes fought each other in this region. Aklavik was for a time the administrative centre for the area, but serious flooding and erosion prompted the federal government to move in the 1950s to a new site at Inuvik. The Mad Trapper Jamboree, held at Easter, keeps alive the memory of Albert Johnson, the Mad Trapper of Rat River. He murdered other trappers for their gold fillings, but was finally gunned down in a shoot-out at Eagle River in 1932 by the mounties, after he'd killed one of their officers.

### Paulatuk

This small Karngmalit community is on the Arctic coast at the southern end of Darnley Bay near the mouth of the Hornaday River, about 400 km east of Inuvik. The town's name means 'soot of coal' and one of the main local attractions are the **Smoking Hills**, which contain smouldering sulphide-rich slate and seams of coal. It's also possible to see caribou, musk ox and polar bears in the surrounding lands.

### Banks Island

Lying in the Arctic Ocean to the north of Paulatuk, Banks Island may have been inhabited for nearly 3500 years. **Sachs Harbour**, a small Inavaluit community, is the only settlement on the island. Wildlife is abundant and the island has two bird sanctuaries where you can see flocks of snowgeese and sea birds in the summer. In **Aulavik National Park**, on the north of the island, you can canoe or raft the Thomsen River.

### Victoria Island

The site of **Cambridge Bay**, in the southeast of the island, was a traditional meeting place of the Inuit who came here for the excellent fishing. Explorers in search of the Northwest Passage often took shelter here and you can see the remains of Roald Amundsen's schooner, *Maud* on the beach in the harbour.

Today Cambridge Bay is a transport and service centre for communities along the Arctic coast. From the town you can hike to **Mt Pelly** to view the birds and other wildlife.

## DISTRICT OF FRANKLIN

The District of Franklin is the most northerly and has many islands, including Baffin Island, one of the world's largest, which contains Auyuittuq National Park. Ellesmere Island National Park consists of the northern section of Ellesmere Island way up at the peak of the Canadian Arctic, not far from Greenland's north-western edge. Not one tree grows in the entire District of Franklin but many flowers bloom during the short summer. The northern regions are almost completely uninhabited. There is the odd weather station, military installation or biological research centre.

Access to the district is by boat or plane.

### Baffin Island

**Iqaluit** This town, formerly called Frobisher Bay, is on the east coast of Baffin Island in the eastern section of the territories. In 1984 the town voted to change the name back to Iqaluit (pronounced 'ee-KAL-oo-it'), its original Inuit name meaning 'the place of fish'. It was established in 1942 as a US Air Force base and is now a fairly large settlement of 2600. It's the first stop on the fly-in trip to Auyuittuq National Park. There is not much to see or do here but a variety of side trips is possible and there are a number of hiking trails marked by inukshuks (humanlike figures made of rocks), which take you past archaeological sites and out into the tundra. Most people coming here stop off as part of a package tour en route to somewhere else.

*Places to Stay* Accommodation is expensive. *Mariner Lodge* (☎ 979-0344) is one of the cheapest places, with rooms starting at $55. *Kamotiq B&B* (☎ 979-5937/6327), in the suburb of Apex, has singles/doubles for $75/95 and is open year round, while the *Bayshore Inn* (☎ 979-6733) has doubles for $95. There is a campground as well.

**Getting There & Away** Canadian Airlines (☎ 979-5331) has an office in Iqaluit. Once a week in the summer, First Air (☎ 979-5810) flies from here to Nuuk, the capital of Greenland. It also has scheduled air services from Montreal, Ottawa, Yellowknife and Edmonton.

**Auyuittuq National Park** Covering an area of 21,470 sq km, this is Canada's third largest national park and one of the world's few national parks north of the Arctic Circle. Pronounced 'ah-you-EE-tuk', the word means 'the land that never melts'. Most of the park is a beautiful, pristine wilderness consisting of mountains, valleys, fjords and meadows. Most visitors go for the hiking along 96-km **Pangnirtung Pass** – between late June and early September when it's free of snow. Cross-country skiing in the spring and climbing are also good. Being north of the Arctic Circle the park has 24 hours of daylight each day from May to the end of

July, although the weather is unpredictable and temperatures remain low.

Many tour companies offer trips in the park – see the Northwest Territories *Explorers' Guide*.

**Places to Stay** There are two primitive campgrounds in the park: at Overlord and Summit Lake. There are also seven emergency shelters along the Pangnirtung Pass. Hikers should be in good condition as the trail is considered hard going. Most visitors spend four to seven days. For more information on the park, contact the Superintendent (☎ 473-8828), Auyuittuq National Park, Pangnirtung, NWT, X0A 0R0.

**Getting There & Away** The problem with the place is getting there – it's expensive. First you must fly from one of the major cities to Iqaluit, which is nearly 300 km from the park. Canadian Airlines and First Air fly to Iqaluit from where you have to catch

Timber wolf

another flight to Pangnirtung near the southern edge of the park or to Broughton Island, at the eastern edge. First Air flies from Iqaluit to both places and from either point you walk or go by canoe (after the ice breaks up in July) into the park.

**Pangnirtung** Pang, as it's often referred to, is a town with about 1100 residents, beautifully set alongside a fjord amidst mountains at the entrance to Auyuittuq National Park. It lies at the southern end of Pangnirtung Pass 40 km south of the Arctic Circle and acts as the jumping-off point for park visitors. No alcohol is permitted in the town: this is one of several northern communities that have voted themselves 'dry' to help alleviate alcohol-related problems. First Air has daily flights to Iqaliut.

***Things to See & Do*** Two walking trails begin in town. One, following the Duval River takes about three hours. The other, following the Ikuvik River uphill offers a fine view of the fjord and takes about six hours. Good boots are recommended for both.

About 50 km south of town is the **Kekerten National Historic Park**, an old whaling station. A trail leads around parts of the island past the remains of the 19th-century houses, tools and graves. An interpretive centre provides background information. The park is about two hours by boat from Pangnirtung.

***Places to Stay*** There's camping at the *Pisuktinu-Tungavik* campground or you can stay at the *Auyuittuq Lodge* (☎ 473-8955) for $120; the lodge also has a dining room.

***Things to Buy*** The town has a reputation for its woven tapestries which can be seen and purchased at several shops or at the Inuit Co-op in town. Most of the tapestries are pictorial, depicting scenes from the traditional lifestyle of the region. Prices range from the high hundreds to several thousand dollars. Less costly items such as sweaters,

scarves and the popular crocheted Pang hats are also available.

**Cape Dorset** At Cape Dorset, on the south-west coast of Baffin Island, the remains of an ancient Inuit civilisation which existed between 1000 BC and 1100 AD, were first found. Nowadays it is most noted as a centre for contemporary Inuit art. It's also a good place from which to go hiking, or birdwatching in the **Dewey Soper Bird Sanctuary**.

### Bylot Island
Off the north-east of Baffin Island in Lancaster Sound, is this island bird sanctuary, a summer nesting ground for snow geese and home to other birds like the murres and kittiwakes. The waters around the island are also rich in marine life. Access is by boat from Pond Inlet.

### Ellesmere Island
**Ellesmere Island National Park** This national park, way up at the northern tip of Ellesmere Island at the top of the world, is for wealthy wilderness seekers only. It features **Cape Columbia**, the northernmost point of North America, **Mt Barbeau**, one of the highest peaks on the eastern side of the continent, **Lake Hazen** and numerous glaciers. Around the park are thermal oases where plants and animals are able to survive despite the harsh climate.

### DISTRICT OF KEEWATIN
To the west, the District of Keewatin consists of a vast, rocky, barren plateau, part of the Canadian Shield, with only 4800 people; to the east its official boundaries incorporate much of Hudson Bay and James Bay. Most of the Inuit population lives in this district, in settlements along the western shores of Hudson Bay. As well as English, the main language of the area is Inuktitut which means 'language of the people' and is written in a series of symbols.

Farley Mowat's *Never Cry Wolf* tells of a man who lived among the wolves in Keewatin; another, *People of the Deer*, tells of the hardship inflicted on the Padlirmiut

Inuit as a result of the change in migration patterns of the caribou in the 1940s and 1950s.

Accommodation is available in all the communities, but it is expensive and you'll need to book ahead. Calm Air (☎ 645-2746) has scheduled flights to Rankin Inlet from Churchill in Manitoba and serves other communities in the district. NWT Air connects Rankin Inlet with Yellowknife and Iqaluit.

### Arviat

Arviat, formerly called Eskimo Point, is Keewatin's most southerly settlement. This was originally the site of a summer camp used by several groups of Inuit who lived along the western coast of Hudson Bay and on the mainland tundra. The Hudson's Bay Company established a trading post here in the 1920s and the community now has a population of about 1100. Many people still make a living from fishing, hunting and trapping.

From Arviat you can arrange a trip south to **McConnell River Bird Sanctuary** where from June onwards about 400,000 snow geese nest, together with snowy owls, Arctic terns, falcons and others.

### Rankin Inlet

Founded in 1955 as a mining centre, Rankin Inlet, with a population of 1500, is Keewatin's largest community and the government and transport centre for the district.

From here you can go fishing in the bay or in the many rivers and lakes. In Hudson Bay, about 50 km from Rankin Inlet, is **Marble Island**, a graveyard for James Knight and his crew who were seeking the Northwest Passage in the 18th century. Some 19th-century whaling ships are there too. You can also hike to the **Ijiraliq Archaeological Site**, at the mouth of the Meliadine River, and explore the 15th-century underground houses of the Thule Inuit.

### Baker Lake

Geographically, Baker Lake lies at the centre of Canada. It's good for fishing and is the departure point for canoe or raft trips on the Dubawnt, Kazan and Hanbury-Thelon rivers. From Baker Lake you can arrange a visit west to **Thelon Game Sanctuary**, founded in 1927 by the federal government to save the then-endangered musk ox, and where many indigenous animals are now protected. Baker Lake is also noted for its Inuit artwork.

### Repulse Bay

Sitting on the Arctic Circle at the southern end of Melville Peninsula, Repulse Bay is a natural harbour. For centuries whaling ships set off from there. Today you can go whale-watching to see beluga or narwhal whales (August is the best time) or take a boat out fishing.

# Glossary

**Acadians** – The first French settlers from France in Nova Scotia were known as Acadians.

**Atlantic Provinces** – The Atlantic Provinces refers to: New Brunswick, Nova Scotia, Prince Edward Island and Newfoundland. See Maritime Provinces entry later.

**aurora borealis** – Also called the northern lights, they are charged particles from the sun which are trapped in the earth's magnetic field. They appear as other-worldly coloured, waving beams.

**badlands** – A dry, barren, arid region of unusual, irregular features of erosion and prehistoric fossils. In Canada, the main such region is found in southern Alberta.

**bakeapple** – Also called the golden bakeapple and a speciality of Newfoundland, it's a type of berry which is often used for jam.

**beaver fever (giardiasis)** – The bacteria which causes this disease is found in many freshwater streams and lakes. It affects the digestive tract and can be avoided by boiling drinking water.

**boîtes à chanson** – Generally cheap, casual and relaxed folk clubs, popular in Quebec.

**boreal** – Refers to the Canadian north and its character as in the boreal forest, the boreal wind, etc.

**Bluenose II** – A well-known, widely travelled replica of Canada's famous sailing vessel.

**brew pub** – A pub that brews and sells one or more of its own beers

**cabin fever** – A traditional term still used to indicate a stir-crazy, frustrated state of mind due to being cooped up indoors over the long winter. By extension, it's used to denote the same feelings due to being forced to remain in the house, cottage, tent, etc for a period of time because of inclement weather, bad health, etc.

**calèche** – Horse-drawn carriages which can be taken around parts of Montreal and Quebec City.

**Canadian Shield** – Also known as the Precambrian or Laurentian Shield, it is a plateau of rock that was formed 2.5 billion years ago and covers much of the north of the country.

**ceilidh** – Pronounced KAY-lee; a Gaelic word meaning an informal gathering for song, dance and story. It is sometimes known as a house party; especially popular in Prince Edward Island.

**clearcut** – A hated sight for environmentalists, this is an area where loggers have cut every tree, large and small, leaving nothing standing. A traveller's first view of one is often shocking.

**coulees** – Gulches, usually dry

**Cowichan** – The name of a Native Indian people originally from the Lake Cowichan area on Vancouver Island; also the name given to the hand-knitted, 100% wool sweaters they made famous.

**dome car** – The two-levelled, glass-topped observation car of a train.

**Doukhobours** – A Russian Christian pacifist sect, some of whom settled in Canada during the 19th century.

**Father Pandosy** – Canada's lesser known equivalent of the USA's Johnny Appleseed.

**First Nations** – A term used to denote Canada's aboriginal peoples. It can be used instead of Indians or Native peoples.

**flowerpots** – Unusual rock formations, these irregular geological forms are created by erosion effects of waves. Examples can be seen at Tobermory in Ontario and at The Rocks in New Brunswick.

**fruit leather** – A blend of fruit purees dried into thin sheets and pressed together. It's great for backpacking and hiking.

**gasoline** – Petrol, known as gasoline or simply gas (gaz in Quebec). Almost all gas in Canada is termed unleaded and comes in regular and more costly higher octane versions.

**Great Explosion** – In 1917 a French munitions ship carrying an enormous cargo of TNT collided with another foreign ship in Halifax harbour. The result was the biggest unnatural explosion ever, prior to the A-bombs' being dropped on Japan in 1945.

**Group of Seven** – A collective term used to refer to Canada's best known painters active primarily between 1920 and 1930.

**Haligonians** – Residents of Halifax

**Halloween** – A celebration occurring annually on 31 October originating with ancient Celtic beliefs. Now mainly for children it features dressing in costume often based on the supernatural.

**hoodoos** – Fantastically shaped pillars of sandstone rock formed by erosion found in badland regions mainly in southern Alberta.

**Hudson's Bay Company** – An English trading-company begun in 1670 which traded in all areas which had rivers draining into Hudson Bay. In the 18th century the Hudson's Bay Company and its main rival the Northwest Company; both set up forts and trading posts over a vast area including parts of what were to become the various provinces between at least Quebec and Alberta. The two companies amalgamated in 1821 and the Hudson's Bay Company administered the area until 1870 when the territory became part of the Dominion of Canada. The Bay department store, seen across the country is the contemporary link in this Canada's oldest company.

**igloo** – The traditional Inuit houses made of blocks of ice.

**information chalets** – Tourist information booths across Newfoundland Province.

**Innu** – Another name for the Montagnais and Naskapi peoples.

**inukshuk** – Inuit preferred to trap caribou in water where they could be hunted from a kayak. For this reason they built stone figures called 'inukshuks', next to lakes to direct the animals into the water.

**Inside Passage** – The sea route between the Alaskan Panhandle and Washington state along the west coast of British Columbia.

**interior camping** – This refers to usually lone, individual sites accessible only by foot or canoe. When found in provincial or national parks pre-registering with park authorities is required for your own safety.

**Loyalists** – They were residents of America who maintained their allegiance to Britain during the American Revolution and who fled to Canada.

**Liveyers** – European descendants living along the Strait of Belle Isle in Labrador were known as 'liveyers'. They lived in little villages dotted along the rocky coasts, fishing and hunting.

**mall** – A shopping centre, usually enclosed and containing a range of retail stores. The larger ones generally include a number of low-cost fast-food places at which to eat.

**Maritime Provinces** – The Maritime Provinces also known as the Maritimes refer to the three provinces: New Brunswick, Nova Scotia and Prince Edward Island.

**Mennonites** – A religious Utopian group originating in Europe. They are found in number in the Kitchener-Waterloo region of southern Ontario.

**Métis** – Canadians of French and Native Indian stock.

**Mounties** – Royal Canadian Mounted Police (RCMP)

**mukluks** – Moccasins or boots made from sealskin and often trimmed with fur; usually made by Inuit people.

**muskeg** – The bogs of northern Canada where the layers of matted plant life, grasses and sometimes trees float on top of stagnant water.

**Naskapi** – A group of Native Canadians, also called the Innu. They are found in north-eastern Quebec.

**Newfie** – Humorous term applying to residents of Newfoundland or 'The Rock' as it is sometimes known.

**no-see-um** – Any of various tiny biting

insects which are difficult to see and which can annoy hikers, campers, canoeists, etc when out in the woods or along some beaches. No-see-um netting, a very fine mesh screen on a tent is designed to keep them out and allow the occupants a sound night's sleep.

**Northwest Passage** – The water route across North America from the Atlantic to the Pacific Ocean. Assuming there must be such a route, which would aid trading, explorers from around the world searched for almost 300 years before Roald Amundsen successfully navigated it in 1906.

**Ogopogo** – A monster, similar to the Loch Ness monster, thought to reside within the waters of Okanagan Lake (BC). It has never been photographed.

**outports** – Small, isolated coastal villages of Newfoundland, connected with the rest of the province by boat.

**permafrost** – Permanently frozen subsoil that covers the far north of Canada.

**petroglyphs** – Ancient paintings or carvings on rock.

**potlatch** – A traditional gathering of some West Coast indigenous peoples held to commemorate any memorable occasion.

**public/separate schools** – The two basic school systems. Both are free and essentially the same but the latter is designed for Catholics and offers more religious education along with the three 'r's.

**pysankas** – Ukrainian term for painted Easter eggs.

**qiviut** – The wool of the musk ox that was traditionally woven into garments by some Inuit groups in the far north.

**Québecois** – The local tongue of Quebec

where the vast majority of the population is French; also known as *joual*. The term also refers to the residents of Quebec although it is only applied to the French, not English Quebeckers.

**rock hounds** – Rock collectors.

**RV** – Recreational vehicle (usually a motorhome)

**screech** – A particularly strong rum once available only in Newfoundland, but now widely available across Canada but in diluted form.

**sourdough** – Refers to a person who has completed one year's residency in the north.

**spelunking** – Caving

**steamies** – Hot dogs in Quebec are sometimes known as steamies because of the way they're cooked.

**sub-compact cars** – These are the smallest cars available either for purchase or rent. They are smaller than compacts which are one size down from standard cars.

**sugar-making moon** – A former Indian term for the spring date when the maple tree's sap begins to run.

**sugar shack** – The place where the collected maple sap is distilled in large kettles and boiled as part of the production of maple syrup.

**taiga** – The sub-arctic, evergreen forests of the far north.

**tundra** – The vast, treeless Arctic plains, north of the treeline and with a perpetually frozen subsoil.

**649** – The country's most popular, highest paying lottery.

# Index

913

## TEXT

Map references are in **bold** type.

922  Index

928

## THANKS

Thanks to all the following travellers and others (apologies if we've misspelt your name) who took time to write to us about their experiences of Canada.

To those whose names have been omitted through oversight – your time and efforts are appreciated.

Sue Allen (UK), Nick Anning (UK), Maya Araki (C), Renee Auer (C), Glenn Barker (UK), Alex Gatey (USA), Ann Benueniste (C), Sven-Goran Bergh (S), Ernest Beyl (USA), John Bingeman (C), Marina Biral (I), Glenn Brady (USA), Alison Breugger (C), Linda Broschofsky (Aus), Steven D Brown (USA), Mrs JF Brown, Steven Brown (USA), Jonathan Buchanan (C), John Burchfield (UK), Helen Burich (C), John Butcher (UK), David Callan (C), John F Campbell (C), Caroline Casselman (C), L Chisholm (C), Jean Christie (Aus), Leonard Clarke (C), Mike Coburn (C), Cathryn Craik-Hugh (C), Jacqueline Dale (UK), Seann Day (USA), Peter de Wit (NL), Farida Deeming (D), Jean Dery (C), Linda B Deveau (C), Patricia Doucette (C), Isabelle Dumont, Christopher Eich (D), James Evans (C), Nancy Farley (C), Louise Faure (C), Ruth & Bernard Finkelstein (USA), Jette Finsborg (C), Mike Fisher (USA), Maria Fleuren (NL), Fiona Forrest (UK), Suzi Fraser (C), Aline Gillespie (Aus), Jane Gogarty (UK), Vera Gould (C), Julian Green (UK), Clarke Green (USA), Susan Harrison (C), Mats Heder (S), Erik Heegaard (Dk), Sarah Honisett (C), Mark Horobin (UK), Sally Hughes (Aus), Anne Hughes (C), David & Greeba Hughes (UK), Brigitte Jacobs (USA), Chris Jeffries (USA), Lloyd Jones (C), Suzanne Jongeneel (C), David & Liz Joseph (UK), Karout Famil (NL), R J Keir (C), Donna Ketchen (C), Marjclei Kistemake (NL), Suzanne Kolmer (C), Kathleen Krauss (B), Rene Kreeftenberg (NL), Pat Lee (C), J Leishman (C), Jeffrey Levitz (C), Andrew D Lindenauer (USA), Bill Macdonald (C), Duff Malkin (C), Peter Mok (C), Chris Molisch (A), Jean-Guy Monette (C), Donna Murphy (Aus), P Nesbit (UK), Sue Norman (C), Shiela O'Brien (USA), Joe O'Grady (C), B Osborne (NZ), Shirley Pelletier (C), Roland Perrin (C), Roger & Shirley Randall (C), Lois Rockcastle (USA), Rosalia Salpeter (Aus), Mrs H Scholte (NL), Kelly Shaver (C), Carl & Mari Shepherd (C), Heidi Sigmond (T), Jan & Dave Smith (NZ), John S Sparks (USA), Richard Stadler (USA), S Steele (UK), Cindy Storie (C), Verdun Thomson (C), Nancy & Paul Travis (C), Leopold Unger (A), Cheryl Upright (C), Heather van Doorninck (C), Astrid van Duin (NL), Mark Varley (UK), Ivan Volund (Dk), Ly Warde (C), Carol Waters (C), Basil Wetters (UK), Mrs P Whitear (UK), Caroline Whiting (Aus), Peter Wickenden (UK), Judit Zeita (UK)

Aus - Australia, A - Austria, B - Belgium, Bra - Brazil, C - Canada, CH - Switzerland, D - Germany, Dk - Denmark, Fr - France, It - Italy, Ken - Kenya, N - Norway, NL - Netherlands, NZ - New Zealand, Sp - Spain, Sw - Sweden, UK- United Kingdom, USA - United States of America

# LONELY PLANET JOURNEYS

JOURNEYS is a unique collection of travellers' tales – published by the company that understands travel better than anyone else. It is a series for anyone who has ever experienced – or dreamed of – the magical moment when they encountered a strange culture or saw a place for the first time. They are tales to read while you're planning a trip, while you're on the road or while you're in an armchair, in front of a fire.

JOURNEYS books will catch the spirit of a place, illuminate a culture, recount a crazy adventure, or introduce a fascinating way of life. They will always entertain, and always enrich the experience of travel.

## ISLANDS IN THE CLOUDS
### Travels in the Highlands of New Guinea
*Isabella Tree*

This is the fascinating account of a journey to the remote and beautiful Highlands of Papua New Guinea and Irian Jaya. The author travels with a PNG Highlander who introduces her to his intriguing and complex world. *Islands in the Clouds* is a thoughtful, moving book, full of insights into a region that is rarely noticed by the rest of the world.

*'One of the most accomplished travel writers to appear on the horizon for many years . . . the dialogue is brilliant'* – Eric Newby

## LOST JAPAN
*Alex Kerr*

*Lost Japan* draws on the author's personal experiences of Japan over a period of 30 years. Alex Kerr takes his readers on a backstage tour: friendships with Kabuki actors, buying and selling art, studying calligraphy, exploring rarely visited temples and shrines . . . The Japanese edition of this book was awarded the 1994 Shincho Gakugei Literature Prize for the best work of non-fiction.

*'This deeply personal witness to Japan's wilful loss of its traditional culture is at the same time an immensely valuable evaluation of just what that culture was'*
– Donald Richie of the Japan Times

## THE GATES OF DAMASCUS
*Lieve Joris*
*Translated by Sam Garrett*

This best-selling book is a beautifully drawn portrait of day-to-day life in modern Syria. Through her intimate contact with local people, Lieve Joris draws us into the fascinating world that lies behind the gates of Damascus.

*'A brilliant book . . . Not since Naguib Mahfouz has the everyday life of the modern Arab world been so intimately described'* – William Dalrymple

## SEAN & DAVID'S LONG DRIVE
*Sean Condon*

Sean and David are young townies who have rarely strayed beyond city limits. One day, for no good reason, they set out to discover their homeland, and what follows is a wildly entertaining adventure that covers half of Australia. Sean Condon has written a hilarious, offbeat road book that mixes sharp insights with deadpan humour and outright lies.

*'Funny, pithy, kitsch and surreal . . . This book will do for Australia what Chernobyl did for Kiev, but hey you'll laugh as the stereotypes go boom'* – Andrew Tuck, Time Out

# LONELY PLANET TRAVEL ATLASES

Lonely Planet has long been famous for the number and quality of its guidebook maps. Now we've gone one step further and in conjunction with Steinhart Katzir Publishers produced a handy companion series: Lonely Planet travel atlases – maps of a country produced in book form.

Unlike other maps, which look good but lead travellers astray, our travel atlases have been researched on the road by Lonely Planet's experienced team of writers. All details are carefully checked to ensure the atlas corresponds with the equivalent Lonely Planet guidebook.

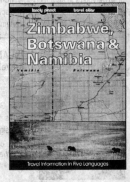

The handy atlas format means no holes, wrinkles, torn sections or constant folding and unfolding. These atlases can survive long periods on the road, unlike cumbersome fold-out maps. The comprehensive index ensures easy reference.

- full-colour throughout
- maps researched and checked by Lonely Planet authors
- place names correspond with Lonely Planet guidebooks
  – no confusing spelling differences
- legend and travelling information in English, French, German, Japanese and Spanish
- size: 230 x 160 mm

**Available now:**
Thailand; India & Bangladesh; Vietnam; Zimbabwe, Botswana & Namibia

**Coming soon:**
Chile; Egypt; Israel; Laos; Turkey

---

# LONELY PLANET TV SERIES & VIDEOS

Lonely Planet travel guides have been brought to life on television screens around the world. Like our guides, the programmes are based on the joy of independent travel, and look honestly at some of the most exciting, picturesque and frustrating places in the world. Each show is presented by one of three travellers from Australia, England or the USA and combines an innovative mixture of video, Super-8 film, atmospheric soundscapes and original music.

Videos of each episode – containing additional footage not shown on television – are available from good book and video shops, but the availability of individual videos varies with regional screening schedules.

*Video destinations include:* Alaska; Australia (Southeast); Brazil; Ecuador & the Galápagos Islands; Indonesia; Israel & the Sinai Desert; Japan; La Ruta Maya (Yucatán, Guatemala & Belize); Morocco; North India (Varanasi to the Himalaya); Pacific Islands; Vietnam; Zimbabwe, Botswana & Namibia.

*Coming soon:* The Arctic (Norway & Finland); Baja California; Chile & Easter Island; China (Southeast); Costa Rica; East Africa (Tanzania & Zanzibar); Great Barrier Reef (Australia); Jamaica; Papua New Guinea; the Rockies (USA); Syria & Jordan; Turkey.

*The Lonely Planet TV series is produced by:*
**Pilot Productions**
Duke of Sussex Studios
44 Uxbridge St
London W8 7TG UK

*Lonely Planet videos are distributed by:*
**IVN Communications Inc**
2246 Camino Ramon
California 94583, USA

107 Power Road, Chiswick
London W4 5PL UK

*Music from the TV series is available on CD & cassette.*
*For ordering information contact your nearest Lonely Planet office.*

# PLANET TALK

## *Lonely Planet's FREE quarterly newsletter*

We love hearing from you and think you'd like to hear from us.

**When**...is the right time to see reindeer in Finland?
**Where**...can you hear the best palm-wine music in Ghana?
**How**...do you get from Asunción to Areguá by steam train?
**What**...is the best way to see India?

*For the answer to these and many other questions read PLANET TALK.*

Every issue is packed with up-to-date travel news and advice including:

- a letter from Lonely Planet co-founders Tony and Maureen Wheeler
- go behind the scenes on the road with a Lonely Planet author
- feature article on an important and topical travel issue
- a selection of recent letters from travellers
- details on forthcoming Lonely Planet promotions
- complete list of Lonely Planet products

To join our mailing list contact any Lonely Planet office.

*Also available: Lonely Planet T-shirts. 100% heavyweight cotton..*

---

# LONELY PLANET ONLINE

## *Get the latest travel information before you leave or while you're on the road*

Whether you've just begun planning your next trip, or you're chasing down specific info on currency regulations or visa requirements, check out the Lonely Planet World Wide Web site for up-to-the-minute travel information.

As well as travel profiles of your favourite destinations (including interactive maps and full-colour photos), you'll find current reports from our army of researchers and other travellers, updates on health and visas, travel advisories, and the ecological and political issues you need to be aware of as you travel.

There's an online travellers' forum (the Thorn Tree) where you can share your experiences of life on the road, meet travel companions and ask other travellers for their recommendations and advice. We also have plenty of links to other Web sites useful to independent travellers.

With tens of thousands of visitors a month, the Lonely Planet Web site is one of the most popular on the Internet and has won a number of awards including GNN's Best of the Net travel award.

## http://www.lonelyplanet.com

# LONELY PLANET PRODUCTS

Lonely Planet is known worldwide for publishing practical, reliable and no-nonsense travel information in our guides and on our web site. The Lonely Planet list covers just about every accessible part of the world. Currently there are eight series: *travel guides, shoestring guides, walking guides, city guides, phrasebooks, audio packs, travel atlases* and *Journeys* – a unique collection of travellers' tales.

---

## EUROPE

Austria • Baltic States & Kaliningrad • Baltic States phrasebook • Britain • Central Europe on a shoestring • Central Europe phrasebook • Czech & Slovak Republics • Denmark • Dublin city guide • Eastern Europe on a shoestring • Eastern Europe phrasebook • Finland • France • Greece • Greek phrasebook • Hungary • Iceland, Greenland & the Faroe Islands • Ireland • Italy • Mediterranean Europe on a shoestring • Mediterranean Europe phrasebook • Poland • Prague city guide • Russia, Ukraine & Belarus • Russian phrasebook • Scandinavian & Baltic Europe on a shoestring • Scandinavian Europe phrasebook • Slovenia • St Petersburg city guide • Switzerland • Trekking in Greece • Trekking in Spain • Ukranian phrasebook • Vienna city guide • Walking in Switzerland • Western Europe on a shoestring • Western Europe phrasebook

## NORTH AMERICA

Alaska • Backpacking in Alaska • Baja California• California & Nevada • Canada • Hawaii • Honolulu city guide • Los Angeles city guide • Mexico • Pacific Northwest USA • Rocky Mountain States • San Francisco city guide • Southwest USA • USA phrasebook

## CENTRAL AMERICA & THE CARIBBEAN

Central America on a shoestring • Costa Rica • Eastern Caribbean • Guatemala, Belize & Yucatán: La Ruta Maya • Jamaica

## SOUTH AMERICA

Argentina, Uruguay & Paraguay • Bolivia • Brazil • Brazilian phrasebook • Buenos Aires city guide • Chile & Easter Island • Colombia • Ecuador & the Galápagos Islands • Latin American Spanish phrasebook • Peru • Quechua phrasebook • Rio de Janeiro city guide • South America on a shoestring • Trekking in the Patagonian Andes • Venezuela

## ALSO AVAILABLE:

Travel with Children • Traveller's Tales

## AFRICA

Arabic (Moroccan) phrasebook • Africa on a shoestring • Cape Town city guide • Central Africa • East Africa • Egypt & the Sudan • Ethiopian (Amharic) phrasebook • Kenya • Morocco • North Africa • South Africa, Lesotho & Swaziland • Swahili phrasebook • Trekking in East Africa • West Africa • Zimbabwe, Botswana & Namibia • Zimbabwe, Botswana & Namibia travel atlas

# MAIL ORDER

Lonely Planet products are distributed worldwide. They are also available by mail order from Lonely Planet, so if you have difficulty finding a title please write to us. North American and South American residents should write to Embarcadero West, 155 Filbert St, Suite 251, Oakland CA 94607, USA; European and African residents should write to 10 Barley Mow Passage, Chiswick, London W4 4PH; and residents of other countries to PO Box 617, Hawthorn, Victoria 3122, Australia.

## NORTH-EAST ASIA

Beijing city guide • Cantonese phrasebook • China • Hong Kong, Macau & Canton • Hong Kong city guide • Japan • Japanese phrasebook • Japanese audio pack • Korea • Korean phrasebook • Mandarin phrasebook • Mongolia • Mongolian phrasebook • North-East Asia on a shoestring • Seoul city guide • Taiwan • Tibet • Tibet phrasebook • Tokyo city guide

## INDIAN SUBCONTINENT

Bengali phrasebook • Bangladesh • Delhi city guide • Hindi/Urdu phrasebook • India • India & Bangladesh travel atlas • Karakoram Highway • Kashmir, Ladakh & Zanskar • Nepal • Nepali phrasebook • Pakistan • Sri Lanka • Sri Lanka phrasebook • Trekking in the Indian Himalaya • Trekking in the Nepal Himalaya

## SOUTH-EAST ASIA

Bali & Lombok • Bangkok city guide • Burmese phrasebook • Cambodia • Ho Chi Minh city guide • Indonesia • Indonesian phrasebook • Indonesian audio pack • Jakarta city guide • Java • Laos • Lao phrasebook • Malaysia, Singapore & Brunei • Myanmar (Burma) • Philippines • Pilipino phrasebook • Singapore city guide • South-East Asia on a shoestring • Thailand • Thailand travel atlas • Thai phrasebook • Thai audio pack • Thai Hill Tribes phrasebook • Vietnam • Vietnamese phrasebook • Vietnam travel atlas

## MIDDLE EAST & CENTRAL ASIA

Arab Gulf States • Arabic (Egyptian) phrasebook • Central Asia • Iran • Israel • Jordan & Syria • Middle East • Turkey • Turkish phrasebook • Trekking in Turkey • Yemen
*Travel Literature:* The Gates of Damascus

## ISLANDS OF THE INDIAN OCEAN

Madagascar & Comoros • Maldives & Islands of the East Indian Ocean • Mauritius, Réunion & Seychelles

## AUSTRALIA & THE PACIFIC

Australia • Australian phrasebook • Bushwalking in Australia • Bushwalking in Papua New Guinea • Fiji • Fijian phrasebook • Islands of Australia's Great Barrier Reef • Melbourne city guide • Micronesia • New Caledonia • New South Wales & the ACT • New Zealand • Outback Australia • Papua New Guinea • Papua New Guinea phrasebook • Queensland • Rarotonga & the Cook Islands • Samoa • Solomon Islands • South Australia • Sydney city guide • Tahiti & French Polynesia • Tonga • Tramping in New Zealand • Vanuatu • Victoria • Western Australia
*Travel Literature:* Islands in the Clouds • Sean & David's Long Drive

# THE LONELY PLANET STORY

Lonely Planet published its first book in 1973 in response to the numerous 'How did you do it?' questions Maureen and Tony Wheeler were asked after driving, bussing, hitching, sailing and railing their way from England to Australia.

Written at a kitchen table and hand collated, trimmed and stapled, *Across Asia on the Cheap* became an instant local bestseller, inspiring thoughts of another book.

Eighteen months in South-East Asia resulted in their second guide, *South-East Asia on a shoestring*, which they put together in a backstreet Chinese hotel in Singapore in 1975. The 'yellow bible', as it quickly became known to backpackers around the world, soon became *the* guide to the region. It has sold well over half a million copies and is now in its 8th edition, still retaining its familiar yellow cover.

Today there are over 180 titles, including travel guides, walking guides, language kits & phrasebooks, travel atlases and travel literature. The company is one of the largest travel publishers in the world. Although Lonely Planet initially specialised in guides to Asia, we now cover most regions of the world, including the Pacific, North America, South America, Africa, the Middle East and Europe.

The emphasis continues to be on travel for independent travellers. Tony and Maureen still travel for several months of each year and play an active part in the writing, updating and quality control of Lonely Planet's guides.

They have been joined by over 70 authors and 170 staff at our offices in Melbourne (Australia), Oakland (USA), London (UK) and Paris (France). Travellers themselves also make a valuable contribution to the guides through the feedback we receive in thousands of letters each year.

The people at Lonely Planet strongly believe that travellers can make a positive contribution to the countries they visit, both through their appreciation of the countries' culture, wildlife and natural features, and through the money they spend. In addition, the company makes a direct contribution to the countries and regions it covers. Since 1986 a percentage of the income from each book has been donated to ventures such as famine relief in Africa; aid projects in India; agricultural projects in Central America; Greenpeace's efforts to halt French nuclear testing in the Pacific; and Amnesty International.

*'I hope we send the people out with the right attitude about travel. You realise when you travel that there are so many different perspectives about the world, so we hope these books will make people more interested in what they see. These are guidebooks, but you can't really guide people. All you can do is point them in the right direction.'*
– Tony Wheeler

# LONELY PLANET PUBLICATIONS

**Australia**
PO Box 617, Hawthorn 3122, Victoria
tel: (03) 9819 1877  fax: (03) 9819 6459
e-mail: talk2us@lonelyplanet.com.au

**USA**
Embarcadero West, 155 Filbert St, Suite 251,
Oakland, CA 94607
tel: (510) 893 8555  TOLL FREE: 800 275-8555
fax: (510) 893 8563
e-mail: info@lonelyplanet.com

**UK**
10 Barley Mow Passage, Chiswick,
London W4 4PH
tel: (0181) 742 3161  fax: (0181) 742 2772
e-mail: 100413.3551@compuserve.com

**France:**
71 bis rue du Cardinal Lemoine, 75005 Paris
tel: 1 44 32 06 20  fax: 1 46 34 72 55
e-mail: 100560.415@compuserve.com

**World Wide Web: http://www.lonelyplanet.com**